Rick Steves'

ENGLAND

D0109124

CONTENTS

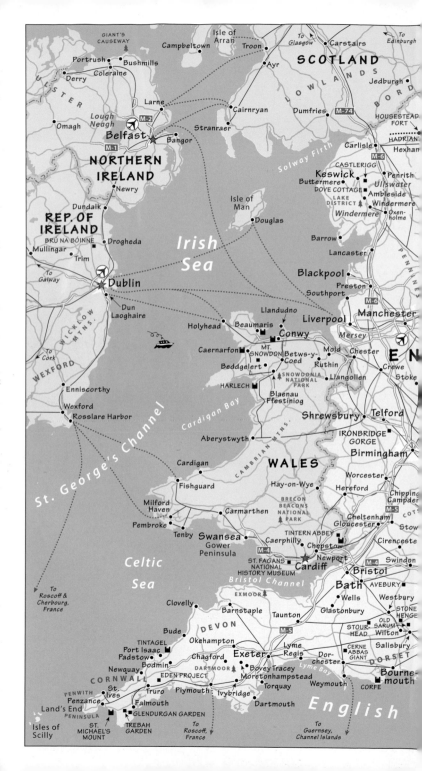

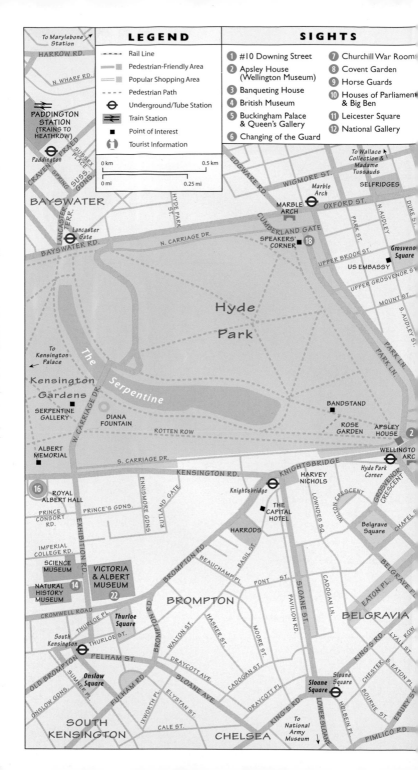

LEGEND

- - - - Rail Line
━━━ Pedestrian-Friendly Area
━━━ Popular Shopping Area
- - - Pedestrian Path
⊖ Underground/Tube Station
⇌ Train Station
■ Point of Interest
ℹ Tourist Information

0 km   0.5 km
0 mi   0.25 mi

SIGHTS

1 #10 Downing Street
2 Apsley House (Wellington Museum)
3 Banqueting House
4 British Museum
5 Buckingham Palace & Queen's Gallery
6 Changing of the Guard
7 Churchill War Rooms
8 Covent Garden
9 Horse Guards
10 Houses of Parliament & Big Ben
11 Leicester Square
12 National Gallery

To Marylebone Station
HARROW RD.
N. WHARF RD.

PADDINGTON STATION (TRAINS TO HEATHROW)
Paddington
CRAVEN RD. SPRING ST. SUSSEX GDNS. SUSSEX PLACE

BAYSWATER
Lancaster Gate
LANCASTER TERR.
BAYSWATER RD.

To Kensington Palace

Kensington Gardens

The Serpentine

SERPENTINE GALLERY

DIANA FOUNTAIN

W. CARRIAGE DR.

N. CARRIAGE DR.

HYDE ST.

Hyde Park

EDGWARE RD.

WIGMORE ST.
Marble Arch
SELFRIDGES
MARBLE ARCH ⊖ OXFORD ST.

To Wallace Collection & Madame Tussauds

CUMBERLAND GATE
SPEAKERS' CORNER 18

UPPER BROOK ST.
US EMBASSY
UPPER GROSVENOR ST.
Grosvenor Square

MOUNT ST.

PARK LN.
PARK LN.
S. AUDLEY ST.
N. AUDLEY ST.
PARK ST.
DUKE ST.

BANDSTAND

ROTTEN ROW

ROSE GARDEN

APSLEY HOUSE 2

WELLINGTON ARCH
Hyde Park Corner ⊖
GROSVENOR CRESCENT

ALBERT MEMORIAL

S. CARRIAGE DR.
KENSINGTON RD.
KNIGHTSBRIDGE
HARVEY NICHOLS

16 ROYAL ALBERT HALL
PRINCE CONSORT RD.
IMPERIAL COLLEGE RD.
SCIENCE MUSEUM
NATURAL HISTORY MUSEUM 14

EXHIBITION RD.
PRINCE'S GDNS.
ENNISMORE GDNS.
RUTLAND GATE

Knightsbridge ⊖
THE CAPITAL HOTEL

HARRODS
BROMPTON RD.
BEAUCHAMP PL.
BASIL ST.
PONT ST.
LOWNDES SQ.
LOWNDES ST.
WILTON CRESCENT
Belgrave Square

BELGRAVIA

CHAPEL ST.
BELGRAVE PL.
EATON PL.
LYALL ST.

VICTORIA & ALBERT MUSEUM 22

CROMWELL ROAD
THUROE PL.
Thurloe Square
South Kensington ⊖
THURLOE ST.
PELHAM ST.
ONSLOW SQUARE
ONSLOW GDNS.
SUMNER PL.
OLD BROMPTON RD.

BROMPTON

WALTON ST.
HASKER ST.
MOORE ST.
DRAYCOTT AVE.
SLOANE AVE.
FULHAM RD.
PELHAM ST.
CADOGAN ST.
PAVILION RD.
SLOANE ST.
CADOGAN LN.

SOUTH KENSINGTON
CALE ST.
ELYSTAN ST.
WORTH PL.
DRAYCOTT PL.

CHELSEA
KING'S RD.
To National Army Museum

Sloane Square
Sloane Square ⊖
LOWER SLOANE ST.
HOLBEIN PL.
PIMLICO RD.

KING'S RD.
CHESTER ROW
S. EATON PL.
BOURNE ST.
EBURY ST.

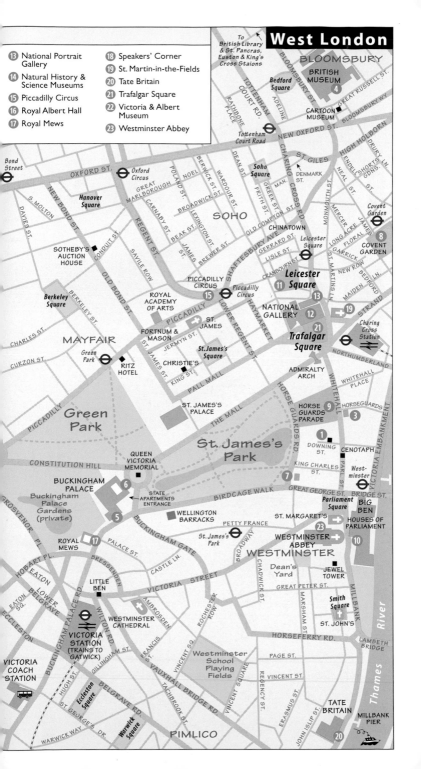

West London

To British Library & St. Pancras, Euston & King's Cross Staions

13 National Portrait Gallery
14 Natural History & Science Museums
15 Piccadilly Circus
16 Royal Albert Hall
17 Royal Mews
18 Speakers' Corner
19 St. Martin-in-the-Fields
20 Tate Britain
21 Trafalgar Square
22 Victoria & Albert Museum
23 Westminster Abbey

BLOOMSBURY
BRITISH MUSEUM
Bedford Square
CARTOON MUSEUM

Bond Street
OXFORD ST.
Oxford Circus
Hanover Square
SOTHEBY'S AUCTION HOUSE
Berkeley Square
MAYFAIR
Green Park
CHARLES ST.
CURZON ST.
RITZ HOTEL
Green Park

Tottenham Court Road
NEW OXFORD ST.
ST. GILES
Soho Square
SOHO
CHINATOWN
Leicester Square
PICCADILLY CIRCUS
15
ROYAL ACADEMY OF ARTS
PICCADILLY
ST. JAMES
FORTNUM & MASON
St. James's Square
CHRISTIE'S
PALL MALL
ST. JAMES'S PALACE
THE MALL

Covent Garden
8
COVENT GARDEN
13
NATIONAL GALLERY
12
19
Trafalgar Square
21
Charing Cross Station
ADMIRALTY ARCH
NORTHUMBERLAND

Green Park
CONSTITUTION HILL
BUCKINGHAM PALACE
Buckingham Palace Gardens (private)
6
QUEEN VICTORIA MEMORIAL
STATE APARTMENTS ENTRANCE
5
WELLINGTON BARRACKS
St. James's Park
ROYAL MEWS
17

St. James's Park
BIRDCAGE WALK
7
GREAT GEORGE ST.
ST. MARGARET'S
PETTY FRANCE
BROADWAY
23
WESTMINSTER ABBEY
WESTMINSTER

HORSE GUARDS PARADE
HORSEGUARDS
9
3
1
DOWNING ST.
CENOTAPH
Westminster
KING CHARLES ST.
Parliament Square
BIG BEN
HOUSES OF PARLIAMENT
10
JEWEL TOWER
Dean's Yard
GREAT PETER ST.
Smith Square
ST. JOHN'S
MILLBANK

GROSVENOR PL.
HOBART PL.
EATON
LOWER BELGRAVE
ECCLESTON
EATON SQ.
VICTORIA COACH STATION
PALACE ST.
BRESSENDEN
LITTLE BEN
WILTON RD.
WESTMINSTER CATHEDRAL
VICTORIA STATION (TRAINS TO GATWICK)
CASTLE LN.
VICTORIA STREET
ROCHESTER ROW
CHADWICK ST.

HORSEFERRY RD.
LAMBETH BRIDGE
PAGE ST.
Westminster School Playing Fields
VINCENT ST.
TATE BRITAIN
MILLBANK PIER
20

Thames River

ECCLESTON
ST. GEORGE'S DR.
WARWICK WAY
Eccleston Square
BELGRAVE RD.
Warwick Square
VAUXHALL BRIDGE RD.
PIMLICO

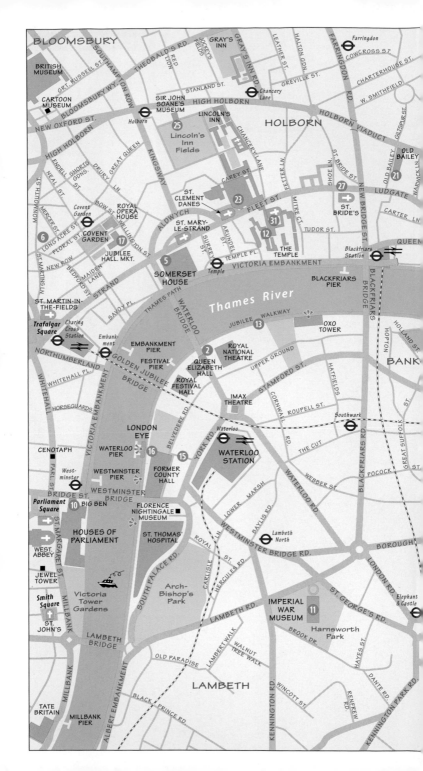

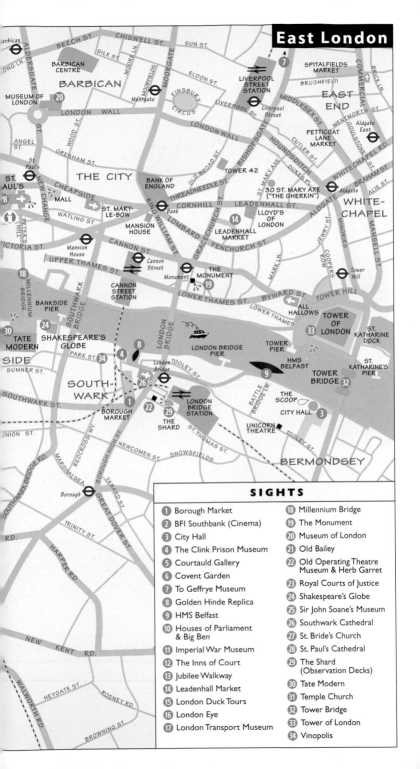

East London

BEECH ST. · **CHISWELL ST.** · SUN ST. · **BARBICAN CENTRE** · SILK ST. · MOORE LN. · MOORGATE · ELDON ST. · **SPITALFIELDS MARKET** · BRUSHFIELD · **EAST END** · COMMERCIAL · BRICK LN.

BARBICAN · Moorfields · FINSBURY CIRCUS · **LIVERPOOL STREET STATION** · Liverpool Street · MIDDLESEX ST. · **⑦**

MUSEUM OF LONDON ⑳ · Moorgate · LONDON WALL · LIVERPOOL ST. · WENTWORTH · Aldgate East

LONDON WALL · PETTICOAT LANE MARKET · GOULSTONE ST. · WHITECHAPEL RD.

ANGEL ST. · GRESHAM ST. · OLD BROAD ST. · TOWER 42 · CUTLER ST. · HOUNDSDITCH · DUKE'S PL. · **WHITE-CHAPEL**

St. Paul's · **ST. PAUL'S** · **THE CITY** · BANK OF ENGLAND · THREADNEEDLE ST. · 30 ST. MARY AXE ("THE GHERKIN") · Aldgate · BRAHAM ST. · ALIE ST.

⑧ · NEW CHANGE · CHEAPSIDE · MALL · ST. MARY-LE-BOW · CORNHILL · LEADENHALL ST. · LLOYD'S OF LONDON · MINORIES

PETER'S HILL · WATLING ST. · MANSION HOUSE · Bank · LOMBARD ST. · ⑭ · LEADENHALL MARKET · JEWRY ST. · MANSELL ST.

VICTORIA ST. · Mansion House · KING WILLIAM ST. · GRACECHURCH ST. · FENCHURCH ST. · MARK LN. · COOPER'S ROW · Tower Hill

⑱ · CANNON ST. · UPPER THAMES ST. · Cannon Street · CANNON STREET STATION · Monument · **THE MONUMENT** · LOWER THAMES ST. · BYWARD ST. · TOWER HILL · Tower Hill

MILLENNIUM BRIDGE · BANKSIDE PIER · ⑲ · LOWER THAMES · ALL HALLOWS · **TOWER OF LONDON** · ST. KATHARINE DOCK

⑳ · ㉔ · SHAKESPEARE'S GLOBE · LONDON BRIDGE · LONDON BRIDGE PIER · TOWER PIER · ㉝ · ST. KATHARINE'S PIER

TATE MODERN · PARK ST. · ㉞ · ④ · ⑧ · TOOLEY ST. · HMS BELFAST · **TOWER BRIDGE** · ㉜

SIDE · SUMNER ST. · London Bridge · ⑨ · ③

SOUTHWARK ST. · **SOUTH-WARK** · ㉖ · ㉒ · **LONDON BRIDGE STATION** · BATTLE BRIDGE LN. · **THE SCOOP** · CITY HALL · ③

① · **BOROUGH MARKET** · ㉙ · **THE SHARD** · UNICORN THEATRE · TOOLEY ST. · **BERMONDSEY**

Borough · ST. THOMAS ST. · SNOWSFIELDS

UNION ST. · REDCROSS WY. · NEWCOMEN ST.

SOUTHWARK BRIDGE RD. · MARSHALSEA · BOROUGH HIGH ST. · TABARD ST. · Borough · GREAT DOVER ST.

TRINITY ST. · HARPER RD. · RD.

NEW KENT RD. · HEYGATE ST. · RODNEY RD. · BROWNING ST.

WALWORTH RD.

SIGHTS

- ① Borough Market
- ② BFI Southbank (Cinema)
- ③ City Hall
- ④ The Clink Prison Museum
- ⑤ Courtauld Gallery
- ⑥ Covent Garden
- ⑦ To Geffrye Museum
- ⑧ Golden Hinde Replica
- ⑨ HMS Belfast
- ⑩ Houses of Parliament & Big Ben
- ⑪ Imperial War Museum
- ⑫ The Inns of Court
- ⑬ Jubilee Walkway
- ⑭ Leadenhall Market
- ⑮ London Duck Tours
- ⑯ London Eye
- ⑰ London Transport Museum
- ⑱ Millennium Bridge
- ⑲ The Monument
- ⑳ Museum of London
- ㉑ Old Bailey
- ㉒ Old Operating Theatre Museum & Herb Garret
- ㉓ Royal Courts of Justice
- ㉔ Shakespeare's Globe
- ㉕ Sir John Soane's Museum
- ㉖ Southwark Cathedral
- ㉗ St. Bride's Church
- ㉘ St. Paul's Cathedral
- ㉙ The Shard (Observation Decks)
- ㉚ Tate Modern
- ㉛ Temple Church
- ㉜ Tower Bridge
- ㉝ Tower of London
- ㉞ Vinopolis

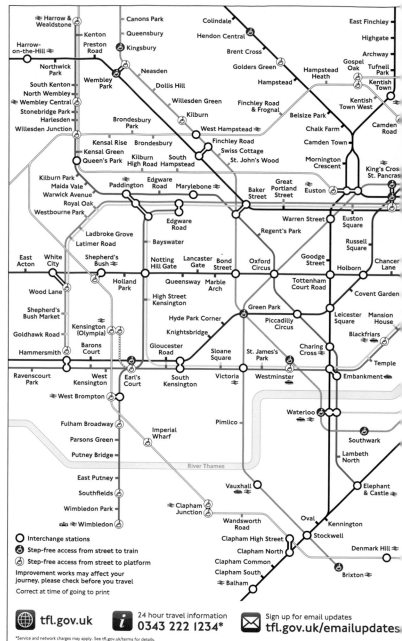

Harrow & Wealdstone
Canons Park
Colindale
East Finchley
Kenton
Queensbury
Hendon Central
Highgate
Preston Road
Kingsbury
Brent Cross
Archway
Harrow-on-the-Hill
Gospel Oak
Tufnell Park
Northwick Park
Neasden
Golders Green
Hampstead Heath
Kentish Town
South Kenton
Wembley Park
Dollis Hill
Hampstead
North Wembley
Willesden Green
Wembley Central
Finchley Road & Frognal
Kentish Town West
Stonebridge Park
Kilburn
Belsize Park
Harlesden
Brondesbury Park
West Hampstead
Camden Road
Willesden Junction
Kensal Rise
Brondesbury
Finchley Road
Chalk Farm
Kensal Green
Kilburn High Road
Swiss Cottage
Camden Town
Queen's Park
South Hampstead
St. John's Wood
Mornington Crescent
Kilburn Park
Edgware Road
Marylebone
Baker Street
Great Portland Street
Euston
King's Cross St. Pancras
Maida Vale
Paddington
Warwick Avenue
Royal Oak
Warren Street
Euston Square
Westbourne Park
Edgware Road
Regent's Park
Russell Square
Ladbroke Grove
Bayswater
Latimer Road
East Acton
White City
Shepherd's Bush
Notting Hill Gate
Lancaster Gate
Bond Street
Oxford Circus
Goodge Street
Holborn
Chancery Lane
Wood Lane
Holland Park
Queensway
Marble Arch
Tottenham Court Road
Covent Garden
Shepherd's Bush Market
High Street Kensington
Green Park
Piccadilly Circus
Leicester Square
Mansion House
Goldhawk Road
Kensington (Olympia)
Hyde Park Corner
Blackfriars
Hammersmith
Barons Court
Knightsbridge
Charing Cross
Ravenscourt Park
West Kensington
Gloucester Road
Sloane Square
St. James's Park
Temple
Earl's Court
South Kensington
Victoria
Westminster
Embankment
West Brompton
Pimlico
Waterloo
Fulham Broadway
Imperial Wharf
Southwark
Parsons Green
Lambeth North
Putney Bridge
River Thames
East Putney
Vauxhall
Elephant & Castle
Southfields
Clapham Junction
Oval
Kennington
Wimbledon Park
Wandsworth Road
Stockwell
Wimbledon
Clapham High Street
Denmark Hill
Clapham North
Clapham Common
Brixton
Clapham South
Balham

○ Interchange stations
♿ Step-free access from street to train
♿ Step-free access from street to platform
Improvement works may affect your journey, please check before you travel
Correct at time of going to print

🌐 **tfl.gov.uk**

ℹ 24 hour travel information **0343 222 1234***

✉ Sign up for email updates **tfl.gov.uk/emailupdates**

*Service and network charges may apply. See tfl.gov.uk/terms for details.

MAYOR OF LONDON

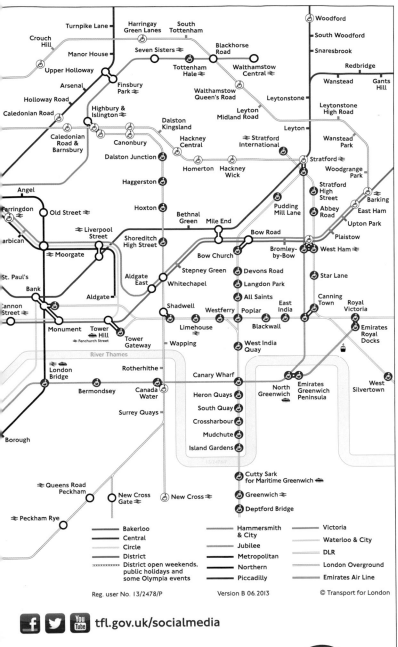

▬▬▬ Bakerloo	▬▬▬ Hammersmith & City	▬▬▬ Victoria
▬▬▬ Central	▬▬▬ Jubilee	▬▬▬ Waterloo & City
▬▬▬ Circle	▬▬▬ Metropolitan	▬▬▬ DLR
▬▬▬ District	▬▬▬ Northern	▬▬▬ London Overground
░░░ District open weekends, public holidays and some Olympia events	▬▬▬ Piccadilly	▬▬▬ Emirates Air Line

Reg. user No. 13/2478/P   Version B 06.2013   © Transport for London

 tfl.gov.uk/socialmedia

Transport for London   **UNDERGROUND**

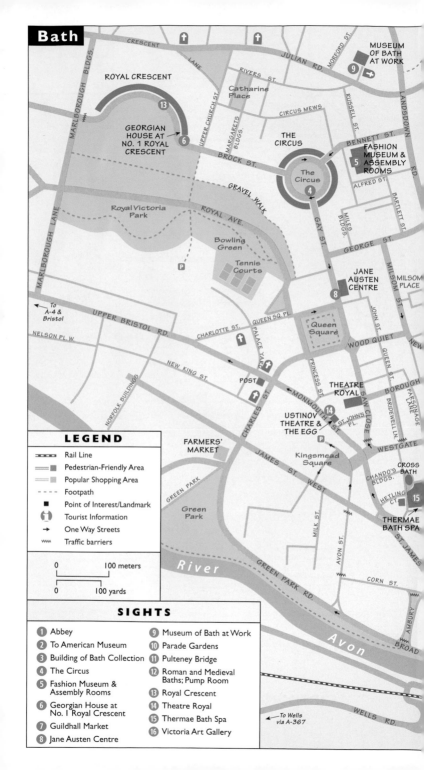

Bath

MUSEUM OF BATH AT WORK

ROYAL CRESCENT

GEORGIAN HOUSE AT NO. 1 ROYAL CRESCENT

THE CIRCUS

FASHION MUSEUM & ASSEMBLY ROOMS

Royal Victoria Park

Bowling Green

Tennis Courts

JANE AUSTEN CENTRE

MILSOM PLACE

To A-4 & Bristol

Queen Square

THEATRE ROYAL

USTINOV THEATRE & THE EGG

CROSS BATH

FARMERS' MARKET

Kingsmead Square

THERMAE BATH SPA

Green Park

River Avon

To Wells via A-367

WELLS RD.

LEGEND

- ▬▬▬ Rail Line
- ▬▬ Pedestrian-Friendly Area
- ▬▬ Popular Shopping Area
- - - - Footpath
- ■ Point of Interest/Landmark
- ✆ Tourist Information
- → One Way Streets
- ⌇⌇⌇ Traffic barriers

0   100 meters

0   100 yards

SIGHTS

1. Abbey
2. To American Museum
3. Building of Bath Collection
4. The Circus
5. Fashion Museum & Assembly Rooms
6. Georgian House at No. 1 Royal Crescent
7. Guildhall Market
8. Jane Austen Centre
9. Museum of Bath at Work
10. Parade Gardens
11. Pulteney Bridge
12. Roman and Medieval Baths; Pump Room
13. Royal Crescent
14. Theatre Royal
15. Thermae Bath Spa
16. Victoria Art Gallery

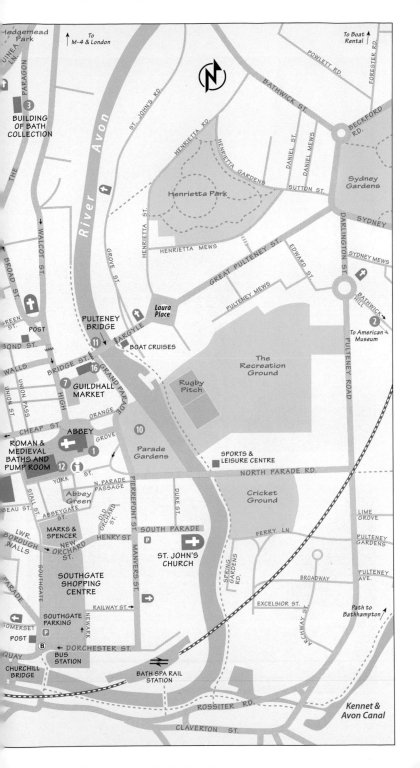

London Eye

Swan Hotel in Bibury

Beachy Head

London's Guard

Castlerigg Stone Circle

Rick Steves'®

ENGLAND

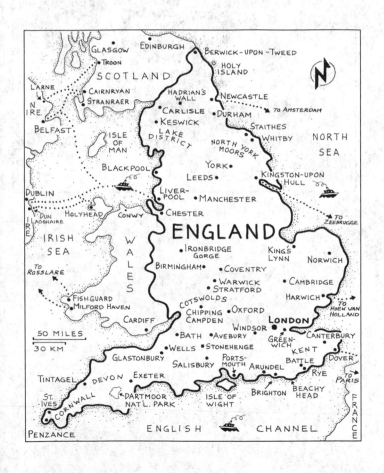

Top Destinations in England

INTRODUCTION

From the grandeur and bustle of London, to the pastoral countryside that inspired Shakespeare, to some of the quaintest towns
you'll ever experience, England delights. Stand in a desolate field
and ponder an ancient stone circle. Strike up a conversation just to
hear the Queen's English. Bite into a scone smothered with clotted
cream, sip a cup of tea, and wave your pinky as if it's a Union Jack.

This book breaks England into its top big-city, small-town,
and rural destinations. It gives you all the information and opinions
necessary to wring the maximum value out of your limited time
and money in each of these locations.

Note that this book covers only England, which occupies the
southern two-thirds of the island of Great Britain. If you want to
visit Wales and Scotland too, pick up a copy of *Rick Steves' Great
Britain* instead.

Experiencing English culture, people, and natural wonders
economically and hassle-free has been my goal for more than three
decades of traveling, tour guiding, and travel writing. With this
new edition, I pass on to you the lessons I've learned, updated for
your trip.

While including the predictable biggies (such as Big Ben,
Stratford-upon-Avon, and Stonehenge), the book also mixes in a
healthy dose of Back Door intimacy (windswept Roman lookouts,
angelic boys' choirs, and nearly edible Cotswold villages). This
book is selective. For example, while Hadrian's Wall is more than
70 miles long, I recommend visiting just the best six-mile stretch.

The best is, of course, only my opinion. But after spending half
my adult life researching Europe, I've developed a sixth sense for
what travelers enjoy. The places featured in this book will knock
your spots off.

Map Legend

⚐ Viewpoint	✈ Airport		Tunnel
⬆ Entrance	Ⓣ Taxi Stand		Pedestrian Zone
ⓘ Tourist Info	⊤ Tram Stop		Railway
WC Restroom	Ⓑ Bus Stop		Ferry/Boat Route
⛫ Castle	Ⓟ Parking		Tram
⛪ Church	⊖ Tube		Stairs
▪ Statue/Point of Interest	)(Mtn. Pass		Walk/Tour Route
☗ Pub	Park		Trail

Use this legend to help you navigate the maps in this book.

About This Book

Rick Steves' England is a personal tour guide in your pocket. The book is organized by destinations. Each is a mini-vacation on its own, filled with exciting sights, strollable neighborhoods, homey and affordable places to stay, and memorable places to eat. In the following chapters, you'll find these sections:

Planning Your Time suggests a schedule for how to best use your limited time.

Orientation includes specifics on public transportation, helpful hints, local tour options, easy-to-read maps, and tourist information.

Sights describes the top attractions and includes their cost and hours.

Self-Guided Walks take you through interesting neighborhoods, with a personal tour guide in hand.

Sleeping describes my favorite hotels, from good-value deals to cushy splurges.

Eating serves up a range of options, from inexpensive pubs to fancy restaurants.

Connections outlines your options for traveling to destinations by train, bus, and plane, plus route tips for drivers.

The **Britain: Past and Present** chapter is a quick overview of British history and culture.

The **appendix** is a traveler's tool kit, with telephone tips, useful phone numbers and websites, transportation basics (on trains, buses, car rentals, driving, and flights), recommended books and films, a festival list, a climate chart, a handy packing checklist, and a fun British-Yankee dictionary.

Browse through this book, choose your favorite destinations, and link them up. Then have a brilliant trip! Traveling like a temporary local, you'll get the absolute most out of every mile, minute,

Key to This Book

Updates

This book is updated every year, but things change. For the latest, visit www.ricksteves.com/update, and for a valuable list of reports and experiences—good and bad—from fellow travelers, check www.ricksteves.com/feedback.

Abbreviations and Times

I use the following symbols and abbreviations in this book:

Sights are rated:

▲▲▲	Don't miss
▲▲	Try hard to see
▲	Worthwhile if you can make it
No rating	Worth knowing about

Tourist information offices are abbreviated as **TI,** and bathrooms are **WCs.** To categorize accommodations, I use a **Sleep Code** (described on page 22).

Like Europe, this book uses the **24-hour clock** for schedules. It's the same through 12:00 noon, then keeps going: 13:00, 14:00, and so on. For anything over 12, subtract 12 and add p.m. (14:00 is 2:00 p.m.).

When giving **opening times,** I include both peak season and off-season hours if they differ. So, if a museum is listed as "May-Oct daily 9:00-16:00," it should be open from 9 a.m. until 4 p.m. from the first day of May until the last day of October (but expect exceptions).

For **transit** or **tour departures,** I first list the frequency, then the duration. So, a train connection listed as "2/hour, 1.5 hours" departs twice each hour, and the journey lasts an hour and a half.

and dollar. I'm happy that you'll be visiting places I know and love, and meeting my favorite English people.

Planning

This section will help you get started on planning your trip—with advice on trip costs, when to go, and what you should know before you take off.

Travel Smart

Your trip to England is like a complex play—it's easier to follow and really appreciate on a second viewing. While no one does the same trip twice to gain that advantage, reading this book in its entirety before your trip accomplishes much the same thing.

Design an itinerary that enables you to visit sights at the best possible times. Note festivals, holidays, specifics on sights, and days

England at a Glance

▲▲▲London Thriving metropolis packed with world-class museums, monuments, churches, parks, palaces, theaters, pubs, Beefeaters, telephone boxes, double-decker buses, and all things British.

▲▲Greenwich, Windsor, and Cambridge Easy side-trips from London: famous observatory at the maritime center of Greenwich, the Queen's palace at Windsor, and England's best university town, Cambridge.

▲Canterbury Pleasant pilgrimage town with England's top church.

▲Dover and Southeast England The imposing Dover Castle, famous White Cliffs, lush Sissinghurst Gardens, hill town of Rye, and historic site of the Battle of Hastings.

▲Brighton Flamboyant beach resort on England's south coast, near the rolling hills of South Downs Way and the chalky cliffs at Beachy Head.

▲Portsmouth Newly rejuvenated shipbuilding city with top nautical sights at the Historic Dockyard, plus Roman ruins and stately Arundel Castle nearby.

▲Dartmoor Mysterious, desolate, moor-cloaked national park with wild ponies, hiking paths, and an ancient stone circle.

▲Cornwall Feisty peninsula littered with prehistoric ruins, plus the seaside resort towns of Penzance and St. Ives, King Arthur's supposed Tintagel Castle, the tip of England at Land's End, and other offbeat sights.

▲▲▲Bath Genteel Georgian showcase city, built around the remains of an ancient Roman bath.

▲▲Near Bath England's mysterious heart, including the prehistoric-meets-New Age hill at Glastonbury, spine-tingling stone circles at Stonehenge and Avebury, enjoyable cathedral towns of Wells and Salisbury, and delightful Dorset countryside.

▲**Oxford** Stately university town with Blenheim Palace—one of England's best—on its doorstep.

▲▲**The Cotswolds** Remarkably quaint villages—including the cozy market town Chipping Campden, popular hamlet Stow-on-the-Wold, and handy transit hub Moreton-in-Marsh—scattered over a hilly countryside.

▲**Stratford-upon-Avon** Shakespeare's hometown and top venue for seeing his plays performed.

Warwick and Coventry England's best medieval castle, in pleasant Warwick, and the stirring bombed-out husk of an ancient cathedral, in Coventry.

▲**Ironbridge Gorge** Birthplace of the Industrial Revolution, with sights and museums that tell the earth-changing story.

▲**Liverpool** Rejuvenated port city and the Beatles' hometown.

Blackpool England's tackiest, most fun-loving beach resort.

▲▲**The Lake District** Idyllic lakes-and-hills landscape, with enjoyable hikes and joyrides, time-passed valleys, William Wordsworth and Beatrix Potter sights, and the charming home-base town of Keswick.

▲▲▲**York** Walled medieval town with grand Gothic cathedral, excellent museums (Viking, Victorian, Railway), and atmospheric old center.

▲**North Yorkshire** Smattering of ruined abbeys, desolate moors, seaside towns (including bustling Whitby and tiny Staithes), and other sights near York.

▲**Durham and Northeast England** Youthful working-class town with magnificent cathedral, plus (nearby) an open-air museum, the Roman remains of Hadrian's Wall, Holy Island, and Bamburgh Castle.

when sights are closed. To get between destinations smoothly, read the tips in this book's appendix on taking trains and buses, or renting a car and driving. A smart trip is a puzzle—a fun, doable, and worthwhile challenge.

When you're plotting your itinerary, strive for a mix of intense and relaxed stretches. To maximize rootedness, minimize one-night stands. It's worth a long drive after dinner to be settled into a town for two nights. Hotels and B&Bs are more likely to give a better price to someone staying more than one night. Every trip (and every traveler) needs slack time (laundry, picnics, people-watching, and so on). Pace yourself. Assume you will return.

Reread this book as you travel, and visit local TIs. Upon arrival in a new town, lay the groundwork for a smooth departure; get the schedule for the train or bus that you'll take when you depart. Drivers can study the best route to their next destination.

Get online at Internet cafés or at your hotel, and carry a mobile phone (or use a phone card) to make travel plans: You can find tourist information, learn the latest on sights (special events, tour schedules, etc.), book tickets and tours, make reservations, reconfirm hotels, research transportation connections, check weather, and keep in touch with your loved ones.

Enjoy the friendliness of the British people. Connect with the culture. Set up your own quest for the best pub, cathedral, or chocolate bar. Slow down and be open to unexpected experiences. You speak the language—use it! Ask questions—most locals are eager to point you in their idea of the right direction. Keep a notepad in your pocket for noting directions, organizing your thoughts, and confirming prices. Wear your money belt, learn the currency, and figure out how to estimate prices in dollars. Those who expect to travel smart, do.

Trip Costs

Five components make up your trip costs: airfare, surface transportation, room and board, sightseeing and entertainment, and shopping and miscellany.

Airfare: A basic round-trip US-to-London flight can cost, on average, about $1,000-1,800, depending on where you fly from and when (cheaper in winter). Smaller budget airlines may provide bargain service from several European capitals to many cities in England. If your trip extends beyond England, consider saving time and money by flying into one city and out of another—for instance, into London and out of Amsterdam.

Surface Transportation: For a three-week whirlwind trip of all my recommended English destinations, allow $550 per person for public transportation (train pass, key buses, and Tube fare in London). For a three-week trip by car, allow $300-450 per person (based on two people sharing; not including gas, insurance, or taxes)—or look into leasing, which can save you money on insurance and taxes for trips of this length. Car rentals and leases are cheapest when arranged from the US. Train passes are normally available only outside Europe. You may save money by simply buying tickets as you go. Don't hesitate to consider flying, as budget airlines can be cheaper than taking the train (check Skyscanner.com for intra-European flights). For more on public transportation and car rental, see "Transportation" in the appendix.

Room and Board: Outside of London, you can thrive in England on $120 per day per person for room and board. This allows $15 for lunch, $35 for dinner, and $70 for lodging (based on two people splitting the cost of a $140 double room that includes breakfast). Allow about 15 percent more for your days in London or other big cities. Students and tightwads can enjoy England for as little as $60 ($30 for a bed, $30 for meals and snacks).

Sightseeing and Entertainment: Figure about $15-35 per major sight (Stonehenge-$13, Shakespeare's Birthplace in Stratford-$24, Westminster Abbey-$29, Tower of London-$35), $7 for minor ones (climbing church towers), and $35-40 for splurge experiences (e.g., bus tours, concerts, discounted tickets for plays). For information on various sightseeing passes, see page 20.

Fortunately, many of the best sights in London are free, including the British Museum, National Gallery, National Portrait Gallery, Tate Britain, Tate Modern, British Library, and the Victoria & Albert Museum (though most request donations). An overall average of $30 a day works in most cities (allow $50 for London). Don't skimp here. After all, this category is the driving force behind your trip—you came to sightsee, enjoy, and experience England.

Shopping and Miscellany: Figure roughly $2 per postcard, $3 for tea or an ice-cream cone, and $5 per pint of beer. Shopping can vary in cost from nearly nothing to a small fortune. Good budget travelers find that this has little to do with assembling a trip full of lifelong and wonderful memories.

Sightseeing Priorities

Depending on the length of your trip, and taking geographic proximity into account, here are my recommended priorities:

3 days:	London
5 days, add:	Bath and nearby sights (take a minibus tour or choose some combination of Stonehenge, Avebury, Wells, Glastonbury, and Salisbury)
7 days, add:	Cotswolds
9 days, add:	York
11 days, add:	Lake District

14 days, add: Durham, Stratford, Warwick
17 days, add: Ironbridge Gorge, Liverpool
21 days, add: Cornwall, Dartmoor
24 days, add: Choose two of the following—Cambridge,
Oxford, Blackpool, Coventry, Portsmouth,
Brighton, Canterbury, or Dover

This list includes virtually everything on my "England's Best Three-Week Trip by Car" itinerary and map (see page 10).

Note: Instead of spending the first few days of your trip in busy London, consider a gentler small-town start in Bath (the ideal jet-lag pillow), and let London be the finale of your trip. You'll be more rested and ready to tackle England's greatest city. Heathrow Airport has direct bus connections to Bath and other cities. (Bristol Airport is also near Bath.)

Your itinerary will depend on your interests. Nature lovers will likely put the lovely Lake District and the more remote Dartmoor nearer the top of their list, while engineers are drawn like a magnet to Ironbridge Gorge. Beatlemaniacs make a pilgrimage to Liverpool. Coastal Brighton and Blackpool offer amusement-park fun, refreshing for families and those who've had enough of museums. Literary fans like Cambridge, Oxford, Stratford, Bath, and the South Lake District.

When to Go

In England, July and August are peak season—my favorite time—with very long days, the best weather, and the busiest schedule of tourist fun.

Prices and crowds don't go up during peak times as dramatically in England as they do in much of Europe, except for holidays and festivals (see "Holidays and Festivals" in the appendix). Still, travel during "shoulder season" (May, early June, Sept, and early Oct) is easier and can be a bit less expensive. Shoulder-season travelers usually enjoy smaller crowds, decent weather, the full range of sights and tourist fun spots, and the ability to grab a room almost whenever and wherever they like—often at a flexible price. Winter travelers find absolutely no crowds and soft room prices, but shorter sightseeing hours and reliably bad weather. Some attractions are open only on weekends or are closed entirely in the winter (Nov-Feb). The weather can be cold and dreary, and nightfall draws the shades on sightseeing well before dinnertime. While rural charm falls with the leaves, city sightseeing is fine in the winter.

Plan for rain no matter when you go. Just keep traveling and take full advantage of bright spells. The weather can change several times in a day, but rarely is it extreme. As the locals say, "There is no bad weather, only inappropriate clothing." Bring a jacket and dress in layers. Temperatures below 32°F cause headlines, and days that break 80°F—while more frequent in recent years—are still rare in England. Weather-wise, July and August are not much better than shoulder months. May and June can be lovely anywhere in England. (For more information, see the climate chart in the appendix.) While sunshine may be rare, summer days are very long. The midsummer sun is up from 6:30 until 22:30. It's not uncommon to have a gray day, eat dinner, and enjoy hours of sunshine afterward.

Know Before You Go

Your trip is more likely to go smoothly if you plan ahead. Check this list of things to arrange while you're still at home.

You need a **passport**—but no visa or shots—to travel in Great Britain. You may be denied entry into certain European countries if your passport is due to expire within three to six months of your ticketed date of return. Get it renewed if you'll be cutting it close. It can take up to six weeks to get or renew a passport (for more on passports, see www.travel.state.gov). Pack a photocopy of your passport in your luggage in case the original is lost or stolen.

Book rooms well in advance if you'll be traveling during peak season and any major **holidays** (see list on page 892).

Call your **debit- and credit-card companies** to let them know the countries you'll be visiting, to ask about fees, to request your PIN code (it will be mailed to you), and more. See page 14 for details.

Do your homework if you want to buy **travel insurance.** Compare the cost of the insurance to the likelihood of your using it and your potential loss if something goes wrong. Also, check whether your existing insurance (health, homeowners, or renters) covers you and your possessions overseas. For more tips, see www.ricksteves.com/insurance.

Consider buying a **railpass** after researching your options (see page 870 and www.ricksteves.com/rail for all the specifics). If traveling to continental Europe on the **Eurostar** train, you can order a ticket in advance or buy it in Britain; for details, see page 220.

If you're planning on **renting a car** in Great Britain, bring your driver's license.

If you'll be in London or Stratford and want to **see a play,** check theater schedules ahead of time. For simplicity, I book plays while in England, but if there's something you just have to see, consider buying tickets before you go. For a current schedule of London plays and musicals, visit www.officiallondontheatre.co.uk. Tickets to performances at Stratford's Royal Shakespeare Theatre are likely to sell out (see www.rsc.org.uk), but if it's just Shakespeare you're after—with or without Stratford—you can see his plays in London, too.

At **Stonehenge,** anyone can see the stones from behind the

England's Best Three-Week Trip by Car

Day	Plan	Sleep in
1	Arrive at London's Heathrow Airport, train/bus combo or direct bus to Bath	Bath
2	Bath	Bath
3	Pick up car, Avebury, Wells, Bath	Glastonbury
4	Early drive to Cornwall	Penzance
5	Cornwall	Penzance
6	Dartmoor	Salisbury
7	Salisbury, Portsmouth	Salisbury
8	Oxford, Blenheim	Chipping Campden
9	Explore the Cotswolds	Chipping Campden
10	Stratford, Warwick, Coventry	Ironbridge Gorge
11	Ironbridge Gorge	Liverpool
12	Liverpool, maybe side-trip to Blackpool	Liverpool
13	South Lake District	Keswick area
14	North Lake District	Keswick area
15	Hadrian's Wall and Durham, to York, turn in car	York
16	York	York
17	Early train to London	London
18	London	London
19	London	London
20	Canterbury, Dover	London
21	Greenwich, Windsor, Cambridge, Brighton (choose one)	London
22	Whew!	

While this three-week itinerary is designed to be done by car, it can be done by train and bus or, better yet, with a BritRail & Drive Pass (best car days: Cornwall/Dartmoor, Cotswolds, and Lake District); for more on the pass, see page 868. For three weeks without a car, I'd cut back on the recommended sights with the

rope line (and for most people, this is sufficient), but if you want to go inside the stone circle, you'll need reservations (see page 476); book it when you know the date you'll be there. You can also reserve a tour of the Lennon and McCartney homes in Liverpool (figure on two weeks ahead in peak season, otherwise just a few days; see page 658).

If you plan to hire a **local guide,** reserve ahead by email. Popular guides can get booked up.

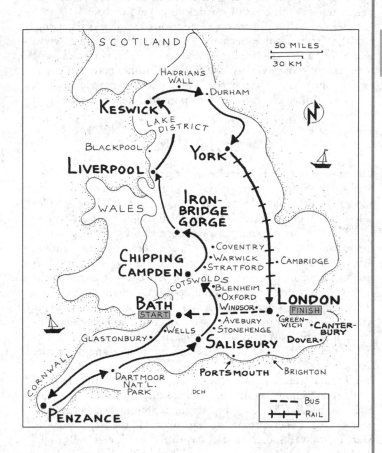

most frustrating public transportation (Cornwall, Dartmoor, and Ironbridge Gorge). Lacing together the cities by train is very slick, and buses get you where the trains don't go. With more time, everything is workable without a car.

If you're bringing a **mobile device,** download any apps you might want to use on the road, such as maps and transit schedules. Check out **Rick Steves Audio Europe,** featuring audio tours of major sights in London, hours of travel interviews on Great Britain, and more (via www.ricksteves.com/audioeurope, iTunes, Google Play, or the Rick Steves Audio Europe smartphone app; for details, see page 885).

Check the **Rick Steves guidebook updates** page for any recent changes to this book (www.ricksteves.com/update).

Because **airline carry-on restrictions** are always changing, visit the Transportation Security Administration's website (www.tsa.gov) for an up-to-date list of what you can bring on the plane with you and what you must check. Some airlines may restrict you to only one carry-on (no extras like a purse or daypack); check with your airline or at Britain's transportation website for the latest (www.dft.gov.uk).

Practicalities

Emergency and Medical Help: In Great Britain, dial 999 for police help or a medical emergency. If you get sick, do as the Brits do and go to a pharmacist for advice. Or ask at your B&B or hotel for help—they'll know the nearest medical and emergency services.

Theft or Loss: To replace a passport, you'll need to go in person to an embassy or consulate (see page 866). If your credit and debit cards disappear, cancel and replace them (see "Damage Control for Lost Cards" on page 16). File a police report, either on the spot or within a day or two; you'll need it to submit an insurance claim for lost or stolen railpasses or travel gear, and it can help with replacing your passport or credit and debit cards. For more information, see www.ricksteves.com/help. Precautionary measures can minimize the effects of loss—back up photos and other files frequently.

Time Zones: Britain, which is one hour earlier than most of continental Europe, is five/eight hours ahead of the East/West coasts of the US. The exceptions are the beginning and end of Daylight Saving Time: Europe "springs forward" the last Sunday in March (two weeks after most of North America), and "falls back" the last Sunday in October (one week before North America). For a handy online time converter, try www.timeanddate.com/world-clock.

Business Hours: In England, most stores are open Monday through Saturday from roughly 10:00 to 17:00. In London, stores stay open later on Wednesday or Thursday (until 19:00 or 20:00), depending on the neighborhood. Saturdays are virtually weekdays, with earlier closing hours. Sundays have the same pros and cons as they do for travelers in the US: Sightseeing attractions are generally open; banks and many shops are closed; public transportation options are fewer (for example, no bus service to or from smaller towns); there's no rush hour. Rowdy evenings are rare on Sundays.

Watt's Up? Europe's electrical system is 220 volts, instead of North America's 110 volts. Most newer electronics (such as laptops, battery chargers, and hair dryers) convert automatically, so

you won't need a converter, but you will need an adapter plug with three square prongs, sold inexpensively at travel stores in the US, and in British airports and drugstores. Avoid bringing older appliances that don't automatically convert voltage; instead, buy a cheap replacement in Europe. Low-cost hairdryers and other small appliances are sold at Superdrug, Boots, and Argos stores (ask your hotelier for the closest branch).

Discounts: Discounts (called "concessions" or "concs" in Britain) are not listed in this book. However, many sights offer discounts for youths (up to age 18), students (with proper identification cards, www.isic.org), families, seniors (loosely defined as retirees or those willing to call themselves a senior), and groups of 10 or more. Always ask. Some discounts are available only for EU citizens.

Money

This section offers advice on how to pay for purchases on your trip (including getting cash from ATMs and paying with plastic), dealing with lost or stolen cards, VAT (sales tax) refunds, and tipping.

What to Bring

Bring both a credit card and a debit card. You'll use the debit card at cash machines (ATMs) to withdraw pounds for most purchases, and the credit card to pay for larger items. Some travelers carry a third card, in case one gets demagnetized or eaten by a temperamental machine.

For an emergency reserve, bring several hundred dollars in hard cash in $20 bills. If you have to exchange the bills, go to a bank; avoid using currency-exchange booths because of their lousy rates and/or outrageous fees.

Cash

Cash is just as desirable in Britain as it is at home. Small businesses (hotels, restaurants, and shops) prefer that you pay your bills with cash. Some vendors will charge you extra for using a credit card, and some won't take credit cards at all. Cash is the best—and sometimes only—way to pay for bus fare, taxis, and local guides.

Throughout Europe, ATMs are the standard way for travelers to get cash. Most ATMs in Britain are located outside a bank. But stay away from "independent" ATMs such as Travelex, Euronet, and Forex, which charge huge commissions and have terrible exchange rates.

Exchange Rate

I list prices in pounds (£) throughout this book.

1 British pound (£1) = about $1.60

While the euro (€) is now the currency of most of Europe, Britain is sticking with its pound sterling. The British pound (£), also called a "quid," is broken into 100 pence (p). Pence means "cents." You'll find coins ranging from 1p to £2, and bills from £5 to £50. Counterfeit pound coins are easy to spot (real coins have an inscription on their outside rims; the rims on the fakes look like tree bark).

London is so expensive that some travelers try to kid themselves that pounds are dollars. But when they get home, that £1,000 Visa bill isn't asking for $1,000...it wants $1,600. (Check www.oanda.com for the latest exchange rates.)

To withdraw money from an ATM (which locals call "cashpoints"), you'll need a debit card (ideally with a Visa or MasterCard logo for maximum usability), plus a PIN code. Know your PIN code in numbers; there are no letters on European keypads. Although you can use a credit card for an ATM transaction, it only makes sense in an emergency, because it's considered a cash advance (borrowed at a high interest rate) rather than a withdrawal. Try to withdraw large sums of money to reduce the number of per-transaction bank fees you'll pay.

For increased security, shield the keypad when entering your PIN code, and don't use an ATM if anything on the front of the machine looks loose or damaged (a sign that someone may have attached a "skimming" device to capture account information). Some travelers make a point of monitoring their accounts while traveling to detect any unauthorized transactions.

Even in jolly olde England, pickpockets target tourists. To safeguard your cash, wear a money belt—a pouch with a strap that you buckle around your waist like a belt and tuck under your clothes. Keep your cash, credit cards, and passport secure in your money belt, and carry only a day's spending money in your front pocket.

Credit and Debit Cards

For purchases, Visa and MasterCard are more commonly accepted than American Express. Just like at home, credit and debit cards work easily at larger hotels, restaurants, and shops. I typically use my debit card to withdraw cash to pay for most purchases. I use my credit card only in a few specific situations: to book hotel reservations by phone, to cover major expenses (such as car rentals, plane tickets, and long hotel stays), and to pay for things near the end of my trip (to avoid another visit to the ATM). While you could use a debit card to make most large purchases, using a credit card offers a greater degree of fraud protection (because debit cards draw funds directly from your account).

Ask Your Credit- or Debit-Card Company: Before your trip, contact the company that issued your debit or credit cards.

• Confirm your card will work overseas, and alert them that you'll be using it in Europe; otherwise, they may deny transactions if they perceive unusual spending patterns.

• Ask for the specifics on transaction **fees.** When you use your credit or debit card—either for purchases or ATM withdrawals—you'll typically be charged additional "international transaction" fees of up to 3 percent (1 percent is normal) plus $5 per transaction. If your card's fees seem high, consider getting a different card just for your trip: Capital One (www.capitalone.com) and most credit unions have low-to-no international fees.

• If you plan to withdraw cash from ATMs, confirm your daily **withdrawal limit,** and if necessary, ask your bank to adjust it. Some travelers prefer a high limit that allows them to take out more cash at each ATM stop (saving on bank fees), while others prefer to set a lower limit in case their card is stolen. Note that foreign banks also set maximum withdrawal amounts for their ATMs.

• Get your bank's emergency phone number in the US (but not its 800 number, which isn't accessible from overseas) to call collect if you have a problem.

• Ask for your credit card's **PIN** in case you need to make an emergency cash withdrawal or encounter Europe's "chip-and-PIN" system; the bank won't tell you your PIN over the phone, so allow time for it to be mailed to you.

Chip and PIN: Europeans are increasingly using chip-and-PIN cards, which are embedded with an electronic security chip (in addition to the magnetic stripe found on American-style cards). With this system, the purchaser punches in a PIN rather than signing a receipt. Your American-style card might not work at automated payment machines, such as those at train and subway stations, toll roads, parking garages, luggage lockers, and self-serve gas pumps.

If you have problems using your American card in a chip-and-PIN machine, here are some suggestions: For either a debit card or credit card, try entering that card's PIN when prompted. (Note that your credit-card PIN may not be the same as your debit-card PIN; you'll need to ask your bank for your credit-card PIN.) If your cards still don't work, look for a machine that takes cash, seek out a clerk who might be able to process the transaction manually, or ask a local if you can pay them cash to run the transaction on their card.

And don't panic. Many travelers who use only magnetic-stripe cards never have a problem. Still, it pays to carry plenty of cash (you can always use an ATM to withdraw cash with your magnetic-stripe debit card).

If you're still concerned, you can apply for a chip card in the US (though I think it's overkill). One option is the no-annual-fee GlobeTrek Visa, offered by Andrews Federal Credit Union in Maryland (open to all US residents; see www.andrewsfcu.org).

Dynamic Currency Conversion: If merchants offer to convert your purchase price into dollars (called dynamic currency conversion, or DCC), refuse this "service." You'll pay even more in fees for the expensive convenience of seeing your charge in dollars.

Damage Control for Lost Cards

If you lose your credit, debit, or ATM card, you can stop people from using your card by reporting the loss immediately to the respective global customer-assistance centers. Call these 24-hour US numbers collect: Visa (tel. 303/967-1096), MasterCard (tel. 636/722-7111), or American Express (tel. 336/393-1111). European toll-free numbers (listed by country) can be found at the websites for Visa and MasterCard.

Providing the following information will allow for a quicker cancellation of your missing card: full card number, whether you are the primary or secondary cardholder, the cardholder's name exactly as printed on the card, billing address, home phone number, circumstances of the loss or theft, and identification verification (your birth date, your mother's maiden name, or your Social Security number—memorize this, don't carry a copy). If you are the secondary cardholder, you'll also need to provide the primary cardholder's identification-verification details. You can generally receive a temporary card within two or three business days in Europe (see www.ricksteves.com/help for more).

If you report your loss within two days, you typically won't be responsible for any unauthorized transactions on your account, although many banks charge a liability fee of $50.

Tipping

Tipping in Britain isn't as automatic and generous as it is in the US, but for special service, tips are appreciated, if not expected. As in the US, the proper amount depends on your resources, tipping philosophy, and the circumstances, but some general guidelines apply.

Restaurants: At pubs where you order at the counter, you don't have to tip. (Regular customers ordering a round sometimes say, "Add one for yourself" as a tip for drinks ordered at the bar—

but this isn't expected.) At a pub or restaurant with waitstaff, check the menu or your bill to see if the service is included; if not, tip about 10 percent. Many restaurants in London now add a 12.5 percent "optional" tip onto the bill—read your bill carefully, and tip only what you think the service warrants.

Taxis: To tip the cabbie, round up. For a typical ride, round up your fare a bit (for instance, if the fare is £4.50, give £5; for a £28 fare, give £30). If the cabbie hauls your bags and zips you to the airport to help you catch your flight, you might want to toss in a little more. But if you feel like you're being driven in circles or otherwise ripped off, skip the tip.

Services: In general, if someone in the service industry does a super job for you, a small tip of a pound or two is appropriate, but not required. If you're not sure whether (or how much) to tip for a service, ask your hotelier or the TI.

Getting a VAT Refund

Wrapped into the purchase price of your British souvenirs is a Value-Added Tax (VAT) of 20 percent. You're entitled to get most of that tax back if you spend a significant amount, set by the retailer (Harrods, for example, won't process a refund unless you spend at least £50). Typically, you must ring up the minimum at a single retailer—you can't add up your purchases from various shops to reach the required amount.

Getting your refund is usually straightforward and, if you buy a substantial amount of souvenirs, well worth the hassle. If you're lucky, the merchant will subtract the tax when you make your purchase. (This is more likely to occur if the store ships the goods to your home.) Otherwise, you'll need to:

Get the paperwork. Have the merchant completely fill out the necessary refund document (either an official VAT customs form, or the shop or refund company's own version of it). You'll have to present your passport at the store. Get the paperwork done before you leave the shop to ensure you'll have everything you need (including your original sales receipt).

Get your stamp at the border or airport. Process your VAT document at your last stop in the European Union (such as at the airport) with the customs agent who deals with VAT refunds. Arrive an additional hour early before you need to check in for your flight, to allow time to find the local customs office—and to stand in line. Keep your purchases readily available for viewing by the customs agent (ideally in your carry-on bag—don't make the mistake of checking the bag with your purchases before you've seen the agent). You're not supposed to use your purchased goods before you leave. If you show up at customs wearing your new

INTRODUCTION

Wellingtons, officials might look the other way—or deny you a refund.

Collect your refund. You'll need to return your stamped document to the retailer or its representative. Many merchants work with a service, such as Global Blue or Premier Tax Free, which have offices at major airports, ports, or border crossings (either before or after security, probably strategically located near a duty-free shop). These services, which extract a 4 percent fee, can refund your money immediately in cash or credit your card (within two billing cycles). If the retailer handles VAT refunds directly, it's up to you to contact the merchant for your refund. You can mail the documents from home, or more quickly, from your point of departure (using an envelope you've prepared in advance or one that's been provided by the merchant). You'll then have to wait—it can take months.

Customs for American Shoppers

You are allowed to take home $800 worth of items per person duty-free, once every 30 days. You can also bring in duty-free a liter of alcohol. As for food, you can take home many processed and packaged foods: vacuum-packed cheeses, dried herbs, jams, baked goods, candy, chocolate, oil, vinegar, mustard, and honey. Fresh fruits and vegetables and most meats are not allowed. Any liquid-containing foods must be packed in checked luggage, a potential recipe for disaster. To check customs rules and duty rates, visit http://help.cbp.gov.

Sightseeing

Sightseeing can be hard work. Use these tips to make your visits to England's finest sights meaningful, fun, efficient, and painless.

Plan Ahead

Set up an itinerary that allows you to fit in all your must-see sights. For a one-stop look at opening hours in the bigger cities, see the "At a Glance" sidebars throughout this book. Most sights keep stable hours, but you can easily confirm the latest by checking with the TI or visiting museum websites.

Don't put off visiting a must-see sight—you never know when a place will close unexpectedly for a holiday, strike, or restoration. Many museums are closed or have reduced hours at least a few days a year, especially on holidays such as Christmas, New Year's, and Bank holidays in May and August. A list of holidays is on page 892; check museum websites for possible closures during your trip. Off-season, many museums have shorter hours.

Going at the right time helps avoid crowds. This book offers tips on specific sights. Try visiting popular sights very early, at lunch, or very late. Evening visits are usually peaceful, with fewer crowds. For specifics on London at night, see the sidebar on page 102.

Study up. To get the most out of the self-guided walks and sight descriptions in this book, read them before you visit.

At Sights

Here's what you can typically expect:

Entering: Be warned that you may not be allowed to enter if you arrive 30 to 60 minutes before closing time. And guards start ushering people out well before the actual closing time, so don't save the best for last.

Some important sights have a security check, where you must open your bag or send it through a metal detector. Some sights require you to check daypacks and coats. (If you'd rather not check your daypack, try carrying it tucked under your arm like a purse as you enter.)

At ticket desks, you'll constantly see references to "Gift Aid"— a complicated tax-deduction scheme that benefits both museums (which are often classified as charities) and their patrons who are British taxpayers. But unless you pay taxes in Britain, you can ignore this.

Photography: If the museum's photo policy isn't clearly posted, ask a guard. Generally, taking photos without a flash or tripod is allowed. Some sights ban sights ban photos altogether.

Temporary Exhibits: Museums may show special exhibits in addition to their permanent collection. Some exhibits are included in the entry price, while others come at an extra cost (which you may have to pay even if you don't want to see the exhibit).

Expect Changes: Artwork can be on tour, on loan, out sick, or shifted at the whim of the curator. To adapt, pick up a floor plan as you enter, and ask museum staff if you can't find a particular item.

Audioguides: Many museums rent audioguides, which generally offer excellent recorded descriptions (about £3.50; sometimes included with admission). If you bring your own earbuds, you can enjoy better sound and avoid holding the device to your ear. To save money, bring a Y-jack and share one audioguide with your travel partner. Increasingly, museums are offering apps (often free) that you can download to your mobile device. I've produced free downloadable audio tours of the major sights in London; see page 51.

Guided tours are most likely to be available during peak season (they can be included with your admission or cost up to £8, and range widely in quality). If sights offer short films featuring their highlights and history, they're generally well worth your time.

Services: Important sights and cathedrals may have an on-site café or cafeteria (usually a good place to rejuvenate during a long visit). The WCs are usually free and nearly always clean.

Before Leaving: At the gift shop, scan the postcard rack or thumb through a guidebook to be sure you haven't overlooked something that you'd like to see.

Every sight or museum offers more than what is covered in this book. Use the information in this book as an introduction—not the final word.

Sightseeing Memberships

Many sights in England are managed by either English Heritage or the National Trust (the sights don't overlap). Both organizations sell annual memberships that allow free or discounted entry to the sights they supervise; the English Heritage also sells passes for overseas visitors. You can join the National Trust or English Heritage online or at just about any of their sights.

Membership in **English Heritage** includes free entry to more than 400 sights in England and half-price admission to about 100 more sights in Scotland and Wales. For most travelers, the **Overseas Visitor Pass** is a better choice than the pricier one-year membership (Visitor Pass: £24/9 days, £28/16 days, discounts for couples and families; Membership: £48 for one person, £84 for two, discounts for seniors and students, children under 19 free; toll tel. 0870-333-1182, www.english-heritage.org.uk).

Membership in the **National Trust** is best suited for garden-and-estate enthusiasts, ideally those traveling by car. It covers more than 350 historic houses, manors, and gardens throughout Great Britain. From the US, it's easy to join online through the Royal Oak Foundation, the National Trust's American affiliate (one-year membership: $65 for one person, $95 for two, family and student memberships, www.royal-oak.org). Children under age five are always admitted free to National Trust properties (www.national-trust.org.uk).

Factors to Consider: If you have children over the age of five and you're all avid sightseers, consider the National Trust family membership—but remember that your kids get in free or cheaply at most sights. Similarly, people over 60 get "concessions" (discounted prices) at many English sights (and can get a senior discount on an English Heritage membership). If you're traveling by car and can get to the more remote sights, you're more likely to get your money's worth out of a pass or membership, especially during peak season (Easter-Oct). If you're traveling off-season (Nov-Easter) when many of the sights are closed, the deals are a lesser value.

The Bottom Line: These various deals can save a busy sightseer money, but only if you choose carefully. Make a list of the sights you plan to see, check which ones are covered (visit the websites for each pass), and then add up the total if you were to pay individual admissions to the covered sights. Compare the total to the cost of the pass or membership. Keep in mind that an advantage to any of these deals is that you'll feel free to dip into lesser sights that normally aren't worth the cost of their admission.

Sleeping

I favor hotels and restaurants that are handy to your sightseeing activities. In England, small bed-and-breakfast places (B&Bs) generally provide the best value, though I also include some bigger hotels. Rather than list lodgings scattered throughout a city, I describe two or three favorite neighborhoods and recommend the best accommodations values in each, from dorm beds to fancy doubles with all the comforts. Outside of pricey London, you can expect to find good doubles for £50-100 ($80-160), including cooked breakfasts and tax. (For specifics on London, see page 167.)

A major feature of this book is its extensive and opinionated listing of good-value rooms. I like places that are clean, central, relatively quiet at night, reasonably priced, friendly, small enough to have a hands-on owner and stable staff, run with a respect for British traditions, and not listed in other guidebooks. (In Britain, for me, six of these eight criteria means it's a keeper.) I'm more impressed by a convenient location and a fun-loving philosophy than flat-screen TVs and a pricey laundry service.

Book your accommodations well in advance if you'll be traveling during busy times. Mark these dates in red on your travel calendar: New Year's Day, Good Friday through Easter Monday, the Bank Holidays that occur on the first and last Mondays in May and on the last Monday in August, Christmas, and December 26 (Boxing Day). See page 892 for a list of major holidays and festivals in England; for tips on making reservations, see page 28.

England has a rating system for hotels and B&Bs. Its diamonds and stars are supposed to imply quality, but I find that they mean only that the place sporting these symbols is paying dues to the tourist board. Rating systems often have little to do with value.

Rates and Deals

I've described my recommended accommodations using a Sleep Code (see sidebar). Prices listed are for one-night stays in peak

Sleep Code

(£1 = about $1.60, country code: 44)

Price Rankings

To help you easily sort through my listings, I've divided the accommodations into three categories based on the price for a double room with bath during high season:

> $$$ **Higher Priced**
> $$ **Moderately Priced**
> $ **Lower Priced**

I always rate hostels as $, whether or not they have double rooms, because they have the cheapest beds in town. Prices can change without notice; verify the hotel's current rates online or by email.

Abbreviations

To pack maximum information into minimum space, I use the following code to describe accommodations in this book. Prices listed are per room, not per person. When a price range is given for a type of room (such as double rooms listing for £80-120), it means the price fluctuates with the season, size of room, or length of stay; expect to pay the upper end for peak-season stays.

S = Single room (or price for one person in a double).

D = Double or twin room. "Double beds" can be two twins sheeted together and are usually big enough for non-romantic couples.

T = Triple (generally a double bed with a single).

Q = Quad (usually two double beds; adding an extra child's bed to a T is usually cheaper).

b = Private bathroom with toilet and shower or tub.

s = Private shower or tub only. (The toilet is down the hall.)

According to this code, a couple staying at a "Db-£80" B&B would pay a total of £80 (about $130) for a double room with a private bathroom. Unless otherwise noted, breakfast is included and credit cards are accepted. For most places, the rates I list include the 20 percent VAT tax—but it's smart to ask when you book your room.

There's almost always Wi-Fi and/or a guest computer available, either free or for a fee.

season, usually include a hearty breakfast, and assume you're booking directly (not through an online hotel-booking engine or TI). Booking services extract a commission from the hotel, which logically closes the door on special deals. Book direct.

Many hotels use "dynamic pricing," which means room rates change from day to day depending on demand. This makes it extremely difficult to predict what you will pay. When possible, I've tried to list just one price, which is what you'll most likely pay for a standard room during the busy season (but ignoring the dramatically inflated rates hotels charge for special events a few days each year). This rate is intended as a rough guideline, and may vary significantly based on demand—check the hotel's website, or email them, to find out specifics for the date of your visit. For other hotels, I list a range of prices. If the rate you're offered is at or near the bottom of my printed range, it's likely a good deal.

Given the economic downturn, hoteliers and B&B operators are often willing and eager to make a deal. I'd suggest emailing several hotels or B&Bs to ask for their best price. Comparison-shop and make your choice.

As you look over the listings, you'll notice that some accommodations promise special prices to Rick Steves readers who book directly with the hotel. To get these rates, you must book direct (that is, *not* through a booking site like TripAdvisor or Booking. com), mention this book when you reserve, and then show the book upon arrival. Rick Steves discounts apply to readers with ebooks as well as printed books. Because we trust hotels to honor this, please let me know if you don't receive a listed discount. Note, though, that discounts understandably may not be applied to promotional rates.

In general, prices can soften if you do any of the following: offer to pay cash, stay at least three nights, or mention this book. You can also try asking for a cheaper room or a discount, or offer to skip breakfast. When establishing prices, confirm if the charge is per person or per room (if a price is too good to be true, it's probably per person). Because many places in Britain charge per person, small groups often pay the same for a single and a double as they would for a triple. In this book, however, room prices are listed per room, not per person.

Types of Accommodations

Hotels

Many of my recommended hotels have three floors of rooms and steep stairs; expect good exercise and be happy you packed light. You'll generally find an elevator (called a "lift" here) only at larger hotels. If you're concerned about stairs, call and ask about ground-floor rooms or pay for a hotel with a lift. Air-conditioning is rare

(I've noted which of my listings have it), but most places have fans. On hot summer nights, you'll want your window open—though in big cities, you may have to put up with street noise.

"Twin" means two single beds, and "double" means one double bed (but in my listings, I list all two-person rooms as "doubles," regardless of bed type). If you will take either bed configuration, let the hotel know, or you might be needlessly turned away. Most hotels offer family deals, which means that parents with young children can easily get a room with an extra child's bed or a discount for larger rooms. Call to negotiate the price. Teenage kids are generally charged as adults. Kids under five almost always sleep free.

Understand the terminology: "En suite" (pronounced "on sweet") means the room has a bathroom (toilet and either a tub or shower). Hotels sometimes call a basic en suite room a "standard" room to differentiate it from a fancier "superior" or "deluxe" room—if you're not sure, ask for clarification.

Note that to be called a "hotel," a place technically must have certain amenities, including a 24-hour reception (though this rule is loosely applied). TVs are standard in rooms, but may come with only the traditional five British channels (no cable). All of Britain's accommodations are now non-smoking.

If you're arriving early in the morning, your room probably won't be ready. You should be able to safely check your bag at the hotel and dive right into sightseeing.

Hoteliers (and B&B hosts) can be a great help and source of advice. Most know their city well and can assist you with everything from public transit and airport connections to finding a good restaurant, the nearest Internet café, or a self-service launderette.

Even at the best places, mechanical breakdowns occur: Air-conditioning malfunctions, sinks leak, hot water turns cold, and toilets gurgle and smell. Report your concerns clearly and calmly at the front desk. For more complicated problems, don't expect instant results.

If you suspect night noise will be a problem (if, for instance, your room is over a pub), ask for a quiet room in the back or on an upper floor. To guard against theft in your room, keep valuables out of sight. Some rooms come with a safe, and other hotels have safes at the front desk. I've never bothered using one.

Checkout can pose problems if surprise charges pop up on your bill. If you settle up your bill the afternoon before you leave, you'll have time to discuss and address any points of contention (before 19:00, when the night shift usually arrives).

Above all, keep a positive attitude. Remember, you're on vacation. If your hotel is a disappointment, spend more time out enjoying the city you came to see.

Modern Hotel Chains: While most travelers prefer the

classic British hotel or B&B experience, chain hotels—which are popping up in bigger cities all over Britain—can be a great value. They offer simple, clean, and modern rooms for up to four people (two adults/two children) for £60-100, depending on the location (more expensive in London). Rooms come with a private shower, WC, and TV. Some hotels are located near the train station, on major highways, or outside the city center. What you lose in charm, you gain in savings.

These hotels are as cozy as a Motel 6, but they are especially worth considering for families, as kids sometimes stay for free. There's usually an attached restaurant, good security, an elevator, and a 24-hour staffed reception desk. Breakfast is always extra.

Book through the hotel's website, as it is often the easiest way to make reservations, and will generally net you a discount. To find the going rate, punch in your dates on the hotel's online reservation form. Like airline tickets, pricing changes from day to day or week to week according to demand. Expect higher rates on weekdays in business-travel destinations, and pricier weekends in tourist-oriented places. Either way, Sunday nights can be shockingly cheap. The best deals typically require a prepaid, nonrefundable, three-week advance purchase.

The biggest chains are **Premier Inn** (www.premierinn.com, reservations tel. 0870-242-8000) and **Travelodge** (www.travelodge.co.uk, reservations tel. 0870-085-0950). Both have attractive deals for prepaid or advance bookings. Other chains operating in Britain include the Irish **Jurys Inn** (www.jurysinns.com) and the French-owned **Ibis** (www.ibishotel.com). Couples can consider **Holiday Inn Express,** which is spreading throughout England. Like a Holiday Inn lite, with cheaper prices and no restaurant, many of these hotels allow only two per room, although some take up to four (make sure Express is part of the name or you'll be paying more for a regular Holiday Inn, www.hiexpress.co.uk).

EasyHotel is a different animal—an extremely basic, pay-as-you-go bargain chain with several branches in London (see page 184 for details).

For recommendations for online hotel deals in London, as well as using auction-type sites, see page 167.

Hotels Beyond This Book: If you're traveling beyond my recommended destinations, you'll find accommodations where you need them. Any town with tourists has a TI that books rooms or can give you a list and point you in the right direction—but book direct for the best prices. In the absence of a TI, ask people on the street or in pubs or restaurants for help. Online, visit www.smoothhound.co.uk, which offers a range of accommodations for towns throughout the UK (searchable by town, airport, hotel name, or price range).

Small Hotels and B&Bs

Places with "townhouse" or "house" (such as "London House") are like big B&Bs or small family-run hotels—with fewer amenities but more character than a hotel. B&Bs range from large guest-houses with 15-20 rooms to small homes renting out a spare bedroom, but they typically have six rooms or fewer. The philosophy of the management determines the character of a place more than its size and facilities offered. I avoid places run as a business by absentee owners. My top listings are run by people who enjoy welcoming the world to their breakfast table.

Compared to hotels, B&Bs give you double the cultural intimacy for half the price. While you may lose some of the conveniences of a hotel—such as fancy lobbies, in-room phones, and frequent bedsheet changes—I happily make the trade-off for the lower rates and personal touches. If you have a reasonable but limited budget, skip hotels and go the B&B way. Many B&Bs now take credit cards, but may add the card service fee to your bill (about 3 percent).

You'll generally pay £30-50 (about $45-80) per person for a double room in a B&B in Britain. When considering the price of a B&B or small hotel, remember you're getting two breakfasts (up to a £25 value) for each double room.

Remember, "en suite" means a room with an attached bathroom. A room with a "private bathroom" can mean that the bathroom is all yours, but it's across the hall. Some B&Bs have rooms with access to a bathroom that's down the hall and shared with other guests. Figuring there's little difference between en suite and private rooms, some places charge the same for both. If you want your own bathroom inside the room, request en suite.

B&Bs are not hotels. Think of your host as a friendly acquaintance who's invited you to stay in her home, rather than someone you're paying to wait on you.

B&B proprietors are selective as to whom they invite in for the night. At many B&Bs, children are not welcome. If you'll be staying for more than one night, you are a "desirable." In popular weekend-getaway spots, you're unlikely to find a place to take you for Saturday night only. If my listings are full, ask for guidance. Mentioning this book can help. Owners usually work together and can call up an ally to land you a bed.

Small places usually serve a hearty fried breakfast of eggs and much more (for details on breakfast, see page 34). Because your B&B owner is also the cook, the time span when breakfast is served is usually limited (typically about an hour—confirm before you turn in for the night). It's an unwritten rule that guests shouldn't show up at the very end of the breakfast period and expect a full cooked breakfast (try to arrive at least 15 minutes before the ending time). If you do arrive late (or need to leave before breakfast is served), most hosts are happy to let you help yourself to cereal, fruit, juice, and coffee; ask if it's possible.

Most B&Bs stock rooms with an electric kettle, along with cups, tea bags, and coffee packets.

Americans sometimes assume they'll get new towels each day. The English don't, and neither should you. Hang towels up to dry and reuse.

Be aware of luggage etiquette. A large bag in a compact older building can easily turn even the most graceful of us into a bull in an English china shop. If you've got a backpack, don't wear it indoors. If your host offers to carry your bag upstairs, accept—they're adept at maneuvering luggage up tiny staircases without damaging the walls and banisters. Finally, use your room's luggage racks—putting bags on empty beds can dirty and scuff nice comforters. Treat these lovingly maintained homes as you would a friend's house.

Electrical outlets sometimes have switches that turn the current on or off; if your electrical appliance isn't working, flip the switch at the outlet. When you unplug your appliance, don't forget your adapter—most B&Bs have boxes of various adapters left behind by guests (which is handy if you left yours at the last place).

You're likely to encounter unusual bathroom fixtures. The "pump toilet" has a flushing handle that doesn't kick in unless you push it just right: too hard or too soft, and it won't go. (Be decisive but not ruthless.) There's also the "dial-a-shower," an electronic box under the showerhead where you'll turn a dial to select the heat of the water and (sometimes with a separate dial or button) turn on or shut off the flow of water. If you can't find the switch to turn on the shower, it may be just outside the bathroom.

Many B&Bs and small hotels are in older buildings, with thin walls and doors, and sometimes creaky floorboards. This can make for a noisy night, especially with people walking down the hall to use the bathroom. If you're a light sleeper, bring earplugs. And please be quiet in the halls and in your rooms (talk softly, and keep the TV volume low). Those of us getting up early will thank you for it.

Your B&B bedroom probably won't include a phone. In this mobile-phone age, street phone booths can be few and far between. Some B&B owners will allow you to use their phone, but many are disinclined to let you ring up charges. That's because most British people pay for each local call, and rates are expensive. Therefore, to be polite, ask to use their phone only in an emergency—and offer to use an international calling card or to pay for the call. If you plan to be staying in B&Bs and making frequent calls, consider buying a British mobile phone (see page 859).

Making Hotel Reservations

Reserve your rooms several weeks in advance—or as soon as you've pinned down your travel dates—particularly if you'll be traveling during peak times. Note that some national holidays jam things up and merit your making reservations far in advance (see "Holidays and Festivals" on page 892).

Requesting a Reservation: It's usually easiest to book your room through the hotel's website. Many have a reservation-request form built right in. (For the best rates, be sure to use the hotel's official site and not a booking agency's site.) Simpler websites will generate an email to the hotelier with your request. If there's no reservation form, or for complicated requests, send an email (see below for a sample request). The hotelier wants to know:

- the number and type of rooms you need
- the number of nights you'll stay
- your date of arrival
- your date of departure
- any special needs (such as bathroom in the room or down the hall, cheapest room, twin beds vs. double bed, crib, air-conditioning, quiet, view, ground floor or no stairs, and so on)

If you request a room by email, use the European style for writing dates: day/month/year. For example, for a two-night stay in July 2015, ask for "1 double room for 2 nights, arrive 16/07/15, depart 18/07/15." Make sure you mention any discounts—for Rick Steves readers or otherwise—when you make the reservation.

Confirming a Reservation: When the hotel replies with its room availability and rates, just email back to confirm your reservation. Most places will request a credit-card number to hold your room. While you can email it (I do), it's safer to share that confidential info via a phone call, two emails (splitting your number between them), or the hotel's secure online reservation form. On the small chance that a hotel loses track of your reservation, bring along a hard copy of their confirmation.

Canceling a Reservation: If you must cancel your reservation, it's courteous—and smart—to do so with as much notice as possible, especially for smaller family-run places. Simply make a quick phone call or send an email. Request confirmation of your cancellation in case you are accidentally billed.

Be warned that cancellation policies can be strict; read the

With so many people traveling these days with a laptop or mobile device, nearly every B&B comes equipped with free Wi-Fi (as noted in my accommodations listings); however, the signal frequently won't reach up many stairs, so you may have to sit in the lounge to access it.

Many B&B owners are also pet owners. And, while pets are

From:	rick@ricksteves.com
Sent:	Today
To:	info@hotelcentral.com
Subject:	Reservation request for 19-22 July

Dear Hotel Central,

I would like to reserve a room for 2 people for 3 nights, arriving 19 July and departing 22 July. If possible, I would like a quiet room with a double bed and a bathroom inside the room.

Please let me know if you have a room available and the price.

Thank you!
Rick Steves

fine print or ask about these before you book. For example, if you cancel on short notice, you could lose your deposit, or be billed for one night or even your entire stay. Internet deals may require prepayment, with no refunds for cancellations.

Reconfirming a Reservation: Call to reconfirm your room reservation a few days in advance. Smaller hotels and B&Bs appreciate knowing your estimated time of arrival. If you'll be arriving late (after 17:00), let them know.

Reserving Rooms as You Travel: You can make reservations as you travel, calling hotels and B&Bs a few days to a week before your arrival. If you'd rather travel without any reservations at all, you'll have greater success snaring rooms if you arrive at your destination early in the day. When you anticipate crowds (weekends are worst), call hotels at about 9:00 or 10:00 on the day you plan to arrive, when the receptionist knows who'll be checking out and which rooms will be available.

Although most TIs in Britain can book you a room in their town, and also often in nearby towns, they generally charge a booking fee, and you'll pay a small deposit. While this can be useful in a pinch, but it's a better deal for everyone (except the TIs) to book direct, using the listings in this book.

Phoning: For tips on how to call hotels overseas, see page 858.

rarely allowed into guest rooms, and B&B proprietors are typically very tidy, visitors with pet allergies might be bothered. I've tried to list which B&Bs have pets, but if you're allergic, ask about pets when you reserve.

Remember that you may need to pay cash for your room. Plan ahead so you have enough cash to pay up when you check out.

Hostels

England has hundreds of hostels of all shapes and sizes. Choose your hostel selectively. Hostels can be historic castles or depressing tenements, serene and comfy or overrun by noisy school groups. You'll pay about £20-25 ($32-40) for a bed. Travelers of any age are welcome if they don't mind dorm-style accommodations and meeting other travelers. Most hostels offer kitchen facilities, guest computers, Wi-Fi, and a self-service laundry. Nowadays, concerned about bedbugs, hostels are likely to provide all bedding, including sheets. Family and private rooms may be available on request.

Independent hostels tend to be easygoing, colorful, and informal (no membership required); Hostelworld.com is the standard way backpackers search and book hostels these days, but also try www.hostelz.com, www.hostels.com, and www.hostelbookers.com.

Official hostels are part of Hostelling International (HI) and share an online booking site (www.hihostels.com). HI hostels typically require that you either have a membership card or pay extra per night. For more England hostel listings, consult www.yha.org.uk.

Other Options

Whether you're in a city or the countryside, renting an apartment, house, or villa can be a fun and cost-effective way to delve into Europe. Websites such as HomeAway.com and its sister site VRBO.com let you correspond directly with European property owners or managers.

Airbnb.com makes it reasonably easy to find a place to sleep in someone's home. Beds range from air-mattress-in-living-room basic to plush-B&B-suite posh. If you want a place to sleep that's free, Couchsurfing.com is a vagabond's alternative to Airbnb. It lists millions of outgoing members, who host fellow "surfers" in their homes.

Eating

England's reputation for miserable food, while once well-deserved, is now sorely dated. A few names familiar stateside—Jamie Oliver, Gordon Ramsay, Nigella Lawson—are just the tip of the culinary iceberg of British celebrity chefs prodding their national cuisine forward. Over the last generation, British cooking has embraced international influences and good-quality ingredients, making "modern British" food something to be truly proud of. While some dreary pub food still exists, you'll generally find the cuisine scene here lively, trendy, and pleasantly surprising. (Unfortunately, it's also expensive.) Even the basic, traditional pub grub has gone up-

---

Sounds Bad, Tastes Good

The English have a knack for making food sound funny. Here are a few examples:

Toad in the Hole: Sausage dipped in batter and fried
Bubble and Squeak: Leftovers, usually potatoes, veggies, and meat, all fried up together
Bap: Small roll
Treacle: Golden syrup, similar to light molasses

---

market—more and more "gastropubs" are serving locally sourced meats and fresh vegetables. Even basic pubs are more likely to dish up homemade, creative dishes rather than microwaved pies, soggy fries, and mushy peas.

All indoor English eateries are now smoke-free. Establishments keep their smokers contented by allowing them to light up in doorways and on outdoor patios.

When restaurant-hunting, choose a spot filled with locals, not tourists. Venturing even a block or two off the main drag leads to higher-quality food for less. Locals know they can eat better at lower-rent locales.

Budget Eating Tips

You have plenty of inexpensive choices: pub grub, daily lunch and early-bird specials, ethnic restaurants, cafeterias, fast food, picnics, fish-and-chips, greasy-spoon cafés, pizza, and more.

I've found that portions are huge and, with locals feeling the economic pinch, **sharing plates** is generally just fine. Ordering two drinks, a soup or side salad, and splitting a £10 meat pie can make a good, filling meal. If you are on a limited budget, share a main course in a more expensive place for a nicer eating experience.

Pub grub is the most atmospheric budget option. You'll usually get hearty lunches and dinners priced reasonably at £6-10 under ancient timbers (see "Pubs," later). Gastropubs, with better food, are more expensive.

Classier restaurants have some affordable deals. Lunch is usually cheaper than dinner; a top-end, £25-for-dinner-type restaurant often serves the same quality two-course lunch deals for £10-12. Look for early-bird dinner specials, allowing you to eat well and affordably (usually last order by 18:30 or 19:00).

Ethnic restaurants from all over the world add spice to England's cuisine scene. Eating Indian, Bangladeshi, Chinese, or Thai is cheap (even cheaper if you do takeout). Middle Eastern stands sell gyro sandwiches, falafel, and *shwarmas* (lamb in pita bread). An Indian samosa (greasy, flaky meat-and-vegetable pie) costs £2, can be microwaved, and makes a very cheap, if small, meal. (For more, see "Indian Food," later.) You'll find all-you-can-eat Chinese and Thai places serving £5-7 meals and offering even cheaper take-away boxes. While you can't "split" a buffet, you can split a take-away box. Stuff the box full, and you'll have England's cheapest hot meal.

Fish-and-chips are a heavy, greasy, but tasty English classic. Every town has at least one "chippy" selling a takeaway box of fish-and-chips in a cardboard box or (more traditionally) wrapped in paper for about £4-7. You can dip your fries in ketchup, American-style, or "go English" and drizzle the whole thing with vinegar.

Most large **museums** (and some historic **churches**) have handy, moderately priced cafeterias.

Fast food places, both American and British, are everywhere.

Inexpensive chain restaurants serve middle-of-the-road food in family-friendly settings (£7-12 meals). For specific chains to keep an eye out for, see "Good Chain Restaurants," later.

Bakeries sell yogurt, cartons of "semi-skimmed" milk, pastries, meat pies, and pasties (PASS-teez). Pasties are heavy, savory meat pies that originated in the Cornish mining country; they had big crust handles so miners with filthy hands could eat them and toss the crust. The most traditional filling is beef stew, but you'll also find them with chicken, vegetable, lamb and mint, and even Indian flavors inside (see sidebar on page 396).

Picnicking saves time and money. You can easily get prepared food to go. Munch a relaxed "meal on wheels" picnic during your open-top bus tour or river cruise to save 30 precious minutes for sightseeing.

Stop at a good **sandwich shop** or corner **grocery store** for boxes of orange juice (pure, by the liter), fresh bread, tasty English cheese, meat, a tube of Colman's English mustard, local eatin' apples, bananas, small tomatoes, a small tub of yogurt (drinkable), trail mix, nuts, plain or chocolate-covered digestive biscuits, and any local specialties. At **open-air markets** and **supermarkets,** you can get produce in small quantities. Supermarkets often have  good deli sections, even offering Indian dishes, and sometimes salad bars. Decent packaged sandwiches (£3-4) are sold everywhere (for a few options, see "Carryout Chains," later).

Good Chain Restaurants

I know—you're going to London to enjoy characteristic little hole-in-the-wall pubs, so mass-produced food is the furthest thing from your mind. But several excellent chains with branches across the UK can be a nice break from pub grub.

Sit-Down Chains

Most branches of the chains listed here open daily no later than noon (several at 8:00 or 9:00), and close sometime between 22:00 and midnight. Occasionally a place may close on Sundays or in the afternoon between lunch and dinner, but these are rare exceptions.

Wagamama Noodle Bar, serving up pan-Asian cuisine (udon noodles, fried rice, and curry dishes), is a noisy, organic slurpathon. Portions are huge and splittable. There's one in almost every mid-size city in the UK, usually located in sprawling halls filled with long shared tables and busy servers who scrawl your order on the placemat. While the quality has gone downhill a bit as they've expanded, this remains a reliable choice with reasonable prices (£8-12 main dishes big enough for light eaters to share, good veggie options, www.wagamama.com).

Côte Brasserie is a contemporary French chain serving good-value French cuisine in reliably pleasant settings, and at the right prices (£9-14 main dishes, early dinner specials, www.cote-restaurants.co.uk).

Byron, an upscale-hamburger chain with hip interiors, is worth seeking out if you need a burger fix. While British burgers aren't exactly like American ones—they tend to be a bit overcooked by our standards—Byron's burgers are your best bet (£7-10 burgers, www.byronhamburgers.com). **Gourmet Burger Kitchen (GBK)** provides a cheaper alternative, serving burgers that are, if not quite gourmet, very good. Choices range from a simple cheeseburger to more elaborate options, such as Jamaican. Choose a table and order at the counter—they'll bring the food to you (£7-11 burgers).

Loch Fyne Fish Restaurant is part of a Scottish chain that raises its own oysters and mussels. Its branches offer an inviting, lively atmosphere with a fine fishy energy and no pretense (£10-18 main dishes, two- and three-course specials often available before 19:00, www.lochfyne-restaurants.com).

Nando's is understandably popular as a casual, affordable place to get flame-broiled chicken with a range of Portuguese and South African flavors (£10 meals, www.nandos.co.uk).

At **Yo! Sushi,** sushi dishes trundle past on a conveyor belt. Color-coded plates tell you how much each dish costs (£1.90-5), and a picture-filled menu explains what you're eating. For £1.50, you get unlimited green tea (water for £1.05). Snag a bar stool and grab dishes as they rattle by (www.yosushi.com).

Ask and **Pizza Express** serve quality pasta and pizza in a pleasant, sit-down atmosphere that's family-friendly. **Jamie's**

INTRODUCTION

Italian (from celebrity chef Jamie Oliver) is hipper and pricier, and feels more upmarket.

Carry-Out Chains

While the following places may have some seating, they're best as an easy place to grab some prepackaged food on the run.

Major supermarket chains have smaller, offshoot branches that specialize in sandwiches, salads, and other prepared foods to go. These can be a picnicker's dream come true. Some shops are stand-alone, while others are located inside a larger store. The most prevalent—and best—is **M&S Simply Food** (an offshoot of the Marks & Spencer department-store chain; there's one in every major train station). **Sainsbury's Local** grocery stores also offer some decent prepared food; **Tesco Express** and **Tesco Metro** run a distant third.

Some "cheap and cheery" chains, such as **Pret à Manger, Eat, Apostróphe,** and **Pod,** provide office workers with good, healthful sandwiches, salads, and pastries to go. Among these, Eat has a reputation for slightly higher quality...and higher prices.

West Cornwall Pasty Company and **Cornish Bakehouse** sell a variety of these traditional savory pies for around £3—as do many smaller, independent bakeries.

The Great English Breakfast

The traditional "fry," or "full English breakfast"—generally included in the cost of your room—is famous as a hearty way to start the day. Also known as a "heart attack on a plate," the breakfast is especially feast-like if you've just come from the land of the skimpy continental breakfast across the Channel.

The standard fry gets off to a healthy start with juice and cereal or porridge. (Try Weetabix, a soggy English cousin of shredded wheat and perhaps the most absorbent material known to humankind.) Next, with tea or coffee, you get a heated plate with eggs (cooked to order—poached is the only style not floating in grease), Canadian-style bacon or sausage, a grilled tomato, sautéed mushrooms, baked beans, and sometimes hash browns, kippers (herring), or fried bread (sizzled in a greasy skillet). Toast comes in a rack (to cool quickly and crisply) with butter and marmalade. This protein-stuffed meal is great for stamina and tides many travelers over until dinner.

You'll figure out quickly which parts of the fry you like and don't like. Your host will likely ask you this up front, rather than serve you the whole shebang and risk having to throw out uneaten food. There's nothing wrong with skipping some or all of the fry—few Brits actually start their day with this heavy breakfast. Many progressive B&B owners offer vegetarian, organic, or other creative variations on the traditional breakfast.

These days, the best coffee is served in a *cafetière* (a French press). When your coffee has steeped as long as you like, plunge down the filter and pour.

Afternoon Tea

People of leisure punctuate their day with an afternoon tea at a tearoom. You'll get a pot of tea, small finger foods (like sandwiches with the crusts cut off), homemade scones, jam, and thick clotted cream. A lighter "cream tea" gets you tea and a scone or two. Tearooms, which often serve appealing light meals, are usually open for lunch and close at about 17:00, just before dinner. For more on this most English of traditions, see page 208.

Pubs

Pubs are a basic part of the British social scene, and, whether you're a teetotaler or a beer guzzler, they should be a part of your travel here. "Pub" is short for "public house." It's an extended living room where, if you don't mind the stickiness, you can feel the pulse of England.

People go to a public house to be social. They want to talk. Get vocal with a local. This is easiest at the bar, where people assume you're in the mood to talk (rather than at a table, where you're allowed a bit of privacy). The pub is the next best thing to having relatives in town. A cup of darts is free for the asking.

Smart travelers use the pubs to eat, drink, get out of the rain, watch sporting events, and make new friends. Unfortunately, many city pubs have been afflicted with an excess of brass, ferns, and video slot machines. The most traditional, atmospheric pubs are in the countryside and in smaller towns.

Pub hours vary. Pubs generally serve beer (and food for shorter hours; see next page) Monday to Saturday 11:00-23:00 and Sunday 12:00-22:30, though many are open later, particularly on Friday and Saturday. As it nears closing time, you'll hear shouts of "Last orders." Then comes the 10-minute warning bell. Finally, they'll call "Time!" to pick up your glass, finished or not, when the pub closes.

Pub Grub

Pub grub gets better each year. In London, it offers the best indoor eating value. For £6-10, you'll get a basic budget hot lunch or dinner in friendly surroundings. The *Good Pub Guide* is excellent (www.thegoodpubguide.co.uk). Pubs that are attached to restaurants, advertise their food, and are crowded with locals are more likely to have fresh food and a chef—and less likely to be the kind of pub that sells only lousy microwaved snacks.

Pubs generally serve traditional dishes, such as fish-and-chips, vegetables, "bangers and mash" (sausages and mashed potatoes), roast beef with Yorkshire pudding (batter-baked in the oven), gammon (ham steak), and assorted meat pies, such as steak-and-kidney pie or shepherd's pie (stewed lamb topped with mashed potatoes). Side dishes include salads (sometimes even a nice self-serve salad bar), vegetables, and—invariably—"chips" (French fries). "Crisps" are potato chips. A "jacket potato" (baked potato stuffed with fillings of your choice) can almost be a meal in itself. A "ploughman's lunch" is a traditional English meal of bread, cheese, and sweet pickles that nearly every tourist tries...once. These days, you'll likely find more Italian pasta, curried dishes, and quiche on the menu than traditional fare.

Meals are usually served from 11:00 or 12:00 until 21:00 or later, although some pubs close the kitchen between lunch and dinner. There's often no table service. Order at the bar, then take a seat and they'll bring the food when it's ready (or sometimes you pick it up at the bar). Pay at the bar (sometimes when you order, sometimes after you eat). Don't tip unless it's a place with full table service. Servings are hearty, service is quick, and you'll often eat for £10 or less per person. (If you're on a tight budget, consider sharing a meal—note the size of portions around you before ordering.) A beer or cider adds another couple of pounds. (Free tap water is always available.)

If you want food that's a notch above, seek out a **gastropub.** Although similar to a regular pub, a gastropub pays more attention to the quality of its menu—with accordingly higher prices (£10-15 meals). You'll find a few gastropubs in the towns and cities, but some of the best are in countryside villages.

Beer and Other Beverages

The British take great pride in their beer. Many Brits think that drinking beer cold and carbonated, as Americans do, ruins the taste. Most pubs will have **lagers** (cold, refreshing, American-style beer), **ales** (amber-colored, cellar-temperature beer), **bitters** (hop-flavored ale, perhaps the most typical British beer), and **stouts** (dark and somewhat bitter, like Guinness).

Order your beer at the bar and pay as you go, with no need to tip. An average beer costs £3. Part of the experience is standing before a line of "hand pulls," or taps, and wondering which beer to choose. Long-handled pulls are used to draw traditional, rich-flavored "real ales" up from the cellar. Short-handle pulls at the bar mean colder, fizzier, mass-produced, and less interesting keg beers. Mild beers are sweeter, with a creamy malt flavoring. Irish cream ale is a smooth, sweet experience. Try the draft cider (sweet or dry)...carefully.

Even if you enjoy fizzy beer, you should at least sample a **real ale** while in Britain. These are the connoisseur's favorites and often come with fun names. Served straight from the brewer's cask at cellar temperature, real ales finish fermenting naturally and are not pasteurized or filtered, so they must be consumed within two or three days after the cask is tapped. Naturally carbonated, real ales have less gassiness and head; they vary from sweet to bitter, often with a hoppy or nutty flavor.

As dictated by British law, draft beer and cider are served by the pint (20-ounce imperial size) or the half-pint (9.6 ounces). (It's almost feminine for a man to order just a half; I order mine with quiche.) The government recently sanctioned an in-between serving size—the two-thirds pint—hoping that more choice will woo more beer drinkers (a steady decline in beer consumption, which is taxed, has had a negative effect on tax revenues). Proper English ladies like a **shandy** (half beer and half 7-Up).

Besides beer, many pubs actually have a good selection of wines by the glass, a fully stocked bar for the gentleman's "G and T" (gin and tonic), and the increasingly popular bottles of alcohol-plus-sugar (such as Bacardi Breezers) for the younger, working-class set. **Pimm's** is a refreshing and fruity summer liqueur, traditionally popular during Wimbledon. It's an upper-class drink—a rough bloke might insult a pub by claiming it sells more Pimm's than beer.

Teetotalers can order from a wide variety of soft drinks—both the predictable American sodas and other more interesting bottled drinks, such as ginger beer (similar to ginger ale but with more bite), root beers, or other flavors (Fentimans brews some unusual options that are stocked in many English pubs). Note that in Britain, "lemonade" is lemon-lime soda (like 7-Up). Children are served food and soft drinks in pubs, but you must be 18 to order a beer.

British Chocolate

My chocoholic readers are enthusiastic about British choco-lates. As with other dairy products, chocolate seems richer and creamier here than it does in the US, so even the basics like Kit Kat (which was actually invented in York—see page 750) and Twix have a different taste. Some favorites include Cadbury Gold bars (filled with liquid caramel), Cadbury Crunchie bars, Nestlé's Lion bars (layered wafers covered in caramel and chocolate), Cadbury's Boost bars (a shortcake biscuit with caramel in milk chocolate), Cadbury Flake (crum-bly folds of melt-in-your-mouth chocolate), Galaxy chocolate bars (especially the ones with hazelnuts), and Aero (a light-as-air chocolate bar filled with little bubbles). Thornton shops (in larger train stations) sell a box of sweets called the Con-tinental Assortment, which comes with a tasting guide. The highlight is the mocha white-chocolate truffle. British M&Ms, called Smarties, are better than American ones. At ice-cream vans, look for the beloved traditional "99p"—a vanilla soft-serve cone with a small Flake bar stuck right into the middle. For a break from chocolate, buy a roll of wine gums—similar to Jujubes, but tangier and less sweet (Maynards is the biggest brand).

Indian Food

Eating Indian food is "going local" in cosmopolitan, multiethnic England. You'll find recommended Indian restaurants in most English cities, and even in small towns. Take the opportunity to sample food from Britain's former colony. Indian cuisine is as var-ied as the country itself. In general, they use more exotic spices than British or American cuisine—some hot, some sweet. (But if you like your food very hot, you'll find that Indian restaurants dull the spice for timid British palates—you'll have to be insistent if you want four-star heat.) Indian food is very vegetarian-friendly, offering many meatless dishes to choose from on any given menu.

For a simple meal that costs about £12-14, order one dish with rice and naan (Indian flatbread that can be served plain, with gar-lic, or other ways—usually one order is plenty for two people to share). You'll generally pay £2-3 extra for an order of rice (it's not included in the price of the main dish). Many restaurants have a fixed-price combination meal that offers more variety, and is sim-pler and cheaper than ordering à la carte. For about £20, you can make a mix-and-match platter out of several sharable dishes, in-cluding *dal* (simmered lentils) as a starter; one or two meat or veg-etable dishes with sauce (for example, chicken curry, chicken *tikka masala* in a creamy tomato sauce, grilled fish tandoori, chickpea *chana masala*, or a spicy *vindaloo* dish); *raita* (a cooling yogurt that's added to spicy dishes); rice; naan; and an Indian beer (wine and Indian food don't really mix) or chai (a cardamom- and cinnamon-spiced tea, usually served with milk). An easy way to taste a variety of dishes (especially for a single diner) is to order a *thali*—a sort of sampler plate, generally served on a metal tray, with small servings of various specialties.

Desserts

To the British, the traditional word for dessert is "pudding," although it's also referred to as "sweets" these days. Sponge cake, cream, fruitcake, and meringue are key players.

Trifle is the best-known British concoction, consisting of sponge cake soaked in brandy or sherry (or orange juice for children), then covered with jam and/or fruit and custard cream. Whipped cream can sometimes put the final touch on this "light" treat.

Castle puddings are sponge puddings cooked in small molds and topped with Golden Syrup (a popular brand and a cross between honey and maple syrup). Bread-and-butter pudding consists of slices of French bread baked with milk, cream, eggs, and raisins (similar to the American preparation), served warm with cold cream. Hasty pudding, supposedly the invention of people in a hurry to avoid the bailiff, is made from stale bread with dried fruit and milk. Queen of puddings is a breadcrumb pudding topped with warm jam, meringue, and cream. Treacle pudding is a popular steamed pudding whose "sponge" mixture combines flour, suet (animal fat), butter, sugar, and milk. Christmas pudding (also called plum pudding) is a dense mixture with dried and candied fruit served with brandy butter or hard sauce. Sticky toffee pudding is a moist cake made with dates, heated and drizzled with toffee sauce, and served with ice cream or cream. Banoffee pie is the delicious British answer to banana cream pie.

The English version of custard is a smooth, yellow liquid. Cream tops most everything custard does not. There's single cream for coffee. Double cream is really thick. Whipped cream is familiar, and clotted cream is the consistency of whipped butter.

Fool is a dessert with sweetened pureed fruit (such as rhubarb, gooseberries, or black currants) mixed with cream or custard and chilled. Elderflower is a popular flavoring for sorbet.

Scones are tops, and many inns and restaurants have their secret recipes. Whether made with fruit or topped with clotted cream, scones take the cake.

INTRODUCTION

How Was Your Trip?

Were your travels fun, smooth, and meaningful? If you'd like to share your tips, concerns, and discoveries, please fill out the survey at www.ricksteves.com/feedback. I value your feedback. Thanks in advance—it helps a lot.

Traveling as a Temporary Local

We travel all the way to England to enjoy differences—to become temporary locals. You'll experience frustrations. Certain truths that we find "God-given" or "self-evident," such as cold beer, ice in drinks, bottomless cups of coffee, and bigger being better, are suddenly not so true. One of the benefits of travel is the eye-opening realization that there are logical, civil, and even better alternatives. A willingness to go local ensures that you'll enjoy a full dose of English hospitality.

Europeans generally like Americans. But if there is a negative aspect to the English image of us, it's that we are loud, wasteful, ethnocentric, too informal (which can seem disrespectful), and a bit naive.

The English (and Europeans in general) place a high value on speaking quietly in restaurants and on trains. Listen while on the bus or in a restaurant—the place can be packed, but the decibel level is low. Try to adjust your volume accordingly to show respect for their culture.

While the English look bemusedly at some of our Yankee excesses—and worriedly at others—they nearly always afford us individual travelers all the warmth we deserve.

Judging from all the happy feedback I receive from travelers who have used this book, it's safe to assume you'll enjoy a great, affordable vacation—with the finesse of an independent, experienced traveler.

Thanks, and have a brilliant holiday!

Back Door Travel Philosophy

From *Rick Steves' Europe Through the Back Door*

Travel is intensified living—maximum thrills per minute and one of the last great sources of legal adventure. Travel is freedom. It's recess, and we need it.

Experiencing the real Europe requires catching it by surprise, going casual..."through the Back Door."

Affording travel is a matter of priorities. (Make do with the old car.) You can eat and sleep—simply, safely, and enjoyably—anywhere in Europe for $120 a day plus transportation costs. In many ways, spending more money only builds a thicker wall between you and what you traveled so far to see. Europe is a cultural carnival, and time after time, you'll find that its best acts are free and the best seats are the cheap ones.

A tight budget forces you to travel close to the ground, meeting and communicating with the people. Never sacrifice sleep, nutrition, safety, or cleanliness to save money. Simply enjoy the local-style alternatives to expensive hotels and restaurants.

Connecting with people carbonates your experience. Extroverts have more fun. If your trip is low on magic moments, kick yourself and make things happen. If you don't enjoy a place, maybe you don't know enough about it. Seek the truth. Recognize tourist traps. Give a culture the benefit of your open mind. See things as different, but not better or worse. Any culture has plenty to share.

Of course, travel, like the world, is a series of hills and valleys. Be fanatically positive and militantly optimistic. If something's not to your liking, change your liking.

Travel can make you a happier American, as well as a citizen of the world. Our Earth is home to seven billion equally precious people. It's humbling to travel and find that other people don't have the "American Dream"—they have their own dreams. Europeans like us, but with all due respect, they wouldn't trade passports.

Thoughtful travel engages us with the world. In tough economic times, it reminds us what is truly important. By broadening perspectives, travel teaches new ways to measure quality of life.

Globetrotting destroys ethnocentricity, helping us understand and appreciate other cultures. Rather than fear the diversity on this planet, celebrate it. Among your most prized souvenirs will be the strands of different cultures you choose to knit into your own character. The world is a cultural yarn shop, and Back Door travelers are weaving the ultimate tapestry. Join in!

ENGLAND

ENGLAND

England (pop. 53 million) is a hilly country the size of Louisiana (50,346 square miles) and located in the lower two-thirds of the isle of Britain. Scotland is to the north and the English Channel to the south, with the North Sea to the east and Wales (and the Irish Sea) to the west. Fed by ocean air from the southwest, the climate is mild, with a chance of cloudy, rainy weather almost any day of the year.

England has an economy that can stand alongside many much larger nations. It boasts high-tech industries (software, chemicals, aviation), international banking, and textile manufacturing, and is a major exporter of beef. While farms and villages remain, England is now an urban, industrial, and post-industrial colossus.

England traditionally has been very class-conscious, with the wealthy landed aristocracy, the middle-class tradesmen, and the lower-class farmers and factory workers. While social stratification is fading with the new global economy, regional differences remain strong. Locals can often identify where someone is from by their dialect or local accent—Geordie, Cockney, or Queen's English.

One thing that sets England apart from its fellow UK countries (Scotland, Wales, and Northern Ireland) is its ethnic makeup. Traditionally, those countries had Celtic roots, while the English mixed in Saxon and Norman blood. In the 20th century, England welcomed many Scots, Welsh, and Irish as low-wage workers. More recently, it's become home to immigrants from former colonies of its worldwide empire—particularly from India/Pakistan/Bangladesh, the

Caribbean, and Africa—and to many workers from poorer Eastern European countries. These days it's not a given that every "English" person speaks English. Nearly one in three citizens does not profess the Christian faith. As the world becomes interconnected by communications technology, it's possible for many immigrants to physically inhabit the country while remaining closely linked to their home culture—rather than truly assimilating into England.

This is the current English paradox. England—the birthplace and center of the extended worldwide family of English-speakers—is losing its traditional Englishness. Where Scotland, Wales, and Northern Ireland have cultural movements to preserve their local languages and customs, England does not. Politically, there is no "English" party in the UK Parliament. While Scotland, Wales, and Northern Ireland have their own parliaments to decide local issues, England must depend on the decisions of the UK government at large. Except for the occasional display of an English flag at a soccer match (the red St. George's cross on a white background), many English people don't really think of themselves as "English"—more as "Brits," a part of the wider UK.

Today, England tries to preserve its rich past as it races forward as a leading global player. There are still hints of its legacy of farms, villages, Victorian lamplighters, and upper-crust dandies. But it's also a jostling world of unemployed factory workers, investment bankers, soccer matches, rowdy "stag parties," and faux-Tudor suburbs. Modern England is a culturally diverse land in transition. Catch it while you can.

LONDON

London is more than 600 square miles of urban jungle—a world in itself and a barrage on all the senses. On my first visit, I felt extremely small.

London is more than its museums and landmarks. It's the L.A., D.C., and N.Y.C. of Britain—a living, breathing, thriving organism...a coral reef of humanity. The city has changed dramatically in recent years, and many visitors are surprised to find how "un-English" it is. ESL (English as a second language) seems like the city's first language, as white people are now a minority in major parts of the city that once symbolized white imperialism. Arabs have nearly bought out the area north of Hyde Park. Chinese takeouts outnumber fish-and-chips shops. Eastern Europeans pull pints in British pubs. Many hotels are run by people with foreign accents (who hire English chambermaids), while outlying suburbs are home to huge communities of Indians and Pakistanis. London is a city of eight million separate dreams, inhabiting a place that tolerates and encourages them. With the English Channel Tunnel and discount airlines making travel between Britain and the Continent easier than ever, London is learning—sometimes fitfully—to live as a microcosm of its formerly vast empire.

The city, which has long attracted tourists, seems perpetually at your service, with an impressive slate of sights, entertainment, and eateries, all linked by a great transit system. With just a few days here, you'll get no more than a quick splash in this teeming human tidal pool. But with a good orientation, you'll find London manageable and fun. You'll get a sampling of the city's top sights, history, and cultural entertainment, and a good look at its ever-changing human face.

Blow through the city on the open deck of a double-decker orientation tour bus, and take a pinch-me-I'm-in-London walk through the West End. Ogle the crown jewels at the Tower of London, hear the chimes of Big Ben, and see the Houses of Parliament in action. Cruise the Thames River, and take a spin on the London Eye. Hobnob with poets' tombstones in Westminster Abbey, and visit with Leonardo, Botticelli, and Rembrandt in the National Gallery. Enjoy Shakespeare in a replica of the Globe theater and marvel at a glitzy, fun musical at a modern-day theater. Whisper across the dome of St. Paul's Cathedral, then rummage through our civilization's attic at the British Museum. And sip your tea with pinky raised and clotted cream dribbling down your scone.

Planning Your Time

The sights of London alone could easily fill a trip to England. It's a great one-week getaway. But on a three-week tour of England, I'd give London three busy days. You won't be able to see everything, so don't try. You'll keep coming back to London. After dozens of visits myself, I still enjoy a healthy list of excuses to return. If you're flying in to one of London's airports, consider starting your trip in Bath and making London your English finale. Especially if you hope to enjoy a play or concert, a night or two of jet lag is bad news.

Here's a suggested three-day schedule:

Day 1

9:00	Tower of London (crown jewels first, then Beefeater tour and White Tower; note that on Sun-Mon, the Tower opens at 10:00).
13:00	Grab a picnic, catch a boat at Tower Pier, and relax with lunch on the Thames while cruising to Westminster Pier.
14:30	Tour Westminster Abbey, and consider their evensong service (usually at 17:00, at 15:00 on Sun and off-season Sat, never on Wed).
17:00 (or after evensong)	Follow my self-guided Westminster Walk. When you're finished, if it's a Monday or Tuesday, you could return to the Houses of Parliament and possibly pop in to see the House of Commons in action.

Day 2

8:30	Take a double-decker hop-on, hop-off London

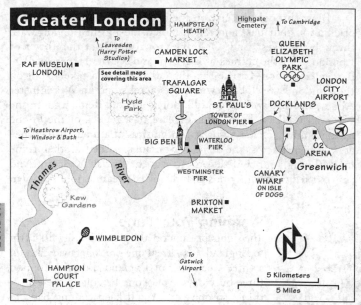

sightseeing bus tour (from Green Park or Victoria
Station), and hop off for the Changing of the Guard.

11:00   Buckingham Palace (guards change most days May-
        July at 11:30, alternate days Aug-April—confirm
        online).

12:00   Walk through St. James's Park to enjoy London's
        delightful park scene.

13:00   After lunch, tour the Churchill War Rooms.

16:00   Tour the National Gallery.

Evening Have a pub dinner before a play, concert, or evening
         walking tour.

Day 3 (or More)

Choose among these remaining London highlights: British Library, Imperial War Museum, the two Tates (Tate Modern on the South Bank for modern art, Tate Britain on the North Bank for British art), St. Paul's Cathedral, Victoria and Albert Museum, National Portrait Gallery, Natural History Museum, Courtauld Gallery, or the Museum of London; take a spin on the London Eye or a cruise to Kew Gardens or Greenwich; enjoy a play at Shakespeare's Globe; do some serious shopping at one of London's elegant department stores or open-air markets; or take another historic walking tour.

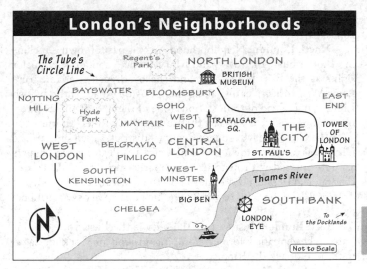

London's Neighborhoods

The Tube's Circle Line

Regent's Park

NORTH LONDON

BRITISH MUSEUM

BAYSWATER

NOTTING HILL

Hyde Park

BLOOMSBURY

SOHO

MAYFAIR

WEST END

TRAFALGAR SQ.

EAST END

THE CITY

TOWER OF LONDON

WEST LONDON

BELGRAVIA

PIMLICO

CENTRAL LONDON

ST. PAUL'S

SOUTH KENSINGTON

WEST-MINSTER

Thames River

CHELSEA

BIG BEN

SOUTH BANK

LONDON EYE

To the Docklands

Not to Scale

LONDON

Orientation to London

To grasp London more comfortably, see it as the old town in the city center without the modern, congested sprawl. (Even from that perspective, it's still huge.)

The Thames River (pronounced "tems") runs roughly west to east through the city, with most of the visitor's sights on the North Bank. Mentally, maybe even physically, trim down your map to include only the area between the Tower of London (to the east), Hyde Park (west), Regent's Park (north), and the South Bank (south). This is roughly the area bordered by the Tube's Circle Line. This four-mile stretch between the Tower and Hyde Park (about a 1.5-hour walk) looks like a milk bottle on its side (see map above), and holds 80 percent of the sights mentioned in this chapter.

With a core focus and a good orientation, you'll get a sampling of London's top sights, history, and cultural entertainment, and a good look at its ever-changing human face.

The sprawling city becomes much more manageable if you think of it as a collection of neighborhoods.

Central London: This area contains Westminster and what Londoners call the West End. The Westminster district includes Big Ben, Parliament, Westminster Abbey, and Buckingham Palace—the grand government buildings from which Britain is ruled. Trafalgar Square, London's gathering place, has many major museums. The West End is the center of London's cultural life, with bustling squares: Piccadilly Circus and Leicester Square host cinemas, tourist traps, and nighttime glitz. Soho and Covent Garden are thriving people zones with theaters, restaurants, pubs, and boutiques. And Regent and Oxford streets are the city's main shopping zones.

North London: Neighborhoods in this part of town—including Bloomsbury, Fitzrovia, and Marylebone—contain such major sights as the British Museum and the overhyped Madame Tussauds Waxworks. Nearby, along busy Euston Road, is the British Library, plus a trio of train stations (one of them, St. Pancras International, is linked to Paris by the Eurostar "Chunnel" train).

The City: Today's modern financial district, called simply "The City," was a walled town in Roman times. Gleaming skyscrapers are interspersed with historical landmarks such as St. Paul's Cathedral, legal sights (Old Bailey), and the Museum of London. The Tower of London and Tower Bridge lie at The City's eastern border.

East London: Just east of The City is the East End—the increasingly gentrified former stomping ground of Cockney ragamuffins and Jack the Ripper.

The South Bank: The South Bank of the Thames River offers major sights (Tate Modern, Shakespeare's Globe, London Eye) linked by a riverside walkway. Within this area, Southwark (SUTH-uck) stretches from the Tate Modern to London Bridge. Pedestrian bridges connect the South Bank with The City and Trafalgar Square.

West London: This huge area contains neighborhoods such as Mayfair, Belgravia, Pimlico, Chelsea, South Kensington, and Notting Hill. It's home to London's wealthy and has many trendy shops and enticing restaurants. Here you'll find a range of museums (Victoria and Albert Museum, Tate Britain, and more), my top hotel recommendations, lively Victoria Station, and the vast green expanses of Hyde Park and Kensington Gardens.

Outside the Center: The Docklands, London's version of Manhattan, is farther east than the East End; Queen Elizabeth Olympic Park is just north of the Docklands. Historic Greenwich is southeast of London and across the Thames. Kew Gardens and Hampton Court Palace are southwest of London.

Tourist Information

For such a big and important city, it's amazing how hard it can be to find unbiased sightseeing information and advice in London. You'll see "Tourist Information" offices advertised everywhere, but most of them are private agencies that make a big profit selling tours and advance sightseeing and/or theater tickets; others are run by Transport for London (TFL) and are primarily focused on providing public-transit advice.

The only publicly funded (and therefore impartial) "real" TI is the **City of London Information Centre** (Mon-Sat 9:30-17:30,

---

Rick Steves Audio Europe

If you're bringing a mobile device, be sure to check out **Rick Steves Audio Europe,** where you can download free audio tours and hours of travel interviews (via the Rick Steves Audio Europe smartphone app, www.ricksteves.com/audioeurope, iTunes, or Google Play).

My self-guided **audio tours** are user-friendly, easy to follow, fun, and informative, covering the major sights and neighborhoods in London: the British Museum, British Library, St. Paul's Cathedral, The City, and the Westminster Walk. Compared with live tours, my audio tours are hard to beat: Nobody will stand you up, the quality is reliable, you can take the tour exactly when you like, and they're free.

Rick Steves Audio Europe also offers a far-reaching library of intriguing **travel interviews** with experts from around the globe.

Sun 10:00-16:00; across the busy street from St. Paul's Cathedral—around the right side as you face the main staircase, in the modern, angular building just toward the Millennium Bridge; Tube: St. Paul's, tel. 020/7332-1456, www.visitthecity.co.uk). While officially a service of The City (London's financial district), this office also provides information about the rest of London. It sells Oyster cards, London Passes, and advance "Fast Track" sightseeing tickets (all described later), and stocks various free publications: *London Planner* (a free monthly that lists all the sights, events, and hours), some walking-tour brochures, the *Official London Theatre Guide,* a free Tube and bus map, the *Guide to River Thames Boat Services,* and brochures describing self-guided walks in The City (various themes, including Dickens, modern architecture, and film locations). They give out a free map of The City, and sell several city-wide maps; ask if they have yet another, free map with a coupon good for 20 percent off admission to St. Paul's. I'd skip their room-booking service (charges a commission) and theater box office (may charge a commission).

Visit London, which serves the greater London area, doesn't have an office you can visit in person—but does operate a call center and website (tel. 0870-156-6366, www.visitlondon.com).

Fast Track Tickets: To skip the ticket-buying queues at certain London sights, you can buy Fast Track tickets in advance—and they can be cheaper than tickets sold right at the sight. They're particularly smart for the Tower of London, the London Eye, and Madame Tussauds Waxworks, all of which get very busy in high season. They're available through various sales outlets around

London (including the City of London TI, souvenir stands, and faux-TIs scattered throughout touristy areas).

London Pass: This pass, which covers many big sights and lets you skip some lines, is expensive but potentially worth the investment for extremely busy sightseers (£47/1 day, £64/2 days, £77/3 days, £102/6 days; days are calendar days rather than 24-hour periods; comes with 160-page guidebook, also sold at major train stations and airports, tel. 0870-242-9988, www.london-pass.com). Among the many sights it includes are the Tower of London, Westminster Abbey, St. Paul's Cathedral, and Windsor Castle, as well as many temporary exhibits and audioguides at otherwise "free" biggies. Think through your sightseeing plans, study their website to see what's covered, and do the math before you buy.

Arrival in London

For more information on getting to or from London by train, bus, plane, and cruise ship, see "London Connections," near the end of this chapter.

By Train: London has nine major train stations, all connected by the Tube (subway). All have ATMs, and many of the larger stations also have shops, fast food, exchange offices, and luggage storage. From any station, you can ride the Tube or taxi to your hotel. For more info on train travel, see www.nationalrail.co.uk.

By Bus: The main intercity bus station is Victoria Coach Station, one block southwest of Victoria train/Tube station. For more on bus travel, see www.nationalexpress.com.

By Plane: London has six airports. Most tourists arrive at Heathrow or Gatwick airport, although flights from elsewhere in Europe may land at Stansted, Luton, Southend, or London City airport. For specifics on getting from London's airports to downtown, see "London Connections" near the end of this chapter; for hotels near Heathrow and Gatwick, see page 185.

Helpful Hints

Theft Alert: Wear your money belt. The Artful Dodger is alive and well in London. Be on guard, particularly on public transportation and in places crowded with tourists, who, considered naive and rich, are targeted. The Changing of the Guard scene is a favorite for thieves. And more than 7,500 purses are stolen annually at Covent Garden alone.

Pedestrian Safety: Cars drive on the left side of the road—which can be as confusing for foreign pedestrians as for foreign drivers. Before crossing a street, I always look right, look left, then look right again just to be sure. Most crosswalks are even painted with instructions, reminding foreign guests to "Look right" or "Look left." While locals are champion jaywalkers, you shouldn't try it; jaywalking is treacherous when you're disoriented about which direction traffic is coming from.

Medical Problems: Local hospitals have good-quality 24-hour-a-day emergency care centers, where any tourist who needs help can drop in and, after a wait, be seen by a doctor. Your hotel has details. St. Thomas' Hospital, immediately across the river from Big Ben, has a fine reputation.

Getting Your Bearings: London is well-signed for visitors. Through an initiative called Legible London, the city is erecting thoughtfully designed, pedestrian-focused maps around town. In this sprawling city—where predictable grid-planned streets are relatively rare—it's also smart to buy and use a good map. *Benson's London Street Map*, sold at many newsstands and bookstores, is my favorite for efficient sightseeing.

Festivals: For one week in February and another in September, fashionistas descend on the city for **London Fashion Week** (www.londonfashionweek.co.uk). The famous **Chelsea Flower Show** blossoms in late May (book ahead for this popular event at www.rhs.org.uk/chelsea). During the annual **Trooping the Colour** in June, there are military bands and pageantry, and the Queen's birthday parade (www.trooping-the-colour.co.uk). Tennis fans pack the stands at the **Wimbledon Tennis Championship** in late June to early July (www.wimbledon.org), and partygoers head for the **Notting Hill Carnival** in late August.

Traveling in Winter: London dazzles year-round, so consider visiting in winter, when airfares and hotel rates are generally cheaper and there are fewer tourists. For ideas on what to do, see the "Winter Activities in London" article at www.ricksteves.com/winteracts.

Getting Online with a Mobile Device: In addition to the Wi-Fi that's likely available at your hotel, it's smart to get a free account with **The Cloud,** a free Wi-Fi service found in many convenient spots around London, including most train stations and many museums, coffee shops, cafés, and shopping centers. Sign up at www.thecloud.net/free-wifi, where you'll have to enter a street address and postal code; it doesn't matter which one (use your hotel's, or the Queen's: Buckingham Palace, SW1A 1AA). Your Wi-Fi may be limited to 15 or 30 minutes at a time; if you max out, simply log in again.

Most **Tube stations** and trains have Wi-Fi, but it's free only to those with a British cellular account. However, the Tube's Wi-Fi always lets you access Transport for London's Journey Planner (www.tfl.gov.uk), making it easy to look up your city transit options—and get real-time updates on delays—once you're in a station. To access the rest of the

Affording London's Sights

London is one of Europe's most expensive cities, with the dubious distinction of having some of the world's steepest admission prices. Fortunately, many sights are free.

Free Museums: Many of the city's biggest and best museums won't charge you a dime. Free sights include the British Museum, British Library, National Gallery, National Portrait Gallery, Tate Britain, Tate Modern, Wallace Collection, Imperial War Museum, Victoria and Albert Museum, Natural History Museum, Science Museum, Sir John Soane's Museum, the Museum of London, and the Geffrye Museum.

About half of these museums request a donation of a few pounds, but whether you contribute or not is up to you. If I spend money for an audioguide, I feel fine about not otherwise donating. If you can afford it, donate.

Free Churches: Smaller churches let worshippers (and tourists) in free, although they may ask for a donation. The big sightseeing churches—Westminster Abbey and St. Paul's—charge higher admission fees, but offer free evensong services nearly daily (though you can't stick around afterward to sightsee). Westminster Abbey also offers free organ recitals most Sundays at 17:45.

Other Freebies: London has plenty of free performances, such as lunch concerts at St. Martin-in-the-Fields (see page 101) and summertime movies at The Scoop amphitheater near City Hall (see page 166). For other freebies, check out www.freelondonlistings.co.uk. There's no charge to enjoy the pageantry of the Changing of the Guard, rants at Speakers' Corner in Hyde Park (on Sun afternoon), displays at Harrods, the people-watching scene at Covent Garden, and the colorful streets of the East End. It's free to view the legal action at the Old Bailey and the legislature at work in the Houses of Parliament. And you can get into a bit of the Tower of London and Windsor Castle by attending Sunday services in each place's chapel (chapel access only).

Greenwich makes for an inexpensive day trip (see next chapter). Many of its sights are free, and the journey there is covered by a cheap Zones 1-2 Tube ticket or pass.

Sightseeing Deals: If you buy a paper One-Day Travelcard at a National Rail station (such as Paddington or Victoria), you may be eligible for two-for-one discounts at many popular sights, such as the Churchill War Rooms, London Eye, Tower of London, and Madame Tussauds. (This also works with paper train tickets bought in person at the station—if you'll be riding into London and visiting one of these sights later in the day.) See page 59 for details.

Good-Value Tours: The city walking tours with professional guides (£6-9) are one of the best deals going. (Note that the guides for the "free" walking tours are unpaid by their companies, and they expect tips—I'd pay up front for an expertly guided

LONDON

tour instead.) Hop-on, hop-off big-bus tours, while expensive (£24-30), provide a great overview and include free boat tours as well as city walks. (Or, for the price of a transit ticket, you could get similar views from the top of a double-decker public bus.) A one-hour Thames ride to Greenwich costs £12 one-way, but most boats come with entertaining commentary. A three-hour bicycle tour is about £20.

Pricey...but Worth It? Big-ticket sights worth their hefty admission fees (£13.50-17.50) are Kew Gardens, Shakespeare's Globe, the Churchill War Rooms, and Kensington Palace.

The London Eye has become a London must-see—though if you're on a tight budget, it's difficult to justify its very high cost (£19). While Hampton Court Palace (£18) is expensive, it is well presented and a reasonable value if you have an interest in royal history. The Queen charges royally for a peek inside Buckingham Palace (£19, open Aug-Sept only), and her art gallery and carriage museum (adjacent to the palace, about £9 each) are expensive but interesting. Madame Tussauds Waxworks is pricey but still hard for many to resist (£30, see page 117 for info on discounts). Harry Potter fans gladly pay the Hagrid-sized £29 fee to see the sets and props at the Warner Bros. Studio Tour (but those who wouldn't know a wizard from a Muggle shouldn't waste the time or money).

Many smaller museums charge relatively low admission. My favorites include the Courtauld Gallery (£6, £3 on Mon) and the Wellington Museum at Apsley House (£6.70).

Totally Pants (Brit-speak for Not Worth It): The London Dungeon, at £24.60, is gimmicky, overpriced, and a terrible value...despite the long line at the door. It doesn't make sense to spend your pounds on Winston Churchill's Britain at War Experience (£14.50) when the Churchill War Rooms (£17.50) and the Imperial War Museum (free) cover the same themes much better.

Theater: Compared with Broadway's prices, London's theater is a bargain. Seek out the freestanding tkts booth at Leicester Square to get discounts from 25 to 50 percent on good seats (and full-price tickets to the hottest shows with no service charges; see page 158). Buying direct at the theater box office can score you a great deal on same-day tickets, and even the most popular shows generally have some seats under £20 (possibly with obstructed views)—ask. A £5 "groundling" ticket for a play at Shakespeare's Globe is the best theater deal in town (see page 163). Tickets to the Open Air Theatre at north London's Regent's Park start at £15 (see page 165).

London doesn't come cheap. But with its many free museums and affordable plays, this cosmopolitan, cultured city offers days of sightseeing thrills without requiring you to pinch your pennies (or your pounds).

Web using the Tube's Wi-Fi, you can pay £2 for a one-day pass, or £5 for a one-week pass (easy sign-up and credit-card payment at http://my.virginmedia.com/wifi). The Wi-Fi can falter inside Tube tunnels, but generally comes right back as you approach the next station.

Useful Apps: While the Transport for London's Journey Planner works great for people with access to the Internet, the **MX Apps free Tube map** works even when you're not online, showing the easiest way to connect station A to station B. When you are online, the app provides live updates about Tube delays and closures. (It doesn't, however, look up bus connections, and MX Apps' "Bus London" map isn't very useful offline.) **City Maps 2Go** ($2) lets you download searchable offline maps; their London version is quite good. **Time Out London's** free app has reviews and listings for theater, museums, movies, and more (download the "Things to Do" version, which is updated weekly, rather than the boilerplate "Travel Guide" version).

Travel Bookstores: Located between Covent Garden and Leicester Square, the very good **Stanfords Travel Bookstore** stocks current editions of many of my books (Mon and Wed-Fri 9:00-20:00, Tue 9:30-20:00, Sat 10:00-20:00, Sun 12:00-18:00, 12-14 Long Acre, second entrance on Floral Street, Tube: Leicester Square, tel. 020/7836-1321, www.stanfords.co.uk).

Two impressive **Waterstones** bookstores have the biggest collection of travel guides in town: on Piccadilly (Mon-Sat 9:00-22:00, Sun 11:30-18:00, Costa Café, great views from top-floor bar—see sidebar on page 124, 203 Piccadilly, tel. 0843-290-8549) and on Trafalgar Square (Mon-Sat 9:30-21:00, Sun 12:00-18:00, Costa Café on second floor, tel. 0843-290-8651).

Baggage Storage: Train stations have replaced lockers with more secure left-luggage counters. Each bag must go through a scanner (just like at the airport), so lines can be slow. Expect long waits in the morning to check in (up to 45 minutes) and in the afternoon to pick up (each item-£8.50/24 hours, most stations daily 7:00-23:00). You can also store bags at the airports (similar rates and hours, www.excess-baggage.com). If leaving London and returning later, you may be able to store a box or bag at your hotel for free—assuming you'll be staying there again.

"Voluntary Donations": About a half-dozen sights automatically add a "voluntary donation" of about 10 percent to their admission fees (these are noted in the listings). The price posted and quoted includes the donation, though it's perfectly fine to say you want to pay a cheaper price without the donation.

Updates to This Book: Check www.ricksteves.com/update for any significant changes that have occurred since this book was published.

Getting Around London

To travel smart in a city this size, you must get comfortable with public transportation. London's excellent taxis, buses, and subway (Tube) system make a car unnecessary (see page 67 for details on driving in London—and why it's a bad idea).

The helpful *Welcome to London* brochure, produced by the mayor's office and Transport for London (TFL), includes both a Tube map and a handy schematic map of the best bus routes (available free at TFL offices—such as the one in Victoria Station, the City of London TI, and at museums and hotels all over town). For specific directions on how to get from point A to point B on London's transit, call TFL's automated info line at 0843-222-1234.

Public-Transit Passes

London has the most expensive public transit in the world—save money on your Tube and bus rides using a multiride pass. You have three options: Pay double by buying individual tickets as you go; buy a £5 Oyster card and top it up as needed to travel like a local for about £1-2 per ride; or get a Travelcard for unlimited travel on either one or seven days.

The transit system has six zones. Since almost all of my recommended accommodations, restaurants, and sights are within Zones 1 and 2, those are the prices I've listed here; you'll pay more to go farther afield. Specific fares and other details change constantly; for a complete and updated list of prices, check www.tfl.gov.uk.

Individual Transit Tickets

These days in London, individual paper tickets are obsolete; there's no point buying one unless you're literally taking just one ride your entire time in the city. Because individual fares (£4.50 per Tube ride, £2.40 per bus ride) are about double the cost of using a pay-as-you-go Oyster card, in just two or three rides you'll recoup the £5 added deposit for the Oyster. If you do buy a single ticket, avoid ticket-window lines in Tube stations by using the coin-op machines; practice on the punchboard to see how the system works (hit "Adult Single" and your destination). These tickets are valid only on the day of purchase.

LONDON

Oyster Cards

A pay-as-you-go Oyster card (a plastic card embedded with a computer chip) is the standard, smart way to economically ride the Tube, buses, Docklands Light Railway (DLR), and Overground. On each type of transport, you simply lay the card flat against (or sufficiently near) the yellow card reader at the turnstile or entrance, it flashes green, and the fare is automatically deducted. (You'll also tap your card again to "touch out" as you exit the Tube and DLR turnstiles, but not to exit buses.)

With an Oyster card, rides cost about half the price of individual paper tickets (£2.10 or £2.80 per Tube ride—depending on time of day, £1.40 per bus ride). You buy the card itself at any Tube station ticket window for a refundable £5 deposit, then load it up with as much credit as you want. (For extra peace of mind, ask about registering your card against theft or loss.) When your balance gets low, simply add credit—or "top up"—at a ticket window or machine. A price cap on the pay-as-you-go Oyster card guarantees you'll never pay more than the One-Day Travelcard price within a 24-hour period.

You can see how much credit remains on your card by touching it to the pad at any ticket machine. Oyster card balances never expire (though they need reactivating at a ticket window every two years), so you can use the card whenever you're in London, or lend it to someone else.

When you're finished with the card (and if you don't mind a short wait), you should be able to reclaim your £5 deposit at any ticket window. However, to make it as easy as possible to recoup your deposit, you should always use the same mode of payment: For example, if you pay the deposit in cash, you need to top up with cash. If you pay the deposit in cash and top up with a credit card, or vice versa, it can be more difficult (or impossible) to get your deposit back.

Transfers: You can change from one Tube line to another on the same Oyster journey (as long as you don't leave the station); however, if you change between buses, or change between bus and Tube, you'll pay a new fare.

Travelcards

Like the Oyster card, Travelcards are valid on the Tube, buses, Docklands Light Railway (DLR), and Overground. The difference is that Travelcards let you ride as many times as you want within a one- or a seven-day period, for one fixed price.

Before you buy a card, estimate where you'll be going; there's a card for Zones 1 and 2, and another for Zones 1-6 (which includes Heathrow Airport). If Heathrow is the only ride you're taking outside Zones 1-2 (which is likely), you can pay a small supplement to make the Zones 1-2 Travelcard stretch to cover that one ride.

The **One-Day Travelcard** gives you unlimited travel for a day (Zones 1-2: £8.80, off-peak version £7.30; Zones 1-6: £16.40, off-peak version £8.90; off-peak cards are good for travel after 9:30 on weekdays and anytime on weekends). This Travelcard works like a traditional paper ticket: Buy it at any Tube station ticket window or machine, then feed it into a turnstile (and retrieve it) to enter and exit the Tube. On a bus, just show it to the driver when you get on.

The **Seven-Day Travelcard** is a great option if you're staying four or more days and plan to use buses and the Tube a lot. It's issued as credit on your plastic Oyster card, and gives you unlimited travel anytime, anywhere in Zones 1 and 2 for a week (£30.40 plus the refundable £5 deposit for the Oyster card). As with a standard Oyster card, you'll touch it to the yellow card reader when entering or exiting a Tube turnstile, or when boarding a bus. It's smart to keep an extra £5-6 worth of credit on your Oyster card on top of the Travelcard to cover travel outside zones 1-2 or after your Travelcard runs out.

LONDON

Discounts

Groups: A gang of 10 or more adults can travel all day on the Tube for £4.50 each (but not on buses). Kids ages 11-17 pay £1.70 when part of a group of 10.

Families: A paying adult can take up to four kids (ages 10 and under) for free on the Tube, Docklands Light Railway (DLR), and Overground all day, every day (kids 10 and under are always free on buses). At the Tube station, use the manual gate, rather than the turnstiles, to be waved in. Other child and student discounts are explained at www.tfl.gov.uk/tickets. Or simply show up at a Tube ticket window with your family; the clerk will tell you which deal is best.

River Cruises: A Travelcard gives you a 33 percent discount on most Thames cruises (see "Cruises," later). If you pay for Thames Clippers (including the Tate Boat museum ferry) with your pay-as-you go Oyster card, you'll get a 10 percent discount.

Sightseeing Deal: By buying a paper One-Day Travelcard at a train station, you can qualify for two-for-one discounts at many popular sights. If two of you will be visiting a pricey sight (such as the Tower of London, Churchill War Rooms, London Eye, or Madame Tussauds) and getting a One-Day Travelcard anyway, this is a smart move. But it only works if your paper Travelcard is issued through a National Rail train-station machine or ticket counter, and the sight discount must be used on the day the ticket is valid. It doesn't work if your Travelcard is loaded onto an Oyster card, or if you get your Travelcard in a Tube station. Look for brochures with coupons at major train stations, or print vouchers at www.daysout-guide.co.uk.

The Bottom Line

Struggling to choose which pass works best for your trip? First of all, skip the individual tickets. On a short visit (three days or fewer), get an Oyster card and pay as you go (remember, even if you'll be zipping around a lot, using an Oyster card means you'll never pay more per day than the cost of a One-Day Travelcard). If you're in London four days or longer, the Seven-Day Travelcard will likely pay for itself.

By Tube

London's subway system is called the Tube or Underground (but never "subway," which, in Britain, refers to a pedestrian underpass).

The Tube is one of this planet's great people-movers and usually the fastest long-distance transport in town (runs Mon-Sat about 5:00-24:00, Sun about 7:00-23:00). Two other commuter rail lines, while technically not part of the Tube, are tied into the network and use the same tickets: the Docklands Light Railway (called DLR, runs to the Docklands, Greenwich, and Olympic Park) and the Overground.

Get your bearings by studying a map of the system (free at any station).

Each line has a name (such as Circle, Northern, or Bakerloo) and two directions (indicated by the end-of-the-line stops). Find the line that will take you to your destination, and figure out roughly which direction (north, south, east, or west) you'll need to go to get there.

You can use an Oyster card, Travelcard, or individual tickets (all explained earlier) to pay for your journey. At the Tube station, touch your Oyster card flat against the turnstile's yellow card reader, both when you enter and exit the station. If you have a regular paper ticket or a One-Day Travelcard, feed it into the turnstile, reclaim it, and hang on to it—you'll need it later.

Find your train by following signs to your line and the (general) direction it's headed (such as Central Line: east). Since some tracks are shared by several lines, double-check before boarding a

train: First, make sure your destination is one of the stops listed on the sign at the platform. Also, check the electronic signboards that announce which train is next, and make sure the destination (the end-of-the-line stop) is the direction you want. Some trains, particularly on the Circle and District lines, split off for other directions, but each train has its final destination marked above its windshield.

Trains run about every 3-10 minutes. For a rough idea of how long it takes to get from point A to point B by Tube, estimate five minutes per stop (which includes time to walk into and out of stations, and to change trains). So a destination six stops away will take you about 30 minutes.

If one train is absolutely packed and another to the same destination is coming in three minutes, wait to avoid the sardine routine. Rush hours (8:00-10:00 and 16:00-19:00) can be packed and sweaty. Bring something to do to make your waiting time productive. If you get confused, ask for advice from a local, a blue-vested staff person, or at the information window located before the turnstile entry.

At most stations, you can't leave the system without touching your Oyster card to an electronic reader, or feeding your ticket or One-Day Travelcard into the turnstile. (If you have a single-trip paper ticket, the turnstile will eat your now-expired ticket; if it's a One-Day Travelcard, it will spit out your still-valid card.) Some stations, such as Hampton Court, do not have a turnstile, so you'll have to locate a reader to "touch out" your Oyster card. If you skip this step and leave the station, the system assumes you've ridden to the most remote station, and highest fare will be deducted from your card. When leaving a station, save walking time by choosing the best street exit—check the maps on the walls or ask any station personnel.

The system can be fraught with construction delays and breakdowns (the Circle Line is notorious for problems). Most construction is scheduled for weekends. Closures are publicized in advance (online at www.tfl.gov.uk and with posters in the Tube; Google Maps also has real-time service alerts for the Tube, and TFL does a fine job of tweeting updates). Pay attention to signs and announcements explaining necessary detours. Closed Tube lines are often replaced by temporary bus service, but it can be faster to figure out alternate routes on the Tube; since the lines cross each other constantly, there are several ways to make any journey. For help, check out the "Journey Planner" at www.tfl.gov.uk, which is accessible (for free) on any mobile device within most Tube stations.

Tube Etiquette

- When your train arrives, stand off to the side and let riders exit before you try to board.
- Avoid using the hinged seats near the doors of some trains when the car is jammed; they take up valuable standing space.
- If you're blocking the door when the train stops, step out of the car and off to the side, let others off, then get back on.
- Talk softly in the cars. Listen to how quietly Londoners communicate and follow their lead.
- On escalators, stand on the right and pass on the left. But note that in some passageways or stairways, you might be directed to walk on the left (the direction Brits go when behind the wheel).
- When leaving a station, it's polite to hold the door for the person behind you.
- Discreet eating and drinking are fine (nothing smelly); drinking alcohol and smoking are not.

By Bus

If you figure out the bus system, you'll swing like Tarzan through the urban jungle of London (see sidebar for a list of handy routes). Pick up a free bus map; the most user-friendly is in the *Welcome to London* brochure (mentioned earlier). You can also find thicker, more in-depth maps of various sectors of the city (most useful is the Central London Bus Guide). Bus maps are available at Transport for London offices, the City of London TI, and other tourist spots around town. With a mobile phone, you can find out the arrival time of the next bus by texting your bus stop's five-digit code (posted at the stop, above the timetable) to 87287 (if you're using your US phone's SIM card, text the code to 011-44-7797-800-287).

O			
Oakwood ⊖	N91	❶ ❽	
Old Coulsdon	N68	Aldwych	
Old Ford	N8	Oxford Circus	
Old Kent Road Canal Bridge	53, N381		
	453	❹ ❼	
	N21	❻	
Old Street ⊖ ⇌	243	Aldwych	
Orpington ⇌	N47	❻	
Oxford Circus ⊖	Any bus	❼	
	N18	❺	
P			
Paddington ⊖ ⇌	23, N15	❻ ❼ ❼	
Palmers Green ⇌	N29	❻	
Park Langley	N3	❹ ❻	
Peckham	12	❹ ❼	
	N89, N343	❻	
	N136	❹ ❻	
	N381	❼	
Penge Pawleyne Arms	176	❻	
	N3	❹ ❻	
Petts Wood ⇌	N47	❻	
Pimlico Grosvenor Road	24	❹ ❻	
Plaistow Greengate	N15	❻ ❼	
Plumstead ⇌	53	❼	
Plumstead Common	53	❼	

Buses are covered by Travelcards and Oyster cards. You can also buy individual tickets from a machine at bus stops (no change given), but you can't buy tickets on board. Any bus ride in downtown London costs £2.40 for those paying cash, or £1.40 if using an Oyster card (with a cap of £4.40 per day).

The first step in mastering London's bus system is learning how to decipher the bus stop signs (see photo). In the first column, find your destination on the list—e.g., Paddington. In the next column, find a bus that goes there—the #23. The final column has a letter within a circle (e.g., "H") that tells you exactly which bus stop you need to stand at to catch your bus. (You'll find the same letter marked on a neighborhood map nearby.) Make your way to that stop—you'll know it's yours because it will have the same letter on its pole—and wait for the bus with your number on it to arrive. Hop on, and you're good to go.

As you board, touch your Oyster card to the card reader, or, if you have a paper ticket or a One-Day Travelcard, show it to the driver. On "Heritage Routes" #9 and #15 (some of which use older double-decker buses), you may still pay a conductor; take a seat, and he or she will come around to collect your fare or verify your pass. There's no need to tap your card or show your ticket when you hop off.

If you have an Oyster card or Travelcard, save your feet and get in the habit of hopping buses for quick little straight shots, even just to get to a Tube stop. During bump-and-grind rush hours (8:00-10:00 and 16:00-19:00), you'll usually go faster by Tube.

By Taxi

London is the best taxi town in Europe. Big, black, carefully regulated cabs are everywhere. (While historically known as "black cabs," some of London's official taxis are covered with wildly colored ads.) Some cabs now run on biofuels—a good way to dispose of all that oil used to fry fish-and-chips.

I've never met a crabby cabbie in London. They love to talk, and they know every nook and cranny in town. I ride in a taxi each day just to get my London questions answered (drivers must pass a rigorous test on "The Knowledge" of London geography to earn their license).

If a cab's top light is on, just wave it down. Drivers flash lights when they see you wave. They have a tight turning radius (on new cabs, the back tires actually pivot), so you can hail cabs going in either direction. If waving doesn't work, ask someone where you can find a taxi stand. Telephoning a cab will get you one in a few

Handy Bus Routes

Ever since London instituted a congestion charge for cars, the bus system has gotten faster, easier, and cheaper. Tube-oriented travelers need to get over their tunnel vision, learn the bus system, and get around fast and easy. The best views are upstairs on a double-decker.

Here are some of the most useful routes:

Route #9: High Street Kensington to Knightsbridge (Harrods) to Hyde Park Corner to Piccadilly Circus to Trafalgar Square. This is one of two "Heritage Routes," using some old-style double-decker buses.

Route #11: Victoria Station to Westminster Abbey to Trafalgar Square to St. Paul's and Liverpool Street Station and the East End.

Route #15: Regent Street to Piccadilly Circus to Trafalgar Square to St. Paul's to Tower of London. This is the other "Heritage Route," also with old-style double-decker buses.

Routes #23 and #159: Paddington Station to Oxford Circus to Piccadilly Circus to Trafalgar Square; from there, #23 heads east to St. Paul's and Liverpool Street Station, while #159 heads to Westminster and the Imperial War Museum.

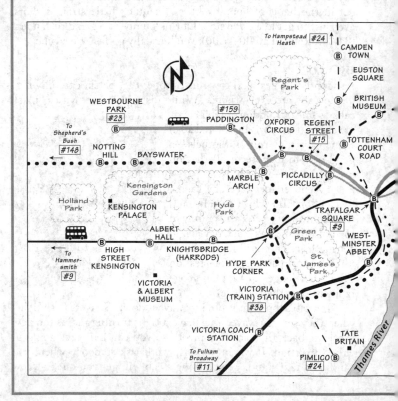

In addition, several buses (including #6, #13, and #139) also make the corridor run between Marble Arch, Oxford Circus, Piccadilly Circus, and Trafalgar Square.

Route #24: Pimlico (near Tate Britain) to Victoria Station to Westminster Abbey to Trafalgar Square to Euston Square, then all the way north to Camden Town (Camden Lock Market) and Hampstead Heath.

Route #38: Victoria Station to Hyde Park Corner to Piccadilly Circus to British Museum.

Route #RV1 (a scenic South Bank joyride): Tower of London to Tower Bridge to Southwark Street (five-minute walk behind Tate Modern/ Shakespeare's Globe) to London Eye/Waterloo Station, then over Waterloo Bridge to Aldwych and Covent Garden.

Route #148: Westminster Abbey to Victoria Station to Notting Hill and Bayswater (by way of the east end of Hyde Park and Marble Arch).

Check the bus stop closest to your hotel—it might be convenient to your sightseeing plans.

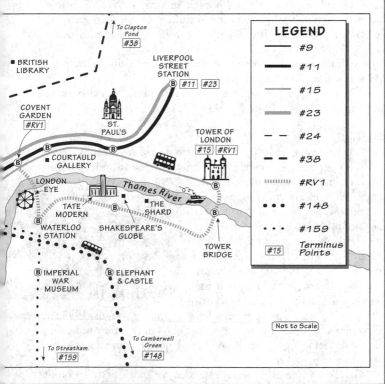

minutes, but costs a little more (tel. 0871-871-8710; £2 surcharge, plus extra fee to book ahead by credit card).

Rides start at £2.40. The regular tariff #1 covers most of the day (Mon-Fri 6:00-20:00), tariff #2 is during "unsociable hours" (Mon-Fri 20:00-22:00 and Sat-Sun 6:00-22:00), and tariff #3 is for nighttime (22:00-6:00) and holidays. Rates go up about 15-20 percent with each higher tariff. All extra charges are explained in writing on the cab wall. Tip a cabbie by rounding up (maximum 10 percent).

Connecting downtown sights is quick and easy, and will cost you about £6-10 (for example, St. Paul's to the Tower of London, or between the two Tate museums). For a short ride, three adults in a cab generally travel at close to Tube prices—and groups of four or five adults should taxi everywhere. All cabs can carry five passengers, and some take six, for the same cost as a single traveler.

Don't worry about meter cheating. Licensed British cab meters come with a sealed computer chip and clock that ensures you'll get the correct tariff. The only way a cabbie can cheat you is by taking a needlessly long route. One serious pitfall, however, is taking a cab when traffic is bad to a destination efficiently served by the Tube. On one trip to London, I hopped in a taxi at South Kensington for Waterloo Station and hit bad traffic. Rather than spending 20 minutes and £2 on the Tube, I spent 40 minutes and £16 in a taxi.

If you overdrink and ride in a taxi, be warned: Taxis charge £40 for "soiling" (a.k.a., pub puke).

If you forget this book in a taxi, call the Lost Property office and hope for the best (tel. 0845-330-9882).

By Bike

London is keeping up its push to become more bike-friendly. Since 2010, it's operated a citywide bike-rental program similar to ones in other major European cities, and new bike lanes are still cropping up around town. Still, London isn't (yet) ideal for biking. Although the streets are relatively uncongested, the network of designated bike lanes is far from complete, and the city's many one-way streets (not to mention the need to bike on the "wrong" side) can  make biking here a bit more challenging than it sounds. If you're accustomed to urban biking, it can be a good option for connecting your sightseeing stops, but if you're just up for a joyride, stick to London's large parks.

Barclays Cycle Hire bikes, intended for quick point-to-point trips, are fairly easy to rent and a giddy joy to use, even for the most jaded London tourist. These "Boris Bikes" (as they are affectionately called by locals, after cycle enthusiast and mayor Boris Johnson) are cruisers with big, cushy seats, a bag rack with elastic straps, and three gears.

Approximately 600 bike-rental stations are scattered throughout the city, each equipped with a computer kiosk. To rent a bike, you need to pay an access fee (£2/day or £10/week). The first 30 minutes are free; if you hang on to the bike for longer, you'll be charged (£1 for 1 hour, £4 for 1.5 hours, £6 for 2 hours, and much steeper beyond that).

When you're ready to ride, press "Hire a Cycle" and insert your credit card when prompted. You'll then get a ticket with a five-digit code (using a combination of 1s, 2s, and 3s). Take the ticket to any bike, then wake up the machine by pressing any button on the panel near the front tire. When the light comes on, punch in the number. After the yellow light blinks, a green light will appear: Now you can (firmly) pull the bike out of the slot.

When your ride is over, find a station with an empty slot, then push your bike in until it locks and the green light flashes.

You can hire bikes as often as you like (which will start your free 30-minute period over again), as long as you wait five minutes between each use. There can be problems, of course—stations at popular locations (such as entrances to parks) can temporarily run out of bikes, and you may have trouble finding a place to return a bike—but for the most part, this system works great. To make things easier, get a map of the docking stations—pick one up at any major Underground station. It's also available online at www.tfl.gov.uk (click on "Barclays Cycle Hire") and as a free smartphone app (http://cyclehireapp.com).

Helmets are not provided, so ride carefully. Stay to the far-left side of the road and watch closely at intersections for *left*-turning cars. If riding on crowded streets feels intimidating, stick to parks and quiet back lanes. Be aware that in most parks (including Hyde Park/Kensington Gardens) only certain paths are designated for bike use—you can't ride just anywhere. Maps posted at park entrances identify bike paths, and non-bike paths are generally clearly marked.

Some bike tour companies also rent bikes—for details, see page 74.

By Car

If you have a car, stow it—you don't want to drive in London. If you need convincing, here's one more reason: A £10 **congestion charge** is levied on any private car entering the city center during peak hours (Mon-Fri 7:00-18:00, no charge Sat-Sun and holidays,

LONDON

fee payable at gas stations, convenience stores, and self-service machines at public parking lots, or online at www.cclondon.com). Traffic cameras photograph and identify every vehicle that enters the fee zone; if you get spotted and don't pay up by midnight that day (or pay £12 before midnight of the following day), you'll get socked with a penalty of at least £60. The system has been effective in cutting down traffic jam delays and bolstering London's public transit. The revenue that's raised subsidizes the buses, which are now cheaper, more frequent, and even more user-friendly than before. Today, the vast majority of vehicles in the city center are buses, taxis, and service trucks.

Tours in London

To sightsee on your own, download my series of free audio tours that illuminate some of London's top sights and neighborhoods (see sidebar on page 51 for details).

▲▲▲Hop-On, Hop-Off Double-Decker Bus Tours

Two competitive companies (Original and Big Bus) offer essentially the same two tours of the city's sightseeing highlights, with nearly 30 stops on each route. Big Bus tours are a little more expensive (£30), while Original tours are cheaper (£24 with this book) and nearly as good.

These two-to-three hour, once-over-lightly bus tours drive by all the famous sights, providing a stress-free way to get your bearings and see the biggies. They stop at the same core group of sights regardless of which overview tour you're on: Piccadilly Circus, Trafalgar Square, Big Ben, St. Paul's, the Tower of London, Marble Arch, Victoria Station, and elsewhere. With a good guide and nice weather, I'd sit back and enjoy the entire tour. (If you don't like your guide, you can hop off and try your luck with the next departure.)

Each company offers at least one route with live (English-only) guides, and a second (sometimes slightly different route) comes with recorded, dial-a-language narration. In addition to the overview tours, both Original and Big Bus include the Thames River boat trip by City Cruises (between Westminster and the Tower of London) and three 1.5-hour walking tours.

Pick up a map from any flier rack or from one of the countless salespeople, and study the complex system. Sunday morning—when the traffic is light and many museums are closed—is a fine time for a tour. Unless you're using the bus tour mainly for hop-on, hop-off transportation, consider saving time and money by taking a night tour (described later).

Combining a London Bus Tour and the Changing of the Guard

For a grand and efficient intro to London, consider catching either of the bus companies' overview tours at 8:30, riding 90 percent of the loop (which takes just over two hours, depending on traffic), and hopping off at Buckingham Palace in time to catch the Changing of the Guard ceremony. Choose between the Big Bus Tour (catch it at the Green Park Tube station) or the Original Bus Tour (catch it at Grosvenor Gardens a block from Victoria Station). If you miss the 8:30 bus, you could catch the next one (generally about 20 minutes later), though it may get you to the ceremony a bit late (check with the driver).

Buses run about every 10-15 minutes in summer, every 10-20 minutes in winter, and operate daily. They start at about 8:30 and run until early evening in summer or late afternoon in winter. The last full loop usually leaves Victoria Station at about 19:00 in summer, and at about 17:00 in winter (confirm by checking the schedule or asking the driver).

You can buy tickets from drivers or from staff at street kiosks (credit cards accepted at kiosks at major stops such as Victoria Station, ticket good for 24 hours).

Original London Sightseeing Bus Tour

They offer two versions of their basic highlights loop: **The Original Tour** (live guide, marked with a yellow triangle on the front of the bus) and the **City Sightseeing Tour** (essentially the same route but with recorded narration, a kids' soundtrack option, and a stop at Madame Tussauds; bus marked with a red triangle). Other routes include the blue-triangle **Museum Tour** (connecting far-flung museums and major shopping stops), and green, black, and purple triangle routes (linking major train stations to the central route). All routes are covered by the same ticket. Keep it simple and just take one of the city highlights tours (£28, £4 less with this book, limit four discounts per book, they'll rip off the corner of this page—raise bloody hell if the staff or driver won't honor this discount; also online deals, info center at 17 Cockspur Street, tel. 020/8877-1722, www.theoriginaltour.com).

Big Bus London Tours

For £30 (up to 30 percent discount online—requires printer), you get the same basic overview tours: Red buses come with a live guide, while the blue route has a recorded narration and a one-hour longer path that goes around Hyde Park. These pricier Big Bus tours tend to have better, more dynamic guides than the Original tours, and more departures—meaning shorter waits for those hopping on and

LONDON

Daily Reminder

Sunday: The Tower of London and British Museum are both especially crowded today. Speakers' Corner in Hyde Park rants from early afternoon until early evening. These places are closed: Sir John Soane's Museum, and legal sights (Houses of Parliament, City Hall, and Old Bailey; the neighborhood called The City is dead). Westminster Abbey and St. Paul's are open during the day for worship but closed to sightseers. With all these closures, this morning is a good time to take a bus tour. Most big stores open late (around 11:30) and close early (18:00). Street markets are flourishing at Camden Lock, Spitalfields (at its best today), Petticoat Lane, Brick Lane, and Greenwich, but Portobello Road and Brixton markets are closed (though the Brixton farmers' market is open 10:00-14:00). Theaters are quiet, as most actors take today off. (There are a few exceptions, such as Shakespeare's Globe, which offers Sunday performances in summer, and family-oriented fare, including *The Lion King*, offered year-round.)

Monday: Virtually all sights are open, except Apsley House, Sir John Soane's Museum, Vinopolis, and a few others. The Houses of Parliament may be open as late as 22:00.

Tuesday: Virtually all sights are open, except Vinopolis and Apsley House. The British Library is open until 20:00, and the Houses of Parliament may be open as late as 22:00. On the first Tuesday of the month, Sir John Soane's Museum is also open 18:00-21:00.

Wednesday: Virtually all sights are open. Vinopolis is open until 21:30 and the Houses of Parliament may be open as late as 22:00.

Thursday: All sights are open, plus evening hours at the National Portrait Gallery (until 21:00) and Vinopolis (until 21:30).

off (daily 8:30-18:00, winter until 16:30, info center at 48 Buckingham Palace Road, tel. 020/7233-9533, www.bigbustours.com).

London by Night Sightseeing Tour

This tour offers a 1.5-hour circuit, but after hours, with no extras (e.g., walks, river cruises), and at a lower price. While the narration can be pretty lame, the views at twilight are grand—though note that it stays light until late on summer nights, and London just doesn't do floodlighting as well as, say, Paris (£19, £15 online). From June through late September, open-top buses depart at 19:00, 20:00, 20:45, 21:30, 22:10, and 22:55 from Victoria Station (Jan-May and late Sept-late Dec departs at 19:00, 20:45, and 22:10 only with closed-top bus, no tours between Christmas and New Year). Buses leave from near Victoria Station (in front of Grosvenor Hotel on Buckingham Palace Road; or you can board at any stop, such as

Friday: All sights are open, except the Houses of Parliament. Sights open late include the British Museum (selected galleries until 20:30), National Gallery (until 21:00), National Portrait Gallery (until 21:00), Vinopolis (until 21:30), Victoria and Albert Museum (selected galleries until 22:00), and Tate Modern (until 22:00). The Tate Britain is open until 22:00 on select Fridays.

Saturday: Most sights are open, except legal ones (Old Bailey, City Hall; skip The City). The Houses of Parliament are open only with a tour. Vinopolis is open until 21:30 and the Tate Modern until 22:00. The Tower of London is especially crowded today. Today's the day to hit the Portobello Road street market; the Camden Lock and Greenwich markets are also good.

Notes: St. Martin-in-the-Fields church offers concerts at lunchtime (Mon, Tue, and Fri at 13:00) and in the evening (several nights a week at 19:30, jazz Wed at 20:00).

Evensong occurs nearly daily at St. Paul's (Sun at 15:15 and Tue-Sat at 17:00), Westminster Abbey (Sun at 15:00, Mon-Tue and Thu-Sat at 17:00 except Sat at 15:00 Sept-April), and Southwark Cathedral (Sun at 15:00, Tue-Fri 17:30, Sat at 16:00). For a description of evensong services, see page 164.

London by Night Sightseeing Tour buses leave from Victoria Station each evening (six departures 19:00-22:55; at 19:00, 20:45, and 22:10 in winter).

The London Eye spins nightly (last departure between 20:30 and 21:30, depending on the season).

In winter, Apsley House is open only on weekends (closed Mon-Fri).

Marble Arch, Trafalgar Square, London Eye, or Tower of London; tel. 020/8545-6110, www.london-by-night.net). For a memorable and economical evening, munch a scenic picnic dinner on the top deck. (There are plenty of takeaway options within the train stations and near the various stops.)

▲▲Walking Tours

Several times a day, top-notch local guides lead (sometimes big) groups through specific slices of London's past. Look for brochures at TIs or ask at hotels, although the latter usually push higher-priced bus tours. *Time Out,* the weekly entertainment guide, lists some, but not all, scheduled walks. Check with the various tour companies by phone or online to get their full picture.

To take a walking tour, simply show up at the announced

location and pay the guide. Then enjoy two chatty hours of Dickens, Harry Potter, the Plague, Shakespeare, Legal London, the Beatles, Jack the Ripper, or whatever is on the agenda.

London Walks

This leading company lists its extensive and creative daily schedule on their amusing website, as well as in a beefy, plain *London Walks* brochure (available at St. Martin-in-the-Fields' Café in the Crypt on Trafalgar Square and at the City of London TI). Just perusing their fascinating lineup of tours inspires me to stay longer in London. Their two-hour walks, led by top-quality professional guides (ranging from archaeologists to actors), cost £9 (cash only, walks offered year-round, private tours for groups-£130, tel. 020/7624-3978 for a live person, tel. 020/7624-9255 for a recording of today's or tomorrow's walks and the Tube station they depart from, www.walks.com).

London Walks also offers day trips into the countryside, a good option for those with limited time and transportation (£12-16 plus £10-50 for transportation and any admission costs, cash only: Stonehenge/Salisbury, Oxford/Cotswolds, Cambridge, Bath, and so on). These are economical in part because everyone gets group discounts for transportation and admissions.

Sandemans New London "Free Royal London Tour"

This company employs students (rather than licensed guides) who recite three-hour spiels covering the basic London sights. While the fast-moving, youthful tours are light and irreverent, and can be both entertaining and fun, it's misleading to call the tours "free," as tips are expected (the guides actually pay the company for the privilege of asking for tips). Given that London Walks offers daily tours at a reasonable price, taking this "free" tour makes no sense to me (daily at 11:00 and 13:00, meet at Wellington Arch, Tube: Hyde Park Corner, Exit 2). Sandemans also has other guided tours for a charge, including a Pub Crawl (£20, nightly at 19:30, meet at Verve Bar at 1 Upper St. Martin's Lane, Tube: Leicester Square, www.newlondon-tours.com).

Beatles Walks

Fans of the still-Fab Four can take one of three Beatles walks (London Walks has two that run 5 days/week; Big Bus includes a daily walk with their bus tour; both listed earlier). For more on Beatles sights, see page 118.

Jack the Ripper Walks

Each walking tour company seems to make most of its money with "haunted" and Jack the Ripper tours. Many guides are historians and would rather not lead these lightweight tours—but, in tourism as in journalism, "if it bleeds, it leads" (which is why the juvenile London Dungeon is one of the city's busiest sights).

Two reliably good two-hour tours start every night at the

Tower Hill Tube station exit. **London Walks'** leave nightly at 19:30 (£9, pay at the start, tel. 020/7624-3978, recorded info tel. 020/7624-9255, www.jacktheripperwalk.com). **Ripping Yarns',** which leave earlier, are guided by off-duty Yeoman Warders—the Tower of London "Beefeaters" (£7, pay at end, nightly at 18:45, no tours between Christmas and New Year, mobile 07813-559-301, www.jack-the-ripper-tours.com). After taking both, I found the London Walks tour more entertaining, informative, and with a better route (along quieter, once-hooker-friendly lanes, with less traffic), starting at Tower Hill and ending at Liverpool Street Station rather than returning to Tower Hill. Groups can be huge for both, but there's always room—just show up.

Private Walks with Local Guides

Standard rates for London's registered Blue Badge guides are about £150-165 for four hours and £250 or more for nine hours (tel. 020/7611-2545, www.guidelondon.org.uk or www.britainsbest-guides.org). I know and like four fine local guides: **Sean Kelleher** (tel. 020/8673-1624, mobile 07764-612-770, seankelleher@btint-ernet.com), **Britt Lonsdale** (£230/half-day, £330/day, great with families, generous with pre-trip advice, tel. 020/7386-9907, mobile 07813-278-077, brittl@btinternet.com), and two others who work in London when they're not on the road leading my Britain tours, **Tom Hooper** (mobile 07986-048-047, tomh@ricksteves.net) and **Gillian Chadwick** (mobile 07889-976-598, gillychad@hotmail. co.uk).

Driver-Guides

These two guides have cars or a minibus (particularly helpful for travelers with limited mobility): **Robina Brown** (£330/half-day, £475/day, £660 outside London, £40 more for groups of 4-6 people, also does overnight tours farther afield, tel. 020/7228-2238, www. driverguidetours.com, robina@driverguidetours.com) and **Janine Barton** (£350/half-day, £470/day within London, £550 outside London, tel. 020/7402-4600, http://seeitinstyle.synthasite.com, jbsiis@aol.com).

London Duck Tours

A bright-yellow amphibious WWII-vintage vehicle (the model that landed troops on Normandy's beaches on D-Day) takes a gang of 30 tourists past some famous sights on land—Big Ben, Trafal-gar Square, Piccadilly Circus—then splashes into the Thames for a cruise. All in all, it's good fun at a rather steep price. The live guide works hard, and it's kid-friendly to the point of goofiness. Beware: These book up in advance (£21, April-Sept daily, first tour 9:30 or 10:00, last tour usually 18:00, shorter hours Oct-March, 1-4/hour, 1.25 hours—45 minutes on land and 30 minutes in the river, £3 booking fee by phone or online, departs from Chicheley

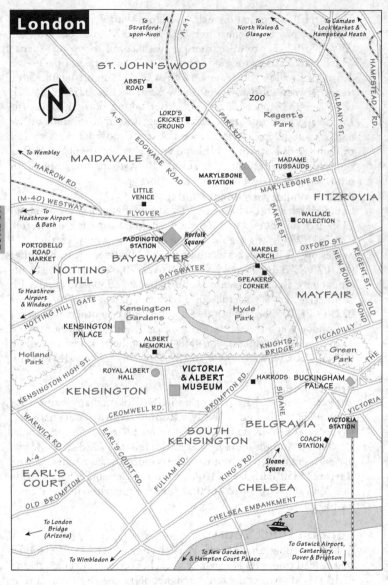

LONDON

Street—you'll see the big, ugly vehicle parked 100 yards behind the London Eye, Tube: Waterloo or Westminster, tel. 020/7928-3132, www.londonducktours.co.uk).

Bike Tours

London, like Paris, is committed to creating more bike paths, and many of its best sights can be laced together with a pleasant pedal

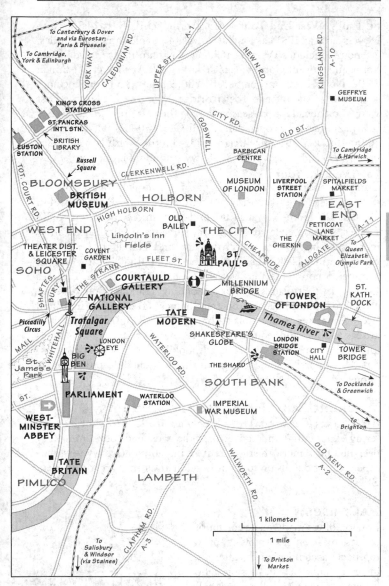

LONDON

through its parks. A bike tour is a fun way to see the sights and enjoy the city on two wheels.

London Bicycle Tour Company

Three tours covering London are offered daily from their base at Gabriel's Wharf on the South Bank of the Thames. Sunday is the best, as there is less car traffic (**Central Tour**—£19, daily at 10:30, 6 miles, 2.5 hours, includes Westminster, Covent Garden, and

St. Paul's; **West End Tour**—£19, April-Oct daily at 14:30, Nov-March daily at 12:00 as long as at least 4 people show up, 7 miles, 2.5 hours, includes Westminster, Buckingham Palace, Hyde Park, Soho, and Covent Garden; **East Tour**—£22, April-Oct Sat-Sun at 14:00, Nov-March only on Sat at 12:00, 9 miles, 3.5 hours, includes south side of the river to Tower Bridge, then The City to the East End; book ahead for off-season tours). They also rent bikes (£3.50/hour, £20/day; office open daily April-Oct 9:30-18:00, Nov-March 10:00-16:00, west of Blackfriars Bridge on the South Bank, 1a Gabriel's Wharf, tel. 020/3318-3088, www.londonbicycle.com).

Fat Tire Bike Tours

Daily bike tours cover the highlights of downtown London, on two different itineraries (£2 discount with this book): **Royal London** (£20, daily March-Nov at 11:00, mid-May-mid-Sept also at 15:30, 7 miles, 4 hours, meet at Queensway Tube station; includes Parliament, Buckingham Palace, Hyde Park, and Trafalgar Square) and **River Thames** (£28, March-Nov Thu-Sat at 10:30, nearly daily in summer, 5 hours, meet at Waterloo Tube station—exit 2; includes London Eye, St. Paul's, Tower of London, Trafalgar Square, Covent Garden, and boat trip on the Thames). The spiel is light and irreverent rather than scholarly, but the price is right. Reservations are easy online, and required for River Thames tours and kids' bikes (off-season tours can be arranged, mobile 078-8233-8779, www.fattirebiketourslondon.com). Confirm the schedule online or by phone.

Weekend Tour Packages for Students

Andy Steves (Rick's son) runs **Weekend Student Adventures,** offering experiential and active three-day weekend tours from €199 designed for American students studying abroad (see www.wsaeurope.com for details on tours of London and other great European cities).

▲▲Cruises

London offers many made-for-tourist cruises, most on slow-moving, open-top boats accompanied by entertaining commentary about passing sights. Several companies offer essentially the same trip. Generally speaking, you can either do a **short city-center cruise** by riding a boat 30 minutes from Westminster Pier to Tower Pier (particularly handy if you're interested in visiting the Tower of London anyway), or take a **longer cruise**

Thames Boat Piers

While Westminster Pier is the most popular, it's not the only dock in town. Consider all the options (listed from west to east, as the Thames flows—see the color maps in the front of this book):

Millbank Pier (North Bank), at the Tate Britain Museum, is used primarily by the Tate Boat service (express connection to Tate Modern at Bankside Pier).

Westminster Pier (North Bank), near the base of Big Ben, offers round-trip sightseeing cruises and lots of departures in both directions (though the Thames Clippers boats don't stop here). Nearby sights include Parliament and Westminster Abbey.

Waterloo Pier (a.k.a. **London Eye Pier,** South Bank), right at the base of the London Eye, is a good, less-crowded alternative to Westminster, with many of the same cruise options (Waterloo Station is nearby).

Embankment Pier (North Bank) is near Covent Garden, Trafalgar Square, and Cleopatra's Needle (the obelisk on the Thames). This pier is used mostly for special boat trips (such as some RIB—rigid inflatable boat—trips, and lunch and dinner cruises).

Festival Pier (South Bank) is next to the Royal Festival Hall, just downstream from the London Eye.

Blackfriars Pier (North Bank) is in The City, not far from St. Paul's.

Bankside Pier (South Bank) is directly in front of the Tate Modern and Shakespeare's Globe.

London Bridge Pier (a.k.a. **London Bridge City Pier,** South Bank) is near the HMS *Belfast*.

Tower Pier (North Bank) is at the Tower of London, at the east edge of The City and near the East End.

St. Katharine's Pier (North Bank) is just downstream from the Tower of London.

Canary Wharf Pier (North Bank) is at the Docklands, London's new "downtown."

In outer London, you might also use the piers at **Greenwich, Kew Gardens,** and **Hampton Court.**

that includes a peek at the East End, riding from Westminster all the way to Greenwich (save time by taking the Tube back).

Each company runs cruises daily, about twice hourly, from morning until dark; many reduce frequency off-season. Boats come and go from various docks in the city center (see sidebar). The most popular places to embark are Westminster Pier (at the base of Westminster Bridge across the street from Big Ben) and Waterloo Pier (at the London Eye, across the river).

A one-way trip within the city center costs about £10; going all the way to Greenwich costs about £2 more. Most companies charge around £3 more for a round-trip ticket, and others sell hop-on, hop-off day tickets (around £19). But I'd rather just savor one cruise, then zip home by Tube—making these return tickets not usually worthwhile.

You can buy tickets at kiosks on the docks. A Travelcard can snare you a 33 percent discount on most cruises (just show the card when you pay for the cruise); the pay-as-you-go Oyster card only nets you a discount on Thames Clippers. Because companies vary in the discounts they offer, always ask. Children and seniors generally get discounts. You can purchase drinks and scant, overpriced snacks on board. Clever budget travelers pack a picnic and munch while they cruise.

The three dominant companies are **City Cruises** (handy 30-minute cruise from Westminster Pier to Tower Pier; www.citycruises.com), **Thames River Services** (fewer stops, classic boats, friendlier and more old-fashioned feel; www.thamesriverservices.co.uk), and **Circular Cruise** (full cruise takes about an hour, operated by Crown River Services, www.crownriver.com). I'd skip the **London Eye**'s River Cruise from Waterloo Pier—it's about the same price as Circular Cruise, but 20 minutes shorter. The speedy **Thames Clippers** (described later) are designed more for no-nonsense transport than lazy sightseeing.

For details—including prices, schedules, and exactly which piers each company uses—check their websites or look for ticket kiosks at the docks. If you'd like to compare all of your options in one spot, head to Westminster Pier, which has a row of kiosks for all of the big outfits.

Cruising Downstream, to Greenwich: Both **City Cruises** and **Thames River Services** head from Westminster Pier to Greenwich. The cruises are usually narrated by the captain, with most commentary given on the way to Greenwich. The companies' prices are the same, though their itineraries are slightly different (Thames River Services makes only one stop en route and takes just an hour, while City Cruises makes two stops and adds about 10 minutes). The **Thames Clippers** boats, described later, are cheaper and faster (about 45 minutes to Greenwich), but have no commentary and no seating up top. To maximize both efficiency and sightseeing, I'd take a narrated cruise to Greenwich one way, and go the other way on the DLR (Docklands Light Railway), with a stop in the Docklands (Canary Wharf station).

Cruising Upstream, to Kew Gardens and Hampton Court Palace: Boats operated by the **Westminster Passenger Services Association** leave for Kew Gardens from Westminster Pier (£12 one-way, £18 round-trip, cash only, 2-4/day, 1.5 hours, about half the trip is narrated, www.wpsa.co.uk). Most boats continue on to Hampton Court Palace for an additional £3 (and another 1.5 hours). Because of the river current, you can save 30 minutes cruising from Hampton Court back into town (depends on the tide—ask before you commit to the boat). Romantic as these rides sound, it can be a long trip...especially upstream.

Commuting by Clipper

Thames Clippers, which uses fast, sleek, 220-seat catamarans, is designed for commuters rather than sightseers. Think of the boats as express buses on the river—they zip through London every 20-30 minutes, stopping at most of the major docks en route (including Canary Wharf/Docklands and Greenwich). They're fast: roughly 20 minutes from Embankment to Tower, 10 more minutes to Docklands, and 10 more minutes to Greenwich. However, the boats are less pleasant for joyriding than the cruises described earlier, with no commentary and no open deck up top (the only outside access is on a crowded deck at the exhaust-choked back of the boat, where you're jostling for space to take photos). Any one-way ride costs £6.50, and a River Roamer all-day ticket costs £15 (discounts with Travelcard and Oyster card, www.thamesclippers.com).

Thames Clippers also offers two express trips. The **Tate Boat** ferry service, which directly connects the Tate Britain (Millbank Pier) and the Tate Modern (Bankside Pier), is made for art lovers (£5.50 one-way, covered by River Roamer day ticket; buy ticket at gallery desk or on board; for frequency and times, see the Tate Britain and Tate Modern listings, later, or www.tate.org.uk/visit/tate-boat). The **O2 Express** runs only on nights when there are events at the O2 arena (departs from Waterloo Pier).

Self-Guided Walk

Westminster Walk

Just about every visitor to London strolls along historic Whitehall from Big Ben to Trafalgar Square. This walk gives meaning to that touristy ramble (most of the sights you'll see are described in more detail later). Under London's modern traffic and big-city bustle lie 2,000 fascinating years of history. You'll get a whirlwind tour as well as a practical orientation to London. (You can download a free, extended audio version of this walk to your mobile device; see page 51.)

Start halfway across ❶ **Westminster Bridge** for that "Wow, I'm really in London!" feeling. Get a close-up view of the **Houses of Parliament** and **Big Ben** (floodlit at night). Downstream you'll see the **London Eye.** Down the stairs to Westminster Pier are boats to the Tower of London and Greenwich (downstream) or Kew Gardens (upstream).

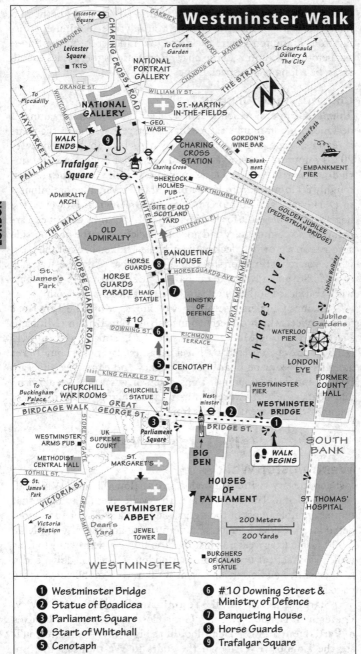

Westminster Walk

Leicester Square
Leicester Square
CRANBOURN
TKTS

CHARING CROSS ROAD
ORANGE ST.
WHITCOMB ST.
WALK ENDS
NATIONAL GALLERY

HAYMARKET
PALL MALL
Trafalgar Square

To Piccadilly

GARRICK
To Covent Garden
NATIONAL PORTRAIT GALLERY
BEDFORD
MAIDEN LN.
CHANDOS PL.
THE STRAND
WILLIAM IV ST.
ST.-MARTIN-IN-THE-FIELDS
GEO. WASH.
To Courtauld Gallery & The City

VILLIERS
CHARING CROSS STATION
GORDON'S WINE BAR
Charing Cross
Embankment
EMBANKMENT PIER
Thames Path

SHERLOCK HOLMES PUB
NORTHUMBERLAND

ADMIRALTY ARCH
THE MALL
OLD ADMIRALTY
WHITEHALL
SITE OF OLD SCOTLAND YARD
WHITEHALL PL.

GOLDEN JUBILEE (PEDESTRIAN BRIDGE)

St. James's Park

HORSE GUARDS ROAD
HORSE GUARDS PARADE
HAIG STATUE
Horse Guards
BANQUETING HOUSE
HORSEGUARDS AVE.
MINISTRY OF DEFENCE

Thames River

Jubilee Walkway

#10
DOWNING ST.
RICHMOND TERRACE
Jubilee Gardens
WATERLOO PIER
LONDON EYE

CENOTAPH
KING CHARLES ST.
PARL. ST.

To Buckingham Palace
CHURCHILL WAR ROOMS
GREAT GEORGE ST.
BIRDCAGE WALK
CHURCHILL STATUE
Parliament Square
Westminster
WESTMINSTER PIER
FORMER COUNTY HALL

WESTMINSTER ARMS PUB
STOREY'S GATE
UK SUPREME COURT
ST. MARGARET'S
BRIDGE ST.
BIG BEN
WESTMINSTER BRIDGE
WALK BEGINS
SOUTH BANK

METHODIST CENTRAL HALL
TOTHILL ST.
VICTORIA ST.
GREAT SMITH ST.
St. James's Park
To Victoria Station
Dean's Yard
WESTMINSTER ABBEY
JEWEL TOWER
HOUSES OF PARLIAMENT
ST. THOMAS' HOSPITAL

WESTMINSTER
BURGHERS OF CALAIS STATUE

200 Meters
200 Yards

❶ Westminster Bridge
❷ Statue of Boadicea
❸ Parliament Square
❹ Start of Whitehall
❺ Cenotaph
❻ #10 Downing Street & Ministry of Defence
❼ Banqueting House
❽ Horse Guards
❾ Trafalgar Square

En route to Parliament Square, you'll pass a ❷ **statue of Boadicea,** the Celtic queen defeated by Roman invaders in A.D. 60.

For fun, call home from near Big Ben at about three minutes before the hour to let your loved one hear the bell ring. You'll find four red phone booths lining the north side of ❸ **Parliament Square** along Great George Street—also great for a phone-box-and-Big-Ben photo op.

Wave hello to Winston Churchill and Nelson Mandela in Parliament Square. To Churchill's right is **Westminster Abbey,** with its two stubby, elegant towers. The white building (flying the Union Jack) at the far end of the square houses Britain's **Supreme Court.**

Head north up Parliament Street, which turns into ❹ **Whitehall,** and walk toward Trafalgar Square. You'll see the thought-provoking ❺ **Cenotaph** in the middle of the boulevard, reminding passersby of the many Brits who died in the last century's world wars. To visit the **Churchill War Rooms,** take a left before the Cenotaph, on King Charles Street.

Continuing on Whitehall, stop at the barricaded and guarded ❻ **#10 Downing Street** to see the British "White House," home of the prime minister. Break the bobby's boredom and ask him a question. The huge building across Whitehall from Downing Street is the **Ministry of Defence** (MOD), the "British Pentagon."

Nearing Trafalgar Square, look for the 17th-century ❼ **Banqueting House** across the street and the ❽ **Horse Guards** behind the gated fence.

The column topped by Lord Nelson marks ❾ **Trafalgar Square.** The stately domed building on the far side of the square is the **National Gallery,** which has a classy café in the Sainsbury wing. To the right of the National Gallery is **St. Martin-in-the-Fields Church** and its Café in the Crypt.

To get to Piccadilly from Trafalgar Square, walk up Cockspur Street to Haymarket, then take a short left on Coventry Street to colorful **Piccadilly Circus** (see map on page 104).

Near Piccadilly, you'll find a number of theaters. **Leicester Square** (with its half-price "tkts" booth for plays—see page 160) thrives just a few blocks away. Walk through seedy **Soho** (north of Shaftesbury Avenue) for its fun pubs. From Piccadilly or Oxford Circus, you can take a taxi, bus, or the Tube home.

LONDON

Sights in Central London

Westminster

These sights are listed roughly in geographical order from Westminster Abbey to Trafalgar Square, and are linked in my self-guided Westminster Walk.

▲▲▲Westminster Abbey

The greatest church in the English-speaking world, Westminster Abbey is where the nation's royalty has been wedded, crowned, and buried since 1066. Indeed, the histories of Westminster Abbey and England are almost the same. A thousand years of English history—3,000 tombs, the remains of 29 kings and queens, and hundreds of memorials to poets, politicians, scientists, and warriors—lie within its stained-glass splendor and under its stone slabs.

Cost and Hours: £18, £36 family ticket (covers 2 adults and 1 child), cash or credit cards accepted (line up in the correct queue to pay), ticket includes audioguide and entry to cloisters and Abbey Museum; abbey—Mon-Fri 9:30-16:30, Wed until 19:00 (main church only), Sat 9:30-14:30, last entry one hour before closing, closed Sun to sightseers but open for services; museum—daily 10:30-16:00; cloisters—daily 8:00-18:00; no photos, café in cellar, Tube: Westminster or St. James's Park, tel. 020/7222-5152, www.westminster-abbey.org. It's free to enter just the cloisters and Abbey Museum (through Dean's Yard, around the right side as you face the main entrance), but if it's too crowded inside, the marshal at the cloister entrance may not let you in.

When to Go: The place is most crowded every day at mid-morning and all day Saturdays and Mondays. Visit early, during lunch, or late to avoid tourist hordes. Weekdays after 14:30 are less congested; come after that time and stay for the 17:00 evensong. The main entrance, on the Parliament Square side, often has a sizable line. Of the two queues (cash or credit) at the admissions desk, the cash line is probably moving faster.

Music and Services: Mon-Fri at 7:30 (prayer), 8:00 (communion), 12:30 (communion), 17:00 evensong (except on Wed, when the evening service is generally spoken—not sung); Sat at 8:00 (communion), 9:00 (prayer), 15:00 (evensong; May-Aug it's at 17:00); Sun services generally come with more music: at 8:00 (communion), 10:00 (sung Matins), 11:15 (sung Eucharist), 15:00 (evensong), 18:30 (evening service). For more on evensong, see page 164. Services are free to anyone, though visitors who haven't paid

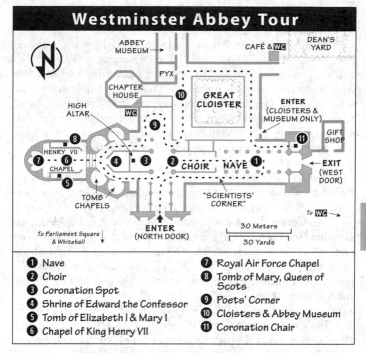

Westminster Abbey Tour

1. Nave
2. Choir
3. Coronation Spot
4. Shrine of Edward the Confessor
5. Tomb of Elizabeth I & Mary I
6. Chapel of King Henry VII
7. Royal Air Force Chapel
8. Tomb of Mary, Queen of Scots
9. Poets' Corner
10. Cloisters & Abbey Museum
11. Coronation Chair

church admission aren't allowed to linger afterward. Free organ recitals are usually held Sun at 17:45 (30 minutes). For a schedule of services or recitals on a particular day, look for posted signs with schedules or check the Abbey's website.

Tours: Entertaining guided tours of the Abbey (£3, 1.5 hours, schedule posted outside and inside entry) are offered up to 5/day in summer, 4/day in winter.

❍ Self-Guided Tour: You'll have no choice but to follow the steady flow of tourists through the church, following the route laid out for the audioguide. My tour covers the Abbey's top stops.

• *Walk straight in through the north transept. Follow the crowd flow to the right and enter the spacious...*

Nave: Look down the long and narrow center aisle of the church. Lined with the praying hands of the Gothic arches, glowing with light from the stained glass, it's clear that this is more than a museum. With saints in stained glass, heroes in carved stone, and the bodies of England's greatest citizens under the floor stones, Westminster Abbey is the religious heart of England.

The king who built the Abbey was Edward the Confessor. Find him in the stained glass windows on the left side of the nave (as you face the altar). He's in the third bay from the end (marked

S: Edwardus rex...), with his crown, scepter, and ring. The Abbey's 10-story nave is the tallest in England.

On the floor near the west entrance of the Abbey is the flower-lined Tomb of the Unknown Warrior, one ordinary WWI soldier buried in soil from France with lettering made from melted-down weapons from that war. Contemplate the million-man army from the British Empire, and all those who gave their lives. Their memory is so revered that, when Kate Middleton walked up the aisle on her wedding day, by tradition she had to step around the tomb (and her wedding bouquet was later placed atop this tomb, also in accordance with tradition).

• *Walk up the nave toward the altar. This is the same route every future monarch walks on the way to being crowned. Midway up the nave, you pass through the colorful screen of an enclosure known as...*

LONDON

The Choir: These elaborately carved-wood and gilded seats are where monks once chanted their services in the "quire"—as it's known in British churchspeak. Today, it's where the Abbey boys' choir sings the evensong. The "high" (main) altar, which usually has a cross and candlesticks atop it, sits on the platform up the five stairs in front of you.

• *It's on this platform—up the five steps—that the monarch is crowned.*

The Coronation Spot: The area immediately before the high altar is where every English coronation since 1066 has taken place. Royalty are also given funerals here. Princess Diana's coffin was carried to this spot for her funeral service in 1997. The "Queen Mum" (mother of Elizabeth II) had her funeral here in 2002. This is also where most of the last century's royal weddings have taken place, including the unions of Queen Elizabeth II and Prince Philip (1947), Prince Andrew and Sarah Ferguson (1986), and Prince William and Kate Middleton (2011).

• *Veer left and follow the crowd. Pause at the wooden staircase on your right.*

Shrine of Edward the Confessor: Step back and peek over the dark coffin of Edward I to see the tippy-top of the green-and-gold wedding-cake tomb of King Edward the Confessor—the man who built Westminster Abbey. God had told pious Edward to visit St. Peter's Basilica in Rome. But with the Normans thinking conquest, it was too dangerous for him to leave England. Instead, he built this grand church and dedicated it to St. Peter. It was finished just in time to bury Edward and to crown his foreign successor, William the Conqueror, in 1066. After Edward's death, people prayed at his tomb, and, after getting good results, Pope Alexander III canonized him. This elevated, central tomb—which lost some of its luster when Henry VIII melted down the gold coffin-case—is surrounded by the tombs of eight kings and queens.

• *At the top of the stone staircase, veer left into the private burial chapel of Queen Elizabeth I.*

Tomb of Queens Elizabeth I and Mary I: Although there's only one effigy on the tomb (Elizabeth's), there are actually two

queens buried beneath it, both daughters of Henry VIII (by different mothers). Bloody Mary—meek, pious, sickly, and Catholic—enforced Catholicism during her short reign (1553-1558) by burning "heretics" at the stake.

Elizabeth—strong, clever, and Protestant—steered England on an Anglican course. She holds a royal orb symbolizing that she's queen of the whole globe. When 26-year-old Elizabeth was crowned in the Abbey, her right to rule was questioned (especially by her Catholic subjects) because she was considered the bastard seed of Henry VIII's unsanctioned marriage to Anne Boleyn. But Elizabeth's long reign (1559-1603) was one of the greatest in English history, a time when England ruled the seas and Shakespeare explored human emotions. When she died, thousands turned out for her funeral in the Abbey. Elizabeth's face on the tomb, modeled after her death mask, is considered a very accurate take on this hook-nosed, imperious "Virgin Queen."

• *Continue into the ornate, flag-draped room up a few more stairs, directly behind the main altar.*

Chapel of King Henry VII (a.k.a. the Lady Chapel): The light from the stained-glass windows; the colorful banners overhead; and the elaborate tracery in stone, wood, and glass give this room the festive air of a medieval tournament. The prestigious Knights of the Bath meet here, under the magnificent ceiling studded with gold pendants. The ceiling—of carved stone, not plaster (1519)—is the finest English Perpendicular Gothic and fan vaulting you'll see (unless you're going to King's College Chapel in Cambridge). The ceiling was sculpted on the floor in pieces, then jigsaw-puzzled into place. It capped the Gothic period and signaled the vitality of the coming Renaissance.

• *Go to the far end of the chapel and stand at the banister in front of the modern set of stained-glass windows.*

Royal Air Force Chapel: Saints in robes and halos mingle with pilots in parachutes and bomber jackets. This tribute to WWII flyers is for those who earned their angel wings in the Battle of Britain (July-Oct 1940). A bit of bomb damage has been preserved—look for the little glassed-over hole in the wall below the windows in the lower left-hand corner.

• *Exit the Chapel of Henry VII. Turn left into a side chapel with the tomb (the central one of three in the chapel).*

Tomb of Mary, Queen of Scots: The beautiful, French-educated queen (1542-1587) was held under house arrest for 19 years by Queen Elizabeth I, who considered her a threat to her sovereignty. Elizabeth got wind of an assassination plot, suspected Mary was behind it, and had her first cousin (once removed) beheaded. When Elizabeth—who was called the "Virgin Queen"—died heirless, Mary's son, James VI, King of Scots, also became King James I of England and Ireland. James buried his mum here (with her head sewn back on) in the Abbey's most sumptuous tomb.

• *Exit Mary's chapel. Continue on, until you emerge in the south transept. You're in...*

Poets' Corner: England's greatest artistic contributions are in the written word. Here the masters of arguably the world's

most complex and expressive language are remembered: Geoffrey Chaucer *(Canterbury Tales)*, Lord Byron, Dylan Thomas, W. H. Auden, Lewis Carroll *(Alice's Adventures in Wonderland)*, T. S. Eliot *(The Waste Land)*, Alfred, Lord Tennyson, Robert Browning, and Charles Dickens. Many writers are honored with plaques and monuments; relatively few are actually buried here. Shakespeare is commemorated by a fine statue that stands near the end of the transept, overlooking the others.

• *Exit the church (temporarily) at the south door, which leads to the...*

Cloisters and Abbey Museum: The buildings that adjoin the church housed the monks. Cloistered courtyards gave them a place to meditate on God's creations.

The small Abbey Museum, formerly the monks' lounge, is worth a peek for its fascinating and well-described exhibits. Look into the impressively realistic eyes of Elizabeth I, Charles II, Admiral Nelson, and a dozen others, part of a compelling series of wax-and-wood statues that, for three centuries, graced coffins during funeral processions. The once-exquisite, now-fragmented Westminster Retable, which decorated the high altar in 1270, is the oldest surviving altarpiece in England.

• *Go back into the church for the last stop.*

Coronation Chair: A gold-painted oak chair waits here under a regal canopy for the next coronation. For every English coronation since 1308 (except two), it's been moved to its spot before the high altar to receive the royal buttocks. The chair's legs rest on lions, England's symbol.

▲▲Houses of Parliament (Palace of Westminster)

This Neo-Gothic icon of London, the royal residence from 1042 to 1547, is now the meeting place of the legislative branch of government. Like the US Capitol in Washington, DC, the complex is open to visitors. You can view parliamentary sessions in either the bickering House of Commons or the sleepy House of Lords. Or you can simply wander on your own (through a few closely monitored rooms) to appreciate the historic building itself.

LONDON

The Palace of Westminster has been the center of political power in England for nearly a thousand years. In 1834, a horrendous fire gutted the Palace. It was rebuilt in a retro style that recalled England's medieval Christian roots—pointed arches, stained-glass windows, spires, and saint-like statues. At the same time, Britain was also retooling its government. Democracy was on the rise, the queen became a constitutional monarch, and Parliament emerged as the nation's ruling body. The Palace of Westminster became a symbol—a kind of cathedral—of democracy. A visit here gives both UK residents and foreign tourists alike a chance to tour a piece of living history and see the British government in action.

Cost and Hours: Free, open to visitors whenever Parliament is in session—generally Oct-July, Mon-Thu. If you see a light on above Big Ben's clock and a flag atop Victoria Tower (at the south end of the building), then Parliament is in session.

The House of Commons is usually in session Oct-July Mon 14:30-22:00, Tue-Wed 11:30-19:00, Thu 9:30-17:30; House of Lords is typically in session Oct-July Mon-Tue 14:30-22:00, Wed 15:00-22:00, Thu 11:00-19:00; last entry usually around 20:00, both houses closed Fri-Sun except for Sat tours. During the Aug-Sept recess, the only way to visit is on a guided tour (see next page). Tube: Westminster, tel. 020/7219-4272 or 020/7219-3107, see www.parliament.uk for schedule, or visit www.parliamentlive.tv for a preview.

Dealing with Lines: Expect lines—it may take a while to get through security, plus another 20-60 minutes once inside to be admitted to the house chambers. Lines are longest at the start of each day's session (when the most fiery debate often occurs), and especially bad on Wednesdays, when the prime minister normally attends. The later in the day you enter, the less crowded (and less exciting) it is. Visiting after 18:00 is risky, as sessions tend to end well before their official closing time, and visitors aren't allowed in after the politicians call it a day.

If you only visit one of the bicameral legislative bodies, I'd choose the House of Lords. Though less important politically, the lords meet in a more ornate room, and the waiting time is shorter (likely less than 30 minutes). The House of Commons is where major policy is made, but the room itself is sparse, and waiting times are longer (30-60 minutes or more). If you just want to see the grand halls of this majestic building (without visiting either of the legislative chambers), you won't have any waiting once you're through security.

Tours: When Parliament is in recess during much of August and September, you can get a behind-the-scenes peek at the royal chambers of both houses by taking a tour (£15, 1.25 hours, generally Mon-Sat, times vary, so confirm in advance; book ahead by calling 0844-847-1672 or through www.ticketmaster.co.uk). The same tours are offered Saturdays year-round 9:15-16:30.

◑ Self-Guided Tour: Enter midway along the west side of the building (across the street from Westminster Abbey), where there's a tourist ramp leading to the visitor entrance. As you enter, you'll be asked if you want to visit the House of Commons or the House of Lords. I choose "Lords" (because the line is shorter), but it really doesn't matter. Once inside, you'll be able to do whatever you please: switch houses, see them both, or see neither and just browse through the other public spaces. If you have questions, the attendants are extremely helpful.

At the airport-style security, you're photographed and given a (Lords or Commons) badge. Continue past the Jubilee Café (which has live video feeds of Parliament in session), pick up helpful brochures at the information desk, and take in the cavernous...

Westminster Hall: This vast hall—covering 16,000 square feet—survived the 1834 fire, and is one of the oldest and most important buildings in England. Begun in 1097, the hall was greatly remodeled around 1380 by Richard II, who made it the grandest space in Europe. His self-supporting oak-timber roof (1397) wowed everyone. Unlike earlier roofs that spanned the hall with long beams, this "hammer-beam" roof uses short beams that jut horizontally out from the walls. England's vaunted legal system was

invented in this hall, as this was the major court of the land for 700 years. King Charles I was tried and sentenced to death here. Guy Fawkes was condemned for plotting to blow up the Halls of Parliament in 1605. (He's best remembered today for the sly-smiling "Guy Fawkes mask" that has become the symbol of 21st-century anarchists.)

Walking through the hall and up the stairs, you'll enter the busy world of today's government. You soon reach St. Stephen's Hall, where visitors wait to enter the House of Commons Chamber.

St. Stephen's Hall: This long, beautifully lit room was the original House of Commons for three centuries (from 1550 until the fire of 1834). MPs sat in church pews on either side of the hall—the ruling party on one side, the opposition on the other—a format they'd keep when they moved into the new chambers.

Next, you reach the...

Central Lobby: This ornate, octagonal, high-vaulted room is often called the "heart of British government," because it sits midway between the House of Commons (to the left) and House of Lords (right). Constituents come to this lobby to petition, or "lobby," their MPs (from which the term may derive). Video monitors list the schedule of meetings and events in this vast 1,100-room governmental hive. This is the best place to admire the Palace's carved wood, chandeliers, statues, and floor tiles.

This lobby marks the end of the public space where you can wander freely. To see the House of Lords or House of Commons, you must wait in line. Just before entering either chamber, you'll need to check your belongings—bag, camera, phone, even this guidebook. Read up on the info below while you wait, and ask the attendant for any brochures.

When you're done visiting the chambers, you'll backtrack through the same halls, where you can sightsee leisurely on your way back out into a well-governed London.

House of Lords: When you're called, you'll walk to the Lords Chamber by way of the long Peers' Corridor. Paintings on the corridor walls depict the anti-authoritarian spirit brewing under the reign of Charles I. When you reach the House of Lords Chamber, you watch the proceedings from an upper-level gallery.

The House of Lords consists of 750 members, called "Peers." They are not elected by popular vote. Some are nobles who've inherited the position; others are appointed by the Queen. These days, their role is largely advisory. They can propose, revise, and filibuster laws, but they have no real power to pass laws on their own. On any typical day, only a handful of the 750 lords actually show up to debate.

The Lords Chamber is church-like and impressive, with

London at a Glance

▲▲▲**Westminster Abbey** Britain's finest church and the site of royal coronations and burials since 1066. **Hours:** Mon-Fri 9:30-16:30, Wed until 19:00, Sat 9:30-14:30, closed Sun to sightseers except for worship. See page 82.

▲▲▲**Churchill War Rooms** Underground WWII headquarters of Churchill's war effort. **Hours:** Daily 9:30-18:00. See page 93.

▲▲▲**National Gallery** Remarkable collection of European paintings (1250-1900), including Leonardo, Botticelli, Velázquez, Rembrandt, Turner, Van Gogh, and the Impressionists. **Hours:** Daily 10:00-18:00, Fri until 21:00. See page 95.

▲▲▲**British Museum** The world's greatest collection of artifacts of Western civilization, including the Rosetta Stone and the Parthenon's Elgin Marbles. **Hours:** Daily 10:00-17:30, Fri until 20:30 (selected galleries only). See page 111.

▲▲▲**British Library** Impressive collection of the most important literary treasures of the Western world. **Hours:** Mon-Fri 9:30-18:00, Tue until 20:00, Sat 9:30-17:00, Sun 11:00-17:00. See page 115.

▲▲▲**St. Paul's Cathedral** The main cathedral of the Anglican Church, designed by Christopher Wren, with a climbable dome and daily evensong services. **Hours:** Mon-Sat 8:30-16:30, closed Sun except for worship. See page 120.

▲▲▲**Tower of London** Historic castle, palace, and prison housing the crown jewels and a witty band of Beefeaters. **Hours:** March-Oct Tue-Sat 9:00-17:30, Sun-Mon 10:00-17:30; Nov-Feb Tue-Sat 9:00-16:30, Sun-Mon 10:00-16:30. See page 126.

▲▲▲**Victoria and Albert Museum** The best collection of decorative arts anywhere. **Hours:** Daily 10:00-17:45, Fri until 22:00 (selected galleries only). See page 147.

▲▲**Houses of Parliament** London's Neo-Gothic landmark, famous for Big Ben and occupied by the Houses of Lords and Commons. **Hours:** Generally Mon-Tue 14:30-22:00, Wed 11:30-22:00, Thu 9:30-19:00, closed Fri-Sun and most of Aug-Sept. Can visit on Sat via guided tour only. See page 87.

▲▲**Trafalgar Square** The heart of London, where Westminster, The City, and the West End meet. **Hours:** Always open. See page 95.

▲▲**National Portrait Gallery** A *Who's Who* of British history, featuring portraits of this nation's most important historical figures. **Hours:** Daily 10:00-18:00, Thu-Fri until 21:00, first and second floors open Mon at 11:00. See page 100.

▲▲**Covent Garden** Vibrant people-watching zone with shops, cafés, street musicians, and an iron-and-glass arcade that once hosted a produce market. **Hours:** Always open. See page 103.

▲▲**Changing of the Guard at Buckingham Palace** Hour-long spectacle at Britain's royal residence. **Hours:** Generally May-July daily at 11:30, Aug-April every other day. See page 108.

▲▲**London Eye** Enormous observation wheel, dominating—and offering commanding views over—London's skyline. **Hours:** Daily July-Aug 10:00-21:30, April-June 10:00-21:00, Sept-March 10:00-20:30. See page 133.

▲▲**Imperial War Museum** Exhibits examining the military history of the bloody 20th century. **Hours:** Daily 10:00-18:00. See page 136.

▲▲**Tate Modern** Works by Monet, Matisse, Dalí, Picasso, and Warhol displayed in a converted powerhouse. **Hours:** Daily 10:00-18:00, Fri-Sat until 22:00. See page 137.

▲▲**Shakespeare's Globe** Timbered, thatched-roofed reconstruction of the Bard's original "wooden O." **Hours:** Theater complex, museum, and actor-led tours generally daily 9:00-17:00; in summer, morning theater tours only. Plays are also staged here. See page 138.

▲▲**Tate Britain** Collection of British painting from the 16th century through modern times, including works by William Blake, the Pre-Raphaelites, and J. M. W. Turner. **Hours:** Daily 10:00-18:00, select Fridays until 22:00. See page 144.

▲▲**Kensington Palace** Recently restored former home of British monarchs, with appealing exhibits on Queen Victoria, as well as William and Mary. **Hours:** Daily 10:00-18:00, until 17:00 Nov-Feb. See page 146.

▲▲**Natural History Museum** A Darwinian's delights, packed with stuffed creatures, engaging exhibits, and enthralled kids. **Hours:** Daily 10:00-17:50. See page 148.

▲**Courtauld Gallery** Fine collection of paintings filling one wing of the Somerset House, a grand 18th-century palace. **Hours:** Daily 10:00-18:00. See page 106.

LONDON

stained glass and intricately carved walls. Once you're seated in the galleries, your gaze will likely go to the Queen's gilded throne at the far end of the room. She's the only one who may sit there, and only once a year, when she gives a speech to open Parliament.

The benches where the lords sit are always upholstered red. (The House of Commons is green.) The ruling party sits on one side, the opposition on the other, and unaffiliated "crossbenchers" in between. In the center of the room sits the "Woolsack"—a cushion stuffed with wool. Here the Lord Speaker presides, with his/her ceremonial mace placed behind the backrest.

House of Commons: On the way to the House of Commons Chamber, you first pass through the long Commons Corridor, which spills into the Members' Lobby. In the lobby, MPs check their message box with its state-of-the-art 1960s technology; they enter the chamber through a stone archway that still bears bomb damage from the Nazi Blitz; and as they enter, many rub the Churchill statue's golden toe for good luck.

The Commons Chamber may be much less grandiose than the Lords Chamber, but this is where the sausage gets made. The House of Commons is as powerful as the lords, prime minister, and Queen combined. It was destroyed in the Blitz, and Churchill rebuilt the surprisingly small chamber with the same cube-shaped floor plan. Of today's 650-plus MPs, only 450 can sit—the rest have to stand at the ends.

As in the House of Lords, the ruling party sits on the left, opposition on the right. Keep an eye out for two red lines on the floor, which cannot be crossed when debating the other side. (They're supposedly two sword-lengths apart, to prevent a literal clashing of swords.) Between the benches is the canopied Speaker's Chair, for the chairman who keeps order and chooses who can speak next. The clerks sit at a central table that holds the ceremonial mace, a symbol of the power given Parliament by the monarch. Also on the table are the two "dispatch boxes"—old wooden chests that serve as lecterns, one for each side.

The Queen is not allowed in the Commons Chamber. When the prime minister visits, he speaks from one of the boxes. His ministers (or cabinet) join him on the front bench, while lesser MPs (the "backbenchers") sit behind. It's often a fiery spectacle, as the prime minister defends his policies, while the opposition grumbles and harrumphs in displeasure. It's not unheard of for MPs to get out of line and be escorted out by the Serjeant at Arms. One furious MP even grabbed the Serjeant's hallowed mace and threw it to the ground. His career was over.

Nearby: Across the street from the Parliament building's St. Stephen's Gate, the **Jewel Tower** is a rare remnant of the old Palace of Westminster, used by kings until Henry VIII. The crude stone tower (1365-1366) was a guard tower in the palace wall, over-looking a moat. It contains a fine little exhibit on Parliament and the tower (£4, April-Oct daily 10:00-17:00; Nov-March Sat-Sun 10:00-16:00, closed Mon-Fri; tel. 020/7222-2219). Next to the tower (and free) is a quiet courtyard with picnic-friendly benches.

Big Ben, the 315-foot-high clock tower at the north end of the Palace of Westminster, is named for its 13-ton bell, Ben. The light above the clock is lit when Parliament is in session. The face of the clock is huge—you can actually see the minute hand moving. For a good view of it, walk halfway over Westminster Bridge.

Other Sights in Westminster
▲▲▲Churchill War Rooms

This excellent sight offers a fascinating walk through the under-ground headquarters of the British government's fight against the Nazis in the darkest days of the Battle for Britain. It has two parts: the war rooms themselves, and a top-notch museum dedicated to the man who steered the war from here, Winston Churchill. For details on all the blood, sweat, toil, and tears, pick up the excellent,

essential, and included audioguide at the entry, and dive in. Allow yourself 1-2 hours for this sight.

Cost and Hours: £17.50 (includes 10 percent optional dona-tion), £5 guidebook, daily 9:30-18:00, last entry one hour before closing; on King Charles Street, 200 yards off Whitehall, follow the signs, Tube: Westminster, tel. 020/7930-6961, www.iwm.org.uk/churchill. The museum's gift shop is great for anyone nostalgic for the 1940s.

Cabinet War Rooms: The 27-room, heavily fortified nerve center of the British war effort was used from 1939 to 1945. Churchill's room, the map room, and other rooms are just as they were in 1945. As you follow the one-way route, be sure to take advantage of the audioguide, which explains each room and offers first-person accounts of wartime happenings here (it takes about 45 minutes, not counting the Churchill Museum). Be patient—it's well worth it. While the rooms are spartan, you'll see how British gentility survived even as the city was bombarded—posted signs informed those working underground what the weather was like outside, and a cheery notice reminded them to turn off the light switch to conserve electricity.

Churchill Museum: Don't bypass this museum, which occu-pies a large hall amid the war rooms. It dissects every aspect of the man behind the famous cigar, bowler hat, and V-for-victory sign. It's extremely well-presented and engaging, using artifacts, quotes, political cartoons, clear explanations, and high-tech interactive exhibits to bring the colorful statesman to life; this museum alone deserves an hour. You'll get a taste of Winston's wit, irascibility, work ethic, passion for painting, American ties, writing talents, and drinking habits. The exhibit shows Winston's warts as well: It questions whether his party-switching was just political opportunism, examines the basis for his opposition to Indian self-rule, and reveals him to be an intense taskmaster who worked 18-hour days and was brutal to his staffers (who deeply respected him nevertheless).

A long touch-the-screen timeline lets you zero in on events in his life from birth (November 30, 1874) to his first appointment as prime minister in 1940. Many of the items on display—such as a European map divvied up in permanent marker, which Churchill brought to England from the postwar Potsdam Conference—drive home the remarkable span of history this man lived through. Imagine: Churchill began his military career riding horses in the cavalry and ended it speaking out against the proliferation of nuclear armaments. It's all the more amazing considering that, in the 1930s, the man who would become my vote for greatest statesman of the 20th century was considered a washed-up loony ranting about the growing threat of fascism.

Eating: Get your rations at the Switch Room café (in the museum), or for a nearby pub lunch, try Westminster Arms (food served downstairs, on Storey's Gate, a couple of blocks south of the museum).

Horse Guards

The Horse Guards change daily at 11:00 (10:00 on Sun), and a colorful dismounting ceremony takes place daily at 16:00. The rest of the day, they just stand there—terrible for video cameras (on Whitehall, between Trafalgar Square and #10 Downing Street, Tube: Westminster, www.changing-the-guard.com). Buckingham Palace pageantry is canceled when it rains, but the Horse Guards change regardless of the weather.

▲Banqueting House

England's first Renaissance building (1619-1622) is still standing. Designed by Inigo Jones, built by King James I, and decorated by his son Charles I, the Banqueting House came to symbolize the Stuart kings' "divine right" management style—the belief that God himself had anointed them to rule. The house is one of the few London landmarks spared by the 1698 fire and the only surviving part of the original Palace of Whitehall. Today it opens its doors to visitors, who enjoy a restful 20-minute audiovisual history, a 30-minute audioguide, and a look at the exquisite banqueting hall itself. As a tourist attraction, it's basically one big room, with sumptuous ceiling paintings by Peter Paul Rubens. At Charles I's request, these paintings drove home the doctrine of the legitimacy of the divine right of kings. Ironically, in 1649—divine right ignored—King Charles I was famously executed right here.

Cost and Hours: £5 (includes 10 percent optional donation), includes audioguide, daily 10:00-17:00, last entry at 16:30, may close for government functions—though it promises to stay open at least until 13:00 (call ahead for recorded information about closures), aristocratic WC, immediately across Whitehall from the Horse Guards, Tube: Westminster, tel. 020/3166-6154, www.hrp.org.uk.

LONDON

▲▲Trafalgar Square

London's central square—at the intersection of Westminster, The City, and the West End—is the climax of most marches and demonstrations, and a thrill-

ing place to simply hang out. A recent remodeling of the square has rerouted car traffic, helping reclaim the area for London's citizens. At the top of Trafalgar Square (north) sits the domed National Gallery with its grand staircase, and to the right, the steeple of St. Martin-in-the-Fields, built in 1722, inspiring the steeple-over-the-entrance style of many town churches in New England. In the center of the square, Lord Horatio Nelson stands atop his 185-foot-tall fluted granite column, gazing out toward Trafalgar, where he lost his life but defeated the French fleet. Part of this 1842 memorial is made from his victims' melted-down cannons. He's surrounded by spraying fountains, giant lions, hordes of people, and—until recently—even more pigeons. A former London mayor decided that London's "flying rats" were a public nuisance and evicted Trafalgar Square's venerable seed salesmen (Tube: Charing Cross).

▲▲▲National Gallery

Displaying Britain's top collection of European paintings from 1250 to 1900—including works by Leonardo, Botticelli, Velázquez, Rembrandt, Turner, Van Gogh, and the Impressionists—this is one of Europe's great galleries. You'll peruse 700 years of art—from gold-backed Madonnas to Cubist bathers.

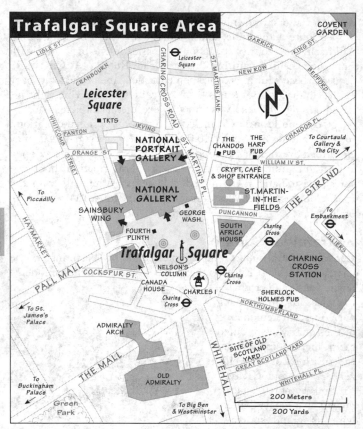

Trafalgar Square Area

Cost and Hours: Free, but suggested donation of £4, temporary (optional) exhibits extra, daily 10:00-18:00, Fri until 21:00, last entry to special exhibits 45 minutes before closing, no photos, on Trafalgar Square, Tube: Charing Cross or Leicester Square.

Information: Helpful £1 floor plan available from information desk; free one-hour overview tours leave from Sainsbury Wing info desk daily at 11:30 and 14:30, plus Fri at 19:00; excellent £3.50 audioguides—choose from one-hour highlights tour, several theme tours, or tour option that lets you dial up info on any painting in the museum; ArtStart computer terminals help you study any artist, style, or topic in the museum, and print out a tailor-made tour map (located in the comfy Espresso Bar on the ground floor of the main building; a few more non-printing terminals are inside the entrance to the Sainsbury Wing); info tel. 020/7747-2885, switchboard tel. 020/7839-3321, www.national-gallery.org.uk.

Eating: Consider splitting afternoon tea at the excellent-but-pricey National Dining Rooms, on the first floor of the Sainsbury Wing. The National Café, located near the Getty Entrance, also has afternoon tea (see page 208 for more info on both).

Ɔ Self-Guided Tour: Go in through the Sainsbury Entrance (in the smaller building to the left of the main entrance), and approach the collection chronologically.

Medieval and Early Renaissance: In the first rooms, you see shiny paintings of saints, angels, Madonnas, and crucifixions floating in an ethereal gold never-never land.

After leaving this gold-leaf peace, you'll stumble into Uccello's *Battle of San Romano* and Van Eyck's *The Arnolfini Portrait*,

called by some "The Shotgun Wedding." This painting—a masterpiece of down-to-earth details—was once thought to depict a wedding ceremony forced by the lady's swelling belly. Today it's understood as a portrait of a solemn, well-dressed, well-heeled couple, the Arnolfinis of Bruges, Belgium (she likely was not pregnant—the fashion of the day was to gather up the folds of one's extremely full-skirted dress).

Renaissance: In painting, the Renaissance meant realism. Artists rediscovered the beauty of nature and the human body, expressing the optimism and confidence of this new age. Look for Botticelli's *Venus and Mars,* Michelangelo's *The Entombment,* Raphael's *Pope Julius II,* and Leonardo's *The Virgin of the Rocks.*

Hans Holbein the Younger's *The Ambassadors* depicts two well-dressed, suave men flanking a shelf full of books, globes, navigational tools, and musical instruments—objects that symbolize the secular knowledge of the Renaissance. So what's with the gray, slanting blob at the bottom? If you view the blob from the right-hand edge of the painting (get real close, right up to the frame), the blob suddenly becomes...a skull, a reminder that—despite the fine clothes, proud poses, and worldly knowledge—we will all die.

In *The Origin of the Milky Way* by Venetian Renaissance painter Tintoretto, the god Jupiter places his illegitimate son, baby Hercules, at his wife's breast. Juno says, "Wait a minute. That's not my baby!" Her milk spurts upward, becoming the Milky Way.

Northern Protestant: Greek gods and Virgin Marys are out, and hometown folks and hometown places are in. Highlights in-

MEDIEVAL & EARLY RENAISSANCE

1 ANONYMOUS – The Wilton Diptych
2 UCCELLO – Battle of San Romano
3 VAN EYCK – The Arnolfini Portrait

ITALIAN RENAISSANCE

4 LEONARDO – The Virgin of the Rocks
5 BOTTICELLI – Venus and Mars
6 CRIVELLI – The Annunciation, with Saint Emidius
7 LEONARDO – Virgin and Child with St. Anne and St. John the Baptist

VENETIAN RENAISSANCE

8 TITIAN – Bacchus and Ariadne
9 TINTORETTO – The Origin of the Milky Way

HIGH RENAISSANCE

10 MICHELANGELO – The Entombment
11 RAPHAEL – Pope Julius II
12 BRONZINO – An Allegory with Venus and Cupid
13 HOLBEIN – The Ambassadors

NORTHERN PROTESTANT ART

14 VERMEER – A Young Woman Standing at a Virginal
15 VAN HOOGSTRATEN – A Peepshow with Views of the Interior of a Dutch House
16 REMBRANDT – Belshazzar's Feast
17 REMBRANDT – Self-Portrait at the Age of 63

BAROQUE & FRENCH ROCOCO

18 RUBENS – The Judgment of Paris
19 VELÁZQUEZ – The Rokeby Venus
20 VAN DYCK – Equestrian Portrait of Charles I
21 CARAVAGGIO – The Supper at Emmaus
22 BOUCHER – Pan and Syrinx

BRITISH

23 CONSTABLE – The Hay Wain
24 TURNER – The Fighting Téméraire
25 DELAROCHE – The Execution of Lady Jane Grey

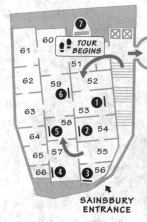

To Leicester Square (5 min. walk)

SAINSBURY WING

ENTRANCE ON LEVEL 0

SELF-GUIDED TOUR STARTS ON LEVEL 2

TOUR BEGINS

SAINSBURY ENTRANCE

LONDON

clude Vermeer's *A Young Woman Standing at a Virginal* and Rembrandt's *Belshazzar's Feast*.

Rembrandt painted his *Self-Portrait at the Age of 63* in the year he would die. He was bankrupt, his mistress had just passed away, and he had also buried several of his children. We see a disillusioned, well-worn, but proud old genius.

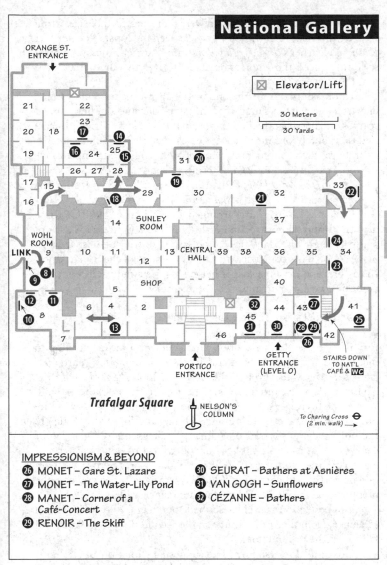

National Gallery

ORANGE ST. ENTRANCE

⊠ Elevator/Lift

30 Meters
30 Yards

WOHL ROOM

LINK

SUNLEY ROOM

CENTRAL HALL

SHOP

PORTICO ENTRANCE

GETTY ENTRANCE (LEVEL 0)

STAIRS DOWN TO NAT'L CAFÉ & **WC**

Trafalgar Square

NELSON'S COLUMN

To Charing Cross ⊖ (2 min. walk) →

LONDON

IMPRESSIONISM & BEYOND

26 MONET – *Gare St. Lazare*
27 MONET – *The Water-Lily Pond*
28 MANET – *Corner of a Café-Concert*
29 RENOIR – *The Skiff*

30 SEURAT – *Bathers at Asnières*
31 VAN GOGH – *Sunflowers*
32 CÉZANNE – *Bathers*

Baroque: The museum's outstanding Baroque collection includes Van Dyck's *Equestrian Portrait of Charles I* and Caravaggio's *The Supper at Emmaus*. In Velázquez's *The Rokeby Venus,* Venus lounges diagonally across the canvas, admiring herself, with flaring red, white, and gray fabrics to highlight her rosy white skin and inflame our passion. This work by the king's personal court painter is a rare Spanish nude from that ultra-Catholic country.

British: The reserved British were more comfortable cavorting with nature than with the lofty gods, as seen in Constable's *The Hay Wain* and Turner's *The Fighting Téméraire*. Turner's messy, colorful style influenced the Impressionists and gives us our first glimpse into the modern art world.

Impressionism: At the end of the 19th century, a new breed of artists burst out of the stuffy confines of the studio. They donned scarves and berets and set up their canvases in farmers' fields or carried their notebooks into crowded cafés, dashing off quick sketches in order to catch a momentary...impression. Check out Impressionist and Post-Impressionist masterpieces such as Monet's *Gare St. Lazare* and *The Water-Lily Pond*, Renoir's *The Skiff*, Seurat's *Bathers at Asnières*, and Van Gogh's *Sunflowers*.

Cézanne's *Bathers* are arranged in strict triangles. Cézanne uses the Impressionist technique of building a figure with dabs of paint (though his "dabs" are often larger-sized "cube" shapes) to make solid, 3-D geometrical figures in the style of the Renaissance. In the process, his cube shapes helped inspire a radical new style—Cubism—bringing art into the 20th century.

Other Sights on Trafalgar Square

▲▲National Portrait Gallery

Put off by halls of 19th-century characters who meant nothing to me, I used to call this "as interesting as someone else's yearbook." But a selective walk through this 500-year-long *Who's Who* of British history is quick and free, and puts faces on the story of England.

Some highlights: Henry VIII and wives; portraits of the "Virgin Queen" Elizabeth I, Sir Francis Drake, and Sir Walter Raleigh; the only real-life portrait of William Shakespeare; Oliver Cromwell and Charles I with his head on; portraits by Gainsborough and Reynolds; the Romantics (William Blake, Lord Byron, William Wordsworth, and company); Queen Victoria and her era; and the present royal family, including the late Princess Diana.

The collection is well-described, not huge, and in historical sequence, from the 16th century on the second floor to today's royal family on the ground floor.

Cost and Hours: Free, but suggested donation of £5, temporary (optional) exhibits extra, floor plan-£1; daily 10:00-18:00, Thu-Fri until 21:00, first and second floors open Mon at 11:00, last entry to special exhibits one hour before closing; audioguide-£3, no photos, basement café and top-floor view restaurant, entry 100 yards off Trafalgar Square (around the corner from National Gallery, opposite Church of St. Martin-in-the-Fields), Tube: Charing Cross or Leicester Square, tel. 020/7306-0055, recorded info tel. 020/7312-2463, www.npg.org.uk.

▲St. Martin-in-the-Fields

The church, built in the 1720s with a Gothic spire atop a Greek-type temple, is an oasis of peace on wild and noisy Trafalgar Square. St. Martin cared for the poor. "In the fields" was where the first church stood on this spot (in the 13th century), between Westminster and The City. Stepping inside, you still feel a compassion for the needs of the people in this neighborhood—the church serves the homeless and houses a Chinese community center. The modern east window—with grillwork bent into the shape of a warped cross—was installed in 2008 to replace one damaged in World War II.

A freestanding glass pavilion to the left of the church serves as the entrance to the church's underground areas. There you'll find the concert ticket office, a gift shop, brass-rubbing center, and the recommended support-the-church Café in the Crypt.

Cost and Hours: Free, but donations welcome; hours vary but generally Mon-Fri 8:30-13:00 & 14:00-18:00, Sat 9:30-13:00 & 14:00-18:00, Sun 15:30-17:00; £3.50 audioguide at shop downstairs, Tube: Charing Cross, tel. 020/7766-1100, www.smitf.org.

Music: The church is famous for its concerts. Consider a free lunchtime concert (suggested £3 donation; Mon, Tue, and Fri at 13:00), an evening concert (£8-28, several nights a week at 19:30), or Wednesday night jazz at the Café in the Crypt (£5.50 or £9, at 20:00). See the church's website for the concert schedule.

The West End and Nearby

To explore this area during dinnertime, see my recommended restaurants on page 188.

Piccadilly and Soho
▲Piccadilly Circus

Although this square is slathered with neon billboards and tacky attractions (think of it as the Times Square of London), the surrounding streets are packed with great shopping opportunities and swimming with youth on the rampage.

Nearby Shaftesbury Avenue and Leicester Square teem with fun-

London for Early Birds and Night Owls

Most sightseeing in London is restricted to the hours between 10:00 and 18:00. Here are a few exceptions:

Sights Open Early

Every day, several sights open at 9:30 or earlier.

St. Paul's Cathedral: Mon-Sat at 8:30.

Shakespeare's Globe: Daily at 9:00.

Madame Tussauds Waxworks: Daily mid-July-Aug at 9:00, Sept-mid-July Mon-Fri at 9:30, Sat-Sun at 9:00.

Tower of London: Tue-Sat at 9:00.

Churchill War Rooms: Daily at 9:30.

Kew Gardens: Daily at 9:30.

Westminster Abbey: Mon-Sat at 9:30.

British Library: Mon-Sat at 9:30.

Buckingham Palace: Aug-Sept daily at 9:30.

Sights Open Late

Every night in London, at least one sight is open late (in addition to the London Eye and Madame Tussauds). Keep in mind, however, that many of these sights stop admitting visitors well before their posted closing times.

London Eye: Last ascent July-Aug daily at 21:30, April-June at 21:00, Sept-March at 20:30.

Madame Tussauds: Mid-July-Aug daily until 19:00.

Clink Prison Museum: July-Sept daily until 21:00, Oct-June Sat-Sun until 19:30.

British Library: Tue until 20:00.

Sir John Soane's Museum: First Tue of month until 21:00.

British Museum (some galleries): Fri until 20:30.

National Portrait Gallery: Thu-Fri until 21:00.

Vinopolis: Thu-Sat until 21:30.

National Gallery: Fri until 21:00.

Victoria and Albert Museum: Fri until 22:00 (selected galleries).

Tate Modern: Fri-Sat until 22:00.

Tate Britain: Select Fridays until 22:00 (check online or call to confirm).

seekers, theaters, Chinese restaurants, and street singers. To the northeast is London's Chinatown and, beyond that, the funky Soho neighborhood (described next). And curling to the northwest from Piccadilly Circus is genteel Regent Street, lined with the city's most exclusive shops.

▲Soho

North of Piccadilly, seedy Soho has become trendy—with many recommended restaurants—and is well worth a gawk. It's the epicenter of London's thriving, colorful youth scene, a fun and funky *Sesame Street* of urban diversity.

Soho is also London's red light district (especially near Brewer and Berwick Streets), where "friendly models" wait in tiny rooms up dreary stairways, voluptuous con artists sell strip shows, and eager male tourists are frequently ripped off. But it's easy to avoid trouble if you're not looking for it. In fact, the sleazy joints share the block with respectable pubs and restaurants, and elderly couples stroll past neon signs that flash *Licensed Sex Shop in Basement*.

Covent Garden and Nearby

▲▲Covent Garden

This large square teems with people and street performers—jugglers, sword swallowers, and guitar players. London's buskers (including those in the Tube) are auditioned, licensed, and assigned times and places where they are allowed to perform.

The square's centerpiece is a covered marketplace. A market has been here since medieval times, when it was the "convent" garden owned by Westminster Abbey. In the 1600s, it became a housing development with this courtyard as its center, done in the Palladian style by Inigo Jones. Today's fine iron-and-glass structure was built in 1830 (when such buildings were all the Industrial Age rage) to house the stalls of what became London's chief produce market. Covent Garden remained a produce market until 1973, when its venerable arcades were converted to boutiques, cafés, and antique shops. A market still thrives here today (for details, see page 155).

The "Actors' Church" of St. Paul, the Royal Opera House, and the London Transport Museum (described next) all border the square, and theaters are nearby. The area is a people-watcher's delight, with cigarette eaters, Punch-and-Judy acts, food that's good for you (but not your wallet), trendy crafts, and row after row of boutique shops and market stalls. For better Covent Garden lunch deals, walk a block or two away from the eye of this touristic hurricane (check out the places north of the Tube station, along Endell and Neal streets).

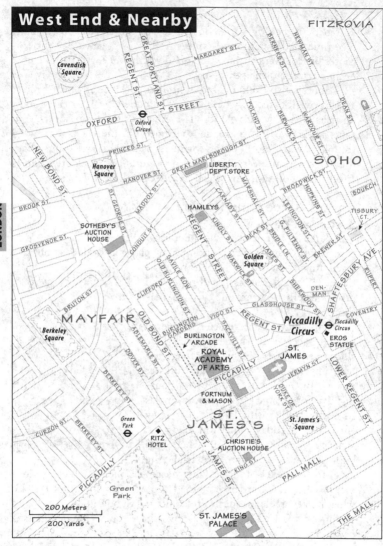

West End & Nearby

FITZROVIA

Cavendish Square

GREAT PORTLAND STREET

REGENT ST.

MARGARET ST.

BERNERS RD.
NEWMAN ST.

OXFORD

Oxford Circus

POLAND ST.
BERWICK ST.
WARDOUR ST.
DEAN ST.

PRINCES ST.

SOHO

NEW BOND ST.

Hanover Square

HANOVER ST.

GREAT MARLBOROUGH ST.

LIBERTY DEP'T.STORE

BROADWICK ST.

HOPKINS ST.

BROOK ST.

MADDOX ST.

ST. GEORGE'S

CONDUIT ST.

HAMLEYS

CARNABY ST.

KINGLY ST.

MARSHALL ST.

LEXINGTON ST.

G. PULTENEY ST.
BREWER ST.

BOURCH

TISBURY CT.

SOTHEBY'S AUCTION HOUSE

GROSVENOR ST.

REGENT STREET

WARWICK ST.

BEAK ST.

BRIDLE LN.

JAMES ST.

SHERWOOD ST.

SHAFTESBURY AVE.

RUPERT

Golden Square

BRUTON ST.

MAYFAIR

Berkeley Square

OLD BURLINGTON ST.

CLIFFORD ST.

SAVILE ROW

BURLINGTON GARDENS

VIGO ST.

SACKVILLE ST.

GLASSHOUSE ST.

DEN-MAN

REGENT ST.

COVENTRY

Piccadilly Circus

Piccadilly Circus

EROS STATUE

ARTEMELE ST.

DOVER ST.

BURLINGTON ARCADE

ROYAL ACADEMY OF ARTS

PICCADILLY

ST. JAMES

JERMYN ST.

LOWER REGENT ST.

BERKELEY ST.

CURZON ST.

Green Park

RITZ HOTEL

FORTNUM & MASON

ST. JAMES'S

CHRISTIE'S AUCTION HOUSE

DUKE OF YORK ST.

St. James's Square

ST. JAMES ST.

KING ST.

PALL MALL

PICCADILLY

Green Park

200 Meters
200 Yards

ST. JAMES'S PALACE

THE MALL

LONDON

▲**London Transport Museum**

This modern, well-presented museum, located right at Covent Garden, is fun for kids and thought-provoking for adults (if a bit overpriced). Whether you're cursing or marveling at the buses and Tube, the growth of Europe's third-biggest city (after Moscow and Istanbul) has been made possible by its public transit system.

After you enter, take the elevator up to the top floor...and the year 1800, when horse-drawn vehicles ruled the road. Next, you descend to the first floor and the world's first underground Metro

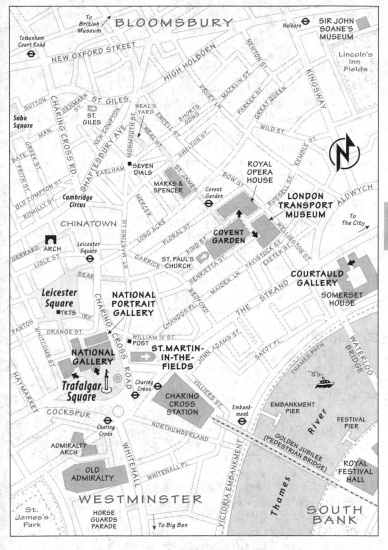

system, which used steam-powered locomotives (the Circle Line, c. 1865). On the ground floor, horses and trains are replaced by motorized vehicles (cars, taxis, double-decker buses, streetcars), resulting in 20th-century congestion. How to deal with it? In 2003, car drivers in London were slapped with a congestion charge, and today, a half-billion people ride the Tube every year.

Cost and Hours: £15, ticket good for one year, kids under 16 free, Sat-Thu 10:00-18:00, Fri 11:00-18:00, last entry 45 minutes before closing, pleasant upstairs café with Covent Garden view, in southeast corner of Covent Garden courtyard, Tube: Covent Garden, switchboard tel. 020/7379-6344, recorded info tel. 020/7565-7299, www.ltmuseum.co.uk.

▲Courtauld Gallery

While less impressive than the National Gallery, this wonderful and compact collection of paintings is still a joy. The gallery is part of the Courtauld Institute of Art, and the thoughtful description of each piece of art reminds visitors that the gallery is still used for teaching. You'll see medieval European paintings and works by Rubens, the Impressionists (Manet, Monet, and Degas), Post-Impressionists (such as Cézanne and an intense Van Gogh self-portrait), and more. Besides the permanent collection, a quality selection of loaners and temporary exhibits are often included in the entry fee. The gallery is located within the grand Somerset House; enjoy the riverside eateries and the courtyard featuring a playful fountain.

Cost and Hours: £6 (£3 on Mon); open daily 10:00-18:00, last entry 30 minutes before closing, occasionally open Thu until 21:00—check website, café, at Somerset House along the Strand, Tube: Temple or Covent Garden, recorded info tel. 020/7848-2526, shop tel. 020/7848-2579, www.courtauld.ac.uk.

Buckingham Palace

Three palace sights require admission: the State Rooms (Aug-Sept only), Queen's Gallery, and Royal Mews. You can pay for each separately, or buy a combo-ticket. A combo-ticket for £32 admits you to all three sights; a cheaper version for £16 covers the Queen's Gallery and Royal Mews. Many tourists are more interested in the Changing of the Guard, which costs nothing at all to view.

▲State Rooms at Buckingham Palace

This lavish home has been Britain's royal residence since 1837. When the Queen's at home, the royal standard flies (a red, yellow, and blue flag); otherwise, the Union Jack flaps in the wind. The Queen opens her palace to the public—but only in August and September, when she's out of town.

Cost and Hours: £19 for lavish State Rooms and throne room, includes audioguide; Aug-Sept only, daily 9:30-18:30, until 19:00 in Aug, last admission 16:45 in Aug, 15:45 in Sept; limited to 8,000 visitors a day by timed entry; come early to the palace's Visitor Entrance (opens 9:15), or book ahead in person, by phone, or online (£2.50 extra); Tube: Victoria, tel. 020/7766-7300, www.royalcollection.org.uk.

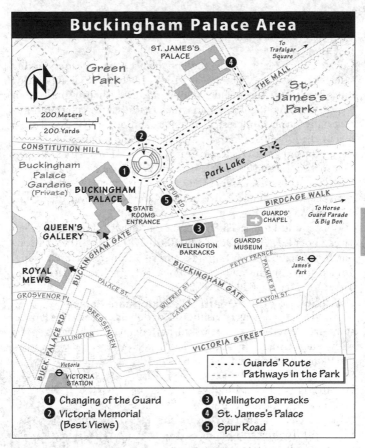

Buckingham Palace Area

To Trafalgar Square

ST. JAMES'S PALACE

THE MALL

St. James's Park

Green Park

200 Meters
200 Yards

CONSTITUTION HILL

Park Lake

Buckingham Palace Gardens (Private)

BUCKINGHAM PALACE

SPUR RD.

BIRDCAGE WALK

To Horse Guard Parade & Big Ben

STATE ROOMS ENTRANCE

GUARDS' CHAPEL

QUEEN'S GALLERY

WELLINGTON BARRACKS

GUARDS' MUSEUM

ROYAL MEWS

BUCKINGHAM GATE

PETTY FRANCE

PALMER ST.

St. James's Park

PALACE ST.

WILFRED ST.

GROSVENOR PL.

BRESSENDEN

CASTLE LN.

CAXTON ST.

ALLINGTON

VICTORIA STREET

BUCK. PALACE RD.

Victoria

VICTORIA STATION

- - - - - Guards' Route
- - - - Pathways in the Park

❶ Changing of the Guard
❷ Victoria Memorial (Best Views)
❸ Wellington Barracks
❹ St. James's Palace
❺ Spur Road

LONDON

Queen's Gallery at Buckingham Palace

A small sampling of Queen Elizabeth's personal collection of art is on display in five rooms in a wing adjoining the palace. Her 7,000 paintings, one of the largest private art collections in the world, are actually a series of collections, which have been built upon by each successive monarch since the 16th century. The Queen rotates the paintings, enjoying some privately in her many palatial residences while sharing others with her subjects in public galleries in Edinburgh and London. The exhibits change two or three times a year and are lovingly described by the included audioguide.

Because the gallery is small and security is tight (involving lines), I'd suggest visiting this gallery only if you're a patient art lover interested in the current exhibit.

Cost and Hours: £9.25 but can change depending on exhibit, combo-ticket with Royal Mews saves about £2, daily 10:00-17:30, opens at 9:30 Aug-Sept, last entry one hour before closing, Tube:

Victoria, tel. 020/7766-7301—but Her Majesty rarely answers. Men shouldn't miss the mahogany-trimmed urinals.

Royal Mews

Located to the left of Buckingham Palace, the Queen's working stables are open to visitors. The visit is likely to be disappointing unless you follow the included audioguide or the hourly guided tour (April-Oct only, 45 minutes), in which case it's fairly entertaining—especially if you're interested in horses and/or royalty. You'll see a few of the Queen's 30 horses, a fancy car, and a bunch of old carriages, finishing with the Gold State Coach (c. 1760, 4 tons, 4 mph). Queen Victoria said absolutely no cars. When she died, in 1901, the mews got its first Daimler. Today, along with the hay-eating transport, the stable is home to five Bentleys and Rolls-Royce Phantoms, with one on display.

Cost and Hours: £8.50, combo-ticket with Queen's Gallery saves about £2, April-Oct daily 10:00-17:00, Nov-March Mon-Sat 10:00-16:00, closed Sun, last entry 45 minutes before closing, guided tours on the hour in summer, Buckingham Palace Road, Tube: Victoria, tel. 020/7766-7302.

▲▲Changing of the Guard at Buckingham Palace

This is the spectacle every visitor to London has to see at least once: stone-faced, red-coated, bearskin-hatted guards changing posts with much fanfare, in an hour-long ceremony accompanied by a brass band.

It's 11:00 at Buckingham Palace, and the on-duty guards (the "Queen's Guard") are ready to finish their shift. Nearby at St. James's Palace (a half-mile northeast), a second set of guards is also ready for a break. Meanwhile, fresh replacement guards (the "New Guard") gather for a review and inspection at Wellington Barracks, 500 yards east of the palace (on Birdcage Walk).

At 11:15, the tired St. James's guards head out to the Mall, and then take a right turn for Buckingham Palace. At 11:30, the replacement troops, led by the band, also head for Buckingham Palace. Meanwhile, a fourth group—the Horse Guard—passes by along the Mall on its way back to Hyde Park Corner from its own changing-of-the-guard ceremony on Whitehall (which just took place at Horse Guards Parade at 11:00, or 10:00 on Sun).

At 11:45, the tired and fresh guards converge on Buckingham Palace in a perfect storm of Red Coat pageantry. Everyone parades around, the guard changes (passing the regimental flag, or "colour") with much shouting, the band plays a happy little concert, and then they march out. At noon, two bands escort two detach-

Changing of the Guard Timeline

When	What	Where
10:30	Tourists begin to gather (arrive now for a spot by the fence)	Fence outside the palace
11:00	Victoria Monument gets crowded	Middle of traffic circle in front of palace
11:00-11:15	"New Guard" gathers for inspection	Wellington Barracks
11:00 (10:00 Sun)	Horse Guard changing of the guard	Horse Guards Parade (opposite end of St. James's Park)
11:15-11:30	Tired St. James's Palace guards and Horse Guard both head for the palace	Down the Mall
11:15-11:30	Fresh replacement troops head from Wellington Barracks to Buckingham Palace	Down Spur Road
11:30-11:45	All guards gradually converge	Around Victoria Monument in front of the palace
11:45-12:00	The Changing of the Guard ceremony	Inside fenced courtyard of Buckingham Palace
12:00-12:10	Tired guards head for Wellington Barracks	Up the Mall
12:00-12:10	Fresh guards head for St. James's Palace	Up Spur Road
12:15	Smaller changing of the guard ceremony	In front of St. James's Palace

ments of guards away: the tired guards to Wellington Barracks and the fresh guards to St. James's Palace. As the fresh guards set up at St. James's Palace and the tired ones dress down at the barracks, the tourists disperse.

Cost and Hours: Free, daily May-July at 11:30, every other day Aug-April, no ceremony in very wet weather; exact schedule subject to change—call 020/7766-7300 for the day's plan, or check www.royalcollection.org.uk; Buckingham Palace, Tube: Victoria, St. James's Park, or Green Park. Or hop into a big black taxi and say, "Buck House, please."

Sightseeing Strategies: Most tourists just show up and get lost in the crowds, but those who know the drill will enjoy the event more. The action takes place in stages over the course of an hour, at several different locations. The main event is in the forecourt right in front of Buckingham Palace (between Buckingham Palace and the fence) from 11:30 to 12:00. To see it close up, you'll need to get here no later than 10:30 to get a place right next to the fence.

But there's plenty of pageantry elsewhere. Get out your map and strategize. You could see the guards mobilizing at Wellington Barracks or St. James's Palace (11:00-11:15). Or watch them parade with bands down The Mall and Spur Road (11:15-11:30). After the ceremony at Buckingham Palace is over (and many tourists have gotten bored and gone home), the parades march back along those same streets (12:10).

Pick one event and find a good, unobstructed place from which to view it. The key is to get either right up front along the road or fence, or find some raised elevation to stand or sit on—a balustrade or a curb—so you can see over people's heads.

If you get there too late to score a premium spot right along the fence, head for the high ground on the circular Victoria Memorial, which provides the best overall view (come before 11:00 to get a place). From the memorial, you have good (if more distant) views of the palace as well as the arriving and departing parades along The Mall and Spur Road. The actual Changing of the Guard in front of the palace is a nonevent. It is interesting, however, to see nearly every tourist in London gathered in one place at the same time.

If you arrive too late to get any good spot at all, or you just don't feel like jostling for a view, stroll down to St. James's Palace and wait near the corner for a great photo-op. At about 12:15, the parade marches up The Mall to the palace and performs a smaller changing ceremony—with almost no crowds. Afterward, stroll through nearby St. James's Park.

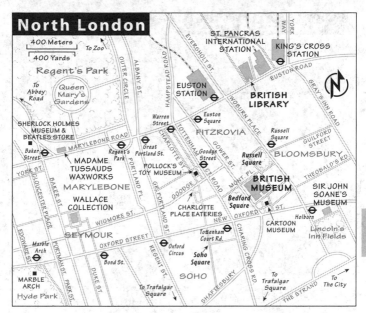

Sights in North London

▲▲▲British Museum

Simply put, this is the greatest chronicle of civilization...anywhere. A visit here is like taking a long hike through *Encyclopedia Britannica* National Park. While the vast British Museum wraps around its Great Court (the huge entrance hall), the most popular sections of the museum fill the ground floor: Egyptian, Assyrian, and ancient Greek, with the famous frieze sculptures from the Parthenon  in Athens. The museum's stately Reading Room—famous as the place where Karl Marx hung out while formulating his ideas on communism and writing *Das Kapital*—sometimes hosts special exhibits.

   Cost and Hours: Free but a £5 donation requested, temporary exhibits usually extra (and with timed ticket); daily 10:00-17:30, Fri until 20:30 (selected galleries only), least crowded weekday late afternoons; multimedia guide—£5, free Rick Steves audio tour available—see page 51, Great Russell Street, Tube: Tottenham Court Road, general info tel. 020/7323-8000,

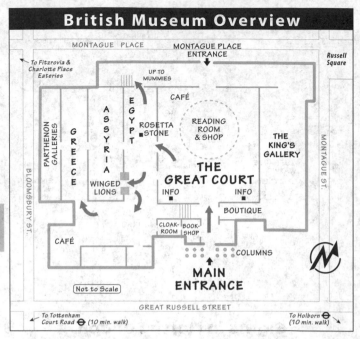

British Museum Overview

MONTAGUE PLACE

MONTAGUE PLACE ENTRANCE

Russell Square

To Fitzrovia & Charlotte Place Eateries

UP TO MUMMIES

CAFÉ

EGYPT

ASSYRIA

PARTHENON GALLERIES

GREECE

ROSETTA STONE

READING ROOM & SHOP

THE KING'S GALLERY

MONTAGUE ST.

BLOOMSBURY ST.

WINGED LIONS

THE GREAT COURT

INFO

INFO

BOUTIQUE

CLOAK-ROOM

BOOK-SHOP

CAFÉ

COLUMNS

Not to Scale

MAIN ENTRANCE

GREAT RUSSELL STREET

To Tottenham Court Road ⊖ (10 min. walk)

To Holborn ⊖ (10 min. walk)

LONDON

ticket desk tel. 020/7323-8181, collection questions tel. 020/7323-8838, www.britishmuseum.org.

Information: Information desks offer a £1 basic map or £2 version highlighting important pieces, but neither is essential; the *Visitor's Guide* (£3.50) offers 15 different tours and skimpy text. Free 30-minute **eyeOpener tours** are led by volunteers, who focus on select rooms (daily 11:00-15:45, generally every 15 minutes). Free 45-minute **gallery talks** on specific subjects are offered Tue-Sat at 13:15; a free 20-minute highlights tour is available on Friday evening. The £5 **multimedia guide** offers dial-up audio commentary and video on 200 objects, as well as several theme tours (must leave photo ID). There's also a fun children's audioguide (£3.50). General info tel. 020/7323-8000, ticket desk tel. 020/7323-8181, collection questions tel. 020/7323-8838, www.britishmuseum.org.

○ Self-Guided Tour: From the Great Court, doorways lead to all wings. To the left are the exhibits on Egypt, Assyria, and Greece—the highlights of your visit.

Egypt: Start with the Egyptian section. Egypt was one of the world's first "civilizations"—a group of people with a government, religion, art, free time, and a written language. The Egypt we think of—pyramids, mummies, pharaohs, and guys who walk funny—lasted from 3000 to 1000 B.C. with hardly any change in the government, religion, or arts. Imagine two millennia of Nixon.

The first thing you'll see in the Egypt section is the **Rosetta Stone.** When this rock was unearthed in the Egyptian desert in 1799, it was a sensation in Europe. This black slab, dating from 196 B.C., caused a quantum leap in the study of ancient history. Finally, Egyptian writing could be decoded. It contains a single inscription repeated in three languages. The bottom third is plain old Greek, while the middle is medieval Egyptian. By comparing the two known languages with the one they didn't know, translators figured out the hieroglyphics.

Next, wander past the many **statues,** including a seven-ton Ramesses, with the traditional features of a pharaoh (goatee, cloth headdress, and cobra diadem on his forehead). When Moses told the king of Egypt, "Let my people go!" this was the stony-faced look he got. You'll also see the Egyptian gods as animals—these include Amun, king of the gods, as a ram, and Horus, the god of the living, as a falcon.

At the end of the hall, climb the stairs to **mummy** land (use the elevator if it's running). To mummify a body, you first disembowel it (but leave the heart inside), then pack the cavities with pitch, and dry it with natron, a natural form of sodium carbonate (and, I believe, the active ingredient in Twinkies). Then carefully bandage it head to toe with hundreds of yards of linen strips. Let it sit 2,000 years, and...*voilà!* The mummy was placed in a wooden coffin, which was put in a stone coffin, which was placed in a tomb. The result is that we now have Egyptian bodies that are as well preserved as Joan Rivers. Many of the mummies here are from the time of the Roman occupation, when fine memorial portraits painted in wax became popular. X-ray photos in the display cases tell us more about these people. Don't miss the animal mummies. Cats were popular pets. They were also considered incarnations of the cat-headed goddess Bastet. Worshipped in life as the sun god's allies, preserved in death, and memorialized with statues, cats were given the adulation they've come to expect ever since.

Assyria: Long before Saddam Hussein, Iraq was home to other palace-building, iron-fisted rulers—the Assyrians, who conquered their southern neighbors and dominated the Middle East for 300 years (c. 900-600 B.C.). Their strength came from a superb army (chariots, mounted cavalry, and siege engines), a policy of terrorism against enemies ("I tied their heads to tree trunks all around the city," reads a royal inscription), ethnic cleansing and mass deportations of the vanquished, and efficient administration (roads and express postal service). They have been called the "Romans of the East."

Standing guard over the Assyrian exhibit halls are two human-headed **winged lions.** These stone lions guarded an Assyrian palace (11th-8th century B.C.). With the strength of a lion, the wings of an eagle, the brain of a man, and the beard of ZZ Top, they protected the king from evil spirits and scared the heck out of foreign ambassadors and left-wing newspaper reporters. (What has five legs and flies? Take a close look. These quintupeds, which appear complete from both the front and the side, could guard both directions at once.)

Carved into the stone between the bearded lions' loins, you can see one of civilization's most impressive achievements—writing. This wedge-shaped **(cuneiform)** script is the world's first written language, invented 5,000 years ago by the Sumerians (of southern Iraq) and passed down to their less-civilized descendants, the Assyrians.

The **Nimrud Gallery** is a mini version of the throne room and royal apartments of King Ashurnasirpal II's Northwest Palace at Nimrud (9th century B.C.). It's filled with royal propaganda reliefs, 30-ton marble bulls, and panels depicting wounded lions (lion-hunting was Assyria's sport of kings).

Greece: During their civilization's Golden Age (500-430 B.C.), the ancient Greeks set the tone for all of Western civilization to follow. Democracy, theater, literature, mathematics, philosophy, science, gyros, art, and architecture, as we know them, were virtually all invented by a single generation of Greeks in a small town of maybe 80,000 citizens.

Your walk through Greek art history starts with **pottery,** usually painted red and black and a popular export product for the sea-trading Greeks. The earliest featured geometric patterns (eighth century B.C.), then a painted black silhouette on the natural orange clay, then a red figure on a black background. Later, painted vases show a culture really into partying.

The highlight is the **Parthenon Sculptures,** taken from the temple dedicated to Athena, goddess of wisdom and the patroness of

Athens—the crowning glory of an enormous urban-renewal plan during Greece's Golden Age. The sculptures are also called the Elgin Marbles, for the shrewd British ambassador who had his men hammer, chisel, and saw them off the Parthenon in the early 1800s. Though the Greek government complains about losing its marbles, the Brits feel they rescued and preserved the sculptures. These much-wrangled-over bits of the Parthenon (from about 450 B.C.) are indeed impressive. The marble panels you see lining the walls of this large hall are part of the frieze that originally ran around the exterior of the Parthenon, under the eaves. The statues at either end of the hall once filled the Parthenon's triangular-shaped pediments and showed the birth of Athena. The relief panels known as metopes tell the story of the struggle between the forces of human civilization and animal-like barbarism.

The Rest of the Museum: Be sure to venture upstairs to see artifacts from **Roman Britain** that surpass anything you'll see at Hadrian's Wall or elsewhere in the country. Also look for the Sutton Hoo Ship Burial artifacts from a seventh-century royal burial on the east coast of England (Room 41). A rare Michelangelo cartoon (preliminary sketch) is in Room 90 (level 4).

Other Sights in North London

▲▲▲British Library

The British Empire built its greatest monuments out of paper; it's through literature that England has made her lasting contribution to history and the arts. Here, in just two rooms, are the literary treasures of Western civilization, from early Bibles, to the Magna Carta, to Shakespeare's *Hamlet*, to Lewis Carroll's *Alice's Adventures in Wonderland*. You'll see the Lindisfarne Gospels transcribed on an illuminated manuscript, as well as Beatles lyrics scrawled on the back of a greeting card. Pages from Leonardo da Vinci's notebook show his powerful curiosity, his genius for invention, and his famous backward and inside-out handwriting, which makes sense only if you know Italian and have a mirror. A *Beowulf* manuscript from A.D. 1000, *The Canterbury Tales*, and Shakespeare's First Folio also reside here. (If the First Folio is not out, the library should have other Shakespeare items on display.)

Exhibits change often, and many of the museum's old, fragile manuscripts need to "rest" periodically in order to stay well-preserved. If your heart's set on seeing that one particular rare Dickens book or letter penned by Gandhi, call ahead to make sure it's on display.

Cost and Hours: Free, but £5 suggested donation, admission charged for some (optional) temporary exhibits; Mon-Fri 9:30-18:00, Tue until 20:00, Sat 9:30-17:00, Sun 11:00-17:00;

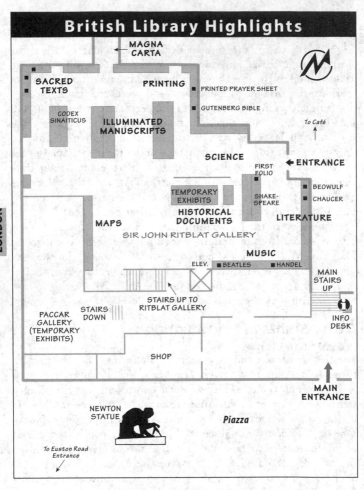

British Library Highlights

MAGNA CARTA

SACRED TEXTS

PRINTING

PRINTED PRAYER SHEET

GUTENBERG BIBLE

CODEX SINAITICUS

ILLUMINATED MANUSCRIPTS

To Café

SCIENCE

FIRST FOLIO

◄ ENTRANCE

BEOWULF

CHAUCER

TEMPORARY EXHIBITS

SHAKE-SPEARE

HISTORICAL DOCUMENTS

LITERATURE

MAPS

SIR JOHN RITBLAT GALLERY

MUSIC

ELEV.   ■ BEATLES   ■ HANDEL

MAIN STAIRS UP

STAIRS UP TO RITBLAT GALLERY

STAIRS DOWN

PACCAR GALLERY (TEMPORARY EXHIBITS)

INFO DESK

SHOP

MAIN ENTRANCE

NEWTON STATUE

Piazza

To Euston Road Entrance

LONDON

96 Euston Road, Tube: King's Cross St. Pancras or Euston, tel. 019/3754-6060 or 020/7412-7676, www.bl.uk.

Tours: While the British Library doesn't offer an audioguide or guided tours of the permanent collection, you can download a free Rick Steves **audio tour** that describes its highlights (see page 51). Guided tours are offered of the building itself—the archives and reading rooms.

▲Wallace Collection

Sir Richard Wallace's fine collection of 17th-century Dutch Masters, 18th-century French

Rococo, medieval armor, and assorted aristocratic fancies fills the sumptuously furnished Hertford House on Manchester Square. From the rough and intimate Dutch lifescapes of Jan Steen to the pink-cheeked Rococo fantasies of François Boucher, a wander through this little-visited mansion makes you nostalgic for the days of the empire. While this collection would be a big deal in a mid-sized city, it's small potatoes here in London...but enjoyable nevertheless.

Cost and Hours: Free, daily 10:00-17:00, audioguide-£3, free guided tours or lectures almost daily—call to confirm times, just north of Oxford Street on Manchester Square, Tube: Bond Street. Tel. 020/7563-9500, www.wallacecollection.org.

▲Madame Tussauds Waxworks

This waxtravaganza is gimmicky, crass, and crazily expensive, but dang fun...a hit with the kind of tourists who skip the British Museum. The original Madame Tussaud did wax casts of heads lopped off during the French Revolution (such as Marie-Antoinette's). She took her show on the road and ended up in London in 1835. Now it's all about squeezing Tom Cruise's bum, gambling with George Clooney, and partying with Beyoncé and Brangelina. In addition to posing with all the eerily realistic wax dummies— from Johnny Depp to Barack Obama to the Beatles—you'll have the chance to tour a hokey haunted-house exhibit; learn how they created this waxy army; hop on a people-mover and cruise through a kid-pleasing "Spirit of London" time trip; and visit with Spider-Man, the Hulk, and other Marvel superheroes. A nine-minute "4-D" show features a 3-D movie heightened by wind, "back ticklers," and other special effects.

Cost: £30, 10 percent discount and no waiting in line if you buy tickets on their website (also consider combo-deal with London Eye, sold cheaper online), £25.50 Fast Track ticket (see page 51), often even bigger discount—up to 50 percent—if you get "Late Saver" ticket online for visits later in the day, 2-for-1 rail vouchers accepted (see page 59). Kids also get a discount of about £4, and those under 5 are free.

Hours: Mid-July-Aug and school holidays daily 9:00-19:00, Sept-mid-July Mon-Fri 9:30-17:30, Sat-Sun 9:00-18:00, these are last entry times—place stays open roughly two hours later; Marylebone Road, Tube: Baker Street, tel. 0871-894-3000, www. madametussauds.com.

Crowd-Beating Tips: This popular attraction can be swamped with people. To avoid the ticket line, buy a Fast Track ticket or reserve online. If you wait to buy tickets at the attraction, you'll discover that the ticket-buying line twists endlessly once inside the door (believe the posted signs warning you how long the wait will be—an hour or more is not unusual at busy times). If you buy your tickets at the door, try to arrive after 15:00—a smart move even with advance tickets, as the crowds inside thin out later in the day.

▲Sir John Soane's Museum

Architects love this quirky place, as do fans of interior decor, eclectic knickknacks, and Back Door sights. Tour this furnished home

on a bird-chirping square and see 19th-century chairs, lamps, and carpets, wood-paneled nooks and crannies, and stained-glass skylights. (While some sections may be closed for restoration through 2014, the main part of the house will be open.) The townhouse is cluttered with Soane's (and his wife's) collection of ancient relics, curios, and famous paintings, including Hogarth's series on *The Rake's Progress* (read the fun plot) and several excellent Canalettos. In 1833, just before his death, Soane established his house as a museum, stipulating that it be kept as nearly as possible in the state he left it. If he visited today, he'd be entirely satisfied. You'll leave wishing you'd known the man.

Cost and Hours: Free, but donations much appreciated, Tue-Sat 10:00-17:00, open and candlelit the first Tue of the month 18:00-21:00, closed Sun-Mon, last entry 30 minutes before closing, long entry lines on Sat and first Tue, good £1 brochure, £10 guided tour Sat at 11:00, free downloadable audio tours on their website, 13 Lincoln's Inn Fields, quarter-mile southeast of British Museum, Tube: Holborn, tel. 020/7405-2107, www.soane.org.

Beatles Sights

London's city center is surprisingly devoid of sights associated with the famous '60s rock band. To see much of anything, consider taking a guided walk (see page 72).

For a photo op, go to **Abbey Road** and walk the famous crosswalk pictured on the *Abbey Road* album cover (Tube: St. John's Wood, get information and buy Beatles memorabilia at the small kiosk in the station). From the Tube station, it's a five-minute walk west down Grove End Road to the intersection with

Abbey Road. The Abbey Road recording studio is the low-key, white building to the right of Abbey House (it's still a working studio, so you can't go inside). Ponder the graffiti on the low wall outside, and...imagine. To re-create the famous cover photo, shoot the crosswalk from the roundabout as you face north up Abbey Road. Shoes are optional.

Nearby is **Paul McCartney's current home** (7 Cavendish Avenue): Continue down Grove End Road, turn left on Circus Road, and then right on Cavendish. Please be discreet.

The **Beatles Store** is at 231 Baker Street (Tube: Baker Street). It's small—some Beatles-logo T-shirts, mugs, pins, and old vinyl like you might have in your closet—and has nothing of historic value (open eight days a week, 10:00-18:30, tel. 020/7935-4464, www.beatlesstorelondon.co.uk; another rock memorabilia store is across the street).

Sherlock Holmes Museum

A few doors down from the Beatles Store, this meticulous re-creation of the (fictional) apartment of the (fictional) detective sits at the (real) address of 221b Baker Street. The first-floor replica (so to speak) of Sherlock's study delights fans with the opportunity to play Holmes and Watson while sitting in authentic 18th-century chairs. The second and third floors offer fine exhibits on daily Victorian life, showing off furniture, clothes, pipes, paintings, and chamber pots; in other rooms, models are posed to enact key scenes from Sir Arthur Conan Doyle's famous books.

Cost and Hours: £8, daily 9:30-18:00, last entry at least 30 minutes before closing, expect to wait 15 minutes or more, large gift shop for Holmes connoisseurs, Tube: Baker Street, tel. 020/7935-8866, www.sherlock-holmes.co.uk.

Sights in The City

When Londoners say "The City," they mean the one-square-mile business center in East London that 2,000 years ago was Roman Londinium. The outline of the Roman city walls can still be seen in the arc of roads from Blackfriars Bridge to Tower Bridge. Within The City are 23 churches designed by Sir Christopher Wren, mostly just ornamentation around St. Paul's Cathedral. Today, while home to only 7,000 residents, The City thrives with nearly 300,000 office workers coming and going daily. It's a fascinating district to

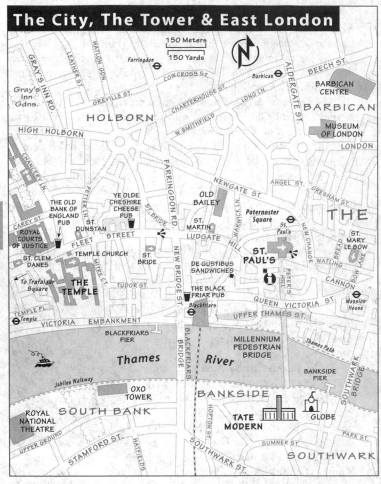

The City, The Tower & East London

wander on weekdays, but since almost nobody actually lives there, it's dull in the evenings and on Saturday and Sunday.

You can download a free Rick Steves **audio tour** of The City, which peels back the many layers of history in this oldest part of London (see page 51).

▲▲▲St. Paul's Cathedral

Sir Christopher Wren's most famous church is the great St. Paul's, its elaborate interior capped by a 365-foot dome. There's been a church on this spot since 604. After the Great Fire of 1666 destroyed the old cathedral, Wren created this Baroque masterpiece. And since World War II, St. Paul's has been Britain's symbol of resilience. Despite 57 nights of bombing, the Nazis failed to destroy

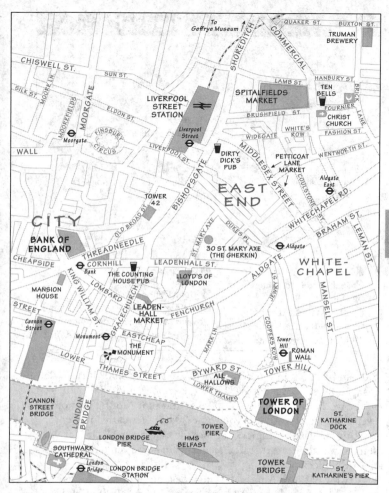

the cathedral, thanks to the St. Paul's volunteer fire watchmen, who stayed on the dome.

Cost and Hours: £16, includes church entry, dome climb, crypt, tour, and audioguide; Mon-Sat 8:30-16:30, last entry for sightseeing 16:00 (dome opens at 9:30, last entry at 16:15), closed Sun except for worship, sometimes closed for special events, no photos, café and restaurant in crypt, Tube: St. Paul's.

Music and Services: If interested, check the website for worship times the day of your visit. Communion is generally Mon-Sat at

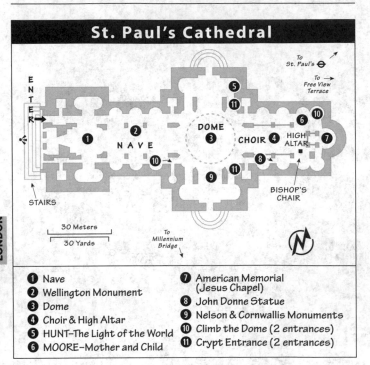

St. Paul's Cathedral

E N T E R

To St. Paul's ⊖

To Free View Terrace

DOME

NAVE

CHOIR

HIGH ALTAR

BISHOP'S CHAIR

STAIRS

30 Meters
30 Yards

To Millennium Bridge

1 Nave
2 Wellington Monument
3 Dome
4 Choir & High Altar
5 HUNT—The Light of the World
6 MOORE—Mother and Child
7 American Memorial (Jesus Chapel)
8 John Donne Statue
9 Nelson & Cornwallis Monuments
10 Climb the Dome (2 entrances)
11 Crypt Entrance (2 entrances)

LONDON

8:00 and 12:30. On Sunday, services are held at 8:00, 10:15 (Matins), 11:30 (sung Eucharist), 15:15 (evensong), and 18:00. The rest of the week, evensong is at 17:00 Tue-Sat (not Mon). For more on evensong, see page 164. If you come 20 minutes early for evensong worship (under the dome), you may be able to grab a big wooden stall in the choir, next to the singers. On some Sundays, there's a free organ recital at 16:45.

Information: Admission includes an **audioguide** as well as a 1.5-hour guided tour (Mon-Sat at 10:00, 11:00, 13:00, and 14:00; confirm schedule at church or call 020/7246-8357). Free 15-minute talks are offered throughout the day, and a stand-up, wrap-around **film** program titled *Oculus: An Eye into St. Paul's* gives some historical background and shows the view from atop the dome (find it near Nelson's tomb). You can also download a free Rick Steves **audio tour** of St. Paul's (see page 51). Recorded info tel. 020/7236-4128, reception tel. 020/7246-8350, www.stpauls.co.uk.

◑ Self-Guided Tour: Even now, as skyscrapers encroach, the 365-foot-high dome of St. Paul's rises majestically above the rooftops of the neighborhood. The tall dome is set on classical columns, capped with a lantern, topped by a six-foot ball, and iced with a cross. As the first Anglican cathedral built in London after the Reformation, it is Baroque: St. Peter's in Rome filtered through clear-eyed English reason. Often the site of historic funerals (Queen Victoria and Winston Churchill), St. Paul's most famous ceremony was a wedding—when Prince Charles married Lady Diana Spencer in 1981.

Inside, this big church feels big. At 515 feet long and 250 feet wide, it's Europe's fourth largest, after Rome (St. Peter's), Sevilla, and Milan. The spaciousness is accentuated by the relative lack of decoration. The simple, cream-colored ceiling and the clear glass in the windows light everything evenly. Wren wanted this: a simple, open church with nothing to hide. Unfortunately, only this entrance area keeps his original vision—the rest was encrusted with 19th-century Victorian ornamentation.

The **dome** you see from here, painted with scenes from the life of St. Paul, is only the innermost of three. From the painted interior of the first dome, look up through the opening to see the light-filled lantern of the second dome. Finally, the whole thing is covered on the outside by the third and final dome, the shell of lead-covered wood that you see from the street. Wren's ingenious three-in-one design was psychological as well as functional—he wanted a low, shallow inner dome so worshippers wouldn't feel diminished.

Do a quick clockwise spin around the church. In the north transept (to your left as you face the altar), find the big painting *The Light of the World* (1904), by the Pre-Raphaelite William Holman Hunt. Inspired by Hunt's own experience of finding Christ during a moment of spiritual crisis, the crowd-pleasing work was criticized by art highbrows for being "syrupy" and "simple"—even as it became the most famous painting in Victorian England.

Along the left side of the choir is the modern statue *Mother and Child*, by the great modern sculptor Henry Moore. Typical of Moore's work, this Mary and Baby Jesus—inspired by the sight of British moms nursing babies in WWII bomb shelters—renders a traditional subject in an abstract, minimalist way.

The area behind the altar, with three bright and modern stained-glass windows, is the **American Memorial Chapel**—honoring the Americans who sacrificed their lives to save Britain in World War II. In colored panes that arch around the big windows, spot the American eagle (center window, to the left of Christ), George Washington (right window, upper-right corner), and symbols of all 50 states (find your state seal). In the carved wood beneath the windows, you'll see birds and foliage native to the US. The Roll of Honor (a 500-page book under glass, immediately behind the altar) lists the names of 28,000 US servicemen and women based in Britain who gave their lives during the war.

Around the other side of the choir is a shrouded statue honoring **John Donne** (1621–1631), a passionate preacher in old St.

London's Best Views

Though London is a height-challenged city, you can get lofty perspectives on it from several high-flying places. For some viewpoints, you need to pay admission (cheapest at The Monument), and at the bars or restaurants, you'll need to buy a drink; the only truly free spots are Primrose Hill, the rooftop terrace of a shopping mall next to St. Paul's Cathedral, and the viewpoint in front of Greenwich's Royal Observatory.

London Eye: Ride the giant Ferris wheel for stunning London views. See page 133.

St. Paul's Dome: You'll earn a striking, unobstructed view by climbing hundreds of steps to the cramped balcony of the church's cupola. See page 120.

Rooftop Terrace: Get fine, free views of St. Paul's Cathedral and surroundings—nearly as good as those from St. Paul's Dome—from the rooftop terrace of the shopping mall just behind and east of the church.

Tate Modern: Take in a classic vista across the Thames from the museum's level-6 restaurant and bar. See page 137.

The Monument: Though surrounded by modern buildings in the financial district, this 202-foot column memorializing the Great Fire of 1666 affords a nice view of The City. See page 126.

National Portrait Gallery: A mod top-floor restaurant peers over Trafalgar Square and the Westminster neighborhood. See page 100.

Waterstones Bookstore: Its hip, low-key, top-floor café/bar has reasonable prices and sweeping views of the London Eye,

Paul's, as well as a great poet ("never send to know for whom the bell tolls—it tolls for thee").

In the south transept are monuments to military greats **Horatio Nelson,** who fought Napoleon, and **Charles Cornwallis,** who was finished off by George Washington at Yorktown.

Climbing the Dome: During your visit, you can climb 528 steps to reach the dome and great city views. Along the way, have some fun in the Whispering Gallery (257 steps up). Whisper sweet nothings into the wall, and your partner (and anyone else) standing far away can hear you. For best effects, try whispering (not talking) with your mouth close to the wall, while your partner stands a few dozen yards away with his or her ear to the wall.

Visiting the Crypt: The crypt is a world of historic bones and interesting cathedral models. Many legends are buried here— Horatio Nelson, who wore down Napoleon; the Duke of Wellington, who finished Napoleon off; and even Wren himself. Wren's actual tomb is marked by a simple black slab with no statue, though he considered this church to be his legacy. Back up in the nave, on

Big Ben, and the Houses of Parliament (see page 56, on Sun bar closes one hour before bookstore, www.5thview.co.uk).

OXO Tower: Perched high over the Thames River, the building's upscale restaurant/bar boasts views over London and St. Paul's, with al fresco dining in good weather (Barge House Street, Tube: Blackfriars, tel. 020/7803-3888, www.harveynichols.com/restaurants/oxo-tower-london).

London Hilton, Park Lane: You'll spot Buckingham Palace, Hyde Park, and the London Eye from Galvin at Windows, a 28th-floor restaurant/bar in an otherwise nondescript hotel (22 Park Lane, Tube: Hyde Park Corner, tel. 020/7208-4021, www.galvinatwindows.com).

The Shard: The observation decks that cap this 1,020-foot-tall skyscraper offer London's most commanding views, but at an outrageously high price. See page 142.

Primrose Hill: For dramatic 360-degree city views, head to the huge grassy expanse at the summit of Primrose Hill, just north of Regent's Park (off Prince Albert Road, Tube: Chalk Farm or Camden Town, www.royalparks.gov.uk/The-Regents-Park).

The Thames River: Various companies run boat trips on the Thames, offering a unique vantage point and unobstructed, ever-changing views of great landmarks (see page 76).

Royal Observatory Greenwich: Enjoy sweeping views of Greenwich's grand buildings in the foreground, the Docklands' skyscrapers in the middle ground, and The City and central London in the distance.

the floor directly under the dome, is Christopher Wren's name and epitaph (written in Latin): "Reader, if you seek his monument, look around you."

Near St. Paul's Cathedral
▲Old Bailey

To view the British legal system in action—lawyers in little blond wigs speaking legalese with an upper-crust accent—spend a few minutes in the visitors' gallery at the Old Bailey, called the "Central Criminal Court." Don't enter under the dome; continue down the block about halfway to the modern part of the building—the entry is at Warwick Passage.

Cost and Hours: Free, generally Mon-Fri 9:45-13:00 & 14:00-16:00 depending on caseload, last entry at 15:40 but often closes an hour or so earlier, closed Sat-Sun, fewer cases in Aug; no kids under 14; no bags, mobile phones, cameras, iPods, or food, but small purses OK; you can check bags at the Capable Travel agency just down the street at Old Bailey 4—£5/bag, £1 per phone or camera;

2 blocks northwest of St. Paul's on Old Bailey Street, follow signs to public entrance, Tube: St. Paul's, tel. 020/7248-3277.

▲Museum of London

This museum tells the fascinating story of London, taking you on a walk from its pre-Roman beginnings to the present. It features London's distinguished citizens through history—from Neanderthals, to Romans, to Elizabethans, to Victorians, to Mods, to today. The museum's displays are chronological, spacious, and informative without being overwhelming. Scale models and costumes help you visualize everyday life in the city at different periods. In the last room, you'll see the museum's prized possession: the Lord Mayor's Coach, a golden carriage pulled by six white horses, looking as if it had pranced right out of the pages of *Cinderella*. There are enough whiz-bang multimedia displays (including the Plague and the Great Fire) to spice up otherwise humdrum artifacts. This regular stop for the local school kids gives the best overview of London history in town.

Cost and Hours: Free, daily 10:00-18:00, galleries shut down 30 minutes before closing, see the day's events board for special talks and tours, café, £1 lockers, on London Wall at Aldersgate Street, Tube: Barbican or St. Paul's plus a five-minute walk, tel. 020/7001-9844, www.museumoflondon.org.uk.

The Monument

Wren's 202-foot-tall tribute to London's Great Fire was restored a few years ago. Climb the 331 steps inside the column for a view of The City that is still monumental.

Cost and Hours: £3, daily 9:30-18:00, until 17:30 Oct-March, last entry 30 minutes before closing, junction of Monument Street and Fish Street Hill, Tube: Monument, tel. 020/7626-2717, www.themonument.info.

▲▲▲Tower of London

The Tower has served as a castle in wartime, a king's residence in peacetime, and, most notoriously, as the prison and execution site of rebels. You can see the crown jewels, take a witty Beefeater tour, and ponder the executioner's block that dispensed with Anne Boleyn, Sir Thomas More, and troublesome heirs to the throne.

Cost and Hours: £22, family-£57 (both prices include a 10 percent optional donation), entry fee includes Beefeater tour (described later); March-Oct Tue-Sat 9:00-17:30, Sun-Mon 10:00-17:30; Nov-Feb Tue-Sat

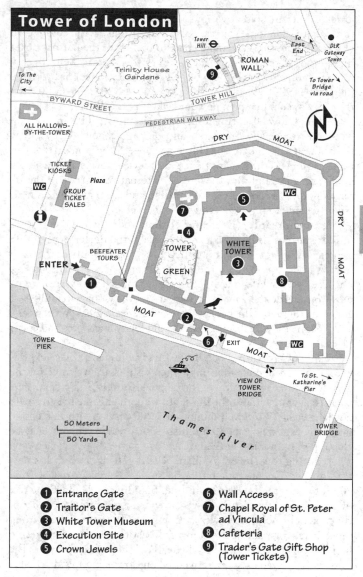

Tower of London

Legend:

1. Entrance Gate
2. Traitor's Gate
3. White Tower Museum
4. Execution Site
5. Crown Jewels
6. Wall Access
7. Chapel Royal of St. Peter ad Vincula
8. Cafeteria
9. Trader's Gate Gift Shop (Tower Tickets)

9:00-16:30, Sun-Mon 10:00-16:30; last entry 30 minutes before closing; skippable audioguide-£4, Tube: Tower Hill, switchboard tel. 0844-482-7777, www.hrp.org.uk.

Advance Tickets: To avoid the long ticket-buying lines at the Tower, buy your ticket at the Trader's Gate gift shop, located down the steps from the Tower Hill Tube stop (tickets here are generally slightly cheaper than at the gate; similar, discounted Fast

Track tickets are sold at various locations (such as travel agencies) throughout London. You can also buy tickets, with credit card only, at the Tower Welcome Centre to the left of the normal ticket lines—though on busy days, it can be crowded here as well. It's easy to book online (www.hrp.org.uk, £1 discount, no fee) or by phone (tel. 0844-482-7799 within UK or tel. 011-44-20-3166-6000 from the US; £2 fee), then pick up your tickets at the Tower.

More Crowd-Beating Tips: It's most crowded in summer, on weekends (especially Sundays), and during school holidays. Any time of year, the line for the crown jewels—the best on earth—can be just as long as the line for tickets. For fewer crowds, arrive before 10:00 and go straight for the jewels. Alternatively, arrive in the afternoon, tour the rest of the Tower first, and see the jewels an hour before closing time, when crowds die down.

Yeoman Warder (Beefeater) Tours: Today, while the Tower's military purpose is history, it's still home to the Beefeaters—the 35 Yeoman Warders and their families. (The original duty of the Yeoman Warders was to guard the Tower, its prisoners, and the jewels.) The free, worthwhile, one-hour Beefeater tours leave every 30 minutes from inside the gate (first tour at 10:00, last one at 15:30—or 14:30 in Nov-Feb). The boisterous Beefeaters are great entertainers, and their historical talks include lots of bloody anecdotes and corny jokes.

Sunday Worship: For a refreshingly different Tower experience, come on Sunday morning, when visitors are welcome on the grounds for free to worship in the Chapel Royal of St. Peter ad Vincula. You get in without the lines, but you can only see the chapel—no sightseeing (9:15 Communion or 11:00 service with fine choral music, meet at west gate 30 minutes early, dress for church, may be closed for ceremonies—call ahead).

Visiting the Tower: William I, still getting used to his new title of "the Conqueror," built the stone "White Tower" (1077-1097) to keep the Londoners in line. Standing high above the rest of old London, the White Tower provided a gleaming reminder of the monarch's absolute power over subjects. If you made the wrong move here, you could be feasting on roast boar in the banqueting hall one night and chained to the walls of the prison the next. The Tower also served as an effective lookout for seeing invaders coming up the Thames.

This square, 90-foot-tall tower was the original structure that gave this castle complex of 20 towers its name. William's successors enlarged the complex to its present 18-acre size. Because of the security it provided, the Tower of London served over the centuries as a royal residence, the Royal Mint, the Royal Jewel House, and, most famously, as the prison and execution site of those who dared oppose the Crown.

You'll find more bloody history per square inch in this original tower of power than anywhere else in Britain. Inside the White Tower is a **museum** with exhibits re-creating medieval life and chronicling the torture and executions that took place here. In the Royal Armory, you'll see some suits of armor of Henry VIII—slender in his youth (c. 1515), heavyset by 1540—with his bigger-is-better codpiece. On the top floor, see the Tower's actual execution ax and chopping block.

The **execution site,** however, in the middle of Tower Green, looks just like a lawn. It was here that enemies of the crown would kneel before the king for the final time. With their hands tied behind their backs, they would say a final prayer, then lay their heads on a block, and—*shlit*—the blade would slice through their necks, their heads tumbling to the ground. Tower Green was the most prestigious execution site at the Tower. Henry VIII axed a couple of his ex-wives here (divorced readers can insert their own joke), including Anne Boleyn and his fifth wife, teenage Catherine Howard (for more on Henry, see the sidebar on page 130).

The Tower's hard stone and glittering **crown jewels** represent the ultimate power of the monarch. The Sovereign's Scepter is encrusted with the world's largest cut diamond—the 530-carat Star of Africa, beefy as a quarter-pounder. The Crown of the Queen Mother (Elizabeth II's famous mum, who died in 2002) has the 106-carat Koh-I-Noor diamond glittering on the front (considered unlucky for male rulers, it only adorns the crown of the king's wife). The Imperial State Crown is what the Queen wears for official functions such as the State Opening of Parliament. Among its 3,733 jewels are Queen Elizabeth I's former earrings (the hanging pearls, top center), a stunning 13th-century ruby look-alike in the center, and Edward the Confessor's ring (the blue sapphire on top, in the center of the Maltese cross of diamonds).

The Tower was defended by state-of-the-art **walls** and fortifications in the 13th century. Walking along them offers a good look at the walls, along with a fine view of the famous Tower Bridge, with its twin towers and blue spans (described next).

After your visit, consider taking the boat to Greenwich from here (see cruise info on page 76).

Near the Tower of London
Tower Bridge
The iconic Tower Bridge (often mistakenly called London Bridge) has been recently painted and restored. The hydraulically powered drawbridge was built in 1894 to accommodate the growing East End. While fully modern, its design was a retro Neo-Gothic look.

You can tour the bridge at the **Tower Bridge Exhibition,** with a history display and a peek at the Victorian engine room that lifts

Henry VIII (1491-1547)

The notorious king who single-handedly transformed England was a true Renaissance Man—six feet tall, handsome, charismatic, well-educated, and brilliant. He spoke English, Latin, French, and Spanish. A legendary athlete, he hunted, played tennis, and jousted with knights and kings. He played the lute and wrote folk songs; his "Pastime with Good Company" is still being performed. When 17-year-old Henry, the second monarch of the House of Tudor, was crowned king in Westminster Abbey, all of England rejoiced.

Henry left affairs of state in the hands of others, and filled his days with sports, war, dice, women, and the arts. But in 1529, Henry's personal life became a political atom bomb, and it changed the course of history. Henry wanted a divorce, partly because his wife had become too old to bear him a son, and partly because he'd fallen in love with Anne Boleyn, a younger woman who stubbornly refused to be just the king's mistress. Henry begged the pope for an annulment, but—for political reasons, not moral ones—the pope refused. Henry went ahead and divorced his wife anyway, and he was excommunicated.

The event sparked the English Reformation. With his defiance, Henry rejected papal authority in England. He forced monasteries to close, sold off some church land, and confiscated everything else for himself and the Crown. Within a decade, monastic institutions that had operated for centuries were left empty and gutted (many ruined sites, including the abbeys of Glastonbury, St. Mary's at York, Rievaulx, and Lindisfarne, can be visited today). Meanwhile, the Catholic Church was reorganized into the (Anglican) Church of England, with Henry as its head. Though Henry himself basically adhered to Catholic doctrine, he discouraged the veneration of saints and relics, and commissioned an English translation of the Bible. Hard-core Catholics had to assume a low profile. Many English welcomed this break from Italian religious influence, but others rebelled. For the next few generations, England would suffer through bitter Catholic-Protestant differences.

Henry famously had six wives. The issue was not his love life (which could have been satisfied by his numerous mistresses), but the politics of royal succession. To guarantee the Tudor family's dominance, he needed a male heir born by a recognized queen.

Henry's first marriage, to Catherine of Aragon, had been arranged to cement an alliance with her parents, Ferdinand and Isabel of Spain. Catherine bore Henry a daughter, but no sons. Next came Anne Boleyn, who also gave birth to a daughter. After a turbulent few years with Anne and several miscarriages, a frustrated Henry had her beheaded at the Tower of London. His next wife, Jane Seymour, finally had a son (but Jane died soon after giving birth). A blind-marriage with Anne of Cleves ended quickly when she proved to be both politically useless and ugly—the "Flanders Mare." Next, teen bride Catherine Howard ended up cheating on Henry, so she was executed. Henry finally found comfort—but no children—in his later years with his final wife, Catherine Parr.

In 1536, Henry suffered a serious accident while jousting. His health would never be the same. Increasingly, he suffered from festering boils and violent mood swings, and he became morbidly obese, tipping the scales at 400 pounds with a 54-inch waist.

Henry's last years were marked by paranoia, sudden rages, and despotism. He gave his perceived enemies the pink slip in his signature way—charged with treason and beheaded. (Ironically, Henry's own heraldic motto was "Coeur Loyal"—true heart.) Once-wealthy England was becoming depleted, thanks to Henry's expensive habits, which included making war on France, building and acquiring palaces (he had 50), and collecting fine tapestries and archery bows.

Henry forged a large legacy. He expanded the power of the monarchy, making himself the focus of a rising, modern nation-state. Simultaneously, he strengthened Parliament—largely because it agreed with his policies. He annexed Wales, and imposed English rule on Ireland (provoking centuries of resentment). He expanded the navy, paving the way for Britannia to soon rule the waves. And—thanks to Henry's marital woes—England would forever be a Protestant nation.

When Henry died at age 55, he was succeeded by his nine-year-old son by Jane Seymour, Edward VI. Weak and sickly, Edward died six years later. Next to rule was Mary, Henry's daughter from his first marriage. A staunch Catholic, she tried to brutally reverse England's Protestant Reformation, earning the nickname "Bloody Mary." Finally came Henry's daughter with Anne Boleyn—Queen Elizabeth I, who ruled a prosperous, expanding England, seeing her father's seeds blossom into the English Renaissance.

London abounds with "Henry" sights. He was born in Greenwich (at today's Old Royal Naval College) and was crowned in Westminster Abbey. He built a palace along Whitehall and enjoyed another at Hampton Court. At the National Portrait Gallery, you can see portraits of some of Henry's wives, and at the Tower you can see where he executed them. Henry is buried alongside his final wife at Windsor Castle.

the span. It's overpriced at £8, though the city views from the walkways are spectacular (daily 10:00-18:00 in summer, 9:30-17:30 in winter, last entry 30 minutes before closing, enter at the northwest tower, Tube: Tower Hill, tel. 020/7403-3761, www.towerbridge.org.uk).

The bridge is most interesting when the drawbridge lifts to let ships pass, as it does a thousand times a year, but it's best viewed from outside the museum. For the bridge-lifting schedule, check the website or call (see above for contact info).

Nearby: The best remaining bit of London's **Roman Wall** is just north of the Tower (at the Tower Hill Tube station). The chic **St. Katharine Dock,** just east of Tower Bridge, has private yachts, mod shops, the recommended medieval banquet, and the classic Dickens Inn, fun for a drink or pub lunch. Across the bridge, on the South Bank, is the upscale Butlers Wharf area, as well as City Hall, museums, the Jubilee Walkway, and, towering overhead, The Shard. Or you can head north to Liverpool Street Station, and stroll London's East End (described next).

Sights in East London

▲East End

The East End has a long history as London's poorer side of town—even in medieval times. These days, it still lacks the posh refinement of the West End—but the area just beyond Liverpool Street Station is now one of London's hippest, most fun spots. It boasts a colorful mix of bustling markets, late-night dance clubs, the Bangladeshi ghetto (called "Banglatown"), and tenements of Jack the Ripper's London, all in the shadow of glittering new skyscrapers. Head up Brick Lane for a meal in "the curry capital of Europe," or check out the former Truman Brewery, which now houses a Sunday market, cool shops, and Café 1001 (good coffee). This neighborhood is best on Sunday afternoons, when the Spitalfields, Petticoat Lane, and Backyard markets thrive (for more on these markets, see page 154).

▲Geffrye Museum

This low-key but well-organized museum—housed in an 18th-century almshouse—is located north of Liverpool Street Station in the hip Shoreditch area. Its displays give a historical overview of the "middling sort" (middle class), as seen through the prism of home decor. Walk past 11 English living rooms, furnished and decorated in styles from 1600 to 2000, then descend the circular stairs to see changing exhibits. In summer, explore the fragrant herb garden.

Cost and Hours: Free, fees for (optional) special exhibits, Tue-Sat 10:00-17:00, Sun 12:00-17:00, closed Mon, garden open April-Oct, 136 Kingsland Road, tel. 020/7739-9893, www.geffrye-museum.org.uk.

Getting There: Take the Tube to Liverpool Street, then ride the bus 10 minutes north (bus #149 or #242—leave station through Bishopsgate exit and head left a few steps to find stop; hop off at the Hoxton Station stop, just after passing the brick museum on the right). Or take the East London line on the Overground to the Hoxton stop, which is right next to the museum (Tube tickets and Oyster cards also valid on Overground).

Sights on the South Bank

The South Bank of the Thames is a thriving arts and cultural center, tied together by the riverfront Jubilee Walkway.

▲Jubilee Walkway

This riverside path is a popular, pub-crawling pedestrian promenade that stretches all along the South Bank, offering grand views

of the Houses of Parliament and St. Paul's. On a sunny day, this is the place to see Londoners out strolling. The Walkway hugs the river except just east of London Bridge, where it cuts inland for a couple of blocks. It was recently expanded into a 60-mile "Greenway" circling the city, including the 2012 Olympics site.

▲▲London Eye

This giant Ferris wheel, towering above London opposite Big Ben, is one of the world's highest observational wheels and London's an-

swer to the Eiffel Tower. Riding it is a memorable experience, even though London doesn't have much of a skyline, and the price is borderline outrageous. Whether you ride or not, the wheel is a sight to behold.

The experience starts with a brief (four-minute) and engaging show combining a 3-D movie with wind and water effects. Then it's time to spin around the Eye. Designed like a giant bicycle wheel, it's a pan-European undertaking: British steel and Dutch engineering, with Czech, German, French, and Italian mechanical parts. It's also very "green," running extremely efficiently and virtually silently. Twenty-five people ride in each of

The South Bank

LONDON

its 32 air-conditioned capsules for the 30-minute rotation (you go around only once). Each capsule has a bench, but most people stand. From the top of this 443-foot-high wheel—the second-highest public view-point in the city—even Big Ben looks small.

Cost: £19, family ticket available, about 10 percent cheaper if bought online. Buy tickets in advance at www.londoneye.com, by calling 0870-500-0600, or in person at the box office (in the corner of the County Hall building nearest the Eye). Combo-tickets that also cover Madame Tussauds Waxworks cost roughly twice as much (also cheaper online).

Hours: Daily April-June 10:00-21:00, July-Aug 10:00-21:30, Sept-March 10:00-20:30, these are last-ascent times, closed Dec 25 and a few days in Jan for annual maintenance, Tube: Waterloo or Westminster. Thames boats come and go from Waterloo Pier at the foot of the wheel.

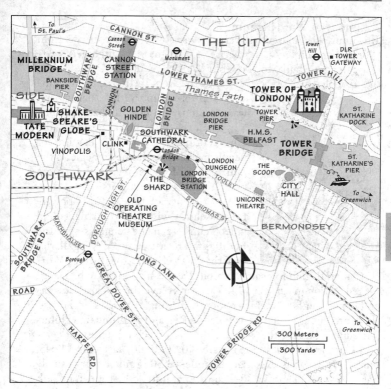

LONDON

Crowd-Beating Tips: The London Eye is busiest between 11:00 and 17:00, especially on weekends year-round and every day in July and August. When it's crowded, you might have to wait up to 30 minutes to buy your ticket, then another 30-45 minutes to board your capsule. If you plan to visit during a busy time, call ahead or go online to pre-book your ticket. Once at the sight, you punch your confirmation code into the automated machine in the ticket office (otherwise, you can pick up your ticket in the short "Groups and Ticket Collection" line at desk #5). Even if you pre-reserve, you still have to wait a bit to board the wheel. You can pay an extra £7-10 for a Fast Track ticket that lets you jump the queue, but the time you save is probably not worth the expense.

By the Eye: The area next to the London Eye has developed a cotton-candy ambience of kitschy, kid-friendly attractions. There's an aquarium, game arcade, and London Film Museum dedicated to movies filmed in London, from *Harry Potter* to *Star Wars* (not to be confused with the far-superior British Film Institute, a.k.a. the BFI Southbank, just to the east).

▲▲Imperial War Museum

This impressive museum covers the wars of the last century—from World War I biplanes, to the rise of fascism, to Montgomery's Africa campaign tank, to the Cold War, the Cuban Missile Crisis, the Troubles in Northern Ireland, the wars in Iraq and Afghani-

stan, and terrorism. Rather than glorify war, the museum does its best to shine a light on the 100 million deaths of the 20th century. It shows everyday life for people back home and never neglects the human side of one of civilization's more uncivilized, persistent traits.

Allow plenty of time, as this powerful museum—with lots of artifacts and video clips—can be engrossing. The highlights are the new WWI galleries and the WWII area, the "Secret War" section, and the Holocaust exhibit. (Some sections may be closed for renovation in early 2014.) War wonks love the place, as do general history buffs who enjoy patiently reading displays. For the rest, there are enough interactive experiences and multimedia exhibits and submarines for the kids to climb in to keep it interesting.

Cost and Hours: Free, daily 10:00-18:00, last entry 17:45, temporary exhibits extra, audioguide-£3.50, guided tours usually Sat-Sun at 11:30 and 13:30—confirm at info desk, Tube: Lambeth North or Elephant and Castle; buses #3, #12, and #159 come here from Westminster area; tel. 020/7416-5000, www.iwm.org.uk.

Visiting the Museum: Start with the museum's latest pride and joy: the **WWI galleries,** newly souped up for the centennial anniversary of the start of the "Great War." Exhibits cover the various theaters and the war at sea, as well as the home front, and the Treaty of Versailles and interwar years. The Trench Experience lets you walk through a dark, chaotic, smelly WWI trench. Then head into the **WWII section** that explains Blitzkrieg and its effects (see an actual Nazi parachute bomb like the ones that devastated London). The Blitz Experience is a walk-through simulator that assaults the senses with the noise and intensity of a WWII air raid on London (begins every 10 minutes). End with a visit to a special exhibit celebrating Field Marshal Bernard Montgomery, and the displays about conflicts since 1945.

The **cinema** on the ground floor shows a rotating selection of films. Up on the first floor, you'll get the best view of the entry hall's **large exhibits**—including Monty's tank, several field guns, and, dangling overhead, vintage planes. Imagine the awesome power of the 50-foot V-2 rocket (towering up from the ground

floor)—the kind the Nazis
rained down on London,
which could arrive silently
and destroy a city block.

Near the first-floor
stairwell is the **"Secret
War"** exhibit, which peeks
into the intrigues of espio-
nage and poses challeng-
ing questions about the
role of secrecy in government.

The second floor has temporary exhibits and the **John Singer
Sargent room,** an art gallery of military-themed works; hiding
behind the entryway is Sargent's *Gassed* (1919) and other giant
canvases. Across the hall is a provocative 30-minute **film** about
genocide, *Crimes Against Humanity.* The third-floor section on the
Holocaust, one of the best on the subject anywhere, tells the story
with powerful videos, artifacts, and fine explanations.

The museum (which sits in an inviting park equipped with an
equally inviting café) is housed in what had been the Royal Bethlam
Hospital. Also known as "the Bedlam asylum," the place was so
wild that it gave the world a new word for chaos. Back in Victorian
times, Londoners—without reality shows and YouTube—paid admission to visit the asylum on weekends for entertainment.

From Tate Modern to City Hall

These sights are in Southwark (SUTH-uck), the core of the tourist's South Bank. Southwark was for centuries the place Londoners would go to escape the rules and decency of the city and let
their hair down. Bearbaiting, brothels, rollicking pubs, and theater—you name the dream, and it could be fulfilled just across the
Thames. A run-down warehouse district through the 20th century,
it's been gentrified with classy restaurants, office parks, pedestrian
promenades, major sights (such as the Tate Modern and Shakespeare's Globe), and a colorful collection of lesser sights. The area is
easy on foot and a scenic—though circuitous—way to connect the
Tower of London with St. Paul's.

▲▲Tate Modern
Dedicated in the spring of 2000, the striking museum across the
river from St. Paul's opened the new century with art from the
previous one. Its powerhouse collection of Monet, Matisse, Dalí,
Picasso, Warhol, and much more is displayed in a converted powerhouse.

The permanent collection is on levels 2 through 4. Paintings
are arranged according to theme, not chronologically or by artist.

Paintings by Picasso, for example, are scattered all over the
building. Don't just come to see
the Old Masters of modernism.
Push your mental envelope with
more recent works by Pollock,
Miró, Bacon, Picabia, Beuys,
Twombly, and others.

Of equal interest are the
many temporary exhibits featur-
ing cutting-edge art. Each year, the main hall features a different
monumental installation by a prominent artist—always one of the
highlights of the art world. The Tate is constructing a new wing to
the south, which will double the museum's exhibition space. The
new wing is opening bit by bit and, once it's finished, the permanent exhibits will likely be rearranged, with some pieces moving to
the new section.

Cost and Hours: Free, but £4 donation appreciated, fee for
special exhibitions, open daily 10:00-18:00, Fri-Sat until 22:00,
last entry to temporary exhibits 45 minutes before closing, especially crowded on weekend days (crowds thin out on Fri and Sat
evenings), audioguide-£4, free 45-minute guided tours are offered
about four times daily (ask for schedule at info desk), no photos
beyond entrance hall, coffee shops and restaurant, tel. 020/7887-
8888, www.tate.org.uk.

Getting There: Cross the Millennium Bridge from St. Paul's;
take the Tube to Southwark, London Bridge, or Mansion House
and walk 10-15 minutes; or catch Thames Clippers' Tate Boat ferry
service from the Tate Britain (£5.50 one-way or £15 for day ticket,
discounts with Travelcard or Oyster card, buy ticket at gallery desk
or on board, departs every 40 minutes from 9:55 to 17:00, about 15
minutes, check schedule at www.tate.org.uk/visit/tate-boat).

▲Millennium Bridge

The pedestrian bridge links St. Paul's Cathedral and the Tate Modern across the Thames. This is London's first new bridge in a century. When it first opened, the $25 million bridge wiggled when
people walked on it, so it promptly closed for repairs; 20 months
and $8 million later, it reopened. Nicknamed the "blade of light"
for its sleek minimalist design (370 yards long, four yards wide,
stainless steel with teak planks), its clever aerodynamic handrails
deflect wind over the heads of pedestrians.

▲▲Shakespeare's Globe

This replica of the original Globe Theatre was built, half-timbered
and thatched, as it was in Shakespeare's time. (This is the first
thatched roof constructed in London since they were outlawed
after the Great Fire of 1666.) The Globe originally accommodated

2,200 seated and another 1,000 standing. Today, slightly smaller and leaving space for reasonable aisles, the theater holds 800 seated and 600 groundlings. Its promoters brag that the theater melds "the three A's"—actors, audience, and architecture—with each contrib-  uting to the play. The working theater hosts authentic performances of Shakespeare's plays with actors in period costumes, modern interpretations of his works, and some works by other playwrights. For details on attending a play, see page 163.

Cost: £13.50, includes Exhibition, audioguide, and 40-minute tour of the Globe; tickets good all day; when the Globe theater is closed, you can tour the Exhibition only for £10, or take a guided tour of the nearby Rose Theatre (also £10, only available some afternoons).

Hours: The complex is open daily 9:00-17:00. Exhibition and tours: May-Sept—Globe tours offered mornings only with Rose Theatre tours some afternoons; Oct-April—Globe tours run all day, tours start every 15-30 minutes. Located on the South Bank directly across Thames over Southwark Bridge from St. Paul's, Tube: Mansion House or London Bridge plus a 10-minute walk; tel. 020/7902-1400 or 020/7902-1500, www.shakespearesglobe.com.

Visiting the Globe: The complex has four parts: the Globe theater itself, the box office, a museum (the Exhibition), and the new Sam Wanamaker Playhouse (an indoor Jacobean theater). The Globe Exhibition ticket includes both a tour of the Globe theater and the Exhibition.

Exhibition: You browse on your own (with the included audioguide) through displays of Elizabethan-era costumes and makeup, music, script-printing, and special effects (the displays change). There are early folios and objects that were dug up on site. Videos and scale models help put Shakespearean theater within the context of the times. (The Globe opened one year after England mastered the seas by defeating the Spanish Armada. The debut play was Shakespeare's *Julius Caesar*.) You'll also learn how they built the replica in modern times, using Elizabethan materials and techniques. Take advantage of the touch screens to delve into specific topics.

Theater: You must tour the theater at the time stamped on your ticket, but you can come back to the Exhibition museum afterward; tickets are good all day. A guide (usually an actor) leads you into the theater to see the stage and the various seating areas for the

different classes of people. You take
a seat and learn how the new Globe
is similar to the old Globe (open-air
performances, standing-room by the
stage, no curtain) and how it's different (female actors today, lights for
night performances, concrete floor).
It's not a backstage tour—you don't
see dressing rooms or costume shops

or sit in on rehearsals, though you may see workers building sets
for a new production. You mostly sit and listen. The guides are energetic, theatrical, and knowledgeable, bringing the Elizabethan
period to life.

When matinee performances are going on, you can't tour the
theater. But you can see the Exhibition museum, or possibly tour
the nearby Rose Theatre (occasionally open and less interesting).

Sam Wanamaker Playhouse: The indoor Jacobean theater,
which is attached to the back of the Globe complex, allows performances to continue through the winter. The intimate venue is
horseshoe-shaped, seats fewer than 350, and is designed to use
authentic candle-lighting for period performances. The repertoire
focuses less on Shakespeare and more on the work of his contemporaries (Jonson, Marlow, Fletcher), as well as concerts. (For details
on getting tickets, go to www.shakespearesglobe.com.) There may
be tours of this new theater, but—as at the Globe itself—tours always come second to the performance schedule.

Eating: The Swan at the Globe café offers a sit-down restaurant (for lunch and dinner, reservations recommended, tel.
020/7928-9444), a drinks-and-plates bar, and a sandwich-and-
coffee cart (daily 9:00-closing, depending on performance times).

Vinopolis

While it seems illogical to have a huge wine museum in beer-loving
London, Vinopolis makes a good case. Built over a Roman wine
store and filling the massive vaults of an old wine warehouse, the

museum offers interactive exhibits
that give a light yet earnest history of
wine to accompany your sips of various mediocre reds and whites, ports,
and champagnes. A few varieties of
spirits help keep it interesting. Your
visit starts with a 15-minute wine-
tasting lesson, then you're let loose.
Ticket prices vary according to how

many virtual "tokens" you load onto a card, which you use to
dispense your samples through their "enomatic" machines (most
wines cost 1-4 tokens). Tapas-style snacks are available, in addi-

tion to the five restaurants on site. Booking ahead for Friday and Saturday nights is smart.

Cost and Hours: Self-guided tour options range from £27 (7 tokens) to £38 (16 tokens), also offer packages that include a meal, Wed 18:00-21:30, Thu-Fri 14:00-21:30, Sat 12:00-21:30, Sun 12:00-16:00, closed Mon-Tue, last entry 2 hours before closing, between Shakespeare's Globe and Southwark Cathedral at 1 Bank End, Tube: London Bridge, tel. 020/7940-3000, www.vinopolis. co.uk.

The Clink Prison Museum

Proudly the "original clink," this was, until 1780, where law-abiding citizens threw Southwark troublemakers. Today, it's a low-tech torture museum filling grotty old rooms with papier-mâché gore. Unfortunately, there's little that seriously deals with the fascinating problem of law and order in Southwark, where 18th-century Londoners went for a good time.

Cost and Hours: Overpriced at £7.50; July-Sept daily 10:00-21:00; Oct-June Mon-Fri 10:00-18:00, Sat-Sun until 21:00, last entry 30 minutes before closing; 1 Clink Street, Tube: London Bridge, tel. 020/7403-0900, www.clink.co.uk.

Golden Hinde Replica

This is a full-size replica of the 16th-century warship in which Sir Francis Drake circumnavigated the globe from 1577 to 1580. Commanding the original ship (now long gone), Drake earned his reputation as history's most successful pirate. This replica, however, has logged more than 100,000 miles, including a voyage around the world. While the ship is fun to see, its interior is not worth touring.

Cost and Hours: £6, daily 10:00-17:30, last entry at 16:45, sometimes closed for private events, Tube: London Bridge, ticket office just up Pickfords Wharf from the ship, tel. 020/7403-0123, www.goldenhinde.com.

▲Southwark Cathedral

While made a cathedral only in 1905, it's been the neighborhood church since the 13th century, and comes with some interesting history. The enthusiastic docents give impromptu tours if you ask.

Cost and Hours: Free, but £4 donation requested (you'll likely be approached about the donation, so be prepared with at least £1 or a simple "No"), daily 8:00-18:30—though only the back of the nave is open to discreet sightseers during frequent services, last entry 30 minutes before closing, £3.50 guidebook, no photos without permission (£2), Tube: London Bridge. Tel. 020/7367-6700, http://cathedral.southwark.anglican.org.

Music: The cathedral hosts evensong Sun at 15:00, Tue-Fri 17:30, Sat at 16:00; they also host organ recitals Mon at 13:00 and music recitals Tue at 15:15 (call or check website to confirm times of evensong and recitals).

▲Old Operating Theatre Museum and Herb Garret

Climb a tight and creaky wooden spiral staircase to a church attic where you'll find a garret used to dry medicinal herbs, a fascinating exhibit on Victorian surgery, cases of well-described 19th-century medical paraphernalia, and a special look at "anesthesia, the defeat of pain." Then you stumble upon Britain's oldest operating theater, where limbs were sawed off way back in 1821.

Cost and Hours: £6.20, cash only, borrowable laminated descriptions, daily 10:30-16:45, closed Dec 15-Jan 5, £1 audioguide tries hard but is not quite worthwhile, 9a St. Thomas Street, Tube: London Bridge, tel. 020/7188-2679, www.thegarret.org.uk.

The Shard

Rocketing dramatically 1,020 feet above the south end of the London Bridge, this recent addition to London's skyline is by far the tallest building in Western Europe (for now). Designed by Renzo Piano (best known as the co-architect of Paris' Pompidou Center), the glass-clad pyramid shimmers in the sun and its prickly top glows like the city's nightlight after dark. Its uppermost floors are set aside as public viewing galleries, but the ticket price is as outrageously high as the building itself, especially given that it's a bit far from London's most exciting landmarks. For a list of cheaper view opportunities in London, see the sidebar on page 124.

Cost and Hours: £25 if booked at least a day in advance, £29 for same-day reservations, book as soon as you have reasonable chance of assuring decent weather, least crowded on weekday mornings, daily 9:00-22:00, last entry slot at 20:30, Tube: London Bridge—use London Bridge exit, tel. 0844-499-7111, www.theviewfromtheshard.com.

Ascending the Tower: From the entrance on Joiner Street (just off St. Thomas Street) you'll take a two-part elevator ride up to the 68th floor, then climb up one story to the main observation platform. It's equipped with cool telescopes that label major landmarks, and even let you see how the view from here would appear at other times of the day. From here you've got great views of St. Paul's, the Tower of London, Southwark Cathedral (straight down), and, in the distance, the 2012 Olympic stadium in one direction, and the Houses of Parliament in the other (find Buckingham Palace, just left of the Eye). On the clearest days, you can see 40 miles out, and a few people say they've been able to make out ships on the North Sea. Even in bad weather it's mesmerizing to watch the constant movement of the city's transit system, which looks like a model-train set from this height. Climbing up to the 72nd floor gets you to the open-air deck, where the wind roars over the glass enclosure. As you look up, try to picture Prince Andrew rappelling off the very top, which he and 40 others did in 2012 as a charity fundraising stunt.

HMS *Belfast*

"The last big-gun armored warship of World War II" clogs the Thames just upstream from the Tower Bridge. This huge vessel—now manned with wax sailors—thrills kids who always dreamed of sitting in a turret shooting off their imaginary guns. If you're into WWII warships, this is the ultimate. Otherwise, it's just lots of exercise with a nice view of the Tower Bridge.

Cost and Hours: £15 including 9 percent voluntary donation, includes audioguide, kids under 15 free, daily March-Oct 10:00-18:00, Nov-Feb 10:00-17:00, last entry one hour before closing, Tube: London Bridge, tel. 020/7940-6300, www.iwm.org.uk/visits/hms-belfast.

City Hall

The glassy, egg-shaped building near the south end of Tower Bridge is London's City Hall, designed by Sir Norman Foster, the architect who worked on London's Millennium Bridge and Berlin's Reichstag. Nicknamed "the Armadillo," City Hall houses the office of London's mayor—the blond, flamboyant, conservative former journalist and author Boris Johnson. He consults here with the Assembly representatives of the city's 25 districts. An interior spiral ramp allows visitors to watch and hear the action below in the Assembly Chamber—ride the lift to floor 2 (the highest visitors can go) and  spiral down. On the lower ground floor is a large aerial photograph of London and a handy cafeteria. Next to City Hall is the outdoor amphitheater called The Scoop (see page 166).

Cost and Hours: Free, open to visitors Mon-Thu 8:30-18:00, Fri 8:30-17:30, closed Sat-Sun; Tube: London Bridge station plus 10-minute walk, or Tower Hill station plus 15-minute walk; tel. 020/7983-4000, www.london.gov.uk.

Sights in West London

▲▲Tate Britain

One of Europe's great art houses, Tate Britain specializes in British painting from the 16th century through modern times. This is people's art, with realistic paintings rooted in the people, landscape, and stories of the British Isles.

The recently renovated Tate shows off Hogarth's stage sets, Gainsborough's ladies, Blake's angels, Constable's clouds, Turner's tempests, the swooning realism of the Pre-Raphaelites, and the camera-eye portraits of Hockney and Freud. Even if these names are new to you, don't worry. You'll likely see a few "famous" works you didn't know were British and exit the Tate Britain with at least one new favorite artist.

Cost and Hours: Free but £4 donation requested, admission fee for (optional) temporary exhibits, map-£1 suggested donation, ask if audioguide is available; daily 10:00-18:00, sometimes Fri until 22:00 (check online or call to confirm), last entry 45 minutes before closing; free tours generally offered daily—ask at the information desk or call ahead; café and restaurant, tel. 020/7887-8888, www.tate.org.uk.

Getting There: It's on the Thames River, south of Big Ben and north of Vauxhall Bridge. Take the Tube to Pimlico, then walk seven minutes. Or hop on the Tate Boat museum ferry from the Tate Modern (for details, see page 137).

Hyde Park and Nearby

A number of worthwhile sights border this grand park, from Apsley House on the east to the newly renovated Kensington Palace on the west.

▲Apsley House (Wellington Museum)

Having beaten Napoleon at Waterloo, Arthur Wellesley, the First Duke of Wellington, was once the most famous man in Europe.

He was given a huge fortune, with which he purchased London's ultimate address, #1 London. His refurbished mansion offers a nice interior, a handful of world-class paintings, and a glimpse at the life of the great soldier and two-time prime minister. The highlight is the large ballroom, the Waterloo Gallery, decorated with

West London

NOTTING HILL
BAYSWATER
Queensway
Notting Hill Gate
NOTTING HILL GATE
Holland Park
PLAYGROUND
Kensington Gardens
KENSINGTON PALACE
ALBERT MEMORIAL
Holland Park
KENS. HIGH ST.
High St. Kensington
KENSINGTON RD.
ROYAL ALBERT HALL
VICTORIA & ALBERT MUSEUM
SCIENCE & NAT'L HISTORY MUSEUMS
KNIGHTSBRIDGE RD.
HARRODS
EARL'S CT. RD.
CROMWELL RD.
South Kens.
Gloucester Road
OLD BROMPTON RD.
SOUTH KENSINGTON
FULHAM RD.
KING'S RD.
CHELSEA
NATIONAL ARMY MUSEUM
CHELSEA EMBANKMENT
Paddington Station
MARBLE ARCH
Marble Arch
BAYSWATER RD.
Lancaster Gate
SPEAKERS' CORNER
Hyde Park
DIANA FOUNTAIN
APSLEY HOUSE
Hyde Park Corner
Knights-bridge
BROMPTON RD.
SLOANE ST.
Sloane Square
Sloane Square
OXFORD ST.
Bond Street
Oxford Circus
Old Bond St.
Green Park
PARK LN.
MAYFAIR
PICCADILLY
Green Park
BUCKINGHAM PALACE
BELGRAVIA
VICTORIA ST.
Victoria
VICTORIA STATION
COACH STATION
PIMLICO
To Tate Britain
VAUXHALL BRIDGE
BELGRAVE RD.
GROSVENOR RD.
Pimlico
REGENT ST.
SHAFTS.
Piccadilly Circus
St. James's Park
St. James's Park
WEST-MINSTER CATH.

500 Meters
1/2 Mile

LONDON

Thames River

Anthony van Dyck's *Charles I on Horseback* (over the main fireplace), Diego Velázquez's earthy *Water-Seller of Seville* (to the left of Van Dyck), and Jan Steen's playful *Dissolute Household* (to the right). Just outside the door, in the Portico Room, is a large portrait of Wellington by Francisco Goya.

Those who know something about Wellington ahead of time will appreciate the place much more than those who don't, as there's scarce biographical background. The place is well-described by the included audioguide, which has sound bites from the current Duke of Wellington (who still lives at Apsley).

Cost and Hours: £6.70, free on June 18—Waterloo Day; April-Oct Wed-Sun 11:00-17:00, closed Mon-Tue; Nov-March Sat-Sun 10:00-16:00, closed Mon-Fri; no photos, 20 yards from Hyde Park Corner Tube station, tel. 020/7499-5676, www.english-heritage.org.uk.

Nearby: Hyde Park's pleasant rose garden is picnic-friendly. **Wellington Arch,** which stands just across the street, is open to the public (except closed Mon-Tue) but not worth the £4 charge (or £8.60 combo-ticket with Apsley House; elevator up, lousy views and boring exhibits).

▲Hyde Park and Speakers' Corner

London's "Central Park," originally Henry VIII's hunting grounds, has more than 600 acres of lush greenery, "Boris Bikes" rental stations, the huge man-made Serpentine Lake

(with rental boats and a lakeside swimming pool), the royal Kensington Palace (described later), and the ornate Neo-Gothic Albert Memorial across from the Royal Albert Hall (for more about the park, see www.royalparks.org.uk/parks/hyde-park). The western half of the park is known as Kensington Gardens. The park is huge—study a Tube map to choose the stop nearest to your destination.

On Sundays, from just after noon until early evening, **Speakers' Corner** offers soapbox oratory at its best (northeast corner of the park, Tube: Marble Arch). Characters climb their stepladders, wave their flags, pound emphatically on their sandwich boards, and share what they are convinced is their wisdom. Regulars have resident hecklers who know their lines and are always ready with a verbal jab or barb. "The grass roots of democracy" is actually a holdover from when the gallows stood here and the criminal was allowed to say just about anything he wanted to before he swung. I dare you to raise your voice and gather a crowd—it's easy to do.

The **Princess Diana Memorial Fountain** honors the "People's Princess," who once lived in nearby Kensington Palace. The low-key circular stream, great for cooling off your feet on a hot day, is in the south-central part of the park, near the Albert Memorial and Serpentine Gallery (Tube: Knightsbridge). A similarly named but different sight, the **Diana, Princess of Wales Memorial Playground,** is in the park's northwest corner and fun for kids (Tube: Queensway).

▲▲Kensington Palace

For nearly 150 years (1689-1837), Kensington was the royal residence, before Buckingham Palace became the official home of the

monarch. Sitting primly on its pleasant parkside grounds, the palace is immaculately restored and creatively presented, with exhibits designed to appeal to adults and kids alike. It gives a fun glimpse into the lives of several important residents, especially Queen Victoria, who was born and raised here.

Cost and Hours: £16.50 (includes 10 percent optional donation), save £1 by booking online, daily 10:00-18:00, until 17:00 Nov-Feb, last entry one hour before closing, least crowded in mornings, £5 guidebook but friendly "explainers" will answer questions for free, lockers take £1 coin deposit, a 10-minute stroll through Kensington Gardens from either High Street Kensing-

ton or Queensway Tube stations, tel. 0844-482-7788, www.hrp.
org.uk.

Background: After Queen Victoria moved the monarchy to
Buckingham Palace, lesser royals bedded down at Kensington.
Princess Diana lived here both during and after her marriage to
Prince Charles (1981-1997). More recently, Will and Kate moved
into a thoroughly renovated Apartment 1A (the southern flank of
the palace complex, with four stories and 20 rooms). And Prince
Harry lives in their old digs, a "cottage" on the other side of the
main building. However—as many disappointed visitors discover—
none of these more recent apartments are open to the public.

Visiting the Palace: After buying your ticket, head into the
vestibule. From here, you can reach any of the three main exhibits.
To see them chronologically, head to the right, starting with the
Queen's State Apartments (with highly conceptual exhibits focusing on the later Stuart dynasty—William and Mary, and Mary's
sister, Queen Anne). Then move on to the **King's State Apartments** (the grandest spaces, from Hanoverian times), and finish
with the **"Victoria Revealed"** exhibit (telling the story, through
quotes and artifacts, of Britain's longest-ruling monarch).

Nearby: Garden enthusiasts enjoy popping into the secluded
Sunken Garden, 50 yards from the exit. Consider afternoon tea
at the nearby Orangery (see page 208), built as a greenhouse for
Queen Anne in 1704. On the south side of the palace are the gold-
en gates that became famous in 1997 as the backdrop to the sea of
flowers left here by Princess Diana's mourners.

▲▲▲Victoria and Albert Museum
The world's top collection of decorative arts (vases, stained glass,
fine furniture, clothing, jewelry, carpets, and more), "the V&A" is a
surprisingly interesting assortment of crafts from the West, as well
as Asian and Islamic cultures. Highlights include Raphael's tapestry cartoons, a cast of Trajan's Column that depicts the emperor's
conquests, one of Leonardo da Vinci's notebooks, ladies' underwear through the ages, a Chihuly chandelier, a life-size *David* with
detachable fig leaf, Henry VIII's quill pen, and Mick Jagger's se-
quined jumpsuit. From the worlds of Islam and India, there are
stunning carpets, the ring of the man who built the Taj Mahal,
and a mechanical tiger that eats Brits. Best of all, the objects are
all quite beautiful. You could spend days in the place. Pick up a
museum map and wander at will.

Cost and Hours: Free, but £3 donation requested, sometimes
pricey fees for (optional) special exhibits, £1 suggested donation for
much-needed museum map, daily 10:00-17:45, some galleries open
Fri until 22:00, free one-hour tours daily on the half-hour 10:30-
15:30, on Cromwell Road in South Kensington, Tube: South

Kensington, from the Tube station a long tunnel leads directly to museum, tel. 020/7942-2000, www.vam.ac.uk.

▲▲Natural History Museum

Across the street from Victoria and Albert, this mammoth museum is housed in a giant and wonderful Victorian, Neo-Romanesque building. In the main hall, above a  big dinosaur skeleton and under a massive slice of sequoia tree, Charles Darwin sits as if upon a throne over-seeing it all. Built in the 1870s spe-cifically for the huge collection (50 million specimens), the building has several color-coded "zones" that cover everything from life ("creepy crawlies," human biology, "our place in evolution," and awe-inspir-ing dinosaurs) to earth science (meteors, volcanoes, earthquakes, and so on). Use the helpful map (£1 suggested donation) to find your way through the collection. Exhibits are wonderfully ex-plained, with lots of creative, interactive displays.

Cost and Hours: Free, but £3 donation requested, fees for (optional) special exhibits, daily 10:00-17:50, open later last Fri of the month, last entry 20 minutes before closing, long tunnel leads directly from South Kensington Tube station to museum, tel. 020/7942-5000, exhibit info and reservations tel. 020/7942-5011, www.nhm.ac.uk.

▲Science Museum

Next door to the Natural History Museum, this sprawling won-derland for curious minds is kid-perfect, with themes such as mea-suring time, exploring space, climate change, and the evolution of modern medicine. It offers hands-on fun, from moonwalks to deep-sea exploration, with trendy technology exhibits and a state-of-the-art IMAX theater (shows-£10, £8 for kids, £27 family ticket).

Cost and Hours: Free, daily 10:00-18:00, until 19:00 during school holidays, last entry 45 minutes before closing, Exhibition Road, Tube: South Kensington, tel. 0870-870-4868, www.sci-encemuseum.org.uk.

Sights in Greater London

East of London

▲▲The Docklands

Once the primary harbor for the Port of London, the Docklands has been transformed into a vibrant business center, with ultra-tall skyscrapers, subterranean supermalls, trendy pubs, and peaceful parks with pedestrian bridges looping over canals. While not full of the touristy sights that many are seeking in London, the Docklands offers a refreshing look at the British version of a 21st-century city. It's best at the end of the workday, when it's lively with office workers. It's ideal to see on your way back from Greenwich, since both line up on the same train tracks.

Getting to the Docklands from the City Center: Take the Tube's Jubilee Line to the Canary Wharf station (15 minutes from Westminster, frequent departures). Or catch the Thames Clippers boat to Canary Wharf Pier (£6.50 one-way, £15 all-day pass; boats leave every 20-30 minutes from major London docks; 10-30-minute trip).

Combining the Docklands with Greenwich: It's easy to connect the Docklands with Greenwich—by Docklands Light Rail (DLR) or by boat (for details, see "Getting to Greenwich" on page 229). You could sightsee Greenwich in the morning and early afternoon, then make a brief stop at the Docklands (Canary Wharf station) on your way back to the city center.

LONDON

▲Museum of London Docklands

Illuminating the gritty and fascinating history of this site, this museum traces the story of what was London's primary harbor. You'll see fascinating models of Old London Bridge, crammed with little houses and shops (not unlike how Florence's Ponte Vecchio still looks); a reconstruction of a "Legal Quay," where cargo was processed; and a re-creation of the fuel pipeline that was laid under the English Channel to supply the Allies on the Continent during WWII. You'll also walk through gritty "Sailortown," listening to the salty voices of those who lived and worked in quarters like these.

Cost and Hours: Free, daily 10:00-18:00, last entry 30 minutes before closing, West India Quay, Tube: West India Quay or Canary Wharf, tel. 020/7001-9844, www.museumoflondon.org.uk/docklands.

West of London

▲▲Kew Gardens

For a fine riverside park and a palatial greenhouse jungle to swing through, take the Tube or the boat to every botanist's favorite escape, Kew Gardens. While to most visitors the Royal Botanic Gardens of Kew are simply a delightful opportunity to wander among 33,000 different types of plants, to the hardworking organization that runs them, the gardens are a way to promote the understanding and preservation of the botanical diversity of our planet. From the Kew Tube station, cross the foot-bridge over the tracks, which drops you in a little community of plant-and-herb shops, a two-block walk from Victoria Gate (the main garden entrance). Pick up a map brochure and check at the gate for a monthly listing of best blooms.

Garden lovers could spend days exploring Kew's 300 acres. For a quick visit, spend a fragrant hour wandering through three buildings: the Palm House, a humid Victorian world of iron, glass, and tropical plants that was built in 1844; a Waterlily House that Monet would swim for (see photo); and the Princess of Wales Conservatory, a meandering modern greenhouse with many different climate zones growing countless cacti, bug-munching carnivorous plants, and more. With extra time, check out the Xstrata Treetop Walkway, a 200-yard-long scenic steel walkway that puts you high in the canopy 60 feet above the ground. Young kids will love the Climbers and Creepers indoor/outdoor playground and little zip line, as well as a slow and easy ride on the

hop-on, hop-off Kew Explorer tram (£4 for narrated 40-minute ride, departs on the hour from 11:00 from near Victoria Gate, 2/hour in summer).

Cost: £16 (includes £1.50 voluntary donation), discounted to £14 45 minutes before glasshouses close, kids under 17 free.

Hours: April-Aug Mon-Fri 9:30-18:30, Sat-Sun 9:30-19:30, closes earlier Sept-March—check schedule online, last entry to gardens 30 minutes before closing, glasshouses close at 17:30 in high season—earlier off-season, free one-hour walking tours daily at 11:00 and 13:30, Tube: Kew Gardens, boats run April-Oct between Kew Gardens and Westminster Pier—see page 76, switchboard tel. 020/8332-5000, recorded info tel. 020/8332-5655, www.kew.org.

Eating: For a sun-dappled lunch or snack, walk 10 minutes from the Palm House to the Orangery Cafeteria (£4 sandwiches, £8-12 lunches, daily 10:00-17:30, until 15:15 in winter, closes early for events).

▲Hampton Court Palace

Fifteen miles up the Thames from downtown, the 500-year-old palace of Henry VIII is worth ▲▲ for palace aficionados. Actually, it was originally the palace of his minister, Cardinal Wolsey. When Wolsey, a clever man, realized Henry VIII was experiencing a little palace envy, he gave the mansion to his king. The Tudor palace was also home to Elizabeth I and Charles I. Sections were updated by Christopher Wren for William and Mary. The stately palace stands

overlooking the Thames and includes some impressive Tudor rooms, including a Great Hall with a magnificent hammer-beam ceiling. The industrial-strength Tudor kitchen was capable of keeping 600 schmoozing courtiers thoroughly—if not well—fed. The sculpted garden features a rare Tudor tennis court and a popular maze.

The palace tries hard to please, but it doesn't quite sparkle. From the information center in the main courtyard, you can pick up audioguides for self-guided tours of various wings of the palace (free but slow, aimed mostly at school-aged children). For more in-depth information, strike up a conversation with the costumed characters or docents posted in each room. The Tudor portions of the castle, including the rooms dedicated to the young Henry, are most interesting; the Georgian rooms are pretty dull. The maze in the nearby garden is a curiosity some find fun (maze free with palace ticket, otherwise £5).

Cost and Hours: £18, family-£45 (both prices include a 10 percent optional donation); online discounts, daily April-Oct 10:00-18:00, Nov-March 10:00-16:30, last entry one hour before closing, café, tel. 0844-482-7777 or 020/3166-6000, www.hrp. org.uk.

Getting There: The train (2/hour, 35 minutes, Oyster cards OK) from London's Waterloo Station drops you across the river from the palace (just walk across the bridge). Consider arriving at or departing from the palace by boat (connections with London's Westminster Pier, see page 76); it's a relaxing and scenic three- to four-hour cruise past two locks and a fun new/old riverside mix.

Kew Gardens/Hampton Court Blitz: Because these two sights are in the same general direction (about £20 for a taxi between the two), you can visit both in one day. Here's a game plan: Start your morning at Hampton Court, tour the palace and garden, and have a Tudor-style lunch in the atmospheric dining hall. After lunch, take bus #R68 from Hampton Court Station to Richmond (40 minutes), then transfer to bus #65, which will drop you off at the Kew Gardens gate (5 minutes). After touring the gardens, have tea in the Orangery, then Tube or boat back to London.

North of London

The Making of Harry Potter: Warner Bros. Studio Tour

A nirvana for Potterphiles, this attraction lets fans young and old see the actual sets and props that were used to create the Harry Potter films, video interviews with the actors and filmmakers, and exhibits about how the films' special effects were created. Visitors must book a time slot in advance—it's essential to reserve your visit online as far ahead as possible. Since it's located in Leavesden, a 20-minute train ride from London, and takes about three hours to experience, a visit here will eat up the better part of a day.

Cost and Hours: £29, kids ages 5 to 15-£21.50, family ticket for 2 adults and 2 kids-£85, audio/videoguide—£5; opening hours flex with season—first tour at 9:00 or 10:00, last tour as early as 16:00 or as late as 18:30; café, still photography allowed, tel. 0845-084-0900, www.wbstudiotour.co.uk.

Getting There: Reaching the studio requires a **train and shuttle bus** connection. First, take the frequent train from London Euston to Watford Junction (about 5/hour, 15-20 minutes). From there, you can take a Mullany's Coaches shuttle bus to the studio tour (2-4/hour, 15 minutes, arrive at Watford Junction at least 45 minutes before your tour entrance time, £1.50 one-way, £2 round-trip). Golden Tours runs three more direct (and more expensive) **buses** per day between their office near Victoria Station in central London and the studio (price includes round-trip bus and entrance: adults-£57, kids-£52; leaves London at 8:00, 11:00, and 14:00, tour begins 2 hours after bus departs, reserve ahead at www.golden-tours.com).

Shopping in London

Most stores are open Monday through Saturday from roughly 10:00 to 18:00, and many close Sundays. Large department stores stay open later during the week (until 20:00 or 21:00) and are open shorter hours on Sundays. If you're looking for bargains, you can visit one of the city's many street markets.

Shopping Streets

London is famous for its shopping. The best and most convenient shopping streets are in the West End and West London (roughly between Soho and Hyde Park).  You'll find mid-range shops along **Oxford Street** (running east from Tube: Marble Arch), and fancier shops along **Regent Street** (stretching south from Tube: Oxford Circus to Piccadilly Circus) and **Knightsbridge** (where you'll find Harrods and Harvey Nichols, described later; Tube: Knightsbridge). Other streets are more specialized, such as **Jermyn Street** for old-fashioned men's clothing (just south of Piccadilly Street) and **Charing Cross**

Road for books. **Floral Street,** connecting Leicester Square to Covent Garden, is lined with fashion boutiques.

Fancy Department Stores in West London

Harrods

Harrods is London's most famous and touristy department store. With more than four acres of retail space covering seven floors, it's a place where some shoppers could spend all day. (To me, it's still just a department store.) Big yet classy, Harrods has everything from elephants to toothbrushes (Mon-Sat 10:00-20:00, Sun 11:30-18:00, pay lockers for big backpacks, on Brompton Road, Tube: Knightsbridge, tel. 020/7730-1234, www.harrods.com).

Harvey Nichols

Once Princess Diana's favorite, "Harvey Nick's" remains the department store *du jour* (Mon-Sat 10:00-20:00, Sun 11:30-18:00, near Harrods, 109-125 Knightsbridge, Tube: Knightsbridge, tel. 020/7235-5000, www.harveynichols.com).

Fortnum & Mason

The official department store of the Queen, Fortnum & Mason embodies old-fashioned, British upper-class taste. While some may find it too stuffy, you won't find another store with the same storybook atmosphere (Mon-Sat 10:00-20:00, Sun 12:00-18:00, elegant tea served in their Diamond Jubilee Tea Salon—see page 209, 181 Piccadilly, Tube: Green Park, tel. 020/7734-8040, www.fortnumandmason.com.

Liberty

Known for its gorgeous floral fabrics and well-stocked crafts department, Liberty is fun to stroll through just for a look at its hip, artful displays and castle-like interior (Mon-Sat 10:00-20:00, Sun 12:00-18:00, Great Marlborough St, Tube: Oxford Circus, tel. 020/7734-1234, www.liberty.co.uk.

Street Markets

Antique buffs, people-watchers, and folks who brake for garage sales love London's street markets. There's good early-morning market activity somewhere any day of the week. The best markets—which combine lively stalls and a colorful neighborhood with cute and characteristic shops of their own—are Portobello Road and Camden Lock Market. Any London TI has a complete, up-to-date list. Hagglers will enjoy the no-holds-barred bargaining encouraged in London's street markets.

Warning: Markets attract two kinds of people—tourists and pickpockets.

In Notting Hill

Portobello Road Market

Arguably London's best street market, Portobello Road stretches for several blocks through the delightful, colorful, funky-yet-quaint Notting Hill neighborhood. Already charming streets lined with pastel-painted houses and offbeat antique shops are enlivened on Saturdays with 2,000 additional stalls (8:30-19:00), plus food, live music, and more. (It's also extremely crowded.) If you start at Notting Hill Gate and work your way north, you'll find these general sections: antiques, new goods, produce, more new goods, and a flea market. While Portobello Road is best on Saturdays, it's enjoyable to stroll this street on most other days as well, since the quirky shops are fun to explore—but skip it on Sundays, when virtually everything is closed (Tube: Notting Hill Gate, near recommended accommodations, tel. 020/7727-7684, www.portobelloroad.co.uk).

In Camden Town

Camden Lock Market

This huge, trendy arts-and-crafts festival is divided into three areas, each with its own vibe. The main market, set alongside the

picturesque canal, features a mix of shops and stalls selling boutique crafts and artisanal foods. The market on the opposite side of Chalk Farm Road is edgier, with cheap ethnic food stalls, lots of canalside seating, and punk crafts. The Stables, a sprawling, incense-scented complex, is decorated with fun statues of horses and squeezed into tunnels under the old rail bridge just behind the main market. It's a little lowbrow and wildly creative, with cheap clothes, junk jewelry, and loud music (daily 10:00-18:00, busiest on weekends, Tube: Chalk Farm, bus #24 heads from Pimlico to Victoria Station to Trafalgar Square and then straight up to Camden—before continuing on to Hampstead Heath, tel. 020/7485-7963, www.camdenlockmarket.com). Avoid the tacky, crowded area between the market and the Camden Town Tube station (which bills itself as "The Camden Market," but lacks the real one's canalside charm) by getting off at the Chalk Farm stop; better yet, consider arriving via a scenic waterbus ride from Little Venice (tel. 020/7482-2660, www.londonwaterbus.com).

In the East End

All three of these East End markets are busiest and most interesting on Sundays.

Spitalfields Market

This huge, mod-feeling market hall (pronounced "spittle-fields") combines a shopping mall with old brick buildings and sleek modern ones, all covered by a giant glass roof. While the shops and a rainbow of restaurant options are open every day, the open space between them is filled with stalls Tuesdays through Fridays. It's best on Sundays (9:00-17:00), when all stalls and shops are open; you'll find a lively organic food market, many ethnic eateries, crafts, trendy clothes, bags, and an antique-and-junk market. It's quietest on Saturdays, when only the shops are open—no stalls (shops open daily 10:00-19:00, Tube: Liverpool Street; from the Tube stop, take Bishopsgate East exit, turn left, walk to Brushfield Street, and turn right; www.visitspitalfields.com).

Petticoat Lane Market

Just a block from Spitalfields Market, this line of stalls sits on the otherwise dull, glass-skyscraper-filled Middlesex Street; adjoining Wentworth Street is grungier and more characteristic. Expect budget clothing, leather, shoes, watches, jewelry, and crowds (Sun 9:00-14:00, sometimes later; smaller market Mon-Fri 8:00-16:00 on Wentworth Street only; closed Sat; Middlesex Street and Wentworth Street, Tube: Liverpool Street). The Columbia Road flower market is nearby (Sun 8:00-15:00, http://columbiaroad.info).

Brick Lane Markets

Housed in the former Truman Brewery, this cluster of markets is in the heart of the "Banglatown" Bangladeshi community. Of the three East End market areas, Brick Lane's markets are the grittiest and most avant-garde, selling handmade clothes and home decor as well as ethnic street food. The markets are in full swing on Sundays (roughly 10:00-17:00), though you'll still see some action on Saturdays (11:00-18:00). The Boiler House Food Hall and the Backyard Market (hipster arts & crafts) go all weekend—and the Vintage Market (clothes) even operates on Fridays (11:00-17:30). (Tube: Liverpool Street or Aldgate East, tel. 020/7770-6028, www.brick-lanemarket.com).

In the West End

Covent Garden Market

Originally the convent garden for Westminster Abbey, the iron-and-glass market hall hosted a produce market until the 1970s (earning it the name "Apple Market"). Now it's a mix of fun shops, eateries, and markets. Mondays are for antiques, while arts and crafts dominate the rest of the week. Yesteryear's produce stalls are open daily (10:00-19:00), and on Thursdays, a food market brightens up the square (Tube: Covent Garden, tel. 0870-780-5001, www.coventgardenlondonuk.com. The **Jubilee Hall Market** to the south follows a similar schedule (antiques Mon 5:00-16:00, general market Tue-Fri 9:30-18:30, handcrafts Sat-Sun 9:30-17:30, tel. 020/7836-2139, www.jubileemarket.co.uk).

In South London

Borough Market
The Southwark neighborhood hosts a carnival of food under the Borough Bridge, with stalls selling produce, baked goods, cheeses, and other delicacies (Mon-Wed 10:00-15:00, Thu 11:00-17:00, Fri 12:00-18:00, Sat 8:00-17:00, closed Sun, Tube: London Bridge, tel. 020/7407-1002, www.boroughmarket.org.uk.

Brixton Market
This seedy neighborhood south of the Thames features yet another thriving market. Here the food, clothing, records, and hair-braiding throb with an Afro-Caribbean beat (stalls open Mon-Sat 8:00-18:00, Wed until 15:00, farmers' market Sun 10:00-14:00 but otherwise dead on Sun; Tube: Brixton, www.brixtonmarket.net).

In Greenwich
With several sightseeing treats just a quick DLR ride from central London, Greenwich has its share of great markets, especially lively on weekends. For details, see page 230.

Entertainment in London

For the best list of what's happening and a look at the latest London scene, check www.timeout.com/london. (Unfortunately, the once-dominant print version of *Time Out London*, though free, is thin, paltry, and hard to find.) The free monthly *London Planner* covers sights, events, and plays, though generally not as well as *Time Out* does.

Theater (a.k.a. "Theatre")
London's theater scene rivals Broadway's in quality and usually beats it in price. Choose from 200 offerings—Shakespeare, musicals, comedies, thrillers, sex farces, cutting-edge fringe, revivals starring movie celebs, and more. London does it all well.

   Seating Terminology: Just like at home, London's theaters sell seats in a range of levels—but the Brits use different terms: stalls (ground floor), dress circle (first balcony), upper circle (second balcony), balcony (sky-high third balcony), slips (cheap seats on the fringes). For floor plans of the various theaters, see www.theatremonkey.com.

Big West End Shows

Nearly all big-name shows are hosted in the commercial (non-subsidized) theaters of the West End, clustering around Soho (especially along Shaftesbury Avenue) between Piccadilly and Covent Garden. With a centuries-old tradition of pleasing the masses, they present London theater at its grandest.

I prefer big, glitzy—even bombastic—musicals over serious chamber dramas, simply because London can deliver the lights, booming voices, dancers, and multimedia spectacle I rarely get back home. If that's not to your taste—or you already have access to similar spectacles at home—you might prefer some of London's more low-key offerings.

Well-known musicals may draw the biggest crowds, but the West End offers plenty of other crowd-pleasers, from revivals of classics to cutting-edge works by the hottest young playwrights. These productions tend to have shorter runs than famous musicals. A few relatively recent cinematic hits (including *The King's Speech* and *War Horse*) started out as London plays. Many productions star huge-name celebrities—London is a magnet for movie stars who want to stretch their acting chops.

You'll see the latest offerings advertised all over the Tube and elsewhere. The free *Official London Theatre Guide,* updated weekly, is a handy tool (find it at hotels, box offices, the City of London TI, and online at www.officiallondontheatre.co.uk). If you're picky, check the reviews at www.timeout.com/london.

Most performances are nightly except Sunday, usually with one or two matinees a week. The few shows that run on Sundays are mostly family fare (*Matilda, The Lion King,* and so on). Tickets range from about £15 to £65. Matinees are generally cheaper and rarely sell out.

Buying Tickets for West End Shows

For most visitors, it makes the most sense to simply buy tickets in London. But if your time in London is limited and you have your heart set on a particular show that's likely to sell out (usually the newest shows), you can buy peace of mind by pre-booking your tickets from home.

Before You Go

Once you know what show you want to see, buy your tickets directly from its theater's website (which may reroute you to a third-party ticket vendor such as Ticketmaster). You can also call the theater box office (which may ring through to a central ticketing office).

Whether you book online or over the phone, you'll pay with your credit card. A service charge of £3 per ticket is typical if you book direct with the theater. You may be offered the option

LONDON

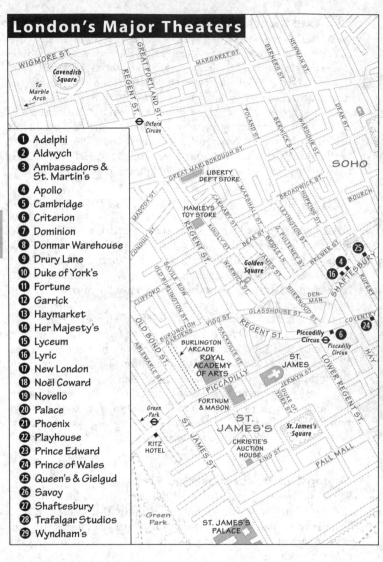

London's Major Theaters

1. Adelphi
2. Aldwych
3. Ambassadors & St. Martin's
4. Apollo
5. Cambridge
6. Criterion
7. Dominion
8. Donmar Warehouse
9. Drury Lane
10. Duke of York's
11. Fortune
12. Garrick
13. Haymarket
14. Her Majesty's
15. Lyceum
16. Lyric
17. New London
18. Noël Coward
19. Novello
20. Palace
21. Phoenix
22. Playhouse
23. Prince Edward
24. Prince of Wales
25. Queen's & Gielgud
26. Savoy
27. Shaftesbury
28. Trafalgar Studios
29. Wyndham's

of having your tickets emailed to you (you print them out); otherwise, arrive about 30 minutes before the show starts to pick up your tickets at Will Call.

Avoid buying tickets through third-party middleman agencies, which mark up their prices dramatically (explained in "Booking Through Other Agencies," later). See www.londontheatretickets.org and www.timeout.com/london for even more cheap-ticket advice.

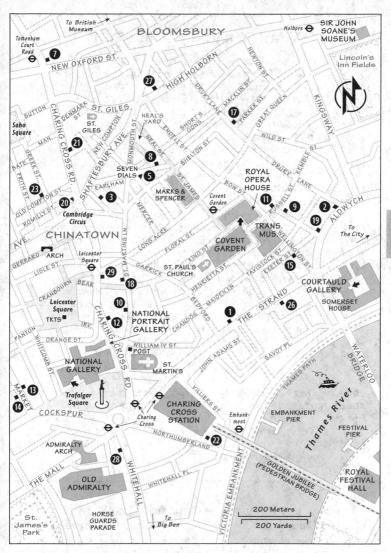

LONDON

In London

Most shows have tickets available on short notice—likely at a discount. While very recent and/or popular shows sell out early (especially for weekend performances), nearly-as-popular shows may offer discounted tickets to fill seats.

You have two good options for booking tickets—the official discount tkts booth at Leicester Square and the theater's box office...and one bad option—a middleman ticket agency (only worthwhile if you're desperate). All three alternatives are described next.

What's On in the West End

Here are some of the perennial favorites that you're likely to find among the West End's evening offerings. If spending the time and money for a London play, I like a full-fledged, high-energy musical (which all of these are). Generally you can book tickets for free at the box office or for a £2-3 fee by phone or online. See the map on page 158 for locations.

Billy Elliot—This adaptation of the popular British film is part family drama, part story of a boy who just has to dance, set to a score by Elton John (£20-68, Mon-Sat 19:30, matinees Thu and Sat 14:30, Victoria Palace Theatre, Victoria Street, Tube: Victoria, tel. 0844-248-5000, www.billyelliotthemusical.com).

Jersey Boys—This fast-moving, easy-to-follow show tracks the rough start and rise to stardom of Frankie Valli and the Four Seasons. It's light, but the music is so catchy that everyone leaves whistling the group's classics (£20-68; Tue-Sat 19:30; matinees Tue and Sat 15:00, Sun 17:00; Prince Edward Theatre, Old Compton Street, Tube: Leicester Square, box office tel. 0844-482-5151, www.jerseyboyslondon.com).

Les Misérables—Claude-Michel Schönberg's musical adaptation of Victor Hugo's epic follows the life of Jean Valjean as he struggles with the social and political realities of 19th-century France. This inspiring mega-hit takes you back to the days of France's struggle for a just and modern society (£20-68, Mon-Sat 19:30, matinees Wed and Sat 14:30, Queen's Theatre, Shaftesbury Avenue, Tube: Piccadilly Circus, box office tel. 0844-482-5160, www.lesmis.com).

The Lion King—In this Disney extravaganza, Simba the lion learns about the delicately balanced circle of life on the savanna (£25-68; Tue-Sat 19:30; matinees Wed, Sat, and Sun 14:30; Lyceum Theatre, Wellington Street, Tube: Charing Cross or Covent Garden, theater info tel. 020/7420-8100, box office tel. 0844-871-3000, www.thelionking.co.uk).

Discount tkts Booth: This famous ticket booth at Leicester (LESS-ter) Square, run by the Society of London Theatre, sells discounted tickets for top-price seats to shows on the push list. Big-name shows frequently turn up on this list. Most tickets are around half-price; other shows are discounted 25 percent (in either case, you'll pay a £3 service charge per ticket). For some extremely popular shows, they sell full-price tickets without the service charge (so it costs the same as at the box office). For about half of the shows, discounted tickets are available only on the day of the performance, although theaters are beginning to offer discounted tickets through tkts up to a week ahead. Their website (www.tkts.co.uk) lists ticket availability and prices, and is updated throughout the day—but you must buy in person at their kiosk. A similar list is posted next to

Mamma Mia!—This energetic, spandex-and-platform-boots musical weaves together a slew of ABBA hits to tell the story of a bride in search of her real dad as her promiscuous mom plans her Greek Isle wedding. The production has the audience dancing in their seats (£15-68, Mon-Sat 19:30, matinees Thu and Sat 15:00, Prince of Wales Theatre, Coventry Street, Tube: Piccadilly Circus, box office tel. 0844-482-5115, www.mamma-mia.com).

Matilda—Based on the Roald Dahl children's book, this hit is a family favorite for its tale of a precocious young girl who's unappreciated by her parents (£20-68, Tue 19:00, Wed-Sat 19:30, matinees Wed and Sat 14:30 and Sun 15:00, Cambridge Theatre, Seven Dials, Tube: Covent Garden or Leicester Square, box office tel. 0844-412-4652, www.matildathemusical.com).

Phantom of the Opera—A mysterious masked man falls in love with a singer in this haunting Andrew Lloyd Webber musical about life beneath the stage of the Paris Opera (£21-65, Mon-Sat 19:30, matinees Thu and Sat 14:30, Her Majesty's Theatre, Haymarket, Tube: Piccadilly Circus or Leicester Square, US toll-free tel. 800-334-8457, box office tel. 0844-412-2707, www.thephantomoftheopera.com).

We Will Rock You—This musical tribute to Queen (more to the band than to Freddie Mercury) is an understandably popular celebration of their work (£32-64, Mon-Sat 19:30, matinees Wed and Sat 14:30, Dominion Theatre, Tottenham Court Road, Tube: Tottenham Court Road, Ticketmaster tel. 0844-847-1775, www.wewillrockyou.co.uk).

Wicked—This lively prequel to The Wizard of Oz examines how the Witch of the West met Glinda the Good Witch, and later became so, you know...(£15-65, Mon-Sat 19:30, matinees Wed and Sat 14:30, Apollo Victoria Theatre, just east of Victoria Station, Tube: Victoria, Ticketmaster tel. 0844-826-8000, www.wickedthemusical.co.uk).

the kiosk—survey your options before you queue (or, if the line is long, while you're in the queue). It's smart to have two or three options in mind, just in case your first choice is sold out when you reach the counter. While the line forms early, it tends to move fast. Unless you have your heart set on a particular show that has only same-day tickets, consider dropping by later in the day, when it's a bit less crowded—many tickets will still be available (open Mon-Sat 9:00-19:00, Sun 10:30-16:30). Note: If tkts runs out of its ticket allotment for a certain show, it doesn't necessarily mean that the show is sold out—you can still try the theater's box office.

Warning: The real booth (with its prominent *tkts* sign) is a freestanding kiosk at the south edge of the garden in Leicester Square. Several dishonest outfits nearby advertise "official half-price tickets"—avoid these, where you'll rarely pay anything close to half-price.

Booking Direct (at the Theater's Box Office): While tkts generally has seats that are as cheap or cheaper than at the theater itself, the advantage of buying direct is that you may have access to deals that you can't get anywhere else. Most theaters offer cheap returned tickets, standing-room, matinee, senior or student standby deals, and more. (Discounted tickets, called "concessions," are indicated with a "conc" or "s" in the listings.) Picking up a late return can get you a great seat at a cheap-seat price.

A good plan for same-day deals is to arrive at the box office right when it opens (most open at 10:00; a few open at 9:00). For example, the popular show *Wicked* saves its front-row tickets to sell at half-price at 10:00 on the day of the show, but you must buy them in person at the box office...and on busy days, people line up early. (Restrictions may apply—for example, you may be limited to two half-price tickets, and even if you can buy more, the seats may not be together.) To find deals, look at the show's website, call the box office, or simply drop by (the theaters are mostly in highly trafficked tourist areas, so you're likely to pass your chosen theater at some point during your visit). Even if a show is "sold out," there's usually a way to get a seat. Call the theater box office and ask how, or check www.timeout.com/London for show-by-show info on same-day tickets at West End theaters.

If you don't care where you sit, you can often buy the absolute cheapest seats at the box office; these tickets usually cost £20 or less. These seats tend to be either in the nosebleed rows and/or have a restricted view (behind a pillar or extremely far to one side), and are often available only as same-day tickets. (For smaller theaters where every seat's a decent one, tkts may indeed beat the best box-office price: Compare online before heading out.) After the lights go down, scooting up is less than a capital offense. Shakespeare did it.

Booking Through Other Agencies: Although booking through a middleman (such as your hotel or a ticket agency) is quick and easy, prices are inflated by a standard 25 percent fee. Ticket agencies (whether in the US or in London) are just scalpers with an address. As a rule of thumb, if anyone other than the box office charges you more than £75 per ticket, you're almost certainly getting ripped off. If you're buying from an agency, look at the ticket carefully (your price should be no more than 30 percent over the printed face value; the 20 percent VAT is already included in the face value) and understand where you're sitting according to the floor plan (if your view is restricted, it will state this on the ticket).

Agencies are worthwhile only if a show you've just got to see is sold out at the box office. They scarf up hot tickets, planning to make a killing after the show is sold out. US booking agencies get their tickets from another agency, adding to your expense by involving yet another middleman. Many tickets sold on the street are forgeries. Although some theaters use booking agencies to handle their advance sales, you'll likely save money by avoiding the middleman.

Beyond the West End

Tickets for lesser-known shows tend to be cheaper (figure £15-30), in part because most of the smaller theaters are subsidized. Remember that plays don't need a familiar title or famous actor to be a worthwhile experience—read up on the latest offerings online; Time Out's site is a great place to start.

Major Noncommercial Theaters: One particularly good venue is the **National Theatre,** which has a range of impressive options, often starring recognizable names; while ugly on the outside, the acts that play out upon its stage are beautiful—as are the deeply discounted tickets it commonly offers (looming on the South Bank by Waterloo Bridge, Tube: Waterloo, www.nationaltheatre.org. uk). The **Barbican Centre** puts on high-quality, often experimental work (right by the Museum of London, just north of The City, Tube: Barbican, www.barbican.org.uk), as does the **Royal Court Theatre,** which has £10 tickets for its Monday shows (west of the West End in Sloane Square, Tube: Sloane Square, www.royal-courttheatre.com).

Royal Shakespeare Company: If you'll ever enjoy Shakespeare, it'll be in Britain. The RSC performs at various theaters around London and in Stratford-upon-Avon year-round (for details, see page 590 in the Stratford-upon-Avon chapter). To get a schedule, contact the RSC (Royal Shakespeare Theatre, Stratford-upon-Avon, tel. 0844-800-1110, www.rsc.org.uk).

Shakespeare's Globe: To see Shakespeare in a replica of the theater for which he wrote his plays, attend a play at the Globe. In this round, thatch-roofed, open-air theater, the plays are performed much as Shakespeare intended—under the sky, with no amplification.

The play's the thing from late April through early October (usually Mon 19:30, Tue-Sat 14:00 and 19:30, Sun either 13:00 and/or 18:30, tickets can be sold out months in advance). You'll pay £5 to stand and £15-39 to sit, usually on a backless bench. Because only a few rows and the pricier Gentlemen's Rooms have seats with backs, £1 cushions and £3 add-on back rests are considered a good investment by many. Dress for the weather.

The £5 "groundling" tickets—which are open to rain—are most fun. Scurry in early to stake out a spot on the stage's edge, where the most interaction with the actors occurs. You're a crude peasant. You can lean your elbows on the stage, munch a picnic dinner (yes, you can bring in food), or walk around. I've never

LONDON

Evensong

One of my favorite experiences in England is to attend evensong at a great church. Evensong is an evening worship service that is typically sung rather than said (though some parts—including scripture readings, a few prayers, and a homily—are spoken). It follows the traditional Anglican service in the Book of Common Prayer, including prayers, scripture readings, canticles (sung responses), and hymns that are appropriate for the early evening—traditionally the end of the working day and before the evening meal. In major churches with resident choirs, this service is filled with quality, professional musical elements. A singing or chanting priest leads the service, and a choir—usually made up of both men's and boys' voices (to sing the lower and higher parts, respectively)—sings the responses. The choir often sings a cappella, or is accompanied by organ. While regular attendees follow the service from memory, visitors—who are welcome—are given an order of service or a prayer book to help them follow along. (If you're not familiar with the order of service, watch the congregation to know when to stand, sit, and kneel.)

The most impressive places for evensong include London (Westminster Abbey, St. Paul's, Southwark Cathedral, or St. Bride's Church), Cambridge (King's College Chapel), Canterbury Cathedral, Wells Cathedral, Oxford (Christ Church Cathedral), York Minster, and Durham Cathedral. While this list includes many of the grandest churches in England, be aware that evensong typically takes place in the small choir area—which is far more intimate than the main nave. (To see the full church in action, a concert is a better choice.) Evensong generally occurs daily between 17:00 and 18:00 (often two hours earlier on Sundays)—check with individual churches for specifics. At smaller churches, evensong is sometimes spoken, not sung.

Note that evensong is not a performance—it's a somewhat somber worship service. If you enjoy worshipping in different churches, attending evensong can be a trip-capping highlight. But if regimented church services aren't your thing, consider getting a different music fix. Most major churches also offer organ or choral concerts—look for posted schedules or ask at the information desk or gift shop.

enjoyed Shakespeare as much as here, performed as it was meant to be in the "wooden O." If you can't get a ticket, consider waiting around. Plays can be long, and many groundlings leave before the end. Hang around outside and beg or buy a ticket from someone leaving early (groundlings are allowed to come and go). A few non-Shakespeare plays are also presented each year. If you can't attend a show, you can take a guided tour of the theater and museum by day (see page 138).

In 2014, the Globe opens a new, indoor theater within the Globe complex. The Sam Wanamaker Playhouse allows Shakespearean-era plays and early-music concerts to be performed through the winter. Tickets for this more intimate venue are somewhat pricier than for the Globe (check online or call the Globe box office for details).

To reserve tickets for plays at the Globe, call or drop by the box office (Mon-Sat 10:00-18:00, Sun 10:00-17:00, open one hour later on performance days, New Globe Walk entrance, no extra charge to book by phone, tel. 020/7401-9919). You can also reserve online (www.shakespearesglobe.com, £2.50 booking fee). If the tickets are sold out, don't despair; a few often free up at the last minute. Try calling around noon the day of the performance to see if the box office expects any returned tickets. If so, they'll advise you to show up a little more than an hour before the show, when these tickets are sold (first-come, first-served).

The theater is on the South Bank, directly across the Thames over the Millennium Bridge from St. Paul's Cathedral (Tube: Mansion House or London Bridge). The Globe is inconvenient for public transport, but the courtesy phone in the lobby lets you get a minicab in minutes. (These minicabs have set fees—e.g., £8 to South Kensington—but generally cost less than a metered cab and provide fine and honest service.) During theater season, there's a regular supply of black cabs outside the main foyer on New Globe Walk.

Outdoor Theater in Summer: Enjoy Shakespearean drama and other plays under the stars at the Open Air Theatre, in leafy Regent's Park in north London. Food is allowed: You can bring your own picnic, order à la carte from the theater menu, or pre-order a picnic supper from the theater at least 48 hours in advance (season runs late May-mid-Sept, tickets available beginning in mid-Jan; book at www.openairtheatre.org or—for an extra booking fee—by calling 0844-826-4242; grounds open 1.5 hours prior to evening performances, one hour prior to matinees; 10-minute walk north of Baker Street Tube, near Queen Mary's Gardens within Regent's Park; detailed directions and more info at www.openairtheatre.org).

Fringe Theater: London's rougher evening-entertainment scene is thriving. Choose from a wide range of fringe theater and comedy acts (generally £12).

Music at Churches

For easy, cheap, or free concerts in historic churches, attend a **lunch concert** (listed on *Time Out*'s website). Good options include St. Bride's Church, with free half-hour lunch concerts twice a week at 13:15 (usually Tue and Fri—confirm in advance, church tel. 020/7427-0133, www.stbrides.com); St. James's at Piccadilly, with 50-minute concerts on Mon, Wed, and Fri at 13:10 (suggested £3.50 donation, info tel. 020/7381-0441, www.st-james-piccadilly. org); and St. Martin-in-the-Fields, offering concerts on Mon, Tue, and Fri at 13:00 (suggested £3 donation, church tel. 020/7766-1100, www.smitf.org).

St. Martin-in-the-Fields also hosts fine **evening concerts** by candlelight (£8-28, several nights a week at 19:30) and live jazz in its underground Café in the Crypt (£5.50 or £9, Wed at 20:00).

Evensong services are held at several churches, including St. Paul's Cathedral (see details on page 120), Westminster Abbey (see page 82), Southwark Cathedral (see page 141), and St. Bride's Church (Sun at 17:30, tel. 020/7427-0133, www.stbrides.com).

Free **organ recitals** are usually held on Sunday at 17:45 in Westminster Abbey (30 minutes, tel. 020/7222-5152). Many other churches have free concerts; ask for the *London Organ Concerts Guide* at the City of London TI.

Summer Evenings Along the South Bank

If you're visiting London in summer, consider hitting the South Bank neighborhood after hours.

Take a trip around the **London Eye** while the sun sets over the city (the wheel spins until late—last ascent at 21:00 April-June, 21:30 July-Aug, 20:30 Sept-March). Then cap your night with an evening walk along the pedestrian-only **Jubilee Walkway,** which runs east-west along the river. It's where Londoners go to escape the heat. This pleasant stretch of the walkway—lined with pubs and casual eateries—goes from the London Eye past Shakespeare's Globe to Tower Bridge (you can walk in either direction).

If you're in the mood for a movie, take in a flick at the **BFI Southbank,** located just across the river, alongside Waterloo Bridge. Run by the British Film Institute, the state-of-the-art theater shows mostly classic films, as well as art cinema (Tube: Waterloo or Embankment, check www.bfi.org.uk for schedules and prices).

Farther east along the South Bank is **The Scoop**—an outdoor amphitheater next to City Hall. It's a good spot for movies, concerts, dance, and theater productions throughout the summer—with Tower Bridge as a scenic backdrop. These events are free, nearly nightly, and family-friendly. For the latest event schedule, see www.morelondon.com and click on "The Scoop at More London" (next to City Hall, Riverside, The Queen's Walkway, Tube: London Bridge).

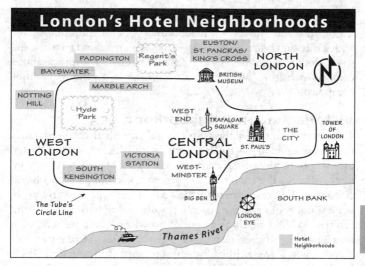

London's Hotel Neighborhoods

- PADDINGTON
- BAYSWATER
- NOTTING HILL
- MARBLE ARCH
- Regent's Park
- EUSTON/ST. PANCRAS/KING'S CROSS
- NORTH LONDON
- BRITISH MUSEUM
- Hyde Park
- WEST LONDON
- WEST END
- TRAFALGAR SQUARE
- CENTRAL LONDON
- ST. PAUL'S
- THE CITY
- TOWER OF LONDON
- VICTORIA STATION
- SOUTH KENSINGTON
- WEST-MINSTER
- BIG BEN
- The Tube's Circle Line
- LONDON EYE
- SOUTH BANK
- Thames River
- Hotel Neighborhoods

Sleeping in London

London is an expensive city for lodging. Cheaper rooms are relatively dumpy. Don't expect £130 cheeriness in an £70 room. For £70, you'll get a double with breakfast in a safe, cramped, and dreary place with minimal service and the bathroom down the hall. For £90, you'll get a basic, clean, reasonably cheery double with a private bath in a usually cramped, cracked-plaster building, or a soulless but comfortable room without breakfast in a huge Motel 6-type place. My London splurges, at £160-290, are spacious, thoughtfully appointed places good for entertaining or romancing.

Looking for Hotel Deals Online: Given London's high hotel prices, using the Internet can help you score a deal. Various websites list rooms in high-rise, three- and four-star business hotels. You'll give up the charm and warmth of a family-run establishment, and breakfast probably won't be included, but you might find that the price is right.

Start by browsing the websites of several chains to get a sense of typical rates and online deals. For listings of no-frills, Motel 6-type places, see "Big, Good-Value, Modern Hotels," later.

Pricier London hotel chains include Millennium/Copthorne (www.millenniumhotels.com), Thistle (www.thistle.com), Inter-Continental/Holiday Inn (www.ichotelsgroup.com), Radisson (www.radisson.com), Hilton (www.hilton.com), and Red Carnation (www.redcarnationhotels.com).

Auction-type sites (such as www.priceline.com and www.hotwire.com) match flexible travelers with empty hotel rooms, often at prices well below the hotel's normal rates.

My readers report good experiences with these accommodation discount sites: www.londontown.com (an informative site with a discount booking service), http://athomeinlondon.co.uk and www.londonbb.com (both list central B&Bs), www.lastminute.com, www.visitlondon.com, http://roomsnet.com, and www.eurocheapo.com.

Victoria Station Neighborhood

The streets behind Victoria Station teem with little, moderately priced-for-London B&Bs. It's a safe, surprisingly tidy, and decent area without a hint of the trashy, touristy glitz of the streets in front of the station. I've divided these accommodations into two broad categories: Belgravia, west of the station, feels particularly posh, while Pimlico, to the east, is still upscale and dotted with colorful eateries. While I wouldn't go out of my way just to dine here, each area has plenty of good restaurants (see page 201). All of my recommended hotels are within a five-minute walk of the Victoria Tube, bus, and train stations. On hot summer nights, request a quiet back room; most of these B&Bs lack air-conditioning and may front busy streets.

The nearest laundry option is **Pimlico Launderette,** on the east—Pimlico—side about five blocks southwest of Warwick Square. Low prices and friendly George brighten your chore (£7.40 same-day full service, £5-6 self-service, daily 8:00-19:00; 3 Westmoreland Terrace—go down Clarendon Street, turn right on Sutherland, and look for the launderette on the left at the end of the street; tel. 020/7821-8692).

Drivers like the 400-space Semley Place NCP **parking garage,** near the hotels on the west—Belgravia—side (£40/day, possible discounts with hotel voucher, just west of Victoria Coach Station at Buckingham Palace Road and Semley Place, tel. 0845-050-7080, www.ncp.co.uk).

West of Victoria Station (Belgravia)

Here in Belgravia, the prices are a bit higher and your neighbors include some of the world's wealthiest people. These two places sit nearly kitty corner from each other on tranquil Ebury Street, two blocks over from Victoria Station (or a slightly shorter walk from the Sloane Square Tube stop). You can cut the walk from Victoria Station to nearly nothing by taking a short ride on frequent bus #C1 (leaves from Buckingham Palace Road side of Victoria Station and drops you off directly in front of Morgan House).

$$$ Lime Tree Hotel, enthusiastically run by Charlotte and Matt, is a gem, with 25 spacious, stylish, comfortable, thoughtfully decorated rooms, a helpful staff, and a fun-loving breakfast room (Sb-£99, Db-£160, larger superior Db-£185, Tb-£205, family

LONDON

room–£220, usually cheaper Jan-Feb, free guest computer and Wi-Fi, small lounge opens onto quiet garden, 135 Ebury Street, tel. 020/7730-8191, www.limetreehotel.co.uk, info@limetreehotel.co.uk, Alex manages the office).

$$ Morgan House, a great budget choice in this neighborhood, has 11 nicely decorated rooms with far more character than you'll find in other nearby hotels in this price range. It's also entertainingly run, with lots of travel tips and friendly chat from owner Rachel Joplin and her staff (S-£58, D-£84, Db-£108, T-£108, family suites: Tb-£148, Qb-£158, free Wi-Fi can be spotty, 120 Ebury Street, tel. 020/7730-2384, www.morganhouse.co.uk, morganhouse@btclick.com).

East of Victoria Station (Pimlico)

This area is a bit less genteel-feeling than Belgravia, but still plenty inviting, with eateries and grocery stores. Most of these hotels are on or near Warwick Way, the main drag through this area. Generally the best Tube stop for this neighborhood is Victoria (though the Pimlico stop works equally well for the Luna Simone). Bus #24 runs right through the middle of Pimlico, connecting Tate Britain to the south with Victoria Station, the Houses of Parliament, Trafalgar Square, and much more to the north.

$$ Luna Simone Hotel rents 36 fresh, spacious, remodeled rooms with modern bathrooms. It's a smartly managed place, run for more than 40 years by twins Peter and Bernard—and Bernard's son Mark—and they still seem to enjoy their work (Sb-£75, Db-£110, Tb-£135, Qb-£165, these prices with cash and this book in 2014, free guest computer and Wi-Fi, at 47 Belgrave Road near

Victoria Station Neighborhood

1 Lime Tree Hotel
2 Morgan House
3 Luna Simone Hotel
4 Bakers Hotel
5 New England Hotel
6 Best Western Victoria Palace
7 Jubilee Hotel
8 Cherry Court Hotel
9 easyHotel Victoria
10 Ebury Wine Bar
11 Jenny Lo's Tea House
12 La Bottega Deli
13 The Thomas Cubitt Pub
14 To The Duke of Wellington Pub
15 The Orange Pub & Daylesford Deli
16 Grumbles Restaurant
17 Pimlico Fresh
18 Seafresh Fish Restaurant
19 The Jugged Hare Pub
20 St. George's Tavern
21 Nando's
22 Grocery Stores (4)
23 To Launderette
24 Bus Tours – Day (2)
25 Bus Tours – Night
26 Tube, Taxis, City Buses
27 Green Line Coach Terminal
28 Buses to Luton & Stansted Airports

LONDON

200 Meters
200 Yards

the corner of Charlwood Street, handy bus #24 to Victoria Station and Trafalgar Square stops out front, tel. 020/7834-5897, www.lunasimonehotel.com, stay@lunasimonehotel.com).

$$ Bakers Hotel shoehorns 11 brightly painted rooms into a small building, but it's conveniently located and offers modest prices and a small breakfast (S-£45-55, Sb-£70-80, D-£70-85, Db-£85-90, T-£90, Tb-£110-120, family room-£135, can be about £5-8 cheaper per person off-season, discounts for stays of at

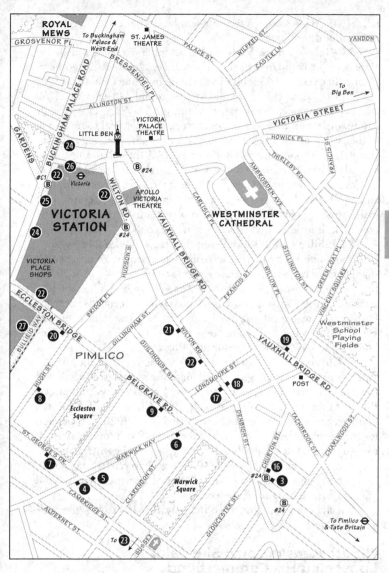

least a week, ask for Rick Steves discount when booking direct, free Wi-Fi, 126 Warwick Way, tel. 020/7834-0729, www.bakershotel. co.uk, reservations@bakershotel.co.uk, Amin Jamani).

$$ New England Hotel, run by Jay and the Patel family, has rather worn public spaces and somewhat faded but well-priced rooms in a tight old corner building (small Sb-£69-79, Db-£89-99, Tb-£119-129, Qb-£129-139, prices soft during slow times, breakfast is very basic, pay Wi-Fi, 20 Saint George's Drive, tel. 020/7834-8351, www.newenglandhotel.com, mystay@newenglandhotel.com).

$$ Best Western Victoria Palace offers modern business-class comfort compared to the other creaky old hotels listed here. Choose between the 43 rooms in the main building (Db-£120, Tb-£200, prices flex with demand—often around Db-£90/Tb-£160 off-season, includes breakfast, elevator, 60-64 Warwick Way), or pay about 20 percent less by booking a nearly identical room in one of the two annexes, each a half-block away—an excellent value for this neighborhood if you skip breakfast. All three buildings were recently renovated (annex Db-£85-90, breakfast-£12.50, air-con, no elevator). Book in advance for the best rates (free guest computer and Wi-Fi, 17 Belgrave Road and 1 Warwick Way, reception at main building, tel. 020/7821-7113, www.bestwesternvictoriapalace.co.uk, info@bestwesternvictoriapalace.co.uk).

$$ Jubilee Hotel is a well-run slumbermill with 24 tiny, simple rooms and many tiny, neat beds. The cheapest rooms, which share bathrooms, are just below street level (S-£39-45, Sb-£59-65, tiny twin D-£55-65, Db-£79-89, T-£65, Tb-£89-95, Qb-£99-109, rates depend on season and length of stay, 5 percent discount for Rick Steves readers if you book direct, free guest computer, pay Wi-Fi, 31 Eccleston Square, tel. 020/7834-0845, www.jubilee-hotel.co.uk, stay@jubileehotel.co.uk, Bob Patel).

$ Cherry Court Hotel, run by the friendly and industrious Patel family, rents 12 very small but bright and well-designed rooms in a central location. Considering London's sky-high prices, this is a fine budget choice (Sb-£60, Db-£68, Tb-£105, Quint/b family room-£130, these prices with this book in 2014, 5 percent fee to pay with credit card, fruit-basket breakfast in room, air-con, free guest computer and Wi-Fi, laundry, peaceful garden patio, 23 Hugh Street, tel. 020/7828-2840, www.cherrycourthotel.co.uk, info@cherrycourthotel.co.uk, daughter Neha answers emails and offers informed restaurant advice).

$ easyHotel Victoria, at 36 Belgrave Road, is part of the budget chain described on page 184.

"South Kensington," She Said, Loosening His Cummerbund

To stay on a quiet street so classy it doesn't allow hotel signs, surrounded by trendy shops and colorful restaurants, call "South Ken" your London home. Shoppers like being a short walk from Harrods and the designer shops of King's Road and Chelsea. When I splurge, I splurge here. Sumner Place is just off Old Brompton Road, 200 yards from the handy South Kensington Tube station (on Circle Line, two stops from Victoria Station; and on Piccadilly Line, direct from Heathrow). A handy **launderette** is on the corner

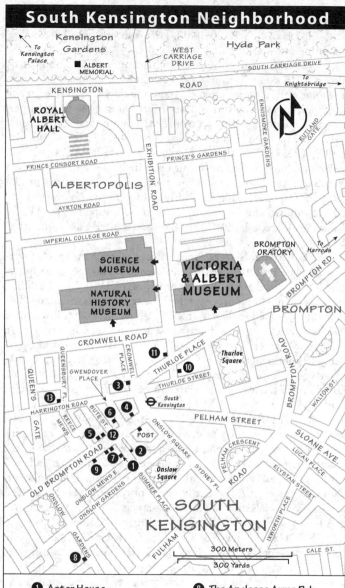

South Kensington Neighborhood

① Aster House
② Number Sixteen Hotel
③ The Pelham Hotel
④ Brompton Hotel
⑤ La Bouchée Bistro Café
⑥ Moti Mahal Indian Rest.
⑦ Bosphorus Kebabs & Beirut Express
⑧ The Anglesea Arms Pub
⑨ Rocca di Papa
⑩ Fernandez & Wells
⑪ Thai Square
⑫ Tesco Express
⑬ Launderette

of Queensberry Place and Harrington Road (Mon-Fri 8:00-20:00, Sat 9:00-19:00, Sun 10:00-18:00, last wash one hour before closing, bring 50p and £1 coins).

$$$ Aster House, well-run by friendly and accommodating Simon and Leonie Tan, has a cheerful lobby, lounge, and breakfast room. Its 13 rooms are comfy and quiet, with TV, phone, and air-conditioning. Enjoy breakfast or just lounging in the whisper-elegant Orangery, a glassy greenhouse. Simon and Leonie offer free loaner mobile phones to their guests (Sb-£125, Db-£190, bigger Db-£235 or £270, does not include 20 percent VAT; significant discount offered to readers of this book in 2014—up to 20 percent discount if you book three or more nights, up to 25 percent discount for five or more nights; additional 5 percent off when you pay cash, check website for specials, pay guest computer, free Wi-Fi, 3 Sumner Place, tel. 020/7581-5888, www.asterhouse.com, asterhouse@gmail.com).

$$$ Number Sixteen, for well-heeled travelers, packs over-the-top class into its 41 artfully imagined rooms, plush designer-chic lounges, and tranquil garden. It's in a labyrinthine building, with boldly modern decor—perfect for an urban honeymoon (Sb-from £180, "superior" Db-from £235—but soft, ask for discounted "seasonal rates," especially on weekends and in Aug—subject to availability, larger "luxury" Db-£285, breakfast buffet in the garden-£19 continental or £20 full English, elevator, free guest computer and Wi-Fi, 16 Sumner Place, tel. 020/7589-5232, US tel. 800-553-6674, www.numbersixteenhotel.co.uk, sixteen@firmdale.com).

$$$ The Pelham Hotel, a 51-room business-class hotel with crisp service and a pricey mix of pretense and style, is genteel, with low lighting and a pleasant drawing room among the many perks (Db-£190-290, rate depends on room size and season, breakfast-£15 continental or £19 full English, does not include 20 percent VAT, slightly lower prices on weekends and in Aug, Web specials can include free breakfast; air-con, elevator, free guest computer, pay Wi-Fi, fitness room, 15 Cromwell Place, tel. 020/7589-8288, US tel. 1-888-757-5587, www.pelhamhotel.co.uk, reservations@pelhamhotel.co.uk, Jamie will take good care of you).

$$ Brompton Hotel is a humble place with 26 rooms above a jumble of cafés and clubs. There's a noisy bar and some street noise, so ask for a room in the back if you want quiet. Since it has no public spaces, they serve breakfast in your room. However, its rates are reasonable for this upscale neighborhood (Sb-£100, Db-£110—but can fall to £75 when demand is down, Tb-£140-150, "deluxe" rooms are just like the others but with a tub, save a little by booking via their website, includes continental breakfast, free Wi-Fi, across from the South Kensington Tube station at 30 Old

Brompton Road, tel. 020/7584-4517, www.bromhotel.com, book@ bromhotel.com).

North of Kensington Gardens and Hyde Park

From the core of the tourist's London, the vast Hyde Park spreads west, eventually becoming Kensington Gardens. Three good accommodations neighborhoods line up side-by-side along the northern edge of the park: Bayswater (with the highest concentration of good hotels) anchors the area, and is bordered by Notting Hill to the west and Paddington to the east. This area has quick bus and Tube access to downtown, and, for London, is very "homely" (Brit-speak for cozy).

Bayswater

Most of my Bayswater accommodations flank a tranquil, tidy park called Kensington Gardens Square (not to be confused with the much bigger Kensington Gardens adjacent to Hyde Park), a block west of bustling Queensway, north of Bayswater Tube station. These hotels are quiet for central London, but the area feels a bit sterile, and the hotels here tend to be impersonal.

Popular with young international travelers, the Bayswater street called **Queensway** is a multicultural festival of commerce and eateries. The neighborhood does its dirty clothes at **Galaxy Launderette** (£6-8 self-service, £10-12 full-service, Mon-Sat 8:00-20:00, Sun 9:00-20:00, last wash at 19:00, staff on hand with soap and coins, 65 Moscow Road, near corner of St. Petersburgh Place and Moscow Road, tel. 020/7229-7771). For **Internet access,** you'll find several stops along busy Queensway, and a self-serve bank of computer terminals on the food-circus level—third floor—of Whiteleys Shopping Centre (long hours daily, corner of Queensway and Porchester Gardens—see page 206).

$$$ Vancouver Studios offers one of the best values in this neighborhood. Its 45 modern, tastefully furnished rooms come with fully equipped kitchenettes (utensils, stove, microwave, and fridge) rather than breakfast. It's nestled between Kensington Gardens Square and Princes Square, and has its own tranquil garden patio out back (Sb-£97, Db-£140, Tb-£179, extra bed-£20, 10 percent discount for seven or more nights, pay guest computer, free Wi-Fi, welcoming lounge, 30 Princes Square, tel. 020/7243-1270, www.vancouverstudios.co.uk, info@vancouverstudios.co.uk).

$$$ Garden Court Hotel is understated, with 37 simple, homey-but-tasteful rooms (prices vary seasonally with demand—these are normal/low-demand rates: Sb-£70-75/£50-65, D-£125, Db-£125/£75-90, Tb-£150/£105, Qb-£175/£120, all rooms can be £20 more when demand is especially high, breakfast-£5, elevator, pay guest computer, free Wi-Fi, 30-31 Kensington Gardens

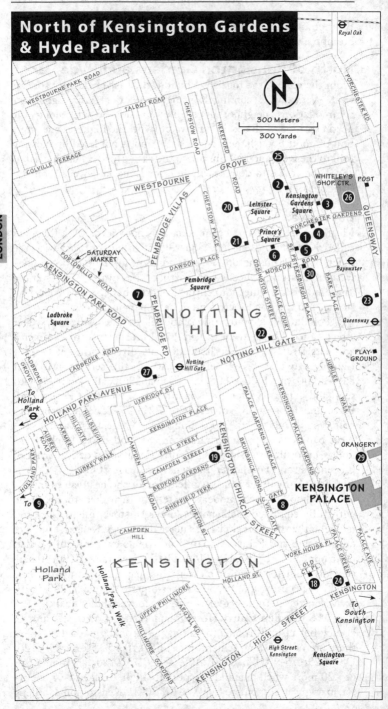

North of Kensington Gardens & Hyde Park

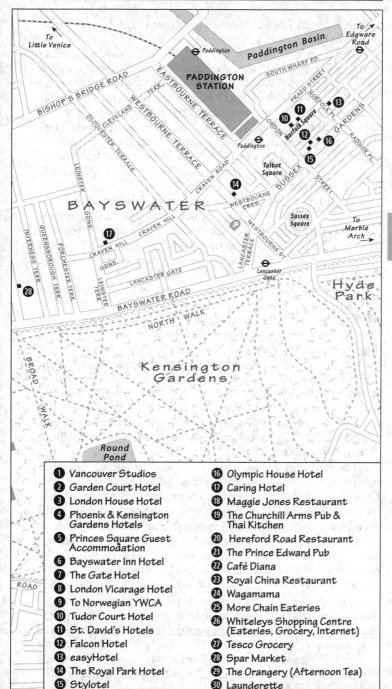

1. Vancouver Studios
2. Garden Court Hotel
3. London House Hotel
4. Phoenix & Kensington Gardens Hotels
5. Princes Square Guest Accommodation
6. Bayswater Inn Hotel
7. The Gate Hotel
8. London Vicarage Hotel
9. To Norwegian YWCA
10. Tudor Court Hotel
11. St. David's Hotels
12. Falcon Hotel
13. easyHotel
14. The Royal Park Hotel
15. Stylotel
16. Olympic House Hotel
17. Caring Hotel
18. Maggie Jones Restaurant
19. The Churchill Arms Pub & Thai Kitchen
20. Hereford Road Restaurant
21. The Prince Edward Pub
22. Café Diana
23. Royal China Restaurant
24. Wagamama
25. More Chain Eateries
26. Whiteleys Shopping Centre (Eateries, Grocery, Internet)
27. Tesco Grocery
28. Spar Market
29. The Orangery (Afternoon Tea)
30. Launderette

LONDON

Square, tel. 020/7229-2553, www.gardencourthotel.co.uk, info@gardencourthotel.co.uk).

$$$ London House Hotel has 103 spiffy, modern cookie-cutter rooms on Kensington Gardens Square. Its rates are great considering the quality and fine location (rates fluctuate, but generally Db-£105 weekdays and £130 on weekends, expect to pay more during busiest times and less in winter, smaller rooms not facing the square are about £10-20 cheaper, basement family rooms-£140, check online for specific rates and last-minute deals, continental breakfast-£7, elevator, free Wi-Fi, 81 Kensington Gardens Square, tel. 020/7243-1810, www.londonhousehotels.com, reservations@londonhousehotels.com).

$$$ Phoenix Hotel, a Best Western modernization of a 125-room hotel, offers American business-class comforts; spacious, plush public spaces; and big, modern-feeling rooms. Its prices—which range from fine value to rip-off—are determined by a greedy computer program, with huge variations according to expected demand. Book online to save money (Sb-£80-110, Db-£110-140, Tb-£150-180, elevator, free guest computer and Wi-Fi, 1-8 Kensington Gardens Square, tel. 020/7229-2494, US tel. 800-528-1234, www.phoenixhotel.co.uk, info@phoenixhotel.co.uk).

$$ Princes Square Guest Accommodation is a crisp (if impersonal) place renting 50 businesslike rooms with pleasant, modern decor. It's well-located, practical, and a very good value, especially if you can score a good rate (prices fluctuate with demand, but generally Db-£80-90, £20 less for a single, £40 more for a triple; email to ask for best price, breakfast likely included if you book direct—ask, elevator, pay Wi-Fi, 23-25 Princes Square, tel. 020/7229-9876, www.princessquarehotel.co.uk, info@princessquarehotel.co.uk).

$$ Kensington Gardens Hotel laces 17 pleasant, slightly scuffed rooms together in a tall, skinny building (Ss-£59, Sb-£66, Db-£92, Tb-£115; book by phone or email for these special Rick Steves prices—and if booking on their website be sure to ask for the Rick Steves discount under "Additional Information"; continental breakfast served at Phoenix Hotel, free Wi-Fi, 9 Kensington Gardens Square, tel. 020/7243-7600, www.kensingtongardenshotel.co.uk, info@kensingtongardenshotel.co.uk, Rowshanak).

$$ Bayswater Inn Hotel's 140 tidy, perfectly adequate rooms come with dated style, an impersonal feel, and outrageously high official rack rates. But rooms commonly go for much lower prices, making this a decent—sometimes great—budget option (if booked in advance roughly Sb-£60, Db-£90, Tb-£125, Qb-£150, stay for free on fifth consecutive night, elevator, pay guest computer and Wi-Fi, 8-16 Princes Square, tel. 020/7727-8621, www.bayswater-innhotel.com, reservations@bayswaterinnhotel.com).

Notting Hill and Nearby

The Notting Hill neighborhood, just west of Bayswater (spreading out from the northwest tip of Kensington Gardens), is famous for two things: It's the site of the colorful Portobello Road Market (see "Shopping in London," earlier), and the setting of the 1999 Hugh Grant/Julia Roberts film of the same name. While the neighborhood is now a bit more upscale and less funky than the one seen in that film, it's still a pleasant place to stay.

$$ The Gate Hotel has seven cramped but decent rooms on a delightful curved street near the start of the Portobello Road Market, in the heart of charming Notting Hill. The lodgings are basic and could be cleaner, but the prices are low for this area and the romantic setting might be worth it for some (Sb-£60, Db-£85, bigger "luxury" Db-£95, Tb-£115; £10-20 more Fri-Sat; 5 percent fee to pay with credit card, continental breakfast in room, pay Wi-Fi, 6 Portobello Road, Tube: Notting Hill Gate, tel. 020/7221-0707, www.gatehotel.co.uk, bookings@gatehotel.co.uk, Jasmine).

West of Kensington Gardens: **$$$ London Vicarage Hotel** is family-run, understandably popular, and located in a quiet, classy neighborhood just south of the core of Notting Hill. It has 17 quality rooms, a modest TV lounge, a grand staircase, and facilities on each floor. Mandy and Monika maintain a homey atmosphere (S-£67, Sb-£112, D-£112, Db-£140, T-£143, Tb-£184, Q-£155, Qb-£205, 20 percent less in winter—check website, free Wi-Fi; 8-minute walk from Notting Hill Gate and High Street Kensington Tube stations, near Kensington Palace at 10 Vicarage Gate; tel. 020/7229-4030, www.londonvicaragehotel.com, vicaragehotel@btconnect.com).

Near Holland Park: **$ Norwegian YWCA (Norsk K.F.U.K.)**—where English is definitely a second language—is open to any Norwegian woman, and to non-Norwegian women under 30. (Men must be under 30 with a Norwegian passport.) Located on a quiet, stately street, it offers a study, TV room, piano lounge, and an open-face Norwegian ambience (goat cheese on Sundays!). They have mostly quads, so those willing to share with strangers are most likely to get a bed (July-Aug: Ss-£46, shared double-£45/bed, shared triple-£40/bed, shared quad-£37/bed, includes sheets and towels, includes breakfast year-round plus sack lunch and dinner Sept-June, £20 key deposit and £3 membership fee required, pay Wi-Fi, 52 Holland Park, Tube: Holland Park, tel. 020/7727-9346 or 020/7727-9897, www.kfukhjemmet.org.uk, kontor@kfukhjemmet.org.uk). With each visit, I wonder which is easier to get—a sex change or a Norwegian passport?

Paddington Station Neighborhood

Just to the east of Bayswater, the neighborhood around Paddington Station—while much less charming than the other areas I've recommended—is pleasant enough, and very convenient to the Heathrow Express airport train. The area is flanked by the Paddington and Lancaster Gate Tube stops. Most of my recommendations circle Norfolk Square, just two blocks in front of Paddington Station, yet are still quiet and comfortable. The main drag, London Street, is lined with handy eateries—pubs, Indian, Italian, Moroccan, Greek, Lebanese, and more—plus convenience stores and an Internet café. (Better restaurants are a short stroll to the west, near Queensway and Notting Hill—see page 205.) To reach this area, exit the station toward Praed Street (with your back to the tracks, it's to the left). Once outside, continue straight across Praed Street and down London Street; Norfolk Square is a block ahead on the left.

On Norfolk Square

These places (and many more on the same street) are similar; all offer small rooms at a reasonable price, in tall buildings with lots of stairs and no elevator. I've chosen the ones that offer the most reasonable prices and the warmest welcome.

$$ Tudor Court Hotel has 38 colorful rooms conscientiously run by Connan and the Gupta family. While the tiny rooms are tight (with prefab plastic bathrooms) and the rates are a bit high, this place distinguishes itself with its warm welcome and attention to detail. If you smell them cooking up a big batch of curry rice, the Guptas are getting ready to take it to the homeless shelter, where they volunteer each week (S-£54-63, Sb-£95-108, "compact" Db-£99-120, larger "standard" Db-£135-165, "compact" Tb-£144-180, larger "standard" Tb-£162-198, family room-£180-225, higher rates are for Fri-Sat and other busy times, pay Wi-Fi, 10-12 Norfolk Square, tel. 020/7723-5157, www.tudorcourtpaddington.co.uk, reservations@tudorcourtpaddington.co.uk).

$$ St. David's Hotels, run by the Neokleous family, has 60 rooms in several adjacent buildings. The rooms are small—as is typical for less-expensive hotels in London—and scruffy, with minimal amenities, but the staff is friendly, and their non-en suite rooms are a workable budget option (S-£50-60, Sb-£70-85, D-£70-85, Db-£90-120, Tb-£100-130, pay Wi-Fi in rooms, free Wi-Fi in lobby, 14-20 Norfolk Square, tel. 020/7723-3856, www.stdavidshotels.com, info@stdavidshotels.com).

$$ Falcon Hotel, a lesser value, has less personality and 19 simple, old-school, faded rooms (S-£59, Sb-£69, D-£85, Db-£95, twin Db-£99, Tb-£139, Qb-£149, rates flex with demand, free guest computer, pay Wi-Fi, 11 Norfolk Square, tel. 020/7723-8603, www.falcon-hotel.com, info@falcon-hotel.com).

$ easyHotel, the budget chain described on page 184, has a branch at 10 Norfolk Place.

Elsewhere near Paddington Station

To reach these hotels, follow the directions on the previous page, but continue away from the station past Norfolk Square to the big intersection with Sussex Gardens; the Royal Park is a couple of blocks to the right, and the others are immediately to the left.

$$$ The Royal Park is the neighborhood's classy splurge, with 48 plush rooms, polished service, a genteel lounge (free champagne for guests nightly 19:00-20:00), and all the little extras ("classic" Db-official rates-£189-279, but prepaid/nonrefundable offers are as low as £140-190, bigger "executive" Db for £20 more, prices vary with demand, does not include 20 percent VAT, breakfast-£14-18, elevator, free guest computer and Wi-Fi, 3 Westbourne Terrace, tel. 020/7479-6600, www.theroyalpark.com, info@theroyalpark.com).

$$ Stylotel feels like the stylish, super-modern, aluminum-clad big sister of the easyHotel chain. Instead of peeling wallpaper and ancient carpets held together with duct tape, they've opted for sleek styling in their 39 rooms, all with clean, hard surfaces—hardwood floors, prefab plastic bathrooms, and metallic walls. While rooms can be a little cramped, the beds have space for your luggage underneath. You may feel like an astronaut in a retro science-fiction film, but if you don't need ye olde doilies, this place offers a good value (Sb-£65, Db-£95, Tb-£115, Qb-£135, prices go up with demand—book early and direct to get these rates, elevator, pay Wi-Fi, 160-162 Sussex Gardens, tel. 020/7723-1026, www.stylotel.com, info@stylotel.com, well-run by Andreas). They also have eight fancier, pricier, air-conditioned suites across the street (£180-220 for 2-4 people, kitchenettes, no breakfast).

$$ Olympic House Hotel has stark public spaces and a stern welcome, but its 38 business-class rooms offer predictable comfort and fewer old-timey quirks than many hotels in this price range (Sb-£75, Db-£105, Tb-£120, rates vary with demand, air-con in most rooms costs extra, elevator, pay Wi-Fi, 138-140 Sussex Gardens, tel. 020/7723-5935, www.olympichousehotel.co.uk, olympichousehotel@btinternet.com).

Between Paddington and Bayswater: About halfway between these two hotel neighborhoods, **$$ Caring Hotel,** plain but affordable, has 25 tidy, nondescript-bordering-on-depressingly dull rooms in a nice, quiet location just off Hyde Park (basic D-£75, Ds-£80, small Db-£90, standard Db-£100, extra bed-£15, these rates are approximate—prices change with demand, free Wi-Fi,

LONDON

24 Craven Hill Gardens—it's the second road with this name as you come from the park, Tube: Queensway, tel. 020/7262-8708, www.caringhotel.co.uk, enquiries@caringhotel.co.uk).

Elsewhere in Central London

$$$ **The Sumner Hotel** rents 19 rooms in a 19th-century Georgian townhouse sporting a lounge decorated with fancy modern Italian furniture. This swanky place packs in all the extras and is conveniently located north of Hyde Park and near Oxford Street, a busy shopping destination—with a convenient Marks & Spencer (see page 207) within walking distance (queen Db-£178, king Db-£197, "deluxe" Db-£216, mention this book to get these Rick Steves rates, can be cheaper off-season, extra bed-£60, air-con, elevator, free Wi-Fi, 54 Upper Berkeley Street, a block and a half off Edgware Road, Tube: Marble Arch, tel. 020/7723-2244, www.thesumner.com, hotel@thesumner.com).

$$$ **The 22 York Street B&B** offers a casual alternative in the city center, renting 10 traditional, hardwood, comfortable rooms, each named for a notable London landmark (Sb-£95, Db-£129, free guest computer and Wi-Fi, inviting lounge; near Marylebone/Baker Street: from Baker Street Tube station, walk 2 blocks down Baker Street and take a right to 22 York Street—since there's no sign, just look for #22; tel. 020/7224-2990, www.22yorkstreet.co.uk, mc@22yorkstreet.co.uk, energetically run by Liz and Michael Callis).

$$ **Seven Dials Hotel**'s 18 no-nonsense rooms are plain and fairly tight, but also clean, reasonably priced, and incredibly well-located. Since their doubles all cost the same, request one of their larger rooms when you book (Sb-£95, Db-£105 but £10 more for twin beds, Tb-£130, Qb-£150, free Wi-Fi, 7 Monmouth Street, Tube: Leicester Square or Covent Garden—see map on page 192, tel. 020/7681-0791, www.sevendialshotellondon.com, info@sevendialshotel.co.uk, Hanna).

Big, Good-Value, Modern Hotels

London has an abundance of modern, impersonal, American-style chain hotels. I've listed and briefly described a few of the dominant chains below, along with a quick rundown on their more convenient London locations. Many of these hotels sit on busy streets in dreary train-station neighborhoods, so use common sense after dark and wear your money belt. For a sneak preview, try looking up the "Street View" for the address in Google Maps.

Premier Inn's locations include a branch inside **London County Hall** (next door to the London Eye), at **Southwark/Borough Market** (near Shakespeare's Globe on the South Bank, 34 Park Street, Tube: London Bridge), **Southwark/Tate Modern** (on Great

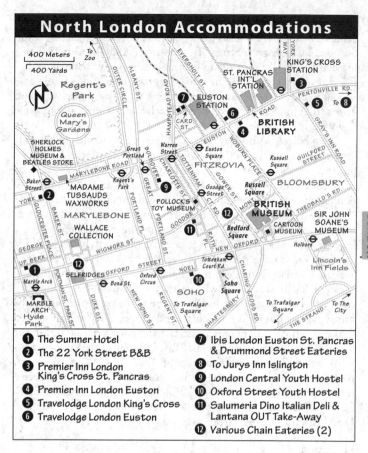

North London Accommodations

400 Meters
400 Yards

To Zoo

Regent's Park

Queen Mary's Gardens

KING'S CROSS STATION

ST. PANCRAS INT'L STATION

EUSTON STATION

PENTONVILLE RD.

To 8

BRITISH LIBRARY

SHERLOCK HOLMES MUSEUM & BEATLES STORE

Great Portland Street

Warren Street

Euston Square

FITZROVIA

Russell Square

BLOOMSBURY

Baker Street

MADAME TUSSAUDS WAXWORKS

Regent's Park

Goodge Street

Russell Square

BRITISH MUSEUM

SIR JOHN SOANE'S MUSEUM

MARYLEBONE

POLLOCK'S TOY MUSEUM

CARTOON MUSEUM

Bedford Square

WALLACE COLLECTION

Holborn

Lincoln's Inn Fields

SELFRIDGES

Bond St.

Oxford Circus

Tottenham Court Rd.

MARBLE ARCH

Marble Arch

SOHO

Soho Square

To Trafalgar Square

SHAFTESBURY

To Trafalgar Square

To The City

THE STRAND

MARBLE ARCH Hyde Park

LONDON

❶ The Sumner Hotel
❷ The 22 York Street B&B
❸ Premier Inn London King's Cross St. Pancras
❹ Premier Inn London Euston
❺ Travelodge London King's Cross
❻ Travelodge London Euston

❼ Ibis London Euston St. Pancras & Drummond Street Eateries
❽ To Jurys Inn Islington
❾ London Central Youth Hostel
❿ Oxford Street Youth Hostel
⓫ Salumeria Dino Italian Deli & Lantana OUT Take-Away
⓬ Various Chain Eateries (2)

Suffolk Street), **London King's Cross St. Pancras** (across the street from the east end of King's Cross Station and near the Eurostar terminus at St. Pancras), **London Euston** (handy but noisy location at corner of Euston Road and Dukes Road), **Kensington/Earl's Court** (11 Knaresborough Place, Tube: Earl's Court or Gloucester Road), **Victoria** (82-83 Eccleston Square, Tube: Victoria), and **Putney Bridge** (farther out, 3 Putney Bridge Approach). Avoid the **Tower Bridge** location, which is an inconvenient 15-minute walk from the nearest Tube stop. Book online at www.premierinn.com or call 0871-527-9222; from North America, dial 011-44-1582-567-890.

Travelodge has quite a few locations in London, including at **King's Cross** (200 yards in front of King's Cross Station, Grays Inn Road, Tube: King's Cross St. Pancras), **Kings Cross Royal Scot, Euston, Marylebone, Covent Garden, Liverpool Street,** and **Farringdon** (www.travelodge.co.uk).

Ibis has only two locations that are convenient to London's center: **Euston St. Pancras** (on a quiet street a block west of Euston Station, 3 Cardington Street, Tube: Euston) and **The City** (5 Commercial Street, Tube: Aldgate East); book at www.ibishotel.com.

Jurys Inn's locations include **Islington** (near King's Cross Station, 60 Pentonville Road, Tube: Angel), **Chelsea** (Imperial Road, Tube: Imperial Wharf), and near **Heathrow Airport,** all bookable at www.jurysinns.com.

easyHotel: With several branches in good neighborhoods around London, easyHotel (www.easyhotel.com) has a unique business model inspired by its parent company, the easyJet budget airline. The generally tiny, super-efficient, no-frills rooms feel popped out of a plastic mold, down to the prefab ship's head-type "bathroom pod." Rates can be surprisingly low (with doubles as cheap as £30 if you book early enough)—but you'll be charged à la carte for add-ons that are included at most hotels, such as TV use, luggage storage, fresh towels, and daily cleaning (breakfast, if available, comes from a vending machine). If you go with the basic package, it's like hosteling with privacy—a hard-to-beat value. But you get what you pay for (walls can be thin, construction can be flimsy, fellow guests can be noisy, and so on). They're only a good deal if you book far enough ahead to get a good price, and skip the many extras...which add up fast. Locations include **Victoria** (34-40 Belgrave Road—see map on page 170, Tube: Victoria), **South Kensington** (14 Lexham Gardens, Tube: Earl's Court or Gloucester Road), **Earl's Court** (44-48 West Cromwell Road, Tube: Earl's Court), **Paddington** (10 Norfolk Place, Tube: Paddington), and **Heathrow** and **Luton** airports.

Hostels

Hostels can slash accommodation costs while meeting your basic needs. Prices listed here include sheets and lockers (bring your own lock), but you'll likely have to rent towels and pay a bit extra for breakfast. All of these places are open 24 hours, give members a £3 discount, and have guest computers and Wi-Fi (usually for a fee).

$ London Central Youth Hostel is the flagship of London's hostels, with 300 beds and all the latest in security and comfortable efficiency. Families and travelers of any age will feel welcome in this wonderful facility. You'll pay the same price for any bed in a four- to eight-bed single-sex dorm—with or without private bathroom—so try to grab one with a bathroom (£16-30/bunk depending on demand, twin D-£40-60, families welcome to book an entire room, members' kitchen, book long in advance, between Oxford Circus and Great Portland Street Tube stations at 104 Bolsover Street—see map on page 183, tel. 0845-371-9154, www.yha. org.uk, londoncentral@yha.org.uk).

$ Oxford Street Youth Hostel is right in the shopping and clubbing zone in Soho, with 90 beds (£20-30/bunk, twin D-£50-60, members' kitchen, 14 Noel Street, Tube: Oxford Street, tel. 0845-371-9133, www.yha.org.uk, oxfordst@yha.org.uk).

$ St. Paul's Youth Hostel, near St. Paul's Cathedral, is modern, friendly, well-run, and a bit scruffy. Most of the 210 beds are in shared, single-sex 3- to 11-bunk rooms (£20-30/bunk depending on demand, twin D-£50-60, cheap meals, 36 Carter Lane, Tube: St. Paul's, tel. 020/7236-4965 or 0845-371-9012, www.yha.org.uk, stpauls@yha.org.uk).

$ A cluster of three **St. Christopher's Inn** hostels, south of the Thames near London Bridge, have cheap dorm beds; one branch (the Oasis) is for women only. All have loud and friendly bars attached (£22-36, higher price is for weekends, less in off-season, D-£60 or thereabouts, small breakfast included, must be over 18 years old, free Wi-Fi, 161-165 Borough High Street, Tube: Borough or London Bridge, reservations tel. 020/8600-7500, www.st-christophers.co.uk).

Heathrow and Gatwick Airports

At or near Heathrow Airport

It's so easy to get to Heathrow from central London, I see no reason to sleep there. But if you do, here are some options. The Yotel is actually inside the airport, while the rest are a short bus or taxi ride away. In addition to public buses, the cutely named £4 "Hotel Hoppa" shuttle buses connect the airport to many nearby hotels (different routes serve the various hotels and terminals—may take a while to spot your particular bus at the airport).

$$ Yotel, at the airport inside Terminal 4, has small sleep dens good for a quick nap (four hours-£35-70), or an overnight stay (tiny "standard cabin"—£70/8 hours, "premium cabin"—£93/8 hours; cabins sleep 1-2 people; price is per cabin—not person, these prices include £3 credit-card fee). Prices vary by day, week, and time of year, so check their website. The windowless rooms are only slightly larger than a double bed, with weirdly purplish lighting, private bathrooms, and free guest computers and Wi-Fi (tel. 020/7100-1100, www.yotel.com, customer@yotel.com).

$$ Jurys Inn, another hotel chain, tempts tired travelers with 300-plus cookie-cutter rooms (Db-£55-105, cheapest when booked at least a week in advance, check website for deals, breakfast extra; on Eastern Perimeter Road, Tube: Hatton Cross plus 5-minute walk; take the Tube one stop from Terminals 1 or 3; or two stops from Terminals 4 or 5; or the Hotel Hoppa #H9 from Terminals 1 or 3, or #H53 or #H56 from Terminals 4 or 5; tel. 020/8266-4664, www.jurysinns.com).

$ easyHotel, your cheapest bet, is in a low-rent residential neighborhood a £5 taxi ride from the airport. Its 53 no-frills, pod-like rooms are on two floors (Db-£40-55 including 20 percent VAT, no breakfast, no elevator, pay guest computer and Wi-Fi, see page 184 for more on easyHotel, Brick Field Lane; take free local bus #140 from airport's Central Bus Station or the Hotel Hoppa #H8 from Terminals 1 or 3—or #H3 after 20:00, or ask the hotel to arrange a taxi; www.easyhotel.com, enquiries@heathrow.easyhotel.com).

$ Hotel Ibis London Heathrow offers predictable value (Db-£40-55, cheapest when booked 3 weeks ahead, website specials as low as £35, breakfast-£9, pay guest computer and Wi-Fi; 112-114 Bath Road, take free local bus #105, #111, #140, or #285 from airport's Central Bus Station or Terminal 4, or the Hotel Hoppa #H6 from Terminals 1 or 3—or #H56 from Terminals 4 or 5; tel. 020/8759-4888, www.ibishotel.com, h0794@accor.com).

At or near Gatwick Airport

$$ Yotel, with small rooms, has a branch right at the airport (Gatwick South Terminal; see prices and contact info in Heathrow listing, previous page).

$ Gatwick Airport Central Premier Inn rents cheap rooms 350 yards from the airport (Db-£45-65, breakfast-£5-9, £3 shuttle bus from airport—must reserve in advance, Longbridge Way, North Terminal, tel. 0871-527-8406, frustrating phone tree, www.premierinn.com). Five more Premier Inns are within a five-mile radius of the airport.

$ Gatwick Airport Travelodge has budget rooms about two miles from the airport (Db-£30-60, breakfast extra, pay Wi-Fi, Church Road, Lowfield Heath, Crawley, £3.20 shuttle bus to/from airport, tel. 0871-984-6031, www.travelodge.co.uk).

Apartment Rentals

Consider the advantages that come with renting a furnished apartment—or "flat," as the British say. Complete with a small, equipped kitchen and living room, this option can also work for families or groups on shorter visits.

Cross-Pollinate is an online booking agency representing B&Bs and apartments in a handful of European cities, including London. Search their website for a listing you like, then submit your reservation online. If the place is available, you'll be charged a small deposit and emailed the location and check-in details. Policies vary from owner to owner, but in most cases you'll pay the balance on arrival in cash. London listings range from a Chelsea B&B room for two for £100 per night to a two-bedroom Marble Arch apartment sleeping four for £280 per night. Minimum stays vary from one to five nights (US tel. 800-270-1190, UK tel. 020/3514-0083, www.cross-pollinate.com, info@cross-pollinate.com).

Coach House Rentals offers a range of hand-selected apartments around the city, nearly all of them in real homes. As with any apartment rental, these can be an especially smart option if you're traveling as a group of four or more. Generally speaking, the more central the apartment, the more you pay (around £200/night for place in Pimlico, £425/night right by Westminster Abbey, £120-150/night farther afield). Each comes with a packet of neighborhood info, a "starter pack" of breakfast snacks, and usually either cable Internet access or Wi-Fi. A staff member meets you when you first arrive, and someone's always available over the phone (5-night minimum, £90 fee on top of quoted rental, tel. 020/8133-8332, http://rentals.chslondon.com, rentals@chslondon.com).

Many other organizations are ready to help; the following have been recommended by local guides and readers: www.perfectplaces.com, www.homefromhome.co.uk, www.london-house.com, www.gowithit.co.uk, www.aplacelikehome.co.uk, and www.regentsuites.com. You can also rent directly from the apartment owner (check reputable websites such as www.airbnb.com, www.HomeAway.com, and www.vrbo.com).

No matter whom you rent through, be very careful to avoid getting scammed: Follow all of the website's safety advice and use their internal payment procedures. Never wire money directly to an apartment owner, or you may find yourself with no place to stay—and no hope of getting your money back.

Read the rental conditions carefully and ask lots of questions. If a certain amenity is important to you (such as Wi-Fi or a washing machine in the unit), ask specifically about it and what to do if it stops working. Plot the location carefully (plug the address into http://maps.google.com), and remember to factor in travel time and costs from outlying neighborhoods to central London. Finally, it's a good idea to buy trip cancellation/interruption insurance, as many weekly rentals are nonrefundable.

LONDON

Eating in London

With "modern English" cuisine on the rise, you could try a different cuisine for each meal in London and never eat "local" English food, even on a lengthy stay. The sheer variety of foods—from every corner of its former empire and beyond—is astonishing. You'll be amazed at the number of hopping, happening new restaurants of all kinds.

If you want to dine (as opposed to eat), drop by a London newsstand to get a weekly entertainment guide or an annual restaurant guide (both have extensive restaurant listings). Visit www.london-eating.co.uk or www.squaremeal.co.uk for more options.

The thought of a £50 meal in Britain generally ruins my appetite, so my London dining is limited mostly to easygoing, fun, moderately priced alternatives. I've listed places by neighborhood—handy to your sightseeing or hotel. Considering how expensive London can be, if there's any good place to cut corners to stretch your budget, it's by eating cheaply. Pub grub (at one of London's 7,000 pubs) and ethnic restaurants (especially Indian and Chinese) are good low-cost options. Of course, picnicking is the fastest and cheapest way to go. Good grocery stores and sandwich shops, fine park benches, and polite pigeons abound in Britain's most expensive city. Affordable chain restaurants (such as those noted in the sidebar) are another good option.

London (and all of Britain) is smoke-free. Expect restaurants and pubs that sell food to be non-smoking indoors, with smokers occupying patios and doorways outside. When ready to pay, Brits generally ask for the "bill" rather than the "check."

Central London

I've arranged these options by neighborhood, but they're all within about a 15-minute walk of each other. Survey your options before settling on a place.

Near Soho and Chinatown

London has a trendy scene that most Beefeater-seekers miss entirely. Foodies who want to eat well skip the more staid and touristy zones near Piccadilly and Trafalgar Square, and head to Soho instead. Make it a point to dine in Soho at least once, to feel the pulse of London's eclectic urban melting pot of international flavors. These restaurants are scattered throughout a chic, creative, and borderline-seedy zone that teems with hipsters, theatergoers,

London's Chain Restaurants

One good way to save money and still eat well is by dining at one of London's excellent chain restaurants. Most of the branches listed here open daily no later than noon (several at 8:00 or 9:00), and close sometime between 22:00 and midnight. Occasionally a place may close on Sundays or in the afternoon between lunch and dinner, but these are rare exceptions.

Busaba Eathai is a hit with Londoners for its snappy (sometimes rushed) service, boisterous ambience, and good, inexpensive Thai cuisine. Wedge yourself at one of the 16-person hardwood tables or at a two-person table by the window—with everyone in the queue staring at your noodles (£7-12 meals, www.busaba.com). New locations pop up often, with outlets in Soho, Covent Garden, near the British Museum, and across from the Bond Street Tube stop.

Thai Square is another dependable Thai option with a much swankier atmosphere (£8-10 salads, noodle dishes, and curries; £13-16 meat dishes, www.thaisquareserver.co.uk). Handy locations include Soho, Trafalgar Square, Covent Garden, the Strand, South Kensington, near Oxford Circus, and The City (one on The Strand at Fleet Street and another near the Mansion House Tube stop).

Masala Zone, serving accessible and Indian food, makes a predictable, good alternative to the many one-off, hole-in-the-wall Indian joints around town. Try a curry-and-rice dish, a *thali* (platter with several small dishes), or their street food specials. Each branch has its own personality (£8-12 meals, www.masalazone.com). Locations include Soho, Covent Garden, Bayswater, and in the Selfridges department store on Oxford Street.

Byron, an upscale-hamburger chain with hip interiors, is worth seeking out if you need a burger fix. While British burgers tend to be a bit overcooked by our standards, Byron's burgers are your best bet (£7-10 burgers, www.byronhamburgers.com). Locations are in Soho, Covent Garden, Leicester Square, between Piccadilly Circus and Trafalgar Square, near St. Paul's, Fitzrovia, South Kensington, Kensington, and Greenwich.

Other quality chain restaurants—which you'll also find across the UK—are **Wagamama Noodle Bar, Côte Brasserie, Gourmet Burger Kitchen (GBK), Loch Fyne Fish Restaurant, Nando's, Yo! Sushi, Ask, Pizza Express,** and **Jamie's Italian.** (For descriptions of these eateries, see page 33.)

and London's gay community. Even if you plan to have dinner elsewhere, it's a treat just to wander around Soho.

Note: While gentrification has mostly stripped this area (no pun intended) of its former "red light district" vibe, a few pockets of sex for sale survive. Beware of the extremely welcoming women standing outside the strip clubs (especially on Great Windmill Street). Enjoy the sales pitch—but know that only fools fall for the "£5 drink and show" lure.

On and near Wardour Street, in the Heart of Soho

Running through the middle of Soho, rumbling past what's left of the strip-club zone, Wardour Street is ground zero for creative restaurateurs hoping to break into the big leagues. Strolling up this street—particularly from Brewer Street northward—you can take your pick from a world of options: Thai, Indonesian, Vietnamese, Italian, French and even...English. Not yet tarnished by the corporatization creeping in from areas to the south, this drag still seems to hit the right balance between trendy and accessible. While I've listed several choices below (including some that are a block or two off Wardour Street), simply strolling the length of the street and following your appetite to the place that looks best is a great plan.

Princi is a vast, bright, efficient, wildly popular Italian deli/ bakery with Milanese flair. Along one wall is a long counter with display cases offering a tempting array of pizza rustica, panini sandwiches, focaccia, a few pasta dishes, and desserts (look in the window from the street to see their wood-fired oven in action). Order your food at the counter, then find a space at a long shared table; or get it to go for an affordable and fast meal (£7-13 meals, Mon-Sat 8:00-24:00, Sun 8:30-22:00, 135 Wardour Street, tel. 020/7478-8888).

Bi Bim Bap is named for what it sells: *bibimbap* (literally "mixed rice"), a scalding stone bowl filled with rice and thinly sliced veggies, topped with a fried egg. Mix it up with your spoon, flavor it to taste with the two sauces, then dig in with your chopsticks. While purists go with the straightforward rice bowl, you can pay a few pounds extra to add other toppings—including chicken, *bulgogi* (marinated beef strips), and mushrooms. Though the food is traditional Korean, the stylish, colorful interior lets you know you're in Soho (£7-10 meals, Mon-Fri 12:00-15:00 & 18:00-23:00, Sat 12:00-23:00, closed Sun, 11 Greek Street, tel. 020/7287-3434).

Mooli's, which may close or move to a new location in 2014, is made-to-order for a quick, affordable, flavorful jolt of Indian street food. Their £5-6 *mooli* wraps, sort of like an Indian burrito, are filled with pork, chicken, beef, *paneer* (cheese), chickpea, or spicy goat. Top it with your choice of chutneys and Indian salsas. Eat in or grab one to go; their "mini" version makes a good £3.50 snack

(Mon-Sat 8:30-23:30, closed Sun, 50 Frith Street, tel. 020/7494-9075).

Bocca di Lupo, a pricey and popular splurge, serves small portions of classic regional Italian food. Dressy and a bit snooty, it's a place where you're glad you made a reservation. The counter seating, on cushy stools with a view into the open kitchen, is particularly memorable. Most diners assemble a sampler meal with a series of £7-10 small plates—but be careful, because at these prices, your bill can add up. A short selection of more affordable £10-15 "one-dish meals" is available for lunch and until 19:00 (Mon-Sat 12:00-15:00 & 17:30-23:00, Sun 12:30-15:15 & 17:00-21:00, 12 Archer Street, tel. 020/7734-2223, www.boccadilupo.com).

Gelupo, Bocca di Lupo's sister gelateria across the street, has a wide array of ever-changing but always creative and delicious dessert favorites—ranging from popular standbys like the incredibly rich chocolate sorbet to fresh-mint *stracciatella* to hay (yes, hay). A £3 sampler cup or cone gets you two flavors (and little taster spoons are generously offered to help you choose). Everything is homemade, and the white subway-tile interior feels clean and bright. They also have espresso drinks and—at lunchtime—£5-6 deli sandwiches (daily 12:00 until late, 7 Archer Street, tel. 020/7287-5555).

Yalla Yalla is a hole-in-the-wall serving up high-quality Beirut street food—hummus, baba ghanoush, tabbouleh, and *shawarmas*. Stylish as you'd expect for Soho, it's tucked down a seedy alley across from a sex shop. Eat in the cramped and cozy interior or at one of the few outdoor tables, or get your food to go (£3-4 sandwiches, £4-6 *mezes*, £7 *meze* platter available until 17:00, £10-12 bigger dishes, Mon-Sat 10:00-23:00, Sun 10:00-22:00, 1 Green's Court—just north of Brewer Street, tel. 020/7287-7663).

Ducksoup, a short block over from Wardour Street, is an upscale-feeling yet cool and relaxed little bar, with a small but thoughtful menu of well-executed international and modern British dishes (£7 small plates, £14 big plates—sharing several items can add up). The menu is handwritten, the music is on vinyl, and the rough woodwork and cramped-but-convivial atmosphere give it the feeling of a well-loved wine bar. While a bit overpriced, the atmosphere is memorable (Mon-Sat 12:00-24:00, food served until 22:30, Sun 13:00-16:00, 41 Dean Street, tel. 020/7287-4599).

And for Dessert: In addition to the outstanding gelato at **Gelupo** and the treats at **Princi** (both described earlier), several other places along Wardour Street boast window displays that tickle the sweet tooth. In just a couple of blocks, you'll see pastry shops, a *crêperie,* and a Hummingbird cupcake shop.

Soho Chain Restaurants: Some of Britain's most popular chain restaurants started out here in Soho, but in this fast-evolving

LONDON

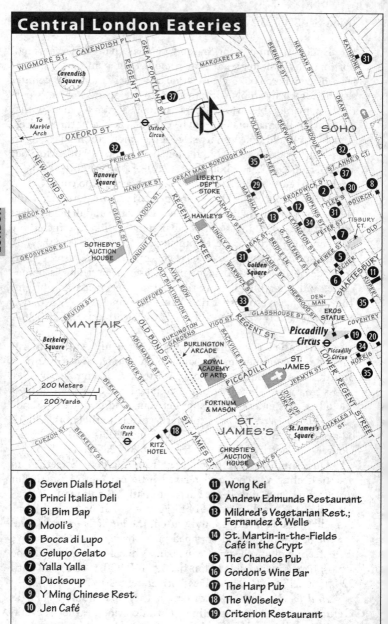

Central London Eateries

1. Seven Dials Hotel
2. Princi Italian Deli
3. Bi Bim Bap
4. Mooli's
5. Bocca di Lupo
6. Gelupo Gelato
7. Yalla Yalla
8. Ducksoup
9. Y Ming Chinese Rest.
10. Jen Café
11. Wong Kei
12. Andrew Edmunds Restaurant
13. Mildred's Vegetarian Rest.; Fernandez & Wells
14. St. Martin-in-the-Fields Café in the Crypt
15. The Chandos Pub
16. Gordon's Wine Bar
17. The Harp Pub
18. The Wolseley
19. Criterion Restaurant

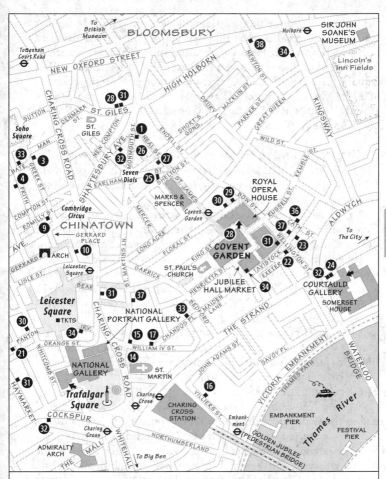

LONDON

20 Stockpot & Woodlands South Indian Vegetarian Restaurant
21 West End Kitchen
22 Joe Allen
23 Sofra Turkish Restaurant
24 Sitar Indian Restaurant
25 Belgo Centraal
26 Neal's Yard Eateries
27 Food for Thought Café
28 Union Jacks (2)

29 Masala Zone (2)
30 Busaba Eathai (3)
31 Byron (7)
32 Thai Square (5)
33 Nando's (3)
34 Wagamama Noodle Bar (5)
35 Yo! Sushi (3)
36 Loch Fyne Fish Restaurant
37 Côte Brasserie (4)
38 The Princess Louise Pub

neighborhood, they're now a little like stale sushi. While I wouldn't waste a Soho meal on one of these places, they're a convenient fallback: **Byron** (particularly appealing industrial-mod branch at 97-99 Wardour Street), **Busaba Eathai** (106 Wardour Street), **Thai Square** (27-28 St. Anne's Court, plus one near Trafalgar Square at 21-24 Cockspur Street), **Wagamama** (10A Lexington Street), **Masala Zone** (9 Marshall Street), **Côte** (124-126 Wardour Street), and **Nando's** (10 Frith Street).

Authentic Chinese Food in and near Chinatown

The main drag of Chinatown (Gerrard Street, with the ornamental archways) is lined with touristy, interchangeable Chinese joints. But these places seem to have an edge.

Y Ming Chinese Restaurant—across Shaftesbury Avenue from the ornate gates, clatter, and dim sum of Chinatown—has dressy European decor, serious but helpful service, and authentic Northern Chinese cooking. London's food critics consider this well worth the short walk from the heart of Chinatown for food that's a notch above (good £12 meal deal offered 12:00-18:00, £8-12 plates, open Mon-Sat 12:00-23:45, closed Sun, turquoise corner shop at 35-36 Greek Street, tel. 020/7734-2721).

Jen Café, across the little square called Newport Place, is a humble Chinese corner eatery much loved for its homemade dumplings. It's just stools and simple seating, with fast service, a fun, inexpensive menu, and a devoted following (£6-8 plates, daily 10:30-21:00, cash only, 4 Newport Place, tel. 020/7287-9708).

Wong Kei Chinese restaurant, at the Wardour Street (west) end of the Chinatown drag, offers a bewildering variety of dishes served by notoriously brusque waiters in a setting that feels like a hospital cafeteria. Londoners put up with the abuse to enjoy one of the satisfying BBQ rice dishes or hot pots. Individuals and couples are usually seated at communal tables, while larger parties are briskly shuffled up or down stairs (£7-12 main dishes, £10-15 fixed-price meals, cash only, Mon-Sat 12:00-23:30, Sun 12:00-22:30, 41-43 Wardour Street, tel. 020/7437-8408).

Sedate and Upscale Options in Soho

Andrew Edmunds Restaurant is a tiny, candlelit space where you'll want to hide your camera and guidebook and not act like a tourist. This little place—with a jealous and loyal clientele—is the closest I've found to Parisian quality in a cozy restaurant in London. The extensive wine list, modern European cooking, and creative seasonal menu are worth the splurge (£5-7 starters, £12-20 main dishes, Mon-Sat 12:00-15:30 & 17:30-22:45, Sun 13:00-16:00 & 18:00-22:30, these are last-order times, come early or call ahead, request ground floor rather than basement, 46 Lexington Street, tel. 020/7437-5708, www.andrewedmunds.com).

Mildred's Vegetarian Restaurant, across from Andrew Edmunds, has cheap prices, an enjoyable menu, and a pleasant interior filled with happy eaters (£8-11 meals, Mon-Sat 12:00-23:00, closed Sun, vegan options, 45 Lexington Street, tel. 020/7494-1634).

Fernandez & Wells is a cozy, convivial, delightfully simple little wine, cheese, and ham bar. Drop in and grab a stool as you belly up to the big wooden bar. Share a plate of top-quality cheeses and/or Spanish, Italian, or French hams with fine bread and oil, while sipping a nice glass of wine (Mon-Fri 11:00-22:00, Sat-Sun 12:00-22:00, quality sandwiches at lunch, 43 Lexington Street, tel. 020/7734-1546).

Traditional Choices near Trafalgar Square

These places, all of which provide a more "jolly olde" experience than high cuisine, are within about 100 yards of Trafalgar Square.

St. Martin-in-the-Fields Café in the Crypt is just right for a tasty meal on a monk's budget—maybe even on a monk's tomb. You'll dine sitting on somebody's gravestone in an ancient crypt. Their enticing buffet line is kept stocked all day, serving breakfast, lunch, and dinner (£7-10 cafeteria plates, hearty traditional desserts, free jugs of water). They also serve a restful cream tea (£6, daily 14:00-18:00). You'll find the café directly under the St. Martin-in-the-Fields Church, facing Trafalgar Square—enter through the glass pavilion next to the church (Mon-Tue 8:00-20:00, Wed 8:00-22:30, Thu-Sat 8:00-21:00, Sun 11:00-18:00, profits go to the church, Tube: Charing Cross, tel. 020/7766-1158 or 020/7766-1100). Wednesday evenings at 20:00 come with a live jazz band (£5.50-9 tickets). While here, check out the concert schedule for the busy church upstairs (or visit www.smitf.org).

The Chandos Pub's Opera Room floats amazingly apart from the tacky crush of tourism around Trafalgar Square. Look for it opposite the National Portrait Gallery (corner of William IV Street and St. Martin's Lane) and climb the stairs (to the right of the pub entrance) to the Opera Room. This is a fine Trafalgar rendezvous point and wonderfully local pub. They serve £4 sandwiches and a better-than-average range of traditional pub meals for under £10—meat pies and fish-and-chips are their specialty. The ground-floor pub is stuffed with regulars and offers snugs (private booths), the same menu, and more serious beer drinking. Chandos proudly serves the local Samuel Smith beer at £4 a pint (kitchen open daily 11:00-19:00, Fri and Sun until 18:00, order and pay at the bar, 29 St. Martin's Lane, Tube: Leicester Square, tel. 020/7836-1401).

Gordon's Wine Bar, with a simple, steep staircase leading into a candlelit 15th-century wine cellar, is filled with dusty

Pub Appreciation

The pub is the heart of the people's England, where all manner of folks have, for generations, found their respite from work and a home-away-from-home. England's classic pubs are national treasures, with great cultural value and rich history, not to mention good beer and grub.

The Golden Age for pub-building was in the late Victorian era (c. 1880-1905), when pubs were independently owned and land prices were high enough to make it worthwhile to invest in fixing up pubs. The politics were pro-pub as well: Conservatives, backed by Big Beer, were in, and temperance-minded Liberals were out.

Especially in class-conscious Victorian times, traditional pubs were divided into sections by elaborate screens (now mostly gone), allowing the wealthy to drink in a more refined setting, while commoners congregated on the pub's rougher side. These were really "public houses," featuring nooks (snugs) for groups and clubs to meet, friends and lovers to rendezvous, and families to get out of the house at night. Because many medieval pub-goers were illiterate, pubs were simply named for the picture hung outside (e.g., The Crooked Stick, The Queen's Arms—meaning her coat of arms).

Historic pubs still dot the London cityscape. The only place to see the very oldest-style tavern in the "domestic tradition" is at **Ye Olde Cheshire Cheese,** which was rebuilt in 1667 (after the Great Fire) from a 16th-century tavern (£5-10 pub grub, £9-14 meals in the restaurant, open daily, 145 Fleet Street, Tube: Blackfriars, tel. 020/7353-6170). Imagine this mazelike place, with three separate bars, in the pre-Victorian era: With no bar, drinkers gathered around the fireplaces, while tap boys shuttled tankards up from the cellar. (This was long before barroom taps were connected to casks in the cellar. Oh, and don't say "keg"—that's a gassy modern thing.)

Late-Victorian pubs are more common, such as the lovingly restored 1897 **Princess Louise** (daily midday until 23:00, lunch and dinner served in less atmospheric upstairs lounge Mon-Thu, Fri lunch only, no food Sat-Sun, 208 High Holborn, see map on page 192, Tube: Holborn, tel. 020/7405-8816). These places are fancy, often with heavy embossed wallpaper ceilings, decorative tile work, fine-etched glass, ornate carved stillions (the big central hutch for storing bottles and glass), and even urinals equipped with a place to set your glass.

London's best Art Nouveau pub is **The Black Friar** (c. 1900-1915), with fine carved capitals, lamp holders, and quirky phrases worked into the decor (£8-11 meals, daily 10:00-23:30, outdoor seating, 174 Queen Victoria Street, Tube: Blackfriars, tel. 020/7236-5474).

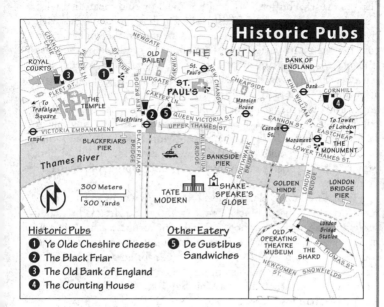

Historic Pubs

Historic Pubs
1 Ye Olde Cheshire Cheese
2 The Black Friar
3 The Old Bank of England
4 The Counting House

Other Eatery
5 De Gustibus
Sandwiches

The "former-bank pubs" represent a more modern trend in pub-building. As banks increasingly go electronic, they're moving out of lavish, high-rent old buildings. Many of these former banks are being refitted as pubs with elegant bars and freestanding stillions, which provide a fine centerpiece. Three such pubs are **The Old Bank of England** (£7-10 meals, Mon-Fri 11:00-23:00, food served 12:00-21:00, closed Sat-Sun, 194 Fleet Street, Tube: Temple, tel. 020/7430-2255), **The Jugged Hare** (open daily, 172 Vauxhall Bridge Road—see map on page 170, Tube: Victoria, tel. 020/7828-1543, also see listing on page 203), and **The Counting House** (Mon-Fri 11:00-23:00, closed Sat-Sun, 50 Cornhill, Tube: Bank, tel. 020/7283-7123, see listing on page 207).

Go pubbing in the evening for a lively time, or drop by during the quiet late morning (from 11:00), when the pub is empty and filled with memories.

old bottles, faded British memorabilia, and nine-to-fivers. At the "English rustic" buffet, choose a hot meal or cold meat dish with a salad (figure around £7-8/dish); the £9 cheese plate comes with two cheeses, bread, and a pickle. Then step up to the wine bar and consider the many varieties of wine and port available by the glass (this place is passionate about port). The low carbon-crusted vaulting deeper in the back seems to intensify the Hogarth-painting atmosphere. Although it's crowded, you can normally corral two chairs and grab the corner of a table. On hot days, the crowd spills out onto a leafy back patio, where a barbecue cooks for a long line of tables (arrive before 17:00 to get a seat, Mon-Sat 11:00-23:00, Sun 12:00-22:00, 2 blocks from Trafalgar Square, bottom of Villiers Street at #47, Tube: Embankment, tel. 020/7930-1408, manager Gerard Menan).

LONDON

Ales: **The Harp,** clearly a local favorite, is a crowded and cluttered little pub just a block above Trafalgar Square. While they serve no food, this is a good, central spot to nurse a fine ale and make a new friend with one of the Londoners crowded around the coaster-coated bar. This is a top choice for an après-work pint among nine-to-fivers, who stand in the dozens out front after the workday, sipping their beers (Mon-Sat 10:30-23:30, Sun 12:00-22:30, 47 Chandos Place, tel. 020/7836-0291).

Near Piccadilly

The first two places are upscale and snooty—but if you want something cheaper in this same area, you'll find plenty of other options.

Swanky Splurges

The Wolseley is the grand 1920s showroom of a long-defunct British car. The last Wolseley drove out with the Great Depression, but today this old-time bistro bustles with formal waiters serving traditional Austrian and French dishes in an elegant black-marble-and-chandeliers setting fit for its location next to the Ritz. Although the food can be unexceptional, prices are reasonable, and the presentation and setting are grand. Reservations are a must (£13-30 main courses; cheaper soup, salad, and sandwich "café menu" available; both menus available in all areas of restaurant, Mon-Fri 7:00-24:00, Sat 8:00-24:00, Sun 8:00-23:00, 160 Piccadilly—see map on page 192, tel. 020/7499-6996, www.thewolseley.com). They're popular for their fancy cream or afternoon tea (for details, see page 208).

The palatial **Criterion** offers grand-piano ambience beneath gilded tiles and chandeliers in a dreamy Byzantine church setting from 1880. It's right on Piccadilly Circus but a world away from the punk junk. It's a deal for the visual experience during lunch and if you order the £19-23 fixed-price meal (except on Sun, when you must order from the expensive à la carte menu). At any hour, the service couldn't care less. Anyone can drop in for coffee or a drink (Mon-Sat 12:00-14:30 & 17:30-23:30, Sun 12:00-15:30 & 17:30-22:30, 224 Piccadilly, tel. 020/7930-0488, www.criterion-restaurant.com).

Cheaper Options near Piccadilly
Hungry and broke in the theater district? Head for Panton Street (off Haymarket, two blocks southeast of Piccadilly Circus), where several hardworking little places compete, all seeming to offer a three-course meal for about £9. Peruse the entire block (vegetarian, Pizza Express, Moroccan, Chinese, and two famous diners) before making your choice.

Stockpot is a meat, potatoes, gravy, and mushy-peas kind of place, famous and rightly popular for its edible, cheap English meals (£6-12, daily 7:00-23:00, 38 Panton Street, tel. 020/7839-5142). The **West End Kitchen** (across the street at #5, same hours and menu) is a direct competitor that's also well-known and just as good (£5-11 meals). Vegetarians may prefer the **Woodlands South Indian Vegetarian Restaurant,** which serves an impressive £19 *thali* combination plate (otherwise £7 main courses, 37 Panton Street).

Good Chains near Piccadilly: **Busaba Eathai** (35 Panton Street), **Wagamama** (8 Norris Street and another in Leicester Square at 14 Irving Street), **Byron** (11 Haymarket), and **Nando's** (46 Glasshouse Street).

Near Covent Garden
Covent Garden bustles with people and touristy eateries. The area feels overrun, but if you must eat around here, you have some good choices.

Joe Allen, tucked in a brick cellar a block away from the market, serves modern international and American cuisine with both style and hubbub. Downstairs off a quiet street with candles and white tablecloths, it's comfortably spacious and popular with the theater crowd. It feels a bit old-fashioned and cluttered, but in a welcoming way (£7 starters, £10-22 main courses, £16 two-course specials and £20 three-course specials available at lunch and 17:00-18:45, open Mon-Fri 12:00-24:00, Sat-Sun 10:00-24:00, piano music after 19:00, 13 Exeter Street, tel. 020/7836-0651).

Sofra Turkish Restaurant is good for quality Turkish with a touch of class. They have several menus: *meze* (Turkish tapas, £4-7), vegetarian, and £10 fixed-price meals (also £10-15 main dishes, daily 9:00-23:00, 36 Tavistock Street, tel. 020/7240-3773).

Sitar Indian Restaurant is a well-respected Indian/Bangladeshi place serving dishes from many regions, fine fish, and a tasty

£15 vegetarian *thali* (combo plate). It's small and dressy, with snappy service (£10-17 main dishes, Mon-Fri 12:00-24:00, Sat-Sun 15:00-23:00, next to Somerset House at 149 Strand, tel. 020/7836-3730).

Belgo Centraal serves hearty Belgian specialties in a vast 400-seat underground lair. It's a mussels, chips, and beer emporium dressed up as a mod-monastic refectory—with noisy acoustics and waiters garbed as Trappist monks. The classy restaurant section is more comfortable and less rowdy, but usually requires reservations. It's often more fun just to grab a spot in the boisterous beer hall, with its tight, communal benches (no reservations accepted). Both sides have the same menu and specials. Belgians claim they eat as well as the French and as heartily as the Germans. This place, which offers a stunning array of dark, blonde, and fruity Belgian beers, actually makes Belgian things trendy—a formidable feat (£10-14 main dishes, open daily 12:00-23:00; Mon-Fri £5-6.30 "beat the clock" meal specials 17:00-18:30—the time you order is the price you pay—including main dishes and fries; no meal-splitting after 18:30, and you must buy food with beer; daily £8 lunch special 12:00-17:00; 1 kid eats free for each parent ordering a regular entrée; 1 block north of Covent Garden Tube station at 50 Earlham Street, tel. 020/7813-2233).

Neal's Yard is a surprisingly colorful courtyard full of cheap, hip, and healthy eateries near Covent Garden. The neighborhood is a tabbouleh of fun, hippie-type cafés. One of the best—nearby—is the venerable and ferociously vegetarian **Food for Thought,** packed with local health nuts (good £5 vegetarian meals, Mon-Sat 12:00-20:30, Sun 12:00-17:30, 2 blocks north of Covent Garden Tube station at 31 Neal Street, tel. 020/7836-9072).

Union Jacks, the latest venture of British celebrity chef Jamie Oliver, fuses traditional British ingredients to make inventive modern dishes. Jamie's wood-fired flatbreads are topped not with cheese and tomatoes, but roast pig shoulder or oxtail and brisket. While this sounds risky, he pulls it off with great flavors, plus fun "fizzy drinks." The more charming of its two London branches sits right inside the Covent Garden market hall; a second restaurant is several blocks away (past Neal's Yard in a glass office building across from St. Giles Church). Each dish costs a few pounds more at the Covent Garden restaurant—this kind of location doesn't come cheap (£5-7 small plates are very small, £10-13 flatbreads, £9-15 classic British dishes, daily 12:00-23:00, Covent Garden, tel. 020/3640-7086, St. Giles tel. 020/3597-7888).

Good Chains near Covent Garden: This area seems to have a branch of nearly every London chain, including **Masala Zone** (particularly fun branch at the top end of the market has giant, colorful marionettes suspended from the ceiling, 48 Floral Street),

Côte (17-21 Tavistock Street and one closer to Leicester Square at 50-51 St. Martin's Lane), **Busaba Eathai** (44 Floral Street), **Thai Square** (166-170 Shaftesbury Avenue, plus one next to Sitar Indian Restaurant at 148 The Strand), **Wagamama** (1 Tavistock Street), **Byron** (behind the London Transport Museum at 33-35 Wellington Street), **Loch Fyne** (a couple of blocks behind the square at 2 Catherine Street), and **Nando's** (66-68 Chandos Place).

Near the British Museum, in Fitzrovia

To avoid the touristy crush right around the museum (and just southwest, in Soho), Londoners head a few blocks west, to the Fitzrovia area. Here, tiny Charlotte Place is lined with small eateries (including the first two listed below); nearby, the much bigger Charlotte Street has several more good options. The higher street signs you'll notice on Charlotte Street are a holdover from a time when they needed to be visible to carriage drivers. This area is a short walk from the Goodge Street Tube station—convenient to the British Museum.

Salumeria Dino serves up hearty sandwiches, pasta, and Italian coffee. Dino, a native of Naples, has run his little shop for more than 30 years and has managed to create a classic Italian deli that's so authentic, you'll walk out singing "O Sole Mio" (£3-5 sandwiches, £1 takeaway cappuccinos, Mon-Fri 9:00-17:00, closed Sat-Sun, 15 Charlotte Place, see map on page 181, tel. 020/7580-3938).

Lantana OUT, next door to Salumeria Dino, is an Australian coffee shop that sells modern soups, sandwiches, and salads at their takeaway window (£3-7 meals, pricier sit-down café next door, Mon-Fri 7:30-15:00, café also open Sat-Sun 9:00-17:00, 13 Charlotte Place, see map on page 183, tel. 020/7637-3347).

Nearby Chains: Several recommended chain restaurants are a short walk from the museum, including **Busaba Eathai** (22 Store Street), **Wagamama** (4 Streatham Street and near Holborn Tube stop at 123 Kingsway), **Côte** (5 Charlotte Street), **Byron** (6 Store Street, with another at 6 Rathbone Place), and **Nando's** (9-10 Southampton Place).

West London

Near Victoria Station Accommodations

These restaurants are within a few blocks of Victoria Station—and all are places where I've enjoyed eating. As with the accommodations in this area, I've grouped them by location: east or west of the station (see the map on page 170).

Cheap Eats: For groceries, a handy **M&S Simply Food** is inside Victoria Station (Mon-Sat 7:00-24:00, Sun 8:00-23:00, near the front, by the bus terminus), along with a **Sainsbury's Local** (daily 6:00-23:00, at rear entrance, on Eccleston Street). A larger

Sainsbury's is on Wilton Road near Warwick Way, a couple of blocks southeast of the station (Mon-Fri 7:00-23:00, Sat 7:00-22:00, Sun 11:00-17:00). A string of good ethnic restaurants lines Wilton Road, including this neighborhood's obligatory branch of **Nando's**. For affordable if forgettable meals, try the row of cheap little eateries on Elizabeth Street.

West of Victoria Station (Belgravia)

Ebury Wine Bar, filled with young professionals, provides a cut-above atmosphere (rumor has it that Prince William held his bachelor party here). In the delightful back room, the fancy menu features modern European cuisine with a French accent, including delicious £15-20 main dishes and a £19 two-course and £25 three-course special (available Mon-Fri at lunch and daily 18:00-20:00; three-course meal includes a glass of champagne that you're welcome to swap for house wine). At the wine bar, find a cheaper bar menu that's better than your average pub grub (£8-15 meals). This is emphatically a "traditional wine bar," with no beers on tap (restaurant open daily 12:00-15:00 & 18:00-22:30, wine bar open all day long, reservations smart, at intersection of Ebury and Elizabeth Streets, 139 Ebury Street, tel. 020/7730-5447, www.eburyrestaurant.co.uk).

Jenny Lo's Tea House is a simple budget place serving up a short menu of £8-9 eclectic Chinese-style meals to locals in the know. Jenny clearly learned from her father, Ken Lo, one of the most famous Cantonese chefs in Britain, whose fancy place is just around the corner (Mon-Fri 12:00-14:45 & 18:00-21:00, closed Sat-Sun, cash only, 14 Eccleston Street, tel. 020/7259-0399).

La Bottega is an Italian delicatessen that fits its upscale Belgravia neighborhood. It offers tasty, freshly cooked pastas (£6), lasagnas, and salads (£8 lasagna-and-salad meal), along with great sandwiches (£3) and a good coffee bar with pastries. While not cheap, it's fast (order at the counter), and the ingredients would please an Italian chef. Grab your meal to go, or enjoy the Belgravia good life with locals, either sitting inside or on the sidewalk (Mon-Fri 8:00-19:00, Sat 9:00-18:00, Sun 9:00-17:00, on corner of Ebury and Eccleston Streets, tel. 020/7730-2730, www.labottega65.com).

The Thomas Cubitt pub, named for the urban planner who designed much of Belgravia, is a trendy neighborhood gastropub packed with young professionals. It's pricey and a pinch pretentious, and prides itself on using sustainable ingredients in its modern English cooking. With a bright but slightly cramped interior and fine sidewalk seating, it's great for a drink or meal (£6 small plates, £14-17 main dishes, 44 Elizabeth Street). Upstairs is a more refined restaurant with the same kitchen, but an emphasis on finer technique and presentation (£8-11 starters, £17-25 main courses, reservations recommended, food served daily 12:00-22:00, tel. 020/7730-6060, www.thethomascubitt.co.uk).

The Duke of Wellington pub is a classic neighborhood place with forgettable grub, sidewalk seating, and an inviting interior. A bit more lowbrow than my other Belgravia listings, this may be your best shot at meeting a local (£5 sandwiches, £7-10 meals, food served Mon-Sat 12:00-15:00 & 18:00-21:00, Sun lunch only, 63 Eaton Terrace, tel. 020/7730-1782).

South End of Ebury Street: A five-minute walk down Ebury Street, where it intersects with Pimlico Road, you'll find a pretty square with a few more eateries to consider—including **The Orange,** a high-priced gastropub with the same owners and a similar menu to The Thomas Cubitt (described earlier); and **Daylesford,** the deli and café of an organic farm (£3-5 light meals to go—a good picnic option).

East of Victoria Station (Pimlico)

Grumbles brags it's been serving "good food and wine at nonscary prices since 1964." Offering a delicious mix of "modern eclectic French and traditional English," this unpretentious little place with cozy booths inside (on two levels, including a cellar) and four nice sidewalk tables is the best spot to eat well in this otherwise workaday neighborhood. Their traditional dishes are their forte (£10-16 plates, £11 early-bird specials 18:00-19:00, open Mon-Sat 12:00-14:30 & 18:00-23:00, Sun 12:00-22:30, reservations wise, half a block north of Belgrave Road at 35 Churton Street, tel. 020/7834-0149, www.grumblesrestaurant.co.uk).

Pimlico Fresh's breakfasts and lunches feature fresh, organic ingredients, served up with good coffee and/or fresh-squeezed juices. Choose from the dishes listed on the wall-sized chalkboard that lines the small eating area, then order at the counter. This place is heaven if you've slept through your hotel's breakfast hour, or if you just need a break from the bacon-eggs-beans routine (£5-10 meals, take-out lunches, plenty of vegetarian options; Mon-Fri 7:30-19:30, breakfast served until 15:00; Sat-Sun 9:00-18:00, breakfast until 17:00; 86 Wilton Road, tel. 020/7932-0030).

Seafresh Fish Restaurant is the neighborhood place for plaice—and classic and creative fish-and-chips cuisine. You can either take out on the cheap or eat in, enjoying a white fish ambience. Though Mario's father started this place in 1965, it feels like the chippy of the 21st century (meals-£5-8 to go, £12-17 to sit, Mon-Sat 12:00-15:00 & 17:00-22:30, closed Sun, 80-81 Wilton Road, tel. 020/7828-0747).

The Jugged Hare pub, a 10-minute walk from Victoria Station, sits in a lavish old bank building, with vaults replaced by tankards of beer and a fine kitchen. They have a fun, traditional menu with more fresh veggies than fries, and a plush, vivid pub scene good for a meal or just a drink (£6.50 sandwiches, £10 meals; Mon-Sat 11:00-23:00, food served 12:00-22:00; Sun 12:00-23:30, food served until 21:30; quiz night Wed at 19:00, 172 Vauxhall Bridge Road, tel. 020/7828-1543).

St. George's Tavern is the neighborhood's best pub for a full meal. They serve dinner from the same fun menu in three zones: on the sidewalk to catch the sun and enjoy some people-watching, in the ground-floor pub, and in a classier downstairs dining room. They're proud of their sausages and "toad in the hole." The scene is inviting for just a beer, too (£8-14 meals, food served Mon-Sat 10:00-22:00, Sun until 21:30, corner of Hugh Street and Belgrave Road, tel. 020/7630-1116).

South Kensington

Popular eateries line Old Brompton Road and Thurloe Street (Tube: South Kensington), and a good selection of cheap eateries are clumped around the Tube station. For locations, see the map on page 173.

La Bouchée Bistro Café is a classy hole-in-the-wall touch of France. This candlelit and woody bistro, with very tight seating, serves a special fixed-price meal (£14.50/2 courses, £16.50/3 courses) on weekdays during lunch and 17:00-19:00, and £15 *plats du jour* all *jour* (also £15-20 à la carte main courses). Reservations are smart in the evening (daily 12:00-15:00 & 17:00-23:00, 56 Old Brompton Road, tel. 020/7589-1929).

Moti Mahal Indian Restaurant, with minimalist-yet-upscale mod ambience and attentive service, serves mostly Bangladeshi cuisine that's delicious. Consider chicken *jalfrezi* if you like spicy food, and buttery chicken if you don't (£8-21 main courses, daily 12:00-15:00 & 17:30-23:00, 3 Glendower Place, tel. 020/7584-8428).

Bosphorus Kebabs is the student favorite for a quick, fast, and hearty Turkish dinner. While mostly for takeaway, they have a few tight tables indoors and on the sidewalk (£5-6 meals, Turkish kebabs, daily 10:30-24:00, 59 Old Brompton Road, tel. 020/7584-4048).

Beirut Express has fresh, well-prepared Lebanese cuisine. In the front, you'll find takeaway service as well as barstools for quick service (£4.50 sandwiches). In the back is a sit-down restaurant with £14-16 plates and £5-8 *mezes* (daily 12:00-24:00, 65 Old Brompton Road, tel. 020/7591-0123).

The Anglesea Arms, with a great terrace surrounded by classy South Kensington buildings, is a destination pub that feels like the classic neighborhood favorite. It's a thriving and happy place, with a woody ambience and a mellow step-down back dining room a world away from any tourism. While the food is the main draw, this is also a fine place to just have a beer (£6-8 starters, £12-17 main dishes, meals served daily 12:00-15:00 & 18:00-22:00; from Old Brompton Road, turn left at Onslow Gardens and go down a few blocks to 15 Selwood Terrace; tel. 020/7373-7960).

Rocca di Papa is a bright and dressy Italian place with a heated terrace (£6-8 pizza, pasta, and salads; daily 11:30-23:30, 73 Old Brompton Road, tel. 020/7225-3413).

Fernandez & Wells has a second outpost just north of the South Kensington Tube station (8 Exhibition Road; similar menu and hours as Soho location—see listing on page 195). Just up Exhibition Road (at #19) is a branch of **Thai Square** (described on page 189).

Supermarket: **Tesco Express** is handy for picnics (daily 7:00-24:00, 50-52 Old Brompton Road).

Near Bayswater and Notting Hill Accommodations

For locations, see the map on page 176.

Maggie Jones's, a Charles Dickens-meets-Ella Fitzgerald splurge, is exuberantly rustic and very English, with a 1940s-jazz soundtrack. It's a longer walk than most of my recommendations, but worth the hike. You'll get solid English cuisine, including huge plates of crunchy vegetables, served by a young and casual staff. It's pricey, but the portions are huge (especially the meat-and-fish pies, their specialty). You're welcome to save lots by splitting your main course. The candlelit upstairs is the most romantic, while the basement is kept lively with the kitchen, tight seating, and lots of action. If you eat well once in London, eat here—and do it quick, before it burns down (lunch—£5 starters, £7 main dishes; dinner—£6-9 starters, £15-24 main dishes; daily 12:00-14:30 & 18:00-23:00, reservations recommended, 6 Old Court Place, just east of Kensington Church Street, near High Street Kensington Tube stop, tel. 020/7937-6462, www.maggie-jones.co.uk).

The Churchill Arms pub and **Thai Kitchen** (same location) are local hangouts, with good beer and a thriving old-English ambience in front, and hearty £8 Thai plates in an enclosed patio in the back. You can eat the Thai food in the tropical hideaway (table service) or in the atmospheric pub section (order at the counter and they'll bring it to you). They also serve basic English pub food at lunch (£3 sandwiches, £5-7 meals). The place is festooned with Churchill memorabilia and chamber pots (including one with Hitler's mug on it—hanging from the ceiling farthest from Thai Kitchen—sure to cure the constipation of any Brit during World War II). Arrive by 18:00 or after 21:00 to avoid a line. During busy times, diners are limited to an hour at the table (food served daily 12:00-22:00, 119 Kensington Church Street, tel. 020/7727-4242).

Hereford Road is a cozy, mod eatery tucked at the far end of Prince's Square. It's stylish but not pretentious, serving heavy, meaty English cuisine executed with modern panache. Cozy two-person booths face the open kitchen up top; the main dining room is down below. There are also a few sidewalk tables (£6-8 starters, £14-16 main courses, reservations smart, Mon-Sat 12:00-15:00 & 18:00-22:00, Sun 12:00-16:00 & 18:00-22:30, 3 Hereford Road, tel. 020/7727-1144, www.herefordroad.org).

The Prince Edward serves good grub in a plush, upscale-pub setting and at its sidewalk tables (£10-15 meals, Mon-Fri 10:30-23:00, Sat 10:00-23:30, Sun 10:00-22:30, family-friendly, 2 blocks north of Bayswater Road at the corner of Dawson Place and Hereford Road, 73 Prince's Square, tel. 020/7727-2221).

Café Diana is a healthy little eatery serving sandwiches, salads, and Middle Eastern food. It's decorated—almost shrine-like—with photos of Princess Diana, who used to drop by for pita sandwiches. You can dine in the simple interior, or order some food from the counter to go (£3-5 sandwiches, £6-10 meat dishes, daily 8:00-23:00, cash only, 5 Wellington Terrace, on Bayswater Road, opposite Kensington Palace Garden Gates, where Di once lived, tel. 020/7792-9606, Abdul).

On Queensway: The road called Queensway is a multiethnic food circus, lined with lively and inexpensive eateries—browse the options along here and choose your favorite. For a cut above, head for **Royal China Restaurant**—filled with London's Chinese, who consider this one of the city's best eateries. It's dressed up in black, white, and gold, with candles and brisk waiters. While it's pricier than most neighborhood Chinese restaurants, the food is noticeably better (£9-13 dishes, Mon-Sat 12:00-23:00, Sun 11:00-22:00, dim sum until 17:00, 13 Queensway, tel. 020/7221-2535). For a lowbrow alternative, **Whiteleys Shopping Centre Food Court**—at the top end of Queensway—offers a fun selection of ethnic and fast-food chain eateries among Corinthian columns, and a multi-screen theater in a delightful mall (most restaurants daily 12:00-23:00, some eateries open shorter hours; options include Yo! Sushi, good salads at Café Rouge, pizza, Starbucks, and a coin-op Internet place; third floor, corner of Porchester Gardens and Queensway).

Supermarkets: **Tesco** is a half-block from the Notting Hill Gate Tube stop (Mon-Fri 7:00-24:00, Sat 7:00-23:00, Sun 12:00-18:00, near intersection with Pembridge Road, 114-120 Notting Hill Gate). Queensway is home to several supermarkets, including the smaller **Spar Market** at #18 (Mon-Sat 7:00-24:00, Sun

8:00-24:00). Nearby, **Marks & Spencer** can be found in Whiteleys Shopping Centre (Mon-Sat 8:30-22:00, Sun 12:00-18:00).

Elsewhere in London

Between St. Paul's and the Tower: **The Counting House,** formerly an elegant old bank, offers great £7-11 meals, nice homemade £10-11 meat pies, fish, and fresh vegetables. The fun "nibbles menu," with £3-6 snacks, is available starting in the early evening until 22:00 (or until 21:00 on Mon; open Mon-Fri 11:00-23:00, gets really busy with the buttoned-down 9-to-5 crowd after 12:15 especially Thu-Fri, closed Sat-Sun, near Mansion House in The City, 50 Cornhill—see map on page 197, tel. 020/7283-7123).

Near St. Paul's: **De Gustibus Sandwiches** is where an artisan bakery meets the public, offering fresh, you-design-it sandwiches, salads, and soups. Communication can be difficult, but it's worth the effort. Just one block below St. Paul's, it has simple seating or take-out picnic sacks for lugging to one of the great nearby parks (£4-8 sandwiches, £6 hot dishes, Mon-Fri 7:00-17:00, closed Sat-Sun, from church steps follow signs to youth hostel a block down-hill—see map on page 197, 53-55 Carter Lane, tel. 020/7236-0056; another outlet is inside the Borough Market in Southwark).

Near the British Library: Drummond Street (running just west of Euston Station—see map on page 183) is famous for cheap and good Indian vegetarian food (£5-10 dishes, £7 lunch buffets). For a good *thali* (combo plate) consider **Chutneys** (124 Drummond, tel. 020/7388-0604) and **Ravi Shankar** (133-135 Drummond, tel. 020/7388-6458, both open long hours daily).

Near the Tower of London: In **The Medieval Banquet**'s underground, brick-arched room, costumed wenches bring you a tasty four-course medieval-themed meal (includes ale and red wine) as minstrels, knights, jesters, and contortionists perform. If you enjoy an act, pound on the table. Reserve in advance online or by phone (adult-£50, child-£30, family deal for 2 adults and 2 kids-£110—Sun-Thu only, 15 percent discount for Rick Steves readers—can't combine with family deal, Mon-Sat around 20:00, Sun around 18:00, veggie option possible, rentable medieval garb, The Medieval Banquet Ivory House, St. Katharine Docks, enter docks off East Smithfield Street, Tube: Tower Hill, tel. 020/7480-5353, www.medievalbanquet.com).

Taking Tea in London

Once the sole province of genteel ladies in fancy hats, afternoon tea has become more democratic in the 21st century. While some tearooms—such as the wallet-draining £42-a-head tea service at the Ritz and the finicky Fortnum & Mason—still require a jacket and tie (and a bigger bank account), most happily welcome tourists in jeans and sneakers.

Tea Terms

The cheapest "tea" on the menu is generally a "cream tea"; the most expensive is the "champagne tea." **Cream tea** is simply a pot of tea and a homemade scone or two with jam and thick clotted cream. (For maximum pinkie-waving taste per calorie, slice your scone thin like a miniature loaf of bread.) **Afternoon tea**—what many Americans would call "high tea"—generally is a cream tea plus a tier of three plates holding small finger foods (such as cucumber sandwiches) and an assortment of small pastries. **Champagne tea** includes all of the goodies, plus a glass of bubbly. **High tea** to the English generally means a more substantial late-afternoon or early-evening meal, often served with meat or eggs.

Tearooms, which often also serve appealing light meals, are usually open for lunch and close about 17:00, just before dinner. At all the places listed below, it's perfectly acceptable for two people to order one afternoon tea and one cream tea (at about £5) and share the afternoon tea's goodies.

Places to Sip Tea

The Wolseley serves a good afternoon tea between their meal service. Split one with your companion and enjoy two light meals at a great price in classic elegance (£10 cream tea, £22.50 afternoon tea, served Mon-Fri 15:00-18:30, Sat 15:30-17:30, Sun 15:30-18:30, see full listing on page 198).

The Orangery at Kensington Palace serves a £20 "Orangery tea" and a £25-30 champagne tea in its bright white hall near Princess Di's former residence. You can also order treats à la carte. The portions aren't huge, but who can argue with eating at a princess' orangery or on the terrace? (Tea served 14:00-18:00, until 17:00 Nov-Feb, no reservations taken; a 10-minute walk through Kensington Gardens from either Queensway or High Street Kensington Tube stations to the orange brick building, about 100 yards from Kensington Palace—see map on page 176; tel. 020/3166-6113, www.hrp.org.uk.)

The Capital Hotel, a luxury hotel a half-block from Harrods, caters to weary shoppers with its intimate five-table, linen-tablecloth tearoom. It's where the ladies-who-lunch meet to decide whether to buy that Versace gown they've had their eye on. Even so, casual clothes, kids, and sharing plates are all OK (£30 afternoon tea, daily 14:30-17:30, call to book ahead—especially on weekends, 22 Basil Street—see map on page vi, Tube: Knightsbridge, tel. 020/7591-1202, www.capitalhotel.co.uk).

The **Fortnum & Mason** department store offers tea at several different restaurants within its walls. You can "Take Tea in the Parlour" for £18 (including ice-cream cakes; Mon-Sat 10:00-20:00, Sun 11:30-18:00), or try the all-out "Gallery Tea" for £26 (daily 15:00-18:00). But the pièce de resistance is their Diamond Jubilee Tea Salon, named in honor of the Queen's 60th year on the throne (and, no doubt, to remind visitors of Her Majesty's visit for tea here in 2012 with Camilla and Kate). At these royal prices, consider it dinner (£40-44, Mon-Sat 12:00-21:00, Sun 12:00-20:00, dress up a bit—no shorts, "children must be behaved," 181 Piccadilly—see map on page 192, smart to reserve online or by phone at least a week in advance, tel. 0845-602-5694, www.fortnumandmason. com).

Other Places Serving Good Tea: The **National Dining Rooms,** within the National Gallery on Trafalgar Square, offers a £17 afternoon tea (served 14:30-16:30, in Sainsbury Wing of National Gallery, Tube: Charing Cross or Leicester Square, tel. 020/7747-2525, www.peytonandbyrne.co.uk). The **National Café,** at the other end of the building, is a bit cheaper (£15 afternoon tea served 14:30-17:30). The **Café at Sotheby's,** on the ground floor of the auction giant's headquarters, gives shoppers a break from fashionable New Bond Street (£8-23, tea served Mon-Fri only 15:00-16:45, reservations smart, 34-35 New Bond Street—see map on page 190, Tube: Bond Street or Oxford Circus, tel. 020/7293-5077, www.sothebys. com/cafe).

Cheaper Options: Taking tea is not just for tourists and the wealthy—it's a true English tradition. If you want the teatime experience but are put off by the price, most department stores on Oxford Street (including those between Oxford Circus and Bond Street Tube stations) offer an afternoon tea. **John Lewis'** mod third-floor brasserie serves a nice afternoon tea platter from 15:30 (£12, on Oxford Street one block west of the Bond Street Tube station, tel. 020/7629-7711, www.johnlewis.com). Many museums and bookstores have cafés serving afternoon tea goodies à la carte, where you can put together a spread for less than £10—**Waterstones'** fifth-floor café and the **Victoria and Albert Museum** café are two of the best. **Teapod,** a modern place near the Tower Bridge, serves cream tea for £5.50 and afternoon tea for £13.50 (Mon-Fri 8:00-18:00, Sat-Sun 10:00-19:00, 31 Shad Thames, tel. 020/7407-0000).

In Bath: The **Pump Room** is reason enough to put off tea in

London—assuming you'll be visiting the city of Bath. This historic, elegant Georgian hall with live music lets anyone enjoy the ritual of tea in grand style (see page 419).

London Connections

By Plane

London has six airports; I've focused my coverage on the two most widely used—Heathrow and Gatwick—with a few tips for using the others (Stansted, Luton, London City, and Southend).

Phone numbers and websites for major airlines are listed in the appendix. For accommodations at or near the major airports, see page 185. A number of discount airlines fly into and out of London's smaller airports, making London a great jumping-off point for other destinations (see "Cheap Flights" on page 883).

Heathrow Airport

Heathrow Airport is one of the world's busiest airports. Think about it: 70 million passengers a year on 470,000 flights from 190 destinations riding 85 airlines, like some kind of global maypole dance. For Heathrow's airport, flight, and transfer information, call the switchboard at 0844-335-1801, or visit the helpful website at www.heathrowairport.com (airport code: LHR).

Heathrow has five terminals, numbered T-1 through T-5 (though T-2 is closed for renovation through mid-2014). Each terminal is served by different airlines and alliances; for example, T-5 is exclusively for British Air and Iberia Air flights, while T-1 serves mostly Star Alliance flights, such as United and Lufthansa. Screens posted throughout the airport identify which terminal each airline uses; this information should also be printed on your ticket or boarding pass.

To navigate, read signs and ask questions. You can walk between T-1, T-2 (when it's open), and T-3. From this central hub (called "Heathrow Central"), T-4 and T-5 split off in opposite directions (and are not walkable). To travel between the T-1/T-2/T-3 cluster and either T-4 or T-5, you can take a shuttle bus (free, serves all terminals), or the Tube (requires a ticket, serves all terminals). You can also connect T-1/T-2/T-3 and T-5 by Heathrow Express train (free, every 15-20 minutes, does not serve T-4).

If you're flying out of Heathrow, it's critical to confirm which terminal your flight will use (look carefully at your ticket/boarding pass, check online, or call your airline in advance)—because if it's

London's Airports

Luton
✈ **Luton**

✈ **Stansted**

N
Not to Scale

M25

ST. PANCRAS

PADDINGTON

LIVERPOOL STREET

Southend

✈ Southend

Reading

Windsor
#71 & #77

Rail Air Link

To Bath

✈ **Heathrow**

Thames

Tube

VICTORIA COACH STN.

VICTORIA

D.L.R.

London City

L o n d o n

EUROSTAR

Guildford

········· Rail
━━━━━ Eurostar Rail
──── Tube & D.L.R.
----- Bus

ALL BUSES ARE NATIONAL EXPRESS
UNLESS NOTED

✈ **Gatwick**

Ashford

To Paris →

↓ To Brighton

English Channel

LONDON

T-4 or T-5, you'll need to allow extra time. Taxi drivers generally know which terminal you'll need based on the airline, but bus drivers may not.

Services: Each terminal has an airport information desk (generally daily 5:00–22:00), car-rental agencies, exchange bureaus, ATMs, a pharmacy, a VAT refund desk (tel. 0845-872-7627, you must present the VAT claim form from the retailer here to get your tax rebate on items purchased in Britain—see page 17 for details), room-booking services, and baggage storage (£5/item for up to 4 hours, £8.50/item for 24 hours, daily 6:00–23:00, opens 30-60 minutes earlier in some terminals, www.excess-baggage.co.uk). Get online 24 hours a day at Heathrow's Internet access points (at each terminal—T-4's is up on the mezzanine level). Pay Wi-Fi is available throughout the airport (provided by Boingo, www.boingo.com). A post office is on the first floor of T-3 (departures area). Each terminal has cheap eateries.

Heathrow's small **"TI"** (tourist info shop), even though it's a for-profit business, is worth a visit if you're nearby and want to pick up free information: a simple map, the *London Planner,* and brochures (daily 6:30–22:00, 5-minute walk from T-3 in Tube station, follow signs to Underground; bypass queue for transit info to reach window for London questions).

Getting to London from Heathrow Airport

You have five basic options for traveling the 14 miles between Heathrow Airport and downtown London: Tube (£5.50/person), bus (£6-9/person), direct shuttle bus (£18/person), express train with connecting Tube or taxi (including connecting Tube fare, about £12/person for slower train, £23/person for faster train), or taxi (about £70/group).

By Tube (Subway): The Tube takes you from any Heathrow terminal to downtown London in 50-60 minutes on the Picca-

dilly Line (6/hour, buy ticket at Tube station ticket window or self-service machine). Depending on your destination in London, you may need to transfer (for example, if headed to the Victoria Station neighborhood, transfer at Earl's Court to the District line and ride two more stops). If you plan to use the Tube for transport in London, it may make sense to buy a Travelcard or pay-as-you-go Oyster card at the airport's Tube station ticket window. (For details on these passes, see page 57.) If your Travelcard covers only Zones 1-2, it does not include Heathrow (Zone 6); however, you can pay a small supplement for the initial trip from Heathrow to downtown.

If you're taking the Tube from downtown London *to* the airport, note that Piccadilly Line trains don't stop at every terminal. Trains either stop at T-4, then T-1/T-2/T-3 (also called Heathrow Central), in that order; or T-1/T-2/T-3, then T-5. When leaving central London on the Tube, allow extra time if going to T-4 or T-5; to ensure you get on a train going to your terminal, carefully check the destination before you board.

By Bus: Most buses depart from the outdoor common area called the Central Bus Station, located a five-minute walk from the T-1/T-2/T-3 complex. To connect between T-4 or T-5 and the Central Bus Station, use Heathrow's free shuttle buses; to reach T-5 only, you can ride the free Heathrow Express train.

National Express has regular service from Heathrow's Central Bus Station to Victoria Coach Station in downtown London, near several of my recommended hotels. While slow, the bus is affordable and convenient for those staying near Victoria Station (£6-9, 1-2/hour, less frequent from Victoria Station to Heathrow, 45-75 minutes depending on time of day, tel. 0871-781-8178, www.nationalexpress.com). A less-frequent National Express bus goes from T-5 directly to Victoria Coach Station.

By Shuttle: Heathrow Shuttle is an economical shuttle-bus service that goes to/from your hotel and your terminal at Heathrow. You'll share a minivan with other travelers who are also being picked up or dropped off, so it's not much of a time savings over taking the Tube (£18/person, progressive discounts for groups of two or more, 1 child under age 10 travels free with 2 adults, runs daily 4:00-18:00, book at least 24 hours in advance, office open daily 7:00-20:00, tel. 0845-257-8068, www.heathrowshuttle.com, info@heathrowshuttle.com). The rival **Hotel by Bus** service is pricey in comparison (£22.50/person).

By Train: Two different trains run between Heathrow Airport and London's Paddington Station. At Paddington Station, you're in the thick of the Tube system, with easy access to any of my recommended neighborhoods—my Paddington hotels are just outside the front door, and Notting Hill Gate is just two Tube stops away. The **Heathrow Connect** train is the slightly slower, much cheaper option, serving T-1/T-2/T-3 at a single station called Heathrow Central; use free transfers if you're coming from either T-4 or T-5 (£9.50 one-way, £19 round-trip, 2/hour Mon-Sat, 1-2/hour Sun, 40 minutes, tel. 0845-678-6975, www.heathrowconnect.com). The **Heathrow Express** train is fast and runs more frequently, but it's pricey (£20 one-way, £34 round-trip, £5 more if you buy ticket on board, 4/hour; 15 minutes to downtown from T-1/T-2/T-3, 21 minutes from T-5; transfer by shuttle required from T-4; covered by BritRail pass, daily 5:10-23:25, tel. 0845-600-1515, www.heathrowexpress.co.uk). At the airport, you can use the Heathrow Express as a free transfer between T-1/T-2/T-3 and T-5 (but not T-4).

By Taxi: Taxis from the airport cost £45-75 to west and central London (one hour). For four people traveling together, this can be a reasonable option. Hotels can often line up a cab back to the airport for about £40. For the cheapest taxi to the airport, don't order one from your hotel. Simply flag down a few and ask them for their best "off-meter" rate. Locals refer to hired cars that do the trip off-meter as "mini-cabs." These are reliable and generally cost about what you'd pay for a taxi in good traffic, but—with a fixed price—they can save you money when taxis are snarled in congestion with the meter running.

Getting to Bath from Heathrow Airport

Heathrow is well-connected by train to London, but it isn't tied directly into the regional rail network. You have several options for reaching Bath: train via London (fastest but expensive without a railpass), direct bus (cheaper but slower and relatively infrequent), train-and-bus combination (more frequent and sometimes shorter than the direct bus, can be cheaper than the direct train), or tour-company minibus. For details on all of these, see "Bath Connections" on page 444.

Gatwick Airport

More and more flights land at Gatwick Airport, which is half-way between London and the south coast (airport code: LGW, tel. 0844-892-0322, www.gatwickairport.com). Gatwick has two terminals, North and South, which are easily connected by a free monorail (two-minute trip, runs 24 hours daily). Note that boarding passes say "Gatwick N" or "Gatwick S" to indicate your terminal. British Airways flights generally use Gatwick North. The Gatwick Express trains (described next) stop only at Gatwick South. Schedules in each terminal show only arrivals and departures from that terminal.

Getting to London: Gatwick Express trains are clearly the best way into London from this airport. They shuttle conveniently between Gatwick South and London's Victoria Station, with many of my recommended hotels close by (£20 one-way, £35 round-trip, at least 10 percent cheaper if purchased online, 4/hour, 30 minutes, runs 5:00-24:00 daily, a few trains as early as 3:30, tel. 0845-850-1530, www.gatwickexpress.com). If you buy your tickets at the station before boarding, ask about their deal where three or four adults travel for the price of two. (If you see others in the ticket line, suggest buying your tickets together—you'll save up to 50 percent.) When going *to* the airport, at Victoria Station note that Gatwick Express has its own ticket windows right by the platform (tracks 13 and 14).

A train also runs between Gatwick South and **St. Pancras International Station** (£10, 3-5/hour, 45-60 minutes, www.firstcapitalconnect.co.uk)—useful for travelers taking the Eurostar train (to Paris or Brussels) or staying in the St. Pancras/King's Cross neighborhood.

Even slower, but cheap and handy to the Victoria Station neighborhood, you can take the **bus** (1.5 hours). National Express runs a bus from Gatwick direct to Victoria Station (£8, at least hourly, tel. 0871-781-8178, www.nationalexpress.com); easyBus has one going to near the Earls Court Tube stop (£2-10 depending on how far ahead you book, 2-3/hour, www.easybus.co.uk).

Getting to Bath: To get to Bath from Gatwick, you can go by train via Reading, or by bus via Heathrow. For details see page 444.

London's Other Airports

Stansted Airport: If you're using Stansted (airport code: STN, tel. 0844-335-1803, www.stanstedairport.com), you have several options for getting into or out of London. Two different **buses** connect the airport and London's Victoria Station neighborhood: National Express (£7-10, every 20 minutes, 1.75 hours, runs 24 hours a day, picks up and stops throughout London, ends at Victoria Coach Station, tel. 0871-781-8178, www.nationalexpress.com) and

Terravision (£9, 2-3/hour, 1.25 hours, ends at Green Line Coach Station just south of Victoria Station). Or you can take the faster, pricier Stansted Express **train** (£23.50, connects to London's Tube system at Tottenham Hale and Liverpool Street, 4/hour, 45 minutes, 4:30-23:00, www.stanstedexpress.com). Stansted is expensive by **cab**; figure £100-120 one-way from central London.

Luton Airport: For Luton (airport code: LTN, airport tel. 01582/405-100, www.london-luton.co.uk), there are two choices into or out of London. The fastest way to go is by **train** to London's St. Pancras International Station (£9.50-13.50 one-way, 1-5/hour, 25-45 minutes—check schedule to avoid slower trains, tel. 0845-712-5678, www.eastmidlandstrains.co.uk); catch the 10-minute shuttle bus (every 10 minutes, £1.50) from outside the terminal to the Luton Airport Parkway Station. The Green Line express **bus** #757 runs to Buckingham Palace Road, just south of Victoria Station, and stops en route near the Baker Street Tube station—best if you're staying near Paddington Station or in North London (£17, small discount for easyJet passengers who buy online, 2-4/hour, 1-1.5 hours, runs 24 hours, tel. 0844-801-7261, www.greenline.co.uk). If you're sleeping at Luton, consider easyHotel (see listing on page 184).

Other Airports: There's a slim chance you might use **London City Airport** (airport code: LCY, tel. 020/7646-0088, www.londoncityairport.com). To get into London, take the Docklands Light Railway (DLR) to the Bank Tube station, which is one stop east of St. Paul's on the Central Line (less than £5 one-way, covered by Travelcard, a bit cheaper with an Oyster card, 22 minutes, www.tfl.gov.uk/dlr). Some easyJet flights land even farther out, at **Southend Airport** (airport code: SEN, tel. 01702/608-100, www.southendairport.com). Trains connect this airport to London's Liverpool Street Station (£15 one-way, 3-8/hour, 55 minutes, www.greateranglia.co.uk).

Connecting London's Airports by Bus

A handy **National Express bus** runs between Heathrow, Gatwick, Stansted, and Luton airports—easier than having to cut through the center of London—although traffic can be bad and can increase travel times (tel. 0871-781-8178, www.nationalexpress.com).

From Heathrow Airport to: Gatwick Airport (1-6/hour, about 1.25 hours—but allow at least three hours between flights, £25), **Stansted Airport** (1-2/hour, about 1.5 hours, £25), **Luton Airport** (roughly hourly, 1-1.5 hours, £21).

By Train

Britain is covered by myriad rail systems (owned by different companies), which together are called National Rail. London, the country's major transportation hub, has a different train station for each region. There are nine main stations (see the map):

Euston—Serves northwest England, North Wales, and Scotland.

St. Pancras International—Serves north and south England, plus the Eurostar to Paris or Brussels (see "Crossing the Channel," later).

King's Cross—Serves northeast England and Scotland, including York and Edinburgh.

Liverpool Street—Serves east England, including Essex and Harwich.

London Bridge—Serves south England, including Brighton.

Waterloo—Serves south England, including Salisbury and Southampton.

Victoria—Serves Gatwick Airport, Canterbury, Dover, and Brighton.

Paddington—Serves south and southwest England, including Heathrow Airport, Windsor, Bath, South Wales, and the Cotswolds.

Marylebone—Serves southwest and central England, including Stratford-upon-Avon.

In addition, London has several smaller train stations that you're less likely to use, such as **Charing Cross** (serves southeast England, including Dover) and **Blackfriars.**

Any train station has schedule information, can make reservations, and can sell tickets for any destination. Most stations offer a baggage-storage service (£8.50/bag for 24 hours, look for *left luggage* signs); because of long security lines, it can take a while to check or pick up your bag (www.excess-baggage.com). For more details on the services available at each station, see www.national-rail.co.uk/stations.

For tips on buying train tickets—as well as your railpass options—see "Trains" on page 870 of the Appendix.

Train Connections from London

To Points West

From Paddington Station to: Bath (2/hour, 1.5 hours; also consider a guided Evan Evans tour by bus—see page 218), **Windsor** (2-3/hour, 30-40 minutes, easy change at Slough; or slower but direct from Waterloo Station, 2/hour, 50 minutes), **Oxford** (2/hour direct, 1 hour, more possible with transfer in Reading), **Penzance** (every 1-2 hours, 5-5.5 hours, possible change in Plymouth), and **Cardiff** (2/hour, 2 hours).

To Points North

From King's Cross Station: Trains run at least hourly, stopping

London's Major Train Stations

To North Wales & Glasgow

To Cambridge, York & Edinburgh

To Harwich

To Stratford-upon-Avon

To Canterbury & Dover and via Eurostar: Paris & Brussels

RAF MUSEUM LONDON

ST. PANCRAS INT'L

STRATFORD INT'L

To Heathrow Airport, Windsor (via Slough), Bath, S. Wales & Cotswolds

MARYLE-BONE

EUSTON

KING'S CROSS

PADDINGTON

TRAF. SQ.

LIVERPOOL STREET

DOCKLANDS

LONDON CITY AIRPORT

LONDON

VICTORIA

WATER-LOO

LONDON BRIDGE

O2 ARENA

CANARY WHARF ON ISLE OF DOGS

GREENWICH

Thames River

Kew Gardens

To Brighton

WIMBLEDON

HAMPTON COURT PALACE

To Gatwick Airport, Canterbury, Dover & Brighton

To Salisbury & Windsor (via Staines)

= Central London

5 Kilometers

5 Miles

LONDON

in **York** (2 hours), **Durham** (3 hours), and **Edinburgh** (4.5 hours). Trains to **Cambridge** also leave from here (2/hour, 45 minutes–1.25 hours).

From **Euston Station** to: **Conwy** (nearly hourly, 3.25 hours, transfer in Chester), **Liverpool** (at least hourly, 2 hours, more with transfer), **Blackpool** (hourly, 3-3.5 hours, transfer at Preston), **Keswick** (hourly, 4-4.5 hours, transfer to bus at Penrith), and **Glasgow** (1-2/hour, 4.5-5 hours).

From London's Other Stations

Trains run between London and **Canterbury,** leaving from St. Pancras International Station and arriving in Canterbury West (1-2/hour, 1 hour), as well as from London's Victoria Station and arriving in Canterbury East (2/hour, 1.25 hours).

Direct trains leave for **Stratford-upon-Avon** from Marylebone Station, located near the southwest corner of Regent's Park (5/day direct, more with transfers, 2.25 hours).

To Other Destinations: Dover (hourly, 1.25 hours, from St. Pancras International Station; also 2/hour, 2 hours, direct from Victoria Station or Charing Cross Station), **Brighton** (4-5/hour,

Public Transportation near London

LONDON

1 hour, from Victoria Station and London Bridge Station), **Portsmouth** (5/hour, 1.5-2 hours, most from Waterloo Station, a few from Victoria Station), and **Salisbury** (1-2/hour, 1.25 hours, from Waterloo Station).

By Bus

Buses are slower but considerably cheaper than trains for reaching destinations around Britain, and beyond. Most depart from **Victoria Coach Station,** which is one long block south of Victoria Station (near many recommended accommodations and Tube: Victoria). Inside the station, you'll find basic eateries, kiosks, and a helpful information desk stocked with schedules and ready to point you to your bus or answer any questions. Watch your bags carefully—luggage thieves thrive at the station.

Most domestic buses are operated by **National Express** (tel. 0871-781-8178, www.nationalexpress.com); their international departures are called **Eurolines** (www.eurolines.co.uk).

A smaller company called **Megabus** undersells National Express with deeply discounted promotional fares—the farther ahead you buy, the less you pay (some trips for just £1.50, toll tel. 0900-160-0900, www.megabus.com). While Megabus can be much cheaper than National Express—even half the price—they tend to be slower than their competitor and their routes mainly connect cities, not smaller towns). They also sell discounted train tickets on selected routes.

Try to avoid bus travel on Friday and Sunday evenings, when weekend travelers are more likely to make buses sell out.

To ensure getting a ticket—and to save money with special promotions—you can book your ticket in advance online (National Express charges a £1 fee) or over the phone (£2 surcharge). The cheapest pre-purchased tickets can be changed (for a £5 fee), but they're usually nonrefundable within 72 hours of travel. If you have a British mobile phone, you can order online and have a "text ticket" sent right to your phone.

Ideally you'll buy your tickets online. But if you must buy one at the station, try to arrive an hour before the bus departs—or drop by the day before. Ticketing machines are scattered around the station (separate machines for National Express/Eurolines and Megabus; you can buy either for today or for tomorrow); there's also a ticket counter near gate 21.

To Bath: The National Express bus leaves from Victoria Coach Station (nearly hourly, 3.5 hours, sample fares: one-way-£7-25, round-trip-£12-34). To get to Bath via Stonehenge, consider taking a guided bus tour from London to Stonehenge, Salisbury, and Bath, and abandoning the tour in Bath (confirm that Bath is the last stop on that particular tour; you can stow your bag in a compartment under the bus). **Evan Evans'** tour leaves from Victoria Coach Station every morning, stops in Salisbury (for a look at its magnificent cathedral) and Stonehenge, and then stops in Bath before returning to London (offered year-round—but order of stops can vary per day of week; they also offer another tour to Stonehenge and Bath via Windsor Castle; www.evanevanstours.co.uk). **Golden Tours** also runs a Stonehenge-Bath tour (departs from Fountain Square, located across from Victoria Coach Station, www.goldentours.com).

To Other Destinations: National Express buses go to **Oxford** (2/hour, about 2 hours; see page 518 for other bus options), **Cambridge** (every 60-90 minutes, 2-2.5 hours), **Canterbury** (about hourly, 2-2.5 hours), **Dover** (about hourly, 2.5-3.25 hours), **Brighton** (hourly, 2.5 hours), **Penzance** (5/day, 8.5-10 hours, overnight available), **Cardiff** (hourly, 3.25 hours), **Stratford-upon-Avon** (3/day, 3.5 hours), **Liverpool** (8/day direct, 5.25-6 hours, overnight available), **Blackpool** (4/day direct, 6.25-7 hours, overnight available), **York** (4/day direct, 5.25 hours), **Durham** (3/day direct, 6.5-7.5 hours, train is better), **Glasgow** (2-4/day direct, 8-9 hours, train is a much better option), **Edinburgh** (2/day direct, 8.75-9.75 hours, go by train instead).

To Dublin, Ireland: This bus/boat journey, operated by

National Express, takes 10-12 hours (£52, 1/day, departs Victoria Coach Station at 18:00, check in with passport one hour before). Consider a cheap 1.25-hour Ryanair flight instead (www.ryanair.com).

To the Continent: Especially in summer, buses run to destinations all over Europe, including Paris, Amsterdam, Brussels, and Germany (sometimes crossing the Channel by ferry, other times through the Chunnel). For any international connection, you need to check in with your passport one hour before departure. For details, call 0871-781-8178 or visit www.eurolines.co.uk. For information on crossing the Channel by bus, see "By Bus and Boat," later.

Crossing the Channel

By Eurostar Train

The fastest and most convenient way to get from Big Ben to the Eiffel Tower is by rail. Eurostar is the speedy passenger train that zips you (and up to 800 others in 18 sleek cars) from downtown London to downtown Paris or Brussels (1-2/hour, 2.5 hours) faster and more easily than flying. The train goes 190 mph both before and after the English Channel crossing. The actual tunnel crossing is a 20-minute, silent, 100-mile-per-hour nonevent. Your  ears won't even pop. Get ready for more high-speed connections: Germany's national railroad is negotiating to run bullet trains between Frankfurt, Amsterdam, and London by 2016.

Eurostar Fares

Unlike most trains in Western Europe, Eurostar is not covered by railpasses and always requires a separate, reserved train ticket. Eurostar fares (essentially the same between London and Paris or Brussels) vary depending on how far ahead you reserve, whether you can live with restrictions, and whether you're eligible for any discounts.

A **one-way, full-fare ticket** (with no restrictions on refundability) runs about $460 for first class and $300 for second class. **Discounts** can lower fares substantially (figure $60-160 for second class, one-way, usually not refundable or changeable) for children under age 12, youths under age 26, seniors age 60 or older, adults booking months ahead or traveling roundtrip, and railpass holders. The early bird gets the best price in each category. If you're ready to commit, you can book tickets as early as 4-9 months in advance at www.eurostar.com.

A tour company called BritainShrinkers sells one- or two-day tours to Paris, Brussels, or Bruges, enabling you to side-trip to these cities from London for less than most train tickets alone. For example, you'll pay £129 for a one-day Paris "tour" (unescorted Mon-Sat day trip with Métro pass; tel. 020/7404-5100, www.britainshrinkers.com). This can be a particularly good option if you need to get to Paris from London on short notice, when only the costliest Eurostar fares are available.

Buying Eurostar Tickets

Because only the most expensive (full-fare) ticket is fully refundable, don't reserve until you're sure of your plans. But if you wait too long, the cheapest tickets will get bought up.

Once you're confident about the time and date of your crossing, you can check and book fares by phone or online. Ordering online through Eurostar or major agents offers a print-at-home eticket option. You can also order by phone through Rail Europe at US tel. 800-387-6782 for home delivery before you go, or through Eurostar (tel. 0843-218-6186, priced in euros) and pick up your ticket at the train station. In Britain, tickets can be issued only at the Eurostar office in St. Pancras International Station. In continental Europe, you can buy your Eurostar ticket at any major train station in any country or at any travel agency that handles train tickets (expect a booking fee). You can purchase passholder discount tickets at Eurostar departure stations, through US agents, or by phone with Eurostar, but they may be harder to get at other train stations and travel agencies, and are a discount category that can sell out.

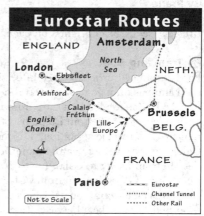

Remember that Britain's time zone is one hour earlier than France and Belgium's. Times listed on tickets are local times (departure from London is British time, arrival in Paris is French time).

Taking the Eurostar

Eurostar trains depart from and arrive at London's St. Pancras International Station. Check in at least 30 minutes in advance for your Eurostar trip. It's very similar to an airport check-in: You pass through airport-like security, show your passport to customs officials, and find a TV monitor to locate your departure gate. There are a few airport-like shops, newsstands, horrible snack bars, and cafés (bring food for the trip from elsewhere), pay-Internet terminals, and a currency-exchange booth with rates about the same as you'll find on the other end.

Crossing the Channel Without Eurostar

For speed and affordability, look into cheap flights. The old-fashioned ways of crossing the Channel are cheaper than Eurostar (taking the bus is cheapest). They're also twice as romantic, complicated, and time-consuming.

By Plane

Check with budget airlines for cheap round-trip fares to Paris or Brussels (see "Cheap Flights" on page 883).

By Train and Boat

For additional European ferry info, visit www.aferry.to. For UK train and bus info, go to www.traveline.org.uk.

To Paris: You'll take a train from London to the port of Dover (trains depart hourly from London's St. Pancras International Station to Dover's Priory Station, 1.25 hours), then catch a ferry to Calais, France, before boarding another train for Paris. P&O Ferries sail from Dover to Calais (up to 2/hour, 1.5 hours, www.poferries.com); TGV trains run from Calais to Paris.

To Amsterdam: Stena Line's Dutchflyer service combines train and ferry tickets between London and Amsterdam via the ports of Harwich and Hoek van Holland. Trains go from London's Liverpool Street Station to **Harwich** (hourly, 1.75 hours, most transfer in Manningtree). From Harwich, Stena Line ferries sail to Hoek van Holland (8 hours), where you can catch a train to Amsterdam (book ahead for best price, 13 hours total travel time, www.stenaline.co.uk, Dutch train info at www.ns.nl).

By Bus and Boat

You can take the bus from London direct to **Paris** (4/day, 8.25-9.75 hours), **Brussels** (4/day, 9 hours), or **Amsterdam** (4/day, 12 hours) from Victoria Coach Station (via ferry or Chunnel, day or overnight). Prices are the same to Paris, Brussels, or Amsterdam (around £60-70 one-way, cheaper in advance, tel. 0870-514-3219, www.eurolines.co.uk).

London's Cruise Ports

Many cruises begin, end, or call at one of several English ports offering easy access to London. Cruise lines favor two ports in particular: **Southampton**, 80 miles southwest of London; and **Dover**, 80 miles southeast of London (each one within about a 1.5-hour drive or train ride into the city).

While London offers plenty of public-transportation connections for getting you from your ship into town (explained below), most cruise lines offer an **"On Your Own" excursion** that includes an unguided bus trip from your ship to downtown London (usually Piccadilly Circus), then back again at an appointed time. While a bit pricey (usually around £65, compared to about £40 round-trip by train from Southampton, or about £36 from Dover), this can be efficient and avoids the potential stress of doing it on your own. Ask your cruise line for details.

Southampton Cruise Port

An important English port city for centuries, Southampton is best known for three ships that set sail from here and gained fame for very different reasons: the *Mayflower* in 1620, the *Titanic* in 1912, and the *Queen Mary* in 1936. Like many port cities, Southampton was badly damaged by WWII bombs, obliterating whatever cobbled charm it once had. These days, if Southampton is known for anything, it's for cruising. In 2012, 1.4 million cruise passengers passed through here.

Services: With 240,000 people, Southampton is a sprawling port town with a relatively compact downtown core. Everything is, to a point, walkable—though most of the cruise terminals (described later) are a long walk from the train station. The main drag stretching up from the waterfront, High Street (which becomes Above Bar higher up), is the easiest place to find ATMs, Wi-Fi hotspots, and a Boots pharmacy.

Transit Within Town: To reach the train station from your cruise ship, the easiest solution is to take a **taxi** (figure £5-8; around £125 one-way into central London). To save a bit of money, you can walk partway or all the way to the station; to shave some time off the walk, consider the free **Citylink bus,** which goes from the public ferry dock at Town Quay (between the two cruise port areas, where High Street meets the water, in front of the Red Funnel ticket office) up to the train station about every 15 minutes. As this bus doesn't stop at the cruise terminals themselves, you must walk to meet it: Figure 10 minutes from the Ocean Cruise Terminal, 15 minutes from the City Cruise Terminal, and even farther from the other terminals (from those, I'd take a taxi instead).

Cruise Terminals: Within Southampton's sprawling port (www.cruisesouthampton.com), cruises use two separate dock areas, each with two different terminals. All four terminal buildings have WCs, a rack of tourist brochures and maps, a basic café, a taxi stand out front, and possibly Wi-Fi (ask for the password). Most don't have ATMs or TIs.

Eastern Docks: The long piers jabbing straight out from Southampton have two cruise terminals (accessed through Dock Gate 4): **Ocean Cruise Terminal** at the near end (Berth 46, about a 5-minute walk to the mainland), and **QEII Cruise Terminal** at the tip (Berth 38/39, about a 15-minute walk to the mainland). From the QEII Terminal, I'd take a taxi; from Ocean Cruise Terminal, the walk-plus-bus combo is worth considering, though it takes longer: Walk down the pier and through Dock Gate 4, turn left, and follow the busy road (with the port on your left) about five more minutes to the Citylink bus stop at Town Quay.

Western Docks: This gloomy industrial zone, accessed through Dock Gate 8 (closer to town) or 10 (closer to the train station), hugs Southampton's coastline west of downtown. Shuffled between the endless parking lots and container shipping berths are two cruise terminals: **City Cruise Terminal,** close to the town center (Berth 101); and **Mayflower Cruise Terminal,** farther out (Berth 106). As Mayflower is a distant and dreary walk from the port gate, I'd spring for a taxi. From City Cruise Terminal, the walk-plus-bus combo may be worth considering: Exit the terminal to the right, then continue straight about 10 minutes through Dock Gate 8 and along the port to Town Quay and the free Citylink bus.

Trains to London: From Southampton Central Station, trains depart every 30 minutes to London's **Waterloo Station** (1.25 hours; additional departures require a change in Basingstoke and take 1.5 hours; slower trains go to London's Victoria Station in 2.5 hours). A same-day return (round-trip) ticket to London costs £39; a one-way ticket costs £34.10.

When returning to Southampton, be sure to get off at **Southampton Central Station;** the stop called Southampton Airport Parkway is much farther from the cruise port.

Sights in Southampton: While most people will make a beeline for London, the port city does have one sight worth considering: its excellent **SeaCity Museum,** with a beautifully presented exhibit about the *Titanic*. "Southampton's *Titanic* Story" explores every facet of the ill-fated ocean liner that set sail from here on April 10, 1912, and sank in the North Atlantic a few days later. Three-quarters of the *Titanic's* 897 crew members lived in Southampton (£8.50, daily 10:00-17:00, last entry at 15:00, next to the Civic Centre along Havelock Road, tel. 023/8083-3007, www.seacitymuseum.co.uk).

Dover Cruise Port

For generations, Dover—with its easy ferry connections across the English Channel to the Continent—was the place where many travelers first set foot in Britain. But since the advent of cheap flights and the high-speed Eurostar train beneath the Channel, Dover is most useful these days for its cruise port. If your cruise arrives in Dover, be sure to read the Dover chapter. If you'd rather stick around Dover, you can tour its impressive castle, described on page 286.

Services: Like much of southern England, Dover sits on a foundation of chalk; its famous white cliffs are visible from your cruise ship. The workaday city center is anchored by Market Square, with a handy **TI** (inside the Dover Museum). Across the square begins the mostly pedestrianized (but not particularly charming) main shopping drag, Cannon Street/Biggin Street, with ATMs, Wi-Fi hotspots, and a Boots pharmacy.

Cruise Terminals: Little Dover has a huge port, and cruises put in at its far western edge—at the **Western Docks,** along the extremely long Admiralty Pier (www.whitecliffscountry.org.uk). Near the port gate at the base of the pier, Terminal 1 is a converted old railway station; farther out at the tip, Terminal 2 is a modern facility.

Getting into Town: From either terminal, the best way into town (or to the train station) is by shuttle bus or taxi. The bright-blue **shuttle bus** makes a loop connecting the cruise terminals, Market Square, and Dover Castle (bus costs £3 one-way into town; add £1 to continue up to the castle; www.opentopbus.co.uk). From Market Square, it's a 15-minute walk to the train station: Head up Cannon Street (directly across the square from the TI) for three blocks, turn left onto Priory Street, continue straight through the big roundabout, and head slightly uphill on Folkestone Road; a half-block after the gas station, watch for *Dover Priory* signs on the right marking the station.

For more than two people, it's cheaper to take a **taxi,** which will run you about £7-8 whether you're going downtown, to the train station, or up to Dover Castle (figure around £150 one-way to central London).

I'd avoid the long, dreary, 30-minute **walk** from the cruise terminals into town (you'll have to go down the entire length of the pier to the mainland, turn right along the busy road, and trudge the rest of the way into town; to reach the train station, turn left up York Street, then left again on Folkestone Road).

Trains to London: From Dover Priory Station, you can choose between the faster "Javelin" train (hourly, 1.25 hours to London's **St. Pancras International Station;** £38.10 one-way, £40.60 same-day return, £71.20 anytime return) and the slower train (hourly to **Victoria Station** or hourly to **Charing Cross Station,** each 2 hours; £31.20 one-way, £31.40 same-day return). When choosing a train, consider this: St. Pancras International and Victoria stations are both well-connected to any point in the city by Tube or bus (and St. Pancras International is right next to the British Library), but Charing Cross Station is within easy walking distance of the sights many first-timers want to see (Trafalgar Square, National Gallery, West End, Whitehall, Houses of Parliament)—so the extra time spent on that train could save you time commuting to your sightseeing in London.

Returning to Dover, you'll get off at the **Dover Priory** train station.

GREENWICH, WINDSOR & CAMBRIDGE

Three of the best day-trip possibilities near London are Greenwich, Windsor, and Cambridge. Greenwich, which actually lies within London's city limits, is England's maritime capital; Windsor, west of the city, has a very famous castle; and Cambridge, an hour to the north, is England's best university town.

Other worthwhile destinations within day-tripping range of London include Stonehenge, Salisbury, Canterbury, Oxford, and York—all covered in other chapters in this book.

Getting Around

By Train: If day-tripping from London, take advantage of British Rail's discounts. The "off-peak day return" ticket is a round-trip fare that costs virtually the same as one-way, provided you depart London outside rush hour (usually after 9:30 on weekdays and anytime Sat-Sun). Be sure to specifically ask for the "day return" ticket (round-trip within a single day) rather than the more expensive standard "return." You can also save a little money if you purchase tickets before 18:00 the day before your trip.

By Train Tour: London Walks offers a variety of "Daytrips from London" tours year-round by train, including a Cambridge itinerary (£16 plus transportation and admissions costs, pick up their brochure at the TI or hotels, tel. 020/7624-3978, www.walks.com).

London Day Trips

50 Kilometers
50 Miles

ENGLAND

Luton

Cambridge

Stansted

Southend

North Sea

London

London City

WALES

Bath

Windsor

Greenwich

Heathrow

STONEHENGE

Gatwick

BUS

Salisbury

CHANNEL TUNNEL

To Paris & Brussels

English Channel

Greenwich

Tudor kings favored the palace at Greenwich (GREN-ich). Henry VIII was born here. Later kings commissioned architects Inigo Jones and Christopher Wren to beautify the town and palace, and William and Mary built a grand hospital to care for retired seamen (which later became a college for training naval officers).

Greenwich is England's maritime capital. Visitors come here for all things salty, including the *Cutty Sark* clipper ship, the area's premier attraction. The town is synonymous with timekeeping and astronomy, and at the Royal Observatory Greenwich, you can learn how those pursuits relate to seafaring. Greenwich also has stately Baroque architecture, appealing markets, a fleet of nautical shops, plenty of parks, kid-friendly museums, and hordes of tourists. Since many of the major sights here are free to enter, and you can travel between central London and Greenwich on a cheap Tube ticket, it's a wonderfully inexpensive day out. And where else can you set your watch with such accuracy?

Planning Your Time

Note that the town's popular market is closed Monday. Before or after the *Cutty Sark,* stroll to the Discover Greenwich exhibit and TI, drop into the grand buildings of the Old Royal Naval College, and walk the shoreline promenade. Greenwich's parks are picnic-perfect: Consider gathering picnic supplies before heading to the National Maritime Museum, and on through the park to the Royal Observatory Greenwich.

If you like to mix and match public transit, I'd suggest taking the boat to Greenwich for the scenery and commentary, and the Docklands Light Railway (DLR) back, especially if you want to stop at the Docklands on the way home. To visit the Docklands—the glittering forest of skyscrapers rising from a once-derelict port—hop off the train at the Canary Wharf stop for a quick stroll (see page 148).

Getting to Greenwich

It's a joy by boat or a snap by DLR.

By Boat: From central London, you can cruise scenically down the Thames to Greenwich. Various tour boats—with commentary and open-deck seating up top—leave from the piers at Westminster, Waterloo, and the Tower of London (2/hour, 1-1.25 hours); most boats have commentary only on the way to Greenwich, not on the way back.

Thames Clippers offers faster trips, with no commentary and only a small deck at the stern (departs every 20-30 minutes from several piers in central London, 40 minutes). Thames Clippers also connects Greenwich to the Docklands' Canary Wharf Pier (2-3/hour, 10 minutes).

For cruising details, see page 76.

By DLR Train: From Bank Station in central London (also accessible from the Monument Tube station), take the DLR to Cutty Sark Station in central Greenwich; it's one stop before the main—but less central—Greenwich Station (departs at least every 10 minutes, 20 minutes, all in Zone 2, covered by any Tube pass). Many DLR trains terminate at Canary Wharf, so make sure you get on one that continues to Lewisham or Greenwich.

Some DLR trains terminate at Island Gardens—you can generally catch another train to Greenwich's Cutty Sark Station within a few minutes. Or, disembark at Island Gardens for the unique experience of walking under the Thames into Greenwich: To reach the pedestrian tunnel, exit the station, cross the street and follow signs to *Island Gardens* for a good photo op. Then enter the red-brick Greenwich Foot Tunnel (opened in 1902), descend 86 spiral stairs (or ride the lift), hold your breath, and re-emerge on dry land at the bow of the *Cutty Sark*.

By Train: Mainline trains also go from London (Cannon Street and London Bridge stations) several times an hour to Greenwich Station (10-minute walk from the sights). Although the train is fast and cheap, the DLR is preferable because it drops you right in the heart of town.

By Bus: Catch bus #188 from Russell Square near the British Museum (about 45 minutes to Greenwich).

Orientation to Greenwich

Still well within the city limits of London, the Royal Borough of Greenwich—a title bestowed by the Queen in honor of her Diamond Jubilee—feels like a small town all its own. Covered markets and outdoor stalls make for lively weekends. Save time to browse the town. Wander beyond the touristy Church Street and Greenwich High Road to where flower stands spill onto the side streets and antique shops sell brass nautical knickknacks. King William Walk, College Approach, Nelson Road, and Turnpin Lane (all in the vicinity of Greenwich Market) are all worth a look. If you need pub grub, Greenwich has almost 100 pubs, with some boasting that they're mere milliseconds from the prime meridian.

Markets: Thanks to its markets, Greenwich throbs with day-trippers on weekends. The **Greenwich Market** is an entertaining mini-Covent Garden, located in the middle of the block between the Cutty Sark DLR station and the Old Royal Naval College—right on your way to the sights (Tue-Sun 10:00-17:30, closed Mon; farmers' market, arts and crafts, and food stands; antiques-only on Thu, www.greenwichmarket.net). The **Clocktower Market** sells old odds and ends at high prices on Greenwich High Road, near the post office (Sat-Sun and bank holidays only 10:00-17:00, www.clocktowermarket.co.uk).

Tourist Information

The TI is inside the Discover Greenwich visitors center (described later, under "Sights in Greenwich"), right next to the *Cutty Sark* entrance. From the DLR station, turn left, pass under the brick archway, cross the street, and continue straight ahead to the monumental gateway for the Old Royal Naval College complex; Discover Greenwich is just inside the gate on the left (daily 10:00-17:00, Pepys House, 2 Cutty Sark Gardens, tel. 0870-608-2000, www.visitgreenwich.org.uk).

Guided walks, which depart from the TI, offer an overview of the town and go past most of the big sights (£8, daily at 12:15 and 14:15, 1.5 hours; the only sights you enter are the Painted Hall and

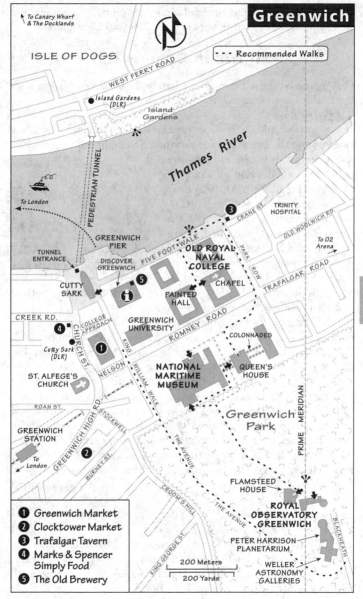

Greenwich

To Canary Wharf & The Docklands

---- Recommended Walks

ISLE OF DOGS

WEST FERRY ROAD

Island Gardens (DLR)

Island Gardens

Thames River

PEDESTRIAN TUNNEL

To London

GREENWICH PIER

TUNNEL ENTRANCE

DISCOVER GREENWICH

CUTTY SARK

FIVE FOOT WALK

OLD ROYAL NAVAL COLLEGE

CRANE ST.

TRINITY HOSPITAL

OLD WOOLWICH RD.

To O2 Arena

PARK ROW

TRAFALGAR ROAD

CHAPEL

PAINTED HALL

CREEK RD.

COLLEGE APPROACH

CHURCH ST.

Cutty Sark (DLR)

ST. ALFEGE'S CHURCH

ROAN ST.

GREENWICH STATION

To London

GREENWICH HIGH RD.

NELSON

KING WILLIAM WALK

STOCKWELL

BURNEY ST.

GREENWICH UNIVERSITY

ROMNEY ROAD

NATIONAL MARITIME MUSEUM

COLONNADES

QUEEN'S HOUSE

Greenwich Park

PRIME MERIDIAN

THE AVENUE

CROOM'S HILL

THE AVENUE

KING GEORGE ST.

FLAMSTEED HOUSE

ROYAL OBSERVATORY GREENWICH

PETER HARRISON PLANETARIUM

BLACKHEATH

WELLER ASTRONOMY GALLERIES

200 Meters
200 Yards

1 Greenwich Market
2 Clocktower Market
3 Trafalgar Tavern
4 Marks & Spencer Simply Food
5 The Old Brewery

GREENWICH

Chapel of St. Peter and St. Paul, and only on the 14:15 tour; the 12:15 tour leaves you at the door of the Naval Observatory).

Sights in Greenwich

I've organized these listings as a handy sightseeing walk through town, starting near the Cutty Sark DLR station.

▲▲Cutty Sark

The Scottish-built *Cutty Sark* was the last of the great China tea clippers and the queen of the seas when first launched in 1869. She

was among the fastest clippers ever built, the culmination of centuries of ship design. With 32,000 square feet of sail—and favorable winds— she could travel 300 miles in a day. But as a new century dawned, steamers began to outmatch sailing ships for speed, and by the mid-1920s the *Cutty Sark* was the world's last oper-

ating clipper ship. After a stint as a training ship, she was retired and turned into a museum in the 1950s.

Following a five-year-long restoration, interrupted by a devastating fire, the ship reopened to the public in the spring of 2012. The spectacular new display space has one major drawback: The glass building obscures the elegant lines of the hull that gave the *Cutty Sark* her record-breaking speed (one critic groused that the ship now "looks like it has run aground in a giant greenhouse"). On the plus side, the building allows visitors to walk directly below the ship, which has been raised 11 feet above her dry dock. Above deck, the ship's rigging has been restored to original specifications, while below deck, displays explore the *Cutty Sark*'s 140-year history and the cargo she carried—everything from tea to wool to gunpowder—as she raced between London and ports all around the world.

Cost and Hours: £12, includes voluntary 10 percent donation, kids ages 5-15-£6.50, free for kids under age 5, family tickets available; daily 10:00-17:00 but occasionally closed Mon, may stay open until 18:00 at busiest times; last entry one hour before closing; £5 guidebook available but hardly necessary, reservation tel. 020/8312-6608, www.rmg.co.uk/cuttysark).

Crowd-Beating Tips: The ship can get busy on school holidays and on weekends. To skip the line, you can reserve ahead online or by phone, or just try showing up around 13:00, when there's often a lull in visitors.

Visiting the *Cutty Sark:* The first deck you'll visit harkens back to the ship's days in the Chinese tea trade...which didn't last long,

GREENWICH

as the Suez Canal soon opened, allowing steam-powered ships to reach China much faster than sailboats. The *Cutty Sark* turned to trading wool with Australia, as explored on the next deck up. This "Tween Deck" is full of not-quite-gimmicky displays that mostly succeed in making the ship's history come alive, even for adults. Find the fun video game that lets you attempt to beat Captain Woodget's record voyage sailing a wool-laden *Sark* from Sydney to London. Sit on the tilting benches of tea crates for a seaborne feel, try your hand at some knots, enjoy the oddly mesmerizing video at the stern, and get the figurehead's take on *Sark* history in the bow.

Sailing fans will like the gorgeously restored top deck best. Notice how pathetic the crew's mattresses were, and don't miss the video showing the rigger's-eye-view as he climbs high above the deck. Your visit ends down below, where you can take a coffee break directly under the shiny stern (it may gleam like gold, but the hull's covering is actually an alloy of copper and zinc). Near the bow is a colorful collection of figureheads from other ships. On the floor directly under the front of the hull, note the compass rose that shows how many days at sea it'd take to reach major ports from here.

Discover Greenwich

This visitors center is located at the corner of the Old Royal Naval College closest to the *Cutty Sark*. While it's hardly a museum, it offers a decent introduction to Greenwich and some fun exhibits for kids. In the center, a model of the town lights up to tell its history. Surrounding the model are displays and artifacts from various people who have left their mark on the town, along with exhibits about the architecture and construction of Greenwich's fine buildings. Tours of the Royal Naval College (described next) leave from the reception desk. Adjoining Discover Greenwich are the TI and a recommended pub, The Old Brewery.

Cost and Hours: Free, daily 10:00-17:00, tel. 020/8269-4799, www.oldroyalnavalcollege.org.

▲Old Royal Naval College

The college was originally a hospital founded by Queen Mary II and King William III in 1692 as a charity to care for retired or injured naval officers (called pensioners). William and Mary spared no expense, hiring the great Christopher Wren to design the complex (though other architects completed it). Its days as a hospital ended in 1869, and it served as a college for training naval officers from 1873 to 1998. Now that the Royal Navy has moved out, the public is invited to view the college's elaborate Painted Hall and Chapel of St. Peter and St. Paul, which are in symmetrical buildings that face each other overlooking a broad riverfront park.

Cost and Hours: Free, daily 10:00-17:00, sometimes closed for private events, service Sun at 11:00 in chapel—all are welcome, www.ornc.org.

Tours: Guides give one-hour tours covering the hall and chapel, along with other areas not open to the general public (£5, daily at 14:00, departs from Discover Greenwich, call ahead to check availability, tel. 020/8269-4799).

❍ **Self-Guided Tour:** Each building sells a descriptive guide (50p-£1), or you can buy the fun *Nasty Naval College* brochure, with offbeat facts about the place (£1). Volunteers are often standing by to answer questions.

Painted Hall: Originally intended as a dining hall for pensioners, this sumptuously painted room was deemed too glorious (and, in the winter, too cold) for that purpose. So almost as soon as it was completed, it became simply a place to impress visitors.

Enter the hall, climb the stairs, and gape up at one of the largest painted ceilings in Europe—112 feet long. It's a big propaganda scene, glorifying the building's founders, Queen Mary II and King William III (who, as a Protestant monarch, had recently trounced the Catholic French King Louis XIV in a pivotal bat-

tle). Crane your neck—or use the clever wheeled mirrors—to examine the scene. In the center are William and Mary. Under his foot, William is crushing a dark figure with a broken sword...Louis XIV. William is handing a red cap (representing liberty) to the woman on the right, who holds the reins of a white horse (symbolizing Europe). On the left, a white-robed woman hands him an olive branch, a sign of peace. The message: William has granted Europe liberty by saving it from the tyranny of Louis XIV. Below the royal couple, the Spirit of Architecture shows them the plans for this very building (commemorating the sad fact that Mary died before its completion). Ringing the central image are the four seasons (represented by Zodiac signs), the four virtues, and—at the top and bottom—a captured Spanish galleon and a British man-of-war battleship.

Up the steps at the end of the room, along the wall of the **upper hall,** is a portrait of the family of King George I. On the right is the artist who spent 19 years of his life painting this hall,

James Thornhill (he finally finished it in 1727). He's holding out his hand—reportedly, he didn't feel he was paid enough for this Sistine-sized undertaking.

• *Exit the hall, and cross the field to enter the...*

Chapel of St. Peter and St. Paul: Not surprisingly, you'll sense a nautical air in this fine chapel. Notice the rope motif in the floor tiles down the aisle. The painting above the altar, by American Benjamin West, depicts the shipwreck of St. Paul on the island of Malta. According to the Bible, Paul disturbed a poisonous viper but managed to throw it in a fire, miraculously without being harmed. Soon after the chapel was completed, it was gutted by a fire and had to be redecorated all over again. The plans were too ambitious, so the designers cut corners. Some of the columns and capitals are fake, and the "sculptures" lining the nave high above are actually *trompe l'oeil*—3-D paintings meant to look real. But some items, such as the marble frame around the main door, are finely crafted from expensive materials.

• *Leave the chapel, and walk straight down to the water—enjoying the sweeping views across to the Docklands. When you hit the river, turn right for a quick...*

Riverside Stroll

Looking back toward the Old Royal Naval College, notice how it's split into two parts; reportedly, Queen Mary didn't want the view from the Queen's House blocked. The college's twin-domed towers (one giving the time, the other the direction of the wind) frame the Queen's House, and the Royal Observatory Greenwich crowns the hill beyond.

Wander east along the Thames on Five Foot Walk (named for the width of the path). From here you can see the big, white, spiky

O2 dome a mile downstream. This stadium languished for nearly a decade after its controversial construction and brief life as the Millennium Dome. Intended to be a world's fair-type site and the center of London's year 2000 celebration, it ended up as the topic of heated debates about cost overruns and its controversial looks.

The site was finally bought by a developer a few years ago and re-christened "The O2" (a telecommunications company paid for the naming rights). Today it hosts sporting events and concerts. Next to the O2 are the towers of the Emirates Air Line aerial gondola, which ferries passengers between the O2 and across the Thames to, essentially, nowhere.

Continuing downstream, just past the college, you'll find the recommended **Trafalgar Tavern.** Dickens knew the pub well, and he used it as the setting for the wed-

ding breakfast in *Our Mutual Friend.* Built in 1837 in the Regency style to attract Londoners downriver, the up-stairs Nelson Room is still used for weddings. Its formal moldings and elegant windows with balconies over the Thames are a step back in time and worth a peek.

• *From the Trafalgar Tavern, walk two long blocks up Park Row. After crossing busy Romney Road, turn right (through the gate near the corner) into the park. The palatial buildings in the middle of the park are the Queen's House and the National Maritime Museum; the Royal Observatory Greenwich is on the hilltop beyond. Together, this trio is known as the Royal Museums of Greenwich.*

Queen's House

This building, the first Palladian-style villa in Britain, was de-signed in 1616 by Inigo Jones for James I's wife, Anne of Denmark. All traces of the queen are long gone, and the Great Hall and Royal Apartments now serve as an art gallery for the National Maritime Museum. Predictably, most of the art is nautical-themed, with plenty of paintings of ships and sea battles, and portraits of admirals and captains. Among these is the great J. M. W. Turner painting *The Battle of Trafalgar* (1824), the artist's only royal commission. The painting is often out on loan, so ask at the entry before you look for it. If you're short on time or energy, skip this sight.

Cost and Hours: Free, daily 10:00-17:00, last entry 30 minutes before closing, tel. 020/8858-4422, www.rmg.co.uk.

Tours: Skip the free (and outdated) audioguide and instead ask about the daily tour (free, 2-3/day).

• *Exiting the Queen's House, walk toward the hill and turn right. About 300 yards farther on you'll find the...*

▲National Maritime Museum

Great for anyone interested in the sea, this museum holds everything from a giant working paddlewheel to the uniform Admiral Horatio Nelson wore when he was killed at Trafalgar (look for the bullet hole, in the left shoulder). A big glass roof tops three levels of slick, modern, kid-friendly exhibits about all things seafaring.

Cost and Hours: Free, daily 10:00-17:00, ground floor until 20:00 on Thu, last entry 30 minutes before closing, tel. 020/8858-

4422, www.rmg.co.uk. The museum hosts frequent family-oriented events—singing, treasure hunts, and storytelling—particularly on weekends; ask at the desk. Inside, listen for announcements alerting visitors to free tours on various topics.

Visiting the Museum: The Explorers exhibit covers early expeditions and an ill-fated Arctic trip, complete with a soundtrack of creaking wooden ships and crashing waves. One room displays stained-glass windows honoring members of London's Baltic Exchange (an important shipping consortium) killed in World War I, while the somber Atlantic Worlds hall thoughtfully describes how the movements of goods, ideas, and enslaved people shaped the 17th to 19th centuries. Kids like the All Hands and Bridge galleries, where they can send secret messages by Morse code and operate a miniature dockside crane. Along with displays of lighthouse technology and a whaling cannon, you'll see model ships, nautical paintings, and various salty odds and ends. While some parts of the museum are closed for ongoing renovation, there's still plenty to see.

• *The final sight in town—the Royal Observatory Greenwich—is at the top of the hill just behind the National Maritime Museum. To reach it, cross through the colonnade connecting the museum and the Queen's House, then follow the crowds as they huff up the steep hill (allow 10-15 minutes).*

As you hike up, look along the observatory's roof for the red **Time Ball** *(also visible from the Thames), which drops daily at 13:00.*

▲▲Royal Observatory Greenwich

Located on the prime meridian (0° longitude), the observatory is famous as the point from which all time is measured. The observatory's early work, however, had nothing to do with coordinating the world's clocks to Greenwich Mean Time (GMT). The observatory was founded in 1675 by Charles II for the purpose of improving navigation by more accurately charting the night sky. Today, the Greenwich time signal is linked with the BBC (which broadcasts the famous "pips" worldwide at the top of the hour). A visit here gives you a taste of the sciences of astronomy, timekeeping, and seafaring—and how they all meld together—along with great views over Greenwich and the distant London skyline. The Royal Observatory grounds are made up of the observatory (with the prime meridian and three worthy exhibits), the Weller Astronomy Galleries, and the Peter Harrison Planetarium.

The Longitude Problem

Around 1700, as the ships of seafaring nations began to venture farther from their home bases, the alarming increase in the number of shipwrecks made it clear that navigational tools had to be improved. Determining latitude—the relative position between the equator and the North or South Pole—was straightforward; sailors needed only to measure the angle of the sun at noon. But figuring out longitude, or their east-west position, was not as easy without a fixed point (such as the equator) from which to measure.

In 1714, the British government offered the £20,000 Longitude Prize. Two successful solutions emerged, and both are tied to Greenwich.

The first approach was to observe the position of the moon, which moves in relation to the stars. Sailors would compare the night sky they saw with the sky over Greenwich by consulting a book of tables prepared by Greenwich astronomers. This told them how far they were from Greenwich—their longitude. Visitors to the Royal Observatory can still see the giant telescopes—under retractable roofs—that were used to carefully chart the heavens to create these meticulous tables.

The second approach was to create a clock that would remain completely accurate on voyages—no easy feat back then, when turbulence and changes in weather and humidity made timepieces notoriously unreliable at sea. John Harrison spent 45 years working on this problem, finally succeeding in 1760 with his fourth effort, the H4 (which won him the Longitude Prize). All four of his attempts are on display at the Royal Observatory.

So, how can a clock determine longitude? Every 15° of longitude equals an hour when comparing the difference in sunrise or sunset times between two places. For example, the time gap between Greenwich and New York City is five hours, which translates into a longitudinal difference of 75°. Equipped with an accurate timepiece set to Greenwich Mean Time, sailors could figure out their longitude by comparing sunset time at their current position with sunset time back in Greenwich.

Notice that both approaches use Greenwich as a baseline—either on an astral map or on a clock. That's why, to this day, the prime meridian and official world time are both centered in this unassuming London suburb.

If your only interest in the Royal Observatory is the famous prime meridian line, you can enter through the iron gate near the entrance for a free, more simplistic (and significantly less crowded) display of the prime meridian. Under the analog clock just outside the courtyard, see how your foot measures up to the foot where the public standards of length are cast in bronze.

Observatory: £7, ticket good for re-entry for one year, £11.50 combo-ticket with planetarium saves money if you visit both, audioguide-£3.50, 1 hour; daily 10:00-17:00, later in summer—can be as late as 19:00, last entry 30 minutes before closing.

Weller Astronomy Galleries: Free, daily 10:00-17:00, last entry at 16:30.

Peter Harrison Planetarium: £6.50, £11.50 combo-ticket with observatory; 30-minute shows generally run every hour (usually Mon-Fri 13:00-16:00, Sat-Sun 11:00-16:00, fewer shows in winter, schedule can change from day to day). Confirm times by calling ahead, checking online, or picking up a flier (which you'll see around the observatory). As these shows can sell out, consider calling ahead to order tickets.

Information: Tel. 020/8858-4422, www.rmg.co.uk.

● **Self-Guided Tour:** Entering the complex, you're directed either to the observatory entrance or the Weller Astronomy Galleries. Since the observatory is more interesting, do that first (but note that the Weller Galleries won't let you in after 16:30).

• *After purchasing your ticket, enter the courtyard.*

Running through the middle of this space is The Line—the **prime meridian.** Visitors wait patiently to have their photographs taken as they straddle the line in front of the monument, with one foot in each hemisphere. While watching all this fuss over a little line, consider that—unlike the equator—the placement of the prime meridian is totally arbitrary. It could well have been at my house, in Timbuktu, or just a few feet over—as, for a time, it was (the trough along the building's roofline shows where one astronomer had placed it). While waiting for your turn, set your wristwatch to the digital clock showing GMT to a tenth of a second.

Three different attractions are scattered around this courtyard. First, hiding in a corner is a **camera obscura.** This thrillingly low-tech device projects a live image from Greenwich onto a flat disc in a darkened room simply by manipulating light, without electricity or machinery (although the image can be pretty dim on cloudy days). Imagine how astonishing it was in the days before television.

The smaller building is the **Flamsteed House,** named for John Flamsteed, the first king-appointed Astronomer Royal (in 1675). It contains the apartments that he lived in and the Wren-designed Octagon Room, where he carried out some of his work.

Downstairs is a fascinating exhibit on the "Longitude Problem" and how it was solved (see sidebar). Also on display are all four of John Harrison's sea clocks. Compared to his other contraptions, the fourth and final attempt looks like an oversized pocket watch. But, in terms of its impact, this little timepiece is right up there with the printing press, the cotton gin, the telegraph, and the money belt on the scale of human achievement.

The **Telescopes Exhibition,** in the larger house, has a wide assortment of historical telescopes, including a couple of room-sized ones. Upstairs from the gift shop, a skippable exhibit explores the role of timekeeping in our society.

• *Now head out back.*

Walk past the giant rusted-copper cone top of the planetarium. The building beyond houses the **Weller Astronomy Galleries,** where interactive, kid-pleasing displays allow you to guide a space mission and touch a 4.5-billion-year-old meteorite. You can also buy tickets for and enter the state-of-the-art, 120-seat **Peter Harrison Planetarium** from here.

Before you leave the observatory grounds, enjoy the **view** from the overlook—the symmetrical royal buildings, the Thames, and the Docklands and its busy cranes (including the prominent Ca-

nary Wharf Tower, with its pyramid cap). You may be able to see—poking up between buildings—the white stadium and red Orbit tower in Queen Elizabeth Olympic Park. To the right is the huge O2 dome and the towers of the Emirates Air Line gondola. To the left lies the square-mile City of London, with skyscrapers and the dome of St. Paul's Cathedral. The Shard is to the far left. At night (17:00-24:00), look for the green laser beam the observatory projects into the sky (best viewed in winter), which extends along the prime meridian for 15 miles.

Eating in Greenwich

The colorful **Greenwich Market** hosts food stalls, great for assembling a picnic (Tue-Sun 10:00-17:30, closed Mon, down the street from Cutty Sark DLR station). Another handy place to pick up ready-made food is **Marks & Spencer Simply Food,** between the

DLR station and the *Cutty Sark* dry dock (Mon-Sat 8:00-20:30, Sun 9:30-20:30, 55 Greenwich Church Street).

The Trafalgar Tavern, with a casual pub and elegant ground-floor dining room, is a historical place for an overpriced meal (£12-17 main courses in restaurant, food served Mon-Sat 12:00-22:00, Sun 12:00-16:00, Park Row, tel. 020/8858-2909).

The Old Brewery, in the Discover Greenwich center on the Old Royal Naval College grounds, is an upscale gastropub decorated with all things beer. An adjacent café serves cheap lunches. A brewery on this site once provided the daily ration of four pints of beer for pensioners at the hospital. Today it's a microbrewery offering 50 different beers, while a beer sommelier suggests the right pairings with food on the menu (£4 bar snacks, £12 lunches, part of the pub becomes a fancier restaurant in the evenings with £5-10 starters and £10-17 main courses; daily 10:00-23:00, lunch 12:00-17:00, dinner from 18:00, tel. 020/3327-1280).

Windsor

Windsor, a compact and easy walking town of about 30,000 people, originally grew up around the royal residence. In 1070, William the Conqueror continued his habit of kicking Saxons out of their various settlements, taking over what the locals called "Windlesora" (meaning "riverbank with a hoisting winch")—which eventually became "Windsor." William built the first fortified castle on a chalk hill above the Thames; later kings added on to his early designs, rebuilding and expanding the castle and surrounding gardens.

By setting up their primary residence here, modern monarchs increased Windsor's popularity and prosperity—most notably, Queen Victoria, whose stern statue glares at you as you approach the castle. After her death, Victoria rejoined her beloved husband, Albert, in the Royal Mausoleum at Frogmore House, a mile south of the castle in a private section of the Home Park (house and mausoleum rarely open). The current Queen considers Windsor her primary residence, and the one where she feels most at home. She generally hangs her crown here on weekends, using it as an escape from her workaday grind at Buckingham Palace in the city. You can tell if Her Majesty is in residence by checking to see which flag is flying above the round tower: If it's the royal standard (a red, yellow, and blue flag) instead of the Union Jack, the Queen is at home.

While 99 percent of visitors just come to tour the castle and go, some enjoy spending the night. Daytime crowds trample Windsor's charm, which is most evident when the tourists are gone. Consider overnighting here—parking and access to Heathrow Airport are easy, and an evening at the horse races (on Mondays) is hoof-pounding, heart-thumping fun.

Getting to Windsor

By Train: Windsor has two train stations—Windsor & Eton Central (5-minute walk to palace; TI in adjacent shopping center) and Windsor & Eton Riverside (5-minute walk to palace and TI). First Great Western trains run between London's Paddington Station and Windsor & Eton Central (2-3/hour, 30-40 minutes, easy change at Slough; £9.50 one-way standard class, £10-13 same-day return, www.firstgreatwestern.co.uk). South West Trains run between London's Waterloo Station and Windsor & Eton Riverside (2/hour, 50 minutes; £9.50 one-way standard class, £10-17.50 same-day return, info tel. 0845-748-4950, www.nationalrail.co.uk). If deciding between these, notice that while Waterloo is more central within London and has a direct connection, it takes nearly twice as long as the alternative from Paddington.

If you're day-tripping into London *from* Windsor, ask at the train station about combining a same-day return train ticket with a One-Day Travelcard—you'll end up with one ticket that covers rail transportation to and from London and doubles as an all-day Tube and bus pass in town (£13-22, lower price for travel after 9:30, rail ticket also qualifies you for some half-price London sightseeing discounts—ask or look for brochure at station, or go to www.daysoutguide.co.uk).

By Bus: Green Line buses #701 and #702 run from London's Victoria Colonnades (between the Victoria train and coach stations) to the Parish Church stop on Windsor's High Street, before continuing on to Legoland (1-2/hour, 1.5 hours to Windsor, £5.50-9.50 one-way, £9-16 round-trip, prices vary depending on time of day, tel. 01753/524-144, www.rainbowfares.com).

By Car: Windsor is about 20 miles from London and just off Heathrow Airport's landing path. The town (and then the castle and Legoland) is well-signposted from the M-4 motorway. It's a convenient first stop if you're arriving at and renting a car from Heathrow, and saving London until the end of your trip.

From Heathrow Airport: Buses #71 and #77 run between

Terminal 5 and Windsor, dropping you in the center of town on Peascod Street (about £8, 1-3/hour, 50 minutes, tel. 01753/524-144). London black cabs can (and do) charge whatever they like from Heathrow to Windsor; avoid them by calling a local cab company, such as Windsor Radio Cars (£25, tel. 01753/677-677, www.windsorcars.com).

Orientation to Windsor

Windsor's pleasant pedestrian shopping zone litters the approach to its famous palace with fun temptations. You'll find most shops and restaurants around the castle on High and Thames streets, and down the pedestrian Peascod Street (PESS-cot), which runs perpendicular to High Street.

Tourist Information

The TI is immediately adjacent to Windsor & Eton Central Station, in the Windsor Royal Shopping Centre's Old Booking Hall (May-Sept Mon-Sat 10:00-17:00, Sun 10:00-16:00; Oct-April Sun-Fri 10:00-16:00, Sat 10:00-17:00; tel. 01753/743-900, www.windsor.gov.uk). The TI sells discount tickets to Legoland (see "More Sights in Windsor," later).

Arrival in Windsor

By Train: The train to Windsor & Eton Central Station from Paddington (via Slough) spits you out into the Windsor Royal shopping pavilion (which houses the TI), only a few minutes' walk from the castle. If you arrive instead at Windsor & Eton Riverside Station (from Waterloo Station), you'll see the castle as you exit—just follow the wall to the castle entrance.

By Car: Follow signs from the M-4 motorway for pay-and-display parking in the center. River Street Car Park is closest to the castle, but pricey and often full. The cheaper, bigger Alexandra Car Park (near the riverside Alexandra Gardens) is farther west. To walk to the town center from the Alexandra Car Park, head east through the tour-bus parking lot toward the castle. At the souvenir shop, walk up the stairs (or take the elevator) and cross the overpass to Windsor & Eton Central Station. Just beyond the station, you'll find the TI in the Windsor Royal Shopping Centre. Yet another, even cheaper option is the King Edward VII Avenue car-park-and-ride, east of the castle on B-470, which includes a shuttle bus into town.

Helpful Hints

Festivals: In addition to the Royal Ascot horse races (described later, under "Beyond Windsor"), Windsor hosts a tattoo for

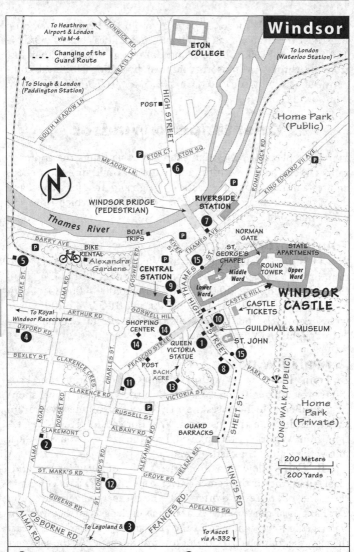

Windsor

To Heathrow
Airport & London
via M-4

- - - Changing of the
Guard Route

ETON
COLLEGE

To London
(Waterloo Station)

To Slough & London
(Paddington Station)

ETONWICK RD.

KEATS LN.

SOUTH MEADOW LN.

HIGH STREET

POST

Home Park
(Public)

MEADOW LN.

ETON CT.

ETON SQ.

ROMNEY LOCK RD.

KING EDWARD VII AVE.

N

WINDSOR BRIDGE
(PEDESTRIAN)

RIVERSIDE
STATION

Thames River

BOAT
TRIPS

THAMES AVE.

NORMAN
GATE

ST.
GEORGE'S
CHAPEL

STATE
APARTMENTS

BARRY AVE.

BIKE
RENTAL

Alexandra
Gardens

GOSWELL RD.

RIVER ST.

THAMES ST.

CENTRAL
STATION

Middle
Ward

ROUND
TOWER

Upper
Ward

DUKE ST.

ALMA RD.

Lower
Ward

WINDSOR
CASTLE

To Royal
Windsor Racecourse

ARTHUR RD.

GOSWELL HILL

CASTLE HILL

CASTLE
TICKETS

OXFORD RD.

SHOPPING
CENTER

PEASCOD STREET

GUILDHALL & MUSEUM

ST. JOHN

BEXLEY ST.

CLARENCE CRES.

CHARLES ST.

QUEEN
VICTORIA
STATUE

HIGH STREET

PARK ST.

Home
Park
(Private)

POST

BACH
ACRE

CLARENCE RD.

VICTORIA ST.

SHEET ST.

CLAREMONT

DORSET RD.

RUSSELL ST.

ALBANY RD.

ALEXANDRA RD.

HELENA RD.

GUARD
BARRACKS

KING'S RD.

LONG WALK (PUBLIC)

ALMA ROAD

ST. MARK'S RD.

ST. LEONARD'S RD.

GROVE RD.

200 Meters

200 Yards

QUEENS RD.

OSBORNE RD.

ALMA RD.

To Legoland &

FRANCES RD.

ADELAIDE SQ.

To Ascot
via A-332

1 Mercure Windsor Castle Hotel
2 Langton House B&B
3 To Park Farm B&B
4 Dee & Steve's B&B
5 76 Duke Street B&B
6 Crown & Cushion Rooms
7 Bel & The Dragon
8 Cornucopia Bistro

9 The Duchess of Cambridge Pub
10 The Crooked House Teahouse
11 Meimo Restaurant
12 Saffron Restaurant
13 Library (Internet Access)
14 Grocery Stores (2)
15 Legoland Bus Stops (2)

WINDSOR

four days in May, when troops march in military regalia at the public Home Park, just northeast of the castle.

Internet Access: Get online at the **library,** located on Bachelors' Acre, between Peascod and Victoria Streets (£1.50/30 minutes, free Wi-Fi, Mon and Thu 9:30-17:00, Tue 9:30-20:00, Wed 14:00-17:00, Fri 9:30-19:00, Sat 9:30-15:00, closed Sun, tel. 01753/743-940, www.rbwm.gov.uk).

Supermarkets: Pick up picnic supplies at **Marks & Spencer** (Mon-Sat 8:00-19:00, closed Sun, 130 Peascod Street, tel. 01753/852-266) or at **Waitrose** (Mon-Fri 8:00-21:00, Sat 8:00-20:00, Sun 11:00-17:00, King Edward Court Shopping Centre, just south of Windsor & Eton Central Station, tel. 01753/860-565). Just outside the castle, you'll find long benches near the statue of Queen Victoria—great for people-watching while you munch.

Bike Rental: Extreme Motion, near the river in Alexandra Gardens, rents 21-speed mountain bikes as well as helmets (£12.50/4 hours, £18/day, helmets-£1-1.50, £150 credit-card deposit required, bring passport as ID, summer daily 10:00-18:00, only open Sat-Sun off-season, tel. 01753/830-220).

Sights in Windsor

▲▲Windsor Castle

Windsor Castle, the official home of England's royal family for 900 years, claims to be the largest and oldest occupied castle in

the world. Thankfully, touring it is simple. You'll see sprawling grounds, lavish staterooms, a crowd-pleasing dollhouse, a gallery of Michelangelo and Leonardo da Vinci drawings, and an exquisite Perpendicular Gothic chapel.

Cost: If everything is open, a ticket costs £18.50 (family-£48); on (relatively rare) days that the Queen is hosting special events in her state rooms, the price is reduced to £10 (family-£26) to make up for the closure. Either ticket is valid for one year of re-entry if you get it stamped at the exit.

Crowd Control: Ticket lines can be long in summer; avoid the wait by purchasing tickets in advance online at www.royalcollection.org.uk or in person at the Buckingham Palace ticket office in London. Tickets in hand, you'll go in through a fast-entry door. There's nowhere in Windsor to buy advance tickets, so once you're here, the ticketless have to stand in line.

Hours: Grounds and most interiors open daily March-Oct

9:45-17:15, Nov-Feb 9:45-16:15, except St. George's Chapel, which is closed Sun to tourists (but open to worshippers). Last entry to grounds and St. George's Chapel 75 minutes before closing. Last entry to State Apartments and Queen Mary's Dolls' House 45 minutes before closing.

Possible Closures: If the queen is entertaining, the State Apartments may be closed—a big disappointment if you're not expecting it, but at least the ticket is cheaper (explained earlier). The entire palace occasionally closes for special events (such as the Garter Service in mid-June). It's smart to call ahead or check the website to make sure everything is open when you want to go. While you're at it, confirm the Changing of the Guard schedule.

Tours: As you enter, you'll pick up the dry, reverent, but informative audioguide, which covers both the grounds and interiors. For a good overview—and an opportunity to ask questions—consider the free 30-minute guided walks around the grounds (usually 2/hour, schedule posted next to audioguide desk). The official £5 guidebook is full of gorgeous images and makes a fine souvenir, but the information within is already covered by the audioguide and tour.

Information: Tel. 020/7766-7304, www.royalcollection.org.uk.

Changing of the Guard: The Changing of the Guard takes place Monday through Saturday at 11:00 (April-July) and on alternating days the rest of the year (check website to confirm

schedule; get there by 10:30, or earlier if you expect a line for tickets). There is no Changing of the Guard on Sundays or in very wet weather. The fresh guards, led by a marching band, leave their barracks on Sheet Street and march up High Street, hanging a right at Victoria, then a left into the castle's Lower Ward, arriving at about 11:00. After about a half-hour, the tired guards march back the way they came. To watch the actual ceremony inside the castle, you'll need to have already bought your ticket, entered the grounds, and staked out a spot. Alternatively, you could wait for them to march by on High Street or on the lower half of Castle Hill.

Evensong: An evensong takes place in the chapel nightly at 17:15 (free for worshippers, line up at exit gate to be admitted).

Best View: While you can get great views of the castle from any direction, the classic views are from the long, wooded walkway called the Long Walk, which stretches south of the palace and is open to the public.

The Order of the Garter

In addition to being the royal residence, Windsor is the home of the Most Noble Order of the Garter—Britain's most prestigious chivalrous order. The castle's history is inexorably tied to this order.

Founded in 1348 by King Edward III and his son (the "Black Prince"), the Order of the Garter was designed to honor returning Crusaders. This was a time when the legends of King Arthur and the Knights of the Round Table were sweeping England, and Edward III fantasized that Windsor could be a real-life Camelot. (He even built the Round Tower as an homage to the Round Table.)

The order's seal illustrates the story of the order's founding and unusual name: a cross of St. George encircled with a belt and a French motto loosely translated as "Shame be upon he who thinks evil of it." Supposedly while the king was dancing with a fair maiden, her garter slipped off onto the floor; in an act of great chivalry, he rescued her from embarrassment by picking it up and uttering those words.

The Order of the Garter continues to the present day as the single most prestigious honor in the United Kingdom. There can be only 24 knights at one time, plus the sitting monarch and the Prince of Wales (perfect numbers for splitting into two 12-man jousting teams). Aside from royals and the nobility, past Knights of the Garter have included Winston Churchill, Bernard "Monty" Montgomery, and Ethiopian Emperor Haile Selassie. In 2008, Prince William became only the 1,000th knight in the order's 660-year history.

The patron of the order is St. George—the namesake of the State Apartments' most sumptuous hall and of the castle's own chapel. Both of these spaces—the grandest in all of Windsor—are designed to celebrate and to honor the Order of the Garter.

WINDSOR

Eating: There are a few shops scattered around the premises, but none sell real food (unless you count gifty boxes of chocolates)—though bottles of water are available. If you'll want a snack during your long castle visit, plan ahead and pack one in from outside.

◆ Self-Guided Tour: After buying your ticket and going through the tight security checkpoint, head into the castle grounds to pick up your audioguide.

The Grounds: Turn right and head up the hill, enjoying the first of many fine castle views you'll see today. The tower-topped, conical hill on your left represents the historical core of the castle. William the Conqueror built this motte (artificial mound) and bailey (fortified stockade around it) in 1080—his first castle in England. Among the later monarchs who spiffed up Windsor were Edward III (flush with French war booty, he made it a palace fit for a 14th-century king), Charles II (determined to restore the monarchy properly in the 1660s), and George IV (Britain's "Bling King," who financed many such vanity projects in the 1820s). On your right, the circular bandstand platform has a seal of the Order of the Garter, which has important ties to Windsor (see sidebar).

Passing through the small gate, you approach the stately St. George's Gate. Peek through here to the Upper Ward's **Quadrangle,** surrounded by the State Apartments (across the field) and the Queen's private apartments (to the right).

Turn left and follow the wall. On your right-hand side, you enjoy great views of the **Round Tower** atop that original motte; running around the base of this artificial hill is the delightful, peaceful garden of the castle governor. The unusual design of this castle has not one "bailey" (castle yard), but three, which today make up Windsor's Upper Ward (where the Queen lives, which we just saw), Middle Ward (the ecclesiastical heart of the complex, with St. George's Chapel, which you'll soon pass on the left), and Lower Ward (residences for castle workers).

Continue all the way around this mini-moat to the **Norman Gate,** which once held a prison. Walking under the gate, look up to see the bottom of the portcullis that could be dropped to seal off the inner courtyard. Three big holes are strategically situated to dump boiling goo or worse on whoever was being kept outside the gate. Past the gate are even finer views of the Quadrangle we just saw from the other side.

Do a 180 and head back toward the Norman Gate, but before you reach it, go down the staircase on the right. You'll emerge onto a fine **terrace** overlooking the flat lands all around. It's easy to understand why this was a strategic place to build a castle. That's Eton College across the Thames. Imagine how handy it's been for royals to be able to ship off their teenagers to an elite prep school so close that they could easily keep an eye on them...literally. The power-plant cooling towers in the distance mark the workaday burg of Slough (rhymes with "plow," immortalized as the setting for Britain's original version of *The Office*).

Turn right and wander along the terrace. You'll likely see two lines: one long and one short. The long line leads to Queen Mary's Dolls' House, then to the State Apartments. The short line skips the dollhouse and lets you proceed directly to the apartments. While the State Apartments are certainly worth seeing, the Dolls' House may not be worth a long wait; read the following descriptions and decide (or return at the end of your castle visit; the dollhouse line tends to ease up at the end of the day). You can see the Drawings Gallery and the China Museum either way.

Queen Mary's Dolls' House: This palace in miniature (1:12 scale, from 1924) is "the most famous dollhouse in the world." It was a gift for Queen Mary (the wife of King George V, and the current Queen's grandmother), who greatly enjoyed miniatures, when she was already a fully grown adult. It's basically one big, dimly lit room with the large dollhouse in the middle, executed with an astonishing level of detail. Each fork, knife, and spoon on the expertly set banquet table is perfect and made of real silver—and the tiny pipes of its plumbing system actually have running water. But you're kept a few feet away by a glass wall, and are constantly jostled by fellow sightseers in this crowded space, making it difficult to fully appreciate. Unless you're a dollhouse devotee, it's probably not worth waiting a half hour for a five-minute peek at this, but if the line is short it's definitely worth a look.

Drawings Gallery and China Museum: Positioned at the exit of the Dolls' House, this collects a changing array of pieces from the Queen's collection—usually including some big names, such as Michelangelo and Leonardo. The China Museum features items from the Queen's many exquisite settings for royal shindigs.

State Apartments: Dripping with chandeliers, finely furnished, and strewn with history and the art of a long line of kings

and queens, they're the best I've seen in Britain. This is where the Queen wows visiting dignitaries. The apartments are even more remarkable considering that many of these grand halls were badly damaged in a fire on November 20, 1992. They've been immaculately restored since. Take advantage of the talkative docents in each room, who are happy to answer your questions.

You'll climb the Grand Staircase up to the **Grand Vestibule,** decorated with exotic items seized by British troops during their missions to colonize various corners of the world. The **Waterloo Chamber** memorializes Wellington and others (from military officers to heads of state to Pope Pius VII) who worked together to defeat Napoleon. You'll pass through various bedchambers, dressing rooms, and drawing rooms of the king and queen (who traditionally maintained separate quarters). Many rooms are decorated with fine canvases by some of Europe's top artists, including Rubens, Van Dyck, and Holbein. Finally you emerge into **St. George's Hall,** decorated with emblems representing the knights of the prestigious Order of the Garter (see sidebar, earlier). This is the site of some of the most elaborate royal banquets—imagine one long table stretching from one end of the hall to the other, seating 160 VIPs. From here, you'll proceed into the rooms that were the most damaged by the 1992 fire, including the "Semi-State Apartments." The **Garter Throne Room** is where new members of the Order of the Garter are invested (ceremonially granted their titles).

Now head down to the opposite end of the terrace, and hook left back into the Middle Ward. From here, you're just above the chapel, with its buttresses; the entrance is about two-thirds of the way down.

St. George's Chapel: Housing numerous royal tombs, this chapel is an exquisite example of Perpendicular Gothic (dating from about 1500), with classic fan-vaulting spreading out from each pillar and with nearly every joint capped with an elaborate and colorful roof boss. Most of these emblems are associated with the Knights of the Garter, which considers St. George's their "mother church." Under the upper stained-glass windows, notice

the continuous frieze of 250 angels, lovingly carved with great detail, ringing the church.

In the corner, take in the melodramatic monument to the popular Princess Charlotte, the only child of King George IV. Heir to the throne, her death (at 21, in childbirth) devastated the nation. Farther along, find the simple chapel containing the tombs of the current Queen's parents, King George VI and "Queen Mum" Elizabeth; the ashes of her younger sister, Princess Margaret, are also kept here (see the marble slab against the wall).

Stepping into the choir area, you're immediately aware that you are in the inner sanctum of the Order of the Garter. The banners lining the nave represent the knights, as do the fancy helmets and half-drawn swords at the top of each wood-carved seat. These symbols honor only living knights; on the seats are some 800 golden panels memorializing departed knights. As you walk up the aisle, notice the marker in the floor: You're walking over the burial site of King Henry VIII and his favorite wife, Jane Seymour (perhaps because she was the only one who died before he could behead her). The body of King Charles I, who was beheaded by Oliver Cromwell's forces at the Banqueting House (see page 94), was also discovered here...with its head sewn back on.

On your way out, you can pause at the door of the sumptuous 13th-century **Albert Memorial Chapel,** redecorated in 1861 after the death of Prince Albert (Queen Victoria's husband) and dedicated to his memory.

Lower Ward: You'll exit the chapel into the castle's Lower Ward. This area is a living town where some 160 people who work for the Queen reside; they include clergy, military, and castle administrators. Just below the chapel, you may be able to enter a tranquil little horseshoe-shaped courtyard ringed with residential doorways—all of them with a spectacular view of the chapels' grand entrance.

Back out in the yard, look for the guard posted at his pillbox. Like those at Buckingham Palace, he's been trained to be a ruthless killing machine...just so he can wind up as somebody's photo op. Click!

More Sights in Windsor

Legoland Windsor

Paradise for Legomaniacs under 12, this huge, kid-pleasing park has dozens of tame but fun rides (often with very long lines) scattered throughout its 150 acres.

The impressive Miniland has 40 million Lego pieces glued together to create 800 tiny buildings and a minitour of Europe; the Creation Centre boasts an 80 percent scale-model Boeing 747 cockpit, made of two million bricks. Several of the more exciting rides involve getting wet, so dress accordingly or buy a cheap disposable poncho in the gift shop. While you may be tempted to hop on the Hill Train at the entrance, it's faster and more convenient to walk down into the park. Food is available in the park, but you can save money by bringing a picnic.

Cost: Adults-£46, children-£37, about 10 percent cheaper if you book online or buy tickets at Windsor TI, free for ages 3 and under; optional Q-Bot ride-reservation gadget allows you to bypass lines (£15-70 depending on when you go and how much time you want to save); coin lockers-£1.

Hours: Convoluted schedule, but generally mid-March-late July and Sept-Oct Mon-Fri 10:00-17:00, Sat-Sun 10:00-18:00, often closed Tue-Wed; late July-Aug daily 10:00-19:00; closed Nov-mid-March. Call or check website for exact schedule, tel. 0871-222-2001, www.legoland.co.uk.

Getting There: A £4.80 round-trip shuttle bus runs from opposite Windsor's Theatre Royal on Thames Street, and from the Parish Church stop on High Street (2/hour). If day-tripping from London, ask about rail/shuttle/park admission deals from Paddington or Waterloo train stations. For drivers, the park is on

B-3022 Windsor/Ascot road, two miles southwest of Windsor and 25 miles west of London. Legoland is clearly signposted from the M-3, M-4, and M-25 motorways. Parking is easy (£3).

Eton College

Across the bridge from Windsor Castle you'll find many post-castle tourists filing toward the most famous "public" (the equivalent of our "private") high school in Britain. Eton was founded in 1440 by King Henry VI; today it educates about 1,300 boys (ages 13-18), who live on campus. Eton has molded the characters of 19 prime ministers as well as members of the royal family, most recently princes William and Harry. The college is sparse on sights, but the public is allowed (via guided tour) into the schoolyard, chapel, cloisters, and the Museum of Eton Life.

Cost and Hours: £7.50, access only by one-hour guided tour at 14:00 and 15:15; tours available late March-Sept, usually Wed and Fri-Sun but daily during spring and summer holiday; closed Oct-late March and about once a month for special events—call ahead; no photos in chapel, no food or drink allowed; tel. 01753/671-177, www.etoncollege.com.

Eton High Street

Even if you're not touring the college, it's worth the few minutes it takes to cross the pedestrian bridge and wander straight up Eton's High Street. A bit more cutesy and authentic-feeling than Windsor (which is given over to shopping malls and chain stores), Eton has a charm that's fun to sample.

Windsor and Royal Borough Museum

Tucked into a small space beneath the Guildhall (where Prince Charles remarried), this little museum does its best to give some insight into the history of Windsor and the surrounding area. They also have lots of special activities for kids. Ask at the desk if tours are running to the Guildhall itself (visits are only possible with a guide); if not, it's probably not worth the admission.

Cost and Hours: £3, includes audioguide, Tue-Sat 10:00-16:00, Sun 12:00-16:00, closed Mon, located in the Guildhall on High Street, tel. 01628/685-686, www.rbwm.gov.uk.

Boat Trips

Cruise up and down the Thames River for classic views of the castle, the village of Eton, Eton College, and the Royal Windsor Racecourse. Choose from a 40-minute or two-hour tour, then relax onboard and nibble a picnic. Boats leave from the riverside promenade adjacent to Barry Avenue.

Cost and Hours: 40-minute tour—£5.70, family pass from £14.25, mid-Feb-Oct 1-2/hour daily 10:00-17:00, Nov hourly Sat-Sun 10:00-16:00; 2-hour tour—£9, family pass from £22.50, late March-Oct only, 1-2/day; closed Dec-mid-Feb; tel. 01753/851-900, www.boat-trips.co.uk.

Horse Racing

The horses race near Windsor every Monday at the Royal Windsor Racecourse (£12-25 entry, online discounts, those under 18 free with an adult, April-Aug and Oct, no races in Sept, sporadic in Aug, off A-308 between Windsor and Maidenhead, tel. 01753/498-400, www.windsor-racecourse.co.uk). The romantic way to get there from Windsor is by a 10-minute shuttle boat (£6 round-trip, www.frenchbrothers.co.uk). The famous Ascot Racecourse (described below) is also nearby.

Near Windsor

Ascot Racecourse

Located seven miles southwest of Windsor and just north of the town of Ascot, this royally owned track is one of the most famous horse-racing venues in the world. The horses first ran here in 1711, and the course is best known for June's five-day Royal Ascot race meeting, attended by the Queen and 299,999 of her loyal subjects. For many, the outlandish hats worn on Ladies Day (Thu) are more interesting than the horses. Royal Ascot is usually the third week in June (June 17-21 in 2014, June 16-20 in 2015). The pricey tickets go on sale the preceding November; while the Friday and Saturday races tend to sell out far ahead, tickets for the other days are often available close to the date (see website). In addition to Royal Ascot, the racecourse runs the ponies year-round—funny hats strictly optional.

Cost: Regular tickets generally £18-30—some may be available at a discount from the TI, Royal Ascot £12-75, online discounts, kids ages 17 and under free; parking £6-8, more for special races; dress code enforced in some areas and on certain days, tel. 0870-722-7227, www.ascot.co.uk.

Sleeping in Windsor

(area code: 01753)

Most visitors stay in London and do Windsor as a day trip. But here are a few suggestions for those staying the night.

$$$ Mercure Windsor Castle Hotel, with 108 business-class rooms and elegant public spaces, is as central as can be, just down the street from Her Majesty's weekend retreat (official rates: Db-£129-169, breakfast-£17; but you'll likely pay around Db-£150 on weekdays and £140 on weekends including breakfast; £30-40 extra for fancy four-poster beds, nonrefundable online deals, air-con, free Wi-Fi, free parking, 18 High Street, tel. 01753/851-577, www. mercure.com, h6618@accor.com).

$$ Langton House B&B is a stately Victorian home with five spacious, well-appointed rooms lovingly maintained by Paul

Sleep Code

(£1 = about $1.60, country code: 44)

S = Single, **D** = Double/Twin, **T** = Triple, **Q** = Quad, **b** = bathroom, **s** = shower only. Unless otherwise noted, credit cards are accepted and breakfast is included.

To help you sort through these listings easily, I've divided the rooms into three categories based on the price for a standard double room with bath:

$$$ **Higher Priced**—Most rooms £100 or more.
  $$ **Moderately Priced**—Most rooms between £60-100.
    $ **Lower Priced**—Most rooms £60 or less.

Prices can change without notice; verify the hotel's current rates online or by email. For the best prices, always book direct.

and Sonja Fogg (S-£73, Sb-£83, D/Db-£103, huge four-poster Db-£113, Tb-£139, Qb-£155, 5 percent extra if paying by credit card, prices can be soft—especially off-season, family-friendly, guest kitchen, free guest computer, free Wi-Fi, 46 Alma Road, tel. 01753/858-299, www.langtonhouse.co.uk, paul@langtonhouse.co.uk).

$$ Park Farm B&B, bright and cheery, is most convenient for drivers. But even if you're not driving, this beautiful place is such a good value, and the welcome is so warm, that you're unlikely to mind the bus ride into town (Sb-£65, Db-£85, Tb-£105, Qb-£120, ask about family room with bunk beds, cash only—credit card solely for reservations, free Wi-Fi, access to shared fridge and microwave, free off-street parking, 1 mile from Legoland on St. Leonards Road near Imperial Road, 5-minute bus ride or 1-mile walk to castle, £5 taxi ride from station, tel. 01753/866-823, www.parkfarm.com, stay@parkfarm.com, Caroline and Drew Youds).

$$ Dee and Steve's B&B is a friendly four-room place above a window shop on a quiet residential street about a 10-minute walk from the castle and station. The rooms are cozy, Dee and Steve are pleasant hosts, and breakfast is served in the contemporary kitchen/lounge (S-£40, Sb-£55-60, Db-£75, free Wi-Fi, 169 Oxford Road, tel. 01753/854-489, www.deeandsteve.com, dee@deeandsteve.com).

$$ 76 Duke Street has two nice rooms, but only hosts one set of guests at a time. While the bathroom is (just) outside your bedroom, you have it to yourself (Db-£80, £5 more for one-night stay, free Wi-Fi, 15-minute walk from station at—you guessed it—76 Duke Street, tel. 01753/620-636, www.76dukestreet.co.uk, bandb@76dukestreet.co.uk, Julia).

$ Crown and Cushion is a good budget option on Eton's High Street, just across the pedestrian bridge from Windsor's waterfront (a short uphill walk to the castle). While the pub it's situated over is worn and drab, you're right in the heart of charming Eton, and the eight creaky rooms—with uneven floors and old-beam ceilings—are nicely furnished (S-£45, Db-£59, Tb-£79, free Wi-Fi, free parking, 84 High Street in Eton, tel. 01753/641-494, info@crownandcushioneton.com, www.crownandcushioneton.co.uk).

Eating in Windsor

Elegant Spots with River Views

Several places flank Windsor Bridge, offering romantic dining after dark. The riverside promenade, with cheap takeaway stands scattered about, is a delightful place for a picnic lunch or dinner with the swans. If you don't see anything that appeals, continue up Eton's High Street, which is also lined with characteristic eateries.

In the Tourist Zone Around the Palace

Strolling the streets and lanes around the palace entrance—especially in the shopping zone near Windsor & Eton Station—you'll find countless trendy and inviting eateries. The central area also has a sampling of dependable British chains (including a Wagamama, Gourmet Burger Kitchen, Thai Square, and Nando's). Residents enjoy a wide selection of unpretentious little eateries (including a fire station turned pub-and-cultural center) just past the end of pedestrian Peascod Street.

Bel & The Dragon is the place to splurge on high-quality, classic British food in a charming half-timbered building with an upscale-rustic dining space (£16-25 mains, food served Mon-Fri 12:00-15:00 & 18:00-22:00, Sat-Sun 10:30-15:00 & 18:00-22:00, afternoon tea served between lunch and dinner, also serves basic pub grub, bar open longer hours, on Thames Street near the bridge to Eton, tel. 01753/866-056).

Cornucopia Bistro, with a cozy, woody atmosphere, serves tasty international dishes (£12 two-course meals available after 19:00 except on Fri-Sat, £12-15 main courses, daily 12:00-14:30 & 18:00-21:30, Fri-Sat until 22:00, closed Sun night, 6 High Street, tel. 01753/833-009).

The Duchess of Cambridge's friendly staff serves up the normal grub in a pub that's right across from the castle walls, and with an open fireplace to boot (£9-12 meals, daily 9:30-22:30 or later, 3-4 Thames Street, tel. 01753/864-405). While the pub predates

Visiting Highclere Castle

If you're a fan of *Downton Abbey,* consider a day trip from London to Highclere Castle, the stately house where much of the show is filmed. Though the hugely popular TV series is set in Yorkshire, the actual house is located in Hampshire, about an hour's train ride west of London. Highclere has been home to the Earls of Carnarvon since 1679 (and the current residents enjoy watching the TV show), but the present, Jacobean-style house was rebuilt in the 1840s by Sir Charles Berry, who also designed London's Houses of Parliament. Noted landscape architect Capability Brown laid out the traditional gardens in the mid-18th century. The castle's Egyptian exhibit features artifacts collected by Highclere's fifth Earl, George Herbert, a keen amateur archaeologist. When Howard Carter discovered King Tut's tomb in 1922, he waited three weeks for his friend and patron Herbert to join him before looking inside. The Earl died unexpectedly a few months later, giving birth to the legend of a "mummy's curse."

Cost and Hours: Entrance is by timed-entry ticket, best bought in advance online (although last-minute afternoon-entry tickets sometimes available—call ahead); £18 for castle, garden, and Egyptian exhibit; £11 for castle and garden only, or Egyptian exhibit and garden only; garden only-£5; July-mid-Sept Sun-Thu 10:30-17:00, closed Fri-Sat and mid-Sept-June except open sporadically April-early June, last entry at 15:30; tickets available online several months ahead—sales begin as early as Feb for following summer; no photos inside, 24-hour info tel. 01635/253-204, www.highclerecastle.co.uk.

Getting There: Highclere is six miles south of Newbury, about 70 miles west of London, off A-34.

By Train and Taxi: First Great Western trains run from London's Paddington Station to Newbury (1-2/hour, 50-70 minutes, £22-50 same-day return, tel. 0845-748-4950, from North America call 011-44-20-7278-5240). From Newbury train station, you'll have to take a taxi (£15-22 one-way, higher price is for Sun, taxis wait outside station or call 01635/33333) or reserve a car and driver (must arrange in advance, £12.50/person round-trip; £25 minimum, WebAir, tel. 07818/430-095, mapeng@msn.com).

By Tour: Brit Movie Tours offer an all-day bus tour of *Downton Abbey* filming locations, including Highclere Castle and the fictional village of Downton (sells out early, £85, includes transport and castle/garden entry, £5 extra for Egyptian exhibit, 9 hours, depart London from outside Gloucester Road Tube Station, reservations required, tel. 0844-247-1007 or 020/7118-1007, http://britmovietours.com).

Kate, it was named in her honor following a recent remodel, and has the photos to prove her endorsement.

The Crooked House is a touristy 17th-century timber-framed teahouse, serving fresh, hearty £8-10 lunches and £8.50 cream teas in a tipsy interior or outdoors on its cobbled lane (daily 10:30-18:00, Wed-Sat until 22:00, in winter daily 11:00-17:00, 51 High Street, tel. 01753/857-534).

Meimo offers "Moroccan/Mediterranean" cuisine in a nicely subdued dining room (£9-14 main dishes, several fixed-price meal options, daily 10:00-22:00, 69-70 Peascod Street, tel. 01753/862-222).

Saffron Restaurant, while a fairly long walk from the castle, is the local choice for South Indian cuisine, with a modern interior and attentive waiters who struggle with English but are fluent at bringing out tasty dishes. Their vegetarian *thali* is a treat (£8-12 dishes, daily 12:00-14:30 & 17:30-23:30, 99 St. Leonards Road, tel. 01753/855-467).

Cambridge

Cambridge, 60 miles north of London, is world famous for its prestigious university. Wordsworth, Isaac Newton, Tennyson, Darwin, and Prince Charles are a few of its illustrious alumni. The university dominates—and owns—most of Cambridge, a historic town of 100,000 people. Cambridge is the epitome of a university town, with busy bikers, stately residence halls, plenty of bookshops, and proud locals who can point out where DNA was originally modeled, the atom first split, and electrons discovered.

In medieval Europe, higher education was the domain of the Church and was limited to ecclesiastical schools. Scholars lived in "halls" on campus. This academic community of residential halls, chapels, and lecture halls connected by peaceful garden courtyards survives today in the colleges that make up the universities of Cambridge and Oxford. By 1350 (Oxford is roughly 100 years older), Cambridge had eight colleges, each with a monastic-type courtyard, chapel, library, and lodgings. Today, Cambridge has 31 colleges, each with its own facilities. In the town center, these grand old halls date back centuries, with ornately decorated facades that try to one-up each other. While students' lives revolve around their independent colleges, the university organizes lectures, presents degrees, and promotes research.

The university schedule has three terms: Lent term from mid-January to mid-March, Easter term from mid-April to mid-June, and Michaelmas term from early October to early December. During exam time (roughly the month of May), the colleges are closed to visitors, which can impede access to all the picturesque little corners of the town. But the main sights—King's College Chapel and Trinity Library—stay open, and Cambridge is never sleepy.

Planning Your Time

Cambridge is worth most of a day. Start by taking the TI's walking tour, which includes a visit to the town's only must-see sight, the King's College Chapel (first tour at 11:00, later on Sun, call ahead to confirm and reserve—see "Tours in Cambridge," later). Spend the afternoon touring the Fitzwilliam Museum (closed Mon), or simply enjoying the ambience of this stately old college town.

Getting to Cambridge

By Train: It's an easy trip from London and less than an hour away. Catch the train from London's King's Cross Station (2/hour, trains leave King's Cross at :15 and :45 past the hour, 45 minutes, £22 one-way standard class, £23 same-day return after 9:30, operated by First Capital Connect, tel. 0845-748-4950, www.firstcapitalc-onnect.co.uk or www.nationalrail.co.uk). Direct trains also run from London's Liverpool Street Station, but take longer (2/hour, 1.25 hours).

By Bus: National Express coaches run from London's Victoria Coach Station to the Parkside stop in Cambridge (every 60-90 minutes, 2-2.5 hours, £11.60, £6 advance fares sometimes available online, tel. 0871-781-8178, www.nationalexpress.co.uk).

Orientation to Cambridge

Cambridge is congested but small. Everything is within a pleasant walk. There are two main streets, separated from the Cam River by the most interesting colleges. The town center, brimming with tearooms, has a TI and a colorful open-air market square. The train station is about a mile to the southeast.

Tourist Information

Cambridge's TI is well-run and well-signposted, just off Market Square in the town center. They book rooms for £5, offer walking tours (see "Tours in Cambridge," later), and sell bus tickets and a £1.50 map/guide (Mon-Sat 10:00-17:00, Easter-Sept also Sun 11:00-15:00—otherwise closed Sun, phones answered from 9:00, Peas Hill, tel. 0871-226-8006, room-booking tel. 01223/457-581, www.visitcambridge.org). In the same building as the TI, you can duck into a former courtroom to catch a free video overview of the town and its history.

Arrival in Cambridge

By Train: Cambridge's train station doesn't have baggage storage, but you can pay to leave your bags at the nearby bike-rental shop (see "Helpful Hints," later). The station does not have a TI, but it does offer free maps and other brochures on an interior wall just before the turnstiles.

To get from the station to downtown Cambridge, you can **walk** for about 25 minutes (exit straight ahead on Station Road, bear right at the war memorial onto Hills Road, and follow it into town); take public **bus** #1, #3, #7, or #8 (buses are referred to as "Citi 1," "Citi 3," and so on in print and online, but only the number is marked on the bus; £1.50, pay driver, runs every 5-10 minutes, turn left when exiting station to find bus stop, get off at Emmanuel Street stop—look for Grand Arcade shopping mall on the left); pay about £6 for a **taxi;** or ride a City Sightseeing **bus tour** (described later).

By Car: To park in the middle of town, follow signs from the M-11 motorway to any of the handy and central short-stay parking lots. Or you can leave the car at one of five park-and-ride lots outside the city, then take the shuttle into town (free parking, shuttle costs £2.50 round-trip if you buy ticket from machine, or £2.80 from driver).

Helpful Hints

Festival: The **Cambridge Folk Festival** gets things humming and strumming in late July (tickets go on sale several months ahead and often sell out quickly; www.cambridgefolkfestival.co.uk).

Bike Rental: Station Cycles, located about a block to your right as you exit the station, rents bikes (£7/4 hours, £10/day, helmets-£1, £60 deposit, cash or credit card) and stores luggage (£3-4/bag depending on size; Mon-Fri 8:00-18:00, Wed until 19:00, Sat 9:00-17:00, Sun 10:00-17:00, tel. 01223/307-125, www.stationcycles.co.uk). A second location is near the center of town (inside the Grand Arcade shopping mall, same hours, tel. 01223/307-655).

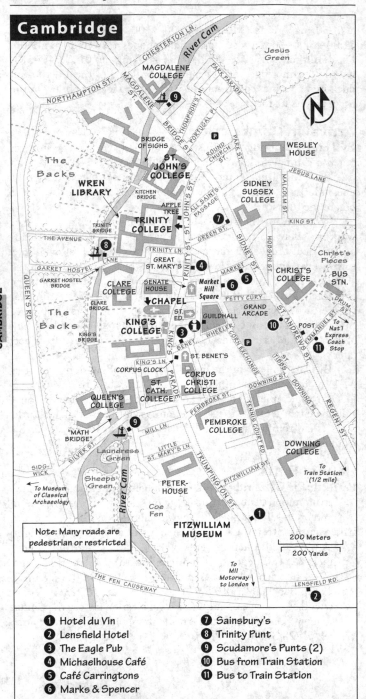

Cambridge

CHESTERTON LN.

River Cam

Jesus Green

MAGDALENE COLLEGE

NORTHAMPTON ST.

MAGDALENE ST.

BRIDGE ST.

THOMPSON'S LN.

PORTUGAL PL.

PARK PARADE

PARK ST.

WESLEY HOUSE

ROUND CHURCH ST.

JESUS LANE

The Backs

BRIDGE OF SIGHS

ST. JOHN'S COLLEGE

ALL SAINTS PASSAGE

ST. JOHN'S ST.

SIDNEY SUSSEX COLLEGE

MALCOLM ST.

KING ST.

WREN LIBRARY

KITCHEN BRIDGE

TRINITY BRIDGE

THE AVENUE

GARRET HOSTEL LANE

APPLE TREE

TRINITY COLLEGE

TRINITY ST.

GREEN ST.

SIDNEY ST.

HOBSON ST.

Christ's Pieces

CHRIST'S COLLEGE

BUS STN.

TRINITY LN.

GREAT ST. MARY'S

MARKET ST.

GARRET HOSTEL BRIDGE

CLARE COLLEGE

SENATE HOUSE

Market Hill Square

PETTY CURY

ST. ANDREWS ST.

DRUM ST.

To Nat'l Express Coach Stop

QUEEN'S RD.

The Backs

CLARE BRIDGE

CHAPEL

KING'S COLLEGE

KING'S BRIDGE

ST. ED.

GUILDHALL

GRAND ARCADE

WHEELER

CORN EXCHANGE

POST

EMMANUEL ST.

KING'S PARADE

ST. BENET'S

BENE'T ST.

CORPUS CLOCK

ST. CATH. COLLEGE

CORPUS CHRISTI COLLEGE

DOWNING ST.

DOWNING PL.

TIBBS

REGENT ST.

QUEEN'S COLLEGE

"MATH BRIDGE"

SILVER ST.

MILL LN.

PEMBROKE ST.

PEMBROKE COLLEGE

TENNIS COURT RD.

DOWNING COLLEGE

SIDG-WICK

Laundress Green

LITTLE ST. MARY'S LN.

TRUMPINGTON ST.

FITZWILLIAM ST.

To Train Station (1/2 mile)

To Museum of Classical Archaeology

Sheeps' Green

River Cam

PETER-HOUSE

Coe Fen

FITZWILLIAM MUSEUM

Note: Many roads are pedestrian or restricted

THE FEN CAUSEWAY

To M11 Motorway to London ↓

LENSFIELD RD.

200 Meters

200 Yards

CAMBRIDGE

① Hotel du Vin
② Lensfield Hotel
③ The Eagle Pub
④ Michaelhouse Café
⑤ Café Carringtons
⑥ Marks & Spencer
⑦ Sainsbury's
⑧ Trinity Punt
⑨ Scudamore's Punts (2)
⑩ Bus from Train Station
⑪ Bus to Train Station

Tours in Cambridge

▲▲Walking Tour of the Colleges

A walking tour is the best way to understand Cambridge's mix of "town and gown." The walks can be more educational (read: dry) than entertaining. But they do provide a good rundown of the historic and scenic highlights of the university, some fun local gossip, and plenty of university trivia. For example, why are entering students called "undergraduates"? Because long ago, new students at Cambridge were assigned to a mentor who already had a degree... so they were "under" the supervision of a "graduate."

The TI offers **daily walking tours** that include the King's College Chapel, as well as another college—usually Queen's College (£17.50, 2 hours, includes admission fees; July-Aug daily at 11:00, 12:00, 13:00, and 14:00, no 11:00 tour on Sun; Sept-June Mon-Sat at 11:00, 13:00, Sun only at 13:00; tel. 01223/457-574, www.visitcambridge.org). It's smart to call ahead to reserve a spot (they'll take your credit-card number), or you can drop by in person (try to arrive 30 minutes before the tour). Notice that the 12:00 tour overlaps with the limited opening times of the Wren Library—so you'll miss out on the library if you take the noon tour.

Private guides are available through the TI (basic 1-hour tour-£4.25/person, £64 minimum; 1.5-hour tour-£4.75/person, £72 minimum; 2-hour tour-£5.25/person, £79 minimum; does not include individual college entrance fees, tel. 01223/457-574, tours@cambridge.gov.uk).

Walking and Punting Ghost Tour

If you're in Cambridge on the weekend, consider a £6 ghost walk to where spooky sightings have been reported, Friday evenings at 18:00, or a creepy £18.50 trip on the River Cam followed by a walk, most Saturdays at dusk (20:00 in summer; book ahead for either tour, organized by the TI, tel. 01223/457-574).

Bus Tours

City Sightseeing hop-on, hop-off bus tours are informative and cover the outskirts, including the American WWII Cemetery. But keep in mind that buses can't go where walking tours can—right into the center (£14, 80 minutes for full 20-stop circuit, buy ticket with credit card at the bus-stop kiosk—or pay cash to driver when you board, departs every 20 minutes in summer, every 40 minutes in winter, first bus leaves train station at 10:06, last bus around 17:30, recorded commentary, tel. 01223/423-250, www.city-sightseeing.com). If arriving by train, you can buy your ticket from the kiosk directly in front of the station, then ride the bus into town.

Sights in Cambridge

Cambridge has many impressive old college buildings to explore, with fancy facades and tranquil grassy courtyards. I've featured the two most interesting (King's and Trinity), but feel free to wander beyond these. You might notice several bricked-up windows on the old buildings around town. This practice dates from a time when taxes were calculated per window...so filling them in saved money.

▲King's Parade and Nearby

The lively street in front of King's College, called King's Parade, seems to be where everyone in Cambridge gathers. Looming across the street from the college is **Great St. Mary's Church,** with a climbable bell tower (£3.50, Mon-Sat 9:30-16:30, Sun 12:30-16:00, 123 stairs). On the street out front, students hawk punting tours on the Cam River (see "Punting on the Cam," later).

Behind the church is the thriving **Market Hill Square.** The big market is on Sunday (9:30-16:30) and features produce, arts, and crafts. On other days, you'll find mostly clothes and food (Mon-Sat roughly 9:30-16:00).

The imposing Neoclassical building at the top (north) end of King's Parade is the **Senate House,** the meeting place of the university's governing body. In June, you might notice green boxes lining the front of this house. Traditionally at the end of the term, students would come to these boxes to see whether or not they'd earned their degree; if a name was not on the list, the student had flunked. Amazingly, until 2010 this was the only notification students received about their status. (Now they also get an email.)

In the opposite direction (south), at Benet Street, look for the strikingly modern **Corpus Clock.** Designed and commissioned by alum John Taylor, the clock was ceremonially unveiled by Stephen Hawking in 2008. It uses concentric golden dials with blue LED lights to tell the time, but it's precise only every five minutes; its otherwise-irregular timekeeping mimics the unpredictability of life. Perched on top is Chronophage, the "eater of time"—a grotesque giant grasshopper that keeps the clock moving and periodically winks at passersby. Creepy and disturbing? Exactly, says Taylor...so is the passage of time.

Just down Benet Street on the left is the recommended **Eagle Pub**—Cambridge's oldest pub and a sight in itself; it's worth poking into the courtyard to learn about its dynamic history, even if you don't eat or drink here. Across the street from the pub stands the oldest surviving building in Cambridgeshire, **St. Benet's Church.**

The Saxons who built the church included circular holes in its bell tower, to encourage owls to roost there and keep the mouse population under control.

▲▲King's College Chapel

Built from 1446 to 1515 by Henrys VI through VIII, England's best example of Perpendicular Gothic architecture is the single most impressive building in town.

Cost and Hours: £7.50, erratic hours depending on school schedule and events; during academic term usually Mon-Fri 9:30-15:30, Sat 9:30-15:15, Sun 13:15-14:30; during breaks (see page 261) usually daily 9:30-16:30; recorded info tel. 01223/331-1212, www.kings.cam.ac.uk/chapel.

Evensong: When school's in session, you're welcome to enjoy an evensong service in this glorious space, with a famous choir made up of men and boys (free, Mon-Sat at 17:30, Sun at 15:30; for more on evensong, see page 164).

Getting There: You'll see the regal front facade of King's College along King's Parade. To enter the chapel, curl around the back: Facing the college on King's Parade, head right and take the first left possible (just after the Senate House, on Senate House passage); at the end, bear left on Trinity Lane to reach the gate where you can pay to enter the chapel.

➲ Self-Guided Tour: Stand inside, look up, and marvel, as Christopher Wren did, at what was then the largest single span of **vaulted roof** anywhere—2,000 tons of incredible fan vaulting, held in place by the force of gravity (a careful balancing act resting delicately on the buttresses visible outside the building).

While Henry VI—who began work on the chapel—wanted it to be austere, his descendants decided it should glorify the House of Tudor (of which his son, Henry VII, was the first king). Lin-

ing the walls are giant **Tudor coats of arms.** The shield includes a fleur-de-lis because an earlier ancestor, Edward III, woke up one day and—citing his convoluted lineage—somewhat arbitrarily declared himself king of France. The symbols on the left (a rose and the red dragon of Wales, holding the shield) represent the Tudors, the family of Henry VII's father. On the right, the greyhound holding the shield and the portcullis (the iron grate) symbolize the family of Henry VII's mother, Lady Margaret Beaufort, who prodded her son for years to complete this chapel.

The 26 **stained-glass windows** date from the 16th century. It's the most Renaissance stained glass anywhere in one spot. (Most

 of the stained glass in English churches dates from Victorian times, but this glass is much older.) The lower panes show scenes from the New Testament, while the upper panes feature corresponding stories from the Old Testament. Considering England's turbulent

history, it's miraculous that these windows have survived for nearly half a millennium in such a pristine state. After Henry VIII separated from the Catholic Church in 1534, many such windows and other Catholic features around England were destroyed. (Think of all those ruined abbeys dotting the English countryside.) However, since Henry had just paid for these windows, he couldn't bear to get rid of them. A century later, in the days of Oliver Cromwell, another wave of iconoclasm destroyed more windows around England. Though these windows were slated for removal, they stayed put. (Historians speculate that Cromwell's troops, who were garrisoned in this building, didn't want the windows removed in the chilly wintertime.) Finally, during World War II, the windows were taken out and hidden away to keep them safe, and then painstakingly replaced after the war ended.

The **choir screen** that bisects the church was commissioned by King Henry VIII to commemorate his marriage to Anne Boleyn. By the time it was finished, so was she (beheaded). But it was too late to remove her initials, which were carved into the screen (look on the far left for *R.A.*, for *Regina Anna*—"Queen Anne").

Behind the screen is the **choir** area, where the King's College Choir performs a daily evensong. On Christmas Eve, a special service is held here and broadcast around the world on the BBC—a tradition near and dear to British hearts.

Walk to the altar and admire Rubens' masterful *Adoration of the Magi* (1634). It's actually a family portrait: The admirer in the front (wearing red) is a self-portrait of Rubens, Mary looks an awful lot like his much-younger wife, and the Baby Jesus resembles their own newborn at the time.

Finally, pop through the door to the left of the altar to find an exhibit with a basic history of the chapel, a nice model showing how the fan vaults were constructed, and an explanation of how the chapel has managed to hang together after all these years.

▲▲Trinity College and Wren Library

More than a third of Cambridge's 83 Nobel Prize winners have come from this richest and biggest of the town's colleges, founded in 1546 by Henry VIII. The college has three sights to see: the entrance gate, the grounds, and the magnificent Wren Library.

Cost and Hours: Grounds—£3, often free off-season, daily 10:00-16:30, last entry 45 minutes before closing; library—free, Mon-Fri 12:00-14:00, Nov-mid-June also Sat 10:30-12:30, closed Sun year-round; only small groups allowed in at a time, tel. 01223/338-400, www.trin.cam.ac.uk.

To see the Wren Library without paying for the grounds, access it from the riverside entrance: Head toward the Garret Hostel Bridge, and, if the gate's open, pass through the parking lot to your right immediately before the bridge. If the gate is not open, it's a long walk across the bridge and around the field to the path that leads back to the college.

Trinity Gate: You'll notice gates like these adorning facades of colleges around town. Above the door is a statue of **King Henry VIII,** who founded Trinity because he feared that Cambridge's existing colleges were too cozy with the Church. Notice Henry's right hand holding a chair leg instead of the traditional crown jewels scepter. This is courtesy of Cambridge's Night Climbers, who first replaced the scepter a century ago, and continue to periodically switch it out for other items. According to campus legend, decades ago some of the world's most talented mountaineers enrolled at Cambridge...in one of the

flattest parts of England. (Cambridge was actually a seaport until Dutch engineers drained the surrounding swamps.) Lacking opportunities to practice their skill, they began scaling the frilly facades of Cambridge's college buildings under cover of darkness (if caught, they'd have been expelled). In the 1960s, climbers actually managed to haul an entire automobile onto the roof of the Senate House. The university had to bring in the army to cut it into pieces

and remove it. Only 50 years later, at a class reunion, did the guilty parties finally fess up.

In the little park to the right, notice the lone **apple tree.** Supposedly, this tree is a descendant of the very one that once stood in the garden of Sir Isaac Newton (who spent 30 years at Trinity). According to legend, Newton was inspired to investigate gravity when an apple fell from the tree onto his head. This tree stopped bearing fruit long ago; if you do see apples, they've been tied on by mischievous students.

• *If you like, head through the gate into the...*

Trinity Grounds: The grounds are enjoyable to explore, if not quite worth the cost of admission. Inside the **Great Court,**
the clock (on the tower on the right) double-rings at the top of each hour. It's a college tradition to take off running from the clock when the high noon bells begin (it takes 43 seconds to clang 24 times), race around the courtyard, touching each of the four corners without setting foot on the cobbles, and try to return to the same

spot by the time the ringing ends. Supposedly only one student (a young lord) ever managed the feat—a scene featured in *Chariots of Fire* (but filmed elsewhere).

The **chapel** (entrance to the right of the clock tower)—which pales in comparison to the stunning King's College Chapel—feels like a shrine to thinking, with statues honoring great Trinity minds both familiar (Isaac Newton, Alfred Lord Tennyson, Francis Bacon) and unfamiliar. Who's missing? The poet Lord Byron, who was such a hell-raiser during his time at Trinity that a statue of him was deemed unfit for Church property; his statue stands in the library instead.

Wren Library: Don't miss the 1695 Christopher Wren-designed library, with its wonderful carving and fascinating original manuscripts. Just outside the library entrance, Sir Isaac Newton clapped his hands and timed the echo to measure the speed of sound as it raced down the side of the cloister and back. In the library's 12 display cases (covered with cloth that you flip back), you'll see handwritten works by Sir Isaac Newton and John Milton, alongside A. A. Milne's original *Winnie the Pooh* (the real Christopher Robin attended Trinity College).

▲▲Fitzwilliam Museum

Britain's best museum of antiquities and art outside of London is the Fitzwilliam, housed in a grand Neoclassical building a 10-minute walk south of Market Square. The Fitzwilliam's broad collection is like a mini-British Museum/National Gallery rolled into one; you're bound to find something you like. Helpful docents—many with degrees or doctorates in art history—are more than willing to answer questions about the collection. The ground floor features an extensive range of antiquities and applied arts—everything from Greek vases, Mesopotamian artifacts, and Egyptian sarcophagi to Roman statues, fine porcelain, and suits of armor.

Upstairs is the painting gallery, with works that span art history: Italian Venetian masters (such as Titian and Canaletto), a worthy English section (featuring Gainsborough, Reynolds, Hogarth, and others), and a notable array of French Impressionist art (including Monet, Renoir, Pissarro, Degas, and Sisley). Rounding out the collection are old manuscripts, including some musical compositions from Handel. Watch your step—in 2006, a visitor tripped and accidentally smashed three 17th-century Chinese vases. Amazingly, the vases were restored (with donations from the community) and are now on display in Gallery 17...in a protective case.

Cost and Hours: Free, £5 donation suggested, Tue-Sat 10:00-17:00, Sun 12:00-17:00, closed Mon except bank holidays, no photos, Trumpington Street, tel. 01223/332-900, www.fitzmuseum.cam.ac.uk.

Museum of Classical Archaeology

Although this museum contains no originals, it offers a unique chance to study accurate copies (19th-century casts) of virtually every famous ancient Greek and Roman statue. More than 450 statues are on display. If you've seen the real things in Greece, Istanbul, Rome, and elsewhere, touring this collection is like a high school reunion..."Hey, I know you!" But since it takes some time to get here, this museum is best left to devotees of classical sculpture.

Cost and Hours: Free, Mon-Fri 10:00-17:00, Sat 10:00-13:00 during term, closed Sun, Sidgwick Avenue, tel. 01223/330-402, www.classics.cam.ac.uk/museum.

Getting There: The museum is a five-minute walk west of Silver Street Bridge; after crossing the bridge, continue straight until you reach a sign reading *Sidgwick Site*. The museum is in the long building on the corner to your right; the entrance is on the opposite side, and the museum is upstairs.

▲Punting on the Cam

For a little levity and probably more exercise than you really want, try hiring one of the traditional flat-bottom punts at the river and pole yourself up and down (or around and around, more likely) the lazy Cam. Once you get the hang of it, it's a fine way to enjoy the scenic side of Cambridge. It's less crowded in late afternoon (and less embarrassing).

Several companies rent punts and offer tours. Hawkers try to snare passengers in the thriving people zone in front of King's College. Prices are soft in slow times—try talking them down a bit before committing.

Trinity Punt, just north of Garret Hostel Bridge, is run by Trinity College students (£14/hour, £40 deposit, 45-minute tours-£40/boat, can share ride and cost with up to 2 others, cash only, ask for quick and free lesson, Easter-mid-Oct Mon-Fri 11:00-17:30, Sat-Sun 10:00-17:30, return punts by 18:30, no rentals mid-Oct-Easter, tel. 01223/338-483). **Scudamore's** has two locations: Mill Lane, just south of the central Silver Street Bridge, and the less convenient Quayside at Magdalene Bridge, at the north end of town (£16-20/hour, credit-card deposit required; 45-minute tours-£16/person, discount if you book at TI; open daily June-Aug 9:00-22:00 or later, Sept-May at least 10:00-17:00, weather permitting, tel. 01223/359-750).

Near Cambridge
Imperial War Museum Duxford
This former airfield, nine miles south of Cambridge, is nirvana for aviation fans and WWII buffs. Wander through seven exhibition halls housing 200 vintage aircraft (including Spitfires, B-17 Flying Fortresses, a Concorde, and a Blackbird) as well as military land vehicles and special displays on Normandy and the Battle of Britain. On many weekends, the museum holds special events, such as air shows (extra fee)—check the website for details.

Cost and Hours: £17.50 (includes small donation), show local bus ticket for discount, daily mid-March-late Oct 10:00-18:00, late Oct-mid-March 10:00-16:00, last entry one hour before closing; Concorde interior open until 17:00, 15:00 off-season; tel. 01223/835-000, http://duxford.iwm.org.uk.

Getting There: The museum is located off A-505 in Duxford. From Cambridge, take bus #7 from the train station (45 minutes) or from Emmanuel Street's Stop A (55 minutes, 2-3/hour daily, www.stagecoachbus.com).

Sleeping in Cambridge

(area code: 01223)
While Cambridge is an easy side-trip from London, its subtle charms might convince you to spend the night. Cambridge has very few accommodations in the city center, and none in the tight maze of colleges and shops where you'll spend most of your time. These recommendations are about a 10- to 15-minute walk south of the town center, toward the train station.

$$$ Hotel du Vin blends France, England, and wine. This worthwhile splurge has 41 comfortable, spacious rooms with all the amenities above a characteristic bistro that offers good deals for guests and non-guests alike. This mod place manages to be classy yet unpretentious (Db-£150-190, fancier suites available, check online for special offers, breakfast-£13-15, air-con, elevator, free Wi-Fi, just down the street from the Fitzwilliam Museum at Trumpington Street 15-18, tel. 01223/227-330 or 0844-736-4253, www.hotelduvin.com, reception.cambridge@hotelduvin.com).

$$$ Lensfield Hotel, popular with visiting professors, has 30 old-fashioned rooms (Sb-£72, Db-£110, Tb-£136, newer "deluxe" Db-£150, pricier suites available, free Wi-Fi, spa and fitness room, 53 Lensfield Road, tel. 01223/355-017, www.lensfieldhotel.co.uk, enquiries@lensfieldhotel.co.uk).

Eating in Cambridge

While picnicking is scenic and saves money, the weather may not always cooperate. Here are a few ideas for fortifying yourself with a lunch in central Cambridge.

The Eagle, near the TI, is the oldest pub in town, and a Cambridge institution with a history so rich that a visit here practically

qualifies as sightseeing. Find your way into the delightful courtyard, with outdoor seating and a good look at the place's past. The second-floor windows once lit guest rooms, back when this was a coachmen's inn as well as a pub. Notice that the window on the right end is open; any local will love to tell you why. Follow the signs into the misnamed "RAF Bar," where US Army Air Corps pilots signed the ceiling while stationed here during World War II. Science fans can celebrate the discovery of DNA—Francis Crick and James Watson first announced their findings here in 1953 (£5-8 lunches, £8-11 dinners, food served daily 10:00-22:00, drinks until 23:00, 8 Benet Street, tel. 01223/505-020).

The **Michaelhouse Café** is a heavenly respite from the crowds, tucked into the repurposed St. Michael's Church, just north of Great St. Mary's Church. At lunch, choose from salads, soups, and sandwiches, as well as a few hot dishes and a variety of tasty baked goods (£7-10 light meals, Mon-Sat 8:00-17:00, breakfast served 8:00-11:00, lunch served 11:30-15:30, hot drinks and baked goods always available, closed Sun, Trinity Street, tel. 01223/309-147). Between 14:30 and 15:30 you can pay £4 to fill your plate with whatever they have left.

Café Carringtons is a cozy cafeteria that serves traditional British food at reasonable prices, including a Sunday roast lunch (£6-8 meals, £5 sandwiches, Mon-Sat 8:00-17:00, Sun 10:00-16:00, down the stairs at 23 Market Street, tel. 01223/361-792).

Supermarkets: There's a **Marks & Spencer Simply Food** at the train station (Mon-Fri 7:00-23:00, Sat 7:00-22:00, Sun 9:00-21:00) and a larger Marks & Spencer department store on Market Hill Square (Mon-Thu 8:00-18:00, Wed until 20:00, Fri-Sat 8:00-19:00, Sun 11:00-17:00, tel. 01223/355-219). **Sainsbury's** supermarket has longer hours (Mon-Sat 8:00-23:30, Sun 11:00-17:00, 44 Sidney Street, at the corner of Green Street).

A good picnic spot is Laundress Green, a grassy park on the river, at the end of Mill Lane near the Silver Street Bridge punts. There are no benches, so bring something to sit on. Remember, the college lawns are private property, so walking or picnicking on the grass is generally not allowed. When in doubt, ask at the college's entrance.

Cambridge Connections

From Cambridge by Train to: York (hourly, 2.5 hours, transfer in Peterborough), **Oxford** (2-3/hour, 2.5-3 hours, change in London involves Tube transfer between train stations), **London** (King's Cross Station: 2/hour, 45 minutes; Liverpool Street Station: 2/hour, 1.25 hours). Train info: Tel. 0845-748-4950, www.nationalrail.co.uk.

By Bus to: London (every 60-90 minutes, 2-2.5 hours), **Heathrow Airport** (hourly, 2-3 hours). Bus info: Tel. 0871-781-8178, www.nationalexpress.com.

CANTERBURY

Canterbury is one of England's most important religious destinations. For centuries, it has welcomed hordes of pilgrims to its grand cathedral and abbey. While these days you'll probably see more iPods than Bibles in this college town, Canterbury's cathedral and medieval core still beckon with rich history and architectural splendor.

Pleasant, walkable Canterbury, like many cities in southern England, was originally founded by the pagan Romans. Then along came St. Augustine, sent by the pope in A.D. 597 to convert England's King Ethelbert of Kent to Christianity. Ethelbert (who had a Christian wife) joined the Church and gave St. Augustine land on which to set up a monastery and an abbey, on the edge of town. As Christianity became more established in England, Canterbury became its center, and the Archbishop of Canterbury emerged as one of the country's most powerful men.

The famous pilgrimages to Canterbury increased in the 12th century, after the assassination of Archbishop Thomas Becket by followers of King Henry II (with whom Becket had been in a long fight). Becket was canonized as a martyr, rumors of miracles at the cathedral spread, and flocks of pilgrims showed up at its doorstep. Along the way, they'd stop off at inns and entertain each other with tales—sometimes bawdy and just for fun, sometimes devout and meaningful.

Today, much of the medieval city—heavily bombed during World War II—exists only in fragments. Miraculously, the cathedral and surrounding streets are fairly well-preserved. Thanks to its huge student population and thriving pedestrian-and-shopper-friendly zone in the center, Canterbury is an exceptionally livable and fun-to-visit town.

Planning Your Time

Because of its impressive cathedral, compact tourist zone, and relaxing break-from-a-big-city ambience, Canterbury is an ideal day trip from London. With more time, it merits an overnight. (You could even come straight from the airport to Canterbury and sleep here for two nights, with a day of sightseeing.) If visiting for just a few hours, head straight for the cathedral, then spend the rest of your time strolling the town's pleasant pedestrian core, and maybe drop into some of Canterbury's other sights (St. Augustine's Abbey is worth a visit). Consider sticking around for evensong in the cathedral (Mon-Fri at 17:30, Sat-Sun generally at 15:15).

Orientation to Canterbury

With about 55,000 people, Canterbury is big enough to be lively but small enough to be manageable. The center of town is enclosed by the old city walls, a ring road, and the Stour River to the west. High Street (also known as St. Peter's Street at one end and St. George's Street at the other) bisects the town center. During the day, the action is on High Street and in the knot of medieval lanes surrounding the cathedral. (At night, the city is quiet all around.) The center is very walkable—it's only about 20 minutes on foot from one end to the other.

Tourist Information

The TI, housed in the atrium of the Beaney Art Museum and Library, assists modern-day pilgrims. Pick up the free Visitors Guide with a map (Mon-Sat 9:00-17:00, Sun 10:00-17:00, on High Street, free Wi-Fi, just past Best Lane, tel. 01227/378-100, www.canterbury.co.uk).

Combo-Ticket: The TI sells a "Canterbury Attractions Passport" that covers the cathedral, Canterbury Tales audiovisual show, Roman Museum, and skippable Canterbury Heritage Museum. It's a good deal only if you plan to see everything (£28, saves about £4, sold only at TI).

Canterbury

200 YARDS
200 METERS

WEST STATION

TO WHITSTABLE VIA A-290

TO LONDON VIA A-2

RHEIMS WAY

STOUR RIVER

ROAD W.

STATION ROAD

NORTH LANE

POUND LANE

ST. DUNSTAN'S

WEST GATE

ST. PETER'S PLACE

ST. PETER'S LANE

ST. PETER'S ST.

THE FRIARS

BLACK GRIFFIN LANE

ST. PETER'S GROVE

CHURCH LANE

STOUR ST.

CASTLE ST.

ST. JOHN'S HOSP.

ST. MARGARET'S ST.

FOUNTAIN

PIN HILL

WINCHEAP

EAST STATION

TO ASHFORD VIA A-28

DCH

CATHEDRAL

ST. RADIGUND

KING ST.

PALACE ST.

SUN ST.

HIGH ST.

MERCER LANE

THE CANTERBURY TALES

ROSE LANE

WATLING ST.

WHITE-FRIARS CENTRE

DANE JOHN PARK

MOUND

RHODAUS TOWN

NORTHGATE

BROAD ST.

MILITARY RD.

CHRIST CHURCH GATE

BURGATE

ROMAN MUSEUM

QUENINGATE

CHURCH BRIDGE

LOWER BRIDGE

LONGPORT

TO ST. AUG. ABBEY & ST. MARTIN'S CHURCH

BUS STN.

ST. GEORGE'S

ST. GEORGE'S PLACE

UPPER BRIDGE

DOVER ST.

OLD DOVER ROAD

TO DOVER VIA NEW DOVER ROAD & A-2

PEDESTRIAN ZONE
--- FOOTPATH
—— CITY WALLS
P PARKING

CANTERBURY

1 The White House
2 Castle House
3 The Miller's Arms
4 The Tudor House B&B
5 To Harriet House
6 St. John's Court Guest House
7 Old Weavers House Restaurant
8 Ask Restaurant
9 Wagamama & Morelli's Restaurants

10 City Fish Bar
11 The Foundry Brew Pub
12 The Dolphin Pub
13 Marks & Spencer (Supermarket)
14 Farmers Market
15 Marlowe Theatre
16 Bike Rental
17 Punting Tours

Arrival in Canterbury

Canterbury's two train stations (East and West) flank the town center. Trains from London's Victoria Station arrive at Canterbury's East Station; trains from London's St. Pancras and Charing Cross stations arrive at Canterbury's West Station. Each train station is about a 10-minute walk or £5 taxi ride from downtown. The bus station is at the end of the High Street pedestrian area, inside the city walls just past the big Whitefriars shopping center.

Helpful Hints

Guided Walk: Canterbury Tourist Guides offer a 1.5-hour walk departing from in front of the cathedral entrance (£6.50, daily at 11:00, April-Sept also at 14:00, www.canterburyguided-tours.com, tel. 01227/459-779).

Internet Access: Many restaurants and cafes, including the recommended **Dolphin Pub,** offer free Wi-Fi for paying customers.

Shopping: A **Marks & Spencer** department store, with a supermarket at the back on the ground floor, is located near the east end of High Street (Mon-Sat 8:00-19:00 except Thu until 20:00, Sun 11:00-17:00, tel. 01227/462-281). Sprawling behind it is a vast shopping complex called **Whitefriars Centre** (most shops open Mon-Sat 9:00-18:00, Sun 11:00-17:00) and a **Tesco** grocery store (Mon-Sat 7:00-23:00, Sun 11:00-17:00). A modest **farmers' market** is held every day except Monday at The Goods Shed (Tue-Sat 9:00-18:00, Sun 10:00-16:00, www.thegoodsshed.co.uk), just to the north of the West Station, adjacent to the parking lot. Another **market,** selling general goods, fills the east end of the city center along St. George's Street on Wednesday (7:00-14:00) and Friday (7:00-17:00).

Bike Rental: Canterbury Cycle Hire rents and repairs bikes (£18/day, helmets-£3, multiple-day discounts, Mon-Sat 9:00-17:30, closed Sun, 71 St. Dunstan's Street, tel. 01227/388-058, www.wcch.co.uk). For a pleasant daylong ride in the countryside, ask for a map of the "Crab and Winkle Way," a popular biking trail from Canterbury to the charming fishing village of Whitstable.

Theater: The **Marlowe Theatre,** named for Christopher Marlowe (Shakespeare's famous competitor and native of Canterbury), offers an array of ballet, Broadway productions, speakers, and musicians in a 21st-century theater (book tickets online, by phone, or at the box office; The Friars, tel. 01227/787-787, www.marlowetheatre.com).

Tours in Canterbury

Canterbury Punting

For a leisurely, water-level view of Canterbury, consider an £8 guided punting tour on the Stour River. The 40-minute outings, including ghost-themed, romantic, and historic options, are offered daily by the Canterbury Punting Company aboard their traditional, pole-propelled boats. Call for times and reservations (Water Lane, next to Browns Coffee Shop, tel. 01227/464-797, www.canterburypunting.co.uk).

Sights in Canterbury

▲▲▲Canterbury Cathedral

This grand landmark of piety, one of the most important churches in England, is the headquarters of the Anglican Church—in terms of church administration, it's something like the English Vatican.

It's been a Christian site ever since St. Augustine, the cathedral's first archbishop, broke ground in 597. In the 12th century, the cathedral became world famous because of an infamous act: the murder of its then-archbishop, Thomas Becket. Canterbury became a prime destination for religious pilgrims, trumped in importance only by Rome and Santiago de Compostela, Spain. The dramatic real-life history of Canterbury Cathedral is the tale of two King Henrys (Henry II and Henry VIII), and of the martyred Becket.

Cost and Hours: £9.50; Easter-Oct Mon-Sat 9:00-17:30, Sun 12:30-14:00; slightly shorter hours Nov-Easter; last entry 30 minutes before closing.

Information: Tel. 01227/762-862, www.canterbury-cathedral.org.

Tours: Knowledgeable guides wearing golden sashes are posted throughout the cathedral to answer your questions. Guided £5 tours are offered Mon-Fri at 10:30, 12:00, and 14:30 (14:00 in winter); and Sat at 10:30, 12:00, and 13:30 (no tours Sun). At the shop inside the cathedral, you can rent a dry but informative £4 audioguide.

Evensong: The choral evensong is easy even for atheists. As you enter, they'll hand you a laminated placard telling you what to say for group responses (you don't have to say anything if you don't want to), when to sit and stand, and when the music begins (free,

Canterbury Cathedral

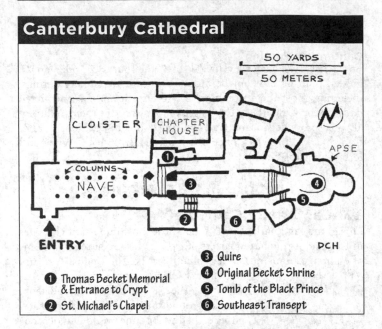

50 YARDS

50 METERS

CLOISTER

CHAPTER HOUSE

APSE

COLUMNS

NAVE

❶

❸

❹

❺

❷

❻

ENTRY

DCH

❶ Thomas Becket Memorial & Entrance to Crypt

❷ St. Michael's Chapel

❸ Quire

❹ Original Becket Shrine

❺ Tomb of the Black Prince

❻ Southeast Transept

Mon-Fri at 17:30, Sat-Sun generally at 15:15). Weekend schedules are subject to change, so it's smart to stop by or call to confirm (tel. 01227/762-862). For more on evensong, see page 164.

❺ Self-Guided Tour: Although guided tours and audioguides are available, it's simple just to wander through on your own.

• *Begin your tour in the pedestrian shopping zone just outside the cathedral grounds. Before going through the passageway (and admission area), take a moment to appreciate the...*

Christ Church Gate: This highly decorated gate is the cathedral yard's main entrance. Find the royal seals and symbols on the gate, including the Tudor rose. This rose was the symbol of Henry VIII, who—shortly after the Christ Church Gate was built—divorced both his wife and the Vatican, establishing the Anglican Church (for more on Henry, see the sidebar on page 130).

• *Go through the gate (where you'll buy your ticket) and walk into the courtyard that surrounds this massive, impressive church. An information booth, where you can get a free map of the building, is to your right. Examine the...*

Cathedral Exterior: Notice the cathedral's length, and how each section is distinctive. The church was already considered large in pre-pilgrim days, but in the 15th century, builders began another 100 years of construction (resulting in a patchwork effect that you'll notice in the interior).

• *Enter the church through the side door—the front doors of English cathedrals tend to be used only for special occasions. Take a seat in the...*

Thomas Becket and Canterbury Cathedral

In the 12th century, Canterbury Cathedral had already been a Christian church for more than 500 years. The king at the

time was Henry II (who rebuilt and expanded nearby Dover Castle, described in the next chapter). Henry was looking for a new archbishop, someone who would act as a yes-man and allow him to gain control of the Church (and its followers). He found a candidate in his drinking buddy and royal chancellor: Thomas Becket (also called Thomas à Becket). In 1162, the king's friend was consecrated as archbishop.

But Becket surprised the king, and maybe even himself. Inspired by his new position—and wanting to be a true religious leader to his mighty flock—he cleaned up his act, became dedicated to the religious tenets of the Church (dressing as a monk), and refused to bow to the king's wishes. As tensions grew, Henry wondered aloud, "Will no one rid me of this turbulent priest?" Four knights took his words seriously, and assassinated Becket during vespers in the cathedral. The act shocked the medieval world. King Henry later submitted to walking barefoot through town while being flogged by priests as an act of pious penitence.

Not long after Becket's death in 1170, word spread that miracles were occurring in the cathedral, prompting the pope to canonize Becket. Soon the pilgrims came, hoping some of Becket's steadfast goodness would rub off (perhaps they also wanted to see the world—just like travelers today).

Nave: The interior of the nave shows the inner workings of this sprawling, eclectic structure. Look around, and you'll see a church that's had many incarnations. Archaeological excavations in the early 1990s showed that the building's core is Roman. Through the ages, new sections were added on, with the biggest growth during the 1400s, when the cathedral had to be expanded to hold all of its pilgrims.

While tourists still flock here, this is also a working church, the headquarters of the Anglican Church, and the seat of the Archbishop of Canterbury. Justin Welby is the new archbishop (as of 2012). A married father of five, he is descended from a German-Jewish family who fled anti-Semitism in the late 19th century.

• *From here, we'll follow the route laid out by the map you picked up when you entered. Head up the left aisle. When you get to the quire (marked by a beautifully carved stone portal in the center of the nave), go down the stairs to your left. Immediately to your right is the...*

Thomas Becket Memorial: This is where Thomas Becket was martyred. You'll see a humble plaque and an overly dramatic wall sculpture of lightning-rod arrows pointing to the place where he died.

• *Continue down the stairs next to the memorial and enter the...*

Crypt: Notice the heavy stone arches. This lower section was started by the Normans, who probably built on top of St. Augustine's original church. Work your way to the other (right) side of the vast crypt. The small chapel marked *Église Protestante Française* celebrates a Mass in French every Sunday at 15:00. This chapel has been used for hundreds of years by French (Huguenot) and Belgian (Walloon) Protestant communities, who fled persecution in their home countries for the more welcoming atmosphere in Protestant England.

• *Facing this chapel, turn right, walk to the end of the crypt, and climb up the stairs. At the landing, turn left to find...*

St. Michael's Chapel: Also known as the Warrior's Chapel, this was built by Lady Margaret Holland (d. 1439) to house family tombs. The chapel, which may be undergoing restoration when you visit, is also associated with the Royal East Kent Regiment ("The Buffs"). Notice the ancient military flags adorning the walls.

• *Head up the stairs across from the tomb, and go through the ornate stone portal we passed earlier. This will bring you into the* **quire,** *where the choir sings evensong. Walk toward the high altar, then turn left through the gate and walk with the quire on your right to the side of the church (the apse). Behind the quire, and to the right (up some steps), you'll see a candle in the center of the floor. This was the site of the...*

Original Becket Shrine: Beginning in the 12th century, hundreds of thousands of pilgrims came to this site to leave offerings. Imagine this site in the Dark Ages. You're surrounded by humble, devout pilgrims who've trudged miles upon miles to reach this spot. (Try to ignore the B.O.) Now that they've finally arrived, they're hoping to soak up just a bit of the miraculous power that's supposed to reside here.

Then came King Henry VIII, who broke away from the pope so he could marry on his own terms. In 1538, he destroyed the original altar (and lots more, including the original abbey of St. Augustine on the edge of town). Dictatorial Henry VIII—no fan of a priest who would stand up to a king—had Thomas Becket's body removed from the cathedral. Legend says that Henry had

Becket's body burned and the ashes scattered as part of his plan to drive religious pilgrims away from the site.

• *Follow the curve of the apse to the...*

Tomb of the Black Prince: Marked by a famous sculpture on his tomb, this is the final resting place of the Black Prince, Edward of Woodstock (d. 1376). The Prince of Wales and the eldest son of Edward III, the Black Prince was famous for his cunning in battle and his chivalry—the original "knight in shining armor."

• *Head downstairs and make your way to the southeast transept (on your left).*

Southeast Transept: The small ship's bell standing to the left may be moved back to St. Michael's Chapel after restoration work is done there. This bell once rang from the HMS *Canterbury*, a ship that waged war against those disobedient colonists during the American Revolution. Each day at 11:00, the bell is rung and a prayer is said here to honor those who have lost their lives in battle.

The stained-glass windows in the transept are actually modern, relatively speaking, created by Hungarian-born artist and refugee Ervin Bossányi, who was commissioned by the Dean of Canterbury to replace earlier windows damaged by WWII bombs.

Our tour is finished. As you leave the cathedral, consider this: Even with all their power, wealth, and influence, two English kings were unable to successfully eradicate Thomas Becket's influence (if they had, the line to get into the cathedral would be shorter). A man of conscience—who once stood up to the most powerful ruler in England—continues to inspire visitors, nearly a thousand years after his death.

More Sights in the Old Town

▲The Canterbury Tales

If your visit to Canterbury gives you English Lit flashbacks, this corny audiovisual show offers a good review—or, if you're unfamiliar with Chaucer, it provides a decent introduction. Making use of live actors, primitive lighting effects, and medieval smells, it dramatizes five of the tales. More hokey than literary, the exhibit is useful as a CliffsNotes to Chaucer's masterpiece.

Cost and Hours: £8.55, includes 35-minute audioguide, daily 10:00-17:00, July-Aug from 9:30, Nov-Feb until 16:30, St. Margaret's Street, tel. 01227/454-888, recorded info tel. 01227/479-227, www.canterburytales.org.uk.

Roman Museum

The colorful displays in this slight museum illustrate Canterbury's Roman origins and end with a view of sections of still-intact foundations and mosaics. Included are several shamelessly self-congratulatory exhibits celebrating the museum archaeologist...nice touch.

Cost and Hours: £6, free for kids, daily 10:00-17:00 except

The Canterbury Tales

"Whan that Aprill, with his shoures soote
The droghte of March hath perced to the roote..."

So begins *The Canterbury Tales,* one of the earliest and most influential works of English literature. In the late 14th century, author and diplomat Geoffrey Chaucer (c. 1343-1400) was so inspired by the cross-section of humanity undertaking the pilgrimage to Canterbury that he penned a collection of 24 fascinating and sometimes bawdy tales told by fictional travelers. *The Canterbury Tales* is arguably the oldest surviving travelogue, and the greatest work written in the Middle English vernacular—a bold move at a time when Latin and French were the literary languages of choice. (Because Middle English is essentially a different language—see the first two lines, above—the work is most often read today in present-day English translation.)

Chaucer demonstrates an impressive range of themes and genres within these tales, ranging from tragedy to romance to humor. *The Canterbury Tales* is a microcosm of human experience, featuring yarns spun by people from diverse walks of life: knight, miller, cook, lawyer, wife, merchant, squire, physician, monk, nun. Despite their obvious differences, all of these travelers were drawn together by a shared faith and the desire to experience the power of the shrine of Thomas Becket...and by a mutual appreciation for a good story.

closed Sun off-season, last entry 45 minutes before closing, Butchery Lane, across from City Arms Inn, tel. 01227/785-575, www.canterbury.co.uk.

East of the Old Town

While historically significant, these two sights—about a 10-minute walk east of the Old Town walls—aren't worth the trek for most visitors. Both are well-marked; if you decide to go, just follow the signs.

St. Augustine's Abbey

The ruins of the original abbey—founded by the man himself, St. Augustine—sit right on the edge of town. At its height, the abbey was a hive of activity, with a large church, cloister, and a cluster of service buildings for the monks. In the 16th century, King Henry VIII grew jealous of the wealth and influence held by England's monks, so he closed down the monasteries, retired the monks, and sold off the land and buildings. The abbey's buildings were converted to houses, while the large church was slowly dismantled and used as a building-material quarry for projects in the area.

A modest museum sets up your visit. Outside, the foundations and some fragments of the original structures (including a standing stone from the Neolithic period) are still visible in a grassy field, and the audioguide manages to bring the site to life. Pace the square of the cloister and imagine yourself as a monk in the early days of Christianity in England. On a sunny day, the abbey grounds are a fine place for a picnic.

Cost and Hours: £5, includes audioguide; April-Sept daily 10:00-18:00; Oct-Nov Wed-Sun 10:00-17:00, closed Mon-Tue; Dec-March Sat-Sun 10:00-16:00, closed Mon-Fri; sometimes closes at 15:00 for concerts, last entry 30 minutes before closing, tel. 01227/767-345, www.english-heritage.org.uk.

St. Martin's Church

Set in the center of an old, slanted graveyard, humble little St. Martin's has the honor of being the oldest parish church in England. In continual use since 650, it sits on the foundations of a Roman temple, and features an elegant Norman-era baptismal font to the right of the entrance.

Cost and Hours: Free; may be open Tue, Thu, and Sat 11:00-15:00; Sun service at 9:50; tel. 01227/768-072, www.martinpaul. org. Because the church is run by volunteers, it has very sporadic hours, so call to confirm. To find the church, continue on the busy road 300 yards past the abbey, and turn down the first real road to the left (North Holmes Road); you'll see the churchyard's wooden entry gate from the main road.

Sleeping in Canterbury

Canterbury is a pleasant college town with lots of shops, restaurants, and pubs, making it a fine home base. There are relatively few options within the old walls, but I've listed my favorites. The roads heading out of town, particularly New Dover Road, have clusters of B&Bs that are slim on charm but suitable for tired drivers.

$$$ The White House is a classy and elegant B&B. Its seven renovated and nicely decorated rooms, on a quiet residential lane just two blocks from the bustle of High Street, offer more modern flair than other Canterbury options in this price range (Sb-£65-80, Db-£95-150 depending on size, 6 St. Peter's Lane, tel. 01227/761-836, www.whitehousecanterbury.co.uk, info@whitehousecanterbury.co.uk, Adrian and Sharon).

$$$ Castle House, a 10-minute walk from the cathedral, has 15 spacious, inn-like rooms. It's next to the city walls and overlooks a major roundabout, but the double-glazed windows keep noise to a minimum (Sb-£60-90, Db-£75-115, family apartment-£85-140, free Wi-Fi, free parking, 28 Castle Street, tel. 01227/761-897, www.castlehousehotel.co.uk, enquiries@castlehousehotel.co.uk).

$$$ The Miller's Arms offers 11 comfy, modern rooms adjacent

Sleep Code

(£1 = about $1.60, country code: 44, area code: 01227)
S = Single, **D** = Double/Twin, **T** = Triple, **Q** = Quad, **b** = bathroom, **s** = shower only. Unless otherwise noted, credit cards are accepted and breakfast is included.

To help you sort easily through these listings, I've divided the accommodations into three categories based on the price for a standard double room with bath:

$$$ Higher Priced—Most rooms £80 or more.
$$ Moderately Priced—Most rooms between £45-80.
$ Lower Priced—Most rooms £45 or less.

Prices can change without notice; verify the hotel's current rates online or by email. For the best prices, always book direct.

to a cozy pub and restaurant, on a quiet street across from the Stour River (Sb-£65, Db-£75-95, pay Wi-Fi, parking-£6/day, 1 Mill Lane, tel. 01227/456-057, www.millerscanterbury.co.uk, millersarms@shepherdneame.co.uk).

$$ The Tudor House B&B has seven slanted-floor, older-feeling, Victorian-wallpaper rooms in a 16th-century home. Located in Canterbury's center, just two blocks from the cathedral, it has a garden with a river view (S-£35, Sb-£50, D-£59, Db-£73, T-£73, free Wi-Fi, 6 Best Lane, tel. 01227/765-650, www.tudorhousecanterbury.co.uk, info@tudorhousecanterbury.co.uk, Mazi Gerogan and Mamad Arabnia).

$$ Harriet House offers seven tidy and comfortable rooms with sophisticated decor, and it's just a 10-minute walk along a scenic river footpath from the town center (Sb-£48-55, Db-£70-85, Tb-from £120, free Wi-Fi, free parking, 3 Broad Oak Road, tel. 01227/457-363, www.harriethouse.co.uk, enquiries@harriethouse.co.uk, Terry and Chris).

$ St. John's Court Guest House is a good value on a quiet street within the walls. No-nonsense Liz Rowe rents eight bright rooms (all with shared bathrooms down the hall) in a quaint brick building (S-£35, D-£50, T-£70, cash only, no young children, parking, St. John's Lane, tel. 01227/456-425, www.stjohnscourtguesthouse.co.uk, nigelnrw@aol.com).

Eating in Canterbury

As a student town, Canterbury is packed with eateries—especially along the pedestrianized shopping zone. However, many places serve only lunch, leaving options pretty thin for dinner.

Old Weavers House serves solid English food in a pleasant, historic building next to the river. Sit inside beneath sunny walls

and creaky beams, or outside on their riverside garden patio. This is the most atmospheric of my listings, and it can get very busy (£6-7 lunch specials, £9-15 dinner plates, daily 12:00-23:00, 1 St. Peter's Street, tel. 01227/464-660).

Ask, over a small bridge from Old Weavers House, is in a renovated home. This chain restaurant offers decent Italian food at moderate prices. The garden in back, while pleasant, lacks the Old Weavers House's river view (£8-12 meals; big and splittable salads, pasta bowls, and meat dishes; daily 11:30-23:00, 24 High Street, tel. 01227/767-617).

Wagamama, part of the wildly popular British chain known for slinging tasty pan-Asian fare, has a convenient location just off the main shopping street (£8-13 main dishes, daily 11:30-22:00, 7-11 Longmarket Street, tel. 01227/454-307).

Morelli's Restaurant serves typical soups, sandwiches, and "jacket potatoes" with takeaway options. You'll find it above the recommended Wagamama on Longmarket Street, with glassy indoor seating and a fine outdoor terrace (£5-7 light lunches, Mon-Sat 8:00-17:00, Sun 9:00-17:00, tel. 01227/784-700).

City Fish Bar is your quintessential British "chippy," serving several kinds of fried fish. Get yours for takeaway or grab a sidewalk table on this charming pedestrian street (£5-8 fish-and-chips, Mon-Sat 10:00-19:00, Sun 11:00-16:00, 30 St. Margaret's Street, tel. 01227/760-873).

The Foundry Brew Pub offers up to 57 home brews on tap (depending on the season) and serves beer-inspired dishes like steak-and-ale pie and BBQ beer ribs. Bartenders happily pour generous samples for curious customers (with the intent of selling you a pint) and explain the inspiration behind the name of their signature draft, Torpedo (£4-7 starters and salads, £9-10 meat pies, £8-14 main dishes, food served daily 12:00-18:00, pub open until 24:00, White Horse Lane, tel. 01227/455-899).

Pub: **The Dolphin,** a local favorite, is a homey 1930s pub with carefully chosen ales. The food is a cut above typical pub grub, with quality local ingredients and daily specials. Sit in the main bar, in the sunroom, or—in nice weather—at a picnic table in the grassy garden (large £8-12 plates, daily 12:00–24:00, free Wi-Fi, 17 St. Radigunds St, tel. 01227/455-963).

Canterbury Connections

Remember that Canterbury has two train stations, East and West.

From Canterbury by Train to: London (1-2/hour, 1-hour direct express trains from Canterbury West Station to St. Pancras International Station; more to Charing Cross station with transfer; also 2/hour, 1.25 hours from Canterbury East Station to Victoria Station), **Dover** (2/hour, 15-30 minutes, from Canterbury East to Dover Priory), **Rye** (hourly, 1 hour, from Canterbury West, transfer at Ashford International), **Hastings** (hourly, 1.25 hours, from Canterbury West, transfer at Ashford International), **Brighton** (hourly, 2.5 hours, 1-3 transfers, can be complicated—best connections through London's St. Pancras or Ashford International, from Canterbury West). Train info: Tel. 0845-748-4950, www.nationalrail.co.uk.

By Bus to: London's Victoria Coach Station (about hourly, 2-2.5 hours), **Dover** (roughly hourly, 45 minutes). Bus info: Tel. 0870-781-8181, www.nationalexpress.com.

CANTERBURY

DOVER AND SOUTHEAST ENGLAND

Dover—like much of southern England—sits on a foundation of chalk. Miles of cliffs stand at attention above the beaches; the most famous are the White Cliffs of Dover. Sitting above those cliffs is the impressive Dover Castle, England's primary defensive stronghold from Roman through modern times. From the nearby port, ferries, hydrofoils, and hovercrafts shuttle people and goods back and forth across the English Channel. France is only 23 miles away—on a sunny day, you can see it off in the distance.

Because of its easy access from the Continent, many travelers have a sentimental attachment to Dover as the first place they saw in England. But in recent years—especially since the opening of the English Channel Tunnel in 1994—this workaday town has lost whatever luster it once had. The run-down town center isn't worth a second look. Focus instead on a fun in-and-out visit to Dover's looming castle, standing guard as it has for almost a thousand years. Geologists and romantics may want to take a cruise to get the best view of the famous white cliffs. (Or, for a more rural and idyllic white cliff experience, visit Beachy Head near Brighton—described on page 318.)

In the southeast English countryside near Dover, you can explore a castle and charming cottage garden at Sissinghurst; stroll the cobbles of the huggable hill town of Rye; and visit the Battle of Hastings site—in the appropriately named town of Battle—where England's future course was charted in 1066.

Planning Your Time

Dover works best as a day trip from Canterbury or London, and is worth a quick visit if you're passing through anyway. Ambitious sightseers can tackle both Dover and Canterbury as a one-day side-trip from London (see page 272).

Orientation to Dover

Gritty, urban-feeling Dover seems bigger than its population of 30,000. The town lies between two cliffs, with Dover Castle on one side and the Western Heights on the other. While the streets stretch longingly toward the water, the core of the town is cut off from the harbor by the rumbling A-20 motorway (connecting Dover with cities to the west) and a long, eyesore apartment building. The workaday city center is anchored by Market Square and the mostly pedestrianized (but not particularly charming) main shopping drag, Cannon Street/Biggin Street, which runs north from Market Square to the old town jail. A short five-minute walk south of Market Square, through a pedestrian underpass ("subway"), takes you to the waterfront—a pleasant pebbly beach lined with a promenade; at its western end, you can enjoy fine views of the castle and white cliffs. But this is only worth it on a gorgeous day—views of the white cliffs are better from out of town, and the beach is pretty tame even by British standards.

Tourist Information

You'll find the TI in the Dover Museum, on Market Square. The TI sells ferry and long-distance bus tickets, and books rooms for a £3 fee (April-Sept Mon-Sat 9:30-17:00, Sun 10:00-15:00; Oct-March Mon-Sat 9:30-17:00, closed Sun; Market Square, tel. 01304/201-066, www.whitecliffscountry.org.uk, tic@doveruk.com).

Arrival in Dover

Trains arrive on the west side of town, a five-minute walk from the main pedestrian area and the TI. **Drivers** find that parking is plentiful close to the water—just follow *P* signs. If you arrive by **boat** at the Eastern Docks, walk about 20 minutes along the base of the cliffs into town (with the sea on your left), or catch a shuttle bus to the train station (3/hour, daily 7:00-21:00).

Dover is also a popular destination (and starting/ending point) for **cruise ships.** For information on Dover's cruise ports—and how to connect to London—see page 222.

Sights in Dover

▲▲Dover Castle

Strategically located Dover Castle—considered "the key to England" by would-be invaders—perches grandly atop the White Cliffs of Dover. English troops were garrisoned within the castle's medieval walls for almost 900 years, protecting the coast from European invaders (a record of military service rivaled only by Windsor Castle and the Tower of London). With a medieval Great Tower as its centerpiece and battlements that survey 360 degrees of windswept coast, Dover Castle has undeniable majesty. Today, the biggest invading menaces are the throngs of school kids on field trips, so it's best to arrive early. While the historic parts of the castle are unexceptional, the exhibits in the WWII-era Secret Wartime Tunnels are unique and engaging—particularly the new, powerful, well-presented tour that tells the story of Operation Dynamo,

a harrowing WWII rescue operation across the English Channel.

Cost and Hours: £17, £44 family ticket; April-Sept daily 10:00-18:00, from 9:30 in Aug; Oct daily 10:00-17:00; Nov-March Sat-Sun 10:00-16:00, closed Mon-Fri; last entry one hour before closing, keep yard may close in high winds.

Information: Ticket kiosks at either entrance distribute helpful maps of the castle grounds. In the middle of the complex, just below the Great Tower, a handy visitors center also dispenses information. Tel. 01304/211-067, www.english-heritage.org.uk/dovercastle.

Avoiding Lines: Arrive early for the fewest crowds (busiest on summer bank holidays and weekends; worst around 11:30). While crowds can impede your progress throughout the site, the biggest potential headaches are lines for the two tours of the Secret Wartime Tunnels: The line for the Operation Dynamo exhibit can be quite long (up to two hours at the worst), while the Underground Hospital line is usually shorter. When you buy your ticket, ask about wait times and organize your visit accordingly (see "Planning Your Time," later).

Getting There: Drivers follow signs from A-20 or the town center. For those without a car, getting up to the castle is tricky. Bus #15 departs hourly from the bus station (on Pencester Road) and heads up to the castle. Otherwise, you can take a taxi from downtown (about £5 one-way) or hoof it up the steep hill (30-45 minutes straight up; 1.5 miles from train station). By the time you get to the top, you'll know why no invading army ever successfully took the castle. The hike back down is easier, of course—ask for walking directions (using shortcut staircases) at the castle's visitors center before you leave.

Entrances: Two entry gates have kiosks where you'll pause to buy your ticket before entering the grounds. The Cannon Gate is closer to the Secret Wartime Tunnels, at the lower end of the cas-

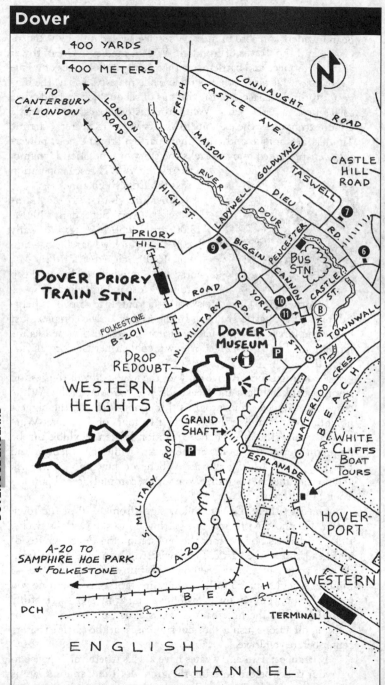

Dover

DOVER & SE ENGLAND

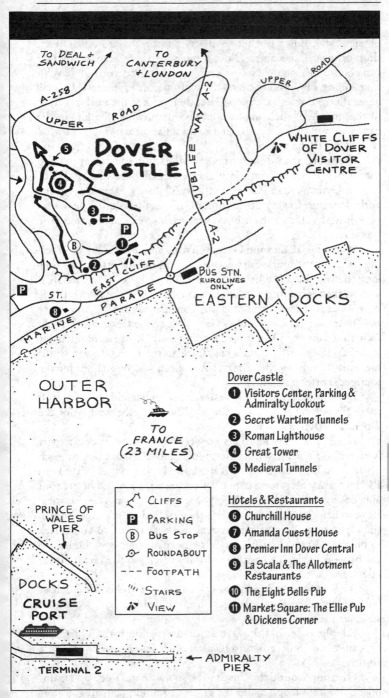

Dover Castle

1. Visitors Center, Parking & Admiralty Lookout
2. Secret Wartime Tunnels
3. Roman Lighthouse
4. Great Tower
5. Medieval Tunnels

Hotels & Restaurants

6. Churchill House
7. Amanda Guest House
8. Premier Inn Dover Central
9. La Scala & The Allotment Restaurants
10. The Eight Bells Pub
11. Market Square: The Ellie Pub & Dickens Corner

tle, while the Constable's Gate is near the Great Tower, at the top of the castle. Buses (including shuttles from Dover's cruise port) drop off near Constable's Gate; walkers or those arriving by taxi can choose either gate. Note that from either gate, you still have to hike quite a bit uphill to reach the main points of interest. Drivers generally go through Cannon Gate, then park at the visitors center in the middle of the complex; on busy days, when the lots in the castle are full, you'll be directed to an adjacent parking lot with a shuttle bus to the grounds.

Planning Your Time: The key is planning your day around the Secret Wartime Tunnels tours—especially the excellent Operation Dynamo tour. Each tour allows 30 people to enter at a time, with departures every 10-15 minutes. Your decision depends on two things: Which entrance you use (see above), and how long the lines are.

If arriving at **Cannon Gate,** you're a short walk from the starting point for the tours. Survey the line and ask the attendants how long the wait is. If it'll be a while, consider hiking up to the Great Tower, then returning here later, in the hope that the lines will die down. But if the wait isn't too long, consider taking the tour now.

If arriving at **Constable's Gate,** ask at the ticket kiosk about wait times for the Operation Dynamo tour. If lines are relatively short, do the tour first, then backtrack to the Great Tower. But if the wait is long, see the Great Tower first, and hope lines for the tour get shorter later on.

Drivers parking at the **visitors center** should ask the staff there for advice; they know roughly how long the wait is for the Operation Dynamo tour.

Note: The lines for the two Secret Wartime Tunnels tours (Operation Dynamo and Underground Hospital) are next to each other. It makes sense to do the Operation Dynamo tour (often with a longer wait) first, for a variety of reasons: it's a much better tour and deserves to be done while you're fresh; it sets the historical stage to help you better appreciate the hospital tour; and you finish the Operation Dynamo tour nearby, making it easy to circle back to do the hospital tour (whereas the hospital tour ends higher up the hill—more logically situated for hiking up to the Great Tower afterward).

Also ask about periodic special events at the castle, such as falconry shows (various activities offered sporadically, especially on summer weekends).

Finally, note that the last departure for both the Operation Dynamo and Underground Hospital tours leaves one hour before closing.

Getting Around the Castle: The sporadic and free "land train" does a constant loop around the castle's grounds, shuttling visitors between the Secret Wartime Tunnels, the entrance to the Great Tower, and the Medieval Tunnels (at the top end of the castle). Though handy for avoiding the ups and downs, the train doesn't run every day. Nothing at the castle is more than a 10-minute walk from anything else—so you'll likely spend more time waiting for the train than you would walking.

Background: Armies have kept a watchful eye on this strategic lump of land since Roman times (as evidenced by the partly standing ancient lighthouse). A linchpin for English defense starting in the Middle Ages, Dover Castle was heavily used in the time of Henry VIII and Elizabeth I. After a period of decline, the castle was reinvigorated during the Napoleonic Wars, and became a central command in World War II (when naval headquarters were buried deep in the cliffside). Part of the tunnels were also used as a hospital and triage station for injured troops. After the war, in the 1960s, the tunnels were converted into a dramatic Cold War bunker—one of 12 designated sites in the UK that would house government officials and a BBC studio in the event of nuclear war. When it became clear that even the stout cliffs of Dover couldn't be guaranteed to stand up to a nuclear attack, Dover Castle was retired from active duty in 1984.

➔ Self-Guided Tour: The sights at Dover Castle basically cluster into two areas: The Secret Wartime Tunnels (with two, very different tunnel tours and a modest exhibit) and the Great Tower and surrounding historical castle features (such as the old Roman lighthouse and the Medieval Tunnels). The order you see these sights depends on where you enter and the crowds—see "Planning Your Time," earlier, for tips.

Secret Wartime Tunnels

In the 1790s, with the threat of Napoleon looming, the castle's fortifications were beefed up again. So many troops were stationed

here that they needed to tunnel into the chalk to provide sleeping areas for up to 2,000 men. These tunnels were vastly expanded during World War II, when operations for the war effort moved into a bomb-proofed, underground air-raid shelter safe from Hitler's feared Luftwaffe planes. Winston Churchill watched air battles from here, while Allied commanders looked out over a battle zone nicknamed "Hellfire Corner." There are three layers of tunnels: Annexe at the top, Casemates in the middle, and Dumpy at the lowest point. Two different tours take you into the tunnels: Operation Dynamo (Casemates tunnels) and Underground Hospital (Annexe

Dover Castle and Operation Dynamo

It was during World War II that Dover Castle lived its most dramatic moments, most notably as the headquarters for the inspiring **Operation Dynamo**—a story you'll hear retold again and again on your visit here.

In the spring of 1940, in the early days of the war, a joint French-British-Dutch-Belgian attack on the Nazis was met by a shockingly aggressive German counteroffensive. While Allied forces were distracted with their eastern front, the Nazis flanked them to the west, pinning them into an ever-narrowing corner of northern France (around the port cities of Calais and Dunkerque, which Brits call Dunkirk). As the Nazis closed in, it became clear that hundreds of thousands of British and other Allied troops being squeezed against the English Channel would soon be captured—or worse. From the tunnels below Dover Castle, Admiral Sir Bertram Ramsay oversaw Operation Dynamo. In 10 days, using a variety of military and civilian ships, Ramsay staged a dramatic evacuation of 338,000 Allied soldiers from the beaches of Dunkirk (several thousand troops, both British and French, were captured).

Because so many survived the desperate circumstances, the operation has been called a "victory in defeat." And although the Allies were forced to leave northern France to Hitler, Operation Dynamo saved an untold number of lives and bolstered morale in a country just beginning the most devastating war it would ever face. This unlikely evacuation is often called the "Miracle at Dunkirk."

tunnels). A small exhibit near the Operation Dynamo exit tells the whole story of the tunnels.

Operation Dynamo: From these tunnels in May of 1940, Admiral Sir Bertram Ramsay oversaw the rescue mission wherein the British managed, in just 10 days, to evacuate some 338,000 Allied soldiers from the beaches of Dunkirk in Nazi-occupied France. In this 45-minute tour, you're led from room to room, where a series of exceptionally well-produced audiovisual shows narrate, step-by-step, the lead-up to World War II and the exact conditions that led to the need for Operation Dynamo. You'll hear fateful radio addresses from Winston Churchill and King George VI (immortalized in the 2010 movie *The King's Speech*) announcing the declaration of war, and watch newsreel footage of Britain preparing its war effort. Imagine learning about war in this somber way (in the days before bombastic 24-hour cable news). Sitting around an animated map, you'll learn how the Allied troops advanced toward Germany and how the strategic tables turned, pinning the Allies down against the English Channel. Then you'll walk slowly down a long tunnel, as footage projected on the wall tells the stirring tale of the evacuation.

At the end of the guided portion, you're set free to explore several rooms still outfitted as they were back in World War II—such as the mapping room, repeater station, and telephone exchange. An unusually clever combination of state-of-the-art technology and good old-fashioned history, the exhibit is one of the best on World War II in this country so full of museums and memorials to that defining struggle.

You'll exit the Operation Dynamo exhibit into the gift shop and café area, where a smaller exhibit, **Wartime Tunnels Uncovered,** uses diaries, uniforms, archival films, and other artifacts to chart the development of the tunnels from the Napoleonic era to the Cold War.

Underground Hospital: Immediately next to the Operation Dynamo tour is the entrance to this shorter, lower-tech, 20-minute tour of the topmost Annexe levels of the tunnels, which were used during World War II as a hospital, then as a triage-type dressing station for wounded troops. Your guide leads you through the various parts of a re-created 1941 operating room and a narrow hospital ward, as you listen to the story of an injured Mosquito (wooden bomber) pilot—with occasional smells and lighting effects to enhance the tale. Finally, you'll climb a 78-step double-helix staircase and pop out next to the Admiralty Lookout (described next). Although the Underground Hospital lacks the excellent storytelling of the (much newer) Operation Dynamo tour, they complement each other well (though if you're triaging, choose Dynamo).

Great Tower and Nearby

• *If you take the Underground Hospital tour, you'll surface right next to the Admiralty Lookout; otherwise, hike up toward the visitors center and follow signs to find it. The lookout is near the grassy slope on the seaward side of the officers' barracks.*

Admiralty Lookout: The White Cliffs of Dover are directly beneath you. Take in the superb view across the Channel. Can you see France from here? The statue is of British Admiral Sir Bertram Ramsay, who heroically orchestrated Operation Dynamo (see sidebar).

• *Backtrack past the visitors center (if you're starting at the lookout, climb up the hill and bear right past the big barracks building to reach the visitors center on the hill above), and hike up the path (following signs to the Great Tower) through the stubby guard tower. Emerging on the other side of the guard tower, you'll be facing the Great Tower. But before going there, look up the hill to your right. The round tower behind the flagpole is the oldest structure at the castle, the...*

Roman Lighthouse: The lighthouse *(pharos)* was built during the first century A.D., when Julius Caesar's Roman fleet for the colony of Britannia was based in the harbor below. To guide the boats, they burned wet wood by day (for maximum smoke), and dry wood by night (for maximum light). When the Romans finally left England 400 years later, the *pharos* is said to have burst into flames as the last ship departed. Adjacent to the lighthouse is the unimpressive St. Mary-in-the-Castle Church, built to guard against invading Saxons in the sixth century.

• *Back at the guard tower, go past the parking lot and head through the archway to enter the courtyard of...*

Henry II's Great Tower: The heart of this frontier fortress first beat in 1066, when a castle was built here after the Battle of Hastings (see page 303). In the 12th century, King Henry II (the bad guy in the Thomas Becket story—see page 277 in the Canterbury chapter) added heavy castle fortifications. For centuries, Dover Castle was the most secure fortress in all of England, and an important symbol of royal might on the coast.

Examine the Tower of London-like central building, which was the original tower (also called a "keep"). The walls are up to 20 feet thick. King Henry II slept on the top floor, surrounded by his best protection against an invading army. Imagine the attempt: As the thundering enemy cavalry makes its advance, the king's defenders throw caltrops (four-starred metal spikes meant to cut through the horses' hooves). His knights unsheathe their  swords, and trained crossbow archers ring the tower, sending arrows into foreign armor. Later kings added buildings near the tower (along the inner bailey, which lines the keep yard) to garrison troops during wartime, to provide extra rooms for royal courtiers during peacetime, and to be filled centuries later with museum exhibits and a gift shop. On summer weekends, and for most of August, costumed actors wandering the grounds add to the fun.

Before going in the tower itself, check out some of the exhibits in the surrounding garrison buildings. To the right as you enter the courtyard, you'll first see the **Great Tower Story** exhibit, which uses colorful displays and animated films to bring meaning to the place. You'll learn how Henry II established the mighty empire of Aquitaine (encompassing much of today's England and France), how his heirs squandered it, and how it evolved into the Plantagenet dynasty that ruled England for some 400 years (including many of the famous Henrys and Richards).

Next door, the **Princess of Wales's Royal Regiment and Queen's Regiment Museum** collects military memorabilia and tells the story of these military units, which have fought in foreign conflicts for centuries—you'll see gritty helmet-cam footage from their recent participation in Afghanistan. (Sorry, no Princess Diana items.)

Now enter the **Great Tower** itself. While fun to poke around, it's somewhat empty-feeling, decorated with brightly colored furnishings from the period—a dining hall, a throne room, a kitchen, a bedroom, and so on. While there's no real exhibit, docents are standing by to answer questions, and the kid-friendly furnishings give a sense of what the castle was like in King Henry VIII's time. Find the well, which helped make the tower even more siege-resistant. Fans of Thomas Becket can look for his chapel, a tiny sacristy called the "upper chapel" (it's hiding down a forgotten hallway high in the building—ask a docent for directions). If you're feeling energetic, climb all the way to the top of the tower's spiral staircase for a sweeping view of the town and sea beyond. The basement holds the medieval kitchen and royal armory.

• *Exit the keep yard at the far end through the King's Gate. Cross a stone bridge and then descend a wooden staircase. Under these stairs is the entrance to the...*

Medieval Tunnels: This system of steep tunnels was originally built in case of a siege. While enjoyable for a kid-in-a-castle experience, there's actually little to see. From here, you can catch the tourist train (if it's running) or do the Battlements Walk. Much of Dover's success as a defendable castle came from these unique concentric walls—the battlements—which protected the inner keep.

• *Our tour of the castle is finished. For a fast return to town, pop out the Constable's Gate near the Medieval Tunnels and follow the path steeply down.*

Other Sights in Dover

Dover Museum

This museum, right off the tiny main square, houses a large, impressive, and well-preserved 3,600-year-old Bronze Age boat unearthed near Dover's shoreline.  The boat is displayed on the top floor along with other finds from the site, an exhibit on boat construction techniques, and a 12-minute film. Nearby, an endearing exhibit fills one big room (the Dover History Gallery) with the story of how this small but strategically located town has shaped history—from Tudor times to the Napoleonic era to World War II. The ground floor has exhibits covering the Roman and Anglo-Saxon periods.

DOVER & SE ENGLAND

Cost and Hours: £3.50; Mon-Sat 9:30-17:00, also Sun 10:00-15:00 April-Sept; tel. 01304/201-066, www.dovermuseum.co.uk.

The Cliffs of Dover

The cliff called **Western Heights**—opposite Dover Castle, just outside of town—provides a sweeping view of Dover (and occasionally of France). The trail along the cliff weaves around former gun posts that were originally installed during Napoleonic times, but were used most extensively during World War II. It was here that the British military amassed huge decoy forces in an effort to fool the Germans into thinking that a Dover-based attack across the Channel was imminent. This fake-out maneuver was meant to disguise the plan for the Normandy D-Day invasion. Today, the bunkers are abandoned, but in decent condition. This is the place where you always wished you could play war as a kid...and with a little imagination, you still can. Peaceniks find it an excellent picnic spot. To drive there, take A-20 west past the harbor to the Western Heights roundabout, take the Aycliff exit onto Military Road, wind uphill for about half a mile, then turn right at the small brown sign onto Drop Redoubt Road. For more information, see www.doverwesternheights.org.

For a different (and many say better) view from the cliffs, as well as a fascinating look at one of the world's busiest ports, head east of town to **The White Cliffs of Dover Visitor Centre** (free, parking-£3.50/day, daily March-Oct 10:00-17:00, Nov-Feb 11:00-16:00, parking lot open longer hours; Upper Road, Langdon Cliffs, tel. 01304/202-756, www.nationaltrust.org.uk/white-cliffs-dover). You'll find exhibits about the cliffs and local flora and fauna, plus a handy  café and ample space for picnicking. You can walk to the visitors center from Dover (about 2.5 miles from the train station—just walk along the base of the cliffs with the sea on your right, following footpath signs from the town center), or you can drive: Head up the Castle Hill Road, pass the castle entrance, then take a sharp right turn onto Upper Road. After crossing over the A-2 motorway, look for the visitors center entrance at the next hairpin turn. If the first parking area is full, keep going—there are several.

If you have the energy, you can walk two miles farther along the cliff top from the visitors center to the **South Foreland Lighthouse,** built in 1843, and enjoy the glorious view. A bus makes the trip on Sundays in summer. Entry to the lighthouse is possible only with the included 30-minute guided tour (lighthouse-£5, round-trip bus-£3, Thu-Mon 11:00-17:30, closed Tue-Wed except Aug and school holidays, last tour 30 minutes before closing, tea room, tel. 01304/852-463, www.nationaltrust.org.uk/south-foreland-lighthouse).

Samphire Hoe

This man-made park, less than two miles south of Dover, makes a good stop for those who wish to see more of the white cliffs—without out the industrial crush of the busy Dover docks. Samphire Hoe, a chalk meadowland beneath the cliffs, was created using more than six million cubic yards of chalk left over from the construction of the Channel Tunnel in the early 1990s. What could have been a  dumping ground is now a grassy expanse hosting a rich variety of plants and wildlife. The park has walking paths and a tea kiosk, as well as a mile-long seawall that attracts anglers, wave watchers, and swimmers aiming for France.

Cost and Hours: Free, parking-£1/day, park open daily 7:00-dusk; tea kiosk daily Easter-Sept, weekends only in winter; tel. 01304/225-649, www.samphirehoe.co.uk.

Getting There: From Dover, drivers take A-20 heading to Folkestone and watch for the Samphire Hoe exit. After waiting for the green light at the 007-style tunnel, you'll emerge at a pay-and-display parking lot. Walkers can follow the North Downs Way footpath, while cyclists can use the National Cycle Network Route 2; both are signposted from Dover—ask the TI for specifics.

Prince of Wales Pier

If it's a sunny day and you want a nice view of the cliffs and castle without heading out of town, stroll to the western end of the beachfront promenade (to the right, as you face the water), then hike out along the Prince of Wales Pier for perfect panoramas back toward the city.

Cost and Hours: Free, daily June-Aug 8:00-21:00, Sept-May 8:00-19:00.

Boat Tours

The famous White Cliffs of Dover are almost impossible to appreciate from town. A 40-minute Dover White Cliffs Boat Tour around the bay gives you all the photo ops you need. It leaves from the Dover Marina—just past the western end of the waterfront promenade, near the Prince of Wales Pier.

Cost and Hours: £8, May-Aug daily at 12:00, 14:00, and 16:00; Sept-April by appointment only—book at least 24 hours ahead, tel. 01303/271-388, mobile 07971/301-379, www.dover-whitecliffetours.com.

Ferries to France

In the mood for a glass of wine and some escargot? A day trip to France is only a short boat ride away (walk-on passengers generally £13-15 round-trip, car prices vary with demand—usually £20-75 but can double on Sat). Two companies make the journey from Dover: P&O Ferries (1.5 hours to Calais, toll tel. 0871-664-2121, www.poferries.com), or DFDS Seaways (cars only; 2 hours to Dunkirk or 1.5 hours to Calais, tel. 0871-574-7235, www.dfds-seaways.co.uk).

Sleeping in Dover

(area code: 01304)

I'd rather sleep in Canterbury, but in a pinch, Dover has a variety of B&Bs spread throughout town (if arriving late at night, take a cab). The guesthouses below can recommend another B&B if they're booked up.

$$ Churchill House, neatly run by Alastair, Betty, and Alex Dimech, is a comfortable, traditional type of place. It's perfectly situated, just at the base of the castle hill, with eight rooms plus a family-friendly flat (Sb-£45-50, Db-£60-80, 5-person basement apartment-£80-140, guest computer, free Wi-Fi, 6 Castle Hill Road, tel. 01304/204-622, www.toastofdover.com, toastofdover@gmail.com).

The homier **$$ Amanda Guest House,** on one of the quietest streets in town, works best for drivers (Db-£65-75, cash only but reserve with credit card, easy parking, 20-minute walk from train station to 4 Harold Street, tel. 01304/201-711, www.amandaguesthouse.com, amandaguesthouse@hotmail.com, Mike and Anne).

Sleeping near the Waterfront: **$$ Premier Inn Dover Central** is handy to the ferry and cruise terminal, with dozens of identical, prefab rooms (Db-£39-86 depending on demand—up to £100 on summer weekends, sleeps up to 2 adults and 2 kids, check website for specials, breakfast-about £5-8, restaurant, pay Wi-Fi, free parking, Marine Court, Marine Parade, tel. 0871-527-8306, www.premierinn.com).

Eating in Dover

Your dining options in downtown Dover are few, and only a handful of places (including the three listed next) are open for dinner. A few more places line the beachfront promenade. Consider having lunch at one of the castle's two cafés.

La Scala is tiny, but in a romantic way, and serves a good variety of Italian dishes (£9-11 pastas, £13-17 meat and fish dishes, Mon-Sat 12:00-15:00 & 18:00-23:00, closed Sun, 19 High Street, tel. 01304/208-044).

The Allotment is trying to bring class to this small town, with an emphasis on locally sourced ingredients (in Brit-speak, an "allotment" is like a community garden). The rustic-chic interior feels a bit like an upscale deli (£3-6 breakfast dishes, £5-6 starters, £8-16 main dishes, Tue-Sat 8:30-23:00, closed Sun-Mon, 9 High Street, tel. 01304/214-467).

The Eight Bells, lively and wood-paneled, is a huge Wetherspoon chain pub that feels like a Vegas lounge (£4-7 "pub classics," bigger £6-10 meals, £8 lunch specials, daily 8:00-24:00, kids OK before 20:00, facing the small church at 19 Cannon Street, tel. 01304/205-030).

Lunch Eateries on Market Square: Dover's main shopping square is surrounded by places for a quick lunch. **The Ellie,** a generic, modern pub at a convenient location (right next door to the Dover Museum), spills out onto Market Square (£4 sandwiches, £6 main dishes, open daily 10:00-24:00, food served April-Sept 11:00-15:00 only, inviting outdoor seating on the square, tel. 01304/215-685). Across the square is the more genteel **Dickens Corner,** a comfy diner with a tearoom upstairs (£3-5 "jacket potatoes," sandwiches, and soups; Mon-Sat 8:00-16:45, closed Sun, 7 Market Square, tel. 01304/206-692).

Dover Connections

While the train will get you to most big destinations on the South Coast, the bus has better connections to smaller towns. Stagecoach offers good one-day "Explorer" (£6) or one-week "Megarider Gold" (£19.50) tickets covering anywhere they go in southeast England (tel. 0871-200-2233, www.stagecoachbus.com).

The Dover train station is called Dover Priory. Most buses stop at the "bus station" (it's more of a lot) on Pencester Road in the town center. Eurolines buses stop at the Eastern Docks, near the ferries to and from France.

From Dover by Train to: London (hourly, 1.25 hours, direct to St. Pancras; also 2/hour, 2 hours, direct to Victoria Station or Charing Cross Station), **Canterbury** (2/hour, 15-30 minutes, arrives at Canterbury East Station), **Rye** (hourly, 1.25 hours, transfer at Ashford International), **Hastings** (hourly, 1.5 hours, transfer at Ashford International), **Brighton** (at least hourly, 2.75-3 hours, transfer at Ashford International or London Bridge Station). Train info: tel. 0845-748-4950, www.nationalrail.co.uk.

By Bus: National Express (tel. 0871-781-8181, www.nationalexpress.com) goes to **London** (roughly hourly, 2.75-3.25 hours) and **Canterbury** (roughly hourly, 45 minutes). Stagecoach (tel. 0871-200-2233, www.stagecoachbus.com) goes to **Rye** (hourly, 2 hours) and **Hastings** (hourly, 3 hours).

Near Dover

Sissinghurst Castle Garden

For a taste of traditional English gardening, this elegant home and well-maintained garden is worth seeking out. Poet and writer

Vita Sackville-West, also known as a socialite and the lover of Virginia Woolf, purchased this castle and land in the early 20th century with her husband, diplomat-author Harold Nicolson. The two of them transformed the grounds into a beautiful English cottage garden. The gardens are laid out in sections, each with a theme, such as the Herb Garden and the Lime Walk. Every section feels like a small outdoor room. There is always something blooming here, but the best show is in June, when the famous "White Garden" bursts with fragrant roses. The castle, formerly a vast and grand affair, has disappeared for the most part, but an Elizabethan tower still stands. Inside are a few small exhibits, and—on the second floor—a series of illustrations that show the development, disintegration, and rebirth of the estate. At the top of the tower, you can survey the garden and orchard from up high. Inside the library wing, a portrait of Vita Sackville-West hangs over the fireplace, along with paintings of other family members, some of whom still live on the property.

Cost and Hours: £12, parking-£2/day; garden open March-Oct Mon-Fri 10:30-17:30, closed Sat-Sun, last entry 45 minutes before closing; shorter hours for castle and library, café, tel. 01580/710-700, www.nationaltrust.org.uk/sissinghurst-castle.

Getting There: Sissinghurst is about 55 miles west of Dover, off A-262, near Cranbrook. **Trains** from London connect to Staplehurst, about six miles away (2/hour, 1 hour from Charing Cross Station, tel. 0845-748-4950, www.nationalrail.co.uk). From Staplehurst, you can take a **taxi** directly to the garden (about £12, tel. 01580/890-003), or a **bus** to the village of Sissinghurst, where you can **walk** along an idyllic footpath about a mile to the garden (path can be muddy; catch bus #5 from Staplehurst, hourly in the afternoon; for more info call 0871-200-2233 or use the journey planner at www.travelinesoutheast.org.uk).

Southeast England

ENGLAND
DOVER & SE ENGLAND

Rye

If you dream of half-timbered pubs and wisteria-covered stone churches, Rye is the photo op you've been looking for. A busy sea-

port village for hundreds of years, Rye was frozen in time as silt built up and the sea retreated in the 16th and 17th centuries, leaving only a skinny waterway to remind it of better days. While shipbuilding and smuggling were the mainstays of the economy back then, antique shops, coffee shops, and expensive B&Bs drive

business these days. Rye is England's version of a hill town, packed with tourists trying to soak up some charm.

Arrival in Rye: As you approach town, notice the canal, often filled with boats. Follow it along to the old quays. The waterline used to come up to this area, and the parking lot on Strand Quay would have been the wharf. Drivers should ignore the confusing *P* signs, which direct you to parking lots away from the town center—instead, navigate the one-way system and try to squeeze into the small lot next to the Rye Heritage Centre (by the antique shops) or the larger one across the street.

Tourist Information: The TI is located at the top of the hill, just below the Church of St. Mary the Virgin. They offer an audioguide of the town for £4 (daily April-Sept 10:00-17:00, Oct-March 10:00-16:00, 4-5 Lion Street, tel. 01797/229-049, www.visitrye.co.uk).

Sights in Rye: Rye's sights try to make too much of this little town, but a stroll along the cobbles is enjoyable. Start at the **Rye Heritage Centre,** which has an impressive scale model of the town, presented in a 20-minute sound-and-light show (£3.50, every 30 minutes, if it's not running you can peek in at the model for free; daily April-Oct 10:00-17:00, Nov-March 10:00-16:00; town audioguide-£4, Strand Quay/A-259, tel. 01797/226-696, www.ryeheritage.co.uk).

From near the Rye Heritage Centre, Mermaid Street leads up into the medieval heart of Rye. Along this street (on the left), look for the **Mermaid Inn,** rebuilt in 1420 after the original burned down. Step inside and have a peek into Rye's heyday, or splurge for an expensive lunch (£20-25 fixed-price lunches, daily 12:00-14:30 & 19:00-21:30, tel. 01797/223-065). Today, it's a pricey upscale hotel with plenty of four-poster beds. Look for photos of recent celebrity customers just inside the door.

Continuing up Mermaid Street, jog right up West Street to Church Square. The old **Church of St. Mary the Virgin** has a pleasant interior, an 84-step tower you can climb for a countryside view, and a red-brick water tower built in 1753 (church—free, daily 9:15-17:15, shorter hours in winter; tower—£2.50, same hours as church but may close in bad weather; tel. 01797/224-935).

Beyond the square is a miniature castle called the Ypres Tower, housing the **Rye Castle Museum,** with a lookout tower and a mod-est collection of items from the town's

past. Striking up a conversation with the museum's custodian, a lifelong resident, may be the museum's most interesting attraction (£3; April-Oct daily 10:30-17:00; Nov-March daily 10:30-15:30; last entry 30 minutes before closing, tel. 01797/226-728, www.ryemuseum.co.uk). On sum-mer weekends you can visit the museum's second location, which features a 1745 fire engine and more about Rye's shipbuilding past (£2.50, £5 combo-ticket with castle museum, April-Oct Sat-Sun 10:30-17:00, closed Mon-Fri and Nov-March, 3 East Street).

Getting There: Rye is about 35 miles southwest of Dover on A-259 (the route to Brighton). **Trains** connect to Rye from London (hourly, 1.25 hours from St. Pancras Station, 2 hours from Charing Cross Station, transfer at Ashford International) and Dover (hourly, 1.25 hours, transfer at Ashford International). Stagecoach **bus** #100 provides a direct connection to Dover (hourly, 2 hours, tel. 0871-200-2233, www.stagecoachbus.com).

Near Rye: Compared to sugary-sweet Rye, modest and medieval **Winchelsea** feels like an antacid. Small, inviting, and just far enough away from the maddening crowd, the town makes a good stop for a picnic lunch. The grocery shop on the square sells all you need for a quiet meal on the little village green. Winchelsea is about three miles southwest of Rye on A-259, toward Hastings (www.winchelsea.net).

▲Battle of Hastings Abbey and Battlefield

Located about an hour southwest of Dover by car, the town of Battle commemorates a fight no Brit can forget—the Battle of Hastings. In 1066, a Norman (French) duke was victorious in the Battle of Hastings and seized control of England, leading to a string of Norman kings and forever changing the course of English history and the English language. The battlefield and adjoining ruined abbey (built soon after the battle to atone for all the spilled blood) are worth ▲▲▲ to British-history buffs, but anyone can appreciate the dramatic story behind the grassy field. Ignore the tourists and take a journey back in time...these fields would have looked almost the same 1,000 years ago. Gaze across the unassuming little valley and imagine thousands of invading troops. Your visit can last from three minutes to three hours, depending on your imagination.

Cost and Hours: £8, includes audioguide, £20 family ticket; April-Sept daily 10:00-18:00; Oct-March Sat-Sun 10:00-16:00, closed Mon-Fri except in Oct; last entry 30 minutes before closing, children's play area, tel. 01424/777-787, www.english-heritage.org.uk/battleabbey.

Getting There: The town of Battle isn't on a major road, but **drivers** find that it's well-signposted from the busy A-259, whether you're coming from the east (Dover), the north (London), or the west (Brighton). There's a pricey £3.50 parking lot next to the abbey (purchase tokens inside the abbey gatehouse).

Battle can be reached by **train** from London's Charing Cross or Cannon Street stations (2/hour, 1.5 hours, some require transfer), Hastings (2/hour, 15 minutes), or Dover (2-3/hour, 2-2.5 hours, 1-2 transfers). The entrance to Battle Abbey is at the south end of High Street; follow signs from the train station.

Background: The most epic of all of Europe's medieval *Lord of the Rings*-style battles took place on the most memorable date of the Middle Ages: October 14, 1066. The pivotal Battle of Hastings came about because the celibate King Edward the Confessor of England had died without an heir, and three nobles claimed the throne.

An Anglo-Saxon noble named Harold Godwinson, Earl of Wessex, claimed that Edward gave him the throne on his deathbed. He was named king by the traditional council, but support for Harold was weak: A Viking king from Norway, Harald Hardrada, had a claim to the throne through his bloodline. And across the English Channel, French-born William, Duke of Normandy, claimed that Edward had personally selected *him* as his successor. As the descendant of Vikings who'd once settled in England, William also claimed to be of royal blood. (His enemies called him William the Bastard—his mother was the former Duke of Normandy's mistress.)

With the pope's blessing, William patiently gathered and trained a large Norman army. Meanwhile, Harold and the English army confronted Hardrada in the north of England. Harold's victory was decisive, but immediately he got word that William had sailed across the Channel and landed in the south. Harold and his exhausted army raced to meet William. Near the town of Hastings in southern England, Harold assembled his troops into a wall atop the highest hill (Senlac Hill).

Early in the morning on October 14th, the Norman soldiers trudged up the hill, and the battle was on. First, Norman archers rained arrows on the English. Next, foot soldiers on both sides fought hand-to-hand. William's army began to retreat (a tactical maneuver, say the French). Seeing them flee, the English charged ahead, pursuing them down the hill. Suddenly, the Normans turned and attacked.

Riding on horseback, the Norman soldiers were armed with a secret weapon: stirrups, which gave them a foothold to put force behind their lances.

The two sides fought a fierce 14-hour battle, with heavy casualties. Ultimately the Normans decimated the English force. In the battle's climactic finale, Harold was killed (supposedly by an arrow through the eye). William—now "the Conqueror"—marched on to London, where he was crowned King of England in Westminster Abbey on Christmas Day, 1066. William commemorated the dead by building an abbey on the spot of the decisive battle.

The Norman Conquest of England propelled the cultured yet isolated isle of Britain into the European mainstream of feudalism. William centralized the government and imported the Romanesque style of architecture—seen at places such as the White Tower at the Tower of London, and Durham Cathedral. The English call this style "Norman." Historians speculate that, were it not for the stirrup, England would have remained on the fringe of Europe (like Scandinavia), French culture and language would have prevailed in the New World…and you'd be reading this book today in French. *Sacré bleu!* William's conquest also muddied the political waters, setting in motion 400 years of conflict between England and France that would not be resolved until the end of the Hundred Years' War, in 1453.

Visiting the Abbey and Battlefield: A small museum, battleground overlook, and remaining Battle Abbey buildings illuminate the historical significance of the Battle of Hastings. After buying your ticket and picking up the essential, included audioguide, head to the nearby **visitors center** to watch an excellent 15-minute film that recounts the story of the battle, with animated scenes from the famous Bayeux Tapestry (pictured on previous page) and impressive live-action reenactments. Also in the center are replicas of weapons used by the fighters—lift them to appreciate how the Brits invented heavy metal long before Led Zeppelin.

Then head outside, where you have two choices with your audioguide: Follow the short tour along a terrace overlooking the **battlefield** (about 15 minutes), or take the longer version out through the woods and across the fateful field (about 40 minutes). With sound effects and a witty but not corny commentary, the audioguide really injects some life into the site. Finally, you'll wind up at the remains of the **abbey,** where the audioguide relates details of monastic lifestyles. It's interesting and a bit more intact than many other ruined abbeys, but it pales in comparison to the drama  of the battle. Walking back to the entrance, notice that the abbey's former Great Hall now houses another famous English institution—a private school.

Eating in Battle: The **Pilgrims Restaurant,** across the street from the abbey, is an atmospherically crooked half-timbered house serving decent but pricey food with outdoor terrace seating (£8-12 soups, sandwiches, and salads, daily 9:00-17:00, 1 High Street, tel. 01424/772-314).

DOVER & SE ENGLAND

BRIGHTON

Brighton—brash and flamboyant, with a carnival flair—is refreshing if you're suffering from an excess of doilies and museums. The city boasts a garish 19th-century Royal Pavilion, a loud and flashy carnival pier, England's most thriving gay community, and a long stretch of cobbled beach. It's no wonder that youthful bohemians and blue-collar Londoners alike make this town their holiday destination of choice.

In the 1790s, with Napoleon's armies running rampant on the Continent, aristocrats could no longer travel abroad on a traditional "Grand Tour" of Europe. King George IV chose the village of Brighthelmstone to build a vacation palace for himself, and royal followers began a frenzy of construction on the seashore. Soon this once-sleepy seaside village was transformed into an elegant resort town. With the rise of train travel, connections to London became quick and cheap, making Brighton an inviting getaway for working-class Londoners.

The countryside near Brighton is packed with tempting sights and worthwhile stopovers for drivers. Go for a breezy walk on the South Downs Way, lick an ice-cream cone in the postcard-pretty village of Alfriston, visit the best white cliffs in England at Beachy Head, and explore the evocative ruins of a Roman fort at Pevensey.

Planning Your Time

Brighton's sights—its Royal Pavilion, Museum and Art Gallery, and pleasure pier—can be seen in just a few hours, making this a doable day trip from London. If you've got a full day and a car, spend the rest of your day at Alfriston and Beachy Head.

Debating between Brighton and Portsmouth? Travelers in-

Brighton

P PARKING
PEDESTRIAN ZONE

100 YARDS
100 METERS

TRAIN STATION

TO A-23, GATWICK AIRPORT & LONDON

TO A-27, LEWES & EASTBOURNE

TERMINUS ROAD

CHEAPSIDE

YORK PLACE

RICHMOND PLACE

ALBION HILL

TRAFALGAR STREET

SURREY STREET

GLOUCESTER ROAD

NORTH LAINE

QUEEN'S ROAD

DYKE ROAD

WINDSOR

PORTLAND

NORTH ROAD

CHURCH STREET

MARLBOROUGH PL.

GLOCESTER PL.

GRAND PARADE

ASHTON RISE

MORLEY

JOHN STREET

SUSSEX ST.

KINGSWOOD

CARLTON ST.

BLAKER ST.

HIGH ST.

BRIGHTON MUSEUM & ART GALLERY

ROYAL PAVILION

EDWARD STREET

KEMPTOWN

NORTH ST.

BOND ST.

NEW RD.

CASTLE SQ.

POST

SHIP STREET

DUKE ST.

PAVILION ST.

MARKET ST.

WEST STREET

DUKE'S LANE

HOUSE ST.

SHIP ST.

SOUTH ST.

THE LANES

ST. BART.

EAST ST.

POOL VALLEY

OLD STEINE

ST. JAMES'S ST.

MADEIRA PL.

MARG. NEW STEINE

ROCK ST.

BROAD ST.

TO WEST PIER RUINS

KING'S ROAD

GRAND JUNCTION ROAD

MARINE PARADE

BEACH

MADEIRA DR.

VOLK'S ELECTRIC RAILWAY

TO BEACH

DCH

BRIGHTON PIER

ENGLISH   CHANNEL

1 New Steine Street B&Bs
2 Guest and the City
3 Kempfield House
4 St. Christoper's Inn
5 English's of Brighton
6 Terre à Terre Veggie Rest.
7 Market Street Eateries
8 Bill's Produce Store

9 Our Cornish Pasty Shop
10 Wagamama
11 Yo! Sushi
12 La Capannina
13 Townhouse Kemptown
14 Launderette
15 To Bike Rental
16 Brighton Wheel

terested in the arts, shopping, and the restaurant scene are more likely to be turned on by lively Brighton, while those interested in maritime and World War II history might prefer traditional Portsmouth (see next chapter). Either destination works as a good day trip from London, but with more time, visiting both is a great plan.

Orientation to Brighton

Brighton is big, with over 160,000 people. It feels surprisingly urban for a seaside resort—like the Nice of England. Most tourists focus on the area near the waterfront. The heart of Brighton is the Brighton Pier and, several blocks inland, the Royal Pavilion. Between these two landmarks is the twisty old center of town called The Lanes, with good restaurants and lots of shopping. North of The Lanes and past the Royal Pavilion is the popular, recently revived neighborhood of North Laine, with more shopping and eateries, plus occasional street-music performances. The best accommodations cluster to the east of The Lanes, within a block of the seafront, in the colorful neighborhood called Kemptown.

Tourist Information

The TI, in the Royal Pavilion's gift shop, has a good, free color map of Brighton. They also book rooms (£1.50/person), sell bus and train tickets, and promote a £2 iPhone app for power-shoppers (daily 10:00-17:00, tel. 01273/290-337, www.visitbrighton.com).

Arrival in Brighton

Trains arrive at Brighton Station, a 15-minute walk from the center. If you're staying at one of my recommended New Steine Street accommodations, hop on bus #7 or #27 (every 10 minutes, 10-minute ride).

Drivers on the A-23 enter town on the tree-lined Grand Parade, which goes straight to the water (ending near Brighton Pier). Parking is tricky and very expensive: Signs will lead you to parking garages near the center, but if you're staying the night, ask your hotelier for the best place to leave your car.

Helpful Hints

Crowd Control: Brighton can overflow with visitors in summer and on weekends. The Brighton Festival (May, www.brightonfestival.org) and the Summer LGBT Pride Festival (second week of Aug, www.brightonpride.org) are the busiest times. Off-season (roughly Oct-March), visitors may find the city quiet, prices slashed, and attractions shuttered.

Laundry: St. James's Laundry is in Kemptown, near my recommended accommodations (self-service open Mon-Fri 7:30-

21:00, Sat 8:30-14:00, or drop off Mon-Fri 8:30-12:00 for same-day full-service, closed Sun, 53 St. James's Street, tel. 01273/672-395).

Bike Rental: Ask at the TI or try **Brighton Sports Company,** down by the water next to the bike path (£6/hour, £12/3 hours, includes helmet, picture ID and £200 credit-card deposit required, daily Easter-Oct 11:00-18:00, closed Nov-Easter, 10-minute walk east of recommended New Steine B&Bs, halfway between Brighton Pier and Brighton Marina, Madeira Drive, mobile 07917-753-794, www.brightonsports. co.uk, Mark).

Getting Around Brighton

Brighton's well-run bus system is handy, especially if you're staying in one of my recommended guesthouses on Kemptown's New Steine Street (£1.70/ride, £3.90 CitySaver day pass; buy from driver, at TI, or online for slight discount; tel. 01273/886-200, www.buses. co.uk).

Sights in Brighton

▲▲Brighton Royal Pavilion

Famous for his scandalous secret marriage to Catholic widow Mrs. Fitzherbert, King George IV was lively, decadent, and trendsetting. He loved to vacation by the sea and host glamorous dinner parties. George was enamored with Asian cultures, styling his vacation home with exotic decorations from the East. Some regard the palace itself as a work of art, furnished with a mix of English, French,

and Chinese pieces and adorned with gilded dragons and carved palm trees. The result is colorful and exuberant...some would say gaudy. Like Brighton itself, the place smacks of faded elegance—but it's fun to tour. It's free to enter the restored Regency gardens surrounding the Pavilion, and the nearby Brighton Museum and Art Gallery (described later).

Cost and Hours: £10.50, includes audioguide, daily April-Sept 9:30-17:45, Oct-March 10:00-17:15, last entry 45 minutes before closing, head up East Street from The Lanes, bus stop on Old Steine Road, tel. 03000-290-900, www.brighton-hove-rpml. org.uk.

➲ **Self-Guided Tour:** Pick up the free and informative

BRIGHTON

audioguide as you enter. It'll tell you more about these highlights (and other points of interest) along the one-way route.

While George IV planned the palace as a royal holiday residence, it was used mainly as a party pad to entertain guests. They'd be suitably impressed by the grand **Long Gallery.** Here and throughout the Pavilion, examine the fine detail work—such as the "bamboo" stairway decoration that's actually carved from wood.

If guests were impressed by the Long Gallery, they were blown away by the **Banqueting Room.** Imagine England's elite nibbling crumpets under the one-ton chandelier...with its dragons exhaling light through lotus-shaped shades. Notice that the ornate table is permanently set for the dessert course.

The elaborate **Kitchen** was one of the most innovative of its time. Smoke from the fireplace rotated a huge rotisserie that could cook enough meat to feed a hundred hungry diners. The king was so particular about his food that he insisted his kitchen be attached to the dining room (unheard-of at the time). He also had a warming table built to keep food at the optimum temperature.

Head through the gallery and salon into a room dedicated to George's true passion: music. In the massive **Music Room,** the royal band serenaded guests. The room's gilded, domed ceiling is made up of hundreds of plaster cockleshells, creating an illusion of height. Take a moment to appreciate the Chinese-inspired decor here and throughout the palace. Known as *chinoiserie*, it was the height of fashion in those days.

The **Private Apartments** were on the ground floor, to more easily accommodate the ailing king (who spent less and less time here near the end of his life). Note that this space is more intimate and cozy than the showpiece halls we've seen elsewhere. (If you're intrigued by all this, dip into the dry but informative 18-minute film about the Pavilion's history.)

Continuing upstairs, you'll stroll through the restored **Yellow Bow Rooms,** then **Queen Victoria's Apartments,** where you'll learn the epilogue to the story of George's party palace. Queen Victoria first visited the Royal Pavilion in 1837 and felt it was a "strange and odd-looking place, both outside and inside." Uncle George was a big spender and had piled up huge debts. No expense was spared. Prudish Queen Victoria, who took the throne seven years after George's death, wanted more privacy than the Pavilion provided and scorned the excesses in George's court—so she quickly off-loaded the decadent Pavilion to the local town council (which still owns it today). Only recently did Queen Elizabeth II bring the original furniture out of storage and loan it to the Pavilion.

Brighton Museum and Art Gallery

This gallery, similar to the Victoria and Albert Museum in London, displays decorative arts with a heavy focus on 20th-century art and design. The modern pseudo-kitsch includes the Dalí-inspired *Mae West Lips Sofa* and Frank Gehry's *Wiggle Chair*. The café above the gallery has a pleasant view of the action.

Cost and Hours: Free, Tue-Sun 10:00-17:00, closed Mon except holidays, just north of the Royal Pavilion, tel. 03000-290-900, www.brighton-hove-rpml.org.uk.

Brighton Pier

Glittering and shiny with amusement rides and carnival games, Brighton Pier is *the* place to go for a fix of "candy floss" (cotton

candy), fortune-tellers, slot machines, and tacky souvenirs. The pier, opened in 1899 and long known as Palace Pier, has gone in and out of fashion; in recent years, it's come back to life, thanks to an expensive restoration. The main pavilion is a 19th-century gem. If you ignore the fancy video games, you might be able to imagine yourself as a Victorian Londoner out on holiday, seeing brilliant electric lights for the first time.

Cost and Hours: Free entry to pier, rides run Mon-Fri 10:00-17:00, Sat-Sun 11:00-19:00, arcade usually open until 22:00, closing time depends on crowds, tel. 01273/609-361, www.brighton-pier.co.uk.

Nearby: Check out the ruins of the pier to the west. Due to disrepair, the shorter but once equally festive **West Pier** disintegrated into the water in the 1970s. Watch for the long-planned construction of a new observation tower here. Designed by the architects of the London Eye, the **i360** tower's doughnut-like elevator will someday lift tourists to a bird's-eye view over the town. After years of construction delays, it may open sometime in 2015 (for the latest, see www.brightoni360.co.uk).

Until the tower opens, take a spin on the **Brighton Wheel.** Similar to its big brother in London, it has 36 closed gondolas that take you on a 10-minute, three-revolution ride, up to 160 feet above the seafront (£8, daily 10:00-23:00, located east of the Brighton Pier but pretty hard to miss, tel. 01273/722-822, www.brighton-wheel.com).

Beach

OK, so it isn't Hawaii, but you can walk along the large, flattened cobbles, called "shingles," and get your feet wet.

BRIGHTON

Sleep Code

(£1 = about $1.60, country code: 44, area code: 01273)
S = Single, **D** = Double/Twin, **T** = Triple, **Q** = Quad, **b** = bath-room, **s** = shower only. Unless otherwise noted, credit cards are accepted and breakfast is included.

To help you sort easily through these listings, I've divided the accommodations into three categories based on the price for a standard double room with bath:

$$$ Higher Priced—Most rooms £100 or more.
  $$ Moderately Priced—Most rooms between £60-100.
   $ Lower Priced—Most rooms £60 or less.

Prices can change without notice; verify the hotel's cur-rent rates online or by email. For the best prices, always book direct.

Sleeping in Brighton

Brighton's bohemian character is fun during the day, but the town can be a little shady at night. The recommended accommodations are in the gay-friendly Kemptown neighborhood, about a block from the beach and within a 10-minute walk of the Brighton Pier and Royal Pavilion.

The best Brighton accommodations are variations on the same theme: a guesthouse with about a dozen rooms. A guesthouse of-fers more professionalism and anonymity than a B&B, and more character(s) than a hotel. As rooms vary in size, one hotel can have four or five different prices for their doubles. ("Sea views" here are unimpressive, and not worth paying extra for.) In summer, prices skyrocket by £15-30 on weekends, making otherwise good-value places suddenly way overpriced. Summer weekends are also plagued with noisy partygoers roaming the streets until dawn. Avoid sleeping in Brighton on a summer weekend if you can help it—but if you must sleep here, ask for a quieter room away from the road. I've listed the summer ranges; you can assume the lower rates are for weeknights and smaller rooms, while the higher rates are for weekends and fancier and/or view rooms. You'll often get a better deal off-season (especially on weeknights).

On New Steine Street

Kemptown's New Steine Street— essentially a long square with a park in the middle—is lined with about a dozen different guesthouses. After visiting all of them, these are my favorites. Marine View is more traditional; Sea Spray, New Steine, and Gulliver's are mod and stylish; and Strawberry Fields is somewhere in between.

$$$ Sea Spray is an innovative concept hotel: Each of the 16 rooms has a different theme, from the Renaissance to New York to Elvis. It's a memorable place to spend the night, with art-filled public spaces (Db-£50-170, some sea views, some with balconies, pricier suites including one with a private hot tub, free Wi-Fi, sauna and massage, at #26, tel. 01273/680-332, www.seaspraybrighton. co.uk, seaspray@brighton.co.uk, Neil).

$$$ New Steine B&B, with 20 well-decorated rooms, combines Old World charm with contemporary chic (S-£35-59, Db-£65-139, Tb-£79-160, Qb-£90-180, check website for discounts, dinner option, free Wi-Fi, bistro, at #10-11, tel. 01273/681-546, www.newsteinehotel.com, reservation@newsteinehotel.com).

$$$ Gulliver's, their sister hotel two doors down, has similar decor and slightly cheaper prices (S-£30-55, Db-£50-139, Tb-£78-145, at #12a, tel. 01273/695-415, www.gulliversshotel.com, reservation@gulliversshotel.com).

$$ Strawberry Fields Hotel has 27 rooms with a fun strawberry theme. Sharon and her friendly and competent assistant, Anna, look after you (Ss-£33-55, D-£55-79, Db-£70-110, T-£90-105, free Wi-Fi, at #6-7, tel. 01273/681576, www.strawberry-fields-hotel.com, strawberryfields@pavilion.co.uk).

$$ Marine View has 22 comfortable rooms (S-£55-65, Db-£65-105, family room-£85-220, some with sea and pier views, 2-night minimum on weekends, free Wi-Fi, at #24, tel. 01273/603-870, www.marineviewhotelbrighton.co.uk).

Elsewhere in Brighton

$$$ Guest and the City is a comfortably stylish B&B close to the pier that features stained-glass windows in its rooms (Sb-£70-90, Db-£95-140, 2 Broad Street, tel. 01273/698-289, www.guestandthecity.co.uk, info@guestandthecity.co.uk).

Madeira Place, a few blocks closer to the town center than New Steine Street, has its own stretch of guesthouses. The best of these is **$$ Kempfield House,** tastefully run in a Georgian townhouse. The 13 rooms are elegantly simple and nicely appointed (Sb-£50-75, Db-£70-110, huge Db-£85-125, check website for discounts, 2-night minimum on weekends, free Wi-Fi, 18 Madeira Place, tel. 01273/567-521, www.kempfieldhouse.co.uk, info@kempfieldhouse.co.uk).

$ St. Christopher's Inn is your budget hostel option. Smackdab in the middle of the action, on the main seafront road across from the Brighton Pier, this self-described "party hostel" offers cheap doubles and dorm beds for young people wanting to live it up in Brighton. The ground-floor bar and basement disco can be noisy—light sleepers can try requesting a higher floor (£14-28 for a bunk in 4- to 8-bed dorms, Db-£55-110, prices change dramatically by day and season—check online for best deals, elevator, 10-12 Grand Junction Road, booking tel. 020/8600-7500, reception tel. 01273/202-035, www.st-christophers.co.uk).

Eating in Brighton

If you haven't filled yourself up with greasy boardwalk fare, you'll find plenty of good, affordable restaurants around town.

In The Lanes

The area known as The Lanes has the best concentration of both trendy and traditional restaurants. My first two listings are pricey, while the Market Street eateries are easier on a tight budget.

English's of Brighton, hiding on the side of the little square on East Street, is a venerable local institution that's been serving seafood specialties for more than 150 years to luminaries such as Charlie Chaplin and Laurence Olivier. The crisp, white-tablecloth-classy interior sprawls through several rooms on two floors, and there's seating out on the square (£13-15 fixed-price lunches, £15-20 fixed-price dinners, £17-25 main dishes, Mon-Sat 12:00-22:00, reservations smart, 29-31 East Street, tel. 01273/327-980, www.englishs.co.uk).

Terre à Terre keeps vegetarians and healthy eaters happy with imaginative dishes and friendly service (£15 main dishes, Mon-Fri 12:00-22:30, Sat 11:00-23:00, Sun 11:00-22:00, closed Mon in winter, 71 East Street, tel. 01273/729-051).

On Market Street: This bustling area—more a long, wide square than a "street"—is packed with affordable eateries. Take a spin around to choose your favorite, but check out the following: **Fat Leo** gets high marks from locals for big portions of pasta and the best bang-for-your-pound in a bright, modern interior with seating on two levels. It's not haute cuisine, but it's cheap (£4-10 main dishes, daily 12:00-22:00, at #16-17, tel. 01273/325-135). For a seafront picnic, pick up some pastries and pasties at **Forfars Fresh,** baking in Brighton since 1818 (eat at their upstairs café for a few pence more, Mon-Fri 7:30-16:30, Sat until 16:00, closed Sun, café closes one hour before store, at #44, tel. 01273/601-404). **Giggling Squid** serves up tasty Thai dishes in a simple, two-story interior (£4-8 light "Thai tapas" lunch dishes or £10 three-course lunches, bigger £7-13 dinners, Mon-Fri 12:00-16:00 & 17:30-23:00, Sat-Sun 12:00-22:00, at #11, tel. 01273/737-373). **The Burger Bar** is a cute little quasi-diner slinging burgers and all-day breakfast fare. As there's no interior seating, you'll have to grab a table on the square (£3-4 grub, cash only, open daily 9:00-17:00, at #11a, tel. 01273/205-979).

In North Laine

Just north of The Lanes and the Royal Pavilion, this former warehouse district is now the cool place to explore, with new restaurants and fun, quirky shops popping up all the time.

Bill's Produce Store is a unique café (and, yes, produce store) that's immensely popular with locals for its fresh, inventive dishes and smoothies. Get here before the lunch rush to nab a seat and ogle the surroundings—and the fresh-flower-bedecked cakes behind the counter (£4-8 breakfasts, £5-12 lunches and dinners, takeaway sandwiches, Mon-Sat 8:00-23:00, Sun 9:00-22:30, 100 North Road, tel. 01273/692-894).

Our Cornish Pasty Shop offers excellent versions of its namesake, including vegetarian and curry varieties. There are also delicious homemade desserts with gluten-free options. After 18:00, all pasties are sold two-for-one (Mon-Sat 9:30-19:00, Sun 11:00-17:30, 24 Gardner Street, tel. 01273/688-063, Ian and Nese).

Two reliable Asian chains have branches here (a block apart from each other, off North Road). At **Wagamama,** diners slurp pan-fried, pan-Asian noodles at long, shared tables in a single hall as the harried waitstaff scurries around (£6-12 main dishes, Mon-Sat 12:00-23:00, Sun 11:30-22:00, 30 Kensington Street, tel. 01273/688-892). **Yo! Sushi** features a conveyor belt of tasty and creative raw fish (£2-5/plate, Mon-Sat 12:00-23:00, Sun 12:00-22:30, last orders 30 minutes before closing, 6-7 Jubilee Street, tel. 01273/258-711).

In Kemptown

To dine closer to home, simply wander the lively streets of Kemptown. St. James's Street, running parallel to the seafront a block inland, is lined with all types of cuisine: cheap burgers and fish-and-chips, Thai, Mediterranean, pub grub, and more.

For Italian, try **La Capannina,** a cozy restaurant with a run-by-an-Italian-family feel. If it looks full, ask about additional seating downstairs (£6-10 pizzas and pastas, daily 12:00-14:30 & 18:00-23:00, just off St. James's Street at 15 Madeira Place, tel. 01273/680-839).

Townhouse Kemptown features contemporary English cuisine, including steaks, fish, and vegetarian options. Run by a top London chef, the food is fresh and local. Contemporary decor and live music (most nights) have made it a favorite with locals (£12-15 main dishes, Mon-Fri 12:00-15:00 & 18:00-22:00, Sat-Sun 10:00-

BRIGHTON

23:00, 81-82 St. James's Street, tel. 01273/693-216, www.thetown-housekemptown.co.uk).

Brighton Connections

Brighton is well-connected to London and most coastal towns.

From Brighton by Train to: Gatwick Airport (hourly, 20-40 minutes), **London**'s Victoria Station (1-2/hour direct, 1 hour; also to London Bridge Station, 1-2/hour direct, 1 hour), **Portsmouth** (hourly direct, 1.25 hours, more with transfer), **Hastings** (2/hour direct, 1-1.25 hours), **Dover** (at least hourly, 2.75-3 hours, 1-3 transfers), **Canterbury** (hourly, 2.5 hours, 1-3 transfers). Train info: tel. 0845-748-4950, www.nationalrail.co.uk.

By Bus: National Express (tel. 0871-781-8178, www.nationalexpress.com) runs buses to **Gatwick Airport** (at least hourly, 1 hour), **Heathrow Airport** (at least hourly, 2.5 hours, transfer possible), **London**'s Victoria Coach Station (hourly, 2.5 hours), and **Portsmouth** (1/day direct, 2 hours). Stagecoach buses (tel. 0845-121-0190 or 01243/755-850, www.stagecoachbus.com) go to **Portsmouth** (2/hour Mon-Sat, hourly Sun, 4 hours) and **Arundel** (2/hour, fewer on Sun, 2 hours, some require transfer).

Near Brighton

Stretching east of Brighton is a coastline fringed with broad, rolling green downs, or hills—an area known as the South Downs Way. These hills are an excellent place to practice a favorite sport of the English: walking. Paths, well-tended by local walking clubs, weave through much of the English countryside, attracting weekend and holiday strollers, and anyone looking for fresh air and exercise. On a quick visit, the highlights here are the adorable hamlet of Alfriston and the dramatic chalk cliff of Beachy Head. Just beyond is the ruined Roman fort at Pevensey. I've listed these attractions as you'll reach them, traveling eastward from Brighton.

Planning Your Time

These sights can be combined to make a good half-day side trip from Brighton (better in the morning, when traffic is lighter; allow more time if you want to squeeze in a South Downs Way walk en route). Drive east on the A-27, dip down through Alfriston to stroll the cute village center and poke into the clergy house, then continue on to Beachy Head—and enjoy a drive or walk along the dramatic clifftops. Allow an hour to explore the forbidding castle ruins at Pevensey, just off the main A-27/A-259 road connecting Brighton to points eastward (Dover or Canterbury).

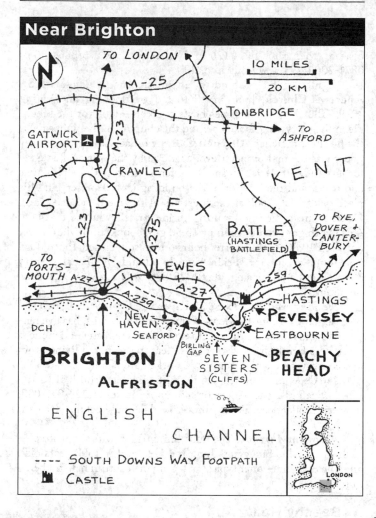

Near Brighton

TO LONDON

M-25

10 MILES
20 KM

TONBRIDGE

GATWICK
AIRPORT

TO
ASHFORD

CRAWLEY

K E N T

S U S S E X

M-23

A-23

A-275

BATTLE
(HASTINGS
BATTLEFIELD)

TO RYE,
DOVER &
CANTER-
BURY

TO PORTS-
MOUTH A-27

LEWES

A-259

A-27

HASTINGS

NEW-
HAVEN

A-259

PEVENSEY

DCH

SEAFORD

EASTBOURNE

BIRLING
GAP

BRIGHTON

SEVEN
SISTERS
(CLIFFS)

BEACHY
HEAD

ALFRISTON

E N G L I S H

C H A N N E L

- - - - SOUTH DOWNS WAY FOOTPATH

CASTLE

LONDON

▲Alfriston

The South Downs Way gently winds inland to Alfriston, set in a

peaceful green valley. This tidy, picturesque little one-street village—half red-brick, half half-timbered, all quaint—is packed with tourists and walkers.

Arrival in Alfriston: Drivers follow *Alfriston* signs south from the A-27. Park in the giant lot at the north end of town, then stroll up the main drag.

Alfriston, while cute, isn't worth the trouble if you don't have a car, but you could take bus #12 or #12A from Brighton south to Seaford, then catch bus #126 to Alfriston (tel. 01273/886-200 or 0871-200-2233, www.buses.co.uk).

Sights: A block behind the main street is the landmark **St. Andrew's Church,** built in 1360 and overlooking an inviting green. The church sometimes hosts concerts—look for the schedule in the entryway. Tucked behind the church (on the right side) is the humble, thatched **Alfriston Clergy House.** This 14th-century house was the first property ever acquired by the National Trust—for just £10—in 1896. Its small garden is filled with delphiniums and roses, and the interior of the building is well-preserved. This place gives you a look at the lifestyles of the medieval and pious. Docents are sometimes waiting inside to tell you more (£4.65, £6.15 with guided tour, skimpy £3.50 guidebook; mid-March-Oct Sat-Wed 10:30-17:00, shorter hours off-season; closed Thu and Fri year-round except open Fri in Aug; closed mid-Dec-Feb; last entry 30 minutes before closing, tel. 01323/870-961, www.nationaltrust.org.uk/alfriston).

Sleeping near Alfriston: **$$$ Riverdale House B&B,** perched on a ridge with beautiful views over the South Downs, has five renovated rooms that tastefully meld traditional character and modern hues. This family-friendly place also features a shared living room and conservatory with lovely views of the garden and beyond (Db-£90-110 depending on size, family suite-£145, just south of Alfriston on Seaford Road—look for sign on right, tel. 01323/871-038, www.riverdalehouse.co.uk, info@riverdalehouse.co.uk, Richard and Judy).

Eating in Alfriston: The pubs lining the town's main street—such as Ye Olde Smugglers Inn, The George Inn (500 years old), and The Star Inn—offer typical pub grub in beautiful half-timbered buildings.

▲▲Beachy Head

The highest chalk sea cliff in England is less well-known but much more dramatic and scenic than the White Cliffs of Dover. If you see one white cliff in England (and one is enough), make it Beachy Head.

The easiest way to appreciate Beachy Head is to drive to the settlement of **Birling Gap,** with easy access to the coastline below the cliff. From Brighton, make your way to the A-259 coastal road. (The most scenic approach is to head east on the speedy A-27, then turn off and head south when you see

South Downs Way

The South Downs Way (often abbreviated SDW) runs for 100 miles along the chalk hills of England's south coast, from Win-

chester (25 miles inland in Hampshire) to Eastbourne (on the coast of East Sussex). This long, scenic ridge has attracted walkers for thousands of years, and in April of 2011, the area surrounding the trail became England's 10th national park. Locals consider these trails a birthright.

The SDW is a bridleway, which means you can walk, bike, or ride a horse. To keep on course, look for the blue arrow signs with a white acorn in the middle or dots of blue paint on posts or trees. It's always a good idea to have a map; the UK Ordnance Survey Explorer maps are excellent and widely available (#123 covers the area around Beachy Head).

Walkers have priority over horses and bicycles, but it's polite to step aside and let them pass. While motorized vehicles are not allowed on the SDW itself, much of the path runs along farm tracks, so you may encounter tractors. Keep a safe distance or you may be plowed under.

While you can walk along almost the entire southern coast, the best part for a day hike is the three-mile stretch out to Beachy Head from Eastbourne (find the path at the west end of King Edward's Parade, also called the B-2103; the small car park is often full, so you may need to park on a nearby street).

Many people walk the entire 100 miles, staying in B&Bs or hostels in towns along the way, or camping in designated areas. The SDW winds its way through or near many towns and villages, including Exton, Buriton, Arundel, Lewes, and Alfriston. Two good websites are www.southdowns.gov.uk and www.nationaltrail.co.uk. You can buy a guidebook at most UK bookshops or online through www.amazon.co.uk. Titles include *South Downs Way* by Jim Manthorpe, *South Downs Way National Trail Guide* by Paul Millmore, and *Walks in the South Downs National Park* by Kev Reynolds.

BRIGHTON

signs for *Alfriston;* you can visit this picturesque town—described previously—on the way to the A-259, which you'll follow east.)

Once on the A-259, you can turn off just past Friston and go directly to Birling Gap, passing through the charming village of East Dean (with a good pub, the Tiger Inn, on the village green). Or—for a slightly longer and more scenic route—continue east on the A-259 to make a loop of it. Just over a mile after leaving East Dean on the A-259, you'll see a turnoff on the right for Beachy

Head. Follow this road as it rises over the hills, with views over wildflower meadows on one side and the English Channel on the other. Soon you'll spot the Countryside Centre on your right, with information for walkers and other visitors (Easter-Oct daily 10:00-16:00, closed Nov-Easter, tel. 01323/737-273). Then continue on Beachy Head Road, which eventually drops you down into Birling Gap.

Once you arrive in Birling Gap, park at the big National Trust pay-and-display lot, and use the staircase to reach the beach. As you stroll under the grand chalky monster, marvel at the otherworldly whiteness of the cliff and the stones underfoot. Pick up a chunk of chalk to feel how soft and crumbly it is—the constant sloughing off is why these cliffs are so steep, dramatic, and pearlywhite (signs warn you to stay away from the immediate base of the cliffs). Stretching to your right (as you face the sea) are the elegant Seven Sisters cliffs, offering chalky splendor as far as the eye can see.

If you have time for a walk, there are two good routes to consider. For a clifftop walk with great sea views, but not the best vistas of the cliff face itself, hike from the lighthouse called Belletout (you can't miss it as you approach the cliffs from the west) to the Countryside Centre. Or, for head-on views of the cliff as you walk, start out in Seaford and hike up the ridge to Hope Gap. Both of these trails are fairly steep, and it's important to watch your step: Long, windblown grass fields come to an abrupt end at the cliff edge, with no barrier between you and the sea crashing hundreds of feet below.

If you don't have a car, take **buses** #12A or #13X, which offer good daily service between Brighton and Birling Gap, Seaford, and Beachy Head (2/hour, 45-90 minutes, tel. 01273/886-200 or 0871-200-2233, www.buses.co.uk).

Pevensey

This nondescript village, 25 miles east of Brighton (where the A-259 coastal route and the faster A-27 inland route intersect), is a one-street town leading up to a massive, brooding fortress—used in Roman, Anglo-Saxon, medieval, and modern times. Originally built as a coastal fortification in the fourth century, **Pevensey Castle**  was also used by the Normans, who landed in 1066 with William the Conqueror at Norman's Bay, just within sight. The moat around the inner castle was probably flushed by the incoming tidewater, although the present coastline has moved farther to the south. The ruins of the castle were also put into action during World War II. While you can pay to go into the castle itself, the best activity—wandering the scenic and grassy field around it—is free.

Cost and Hours: Castle entry-£5, includes informative audioguide; April-Sept daily 10:00-18:00; Oct daily 10:00-16:00; Nov-March Sat-Sun 10:00-16:00, closed Mon-Fri; tel. 01323/762-604, www.english-heritage.org.uk/pevensey.

Getting There: Non-drivers can take the train from Brighton to Pevensey (2/hour, 1 hour, possible change in Lewes, tel. 0845-748-4950, www.nationalrail.co.uk).

PORTSMOUTH

Portsmouth, the age-old home of the Royal Navy and Britain's second-busiest ferry port after Dover, is best known for its Historic Dockyard and many nautical sights. For centuries, Britain, a maritime superpower, relied on the fleets based in Portsmouth to expand and maintain its vast empire and guard against invaders. When sea power was needed, British leaders—from Henry VIII to Winston Churchill to David Cameron—have called upon Portsmouth to ready the ships.

As a major military target, the city of Portsmouth was flattened by WWII bombs (ironically, the Historic Dockyard was relatively unscathed). Postwar reconstruction was hasty and poorly planned, and the city became infamous for its bad architecture. But an impressive gentrification is under way here. Efforts to rejuvenate tourism have included refurbishing Old Portsmouth, building a sprawling new waterfront shopping complex, and adding a sail-like monolith to the skyline. While Brighton rests on its holiday-making laurels—and revels in its shabby-chic—Portsmouth feels increasingly spiffy.

The old nautical sights are more impressive than ever. Visiting landlubbers can tour the HMS *Victory,* which played a key role in Britain's battles with Napoleon's navy, and see the *Mary Rose,* a 16th-century warship that was a favorite of Henry VIII. But the new spirit of Portsmouth is equally enticing. Portsmouth seems to expertly balance its dual status as both a city of the past and one of the future.

Near Portsmouth, on the road to Brighton, are two very different palaces: the ancient remains of Fishbourne Roman Palace, with its striking mosaics; and thriving Arundel Castle, still the proud home of an English duke.

Planning Your Time

Portsmouth works well as a day trip from London, Bath, or Salisbury. The city's top sights—at the Historic Dockyard—can be seen in a few hours. But thanks to the bustling Gunwharf Quays and Spinnaker Tower, the D-Day Museum, and a seaside-holiday atmosphere, you'll have no trouble filling a whole day. Consider spending the night.

Orientation to Portsmouth

Portsmouth, situated on an island, feels smaller than its population of 200,000. Almost all of its visit-worthy sights line up along a two-mile stretch of waterfront, from the Historic Dockyard in the north to the Southsea neighborhood in the south. The walkable core, in the north, contains the top sights: the Historic Dockyard, Spinnaker Tower (views), Gunwharf Quays (shopping complex), Millennium Promenade Walk, and Old Portsmouth; Southsea's D-Day Museum and TI are a 10-minute bus ride away.

Tourist Information

The TI is located inside the D-Day Museum in Southsea, about two miles southeast of the Portsmouth Harbour train station; unless you're going to the museum anyway, it's probably not worth a special trip. They give out a free map and sell discounted tickets for about 10 percent off admission to the Historic Dockyard and the Spinnaker Tower, and a few other less-compelling sights. On most Sundays, the TI offers guided walks, usually at 14:30 for £3; ask for details (open daily April-Sept 10:00-17:30, Oct-March 10:00-17:00, tel. 023/9282-6722, www.visitportsmouth.co.uk, vis@portsmouthcc.gov.uk).

Getting There: From the Hard Interchange bus station, next to the Harbour train station, catch First Bus Company's bus #16 or Stagecoach bus #700 (£2/ride, £4 day pass, 2/hour Mon-Sat, hourly Sun, 10 minutes).

Bus Tours: With vintage double-decker buses and live guides, **Local Haunts** does a 1.5-hour city tour three times a week during the tourist season (£10, buy tickets from guide or at TI, late April-Sept Wed-Thu and Sun at 14:00, leaves from Stand A at The Hard

Portsmouth

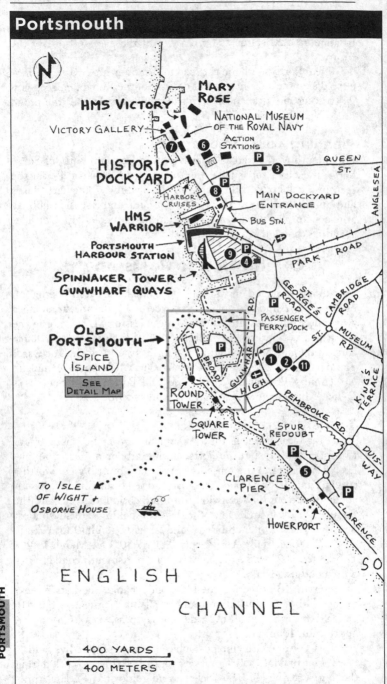

MARY ROSE

HMS VICTORY

VICTORY GALLERY

NATIONAL MUSEUM OF THE ROYAL NAVY

Action Stations

❼ ❻ ❸

QUEEN ST.

HISTORIC DOCKYARD

Harbor Cruises

❽

Main Dockyard Entrance

Bus Stn.

HMS WARRIOR

Portsmouth Harbour Station

❾ ❹

PARK ROAD

ANGLESEA

SPINNAKER TOWER
GUNWHARF QUAYS

ST. GEORGE'S ROAD

ST. CAMBRIDGE ROAD

Passenger Ferry Dock

OLD PORTSMOUTH →
(SPICE ISLAND)
SEE DETAIL MAP

BROAD ST.

GUNWHARF RD.

❿ ❶ ❷ ⓫

MUSEUM RD.

Round Tower

Square Tower

HIGH ST.

PEMBROKE RD.

KING'S TERRACE

Spur Redoubt

DUIS-WAY

TO ISLE OF WIGHT + OSBORNE HOUSE

CLARENCE PIER →

❺

CLARENCE

HOVERPORT

SO

ENGLISH

CHANNEL

400 YARDS

400 METERS

TO LONDON VIA M-3, SALISBURY, CHICHESTER, ARUNDEL & BRIGHTON

1. Lombard House
2. The Duke of Buckingham Pub & Rooms
3. The Royal Maritime Club
4. Express by Holiday Inn
5. Premier Inn Southsea
6. Boathouse No. 7 Cafeteria
7. Georgian Tearooms
8. Costa Coffee & Historic Dockyard Tickets
9. Gunwharf Quays Eateries
10. A Bar Bistro
11. Good Fortune Chinese Restaurant

--- MILLENNIUM PROMENADE
P PARKING
✌ VIEW

PORTSMOUTH + SOUTHSEA STATION

ALFRED — MARKETWAY — COMMERCIAL ROAD — ARUNDEL — EDIN. RD. — ROAD

CHURCHILL AVE.

MIDDLE ST.

KING'S RD. — ELM GROVE — GROVE RD. S.

KENT ROAD

BURG — OSBORNE — CLARENCE PARADE — CLARENDON ROAD — FLORENCE ROAD

UTHSEA — AVE. DE CAEN

ESPLANADE

D-DAY MUSEUM + OVERLORD EMBROIDERY

CASTLE

DCH

PORTSMOUTH

Interchange bus station near Historic Dockyard or 20 minutes earlier from the D-Day Museum, toll-free tel. 0800-389-6897, www.localhaunts.com, info@localhaunts.com).

Arrival in Portsmouth

Portsmouth has two **train** stations. Stay on the train until the final stop at the Portsmouth Harbour Station, conveniently located one long block from the entrance to the Historic Dockyard. The Hard Interchange bus station is just across from the train station (buses #16 and #700 run from here to Southsea). High-speed, passenger-only catamarans to Ryde on the Isle of Wight depart from the waterfront in front of the train station (explained later, under "Portsmouth Connections").

Drivers approach Portsmouth on the M-27 motorway. First take the Portsmouth (W) exit, then follow signs for *Historic Waterfront*. As you get closer, individual parking lots are well-signposted (the one called "Historic Dockyard" is a garage just two blocks from the Dockyard itself).

Sights in Portsmouth

I've listed Portsmouth's sights by neighborhood, from north to south.

▲▲Historic Dockyard

When Britannia ruled the waves, it did so from Portsmouth's Historic Dockyard. Britain's great warships, known as the "Wooden Walls of England," were all that lay between the island nation and invaders from the Continent. Today, this harbor is still the base of the Royal Navy. (If you sneak a peek beyond the guard stations, you can see the British military at work.) The shipyard offers visitors a glimpse of maritime attractions new and old. Marvel at the modern-day warships anchored on the docks, then explore the fantastic collection of historic naval memorabilia and preserved ships.

The museum complex has several parts: HMS *Victory, Mary Rose* Museum, National Museum of the Royal Navy, HMS *Warrior*, Action Stations, and a harbor cruise, as well as numerous merchant marine exhibits. The highlight is the HMS *Victory*, arguably the most important ship in British history. From its deck, Admiral Nelson defeated Napoleon's French fleet at Trafalgar, saving Britain from invasion and escargot. Another top attraction is the ongoing restoration of the *Mary Rose*, one of Henry VIII's favorite warships.

Cost: You can stroll around the Dockyard to see the exteriors of the HMS *Victory* and HMS *Warrior* for free (except during special events), but going inside the attractions requires a £26

Nelson's Victory over Napoleon

Admiral Lord Horatio Nelson (1758-1805), a small man who suffered seasickness throughout his career, was a brilliant military strategist. He developed a new plan for taking on Napoleon's fleet: Instead of pulling parallel to the ships and firing broadside, he would drive a line of ships head-on, perpendicular to his opponent's fleet, cutting them into pieces. When the English attacked the French fleet off the southwest coast of Spain in 1805, they decimated their enemies, who were unable to return adequate fire. Victory was won, but Nelson, who courageously wore his bright uniform to inspire his men, was lost to a sniper's bullet. While sailors are usually buried at sea, Nelson's body was returned to London, where he was given a grand funeral and then entombed in St. Paul's Cathedral. The victory at Trafalgar solidified British dominance of the seas. Although Napoleon would menace Europe for another 10 years, he would never again challenge the British Royal Navy.

ticket that covers everything (a £17 ticket gives you entry to your choice of one attraction). The main TI, across town in Southsea, sells 10-percent-off tickets for this sight (see "Tourist Information," earlier). Day-trippers who arrive by train can save more by purchasing a combined ticket (see "Day-Trip Deal," below).

Hours: The Dockyard is open daily April-Oct 10:00-18:00, Nov-March 10:00-17:30 (last tickets sold 1.5 hours before closing, most attractions close 30 minutes before the Dockyard closes, tel. 023/9283-9766, recorded info tel. 023/9286-1512, www.historic-dockyard.co.uk). Friendly and knowledgeable docents, many who were once seamen, are found throughout the complex, happily answering questions and telling tales of the sea.

Day-Trip Deal: If visiting the Historic Dockyard as a day trip via train from London, knock about £4 off the admission price by buying a combined rail-and-dockyard ticket (most trains depart from London's Waterloo Station, smart to buy at least one day ahead, tel. 0845-600-0650, www.southwesttrains.co.uk).

Crowd-Beating Tips: To skip the line, buy tickets in advance, either at the Southsea TI (which gives a 10 percent discount) or online (www.historicdockyard.co.uk/tickets). Otherwise, you might have to wait 20-45 minutes to buy tickets, especially in July and August, when school is out. Ticket lines are worst at midday, so try to arrive either just before the Dockyard opens or after lunchtime. You can tour the *Victory* on your own in summer, but in winter (Oct-March), you can enter the ship only with a 50-minute tour (you'll get an appointment time for the tour, but as they can fill up by early afternoon, it's best to arrive early in winter).

When entering the Historic Dockyard, you'll be asked to choose a time that you wish to see the *Mary Rose*. Because most visitors slowly plod their way through other exhibits to the *Victory*, the best plan is the opposite: visit the *Victory* first, then work your way over to the *Mary Rose*, and after that, browse the other exhibits on your way back to the entrance. Give yourself at least an hour or two to see the *Victory* before your *Mary Rose* appointment.

▲▲▲HMS *Victory*

This grand historic warship changed the course of world history. At the turn of the 19th century, Napoleon's forces were terrorizing the Continent. In 1805, Napoleon amassed a fleet of French and Spanish ships for the purpose of invading England. The Royal Navy managed to blockade the fleets, but some French ships broke through. Admiral Nelson, commander of the British fleet, pursued the ships aboard the HMS *Victory*, cornering them at Cape Trafalgar, off the coast of Spain (see sidebar). Today, the dry-docked HMS *Victory* is so well-preserved that it feels ready to haul anchor and pull out of the harbor at any moment. In fact, it's still a commissioned warship, the world's oldest. For the British, this ship is more a cathedral than a museum.

⬤ **Self-Guided Tour:** Visitors follow a one-way route that spirals up and down through the ship's six decks, taking at least an hour. Though a 10-year restoration project is underway, the ship remains open. Here are the highlights.

In the **great cabin,** you'll see Admiral Nelson's quarters. Imagine Nelson and his officers dining at the elegant table—or hunched over maps to plan an attack. While it looks like an officer's stately quarters, this space is also designed for action: All of the wood furniture was foldable and could be stowed quickly during battle. The black-and-white checkerboard "tile" flooring—inspired by Nelson's love of southern Italy (and its women)—is actually painted canvas, which could, like the carpets, be rolled up at a moment's notice. It took the crew less than 10 minutes to clear away all the upper-class trappings and turn this space into a fully functional cannon deck. Leaving the Great Cabin, you'll pass Nelson's hanging bunk—even the master of this ship slept on a glorified hammock rather than a bed. (We'll see humbler hammocks soon.)

The **upper gun deck** is filled with original cannons. To prevent the ship from tipping, the lightest were placed higher on the ship, with the heavy ones below. It took a well-trained British sailor two minutes to ready a cannon for firing, compared to the eight minutes French gunners needed to fire their cannons.

Heading up to the **upper deck,** you'll see Captain Hardy's cabin—not quite as posh as his boss Nelson's, but still not bad. Before descending the stairs, notice the small golden plaque on the deck marking the spot where "Nelson fell" during that fateful

Battle of Trafalgar—shot by a sniper. From here, the crew rushed him below deck to care for him during his dying hours.

Down in the **middle gundeck,** you can see how cramped the living conditions were for the sailors. When not in battle, they strung hammocks between the guns and ate at tables wedged under their strung-up beds. Sailors ate from square plates to save space. When a man died, his hammock was his burial cloth—his body was sewn up in the hammock, with a last stitch through the nose to ensure the man was really dead. (Since military service was obligatory, faking death was common.)

As you progress deeper into the bowels of the ship, the space becomes smaller and darker (watch your head). It's down here, in the **orlop deck,** that Nelson died, gasping his final words: "Thank God, I have done my duty." The painting next to the spot of his death shows the admiral glowing like a saint as sailors look on in grief. (Whether or not this is an eyewitness account is suspect; check the size of the ship—either people were much smaller back then, or the painter had never been aboard the *Victory*.) After his death, Nelson was put in a cask filled with brandy to preserve his body. Legend has it that the cask was not quite as full by the time the sailors arrived in London.

▲▲*Mary Rose* Museum

The museum building next to the *Victory* is the home of the *Mary Rose*, which opened in 2013. This 16th-century warship was King Henry VIII's favorite, named after his sister (Mary) and his family emblem (the rose). In July of 1545, when a French fleet approached the English coastline, the *Mary Rose* was sent out to engage the enemy. Suddenly, just two miles offshore, a stiff breeze caught the ship and tipped it over. Since all of the gun bays were open, ready for battle, the water overwhelmed the ship and it began to sink. Netting over the hold was intended to keep boarding parties at bay, but instead trapped 400 sailors as they frantically scrambled to escape. Eventually, the ship and its doomed crew settled, stuck in the mud, in relatively shallow water.

In 1982, about 15 years after the wreck was located, the half of the ship that was encased in mud—and thus protected from voracious shipworms—was raised. Today, the *Mary Rose* is still undergoing conservation. Since allowing the ship to dry out too quickly would cause the structure to disintegrate, for years its remains were constantly sprayed with a sealing wax solution. In 2011, officials finally started to let the hull dry out. Right now, the remains are kept in a "hot box" chamber, but you can view them through windows. When the *Mary Rose* is done drying in a few years, workers will remove the temporary chamber, allowing visitors to see the remains in all their glory.

In the meantime, visitors get to tour the new £36 million

museum—shaped like an oval jewel box—which reunites the preserved hull with thousands of its previously unseen contents. All sorts of Tudor-era items were found inside the wreck, such as clothes, dishes, weapons, a backgammon board, and an oboe-like instrument. There's even the skeleton of Hatch, the ship's dog. It's a fascinating look at everyday shipboard life from almost 500 years ago. Galleries containing these artifacts run along the *Mary Rose's* hull at levels corresponding to the ship's decks, showcasing the items in relation to where they were found. Exhibits at either end focus on crew members' personal stories and their duties aboard ship—and there are re-creations of different parts of the ship such as the surgeon's cabin and the gun deck. Strategically placed high-tech information boards bring it all to life.

National Museum of the Royal Navy

This museum, situated in three buildings, is packed with model ships, paintings, uniforms, and lots more Nelson hero-worship. While interesting, it gets old quickly for all but serious naval history fans. If you dip into only one part, choose the one nearest the *Victory*, called the Victory Gallery. The corny but informative 15-minute Trafalgar Experience multimedia show—with movies, mannequins, sound effects, and smoke—offers a blow-by-blow account of the Battle of Trafalgar. It culminates with a viewing of a panoramic painting of the battle. The new *HMS: Hear My Story* exhibit covers the experiences of ordinary sailors over the last 100 years, from the first days of World War I to recent conflicts in the Middle East.

HMS *Warrior*

This ship, while very impressive, never saw a day of battle...which explains why it's in such good condition. The *Warrior* was the first ironclad warship, a huge technological advance. Compare this ship, built in 1860, with the *Victory*, which was similar to the common warships at the time. The *Warrior* was unbeatable, and the enemy knew it. Its very existence was sufficient to keep the peace. The late 19th century didn't see many sea battles, however, and by  the time warships were needed again, the *Warrior* was obsolete.

Action Stations

Thinly veiled propaganda for the military, this collection of interactive, high-tech exhibits, simulators, and an indoor climbing tower, is aimed mostly at the young and/or prospective Royal Navy recruits. It's like an Army commercial combined with a noisy video arcade—persuasively fun for kids but irritating to weary adults.

Harbor Cruise

You can scoot around the harbor and back to the Historic Dockyard in about 45 minutes by boat. As the boat also stops at Gunwharf Quays, taking this cruise at the very end of your Dockyard visit can be a smart way to eliminate the 10- to 15-minute walk to the Spinnaker Tower and surrounding mall.

Cost and Hours: £7, included in £26 Historic Dockyard ticket, departs about hourly during the summer starting at 11:00, last cruise usually leaves at 16:00 from just inside Dockyard entrance, weather-dependent, tel. 01983/564-602.

Gunwharf Quays and the Spinnaker Tower

If walking to this area from the Historic Dockyard, walk south on the main road past Portsmouth Harbour train station, keeping the water on your right. Then turn right through the archway marked *Gunwharf Quays*, walking under the old brick rail bridge.

Gunwharf Quays

Part of the major (and successful) makeover of Portsmouth, the bustling Gunwharf Quays (pronounced "keys") is an American-style outdoor shopping center on steroids, with restaurants, shops, and entertainment. You'll find all the top shops here, as well as a casino, a bowling alley, a 14-screen cinema, trendy eateries with good views of the water, and an Express by Holiday Inn.

Hours: Mall open Mon-Sat 10:00-19:00, Sun 10:00-17:00, tel. 023/9283-6700, www.gunwharf-quays.com.

Spinnaker Tower

Out at the far end of the shopping zone is this can't-miss-it edifice. Like Seattle's vaguely futuristic Space Needle, the Spinnaker Tower has quickly become an icon of its city. The 557-foot-tall tower is evocative of the billowing ships' sails that have played such a key role in the history of this city and country. You can ride to the 330-foot-high view deck for a panorama of the port and sea beyond, or court acrophobia with a stroll across "Europe's biggest glass floor."

Cost and Hours: £8.55, 10 percent cheaper if bought at Southsea TI; daily 10:00-18:00, last entry 30 minutes before closing; since it can be crowded at midday July-Aug, it's smart to book ahead—and doing so online gets you a 15 percent discount; info tel. 023/9285-7520, booking tel. 023/9285-7521, www.spinnakertower.co.uk.

Old Portsmouth

Portsmouth's historic district—once known as "Spice Island" after the ships' precious cargo—is surprisingly quiet. For a long time, the old sea village was dilapidated and virtually empty. But successful revitalization efforts have brought a few inviting pubs and B&Bs. From the Old Portsmouth promenade, you can watch a procession of 21st-century ferries as they navigate their way into port. It's a pleasant place to stroll around and imagine how different this district was in the old days, when it was filled with salty fishermen and sailors who told tall tales and sang sea shanties in rough-and-tumble pubs.

Getting There: To walk to Old Portsmouth from the Historic Dockyard, first follow the above directions to the Spinnaker Tower. From the tower, head south along the plaza with the water on your right. Cross over the small canal, follow the public pathway to the right around the condo complex, then head inland with the ferry port on your right. When you emerge at busy Gunwharf Road, turn right and follow the decorative chain links in the sidewalk to skirt the ferry port and reach the old town. Eventually you emerge onto Broad Street, with the water in front of you. Head to the right, and in a few blocks, you'll reach the small peninsula of Old Portsmouth.

Old Portsmouth Millennium Promenade Walk

Stylized chain links in the sidewalk mark the Millennium Promenade (also called the Renaissance Trail on some historical markers). The chain symbol recalls the great steel chain that once spanned the mouth of the harbor and was raised to block invading warships. For a pleasant (but often windy) hour-long after-dinner stroll, walk the portion of the well-marked trail south of Old Portsmouth along the oceanfront. Interpretive panels along the way give you insights into Portsmouth's fascinating history.

From the tip of Old Portsmouth, follow the trail around on the ocean side to small **Capstan Square,** where the harbor-spanning chain was raised to keep out enemy ships. Pass through a narrow gate and climb up the stairs to the top of the 15th-century **Round Tower.** A plaque shows where the wreck of the *Mary Rose* was found. After taking in the view, follow the top of the old stone fortifications down to the Square Tower.

The 15th-century **Square Tower,** originally the residence of the governor of Portsmouth, was later used to store gunpowder. South of the Square Tower on the left is the small, roofless **Royal Garrison Church.** Founded in 1212 as a hospice, it was used as a shelter for overseas pilgrims traveling to Canterbury, Chichester, and Winchester. The church was later used by garrisoned troops before the nave lost its roof in a WWII bombing raid.

After walking south about a quarter-mile, you'll see a small moat on the left. You've reached the **Spur Redoubt,** part of the outer fortifications (see interpretive sign down by moat)—and the end of our walk. To avoid the huge crowds that had gathered in town to see him, Admiral Nelson supposedly passed through this area on September 14, 1805, on his way to the Battle of Trafalgar. From the beach, he was rowed out to the *Victory*, waiting off the Isle of Wight. He didn't return to England alive.

Cross the metal bridge over the moat, pass through a tunnel under the earthen fortifications, and immediately turn right and climb up the short path to the top. Walk back along the top of the grassy fortifications. Benches invite you to stop and watch the many passing ferries and other ships or to simply enjoy the sunset. If the weather's clear, you can see the Isle of Wight from here.

Southsea

On a sunny day, this appealing seafront neighborhood—with its long, broad, grassy park stretching for miles in front of fine old townhouses—bustles with locals enjoying their city. While it's studded with some humdrum sights, the main reason to venture to Southsea is for its interesting D-Day Museum, which also houses the TI.

▲D-Day Museum and Overlord Embroidery

This small museum, worth ▲▲ to history buffs, was built to commemorate the 40th anniversary of the D-Day invasions. Though it feels a bit dated and faded, it still does an excellent job of recreating both the atmosphere of WWII England and the detailed planning and execution of the Normandy landing. And its remarkable Overland Embroidery is a world of fascinating details for history buffs to pore over.

Cost and Hours: £6.50, audioguide-£0.50, daily April-Sept 10:00-17:30, Oct-March 10:00-17:00, last entry 30 minutes before closing. A café is on site (open April-Sept). The museum is on the waterfront about two miles south of the Spinnaker Tower (Clarence Esplanade, Southsea, tel. 023/9282-7261, www.ddaymuseum.co.uk).

Getting There: To get from Portsmouth's Hard Interchange bus station to the museum, take First Bus Company's bus #16 or Stagecoach bus #700 (see "Tourist Information," earlier; ask at info booth about last return-bus times). Drivers can park in the pay-and-display parking lot behind the museum.

Visiting the Museum: The centerpiece of the exhibit is the

272-foot long **Overlord Embroidery** (named for the invasion's code name). The 34 appliquéd panels—stitched together over five years by a team of seamstresses, and originally displayed in a brewery's boardroom—were inspired by the Bayeux Tapestry that recorded William the Conqueror's battles during the Norman invasion of England a thousand years earlier. The panels chronologically trace the years from 1940 to 1944, from the first British men receiving their call-up papers in the mail to the successful implementation of D-Day. It celebrates everyone from famous WWII figures to unsung heroes of the home front. An informative audioguide narrates the whole thing, panel by panel (rent when you buy your ticket).

In the center of the embroidery hall, a movie theater shows a good 15-minute film—a montage of archival wartime footage set to period music (included in entry ticket). Then you'll wander through an exhibit that thoughtfully explains the Battle of Britain and D-Day, including some vehicles that were actually used for the landing. Allow at least 1.5 hours for your visit.

Sleeping in Portsmouth

If you just can't get enough of ships and sea air, Old Portsmouth—just a 15-minute walk from the Historic Dockyard (cutting through the outdoor Gunwharf Quays mall)—is charming and fairly quiet, and has several accommodation options.

In Old Portsmouth

$$$ Fortitude Cottage, quaint and cozy, rents six modern-feeling rooms in two adjoining row houses just a block from the water. Everything is done with care, making these some of the best rooms in Portsmouth. The main building has views, and the top-floor room has its own roof terrace. The annex rooms are more spacious, with large modern bathrooms (Sb-£45, Db-£85-150, prices vary by room size and view, Sb pays the Db rate except during slow times, free Wi-Fi, 51 Broad Street, tel. 023/9282-3748, www.fortitude-cottage.co.uk, info@fortitudecottage.co.uk, Maggie and Mike).

$$$ Oyster Cottage is for those who want their B&B to themselves. Witty Carol, who might remind you of Carol Channing, has just one large, light-filled, updated room with a bay-window sitting area, ideal for watching passing boats right up close as you pet her dogs (Db-£70-90, free parking, 9 Bath Square, tel. 023/9282-3683, www.theoystercottage.co.uk, info@theoystercottage.co.uk).

$$ Cecil Cottage is a light and airy, family-run B&B with three rooms, close to Capstan Square (Db-£60-70, Tb-£60-70, free parking, 45 Broad Street, mobile 0789-407-2253, www.cecil-cottage.co.uk).

Sleep Code

(£1 = about $1.60, country code: 44, area code: 023)
S = Single, **D** = Double/Twin, **T** = Triple, **Q** = Quad, **b** = bathroom, **s** = shower only. Unless otherwise noted, credit cards are accepted and breakfast is included.

To help you sort easily through these listings, I've divided the accommodations into three categories based on the price for a standard double room with bath:

  $$$ **Higher Priced**—Most rooms £75 or more.
   $$ **Moderately Priced**—Most rooms between £40-75.
    $ **Lower Priced**—Most rooms £40 or less.

Prices can change without notice; verify the hotel's current rates online or by email. For the best prices, always book direct.

Between Old Portsmouth and Gunwharf Quays

$$ Lombard House rents two rooms on a quiet residential street next to the cathedral, a 10-minute walk from the Historic Dockyard. The public areas are tastefully decorated and feature original artwork. In 2005, as part of the bicentennial of the Battle of Trafalgar, actor-owners Alex and Finni traveled around Europe as Admiral Nelson and his mistress, Lady Emma Hamilton. Alex's museum-quality admiral's uniform is on display in their atmospheric breakfast cellar, which also boasts old oak ship beams (Sb-£55-60, Db-£70, cash only, free Wi-Fi, 9 Lombard Street, tel. 023/9286-2294, mobile 0776-200-1528, finni@victoryfilms.co.uk).

$$ The Duke of Buckingham pub, a few blocks inland from Old Portsmouth, is likely to have rooms when others are full. While the accommodations take a backseat to the popular pub, the 18 basic rooms—some above the bar, some out back in separate cottages—are clean and comfortable (D-£59, Db-£65, no breakfast, free Wi-Fi in the pub, 119 High Street, tel. 023/9282-7067, www.dukeofbuckingham.co.uk, buckingham119@aol.com).

Elsewhere in Portsmouth

$$$ The Royal Maritime Club offers a home away from home to sailors in town who don't want to bunk on the boat. Just two blocks up the road from the Historic Dockyard entrance, it also welcomes tourists, who share its grand public spaces, generous facilities (including a swimming pool, fitness center, game room, self-service laundry, even barbershop) and 100 comfortable, surprisingly newish rooms. The catch: They rent out their ballroom

Old Portsmouth Accommodations & Eateries

1. Fortitude Cottage
2. Oyster Cottage
3. Cecil Cottage
4. The Still & West Country House Pub
5. The Spice Island Inn
6. Spinnaker Café

To Spinnaker Tower

EAST ST.

SEAGER'S CT.

WEST TOWER ST.

ROUND TOWER

BROAD ST. A-3

WHITE HART ROAD

HIGH ST.

P PARKING

To Spur Redoubt

100 YARDS
100 METERS

OLD PORTSMOUTH MILLENNIUM PROMENADE WALK
P PARKING
VIEW

DCH

for parties, which can frequently be noisy into the wee hours—if you're a light sleeper, try requesting a quieter room. It's located two blocks from the Historic Dockyard and four blocks from the train station, opposite the oval-shaped Admiralty Tower (Sb-£52, Db-£98, family suites available, elevator, free Wi-Fi, Queen Street, tel. 023/9282-4231 or 023/9283-7681, www.royalmaritimeclub.co.uk, info@royalmaritimeclub.co.uk).

Big Chain Hotels

The following hotels (with elevators and 24-hour reception) may have rooms when the other accommodations are full.

$$$ Express by Holiday Inn, located in the shadow of the Spinnaker Tower and within the Gunwharf Quays shopping complex, rents 130 cookie-cutter rooms not far from the Portsmouth Harbour train station and Historic Dockyard (£135-190 per room, check website for specials, includes continental breakfast and discounts at some Gunwharf Quays restaurants; free Wi-Fi, free parking for first 24 hours, then £2/day; US reservations tel. 888-465-4329, British reservations toll-free tel. 0800-405-060, reception tel. 023/9289-4240, www.holidayinn-expresssportsmouth. co.uk, portsmouth@kewgreen.co.uk).

$$ Premier Inn Southsea, a half-mile south of Old Portsmouth along the waterfront, offers 48 somewhat tired rooms next to the kitschy, cotton-candy-carnival ambience of Clarence Pier (the noisy pier attractions close down at about 22:30). It's popular with business travelers on weeknights and families on weekends—as the hordes of screaming kids in the family restaurant downstairs can attest (Db for up to two adults and two kids-£70-75, may be up to £119 during special events, check website for specials, continental breakfast-£5.25, full English breakfast-£8, pay Wi-Fi, limited free parking, Long Curtain Road, just off Pier Road, Southsea, tel. 0871-527-9014, www.premierinn.com).

Eating in Portsmouth

At the Historic Dockyard

The Historic Dockyard has an acceptable cafeteria, called **Boathouse No. 7,** with a play area that kids enjoy (£5-8 meals, daily 10:00-15:00). The **Georgian Tearooms** are across the pedestrian street in Storehouse #9, with good sandwich and cake offerings (daily 10:00-17:00). The **Costa Coffee** inside the entrance building offers good grilled sandwiches and coffee drinks to go (daily 10:00-17:00).

At Gunwharf Quays

Eating options abound at this bustling mega-mall. Most restaurants line up along the waterfront by the Spinnaker Tower. You'll pay too much in this high-rent district—and many of the places are chains selling mall food—but it's the most convenient one-stop neighborhood for dining. Familiar restaurant names include **Wagamama, Yo! Sushi, Loch Fyne, Jamie's Italian,** and **Pizza Express** (see descriptions on page 33).

In and near Old Portsmouth

Dinnertime is the best time to head over to Old Portsmouth, eat at a pub, and then stroll along the Millennium Promenade (described earlier, under "Sights in Portsmouth"). The first two pubs listed here sling overpriced pub grub with gorgeous views, within a French fry's toss of the water—the busy maritime traffic makes for a fascinating backdrop. The next two listings are clustered between Old Portsmouth and Gunwharf Quays, along quiet, mostly residential streets. The last listing is a cozy café that closes before dinnertime.

The **Still & West Country House** pub has dining in two appealing zones. Eat from the simpler and cheaper menu on the main floor, or outside on the picnic benches with fantastic views of the harbor (£7 baguette sandwiches and £8 fish-and-chips). Or head upstairs to the dining room with a gorgeous glassed-in conservatory that offers sea views—especially enticing in cold weather (dining room open Mon-Sat 12:00-15:00 & 18:00-21:00, Sun 12:00-19:30, longer hours in the bar, 2 Bath Square, tel. 023/9282-1567).

The **Spice Island Inn,** at the tip of the Old Portsmouth peninsula, has terrific outdoor seating, a family-friendly dining room upstairs, and many vegetarian offerings, although service can be slow (£5-9 lunches, £7-12 dinners, food served daily 11:00-22:00, bar open longer, 1 Bath Square, tel. 023/9287-0543).

The **A Bar Bistro** is a classy but relaxed, seafood-and-wine kind of place, and is handy for those staying near the cathedral or Old Portsmouth (£9-18 main dishes, Mon-Sat 12:00-24:00, Sun 12:00-22:00, 58 White Hart Road, tel. 023/9281-1585).

The **Good Fortune,** across the street from the Duke of Buckingham pub, is a Chinese restaurant favored by locals (£6-10 main dishes, £13-18 multi-course meals, Wed-Mon 18:00-23:00, closed Tue, 21 High Street, tel. 023/9286-3293).

Café: If you're in Old Portsmouth before dinner and could do with a quick snack, visit the **Spinnaker Café,** located at the end of the old quay (£5-8 eggs, burgers, and sandwiches; breakfast served all day, daily 8:00-16:00, 96 Broad Street, mobile 0777-295-3143).

Portsmouth Connections

From Portsmouth by Train to: London (5/hour, 1.5-2 hours, most to Waterloo Station, a few to Victoria Station), **Gatwick Airport** (2/hour, 1.5-2 hours, some require transfer), **Bath** (hourly, 2.25 hours), **Salisbury** (1/hour direct, 1.5 hours), **Oxford** (2-4/hour, 2.5-2.75 hours, 1-2 transfers), **Brighton** (direct trains hourly, 1.25 hours, more with transfer), **Exeter** (hourly, 3-3.5 hours, change in Salisbury). Train info: tel. 0845-748-4950, www.nationalrail.co.uk.

By Bus: For most connections, the train is faster—take the bus only if you're on a tight budget. Stagecoach runs the #700 Coastliner bus to **Brighton** (2/hour Mon-Sat, hourly Sun, 4 hours; tel. 0871-200-2233, www.stagecoachbus.com). National Express buses also go to **Brighton** (1 direct bus/day, 2 hours), **Salisbury** (1 direct bus/day, 1.5 hours), and **Bath** (1 direct bus/day, 3 hours; tel. 0871-781-8181, www.nationalexpress.com).

By Ferry to the Isle of Wight: Wightlink Ferries has service to **Fishbourne** (2/hour, 40 minutes, cars and passengers) and a catamaran to **Ryde** (2/hour, 22 minutes, passengers only, tel. 0871-376-1000, www.wightlink.co.uk). Hovertravel operates a passenger-only hovercraft from Southsea (2 miles south of Portsmouth) to **Ryde** (£16 same-day round-trip, at least 2/hour, 10 minutes, tel. 0843-487-8887, www.hovertravel.co.uk).

Serious royal-family fans can consider a day trip from Portsmouth to the Isle of Wight to see **Osborne House,** a stunning

Italianate palazzo that was Queen Victoria's beloved getaway for 50 years, until her death there in 1901. Today, the house has been lovingly restored and it seems as if she has just stepped away. Be sure to see the Durbar Room, decorated as an over-the-top homage to India, one of Victoria's most valued Colonial prizes. The easiest way to day-trip to the house is to buy a combo-ticket that combines the round-trip boat ride, bus to and from the estate, and admission (£29, buy online at www.hovertravel.co.uk or at Hovertravel's Southsea terminal on the day of travel; Osborne House open daily April-Sept 10:00-17:00, Oct 10:00-16:00; Nov-March open erratically—call first or check online; Osborne House tel. 01983/200-022, www.english-heritage.org.uk).

By International Ferry: Brittany Ferries (tel. 0871-244-0744, www.brittanyferries.com) sails to France: **Caen** (2-4/day, 4 hours on high-speed boat, 6-7 hours on slower boat), **Cherbourg** (1-2/day, 3 hours), **St. Malo** (night crossing, 1/day, 11 hours); and to northern Spain: **Santander** (2/week, 25 hours) and **Bilbao** (2/week, 24-32 hours). LD Lines (toll-free tel. 0800-917-1201 or toll tel. 0844-576-8836, www.ldlines.co.uk) sails to **Le Havre,** France (1/day, 8 hours). **Condor Ferries** (tel. 0845-609-1024, www.condorferries.co.uk) sails to the Channel Islands of **Guernsey** (daily, 7 hours) and **Jersey** (daily, 8-10 hours), and also to **Cherbourg,** France (1/week, 6.5 hours).

Near Portsmouth

These sights are very near the main A-27 road that connects Portsmouth with Brighton. They're worth considering for a stopover if you have time as you pass through.

Fishbourne Roman Palace

In the 1930s, a farmer just outside of Chichester found the remains of an early Roman palace on his land. Wary of archaeologists, he

didn't disclose his find until 1960. The ensuing dig revealed a huge Roman-era villa, probably built around A.D. 50 by a local tribal chief who was loyal to the Roman Empire. In the main museum building, you'll find the collection's impressive centerpiece: well-preserved floor mosaics, which are on display in their original locations (visitors walk above them on an elevated walkway). Also in the main building is a museum telling the story of the palace and Fishbourne's Roman era. The garden outside was reconstructed to resemble the original Roman plan. Across the parking lot, the

Near Portsmouth

Discovery Centre lets you peek into the offices and warehouses of the archaeologists at work—like a zoo for people in lab coats. You'll learn how the artifacts are handled on their long journey from the ground to the display case. The palace is fairly interesting to most, but likely to fascinate true fans of Roman history. Go early to avoid the crush of field-tripping schoolchildren.

Cost and Hours: £8.50, £2 guidebook outlines a very detailed tour, daily March-Oct 10:00-17:00, Nov-mid-Dec and Feb 10:00-16:00, closed mid-Dec-Jan except for Sat-Sun 10:00-16:00, café, tel. 01243/785-859, www.sussexpast.co.uk/fishbourne.

Getting There: It's on the southwestern outskirts of the large town of Chichester, well-signed from the main A-27 motorway connecting Brighton and Portsmouth. First head for the town of Fishbourne, then follow *Roman Palace* signs through a very residential-feeling neighborhood to the museum. From the Fishbourne train station, the palace is a seven-minute walk.

▲Arundel Castle

This impressive castle of Arundel (AIR-uhn-dull) graces the valley below with straight-out-of-a-storybook appeal. The Duke of

Norfolk—the top dog among all English dukes—still lives here, in what amounts to a museum of his own family (the Fitzalan-Howards, who also own Castle Howard in Yorkshire; see page 781). Pompous even for a castle, the self-aggrandizing exhibits, docents who speak in hushed awe of their employers, and opulent interiors offer a somehow off-putting taste of England's affection for its outmoded nobility. Still, castle buffs will find the gorgeous interior worth visiting, and the themed gardens are a delight—check out the Earl's Garden, which is based on 17th-century designs and contains an intriguing "stumpery."

Cost and Hours: Castle interior, chapel, and grounds-£15, private bedrooms-£2 more; grounds and chapel only-£8; £19 during "Joust Week" in late July. The complex is open April-Oct Tue-Sun, closed Mon (except in Aug and on Bank Holidays) and closed Nov-March. Various parts of the castle are open at different times: grounds and Fitzalan Chapel—10:00-17:00; castle keep—10:00-16:30; main castle rooms—12:00-17:00; last entry at 16:00. Parts of the castle can be unexpectedly closed for private events. Tel. 01903/882-173, www.arundelcastle.org.

Getting There: Arundel Castle is right on the A-27 between Brighton and Portsmouth—**drivers** just follow signs to the castle, and park at the pay lot across from the castle gate (£2/3 hours). The town of Arundel is connected by **train** from Portsmouth (2/hour, 1 hour, 1-2 transfers) and Brighton (1-2/hour, 1.25-1.5 hours, 1 transfer); Stagecoach **buses** also run from Brighton to Arundel (2/hour, 2.25 hours, some require transfer).

Background: The castle seems like the perfect medieval fortress. Well, almost...while the castle dates back to the 11th century,

 most of what you see today is actually a Victorian restoration. The owners of the castle, the Catholic Dukes of Norfolk, weren't very popular in this Protestant country, and neither was their castle, which endured multiple sieges. The dukes persevered, however, rebuilding their castle in the 18th and 19th centuries along with a large Catholic church. As you explore the castle, posted explanations fill in the story (such as an English Civil War exhibit with a Catholic spin). For a primer before you begin, consider stopping by the little information room in the gate as you enter the castle grounds (across from the ticket booth).

➋ Self-Guided Tour: The castle is all about its intimidating bulk and opulent interior—so little explanation is necessary. But here are a few tidbits to bring meaning to your visit. Notice that various parts of the castle have different opening times (listed earlier); if you're here in the morning, visit them according to when they open.

Castle Keep: This ancient centerpiece of the castle is a classic motte-and-bailey design, with a stout windowless fortress atop a man-made hill—double defense against attackers. Later, as the castle grew around it, the keep became the last resort in case of an attack. Walking across the bridge to the keep, ponder how easy it would be to keep the keep—it's connected to the outside only by one bridge, and is well defended by strategically placed arrow slits. Inside the keep yard, stairs lead down to a cellar used as both a dungeon and a storehouse for resources in case the keep had to be used for a final stand. If the flag is flying up top, it means the Duke of Norfolk or his heir (the Earl of Arundel) is around.

Main Castle Rooms: This was—and remains—the gorgeously appointed residence of the Duke of Norfolk. As you ogle the decor, docents explain what you're looking at, and they are always eager to tell you about the lineage, heraldry, and personalities of their beloved dukes. You'll pass through a spectacular private **chapel** (19th-century "Catholic Revival") before entering the **Baron's Hall,** with a pair of giant fireplaces and some fine furniture (including a gorgeous inlaid-wood chest). This room is still used for functions...and, occasionally, for filming the British version of *Antiques Roadshow.* Then you'll pass through a **picture gallery** displaying a *Who's Who* of the Dukes of Norfolk (no, really...who *are* these people?) and enjoy strolling through the formal state dining room, bedrooms, and drawing rooms. Finally, you'll reach the highlight: a wonderful old **library** with rich mahogany woodwork and 10,000 musty leather-bound books on two levels.

Fitzalan Chapel: This family church—across a tree-filled garden from the main castle—is the final resting place of many of the Dukes of Norfolk. In the nave of the church, notice the grisly double-decker tomb of a 15th-century earl. Called a *memento mori,* or "reminder of death," this was carved during the earl's lifetime— with his virile, healthy self on the top level, and a rotting corpse on the bottom level—to remind him of his own mortality. Flanking the aisle, find the plaques dedicated to the most recent D.'s of N.: Bernard (who died in 1975) and his cousin Miles Francis (died in 2002). Today's Duke—Edward Fitzalan-Howard—is the 18th to hold the title...and you just walked through his house.

Earl's Garden: From the chapel, follow the signs and walk uphill into the Earl's Garden. Landscaped and maintained by a renowned gardener, the plantings intrigue and impress with their creativity. The stumpery (upturned oak trees), White Garden, and Italianate formal gardens are all lined with herbaceous borders, confirming England's obsession with all things green.

Arundel Town: If you have time to kill, check out the adjacent village of Arundel, where you'll find many fine pubs and shops. The little **TI** is also happy to suggest nearby boat trips and activities in town (daily in summer 10:30-15:00, subject to availability of volunteer staff, 1-3 Crown Yard Mews, off River Road, tel. 01903/882-268, www.sussexbythesea.com).

DARTMOOR

Windswept and desolate, Dartmoor—one of England's best national parks—is one of the few truly wild places you'll find in this densely populated country. Dartmoor's vast medieval commons are still places where all can pass, anyone can graze their sheep, and ponies run wild. Old stone-slab clapper bridges remind hikers that for thousands of years, humans have trod these same paths. In other parts of England, stone circles, stone rows, and standing stones are cause for a tourist frenzy. In Dartmoor, where the terrain is littered with the highest concentration of prehistoric monuments in the UK, they're barely worth a detour.

Great literary minds, perhaps inspired by all that mystery and prehistory, have been drawn to Dartmoor: Sir Arthur Conan Doyle (his masterpiece, *The Hound of the Baskervilles*, was set here), Agatha Christie (who wrote her first mystery novel here), Evelyn Waugh (who wrote *Brideshead Revisited* here), Rosamunde Pilcher, and even Steven Spielberg (whose *War Horse* was filmed here).

Locals brag that Dartmoor is England as it was 50 years ago. Maybe that's why it's increasingly a retreat of the rich and famous. You'll find yourself sharing the narrow roads with luxury SUVs, as many retired CEOs and washed-up celebrities have resettled in this idyllic and remote countryside far from prying eyes. The area around Chagford has become known as the "Golden Triangle."

All that wealth aside, Dartmoor remains first and foremost the terrain of hikers. Dartmoor gives you a chance to be alone with England's history, jittery sheep, stately wild ponies, and seemingly endless moors. It's also a moody place: At sunset on a clear evening, the gold-tinged heather and rolling hills can be romantic; but on a gray and misty day, it's foreboding—and if you listen hard enough, you might just hear the howl of the hound of the Baskervilles.

Planning Your Time

Dartmoor works well as a stopover between Cornwall (see next chapter) and the rest of England. While you could get a taste of Dartmoor with one overnight (after breakfast, do my self-guided driving tour and/or Scorhill Stone Circle before moving on in the afternoon), it really deserves at least one full day and two overnights to fully appreciate its majesty and mystery. This is one of those places where time slows down...and puts a crimp in an ambitious itinerary.

Getting Around Dartmoor

By Car: Drivers have Dartmoor by the tail—but a good map is essential...as is a fair amount of courage. Dartmoor's narrow lanes are the most challenging in England: barely as wide as a single car, and often flanked by tall stone hedges covered in greenery. As most roads are too narrow for two cars to easily pass, you'll often have to pull up or reverse to the nearest wide spot in the road when encountering another car. Just follow the other driver's lead, fold in your mirrors as needed, and don't be shy to wave a thank you. For driving in Dartmoor, rent the smallest car you can tolerate, and you'll breathe easier. The only places to buy gas on or near the moors are in Chagford and Bovey Tracey.

By Bus: Dartmoor is tricky for visitors without a car; bus connections are sparse on weekends and nearly nonexistent during the week (tel. 0871-200-2233, www.dartmoor-npa.gov.uk or http://traveline.info). Okehampton and Ivybridge are both on minor rail lines, but the closest major city is Exeter.

During high season, the **Haytor Hoppa/#271** bus runs Saturdays only to cover the eastern side of Dartmoor (£5 hop-on/hop-off ticket, Easter-Oct 4/day), looping from Bovey Tracey up to Haytor and on to Widecombe-in-the-Moor, before returning to Bovey Tracey. The **Transmoor Link #82** bus runs twice a day on Saturdays and Sundays only June through mid-September. It leaves from Exeter or Plymouth and stops in Moretonhampstead, Postbridge, Princetown, and Yelverton (£2). Two other bus routes from Exeter also connect to Dartmoor towns (Mon-Sat year-round, no buses Sun): Dartline **#173** to Chagford and Moretonhampstead (4/day), and Country Bus **#359** to Moretonhampstead (6/day).

DARTMOOR

Dartmoor National Park

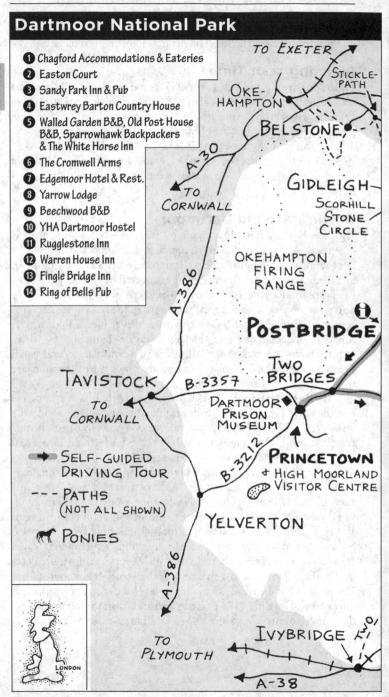

1. Chagford Accommodations & Eateries
2. Easton Court
3. Sandy Park Inn & Pub
4. Eastwrey Barton Country House
5. Walled Garden B&B, Old Post House B&B, Sparrowhawk Backpackers & The White Horse Inn
6. The Cromwell Arms
7. Edgemoor Hotel & Rest.
8. Yarrow Lodge
9. Beechwood B&B
10. YHA Dartmoor Hostel
11. Rugglestone Inn
12. Warren House Inn
13. Fingle Bridge Inn
14. Ring of Bells Pub

TO EXETER

STICKLEPATH

OKEHAMPTON

BELSTONE

A-30

TO CORNWALL

GIDLEIGH

SCORHILL STONE CIRCLE

OKEHAMPTON FIRING RANGE

A-386

POSTBRIDGE

TWO BRIDGES

TAVISTOCK

B-3357

DARTMOOR PRISON MUSEUM

TO CORNWALL

B-3212

PRINCETOWN
+ HIGH MOORLAND VISITOR CENTRE

SELF-GUIDED DRIVING TOUR

--- PATHS (NOT ALL SHOWN)

PONIES

YELVERTON

A-386

LONDON

IVYBRIDGE

TO PLYMOUTH

A-38

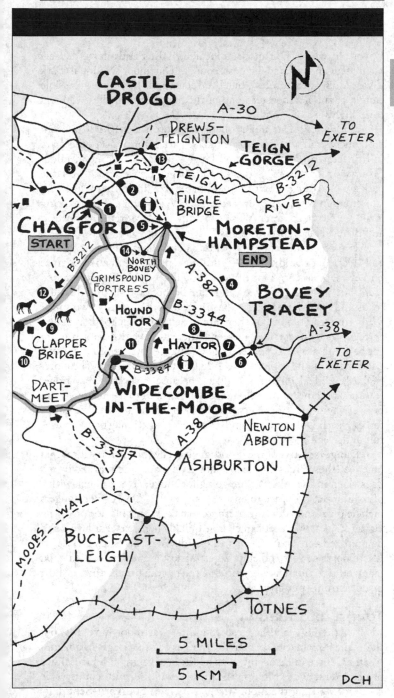

Orientation to Dartmoor

Devon, in which Dartmoor is located, is England's least densely populated and second-biggest county. Dartmoor National Park is vast (368 square miles), but I've focused on the most accessible chunk, at the northeastern end of the park between the A-30 and A-38 highways.

Throughout Dartmoor, there are more than 10,000 ancient monuments, all accessible to walkers. Park information offices are in Princetown, Postbridge, and Haytor (all described later, under "Tourist Information"). The small villages that encroach on the park are charming. Towns of reasonable size (including Chagford, Moretonhampstead, Bovey Tracey, and Widecombe) have parking lots (free or cheap) and WCs (generally free). Moretonhampstead and Bovey Tracey also have TIs.

Two pieces of gear are essential: good shoes (resistant to mud and "Dartmoor landmines"—wild-horse patties) and an Ordnance Survey map (essential for drivers). You'll need this highly detailed map, not just because the land can be boggy, but also because roads and walking paths can be tricky to follow. (Only two major roads cross the moor, but there are dozens of lesser roads twisting through the countryside—it seems there are five different ways to get between any two points.) The Ordnance Survey produces two good maps of the region. The 1:25,000 Dartmoor map (Explorer #OL28) is ideal for serious hikers, because it shows every ridge, feature, and landmark, but—until you get used to it—its detail can be overwhelming for drivers. The 1:50,000 map (called "Okehampton & North Dartmoor," Landranger Map #191) may be more useful for drivers.

Dangers: Parts of the moors are used by the military for target practice. These areas are clearly shown on maps, and marked by red flags when in use—but before going for a hike, always check with a park information office to ensure your route is OK. Other dangers include ticks and adders (a poisonous snake with a black-and-white zigzag stripe). Weather can change quickly here, so wear layers and be prepared for "four seasons in one day" (as locals say). Because Dartmoor is so vast and empty, getting lost is a real threat—a good map and a compass are essential if you're going more than a short distance from your car.

Tourist Information

Most of the bigger villages surrounding Dartmoor have TIs, but the main information center for the park is the **High Moorland Visitor Centre** in Princetown. In addition to hiking info, this office has an interactive exhibit on the history, wildlife, and "countryside code" for walking the moors (free, exhibit-£1.50; April-Sept daily

10:00-17:00; March and Oct daily 10:00-16:00; Nov-Feb Thu-Sun 10:30-15:30, closed Mon-Wed; Tavistock Road, tel. 01822/890-414, www.dartmoor-npa.gov.uk). There are also good branches in **Postbridge** (at the big parking lot near the Clapper Bridge, relaxing video upstairs about Dartmoor ponies, daily April-Sept 10:00-17:00, Oct 10:00-16:00, closed Nov-March, tel. 01822/880-272) and by **Haytor** (on the B-3387 3 miles west of Bovey Tracey, same hours as main branch, tel. 01364/661-520).

At any of these offices, you can buy your Ordnance Survey map and pick up their free information-packed *Enjoy Dartmoor* guide (also downloadable online). These offices are the best source of advice on hikes or driving routes, and each one sells an illustrated £1.50 booklet with suggestions for self-guided walks in that area; they also sell overpriced £4 booklets on other points of interest. If you have a mobile device, you can download free, six-mile audio walks starting at the three park information centers (www.dartmoor-npa.gov.uk; click on "Visiting").

The TIs in **Moretonhampstead** (Easter-Oct daily 9:30-17:00, shorter hours off-season, New Street, tel. 01647/440-043, www.moretonhampstead.com) and **Bovey Tracey** (see page 359) can also be helpful.

Guided Walks: The national park offers guided walks (£5-10/person depending on length, get schedule at www.dartmoor-npa.gov.uk or in the *Enjoy Dartmoor* brochure); many are run by a local guiding collective called **Moorland Guides** (www.moorlandguides.co.uk). You can also go with your own guide for a hike of your choosing at a similar price. **Tom Soby** offers a range of walks, including a popular one exploring the places featured in *The Hound of the Baskervilles* (£7-10/person to join a scheduled walk, 3- to 4-hour private tours-£60, mobile 07516-042-316, tomstors@hotmail.com). **Phil Page,** a former Dartmoor park manager, offers walks all year on topics from butterflies to literary works set in Dartmoor (£10/hour for up to 6 people, can pick you up and drive you to the hike—driving time also chargeable, tel. 07858/421-148, mobile 07849-840-126, www.dartmoornaturetours.co.uk, enquiries@dartmoornaturetours.co.uk). Phil's wife, Hanneke, runs a two-room B&B (see page 364).

Self-Guided Driving Tour

▲▲▲Pony, Lamb, and Moor Joyride

This all-day driving route is a convenient framework for your Dartmoor exploration. Linger at the desolate viewpoints you find most appealing, and don't be afraid to venture off this plan for a walk to a secluded stone row or circle. If you have enough time, chase down leads suggested by locals—there are many hidden gems embedded in Dartmoor. This circular route begins and ends in Chagford, but you can join or leave it wherever you like. If you're in a rush,

you can squeeze this drive into three hours: Skip the optional detours (such as Grimspound and Princetown), choose just one tor to climb, and grab lunch on the go.

• *Begin in the village of...*

▲Chagford

Perched on the edge of the moor, this tiny town is not only charming but actually feels like a real, normal slice of English life (www.chagford-parish.co.uk; park at the pay lot at the far end of town, past the church and Jubilee Hall—follow *P* signs). The small-town ambience here may make you feel like you've stepped into a time warp (or maybe a quaint BBC sitcom). Villages like this one, which was probably established in Saxon times, were built around Dartmoor as bases for the tin-mining industry. In 1305, Chagford became one of four Dartmoor stannary towns, a main center for "weighing and paying" the miners. The eight-sided **Market House** in the village square (known as the "pepper pot") is located on the site of the old stannary court/assayer's office.

St. Michael's Parish Church, at the upper end of town, mostly dates from the 15th century and is built out of the typical stone of the area, gray granite. The hard rock is tough to work, so most buildings here are fairly simple. An incident occurred here that is said to have inspired R. D. Blackmore's *Lorna Doone:* A bride named Mary Whiddon was shot dead by a former suitor as she left the church during her wedding in 1641. Look among the pews at the needlepoint cushions, a few of which bear a tinner's symbol: three rabbits in a circle that each have two ears, but appear to share only three ears among them. (This motif also shows up in the stained-glass window over the door of the wine store on the town square.)

The little **village square**—named simply The Square—has all the essentials: bank, post office, small grocery store, pharmacy, butcher, delicatessen, and a few hardware shops that sell any hiking gear that you might have forgotten (including Ordnance Survey maps). Go gawk inside Bowden's hardware store and "Moorland Centre" to see how everything you could possibly ever need can be neatly  crammed into one place. Don't miss the glassed-in antique-hardware room way in the back, and the loft full of rain gear (Mon-Sat 9:00-17:30, closed Sun, tel. 01647/433-271). Devonshire Dairy sells ice-cream cones, interesting cheeses from the area, and clotted cream by the pound (Mon-Sat 9:00-17:00, closed Sun).

• *Hop in your car and follow* Postbridge *signs directing you to the road south of Chagford, which will take you to the busy B-3212. Soon after you turn right onto B-3212, you'll cross some...*

Cattle Grates

Welcome to wild-pony country. The rumble of your tires over cattle grates—which you'll cross several times on our drive—tells you  that you've entered an area without fences, where livestock of all kinds can roam freely. It's also a reminder to slow down and watch the road closely, especially around blind corners—the animals find cars more interesting than scary, and you may well find some sunning themselves in the middle of the road. I've had to lean on my horn several times to convince a dozing sheep to let me pass. As throughout England, you'll see sheep grazing and fluffy little lambs bounding through the heather. But Dartmoor adds its own unique touch: famously "wild," but remarkably tame, horses. (In fact, the horses are all owned by local farmers, who keep an eye on them as they graze the moors—notice that some horses are branded.) Horses have wandered here for centuries, and the brown ones are probably the most closely related to the ancestral Dartmoor breed. The park discourages people from feeding or even approaching the horses—they get used to mooching, so they often readily come up to people, but may bite or kick without warning.

• *After crossing the cattle grates, you're really into the heart of...*

The Moors

England's green, bucolic landscape is occasionally interrupted by brown, scrubby moorlands like these. It's tricky to define a

DARTMOOR

"moor"—but once you've spent time on one, you'll know them when you see them. A moor is characterized by its relative lack of vegetation, save for high grasses and heather—a dull-brown shrub that thrives here (and briefly turns a brilliant purple when it flowers in late summer). In the springtime, you may see splashes of vibrant yellow flowers on the plant called gorse (closely related to Scotch broom). The long, undulating expanses of open land, almost unbroken by trees but scattered with long-forgotten prehistoric stone monuments, makes Dartmoor feel even more evocative and mysterious than other English moors.

• *On the left, you may notice the first of many tors—hilltop clusters of rocks—we'll see on this trip. This one overlooks the evocative remains of a Bronze Age settlement. If you're up for a hike to get a closer look, consider this optional detour: Turn left at the* Widecombe *sign, and follow the road for a few minutes—keeping an eye on those hilltop rocks above you on the left. The road reaches a steep bend at a place where a mountain stream trickles down the hill; look for a pullout on the right, and four stone steps on the left. You can park and use these steps to climb up to...*

Grimspound

As you face the hilltop pile of rocks, called Hookney Tor, look right to the saddle between the two hills to find the huge, graceful outer ring of Grimspound. Dating from 2000 B.C., this late-Bronze Age fortress was a settlement for 800 years. The outer stone wall enclosed the smaller inner circles, which would have been stone huts. In some of these footprints, the tall stones flanking the entryway are still visible. The outer wall was probably designed to pen animals. Notice that the ring is designed to provide access to the stream. Running water was both useful and (archaeologists believe) spiritually important to prehistoric peoples. Well-populated in ancient times, the moors are thought to have become unlivable in about 1200 B.C. because of climate change, and settlements like these were abandoned. From the settlement, look across the valley; on the left side of the adjacent ridge (to the left of the stone rabbit fence that runs down to the valley), you'll see the faint remains of hillside terraces, called lynchets, created by medieval farmers.

If you have time for a longer hike, consider huffing up to the top of Hookney Tor for a better view down on Grimspound and the surrounding hills. (A standing stone and a stone row are both faintly visible—to those with excellent eyesight—on the top of the ridge across the valley.) The flat hilltop above Grimspound (Hamel Down) was covered with poles during World War II, to prevent German gliders from landing there.

• *Back in your car, backtrack to the main road you were on, and continue south. Very soon on the left, just before the big parking lot, look for the worn and weathered stub of a...*

Celtic Cross

All along the road, look for tall stone crosses like this one. These marked the way for villagers to cross the moor, often for funeral processions. Many of these began life as prehistoric pagan pillars, and were carved into crosses later, after Christianization.

• *Soon after the cross, on the right, you'll see the...*

Warren House Inn

Named for a warrener (rabbit-raiser) who fed bunnies to hungry miners, this pub comes with a fun history. This site has reputedly been occupied by a travelers' rest stop for more than 900 years. In 1845, a pub across the road was falling down from disrepair, so this "new" structure was built. Supposedly embers from the old fire were used to light the fire in the new building—which has burned ever since. While the story is questionable, the food here is good—specializing in (of course) rabbit pie, as well as steak-and-ale pie. The glorious moorside seating, at picnic benches out front and across the road, make it an enticing stop for a meal or drink. If it's chilly, you can take advantage of the cozy interior, with that legendary fireplace still smoldering (£8-12 main dishes, April-Oct Mon-Sat 12:00-21:00, Sun 12:00-20:30, off-season closed Mon and Tue for dinner, tel. 01822/880-208, www.warrenhouseinn.co.uk).

• *There's a lot moor to see (sorry), so let's keep moving. Carry on along the same road into the town of...*

Postbridge

This functional village comes with one of Dartmoor's classic views. As you cross the bridge in the heart of town, on the left

you'll see an ancient bridge parallel to the road. Bridges like this one—essentially a post and a wide, flat stone lintel—dot the moor. Called clapper bridges, they date from the Middle Ages, if not earlier. For a closer look, pull over at the big parking lot on the right soon after the bridge, near the handy and very helpful national park office. If you have time, consider a hike—Postbridge is a good base for moor walks (pick up their £1.50 booklet for walks from here).

• *Continue down to the village of Two Bridges, where you hit B-3357. Our route turns left (east) on this road, but consider detouring to the right (west) to the town of **Princetown** (pronounced "Princeton"), with its High Moorland Visitor Centre (see "Tourist Information," earlier). Princetown is also home to a historic high-security prison that held French prisoners during the Napoleonic Wars, and American POWs during the War of*

1812; today it has a museum (see "Sights in Dartmoor," later). But if you've already gotten your fill of park info from the Postbridge office, and don't care about prison history, Princetown is skippable.

Heading east on B-3357, you'll cross more cattle grates and continue to enjoy moor scenery. Soon the straightforward highway we've been relying on disappears, and you'll have to use narrower back roads to reach our next stop. You'll feel lost, but use your map and track signs closely: Leaving the moor, cut through the forest and carry on straight through Dartmeet, then veer uphill toward (but not all the way to) Ashburton. You'll go back up and down another mini-moor; at this point, watch for the turnoff on the left toward Sherril and Babeny; once on this road, continue straight (skipping the second Sherril/Babeny turnoff) into the village of Ponsworthy, from which signs direct you onward to our next stop...

▲Widecombe-in-the-Moor

Set in the center of the rolling hills, this adorable but often shopper-choked village is a scenic stop—and feels crowded after a drive on the empty moor. There's usually a farmers' market on the fourth Saturday of every month (10:00-16:00), and generally a Thursday craft market during the summer at the 1537 Church House (late May-early Oct 10:00-16:00, www.widecombe-in-the-moor.com). Stroll through the tranquil churchyard—with views of  hilltop tors on the horizon above—and dip into the Church of St. Pancras.

If you're ready for a meal, carry on (turning right at the sign by the Church House) down the country road to the **Rugglestone Inn**—which is more likely to have local farmers drinking a pint than tourists. They serve up heaping plates of good, hearty food... but watch out for the high-powered local cider. Choose between the wonderfully claustrophobic interior, or stroll across the stream to the delightful garden (£11-12 main dishes, food served daily 12:00-14:00 & 18:30-21:00, tel. 01364/621-327, www.ruggle-stoneinn.co.uk).

• Leave Widecombe, following signs for Bovey Tracey and enjoying the sky-high views. (On a clear day, you can see all the way to the English Channel.) Now we'll take a look at two of the better-known "tors" of Dartmoor. If you're tight on time, choose one: Haytor is famous and offers better views, but is more difficult to hike to, while Hound Tor is the more impressive formation.

On the Bovey Tracey road, you'll spot a turnoff on the left toward Hound Tor and Merton, which we'll take later (or now, if you want to skip Haytor). To see Haytor, continue 1.5 miles farther on—you'll spot it on the hilltop above you on the left. Use the giant parking lot on the right (after a smaller one on the left) and hike up to the grand...

▲Haytor

Dartmoor sits up on a granite plateau, and occasionally bare granite "peaks" poke up through the heather. (Technically, these are

the crumbling craters of long-extinct volcanoes—covered by dirt and sediment that has since eroded away.) Like lonesome watchtowers looming above the barren landscape, these tors are Dartmoor's most distinctive landmarks—and Haytor is the most famous and popular, thanks to its excellent vantage point for panoramic views. Tors look like piles of boulders that you can imagine might have been dragged and dropped on hilltops by prehistoric developers, but they're all natural. This area is divided into two parts: Haytor itself, and the adjacent Haytor Rocks.

• *Yet another national park information office is on this same road, less than a minute beyond the parking lot. And if you'd like to detour into the town of **Bovey Tracey** (described under "Sights in Dartmoor," later), now's the time—it's 10 minutes away on B-3387, down in the valley. En route are the gorgeous grounds of The Edgemoor, a picture-perfect place to enjoy a cream tea (see page 366).*

Or, to continue our loop, backtrack to the Hound Tor/Merton turn-off, which you'll now follow north through the moors. Soon you'll see another tor ahead and on the right. When you get to the little fork, follow the P signs to the right and park to walk up to...

▲▲Hound Tor

Perhaps the most striking tor in Dartmoor, and the inspiration for the Sherlock Holmes story *The Hound of the Baskervilles*, this

mighty clump of rocks impresses. According to legend, this stand of stones was once a pack of hunting dogs that had disrupted a witches' coven. As a punishment, the pooches were petrified. (The hunter who owned the dogs was

turned into the nearby tor called Bowerman's Nose, about a mile north of here.) Hike up and scramble over the many levels. In the

Letterboxing

The local pastime of letterboxing began as a way to collect tourist postcards. What has evolved is a secret system of log-books hidden all over Dartmoor—inside metal boxes, squir-reled away under rocks, or stuffed in the brush. Your goal: Find the logbook and stamp, and add your name and stamp to as many books as possible (bring your own inkpad just in case). Since this practice is a bit of a secret, you'll need to en-list a local to help you get started. Ask at a local TI or at the YHA Dartmoor hostel (near Postbridge), or check out www.dartmoorletterboxing.org and www.letterboxingondartmoor.co.uk.

valley beyond this ridge are the faint remains of some old Devon longhouses. These were situated at a gentle angle, with animals in the lower part and people in the upper part—liquids and other waste would run downhill, while the heat generated by the live-stock would warm its owners above.

• *Our tour is nearly finished. From the Hound Tor parking lot, back-track a few yards to the little fork and turn right, following signs to M'hampstead. You'll drive through the countryside before reaching the larger but still charming town of* **Moretonhampstead.** *You'll find parking and free WCs on your left as you enter town (on Court Street). The town's tiny, thatched center is a busy traffic crossroads, with two pubs, two res-taurants (including the recommended White Horse Inn), a Co-op grocery store, a pharmacy, a bakery, a hardware store, and a well-stocked TI.*

Our drive is finished...but there's plenty more Dartmoor to explore. If you still have daylight left, consider heading north out of Moreton-hampstead on A-382 until the turnoff (to the right) for Drewsteignton and the **Fingle Bridge;** *or head back through Chagford and venture to the* **Scorhill Stone Circle** *(both described under "Sights in Dartmoor," next).*

Sights in Dartmoor

▲Walks on the Moors

Pick up your Ordnance Survey map at any local shop or TI and start walking. The Princetown TI also has a map with suggestions for routes through the moors. Postbridge, in the heart of the moor-lands, is a fine launch pad for good walks, and has a park infor-mation center that can suggest well-outlined routes. Other good walking bases include Belstone in the north (for rugged scenery) and Ivybridge in the south (more forested). You can go almost any-where—except the firing ranges. These are technically open for walking when not in use (you'll see red flags if they're closed), but it's probably best to avoid them entirely. For more pointers, read "Orientation to Dartmoor," earlier.

Here are a few ideas for popular, easy-to-moderate, two- to four-hour hikes in the region. Before attempting any of these, get details (and ideally maps) from a local TI or park office:

From **Scorhill Stone Circle** (described next), you can continue through Scorhill Down to the river, where you'll see a tolmen (a doughnut-shaped stone), then proceed through Chagford Common before hooking back up past Kestor Rock toward your car.

From **Postbridge,** consider the hike up to Bellever Tor, then circle around to the youth hostel and back to the bridge.

From **Haytor**'s park information office, circle around the base of Haytor Down to the village of Leighton, then hike back along the road.

From **Grimspound,** the Bronze Age settlement described on my self-guided driving tour (see earlier), you can hike up to Hameldown Tor and along the summit of Hamel Down, then down into the valley and back to your car.

▲▲Scorhill Stone Circle

Thousands of Neolithic ruins dot the landscape of Dartmoor, but the Scorhill (SCO-rill) Stone Circle near Gidleigh may be the best.

Stonehenge, *the* iconic stone circle, is much bigger—but it's also packed with crowds and right off a busy road (described in the Near Bath chapter). Tranquil, forgotten Scorhill is yours alone—the way a stone circle should be. As it comes with a scenic stroll across a moor, it's a great sampling of what Dartmoor is all about—as much about the journey as about the destination.

Once there, you'll be alone with the heather, broom, ancient history...and, often, sheep and wild ponies. Enjoying the solitude at the circle, scan the horizon, noticing other formations all around you—some natural tors, others likely man-made like this one. Places like Scorhill are a rare case in our modern world where we simply don't know the who, what, why, or how.

Getting There: The trailhead is about a 15-minute drive west of Chagford. The trailhead is tricky to find—be patient, use your Ordnance Survey map, and solicit help from a local. (I wouldn't attempt it in a heavy fog—but if you do, take along a compass.) From Chagford, follow signs to *Gidleigh*—you'll drive west out of town, bear right (uphill) at the fork, then turn right at the next intersection; from there, cross over the very narrow bridge, then turn left to go through Murchington. Proceed straight, going up and down the hills through Gidleigh. Keep following the same off-the-beaten-path road through the mossy stone hamlet of Berrydown, until you dead-end at a little parking lot (if in doubt, follow signs for *Scorhill*). Park, then walk through the gate and hike about 15 minutes straight ahead up and over the moor (with long stone fences on either side of you, which gradually widen). After cresting the hill (with 360-degree views), head down into the gentle valley and look for the circle below (when the wide, well-trod path through the heather forks, angle right).

▲Teign Gorge and Fingle Bridge

In the town of Drewsteignton, a narrow road leads down into the Teign River Valley (from B-3219, watch for the easy-to-miss *Fingle Bridge* signs to the right). At the end of

the road is the out-of-the-way but understandably popular **Fingle Bridge Inn,** a pub set along a river and a picturesque old bridge. The food is good and reasonably priced, with daily specials and a hearty ploughman's lunch of open-face sandwiches. While the interior is cozy, on a nice day it can't match the delightful riverside picnic tables (£6-8 lunches and cream tea served 12:00-15:00, £9-12 dinners served Tue-Sat 18:00-21:00, no dinner Sun-Mon; open June-Sept Mon-Sat 11:00-22:00, Sun 11:00-18:00; Oct-May daily 11:00-16:00, until 22:00 Fri-Sat; tel. 01647/281-287, www.finglebridgeinn.com). The bridge is a popular spot for weddings and fly-fishing (though not at the same time). The trail across the road makes for an excellent post-meal amble along the river.

Castle Drogo

Just up the road from the Teign Gorge, you'll come across this elaborate country house—complete with a circular croquet lawn

(you can borrow balls and mallets at the ticket desk) and formal gardens—that has the honor of being the last castle built in England, finished in 1930.

   Cost and Hours: £8.70, grounds only-£5 .50, mid-March-Oct daily 11:00-17:00, grounds and visitors center open at 9:00, closes earlier or open weekends only off-season, closed late Dec-mid-Feb, last entry 30 minutes before closing, on-site café, tel.

01647/433-306, www.nationaltrust.org.uk/castledrogo. Some trails on the estate lead down to Fingle Bridge.

Visiting the Castle: Drogo's megalomaniacal owner, Julius Drewe, demanded a flat roof (to match the medieval castles he was imagining). But the modern building methods of the day couldn't support that unusual design, and the building leaked terribly even before it was completed. Consequently, the castle is undergoing an extensive renovation project (through at least 2018). In the meantime, you can still visit the interior, but the collection of furnishings and noble bric-a-brac has been consolidated in one half of the complex, while the other half has cleverly been turned into a "work in progress" exhibit about the project itself—with knowledgeable docents who can explain exactly what went wrong and what's being done to fix it. The castle wasn't particularly worth visiting even before the project, and even less so now; come here only if this is your best chance to see a noble estate.

Dartmoor Prison Museum

It makes sense that a prison would be set upon the moors near Princetown. To Victorian-age Londoners, this rugged and distant land must have felt like Siberia. Built in the early 1800s to house French military prisoners captured during the Napoleonic Wars (along with some American POWs from the War of 1812), Dartmoor Prison was later converted to incarcerate civilian criminals. Notorious until recently for housing some of the most unsavory convicts alive (sort of a British San Quentin), the prison was also briefly used in 1917 to hold conscientious objectors who refused to join in the Great War. The museum, located in the former dairy across the street from the still-functioning prison, features historical exhibits and artifacts (from shackles to homemade items crafted by inmates) that offer insight into this infamous house of incarceration.

Cost and Hours: £3, daily 9:30-12:30 & 13:30-16:30, Fri and Sun until 16:00, last entry 30 minutes before closing, just north of Princetown on B-3357/Tavistock Road, tel. 01822/322-130, www.dartmoor-prison.co.uk.

Bovey Tracey

This town (pronounced "Buvvy Tracy") on the southeastern side of Dartmoor National Park is too big to be cute (pop. 7,000), but it does offer a few modest indoor options to explore when the rains chase you off the moors (just 10 minutes' drive west of Haytor on B-3387). The **TI** is located on the main street at the main pay-and-display lot on the right as you drive into town (March-Oct Sun-Fri 10:00-16:00, Sat 9:30-15:30, sporadic hours off-season, Station Road, tel. 01626/832-047, www.boveytracey.gov.uk).

Bovey Tracey, a pottery town until the 1950s, is becoming known as a center for fine crafts. Clay was quarried nearby, and

Josiah Wedgwood even nosed around here when deciding where to locate his china factory (he later chose Staffordshire). The **Devon Guild of Craftsmen** has an appealing gallery/museum and shop in a restored riverside mill downtown. The bright, modern interior showcases items for sale by local artists (serious shoppers may find these a pricey but very classy alternative to trinkets); a few temporary exhibits also highlight local crafts (free, daily 10:00-17:30, café, immediately after crossing the river on Station Road, tel. 01626/832-223, www.crafts.org.uk). They also host a contemporary crafts festival in mid-June (www.craftsatboveytracey.co.uk).

The **House of Marbles,** on the outskirts of town, sounds goofy enough that you might want to visit. It's basically a giant gift shop inside a historic pottery with some interesting glassmaking displays. Check out the marble museum displaying antique marbles, ones made of odd materials, and fun, kinetic wire marble mazes in action that always draw a crowd (press the button to make them go). Nearby is a small pottery museum. The place is also home of the Teign Valley Glass Studios, and you can watch artisans at work creating contemporary glassware using traditional and modern techniques (free, artists in action generally Tue-Fri and sometimes also Sat 9:00-16:30, Sun 10:00-15:00, lunch and tea breaks posted). Outside in the courtyard, surrounded by café tables, are old, circa-1900 "muffle" kilns (signs describe their history). Beyond those is a sprawling children's area. In the gift shop, kids of all ages will love digging through the giant bins of multicolored marbles—they're actually made in Mexico, but big piles of them look really cool (free, Mon-Sat 9:00-17:00, Sun 11:00-17:00, café, about 1.5 miles south of town toward Newton Abbot just off the A-382, at The Old Pottery on Pottery Road, tel. 01626/835-358, www. houseofmarbles.com).

Near Dartmoor
▲Exeter Cathedral

The nearest large city to Dartmoor is Exeter, only about 15 miles (a half-hour drive) east of the moor. A pleasant and bustling university city of 120,000, Exeter's claim to fame is its beautiful cathedral, which sits on a charming green facing the old town. With a Norman core later embellished in Decorated Gothic style, the cathedral could be worth a stop if you're passing through Exeter and have time to spare. Highlights of the grand interior include the ribbed vaulting, 400 colorful "bosses" (decorations at the intersection of vaulting spines, including the famous "Becket Boss" showing the execution of Thomas Becket), the unique minstrels' gallery (more commonly seen in palaces than churches), the colorful astronomical clock, and the quire, with its 50 fold-down, carved-wooden seats called misericords.

Cost and Hours: £6, open to tourists Mon-Sat 9:00-16:45, closed Sun, longer hours for worshippers, tel. 01392/285-983, www.exeter-cathedral.org.uk.

Sleeping in Dartmoor

Befitting such a mysterious destination, accommodations in Dartmoor tend to be quirkier than the English norm, with more character(s) than the staid, hotelesque accommodations in more mainline destinations. Sleeping here really feels like "going local." Given the confusing spaghetti of back roads here, it's always smart to call ahead for precise arrival instructions.

In Chagford
(area code: 01647)

For a description of the handy home-base town of Chagford, see page 350. Along Chagford's main street, several pubs rent rooms upstairs. But the best value is the B&B.

$$$ Three Crowns is trying to bring contemporary class to this traditional town, with 21 modern rooms across the street from the churchyard (standard Db-£89, larger "classic" Db-£115, superior Db-£145, can be higher on peak-season weekends, free Wi-Fi, High Street, tel. 01647/433-444, www.threecrowns-chagford. co.uk, threecrowns@staustellbrewery.co.uk). This is also a good place to eat (see "Eating in Dartmoor," later).

Other pub options: **$$$ The Globe Inn,** with seven decent rooms, is a lesser value (Sb-£65, Db-£95, deluxe Db-£150, Tb/ Qb-£120, free Wi-Fi, 9 High Street, pay parking lot nearby, tel. 01647/433-485, www.theglobeinnchagford.co.uk, graham@the-globeinnchagford.co.uk, Graham and Mary). They're also open for meals (£10-15, daily 12:00-14:30 & 18:00-21:00). **$$ Ring O'Bells,** an old-school pub, has four simple but comfortable rooms that are worth considering if other options are booked (Db-£75-95 depending on size, Sb-£20 less, free Wi-Fi, 44 The Square, tel. 01647/432-466, www.ringobellschagford.co.uk, info@ringobells-chagford.co.uk).

$$ Farleigh Cottage, a short walk below the main square, has three tidy, bright, modern rooms rented by charming, pleasant, and proper Lyn (D with private b on the hall-£60, en-suite Db-£65, free Wi-Fi, free parking, 11 Lower Street, tel. 01647/432-600, www.farleighcottage.co.uk, farleighcottage@tiscali.co.uk). Lyn also has a self-catering cottage for longer stays.

Near Chagford

These options—both good values—are within a few minutes of Chagford to the east and north (toward the Teign Gorge).

Sleep Code

(£1 = about $1.60, country code: 44)
S = Single, **D** = Double/Twin, **T** = Triple, **Q** = Quad, **b** = bathroom, **s** = shower only. Unless otherwise noted, credit cards are accepted and breakfast is included.

To help you sort easily through these listings, I've divided the accommodations into three categories based on the price for a standard double room with bath:

$$$ Higher Priced—Most rooms £90 or more.
 $$ Moderately Priced—Most rooms between £50-90.
  $ Lower Priced—Most rooms £50 or less.

Prices can change without notice; verify the hotel's current rates online or by email. For the best prices, always book direct.

$$ Easton Court is a great value, offering five bright, spacious, modern rooms that overlook the gardens where *Brideshead Revisited* was written (decorated with a faux stone circle to ponder). It feels like the ideal thatched-roof English guesthouse. Literature fans can ask to see the rooms where famous writers stayed and wrote back in the 1920s, when this was owned by a local woman who enjoyed fostering the arts (one small classic Db-£75, bigger superior Db with king-size bed-£85, Sb-£15 less, Tb-£15 more, all rooms £5 cheaper off-season or if staying at least 2 nights, guest computer, free Wi-Fi, free parking, tel. 01647/433-469, www.easton.co.uk, stay@easton.co.uk, Debra, Paul, and Diana the housekeeper). It's at the crossroads called Easton, just east of Chagford, right on A-382.

$$ Sandy Park Inn rents four well-appointed but overpriced rooms above a busy upmarket pub. Although it's in a creaky old 16th-century shell, it comes with modern touches (Sb-£59, twin D with private b on the hall-£65, small D with private b on the hall-£69, Db-£79, cheaper for longer stays, free Wi-Fi, tel. 01647/433-267, www.sandyparkinn.co.uk, info@sandyparkinn.co.uk, Matt). It's on A-382 east of Chagford, at the turnoff for the Teign Gorge. For more on the pub, see "Eating in Dartmoor," later.

In Moretonhampstead
(area code: 01647)

Moretonhampstead—larger and less quaint than Chagford or Widecombe-in-the-Moor—is a handy home base with its own share of half-timbered appeal. It feels more like a real, working town and less like a backward, cutesy village.

$$ The Walled Garden is Moretonhampstead's top B&B option, with three crisp, modern rooms in a house in the town center that's within walking distance of everything, and surrounded by the relaxing, namesake garden (Db-£65, one room has private b down the hall, cheaper for 3 or more nights, cash only, free Wi-Fi, free parking, Mount Pleasant, tel. 01647/441-353, www.moretonwalledgarden.co.uk, anne.short@talktalk.net, Anne and Richard).

$$ The Old Post House B&B, right along the main road through Moretonhampstead, has five older, slightly musty rooms at an appealingly affordable price (Db-£60, spacious top-floor family room-£30/adult and £10/child, free Wi-Fi, 18 Court Street, tel. 01647/440-900, www.theoldposthouse.com, info@theoldposthouse.com, Steve and Zoe).

$ Sparrowhawk Backpackers, with an easygoing hippie vibe, rents cheap beds in the Moretonhampstead town center, in the light-filled loft of a restored stone stable (£17 bunks in coed 14-bed slumbermill dorm with curtains, D-£38, family room—add £8/child, bedding provided, no breakfast, communal kitchen, free Wi-Fi, 45 Ford Street, tel. 01647/440-318, mobile 07870-513-570, www.sparrowhawkbackpackers.co.uk, ali@sparrowhawkbackpackers.co.uk, Alison).

In or near Bovey Tracey
(area code: 01626)

Sleep here if you want to be close to a real town on the edge of the national park, rather than the rustic villages inside Dartmoor. For more on Bovey Tracey, see page 359.

$$$ The Edgemoor screams "English countryside destination wedding." Filling a picturesque, ivy-draped 1879 schoolhouse, this family-run hotel has 17 rooms (in an old shell, but with modern style). Aptly named, it sits right at the edge of the moor, just outside Bovey Tracey on the road to Haytor. It's pricey and a bit idiosyncratic, but a memorable splurge (rates are soft, but generally Db-£170, bigger superior Db-£190, free Wi-Fi, free parking, Haytor Road, Lowerdown Cross—leave Bovey Tracey toward Haytor on B-3387 and watch for the ivy-covered building on the right about a mile out of town, tel. 01626/832-466, www.edgemoor.co.uk, reservations@edgemoor.co.uk).

$$$ Eastwrey Barton Country House is set on a terraced lawn halfway up the side of the Wray Valley between Moretonhampstead and Bovey Tracey. It has five warm and spacious rooms in a restored Georgian country house (perfectly fine standard rooms: Sb-£90, Db-£115; larger superior rooms: Sb-£105, Db-£130; all with countryside views, £30 three-course dinners for guests, no children under 10, free Wi-Fi, several nice lounges and an inviting garden, on A-382 near Lustleigh, tel. 01647/277-338, www.eastwreybarton.co.uk, reservations@eastwreybarton.co.uk, friendly Sharon and Patrick).

$$ The Cromwell Arms is a 16th-century coaching inn right in the middle of Bovey Tracey with 12 simple, comfortable rooms (Sb-£55, Db-£75, family Tb or Qb-£100, minimum 2-night stay on weekends, free Wi-Fi, Fore Street, tel. 01626/833-473, www. thecromwellarms.co.uk, info@thecromwellarms.co.uk, Gary and Julie). The pub serves good meals in a traditional atmosphere (£6 lunches, £10-11 dinners, open daily).

At **$$ Yarrow Lodge,** Hanneke and local guide Phil rent two simple rooms (with a shared bath) in their home in the midst of Yarner Wood, a nature reserve within the national park between Bovey Tracey and Haytor (S-£33, D-£65, free Wi-Fi, tel. 01626/836-589, mobile 07849-840-126, www.yarrowlodge.co.uk, enquiries@yarrowlodge.co.uk). It's on the road to the East Dartmoor Nature Park: Leaving Bovey Tracey toward Haytor, turn right immediately after The Edgemoor (described earlier), turn left at the T-junction, then turn left up the next lane, following brown signs for *East Dartmoor.*

Near Postbridge

Postbridge—more a wide spot in the road than a village—is a popular springboard for hikes. While there's not much here beyond a pub, a TI, and a gift shop, there are plenty of services in Princetown, about a 15-minute drive south.

$$ Beechwood B&B, right at the entrance to Postbridge (as you approach from Chagford), is energetically run by Lynette and Adam. This super-cozy guesthouse has five rooms, a comfy lounge, a fine garden, and a glassed-in breakfast area (twin D-£72, Db-£78, large family Db-£84 plus £18/extra person, free Wi-Fi, free parking, Postbridge, tel. 01822/880-332, www.beechwood-dartmoor.co.uk, enquiries@beechwood-dartmoor.co.uk).

$ YHA Dartmoor offers 34 beds in seven rooms on the moors. It's simple and institutional, but it comes with an impressive wildlife area out front so you can learn about the local terrain (£15-22/ bunk in 4- to 8-bed rooms, Q-£50-66, £1/night discount if arriving by bus, bicycle, or on foot; £3 less for members, includes sheets, breakfast-£5, £7-9 dinners, members' kitchen, open all year, reception open 8:00-10:00 & 17:00-22:30, pay Wi-Fi, free parking, kids' game room, tel. 0845-371-9622, www.yha.org.uk, dartmoor@yha. org.uk). It's about a mile south of Postbridge, well-signed from the main road.

Eating in Dartmoor

Like many borderline-touristy English holiday regions, Dartmoor has a surprising array of good-quality eateries—including a few "destination" restaurants that charge big prices to match their big reputations. I've focused my listings on pubs that emphasize their food and are located in charming villages or rustic countryside settings. Note that three of my favorites are actually described earlier in this chapter: **Warren House Inn,** perched atop a moor south of Chagford (see page 353); **Rugglestone Inn,** just outside the village of Widecombe-in-the-Moor (see page 354); and the **Fingle Bridge Inn,** in the Teign Gorge (see page 358).

In or near Chagford

Blacks Delicatessen is the perfect place to grab a quick lunch. Peruse the options—£2-5 quiches, pies, pasties, paninis, and soups—in their display case, and consider supplementing your choice with their carefully selected grocery items. You can sit out on The Square or—better yet—head for the hidden outdoor tables tucked behind the deli, in the churchyard around back (Mon-Sat 8:00-17:30, closed Sun, 28 The Square, tel. 01647/433-535).

Three Crowns, the best of the many pubs lining the main drag, is classy and modern, but with a respect for tradition. For seating, you have several options: traditional pub up front, modern glassed-in courtyard farther back, open-air interior courtyard, or a few outdoor tables (£6-10 lunches, £9-20 dinners, free Wi-Fi, daily 9:00-21:00, High Street, tel. 01647/433-444).

Whiddons Eatery, in a classic old black-and-white thatched house on High Street (across from the churchyard) is a good non-pub option for seasonal, traditional food (lunch: £7-10 meals, Mon-Tue and Thu-Sat 10:30-14:30, Sun 12:00-14:30, closed Wed; dinner: £21/2 courses, £25/3 courses, Fri-Sat only 19:00-21:00, plus Sun in summer; 4-6 High Street, tel. 01647/433-406).

The Birdcage has a cozy, woody interior and a few tables out front, facing The Square. They specialize in £8-10 pizzas (other £5-6 light meals also available, Mon-Thu 9:30-17:00, Fri-Sat 9:30-21:00, Sun 12:00-17:00, 11 The Square, tel. 01647/433-883).

22 Mill Street, pricey and pretentious, is a cut above the other eateries lining Chagford's main street, both in terms of class and quality (lunch-£19/2 courses, £24/3 courses; dinner-£36/2 courses, £42/3 courses; Tue-Sat 12:00-15:00 & 19:00-22:00, closed Sun-Mon, reservations smart, tel. 01647/432-244). They also rent two good rooms upstairs (standard Db-£129, superior Db-£169, ask about dinner package, www.22millst.com).

Near Chagford: **Sandy Park Inn,** which also rents rooms, has a characteristic 16th-century pub and a cozy dining room that serves pricey but good food with great Old World atmosphere (£5-6 sandwiches at lunch, £10-14 main dishes; pub open daily 11:00-23:00, lunch served daily 12:00-14:30, dinner served Mon-Sat 18:00-21:30, no dinner on Sun; tel. 01647/433-267). It's a few minutes from Chagford—for location details, see "Sleeping in Dartmoor," earlier.

In Moretonhampstead

The White Horse Inn, with welcoming, lively decor and a well-respected chef, specializes in tasty, crispy wood-fired pizzas, along with other Mediterranean dishes and traditional pub fare. You can sit in the cozy and convivial pub up front, or a few steps down in the quieter, more modern dining room (£9-11 pizzas, £12-18 main dishes, dining room open Tue-Sat 12:30-14:30 & 18:30-21:00, Sun-Mon only pizzas 18:30-21:00, shorter hours possible in winter, reservations recommended on weekends, 7 George Street, tel. 01647/440-242, http://whitehorse.q-media.com).

In addition to the White Horse Inn, Moretonhampstead has two spit-and-sawdust pubs offering affordable food and drink, plus the upscale (almost pretentious) **White Hart Hotel,** with a pleasantly traditional but spacious hunting-lodge feel (£6-7 lunches, £9-18 dinners, daily 12:30-14:15 & 18:30-20:45, The Square, tel. 01647/440-500). And North Bovey (described next) is a short drive away.

Near Moretonhampstead, in North Bovey

This charming village—just a mile and a half (down narrow country lanes) from Moretonhampstead—has a triangular village green, more than its share of idyllic thatch, and a fine pub: **Ring of Bells** fills a 13th-century building with atmosphere, happy eaters, and good food. Choose between the various indoor dining spaces, or head out to the delightful yard, surrounded by thatched homes (£10-15 meals, daily 12:00-14:30 & 18:00-21:00, tel. 01647/440-375). They also have five rooms upstairs (Db-£85, www.ringofbells.net).

Between Bovey Tracey and Haytor

The Edgemoor, about a mile outside of Bovey Tracey on the way to Haytor (B-3387), has a picture-perfect setting, filling an old ivy-covered schoolhouse. While the interior rooms are worth considering (the "Old School Rooms" have a cheaper menu—£7-8 lunches, £9-12 main courses, daily 12:00-15:00 & 18:30-21:00; the fancier "Library" restaurant is pricier—£17-19 main courses, dinner only, daily 18:30-21:00), in good weather it's hard to resist the perfectly English garden out front, which seems made to order for a £7 cream tea or £11.50 high tea (same menu and hours as Old School Rooms). They also rent rooms (for directions and lodging details, see "Sleeping in Dartmoor," earlier; tel. 01626/832-466).

CORNWALL

*Penzance • St. Ives • The Penwith Peninsula
• East Cornwall*

Set on a rocky peninsula at the southwest tip of England, Cornwall has a Celtic vibe. Its rugged scenery and wild, uncultivated appeal make you feel as if you're approaching the end of the world (and many natives would say it's exactly that). Harboring the remnants of an endangered Celtic culture (Cornish), an extinct tin-mining industry, and a gaggle of visit-worthy sights, this is one of England's most popular holiday regions—especially among the English.

Cornwall—part of the "Celtic fringe" of Britain—grew up as a very different place from England, with its own language, called Cornish, which thrived for centuries. Fishing, shipping, and smuggling were the main businesses here for hundreds of years, but in the 18th century, tin-mining became the major industry. The 20th century dealt a double blow to Cornwall: The local pilchard fish became depleted, and cheap Asian and South American tin put an end to mining. Today's predominant trade is tourism, as evidenced by the many tacky tourist traps littering the landscape.

But visitors flock here for good reason. Not only is the area packed with ancient sites, precious villages, and historic monuments, but the climate is also unusually mild. The Gulf Stream often brings warm, almost tropical weather to Cornwall—making it perfect for gardening, walking, basking on the beach, and generally enjoying life. The region also exerts a pull on fans of British culture—from literature (many of author Rosamunde Pilcher's works are set here), to British television series (the 1970s classic *Poldark* used Cornish locations, and the recent hit *Doc Martin* is shot in Port Isaac), to cuisine (celebrity chef Rick Stein has a mini-empire of restaurants in Padstow).

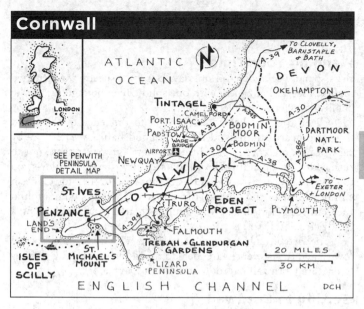

To see Cornwall, set yourself up in a home base (Penzance or St. Ives) and spend most of your time venturing out on day trips. Romantic St. Ives has an artsy beach-bum ambience and is crowded with holidaymakers in summer (leaving many natives jaded and disinterested). Penzance, on the other hand, is a working-class shipping port with a pleasant main-street bustle, enthusiastically welcoming natives, and appealing eateries. Since Cornwall is best suited for day-tripping, Penzance's relative lack of tourist charm is actually an asset—it's much easier to drive into and out of, has better public-transportation connections, and enjoys an impressive array of top-quality accommodations—making it my preferred home base. Sleep in St. Ives only if you're serious about gallery-hopping or surfing.

Venture to quaint seaside villages, a dramatic theater, a telegraph museum, a dead tin mine, the scant remains of an Iron Age village, and a thought-provoking stone circle. Cry "Land Ho!" at Land's End, and consider going by plane or ferry to the castaway Isles of Scilly. Farther northeast, the castle of a king named Arthur tickles travelers' imaginations, the harbor towns of Padstow and Port Isaac offer a taste of workaday (but still cute)

Cornwall, and unusual gardens near Falmouth thrill those with green thumbs.

Planning Your Time

Brits spend weeks here on holiday. But for a speedy traveler, two nights based in Penzance, with one solid day rambling around the peninsula, offer a suitable first taste.

Given that it takes so long to get to this edge of the world from the heart of England (figure a good half-day each way by car or train, not counting sightseeing stops), it makes sense not to rush your visit. Spending three nights and two days here allows you to slow down, see all the sights, and get a better feel for Cornish culture. Most of the noteworthy sights and villages wrap around the Penwith Peninsula, so you can line them up and see them on a handy circular drive.

The attractions farther east—Tintagel Castle, the coastal towns, and the gardens—are ideal for breaking up the long journey to or from Cornwall (en route to Bath or Dartmoor).

Getting to Cornwall

By Car: The drive here is time-consuming: To reach Penzance, figure about five hours from London, four hours from Bath or Salisbury, or two hours from Dartmoor (not counting stops or traffic delays). The M-5 motorway speeds you as far as Exeter, where you'll pick up A-30 the rest of the way (mostly four-lane, partly two-lane). Consider a more scenic, less trafficked route: Partway down M-5 from Bristol, near Tiverton, turn off onto A-361 (a.k.a. the North Devon Link Road), which you can follow through north Devon before hopping on A-39, which parallels the coastline (getting you close to Tintagel Castle, Port Isaac, and Padstow), rejoining the A-30 35 miles east of Penzance. While this is a smaller road, it's more scenic and fewer miles (as it avoids the southerly jog to Exeter), so can be faster if traffic is heavy on the main road.

By Train: Train travelers arrive in Cornwall at Penzance, the most central and largest city on the coast (see "Penzance Connections" on page 382).

By Plane: Cornwall's main airport is Newquay-Cornwall International (airport code: NQY, www.newquaycornwallairport.com), 5 miles from Newquay and 35 miles northeast of Penzance. Airlines that serve Newquay include Flybe (from Edinburgh, Manchester, or London-Gatwick, www.flybe.com), Lufthansa (from Dusseldorf, www.lufthansa.com), and easyJet (from Liverpool, www.easyjet.com). Avis (www.avis.com), Europcar (www.europcar.co.uk), and Hertz (www.hertz.com) rent cars at or near the airport. Public-transportation connections into Penzance can be tricky—contact the Newquay TI for suggestions (tel.

01637/854-020, www.visitnewquay.org). You'll likely find that it's easiest to spring for a taxi (try Newquay-based BioTravel, about £75, tel. 01637/860-006, www.biotravel.co.uk; or, for about £90, Penzance-based Anytime Taxis, tel. 01736/888-888, or Stones Taxi, tel. 01736/363-400).

Getting Around Cornwall

This region is most satisfying by car, which allows you to pack a lot into each day. It's challenging but doable by public transportation, and you'll have to be more selective. Note that all public-transit routes run less frequently off-season (Oct-April). A tour with Western Discoveries (see page 377) is a handy way to get into the countryside.

By Car: The coastal road (B-3315 in the south, and B-3306 in the west and north, connecting via A-30 near Land's End)—which passes through Penzance and above St. Ives—links together almost all of the best sights. Driving in Cornwall is generally easy, but parking is not, especially in summer. Small villages often have tiny parking lots near the water and larger ones outside of town, so it's a good idea to arrive early in the day. Roads can get very congested on Bank Holiday weekends and in August, so allow extra time, especially on main routes such as A-30 and A-38. Narrow, twisty Cornish lanes crisscross the spine of the peninsula, and can save time if the main routes are crowded—but you'll need a good map (try the 1:100,000 Ordnance Survey) and, even more importantly, a good navigator. For current traffic conditions, listen to the radio— many rental-car stereos have a setting for automatic traffic updates (often marked by the letters TA or TP; see page 876).

By Bus: It's slow but possible to reach most Cornwall sights by bus, some of which go topless May through September. Most buses are run by First Bus Company (tel. 0845-600-1420 or Traveline tel. 0871-200-2233, www.firstgroup.com), though Western Greyhound picks up a few routes (tel. 01637/871-871, www.westerngreyhound.com). First has a useful all-day pass called "FirstDay Cornwall" for the region that includes Penzance, St. Ives, Land's End, and the surrounding area (£7.20/1 day, £16.50/3 day, pay driver); Western Greyhound has a similar pass called "Day Explorer" (£8.50, pay driver)—note that these passes only work on the designated company's buses. Yet another pass, called Ride Cornwall, costs £10 for a full day of using trains as well as buses operated by either company.

You'll find the following bus routes useful:

Buses **#1** and **#1A** connect Penzance with Newlyn and Land's End (Mon-Sat 2/hour, Sun 5/day, 10 minutes to Newlyn, 50 minutes to Land's End); #1A also stops at Porthcurno, near the Telegraph

Cornish History

Cornwall's history is almost as old as the history of humanity. Prehistoric huts, stone circles, and other mysterious structures stand witness to the timeless appeal of the area. While a few of these are easy to reach (such as the Merry Maidens and Chysauster), most are hidden away and best uncovered with a local guide (try Western Discoveries tours—described on page 377).

When the Romans arrived in Britain in the first century B.C., the native Celtic inhabitants were forced to the farthest, most inhospitable corners of the island. To this day, a "Celtic fringe" still rings England. This includes several groups struggling to keep alive their fading languages, such as Welsh, Scottish Gaelic, Irish Gaelic, Manx (on the Isle of Man)...and Cornish.

This part of Britain—specifically Penzance—was ideally located for shipping, since boats could launch straight into the Atlantic, rather than having to tack from farther east all the way along the English Channel. It's no wonder that Penzance is best known as the namesake for a Gilbert and Sullivan musical about the high seas. Along with the sailors and pirates, artists love this scenic corner of Britain, which can change from sun-drenched to rainy and windblown in a matter of minutes. Dramatic clouds hit Cornwall like a hammer, and the sea changes color with the sky.

Rich deposits of metals—especially tin—have linked this rugged spit of land to the rest of the world, making Cornwall unexpectedly cosmopolitan. Cornish tin has been found in ancient plumbing as far away as Turkey and Pompeii (Italy). Cornwall wasn't conquered by the Romans, partly because of its remoteness, but also because the Cornish were already Roman trading partners. (You'll find no Roman forts in Cornwall, but you will find Roman goods.) Cornish trading came with an influx of exotic products—Cornish cooking is unique in England for its use of saffron, likely bartered with the Near East for metals.

In the 18th century, Cornwall's tin-mining industry enjoyed a boom (see sidebar on page 396). But when the industry went bust in the late 19th century, many miners had to find work elsewhere. Though tin-mining was a back-breaking, menial job, it

Museum and a steep uphill climb to the Minack Theatre (Mon-Sat 3/day, none on Sun, 40 minutes).

Buses **#2** and **#2A** run between Penzance and Falmouth, stopping at Marazion near St. Michael's Mount (Mon-Sat 1-2/hour, Sun every 2 hours, 10 minutes to Marazion, 1.75 hours to Falmouth). Bus **#302** follows the same route to Marazion, but doesn't continue all the way to Falmouth (about hourly, summer only).

Buses **#6** and **#6A** connect Penzance with Newlyn and Mousehole (2-3/hour, 10 minutes to Newlyn, 20 minutes to Mousehole). Buses **#5** and **#5A** also go to Newlyn.

Buses **#17**, **#17A**, and **#17B** connect Penzance and St. Ives (2/

also required highly skilled miners. Mine owners from around the world began to recruit and relocate unemployed Cornish miners. Throughout the 1860s, 20 percent of Cornish people emigrated, and this "Cornish diaspora" spread the culture from this corner of England across the face of the earth. For example, hundreds of Cornish miners went to California to get in on the Gold Rush. Locals brag, "Anywhere you find a hole in the ground, you'll find a Cornishman at the bottom of it." Similarly, Cornish graveyards read like a geography textbook, as headstones often list the places where the person lived.

The great migration of the late 19th century also left behind many ghost towns, which still dot the Cornish countryside. Today, many of these long-abandoned homes are being bought up by Londoners and converted into holiday villas—driving up prices and forcing out the few remaining locals.

The Cornish language—related to Welsh, and more distantly related to Scottish Gaelic and Irish Gaelic—was widely spoken here through the late 18th century. As the Industrial Revolution shrank England and church leaders refused to offer services in Cornish, the language became obsolete. Cornish survived only among a handful of speakers through the 19th and early 20th centuries. But, remarkably, Cornish held on, and—after a recent EU designation as an official minority language—it's now allowed to be taught in schools again. More people speak Cornish today than two centuries ago, and raising kids to be bilingual is in vogue.

Today, feisty Cornwall, with a half-million residents, is officially and for all practical purposes part of England (unlike Wales or Scotland). But native-born Cornishmen and Cornishwomen still cling to what makes them unique—they're Cornish first, British second. The fledgling Cornish independence movement has never really gotten anywhere, but that doesn't stop locals from displaying the flag of Cornwall: a black field (representing the earth) with a white cross (the tin flowing through the earth). Also look for bumper stickers boasting the Cornish word for "Cornwall": *Kernow.*

hour, 35-50 minutes). Bus **#17B** also stops at Marazion (St. Michael's Mount).

Bus **#300** is a topless tourist bus that does a big, 3.5-hour, loop around the Penwith Peninsula (daily Easter-Sept only, 3/day in each direction—5/day in each direction mid-May-Aug), connecting Penzance, Marazion (St. Michael's Mount), St. Ives, Geevor Tin Mine, Sennen Cove, Land's End, Porthcurno (mid-May-Aug only), and Newlyn.

Bus **#504** connects Penzance to some otherwise difficult-to-reach destinations along the southern edge of Penwith (Mon-Sat 2/day, none on Sun): Newlyn (10 minutes), Merry Maidens (30 minutes), Porthcurno (50 minutes), Minack Theatre (50 minutes), Land's End (1.25 hours), and Sennen Cove (1.5 hours). Bus **#501** does a similar Penzance-Newlyn-Land's End route, but doesn't make all of the stops (alternates between stopping at Porthcurno and Sennen Cove, and does not stop at Merry Maidens or Minack Theatre; runs every 2 hours, 40 minutes).

By Train: A scenic (read: slow) rail line connects Penzance and St. Ives, mostly running along the coast (1/day direct, 20 minutes, departs Penzance at 8:57 and St. Ives at 22:31; otherwise roughly hourly with transfer in St. Erth, 30-60 minutes; tel. 0845-748-4950, www.nationalrail.co.uk).

Penzance

Sure enough, Penzance had its share of pirates. Strategically situated near the very tip of Britain, the town was an ideal spot for pirates to hijack and plunder ships returning from the New World with untold treasures. But today's Penzance is less of a rough-and-tumble pirate smuggler's cove and more of a blue-collar transportation hub. Penzance can't compete with the artsy vibe of St. Ives or the precious jewel-box quality of nearby Mousehole, but it's cornered the market on functionality: Well-located B&Bs, good restaurants, train and bus stations, and easy parking make Penzance the most practical home base for exploring the Cornish coast. And its bustling main street, picturesque waterfront setting, and agreeable natives make it an enjoyable place to "come home to" at the end of a busy sightseeing day.

Orientation to Penzance

Penzance, with about 20,000 people, is situated on a small peninsula. The eastern part of the peninsula has the harbor and the train and bus stations. The southern part has a broad and inviting promenade, with most of the town's B&Bs nearby. Climbing uphill from the water are various streets, including the busy Market Jew Street (derived from the Cornish *Marghas Yow*, meaning "Thursday Market") and the atmospheric, restaurant-lined Chapel Street. The hill is capped by the spire of the Church of St. Mary and the grandly domed Market House, now a bank.

Tourist Information

The **Welcome to West Cornwall Centre** is located between the train and bus stations. They are generous with information on the surrounding region, and also offer free Wi-Fi (Easter-mid-July

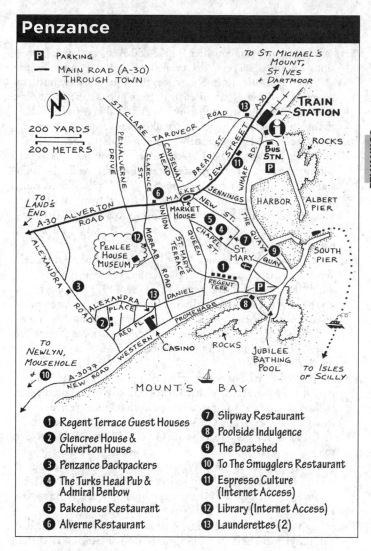

Penzance

🅿 PARKING
— MAIN ROAD (A-30) THROUGH TOWN

🧭 N

200 YARDS
200 METERS

TO ST. MICHAEL'S MOUNT, ST. IVES & DARTMOOR

TRAIN STATION

ROCKS

BUS STN.

ST. CLARE ST.

PENALVERNE DRIVE

TARDVEOR ROAD

CAUSEWAY HEAD

CLARENCE ST.

BREAD ST.

JEW ST.

STREET

WHARF RD.

⓭

⓫

HARBOR

ALBERT PIER

TO LANDS END
← A-30 ALVERTON ROAD

⑥ MARKET ST.

Market House

NEW ST.

JENNINGS

THE QUAY

⑤
④
⑦

CHAPEL ST.

⑨

SOUTH PIER

ALEXANDRA ROAD

PENLEE HOUSE MUSEUM

⑫

MORRAB ROAD

UNION ST.

ST. MARY'S TERRACE

QUEEN ST.

ST. MARY

QUAY

③

⓭

ALEXANDRA PLACE

DANIEL

① REGENT TERR.

🅿

⑧

② RED. PL.

PROMENADE

TO NEWLYN, MOUSEHOLE
⑩ ← A-3077 NEW ROAD WESTERN

CASINO

ROCKS

JUBILEE BATHING POOL

TO ISLES OF SCILLY

⛵ MOUNT'S BAY

① Regent Terrace Guest Houses
② Glencree House & Chiverton House
③ Penzance Backpackers
④ The Turks Head Pub & Admiral Benbow
⑤ Bakehouse Restaurant
⑥ Alverne Restaurant
⑦ Slipway Restaurant
⑧ Poolside Indulgence
⑨ The Boatshed
⑩ To The Smugglers Restaurant
⑪ Espresso Culture (Internet Access)
⑫ Library (Internet Access)
⑬ Launderettes (2)

CORNWALL

and Sept-Oct Mon-Fri 10:00-16:00, Sat 10:00-14:00, closed Sun; mid-July-Aug daily 9:30-17:00; Nov-Easter open fewer days per week—call for specifics; Station Approach, tel. 01736/335-530, www.westcornwall.org.uk).

Helpful Hints

Festival: The annual **Golowan (Midsummer) Festival** engulfs Penzance for 10 days in mid- to late June. Things get especially rowdy on Mazey Day, the last Saturday of the festival, with colorful parades and well-lubricated crowds (tel. 01736/369-686, www.golowan.org).

Art Pass: Art buffs can consider the £14.50 Art Pass, which provides unlimited access for seven days to the Penlee House Gallery and Museum in Penzance; the Tate Gallery, Barbara Hepworth Museum, and Leach Pottery in St. Ives; and a discount at the shops in the Newlyn Art Gallery and the Exchange in Newlyn (www.tate.org.uk/stives).

Internet Access: Wi-Fi is readily available in Penzance, including a free hotspot at the TI (see earlier). If you need to use an Internet terminal, try **Steamers Station Café,** inside the train station (£0.50/10 minutes, Mon-Sat 7:30-17:30, closed Sun, tel. 01736/360-369) or the **library,** just up from the Penlee House Gallery and Museum on Morrab Road (£1.80/30 minutes, Mon-Fri 9:00-17:00, Wed until 18:30, Sat 10:00-16:00, closed Sun, tel. 0300-1234-111).

Baggage Storage: You can stow your luggage at **Longboat Hotel,** across the street from the train station (£2/bag, daily 7:30-24:00, Market Jew Street, tel. 01736/364-137). A long block up the street, **Espresso Culture** also stores bags; though pricier and with shorter hours, it's in a cheery café environment, and the storage fee includes a small coffee (£5/bag, Mon-Fri 9:30-17:00, Sat 8:30-17:00, closed Sun, 83 Market Jew Street, tel. 01736/448-681).

Laundry: Penzance's big waterfront casino, along the promenade past the Regent Terrace B&Bs, has a handy little launderette tucked around the right side (about £6/load self-service or £8/load full-service—takes 2-3 hours, more for bigger loads, daily 7:30-20:00, start last load by 18:45, tel. 01736/333-978). Next to the train station, **Suds & Surf** is another good option (about £7/load self-service or £10/load full-service—takes about 2 hours, also has free Wi-Fi and Internet terminals for £1/30 minutes, daily 8:00-20:00, start last load by 18:30, 4 East Terrace, tel. 01736/364-815).

Taxis: Cabs line up at the train station taxi stand. Or you can call **Anytime Taxis** (tel. 01736/888-888) or **Stones Taxi** (tel. 01736/363-400) for the £3-4 fare to my recommended Regent Terrace accommodations.

Swimming Pool: Take a dip next to the sea in the outdoor, Art Deco **Jubilee Pool,** or just watch the action from the promenade (£4.40, cheaper after 15:30, June-Sept daily 10:30-18:00, closes periodically for events and cleaning so smart to call ahead, tel. 01736/369-224, www.jubileepool.co.uk). The recommended café overlooking the pool—which stays open much later—has the only truly waterfront seating in Penzance (see "Eating in Penzance," later).

Tours in Penzance

▲Western Discoveries Tours

If you want to explore Cornwall's hidden nooks and crannies with a local, a minivan tour is a must. Russ Peake is an enthusiastic, energetic young guide with a broad knowledge of Cornwall's history, geology, and culture. He packs up to eight people into his van and takes them on Cornwall's twistiest back lanes to track down forgotten Neolithic monuments and Iron Age settlements. You won't see any

CORNWALL

of the big attractions listed in this book—Russ takes you way off the beaten path. The route and specific sights covered change based on the weather and the interests of the group. This is a great way to experience the real Cornwall...away from the tourist congestion on the coast (£30/person for 4 hours, departs Penzance train station at 9:30; can also pick up near St. Ives cinema at 9:10 for £5 extra; 5 or more go cheaper with £150 private tour, may also be able to pick up at your Penzance hotel, essential to book ahead by phone or email, tel. 01736/362-763, www.westcornwalltours.co.uk, info@ westcornwalltours.co.uk).

Boat Tours

The beautiful Cornish coast is best seen from the water, and the catamaran sailing trips run by **Marine Discovery** are a fun way to sample it with an ecological emphasis. A variety of tours are offered, with a chance to see seals, dolphins, porpoises, seabirds, and even basking sharks (£18-35 depending on length of tour, less for kids—though some tours have age restrictions, cash or PayPal only, March-Nov, may be canceled in bad weather, depart from either Albert Pier or South Pier depending on tides, best to reserve at least 2 days ahead, tel. 01736/874-907, mobile 07749-277-110, www.marinediscovery.co.uk, info@marinediscovery.co.uk).

Sights in Penzance

▲Penlee House Gallery and Museum

Filling a Victorian house in Penlee Park, the gallery hosts a fine collection from painters of the local Newlyn School. These Post-Impressionists, attracted to Cornwall in the late 1800s by the quality of light and the low cost of living, painted seascapes, portraits, and scenes of daily life. You'll enjoy bucolic, perfectly lit scenes from Cornwall's rocky coast and pasture-striped countryside. The ground floor shows off rotating exhibits, often from the museum's permanent collection. The upstairs has more paintings and a modest museum about Penzance's prehistoric and more recent history (learn how Penzance, Newlyn, and Mousehole were burned by Spanish raiders in 1595). It's smart to call ahead, as the museum closes some or all of its galleries for a week several times a year to rearrange its collection.

Cost and Hours: £4.50, free on Sat, open Easter-Sept Mon-Sat 10:00-17:00, Oct-Easter Mon-Sat 10:30-16:30, closed Sun year-round, last entry 30 minutes before closing, café with inviting garden terrace, Morrab Road, tel. 01736/363-625, www.penleehouse.org.uk.

Waterfront Stroll to Newlyn and Mousehole

A broad pedestrian promenade follows the coast around Mount's Bay, from Penzance to Newlyn—perfect for an early-morning or after-dinner stroll (about 30 minutes one-way). From Newlyn, a coastal footpath extends farther to Mousehole (another 30-minute walk; for more on Mousehole, see page 392). These days, any fishing that happens, goes out of Newlyn.

Sleeping in Penzance

Guesthouses on Regent Terrace

Set just a block off the seashore, the upmarket guesthouses on this street are central and convenient. Rooms in front usually have views of the sea, while those in back overlook a churchyard. Most breakfast rooms are downstairs on the garden level. Though they're all run by friendly proprietors, these places feel more like small hotels than B&Bs. All offer free parking, along with free Wi-Fi and Internet access to guests. Drivers should get precise directions from their hotelier in order to find the narrow and easy-to-miss Regent Terrace.

$$$ Camilla House is relaxed and modern, with contemporary class, neutral colors, a sophisticated black-and-white lounge, and lots of luxurious touches throughout. Friendly, helpful Simon and Susan rent eight comfy, sunny rooms, and are a great source for travel tips (S with private b upstairs-£38, Sb-£40, Db-£75-95 depending on size and view, 3-night minimum April-Oct if booking in advance—but worth checking, at #12, tel. 01736/363-771, www.camillahouse.co.uk, info@camillahouse.co.uk).

$$$ Warwick House has seven fine rooms with a casually posh feel (Sb-£46-48, Db-£82-90, at #17, tel. 01736/363-881, www.warwickhousepenzance.co.uk, enquiry@warwickhousepenzance.co.uk, Chris and Julie). They also rent a two-bedroom seafront cottage in the off-season (www.tremorvahcottage.co.uk).

$$$ Chy-an-Mor Guest House ("House of Sea") has nine rooms that try for elegance—some decorated in a vintage, French-

CORNWALL

Sleep Code

(£1 = about $1.60, country code: 44, area code: 01736)

S = Single, **D** = Double/Twin, **T** = Triple, **Q** = Quad, **b** = bathroom, **s** = shower only. Unless otherwise noted, credit cards are accepted and breakfast is included.

To help you sort easily through these listings, I've divided the accommodations into three categories based on the price for a standard double room with bath:

$$$ Higher Priced—Most rooms £80 or more.
$$ Moderately Priced—Most rooms between £50-80.
$ Lower Priced—Most rooms less than £50.

Prices can change without notice; verify the hotel's current rates online or by email. For the best prices, always book direct.

traditional style. Tea and cakes are ready for you upon arrival (Sb-£45, Db-£80-95 depending on size, no children under 10, closed Dec-mid-March, at #15, tel. 01736/363-441, www.chyanmor.co.uk, reception@chyanmor.co.uk, Louise and Richard).

$$$ Blue Seas Hotel has eight sleek, modern, cheerfully colorful rooms and serves a widely varied breakfast (Sb-£42-46, Db-£85-95, price depends on demand, check website for special discounts, closed mid-Dec-Jan, at #13, tel. 01736/364-744, www.blueseashotel-penzance.co.uk, info@blueseashotel-penzance.co.uk, Arnaud and Fiona).

$$$ Lombard House Hotel, a lesser value, offers old-school chandeliered Georgian townhouse atmosphere. The nine rooms come with older furniture and fixtures than my other listings; the two top-floor attic rooms are cozy and have fine views (Sb-£40, Db-£90, Tb/Qb-£135, cheaper for stays three nights or longer if you book on their website, at #16, tel. 01736/364-897, www.lombardhousehotel.com, rita.kruge@lombardhousehotel.com, Rita and Tom).

Cheaper Options on or near Alexandra Road

Alexandra Road, about a five-minute walk down the promenade from Regent Terrace (and therefore a bit farther from the town center and restaurants), is lined with midrange accommodations and a hostel. All of the below offer free Wi-Fi; additional Internet access is available nearby at the library for a small fee.

$$ Glencree House, with eight rooms in a beautiful granite Victorian townhouse, offers charming antique furniture, thoughtful little touches (such as packed lunches available), and comparable quality to the Regent Terrace guesthouses at a slightly lower price (S-£29-40, Sb-£34-42, Db-£60-86, Tb-£60-88, T-£131-139, price depends on length of stay and season, just off Alexandra Road on quiet Mennaye Road at #2, tel. 01736/362-026, www.glencreehouse.co.uk, stay@glencreehouse.co.uk, Andrew and Lynsey).

$$ Chiverton House is a stone Victorian home with six smallish rooms packed with wood furnishings (Sb-£30-40, Db-£50-70, cash only, just off Alexandra Road at 9 Mennaye Road, tel. 01736/332-733, www.chivertonhousebedandbreakfast.co.uk, alan.waller@sky.com, Alan and Sally).

$ Penzance Backpackers, with 30 beds in seven rooms, is situated in a townhouse on a B&B-studded stretch of Alexandra Road. This is your best bet for budget dorm beds (£16-18 beds in 6-person dorms, D-£36-38, reception open 9:00-12:00 & 17:00-22:00, no lockout, tel. 01736/363-836, www.pzbackpack.com, info@pzbackpack.com).

Eating in Penzance

Wherever you eat, check the daily specials lists—most pubs serve fresh local fish and crab, along with the usual options. Many places also have early-bird specials on weekdays before 19:00.

On or Near Chapel Street

This historic street runs up into town from the waterfront near Regent Terrace, toward Market Jew Street. As Chapel Street doesn't use street numbers, use the map on page 375 to locate the following.

The Turks Head, the oldest pub in Penzance, is a dark, low-beamed gem. It's an all-around pub, serving tasty and good-value food and local ales. This is a popular spot—arrive early. There are dining rooms in the back and downstairs, and a small terrace out back, but the pub in front is ideal for rubbing elbows with locals (£7-10 lunches, £10-14 dinners, food served daily 12:00-14:30 & 18:00-21:30, on Chapel Street near intersection with Abbey Street, tel. 01736/363-093).

Bakehouse Restaurant features Cornish cuisine that tries to keep things simple by highlighting quality ingredients. The service is sharp and cheerful, while the decor is modern and nondescript (£12-16 main dishes, good vegetarian options, steaks, nightly from 18:15 but closed Sun in winter, on Chapel Street, set back on a little courtyard called Old Bakehouse Lane, tel. 01736/331-331).

Alverne, a bit above Chapel Street, dishes up British and Mediterranean food in a casual red interior with a cozy lounge up front (£9-11 lunches, £13-16 dinners, Mon-Sat 9:00-14:30 &

17:00-21:00, closed Sun, also closed for dinner Mon and Tue in Oct-May, 30 Alverton Street, tel. 01736/366-007).

Slipway is innovative, fresh, and a bit overpriced. In a formal-feeling modern/minimalist setting, they feature small £3.50 "international street food" tapas in their casual downstairs bar (in cozy easy chairs) or a more upscale £14-19 menu upstairs. Hiding behind a bookcase is the entrance to their claustrophobic bar, once locally famous as the "Zero Club" where many Penzance couples first began courting (Tue-Sun 12:00-14:30 & 18:00-21:00, Mon 18:00-21:00 only, a few steps off Chapel Street at 2 Abbey Street, tel. 01736/333-714).

Admiral Benbow's interior—memorably crammed with over-the-top nautical decor—screams "tacky holiday," but the pub is mysteriously popular with locals as well as tourists. It's worth poking inside for a lesson on how a theme can be taken to the extreme. If it's crowded in front, head farther back to find a much larger, if less outrageously decorated, back room (£6-10 lunches, £10-13 dinners, food served daily 12:00-14:30 & 18:00-21:30, 46 Chapel Street, tel. 01736/363-448).

Along the Waterfront

Poolside Indulgence owns Penzance's only outdoor waterfront seating. Don't be fooled by the fact that it's a poolside grill, with rustic picnic tables squeezed between the public Jubilee Pool and the rocky beachfront promenade. It has a serious respect for food, and a seriously spectacular setting if the weather's good. The menu is short, unpretentious, and determined by the local catch (£6-7 sandwiches, £9-13 main dishes, daily 10:00-15:00 & 17:30 "until it's too cold to eat," heated indoor section if rain rolls in, Wharf Road—look for café to the right of Jubilee Pool entrance, mobile 0777-999-8590).

The Boatshed is a wine bar/restaurant with gently nautical decor tucked across the road from the South Pier. They pride themselves on their locally caught seafood, but the service can be slow... don't dine here if you're in a hurry (£6-7 sandwiches, £8-9 pizzas, £9-15 dinners, food served daily June-Sept 10:30-15:00 & 18:30-21:00, often closed at lunch in shoulder season and on weekdays off-season, closed entirely Jan-Feb, The Quay/Wharf Road, tel. 01736/368-845).

Out of Town, in Newlyn

The Smugglers Restaurant is the best option for white-tablecloth dining (dinners only). This is where locals go to celebrate special occasions. Located 1.5 miles southwest of my recommended B&Bs, it faces the harbor along the main road in Newlyn. Reservations are wise for dinner (£11-17 main dishes, plus pricier specials; summer daily 19:00-21:30; winter Wed-Sat 19:00-21:30, closed Sun-Tue; 12 Fore Street—pay to park near the harbor, then walk two minutes up the hill; tel. 01736/331-501). They also rent out three rooms (Db-£80-90, www.smugglersnewlyn.co.uk, smugglersnewlyn@bt-connect.com, Stephen and Barbara).

Penzance Connections

For connections within Cornwall, see page 371.

From Penzance by Train to: London's Paddington Station (about hourly, 5-6 hours, possible transfer in Plymouth or Newton Abbot), **Salisbury** (about hourly, 5-6 hours, 1-2 transfers), **Bath** (1-2/hour, 4.5-5 hours, one direct, most 1-2 transfers), **Edinburgh** (every 1-2 hours, 10-17 hours, 1 direct, most transfer in London), **York** (every 1-2 hours, 8-11 hours, 1 direct, most transfer in London), **Exeter** (roughly hourly, 3 hours). Train info: Tel. 0845-748-4950, www.nationalrail.co.uk.

By Bus to: Exeter (1-4/day, 5.5-6 hours, possible transfer in Plymouth), **Brighton** (5/day, 11.5-12 hours, transfers in Plymouth, Heathrow, or London), **Portsmouth** (2-5/day, 11-12.5 hours, transfer in Plymouth), **London** (5/day direct, 8.5-10 hours, overnight available). Bus info: Tel. 0871-781-8181, www.nationalexpress.com.

St. Ives

Picturesque St. Ives enjoys three claims to fame: It's a major artists' colony, a top fun-in-the-Cornish-sun holiday destination, and England's surfing mecca. British bohemians and British surfers—two kinds of people you probably didn't expect to meet in England—both abound in St. Ives. Tourists hit the town like a tidal wave in summer (July-Sept)—when, as a local told me, "You can smell the sweat and suntan oil for miles around." While it's  undeniably picturesque and worth seeing—quickly—it sometimes feels like the worst of both worlds: a tacky, overrun seaside resort as well as a self-important artist town, oozing with pretension. An annual music and arts festival keeps things humming in September (www.stivesseptemberfestival.co.uk).

The town's artsy aura is nothing new. With golden light reflecting off the aquamarine waves and twisty lanes, St. Ives began to attract artists in the early 20th century. The potter Bernard Leach practiced his craft here, as did sculptor Barbara Hepworth, and both have museums in town—along with dozens of other, lesser-known artists. (The TI assured me there are an "untold number" of galleries.) Perhaps for this reason, the Tate Gallery also has an unlikely branch here, which seems a bit too big-league for a little-league town.

Orientation to St. Ives

About half the size of Penzance, with 11,000 people, St. Ives occupies a few steep bits of land between sandy beaches. The town clusters around its sandy harbor, with a bulbous spit of land just beyond called The Island. From the quaint, waterfront old town, newer development sprawls uphill toward the main road. Thanks to its warren of convoluted lanes, small St. Ives can be challenging to navigate.

Tourist Information

The St. Ives TI, tucked inside the Guildhall, offers brochures, charges for town maps, has Internet terminals (£1/15 minutes, £3/ hour), and can book you a room for £5 (July-Sept Mon-Fri 10:00-17:00, Sat-Sun 11:00-16:00; May Mon-Fri 10:00-15:00, Sat 11:00-15:00, closed Sun; June Mon-Fri 10:00-16:00, Sat 11:00-16:00, Sun 11:00-15:00; Oct-April Mon-Fri 10:00-15:00, closed Sat-Sun; Street an Pol, tel. 01736/796-297 or 0905-252-2250, www.stives-tic.co.uk).

Arrival in St. Ives

By Car: St. Ives is a pain for drivers—parking is scarce and distant from town, and those who venture into the center find its streets congested with slow-moving pedestrians. As you approach town, you'll reach a roundabout with a "do not enter" sign (9:30-16:00, except for permitted vehicles). While this isn't usually enforced, driving past here is challenging enough that you'll probably prefer to just to go with the flow and park at one of the outlying lots (all cost about the same: £1.90/2 hours, £4.20/4 hours, £6.40/all day until 18:00). The main option is the huge **Trenwith** car park above town, near the Leisure Centre—turn right just before the round-about. From this lot, it's a steep downhill walk or easy £1 shuttle ride into town (drops off and picks up at the movie theater). A bit closer to town is the **Stennack Surgery** car park, just off Stennack Road past the little doctor's office/old schoolhouse. To reach it, proceed straight through the roundabout at the top of town and watch for the blue *P* sign on the left in the first block. Or you can turn left at the roundabout and loop around to the **Barnoon** pay lot just above the Tate Gallery and Porthmeor Beach (the handiest lot if the Tate is your goal, but still a steep hike above the town center/harbor).

Yet another option—which lets you avoid driving in town entirely—is to leave your car at the park-and-ride lot at Lelant Saltings on the way to St. Ives, then ride the train from there into town (see next). If you use the train park-and-ride, you get a £1 discount at the Tate Gallery.

By Train or Bus: The train and bus stations are conveniently located near the waterfront; just exit and walk with the sea on your right into the heart of town. To get here, you can take the cute, historic St. Ives Bay Line that runs above the coast from St. Erth to St. Ives; if coming from Penzance, aim for the once-daily direct train to St. Ives, or change in St. Erth (Traveline tel. 0871-200-2233 or tel. 0845-748-4950, www.nationalrail.co.uk).

Helpful Hints

Internet Access: You can get online at the **TI** (described earlier) or nearby at the **library,** at the corner of Gabriel and Tregenna, just up from the Guildhall (£1.80/30 minutes, Mon and Thu-Fri 9:30-17:00, Tue 9:30-18:30, Sat 10:00-13:00, closed Wed and Sun, tel. 0300-1234-111).

Surf's Up: Find your inner dude by taking lessons from **St. Ives Surf School** on Porthmeor Beach. Choose between surfing (£30/2 hours), kayaking (£45/2 hours), or stand-up paddleboarding (£35/1.5 hours; all prices are per person and include equipment, equipment rentals also available, daily 9:30-18:00, tel. 01736/793-938, www.stivessurfschool.co.uk).

Sights in St. Ives

Art lovers can save money by buying the Art Pass, which includes the first three sights mentioned here, plus others in Cornwall (see page 376).

Tate Gallery

St. Ives very proudly hosts a branch of the prestigious London art museum. The modern building is big and outwardly impressive, but the galleries are quite small, and the ever-changing exhibits—focusing mostly on modern works by relatively obscure local artists—can be a letdown. Find out what's on before paying the steep entry price.

Cost and Hours: £7, £10 combo-ticket includes Barbara Hepworth Museum and Sculpture Garden, ticket includes art talks twice daily—likely at 11:00 and 14:30; March-Oct daily 10:00-17:20; Nov-Feb Tue-Sun 10:00-16:20, closed Mon; last entry 20 minutes before closing, closes for two weeks about three times a year to change exhibits, tel. 01736/796-226, www.tate.org.uk/stives.

▲**Barbara Hepworth Museum and Sculpture Garden**

Many visitors find this collection more accessible than the Tate's. Barbara Hepworth (1903-1975) was one of the first sculptors to create nonrepresentational art (that is, totally abstract works that didn't attempt to imitate the real world). She lived most of her life in St. Ives, and now her home and workshop—called Trewyn Studio—is a small museum, offering a chance to learn a bit about the artist and see her works: large, solid forms pierced by voids. These curvaceous, undulating works were inspired by, if not quite resembling, the sea, wind, clouds, sand, and light of St. Ives. While a few are inside, most of the pieces are sprinkled throughout the linger-worthy garden. While exploring, peek into her actual studio, with its dusty smocks and rusty chisels.

Cost and Hours: £6, £10 combo-ticket includes the Tate, ticket includes daily art talk—usually at 13:00, same hours and contact info as the Tate, at the corner of Ayr Lane and Barnoon Hill.

Leach Pottery Museum

This museum celebrates Bernard Leach, considered one of the founders of the mid-20th-century British studio-pottery movement. You'll walk through what was his actual studio, with its heavy-duty kilns, then tour a collection of works by Leach and his associates, as well as pieces by leading contemporary potters. The complex also includes an active workshop where potters still work (generally not viewable).

Cost and Hours: £5.50; March-Oct Mon-Sat 10:00-17:00, Sun 11:00-16:00; Nov-Feb Mon-Sat 10:00-17:00, closed Sun; last entry 30 minutes before closing, Higher Stennack/B-3306, tel. 01736/799-703, www.leachpottery.com.

Getting There: The studio is well-marked from the upper outskirts of St. Ives, on the road into town. From Royal Square in the center of town, it's a 15-minute walk. Or park at the Trenwith car park (described earlier under "Arrival in St. Ives"); the studio is a six-minute uphill walk from there (disabled parking only at the studio, but you may find street parking nearby).

Stroll the Town

Besides gallery-hopping, the best way to enjoy St. Ives is by taking an ice-cream cone on a waterfront stroll. The slate-tile-clad High Street and pleasant waterfront have plenty of shops and ice-cream stands to entertain even the pickiest kids. Boats departing from the harbor can take you on trips around the cliffs and to the coves, a good way to appreciate why the Cornish coast was so popular with bootleggers and pirates.

CORNWALL

Hit the Beach

St. Ives is popular with Brits on a "bucket-and-spade" holiday because it's surrounded by sandy beaches. In addition to the sandy, central harbor—home to boats as well as swimmers—you'll find family-friendly Porthminster Beach (west) and surfer-friendly Porthmeor Beach (east). Tiny, secluded Porthgwidden Beach—hiding between the rocks under the high peninsula called The Island—is worth the hike.

Sleeping in St. Ives

(area code: 01736)

The town's charm wears thin with the hordes of tourists in high season, but the evenings are quiet enough to consider staying over. The first two options are in tight, twisty old buildings—climbing to your room can feel like spiraling up through a ship's hull.

$$$ Cornerways rents six rooms with lots of grays, blacks, and exposed beams. It's got a smooth nautical-meets-contemporary vibe, with easygoing and helpful Tim at the helm (Sb-£40-80, Db-£80-95, cheaper off-season, free Wi-Fi and Tate/Hepworth museum passes, 1 Bethesda Place, tel. 01736/796-706, mobile 07815-796-706, www.cornerwaysstives.com, cornerwaysstives@aol.com).

$$$ The Anchorage has four cozy rooms and claustrophobic ceilings (S-£45-80, Db-£75-100, 5 Bunkers Hill, tel. 01736/797-135, mobile 07977-928-540, www.anchoragestives.co.uk, info@anchoragestives.co.uk, Christopher).

$$$ The Queens Hotel, with a recommended gastropub on the ground floor, has 10 scruffy but fine rooms that are an afterthought to the popular pub (Db-£79-109, higher on weekends and in summer, free Wi-Fi, on High Street just up from the harbor, tel. 01736/796-468, www.queenshotelstives.com, info@queenshotelstives.com).

Eating in St. Ives

While a few innovative chefs have tried their hand here in St. Ives, in general the town sees a lot of turnover; most places are glitzy, emphasizing style over substance to lure in the one-time tourist trade. Ask locals what's good right now. Opening times for most St. Ives eateries can change from one day to the next, depending on weather and crowds.

Along the Harborfront: The main drag along the harbor has plenty of dining options—though most are clearly tourist traps. Peruse the menus and views, and choose your favorite. **The Rum & Crab Shack** does serve a wide variety of rums (about 40 types) and locally sourced crab (delivered fresh each morning), but the "shack" is a misnomer—it's an appealingly modern, cozy, informal, upstairs space, with big windows looking out over the harbor (£7-13 meals, daily 9:00-24:00, The Wharf, tel. 01736/796-353).

Above Porthmeor Beach: For the best beach views in town—away from the worst of the tacky tourism—head to the **Porthmeor Beach Café,** across the street from the Tate Gallery. Classy but casual, its outdoor or enclosed seating overlooks Cornwall's most popular surfing beach (£6-10 sandwiches, £3-7 tapas, salads, and pizzas; £11-15 dinners, Easter-Oct daily 9:00-21:00, tel. 01736/793-366).

Pasties on Fore Street: Running parallel to the harbor one block inland, Fore Street is lined with tourist shops and some good budget eateries. It's hard to choose among the many Cornish pasty shops along here; rather than recommend one, I suggest following your nose to the best-looking option.

Gastropub: The **Queens Hotel** is an appealingly scruffy-mod gastropub with a pinch of hipster and a whisper of indifferent service. Their well-priced fare appears on a handwritten chalkboard menu that changes regularly (£6-7 lunches, £9-17 dinners, free Wi-Fi, Mon-Sat 12:00-14:30 & 18:30-21:00, Sun 12:00-16:00 only, straight up High Street from the harbor, tel. 01736/796-468).

Fish-and-Chips: The **Albatross,** tucked away on Chapel Street (uphill from the TI), serves tasty local fish-and-chips to take away (daily 12:00-14:30 & 19:00-21:30, tel. 01736/798-492).

And for Dessert: You'll see places hawking "Cornish Ice Cream"—the frozen version of clotted cream, which means it's richer and creamier than the norm. For something deliciously different, try the lavender-and-honey flavor.

St. Ives Connections

The **bus** is more practical than the train for most connections. The most useful lines are #17 and #17A to Penzance; #17B to Penzance via Marazion (St. Michael's Mount); and #300 to Land's End and Penzance (via Geevor Tin Mine, Sennen Cove, and Marazion, plus Porthcurno late May-late Aug only). For details, see page 371.

All **train** connections from St. Ives to points eastward go through St. Erth, where you'll switch from the cute little St. Ives Bay Line to the main line to Penzance (see "Penzance Connections" on page 382).

Penwith Peninsula

The western tip of Cornwall, called the Penwith Peninsula, is a pincushion of worthwhile stops. Literally meaning "headland," Penwith features rugged, rocky, windblown scenery; the best-preserved bits of traditional Cornish culture; and some of Britain's most ancient sites, to boot. With Penzance or St. Ives as a home base, all of the following destinations are within easy striking distance for a day trip. I've listed them roughly clockwise from Penzance (the first sight, St. Michael's Mount, is east of—and visible from—Penzance). Drivers: Note that B-3315 travels west from Penzance, passing Mousehole, the Merry Maidens stone circle, and Porthcurno en route to Land's End.

▲▲St. Michael's Mount

Bookending the English Channel along with France's Mont St. Michel (but on a smaller scale), this dramatic rock island has

been inhabited for 1,500 years. Originally a Benedictine monastery, it was later turned into a fortified castle, and eventually a stately home, by the St. Aubyn family—who still own it today in partnership with the National Trust. If the tide is out, a pedestrian causeway connects the island to the town of Marazion (mah-rah-ZYE-on). Otherwise, a short ride in a motorboat (April-Oct only) will bring you up to the picturesque vest-pocket harbor just below the castle's lower gates. From there, a steep, uneven, rocky path curves its way up to the castle entrance.

Cost and Hours: Castle and garden-£9.60, castle only-£7.60, garden only-£4; castle open late March-Oct Sun-Fri 10:30-17:00—or until 17:30 in July-Aug, closed Sat, last entry 45 minutes before closing; Nov-late March castle tours run from the mount's café "when tides and weather are favourable," usually Tue and Fri at 11:00 and 14:00—call to confirm; garden open mid-April-June Mon-Fri 10:30-17:00, July-Sept Thu-Fri only 10:30-17:00—or until 17:30 in July-Aug, closed off-season; tel. 01736/710-507, ferry and tide info tel. 01736/710-265, www.stmichaelsmount.co.uk.

Getting There: Buses #2, #2A, #17B, #300, and #302 run from Penzance to Marazion. From there, it depends on the tide: At low tide (about four hours per day—most locals know the time or can show you a tide table), you can walk about a quarter-mile across the causeway to the island. At other times, you'll need to catch the

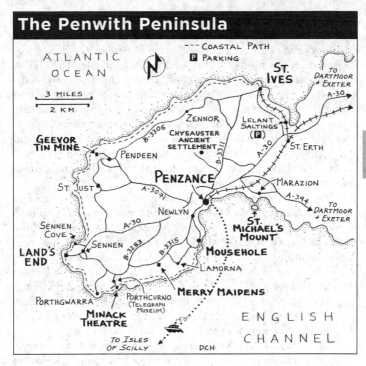

The Penwith Peninsula

boat (£2 one-way, runs continuously—or, in slow times, whenever 12 people show up, April-Oct only, 10 minutes, walk down the path near the post office). Boats don't run on Saturdays, when the castle is closed. Drivers can park in either of two waterfront parking lots (£3.50).

Eating at St. Michael's Mount: For a convenient and good lunch option, try the mount's café or restaurant.

➲ Self-Guided Tour: Contrary to popular belief, most of England's castles are now owned by the state or by charities. The Great Depression bankrupted many noble English families, who were forced to sell off family estates and heirlooms. St. Michael's Mount is one of the few open to the public that has remained associated with the same family since the Middle Ages. Family portraits, some quite recent, adorn the walls.

After buying your ticket, head into the gated entry area. From here, you can enter the **garden** that curls most of the way around the base of the castle, with many tropical plants, a few prehistoric standing stones, and grand views.

But the highlight is the **castle** itself, which you'll reach by hiking steeply upward. Once inside, the castle is surprisingly petite. Docents posted in each room are eager to answer questions. You'll pass through an envy-inducing seaview study and see some historic paintings of the place, before entering one of the building's highlights: the Chevy Chase Room, which was originally the refectory of the monastery that once stood here, and still has that long, somber dining-hall feel. It's named for the circa-1620 frieze that decorates the room, illustrating scenes from a beloved medieval ballad (not for the American comedic actor who knew how to choose a classy stage name). From there, proceed into the smoking room, where men would nurse cigars after dinner, *Downton Abbey*-style. Hanging in the window is a weather gauge, filled with liquid that changes color as barometric conditions change. In the small frame is some nobleman's prized souvenir: a tiny blue scrap from the jacket that Napoleon wore at Waterloo.

Step out onto the breathtaking view terrace (among the newest parts of the castle, it was built to take full advantage of this hilltop's scenic setting). Peer down to see the garden that wraps around the island (described earlier)—and keep an eye out for mysterious prehistoric standing stones, many of which were here before the castle.

Curling around to the landward side of the castle, you'll enter the chapel, built (as the core of that medieval monastery) in the 12th century, then rebuilt after an earthquake in the 13th by Bernard du Bec, the same abbot responsible for France's Mont St. Michel (locals affectionately call him "Bernard the Builder").

The genteel Blue Drawing Room has a vastly different style from what you've seen up to now. Ogling this room, it's easy to imagine the family that owns and lives in this complex hanging out here after-hours. (The painting over the fireplace flips around to reveal a flat-screen TV.) Passing through the map room (with historic maps of this place) and going down the stairs (peer over the bannister to parts of the castle reserved for the residents), you'll reach a small exhibit about the island's history and prehistory.

Before heading back down to the base of the mountain, look out to sea and ponder this: Locals claim that Jesus Christ visited Cornwall during his teen years. Supposedly he landed here at St. Michael's Mount, then traveled up to Glastonbury (near Bath). While this might seem patently bogus, natives persuasively insist that it could have happened: Joseph of Arimathea, who was a wealthy disciple of Jesus, was also a metal trader. He might have brought Jesus to this metal-rich peninsula on a business trip. All that we know of Jesus' life between his adolescence and age 30 is that he traveled in the "wilderness"...which Britain (and most of Europe) certainly was at that time.

Chysauster Iron Age Settlement

Two millennia ago, the granite village of Chysauster (CHIH-zaw-ster) was created high up on a windswept hillside of the Cornish moors. Today, anyone with an interest in prehistory will find it well worth the short drive from Penzance and quarter-mile uphill walk from the parking lot. While many such settlements are scattered around the Penwith Peninsula, Chysauster is relatively easy to find on your own and well set up for visitors.

Cost and Hours: £3.60, Easter-Oct daily 10:00-17:00, July-Aug until 18:00, closed Nov-Easter, tel. 07831/757-934, www. english-heritage.org.uk.

Getting There: The site is accessible only by car. It's tricky to find, hiding on backcountry roads a few miles north of Penzance: Leave town on B-3311 (the back road to St. Ives); about 1.5 miles outside town, at Badgers Cross, turn left, following signs for *Trez-elah* and *Newmill*. Follow that road for about a mile, watching for the parking lot (and WC building) on the left. Park and walk across the road, where a gravel trail leads you up through a field to the ticket kiosk.

Visiting Chysauster: For defensive reasons, the earliest settlements in Cornwall sat upon hilltops, like this one. (Scanning the horizon virtually anywhere on the Penwith Peninsula, you'll notice that the summit of each hill is capped with the scant remains of an old house or fortress.) As life became more civilized and peaceful, people gradually moved down into valleys, and eventually to the coast—abandoning the difficult life at places like Chysauster.

This enigmatic ancient site encompasses nine cloverleaf-shaped homesteads, each one with circular rooms huddled around a central courtyard for protection and comfort. While the buildings were once roofed (most likely either with thatch or turf), it's unclear whether the central courtyard was also covered.

Information boards let you explore and understand each building and imagine how villages like this developed. From the first information board, bear right to #7, then do a counterclockwise loop to see the others. Linger in the two best-preserved houses, #6 and #4. The smaller rooms were used for storage, possibly for game (the people who lived here were hunter-gatherers); the larger rooms were dwellings. A unique feature of this community was an underground passage called a fogou, which may have been used for storage or as a place of refuge (one hides out about 135 yards southeast of house #7).

A place like Chysauster lets fertile imaginations run wild. Looking at the circular shape of each house, ponder the possibility that all of Britain's "mysterious" stone circles (such as Stonehenge)—which have been accounted for by a wide range of wildly creative explanations—may simply be the scant remains of a big, round house. Or try this thought: If Jesus did visit Cornwall in his youth (as local legends suggest), these are the sorts of settlements he'd have seen.

CORNWALL

Mousehole

Tiny and salty as a barnacle on a sloop, Mousehole (MOW-zle) is adorable. Mousehole is typical of the many charming and now touristy fishing villages that sugar this coastline. It's famous for smuggling, for fishing, and for being the last place where the pre-Roman language of Cornish was spoken. Today, Mousehole harvests more tourists than fish. The little harbor maintains a small fleet, but was busier in the past. The tiny passage out of the harbor is said to be what gave the town its curious name.

Looking to the jagged ridge of rocks poking up from the deep just beyond the seawall, imagine how Mousehole (like many such Cornish towns) once specialized in a sort of reverse-piracy called "wrecking." During the rugged days of the late 18th century, townsfolk would place false lighthouse beacons high above town, misleading approaching ships into believing there was safe passage—and luring them right toward these hidden rocks. The ships would wreck, and the less scrupulous residents of Mousehole would rush out to salvage what they could.

Mousehole has a few whitewashed homes, harkening back to Victorian times, when the entire town would have been gleaming white. The lime wash helped waterproof the stone walls and was an excellent insulator (since the sun's heat was reflected away). The best time to enjoy the simple charm of Mousehole is early in the day, when it's enhanced by fresh sea air and noisy seagulls. The beachside path from Newlyn makes an excellent 30-minute stroll (described on page 378).

Getting There: Buses #6 and #6A go from Penzance to Newlyn, then on to Mousehole (2-3/hour, 10 minutes to Newlyn, 20 minutes to Mousehole). Buses #5 and #5A from Penzance also serve Newlyn. Bus #504 provides similar but less frequent service to Newlyn (Mon-Sat 2/day, none on Sun, 10 minutes). Driving into the town—with its narrow and twisty lanes—is stressful, particularly when the town is clogged with pedestrians. While it's possible to park right along the harbor (£3), it's easier to park in the lot at the Penzance end of town (£2) and walk in.

Merry Maidens Stone Circle

In ancient times, stone circles had some sort of significant purpose— probably as a site for religious ceremonies, as a community meeting place, or, most famously, as a calendar. The Merry Maidens feels like a stone circle with training wheels— very easy for drivers to reach, though far simpler than the famous ones at

Stonehenge and Avebury. Still, it's a reminder that the Penwith Peninsula was inhabited in the Neolithic Age (roughly 2000 B.C. or earlier). This is just the beginning of a staggering variety of prehistoric monuments, settlements, and artifacts that still lie just beneath the surface of Cornwall.

The story behind the name, most likely concocted in the Middle Ages, goes like this: A group of village women decided to go into the fields on the Sabbath for some merriment and dancing. This displeased God, who turned the women to stone to serve as a warning to others.

Getting There: The Merry Maidens are in a grassy field just off B-3315 (on the way from Penzance to Land's End). They're easy to miss if you're driving. Coming from Penzance, after passing through Boleigh, look for a pullout on the left near three gates; you'll also see a bus stop and a low-profile stone marker, and, on the right, a green arrow pointing across the road with a faded *Merry Maidens* sign. If you don't have a car, bus #504 takes you from Penzance to the Merry Maidens, but service is so limited that it's impractical (Mon-Sat 2/day, none on Sun, 30 minutes).

Porthcurno

This humdrum hamlet, just off B-3315 between Penzance and Land's End, has two worthwhile sights.

▲Minack Theatre

For good Cornish theater, try the Minack. This local open-air theater has just about the most spectacular setting of any place—

theater or otherwise—in England. This gorgeously landscaped facility can seat up to 750 theatergoers. With seats actually carved into a rocky cliff and a terrace stage perched hundreds of feet over the sea, the Minack is quite a sight. Imagine watching *The Tempest* with only the sunset and crashing waves for scenery. If you aren't a theater buff or don't happen to be here during the theater season, the site is still worth a visit for the unbeatable views of the rocky cliffs. The small exhibit on the history of the Minack includes a short video on Rowena Cade, the visionary theater lover who persevered to build it. There's also a cliff-hanging coffeehouse (accessible only with admission).

Cost and Hours: You can visit the theater just to see it (£4; April-Sept daily 9:30-17:30—except Wed and Fri mid-May-Sept, when it closes at 11:30 for a matinee; call ahead or check website for sporadic closures—a children's festival closes the theater to visitors two weeks each June, and children's matinees close it several mornings each summer; Oct-March daily 10:00-16:00; last entry 30 minutes before closing), or you can attend a **performance** during peak season (£8-9.50, £1 booking fee if you use a credit/debit card, performances generally mid-May-mid-Sept, usually Mon-Fri at 20:00, also Wed and Fri at 14:00, rarely canceled but dress for the weather, tel. 01736/810-181, www.minack.com). As you'll be sitting on the grass, bring a blanket and dress appropriately.

Getting There: The theater is up an extremely narrow and twisty road above Porthcurno, well-signed from town, with free parking. From Penzance, bus #504 goes to the theater (Mon-Sat 2/day, none on Sun, 50 minutes). If you're willing to hike, you can also take buses #1A or #300 from Penzance to the stop in Porthcurno, with a steep, quarter-mile uphill climb to the theater (#1A runs Mon-Sat 3/day, none on Sun, 40 minutes; #300 goes daily 4-5/day late May-late Aug only, 40 minutes); some—but not all—departures of bus #501 from Penzance also stop at Porthcurno (5/day, 40 minutes). During the summer, the last bus #1A leaves Porthcurno for Penzance after the show, at 23:00 (Mon-Sat only).

Telegraph Museum

In 1870, a telegraph cable was laid from Porthcurno to India. By the time World War II broke out, 14 cables tethered this village to the rest of the world. In 1940, defensive tunnels were built to protect the telegraph station and cables from the Nazis—who were then just 80 miles away in France. Today, those tunnels and an adjacent building house a surprisingly interesting museum, tracing the history of the "Victorian Internet." The museum, scheduled to reopen in May of 2014 after an extensive renovation, explains how underwater cables were made possible thanks to a new insulating material (a resin from a Malaysian tree called gutta-percha), how the cables were even more heavily armored in shallower water (where they could be damaged by the anchors of passing ships), and how ruptured cables were repaired in the briny deep. Be sure to ask about the once-hourly presentation about underwater telegraphy, which helps bring the place to life...and, like the museum, is better than it sounds. The tunnels are furnished as they would have been during wartime, when they protected England's very precious connection to the world.

Cost and Hours: £7.20—likely more after the renovation; April-Oct daily 10:00-17:00, Wed until 19:00 in Aug; Nov-March Sun-Mon only 10:00-17:00, closed Tue-Sat; last entry one hour before closing, next to main parking lot in Porthcurno on the road up to Minack Theatre—look for big white building marked *Museum*, tel. 01736/810-966, www.porthcurno.org.uk.

Getting There: Drivers can park in the public lot just below the museum (£2). Bus #1A from Penzance stops in Porthcurno near the museum (Mon-Sat 3/day, none on Sun, 40 minutes), as does #504 (Mon-Sat 2/day, none on Sun), #501 (every 2 hours, 40 minutes), and #300 (daily late May-late Aug only, 4-5/day, 40 minutes).

Land's End

The westernmost point in all of England should seem like a desolate, rugged place. In reality, it's a tacky tourist trap where greedy businesses have chewed up whatever small bit of charm or authenticity this place might once have had. As you approach, you'll see endless signs bragging "the last" (or, in a too-cute spin, "the first and last")... everything: inn, hotel, refreshment stand, postal box, and so on. Come here only if you want to be able to say you've been to Land's End. (Consider lying.)

If you do visit, pay the £3 parking fee (enforced 24 hours/day; coins required 17:00-9:00) and walk straight from the parking lot through the low-budget theme park (stop at your own risk) out to the viewpoint. This was once considered the end of the civilized world, the last (or first) thing to be seen by departing (or arriving) ships. After gazing at the sea and guessing how far away from home you are, find out how close you were by checking your hometown at the picture stand on the right. For £11-14, they'll take your photo with a personalized signpost and mail it to you (tel. 01736/741-222, theme park tel. 0871-720-0044, www.landsend-landmark.co.uk).

"Back Door" Approach to Land's End: To appreciate the majesty of this location while avoiding the tourist logjam, consider hiking in from nearby **Sennen Cove.** From the road just north of Land's End, turn off to drive down the steep and narrow road into the village of Sennen, then park at the harbor (£1/2 hours, £2/4 hours, where the road dead-ends at the end of town). It's a steep, uphill, but rewarding one-mile hike over the windswept headlands to Land's End, following the South West Coast Path, Britain's longest national trail (for a description, see www.southwestcoastpath.com).

Getting There: Buses #1, #1A, #300, #501, and #504 connect Penzance with Land's End (Mon-Sat every 1-2 hours, Sun every 2 hours, no Sun service on #1A or #504; 40 minutes-2.5 hours), while #300, #504, and some #501 departures also stop at Sennen Cove (#300—daily, 4-5/day, 50 minutes; #504—2/day, none on Sun, 1.5 hours; #501—daily, 2/day go to Sennen Cove—check schedule, every 2 hours, 40 minutes).

Cornwall's Tin-Mining Legacy

Cornwall's history is tied to its tin-mining industry. While Cornwall has always been known for its metal deposits, a major tin boom began here in the mid-1700s, as new steam-engine-powered pumps allowed tin to be mined below the water table. The industry peaked 200 years ago, when tin was the cutting edge of technology, and Cornwall was the Silicon Valley of Britain.

Miners would climb down into the narrow shafts, and use a hammer and a long bit to slowly drive deep, skinny holes into a vein of tin. Then they'd insert sticks of dynamite. Before safety fuses were invented, quills from bird feathers were used as fuses, so miners setting off gunpowder never knew how much time they had to reach safety before the explosion.

Deadly cave-ins were frequent. These were supposedly caused by mischievous Tommyknockers, Cornish pixies similar to leprechauns. But these mysterious creatures might simply have been a creation of the oxygen-starved imaginations of exhausted miners.

Mines employed the notorious "company store" system, where workers were paid in tokens that could only be redeemed at the store run by the mine (an obvious conflict of interest—which always worked to the company's advantage). To save money, miners made their own "hardhats." They'd take a felt hat and harden it by dipping it alternately in hot tree resin and soil. Then they'd stick a candle on the brim for light while they worked.

▲Geevor Tin Mine

Once 2,100 feet deep and extending almost a mile under the ocean, the Geevor Mine closed in 1990. Once a huge industry here, tin-mining collapsed in the 1980s, and Margaret Thatcher ended subsidies that were keeping it afloat—effectively prompting the closure of the mine (and earning lots of Cornish enemies). Geevor represents the last hurrah not only of Cornish tin-mining, but, in a sense, of Britain's Industrial Age. Today, considered virtually a shrine by the local community, it's been converted into a museum, exhibiting most of its original buildings and machinery. Exploring the remnants of this recently de-

funct industry, you'll gain an appreciation for the simple, noble life of miners. Even if you're not into heavy metal, this unique look at

Since miners had to buy their own candles (from the company store, of course), they'd extinguish them during their pitch-black lunch break to make them last longer.

After working all morning underground, Cornish tin miners looked forward to their traditional lunch of a **pasty** (PASS-tee). Basically a beef stew wrapped in a pastry crust, pasties had a thick, crimped edge that miners could grab with dirty hands without contaminating their food. Because real flour was expensive, early miners skimped by using barley wheat—making for a very tough package. Leftover chunks of dough were often dropped into the mineshaft to appease the Tommyknockers.

Originally a pasty would be filled half with stew, and the rest with dessert, such as jam or apples. Nowadays there's a nice variety of flavors, like lamb and mint, but the full-meal deal is rare. The British government recently won trademark protection from the European Union for the Cornish pasty. That means the term "Cornish pasty" can only be applied to those pasties made in Cornwall using traditional techniques and recipes (www.cornish-pastyassociation.co.uk). Look for pasties all over Cornwall (and, increasingly, throughout Britain). One of the best places is McFadden and Sons Butchers in St. Just, near Geevor Tin Mine (see page 396).

Other than savory pasties, the crumbling smokestacks that dot the landscape today are the only remnants of Cornwall's now-dead tin-mining industry, which couldn't compete with cheap tin from Asia and South America. The ground underfoot is still honeycombed with forgotten tin mines. Older Cornish natives can still remember being in their houses and hearing the miners working underground.

tin-mining is fascinating—and worth ▲▲▲ to those interested in engineering.

Cost and Hours: £10.50, Sun-Fri 9:00-17:00, until 16:00 Nov-Easter, closed Sat year-round, last entry one hour before closing; self-guided "free flow" visits in summer, guided tours go 3/day in winter—call or check online for exact times; wear good shoes, pick up free map at entry, café, tel. 01736/788-662, www.geevor.com.

Getting There: It's just off the B-3306 road along the north coast of Penwith. Or, if you're driving in from the A-30 Penzance bypass, take A-3071 to St. Just and follow the brown *Historic Mining Area* signs. Take the right fork on B-3318 to Pendeen, turn left at the crossroads to drive through Pendeen, and turn right at the Geevor entrance. You can also get here on buses #10A and #300 from Penzance, or #300 from St. Ives and Land's End (ask your driver about buying a combo-ticket for bus plus mine entry).

Visiting the Mine: Put on your hard hat and wander through the entrance building, keeping an eye out for a giant model that once helped engineers keep track of the network of shafts—making it clear how extensive the mining industry was here. Then head outside, where you'll walk from shed to shed to see the various parts of the day-to-day workings of the mine.

The modern, well-presented **Hard Rock Museum** features exhibits for all ages about mining and the rocks that harbor valuable ores. On the ground floor, you'll find an extensive exhibit about geology (including a 220-pound chunk of tin-embedded stone), display cases with items the miners took down into the shafts with them, and a very loud simulation of what it was like inside the mine shafts (press the button for sound effects). The *Geevor Voices* film (about 20 minutes) uses interviews and news clips to tell the story of the mine's operation, closure, and conversion to a museum. Upstairs are hands-on exhibits about the tin-making process, and a timeline of the mine's history.

The most interesting area is **"The Dry,"** where the miners showered, changed, and dried their uniforms between shifts. Though it closed almost two decades ago, it feels as though the miners could show up at any time to clock in. Enjoy the old time-punch clock, the fun stickers on the miners' lockers, and graffiti showing their sense of humor (such as the *Ear Protection Must Be Worn* sign posted next to the toilets).

In **"The Mill,"** you'll see how a vast warehouse of "shaking tables"—like giant machines panning for gold—separated the miners' haul into its useable parts.

The finale is a 30- to 40-minute **underground tour** of an 18th-century mine (which predates the more recent mine that the current buildings supported, and was discovered by modern miners). A docent, often a former mine employee, gives you a coverall and leads you in. The mines—narrow and low (you'll be hunched for most of the tour, and claustrophobes will be miserable)—give you a sense of the difficult life of miners and the perilous conditions under which they worked. During very busy times in summer, you'll explore this area at your own pace, as docents posted throughout answer questions.

Eating near the Mine: You can get hot, authentic, delicious Cornish pasties on the main square of the humble town of St. Just, at **McFadden and Sons Butchers** (£2.50-4, Mon-Sat 8:00-17:00, closed Sun, 11 Market Square, tel. 01736/788-136). For more on pasties, see the sidebar.

Isles of Scilly

Just off the coast of Cornwall, this group of islands (pronounced "silly") sits right in the path of the Gulf Stream. The warm (or at least warmer) climate is perfect for growing a wide variety of exotic plants, so the islands boast plenty of gardens to visit. While enjoyable, the excursion takes the better part of a day.

Getting There: There are two ways to reach the island: a very slow **boat** called the *Scillonian III* from Penzance (£35 same-day round-trip, £38 one-way, £75 round-trip, 2.75 hours each way, sporadic schedule but generally departs Mon-Sat at 9:15 in summer from the Penzance Quay/Lighthouse Pier, no boats Nov-March, tel. 0845-710-5555, www.ios-travel.co.uk); or a **plane** from the Land's End airport (£100 same-day round-trip, £70 one-way, £140 round-trip, 15-minute flight). As the boat trip to the islands can be quite rough (fighting against the tide), consider flying over and sailing back (this "Air & Sea Day Trip" costs £80 for a same-day round-trip).

East Cornwall

These destinations are a bit farther from Penzance, and closer to Dartmoor National Park (see previous chapter). I've listed them from farthest to nearest to Penzance. Consider visiting them in this order as you approach the tip of Cornwall.

▲▲Tintagel Castle

Wild, rocky, remote, and romantic, Tintagel (tin-TAD-jell) is as dramatic as a castle can be. The real King Arthur—if he actually

existed—was supposedly born here and ruled his lands from this rocky point. While the popular tales of Camelot are flights of fantasy, they may be based on a real person. Even though there's no physical record of King Arthur (other than a pottery shard discovered in the 1990s), the verbal tradition is strong enough that experts think a fifth- or sixth-century ruler by that name probably lived in this area, possibly basing himself in modern Camelford (which might be where "Camelot" comes from). Regardless of whether Arthur is fact or fiction, windblown Tintagel Castle is striking. If you can handle lots of steep hiking up and down, this is one of England's most rewarding ruined-castle experiences. And as a bonus, you get to enjoy a spectacularly scenic stretch of Cornish coastline. Bring a picnic to have lunch with a view, or eat at the on-site café.

Cost and Hours: £6; April-Sept daily 10:00-18:00, Oct daily 10:00-17:00; Nov-March Sat-Sun 10:00-16:00, closed Mon-Fri.

Information: When you buy your ticket, pick up the brochure with a map, which is keyed to numbered plaques around the site. (I've used the same numbers in my self-guided tour, below). For the full story, invest in the £4.50 illustrated guidebook. Tel. 01840/770-328, www.english-heritage.org.uk.

Getting There: The castle clings to the coast below the tacky town of Tintagel. If you're arriving by car, look for *Tintagel* signs from A-39 as it passes through Camelford. Once you enter the village of Tintagel, take your pick of pay parking lots (most charge around £1.50-2). Walk along the main street following brown castle signs, then hike down the steep road to the castle's ticket office, at the rocky bay. Or, if you prefer, take the Land Rover shuttle (£2 each way, runs continuously April-Oct between the top of the trail and the ticket office down at sea level). By public transportation from Penzance, it's a three- to four-hour journey, involving one or more transfers (for specifics, call 0871-200-2233, or use the journey planner at www.travelinesw.com). For bus info, contact National Express (tel. 0871-781-8178, www.nationalexpress.com) or Western Greyhound (tel. 01637/871-871, www.westerngreyhound.com).

➋ Self-Guided Tour: The main part of the castle is on what's called The Island (actually a rocky peninsula attached by a narrow spit; take care on the 100-plus steps); nearby, on the mainland, is a separate section called the Mainland Courtyard. Here are the highlights:

After buying your ticket at the main entrance, watch the seven-minute **film** called *Searching for Arthur,* which considers the historical and legendary underpinnings of this evocative site.

Next, head up to the viewpoint overlooking the cove. As you approach the bridge, look to the right for the holes in the cliff below the ruins. One of these is supposedly **Merlin's cave.** (If the tide is out, you can climb down to explore the famous wizard's former home...and ponder how he managed to keep the carpet dry and prevent seals from climbing on the furniture.)

Now look up to the top of the giant chunk of rock on your left. Appreciate the naturally fortified, easily defensible position of this rock-top castle. Note the narrow and difficult approach to this hunk of land (which was once tethered by a bridge to the mainland), and you can understand why Tintagel—meaning "fortress with narrow entrance"—is aptly named.

Head up the steps, show your ticket, and cross the footbridge, then tackle the very steep climb up to the top of the cliffs, or **The Island.**

As you enter through the Victorian-era back door, you reach

the **Island Courtyard**—castle remnants dating from the Middle Ages (marked *4*). Rather than belonging to Arthur (who would have lived centuries earlier), these structures were built for the brother of a 13th-century king. Notice that the walls are made of stacked sheets of slate, which was mined on this site for many years.

Continue through another evocative doorway, proceed straight along the cliff, and hike up to the viewpoint platform (marked *17*). All around you—including directly below—you'll see the foundations of ruined **Dark Age houses,** which actually date from around the time when Arthur most likely lived (the fifth century A.D.). Here archaeologists have found remains of items from as far away as North Africa and the Eastern Mediterranean—evidence of the wealth and status of this castle's owner. Notice that the farther you get out on the rock, the older the ruins are—Victorian, medieval, Dark Ages.

Climb on up to the top of The Island. While there are precious few ruins to see up here, the 360-degree views are spectacular. Circling around the site, you'll come across several interesting features: In the walled area straight ahead of where you summited the rock—called the **garden** (marked *7*)—medieval residents could relax and entertain visitors in the summer. Just beyond that, the **well** (marked *10*) was the source of water in the Middle Ages, and remains today's last resort in case of fire. The 11th-century **chapel** (marked *12*) is recognizable for the altar at its far end. If you have time, linger up here. The craggy peaks across the tops of the cliffs make a perfect, windblown picnic spot.

After the chapel, you'll head back down the steep steps to the footbridge. From here, for extra credit, consider hiking up the steps across the bridge to the **Mainland Courtyard,** with more medieval remains. If you decide to climb up, you can take a much less steep path behind this courtyard back down to rejoin the main path up the valley.

Villages Just West of Tintagel

If you have some time between the Penwith Peninsula and Tintagel, consider stopping at one or both of these seafront villages.

Padstow

A little Cornish fishing port with a big culinary reputation, Padstow is the home of Michelin-starred chef Rick Stein and several of his fish restaurants. Although largely unknown stateside, this celebrity chef (who has hosted several cooking and travel series for BBC television) is very famous in Britain, and has singlehandedly upped the culinary standards of Cornwall (spawning copycats eager to please foodies who pilgrimage here to dine at Stein's). Some people even call the town "Padstein."

Getting There: Padstow sits on a large estuary about 45 miles northeast of Penzance (roughly on the way to Tintagel Castle). From the main A-30 road, exit at A-39 and follow *Padstow* signs for 12 miles (turning off onto B-3274 about halfway there; total trip from A-30 is about 20 minutes one-way). Entering town, follow *P* signs to the large pay lot along the wharf, a short walk from the harbor and town center.

Visiting Padstow: Ideal for a lunchtime stopover, Padstow is still a working seaport, where local fisherman can sometimes be seen bringing in their daily catch. Tourists now browse the art galleries and enjoy their ice-cream cones, but the town has managed to retain a little of its gritty charm—particularly in the streets behind the harborfront.

Rick Stein's simply named **Seafood Restaurant,** the flagship of his culinary empire, may be worth planning a meal around for curious foodies—but be sure to reserve ahead (£39 three-course lunch, £13-18 starters, £25-45 main courses, daily 12:00-14:30 & 18:30-22:00, between the parking lot and the harbor, tel. 01841-532-700; for details on his eateries and accommodations, see www.rickstein.com).

There's more action along the wharf (near the parking lot), where a large building contains three different, less upscale Rick Stein **eateries:** a fishmonger, a deli (with an antipasti counter, pasties, and pricey picnic fixin's), and expensive but very tasty fish-and-chips (if there's a long line for a table, look for the separate door for takeaway; £8 carry-out, £10 eat-in). Nearby, at the west end of the wharf, is the tourable **National Lobster Hatchery** (www.national-lobsterhatchery.co.uk).

Port Isaac

A pleasantly workaday fishing village tucked in a deep gash of rock just down the coast from Tintagel, Port Isaac offers a good look at the authentic, untouristy Cornwall...only slightly trampled by *Doc Martin* pilgrims. The popular British television series that's set and filmed here has put this otherwise sleepy town on the map. Driving in from the A-389 highway, follow blue *P* signs to the triple-tiered pay parking lot with grand Atlantic Ocean panoramas (including distant views of Tintagel). Then hike back along the main road and climb steeply down into town, pausing periodically to enjoy the views of the deep gorge that protects the town's harbor. On the way into town, you'll pass *Doc Martin*'s old schoolhouse, now cleverly converted into a pub and hotel. (The small cottage where the good doctor resides is across the harbor from the schoolhouse.) Notice how boats are tethered by extremely long lines to the harbor; thanks to the dramatic tides, they're forced to gently beach themselves on sandbars at low tide.

▲The Eden Project

Set in an abandoned china-clay mine, the Eden Project is an ambitious and futuristic work-in-progress—a theme park of global gardening with an environmental conscience.

Exotic plants from all over the world are showcased in two giant biomes, reputedly the largest greenhouses in the world. The displays focus on sustainable farming and eco-conscious planting, but the most interesting thing here is the sheer audacity of the idea. If you're looking for a quaint English cottage garden, this isn't it. Rather than a flowery look at England's past, this "global garden" gives you a sense of how the shrinking of the world will affect us in the future.

Cost and Hours: £23.50, discounts for booking online or arriving by public transport, daily April-Oct 9:00-18:00, Nov-March 10:00-16:30, last entry 1.5 hours before closing, domes can close as early as 15:00 for private events and off-season—check online or call first to confirm closing time, cafés, tel. 01726/811-911, www.edenproject.com.

Crowd Alert: The Eden Project is popular and can be crowded, especially on rainy days and weekdays June-Aug (they told me "wet Wednesdays" are the worst). During peak-of-peak times, you may have to wait up to an hour to get in. To avoid this, consider arriving after 13:00.

Getting There: Drivers will find the Eden Project well-signposted from both A-30 and A-39—you'll be directed to A-391, and follow signs from there. Park at one of the many outlying lots, note your parking lot's fruity symbol, then walk down into the Project (or take the free park-and-ride shuttle bus). By public transit, first take the train to St. Austell, where you'll meet bus #101 (hourly, tel. 0871-200-2233 or 0845-600-1420, www.firstgroup.com). You can also take bus #527 but you'll need to walk a few minutes to the bus stop (see www.travelinesw.com for details; hourly, tel. 01637/871-871, www.westerngreyhound.com). Buses meet most arriving trains for the 20- to 30-minute run to the complex.

Visiting the Eden Project: After buying your ticket, zigzag down into the pit and work your way through the various exhibits, including the enormous, hot, and hazy Rainforest Biome (where my camera completely fogged up; you can seek relief in an air-conditioned hut about halfway through); the smaller and more arid Mediterranean Biome; an eatery-filled walkway connecting them called The Link; The Core, with educational exhibits; and lots of gardens. A land train and an elevator from The Core make it easier to get back up to the visitors center when you're done.

CORNWALL

Kid-oriented programs, rock and pop concerts, and other special events run throughout the year.

It's an impressive concept, and the biomes are striking. But the educational exhibits are a bit too conceptual to be effective—leaving the whole, expensive experience feeling somehow un-moored.

Gardens near Falmouth

Cornwall has many wonderful gardens, some with subtropical varieties of plants that thrive in this mild climate (www.greatgardensofcornwall.co.uk). These two gardens are a few miles apart on the same backcountry road, just south of Falmouth.

Getting There: If you're driving, take A-39 or A-394 into Falmouth until you see brown-and-white *Garden* signs—track these closely for four miles through the countryside to the gardens (Glendurgan is the better-signed of the two). If you're without a car, take buses #500 or #35 from Falmouth toward Helston (15-30 minutes, Traveline tel. 0871-200-2233, www.travelinesw.com).

Sleeping near the Gardens: To maximize your time exploring the gardens, consider spending the night in salty Falmouth, a tidy harbor town nestled near the Tudor fortress of Pendennis Castle. **$$$ Greenbank Hotel** is right on the water with a seagull-eye's view of the many boats moored in the Fal Estuary. Look near the hotel lobby for displays about Kenneth Grahame, who wrote parts of *The Wind in the Willows* while staying here ("classic" Db-£145-185, pricier view rooms and suites also available, check for online deals, guest computer, free Wi-Fi, Harbourside, tel. 01326/312-440, www.greenbank-hotel.co.uk, reception@greenbank-hotel.co.uk).

▲Trebah Garden

The "Garden of Dreams" at Trebah (TREE-bah) is a lush and tropical spectacle. Set on 26 acres that bunny-hop down a ravine to the beach below, this tropical garden is an unexpected treat. While most of England suffers from chilly arctic air, the Cornish peninsula is bathed in warmer air from the Gulf Stream—making average temperatures here much milder (the sea here never drops below 50 degrees Fahrenheit). Palms, succulents, bamboo, large azaleas, giant rhubarbs, and the pre-historic-looking gunnera might make you  think (or wish) that you're in the tropics rather than in Cornwall. The garden's exoticism impresses even non-gardeners. While garden lovers wander in ecstasy, history buffs can ponder the fact that the beach below was used by some US troops in World War II to launch the D-Day attack on Omaha Beach.

Cost and Hours: £8.50 March-Oct, £4 Nov-Feb, show bus ticket for 50 percent discount, open daily 10:00-18:30, until dusk in winter, last entry two hours before closing, colorful year-round but flowers are best late March and April, café, tel. 01326/252-200, www.trebahgarden.co.uk.

Glendurgan Garden

Just up the road from Trebah, Glendurgan has a smaller collection of tropical plants mingled with more traditional English garden fare. Similarly set in a broad basin angled to the sea, Glendurgan is bigger but less striking than its neighbor. However, it comes with an extensive, kid-friendly hedge maze (about waist-high—but still entertaining—for an adult), built by the former owner to amuse his 12 children. Gardeners may appreciate its good orchids and its small "Holy Bank" of biblical-themed plants. And down at the seashore, the fishing hamlet of Durgan makes it feel less like just an overblown backyard for aristocrats.

Cost and Hours: £6.80, worthwhile £3.50 map/guide, mid-Feb-Oct Tue-Sun 10:30-17:30, closed Mon except in Aug, closed Nov-mid-Feb, last entry 30 minutes before closing, best in spring, café, tel. 01326/250-906 or 01326/252-020, www.nationaltrust.org.uk.

BATH

The best city to visit within easy striking distance of London is Bath—just a 1.5-hour train ride away. Two hundred years ago, this city of 85,000 was the trendsetting Hollywood of Britain. If ever a city enjoyed looking in the mirror, Bath's the one. It has more "government-listed" or protected historic buildings per capita than any other town in England. The entire city, built of the creamy warm-tone limestone called "Bath stone," beams in its cover-girl complexion. An architectural chorus line, it's a triumph of the Neoclassical style of the Georgian era—named for the four Georges who sat as England's kings from 1714 to 1830. Proud locals remind visitors that the town is routinely banned from the "Britain in Bloom" contest to give other towns a chance to win. Bath's narcissism is justified. Even with its mobs of tourists (2 million per year) and greedy prices, Bath is a joy to visit.

Bath's fame began with the allure of its (supposedly) healing hot springs. Long before the Romans arrived in the first century, Bath was known for its warm waters. Romans named the popular spa town Aquae Sulis, after a local Celtic goddess. The town's importance carried through Saxon times, when it had a huge church on the site of the present-day abbey and was considered the religious capital of Britain. Its influence peaked in 973 with King Edgar's sumptuous coronation in the abbey. Later, Bath prospered as a wool town.

Bath then declined until the mid-1600s, wasting away to just a huddle of huts around the abbey, with hot, smelly mud and 3,000 residents, oblivious to the Roman ruins 18 feet below their dirt floors. In fact, with its own walls built upon ancient ones, Bath was no bigger than that Roman town. Then, in 1687, Queen Mary, fighting infertility, bathed here. Within 10 months, she gave birth to a son...and a new age of popularity for Bath.

The revitalized town boomed as a spa resort. Ninety percent of the buildings you'll see today are from the 18th century. The classical revivalism of Italian architect Andrea Palladio inspired a local father-and-son team—both named John Wood (the Elder and the Younger)—to build a "new Rome." The town bloomed in the Neoclassical style, and streets were lined not with scrawny sidewalks but with wide "parades," upon which women in their stylishly wide dresses could spread their fashionable tails.

Beau Nash (1673-1762) was Bath's "master of ceremonies." He organized the daily social regimen of aristocratic visitors, and he made the city more appealing by lighting the streets, improving security, banning swords, and opening the Pump Room. Under his fashionable baton, Bath became a city of balls, gaming, and concerts—the place to see and be seen in England. This most civilized place became even more so with the great Neoclassical building spree that followed.

These days, modern tourism has stoked the local economy, as has the fast morning train to London. (A growing number of Bath-based professionals catch the 7:13 train to Paddington Station every morning.) With renewed access to Bath's soothing hot springs at the Thermae Bath Spa, the venerable waters are in the spotlight again, attracting a new generation of visitors in need of a cure or a soak.

Planning Your Time

Bath deserves two nights even on a quick trip. On a three-week England getaway, spend three nights in Bath, with one day for the city and one day for side-trips (see next chapter). Ideally, use Bath as your jet-lag recovery pillow, and do London at the end of your trip.

Consider starting your English vacation this way:

Day 1: Land at Heathrow. Connect to Bath either by train via London Paddington, direct bus, or bus/train combination via Reading (for details, see page 212). You can also consider flying into Bristol. While you don't need or want a car in Bath, those who land early and pick up their cars at the airport can visit Windsor Castle (near Heathrow) and/or Stonehenge on their way to Bath. If you have the evening free in Bath, take a walking tour.

Day 2: 9:00—Tour the Roman Baths; 10:30—Catch the free city walking tour; 12:30—Picnic on the open deck of a tour bus; 14:00—Free time in the shopping center of old Bath; 15:30—Tour the Fashion Museum or Museum of Bath at Work. At night, consider seeing a play, take the evening walking tour (unless you did last night), enjoy the Bizarre Bath comedy walk, consider seeing a play, or go for an evening soak in the Thermae Bath Spa.

Day 3 (and possibly 4): By car, explore nearby sights. Without a car, consider a one-day Avebury/Stonehenge/cute towns minibus tour from Bath (Mad Max tours are best; see "Tours in Bath," later).

Orientation to Bath

Bath's town square, three blocks in front of the bus and train station, is a cluster of tourist landmarks, including the abbey, Roman and Medieval Baths, and the Pump Room. Bath is hilly. In general, you'll gain elevation as you head north from the town center.

Tourist Information

The TI is in the abbey churchyard (Mon-Sat 9:30-17:30, Sun 10:00-16:00, pricey toll tel. 0906-711-2000—50p/minute, www.visitbath.co.uk). The TI sells various visitor guides and maps—survey your options before buying one (£1-1.50). The TI also books rooms with no extra fee (booking tel. 0844-847-5256). If you're a Jane Austen fan, ask about the walking tours that leave from the abbey churchyard on weekends. Entertainment listings from the local paper are posted on the bulletin board.

Arrival in Bath

The Bath Spa **train station** has a staffed ticket desk, ticket machines, and a privately run travel agency masquerading as a TI. Directly in front of the train station is the SouthGate Bath shopping center. To get from the train station to the TI, exit straight ahead and continue up Manvers Street for about five minutes, then turn left at the triangular "square" overlooking the riverfront park, following the small TI arrow on a signpost. The **bus station** is immediately west of the train station, along Dorchester Street.

Helpful Hints

Festivals: The **Bath Literature Festival** is an open book in early March (www.bathlitfest.org.uk). The **Bath International Music Festival** bursts into song in late May (classical, folk, jazz, contemporary; www.bathmusicfest.org.uk), overlapped by the eclectic **Bath Fringe Festival** (theater, walks, talks, bus trips; generally similar dates to the Music Festival, www.bathfringe.co.uk). The **Jane Austen Festival** unfolds genteelly in late September (www.janeausten.co.uk/festivalhome). And for three weeks in December, the squares around the abbey are filled with a **Christmas market.**

Bath's festival **box office** sells tickets for most events (but not for those at the Theatre Royal), and can tell you exactly what's on tonight (housed inside the TI, tel. 01225/463-362, www.bathfestivals.org.uk). The city's weekly paper, the *Bath Chronicle*, publishes a "What's On" events listing each Thursday (www.thisisbath.com).

Internet Access: Plenty of cafés offer free Wi-Fi (as do most of my recommended hotels and B&Bs). You can also get online at the Bath **library** (£1.20/20 minutes, Mon 9:30-18:00, Tue-Thu 9:30-19:00, Fri-Sat 9:30-17:00, Sun 13:00-16:00, 19 Northgate Street near Pulteney Bridge, tel. 01225/394-041, www.bathnes.gov.uk).

Bookstore: Topping & Company, an inviting bookshop, has posters in its windows advertising frequent author readings, free coffee and tea for browsers, a good selection of maps, and tables filled with tidy stacks of carefully selected volumes, including lots of books on Bath and this region (daily 9:00-20:00, near the bottom of the street called "The Paragon"—where it meets George Street, tel. 01225/428-111, www.toppingbooks.co.uk).

Laundry: The **Spruce Goose Launderette** is between the Circus and the Royal Crescent, on the pedestrian lane called Margaret's Buildings. Bring lots of £1 coins for washing and £0.20 coins for drying, as there are no change machines (self-service: about £4-5/load, daily 8:00-20:00, last load at 19:30; full-service: £13.50/load, Mon and Wed-Fri 8:00-12:00 only; tel. 01225/483-309). **Speedy Wash** can pick up your laundry anywhere in town on weekdays before 11:00 for same-day service (£12/small bag, Mon-Fri 7:30-17:30, Sat 8:30-13:00 but no pickup, closed Sun, no self-service, most hotels work with them, 4 Mile End, London Road, tel. 01225/427-616).

Car Rental: Enterprise provides a pickup service for customers to and from their hotels (extra fee for one-way rentals, at Lower Bristol Road outside Bath, tel. 01225/443-311, www.enterprise.com). Others include **Thrifty** (pickup service and one-way rentals available, in the Burnett Business Park in Keynsham—between Bath and Bristol, tel. 01179/867-997, www.thrifty.co.uk), **Hertz** (one-way rentals possible, at Windsor Bridge, tel. 0843-309-3004, www.hertz.co.uk), and **National/Europcar** (one-way rentals available, £7 by taxi from the train station, at Brassmill Lane—go west on Upper Bristol Road, tel. 0871-384-9985, www.europcar.co.uk). Skip **Avis**—it's a mile from the Bristol train station; you'd need to rent a car to get there. Most offices close Saturday afternoon and all day

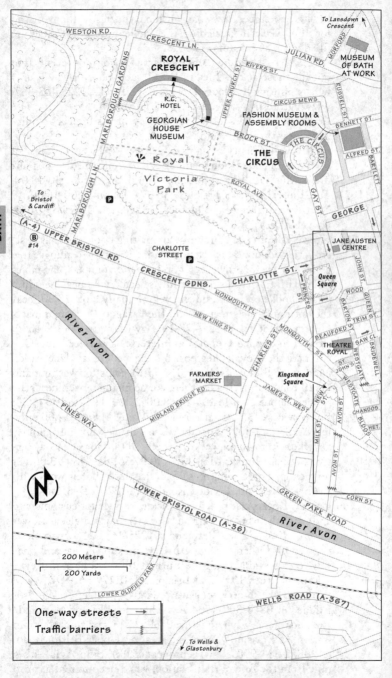

BATH

To Lansdown Crescent

WESTON RD.

CRESCENT LN.

JULIAN RD.

MUSEUM OF BATH AT WORK

ROYAL CRESCENT

R.C. HOTEL

GEORGIAN HOUSE MUSEUM

RIVERS ST.

CIRCUS MEWS

FASHION MUSEUM & ASSEMBLY ROOMS

BROCK ST.

THE CIRCUS

BENNETT ST.

ALFRED ST.

BARTLETT

Royal

Victoria Park

ROYAL AVE.

GAY ST.

GEORGE

To Bristol & Cardiff

(A-4)

B #14

UPPER BRISTOL RD.

CHARLOTTE STREET

CHARLOTTE ST.

CRESCENT GDNS.

MONMOUTH PL.

NEW KING ST.

CHARLES ST.

MONMOUTH ST.

PRINCES

JANE AUSTEN CENTRE

Queen Square

JOHN ST.

WOOD ST.

QUEEN ST.

BARTON ST.

TRIM ST.

BEAUFORD SQ.

SAW CL.

ST. JOHN'S ST.

BRIDEWELL

WESTGATE

THEATRE ROYAL

Kingsmead Square

JAMES ST. WEST

NEW ST.

MILK ST.

AVON ST.

WESTGATE BLDGS.

CHANDOS

HET.

CORN ST.

FARMERS' MARKET

River Avon

PINES WAY

MIDLAND BRIDGE RD.

N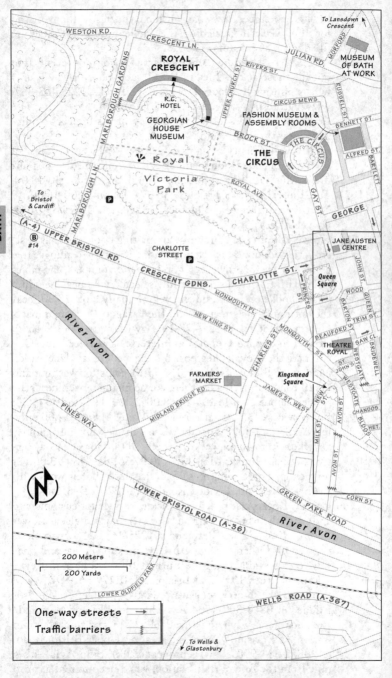

LOWER BRISTOL ROAD (A-36)

River Avon

GREEN PARK ROAD

200 Meters

200 Yards

LOWER OLDFIELD PARK

WELLS ROAD (A-367)

One-way streets →

Traffic barriers

To Wells & Glastonbury

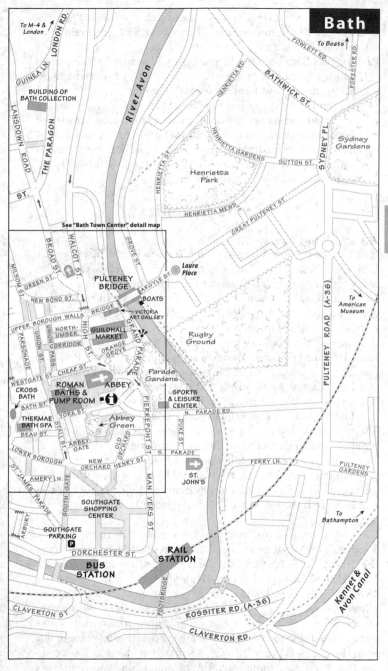

Bath

To M-4 & London

LONDON RD.

GUINEA LN.

LANSDOWN ROAD

THE PARAGON

ST.

BUILDING OF BATH COLLECTION

River Avon

POWLETT RD.

To Boats

BATHWICK ST.

HENRIETTA RD.

FORESTER RD.

SYDNEY PL.

Sydney Gardens

HENRIETTA GARDENS

SUTTON ST.

HENRIETTA ST.

Henrietta Park

HENRIETTA MEWS

GREAT PULTENEY ST.

See "Bath Town Center" detail map

BROAD ST.

WALCOT ST.

GROVE ST.

MILSOM ST.

GREEN ST.

NEW BOND ST.

UPPER BOROUGH WALLS

PARSONAGE

UNION ST.

NORTH-UMBER CORRIDOR

HIGH ST.

BRIDGE

PULTENEY BRIDGE

BOATS

ARGYLE ST.

Laura Place

VICTORIA ART GALLERY

GUILDHALL MARKET

GRAND PARADE

ORANGE GROVE

Rugby Ground

WESTGATE ST.

CHEAP ST.

Parade Gardens

ROMAN BATHS & PUMP ROOM

CROSS BATH

ABBEY

BATH ST.

THERMAE BATH SPA

BEAU ST.

YORK ST.

STALL ST.

Abbey Green

ABBEY GATE

PIERREPONT ST.

SPORTS & LEISURE CENTER

N. PARADE RD.

DUKE ST.

S. PARADE

PULTENEY ROAD (A-36)

To American Museum

PULTENEY GARDENS

LOWER BOROUGH

ST. JAMES PARADE

OLD ORCHARD

NEW ORCHARD

HENRY ST.

AMERY LN.

MAN VERS ST.

ST. JOHN'S

FERRY LN.

To Bathampton

SOUTHGATE SHOPPING CENTER

SOUTH GATE

SOUTHGATE PARKING

ARKBURY

DORCHESTER ST.

RAIL STATION

BUS STATION

FOOTBRIDGE

CLAVERTON ST.

ROSSITER RD. (A-36)

CLAVERTON RD.

Kennet & Avon Canal

BATH

Sunday, which complicates weekend pickups. Ideally, take the train or bus from downtown London to Bath, and rent a car as you leave Bath.

Parking: As Bath becomes increasingly pedestrian-friendly, street parking in the city center is disappearing. Most short-term lots fill up fast (£1.60/hour, 2-4-hour maximum). You'll pay less per hour in long-stay lots. The SouthGate Bath shopping center lot on the corner of Southgate and Dorchester streets is a five-minute walk from the abbey (£4.30/up to 3 hours, £13/24 hours, cash or credit card, open 24/7); the Charlotte Street car park is also handy. For more info on parking, visit the "Travel and Maps" section of http://visitbath.co.uk.

Tours in Bath

▲▲▲Walking Tours

Free two-hour tours are led by **The Mayor's Corps of Honorary Guides,** volunteers who want to share their love of Bath with its many visitors (as the city's mayor first did when he took a group on a guided walk back in the 1930s). These chatty, historical, and gossip-filled walks are essential for your understanding of this town's amazing Georgian social scene. How else would you learn that the old "chair ho" call for your sedan chair evolved into today's "cheerio" farewell? Tours leave from outside the Pump Room in the abbey churchyard (free, no tips, year-round Sun-Fri at 10:30 and 14:00, Sat at 10:30 only; additional evening walks May-Sept Tue and Thu at 19:00; tel. 01225/477-411, www.bathguides.org.uk). Tip for theatergoers: When your guide stops to talk outside the Theatre Royal, skip out for a moment, pop into the box office, and see about snaring a great deal on a play for tonight.

For a **private tour,** call the local guides' bureau, Bath Parade Guides (£85/2 hours, tel. 01225/337-111, www.bathparade-guides.co.uk, bathparadeguides@yahoo.com). For **Ghost Walks** and **Bizarre Bath** tours, see "Nightlife in Bath," later.

▲▲City Bus Tours

City Sightseeing's hop-on, hop-off bus tours zip through Bath. Jump on a bus anytime at one of 17 signposted pickup points, pay the driver, climb upstairs, and hear recorded commentary about Bath. City Sightseeing has two 45-minute routes: a city tour and a "Skyline" route outside town. Try to get one with a live guide (usually at :15 and :45 past the hour for the city tour, and on the hour for the Skyline route); otherwise, bring your own earbuds if you've got 'em (the audio recording on the other buses is barely intelligible with the headsets provided). On a sunny day, this is a multitasking tourist's dream come true: You can munch a sandwich, work on a tan, snap great photos, and learn a lot, all at the same time.

Save money by doing the bus tour first—ticket stubs get you minor discounts at many sights (£13, ticket valid for 24 hours and both tour routes, generally 4/hour daily in summer 9:30-18:30, in winter 10:00-15:00, tel. 01225/330-444, www.city-sightseeing.com).

Taxi Tours
Local taxis, driven by good talkers, go where big buses can't. A group of up to four can rent a cab for an hour (about £40; try to negotiate) and enjoy a fine, informative, and—with the right cabbie—entertaining private joyride. It's probably cheaper to let the meter run than to pay for an hourly rate, but ask the cabbie for advice.

To Stonehenge, Avebury, and the Cotswolds
Bath is a good launchpad for visiting Wells, Avebury, Stonehenge, and more.

Mad Max Minibus Tours
Operating daily from Bath, Maddy offers thoughtfully organized, informative tours run with entertaining guides and limited to 16 people per group. Book ahead—as far ahead as possible in summer—for these popular tours. The **Stone Circles and Villages** full-day tour covers 110 miles and visits Stonehenge, the Avebury Stone Circles, photogenic Lacock (LAY-cock)—featured in parts of the BBC's *Pride and Prejudice* and the Harry Potter movies—and Castle Combe, the southernmost Cotswold village (£35 plus Stonehenge entry fee, tours depart daily at 8:45 and return at 16:30, arrive 15 minutes early, leaves early to beat the Stonehenge hordes). Three days a week (Sun, Tue, Thu) Mad Max offers three-hour tours that skip Stonehenge: a **Villages** tour that includes Lacock and Castle Combe (£16, departs at 11:00) and an **Avebury Mini-Tour** (£16, departs at 14:00). If you combine these as a full-day tour (£30), you get a long lunch break in Lacock, with time to visit its abbey. Their full-day **Cotswold Explorer** tour visits Chipping Campden and other villages, and their full-day **Somerset Explorer** tour includes Wells, Glastonbury, and a rural farm (€35 each, April-Sept only; see website for departure times).

All tours depart from outside the Abbey Hotel on Terrace Walk in Bath, a one-minute walk from the abbey. Arrive 15 minutes before your departure time and bring cash (or book online with a credit card at least 48 hours in advance, 10 percent cash refund on second tour for Rick Steves readers who book two full-day tours; tel. 07990/505-970, phone answered daily 8:00-18:00, www.madmaxtours.co.uk, maddy@madmaxtours.co.uk). Please honor or cancel your seat reservation.

Lion Tours
This well-run outfit gets you to Stonehenge on a half-day tour: Their **Stonehenge and Lacock** tour leaves daily at 12:15 and returns at

Bath at a Glance

▲▲▲Walking Tours Free top-notch tours, helping you make the most of your visit, led by The Mayor's Corps of Honorary Guides. **Hours:** Sun-Fri at 10:30 and 14:00, Sat at 10:30 only; additional evening walks offered May-Sept Tue and Thu at 19:00. See page 412.

▲▲▲Roman and Medieval Baths Ancient baths that gave the city its name, tourable with good audioguide. **Hours:** Daily July-Aug 9:00-22:00, March-June and Sept-Oct 9:00-18:00, Nov-Feb 9:30-17:30 except Sat until 18:00. See page 416.

▲▲Bath Abbey 500-year-old Perpendicular Gothic church, graced with beautiful fan vaulting and stained glass. **Hours:** Mon-Sat 9:00-18:00 except Nov-March until 16:30, Sun 13:00-14:30 & 16:30-17:30. See page 420.

▲▲The Circus and the Royal Crescent Stately Georgian (Neo-classical) buildings from Bath's late-18th-century glory days. **Hours:** Always viewable. See page 422.

▲▲Georgian House at No. 1 Royal Crescent Just reopened after an extensive renovation, this is your best look at the interior of one of Bath's high-rent Georgian beauties. **Hours:** Mon 12:00-17:30, Tue-Sun 10:30-17:30. See page 423.

▲Pump Room Swanky Georgian hall, ideal for a spot of tea or a taste of unforgettably "healthy" spa water. **Hours:** Daily 9:30-12:00 for coffee and breakfast, 12:00-14:30 for lunch, 14:30-17:00 for afternoon tea (open 18:00-21:00 for dinner July-Aug and Christmas holidays only). See page 419.

17:15 (£20 plus Stonehenge entry). In summer this tour also leaves at 9:00 and returns at 13:30, and can be combined with their **Afternoon Villages** tour of Lacock, Biddestone and Castle Combe (£15, £12.50 with morning Stonehenge tour, departs at 13:45, returns at 16:45; runs Mon, Wed, Fri, and Sat). They also offer a **Stonehenge, Wells & Glastonbury** tour (info on website), and a full-day **Cotswold Discovery** tour with stops in Castle Combe, Bibury, Stow-on-the-Wold, Tetbury, the Coln Valley, and The Slaughters (£37.50; runs Sun, Tue, and Thu 8:45-17:30; arrive 15 minutes early). If you ask in advance, you can bring your luggage along and use this tour to get to Stow or, for £5 extra, Moreton-in-Marsh (easy train connections to Oxford and bus connections to Chipping Campden). Lion's tours depart from the same stop as Mad Max Tours—see earlier

▲**Pulteney Bridge and Parade Gardens** Shop-strewn bridge and relaxing riverside gardens. **Hours:** Bridge—always open; gardens—Easter-Sept daily 11:00-17:00, shorter hours off-season. See page 421.

▲**Victoria Art Gallery** Paintings from the late 17th century to today. **Hours:** Tue-Sat 10:00-17:00, Sun 13:30-17:00, closed Mon. See page 422

▲**Fashion Museum** 400 years of clothing under one roof, plus the opulent Assembly Rooms. **Hours:** Daily March-Oct 10:30-18:00, Nov-Feb 10:30-17:00. See page 423.

▲**Museum of Bath at Work** Gadget-ridden circa-1900 engineer's shop, foundry, factory, and office. **Hours:** April-Oct daily 10:30-17:00, Nov and Jan-March weekends only, closed in Dec. See page 424.

▲**American Museum** Insightful look primarily at colonial/early-American lifestyles, with 18 furnished rooms and eager-to-talk guides. **Hours:** Mid-March-Oct Tue-Sun 12:00-17:00, closed Mon except in Aug, closed Nov-mid-March. See page 426.

▲**Thermae Bath Spa** Relaxation center that put the bath back in Bath. **Hours:** Daily 9:00-21:30. See page 427.

Jane Austen Centre Exhibit on 19th-century Bath-based novelist, best for her fans. **Hours:** Mid-March-mid-Nov daily 9:45-17:30, July-Aug Thu-Sat until 19:00; mid-Nov-mid-March Sun-Fri 11:00-16:30, Sat 9:45-18:00. See page 425.

BATH

(mobile 07769-668-668, book online with a credit card, www.lion-tours.co.uk).

Other Tour Options

Scarper Tours runs a minibus tour to Stonehenge (£15, doesn't include £8 Stonehenge entry fee, departs from behind the abbey; daily mid-June-Aug at 9:00, 12:30, and 16:00; mid-March-mid-June and Sept-Oct at 10:00 and 14:00; Nov-mid-March at 13:00; tel. 07739/644-155, www.scarpertours.com). The three-hour tour (two hours there and back, an hour at the site) includes driver narration en route.

Celtic Horizons, run by retired teacher Alan Price, offers tours from Bath to a variety of destinations, such as Stonehenge, Avebury, and Wells. Alan can provide a convenient transfer service (to or from London, Heathrow, Bristol Airport, the Cotswolds, and so on), with or without a tour itinerary en route. Allow about £25/hour for a group (his comfortable minivans seat 4, 6, or 8 people) and £150 for Heathrow-Bath transfers (1-4 persons). It's best to make arrangements and get pricing information by email at alan@celtichorizons.com (cash only, tel. 01373/461-784, www. celtichorizons.com).

Sights in Bath

In the Town Center
▲▲▲Roman and Medieval Baths

In ancient Roman times, high society enjoyed the mineral springs at Bath. From Londinium—and throughout the empire—Romans traveled so often to Aquae Sulis, as the city was called, to "take a bath" that finally it became known simply as Bath. Today, a fine museum surrounds the ancient bath. With the help of a great audioguide, you'll wander past well-documented displays, Roman artifacts, a temple pediment with an evocative bearded face, a bronze head of the goddess Sulis Minerva, excavated ancient foundations, and the actual mouth of the spring. At the end, you'll have a chance to walk around the big pool itself, where Romans once lounged, splished, splashed, and thanked the gods for the gift of naturally hot water.

Cost and Hours: £13.50 (50p more July-Aug), includes audioguide, £18 combo-ticket includes Fashion Museum, family ticket available, daily July-Aug 9:00-22:00, March-June and Sept-Oct 9:00-18:00, Nov-Feb 9:30-17:30 except Sat until 18:00, last entry one hour before closing, tel. 01225/477-785, www.romanbaths.co.uk.

Crowd-Beating Tips: Long lines for tickets typically form on Saturdays and every day in the summer. You can avoid them by either getting your ticket online or, if you'll be visiting the Fashion Museum anyway, buying your combo-ticket there. With voucher or combo-ticket in hand, enter through the "fast track" lane, to the left of the general admission line. On any day, the least crowded time to visit is before 11:00; peak time is between 13:00 and 15:00. If you're here in July or August, the best time is after 19:00, when the baths are romantic, gas-lit, and all yours.

Tours: Take advantage of the included, essential **audioguide,** which makes your visit easy and informative. In addition to the basic commentary, look for posted numbers to key into your audioguide for specialty topics—including a kid-friendly tour and musings from

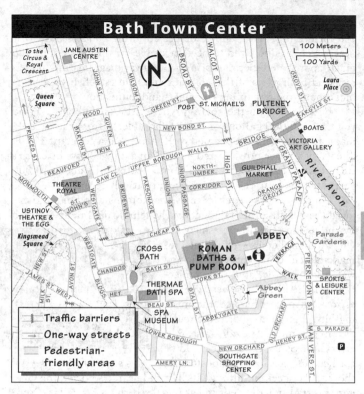

American expat writer Bill Bryson. For those with a big appetite for Roman history, in-depth **guided tours** leave from the end of the museum at the edge of the actual bath (included with ticket, on the hour, a poolside clock is set for the next departure time, 20-40 minutes depending on the guide). You can revisit the museum after the tour.

❷ Self-Guided Tour: Follow the one-way route through the bath and museum complex. This self-guided tour offers a basic overview; for more in-depth commentary, make ample use of the included audioguide.

Begin by walking around the upper **terrace,** overlooking the Great Bath. This terrace—lined with sculptures of VIRs (Very Important Romans)—evokes ancient times but was built in the 1890s. The ruins of the bath complex sat undisturbed for centuries before finally being excavated and turned into a museum in the late 19th century.

Head inside to the **museum,** where exhibits explain the dual purpose of the buildings that stood here in Roman times: a bath complex, for relaxation and for healing; and a temple dedicated to the goddess Sulis Minerva, who was believed to be responsible for the mysterious and much-appreciated thermal springs. Cut-away diagrams and models resurrect both parts of this complex and help establish your bearings among the remaining fragments and foundations.

Peer down into the **spring,** where little air bubbles remind you that 240,000 gallons of water a day emerge from the earth—magically, it must have seemed to Romans—at a constant 115°F. The water you see now, heated more than a mile below the earth's surface, first fell to earth as rain onto nearby hills about 10,000 years ago...making the Romans seem relatively recent.

Go downstairs to get to know the Romans who built and enjoyed these baths. The fragments of the **temple pediment**—carved by indigenous Celtic craftsmen but with Roman themes—represent a remarkable cultural synthesis. Sit and watch for a while, as a slide projection fills in historians' best guesses as to what once occupied the missing bits. The identity of the circular face in the middle puzzles researchers. (God? Santa Claus?) It could be

the head of the Gorgon monster after it was slain by Perseus—are those snakes peeking through its hair and beard? And yet, the Gorgon was traditionally depicted as female. Perhaps instead it's Neptune, the god of water—appropriate for this aquatic site.

The next exhibits examine the importance of Aquae Sulis (the settlement here) in antiquity. Much like the pilgrimage sites of the Middle Ages, this spot exerted a powerful pull on people from all over the realm, who were eager to partake in its healing waters and to worship at the religious site. You'll see some of the small but extremely heavy carved-stone tables that pilgrims hauled here as an offering to the gods.

As you walk through the temple's original foundations, keep an eye out for the sacrificial altar. The gilded-bronze head of the goddess **Sulis Minerva** (in the display case) once overlooked a flaming cauldron inside the temple, where only priests were allowed to enter. Similar to the Greek goddess

Athena, Sulis Minerva was considered to be a life-giving mother goddess. The next room displays some of the requests (inscribed on sheets of pewter or iron) that visitors made of the goddess. Take time to read some of these—many are comically spiteful and petty, offering a warts-and-all glimpse into day-to-day Roman culture.

Engineers enjoy a close-up look at the spring overflow and the original **drain system**—built two millennia ago—that still carries excess water to the River Avon. Marvel at the cleverness and durability of Roman engineering, created in (what we usually imagine to be) a "primitive" time. A nearby exhibit on pulleys and fasteners lets you play with these inventions.

Head outside to the **Great Bath** itself (where you can join one of the included guided tours—look for the clock with the next start time). Take a slow lap (by foot) around the perimeter, imagining the frolicking Romans who once immersed themselves up to their necks in this five-foot-deep pool. (On busy days, when costumed characters hang out by the bath, you may not have to imagine.) The water is greenish because of algae—don't drink it. The best views are from the west end, looking back toward the abbey. Nearby is a giant chunk of roof span, from a time when this was a cavernous covered swimming hall. At the corner, you'll step over a small canal where hot water still trickles into the main pool. Nearby, find a length of original lead pipe, remarkably well preserved since antiquity.

Symmetrical bath complexes branch off at opposite ends of the Great Bath (perhaps dating from a conservative period when the Romans maintained separate facilities for men and women). The **East Baths** show off changing rooms and various bathing rooms, each one designed for a special therapy or recreational purpose (immersion therapy tub, sauna-like heated floor, and so on), as described in detail by the audioguide.

When you're ready to leave, head for the **West Baths** (including a sweat bath and a *frigidarium*, or "cold plunge" pool) and take another look at the spring and more foundations. After returning your audioguide, pop over to the fountain for a free taste of the spa water. Then pass through the gift shop, past the convenient public WCs (which use plain old tap water), and exit through the **Pump Room**—or stay for a spot of tea.

▲Pump Room

For centuries, Bath was forgotten as a spa. Then, in 1687, the previously barren Queen Mary bathed here, became pregnant, and bore a male heir to the throne. A few years later, Queen Anne found the water eased her painful gout. Word of its wonder waters spread, and Bath earned its way back on the aristocratic map. High society soon turned the place into one big pleasure palace. The Pump Room, an elegant Georgian hall just above the Roman Baths, offers visitors their best chance to raise a pinky in Chippendale grandeur. Above the newspaper table and sedan chairs, a statue of Beau Nash himself sniffles down at you. Come for a light meal, or to try a famous (but forgettable) "Bath bun" with your spa water (the same water that's in the fountain at the end of the baths

tour; also free in the Pump Rooms if you present your ticket). The spa water is served by an appropriately-attired waiter, who will tell you the water is pumped up from nearly 100 yards deep and marinated in 43 wonderful minerals. Or for just the price of a coffee, drop in anytime—except during lunch—to enjoy live music and the atmosphere.

Cost and Hours: Daily 9:30-12:00 for coffee and £6-15 breakfast, 12:00-14:30 for £11-16 lunches, 14:30-17:00 for £18.50 traditional afternoon tea (last orders at 16:00), tea/coffee and pastries also available in the afternoons; open 18:00-21:00 for dinner July-Aug and Christmas holidays only; live music daily—string trio or piano, times vary; tel. 01225/444-477.

▲▲Bath Abbey

The town of Bath wasn't much in the Middle Ages, but an important church has stood on this spot since Anglo-Saxon times.

King Edgar I was crowned here in 973, when the church was much bigger (before the bishop packed up and moved to Wells). Dominating the town center, today's abbey—the last great medieval church of England—is 500 years old and a fine example of the Late Perpendicular Gothic style, with breezy fan vaulting and enough stained glass to earn it the nickname "Lantern of the West."

Cost and Hours: £2.50 suggested donation; Mon-Sat 9:00-18:00 except Nov-March until 16:30, Sun 13:00-14:30 & 16:30-17:30; handy flier narrates a self-guided 19-stop tour, schedule of events—including concerts, services, and evensong—posted on the door and online, tel. 01225/422-462, www.bathabbey.org.

Visiting the Abbey: The facade (c. 1500, but mostly restored) is interesting for some of its carvings. Look for the angels going down the ladder. The statue of Peter (to the left of the door) lost its head to mean iconoclasts; it was recarved out of Peter's once super-sized beard. Take a moment to appreciate the abbey's architecture from the Abbey Green square.

Going inside is worth the small suggested contribution. The glass, red-iron gas-powered lamps, and the heating grates on the floor are all remnants of the 19th century. The window behind the altar shows 52 scenes from the life of Christ. A window to the left of the altar shows Edgar's coronation.

Climbing the Tower: You can reach the top of the tower but only with a worthwhile, 50-minute guided tour. You'll hike up 212 steps for views across the rooftops of Bath and a peek down into the Roman and Medieval Baths. In the rafters, you walk right up behind the clock face on the north transept, and get an inside-out look at the fan vaulting. Along the way, you'll hear a brief town history as you learn all about the tower's bells. If you've always wanted to clang a huge church bell for all the town to hear, this is your chance—it's oddly satisfying (£6, sporadic schedule but generally at the top of each hour when abbey is open, more often during busy times; Mon-Sat April-Oct 10:00-16:00, Nov-March 11:00-15:00, these are last tour-departure times; today's tour times usually posted outside abbey entrance, no tours Sun, buy tickets in abbey gift shop).

▲Pulteney Bridge, Parade Gardens, and Cruises

Bath is inclined to compare its shop-lined Pulteney Bridge to Flor-

ence's Ponte Vecchio. That's pushing it. But to best enjoy a sunny day, pack a picnic lunch and pay £1.20 to enter the Parade Gardens below the bridge (Easter-Sept daily 11:00-17:00, shorter hours off-season, includes deck chairs, ask about concerts held some Sun at 15:00 in summer, entrance a block south of bridge). Relaxing peacefully at the riverside provides a wonderful break (and memory).

Across the bridge at Pulteney Weir, tour boat companies run **cruises** (£4 each way, up to 12/day if the weather's good, one hour to Bathampton and back, WCs on board, tel. 01225/312-900). Just take whatever boat is running—all stop in Bathampton—allowing you to hop off and walk back (about 45-60 minutes; for details on the walk, see "Activities in Bath," later). Boats come with picnic-friendly sundecks.

Guildhall Market

The little, old-school shopping mall located across from Pulteney Bridge is a frumpy time warp in this affluent town. It's fun for browsing and picnic shopping, and its recommended Market Café is a cheap place for a bite.

▲Victoria Art Gallery

This gallery, next to Pulteney Bridge, has two parts: The ground floor houses temporary exhibits, while the upstairs is filled with paintings from the late 17th century to the present (find *Bath from the East*—left wall, just below eye level—for a nice look at pre-industrial Bath), along with a small collection of decorative arts.

Cost and Hours: £2 suggested donation, temporary exhibits-£2-4, Tue-Sat 10:00-17:00, Sun 13:30-17:00, closed Mon, WC, tel. 01225/477-233, www.victoriagal.org.uk.

Northwest of the Town Center

Several worthwhile public spaces and museums can be found a slightly uphill 10-minute walk away.

▲▲The Circus and the Royal Crescent

If Bath is an architectural cancan, these are its knickers. These first Georgian "condos"—built in the mid-18th century by the father-and-son John Woods (the Circus by the Elder, the Royal Crescent by the Younger)—are well explained by the city walking tours. "Georgian" is British for "Neoclassical." These two building complexes, conveniently located a block apart from each other, are quintessential Bath.

Circus: True to its name, this is a circular housing complex. Picture it as a coliseum turned inside out. Its Doric, Ionic, and Corinthian capital decorations pay homage to its Greco-Roman origin, and are a reminder that Bath (with its seven hills) aspired to be "the Rome of England." The frieze above the first row of columns has hundreds of different panels representing the arts, sciences, and crafts. The ground-floor entrances were made large enough that aristocrats could be carried right through the door in their sedan chairs, and women could enter without disturbing their sky-high hairdos. The tiny round windows on the top floors were the servants' quarters. While the building fronts are uniform, the backs are higgledy-piggledy, infamous for their "hanging loos" (bathrooms added years later). Stand in the middle of the Circus among the grand plane trees, on the capped old well. Imagine the days when there was no indoor plumbing, and the servant girls gathered here to fetch water—this was gossip central. If you stand on the well, your clap echoes three times around the circle (try it).

Royal Crescent: A long, graceful arc of buildings—impossible to see in one glance unless you step way back to the edge of the big park in front—evokes the wealth and gentility of Bath's glory days. As you

cruise the Crescent, pretend you're rich. Then pretend you're poor. Notice the "ha ha fence," a drop-off in the front yard that acted as a barrier, invisible from the windows, for keeping out sheep and peasants. The refined and stylish **Royal Crescent Hotel** sits unmarked in the center of the Crescent (with the giant rhododendron growing over the door). You're welcome to (politely) drop in to explore its fine ground-floor public spaces and back garden, where a gracious and traditional tea is served (£14.50 cream tea, £25 afternoon tea, daily 15:00-17:00, sharing is OK, reserve a day in advance, tel. 01225/823-333, www.royalcrescent.co.uk).

▲▲Georgian House at No. 1 Royal Crescent

This museum (corner of Brock Street and Royal Crescent) just reopened after an extensive renovation. It takes visitors behind one of those classy Georgian facades, offering your best look into a period house. Take the time to talk with the docents stationed in each room and you'll learn all the fascinating details of Georgian life... like how high-class women shaved their eyebrows and pasted on carefully trimmed strips of furry mouse skin in their place. Look for a bowl of black beauty marks and a head-scratcher from those pre-shampoo days. Fido spent his days on the kitchen treadmill powering the rotisserie.

Cost and Hours: £8.50, Mon 12:00-17:30, Tue-Sun 10:30-17:30, last entry at 16:30, tel. 01225/487-713, www.bath-preservation-trust.org.uk.

▲Fashion Museum

Housed underneath Bath's Assembly Rooms, this museum displays four centuries of fashion on one floor. It's small, but the  fact-filled, included audioguide can stretch a visit to an informative and enjoyable hour. Like fashion itself, the exhibits change all the time. A major feature is the "Dress of the Year" display, for which a fashion expert anoints a new frock each year. Ongoing since 1963, it's a chance to view nearly a half-century of fashion trends in one sweep of the head. (The menswear version—awarded sporadically—shows a bit less variation, but has flashes of creativity.) Many of the exhibits are organized by theme (bags, shoes, underwear, wedding dresses). You'll see how fashion evolved—just like architecture and other arts—from one historical period to the next: Georgian, Regency, Victorian, the Swinging '60s, and so on. If you're intrigued by all those historic garments, go ahead and lace up your own trainer corset (which looks more like a life jacket) and try on a hoop underdress.

Cost and Hours: £8, includes entry to Assembly Rooms when open, £18 combo-ticket also covers Roman Baths, family ticket available, daily March-Oct 10:30-18:00, Nov-Feb 10:30-17:00, last entry one hour before closing, self-service café, Bennett Street, tel. 01225/477-789, www.fashionmuseum.co.uk.

Assembly Rooms

Above the Fashion Museum, these grand, empty rooms—where card games, concerts, tea, and dances were held in the 18th century (before the advent of fancy hotels with grand public spaces made them obsolete)—evoke images of dashing young gentlemen mingling with elegant ladies in a who's who of high society. Note the extreme symmetry (pleasing to the aristocratic eye) and the high windows (assuring privacy). After the Allies bombed the historic and well-preserved German city of Lübeck, the Germans picked up a Baedeker guide and chose a similarly lovely city to bomb: Bath. The Assembly Rooms—gutted in this wartime tit-for-tat by WWII bombs—have since been restored to their original splendor. (Only the chandeliers are original.)

Cost and Hours: Free with Fashion Museum entry, otherwise £2; same hours and contact information as Fashion Museum.

Nearby: Below the Assembly Rooms and Fashion Museum (to the left as you exit, 20 yards away at the door marked *14* and *Alfred House*) is one of the few surviving sets of **iron house hardware.** "Link boys" carried torches through the dark streets, lighting the way for big shots in their sedan chairs as they traveled from one affair to the next. The link boys extinguished their torches in the black conical "snuffers." The lamp above was once gas-lit. The crank on the left was used to hoist bulky things to various windows (see the hooks). Few of these sets survived the dark days of the WWII Blitz, when most were collected and melted down, purportedly to make weapons to feed the British war machine. (Not long ago, these well-meaning Brits finally found out that all of their patriotic extra commitment to the national struggle had been for naught, since the metal ended up in junk heaps.)

Shoppers head down **Bartlett Street,** just below the Fashion Museum, to browse the boutique shops.

▲Museum of Bath at Work

This modest but lovable place explains the industrial history of Bath. The museum is a vivid reminder that there's always been a grimy, workaday side to this spa town. The core of the museum is the well-preserved, circa-1900 fizzy-drink business of one Mr. Bowler. It includes a Dickensian office, engineer's shop, brass foundry, essence room lined with bottled scents (see photo), and

factory floor. It's just a pile of meaningless old gadgets—until the included audioguide resurrects Mr. Bowler's creative genius. Each item has its own story to tell.

Upstairs are display cases featuring other Bath creations through the years, including a 1914 Horstmann car, wheeled sedan chairs (this *is* Bath, after all), and versatile plasticine (colorful proto-Play-Doh—still the preferred medium of Aardman Studios, creators of the stop-motion animated Wallace & Gromit movies). At the snack bar, you can buy your own historic fizzy drink (a descendant of the ones once made here). On your way out, don't miss the intriguing collection of small exhibits on the ground floor, featuring cabinetmaking, the traditional methods for cutting the local "Bath stone," a locally produced six-stroke engine, and more.

Cost and Hours: £5, includes audioguide, April-Oct daily 10:30-17:00, Nov and Jan-March weekends only, closed Dec, last entry at 16:00, Julian Road, 2 steep blocks up Russell Street from Assembly Rooms, tel. 01225/318-348, www.bath-at-work.org.uk.

Sightseeing Tip: Notice the proximity of this museum to the very different Fashion Museum (described earlier). Museum attendants told me that—while open-minded spouses appreciate both places—it's standard for husbands to visit the Museum of Bath at Work while their wives are touring the Fashion Museum. Maybe it's time to divide and conquer?

Jane Austen Centre

This exhibition focuses on Jane Austen's tumultuous, sometimes troubled, five years in Bath (circa 1800, during which time her father died) and the influence the city had on her writing. There's little of historic substance here. You'll walk through a Georgian townhouse that she didn't live in (one of her real addresses in Bath was a few houses up the road, at 25 Gay Street), and you'll see mostly enlarged reproductions of things associated with her writing, but none of that seems to bother the steady stream of happy Austen fans touring through the house.

The museum does describe various places from two novels set in Bath (*Persuasion* and *Northanger Abbey*). Guides give an intro talk (on the first floor, 15 minutes, 3/hour, on the hour and at :20 and :40 past the hour) about the romantic but down-to-earth Austen, who skewered the silly, shallow, and arrogant aristocrats' world, where "the doing of nothing all day prevents one from doing anything." They also show a 15-minute video; after that, you're free to wander through the rest of the exhibit. The well-stocked gift shop—with "I love Mr. Darcy" tote bags and Colin Firth's visage emblazoned on teacups, postcards, and more—is a shopping spree in the making for Austen fans.

Cost and Hours: £8; mid-March-mid-Nov daily 9:45-17:30, July-Aug Thu-Sat until 19:00; mid-Nov-mid-March Sun-Fri

11:00-16:30, Sat 9:45-18:00; these are last tour times, between Queen's Square and the Circus at 40 Gay Street, tel. 01225/443-000, www.janeausten.co.uk.

Tea: Upstairs, the award-winning **Regency Tea Rooms** (free entrance) hits the spot for Austenites with costumed waitstaff and themed teas (£6-10), including the all-out "Tea with Mr. Darcy" for £15 (also £6 sandwiches, same hours as the center, last order taken one hour before closing).

Sightseeing Tip: Jane Austen-themed **walking tours** of the city begin at the KC Change shop near the abbey churchyard and end at the Centre (£8, buy tickets at KC Change shop, 1.5 hours, Sat-Sun at 11:00, no reservation necessary).

Building of Bath Collection

This unique collection offers a geographic introduction to Bath and an intriguing behind-the-scenes look at how the Georgian city was actually built. The interactive model toward the back of the museum traces expansion from the 17th century forward, highlighting town sights. Compare the 1694 Gilmore map, one of Bath's first tourist maps, with the map beside it created 100 years later, which labels Barton's Field as a public space "never to be built upon"...and is now a parking lot.

Cost and Hours: £5, mid-Feb-Nov Tue-Fri 14:00-17:00, Sat-Sun 10:30-17:00, closed Mon and Dec-mid-Feb, last entry 30 minutes before closing, 20-minute film runs upon request or whenever enough people gather, a short walk north of the city center on a street called "The Paragon," tel. 01225/333-895, www.bath-preservation-trust.org.uk.

Outer Bath

▲American Museum

I know, you need this in Bath like you need a Big Mac. The UK's sole museum dedicated to American history, this may be the only place that combines Geronimo and Groucho Marx. It has thoughtful exhibits on the history of Native Americans and the Civil War, but the museum's heart is with the decorative arts and cultural artifacts that reveal how Americans lived from colonial times to the mid-19th century. Each of the 18 completely furnished rooms (from a plain 1600s Massachusetts dining/living room to a Rococo Revival explosion in a New Orleans bedroom) is hosted by eager guides waiting to fill you in on the everyday items that make domestic Yankee history surprisingly interesting. (In the Lee Room, look for the original mouse holes, strategically backlit in the floorboards.) One room is a quilter's nirvana. It's interesting to see your own country through British eyes—but on a nice day, the surrounding gardens and view of the hills might be the best reasons to visit. You could easily spend an afternoon here, enjoying the gardens, arboretum, and trails.

Cost and Hours: £9, mid-March-Oct Tue-Sun 12:00-17:00, closed Mon except in Aug, closed Nov-mid-March, last entry one hour before closing, at Claverton Manor, tel. 01225/460-503, www.americanmuseum.org.

Getting There: The museum is outside of town, but a free hourly shuttle gets you there in 15 minutes (leaves at :15 past the hour from Terrace Walk, just behind the abbey; show up at least 5 minutes early, as shuttle schedule is a little erratic, and the official stop is often blocked by big tour buses—keep your eye out for a white van with the museum's name on it).

Activities in Bath

▲Thermae Bath Spa

After simmering unused for a quarter-century, Bath's natural thermal springs once again offer R&R for the masses. The state-of-

the-art spa is housed in a complex of three buildings that combine historic structures with controversial (and expensive) new glass-and-steel architecture.

Is the Thermae Bath Spa worth the time and money? The experience is pretty pricey and humble compared to similar German and Hungarian spas. The tall, modern building in the city center lacks a certain old-time elegance. Jets in the pools are very limited, and the only water toys are big foam noodles. There's no cold plunge—the only way to cool off between steam rooms is to step onto a small, unglamorous balcony. The Royal Bath's two pools are essentially the same, and the water isn't particularly hot in either—in fact, the main attraction is the rooftop view from the top one (best with a partner or as a social experience).

All that said, this is the only natural thermal spa in the UK and your one chance to bathe in Bath. Bring your swimsuit and come for a couple of hours (Fri night and all day Sat-Sun are most crowded). Consider an evening visit, when—on a chilly day—Bath's twilight glows through the steam from the rooftop pool.

Cost: The cheapest spa pass is £26 for two hours, which gains you access to the Royal Bath's large, ground-floor "Minerva Bath"; four steam rooms and a waterfall shower; and the view-filled, open-air, rooftop thermal pool. Longer stays are £36/4 hours and £56/day (towel, robe, and slippers are an extra £9). If you arrived in Bath by train, your used rail ticket will score you a four-hour session for the price of two hours (£26, Mon-Fri). The much-hyped £42 Twilight Package includes three hours and a meal (one plate, drink, robe, towel, and slippers). The appeal of this package is not the mediocre meal, but being on top of the building at a magical hour (which you can do for less money at the regular rate).

Thermae has all the "pamper thyself" extras: massages, mud wraps, and various healing-type treatments, including "watsu"—water shiatsu (£40-90 extra). Book treatments in advance by phone.

Hours: Daily 9:00-21:30, last entry at 19:00. No kids under age 16 are allowed.

Information: It's 100 yards from the Roman and Medieval Baths, on Beau Street (tel. 01225/331-234, www.thermaebathspa. com). There's a salad-and-smoothies café for guests.

The Cross Bath: Operated by Thermae Bath Spa, this renovated, circular Georgian structure across the street from the main spa provides a simpler and less-expensive bathing option. It has a hot-water fountain that taps directly into the spring, making its water hotter than the spa's (£16/1.5 hours, daily 10:00-20:00, last entry at 18:00, check in at Thermae Bath Spa's main entrance across the street and you'll be escorted to the Cross Bath, changing rooms, no access to Royal Bath, no kids under 12).

Spa Visitor Center: Also across the street, in the Hetling Pump Room, this free, one-room exhibit explains the story of the spa (Mon-Sat 10:00-17:00, Sun 11:00-16:00, audioguide-£2).

Walking

The Bath Skyline Walk is a six-mile wander around the hills surrounding Bath (leaflet at TI). Plenty of other scenic paths are described in the TI's literature. For additional options, get *Country Walks around Bath*, by Tim Mowl (£4.50 at TI or bookstores).

Hiking the Canal to Bathampton

An idyllic towpath leads two miles from the Bath Spa train station, along the Kennet and Avon Canal, to the sleepy village of Bathampton. Immediately behind the station in Bath, cross the footbridge, turn left, and find where the canal hits the River Avon. Head northeast along the small canal, noticing the series of Industrial Age locks and giving thanks that you're not a horse pulling a barge. After the path crisscrosses the canal a few times, you'll mostly walk with the water on your right. You'll be in Bathampton in less than an hour, where The George, a classic pub, awaits with a nice meal and cellar-temp beer (reservations smart, tel. 01225/425-079).

Boating

The Bath Boating Station, in an old Victorian boathouse, rents rowboats, canoes, and punts.

Cost and Hours: £7/person for first hour, then £4/additional hour; all day for £18; Easter-Sept daily 10:00-18:00, closed off-season, intersection of Forester and Rockcliffe roads, one mile northeast of center, tel. 01225/312-900, www.bathboating.co.uk.

Swimming and Kids' Activities

The Bath Sports and Leisure Centre has a fine pool for laps as well as lots of waterslides. Kids have entertaining options in the mini-gym "Active Club" area, which includes a rock wall and a "Zany Zone" indoor playground.

Cost and Hours: Swimming—£4 for adults, £2.60 for kids, family discounts, Mon-Fri 6:30-22:00, Sat 6:30-19:00, Sun 8:00-20:00, kids' hours limited, call for open-swim times, just across the bridge on North Parade Road, tel. 01225/486-905, www.aqua-terra.org.

Shopping

There's great browsing between the abbey and the Assembly Rooms (Fashion Museum). Shops close at about 17:30, and many are open on Sunday (11:00-16:00). Explore the antique shops around Bartlett Street, below the Fashion Museum.

Nightlife in Bath

For an up-to-date list of events, pick up the local weekly newspaper, the *Bath Chronicle,* which includes a "What's On" schedule (www.thisisbath.com). Younger travelers may enjoy the party-ready bar, club, and nightlife recommendations at www.itchybath.co.uk.

▲▲Bizarre Bath Street Theater

For an entertaining walking-tour comedy act "with absolutely no history or culture," follow Dom or Noel Britten on their creative and lively Bizarre Bath walk. This 1.5-hour "tour," which combines stand-up comedy with cleverly executed magic tricks, plays off unsuspecting passersby as well as tour members. It's a belly laugh a minute.

Cost and Hours: £10, £8 if you show this book, April-Oct nightly at 20:00, smaller groups Mon-Thu, promises to insult all nationalities and sensitivities, just racy enough but still good family fun, leaves from The Huntsman pub near the abbey, confirm at TI or call 01225/335-124, www.bizarrebath.co.uk.

▲Theatre Royal Performance

The 18th-century, 800-seat Theatre Royal, recently restored and one of England's loveliest, offers a busy schedule of London West End-type plays, including many "pre-London" dress-rehearsal runs. The Theatre Royal also oversees performances at two other theaters around the corner from the main box office: Ustinov Studio (edgier, more obscure titles, many of which are premier runs in the UK) and "the egg" (for children, young people, and families).

Cost and Hours: £20-40, shows generally start at 19:30 or 20:00, matinees at 14:30, box office open Mon-Sat 10:00-20:00,

Sun 12:00-20:00 if there's a show, £3 extra to book online or by phone with a credit card, on Saw Close, tel. 01225/448-844, www.theatreroyal.org.uk.

Ticket Deals: Forty nosebleed spots on a bench (misnamed "standbys") go on sale at noon Monday through Saturday for that day's evening performance in the main theater (£6, 2 tickets maximum, can book ahead but subject to £3 fee; no fee if bought at box office but cash only). If the show is sold out, same-day "standing places" go on sale at 18:00 (12:00 for matinees) for £4 (2 tickets maximum, cash only). Also at the box office, you can snatch up any "last minute" seats for £15-20 a half-hour before "curtain up" (cash only). Shows in the Ustinov Theatre go for around £20, with no cheap-seat deals.

Sightseeing Tip: During the free Bath walking tour, your guide stops here. Pop into the box office, ask what's playing, and see if there are many seats left for that night. If the play sounds good and plenty of seats remain unsold, you're fairly safe to come back 30 minutes before curtain time to buy a ticket at the cheaper price. Oh...and if you smell jasmine, it's the ghost of Lady Grey, a mistress of Beau Nash.

Evening Walks

Take your choice: comedy (Bizarre Bath, described earlier), history, or ghost tour. The free **city history walks** (a daily standard described on page 412) are offered on some summer evenings (2 hours, May-Sept Tue and Thu at 19:00, leave from Pump Room). **Ghost Walks** are a popular way to pass the after-dark hours (£7, cash only, 1.5 hours, year-round Thu-Sat at 20:00, leave from The Garrick's Head pub—to the left and behind Theatre Royal as you face it, tel. 01225/350-512, www.ghostwalksofbath.co.uk). The cities of York and Edinburgh—which have houses thought to be actually haunted—are better for these walks.

Pubs

Most pubs in the center are very noisy, catering to a rowdy twentysomething crowd. But on the top end of town, you can still find some classic old places with inviting ambience and live music. These are listed in order from closest to farthest away:

The Old Green Tree, the most convenient of all these pubs, is a rare traditional pub right in the town center (locally brewed real ales, no children, 12 Green Street; also recommended for lunch—see "Eating in Bath," later).

The Star Inn is much appreciated by local beer lovers for its fine ale and "no machines or music to distract from the chat." It's a spit-and-sawdust place, and its long bench, nicknamed "death row," still comes with a complimentary pinch of snuff from tins on the ledge. Try the Bellringer Ale, made just up the road (Mon-Fri 12:00-14:30 & 17:30-late, Sat-Sun 12:00-late, no food served,

23 The Vineyards, top of The Paragon/A-4 Roman Road, tel. 01225/425-072, generous and friendly welcome from Paul, who runs the place).

The Bell has a jazzy, pierced-and-tattooed, bohemian feel, but with a mellow older crowd. Some kind of activity is brewing nearly every night, usually live music (Mon-Sat 11:30-23:00, Sun 12:00-22:30, 103 Walcot Street, tel. 01225/460-426, www.thebellinnbath.co.uk).

Summer Nights at the Baths
In July and August, you can stretch your sightseeing day at the Roman Baths, open nightly until 22:00 (last entry 21:00), when the gas lamps flame and the baths are far less crowded and more atmospheric. To take a dip yourself, consider popping over to the Thermae Bath Spa (last entry at 19:00).

Sleeping in Bath

Bath is a busy tourist town. Accommodations are expensive, and low-cost alternatives are rare. By far the best budget option is the YMCA—it's central, safe, simple, very well-run, and has plenty of twin rooms available. To get a good B&B, make a telephone reservation in advance. Competition is stiff, and it's worth asking any of these places for a weekday, three-nights-in-a-row, or off-season deal. Friday and Saturday nights are tightest (with many rates going up by about 25 percent)—especially if you're staying only one night, since B&Bs favor those lingering longer. If staying only Saturday night, you're very bad news to a B&B hostess. If you're driving to Bath, stowing your car near the center will cost you (though some less-central B&Bs have parking)—see "Parking" on page 412, or ask your hotelier. Almost every place provides free Wi-Fi to its guests.

Near the Royal Crescent
These listings are all a 5-10-minute walk from the town center, and an easy 15-minute walk from the train station. With bags in tow you may want to either catch a taxi (£5-6) or (except for Brocks Guest House) hop on bus #14 or #14A (direction: Weston, catch bus inside bus station, pay driver £2.50, get off at the Comfortable Place stop—just after the car dealership on the left, cross street and backtrack 100 yards).

Marlborough, Brooks, and Cornerways all face a busy arterial street; while the noise is minimal by urban standards and these B&Bs have well-insulated windows, those sensitive to traffic noise should request a rear- or side-facing room.

$$$ Marlborough House, exuberantly run by hands-on owner Peter, mixes modern style with antique furnishings and features a

---

Sleep Code

(£1 = about $1.60, country code: 44, area code: 01225)
S = Single, **D** = Double/Twin, **T** = Triple, **Q** = Quad, **b** = bathroom, **s** = shower only. Unless otherwise noted, credit cards are accepted and breakfast is included.

To help you sort easily through these listings, I've divided the rooms into three categories based on the price for a standard double room with bath:

$$$ **Higher Priced**—Most rooms £100 or more.
$$ **Moderately Priced**—Most rooms between £60-100.
$ **Lower Priced**—Most rooms £60 or less.

Prices can change without notice; verify the hotel's current rates online or by email. For the best prices, always book direct.

---

welcoming breakfast room with an open kitchen. Each of the six rooms comes with a sip of sherry (Sb-£75-105, Db-£95-145, Tb-£105-155, rates can vary with demand, mention this book for Rick Steves discount, £5 additional discount when you pay cash, air-con, mini-fridges, organic vegetarian breakfasts and toiletries, free Wi-Fi, free parking, 1 Marlborough Lane, tel. 01225/318-175, www.marlborough-house.net, mars@manque.dircon.co.uk).

$$$ Brooks Guesthouse is the biggest and most polished of the bunch, albeit the least personal, with 21 modern rooms and classy public spaces, including an exceptionally pleasant breakfast room. It's smart to reconfirm your booking a day or two ahead (Sb-£60-90, Db/Tb-£80-120, rates vary with room size and season/demand, great breakfasts with non-traditional and vegetarian options, free Wi-Fi, shared guest fridge, limited parking-£8/day, 1 Crescent Gardens, Upper Bristol Road, tel. 01225/425-543, www.brooksguesthouse.com, info@brooksguesthouse.com).

$$ Brocks Guest House has six rooms in a Georgian townhouse built by John Wood in 1765. Located between the prestigious Royal Crescent and the courtly Circus, it has been redone in a way that would make the great architect proud. Each room has its own Bath-related theme (Db-£99, Db with fireplace-£109, larger Db-£119, Db suite-£129, free Wi-Fi, little top-floor library, 32 Brock Street, tel. 01225/338-374, www.brocksguesthouse.co.uk, brocks@brocksguesthouse.co.uk, Karen and Rachel).

$$ Parkside Guest House has five large, thoughtfully appointed Edwardian rooms. It's tidy, clean, homey, and well-priced—and has a spacious back garden (Sb-£68, Db-£85, these prices for Rick Steves readers, free Wi-Fi, limited free parking,

11 Marlborough Lane, tel. 01225/429-444, www.parksidebandb. co.uk, post@parksidebandb.co.uk, kind Inge Lynall).

$$ Cornerways B&B, just a few blocks from the town center, is simple and pleasant, with three rooms and old-fashioned homey touches (Sb-£45-55, Db-£65-75, 15 percent discount with this book and 3-night stay, free Wi-Fi, DVD library, free parking, 47 Crescent Gardens, tel. 01225/422-382, www.cornerwaysbath. co.uk, info@cornerwaysbath.co.uk, Sue Black).

East of the River

These listings are a 5-10-minute walk from the city center. From the train station, it's best to take a taxi, as there are no good bus connections.

$$$ The Kennard, with 12 rooms immaculately maintained by proud owners Giovanni and Mary Baiano, is a short walk through a genteel neighborhood from the Pulteney Bridge. Each of the rooms is different, but all are colorfully and elaborately decorated (prices are for Sun-Thu/Fri-Sat: S-£65/£70, Sb-£89/£120, Db-£110/£130, superior Db-£140/£160, Tb-£150/£170, free Wi-Fi, free street parking permits, thoughtfully planned Georgian garden out back, 11 Henrietta Street, tel. 01225/310-472, www.kennard. co.uk, reception@kennard.co.uk).

$$$ Villa Magdala rents 20 stately yet modern rooms in a freestanding Victorian townhouse opposite a park. In a city that's so insistently Georgian, it's fun to stay in a mansion that's Victorian (Db-£120-150 depending on size and demand, about £20 more Fri-Sun, family rooms, inviting lounge, free Wi-Fi, free parking when booked direct, in quiet residential area on Henrietta Street, tel. 01225/466-329, www.villamagdala.co.uk, enquiries@villa-magdala.co.uk).

$$$ The Ayrlington, next door to a lawn-bowling green, has 16 attractive rooms, each thoughtfully decorated either in classical or contemporary style and sprinkled with Asian decor. Though this well-maintained hotel fronts a busy street, it's reasonably quiet and tranquil, hinting of a more genteel time. Rooms in the back have pleasant views of sports greens and Bath beyond. For the best value, request a standard top-floor double with a view of Bath (prices are for Mon-Thu/Fri-Sun: twin or standard Db-£110/£130, superior Db-£140/£170, big deluxe Db-£150/£190, extra person-£40, free Wi-Fi, fine garden, free and easy parking, 24-25 Pulteney Road, tel. 01225/425-495, www.ayrlington.com, mail@ayrlington.com, Ling Roper).

$$ At Apple Tree Guesthouse, friendly Les and Lynsay offer six comfortable rooms near a shady canal. You'll think you've clicked your ruby heels three times (Sb-£60-66, Db-£90-110, family/Tb-£135-149, 2-night minimum Fri-Sat nights, free

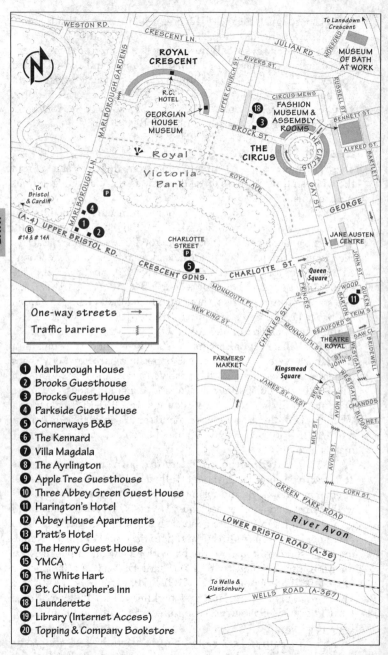

BATH

Legend:

- 1 Marlborough House
- 2 Brooks Guesthouse
- 3 Brocks Guest House
- 4 Parkside Guest House
- 5 Cornerways B&B
- 6 The Kennard
- 7 Villa Magdala
- 8 The Ayrlington
- 9 Apple Tree Guesthouse
- 10 Three Abbey Green Guest House
- 11 Harington's Hotel
- 12 Abbey House Apartments
- 13 Pratt's Hotel
- 14 The Henry Guest House
- 15 YMCA
- 16 The White Hart
- 17 St. Christopher's Inn
- 18 Launderette
- 19 Library (Internet Access)
- 20 Topping & Company Bookstore

One-way streets →
Traffic barriers

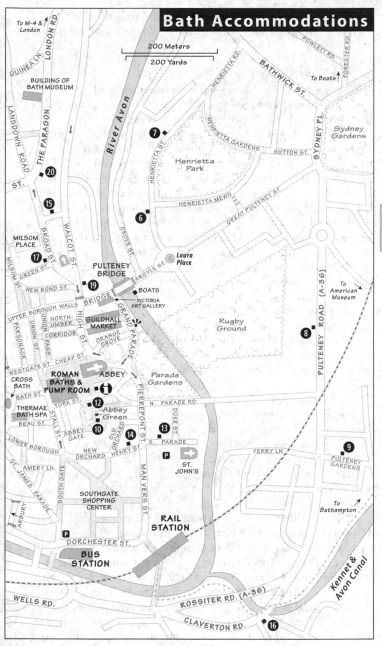

Bath Accommodations

Wi-Fi, free parking, 7 Pulteney Gardens, tel. 01225/337-642, www.appletreeguesthouse.com, enquiries@appletreeguesthouse.co.uk).

In the Town Center

You'll pay a premium to sleep right in the center. And, since Bath is so pleasant and manageable by foot, a downtown location isn't essential. Still, these are particularly well located.

$$$ Three Abbey Green Guest House, with 10 rooms, is bright, cheery, and located in a quiet, traffic-free courtyard only 50 yards from the abbey and the Roman Baths. Its spacious rooms are a fine value (Db-£90-140, four-poster Db-£140-180, family rooms-£140-220, price depends on season and size of room, 2-night minimum on weekends, 3-night minimum on Bank Holiday weekends, free Internet access and Wi-Fi, nice breakfast, limited free parking, 2 ground-floor rooms work well for those with limited mobility, tel. 01225/428-558, www.threeabbeygreen.com, stay@threeabbeygreen.com, Sue, Derek, and daughter Nicola). They also rent self-catering apartments (Db-£140-160, Qb-£170-250, 2-night minimum).

$$$ Harington's Hotel rents 13 fresh, modern rooms on a quiet street in the town center. This stylish place feels like a boutique hotel, but with a friendlier, laid-back vibe (Sb-£78-155, Db-£98-148, large superior Db-£108-168, Tb-£130-198, prices vary substantially with demand—always highest on weekends, free Wi-Fi, hot tub, parking-£11/day, 8-10 Queen Street, tel. 01225/461-728, www.haringtonshotel.co.uk, post@haringtonshotel.co.uk, manager Julian). Owners Melissa and Peter offer a 5 percent discount with this book for two-night stays except on Fridays, Saturdays, and holidays. They also rent two self-catering apartments down the street—one can sleep up to three (Db-£125, Tb-£145, higher on weekends), and the other can sleep up to eight (prices on request; for apartments: 2-night minimum on weekdays, 3-night minimum on weekends).

$$$ At Abbey House Apartments, "Goddess of Rock" Laura watches over five flats on Abbey Green and several others scattered around town—including a former residence of Jane Austen. The apartments called Abbey Green (which comes with a washer and dryer), Abbey View, and Abbey Studio have views of the abbey from their nicely equipped kitchens. These are especially practical and economical if you plan on cooking. Laura provides everything you need for simple breakfasts, and it's fun and cheap to stock the fridge or get takeaway for a meal in your flat. When Laura meets you to give you the keys, you become a local (Sb-£90, Db-£100-175, price depends on size, 2-night minimum, rooms can sleep four with Murphy and sofa beds, apartments clearly described on website, free Wi-Fi, Abbey Green, tel. 01225/464-238, www.laurastownhouseapartments.co.uk, bookings@laurastownhouseapartments.co.uk).

$$$ Pratt's Hotel is as proper and olde English as you'll find in Bath, offering 46 comfy rooms. Its creaks and frays are aristocratic, and even its public places make you want to sip a brandy. Since it's near a busy street, it can occasionally get noisy—request a quiet room, away from the taxi stand and street (Sb-£60-100, Db-£80-150, price depends on size and demand, breakfast-£10, check website for current rates and specials, children under 15 free with 2 adults, elevator, pay Wi-Fi, attached restaurant-bar, 4-6 South Parade, tel. 01225/460-441, www.forestdalehotels.com, pratts@forestdale.com).

$$ The Henry Guest House is a simple, vertical place, renting seven clean rooms. It's friendly, well-run, and just two blocks from the train station (Sb-£75-85, Db-£80-105, premier Db-£95-120, extra bed-£20, family/Tb-£145-165, 2-night minimum on weekends, free Wi-Fi, 6 Henry Street, tel. 01225/424-052, www.thehenry.com, stay@thehenry.com). Liz also rents two self-catering apartments nearby that sleep up to eight with roll-away beds and a sleeper couch (email for rates).

Bargain Accommodations

Bath's Best Budget Beds: **$ The YMCA,** centrally located on a leafy square, has 210 beds in industrial-strength rooms—all with sinks and minimal furnishings. Although it smells a little like a gym, this place is a godsend for budget travelers—safe, secure, quiet, and efficiently run. With lots of twin rooms and a few double beds, this is the only easily accessible budget option in downtown Bath (rates for Sun-Thu/Fri-Sat: S-£32/£36, twin D-£56/£60, D-£60/£64, T-£69/£75, Q-£88/£96, dorm beds-£21/£23, WCs and showers down the hall, includes continental breakfast, cooked breakfast-£3.50, free linens, rental towels, lockers, pay guest computer, free Wi-Fi in lobby, laundry facilities, down a tiny alley off Broad Street on Broad Street Place, tel. 01225/325-900, www.bathymca.co.uk, stay@bathymca.co.uk).

$ White Hart is a friendly and colorful place, offering adults and families good, cheap stays in one of four private rooms, or in one of the two- to six-bed dorms (£15/bed, S-£25, D-£40, Db-£50-70, Wi-Fi, kitchen, fine garden out back, 5-minute walk behind the train station at Widcombe—where Widcombe Hill hits Claverton Street, tel. 01225/313-985, www.whitehartbath.co.uk). The White Hart also has a pub with a reputation for good, although not cheap, food.

$ St. Christopher's Inn, in a prime central location, is part of a chain of low-priced, high-energy hubs for backpackers looking for beds and brews. Their beds are so cheap because they know you'll spend money on their beer. The inn sits above the lively, youthful Belushi's pub, which is where you'll find the reception (54 beds in 6- to 12-bed rooms-£15-25, S-£50-55, D-£110, higher prices are for weekends and walk-ins—it's always cheaper to book online, check website for specials, no guests under 18, free Wi-Fi, laundry facilities, lounge, 9 Green Street, tel. 01225/481-444, www.st-christophers.co.uk).

Eating in Bath

Bath is bursting with eateries. There's something for every appetite and budget—just stroll around the center of town. A picnic dinner of deli food or take-out fish-and-chips in the Royal Crescent Park or down by the river is ideal for aristocratic hoboes. The restaurants I recommend are small and popular—reserve a table on Friday and Saturday evenings. Most pricey little bistros offer big savings with their two- and three-course lunches and "pre-theatre" specials. Restaurants advertise their early-bird specials, and as long as you order within the time window, you're in for a cheap meal.

Romantic, Upscale French and English

Tilleys Bistro serves sophisticated French, English, and vegetarian/gluten-free dishes with candlelit ambience. Owners Dawn and Dave make you feel as if you are guests at a dinner party in their elegant living room. Their menu lets you build your own meal: Start by sharing a couple of small plates, then choose a main course and add sides. Cap things off with homemade desert and a glass of the house port, a passion of Dave's. While it's pricey and the portions are modest, this is a memorable splurge (£6-9 small plates, £10-20 main courses; lunch specials: £6 cream tea, £13.50/2 courses, £16/3 courses, also available 18:00-19:30; open Mon-Sat 12:00-14:30 & 18:00-22:30, Sun 18:00-21:00 only, reservations smart, 3 North Parade Passage, tel. 01225/484-200, www.tilleysbistro.co.uk).

The Circus Café and Restaurant is a relaxing little eatery serving well-executed English cuisine with European flair. Choose between the modern interior—with seating on the main floor or in the cellar—and the four tables on the peaceful street connecting the Circus and the Royal Crescent (£9-13 lunches; set lunch menu: £16/2 courses, £20/3 courses; £7 starters and £15-17 main courses at dinner, open Mon-Sat 10:00-24:00, closed Sun, reservations smart, 34 Brock Street, tel. 01225/466-020, www.thecircuscafeandrestaurant.co.uk).

The Garrick's Head is an elegantly simple gastropub right around the corner from the Theatre Royal, with a pricey restaurant on one side and a bar serving affordable snacks on the other.

You're welcome to eat from the bar menu, even if you're in the fancy dining room or outside enjoying some great people-watching. The word on the street: The fish-and-chips here are the best in town (£7-12 pub grub, £11-17 main courses on the fancier menu; lunch and pre-theater specials: £15/2 courses, £18/3 courses; food served daily 12:00-14:30 & 17:30-20:00, drinks until later, 8 St. John's Place, tel. 01225/318-368).

Casanis French Bistro-Restaurant is a local hit. Chef Laurent, who hails from Nice, cooks "authentic Provençal cuisine" from the south of France, while his wife, Jill, serves. The decor matches the cuisine—informal, relaxed, simple, and top quality. The intimate Georgian dining room upstairs is a bit nicer and more spacious than the ground floor (early dinner specials: £18/2 courses, £22/3 courses; similar specials £2 cheaper at lunchtime; open Tue-Sat 12:00-14:00 & 18:00-22:00, closed Sun-Mon, immediately behind the Assembly Rooms at 4 Saville Row, tel. 01225/780-055).

Casual Alternatives

Whether ethnic food or vegetarian, there are plenty of ways to get some fun culinary variation in this town.

Demuths Vegetarian Restaurant is highly rated and ideal for the well-heeled vegetarian. Its tight, understated interior comes with a vegan vibe (£5-11 lunches, £8 starters and £16 main courses at dinner; dinner specials: £16/2 courses, £19/3 courses, £4 cheaper at lunchtime; daily 12:00-15:00 & 17:30-21:30, 2 North Parade Passage, tel. 01225/446-059).

Yen Sushi is your basic little sushi bar—plain and sterile, with stools facing a conveyor belt that constantly tempts you with a variety of freshly made delights on color-coded plates. When you're done, the waitstaff will tally your plates and give you the bill (£2-5 plates, you can fill up for £14 or so, daily 12:00-15:00 & 17:30-22:30, 11 Bartlett Street, tel. 01225/333-313).

Martini Restaurant, a hopping, purely Italian place, has class and jovial waiters (£11-13 pastas and pizzas, £16-21 meat and fish dishes, daily 12:00-14:30 & 18:00-22:30, open all day long on Sat, veggie options, daily fish specials, extensive wine list, reservations smart on weekends, 9 George Street, tel. 01225/460-818, www. martinirestaurant.co.uk; Nunzio, Franco, and chef Luigi).

Rajpoot Tandoori serves—by all assessments—the best Indian food in Bath. You'll hike down deep into a sprawling cellar, where the plush Indian atmosphere and award-winning cooking make paying the extra pounds palatable. The seating is tight and the ceilings low, but it's air-conditioned (£9 three-course lunch special, £9-16 main courses; figure £20 per person with rice, naan, and drink; daily 12:00-14:30 & 18:00-23:00, 4 Argyle Street, tel. 01225/466-833, Ali).

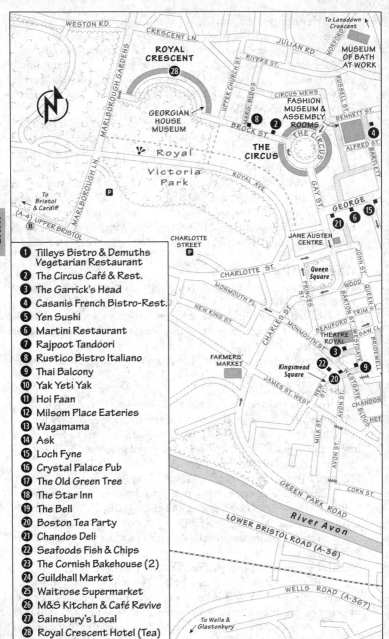

1 Tilleys Bistro & Demuths Vegetarian Restaurant
2 The Circus Café & Rest.
3 The Garrick's Head
4 Casanis French Bistro-Rest.
5 Yen Sushi
6 Martini Restaurant
7 Rajpoot Tandoori
8 Rustico Bistro Italiano
9 Thai Balcony
10 Yak Yeti Yak
11 Hoi Faan
12 Milsom Place Eateries
13 Wagamama
14 Ask
15 Loch Fyne
16 Crystal Palace Pub
17 The Old Green Tree
18 The Star Inn
19 The Bell
20 Boston Tea Party
21 Chandos Deli
22 Seafoods Fish & Chips
23 The Cornish Bakehouse (2)
24 Guildhall Market
25 Waitrose Supermarket
26 M&S Kitchen & Café Revive
27 Sainsbury's Local
28 Royal Crescent Hotel (Tea)

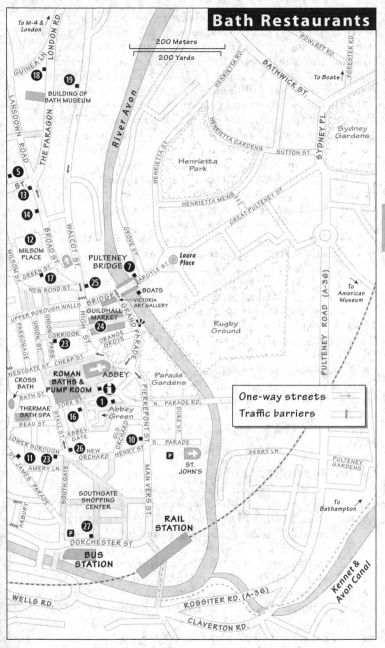

Bath Restaurants

Rustico Bistro Italiano, nestled between the Circus and the Royal Crescent, is precisely what its name implies. Franco and his staff are kept busy by a local crowd (£9-11 pastas, £14-19 *secondi*, no pizza, check chalkboard for specials, Tue-Sun 12:00-14:30 & 18:00-22:00, closed Mon, just off Brock Street at 2 Margaret's Buildings, tel. 01225/310-064).

Thai Balcony Restaurant's open, spacious interior is so plush, it'll have you wondering, "Where's the Thai wedding?" While residents debate which of Bath's handful of Thai restaurants serves the best food or offers the lowest prices, there's no doubt that Thai Balcony's fun and elegant atmosphere makes for a memorable and enjoyable dinner (£10 two-course lunch special, early dinner specials also available, £8-13 plates, daily 12:00-14:00 & 18:00-22:00, Fri-Sat until 22:30, reservations smart on weekends, Saw Close, tel. 01225/444-450, www.thai-balcony.com).

Yak Yeti Yak is a fun Nepalese restaurant with both Western and sit-on-the-floor seating. Sera and his wife, Sarah, along with their cheerful, hardworking Nepali team, cook up great traditional food (including plenty of vegetarian plates) at prices that would delight a sherpa (£7-9 lunches, £5-6 veggie plates, £8-9 meat plates; lunch served daily 12:00-14:00; dinner served Mon-Thu 18:00-22:30, Fri-Sat 17:00-22:30, Sun 17:00-22:00; downstairs at 12 Pierrepont Street, tel. 01225/442-299).

Family-run **Hoi Faan** draws an international crowd by dishing up large portions of traditional Hong Kong-style Chinese food in a bare space. There are plenty of options; if you can't make up your mind, survey nearby tables and point to what looks good (£7 lunch specials include starter and main dish, £7-10 sharable main courses, daily 12:00-23:00, 41-42 St. James Parade, tel. 01225/318-212).

Chain Restaurants

With so many homegrown favorites, I see little reason to frequent a chain restaurant in Bath—but if you're a fan, you'll find plenty of decent choices. **Milsom Place** is a pleasant hidden courtyard with several dependable eateries, including a branch of **Yo! Sushi** and the French-themed **Côte Brasserie.**

Nearby, **Wagamama** specializes in pan-Asian cuisine (£8-11 meals, Mon-Sat 12:00-23:00, Sun 11:30-22:00, 1 York Buildings, corner of George and Broad streets, tel. 01225/337-314) and, just around the corner, **Ask** dishes up Italian comfort food (£8-12 pizzas and pastas, good salads, £11 2-course meal or £14 3-course meal available after 17:00 Sun-Thu, Mon-Sat 11:30-23:00, Sun until 22:00, George Street but entrance on Broad Street, tel. 01225/789-997).

Loch Fyne, a bright, youthful, high-energy place, serves fresh fish at reasonable prices in what was once a lavish bank building (£10-18 meals, £10 two-course special from lunch until 18:00, £5 more after 18:00, daily 12:00-22:00, 24 Milsom Street, tel. 01225/750-120).

Pubs

Bath is not a good pub-grub town, and with so many other tempting options, eating at a pub here isn't as appealing as elsewhere. For the best pub grub, head for **The Garrick's Head** gastropub (described earlier). But if you're looking for a more traditional, lowbrow place, consider these options.

Crystal Palace is an inviting place just a block away from the abbey, facing the delightful little Abbey Green. With a focus on food rather than drink, they serve "pub grub with a Continental flair" in three different spaces, including an airy back patio out back. Be sure to congratulate Toby on completing university (£9-12 meals, food served Mon-Fri 11:00-21:00, Sat 11:00-20:00, Sun 12:00-20:00, last orders for drinks at 22:45, 10-11 Abbey Green, tel. 01225/482-666).

The Old Green Tree, in the old town center, serves satisfying lunches to locals in a characteristic pub setting (real ales on tap, daily for drinks 11:00-23:00 except from 12:00 on Sun, no children, weekend nights can be crowded, 12 Green Street, tel. 01225/448-259).

For a pub to drink and hang out in, rather than eat at, check out **The Star Inn** or **The Bell** (described on pages 430 and 431).

Simple Options

For a fast, handy, and tasty meal on the go, try one of these easy places. If you get takeaway (possible at most of these), you can munch your picnic while watching street musicians from a bench in the abbey churchyard.

The **Boston Tea Party** chain is what Starbucks aspires to be—the neighborhood coffeehouse and hangout. Its extensive breakfasts, light lunches, and salads are fresh and healthy. The outdoor seating overlooks a busy square. Their walls are decorated with works by local artists (£4-7 breakfasts, £5-7 lunches, Mon-Sat 7:30-19:30, Sun 9:00-19:00, free Wi-Fi, 19 Kingsmead Square, tel. 01225/314-826).

Chandos Deli has good coffee, breakfast pastries, and tasty £3-5 sandwiches made on artisan breads plus meats, cheese, baguettes, and wine for assembling a gourmet picnic. Upscale yet casual, this place satisfies dedicated foodies who don't want to pay too much (Mon-Fri 8:00-17:30, Sat 9:00-5:30, Sun 11:00-17:00, 12 George Street, tel. 01225/314-418).

Seafoods Fish & Chips is respected by lovers of greasy fried fish in Bath. There's diner-style and outdoor seating, or you can get your food to go for a bit less (£4-6 takeaway meals, Mon-Wed 11:30-21:00, Thu-Sat 11:30-22:00, closed Sun, 38 Kingsmead Square, tel. 01225/465-190).

The **Cornish Bakehouse** has freshly baked £3 takeaway pasties (Mon-Sat 8:30-17:30, Sun 10:00-17:00, kitty-corner from Marks & Spencer at 1 Lower Borough Walls, second location off High Street at 11A The Corridor, tel. 01225/780-432).

Produce Market and Café: **Guildhall Market,** across from Pulteney Bridge, has produce stalls with food for picnickers. At its inexpensive **Market Café,** you can munch on a homemade meat pie or sip a tea while surrounded by stacks of used books, bananas on the push list, and honest-to-goodness old-time locals (£3-5 traditional English meals including fried breakfasts all day, Mon-Sat 8:00-17:00, closed Sun, tel. 01225/461-593 a block north of the abbey, on High Street).

Supermarkets: **Waitrose** is great for picnics and has a good salad bar (Mon-Fri 7:30-21:00, Sat 7:30-20:00, Sun 11:00-17:00, just west of Pulteney Bridge and across from post office on High Street). **Marks & Spencer,** near the bottom end of town, has a grocery at the back of its department store and two eateries: **M&S Kitchen** on the ground floor and the pleasant, inexpensive **Café Revive** on the top floor (Mon-Sat 8:00-19:00, Sun 11:00-17:00, 16-18 Stall Street). **Sainsbury's Local,** across the street from the bus station, has the longest hours (daily 7:00-23:00, 2-4 Dorchester Street).

Bath Connections

Bath's train station is called Bath Spa (tel. 0845-748-4950). The National Express bus station is just west of the train station (bus info tel. 0871-781-8178, www.nationalexpress.com). For all public bus services in southwestern England, see www.travelinesw.com.

From Bath to London: You can catch a **train** to London's Paddington Station (2/hour, 1.5 hours, best deals for travel after 9:30 and when purchased in advance, www.firstgreatwestern. co.uk), or save money—but not time—by taking the National Express **bus** to Victoria Coach Station (direct buses nearly hourly, 3-3.5 hours, avoid those with layover in Bristol, one-way-£7-25, round-trip-£12-34, cheapest to purchase online several days in advance).

Connecting Bath with London's Airports: To get to or from **Heathrow,** it's fastest and most pleasant to take the **train via London;** with a Britrail pass, it's also the cheapest option, as the whole trip is covered. Without a railpass, it's the most expensive way to go (£50 total for off-peak travel without railpass, £5-10 cheaper bought in advance, up to £60 more for full-fare peak-time ticket; 2/hour, 2-2.25 hours depending on airport terminal, easy change between First Great Western train and Heathrow Express at London's Paddington Station). The **National Express bus** is direct, and often much cheaper for those without a railpass, but it's relatively infrequent, and can take nearly twice as long as the train (10/day, 2.5-4 hours, £22-44 one-way depending on time of day, tel. 0871-781-8178, www.nationalexpress.com). Doing a **train-and-bus combination** via the town of Reading can make sense for non-railpass holders, as it's more frequent, can take less time than the direct bus, and can be much cheaper than the train via London (train to Reading: 2/hour, 1 hour, RailAir Link shuttle bus from there: 2/hour, 45 minutes; allow 2.5 hours total; £26-40 for off-peak, nonrefundable travel booked in advance—but up to £72 for peak-time trains; tel. 0118-957-9425, buy bus ticket from www.railair.com, train ticket from www.firstgreatwestern.co.uk). Another option is the **minibus** operated by recommended tour company Celtic Horizons (see page 415).

You can get to **Gatwick** by train with a transfer in Reading (hourly, 2.5-3 hours, £50-75 one-way depending on time of day, cheaper in advance; avoid transfer in London, where you'll have to change stations; www.firstgreatwestern.co.uk) or by bus with a transfer at Heathrow (8/day, 3.5-4.5 hours, £30 one-way, transfer at Heathrow Airport, www.nationalexpress.com).

Connecting Bath and Bristol Airport: Located about 20 miles west of Bath, this airport is closer than Heathrow, but they haven't worked out good connections to Bath yet. From Bristol Airport, your most convenient options are to take a taxi (£40) or call Alan Price (see "Celtic Horizons" on page 415). Otherwise, at the airport you can hop aboard the Bristol Airport Flyer (bus #A1), which takes you to the Temple Meads train station in Bristol (£7, 3/hour, 30 minutes, buy bus ticket at airport info counter or from driver, tell driver you want the Temple Meads train station). At the Temple Meads Station, check the departure boards for trains going to the Bath Spa train station (4/hour, 15 minutes, £7). To get from Bath to Bristol Airport, take the train to Temple Meads, then catch the Bristol Airport Flyer bus.

From Bath by Train to: Salisbury (1-2/hour, 1 hour), **Portsmouth** (hourly, 2.25 hours), **Exeter** (1-2/hour, 1.5-2 hours, transfer in Bristol or Westbury), **Penzance** (1-2/hour, 4.5-5 hours, one direct, most 1-2 transfers), **Moreton-in-Marsh** (hourly, 2.5-3 hours, 1-2 transfers), **York** (hourly with transfer in Bristol, 4.5 hours, more with additional transfers), **Oxford** (hourly, 1.5 hours, transfer in Didcot), **Cardiff** (hourly, 1-1.5 hours), **Birmingham** (2/hour, 2 hours, transfer in Bristol), and **points north** (from Birmingham, a major transportation hub, trains depart for Blackpool, Scotland,

and North Wales; use a train/bus combination to reach Ironbridge Gorge and the Lake District).

From Bath by Bus to: Salisbury (hourly, 2.75 hours, transfer in Warminster or Devizes; or 1/day direct at 17:05, 1.5 hours on National Express #300), **Portsmouth** (1/day direct, 3 hours), **Exeter** (4/day, 3.5-4 hours, transfer in Bristol), **Penzance** (2/day, 7-8 hours, transfer in Bristol), **Cheltenham** or **Gloucester** (4/day, 2.5 hours, transfer in Bristol), **Stratford-upon-Avon** (1/day, 4 hours, transfer in Bristol), and **Oxford** (1/day direct, 2 hours, more with transfer). For bus connections to **Glastonbury, Avebury,** and **Wells,** see the next chapter.

NEAR BATH

Glastonbury • Wells • Avebury • Stonehenge • Salisbury

Ooooh, mystery, history. The countryside surrounding Bath holds some of England's most goose-pimply prehistoric sites, as well as two particularly fine cathedral towns. Glastonbury, also known as Avalon, is the ancient resting place of King Arthur, and home (maybe) to the Holy Grail. Nearby, medieval Wells gathers around its grand cathedral, where you can enjoy an evensong service. Then get Neolithic at every druid's favorite stone circles, Avebury and Stonehenge. Salisbury is known for its colorful markets and soaring cathedral.

Planning Your Time

Avebury, Glastonbury, and Wells make a wonderful day out from Bath. With a car, you can do all three in a day if you're selective

with your sightseeing in each town (no lingering). If you want to squeeze a little less into each day, choose either the sights to the west (Wells and Glastonbury), or those to the east (Avebury, Stonehenge, and Salisbury). Ideally, try to see Stonehenge on your way from London, saving your Bath side-tripping day for the other sights.

Everybody needs to see **Stonehenge,** but I'll tell you now: It looks just like it looks. You'll know what I mean when you pay to get in and rub up against the rope fence that keeps tourists at a

distance. **Avebury** is the connoisseur's stone circle: more subtle and welcoming.

Wells is simply a cute small town, much smaller and more medieval than Bath, with a uniquely beautiful cathedral that's best experienced at the 17:15 evensong service (Sun at 15:00)—though the service isn't usually held in July and August.

Glastonbury can be covered well in two to three hours: See the abbey, climb the Tor, and ponder your hippie past (and where you are now).

Just an hour from Bath, **Salisbury** makes a pleasant stop, particularly on a market day (Tue, Sat, and every other Wed), though its cathedral is striking anytime. Salisbury is also the logical launchpad for visiting nearby Stonehenge (particularly if you lack a car).

Getting Around the Region

By Car: Drivers can do a 133-mile loop, from Bath to Avebury (25 miles) to Stonehenge (30 miles) to Glastonbury (50 miles) to Wells (6 miles) and back to Bath (22 miles).

By Bus and Train: Wells and Glastonbury are both easily accessible by bus from Bath. Bus #173 goes direct from Bath to **Wells** (nearly hourly, less frequent on Sun, 1.25 hours), where you can continue on to **Glastonbury** by catching bus #375 toward Bridgewater, #377 toward Yeovil, or #29 toward Taunton (3-4/hour, 25 minutes to Glastonbury, drops off directly in front of abbey entrance on Magdalene Street). Note that there are no direct buses between Bath and Glastonbury. First Bus Company offers a £7 day pass that covers all their routes—a good deal if you plan on connecting Glastonbury and Wells from your Bath home base. Wells and Glastonbury are also connected to each other by a 9.5-mile foot and bike path (though only Glastonbury has bike rental).

Many different buses run between Bath and **Avebury,** all requiring one or two transfers (hourly, 2.25 hours, transfer at Trowbridge or Devizes). There is no bus between Avebury and Stonehenge.

A one-hour train trip connects Bath to **Salisbury** (1-2/hour). With the best public transportation of all these towns, Salisbury is a good jumping-off point for Stonehenge or Avebury by bus or car. The Stonehenge Tour runs buses between Salisbury, Old Sarum, and Stonehenge (see page 484). Buses also run from Salisbury to Avebury (hourly, 2-2.5 hours; Wilts & Dorset bus #4 leaves from bus station on Endless Street and also from St. Paul's Church on Fisherton Street, near the train station; transfer in Devizes to Stagecoach's bus #49 to Avebury; other combinations possible, some with 2 transfers).

Various bus companies run these routes, including Stagecoach, Bodmans Coaches, the First Bus Company, and Wilts & Dorset. To find fare information, check with Traveline South West, which combines all the information from these companies into an easy-to-use website that covers all the southwest routes (www.travelinesw.com, tel. 0871-200-2233). Buses run much less frequently on Sundays.

By Tour: From Bath, if you don't have a car, the most convenient and quickest way to see Avebury and Stonehenge is to take an all-day bus tour, or a half-day tour just to Stonehenge. Mad Max is the liveliest of the tours leaving from Bath (see "Tours in Bath" on page 412).

Near Bath at a Glance

Glastonbury

▲▲**Glastonbury Abbey** Once a leading Christian pilgrimage destination, now a lush park with some of England's finest abbey ruins—along with the purported gravesite of Arthur and Guinevere. **Hours:** Daily June-Aug 9:00-20:00, Sept-Nov and March-May 9:00-17:00, Dec-Feb 9:00-16:00. See page 454.

▲**Glastonbury Tor** Holy hill topped with the remnants of a church tower and worth climbing for its sweeping views. **Hours:** Always open. See page 457.

Wells

▲▲**Wells Cathedral** England's first wholly Gothic cathedral, with an ornate facade and heavenly evensong service (except July-Aug). **Hours:** Daily Easter-Sept 7:00-19:00, Oct-Easter 7:00-18:00. See page 460.

▲**Bishop's Palace** Home of the Bishop of Bath and Wells, with spectacular gardens. **Hours:** Daily April-Oct 10:00-18:00, Nov-March 10:00-16:00, often closed on Sat for special events. See page 465.

Avebury

▲▲**Avebury Stone Circle** Giant stone circle, 16 times the size of

Glastonbury

Marked by its hill, or "tor," and located on England's most powerful line of prehistoric sites, the town of Glastonbury gurgles with history and mystery.

In A.D. 37, Joseph of Arimathea—Jesus' wealthy uncle—reputedly brought vessels containing the blood of Jesus to Glastonbury, and with him, Christianity came to England. (Joseph's visit is plausible—long before Christ, locals traded lead and tin to merchants from the Levant.)

While this story is "proven" by fourth-century writings and accepted by the Church, the King-Arthur-and-the-Holy-Grail legends it inspired are not. Those medieval tales came

Stonehenge—but with a fraction of the tourists. **Hours:** Always open. See page 471.

▲**Ritual Procession Way** Double line of stones that once served as a route for ritual processions. **Hours:** Always open. See page 471.

▲**Silbury Hill** Pyramid-shaped chalk mound—and the largest man-made object from prehistoric Europe. **Hours:** Always open. See page 471.

Stonehenge and Salisbury

▲▲**Stonehenge** England's most famous stone circle, unique for its horizontal stones. **Hours:** Daily June-Aug 9:00-20:00, mid-March-May and Sept-mid-Oct 9:30-19:00, mid-Oct-mid-March 9:30-17:00. See page 474.

▲▲**Salisbury Cathedral** Architecturally harmonious Gothic cathedral, boasting the tallest spire in England, surrounded by a huge, peaceful green. **Hours:** April-Oct Mon-Sat 9:00-17:00, Sun 12:00-16:00; Nov-March daily 9:00-17:00. See page 484.

▲**Salisbury and South Wiltshire Museum** Random collection of costumes, art, ceramics, and other historical items, plus a fine exhibit about Stonehenge. **Hours:** Mon-Sat 10:00-17:00, Sun 12:00-17:00 except closed Sun Oct-May. See page 487.

NEAR BATH

when England needed a morale-boosting folk hero for inspiration during a war with France. They pointed to the ancient Celtic sanctuary at Glastonbury as proof enough of the greatness of the fifth-century warlord Arthur. In 1191, after a huge fire, Arthur's supposed remains (along with those of Queen Guinevere) were dug up from the abbey garden. Reburied in the abbey choir, Arthur and Guinevere's gravesite is a shrine today. Many think the Grail trail ends at the bottom of the Chalice Well, a natural spring at the base of the Glastonbury Tor.

By the 10th century, Glastonbury Abbey was England's most powerful and wealthy, and was part of a nationwide network of monasteries that by 1500 owned one-quarter of all English land and had four times the income of the Crown. Then Henry VIII dissolved the abbeys in 1536. He was particularly harsh on Glastonbury—he not only destroyed the abbey but also hung and quartered the abbot, sending the parts of his body on four different national tours...at the same time. This was meant as a warning to other religious clerics, and it worked.

But Glastonbury rebounded. In an 18th-century tourism campaign, thousands signed affidavits stating that they'd been healed

by water from the Chalice Well, and once again Glastonbury was on the tourist map. Today, Glastonbury and its Tor are a center for "searchers"— too creepy for the mainstream Church but just right for those looking for a place to recharge their crystals. Glastonbury is also synonymous with its music and arts festival, an annual long-hair-and-mud Woodstock recreation that's a rite of passage for young music lovers.

Part of the fun of a visit to Glastonbury is just being in a town where every other shop and eatery is a New Age place. Locals who are not into this complain that on High Street, you can buy any kind of magic crystal or incense—but not a roll of TP. But, as this counterculture is their town's bread and butter, they do their best to sit in their pubs and go "Ommmmm."

Orientation to Glastonbury

Tourist Information

The TI is on High Street—as are many of the dreadlocked folks who walk it. It occupies a fine 15th-century townhouse called The Tribunal (Mon-Sat 10:00-16:00, closed Sun, pay Internet terminal, 9 High Street, tel. 01458/832-954, www.glastonburytic.co.uk). The TI sells several booklets about cycling and walking in the area, including the *Glastonbury and Street Guide,* with local listings and a map (£1); and the *Glastonbury Millennium Trail* pamphlet, which sends visitors on a historical scavenger hunt, following 20 numbered marble plaques embedded in the pavement throughout the town (£1). The TI also offers sporadic walking tours (£5, call ahead for schedule).

Above the TI is the marginally interesting **Lake Village Museum,** with two humble rooms featuring tools made of stones, bones, and antlers. Preserved in and excavated from the local peat bogs, these tools offer a look at the lives of marshland people in pre-Roman times (£2.50, extensive descriptions, same hours as TI, tel. 01458/832-954).

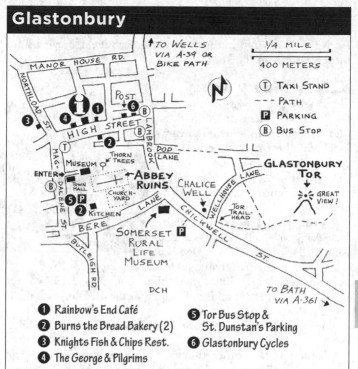

Glastonbury

TO WELLS
VIA A-39 OR
BIKE PATH

¼ MILE
400 METERS

MANOR HOUSE RD.

NORTHLOAD ST.

POST

HIGH STREET

T TAXI STAND
--- PATH
P PARKING
B BUS STOP

LAMBROOK ST.

POP LANE

THORN TREES

MAG. LANE

MUSEUM

ENTER

ABBEY RUINS

TOWN HALL

CHURCH-YARD

CHALICE WELL

GLASTONBURY TOR

WELLHOUSE LANE

GREAT VIEW!

TOR TRAIL-HEAD

KITCHEN

DALELENE ST.

BERE

LANE

CHICKWELL ST.

BUTLEIGH RD.

SOMERSET RURAL LIFE MUSEUM

DCH

TO BATH
VIA A-361

❶ Rainbow's End Café
❷ Burns the Bread Bakery (2)
❸ Knights Fish & Chips Rest.
❹ The George & Pilgrims
❺ Tor Bus Stop &
   St. Dunstan's Parking
❻ Glastonbury Cycles

Near Bath (side tab)

Helpful Hints

Market Day: Tuesday is market day for crafts, knickknacks, and local produce on the main street. There's also a country market Tuesday mornings in the Town Hall.

Glastonbury Festival: Nearly every summer (around the June solstice), the gigantic Glastonbury Festival—billing itself as the "largest music and performing arts festival in the world"—brings all manner of postmodern flower children to its notoriously muddy "Healing Fields." Music fans and London's beautiful people make the trek to see the hottest English and American bands. If you're near Glastonbury during the festival, anticipate increased traffic and crowds (especially on public transportation; more than 165,000 tickets generally sell out), even though the actual music venue is six miles east of town (www.glastonburyfestivals.co.uk).

Bike Rental: Try **Glastonbury Cycles,** at the top of High Street (£10/day, includes lock and tire repair kit, helmets-£2; Mon-Fri 9:30-18:00, Sat 9:30-17:00, closed Sun; deposit required—either cash, credit card, or passport; must return bikes in Glastonbury, 67 High Street, tel. 01458/830-639).

Sights in Glastonbury

I've listed these sights in the order you'll reach them, moving from the town center to the Tor.

▲▲Glastonbury Abbey

The massive and evocative ruins of the first Christian sanctuary in the British Isles stand mysteriously alive in a lush 36-acre park. Be-

cause it comes with a small museum, a dramatic history, and enthusiastic guides dressed in period costume, this is one of the most engaging to visit of England's many ruined abbeys.

Cost and Hours: £6, daily June-Aug 9:00-20:00, Sept-Nov and March-May 9:00-17:00, Dec-Feb 9:00-16:00, last entry 30 minutes before closing.

Getting There: Enter the abbey from Magdalene Street (around the corner from High Street, near the St. Dunstan's parking lot). Pay parking is nearby.

Information: Tel. 01458/832-267, www.glastonburyabbey.com.

Tours and Demonstrations: Costumed guides offer tours and presentations throughout the day (all included with your ticket). These include a fun medieval kitchen demo (described later) and earnest, costumed "Living History" re-enactments (generally daily March-Oct on the hour from 10:00). As you enter, confirm these times, and ask about other tour and show times. Or, if you're coming on a slow day (off-season weekdays), call ahead to get the schedule.

Eating: Picnicking is encouraged—bring something from one of the shops in town (see "Eating in Glastonbury," later), or buy food at the small café on site (open May-Sept).

Background: The space that these ruins occupy has been sacred ground for centuries. The druids used it as a pagan holy site, and during Joseph of Arimathea's supposed visit here, he built a simple place of worship. In the 12th century—because of that legendary connection—Glastonbury was the leading Christian pilgrimage site in all of Britain. The popular abbey grew powerful and very wealthy, employing a thousand people to serve the needs of the pilgrims. Then, in 1171, Thomas Becket was martyred at Canterbury and immediately canonized by the pope (who thanked God for the opportunity to rile up the Christian public in England against King Henry II). This was a classic church-state power struggle. The king was excommunicated. In order to redeem himself, he had to crawl through the streets of London on his knees and submit to a whipping from each bishop in England. Religious pilgrims abandoned Glastonbury for Canterbury, leaving Glastonbury suddenly a backwater.

In 1184, there was a devastating fire in the monastery, and in 1191, the abbot here "discovered"—with the help of a divine dream—the tomb and bodies of King Arthur and Queen Guinevere. Of course, this discovery rekindled the pilgrim trade in Glastonbury, and the new revenues helped to rebuild the abbey.

Then, in 1539, King Henry VIII ordered the abbey's destruction. When Glastonbury Abbot Richard Whiting questioned the king's decision, he was branded a traitor, hung at the top of Glastonbury Tor (after carrying up the plank that would support his noose), and his body cut into four pieces. His head was stuck over the gateway to the former abbey precinct. After this harsh example, the other abbots accepted the king's dissolution of England's abbeys, with many returning to monastic centers in France. Glastonbury Abbey fell into ruin.

Today, the abbey attracts people who find God within and the curious traveler alike. Tie-dyed, starry-eyed pilgrims seem to float through the grounds, naturally high. Others lie on the grave of King Arthur, whose burial site is marked off in the center of the abbey ruins.

❍ **Self-Guided Tour:** After buying your ticket, tour the informative **museum** at the entrance building. A model shows the abbey in its pre-Henry VIII splendor, and exhibits tell the story of a place "grandly constructed to entice the dullest minds to prayer." Knowledgeable, costumed guides are eager to share the site's story and might even offer an impromptu tour.

Then head out to explore the green park, dotted with bits of the **ruined abbey.** You come face-to-face with the abbey's west (entrance) end. The abbey was long and skinny, but vast. Measuring 580 feet, it was the longest in Britain (larger than York Minster is today) and the largest building north of the Alps.

Before poking around the ruins, circle to the left behind the entrance building to find the two **thorn trees.** According to legend, when Joseph of Arimathea came here, he climbed nearby Wearyall Hill and stuck his staff into the soil. A thorn tree sprouted, and its descendant still stands there today; these are its offspring. In 2010, vandals hacked off the branches of the original tree on Wearyall Hill, but miraculously, the stump put out small green shoots the following spring. The trees inside the abbey grounds bloom twice a year, at Easter and at Christmas. If the story seems far-fetched to you, don't tell the Queen—a blossom from the abbey's trees sits proudly on her breakfast table every Christmas morning.

Ahead and to the left of the trees, inside what was the north wall, look for two trap doors in the ground. Lift up the doors to see surviving fragments of the abbey's original tiled floor.

Now hike along the ruins, walking through the remains of the extensive cloisters, to the far end of the abbey. You can stand and, from what was the altar, look down at what was the nave. In this area, you'll find the tombstone (formerly in the floor of the church's choir) marking the spot where the supposed relics of **Arthur and Guinevere** were interred.

Continue around the far side of the abbey ruins, feeling free to poke around the park. Head back toward the front of the church, noticing all of the foundation rubble in the field adjoining the abbey; among these were the former churchyard, where Arthur and Guinevere's bones were originally found.

Head for the only surviving intact building on the grounds—the abbot's conical **kitchen.** Here, you'll often find Matilda the pilgrim (or another costumed docent) demonstrating life in the abbey kitchen in a kind of medieval cooking show.

Near Glastonbury Tor

These sights are about a 15-minute walk from the town center, toward the Tor (see "Getting There," on page 457).

Somerset Rural Life Museum

Exhibits in this free and extremely kid-friendly museum include peat digging and cider- and cheese-making. The abbey farmhouse now houses a collection of domestic and work mementos that illustrate the life of Victorian farm laborer John Hodges "from the cradle to the grave." The fine 14th-century tithe barn (one of 30 such structures that funneled tithes to the local abbey), with its beautifully preserved wooden ceiling, is filled with Victorian farm tools and enthusiastic schoolchildren.

Cost and Hours: Free, Tue-Sat 10:00-17:00, closed Sun-Mon, last entry 30 minutes before closing; parking-£1/2 hours, £2/day; at intersection of Bere Lane and Chilkwell Street, tel. 01823/278-805, www.somerset.gov.uk/museums.

Chalice Well

According to tradition, Joseph of Arimathea brought the chalice from the Last Supper to Glastonbury in A.D. 37. Supposedly it ended up in the bottom of a well, which is now the centerpiece of a peaceful and inviting garden. Even if the chalice is not in the bottom of the well (another legend says it made the trip to Wales), and the water is red from iron ore and not Jesus' blood, the tranquil setting is one where nature's harmony is a joy to ponder. To find the well itself, follow the well-marked path uphill alongside the gurgling stream, passing several places to drink from or wade in the healing water, as well as areas designated for silent reflection. The stones of the well shaft date from the 12th century and are believed to have come from the church in Glastonbury Abbey (which was destroyed by fire). During the 18th century, pilgrims flocked to Glastonbury for the well's healing powers. Have a drink or take some of the precious water home—they sell empty bottles to fill.

Cost and Hours: £3.80, daily April-Oct 10:00-18:00, Nov-March 10:00-16:30, last entry 30 minutes before closing, on Chilkwell Street/A-361, drivers park at Rural Life Museum and walk 5 minutes—see instructions below, tel. 01458/831-154, www.chalicewell.org.uk.

▲Glastonbury Tor

Seen by many as a Mother Goddess symbol, the Tor—a natural plug of sandstone on clay—has an undeniable geological charisma. Climbing the Tor is the essential activity on a visit to Glastonbury. A fine Somerset view rewards those who hike to its 520-foot summit.

Getting There: The Tor is a steep hill at the southeastern edge of the town (it's visible from just about everywhere). The base of the Tor is a 20-minute **walk** from the TI and town center. From the base, a trail leads up to the top (figure another 15-20 uphill minutes, if you keep a brisk pace). While you can hike up the Tor from either end, the less-steep approach (which most people take) starts next to the Chalice Well.

If you have a **car,** drive to the Somerset Rural Life Museum, where you can park, then walk five minutes to the trailhead (walk up the lane between the parking lot and the museum, turn right onto Chilkwell Street, and watch on the left for the Chalice Well, then signs for the trailhead).

If you're without a car and don't want to walk to the Tor trailhead, you have two options: The **Tor Bus** shuttles visitors from the town center to the base of the Tor. If you ask, the bus will also stop at the Somerset Rural Life Museum and the Chalice Well (£3 round-trip, 2/hour, on the half-hour, Easter-Sept daily 9:30-12:30 & 14:00-19:00, doesn't run Oct-Easter, catch bus at St. Dunstan's parking lot in the town center—to the right as you face the abbey entrance, pick up schedule at TI). A **taxi** to the Tor trailhead costs about £5 one-way—an easier and more economical choice for couples or groups. Remember, these take you only to the bottom of the Tor; to reach the top, you have to hike.

Climbing the Tor: Hiking up to the top of the tor, you can survey a former swamp, inhabited for 12,000 years, that is still below sea level at high tide. The ribbon-like man-made drainage canals that glisten as they slice through the farmland are the work of Dutch engineers—Huguenot refugees imported centuries ago to turn the marshy wasteland into something usable.

Looking out, find Glastonbury (at the base of the hill) and Wells (marked by its cathedral) to the right. Above Wells, a TV tower marks the 996-foot high point of the Mendip Hills. It was lead from these hills that attracted the Romans (and, perhaps, Jesus' uncle Joe) so long ago. Stretching to the left, the Mendip Hills define what was the coastline before those Dutch engineers arrived.

The Tor-top tower is the remnant of a chapel dedicated to St. Michael. Early Christians often employed St. Michael, the warrior angel, to combat pagan gods. When a church was built upon a pagan holy ground like this, it was frequently dedicated to Michael. But apparently those pagan gods fought back: St. Michael's Church was destroyed by an earthquake in 1275.

Eating in Glastonbury

Rainbow's End is one of several fine, healthy, vegetarian lunch cafés for hot meals (different every day), salads, herbal teas, soups, yummy homemade sweets, and New Age people-watching. If you're looking for a midwife or a male-bonding tribal meeting, check their notice board (£6-8 meals, cheaper salads sold by the portion, vegan and gluten-free options, counter service, daily 10:00-16:00, free Wi-Fi, a few doors up from the TI, 17 High Street, tel. 01458/833-896).

Burns the Bread has two locations in town, making hearty pasties (savory meat pies) as well as fresh pies, sandwiches, delicious cookies, and pastries. Ask for a sample of the Torsy Moorsy Cake (a type of fruitcake made with cheddar), or try a gingerbread man made with real ginger. Grab a pasty and picnic with the ghosts of Arthur and Guinevere in the abbey ruins (£1.80 pasties and pastries, £2-3 sandwiches, Mon-Sat 6:00-17:00, Sun 11:00-17:00, two locations: 14 High Street and in St. Dunstan's parking lot next to the abbey, tel. 01458/831-532).

Knights Fish and Chips Restaurant has been in the same family since 1909 and is the town's top chippy. It's another fine option for a picnic at the abbey (£6 to go, about £1 more for table service, Mon-Fri 12:00-14:15 & 17:00-21:30, Sat 17:00-21:30 only, closed Sun, 5 Northload Street, tel. 01458/831-882).

The **George & Pilgrims Hotel**'s wonderfully Old World pub might be exactly what the doctor ordered for visitors suffering a New Age overdose. The local owners serve up a traditional pub-grub menu (£5 sandwiches, £8-11 meals, Mon-Sat 11:00-23:00, Sun 12:00-22:30, food served 12:00-14:45 & 18:00-20:45, 1 High Street, tel. 01458/831-146). They also rent rooms (Db-£80, family rooms-£85).

Glastonbury Connections

The nearest train station is in Bath. Local buses are run by First Bus Company (tel. 0845-602-0156, www.firstgroup.com).

From Glastonbury by Bus to: Wells (3-4/hour, 20 minutes, bus #375/#377 or #29), **Bath** (nearly hourly, allow 2 hours, take bus #375/#377 or #29 to Wells, transfer to bus #173 to Bath, 1.25 hours between Wells and Bath). Buses are sparse on Sundays (generally one bus every other hour). If you're heading to points west, you'll likely connect through **Taunton** (which is a transfer point for westbound buses from Bristol).

Wells

Because this well-preserved little town has a cathedral, it can be called a city. It's England's smallest cathedral city (pop. 9,400), with one of its most interesting cathedrals and a wonderful evensong service (generally not offered July-Aug). Wells has more medieval buildings still doing what they were originally built to do than any town you'll visit. Market day fills the town square on Wednesday (farmers' market) and Saturday (general goods).

Orientation to Wells

Tourist Information

The TI is in the lobby of the Wells Museum, across the green from the cathedral. It has useful information about the town's sights and nearby cheese factories (April-Oct Mon-Sat 10:00-17:00, Nov-March Mon-Sat 11:00-16:00, closed Sun year-round, 8 Cathedral Green, tel. 01749/671-770, www.visitsomerset.co.uk). The TI sells town maps for £0.50 and provides information on trails nearby; consider the *Wells City Trail* booklet for £0.60. It also offers a one-hour walking tour of town for £4 on Wednesdays and Saturdays at 11:00 (Easter-Sept only).

Arrival in Wells

If you're coming by **bus,** you can get off in the city center at the Sadler Street stop, around the corner from the cathedral. Or you can disembark at the big, well-organized bus station/parking lot (staffed Mon-Fri 9:00-16:30, closed Sat-Sun), about a five-minute walk from the town center, at the bottom of High Street. (The big church tower you see is *not* the cathedral.) Find the Wells map at the head of the stalls to get oriented; the signpost at the main exit directs you downtown.

Drivers will find pay parking right on the main square, but because of confusing one-way streets, it's hard to reach; instead, it's simpler to park at the Princes Road lot near the bus station (enter on Priory Road) and walk five minutes to the cathedral.

Helpful Hints

Local Guide: Edie Westmoreland, an official cathedral guide, offers town walks in the summer by appointment (£15/group of 2-5 people, £4/person for 8 or more, 1.5-hour tours usually start at Penniless Porch on town square, book three days in advance, tel. 01934/832-350, mobile 07899-836-706, ebwestmoreland@btinternet.com).

Best Views: It's hard to beat the grand views of the cathedral from the green in front of it...but the reflecting pool tucked inside the Bishop's Palace grounds tries hard. For a fine cathedral-and-town view from your own leafy hilltop bench, hike 10 minutes up Tor Hill.

Sights in Wells

▲▲Wells Cathedral

The city's highlight is England's first completely Gothic cathedral (dating from about 1200). Locals claim this church has the largest collection of medieval statuary north of the Alps. It certainly has one of the widest and most elaborate facades I've seen, and unique figure-eight ("scissors arch") that supports in the nave.

Cost and Hours: Free but £6 donation requested—not intended to keep you out, daily Easter-Sept 7:00-19:00, Oct-Easter 7:00-18:00, daily evensong service (except July-Aug)—described later.

Information: Good shop, handy Chapter Two restaurant, tel. 01749/674-483, www.wellscathedral.org.uk.

Tours: Free one-hour tours run April-Oct Mon-Sat at 10:00, 11:00, 13:00, 14:00, and 15:00; Nov-March Mon-Sat usually at

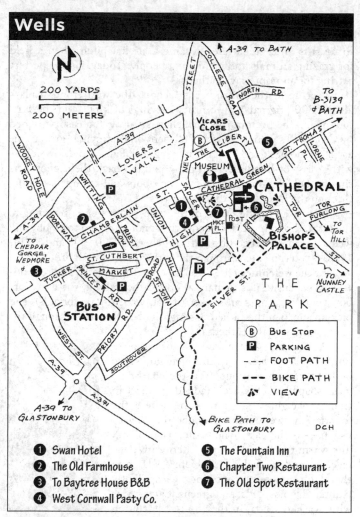

Wells

200 YARDS
200 METERS

A-39 TO BATH

COLLEGE ROAD

NEW STREET

NORTH RD.

TO B-3139 & BATH

VICARS CLOSE

THE LIBERTY

MUSEUM

ST. THOMAS

LORNE

WOOKEY HOLE ROAD

A-39

LOVERS WALK

WHITING

PORTWAY

CHAMBERLAIN

ST. SADLER

UNION

CATHEDRAL GREEN

CATHEDRAL

TOR FURLONG

TO TOR HILL

TO CHEDDAR GORGE, WEDMORE

PRIEST ROW

HIGH ST.

MKT PL.

POST

TOR ST.

BISHOP'S PALACE

TUCKER ST.

ST. CUTHBERT

MARKET

PRINCES RD.

BROAD ST.

ST. JOHN ST.

MILL

SILVER ST.

THE PARK

TO NUNNEY CASTLE

BUS STATION

WEST ST.

PRIORY RD.

SOUTHOVER

A-39

A-371

A-39 TO GLASTONBURY

BIKE PATH TO GLASTONBURY

DCH

Legend:
- Ⓑ Bus Stop
- Ⓟ Parking
- --- Foot Path
- --- Bike Path
- ☆ View

1 Swan Hotel
2 The Old Farmhouse
3 To Baytree House B&B
4 West Cornwall Pasty Co.
5 The Fountain Inn
6 Chapter Two Restaurant
7 The Old Spot Restaurant

12:00 and 14:00—unless other events are going on in the cathedral.

Photography: To take pictures, pay the £3 photography fee at the info desk or at a coin-op machine inside the cathedral. No flash is allowed in the choir.

❂ **Self-Guided Tour:** Begin on the vast, inviting **green** in front of the cathedral. In the Middle Ages, the cathedral was enclosed within "The Liberty," an area free from civil jurisdiction until the 1800s. The Liberty included the green on the west side of the cathedral, which, from the 13th to the 17th centuries, was a burial place for common folk, including 17th-century plague victims. During the Edwardian period, a local character known as Boney Foster used to dig up the human bones and sell them to tourists. The green later became a cricket pitch, then a field for grazing animals and picnicking people. Today, it's the perfect setting for an impressive cathedral.

Peer up at the magnificent **facade.** The west front displays almost 300 original 13th-century carvings of kings and the Last Judgment. The bottom row of niches is empty, too easily reached by Cromwell's men, who were hell-bent on destroying "graven images." Stand back and imagine it as a grand Palm Sunday welcome with a cast of hundreds—all gaily painted back then, choristers singing boldly from holes above the doors and trumpets tooting through the holes up by the 12 apostles.

Now head **inside.** Most of the time, visitors enter by going to the right, through the door under the small spire into the lobby and welcome center. (At certain times—generally 7:00-9:00 and 17:00-19:00—you can enter through the cathedral's main door.)

At the **welcome center,** you'll be warmly greeted and reminded how expensive it is to maintain the cathedral. Pay the donation, buy a photo-permission sticker (if you want to take photos), and pick up a map of the cathedral's highlights. Then head through the cloister and into the cathedral.

At your first glance down the nave, you're immediately struck by the general sense of light and the unique "scissors" or hourglass-shaped **double arch** (added in 1338 to transfer weight from the south—where the foundations were sinking under the tower's weight—to the east, where they were firm). The warm tones of the stone interior give the place a modern feel. Until Henry VIII and the Reformation, the interior was opulently painted in golds, reds, and greens. Later it was whitewashed. Then, in the 1840s, the church experienced the Victorian "great scrape," as locals peeled moldy whitewash off and revealed the bare stone we see today. The floral ceiling painting is based on the original medieval design: A single pattern was discovered under the 17th-century whitewash and repeated throughout.

Small, ornate 15th-century pavilion-like chapels flank the altar, carved in lacy Gothic for wealthy townsmen. The **pulpit** features a post-Reformation, circa-1540 English script—rather than the standard Latin (see where the stonemason ran out of space when carving the inscription). Since this was not a monastery church, the Reformation didn't destroy it as it did the Glastonbury Abbey church.

We'll do a quick clockwise spin around the cathedral's interior. First walk down the left aisle until you reach the north transept.

The medieval **clock** does a silly but much-loved joust on the quarter-hour. If you get to watch the show, notice how—like clockwork—the same rider gets clobbered, as he has for hundreds of years. The clock's face, which depicts the earth at the center of the universe, dates from 1390. The outer ring shows hours, the middle ring shows minutes, and the inner ring shows the dates of the month and phases of the moon. Beneath the clock, the fine **crucifix** (1947) was carved out of a yew tree by English sculptor Estcourt James Clack. Also in the north transept is the door with well-worn steps leading up to the grand, fan-vaulted **Chapter House**—an inspiring architectural achievement and intimate place for the theological equivalent of a huddle among church officials.

Now continue down the left aisle. On the right is the entrance to the **choir** (or "quire," the central zone where the daily services are sung). Go in and take a close look at the embroidery work on the cushions, which celebrate the hometowns of important local church leaders. Up above the east end of the choir is "Jesse's Window," depicting Jesus' family tree. It's also called the "Golden Window," because it's bathed in sunlight each morning.

Head back out to the aisle the way you came in, and continue to the end of the church. In the apse you'll find the **Lady Chapel.**

Examine the medieval stained-glass windows. Do they look jumbled? In the 17th century, Puritan troops trashed the precious original glass. Much was repaired, but many of the broken panes were like a puzzle that was never figured out. That's why today many of the windows are simply kaleidoscopes of colored glass.

Next to the chapel is the oldest piece of wooden furniture in England: a **"cope chest,"** which is still used to store the clergy's garments. It is so large it can't be moved out through any of the cathedral's doors. Historians believe the chest is older than the existing building, and was originally installed around A.D. 800, in the Saxon church that predated the cathedral.

Now circle around and head up the other aisle. As you walk, notice that many of the black **tombstones** set in the floor have decorative recesses that aren't filled with brass (as they once were). After the Reformation in the 1530s, the church was short on cash,

so they sold the brass to raise money for roof repairs.

Once you reach the south transept, you'll find several items of interest. The **old font** survives from the previous church (A.D. 705) and has been the site of Wells baptisms for more than a thousand years. In the far end of this transept, a little of the original green and red wall painting, that wasn't whitewashed, survives.

Nearby, notice the **carvings** at the tops of the pillars, which depict medieval life. On the first pillar, notice the man with a toothache and another man with a thorn in his foot. The second pillar tells a story of medieval justice: On the left, we see thieves stealing grapes; on the right, the woodcutter (with an axe) is warning the farmer (with the pitchfork) what's happening. Circle around to the back of the pillar for the rest of the story: On the left, the farmer chases one of the thieves, grabbing him by the ear. On the right, he clobbers the thief over the head with his pitchfork—so hard the farmer's hat falls off.

Also in the south transept, you'll find the entrance to the cathedral **Reading Room** (free, £0.50 donation requested, April-Oct Fri-Sat 14:30-16:30 only; might also be possible to step in for a quick look on weekday mornings and afternoons). Housing a few old manuscripts, it offers a peek into a real 15th-century library. At the back of the Reading Room, peer through the doors and notice the irons chaining the books to the shelves—a reflection perhaps of the trust in the clergy at that time.

The south transept is where you'll exit the cathedral: Head out into the cloister, then cross the courtyard back to the welcome center, shop, Chapter Two restaurant, and exit. Go in peace.

More Cathedral Sights

▲▲Cathedral Evensong Service

The cathedral choir takes full advantage of heavenly acoustics with a nightly 45-minute evensong service. You'll sit right in the old "quire" as you listen to a great pipe organ and the world-famous Wells Cathedral choir.

Cost and Hours: Free, Mon-Sat at 17:15, Sun at 15:00, generally no service when school is out July-Aug unless a visiting choir performs, to check call 01749/674-483 or visit www.wellscathedral.org.uk. At 17:05 (Sun at 14:50), the verger ushers visitors to their seats. There's usually plenty of room.

Returning to Bath after the Evensong: On weekdays and Saturdays, if you need to catch the 17:40 bus to Bath, request a seat on the north side of the presbytery, so you can slip out the side door without disturbing the service (10-minute walk from cathedral to station, bus also departs from The Liberty stop—a 4-minute walk away—at 17:42; or go at 18:15 via Bristol—explained later, under "Wells Connections").

Other Cathedral Concerts: The cathedral also hosts several evening concerts each month (£10-26, most about £20, generally Thu-Sat at 19:00 or 19:30, buy tickets by phone or at box office in cathedral gift shop; Mon-Sat 10:00-16:30, Sun 11:00-16:30; tel. 01749/672-773). Concert tickets are also available at the TI, along with pamphlets listing what's on.

Vicars Close

Lined with perfectly pickled 14th-century houses, this is the oldest continuously occupied complete street in Europe (since 1348; just a block north of the cathedral—go under the big arch and look left). It was built to house the vicar's choir, and it still houses church officials and choristers (and one of the places, #14, can be rented for a weeklong holiday—from £509; find details on 14 Vicars Close at the cathedral's website, www.wellscathedral.org.uk).

▲Bishop's Palace

Next to the cathedral stands the moated Bishop's Palace, built in the 13th century and still in use today as the residence of the Bishop of Bath and Wells. While the interior of the palace itself is dull, the grounds and gardens surrounding it are spectacular—the most tranquil and scenic spot in Wells, with wonderful views of the cathedral. It's just the place for a relaxing walk in the park. Watch the swans ring the bell when they have an attack of the munchies.

Cost and Hours: £7, daily April-Oct 10:00-18:00, Nov-

NEAR BATH

March 10:00-16:00, often closed on
Sat for special events—call to confirm, last entry one hour before closing.

Information: Tel. 01749/988-
111, www.bishopspalace.org.uk.

Audioguide: A multimedia
guide is available for £3.

**Visiting the Palace and Gar-
dens:** The palace's spring-fed moat
was built in the 14th century to pro-
tect the bishop during squabbles with the borough. Bishops would
generously release this potable water into the town during local
festivals (strangely, nobody asks why the freshwater springs were
walled in to start with). Now the moat serves primarily as a pool
for mute swans. The bridge was last drawn in 1831. Crossing that
bridge, you'll buy your ticket and enter the grounds (past the old-
timers playing a proper game of croquet—daily after 13:30). On
your right, pass through the evocative ruins of the Great Hall
(which was deserted and left to gradually deteriorate), and stroll
through the chirpy south lawn. If you're feeling energetic, hike up
to the top of the ramparts that encircle the property.

Circling around the far side of the mansion, walk through a
door in the rampart wall, cross the wooden bridge, and follow a

path to a smaller bridge and
the wells (springs) that gave the
city its name. Surrounding a
reflecting pool with the cathedral towering overhead, these
flower-bedecked pathways are
idyllic. Nearby are an arboretum, picnic area, and sweet
little pea-patch gardens.

After touring the gardens, the mansion's interior is a letdown—despite the borrowable descriptions that struggle to make
the dusty old place meaningful. Have a spot of tea in the café (with
outdoor garden seating), or climb the creaky wooden staircase to
wander long halls lined with portraits of bishops past.

Near Wells

The following stops are best for drivers.

Cheddar Cheese

If you're in the mood for a picnic, drop by any local aromatic
cheese shop for a great selection of tasty Somerset cheeses. Real
farmhouse cheddar puts Velveeta to shame. The **Cheddar Gorge
Cheese Company,** eight miles west of Wells, gives guests a chance

to see the cheese-making process and enjoy a sample (£1.95, daily 10:00-15:30; take the A-39, then the A-371 to Cheddar Gorge; tel. 01934/742-810, www.cheddargorgecheeseco.co.uk).

Scrumpy Farms

Scrumpy is the wonderfully dangerous hard cider brewed in this part of England. You don't find it served in many pubs because of the unruly crowd it attracts. Scrumpy, at 8 percent alcohol, will rot your socks. "Scrumpy Jack," carbonated mass-produced cider, is not real scrumpy. The real stuff is "rough farmhouse cider." This is potent stuff. It's said some farmers throw a side of beef into the vat, and when fermentation is done only the teeth remain. (Some use a pair of old boots, for the tanin from the leather.)

TIs list cider farms open to the public, such as **Mr. Wilkins' Land's End Cider Farm,** a great Back Door travel experience (free, Mon-Sat 10:00-20:00, Sun 10:00-13:00; west of Wells in Mudgley, take the B-3139 from Wells to Wedmore, then the B-3151 south for 2 miles, farm is a quarter-mile off the B-3151—tough to find, get close and ask locals; tel. 01934/712-385, www.wilkinscider.com).

Apples are pressed from August through December. Hard cider, while not quite scrumpy, is also typical of the West Country, but more fashionable, "decent," and accessible. You can get a pint of hard cider at nearly any pub, drawn straight from the barrel—dry, medium, or sweet.

Nunney Castle

The centerpiece of the charming and quintessentially English village of Nunney (between Bath and Glastonbury, off the A-361) is a striking 14th-century castle surrounded by a fairy-tale moat. Its rare, French-style design brings to mind the Paris Bastille. The year 1644 was a tumultuous one for Nunney. Its noble family was royalist (and likely closet Catholics). They defied Parliament, so Parliament ordered their castle "slighted" (deliberately destroyed) to ensure that it would threaten the order of the land no more. Looking at this castle, so daunting in the age of bows and arrows, you can see how it was no match for the modern cannon. The pretty Mendip village of Nunney, with its little brook, is also worth a wander.

Cost and Hours: Free, visitable at "any reasonable time," tel. 01373/465-757, www.english-heritage.org.uk.

Sleeping in Wells

Wells is a pleasant overnight stop, with a handful of agreeable B&Bs. The first three places are within a short walk of the cathedral.

$$ Swan Hotel, a Best Western facing the cathedral, is a big, comfortable 48-room hotel. Prices for their Tudor-style rooms vary

Sleep Code

(£1 = about $1.60, country code: 44)
S = Single, **D** = Double/Twin, **T** = Triple, **Q** = Quad, **b** = bath-room, **s** = shower only. Unless otherwise noted, credit cards are accepted and breakfast is included.

To help you sort easily through these listings, I've divided the accommodations into two categories based on the price for a standard double room with bath:

$$ **Higher Priced**—Most rooms £90 or more.
$ **Lower Priced**—Most rooms less than £90.

Prices can change without notice; verify the hotel's current rates online or by email. For the best prices, always book direct.

NEAR BATH

based on whether you want extras like a four-poster bed or a view of the cathedral. They also rent five apartments in the village (Sb-£110-124, Db-£144-160, superior Db-£169-179, deluxe Db-£190-207, apartments-£119-155, ask about weekend deals, free Wi-Fi, Sadler Street, tel. 01749/836-300, www.swanhotelwells.co.uk, info@swanhotelwells.co.uk).

$$ The Old Farmhouse, a five-minute walk from the town center, welcomes you with a secluded front garden and two taste-fully decorated rooms (Db-£85-90, 2-night minimum, free Wi-Fi, secure parking, next to the gas station at 62 Chamberlain Street, tel. 01749/675-058, www.wellsholiday.com, theoldfarmhousewells@hotmail.com, charming owners Felicity and Christopher Wilkes).

$ Baytree House B&B is a modern and practical home at the edge of town (on a big road, a 10-minute walk to the bus station) renting five fresh, bright, and comfy rooms. Amanda and Paulo Bellini run the place with Italian enthusiasm (Db-£64-80, Tb-£75-90, two rooms have private bathrooms on the hall, free Wi-Fi, plush lounge, free parking, near where Strawberry Way hits the A-39 road to Cheddar at 85 Portway, tel. 01749/677-933, mobile 07745-287-194, www.baytree-house.co.uk, stay@baytree-house.co.uk).

Eating in Wells

Downtown Wells is tiny. A fine variety of eating options is within a block or two of its market square, including classic pubs; little delis and bakeries serving light meals; and a branch of **West Cornwall Pasty Company,** selling good savory pasties to go (Mon-Sat 8:30-17:00, Sun 10:00-16:30, 1a Sadler Street, tel. 01749/671-616).

The Fountain Inn, on a quiet street 50 yards behind the cathedral, serves good pub grub (£7-14 lunches, £10-14 dinners, daily 12:00-14:00 & 18:00-21:30, pub open until later, St. Thomas Street, tel. 01749/672-317).

Chapter Two, the modern restaurant in the cathedral welcome center, offers a handy if not heavenly lunch (£6-7 lunches, Mon-Sat 10:00-17:00, Sun 11:00-17:00, may close earlier in winter, tel. 01749/676-543).

The Old Spot is a dressy, modern place with a cathedral view. The food is elegant and well-prepared, although pricey (£20-23 fixed-price lunch, £6-7 starters, £14-19 main courses, Tue 19:00-22:30, Wed-Fri and Sat 12:30-14:30 & 19:00-22:30, Sun 12:30-14:30, closed Mon, 12 Sadler Street, tel. 01749/689-099, www.theoldspot.co.uk).

Wells Connections

The nearest train station is in Bath. The bus station in Wells is at a well-organized bus parking lot at the intersection of Priory and Princes roads. Local buses are run by First Bus Company (for Wells, tel. 0845-602-0156, www.firstgroup.com), while buses to and from London are run by National Express (tel. 0871-781-8178, www.nationalexpress.com).

From Wells by Bus to: Bath (nearly hourly, less frequent on Sun, 1.25 hours, last bus #173 leaves at 17:40—except Sun, when there are also buses at 18:46 and 20:03; if you miss the Mon-Sat 17:40 bus to Bath, catch the 18:15 bus to Bristol, then a 15-minute train ride to Bath, arriving 19:35), **Glastonbury** (3-4/hour, 20 minutes, bus #375/#377 or #29), **London**'s Victoria Coach Station (£21-30, 1/day direct, departs Wells at 6:55, arrives London at 11:20; otherwise hourly with a change in Bristol, 4 hours).

Avebury

Avebury is a prehistoric open-air museum, with a complex of fascinating Neolithic sites all gathered around the great stone henge (circle). Because the area sports only a thin skin of topsoil over chalk, it is naturally treeless (similar to the area around Stonehenge). Perhaps this unique landscape—where the land connects with the big sky—made it the choice

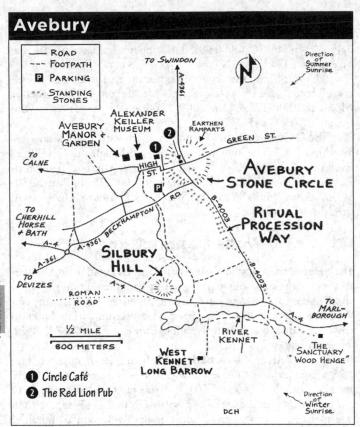

Avebury

Legend:
— ROAD
--- FOOTPATH
P PARKING
:: STANDING STONES

TO SWINDON
A-4361
Direction of Summer Sunrise

ALEXANDER KEILLER MUSEUM
AVEBURY MANOR & GARDEN
EARTHEN RAMPARTS
GREEN ST.
TO CALNE
HIGH ST.
AVEBURY STONE CIRCLE
RITUAL PROCESSION WAY
TO CHERHILL HORSE & BATH
A-4
A-4361
BECKHAMPTON RD.
B-4003
SILBURY HILL
TO DEVIZES
A-361
A-4
ROMAN ROAD
TO MARLBOROUGH
A-4
B-4003
½ MILE
800 METERS
RIVER KENNET
WEST KENNET LONG BARROW
THE SANCTUARY "WOOD HENGE"
Direction of Winter Sunrise

❶ Circle Café
❷ The Red Lion Pub

DCH

of prehistoric societies for their religious monuments. Whatever the case, Avebury dates to 2800 B.C.—six centuries older than Stonehenge. This complex, the St. Peter's Basilica of Neolithic civilization, makes for a fascinating visit. Many enjoy it more than Stonehenge.

Orientation to Avebury

Avebury, just a little village with a big stone circle, is easy to reach by car, but difficult by public transportation (see "Getting Around the Region," page 448).

Tourist Information: The town's TI recently closed due to budget cuts. In the center of the village are signboards with some information provided by the National Trust. For more information on the Avebury sights, see the websites of the English Heritage (www.english-heritage.org.uk) and the National Trust (www.nationaltrust.org.uk).

Arrival by Car: You must pay to park in Avebury, and your only real option is the flat-fee National Trust parking lot, a three-minute walk from the village (£5, £3 after 15:00, £2 in winter; open summer 9:30-18:30, off-season 9:30-16:30). No other public parking is available in the village.

Sights in Avebury

All of Avebury's prehistoric sights are free to visit and always open.

▲▲Avebury Stone Circle

The stone circle at Avebury is bigger (16 times the size), less touristy, and for many, more interesting than Stonehenge. You're free to wander among 100 stones, ditches, mounds, and curious patterns from the past, as well as the village of Avebury, which grew up in the middle of this fascinating 1,400-foot-wide Neolithic circle.

In the 14th century, in frenzy of ignorance and religious paranoia, Avebury villagers buried many of these mysterious pagan stones. Their 18th-century descendants hosted social events in which they broke up the remaining pagan stones (topple, heat up, douse with cold water, and scavenge broken stones as building blocks). In modern times, the buried stones were dug up and re-erected. Concrete markers show where the missing broken-up stones once stood.

To make the roughly half-mile walk around the circle, you'll hike along an impressive earthwork henge—a 30-foot-high outer bank surrounding a ditch 30 feet deep, making a 60-foot-high rampart. This earthen rampart once had stones standing around the perimeter, placed about every 30 feet, and four grand causeway entries. Originally, two smaller circles made of about 200 stones stood within the henge.

▲Ritual Procession Way

Also known as West Kennet Avenue (one of four streets leaving the circle), this double line of stones provided a ritual procession way leading from Avebury to a long-gone wooden circle dubbed "The Sanctuary." This "wood henge," thought to have been 1,000 years older than everything else in the area, is considered to have been the genesis of Avebury and its big stone circle. Most of the stones standing along the procession way today were reconstructed in modern times.

▲Silbury Hill

This pyramid-shaped hill (reminiscent of Glastonbury Tor) is a 130-foot-high, yet-to-be-explained mound of chalk just outside of Avebury. More than 4,000 years old, this mound is considered the largest man-made object in prehistoric Europe (with the surface area of London's Trafalgar Square and the height of the Nelson

Column). It's a reminder that we've only just scratched the surface of England's mysterious and ancient religious landscape.

Inspired by a legend that the hill hid a gold statue in its center, locals tunneled through Silbury Hill in 1830, undermining the structure. Work is currently underway to restore the hill, which remains closed to the public. Archaeologists (who date things like this by carbon-dating snails and other little critters killed in  its construction) figure Silbury Hill took only 60 years to build, in about 2200 B.C. This makes Silbury Hill the last element built at Avebury and contemporaneous with Stonehenge. Some think it may have been an observation point for all the other bits of the Avebury site. You can still see evidence of a spiral path leading up the hill and a moat at its base.

The Roman road detoured around Silbury Hill. (Roman engineers often used features of the landscape as visual reference points when building roads. Their roads would commonly kink at the crest of hills or other landmarks, where they realigned with a new visual point.) Later, the hill sported a wooden Saxon fort, which likely acted as a lookout for marauding Vikings. And in World War II, the Royal Observer Corps stationed men up here to count and report Nazi bombers on raids.

West Kennet Long Barrow
A pullout on the road just past Silbury Hill marks the West Kennet Long Barrow (a 15-minute walk from Silbury Hill). This burial chamber, the best-preserved Stone Age chamber tomb in the UK, stands intact on a ridge. It lines up with the rising sun on the summer solstice. You can walk inside the barrow, or sit on its roof and survey the Neolithic landscape around you.

Cherhill Horse
Heading west from Avebury on the A-4 (toward Bath), you'll see an obelisk (a monument to some important earl) above you on the downs, or chalk hills, near the village of Cherhill. You'll also see a white horse carved into the chalk hillside. Above it are the remains of an Iron Age hill fort known as Oldbury Castle—described on an information board at the roadside pullout. There is one genuinely prehistoric white horse in England (the Uffington White Horse); the Cherhill Horse, like all the others, is just an 18th-century creation. Prehistoric discoveries were all the rage in the 1700s, and it was a fad to make your own fake ones. Throughout southern England, you can cut into the thin layer of topsoil and find chalk. Now, so they don't have to weed, horses like this are cemented and painted white.

Stone Circles: The Riddle of the Rocks

Britain is home to roughly 800 stone circles, most of them rudimentary, jaggedly sparse boulder rings that lack the iconic

upright-and-lintel form of Stonehenge. But their misty, mossy settings provide curious travelers with an intimate and accessible glimpse of the mysterious people who lived in prehistoric Britain.

Bronze Age Britain (2000-600 B.C.) was populated by farming folk who had mastered the craft of smelting heated tin and copper together to produce bronze, which was used to make more durable tools and weapons. Late in the Bronze Age, many of these primitive, clannish communities also chose to put considerable time and effort into gathering huge rocks and arranging them into ceremonial circles for use in rituals with long-forgotten meanings. Some scholars believe that these circles may have been used as solar observatories, to calculate solstices and equinoxes as they planned life-sustaining seasonal crop-planting cycles. Archaeologists have discovered a few ancient remains in the center of some circles, but their primary use seems to have been ceremonial rather than as burial sites. And without any written records, we can only make educated guesses as to their exact purpose.

The superstitious people of the Middle Ages, who hadn't quite perfected their carbon-dating techniques, came up with colorful explanations for the circles. Stonehenge, for example, was believed to have been arranged by giants (makes sense to me). Later, several circles were thought to be petrified partiers who had dared to dance on the Sabbath; nearby standing stones were supposedly the frozen figures of the pipers who had been playing the dance tunes.

England's stone circles generally lie at the fringes of the country, clustering mostly in the southwest (particularly on the Cornwall peninsula) and in the hills north of Manchester. Dedicated travelers seeking stone circles will find them marked in the Ordnance Survey atlas and signposted along rural roads. Ask a local farmer for directions—and savor the experience (wear shoes impervious to grass dew and sheep doo). I've highlighted my favorites in this book: **Stonehenge** and **Avebury** (both described in this chapter), **Castlerigg** (in the Lake District, near Keswick—see page 699), Cornwall's **Merry Maidens** (see page 392), and **Scorhill Stone Circle,** probably the best of the many circles in Dartmoor National Park (see page 357).

Alexander Keiller Museum

This museum, named for the archaeologist who led excavations at Avebury in the late 1930s, is housed in two buildings. The 17th-century Barn Gallery has an interactive exhibit, while the Stables Gallery, across the farmyard, holds artifacts from past digs.

Cost and Hours: £4.90, daily April-Oct 10:00-18:00, Nov-March 10:00-16:00, last entry one hour before closing, tel. 01672/539-250.

Avebury Manor and Garden

Archaeologist Alexander Keiller's former home was the subject of *The Manor Reborn*, a 2011 BBC documentary on the refurbishment of the 500-year-old estate by a team of historians and craftspeople. Nine rooms were decorated in five different styles showing the progression of design, from a Tudor wedding chapel to a Queen Anne-era bedroom to an early-20th-century billiards room. The grounds were also spruced up, with a topiary and a Victorian kitchen garden.

Cost and Hours: £9, limited number of timed tickets sold per day, April-Oct Thu-Tue 11:00-17:00, Nov-mid-Dec and mid-Feb-March Thu-Tue 11:00-15:30, closed Wed and mid-Dec-mid-Feb, last entry one hour before closing, buy tickets at Alexander Keiller Museum's Barn Gallery (listed above) or reserve online in advance (£1 booking fee), tel. 01672/539-250, www.nationaltrust.org.uk.

Eating in Avebury

The pleasant **Circle Café** serves healthy, hearty à la carte lunches, including vegan and gluten-free dishes, and cream teas on most days (daily April-Oct 10:00-17:30, Nov-March 10:00-16:00, no hot food after 14:30, next to National Trust store and the Alexander Keiller Museum, tel. 01672/539-250).

The Red Lion has inexpensive, traditional pub grub; a creaky, well-worn, dart-throwing ambience; and a medieval well in its dining room (£6-12 meals, daily 11:00-21:00, High Street, tel. 01672/539-266).

Stonehenge

As old as the pyramids, and older than the Acropolis and the Colosseum, this iconic stone circle amazed medieval Europeans, who figured it was built by a race of giants. And it still impresses visitors today. As one of Europe's most famous sights, Stonehenge, worth ▲▲, does a valiant job of retaining an air of mystery and majesty (partly because cordons, which keep hordes of tourists from tram-

pling all over it, foster the illusion that it stands alone in a field). Although some people are underwhelmed by Stonehenge, most of its almost one million annual visitors find that it's worth the trip.

The ancient site continues to reveal its mysteries: A laser survey in 2011 found prehistoric carvings on the stones, excavations in 2008 showed that the Romans were active at Stonehenge, and an archaeological dig nearby in 2007 uncovered homes where the circle's builders may have lived.

Expect Changes: A new visitors center/museum and large parking lot opened 1.5 miles to the west of the stone circle in December of 2013. You'll park at the visitors center and ride a shuttle bus or walk to the stones. The highway that previously ran adjacent to the stones has closed, and the old parking lot and ticket booth near the circle are slated for demolition. Call ahead or check the website for updates.

Getting to Stonehenge

Stonehenge is about 90 miles southwest of central London, a two-hour drive.

By Public Transportation: Catch a train to Salisbury, then go by bus or taxi to Stonehenge (for details, see page 481). There is no public transportation between Avebury and Stonehenge.

By Car: Stonehenge is well-signed just off the A-303. It's about 15 minutes north of Salisbury, an hour east of Glastonbury, and an hour south of Avebury. From Salisbury, head north on the A-360 (Devizes Road) for 8.5 miles (13.6 km) to the intersection at Airman's Corner. Watch for signs to the visitor center and parking lot.

By Bus Tour: For tours of Stonehenge from Bath, see page 413 (Mad Max is best); for tours from Salisbury, see page 481.

Orientation to Stonehenge

Cost: £14.90, save £1 if you buy in advance online, covered by English Heritage Pass (see page 20). Entry includes a worthwhile 45-minute audioguide, entry to the visitors center/museum, and the shuttle bus ride to the stone circle. Parking is free with entry to the site (otherwise £3).

Reservations: While not required, buying a ticket in advance online at www.english-heritage.org.uk/stonehenge gives you a guaranteed 30-minute arrival window. Advance ticketholders also have the option of downloading the audio tour directly to their own mobile device.

Hours: Daily June-Aug 9:00-20:00, mid-March-May and Sept-mid-Oct 9:30-19:00, mid-Oct-mid-March 9:30-17:00. Note that last entry is two hours before closing. Expect shorter hours and possible closures June 20-22 due to huge, raucous solstice crowds.

Information: Tel. 0870-333-1181, www.english-heritage.org.uk/stonehenge.

Services: The new visitors center has WCs, a café, and a gift shop. Services at the circle itself are limited to emergency WCs.

Visiting the Inner Stones: Special one-hour access to the stones' inner circle may be available for an extra fee (outside regular visiting hours, no touching allowed, must be reserved well in advance). Details are on the English Heritage website (go to "Visit Stonehenge," then click "Stone Circle Access"), or call 01722/343-834.

Self-Guided Tour

The entrance fee includes a good audioguide, but this commentary will help make your visit even more meaningful. Allow at least two hours to see everything.

Visitors Center: The visitors center and museum are set 1.5 miles away from the circle itself. The new facilities are designed to blend in with the landscape and help make the stone circle feel more pristine.

Once you've bought your ticket and picked up an audioguide, tour the visitors center to learn more about the site and the people who built it. Stand inside a 360-degree projection showing the stones as they are today—and as they were when the monument was first built. The archeological gallery features objects excavated from Stonehenge and other sites nearby, models of the circle, and videos

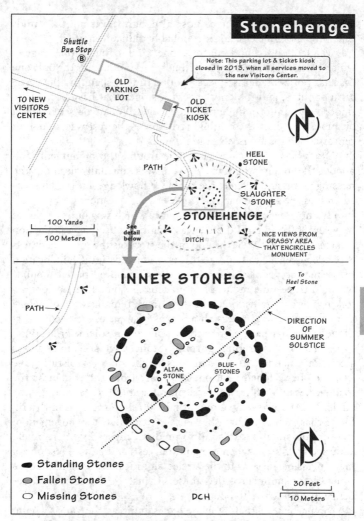

about the site's history. Back outside, you can visit a reconstruction of the prehistoric homes recently unearthed near Stonehenge.

Be sure to use the WCs here, as there are only emergency WCs at the circle.

Stone Circle: Shuttle buses to the stones leave from the back of the visitors center (every 5 minutes, more frequent on busy days, 10-minute trip). You can disembark from the shuttle halfway and walk the remaining 20 minutes to the stones. It's also possible to walk the entire 1.5 miles to the circle.

As you approach the massive structure, walk right up to the knee-high cordon and let your fellow 21st-century tourists melt away. It's just you and the druids...although it was not the druids that built the stone circle (they probably didn't even use it).

England has hundreds of stone circles, but Stonehenge—which literally means "hanging stones"—is unique. It's the only one that has horizontal cross-pieces (called lintels) spanning the vertical monoliths, and the only one with stones that have been made smooth and uniform by human craftsmen. What you see here is a bit more than half the original structure—the rest was carted off centuries ago for use in other buildings.

Now do a slow clockwise spin around the monument, and ponder the following points. As you walk, mentally flesh out the missing pieces and re-erect the rubble. Knowledgeable guides posted around the site are happy to answer your questions.

It's now believed that Stonehenge, which was built in phases between 3000 and 1500 b.c., was originally used as a cremation cemetery. But that's not the end of the story, as the monument was expanded over the millennia. This was a hugely significant location to prehistoric peoples. There are several hundred burial mounds within a three-mile radius of Stonehenge—some likely belonging to kings or chieftains. Some of the human remains were of people from far away, and others show signs of injuries—evidence that Stonehenge may have been used as a place of medicine or healing.

Whatever its original purpose, Stonehenge still functions as a celestial calendar. As the sun rises on the summer solstice (June 21), the "heel stone"—the one set apart from the rest, near the road—lines up with the sun and the altar at the center of the stone circle. A disputed study of more than 300 similar circles in Britain found that each could have been used to calculate the movement of the sun, moon, and stars, and to predict eclipses in order to help early societies know when to plant, harvest, and party—just one of many plausible ideas as to the circles' significance. Even in modern times, as the summer solstice sun sets in just the right slot at Stonehenge, pagans arrive to boogie.

Some believe that Stonehenge is built at the precise point where six "ley lines" intersect. Ley lines are theoretical lines of magnetic or spiritual power that crisscross the globe, often connecting ancient sites. Belief in the power of these lines has gone in and out of fashion. If they were important to prehistoric peoples, they were largely ignored until the early 20th century, when the English writer Alfred Watkins popularized them (to the scorn of serious scientists). More recently, the concept has been embraced by the New Age movement. Without realizing it, you follow these ley lines all the time: Many of England's modern highways, following prehistoric paths, and churches, built over prehistoric monuments, are located where ley lines are thought to intersect. If you're a skeptic, ask one of the guides at Stonehenge to explain the mystique of this paranormal tradition; it's creepy and convincing.

Notice that two of the stones (facing the entry passageway) appear blemished. At the base of one monolith, it looks like someone has pulled back the stone to reveal a concrete skeleton. This is a repair job to fix damage done long ago by souvenir seekers, who actually rented hammers and chisels to take home a piece of Stonehenge. Look to the right of the repaired stone: The back of another stone is missing the same thin layer of protective lichen that covers the others. The lichen—and some of the stone itself—was sandblasted off to remove graffiti. (No wonder they've got Stonehenge roped off now.) The repairs were intentionally done in a different color, so as not to appear like the original stone.

Stonehenge's builders used two different types of stone. The tall, stout monoliths and lintels are sandstone blocks called sarsen stones. Most of the monoliths weigh about 25 tons (the largest is 45 tons), and the lintels are about seven tons apiece. These sarsen stones were brought from "only" 20 miles away. The shorter stones in the middle, called bluestones, came from the south coast of Wales—240 miles away (close if you're taking a train, but far if you're packing a megalith). Imagine the logistical puzzle of floating six-ton stones across Wales' Severn Estuary and up the River Avon, then rolling them on logs about 20 miles to this position...an impressive feat, even in our era of skyscrapers. We know the stones came from Wales because geologists have chemically matched the bluestones to specific outcrops there.

Why didn't the builders of Stonehenge use what seem like perfectly adequate stones nearby? This, like many other questions about Stonehenge, remains shrouded in mystery. Think again about the ley lines. Ponder the fact that many experts accept none of the explanations of how these giant stones were transported. Then imagine congregations gathering here 5,000 years ago, raising thought levels, creating a powerful life force transmitted along the ley lines. Maybe a particular kind of stone was essential for maximum energy transmission. Maybe the stones were levitated here. Maybe psychics really do create powerful vibes. Maybe not. It's as unbelievable as electricity used to be.

Salisbury

Salisbury, set in the middle of the expansive Salisbury Plain, is a favorite stop for its striking cathedral and intriguing history.

Salisbury was originally settled during the Bronze Age, possibly as early as 600 B.C., and later became a Roman town called Sarum. The modern city of Salisbury developed when the old settlement outgrew its boundaries, prompting the townspeople to move the city from a hill to the river valley below. Most of today's visitors come to marvel at the famous Salisbury Cathedral, featuring England's tallest spire and largest cathedral green. Collectors, bargain-hunters, and foodies will savor Salisbury's colorful market days. And archaeologists will dig the region around Salisbury, with England's highest concentration of ancient sites. The town itself is pleasant and walkable, and is a convenient base camp for visiting the ancient sites of Stonehenge and Avebury, or for exploring the countryside.

Orientation to Salisbury

Salisbury (pop. 45,000) stretches along the River Avon in the shadow of its huge landmark cathedral. The heart of the city clusters around Market Square, which is also a handy parking lot on non-market days. High Street, a block to the west, leads to the medieval North Gate of the Cathedral Close. Shoppers can explore the quirkily named streets south of the square. The area north of Market Square is generally residential, with a few shops and pubs.

Tourist Information

The TI, just off Market Square, hands out free city maps, books local rooms for no fee, sells train tickets with a £1.50 surcharge, and offers free Wi-Fi (April-Sept Mon-Sat 10:00-16:00, Sun 10:00-14:00; Oct-March Mon-Sat 9:00-17:00, closed Sun; Fish Row, tel. 01722/342-860, www.visitwiltshire.co.uk).

Ask the TI about 1.5-hour **walking tours** (£5, April-Oct daily at 11:00, Nov-March Sat-Sun only, depart from TI; other itineraries available, including £5 Ghost Walk May-Sept Fri at 20:00; tel. 07873/212-941, www.salisburycityguides.co.uk).

Arrival in Salisbury

By Train: From the train station, it's a 10-minute walk into the town center. Leave the station to the left, and walk about 50 yards down South Western Road. Passing The Railway Tavern on your right, continue onto Mill Road and then onto Fisherton Street. Following signs to the city center, walk up the right side of Fisherton over the river and all the way to High Street. Market Square and the TI are ahead on Queen Street, and it's another two short blocks north (left) on Queen Street to the bus station. The Salisbury Cathedral and recommended Exeter Street B&Bs are to the south (right), down St. John Street (which becomes Exeter Street).

By Bus: The bus station is located in the town center, just off Market Square on Endless Street.

By Car: Drivers will find several pay parking lots in Salisbury—simply follow the blue *P* signs. The "Central" lot, behind the giant red-brick Sainsbury's store, is within a 10-minute walk of the TI or cathedral and is best for overnight stays (enter from Churchill Way West or Castle Street, lot open 24 hours). The "Old George Mall" parking garage is closer to the cathedral and has comparable daytime rates (£1.50/1 hour, £2.20/2 hours, cash only, 1 block north of cathedral, enter from New Street; garage open Mon-Sat 7:00-20:00, Sun 10:00-17:00). Limited parking is available at the cathedral, on the corner of High Street and North Walk (£6/day).

Helpful Hints

Market Days: For centuries, Salisbury has been known for its lively markets. On Tuesdays and Saturdays, Market Square hosts the charter market, with general goods. Every other Wednesday is the farmers' market. There are also special markets, such as one with French products. Ask the TI for a current schedule.

Festivals: The **Salisbury International Arts Festival** runs for just over two weeks at the end of May and beginning of June (www.salisburyfestival.co.uk).

Internet Access: The library has terminals on the first floor for visitors, who can use them free of charge for 30 minutes (Mon 10:00-19:00, Tue and Fri 9:00-19:00, Wed-Thu and Sat 9:00-17:00, closed Sun, show ID at desk to sign in for access number, computers turned off 10 minutes before closing, Market Place, tel. 01722/324-145).

Laundry: **Washing Well** has full-service (£8-15/load depending on size, 2-hour service, Mon-Sat 8:30-17:30) as well as self-service (Mon-Sat 15:30-21:00, Sun 7:00-21:00, last self-service wash one hour before closing; 28 Chipper Lane, tel. 01722/421-874).

Getting to the Stone Circles: You can get to Stonehenge from

Salisbury

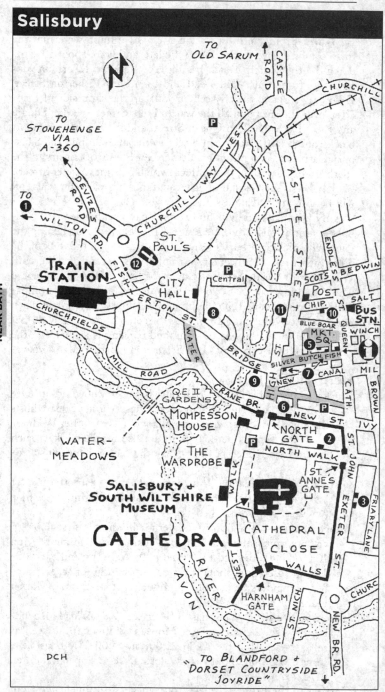

NEAR BATH

TO OLD SARUM

CASTLE ROAD

CHURCHILL

TO STONEHENGE VIA A-360

WEST WAY

CHURCHILL WAY

CASTLE STREET

DEVIZE'S ROAD

TO ①

WILTON RD.

WILTON RD.

FISH

ST. PAUL'S

⑫

TRAIN STATION

CHURCHFIELDS

CITY HALL

Central P

ERTON ST.

WATER

ENDLESS ST.

BEDWIN

SCOTS

Post

CHIP.

Blue Boar

SALT

BUS STN.

WINCH

①

MIL

BROWN

QUEEN ST.

MKT. SQ.

⑪

⑩

⑤

SILVER

BUTCH FISH

⑦

CANAL

MILL ROAD

BRIDGE ST.

HIGH

NEW

⑨

Q.E. II GARDENS

CRANE BR.

⑥

NEW ST.

P

MOMPESSON HOUSE

WATER-MEADOWS

THE WARDROBE

NORTH GATE

②

CATH. ST.

IVY

NORTH WALK

ST. JOHN ST.

EXETER ST.

③

FRIARY LANE

P

WEST WALK

ST. ANNE'S GATE

SALISBURY & SOUTH WILTSHIRE MUSEUM

CATHEDRAL

CATHEDRAL CLOSE

WALLS

CHURC

NEW BR. RD.

RIVER AVON

WEST WALK

HARNHAM GATE

ST. NICH.

ST. NICH.

DCH

TO BLANDFORD & "DORSET COUNTRYSIDE JOYRIDE"

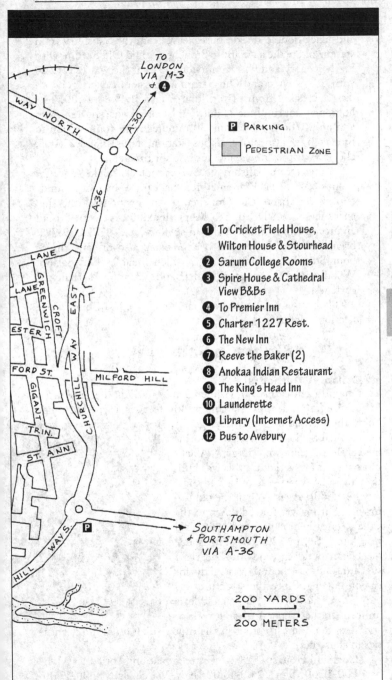

TO
LONDON
VIA M-3
& ❹

WAY NORTH

A-30

A-36

P PARKING

PEDESTRIAN ZONE

LANE

LANE

GREENWICH

CROFT

WAY

EAST

ESTER

FORD ST.

GIGANT

MILFORD HILL

TRIN.

ST. ANN

CHURCHILL WAY

❶ To Cricket Field House,
   Wilton House & Stourhead
❷ Sarum College Rooms
❸ Spire House & Cathedral
   View B&Bs
❹ To Premier Inn
❺ Charter 1227 Rest.
❻ The New Inn
❼ Reeve the Baker (2)
❽ Anokaa Indian Restaurant
❾ The King's Head Inn
❿ Launderette
⓫ Library (Internet Access)
⓬ Bus to Avebury

P

WAY S.

HILL

TO
SOUTHAMPTON
& PORTSMOUTH
VIA A-36

200 YARDS

200 METERS

Salisbury on **The Stonehenge Tour** bus. Their distinctive red-and-black double-decker buses leave from the Salisbury train station and make a circuit to Stonehenge and Old Sarum, with lovely scenery and light commentary along the way (£12, £20 with Stonehenge and Old Sarum admission, tickets good all day, buy ticket from driver, June-Aug daily 9:30-17:00, 1-2/hour, may not run June 21 due to solstice crowds, shorter hours and only 1/hour off-season, 30 minutes from train station to Stonehenge, also stops at bus station, tel. 01983/827-005, check www.thestonehengetour.info for timetable).

A **taxi** from Salisbury to Stonehenge can make sense for groups (£40-50, call or email for exact price, includes round-trip from Salisbury to Stonehenge plus an hour at the site, entry fee not included, 5-6 people maximum, reserve ahead and reconfirm by phone a day in advance, tel. 01722/339-781, briantwort@ntlworld.com, Brian). Brian also offers a three-hour Stonehenge visit for £80, which includes Old Sarum, Woodhenge, Durrington Walls, and Woodford's thatched cottages.

For buses to Avebury's stone circle, see "Salisbury Connections," later.

Sights in Salisbury

▲▲Salisbury Cathedral

This magnificent cathedral, visible for miles around because of its huge spire (the tallest in England at 404 feet), is a wonder to behold. The surrounding enormous grassy field (called a "close") makes the Gothic masterpiece look even larger. What's more impressive is that all this was built in a mere 38 years—astonishingly fast for the Middle Ages. When the old hill town of Sarum was moved down to the valley, its cathedral had to be replaced in a hurry. So, in 1220, the townspeople began building, and in 1258 their sparkling-new cathedral was ready for ribbon-cutting. Since the structure was built in just a few decades, its style is uniform, rather than the patchwork of styles common in cathedrals of the time (which often took centuries to construct).

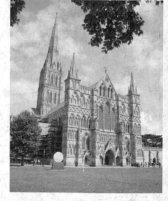

Cost and Hours: £5.50 suggested donation; April-Oct Mon-Sat 9:00-17:00, Sun 12:00-16:00; Nov-March daily 9:00-17:00; Chapter House usually open Mon-Sat 9:30-16:30, Sun 12:45-

Salisbury Cathedral

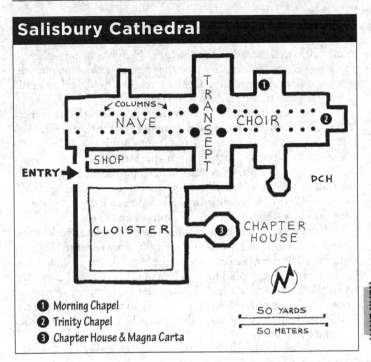

COLUMNS

NAVE

TRANSEPT

CHOIR

SHOP

ENTRY→

DCH

CLOISTER

CHAPTER HOUSE

❶ Morning Chapel
❷ Trinity Chapel
❸ Chapter House & Magna Carta

50 YARDS

50 METERS

15:45, closes entirely for special events; choral evensong Mon-Sat at 17:30, Sun at 15:00. This working cathedral opens early for services: Be respectful if you arrive when one is in session.

Information: Tel. 01722/555-120, recorded info tel. 01722/555-113, www.salisburycathedral.org.uk.

Tower Tours: Imagine building a cathedral on this scale before the invention of cranes, bulldozers, or modern scaffolding. An excellent tower tour (1.5-2 hours) helps visitors understand how it was done. You'll climb in between the stone arches and the roof to inspect the vaulting and trussing; see a medieval winch that was used in the construction; and finish with the 332-step climb up the narrow tower for a sweeping view of the Wiltshire countryside (£10; early April-Sept Mon-Sat at 11:15, 12:15, 13:15, 14:15, and 15:15, Sun at 13:00 and 14:30; fewer off-season but usually one at 13:15, no tours in Dec except Christmas week; maximum 12 people, can reserve by calling 01722/555-156).

Eating: The cathedral's cafeteria is excellent.

❷ **Self-Guided Tour:** Entering the church, you'll instantly feel the architectural harmony. Volunteer guides posted strategically throughout the church stand ready to answer your questions. (Free guided tours of the cathedral nave are offered every hour or so, when enough people assemble.)

As you look down the **nave,** notice how the stone columns march identically down the aisle, like a thick gray forest of tree trunks. The arches overhead soar to grand heights, helping church-goers appreciate the vast and amazing heavens. Now imagine the interior surfaces painted in red, blue, green, and gold, as they would have been prior to the English Reformation.

From the entrance, head to the far wall (the back-left corner). You'll find an interesting **model** showing how this cathedral was built so quickly in the 13th century. Next to that is the "oldest work-ing clock in existence," dating from the 14th century (the hourly bell has been removed, so as not to interrupt worship services). On the wall by the clock is a bell from the decommissioned ship HMS *Salisbury.* Look closely inside the bell to see the engraved names of crew members' children who were baptized on the ship.

Wander down the aisle past monuments and knights' tombs, as well as tombstones set into the floor. When you get to the tran-sept, examine the **columns** where the arms of the church cross. These posts were supposed to support a more modest bell tower, but when a heavy tower was added 100 years later, the columns bent under the enormous weight, causing the tower to lean sideways. Although the posts were later reinforced, the tower still tilts about two and a half feet.

Continue down the left side of the choir and dip into the **Morning Chapel.** At the back of this chapel, find the spectacu-lar glass prism engraved with images of Salisbury—donated to the church in memory of a soldier who died at the D-Day landing at Normandy.

The oldest part of the church is at the apse (far end), where construction began in 1220: the **Trinity Chapel**. The giant, mod-ern stained-glass window ponders the theme "prisoners of con-science."

After you leave the nave, pace the cloister and follow signs to the medieval **Chapter House.** All English cathedrals have a chapter house, so called because it's where the daily Bible verse, or chapter, is read. These spaces often served as gathering places for conducting church or town business. Here you can see a modest display of cathedral items, plus one must-see: the best preserved of the four original copies of the Magna Carta. This document is as important to the English as the Constitution is to Americans. This "Great Charter," dating from 1215, settled a dispute between the slimy King John and some powerful barons. Revolutionary for lim-iting the monarch's power, the Magna Carta constitutionally guar-anteed that the monarch was not above the law. This was one of the first major victories in the long tug-of-war between monarchs and nobles.

▲Cathedral Close

The enormous green surrounding the cathedral is the largest in England, and one of the loveliest. It's cradled in the elbow of the

River Avon and ringed by row houses, cottages, and grand mansions. The church owns the houses on the green and rents them to lucky people with holy connections. A former prime minister, Edward Heath, lived on the green, not because of his political influence, but because he was once the church organist.

The benches scattered around the green are an excellent place for having a romantic moonlit picnic or for gazing thoughtfully at the leaning spire. Although you may be tempted to linger until it's late, don't—this is still private church property...and the heavy medieval gates of the close shut at about 23:00.

A few houses are open to the public, such as the overpriced Mompesson House and the medieval Wardrobe. The most interesting attraction is the...

▲Salisbury and South Wiltshire Museum

Occupying the building just opposite the cathedral entry, this eclectic and sprawling collection was heralded by American expat travel writer Bill Bryson as one of England's best. While that's a stretch, the museum does offer a little something for everyone, including exhibits on local archaeology and social history, a costume gallery, the true-to-its-name "Salisbury Giant" puppet once used by the tailors' guilds during parades, some J. M. W. Turner paintings of the cathedral interior, and a collection of exquisite Wedgwood china and other ceramics. The highlight is the Stonehenge Gallery, with informative and interactive exhibits explaining the prehistoric structure.

Cost and Hours: £8 (includes small donation), Mon-Sat 10:00-17:00, Sun 12:00-17:00 except closed Sun Oct-May, check with desk about occasional tours, 65 The Close, tel. 01722/332-151, www.salisburymuseum.org.uk.

Sleeping in Salisbury

(area code: 01722)

Salisbury's town center has very few affordable accommodations, and I've listed them below—plus a couple of good choices a little farther out. The town gets particularly crowded during the arts festival (late May through early June).

$$ Cricket Field House, outside of town on the A-36 toward

NEAR BATH

Wilton, overlooks a cricket pitch and golf course. It has 17 clean, comfortable rooms, its own gorgeous garden, and plenty of parking (Sb-£50-75, Db-£75-99, deluxe Db-£135, Tb-£75-118, price depends on season, Wilton Road, tel. 01722/322-595, www.cricketfieldhouse.co.uk, cricketfieldcottage@btinternet.com; Brian, Margaret, and Andrew James). While this place works best for drivers, it's just a 20-minute walk from the train station or a five-minute bus ride from the city center.

$$ Sarum College is a theological college that rents 40 rooms in its building right on the peaceful Cathedral Close. Much of the year, it houses visitors to the college, but it usually has rooms for tourists as well—except the week after Christmas, when it closes. The slightly institutional but clean rooms share hallways with libraries, bookstores, and offices, and the five attic rooms come with grand cathedral views (Sb-£64, Db-£99 depending on size, meals available at additional cost, elevator, 19 The Close, tel. 01722/424-800, www.sarum.ac.uk, hospitality@sarum.ac.uk).

$ Cathedral View B&B, with four rooms, offers a good value in an outstanding location just off the Cathedral Close (Db-£85, Tb-£90-105, cash only, 2-night minimum on weekends, no kids under age 10, free Wi-Fi, 83 Exeter Street, tel. 01722/502-254, www.cathedral-viewbandb.co.uk, info@cathedral-viewbandb.co.uk, Wenda and Steve).

$ Spire House B&B, next door, is similar. The four bright, surprisingly quiet rooms come with busy wallpaper, and two have canopied beds (Db-£80-90, Tb-£90-100, no kids under age 8, optional breakfast-£5, free Wi-Fi, 84 Exeter Street, tel. 01722/339-213, www.salisbury-bedandbreakfast.com, spire.enquiries@btinternet.com, friendly Lois and John).

$ Premier Inn, two miles from the city center, offers dozens of prefab and predictable rooms ideal for drivers and families (Db-£70-85, more during special events, 2 kids ages 15 and under sleep free, breakfast-£5-8, pay Wi-Fi, possible noise from nearby trains, off roundabout at A-30 and Pearce Way, tel. 0871-527-8956, www.premierinn.com).

Eating in Salisbury

There are plenty of atmospheric pubs all over town. For the best variety of restaurants, head to the Market Square area. Many places offer great "early bird" specials before 20:00.

Charter 1227, an upstairs eatery overlooking Market Square, is a handy place for a nice meal (£10 two-course lunch, open Tue-Sat 12:00-14:30 & 18:00-21:30, closed Sun-Mon, dinner reservations smart, 6 Ox Row, tel. 01722/333-118, www.charter1227.co.uk).

Reeve the Baker, with a branch just up the street from the TI, crafts an array of high-calorie delights and handy pick-me-ups for a fast and affordable lunch. The long cases of pastries and savory treats will make you drool (Mon-Sat 7:00-17:00, Sun 10:00-16:00, cash only, one location is next to the TI at 2 Butcher Row, another much smaller one is at the corner of Market and Bridge streets at 61 Silver Street, tel. 01722/320-367.

Anokaa is a classy splurge that's highly acclaimed for its up-dated Indian cuisine. You won't find the same old chicken *tikka* here, but clever newfangled variations on Indian themes, dished up in a dressy contemporary setting (£12-19 main dishes, £9 lunch buffet, daily 12:00-14:00 & 17:30-23:00, 60 Fisherton Street, tel. 01722/414-142, www.anokaa.com).

The New Inn serves inventive, game-centered dishes along-side classic pub fare in a 13th-century house rumored to have a tunnel leading directly into the cathedral—perhaps dug while the building housed a brothel? (£5 starters and baguettes, £8-12 main courses, daily 11:00-24:00, food served 12:00-15:00 & 18:00-21:00, 41-43 New Street, tel. 01722/326-662).

The King's Head Inn is a chain pub with an extensive menu, modern interior, and outdoor seating overlooking the pretty little River Avon. It's a bit tired, and so are its servers (£5-6 sandwiches, £5-12 main courses, daily 9:00-24:00, food served until 22:00, kids welcome but must order by 20:30, free Wi-Fi, 1 Bridge Street, tel. 01722/342-050).

Salisbury Connections

From Salisbury by Train to: London's Waterloo Station (1-2/hour, 1.25 hours), **Bath** (1-2/hour, 1 hour), **Oxford** (1-2/hour, 2 hours, transfer in Basingstoke and sometimes also Reading), **Portsmouth** (1/hour direct, 1.5 hours), **Exeter** (1-2/hour, 2 hours, some require transfers), **Penzance** (about hourly, 5.5-6 hours, 1-2 transfers). Train info: tel. 0845-748-4950, www.nationalrail.co.uk.

By Bus to: Bath (hourly, 2.75 hours, transfer in Warminster or Devizes, www.travelinesw.com; or one direct bus/day at 10:35, 1.5 hours on National Express #300, tel. 0871-781-8181, www.nationalexpress.com), **Avebury** (hourly, 2-2.5 hours, transfer in Trowbridge and Devizes, www.travelinesw.com), **Portsmouth** (evenings only at 18:25, 1.5 hours on National Express). Many of Salisbury's long-distance buses are run by Wilts & Dorset (tel. 01722/336-855 or 01983/827-005, www.salisburyreds.co.uk).

Near Salisbury

Old Sarum

Right here, on a hill overlooking the plain below, is where the original town of Salisbury was founded many centuries ago. While little remains of the old town, the view of the valley is amazing... and a little imagination can transport you back to *very* olde England. This is one of the most historically important sites in southern England. Uniquely, it combined both a castle and a cathedral within an Iron Age fortification.

Human settlement in this area stretches back to the Bronze Age, and the Romans, Saxons, and Normans all called this hilltop home. From about 500 B.C. through A.D. 1220, Old Sarum flourished, giving rise to a motte-and-bailey castle, a cathedral, and scores of wooden homes along the town's outer ring. The town grew so quickly that by the Middle Ages, it had outgrown its spot on the hill. In 1220, the local bishop successfully petitioned to move the entire city to the valley below, where space and water was plentiful. So, stone by stone, Old Sarum was packed up and shipped to New Sarum, where builders used nearly all the rubble from the old city to create a brand-new town with a magnificent cathedral.

Old Sarum was eventually abandoned altogether, leaving only a few stone foundations. The grand views of Salisbury from here have in-"spired" painters for ages and provided countless picnickers with a scenic backdrop: Grab a sandwich or snacks from one of the grocery stores in Salisbury or at the excellent Waitrose supermarket at the north end of town—just west of where the A-36 meets the A-345.

Cost and Hours: £3.90, daily July-Aug 9:00-18:00, April-June and Sept 10:00-17:00, Oct and March 10:00-16:00, Nov-Jan 11:00-15:00, Feb 11:00-16:00, last entry 30 minutes before closing, tel. 01722/335-398, www.english-heritage.org.uk.

Getting There: It's two miles north of Salisbury off the A-345, accessible by Wilts & Dorset bus #X5 or via The Stonehenge Tour bus (see page 481). Drivers will find free parking 200 yards from the entrance (on the slope of the original castle's outer bailey).

Wilton House

This sprawling estate, with a grand mansion and lush gardens, has been owned by the Earls of Pembroke since King Henry VIII's time. Long before that, this was the site of a ninth-century nunnery, and later, a Benedictine abbey. Inside the mansion, you'll find a collection of paintings by Rubens, Rembrandt, Van Dyck, and Brueghel, along with quirky odds and ends, such as a lock of Queen Elizabeth I's hair. The perfectly proportioned Double Cube

Near Salisbury

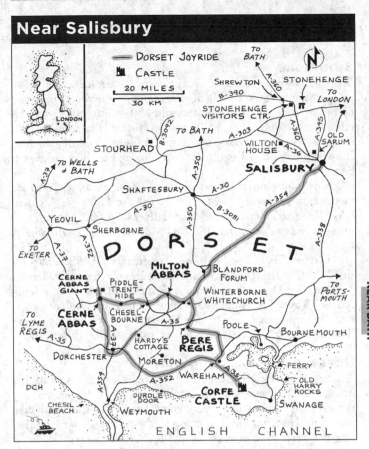

Room has served as everything from a 17th-century state dining room to a secret D-Day planning room during World War II... if only the portraits could talk. The Old Riding School houses a skippable 20-minute film that dramatizes the history of the family. Outside, classic English gardens feature a river lazily winding its way through grasses and under Greek-inspired temples. Jane Austen fans particularly enjoy this stately home, where parts of 2005's Oscar-nominated *Pride and Prejudice* were filmed. But, alas, Mr. Darcy has checked out.

Cost and Hours: House and gardens-£14, gardens only-£5.50; house open Easter weekend and May-Aug Sun-Thu 11:30-17:00, closed Fri-Sat except holiday weekends, closed Sept-April; gardens open May-Aug daily 11:00-17:30, Sept Sat-Sun 11:00-17:30, closed Oct-April; last entry 30 minutes before closing, recorded info tel. 01722/746-729, tel. 01722/746-714, www.wilton-house.com.

Getting There: It's five miles west of Salisbury via the A-36 to Wilton's Minster Street; or bus #R3 from Salisbury to Wilton.

Stourhead

For a serious taste of a traditional English landscape and miles of footpaths, don't miss this 2,650-acre delight. Stourhead, designed by owner Henry Hoare II in the mid-18th century, is a wonderland of rolling hills, meandering paths, placid lakes, and colorful trees, punctuated by classically inspired bridges and monuments. It's what every other English estate aspires to be—like nature, but better.

Cost and Hours: House and garden—£12.50, or £7.70 to see just one; house open mid-March-Oct Fri-Tue 11:00-17:00, closed Wed-Thu; garden open year-round daily 9:00-19:00; last entry 30 minutes before closing, tel. 01747/841-152, www.nationaltrust.org. uk.

Getting There: It's 28 miles (40 minutes) west of Salisbury off the B-3092 in the town of Stourton (3 miles northwest of Mere).

Nearby: Drivers or ambitious walkers can visit nearby **King Alfred's Tower** and climb its 205 steps for glorious views of the estate and surrounding countryside (£3 to climb tower, same opening times as house, 2.5 miles northwest of Stourhead, off Tower Road).

Dorset Countryside Joyride

The region of Dorset, just southwest of Salisbury, is full of rolling fields, winding country lanes, footpaths, quaint cottages, and villages stuffed with tea shops. Anywhere you go in the area will take you someplace charming, so consider this tour only a suggestion and feel free to get pleasantly lost in the English countryside. You'll be taking some less-traveled roads, so bring along a good map.

Starting in Salisbury, take the A-354 through Blandford Forum to Winterborne Whitechurch. From here, follow signs and small back roads to the village of **Bere Regis,** where you'll find some lovely 15th-century buildings, including one with angels carved on the roof. Follow the A-35 and the B-3075 to Wareham, where T. E. Lawrence (a.k.a. Lawrence of Arabia) lived; he's buried in nearby Moreton. Continue south on the A-351 to the dramatic and romantic **Corfe Castle.** This was a favorite residence for medieval kings until it was destroyed by a massive gunpowder blast during a 17th-century siege (£7.70, daily 10:00-18:00, last entry 30 minutes before closing, tel. 01929/481-294, www.nationaltrust.org. uk). Retrace the A-351 to Wareham, and then take the A-352 to Dorchester.

Just northeast of Dorchester on the A-35, near the village of Stinsford, novelist Thomas Hardy was born in 1840; you'll find **Hardy's family's cottage** nearby, in Higher Bockhampton (£5.50,

March-Oct Wed-Sun 11:00-17:00, closed Mon-Tue and Nov-Feb, last entry 30 minutes before closing, tel. 01305/262-366, www. nationaltrust.org.uk). While Hardy's heart is buried in Stinsford with his first wife, Emma, the rest of him is in Westminster Abbey's Poets' Corner. Take the A-35 back to Dorchester. Just west of Dorchester, stay on the A-35 until it connects to the A-37; then follow the A-352 north toward Sherborne.

About eight miles north of Dorchester, on the way to Sherborne, you'll find the little town of **Cerne Abbas** (surn AB-iss), named for an abbey in the center of town. There are only two streets to wander down, so take this opportunity to recharge with a cup of tea and a scone. Abbots Tea Room has a nice cream tea (pot of tea, scone, jam, and clotted cream, 7 Long Street, tel. 01300/341-349). Up the street, you can visit the abbey and its well, reputed to have healing powers.

Just outside of town, a large chalk figure, the **Cerne Abbas Giant,** is carved into the green hillside. Chalk figures such as this one can be found in many parts of the region. Because the soil is only a few inches deep, the overlying grass and dirt can easily be removed to expose the bright white chalk bedrock beneath, creating the outlines. While nobody is sure exactly how old this figure is, or what its original purpose was, the giant is faithfully maintained by the locals, who mow and clear the fields at least once a year. This particular figure, possibly a fertility god, looks friendly... maybe a little too friendly. Locals claim that if a woman who's having trouble getting pregnant sleeps on the giant for one night, she will soon be able to conceive a child. (A few years back, controversy surrounded this giant, as a 180-foot-tall, donut-hoisting Homer Simpson was painted onto the adjacent hillside. No kidding.)

Leaving Cerne Abbas on country roads toward Piddletrenthide (on the aptly named River Piddle), continue through Cheselbourne to **Milton Abbas.** (This area, by the way, has some of the best town names in the country, such as Droop, Plush, Pleck, Folly, and of course, Piddle.) The village of Milton Abbas looks overly perfect. In the 18th century, a wealthy man bought up the town's large abbey and estate. His new place was great...except for the neighbors, a bunch of vulgar villagers with houses that cluttered his view from the garden. So, he had the town demolished and rebuilt a mile away. What you see now is probably the first planned community, with identical houses, a pub, and a church. The estate is now a "public school," which is what the English call an expensive private school. From Milton Abbas, signs lead you back to Winterborne Whitechurch, and the A-354 to Salisbury.

OXFORD

Oxford • Blenheim Palace

For centuries, the University of Oxford's stellar graduates have influenced Western civilization—ever since the first homework was assigned here in 1167. But that doesn't mean that Oxford is stodgy. Although you may see professors in their traditional black robes, this is a fun, young college town, filled with lots of shopping, cheap eats around every corner, and rowdy, rollicking pubs.

While a typical American-style university has one campus, Oxford (like Cambridge) has colleges scattered throughout town. But the sightseers' Oxford is walkable and compact. Many of the streets in the center are pedestrian-only during the day. Stick to the center, and you'll get a feel for workaday Oxford, where knowledge is the town business—and procrastinating over a pint is the students' main hobby. (Local shops sell T-shirts that say, "Don't ask me about my thesis.")

Sample the spirit of Oxford. Step off the busy, urban-feeling High Street into the hushed sanctuary of a grassy college quad. See the dining hall that inspired the one where Harry Potter eats his meals, or the pub where J. R. R. Tolkien first spoke about the hobbits.

If you haven't yet tried pub grub—or sampled a local British ale—make a point to do so in Oxford, just as its famous local writers did. In Oxford, a town known for traditions, the pubs are where the action is.

Perhaps better than anything in Oxford itself is the excellent Blenheim Palace. It's England's best countryside estate, just outside Oxford and described at the end of this chapter. Don't miss it.

Oxford or Cambridge?

England is home to two world-renowned universities: Oxford and Cambridge. Seeing one is enough. While I prefer the town of Cambridge (see page 257), Oxford's historic university makes it a heavyweight sight. If you're choosing between them, consider this: Cambridge feels like a lazy, easygoing small town; Oxford has a slightly more urban vibe, and even more stately buildings than its rival. Cambridge is not really on the way to anything, making it better as a side-trip from London than as a stopover. For convenience, you can't beat Oxford, which sits near the Cotswolds, Stratford-upon-Avon, Warwick, Blenheim Palace, and other major sights.

Planning Your Time

Oxford is a convenient stop for people visiting the Cotswolds, Blenheim Palace (a 30-minute drive away), Stratford-upon-Avon, and Bath. Because of Oxford's proximity to other worthwhile destinations and its relative scarcity of good-value accommodations, a stop-off here on the way to somewhere else is ideal.

Oxford's colleges are generally open to visitors, but each has its own visiting hours (which can be unpredictable). There are three terms: Michaelmas (Oct-Dec), Hilary (Jan-March), and Trinity (April-June). Public spaces in the colleges are more likely to be closed during exams in early to mid-June.

Orientation to Oxford

Oxford was first built where oxen crossed, or forded, the Cherwell and Isis rivers. (The Isis is another name for the Thames. Back then you could row to London from Oxford...in just five days.) Property in the town center is divided about evenly among three different groups: the university, the colleges (which are independent entities), and private shops and homes.

Despite its relatively compact town center, Oxford can be confusing to navigate. All those colleges start to look alike, and streets tend to change names from block to block. Use the biggest buildings as navigational landmarks. If you get confused, don't be shy about asking students for directions.

The main arteries are the north-south Cornmarket/St. Aldate's, and the east-west Queen Street/High Street. At the intersection of these streets stands the stubby, 14th-century Carfax Tower (named for the French *carrefour*, or "crossroads"). From here, pedestrianized Cornmarket—essentially an outdoor mall lined

OXFORD

Oxford

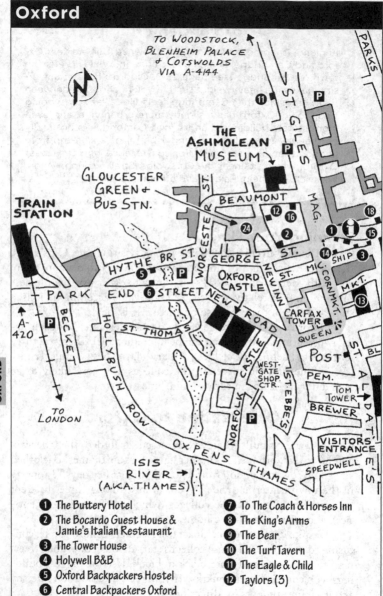

TO WOODSTOCK,
BLENHEIM PALACE
& COTSWOLDS
VIA A-4144

THE ASHMOLEAN MUSEUM

GLOUCESTER GREEN & BUS STN.

TRAIN STATION

BEAUMONT ST.

WORCESTER ST.

ST. GILES

MAG.

PARKS

GEORGE ST.

HYTHE BR. ST.

NEW INN

ST. MIC.

SHIP ST.

OXFORD CASTLE

NEW ROAD

CARFAX TOWER

CORNMKT.

QUEEN ST.

MKT.

PARK END STREET

BECKET

HOLLYBUSH ROW

ST. THOMAS

CASTLE

WEST-GATE SHOP. CTR.

STEBBE'S

POST

PEM.

TOM TOWER

BREWER

ST. ALDATS

A-420

TO LONDON

NORFOLK

OXPENS

THAMES

SPEEDWELL

M's

VISITORS' ENTRANCE

ISIS RIVER (A.K.A. THAMES)

1. The Buttery Hotel
2. The Bocardo Guest House & Jamie's Italian Restaurant
3. The Tower House
4. Holywell B&B
5. Oxford Backpackers Hostel
6. Central Backpackers Oxford
7. To The Coach & Horses Inn
8. The King's Arms
9. The Bear
10. The Turf Tavern
11. The Eagle & Child
12. Taylors (3)

OXFORD

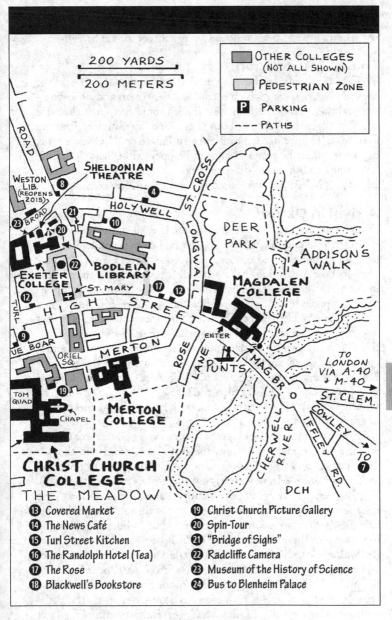

200 YARDS
200 METERS

OTHER COLLEGES (NOT ALL SHOWN)
PEDESTRIAN ZONE
P PARKING
--- PATHS

ROAD

WESTON LIB. (REOPENS 2015)

❽ SHELDONIAN THEATRE

❹

ST. CROSS

❷❸ BROAD

HOLYWELL

❷❶

❷⓿

❿

DEER PARK

ADDISON'S WALK

❷❷

BODLEIAN LIBRARY

EXETER COLLEGE

❶❷ TURL

ST. MARY

❶❷ HIGH STREET

MAGDALEN COLLEGE

LONGWALL

❶❼ ❶❷

❾

UE BOAR

ORIEL SQ.

MERTON

ROSE LANE

ENTER

PUNTS

MAG BR.

TO LONDON VIA A-40 & M-40

ST. CLEM.

COWLEY

IFFELY RD.

TO ❼

❶❾

TOM QUAD

CHAPEL

MERTON COLLEGE

CHERWELL RIVER

CHRIST CHURCH COLLEGE

THE MEADOW

DCH

⓭ Covered Market
⓮ The News Café
⓯ Turl Street Kitchen
⓰ The Randolph Hotel (Tea)
⓱ The Rose
⓲ Blackwell's Bookstore

⓳ Christ Church Picture Gallery
⓴ Spin-Tour
㉑ "Bridge of Sighs"
㉒ Radcliffe Camera
㉓ Museum of the History of Science
㉔ Bus to Blenheim Palace

OXFORD

with shops and chain restaurants—heads north, where it intersects with another pedestrian zone at George Street/Broad Street.

Tourist Information

The TI offers walking tours, a detailed town map (£1.50), and the *Oxford Visitors' Guide*, which includes a basic map and do-it-yourself walking tour (£1). They also book rooms and sell tickets for the City Sightseeing Oxford bus (described later, under "Tours in Oxford"). If you're headed to Blenheim Palace or Warwick Castle, buy your tickets here at a discount (TI open Mon-Sat 9:30-17:00, Sun 10:00-15:00, possibly later in peak season, 15-16 Broad Street, tel. 01865/252-200, www.visitoxfordandoxfordshire.com).

Arrival in Oxford

From the **train** station, the city center is a 10-minute walk (exit straight ahead and follow the signs). A taxi costs around £5-7—but because of the city center's many one-way streets, your cab may have to take a very long way around. The "tourism centre" desk in the train station is actually just a sales outlet for City Sightseeing's skippable hop-on, hop-off bus tours; the real TI (described above) is in the city center. There are no lockers at the station, but day-trippers can leave their luggage at either of two youth hostels 400 yards in front of the train station toward the town center; confusingly, both are called "Backpackers" (Oxford Backpackers Hostel, 9A Hythe Bridge Street, £4/bag, 8:00-23:30; and Central Backpackers, 13 Park End Street, £3/bag, 7:00-23:00). Note: The official Oxford YHA youth hostel, which sits behind the station, does not store bags.

The **bus** station, a bit closer to downtown at Gloucester Green, is just a five-minute walk from the heart of Oxford and the TI: Turn left onto George Street and follow it straight into town (no lockers at station—leave your bags at the hostels mentioned above).

Drivers day-tripping into Oxford have several options. The cheapest but least convenient is to use one of the outlying park-and-ride lots, which are about a 10-minute shuttle-bus ride from the town center. There are some pay parking lots closer to the center (including a handy one between the train station and downtown, and a larger one just southeast of the Oxford Castle, near Westgate Shopping Centre), but they're much more expensive. There's also time-limited pay-and-display street parking north of The Ashmolean Museum, on St. Giles Street (carefully monitored, so get back in time or you're likely to get ticketed).

Helpful Hints

Bookstore: One of the world's largest bookstores, **Blackwell's** boasts miles of shelves in its main location (additional satellite shops around town). The vast Norrington Room in the basement holds stacks of books (Mon and Wed-Sat 9:00-18:30, Tue 9:30-18:30, Sun 11:00-17:00, coffee shop upstairs, WC on top floor, 48-51 Broad Street, tel. 01865/792-792, www.blackwell.co.uk). Ask here about literary walking tours (see "Tours in Oxford," later).

Best Views: At the **University Church of St. Mary the Virgin,** climb the 127 narrow, twisting stairs of the 13th-century bell tower for views of Oxford's many spires and colleges (church—free, tower—£4, daily 9:30-17:00, July-Aug until 18:00, tower opens Sun at 12:30, last entry to tower 30 minutes before closing, coffee shop in vault, High Street, tel. 01865/279-113, www.university-church.ox.ac.uk). For an easier climb, skip up the 99 steps of **Carfax Tower** (£2.30, daily April-Sept 10:00-17:30, March and Oct 10:00-16:30, Nov-Feb 10:00-15:30). Also consider the tower of the **Sheldonian Theatre** (described on page 506). The views from **Oxford Castle's** tower (described on page 513) are underwhelming and only accessible if you pay to join the tour.

Harry Potter Sights: In the movies, the look of Hogwarts School was partially based on a few real-life Oxford sights. For details, see page 890, and consider taking a Harry Potter tour (see below).

Tours in Oxford

▲Walking Tours

The TI's **"City and University" walking tours,** led by Blue Badge guides, explain the local history and traditions and take you inside one or two of the colleges. More informative than entertaining, these dry talks provide a solid historical background (£8, 2 hours, daily at 10:45 and 13:00, additional tours may be offered at 11:00 and/or 14:00 depending on demand—ask at TI for schedule; 10:45 and 14:00 tours generally include Divinity School except on Sat and cost £0.50 extra). They also have a wide variety of themed tours, including **Harry Potter tours** (£15) and **literary tours** about C. S. Lewis, J. R. R. Tolkien, and others (£8.50). All of these tours are popular and often sell out, especially on Saturday; it's smart to book in advance (drop by, call, or go online, TI tel. 01865/252-200, www.visitoxfordandoxfordshire.com; tours depart from sidewalk in front of TI).

Blackwell's Walking Tours, led by proper British gentlemen, focus on literary and historic Oxford. Their Inklings tour visits J. R. R. Tolkien's and C. S. Lewis' former haunts, while their general Literary tour covers a wider range of authors. Check Blackwell's bookstore for current tours and times (£8, mid-April-Oct

Tue-Fri, 1.5 hours, 48-51 Broad Street, tour info tel. 01865/333-602, oxford@blackwell.co.uk).

Other tours include the more casual **Oxford Walking Tours,** which depart hourly from the Trinity College gates, across from the TI (£9.50, daily 11:00-16:00, 1.5 hours, also evening ghost tours, call day before or morning of tour to confirm time, mobile 07790-734-387, www.oxfordwalkingtours.com, Stuart).

Take a pass on the "free" tours led by Footprints Walking Tours. Although led by young, enthusiastic guides, they aren't really free since they expect a tip at the end.

Hop-on, Hop-off Bus Tours

City Sightseeing Oxford runs double-decker buses around town, shuttling tourists from one sight to the next (19 stops in all). Because Oxford is fairly compact, with colleges that have to be seen on foot, consider this tour only if you've missed a walking tour or have tired feet. If you do go, take a seat up top to see over the college walls. The green buses have a live guide, while the red ones have recorded commentary—but both are covered by the same ticket (£13.50, pay driver or buy tickets at TI, runs every 10-15 minutes April-Sept daily 9:30-18:00, less frequent in winter and stops running earlier, tel. 01865/790-522, www.citysightseeingoxford.com).

Sights in Oxford

The Colleges

You could spend a lot of time going from college to college here—but since they all have similar features, frankly, if you've seen one, you've seen them all. If you just take the TI's walking tour, you'll get a sufficient taste of one or two—for most visitors, it's overkill to visit more. Save your time for the excellent Ashmolean Museum, Bodleian Library, or punting.

The entrance to each college is easy to spot—just look for a doorway with crests and a flagpole on the top. Each entry has an office with a porter (live-in caretaker). Inquire there to find out which buildings are open to visitors, and if any plays, music, evensong services, or lectures are scheduled.

▲Christ Church College

This is the alma mater of William Penn (founder of Pennsylvania), John Wesley (influential Methodist leader), Charles Dodgson (a.k.a. Lewis Carroll), and 13 prime ministers. Its grounds include a grand old dining hall, a giant quad, and an impressive chapel that doubles as a cathedral. Of Oxford's colleges, Christ Church is the largest and most prestigious (and, some think, most pretentious). It's also the most popular (and most expensive) for tourists to visit—partly thanks to its historic fame, but mostly because scenes in the Harry Potter movies were filmed here.

Cost and Hours: £8, family ticket-£16, Mon-Sat 10:00-17:00, Sun 14:00-17:00, last entry 30 minutes before closing, church and dining hall close at 16:30, tel. 01865/276-492, www.chch.ox.ac.uk.

Dining Hall Closure: Note that the dining hall—the prime attraction for Harry Potter fans—is closed to outsiders when students are actually eating here. During the term, it's generally open to visitors Mon-Fri 10:30-11:45 & 14:30-16:30, Sat-Sun 14:00-16:30—but it can close on short notice. (Outside the school term, it's open longer hours—typically daily 10:30-16:30.) Call ahead or check the website (go to www.chch.ox.ac.uk, click "Visitor Information," then "Information")—and plan your visit accordingly.

Evensong: Most days in Christ Church Cathedral, an excellent choir of students (sometimes accompanied by fidgety little boys) sings along to the church's pipe organ. This delightful service is open to anyone; linger after the service ends to hear the organist jam (free, Tue-Sun at 18:00, Mon service is spoken rather than sung, enter at Tom Tower). For more on evensong, see page 164.

Getting There: The college is located on St. Aldate's; follow *Visitors' Entrance* signs (past the big tower and all the way to the end of the biggest building, toward the river).

❍ Self-Guided Tour: As you enter the grounds through the visitors' entrance, you'll pass through a bit of countryside spreading out to the river. This is actually part of the college. Called **Christ Church Meadow,** it was the setting Lewis Carroll used for the croquet scenes in *Alice's Adventures in Wonderland* (free, open dawn to dusk). Consider taking a stroll here, either now or after your college visit (though you'll exit at the opposite end of the college complex).

Buy your ticket and pick up the essential self-guided tour booklet with map. Follow the one-way route to be sure you don't miss anything. Gentlemen wearing derby hats, called custodians, are posted around the college to answer questions.

First you'll head into the small **cloister** (WCs outside, in corner), where some Harry Potter scenes were filmed, before reaching the base of the grand staircase leading up to the **dining hall.** Appreciate its grand scale and the splendid, Gothic, hammer-beam roof. While Harry Potter scenes were filmed along the staircase, they never actually filmed in the dining hall itself; set designers merely based their dining hall on this grand space. (Custodians report that astute kids who visit immediately know it's not the "real" Hogwarts—since there are three long rows of tables, not four.)

You'll then enter **Tom Quad,** a grassy field surrounded by college buildings. In the middle is a small fishpond with a statue of

OXFORD

The Colleges of Oxford

While we think of it as one big university, Oxford consists of 38 autonomous, self-funded colleges. The role of the university is to provide lectures, administer exams, and award degrees, but the colleges are where students spend most of their time. Students directly apply to—and study at—one of these colleges, rather than the university (although they can submit an open application and have the university choose the college for them). Most colleges offer all of the traditional majors, but specialized majors have fewer choices. For example, 31 colleges offer history as a major, but only seven offer archaeology. Rivalry among the colleges is fierce, both academically and in sports (rowing is a favorite).

Many of the colleges, dating back hundreds of years, have historic old buildings that are open to the public. While some of these are free to enter, the more famous and interesting ones charge admission. Most are open only in the afternoons, but they can be unexpectedly closed due to exam schedules and special events.

History: The first school is thought to have been founded here in the 11th century, but Oxford really took off in 1167, when, during a period of political tension between England and France, Henry II banned English students from attending the University of Paris. The students—mostly poor peasant kids who'd been fortunate enough to be educated in Latin at monastic schools (the language of higher learning of the day)—gathered in Oxford to pursue their studies. The teachers took students under their wing, rented out boarding houses, and lived with and taught their charges in an almost monastic environment. Students often clashed with residents in this market town, just as university students tussle with "townies" the world over. But in medieval Oxford, these "town-and-gown fights" were often violent and claimed many casualties.

Anatomy of a College: Gradually, little campuses evolved that consisted of four parts: a library, dormitories, a dining hall, and a chapel. In its purest form, a college would have these four buildings surrounding a central courtyard, where students could exercise and which could be locked at night for security—the origin of today's quadrangle (though planting those spaces with golf course-quality grass was a much later innovation). Today, visitors touring a college will still find these same four components.

Notice that many of the chapels are shaped like a capital "T," rather than like a typical cross-shaped church floor plan. One of the earliest chapels (at New College) was planned on a cross shape, but wasn't able to acquire the land they needed. Their

modified, truncated plan (missing the top, or apse) caught on with the other colleges. Many chapels host evensong services at 18:00, which are usually open to the public.

In the Harry Potter-esque dining halls, long rows of tables (for students) lead toward the elevated high table, where the faculty dines. Hanging above the high table is usually a portrait of the college's founder, while portraits of other rectors and important alums also decorate the space. Students still really do eat in these halls at these long tables—which is why, during term periods, you can't enter them at lunchtime (generally from about 11:00 to 14:30, depending on the college).

Oxford Today: About a quarter of applicants are accepted, and about a third of the student body hails from other countries—giving the city an international feel. You'll hear more American accents here than just about anywhere in England. Tuition, room, board, and books run about £10,000 a year for UK and EU residents; non-EU students pay double.

Students enter the college in October and spend their first year (through the following June) preparing for preliminary exams, which they must pass to remain enrolled. Once that hurdle is cleared, they study for two more years preparing for their final exams.

If you visit in June, you might see students wearing traditional academic robes on their way to their finals. (Well, not entirely traditional—while students can be penalized if they're not properly clad, the faculty years ago refused to legislate the length of female students' skirts. Many of today's young women express their individuality amid all that stuffiness by raising their gowns' hemlines...sometimes dramatically.) Students taking their finals wear carnations on their lapels: white on the first day, pink on the second day, and red on the final day. When students emerge from their final exam wearing a red carnation, they're greeted by friends and family who douse them with flour, glitter, and champagne or beer (a tradition called "trashing"). There's usually a happy ending: Among those who remain at Oxford all three years, the graduation rate is nearly 100 percent.

Mercury. Notice the outlines of archways ringing the quad; the architect wanted to create a giant cloister here, but funding ran out.

The tall tower, designed by Christopher Wren, holds a seven-ton bell called **Great Tom.** According to tradition, this clangs out 101 times every night at 21:05. Why not on the hour? When the tradition began, time zones had yet to be standardized—and since Oxford was five minutes of longitude west of Greenwich, clocks here were set five minutes earlier. That means 21:05 Greenwich Mean Time was 21:00 on the dot Oxford time.

Continue a few steps along the quad, and enter the 800-year-old **chapel** (on the right). This is the only university chapel in the world that also serves as a cathedral (bishop's seat). The interior feels dark and mysterious. Pick up the free sheet identifying the highlights, including the shrine to an obscure local saint, St. Frideswide, and a 1320 stained-glass window showing the martyrdom of Thomas Becket (whose face was blacked out to help him survive the Reformation). For information on the musical service that takes place here nightly, see "Evensong," earlier.

Exiting the chapel, you'll be steered back around the cloister, where you can view a 15-minute video about Christ Church. Then circle back around past the base of the dining hall stairs, pass through the Tom Quad again, and head straight to exit out the far end.

Going through the passage, you'll pop out with the grand library on your right; look left for the tall **chestnut tree** behind the wall. Lewis Carroll would watch a cat belonging to a little girl named Alice (the dean's daughter) sitting in the tree. When he later wrote his story about Alice's visit to Wonderland, it inspired him to include the Cheshire Cat character.

Continue past more buildings. On the right just before the exit is Christ Church's final sight, the...

Christ Church Picture Gallery

This sleepy gallery has a good collection that houses a rotating exhibition of drawings and sketches by Albrecht Dürer, Michelangelo, Leonardo da Vinci, Raphael, and other Old Masters. Because the drawings are fragile, they need to "rest" periodically—so don't be disappointed if your favorite is missing. There's also a permanent collection of oil paintings by the likes of Tintoretto, Veronese, Van Dyck, and Frans Hals.

Cost and Hours: £3, £1.50 if you paid to enter the college; June Mon and Wed-Sat 10:30-17:00, Sun 14:00-17:00, closed Tue; July-Sept Mon-Sat 10:30-17:00, Sun 14:00-17:00; Oct-May Mon and Wed-Sat 10:30-13:00 & 14:00-16:30, Sun 14:00-16:30, closed Tue; tel. 01865/276-172, www.chch.ox.ac.uk/gallery.

Getting There: If you're visiting Christ Church College, the one-way tour route will eventually lead you here—look for signs to the *Picture Gallery*. To visit only the gallery—or if the main campus is closed to visitors—you can enter the gallery directly from the street (at Canterbury Gate, off Oriel Square).

Magdalen College

Sitting on the upper edge of town, this college (pronounced "maudlin") has the largest grounds of any of the Oxford colleges (big enough to include its own deer park, with actual deer peacefully browsing the grounds). Visitors can tour the chapel (with a fascinating black-and-white stained-glass window in the antechamber), the dining hall (open 14:00-17:30), and the expansive grounds. Pick up the self-guided walk brochure when you enter. The best-known path through the college, Addison's Walk across the river, was frequented by C. S. Lewis (accessible only if you pay to enter the grounds).

Cost and Hours: £5, daily April-June 13:00-18:00, July-Sept 12:00-19:00, Oct-March 13:00-dusk, last entry 30 minutes before closing; High Street next to Magdalen Bridge, tel. 01865/276-000, www.magd.ox.ac.uk.

Evensong: Evensong services take place Tue-Sun at 18:00 (except July-Sept); while most days feature a mixed chorus of boys and men, Tuesday is generally the renowned boys choir, and Fridays is men only.

Merton College

The third-oldest college (at not quite 750 years old), Merton boasts the oldest quad (Mob Quad, from the 14th century). *The Lord of the Rings* author J. R. R. Tolkien taught here. Visitors have access to the quad and the chapel, but to get inside the superb medieval "chained" library—the oldest in Oxford—you'll have to take a tour.

Cost and Hours: College entry without tour-£3, Mon-Fri 14:00-17:00, Sat-Sun 10:00-17:00, last entry 30 minutes before closing, Merton Street, tel. 01865/276-310, www.merton.ox.ac.uk.

Tours: Guided tours, which are available in the summer for around £5, include the college, chapel, and library; usually run July-Sept at 14:00, 15:00, and 16:00; confirm times at the Porters' Lodge, 45 minutes.

Exeter College

A smaller college, Exeter is centrally located, free to visit, and worth a peek. The highlight is Sir George Gilbert Scott's jewel-like Neo-Gothic chapel. This replica of Paris' Sainte-Chapelle was recently cleaned, so the stone is gleaming. It features William Morris' *The Adoration of the Magi* tapestry (on the right, just before the main altar).

Cost and Hours: Free, usually open daily 14:00-17:00, Turl Street, tel. 01865/279-600.

University Buildings

While each individual college has its own admirable complex of historic buildings, Oxford University's facilities aren't too shabby, either. As if trying to one-up all the colleges, the biggest and best university buildings cluster near the intersection of Broad Street/Holywell Street and Parks Road/Catte Street. These are the classic, iconic Oxford buildings you often see in movies.

▲▲University Buildings Spin-Tour

For a quick look at several grand buildings, begin by making your way to the pebbled courtyard that's squeezed between all of that sandstone beauty (facing Catte Street and the can't-miss-it Bridge of Sighs). Stand in the middle of the courtyard, where the two stone walkways intersect. Begin by facing the building with the white tower.

The **Sheldonian Theatre** is where graduations, matriculations, and other important campus events take place. Before the Sheldonian was built, these ceremonies occurred in a church—but the music and celebratory tone were deemed inappropriate for a sacred space, so this theater was purpose-built. (Despite its name, no theatrical presentations take place here, though music concerts sometimes do.) This was the first major building project designed by Sir Christopher Wren, then an astronomy professor and budding architect who went on to rebuild much of London after the great fire (including the landmark St. Paul's Cathedral). The gate facing the street in front of the theater is lined with the so-called Sheldonian Heads. Each of these 13 hirsute heads illustrates a different style and length of beard. Dating originally from the 17th century (this set—the third round—was carved in the 1970s), these heads are sometimes called "the emperors." (Four more heads stand proudly in front of the Museum of the History of Science—described later—set back just to the right.) Across the street from the heads is the **Weston Library**—recently renovated and due to open in early 2015 with an impressive collection of the Bodleian Library's treasures (see details later).

Turn 90 degrees to the right and face the big Neoclassical building with the columns out front. The **Clarendon Building** was originally built to house the Oxford University Press. Among the books printed here was the Lincoln Bible—used to inaugurate Presidents Lincoln and Obama.

Turn another 90 degrees to the right, and you'll be facing

(through the fence and across the street) the **"Bridge of Sighs,"** modeled and named after the one in Venice. It was built to connect the two parts of Hertford College. A romantic and popular symbol of Oxford, it shows up in many films.

Finally, turn another 90 degrees to face the side of the **Bodleian Library,** with an interior that's well worth touring (described in detail later).

Detours on Foot: Before heading to the Bodleian Library or Sheldonian Theatre, take two detours on foot to appreciate a few more fun details.

First, angle to the right toward the gap between the library and the Sheldonian Theatre, and enter the little courtyard. The ornate buttresses between the large windows support the Divinity School that's attached to the Bodleian Library (also tourable—see later). Look back the way you came (facing the side wing of the Bodleian), look up to just below the roofline, and notice the row of **grotesques** (sculpted heads). While dozens of grotesques line the entire building, this particular row was added in 2009 when Philip Pullman (author of *The Golden Compass*) staged a contest for Oxfordshire children to propose sculpture designs. Scan this row of the nine winners, starting with the dodo bird on the corner. The third shows three men in a boat, honoring Jerome K. Jerome's humorous 1889 travelogue of the same name. The fourth is the head of Aslan, the title feline from C. S. Lewis' *The Lion, the Witch, and the Wardrobe.* The fifth (bravely situated between the lion and a wild boar) shows Thomas Bodley, the library's namesake. The eighth has two chubby figures: Tweedledum and Tweedledee, from *Alice's Adventures in Wonderland.* And the ninth head, a bearded man sipping a mug of beer, is called "From Myths to Monsters," honoring the creations of J. R. R. Tolkien.

Head back to the pebbled square, and turn right to cut straight through the finely decorated courtyard of the Bodleian Library. At the other side, you'll come out onto the quaint, cobblestoned Radcliffe Square, which is dominated by the most distinctive university building of all: the round, columned **Radcliffe Camera.** Built as a medical library, today it's used as a reading room for a gigantic library complex that runs

through tunnels underneath the square. (It's named for the alum who funded it, not for the Harry Potter film star.)

Hook around the Radcliffe Camera to see the tall steeple of the **Church of St. Mary the Virgin,** which is the university church and has a climbable tower (see page 499) and a café in the crypt.

Now that you have your bearings, consider a visit to one or both of the two university facilities that welcome visitors: Bodleian Library and Sheldonian Theatre.

▲Bodleian Library

With some 11 million books and more than 100 miles of shelving in its underground stacks, "the Bod" is one of the world's largest and most famous libraries. Founded by Thomas Bodley in 1602, this is one of six "legal deposit" libraries in the UK—so it must receive a copy of every book printed in the nation (about 6,000 volumes are delivered each week—notice the signs posted for the steady stream of delivery trucks). The palatial building—with a big courtyard and frilly spires along the roofline—has two areas that are open to the public: the Divinity School on the ground floor, and the medieval Duke Humfrey's Library upstairs.

Cost and Hours: You'll pay £1 to enter the Divinity School on your own (Mon-Fri 9:00-17:00, Sat 9:00-16:30, Sun 11:00-17:00), but to see Duke Humfrey's Library you must take a dry but informative **tour** (£5/30-minute tour of Divinity School and library, £7/one-hour version). Tours run several times daily; generally, the one-hour tour runs in the mornings and early afternoons (likely at 10:30, 11:30, 13:00, and 14:00), while the 30-minute version runs later (typically at 15:30, 16:00, and 16:40). On Sundays, it's more of a mix all day long. Specific times can change, so check the schedule and buy your ticket at the kiosk in the passage across the courtyard from the library entrance, or call 01865/277-224, www.bodleian.ox.ac.uk.

Visiting the Library: The **Divinity School,** an impressive fan-vaulted hall, has a ceiling carved with intricately detailed religious symbolism. Above the entry, notice the empty niche where a crucifix once stood (directly over the door), and—just to the left—a defaced statue of St. Peter. These works were victims of Reformation iconoclasts. The colorful stained-glass windows that once lined the hall were another casualty. Above the door at the far end of the

hall is a statue of Mary...holding a book. Students gather here to put on their gowns before walking to their graduation ceremony at the theater next door. Before leaving, imagine hospital beds lining this hall...yes, it's the infirmary from the Harry Potter films.

Upstairs in **Duke Humfrey's Library** are the musty, creaky old shelves of ancient-looking books, stacked neatly under a beautifully painted wooden ceiling. The required tour shows you only a small section of the library—basically one hall, and a view down another—but even at that, it gives you a good feel for the place. You'll learn about the library's history, and about the huge stockpile of books that sits beneath this part of Oxford. Because this is purely a reference library (none of the books can be checked out), they need plenty of space.

Treasures Collection: Nearby (across Broad Street from the Clarendon Building), the newly restored Weston Library is scheduled to re-open in early 2015. It's planned to present (in Blackwell Hall) an extremely impressive "Treasures" exhibition of previously inaccessible items from the Bodleian Library's rare-books collection—with everything from a Shakespearean First Folio to a couple of Magna Cartas. When open, this library will be a must for historians and book lovers. Ask locally for details.

Sheldonian Theatre

While the building's interior isn't too exciting, you'll see the round main hall, with its painted ceiling, gold trim, wood columns marbled to look like stone, and a pipe organ (just for show—music is now played by a digital organ). Your ticket also includes admission to the building's cupola, with 360-degree views over the many spires of Oxford.

Cost and Hours: £3, Mon-Sat 10:00-12:30 & 14:00-16:30, until 15:30 in winter, closed Sun, can close for special events—call ahead, Broad Street, tel. 01865/277-299.

Other Sights

▲▲The Ashmolean Museum of Art and Archaeology

This eclectic museum was founded in 1683 by a royal gardener, John Tradescant, who loved to collect interesting items while traveling in search of plants. All these years later, the collection is huge, and the building recently underwent a thorough £63 million renovation.

Cost and Hours: Free but suggested £3 donation, special exhibits may have entrance fees, audioguide-£3, Tue-Sun 10:00-

OXFORD

Literary Oxford

Oxford's list of alums is almost laughably impressive. A virtual factory for famous politicians—among them a couple dozen prime ministers (including current PM David Cameron), Indira Gandhi, and Bill Clinton (who took classes here as a Rhodes scholar)—it's also the home of some of the most important scientists of the 20th century. Stephen Hawking (*A Brief History of Time*) went to Oxford, Richard Dawkins (*The Selfish Gene*) teaches at Oxford, and Tim Berners-Lee—inventor of the World Wide Web—got in trouble for hacking into Oxford's computers. But Oxford may be most famous for its literary past.

J. R. R. Tolkien (1892-1973) graduated from the university and was a professor at Oxford, teaching the glories of Anglo-Saxon language and English literature through one of his favorite works, the epic poem *Beowulf.* He spent years in Oxford writing the books he's most famous for: *The Hobbit* and the three volumes of *The Lord of the Rings,* beloved by millions of readers.

C. S. Lewis (1898-1963), Tolkien's good friend, was a fellow at Oxford for almost 30 years. Lewis sent generations of children through the back of a wardrobe in his series *The Chronicles of Narnia.* During his time in Oxford, Lewis was also the ringleader of a famous writing society called the Inklings, who met regularly at The Eagle and Child pub (which they called the "Bird and Baby"—see page 516). Picture these literary geniuses sitting in the pub's familiar confines. Lewis orders another round, while Tolkien tells Frodo's tale—with a pipe in hand—for the first time.

The Oxford-educated poet **W. H. Auden** (1907-1973) was a lifelong friend and correspondent of Tolkien's. (He was one of the first critics to publicly praise *The Lord of the Rings.*) Auden may be most familiar to Americans for the lines of his poem "Funeral Blues" that were quoted in the film *Four Weddings and a Funeral:* "He was my North, my South, my East and West, / My working week and my Sunday rest, / My noon, my midnight, my talk, my song; / I thought that love would last for ever: I was wrong."

Lewis Carroll (1832-1898), the pen name of Charles Lutwidge Dodgson, was a mathematician who taught at Oxford, where he met young Alice Liddell, the dean's daughter and the real-life inspiration for his most famous book, *Alice's Adventures in Wonderland.* The author lived at Christ Church College, and Carroll

18:00, closed Mon, rooftop café (same hours as museum except Thu-Fri, when it serves tapas and drinks until 21:00), Beaumont Street, tel. 01865/278-000, www.ashmolean.org.

Visiting the Museum: While the collection doesn't rank with the big-league museums of London, it's very impressive for a small city. The vast collection features everything from antiquities to fine porcelain to paintings by some of the Old Masters. Rather than

and Liddell would regularly play croquet—without the Queen of Hearts—in The Meadow.

Aldous Huxley (1894-1963), a prolific novelist and Oxford student, wrote the early science-fiction classic *Brave New World*, about a disturbing, mindless future. His later book, *The Doors of Perception,* was written under the influence of mescaline. (Jim Morrison, another fan of mind-altering experiences, named his band The Doors after the book.)

Literary great **Virginia Woolf** (1882-1941) was banned from using Oxford's library because she was a woman (Oxford didn't begin admitting women until 1920, though they could attend some classes before that). She later wrote her most important essay, "A Room of One's Own," where she parodied the university she nicknamed "Oxbridge," a combination of Oxford and Cambridge.

Oscar Wilde (1854-1900) did well at Oxford (graduating with the highest grade possible) and went on to become famous for his novels (*The Picture of Dorian Gray),* plays (*The Importance of Being Earnest),* homosexuality (his famous trial sent him to jail), and memorably witty quotes, such as "Men marry because they are tired; women, because they are curious: both are disappointed." Another of his quotes: "I can resist everything except temptation." And another: "We are all in the gutter, but some of us are looking at the stars."

Oxford's other notable literary stars include the poet **Percy Bysshe Shelley, Jonathan Swift** (*Gulliver's Travels),* **T. S. Eliot** (*The Waste Land),* **John le Carré** (*The Spy Who Came in from the Cold),* **Philip Pullman** (*The Golden Compass,* part of his children's book series *His Dark Materials),* **Martin Amis** (*Time's Arrow),* **Helen Fielding** (*Bridget Jones's Diary),* and—maybe most important of all to generations of children's book readers—Theodor Seuss Geisel (a.k.a. **Dr. Seuss**).

In addition to the **Harry Potter** connection, visiting Brits are enthralled by locations relating to the Oxford-set **Inspector Morse** television series, which was an enormous hit in the UK from 1987 to 2000 (the sequel, **Inspector Lewis,** was filmed here and is also a smash hit). Sort of the British Columbo or a modern-day Sherlock Holmes, this fictional police detective was quirky, cultured, and extremely effective.

featuring any particularly famous items, it has a broad range of offbeat bits and pieces (such as Lawrence of Arabia's ceremonial dress, prehistoric Cycladic figurines from Greece, gorgeous Turkish and Middle Eastern tiles, a Stradivarius violin, and so on). What distinguishes this place is that it's all exceptionally well-presented, with engaging descriptions that pull you in to topics you didn't realize were of interest to you.

The museum is loosely organized chronologically, starting in the basement and working up through five floors of history; it's also arranged geographically, with excellent collections of Chinese, Middle Eastern, Indian, Mediterranean, and other regional art and artifacts. As you move up the building, the exhibit shows how these very different civilizations came together as the world shrunk.

For an engaging introduction, head for the basement and peruse the Exploring the Past themed exhibits, which bring together various eras of history and corners of the globe while examining a particular topic (such as money, the human image, and reading and writing). Then browse the collection to your heart's content, and find your own favorites (I enjoyed the paintings of royal elephants from India). The recently renovated Egyptian galleries feature various mummies, including a priest, a two-year-old boy, a cat, and even a baby crocodile, along with an interactive display explaining the process of mummification. The Randolph Sculpture Gallery, near the entrance, features Greek and Roman statues.

The museum's fine painting gallery showcases lesser-known pieces by Degas, Pissarro, Van Gogh, and others. It's fun to see artist J. W. M. Turner's view down High Street in Oxford...then walk a block to see today's version. If nothing else, The Ashmolean provides visitors to this university town a way to see a respectable range of English glass, Chinese porcelain, ancient sculpture, and tapestries without having to ride the train.

▲Museum of the History of Science

Worth ▲▲▲ for scientists, this concise and interesting little museum, conveniently located on the main drag between the TI and the Sheldonian Theatre, is one of Oxford's overlooked gems. Three manageable floors of display cases show off hugely important, well-explained bric-a-brac from Oxford's illustrious scientific history. You'll see a very early pendulum clock, a rare spherical astrolabe, equipment used for first developing penicillin, a sextant belonging to the great English engineer Isambard Brunel, Lewis Carroll's photo-developing kit, and Einstein's chalkboard (still featuring his hand-scrawled equations from a lecture here). As it's free and extremely central, it's well worth a quick visit.

Cost and Hours: Free, Tue-Fri 12:00-17:00, Sat 10:00-17:00, Sun 14:00-17:00, closed Mon, Broad Street, tel. 01865/277-280, www.mhs.ox.ac.uk.

▲Oxford Castle

Originating as a classic Norman motte-and-bailey fort a millennium ago, Oxford's castle gradually evolved into a mighty fortress that was mostly destroyed after the English Civil War. Its surviving St. George Tower was used as a royalist prison, and—a century and a half later—was expanded into a Victorian-era county jail, specializing in demoralizing prisoners with exhausting and humiliating punishments. The facility held prisoners up until 1996. Since then, part of the complex was converted into a posh hotel (its current laundry room was the site of the prison's final execution, in 1952—more than clothes were hung that day), while the rest was recently opened as a tourist attraction. England has far bigger and better castles, but this is an entertaining and educational alternative to all of Oxford's academic sights.

Cost and Hours: £9.25 includes mandatory one-hour tour, daily from 10:00, last tour departs at 16:20; £1 to climb the motte and bailey, open daily 10:00-17:30; 44-46 Oxford Castle, tel. 01865/260-666, www.oxfordcastleunlocked.co.uk.

Visiting the Castle: Although the surviving bits of the castle are small and sparse (basically, the original motte and bailey, one tall tower, and a few cells), this shell is brought to life by a required one-hour tour led by a lively, costumed guide playing the role of a historical figure tied to this place.

The tour includes a climb to the top of the St. George Tower (for distant views over the town) and a visit to the crypt below, with an emphasis on grisly tales of prison life. You'll learn of cruel and unusual punishments and see the deep, circular grooves in the floor where prisoners were forced to work eight-hour shifts trudging around a capstan wheel in silence. The tour provides a strong historical basis—spinning the true tales of Empress Matilda (the usurped queen who dramatically escaped from here and went on to support her son in his quest to become King Henry II), Geoffrey of Monmouth (who first penned tales of King Arthur and Merlin in the 12th century), and other important figures connected to the castle—and also throws in a few silly legends and ghost stories. After the tour, you'll be set free to explore two floors of exhibits about prison history. Admission also includes access to the original motte (hill), where you can wind up the path to the scant remains of the bailey (fort).

Punting

Long, flat boats can be rented for punting (pushing with a long pole) along the River Cherwell. Chauffeurs are available, but the do-it-yourself crowd is having more fun...even if they are a little wet.

Cost and Hours: £18/hour—or £20/hour on weekends, £30 deposit, chauffeured punts-£25/30 minutes, rowboats and paddle

OXFORD

boats available for the less adventurous, cash only, daily Feb-Nov 9:30-dusk, closed Dec-Jan, Magdalen Bridge Boathouse, tel. 01865/202-643, www.oxfordpunting.co.uk).

Sleeping in Oxford

Sleeping cheaply in Oxford is not easy—you'll pay London-size prices for London-size rooms. The colleges and university own much of the town, so boarding space is at a premium. A few B&Bs line the main roads out of town, but they're less convenient for sightseeing; in the town center (where I've focused my listings), you'll find high-priced hotels and guesthouses in very old and poorly maintained buildings. Noise is an issue anywhere in this college town—mostly from students conversing or singing loudly in the streets on the way home from the pub. Try requesting a quiet room, but expect some noise regardless. Given the easy connections by train to the Cotswolds (Moreton-in-Marsh) and London, I'd make Oxford a day trip, and sleep elsewhere. But if you're spending the night, here are some centrally located, reasonable options.

$$$ The Buttery Hotel, up steep steps above a café/bakery (hence the name) and two doors down from the TI, rents 16 comfortable, good-value rooms. The "deluxe" rooms are larger and have big windows overlooking bustling Broad Street—nice for views but not for noise; the cheaper "standard" rooms are quieter (tiny Sb-£69, bigger Sb-£89-95, standard Db-£99-115, deluxe Db-£135-145, Tb-£159-169, higher prices are for Fri-Sat, free Wi-Fi, no parking, 11-12 Broad Street, tel. 01865/811-950, www.thebuttery-hotel.co.uk, enquiries@thebutteryhotel.co.uk, Sally).

$$$ The Bocardo offers modern lodgings along bustling George Street, between the train station and the town center. Rare in this creaky old town, the 10 rooms come with urban style and lots of amenities. It's on a street with lots of nightclubs, so expect noise, and try asking for a quieter room (Sb-£119, bigger "superior" Sb-£125, Db-£136, bigger "superior" Db-£155, no breakfast but lots of cafés nearby, free Wi-Fi, 24-26 George Street, tel. 01865/591-234, www.thebocardo.co.uk, reservations@thebocardo.co.uk).

$$$ The Tower House, with tight spaces and low ceilings, has small, worn-but-sweet rooms, and couldn't be more central. Three of the eight rooms share a bathroom with a spacious shower (S-£70, Sb-£90, D-£80, Db-£110, rates will likely increase after planned renovations, includes breakfast around the corner at Turl Street Kitchen, free Wi-Fi, no parking, request a quieter back room, 15 Ship Street, tel. 01865/246-828, www.towerhouseoxford.co.uk, reservations@towerhouseoxford.co.uk).

$$ Holywell Bed & Breakfast, run by local tour guide Stuart and his American wife Carrie, is hidden away in an ancient row house on quiet Holywell Street, across from New College. Its three rooms share two bathrooms (S-£65-75, D-£85-105, higher prices are for Fri-Sat, book well in advance, no children under age 12, steep stairs, free Wi-Fi, free on-site parking, guests receive discounted walking tour with Stuart-£5, 14 Holywell Street, tel. 01865/721-880, www.holywellbedandbreakfast.com, info@holywellbedandbreakfast.com).

Hostels

This youthful town has two different hostels that are called "Backpackers," at opposite sides of the same block (a 3-minute walk from the train station on the way to the town center). Both are willing to store non-guests' bags for a fee (£4/bag at Oxford Backpackers, £3/bag at Central Backpackers).

$ Oxford Backpackers Hostel rents 92 beds in single-sex and mixed dorms. While the ambience is somewhere between grotty and funky, hard-core hostelers appreciate the cheap beds (£18-23/bed in large dorm, £21-23/bed in 4-person dorm, includes continental breakfast, reception open 8:00-23:30, free Wi-Fi, laundry service, 9A Hythe Bridge Street, tel. 01865/721-761, www.hostels.co.uk, oxford@hostels.co.uk).

$ Central Backpackers Oxford is a Canadian-and-Aussie-run place, with 50 beds in 4- to 12-bed dorms around an inviting covered patio. It feels a bit more tame than Oxford Backpackers (£18-24/bed depending on room size, includes basic continental breakfast, free guest computer and Wi-Fi, laundry service, 13 Park End Street, tel. 01865/242-288, www.centralbackpackers.co.uk).

OXFORD

Near Oxford

$$ The Coach & Horses Inn, a charming 16th-century inn and pub, is located seven miles southeast of Oxford in Chislehampton, across the street from a bus stop that connects the two towns (Sb-£65, Db-£85, free Wi-Fi, tel. 01865/890-255, www.coachhorsesinn.co.uk, enquiries@coachhorsesinn.co.uk).

Eating in Oxford

Pubs

These pubs perfectly conform to what Americans imagine a British pub to be: a rambling series of cozy, well-worn rooms on sloping wooden floors filled with tight clusters of friends enjoying food and ale around ancient-feeling tables. The hours listed below are for when food is served—most stay open later to serve drinks.

The King's Arms, across from the Clarendon Building, has an approachable, open, convivial atmosphere. They offer good, traditional English fare (£5 sandwiches, £9-11 pub grub, food served daily 11:00-21:30, 40 Holywell Street at corner of Parks Road, tel. 01865/242-369).

The Bear, hidden down a side street and close to the Christ Church Picture Gallery, is one of Oxford's oldest and most charming pubs. This teensy place proudly sports no right angles (go ahead—check) since 1242. Peruse the framed collections of amputated clothing on the walls and hold on to your tie if you're wearing one. If you're coming for lunch, arrive before 13:00, when they're typically swamped and tables are in short supply (£9-15 meals, food served daily 12:00-21:00, 6 Alfred Street at corner of Blue Boar Street, tel. 01865/728-164). There are a few picnic tables out back—leave through the pub's side door to find them, or walk to the left as you're facing the front.

The Turf Tavern—big, boisterous, and tucked into a short alley—is popular for its good food, outdoor beer garden, and warren of claustrophobic rooms nestled against the old city wall (£5 sandwiches, £8-13 pub grub and salads, food served daily 11:00-21:00, 4 Bath Place, tel. 01865/243-235). To find it from Holywell Street, listen for the chatter of students enjoying a beer (down Bath Lane); otherwise, head for the gap marked *St. Helen's Passage* under the Bridge of Sighs on New College/Queen's Lane.

The Eagle and Child, a long and thin series of rooms, is subdued, smaller, and more intimate than the other pubs listed. A five-minute walk from the city center, it's famous for its history and ambience. This was the gathering place of the writers known as the Inklings (see sidebar on page 510), and a literary vibe still haunts the place. If you're a fan of Middle-earth and Narnia, stop in for a drink under photos of J. R. R. Tolkien and C. S. Lewis. The food is traditional, with a seasonal, modern twist (£9-13 pub grub, read the history on the menu, food served Mon-Sat 11:00-21:00, Sun 12:00-20:00, 49 St. Giles Street, tel. 01865/302-925).

Eating Cheaply

Taylors is a student favorite for affordable £2.50-5 hot or cold sandwiches with a wide range of fillings. There are a few tables, but most people get food to go and find a scenic spot for a picnic (daily 8:00-17:00, 58 High Street, tel. 01865/723-152). You'll see several Taylors locations around Oxford, including one a few blocks west at 19 High Street and another at Gloucester Green 89 (near the bus station).

The **Covered Market**—a farmers' market maze of shops, fruit stands, deli counters, and cafés—has a fine selection for breakfast, lunch, or a picnic (shops generally open around 8:00-10:00 and close around 16:30-17:30, on Sun generally open 10:00-16:00, between Market Street and High Street, near Carfax Tower).

Other Eateries

Turl Street Kitchen, started by three recent Oxford grads, is a do-gooder eatery focusing on locally and ethically sourced ingredients. Both the lunch and dinner menu change daily, and good vegetarian options are always available. All profits go to the charity Student Hubs, which connects students with various social causes. Service is thoughtful and unhurried (£5-10 lunches, £10-13 dinners, light breakfast also available, food served daily 8:00-11:00 & 12:00-14:30 & 18:00-22:00, 16-17 Turl Street, tel. 01865-264-171).

The **News Café,** with a cheerful and bright interior, serves affordable meals, big salads, and cheaper cream teas than at the large hotels. It's a nice break from the chain eateries on nearby Cornmarket (£7-10 meals, Sun-Fri 9:00-17:30, Sat 9:00-18:00, free Wi-Fi, 1 Ship Street, tel. 01865/242-317).

Chain Restaurants on Cornmarket, George Street, and Nearby: On Cornmarket, you'll find a slew of chain eateries, including **Pret à Manger** and **West Cornwall Pasty Company.** George Street, which intersects Cornmarket on its way to the train station, has another string of reliable chains, including **Ask** (Italian), **Gourmet Burger**

Kitchen and **Byron** (burgers), and **Côte** (French). Also along this street is **Jamie's Italian,** part of a chain owned by British TV's celebrity chef Jamie Oliver and serving up classic Italian cuisine in a sprawling, industrial-mod interior (£6-8 small pastas, £10-14 large pastas, £11-17 main dishes, Mon-Sat 12:00-23:00, Sun 12:00-22:30, 24-26 George Street, tel. 01865/838-383). There's a **Marks & Spencer** on Queen Street, across from Carfax Tower.

Afternoon Tea: The **Randolph Hotel** is a swanky place where proud parents take their graduating students for a fancy afternoon tea (reserve ahead, especially near the end of the term). You'll enjoy impeccable service and classic English afternoon tea under high ceilings and chandeliers (£22 afternoon tea, £16 traditional cream tea, tea served daily 12:00-18:00, Beaumont Street, directly opposite Ashmolean Museum, tel. 01865/256-400). **The Rose,** a more affordable, less crowded alternative, offers good scones in a nondescript, modern atmosphere (£12.50 afternoon tea, £7.50 cream tea, Mon-Sat 9:00-18:00, Sun 10:00-18:00, 51 High Street, tel. 01865/244-429).

Oxford Connections

From Oxford by Train to: London's Paddington Station (2/hour direct, 1 hour, more possible with transfer in Reading), **Bath** (hourly, 1.25 hours, transfer in Didcot), **Moreton-in-Marsh** (every 1-2 hours, 40 minutes), **Stratford-upon-Avon** (every 2 hours, 1.5 hours, transfer in Leamington Spa, Birmingham, or Banbury), **Salisbury** (1-2/hour, 2 hours, transfer in Basingstoke and sometimes also Reading), **Portsmouth** (2-4/hour, 2.5-2.75 hours, 1-2 transfers), **York** (1/hour direct, 3.5 hours, more with transfers). **Train info:** tel. 0845-748-4950, www.nationalrail.co.uk.

By Bus to London: The Oxford Tube bus runs every 12-20 minutes during peak times to London's **Notting Hill Gate, Marble Arch, and Victoria Coach Station** (otherwise 2/hour, free Wi-Fi on bus, tel. 01865/772-250, www.oxfordtube.com). The competing X90 bus runs every 15 minutes during peak times to **Baker Street, Marble Arch, and Victoria Coach Station** (otherwise 2-3/hour, free Wi-Fi on bus, tel. 01865/785-400, www.oxfordbus.co.uk). The trip to London takes about 1.5-1.75 hours, and all buses depart from the Gloucester Green bus station—just show up and ask which bus is leaving first.

By Bus to Other Destinations: An independent bus service called The Airline shuttles students and visitors directly between Oxford and Heathrow Airport 24 hours a day (2/hour, 1.5 hours, £23) and to Gatwick Airport (hourly, 2-2.5 hours, £28; tel. 01865/785-400, www.oxfordbus.co.uk).

National Express runs buses to **Stratford-upon-Avon** (1/day direct, 1 hour) and **Bath** (1/day direct, 2 hours, more with transfer; tel. 0871-781-8181, www.nationalexpress.com). For details on taking a public bus to **Blenheim Palace,** see the next section.

Blenheim Palace

Just 30 minutes' drive from Oxford (and convenient to combine with a drive through the Cotswolds), Blenheim Palace is one of England's best—worth ▲▲▲. Too many palaces can send you into

a furniture-wax coma, but everyone should see Blenheim. The Duke of Marlborough's home—the largest in England—is still lived in, which is wonderfully obvious as you prowl through it. The 2,000-acre yard, well-designed by Lancelot "Capability" Brown, is as majestic to some as the palace itself. The view just past the outer gate as you enter is a classic. Even if you're in a hurry, you'll need two hours to see the basic sights—but if you have more time, you could spend all day here. Note: Americans who pronounce the place "blen-HEIM" are the butt of jokes. It's "BLEN-em."

Cost and Hours: £21, discount tickets that save £2.50-3 are available at TIs in surrounding towns—including Oxford and Moreton-in-Marsh—or on the #S3 bus from Oxford; family ticket for two adults and two kids-£55, £5 guidebook; open mid-Feb-Oct daily 10:30-17:30, last entry at 16:45; Nov-mid-Dec Wed-Sun 10:30-17:30; park open but palace closed Nov-mid-Dec Mon-Tue and mid-Dec-mid-Feb.

Information: Tel. 01993/810-530, recorded info toll-free tel. 0800-849-6500, www.blenheimpalace.com.

Getting There: Blenheim Palace sits at the edge of the cute cobbled town of Woodstock. The train station nearest the palace (Hanborough, 1.5 miles away) has no taxi or bus service.

From **Oxford,** take bus #S3 (2/hour, 30 minutes; bus tel. 01865/772-250, www.stagecoachbus.com). Catch it from the bus station at Gloucester Green (usually stops at Oxford's train station as well; may also pick up in the center on George Street—ask). It stops twice near Blenheim Palace: the "Blenheim Palace Gates" stop is along the main road about a half-mile walk to the palace itself; the "Woodstock/Marlborough Arms" stop puts you right in the heart of the village of Woodstock (handy if you want to poke around town before heading to the palace; this adds just a few more minutes' walking than the other bus stop). The Woodstock gate also offers the most spectacular view of the palace and lake.

If you're coming from the **Cotswolds,** your easiest train connection is from Moreton-in-Marsh to Oxford, where you can catch the bus to Blenheim (note that bus #S3 doesn't always stop at the Oxford train station—you may have to walk five minutes to the bus station).

Drivers head for Woodstock (from the Cotswolds, follow signs for *Oxford* on A-44); the palace is well-signposted once in town, just off the main road. Buy your ticket at the gate, then drive up the long driveway to park near the palace.

Background: John Churchill, first duke of Marlborough, defeated Louis XIV's French forces at the Battle of Blenheim in 1704. This pivotal event marked a turning point in the centuries-long struggle between the English and the French, and some historians claim that if not for his victory, we'd all be speaking French today. (They're probably exaggerating, but *qui sait?*) A thankful Queen Anne rewarded Churchill by building him this nice home, perhaps the finest Baroque building in England (designed by playwright-turned-architect John Vanbrugh). Ten dukes of Marlborough later, it's as impressive as ever. (The current, 11th duke considers the would-be 12th more of an error than an heir, and has largely disowned him.) In 1874, a later John Churchill's daughter-in-law, Jennie Jerome, gave birth at Blenheim to another historic baby in that line...and named him Winston. The history continues.

⊙ Self-Guided Tour: From the parking lot, you'll likely enter at the recently opened East Courtyard Visitors' Center (with café). Pick up a free map and head through the small courtyard. You'll emerge into a grand courtyard in front of the palace's columned yellow facade. Most of the attractions are reached by going through the palace's main entry.

You'll enter into the truly great **Great Hall.** Before taking the well-organized tour, spend some time on your own in the fine **Winston Churchill Exhibition,** which displays letters, paintings, and other artifacts of the great statesman who was born here. The highlight is the bed in which Sir Winston was born in 1874 (prematurely...his mother went into labor suddenly while attending a party here).

When you've had your fill of Churchill, catch the 45-minute guided tour of the **state rooms**—the fancy halls the dukes use to impress visiting dignitaries (tours leave every 10 minutes, included with ticket, last one at 16:45). This fascinating tour lets visitors ogle some of the most sumptuous rooms in the palace, ornamented with fine porcelain, gilded ceilings, portraits of past dukes, photos of the present duke's family, and "chaperone" sofas designed to give courting couples just enough privacy...but not *too* much. When the palace is really busy (most likely on Sun), they dispense with guided tours and go "free flow," allowing those with an appetite for learning to strike up conversations with docents in each room.

Enjoy the series of 10 Brussels tapestries that commemorate military victories of the First Duke of Marlborough, including the Battle of Blenheim. After winning that pivotal conflict, he scrawled a quick note on the back of a tavern bill notifying the queen of his victory (you'll see a replica). The tour offers insights into the quirky ways of England's fading nobility—for example, in exchange for this fine palace, the duke still pays "rent" to the Queen in the form of one ornamental flag per year (called "quit-rent standard").

The palace items come with tales of past dukes of Marlborough and their families. You'll learn about Consuelo Vanderbilt—of the New York Vanderbilts—who was forced against her will to marry into this aristocratic family. She was miserable, but dutifully produced two sons (whom she dubbed "the heir and the spare") before the marriage fell apart after 10 years.

Finish with the remarkable "long library"—with its tiers of books and stuccoed ceilings—before exiting through the chapel, near the entrance to the gardens (described later). But before taking off to explore the gardens, consider two more attractions inside the main palace.

The Untold Story (to the left as you enter the Great Hall) is a modern, 45-minute, multimedia "visitors' experience" (15 people go in every 3 minutes, included in your ticket). You'll travel from room to room—as doors open and close behind you—guided through 300 years of history by a maid named Grace Ridley. (If you have limited time to spend at the palace, this is skippable.)

For a more extensive visit, follow up the general tour with a 30-minute guided walk through the **private apartments** of the duke. Tours leave at the top and bottom of each hour; however, since you'll see where the duke's family actually resides today, tours are cancelled if His Grace is in his jammies (£4.50, irregular schedule but generally daily 12:00-16:30, most likely to be open in summer, tickets are limited, buy from table in library or at main entry, enter in corner of courtyard to left of grand palace entry).

The palace's expansive **gardens** stretch nearly as far as the eye can see in every direction. Access them from the courtyard, by going through the little door near the "Churchill Shop" (as you face the main palace entrance, it's to the right). You'll emerge into the Water Terraces; from there, you can loop around to the left, behind the palace, to see (but not enter) the Italian Garden. Or, head down to the lake to walk along the waterfront trail; going left takes you to the rose gardens and arboretum, while turning right brings you to the Grand Bridge. You can explore on your own (using the map and good signposting), or rent a £3 audioguide that outlines three different walks around the property (40-90 minutes depending on tour; rent it in the "Churchill Shop" next to the door to the gardens). A café sits at the garden exit for basic lunch and teatime treats.

Finally, in the "stables block" (under the gateway to the right, as you face the main palace entrance) is the **Churchill's Destiny exhibit,** which traces the military leadership of two great men who shared that name: John, who defeated Louis XIV at the Battle of Blenheim in the 18th century, and in whose honor this palace was built; and Winston, who was born in this palace, and who won the Battle of Britain and helped defeat Hitler in the 20th century. The exhibit offers a painstaking, blow-by-blow account of each of the battles. It's remarkable that arguably two of the most important military victories in the nation's history were overseen by distant cousins—England is a small island indeed. (Winston Churchill fans can visit his tomb, just over a mile away to the south in the Bladon town churchyard—the church is faintly visible from inside the palace. Look for the footpath across from the White House pub.)

The final attraction is actually on the way out of the palace complex: the kid-friendly **pleasure garden,** where a lush and humid greenhouse flutters with butterflies. A kid zone includes a few second-rate games and the "world's largest symbolic hedge maze." The maze is worth a look if you haven't seen one and want some exercise. If you have a car, you'll pass these gardens as you drive down the road toward the exit; otherwise, you can take the tiny train from the palace parking lot to the garden (2/hour).

Sleeping near Blenheim Palace

(area code: 01993)
These accommodations near Blenheim Palace are in the town of Woodstock.

$$ Blenheim Guest House, charming and 200 years old, has six rooms in the town center. A bit musty, it's located above a tearoom literally next door to the gateway into the palace grounds (Sb-£65, Db-£80-90 depending on size, free Wi-Fi, 17 Park

Street, tel. 01993/813-814, www.theblenheim.co.uk, theblen-heim@aol.com).

$$ The Blenheim Buttery has six modern, comfortable rooms fitted into a half-timbered, slanted-floor building (Sb-£69-115, Db-£89-125, lower prices are for off-season, free cable Internet, 7 Market Place, tel. 01865/811-950, www.theblenheimbuttery.co.uk, info@theblenheimbuttery.co.uk).

THE COTSWOLDS

Chipping Campden • Stow-on-the-Wold
• Moreton-in-Marsh

The Cotswold Hills, a 25-by-90-mile chunk of Gloucestershire, are dotted with enchanting villages. As with many fairy-tale regions of Europe, the present-day beauty of the Cotswolds was the result of an economic disaster. Wool was a huge industry in medieval England, and Cotswold sheep grew the best wool. A 12th-century saying bragged, "In Europe the best wool is English. In England the best wool is Cotswold." The region prospered. Wool money built fine towns and houses. Local "wool" churches are called "cathedrals" for their scale and wealth. Stained-glass slogans say things like "I thank my God and ever shall, it is the sheep hath paid for all."

With the rise of cotton and the Industrial Revolution, the woolen industry collapsed. Ba-a-a-ad news. The wealthy Cotswold towns fell into a depressed time warp; the homes of impoverished nobility became gracefully dilapidated. Today, visitors enjoy a harmonious blend of man and nature—the most pristine of English countrysides decorated with time-passed villages, rich wool churches, tell-me-a-story stone fences, and "kissing gates" you wouldn't want to experience alone. Appreciated by throngs of 21st-century Romantics, the Cotswolds are enjoying new prosperity.

The north Cotswolds are best. Two of the region's coziest towns, Chipping Campden and Stow-on-the-Wold, are eight and four miles, respectively, from Moreton-in-Marsh, which has the best public transportation connections. Any of

these three towns makes a fine home base for your exploration of the thatch-happiest of Cotswold villages and walks.

Planning Your Time

The Cotswolds are an absolute delight by car and, with patience, enjoyable even without a car. On a three-week countrywide trip, I'd spend at least two nights and a day in the Cotswolds. The Cotswolds' charm has a softening effect on many uptight itineraries. You could enjoy days of walking from a home base here.

Home Bases: Chipping Campden and **Stow-on-the-Wold** are quaint without being overrun, and both have good accommodations. Stow has a bit more character for an overnight stay and offers the widest range of choices. The plain town of **Moreton-in-Marsh** is the only one of the three with a train station, and only worth visiting as a transit hub. While Moreton has the most convenient connections, non-drivers can also make it work to home-base in Chipping Campden or Stow—especially if you don't mind sorting through bus schedules or springing for the occasional taxi to connect towns. (This becomes even more challenging on Sundays, when there is essentially no bus service.) With a car, consider really getting away from it all by staying in one of the smaller villages.

Nearby Sights: If you want to take in some Shakespeare, note that Stow, Chipping Campden, and Moreton are only a 30-minute drive from **Stratford,** which offers a great evening of world-class entertainment (see next chapter). And England's top countryside palace, **Blenheim,** is located at the eastern edge of the Cotswolds, between Moreton and Oxford (see previous chapter). For drivers, Blenheim fits well on the way into or out of the region.

One-Day Driver's 100-Mile Cotswold Blitz: Use a good map and reshuffle this plan to fit your home base:

9:00	Browse through Chipping Campden, following my self-guided walk.
10:30	Joyride through Snowshill, Stanway, and Stanton.
12:30	Have lunch in Stow-on-the-Wold, then follow my self-guided walk there.
15:00	Drive to the Slaughters, Bourton-on-the-Water, and Bibury; or, if you're up for a hike instead of a drive, walk from Stow to the Slaughters to Bourton, then catch the bus back to Stow.
18:00	Have dinner at a countryside gastropub (reserve in advance by phone), then head home; or drive 30 minutes to Stratford-upon-Avon for a Shakespeare play.

Two-Day Plan by Public Transportation: This plan is best for any day except Sunday—when virtually no buses run—and assumes you're home-basing in Moreton-in-Marsh.

Cotswold Appreciation 101

History can be read into the names of the area. *Cotswold* could come from the Saxon phrase meaning "hills of sheep's cotes" (shelters for sheep). Or it could mean shelter ("cot" like cottage) on the open upland ("wold").

In the Cotswolds, a town's main street (called High Street) needed to be wide to accommodate the sheep and cattle being marched to market (and today, to park tour buses). Some of the most picturesque cottages were once humble row houses of weavers' cottages, usually located along a stream for their waterwheels (good examples in Bibury and Lower Slaughter). The towns run on slow clocks and yellowed calendars. An entire village might not have a phone booth.

Fields of yellow (rapeseed) and pale blue (linseed) separate pastures dotted with black and white sheep. In just about any B&B, when you open your window in the morning you'll hear sheep baa-ing. The decorative "toadstool" stones dotting front yards throughout the region are medieval staddle stones, which buildings were set upon to keep the rodents out.

Cotswold walls and roofs are made of the local limestone. The limestone roof tiles hang by pegs. To make the weight more bearable, smaller and lighter tiles are higher up. An extremely strict building code keeps towns looking what many locals call "overly quaint."

COTSWOLDS

Day 1: Take the morning bus (likely around 9:30) to Chipping Campden to explore that town. If you want to stretch your legs, hike 30 minutes (each way) into Broad Campden. Then take the bus from Chipping Campden to Moreton and transfer to a Stow-bound bus. After poking around Stow, hike from Stow through the Slaughters to Bourton-on-the-Water (about 3 hours at a relaxed pace), then return by bus or taxi to Moreton for dinner. (For less walking and more time for an early dinner in Stow, do just part of the hike, or take the bus from Stow to Bourton and back.)

Day 2: Take a day trip to Blenheim Palace via Oxford (train to Oxford, bus to palace—explained on page 519); or rent a bike and ride to Chastleton House; or take a daylong countryside walk (best to bus to Stow or Chipping Campden and walk from there).

Tourist Information

Local TIs stock a wide array of helpful resources. Ask for the *Cotswold Lion*, the biannual newspaper, which includes suggestions for walks and hikes (spring/summer); the monthly *Cotswold Events*

While you'll still see lots of sheep, the commercial wool industry is essentially dead. It costs more to shear a sheep than the 50 pence the wool will fetch. In the old days, sheep lived long lives, producing lots of wool. When they were finally slaughtered, the meat was tough and eaten as "mutton." Today, you don't find mutton much because the sheep are raised primarily for their meat, and slaughtered younger. When it comes to Cotswold sheep these days, it's lamb (not mutton) for dinner (not sweaters).

Towns are small, and everyone seems to know everyone. The area is provincial yet ever-so-polite, and people commonly rescue themselves from a gossipy tangent by saying, "It's all very... mmm...yaaa."

In contrast to the village ambience are the giant manors and mansions whose private, gated driveways you'll drive past. Many of these now belong to A-list celebrities, who have country homes here. If you live in the Cotswolds, you can call Madonna, Elizabeth Hurley, and Kate Moss your neighbors.

This is walking country. The English love their walks and vigorously defend their age-old right to free passage. Once a year the Ramblers, Britain's largest walking club, organizes a "Mass Trespass," when each of the country's 50,000 miles of public footpaths is walked. By assuring that each path is used at least once a year, they stop landlords from putting up fences. Any paths found blocked are unceremoniously unblocked.

Questions to ask locals: Do you think foxhunting should have been banned? Who are the Morris men? What's a kissing gate?

guide; bus schedules for the routes you'll be using; and the *Attractions and Events Guide* (with updated prices and hours for Cotswold sights). Each village also has its own assortment of brochures about the place itself, and the surrounding countryside, often for a small fee (£0.50-1). While paying for these items seems chintzy, realize that Cotswold TIs have lost much of their funding and are struggling to make ends meet (some are run by volunteers).

Getting Around the Cotswolds

By Bus

The Cotswolds are so well-preserved, in part, because public transportation to and within this area has long been miserable. Fortunately, larger towns are linked by trains, and a few key buses connect the more interesting villages. Centrally located Moreton-in-the-Marsh is the region's transit hub—with the only train station and several bus lines.

To explore the towns, use the bus routes that hop through the Cotswolds about every 1.5 hours, lacing together main stops and

The Cotswolds

TO WORCESTER

A-44

A-46

TO M-5

B-4084

EVESHAM

HIDCOTE MANOR GARDEN

B-4632

MICKLETON

CHIPPING CAMPDEN

B-

BROADWAY

A-44

A-44

B-4081

BROAD CAMPDEN

STANTON

11

SNOWS-HILL

10

12

BLOCKLEY

7

TO TEWKES-BURY

1

2

STANWAY

STANWAY HOUSE

A-424

WINCHE-COMBE

FORD

6

B-4077

UPPER SWELL

B-4632

COTSWOLD FARM PARK

LOWER SWELL

COTSWOLD WAY FOOTPATH

B-4068

TO CHELTENHAM

UPPER & LOWER SLAUGHTER

9

A-436

A-429

— MAJOR ROAD

— MINOR ROAD

--- FOOTPATH

NOTE: NOT ALL ROADS OR SHEEP ARE SHOWN

TO ❸, BIBURY, NORTHLEACH & CIRENCESTER

COTSWOLDS

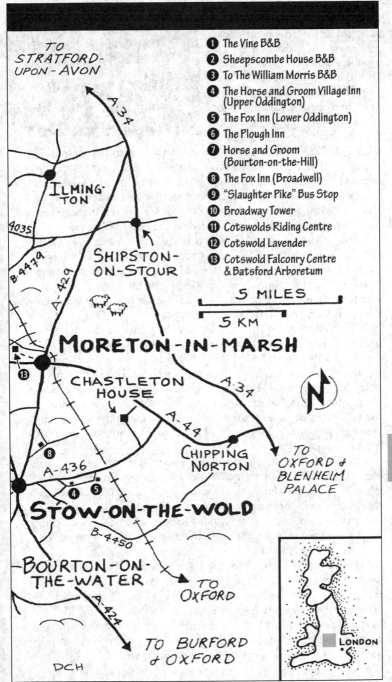

TO STRATFORD-UPON-AVON

A-34

ILMINGTON

4035

B-4479

A-429

SHIPSTON-ON-STOUR

MORETON-IN-MARSH

CHASTLETON HOUSE

A-44

A-34

CHIPPING NORTON

TO OXFORD & BLENHEIM PALACE

A-436

STOW-ON-THE-WOLD

B-4450

BOURTON-ON-THE-WATER

TO OXFORD

A-424

TO BURFORD & OXFORD

DCH

1. The Vine B&B
2. Sheepscombe House B&B
3. To The William Morris B&B
4. The Horse and Groom Village Inn (Upper Oddington)
5. The Fox Inn (Lower Oddington)
6. The Plough Inn
7. Horse and Groom (Bourton-on-the-Hill)
8. The Fox Inn (Broadwell)
9. "Slaughter Pike" Bus Stop
10. Broadway Tower
11. Cotswolds Riding Centre
12. Cotswold Lavender
13. Cotswold Falconry Centre & Batsford Arboretum

5 MILES

5 KM

N

LONDON

COTSWOLDS

ending at rail stations. In each case, the entire trip takes about an hour. Individual fares are around £2-3.

The TI hands out easy-to-read bus schedules for the key lines described below (or check www.traveline.org.uk, or call the Traveline info line, tel. 0871-200-2233). Put together a one-way or return trip by public transportation, making for a fine Cotswold day. If you're traveling one-way between two train stations, remember that the Cotswold villages—generally pretty clueless when it comes to the needs of travelers without a car—have no official baggage-check services. You'll need to improvise; ask sweetly at the nearest TI or business.

Note that no single bus connects the three major towns described in this chapter (Chipping Campden, Stow, and Moreton); to get between Chipping Campden and Stow, you'll have to change buses in Moreton. Since buses can be unreliable and connections aren't timed, it may be better to call a driver or taxi to go between Chipping Campden and Stow.

The following bus lines are operated by Johnsons Coaches (tel. 01564/797-070, www.johnsonscoaches.co.uk): Buses **#21** and **#22** run from Moreton-in-Marsh to Batsford to Bourton-on-the-Hill to Blockley, then either to Broadway (#21) or Broad Campden (#22) on their way to Chipping Campden, and pass through Mickleton before ending at Stratford-upon-Avon. Note that this route is the only one that goes all the way through to Chipping Campden. Bus **#23** goes from Moreton-in-Marsh to Shipston-on-Stour to Stratford-upon-Avon.

The following buses are operated by Pulham & Sons Coaches (tel. 01451/820-369, www.pulhamscoaches.com): Bus **#801** goes from Moreton-in-Marsh to Stow-on-the-Wold to Bourton-on-the-Water; most continue on to Northleach and Cheltenham (limited service on Sun in summer). Bus **#855** goes from Northleach to Bibury to Cirencester and then (in the morning and afternoon) on to the Kemble train station.

Warning: Unfortunately, the buses described here aren't particularly reliable—it's not uncommon for them to show up late, early, or not at all. Leave yourself a huge cushion if using buses to make another connection (such as a train to London), and always have a backup plan (such as the phone number for a few taxis/drivers or for your hotel, who can try calling someone for you). Remember that bus service is essentially nonexistent on Sundays.

By Bike

Despite narrow roads, high hedgerows (blocking some views), and even higher hills, bikers enjoy the Cotswolds free from the constraints of bus schedules. For each area, TIs have fine route planners that indicate which peaceful, paved lanes are particularly scenic for biking. In summer, it's smart to book your rental bike a couple of days ahead.

In **Chipping Campden,** you have two options: **Cycle Cotswolds,** right in town at the Volunteer Inn pub, is the most convenient (£12/day, £15/24 hours, daily 7:00-dusk, Lower High Street, tel. 01789/720-193, www.cyclecotswolds.co.uk). Otherwise, try **Cotswold Country Cycles** (£15/day, tandem-£30/day, includes helmets and route maps, delivery for a fee, daily 9:30-dusk Easter-Sept only, 2 miles north of town at Longlands Farm Cottage, call in advance—tel. 01386/438-706, www.cotswoldcountrycycles.com); they also offer self-led bike tours of the Cotswolds and surrounding areas (2-7 days, see website for details).

In **Moreton-in-Marsh,** the nice folks at the **Toy Shop** rent mountain bikes. You can stop in the shop to rent a bike, or call ahead to pick up or drop off at other times—they're flexible (£15/day with route maps, bike locks, and helmets; shop open Mon and Wed-Fri 9:00-17:00, Sat 10:00-17:00, closed Sun and Tue, High Street, tel. 01608/650-756).

Stow-on-the-Wold does not have any bike-rental shops.

By Foot

Walking guidebooks and leaflets abound, giving you a world of choices for each of my recommended stops (choose a book with clear maps). If you're doing any hiking whatsoever, get the excellent Ordnance Survey Explorer OL #45 map, which shows every road, trail, and ridgeline (£8 at local TIs). Nearly every hotel and B&B has a box or shelf of local walking guides and maps, including Ordnance Survey #45. Don't hesitate to ask for a loaner. For a quick circular hike from a particular village, peruse the books and brochures offered by that village's TI. Villages are generally no more than three miles apart, and most have pubs that would love to feed and water you. For a list of guided walks, ask at any TI for the free *Cotswold Lion* newspaper. The walks range from 2 to 12 miles, and often involve a stop at a pub or tearoom (*Lion* newspaper also online at www.cotswoldsaonb.org.uk—click on "Publications"). Another option is to leave the planning to a company such as Cotswold Walking Holidays, which can provide route instructions and maps, transfer your bags, and arrange lodging (www.cotswoldwalks.com).

There are many options for hikers, ranging from the "Cotswold Way" path that leads 100 miles from Chipping Campden all

The Cotswolds at a Glance

Chipping Campden and Nearby

▲▲**Chipping Campden** Picturesque market town with finest High Street in England, accented by a 17th-century Market Hall, wool-tycoon manors, and a characteristic Gothic church. See page 536.

▲▲**Stanway House** Grand, aristocratic home of the Earl of Wemyss, with the tallest fountain in Britain and a 14th-century tithe barn. **Hours:** June-Aug Tue and Thu only 14:00-17:00, closed Sept-May. See page 548.

▲**Stanton** Classic Cotswold village with flower-filled exteriors and 15th-century church. See page 550.

▲**Snowshill Manor** Eerie mansion packed to the rafters with eclectic curiosities collected over a lifetime. **Hours:** July-Aug Wed-Mon 11:30-16:30, closed Tue; April-June and Sept-Oct Wed-Sun 12:00-17:00, closed Mon-Tue; closed Nov-March. See page 551.

▲**Hidcote Manor Garden** Fragrant garden organized into color-themed "outdoor rooms" that set a trend in 20th-century garden design. **Hours:** May-Aug daily 9:00-19:00; mid-March-April and Sept Sat-Wed 10:00-18:00, closed Thu-Fri; Oct Sat-Wed 10:00-17:00, closed Thu-Fri; Nov-Dec and mid-Feb-mid-March Sat-Sun 11:00-16:00, closed Mon-Fri; closed Jan-mid-Feb. See page 553.

▲**Broad Campden, Blockley, and Bourton-on-the-Hill** Trio of villages with sweeping views and quaint homes, far from the madding crowds. See page 554.

Stow-on-the-Wold and Nearby

▲▲**Stow-on-the-Wold** Convenient Cotswold home base with charming shops and pubs clustered around town square, plus popular day-hikes. See page 554.

COTSWOLDS

the way to Bath, to easy loop trips to the next village. Serious hikers enjoy doing a several-day loop, walking for several hours each day and sleeping in a different village each night. One popular route is the **"Cotswold Ring"**: Day 1—Moreton-in-Marsh to Stow-on-the-Wold to the Slaughters to Bourton-on-the-Water (12 miles); Day 2—Bourton-on-the-Water to Winchcombe (13 miles); Day 3—Winchcombe to Stanway to Stanton (7 miles), or all the way to Broadway (10.5 miles total); Day 4—On to Chipping Campden (just 5.5 miles, but steeply uphill); Day 5—Chipping Campden to

▲**Lower and Upper Slaughter** Inaptly named historic villages—home to a working waterwheel, peaceful churches, and a folksy museum. See page 565.

▲**Bourton-on-the-Water** The "Venice of the Cotswolds," touristy yet undeniably striking, with petite canals and impressive Motor Museum. See page 566.

▲**Cotswold Farm Park** Kid-friendly park with endangered breeds of native British animals, farm demonstrations, and tractor rides. **Hours:** Mid-Feb-mid-Dec daily 10:30-17:00, closed mid-Dec-mid-Feb. See page 568.

▲**Keith Harding's World of Mechanical Music** Tiny museum brimming with self-playing musical instruments, demonstrations, and Victorian music boxes. **Hours:** Daily 10:00-17:00. See page 569.

▲**Bibury** Village of antique weavers' cottages, ideal for outdoor activities like fishing and picnicking. See page 569.

▲**Cirencester** Ancient 2,000-year-old city noteworthy for its crafts center and museum, showcasing artifacts from Roman and Saxon times. See page 570.

Moreton-in-Marsh and Nearby
▲**Moreton-in-Marsh** Relatively flat and functional home base with the best transportation links in the Cotswolds and a bustling Tuesday market. See page 571.

▲**Chastleton House** Lofty Jacobean-era home with a rich family history. **Hours:** April-Sept Wed-Sat 13:00-17:00; mid- to late March and Oct Wed-Sat 13:00-16:00; closed Nov-mid-March and Sun-Tue year-round. See page 575.

COTSWOLDS

Broad Campden, Blockley, Bourton-on-the-Hill or Batsford, and back to Moreton (7 miles).

Realistically, on a short visit, you won't have time for that much hiking. But if you have a few hours to spare, consider venturing across the pretty hills and meadows of the Cotswolds. Each of the home-base villages I recommend has several options. Stow-on-the-Wold, immersed in pleasant but not-too-hilly terrain, is within easy walking distance of several interesting spots and is probably the best starting point. Chipping Campden sits along a ridge, which means that hikes from there are extremely scenic, but also more strenuous. Moreton—true to its name—sits on a marsh, offering flatter and less picturesque hikes.

Here are a few hikes to consider, in order of difficulty (easiest first). I've selected these for their convenience to the home-base towns and because the start and/or end points are on bus lines, allowing you to hitch a ride back to where you started (or on to the next town) rather than backtracking by foot.

Stow, the Slaughters, and Bourton-on-the-Water: Walk from Stow to Upper and Lower Slaughter, then on to Bourton-on-the-Water (which has bus service back to Stow on #801). One big advantage of this walk is that it's mostly downhill (4 miles, about 2-3 hours one-way). For details, see page 559.

Chipping Campden, Broad Campden, Blockley, and Bourton-on-the-Hill: From Chipping Campden, it's an easy mile walk into charming Broad Campden, and from there, a more strenuous hike to Blockley and Bourton-on-the-Hill (which are both connected by buses #21 and #22 to Chipping Campden and Moreton). For more details, see page 537.

Winchcombe, Stanway, Stanton, and Broadway: You can reach the charming villages of Stanway and Stanton by foot, but it's tough going—lots of up and down. The start and end points (Winchcombe and Broadway) have decent bus connections, and in a pinch some buses do serve Stanton (but carefully check schedules before you set out).

Broadway to Chipping Campden: The hardiest hike of those I list here, this takes you along the Cotswold Ridge. Attempt it only if you're a serious hiker (5.5 miles).

Bibury and the Coln Valley are pretty, but limited bus access makes hiking there less appealing.

By Car

Joyriding here truly is a joy. Winding country roads seem designed to spring bucolic village-and-countryside scenes on the driver at every turn. Distances here are wonderfully short—but only if you invest in the Ordnance Survey map of the Cotswolds, sold locally at TIs and newsstands (the £8 Explorer OL #45 map is excellent but almost too detailed for drivers; a £5 tour map covers a wider area in less detail). Here are driving distances from Moreton: **Stow-on-the-Wold** (4 miles), **Chipping Campden** (8 miles), **Broadway** (10 miles), **Stratford-upon-Avon** (17 miles), **Warwick** (23 miles), **Blenheim Palace** (20 miles).

Car hiking is great. In this chapter, I cover the postcard-perfect (but discovered) villages. With a car and the local Ordnance Survey map, you can easily ramble about and find your own gems. The problem with having a car is that you are less likely to walk. Consider taking a taxi or bus somewhere, so that you can walk back to your car and enjoy the scenery (see suggestions earlier).

Car Rental: Two places near Moreton-in-Marsh rent cars by the day. **Value Self Drive,** based in Shipston-on-Stour (about six miles north of Moreton) and run by Steve Bradley, has affordable rates (£23-35/day plus tax, includes insurance, cheaper for longer rentals; open Mon-Sat 8:15-17:30, Sun by appointment only; call ahead to arrange, mobile 07974-805-485, stevebradleycars@ aol.com). Conveniently, Steve will pick you up in Moreton (£8) or Stratford-upon-Avon (£12), and bring you back to Shipston to get your car. **Robinson Goss Self Drive,** also six miles north of Moreton-in-Marsh, is a bit more expensive and won't bring the car to you in Moreton (£31-52/day including everything but gas, Mon-Thu 8:30-17:00, Fri 8:30-17:30, Sat 8:30-12:00, closed Sun, tel. 01608/663-322, www.robgos.co.uk).

By Taxi or Private Driver

Two or three town-to-town taxi trips can make more sense than renting a car. While taking a cab cross-country seems extravagant, the distances are short (Stow to Moreton is 4 miles, Stow to Chipping Campden is 10), and one-way walks are lovely. If you call a cab, confirm that the meter will start only when you are actually picked up. Consider hiring a private driver at the hourly "touring rate" (generally around £30), rather than the meter rate. For a few more bucks, you can have a joyride peppered with commentary. Whether you book a taxi or a private driver, expect to pay about £20-23 between Chipping Campden and Stow and about £18-20 between Chipping Campden and Moreton.

Note that the drivers listed here are not typical city taxi services (with many drivers on call), but are mostly individuals—it's smart to call ahead if you're arriving in high season, since they can be booked in advance on weekends.

To scare up a taxi in Moreton, try Stuart and Stephen at **ETC,** "Everything Taken Care of" (toll-free tel. 0800/955-8584, cotswoldtravel.co.uk) or **Iain Taxis** (mobile 07789-897-966, iaintaxis@ bpinternet.com); see also the taxi phone numbers posted outside the Moreton train station office. In Stow, try Iain (above) or **Tony Knight** (mobile 07887-714-047). In Chipping Campden, call Iain (above), Paul at **Cotswold Private Hire** (mobile 07980-857-833), Barry Roberts at **Chipping Campden Private Hire** (also does tours, mobile 07774-224-684, cotswoldpersonaltours.com), or **Les Proctor,** who offers village tours and station pick-ups (mobile 07580-993-492, Les co-runs Cornerways B&B—see page 544). Tim Harrison at **Tour the Cotswolds** specializes in tours of the Cotswolds and its gardens, but will also do tours outside the area (mobile 07779-030-820, www.tourthecotswolds.co.uk).

By Tour

Departing from Bath, **Lion Tours** offers a Cotswold Discovery full-day tour, and can drop you and your luggage off in Stow at no extra charge or in Moreton-in-Marsh for £2.50/person. If you want to get back to London in time for a show, then ask to be dropped off at Kemble Station; it's best to arrange these drop-offs in advance (see page 413 of the Bath chapter).

While none of the Cotswold towns offer regularly scheduled walks, many have voluntary warden groups who love to meet visitors and give walks for a small donation (see specific contact information below for Chipping Campden).

Chipping Campden

Just touristy enough to be convenient, the north Cotswold town of Chipping Campden (CAM-den) is a ▲▲ sight. This market town, once the home of the richest Cotswold wool merchants, has some incredibly beautiful thatched roofs. Both the great British historian G. M. Trevelyan and I call Chipping Campden's High Street the finest in England.

Orientation to Chipping Campden

To get your bearings, walk the full length of High Street; its width is characteristic of market towns. Go around the block on both ends. On one end, you'll find impressively thatched homes (out Sheep Street, past the public WC, and right on Westington Street). Walking north on High Street, you'll pass the Market Hall, the wavy roof of the first great wool mansion, a fine and free memorial garden, and, finally, the town's famous 15th-century Perpendicular Gothic "wool" church. (This route is the same as my self-guided town walk.)

Tourist Information

Chipping Campden's TI is tucked away in the old police station on High Street. Get the £1.50 town guide with map (April-Oct daily 9:30-17:00; Nov-March Mon-Thu 9:30-13:00, Fri-Sun 9:30-16:00; tel. 01386/841-206, www.chippingcampdenonline.org).

Helpful Hints

Festivals: Chipping Campden's biggest festival is the **Cotswold Olimpicks,** a series of tongue-in-cheek countryside games (such as competitive shin-kicking) atop Dover's Hill, just above town (first Fri-Sat after Late May Bank Holiday, www. olimpickgames.co.uk). They also have a **music festival** in May and an **open gardens festival** the third weekend in June.

Internet Access: Try the occasionally open **library** (closed Thu and Sun; High Street, tel. 08452/305-420) or **Butty's at the Old Bakehouse,** a casual eatery and Internet café (£1.50/15 minutes, £2.50/30 minutes, £4/hour, free Wi-Fi, see page 546 for hours, Lower High Street, tel. 01386/840-401).

Bike Rental: Call **Cycle Cotswolds** or **Cotswold Country Cycles** (see page 531).

Taxi: Try **Cotswold Private Hire, Chipping Campden Private Hire,** or **Tour the Cotswolds** (see page 535).

Parking: Find a spot anywhere along High Street and park for free with no time limit. There's also a pay-and-display lot on High Street, across from the TI (1.5-hour maximum). If those are full, there is free parking on the street called Back Ends.

Tours: The local members of the **Cotswold Voluntary Wardens** would be happy to show you around town for a small donation to their conservation society (suggested donation-£3/person, 1-hour walk, walks June-Sept Tue at 14:30 and Thu at 10:00, meet at Market Hall). Tour guide and coordinator Ann Colcomb can help arrange for a walk on other days as well (tel. 01386/832-131).

Walks and Hikes from Chipping Campden: Since this is a particularly hilly area, long-distance hikes are challenging. The easiest and most rewarding stroll is to the thatch-happy hobbit village of **Broad Campden** (about a mile, mostly level). From there, you can walk or take the bus (#22) back to Chipping Campden.

Or, if you have more energy, continue from Broad Campden up over the ridge and into picturesque **Blockley**—and, if your stamina holds out, all the way to **Bourton-on-the-Hill** (Blockley and Bourton-on-the-Hill are also connected by buses #21 and #22 to Chipping Campden and Moreton).

Alternatively, you can hike up to **Dover's Hill,** just north of the village. Ask locally about this easy circular one-hour walk that takes you on the first mile of the 100-mile-long Cotswold Way (which goes from here to Bath).

For more about hiking, see "Getting Around the Cotswolds—By Foot" on page 531.

Self-Guided Walk

Welcome to Chipping Campden

This stroll through "Campden" (as locals call their town) takes you from the Market Hall west to the old silk mill, and then back east the length of High Street to the church. It takes about an hour.

Market Hall: Begin at Campden's most famous monument—the Market Hall. It stands in front of the TI, marking the

town center. The Market Hall was built in 1627 by the 17th-century Lord of the Manor, Sir Baptist Hicks. (Look for the Hicks family coat of arms in the building's facade.) Back then, it was an elegant—even over-the-top—shopping hall for the townsfolk who'd come here to buy their produce. In the 1940s, it was almost sold to an American, but the townspeople heroically raised money to buy it first, then gave it to the National Trust for its preservation.

The timbers inside are true to the original. Study the classic Cotswold stone roof, still held together with wooden pegs nailed in from underneath. (Tiles were cut and sold with peg holes, and stacked like waterproof scales.) Buildings all over the region still use these stone shingles. Today, the hall, which is rarely used, stands as a testimony to the importance of trade to medieval Campden.

Adjacent to the Market Hall is the sober WWI monument—a reminder of the huge price paid by every little town. Walk around it, noticing how 1918 brought the greatest losses.

The TI is just across the street, in the old police courthouse. If it's open, you're welcome to climb the stairs and peek into the **Magistrate's Court** (free, same hours as TI, ask at TI to go up). Under the open-beamed courtroom, you'll find a humble little exhibit on the town's history.

• *Walk west until you reach the Red Lion Inn. Across High Street (and a bit to the right), look for the house with a sundial, called...*

"Green Dragons": The house's decorative black cast-iron fixtures once held hay and functioned much like salad bowls for horses. Fine-cut stones define the door, but "rubble stones" make up the rest of the wall. The pink stones are the same limestone but have been heated, and likely were scavenged from a house that burned down.

• *At the Red Lion, leave High Street*

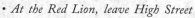

and walk a block down Sheep Street. Just past the public loo, on the right-hand side, is the old...

Silk Mill: The tiny Cam River powered a mill here since about 1790. Today it houses the handicraft workers guild and some interesting history. In 1902, Charles Robert Ashbee (1863-1942) revitalized this sleepy hamlet of 2,500 by bringing a troupe of London artisans and their families (160 people in all) to town. Ashbee was a leader in the romantic Arts and Crafts movement—craftspeople repulsed by the Industrial Revolution who idealized the handmade crafts and preindustrial ways. Ashbee's idealistic craftsmen's guild lasted only until 1908, when most of his men grew bored with their small-town, back-to-nature ideals. Today, the only shop surviving from the originals is that of **silversmith David Hart.** His grandfather came to town with Ashbee, and the workshop (upstairs in the mill building) is an amazing time warp—little changed since 1902. Mr. Hart is a gracious man as well as a fine silversmith, and he welcomes browsers six days a week (Mon-Fri 9:00-17:00, Sat 9:00-12:00, closed Sun, tel. 01386/841-100). (While you could continue 200 yards farther to see some fine thatched houses, this walk doesn't.)

• *Return to High Street, turn right, and walk through town.*

High Street: Chipping Campden's High Street has changed little architecturally since 1840. (The town's street plan and property lines survive from the 12th century.) Notice the harmony of the long rows of buildings. While the street comprises different styles through the centuries, everything you see was made of the same Cotswold stone—the only stone allowed today.

To remain level, High Street arcs with the contour of the hillside. Because it's so wide, you know this was a market town. In past centuries, livestock and packhorses laden with piles of freshly shorn fleece would fill the streets. Campden was a sales and distribution center for the wool industry, and merchants from as far away as Italy would come here for the prized raw wool.

High Street has no house numbers: Locals know the houses by their names. In the distance, you'll see the town church (where this walk ends). Notice that the power lines are buried underground, making the scene delightfully uncluttered.

As you stroll High Street, you'll find the finest houses on the uphill side—which gets more sun. You'll pass several old sundials as you wander. Decorative features (like the Ionic capitals near the TI) are added for non-structural touches of class. Most High Street buildings are half-timbered, but with cosmetic stone facades. You may see some exposed half-timbered walls. Study the crudely beautiful framing, made of hand-hewn oak (you can see the adze marks) and held together by wooden pegs.

Peeking down alleys, you'll notice how the lots are narrow but

COTSWOLDS

Chipping Campden

Self-Guided Walk

- **A** Market Hall
- **B** Magistrate's Court (above TI)
- **C** "Green Dragons" House
- **D** Silk Mill & Silversmith Workshop
- **E** High Street
- **F** Grevel House
- **G** Ernest Wilson Memorial Garden
- **H** Baptist Hicks Land, Ruined Mansion & St. James Church

Hotels & Restaurants

- **1** Noel Arms Hotel
- **2** The Lygon Arms Hotel & Pub
- **3** Badgers Hall Tea Room/B&B
- **4** Bantam Tea Rooms
- **5** Cornerways & Stonecroft B&Bs
- **6** The Old Bakehouse & Butty's (Internet Café)
- **7** Cherry Trees B&B
- **8** The Chance B&B & Bramley House
- **9** Eight Bells Pub
- **10** Michael's Restaurant
- **11** Maharaja Indian Restaurant & Cycle Cotswolds
- **12** La Tradition
- **13** Co-op Grocery

TO BROADWAY

KINGCO

COTSWOLD WAY FOOTPATH

PARK ROAD

THATCHED HOUSES

SILK MILL

WC

TO SNOWSHILL VIA B-4081

WESTINGTON

SHEEP ST.

CATBR

TO MORETON & STOW VIA A-44

COTSWOLDS

very deep. Called "burgage plots," this platting goes back to 1170. In medieval times, rooms were lined up long and skinny like train cars: Each building had a small storefront, followed by a workshop, living quarters, staff quarters, stables, and a pea patch-type garden at the very back. Now the private alleys that still define many of these old lots lead to comfy gardens. While some of today's buildings are wider, virtually all the widths are exact multiples of that basic first unit (for example, a modern building may be three times wider than its medieval counterpart).

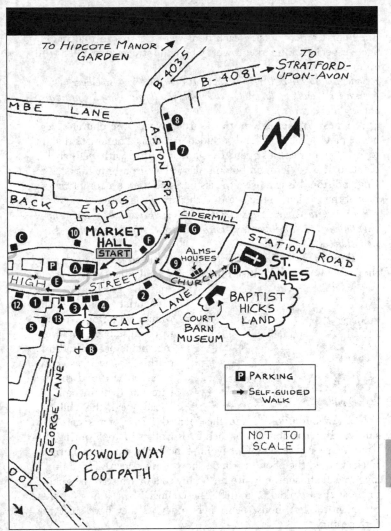

TO HIDCOTE MANOR GARDEN

B-4035

B-4081 → TO STRATFORD-UPON-AVON

MBE LANE

ASTON RD

8

7

BACK ENDS

CIDERMILL

STATION ROAD

C

10 MARKET HALL
START

F

G

ALMS-HOUSES

St. JAMES

HIGH STREET

P

A

E

9

CHURCH

H

BAPTIST HICKS LAND

12 1

3 4

2

LANE

13

5

CALF

B

COURT BARN MUSEUM

GEORGE LANE

P PARKING

→ SELF-GUIDED WALK

NOT TO SCALE

COTSWOLD WAY FOOTPATH

COTSWOLDS

• *Hike up High Street toward the church, to just before the first intersection, to find a house with gargoyles hanging out above. This is the....*

Grevel House: In 1367, William Grevel built what's considered Campden's first stone house (on the left). Sheep tycoons had big homes. Imagine back then, when this fine building was surrounded by humble wattle-and-daub huts. It had newfangled chimneys, rather than a crude hole in the roof. (No more rain inside!) Originally a "hall house" with just one big, tall room, it got its upper floor in the 16th century. The finely carved central bay window is a good early example of the Perpendicular Gothic style.

The gargoyles scared away bad spirits—and served as rain spouts. The boot scrapers outside each door were fixtures in that muddy age—especially in market towns, where the streets were filled with animal dung.

• *Continue up High Street for about 100 yards. Go past Church Street (which we'll walk up later). On the right, you'll find a small Gothic arch leading into a garden.*

Ernest Wilson Memorial Garden: Once the church's vegetable patch, this small and secluded garden is a botanist's delight today. Pop inside if it's open. The garden is filled with well-labeled plants that the Victorian botanist Ernest Wilson brought back to England from his extensive travels in Asia. There's a complete history of the garden on the board to the left of the entry.

• *Backtrack to Church Street. Turn left, walk past the recommended Eight Bells Inn, and hook left with the street. Along your right-hand side stretches...*

Baptist Hicks Land: Sprawling adjacent to the town church, the area known as Baptist Hicks Land held Hicks' huge estate

and manor house. This influential Lord of the Manor was from "a family of substance," who were merchants of silk and fine clothing as well as moneylenders. Beyond the ornate gate (which you'll see ahead, near the church), only a few outbuildings and the charred corner of his **mansion** survive. The mansion was burned by Royalists in 1645 during the Civil War—notice how Cotswold stone turns red when burned. Hicks housed the poor, making a show of his generosity, adding a long row of almshouses (with his family coat of arms) for neighbors to see as they walked to church. These almshouses (lining Church Street on the left) house pensioners today, as they have since the 17th century.

On the right, filling the old **Court Barn,** is a museum about crafts and designs from the Arts and Crafts movement, with works by Ashbee and his craftsmen (£4, April-Sept Tue-Sun 10:00-17:00, Oct-March Tue-Sun 10:00-16:00, closed Mon year-round, tel. 01386/841-951, www.courtbarn.org.uk).

• *Next to the Court Barn, a scenic, tree-lined lane leads to the front door of the church. On the way, notice the 12 lime trees, one for each of the apostles, that were planted in about 1760 (sorry, no limes).*

St. James Church: One of the finest churches in the Cotswolds, St. James Church graces one of its leading towns. Both the town and the church were built by wool wealth. Go inside.

The church is Perpendicular Gothic, with lots of light and strong verticality. Notice the fine vestments and altar hangings (intricate c. 1460 embroidery) behind protective blue curtains (near the back of the church). Tombstones pave the floor in the chancel (often under protective red carpeting)—memorializing great wool merchants through the ages.

At the altar is a brass relief of William Grevel, the first owner of the Grevel House (described earlier), and his wife. But it is Sir Baptist Hicks who dominates the church. His huge, canopied tomb is the ornate final resting place for Hicks and his wife, Elizabeth. Study their faces, framed by fancy lace ruffs (trendy in the 1620s). Adjacent—as if in a closet—is a statue of their daughter, Lady Juliana, and her husband, Lutheran Yokels. Juliana commissioned the statue in 1642, when her husband died, but had it closed until *she* died in 1680. Then, the doors were opened, revealing these two people holding hands and living happily ever after—at least in marble. The hinges were likely used only once.

As you leave the church, look immediately around the corner to the left of the door. A small tombstone reads "Thank you Lord for Simon, a dearly loved cat who greeted everyone who entered this church. RIP 1980."

Sleeping in Chipping Campden

In Chipping Campden—as in any town in the Cotswolds—B&Bs offer a better value than hotels. Try to book well in advance, as rooms are snapped up early in the spring and summer by happy hikers heading for the nearby Cotswold Way. Rooms are also generally tight on Saturdays (when many charge a bit more and are reluctant to rent to one-nighters) and in September, another peak month. Parking is never a problem. Always ask for a discount if staying longer than one or two nights.

On or near High Street

Located on the main street (or just off of it), these places couldn't be more central.

$$$ Noel Arms Hotel, the characteristic old hotel on the main square, has welcomed guests for 600 years. Its lobby was remodeled in a medieval-meets-modern style, and its 28 rooms are well-furnished with antiques (standard Db-£120, bigger Db-£140, fancier four-poster Db-£160-180, deluxe king Db-£180, £10 less for singles, prices are lower midweek or off-season, some ground-

Sleep Code

(£1 = about $1.60, country code: 44)
S = Single, **D** = Double/Twin, **T** = Triple, **Q** = Quad, **b** = bathroom, **s** = shower only. Unless otherwise noted, credit cards are accepted and breakfast is included.

To help you sort easily through these listings, I've divided the accommodations into three categories based on the price for a standard double room with bath:

$$$ **Higher Priced**—Most rooms £100 or more.
 $$ **Moderately Priced**—Most rooms between £75-100.
  $ **Lower Priced**—Most rooms £75 or less.

Prices can change without notice; verify the hotel's current rates online or by email. For the best prices, always book direct.

floor doubles, free Wi-Fi in lobby, attached restaurant/bar and café, free parking, High Street, tel. 01386/840-317, www.noelarmshotel.com, reception@noelarmshotel.com).

$$$ The Lygon Arms Hotel (pronounced "lig-un"), attached to the popular pub of the same name, has small public areas and 10 cheery, open-beamed rooms (one small older Db-£80-85, huge "superior" Db-£115-120, lovely courtyard Db-£145-165, lower prices are for midweek or multi-night stays, family deals, free Wi-Fi, free parking, High Street, go through archway and look for hotel reception on the left, tel. 01386/840-318, www.lygonarms.co.uk, sandra@lygonarms.co.uk, Sandra Davenport).

$$$ Badgers Hall Tea Room, also listed later under "Eating in Chipping Campden," rents three pricey rooms (small low-ceilinged Db-£95, larger Db-£98-115, 2-night minimum, includes breakfast and tea, no kids under age 10, free Wi-Fi, High Street, tel. 01386/840-839, www.badgershall.com, badgershall@talk21.com, Karen).

$$ Cornerways B&B is a fresh, bright, and comfy home (not "oldie worldie") a block off High Street. It's run by the delightful Carole Proctor, who can "look out the window and see the church where we were married." The two huge, light, airy loft rooms are great for families. If you're happy to exchange breakfast for more space, ask about the cottage across the street (Db-£80, Tb-£110, Qb-£130, 2-night minimum; cottage Db-£75, 3-night minimum; cash only, free Wi-Fi, off-street parking, George Lane, just walk through the arch beside Noel Arms Hotel, tel. 01386/841-307, www.cornerways.info, carole@cornerways.info). For a fee, Les can pick you up from the train station, or take you on village tours.

$$ Stonecroft B&B, next to Cornerways (previous listing), has three polished, well-maintained rooms (one with low, slanted ceilings—unfriendly to tall people). The lovely garden with a patio and small stream is a tranquil place for meals or an early-evening drink (Sb-£62, Db-£73, Tb-£110, Qb-£146, no kids under 10, free Wi-Fi, George Lane, tel. 01386/840-486, www.stonecroft-chippingcampden.co.uk, info@stonecroft-chippingcampden.co.uk, Roger and Lesley Yates).

$$ The Old Bakehouse, run by energetic young mom Zoe, rents two small but pleasant twin-bedded rooms in a 600-year-old home with a plush fireplace lounge (Sb-£65, Db-£80, discount for multiple nights, cash only, free Wi-Fi, Lower High Street, near intersection with Sheep Street, tel. 01386/840-979, mobile 07717/330-838, www.theoldbakehouse.org.uk, zoegabb@yahoo.co.uk).

A Short Walk from Town on Aston Road

The B&Bs below are a 10-minute walk from Market Hall. They are listed in the order you would find them when strolling from town (if arriving by bus, ask to be dropped off at Aston Road).

$$ Cherry Trees B&B, set well off the road, is bubbly Angie's spacious, modern home, with two king rooms and one slanty-roof twin room (Sb-£65, Db-£85, discount for multiple nights, free Wi-Fi, free parking, Aston Road, tel. 01386/840-873, www.cherrytreescampden.com, sclrksn7@tiscali.co.uk).

$$ The Chance B&B—a modern home with Cotswold charm—has three tastefully decorated rooms, a small lounge area, and a breakfast room that opens onto a patio. The super-king room has a private garden entry. They also offer a self-catering "Crafty Cottage" in town, next to the silk mill (Sb-£70, Db-£75, super-king Db-£90, call for cottage prices, discounts for stays of 5 nights or longer, cash only, free Wi-Fi, free parking, 1 Aston Road, tel. 01386/849-079, www.the-chance.co.uk, enquiries@the-chance.co.uk, Sally and Paul).

$$ Bramley House, which backs up to a farm, has three rooms including a spacious garden suite with a private outdoor patio and lounge area (bathroom downstairs from bedroom). Crisp white linens and simple country decor give the place a light and airy feel (standard Db-£70-75, king Db-£80-85, garden suite Db-£90-95, 2-night minimum, homemade cake with tea or coffee on arrival, locally sourced/organic breakfast, free Wi-Fi, 6 Aston Road, tel. 01386/840-066, www.bramleyhouse.co.uk, bramleybb@btinternet.com, Jane Povey).

Eating in Chipping Campden

This town—filled with wealthy residents and tourists—comes with many choices. I've listed some local favorites below. If you have a car, consider driving to one of the excellent countryside pubs mentioned in the sidebar on page 562.

The Eight Bells pub is a charming 14th-century inn on Leysbourne with a classy and woody restaurant and a more colorful pub. For more than a decade now, Neil and Julie have enjoyed keeping their seasonal menu as locally sourced as possible. They serve a daily special, are proud of their fish dishes, and always have a good vegetarian dish. As this is rightly considered the best deal going in town for top-end pub dining, reservations are smart (£8-12 lunches, £14-20 dinners, Mon-Thu 12:00-14:00 & 18:30-21:00, later Fri-Sat, Sun 12:00-21:00, tel. 01386/840-371, www.eight-bellsinn.co.uk).

The Lygon Arms pub is cozy and inviting, with a good, basic bar menu. You can order from the same menu in the colorful pub or the more elegant dining room across the passage (£7 sandwiches, £8-15 meals, daily 11:30-14:30 & 18:00-22:00, tel. 01386/840-318).

Michael's, a fun Mediterranean restaurant on High Street, serves hearty portions and breaks plates at closing every Saturday night. Michael, who runs his place with a contagious passion and love of life, is from Cyprus: The forte here is Greek, with plenty of *mezes*—small dishes for £6-10 (also £15-21 larger dishes, £7 *meze* lunch platter, Tue-Sat 11:00-14:30 & 19:00-22:00, Sun 12:00-15:00, closed Mon, tel. 01386/840-826).

Maharaja Indian Restaurant in the Volunteer Inn, while forgettable, is the only Indian place in town (£10-15 meals, daily 17:30-22:30, grassy courtyard out back, Lower High Street, tel. 01386/849-281).

Light Meals

If you want a quick, takeaway sandwich, consider these options. Munch your lunch on the benches on the little green near the Market Hall.

Butty's at the Old Bakehouse offers tasty £3-4 sandwiches and wraps made to order (Mon-Fri 7:30-14:30, Sat 8:00-14:00, closed Sun, Lower High Street, tel. 01386/840-401). They also have Internet access (see "Helpful Hints," earlier).

La Tradition is a hardworking French bakery that serves sausage rolls, quiches, filled croissants, and Cornish pasties (Tue-Sat 8:30-17:00, closed Sun-Mon, 6 High Street, tel. 01386/840-766).

Picnic: The **Co-op** grocery is the town's small "supermarket" (Mon-Sat 7:00-22:00, Sun 8:00-22:00, next to TI on High Street).

Tearooms

To visit a cute tearoom, try one of these places, located in the town center.

Badgers Hall Tea Room is great for a wide selection of savory dishes and desserts. A tempting table of homemade cakes, crumbles, and scones just inside the door lures passersby into its delightful half-timbered dining room. Along with light lunches, they serve a generous afternoon tea—a tall and ritualistic tray of dainty sandwiches, pastries, and scones with tea—for £14, half the London price (£9-13 lunches, daily 10:00-16:30, possibly later in summer, High Street).

Bantam Tea Rooms, near the Market Hall, is also a good value (£8 teas, £6 sandwiches, Mon-Sat 10:00-16:00, Sun 10:30-16:00, slightly shorter hours Nov-March, High Street, tel. 01386/840-386).

Near Chipping Campden

Because the countryside around Chipping Campden is particularly hilly, it's also especially scenic. This is a very rewarding area to poke around and discover little thatched villages.

West of Chipping Campden

Due west of Chipping Campden lies the famous and touristy town of Broadway. Just south of that, you'll find my nominations for the cutest Cotswold villages. Like marshmallows in hot chocolate, Stanway, Stanton, and Snowshill nestle side by side, awaiting your arrival. (Note the Stanway House's limited hours when planning your visit.)

Broadway

This postcard-pretty town, a couple of miles west of Chipping Campden, is filled with inviting shops and fancy teahouses. With a "broad way" indeed running through its middle, it's one of the bigger towns in the area. This means you'll likely pass through at some point if you're driving—but, since all the big bus tours seem to stop here, I usually give Broadway a miss. However, with a new road that allows traffic to skirt the town, Broadway has gotten cuter than ever. Broadway has good bus connections with Chipping Campden (on bus #21).

Just outside Broadway, on the road to Chipping Campden, you might spot signs for the **Broadway Tower,** which looks like a turreted castle fortification stranded in the countryside without a castle in sight. This 55-foot-tall observation tower is a "folly"—a uniquely English term for a quirky, outlandish novelty erected as a giant lawn ornament by some aristocrat with more money than

COTSWOLDS

taste. If you're also weighted down with too many pounds, you can relieve yourself of £4.80 to climb to its top for a view over the pastures (daily 10:00-17:00).

Stanway

More of a humble crossroads community than a true village, sleepy Stanway is worth a visit mostly for its manor house, which offers an intriguing insight into the English aristocracy today. If you're in the area when it's open, it's well worth visiting.

▲▲Stanway House

The Earl of Wemyss (pronounced "Weemz"), whose family tree charts relatives back to 1202, opens his melancholy home and grounds to visitors just two days a week in the summer. Walking

through his house offers a unique glimpse into the lifestyles of England's eccentric and fading nobility.

Cost and Hours: £7 ticket covers house and fountain, £9 ticket also includes watermill; both tickets include audioguide, narrated by the lordship himself; June-Aug Tue and Thu only 14:00-17:00, closed Sept-May, tel. 01386/584-469, www. stanwayfountain.co.uk.

Getting There: By car, leave B-4077 at a statue of (the Christian) George slaying the dragon (of pagan superstition); you'll round the corner and see the manor's fine 17th-century Jacobean gatehouse. There's no public transportation to Stanway.

Visiting the Manor: Start with the grounds, then head into the house.

The Earl restored "the tallest **fountain** in Britain" on the grounds—300 feet tall, gravity-powered, and quite impressive

(fountain spurts for 30 minutes at 14:45 and 16:00 on opening days).

The bitchin' **Tithe Barn** (near where you enter the grounds) dates to the 14th century, and predates the manor. It was originally where monks—in the days before money—would accept one-tenth of whatever the peasants produced. Peek inside: This is a great hall for village hoedowns. While the Tithe Barn is no longer used to greet motley peasants and collect their feudal "rents," the lord still gets rent from his vast landholdings, and hosts community fêtes in his barn.

Stepping into the obviously very lived-in **manor,** you're free to wander around pretty much as you like, but keep in mind that a family does live here. His lordship is often roaming about as well. The place feels like a time warp. Ask a staff member to demonstrate the spinning rent-collection table. In the great hall, marvel at the one-piece oak shuffleboard table and the 1780 Chippendale exercise chair (half an hour of bouncing on this was considered good for the liver).

The manor dogs have their own cutely painted "family tree," but the Earl admits that his last dog, C. J., was "all character and no breeding." Poke into the office. You can psychoanalyze the lord by the books that fill his library, the DVDs stacked in front of his bed (with the mink bedspread), and whatever's next to his toilet.

The place has a story to tell. And so do the docents stationed in each room—modern-day peasants who, even without family trees, probably have relatives going back just as far in this village. Talk to these people. Probe. Learn what you can about this side of England.

A working **watermill,** which produces flour from wheat grown on the estate, is about 100 yards from the house (requires higher-priced ticket to enter).

From Stanway to Stanton: These towns are separated by a row of oak trees and grazing land, with parallel waves echoing the

furrows plowed by medieval farmers. Centuries ago, farmers were allotted long strips of land called "furlongs." The idea was to dole out good and bad land equitably. (One square furlong equals 10 acres.) Over centuries of plowing these, furrows were formed. Let someone else drive, so you can hang out the window under a canopy of oaks, passing stone walls and sheep. Leaving Stanway on the road to Stanton, the first building you'll see (on the left, just outside Stanway) is a thatched cricket pavilion overlooking the village cricket green. Dating only from 1930, it's raised up (as medieval buildings were) on rodent-resistant staddle stones. Stanton is just ahead; follow the signs.

▲Stanton

Pristine Cotswold charm cheers you as you head up the main street of the village of Stanton. Go on a photo safari for flower-bedecked doorways and windows. (A scant few buses serve Stanton, but they're unpredictable—inquire locally.)

Stanton's **Church of St. Michael** (with the pointy spire) betrays a pagan past. It's safe to assume any church dedicated to St. Michael (the archangel who fought the devil) sits upon a sacred pagan site. Stanton is actually at the intersection of two ley lines (a line connecting prehistoric or ancient sights). You'll

see St. Michael's well-worn figure (and, above that, a sundial) over the door as you enter. Inside, above the capitals in the nave, find the pagan symbols for the sun and the moon (see photo). While the church probably dates back to the ninth century, today's building is mostly from the 15th century, with 13th-century transepts. On the north transept (far side from entry), medieval frescoes show faintly through the 17th-century whitewash. (Once upon a time, these frescoes were considered too "papist.") Imagine the church interior colorfully decorated throughout. Original medieval glass is behind the altar. The list of rectors (at the very back of the church, under the organ loft) goes back to 1269. Finger the grooves in the back pews, worn away by sheepdog leashes. (A man's sheepdog accompanied him everywhere.)

Horse Riding: Anyone can enjoy the Cotswolds from the saddle. Jill Carenza's **Cotswolds Riding Centre,** set just outside Stanton village, is in the most scenic corner of the region. The facility's

horses can take anyone from rank beginners to more experienced riders on a scenic "hack" through the village and into the high country (per-hour prices: £30/person for a group hack, £40/person for a semi-private hack, £50 for a private one-person hack; lessons, longer rides, rides for experts, and pub tours available; tel. 01386/584-250, www.cotswoldsriding.co.uk, info@cotswoldsriding.co.uk). From Stanton, head toward Broadway and watch for the riding center on your right after about a third of a mile.

Sleeping and Eating in Stanton: **$$$ The Vine B&B** has five rooms in a characteristic old Cotswold house near the center of town, next to the Cricket Pitch. It's owned by no-nonsense Jill, whose daughter, Sarah Jane, welcomes you to their large, lovingly worn family home. While it suffers from absentee management, the Vine is convenient if you want to ride all day (Ss-£60-80, twin Ds-£80, attic Db-£80, most rooms with four-poster beds, some stairs; for contact info, see listing for riding center, above). For dinner, try **Mount Inn** (£14-17 meals, view terrace, Old Showshill Road).

Snowshill

Another nearly edible little bundle of cuteness, the village of Snowshill (SNOWS-hill) has a photogenic triangular square with a characteristic pub at its base.

▲Snowshill Manor

Dark and mysterious, this old palace is filled with the lifetime collection of Charles Paget Wade. It's one big, musty celebration of

craftsmanship, from finely carved spinning wheels to frightening samurai armor to tiny elaborate figurines carved by prisoners from the bones of meat served at dinner. Taking seriously his family motto, "Let Nothing Perish," Wade dedicated his life and fortune to preserving things finely crafted. The house (whose management made me promise not to promote it as an eccentric collector's pile of curiosities) really shows off Mr. Wade's ability to recognize and acquire fine examples of craftsmanship. It's all very...mmm...yaaa.

COTSWOLDS

Cost and Hours: £10.40; manor house open July-Aug Wed-Mon 11:30-16:30, closed Tue; April-June and Sept-Oct Wed-Sun 12:00-17:00, closed Mon-Tue; closed Nov-March; gardens and ticket window open at 11:00, last entry one hour before closing, restaurant, tel. 01386/852-410, www.nationaltrust.org.uk/snowshillmanor.

Getting There: The manor overlooks the town square, but there's no direct access from the square; instead, the entrance and parking lot are about a half-mile up the road toward Broadway. Park there and follow the long walkway through the garden to get to the house. A golf-cart-type shuttle to the house is available for those who need assistance.

Getting In: This popular sight strictly limits the number of entering visitors by doling out entry times. No reservations are possible; to get a slot, you must report to the ticket desk. It can be up to an hour's wait—even more on busy days, especially weekends (when they can sell out for the day as early as 14:00). Tickets go on sale and the gardens open at 11:00. Therefore, a good strategy is to arrive close to the opening time, and if there's a wait, enjoy the gardens (it's a 10-minute walk to the manor). If you have more time to kill, head into the village of Snowshill itself (a half-mile away) to wander and explore—or get a time slot for later in the day, and return in the afternoon.

Cotswold Lavender

In 2000, farmer Charlie Byrd realized that tourists love lavender. He planted his farm with 250,000 plants, and now visitors come to wander among his 53 acres, which burst with gorgeous lavender blossoms from mid-June through late August. His fragrant fantasy peaks late each July. Lavender—so famous in France's Provence—is not indigenous to this region, but it fits the climate and soil just fine. A free flier in the shop explains the variations of blooming flowers. Farmer Byrd produces lavender oil (an herbal product

valued since ancient times for its healing, calming, and fragrant qualities) and sells it in a delightful shop, along with many other lavender-themed items. In the café, enjoy a pot of lavender-flavored tea with a lavender scone.

Cost and Hours: Free to enter shop and café, £2.50 to walk through the fields and the distillery; generally open June-Aug daily 10:00-17:00; closed Sept-May; schedule changes annually depending on when the lavender blooms—call ahead or check their website, tel. 01386/854-821, www.cotswoldlavender.co.uk.

Getting There: It's a half-mile out of Snowshill on the road toward Chipping Campden (easy parking). Entering Snowshill from the road to the manor (described earlier), take the left fork, then turn left again at the end of the village.

Sleeping near Snowshill: The pretty, one-pub village of Snowshill holds a gem of a B&B. **$$$ Sheepscombe House B&B** is a clean and pristine home on a working sheep farm. It's immersed in the best of Cotswold scenery, with plenty of sheep in the nearby fields. Jacki and Tim Harrison rent two modern, spacious, and thoughtfully appointed rooms. They also offer a holiday cottage (Db-£100-120, call for cottage price, folding cots available, free Wi-Fi, just a third of a mile south of Snowshill—look for signs, tel. 01386/853-769, www.broadway-cotswolds.co.uk/sheepscombe. html, reservations@snowshill-broadway.co.uk). Tim, who's happy to give you a local's perspective on this area, also runs Tour the Cotswolds car service (see page 535).

COTSWOLDS

East of Chipping Campden

Hidcote Manor Garden is just northeast of Chipping Campden, while Broad Campden, Blockley, and Bourton-on-the-Hill lie roughly between Chipping Campden and Stow (or Moreton)—handy if you're connecting those towns.

▲Hidcote Manor Garden

This is less "on the way" between towns than the other sights in this section—but the grounds around this manor house are well

worth a detour if you like gardens. Hidcote is where garden designers pioneered the notion of creating a series of outdoor "rooms," each with a unique theme (such as maple room, red room, and so on) and separated by a yew-tree hedge. The garden's design, inspired by the Arts and Crafts movement, is most formal near the house and becomes more pastoral as it approaches the countryside. Follow your nose through a clever series of small gardens that lead delightfully from one to the next. Among the best in England, Hidcote Gardens are at their fragrant peak from May through August. But don't expect much indoors—the manor house has only a few rooms open to the public.

Cost and Hours: £10.50; May-Aug daily 9:00-19:00; mid-March-April and Sept Sat-Wed 10:00-18:00, closed Thu-Fri; Oct Sat-Wed 10:00-17:00, closed Thu-Fri; Nov-Dec and mid-Feb-mid-March Sat-Sun 11:00-16:00, closed Mon-Fri; closed Jan-mid-Feb; last entry one hour before closing, café, restaurant, tel. 01386/438-333, www.nationaltrust.org.uk/hidcote.

Getting There: If you're driving, it's four miles northeast of Chipping Campden—roughly toward Ilmington. Both gardens are accessible by bus and a 45-minute country walk. Buses #21 and #22 take you to Mickleton (one stop past Chipping Campden), where a footpath begins next to the churchyard. Continuing more or less straight, the path leads uphill through sheep pastures and ends at Hidcote's driveway.

Nearby: Gardening enthusiasts will want to also stop at **Kiftsgate Court Garden,** just across the road from Hidcote. While not as impressive, these private gardens are a fun contrast since they were designed at the same time and influenced by Hidcote (£7.50; May-July Sat-Wed 12:00-18:00, except Aug opens at 14:00, closed Thu-Fri; April and Sept Sun-Mon and Wed only 14:00-18:00; closed Oct-March; tel. 01386/438-777, www.kiftsgate.co.uk).

COTSWOLDS

▲Broad Campden, Blockley, and Bourton-on-the-Hill

This trio of pleasant villages lines up along an off-the-beaten-path road between Chipping Campden and Moreton or Stow. **Broad Campden,** just on the outskirts of Chipping Campden, has some of the cutest thatched-roof houses I've seen. **Blockley,** nestled higher in the picturesque hills, is a popular setting for films. The same road continues on to **Bourton-on-the-Hill** (pictured), with fine views looking down into a valley and an excellent

gastropub (Horse and Groom, described on page 562). All three of these towns are connected to Chipping Campden by bus #22 (#21 goes only to Bourton and Blockley), or you can walk (easy to Broad Campden, more challenging to the other two—see page 531).

Stow-on-the-Wold

Located 10 miles south of Chipping Campden, Stow-on-the-Wold—with a name that means "meeting place on the uplands"—

is the highest point of the Cotswolds. Despite its crowds, it retains its charm, and it merits ▲▲. Most of the tourists are day-trippers, so nights—even in the peak of summer—are peaceful. Stow has no real sights other than the town itself, some good pubs, antiques stores, and cute shops draped seductively around a big town square. Visit the church, with its evocative old door guarded by ancient yew trees and the tombs of wool tycoons. A visit to Stow is not complete until you've locked your partner in the stocks on the village green.

Orientation to Stow-on-the-Wold

Tourist Information

There isn't an official TI in Stow—the nearest is in Moreton-in-Marsh (see page 571). But, you could check in with Andy, who runs Stowi (Stow Info) and Grace Tea & Coffee, located on the ground floor of the Cricket Museum on Sheep Street. He's happy to answer basic questions and hand out brochures (Tue-Sun 9:30-17:00, closed Mon, free Wi-Fi, WC, tel. 01451/830-341, stowinfo.co.uk).

Helpful Hints

Internet Access: Try the erratically open **library** in St. Edwards Hall on the main square (closed Sun, tel. 08452/305-420), or the **youth hostel** (open long hours daily).

Taxi: See "Getting Around the Cotswolds—By Taxi" (page 535).

Parking: Park anywhere on Market Square free for two hours, or overnight between 16:00 and 11:00 (free 18:00-9:00 plus any 2 hours—they note your license, so you can't just move to another spot; £50 tickets for offenders). You can park for free on some streets farther from the center (such as Park Street and Well Lane) for an unlimited amount of time. A pay-and-display lot for longer stays is at the bottom of town (toward the Oddingtons), and there is a free long-stay lot 400 yards north of the town square at the Tesco supermarket (follow the signs).

Self-Guided Walk

Welcome to Stow-on-the-Wold

This little four-stop walk covers about 500 yards and takes about 45 minutes.

Start at the **Stocks on the Market Square.** Imagine this village during the era when people were publicly ridiculed here as a punishment. Stow was born in pre-

Roman times; it's where three trade routes crossed at a high point in the region (altitude: 800 feet). This square was the site of an Iron Age fort, and then a Roman garrison town. This main square hosted an international fair starting in 1107, and people came from as far away as Italy for the wool fleeces. This grand square was a vast, grassy expanse. Picture it in the Middle Ages (before the buildings in the center were added): a public commons and grazing ground, paths worn through the grass, and no well. Until the late 1800s, Stow had no running water; women fetched water from the "Roman Well" a quarter-mile away.

With as many as 20,000 sheep sold in a single day, this square was a thriving scene. And Stow was filled with inns and pubs to keep everyone housed, fed, and watered. A thin skin of topsoil covers the Cotswold limestone, from which these buildings were made. The **Stow Lodge** (next to the church) lies a little lower than the church; the lodge sits on the spot where locals quarried stones for the church. That building, originally the rectory, is now a hotel. The church (where we'll end this little walk) is made of Cotswold stone, and marks the summit of the hill upon which the town was built. The stocks are a great photo op (lock dad up for a great family Christmas card).

• *Walk past the youth hostel and The White Hart Inn to the market, and cross to the other part of the square. Notice how locals seem to be part of a tight-knit little community.*

For 500 years, the **Market Cross** stood in the market reminding all Christian merchants to "trade fairly under the sight of God." Notice the stubs of the iron fence in the concrete base—a reminder of how countless wrought-iron fences were cut down and given to the government to be melted down during World War II. (Recently, it's been disclosed that all that iron ended up in junk heaps—frantic patriotism just wasted.) The plaque on the cross honors the Lord of the Manor, who donated money back to his tenants, allowing the town to finally finance running water in 1878.

Scan the square for a tipsy shop that locals call the "wonky house" (next to The Kings Arms). Because it lists (tilts) so severely, it's a listed building—the facade is protected (but the interior is modern and level). The Kings Arms, with its great gables and scary chimney, was once where travelers parked their horses before spending the night. In the 1600s, this was considered the premium "posting house" between London and Birmingham. Today, The Kings Arms cooks up pub grub and rents rooms upstairs.

During the English Civil War, which pitted Parliamentarians against Royalists, Stow-on-the-Wold remained staunchly loyal to the king. (Charles I is said to have eaten at The Kings Arms before a great battle.) Because of its allegiance, the town has an abundance of pubs with royal names (King's This and Queen's That).

The stately building in the center of the square with the wooden steeple is **St. Edwards Hall.** Back in the 1870s, a bank couldn't locate the owner of an account containing a small fortune, so it donated the funds to the town to build this civic center. It serves as a city hall, library, and meeting place. When it's open for some local event, you can wander around upstairs to see the largest collection of Civil War portrait paintings in England.

• *Walk past The Kings Arms down Digbeth Street to the little triangular park located in front of the Methodist Church and across from the Royalist Hotel. This hotel—along with about 20 others—claims to be the oldest in England, dating from 947.*

Just beyond the small grassy triangle with benches was the

Stow-on-the-Wold

TO
BROADWAY &
CHIPPING CAMPDEN

↑ TO MORETON-IN-MARSH,
STRATFORD-UPON-AVON,
WARWICK

NOT TO
SCALE

A-429

B-4077

TO
UPPER SWELL,
FORD & STANWAY

■ Tesco Supermkt
P Free

PATH TO
BROADWELL

Bus
Stop

HIGH ST.

PARSON'S CORNER

FOSSEWAY

WC

B

START

STOCKS 3

THE
SQUARE

11

1

CHURCH ✠

14

2

ELL LANE

P PARKING
→ SELF-GUIDED
WALK

8

TO
LOWER SWELL

POST

B-4068

13

12

MARKET
CROSS

CHURCH

DIGBETH

TO
UPPER & LOWER
ODDINGTON

4

PARK ST.

SHEEP

ST.

"Go Stow" ℹ

6 7

FLEECE
ALLEY

5

10

WC

DCH

BACK   WALLS

SPRING
GARDENS

→ TO LOWER SLAUGHTER/
BOURTON DAY HIKE

CEM.

A-429

P
Pay &
Display

9

TO

TO BOURTON-ON-THE-WATER &
THE SLAUGHTERS

❶ The Stow Lodge Hotel & Rest.
❷ The Kings Arms Hotel & Pub;
   Co-op Grocery
❸ The Old Stocks Hotel & Rest.
❹ Number Nine B&B;
   Park Street Eateries
❺ Cross Keys Cottage
❻ Chure House
❼ The Pound B&B

❽ Youth Hostel & Café
❾ To Little Broom B&B
❿ The Bell at Stow
⓫ The Queen's Head Pub
⓬ The Talbot Restaurant
⓭ The Coffee House
⓮ St. Edwards Hall
   & Library (Internet)

place where locals gathered for bloody cockfights and bearbaiting (watching packs of hungry dogs tear at bears). Today this is
where—twice a year, in May and October—the Stow Horse Fair
attracts nomadic Roma (Gypsies) and Irish Travellers from far and
wide. They congregate down the street on the Maugersbury Road.
Locals paint a colorful picture of the Roma, Travellers, and horses
inundating the town. The young women dress up because the fair
also functions as a marriage market.

• *Hook right and hike up the wide street.*

As you head up **Sheep Street,** you'll pass a boutique-filled former brewery yard (on the left). Notice its fancy street-front office, with a striking flint facade. Sheep Street was originally not a street, but a staging place for medieval sheep markets. The sheep would be gathered here, then paraded into the Market Square down narrow alleys—just wide enough for a single file of sheep to walk down, making it easier to count them. You'll see several of these so-called "fleece alleys" as you walk up the street.

• *Make a right onto Church Street, which leads past the best coffee shop in town (The Coffee House), and find the church.*

Before entering the **church,** circle it. On the back side, a door is flanked by two ancient yew trees. While many view it as the Christian "Behold, I stand at the door and knock" door, J. R. R. Tolkien fans see something quite different. Tolkien hiked the Cotswolds, and had a passion for sketching evocative trees such as this. *Lord of the Rings* enthusiasts are convinced this must be the inspiration for the door into Moria.

While the church (open daily—apart from services—9:00-18:00) dates from Saxon times, today's structure is from the 15th century. Its history is played up in leaflets and plaques just inside the door. The floor is paved with the tombs of big shots who made their money from wool and are still boastful in death. (Find the tombs crowned with the bales of wool.) Most of the windows are traditional Victorian designs (19th-century), but the two sets high up in the clerestory are from the dreamier Pre-Raphaelite school.

On the right wall as you approach the altar, a monument remembers the many boys from this small town who were lost in World War I (50 out of a population of 2,000). There were far fewer in World War II. The biscuit-shaped plaque remembers an admiral from Stow who lost four sons defending the realm. It's sliced from an ancient fluted column (which locals believe is from Ephesus, Turkey).

During the English Civil War (1615), the church was ransacked, and more than 1,000 soldiers were imprisoned here. The tombstone in front of the altar remembers the Royalist Captain Francis Keyt. His long hair, lace, and sash indicate he was a "cavalier," and true-blue to the king (Cromwellians were called "round heads"—named for their short hair). Study the crude provincial art—childlike skulls and (in the upper corners) symbols of his service to the king (armor, weapons).

Finally, don't miss the kneelers tucked in the pews. These are made by a committed band of women known as "the Kneeler

Group." They meet most Tuesday mornings (except sometimes in summer) at 10:30 in the Church Room to needlepoint, sip coffee, and enjoy a good chat. (The vicar assured me that any tourist wanting to join them would be more than welcome. The help would be appreciated and the company would be excellent.)

Hiking from Stow

Stow/Lower Slaughter/Bourton Day Hike

Stow is made-to-order for day hikes. The most popular is the downhill stroll to Lower Slaughter (3 miles), then on to Bourton-on-the-Water (about 1.5 miles more). It's a two-hour walk if you keep up a brisk pace and don't stop, but dawdlers should allow three to four hours. At the end, from Bourton-on-the-Water, a bus can bring you back to Stow. While those with keen eyes can follow this walk by spotting trail signs, it can't hurt to bring a map (ask to borrow one at your B&B). Note that these three towns are described in more detail starting on page 565.

To reach the trail, find the cemetery (from the main square, head down Church Street, turn left on Sheep Street, right into

Fleece Alley, right onto Back Walls, and left onto Spring Gardens). Walk past the community's big pea patch, then duck right through the cemetery to the far end. Here, go through the gate and walk down the footpath that runs alongside the big A-429 road for about 200 yards, then cross the road and catch the well-marked trail (gravel road with green sign noting *Public Footpath/Gloucestershire Way,* next to Quarwood Cottage). Follow this trail for a delightful hour across farms, through romantic gates, across a fancy driveway, and past Gainsborough-painting vistas. You'll enjoy an intimate backyard look at local farm life. Although it seems like you might lose the trail, tiny, easy-to-miss signs (yellow *Public Footpath* arrows—sometimes also marked *Gloucestershire Way* or *The Monarch's Way*—usually embedded in fence posts) keep you on target—watch for these very carefully to avoid getting lost. Finally, passing a cricket pitch, you reach **Lower Slaughter,** with its fine church and a mill creek leading up to its mill.

Hiking from Lower Slaughter up to **Upper Slaughter** is a worthwhile one-mile detour each way, if you have the time and energy.

From Lower Slaughter, it's a less-scenic 25-minute walk into the bigger town of **Bourton-on-the-Water.** Leave Lower Slaughter along its mill creek, then follow a bridle path back to A-429

COTSWOLDS

and into Bourton. Walking through Bourton's burbs, you'll pass two different bus stops for the ride back to Stow; better yet, to enjoy some time in Bourton itself, continue all the way into town and—when ready—catch the bus from in front of the Edinburgh Woolen Mill (bus #801 departs roughly hourly, none on Sun except May-Aug when it runs about 2/day, 10-minute ride, £1.40).

Sleeping in Stow

$$$ The Stow Lodge Hotel fills the historic church rectory with lots of old English charm. Facing the town square, with its own sprawling and peaceful garden, this lavish old place offers 21 large, thoughtfully appointed rooms with soft beds, stately public spaces, and a cushy-chair lounge (slippery rates but generally Db-£130, £10 extra on Sat, cheaper Nov-April, closed Jan, free Wi-Fi, free parking, The Square, tel. 01451/830-485, www.stowlodge.co.uk, enquiries@stowlodge.co.uk, helpful Hartley family).

$$$ The Kings Arms, with 10 rooms above a pub, manages to keep its historic Cotswold character while still feeling fresh and modern in all the right ways (standard Db-£100, superior Db-£120, steep stairs, three "cottages" out back, free Wi-Fi, free parking, Market Square, tel. 01451/830-364, www.kingsarmsstow.co.uk, info@kingsarmsstow.co.uk, Lucinda and Felicity).

$$ The Old Stocks Hotel, facing the town square, is a good value, even though the building itself is classier than its 18 big, simply furnished rooms. It's friendly and family-run, yet professional as can be. With man-killer beams and all beds equipped with footboards, it's a challenge for anyone over six feet tall (Sb-£45, standard Db-£90, deluxe Db-£100, refurbished "superior" Db-£110, Tb-£120, each room £10 extra on Sat, ground-floor room, free Wi-Fi in common areas, attached bar and restaurant, garden patio, free off-street parking, The Square, tel. 01451/830-666, www.old-stockshotel.co.uk, info@oldstockshotel.co.uk, Allen family).

$$ Number Nine has three large, bright, refurbished, and tastefully decorated rooms. This 200-year-old home comes with watch-your-head beamed ceilings and beautiful old wooden doors (Sb-£45-55, Db-£80, guest computer, free Wi-Fi, 9 Park Street, tel. 01451/870-333, mobile 07779-006-539, www.number-nine.info, enquiries@number-nine.info, James and Carol Brown and their dog Snoop).

$$ Cross Keys Cottage offers four smallish but smartly updated rooms—some bright and floral, others classy white—with modern bathrooms. Kindly Margaret and Roger Welton take care of their guests in this 360-year-old beamed cottage (Sb-£55-65, Db-£70-85, 5 percent Rick Steves discount if you book by phone or email, free Wi-Fi, Park Street, tel. 01451/831-128, www.cross-keyscottage.co.uk, rogxmag@hotmail.com).

$$ Chure House is a new home, built to look as if it's always been there. Tucked off Sheep Street, chatty Kiwi Jill has three light, comfy double rooms and a splendid little garden that begs for a cup of tea (Sb-£60, Db-£80-115, higher rates on weekends and in summer, no children under age 6, free Wi-Fi, limited parking, tel. 01451/832-185, www.bedandbreakfast-stowonthewold.co.uk, churehouse@googlemail.com).

$ The Pound is the quaint, 500-year-old, slanty, cozy, and low-beamed home of Patricia Whitehead. She offers two bright, inviting, twin-bedded rooms and a classic old fireplace lounge (D-£55-65, T-£95, cash only, downtown on Sheep Street next to the Grapevine Bar, tel. 01451/830-229, patwhitehead1@live.co.uk).

$ Hostel: The **Stow-on-the-Wold Youth Hostel,** on Stow's main square, is the only hostel in the Cotswolds. It has 48 beds in nine rooms, a kitchen, and a friendly atmosphere (dorm bed-£18, £3 less for members, includes sheets, some family rooms with private bathrooms, evening meals, pay guest computer and Wi-Fi, reserve long in advance—especially family rooms, tel. 01451/830-497, www.yha.org.uk, stow@yha.org.uk, manager Kayleigh).

Near Stow

$$ Little Broom B&B hides out in the neighboring hamlet of Maugersbury, which enjoys the peace Stow once had. It rents three cozy rooms that share a lush garden and pool (S-£30, Sb-£45-65, D-£55, Db-£60-75, apartment Db-£75 for two people plus £15 for each extra person, cash only, free Wi-Fi, tel. 01451/830-510, www.cotswolds.info/webpage/little-broom.htm, brendarussell1@hotmail.co.uk). Brenda has racehorses, and her greenhouse keeps the pool warm throughout the summer (guests welcome). It's an easy eight-minute walk from Stow: Head east on Park Street and stay right toward Maugersbury. Turn right into Chapel Street and take the first right uphill to the B&B.

Eating in and near Stow

While Stow has several good dining options, consider venturing out of town for a meal. You can walk to the pub in nearby Broadwell, or—better yet—drive to one of the many enticing gastropubs in the surrounding villages (see sidebar on page 562).

COTSWOLDS

Great Country Gastropubs

These places—known for their high-quality meals and fine settings—are very popular. Arrive early or phone in a reservation. (If you show up at 20:00, it's unlikely that they'll be able to seat you for dinner if you haven't called first.) These pubs allow "well-behaved children," and are practical only for those with a car. If you have wheels, make a point to dine at one (or more) of these—no matter where you're sleeping. In addition to these fine choices, other pubs serving worth-a-trip food are **The Eight Bells** in Chipping Camden (described on page 546) and **The Wheatsheaf Inn** in Northleach (see page 569).

Near Stow

The first two (in Oddington, about three miles from Stow) are more trendy and fresh, yet still in a traditional pub setting. The Plough (in Ford, a few miles farther away) is your jolly olde dark pub.

The Fox Inn, a different Fox Inn than the one in Broadwell (see "Pub Dinner Hike from Stow"), has a long history but a fresh approach. It's a popular choice among local foodies for its delicately prepared, borderline-pretentious but still reasonably priced updated pub classics and more-creative dishes. They've perfected their upmarket rustic-chic vibe, with a genteelly Old World interior and a delightful back terrace and garden (£15-21 main dishes, daily 12:00-14:00 & 18:30-21:30, in Lower Oddington, tel. 01451/870-555). They also rent three rooms (Db-£75-95, www.foxinn.net).

The Horse and Groom Village Inn in Upper Oddington is a smart place in a 16th-century inn, serving modern English and Continental food with a good wine list (38 wines by the glass) and serious beer (lunch: £7-10 sandwiches, £10-15 main dishes; dinner: £16-20 main dishes; lunch served daily 12:00-14:00; dinner served Mon-Sat 18:30-21:00, Sun 19:00-21:00, tel. 01451/830-584).

In Stow

These places are all within a five-minute walk of each other, either on the main square or downhill on Queen and Park streets. For dessert, consider munching a treat or fruit (there's plenty for sale at the late-hours grocery on the square) under the trees on the square's benches and watching the sky darken, the lamps come on, and visitors having their photo fun in the stocks.

Restaurants and Pubs

The Stow Lodge is the choice of the town's proper ladies. There are

Between Stow and Chipping Camden

The Plough Inn, in the hamlet of Ford, fills a fascinating old building, once an old coaching inn and later a courthouse. Ask the

bar staff for some fun history—like what "you're barred" means. Eat from the same traditional English menu in the restaurant, bar, or garden. They are serious about both their beer, and serve up heaping portions of stick-to-your-ribs pub-grub classics—a bit more traditional and less refined than others listed here (£11-19 meals, food served daily 12:00-14:00 & 18:00-21:00, all day long Fri-Sun and June-Aug, 6 miles from Stow on the road to Tewkesbury, reservations smart, tel. 01386/584-215, www.the-ploughinnford.co.uk).

Near Moreton-in-Marsh, in Bourton-on-the-Hill

The hill-capping Bourton—about a five-minute drive (or two-mile uphill walk) above Moreton—offers sweeping views over the Cotswold countryside. Perched at the top of this steep, picturesque burg is an enticing destination pub.

Horse and Groom melds a warm welcome with a tempting menu of delicious modern English fare. Of the pubs listed here, they seem to hit the best balance of old and new, combining unassumingly delicious food with a convivial spit-and-sawdust spirit. Choose between the lively, light, spacious interior or—in good weather—the terraced picnic-table garden out back (£13-19 meals, food served Mon-Thu 12:00-14:00 & 19:00-21:00, Fri-Sat 12:00-14:00 & 19:00-21:30, Sun 12:00-14:30 only, tel. 01386/700-413). They also rent rooms (Db-£120-170 depending on size, www.horseandgroom.info, greenstocks@horseandgroom.info). Don't confuse this with The Horse and Groom Village Inn in Upper Oddington, near Stow (described earlier).

COTSWOLDS

two parts: The formal but friendly bar serves fine pub grub (hearty £9-12 lunches and dinners, daily 12:00-14:00 & 19:00-20:30). The restaurant serves a popular £26 three-course dinner (nightly, veggie options, good wines, just off main square, tel. 01451/830-485, Val). On a sunny day, the pub serves lunch in the well-manicured garden, where you'll feel quite aristocratic.

The Old Stocks Hotel Restaurant, which might at first glance seem like a tired and big hotel dining room, is actually a classy place to dine. With attentive service and an interesting menu, they provide tasty and well-presented food. It's good, basic pub grub at pub prices served in a fancy dining room with views of the square. In good weather, the garden out back is a hit (£5-10 lunches, £10-14 dinners, dinner served Sun-Thu 18:30-20:30, Fri-Sat 18:30-21:00, reservations recommended on weekends, tel. 01451/830-666, www.oldstockshotel.co.uk).

The Bell at Stow, at the end of Park Street, serves up classic English dishes with a lighter, sometimes Asian twist. Produce and fish are locally sourced (£7-15 lunches, £12-15 dinners, veggies extra, Mon-Sat full menu served 12:00-14:30 & 18:30-21:30, lighter menu in between, Sun 12:00-21:00, reservations recommended, tel. 01451/870-916, www.thebellatstow.com).

The Queen's Head faces the Market Square, next to the Stow Lodge. With a classic pub vibe, it's a great place to bring your dog and watch the eccentrics while you eat pub grub and drink the local Cotswold brew, Donnington Ale (£5-7 sandwiches, £8-10 lunches, £9-13 dinners, beer garden out back, Mon-Fri 12:00-14:30 & 18:30-21:00, Sat-Sun 12:00-21:00, tel. 01451/830-563, John).

The Talbot has a more contemporary feel, with creative, modern dishes (£6-8 lunches, £12-15 dinners). They serve drinks until midnight or later (lunch served Mon-Sat 12:00-14:30, Sun 12:30-15:30; dinner served Sun-Thu 18:30-21:00, Fri-Sat 18:30-21:30). On Friday and Saturday evenings after 22:00, they crank up the music, making it the liveliest place in town (The Square, tel. 01451/870-934).

Cheaper Options and Ethnic Food

Head to the grassy triangle where Digbeth hits Sheep Street; there you'll find take-out fish-and-chips, Chinese, and Indian food. You can picnic at the triangle, or on the benches by the stocks on Market Street.

Greedy's Fish and Chips, on Park Street, is a favorite with locals for takeout. There's no seating, but they do have benches in front (£5 fish-and-chips, Mon 12:00-14:00 & 16:30-20:30, Tue-Sat 12:00-14:00 & 16:30-21:00, closed Sun, tel. 01451/870-821).

Jade Garden Chinese Take-Away is appreciated by locals who don't want to cook (£3-6 dishes, Wed-Mon 17:00-23:00, closed Tue, 15 Park Street, tel. 01451/870-288).

The Prince of India offers good Indian food to take out or eat in (£8-12 main dishes, nightly 18:00-23:30, 5 Park Street, tel. 01451/830-099).

The Coffee House provides a nice break from the horses-and-hounds traditional cuisine found elsewhere. You can get your food to go, or eat here—there's pleasant garden seating out back (£5 soups, £9-10 salads and sandwiches, good coffee; April-Sept Mon-Wed 9:00-17:00, Thu-Sat 9:00-21:00, Sun 10:00-16:30; off-season Mon-Sat 9:30-17:00, Sun 10:00-16:00; Church Street, tel. 01451/870-802).

The **Youth Hostel Café** (facing the Market Square) serves drinks and meals all day and is family-friendly, with great prices and tables in the backyard garden (£5 breakfast, £7-8 dinner, tel. 01451/830-497).

Even Cheaper: Small grocery stores face the main square (the **Co-op** is open Mon-Sat 7:00-22:00, Sun 8:00-22:00; next to The Kings Arms), and a big **Tesco** supermarket is 400 yards north of town.

Pub Dinner Hike from Stow

From Stow, consider taking a half-hour countryside walk to the village of Broadwell, where you'll find a traditional old pub serving good basic grub in a convivial atmosphere. The **Fox Inn** serves pub dinners and draws traditional ales—including the local Donnington ales (£8-10 meals, food served Mon-Sat 11:30-14:00 & 18:30-21:00, Sun 12:00-14:00 only, outdoor tables in garden out back, on the village green, tel. 01451/870-909, Mike and Carol).

Getting There: If you walk briskly, it's just 20 minutes downhill from Stow. While the walk is not particularly scenic (it's one-third paved lane, and the rest on an arrow-straight bridle path), it is peaceful, and the exercise is a nice way to start and finish your meal. The trail is poorly marked, but it's hard to get lost: Leave Stow at Parson's Corner, continue downhill, pass the town well, follow the bridle path straight until you hit the next road, then turn right at the road and walk downhill into the village of Broadwell. You can often hitch a ride with someone from the pub back to Stow after you eat.

Near Stow-on-the-Wold

These sights are all south of Stow: Some are within walking distance (the Slaughters and Bourton-on-the-Water), and one is 20 miles away (Cirencester). The Slaughters and Bourton are tied together by the countryside walk described on page 559.

▲Lower and Upper Slaughter

"Slaughter" has nothing to do with lamb chops. It comes from the sloe tree (the one used to make sloe gin).

Lower Slaughter is a classic village, with ducks, a charming little church, a working water mill, and usually an artist busy at her easel somewhere. The Old Mill Museum is a folksy ensemble with a tiny museum, shop, and cafe complete with a delightful terrace overlooking the mill pond, enthusiastically run by Gerald and his daughter Laura, who just can't resist giving generous tastes of their homemade ice cream (£2.50, March-Oct daily 10:00-18:00, Nov-Feb daily 10:00-dusk, tel. 01451/822-127, www.oldmill-lowerslaughter.com). Just behind the Old Mill, two kissing gates lead to the path that goes to nearby Upper Slaughter (a 15-minute walk or 2-minute drive away). And if you follow the mill creek downstream, a bridle path leads to Bourton-on-the-Water (described next).

In **Upper Slaughter,** walk through the yew trees (sacred in pagan days) down a lane through the raised graveyard (a buildup of centuries of graves) to the peaceful church. In the back of the fine graveyard, the statue of a wistful woman looks over the tomb of an 18th-century rector (sculpted by his son).

Getting There: Though the stop is not listed on schedules, you should be able to reach these towns on bus #801 (from Moreton or Stow) by requesting the "Slaughter Pike" stop (along the main road, near the villages). Confirm with the driver before getting on. If driving, the small roads from Upper Slaughter to Ford and Kineton (and the Cotswold Farm Park, described later) are some of England's most scenic. Roll your window down and joyride slowly.

▲Bourton-on-the-Water

I can't figure out whether they call this "the Venice of the Cotswolds" because of its quaint canals or its miserable crowds. Either way, it's very pretty. This town—four miles south of Stow and a mile from Lower Slaughter—gets overrun by midday and weekend hordes. Surrounding Bourton's green are sidewalks jammed with disoriented tourists wearing nametags. If you can avoid them, it's worth a drive-through and maybe a short stop. While it can be mobbed with tour groups during the day, it's pleasantly empty in the early evening and after dark.

Getting There: It's conveniently connected to Stow and Moreton by bus #801.

Parking: Finding a spot here is predictably tough. Even during the busy business day, rather than park in the pay-and-display parking lot a five-minute walk from the center, drive right into town and wait for a spot on High Street just past the village green (where the road swings left, turn right to go down High Street;

there's a long row of free two-hour spots in front of the Edinburgh Woolen Mills Shop, on the right).

Tourist Information: The TI is tucked across the stream a short block off the main drag, on Victoria Street, behind Village Hall (Mon-Fri 9:30-17:00, Sat 9:30-17:30, Sun 10:00-14:00 except closed Sun Oct-April, closes one hour earlier Nov-March, tel. 01451/820-211, www.bourtoninfo.com).

Sights: Bourton's attractions are tacky tourist traps, but the three listed below might be worth considering. All are on High Street in the town center. In addition to these, consider Bourton's **leisure center** (big pool and sauna, 5-minute walk from town center off Station Road, open daily, Mon-Fri 6:30-22:00, Sat-Sun 8:00-20:00, tel. 01451/824-024).

▲Motor Museum

Lovingly presented, this good, jumbled museum shows off a lifetime's accumulation of vintage cars, old lacquered signs, threadbare toys, and prewar memorabilia. If you appreciate old cars, this is nirvana. Wander the car-and-driver displays, from the automobile's early days to the stylish James Bond era. Don't miss the back door (marked *Village Life Exhibition*), which leads to old carriage houses filled with even more cars. Talk to an elderly Brit who's touring the place for some personal memories.

Cost and Hours: £4.75, mid-Feb-early Dec daily 10:00-18:00, closed off-season, in the mill facing the town center, tel. 01451/821-255, www.cotswoldmotormuseum.co.uk.

Model Railway Exhibition

This exhibit of three model railway layouts is impressive only to train buffs.

Cost and Hours: £2.75, June-Aug daily 11:00-17:30; Sept-Dec and Feb-May Sat-Sun 11:00-17:00, closed Mon-Fri; closed Jan; located in the back of a hobby shop, in the center of town, tel. 01451/820-686, www.bourtonmodelrailway.co.uk.

Model Village

This light but fun display re-creates the town on a 1:9 scale in a tiny outdoor park, and has an attached room full of tiny models showing off various bits of British domestic life.

Cost and Hours: £3.60 for the park, £1 more for the model room; daily 10:00-18:00, until 16:00 in winter, last entry 15 minutes before closing; at the edge of town, behind The Old New Inn, tel. 01451/820-467.

COTSWOLDS

Walk to the Slaughters

From Bourton-on-the-Water, it's about a 30-minute walk (or a two-minute drive) to Upper and Lower Slaughter (described previously); taken together, they make for an easy two-hour round-trip walk from Bourton. (You could also walk from Stow through the Slaughters to Bourton—hike described on page 559.)

▲Cotswold Farm Park

Here's a delight for young and old alike. This park is the private venture of the Henson family, who are passionate about preserv-  ing rare and endangered breeds of native British animals. While it feels like a kids' zone (with all the family-friendly facilities you can imagine), it's actually a fascinating chance for anyone to get up close and (very) personal with piles of mostly cute animals, including the sheep that made this region famous—the big and woolly Cotswold Lion. The "listening posts" deliver audio information on each rare breed.

A busy schedule of demonstrations gives you a look at local farm life—check the events board as you enter for times for the milking, "farm safari," shearing, and well-done "sheep show." Join the included 20-minute tractor ride, with live narration. Buy a bag of seed (£0.60) upon arrival, or have your map eaten by munchy goats as I did. Tykes love the little tractor rides, maze, and zip line, but the "touch barn" is where it's at for little kids.

Cost and Hours: £8.50, kids-£7.50, family ticket for 2 adults and 2 kids-£29, mid-Feb-mid-Dec daily 10:30-17:00, closed mid-Dec-mid-Feb, last entry 30 minutes before closing, good guidebook (small fee), decent cafeteria, tel. 01451/850-307, www.cotswoldfarmpark.co.uk.

Getting There: It's well-signposted about halfway between Stow and Stanway (15 minutes from either) just off Tewkesbury Road (B-4077, toward Ford from Stow). A visit here makes sense if you're traveling from Stow to Chipping Campden.

Northleach

One of the "untouched and untouristed" Cotswold villages, Northleach is worth a short stop. The town's impressive main square and church attest to its position as a major wool center in the Middle Ages. Park in the square called The Green or the adjoining Market Place. The town

has no TI, but you can pick up a free town map and visitor guide at Keith Harding's World of Mechanical Music (described next) or at the post office on the Market Place (Mon-Fri 9:00-13:00 & 14:00-17:30, Sat 9:00-12:30, closed Sun) and at other nearby shops. Information: www.northleach.gov.uk.

Getting There: Northleach is nine miles south of Stow, down A-429. Bus #801 connects it to Stow and Moreton.

▲Keith Harding's World of Mechanical Music

In 1962, Keith Harding opened this delightful little one-room place. It offers a unique opportunity to listen to 300 years of amazing self-playing musical instruments. It's run by people who are passionate about the restoration work they do on these musical marvels. The curators delight in demonstrating about 20 of the museum's machines with each hour-long tour. You'll hear Victorian music boxes and the earliest polyphones (record players) playing cylinders and then discs—all from an age when music was made mechanically, without the help of electricity. The admission fee includes an essential hour-long tour.

Cost and Hours: £8, daily 10:00-17:00, last entry at 16:00, tours go constantly—join one in progress, High Street, Northleach, tel. 01451/860-181, www.mechanicalmusic.co.uk.

Church of Saints Peter and Paul

This fine Perpendicular Gothic church has been called the "cathedral of the Cotswolds." It's one of the Cotswolds' two finest "wool" churches (along with Chipping Campden's), paid for by 15th-century wool tycoons. Find the oldest tombstone. The brass plaques on the floor memorialize big shots, showing sheep and sacks of wool at their long-dead feet, and inscriptions mixing Latin and the old English.

Eating in Northleach: Tucked along unassuming Northleach's main drag is a foodies' favorite, **The Wheatsheaf Inn.** With a pleasantly traditional dining room and a gorgeous, sprawling garden, it serves up an intriguing, eclectic menu of modern English cuisine. They pride themselves on offering a warm welcome, relaxed service, and a take-your-time approach to top-quality food. Reservations are smart (£16-19 meals, daily, on West End, tel. 01451/860-244, ww.cotswoldswheatsheaf.com).

▲Bibury

Six miles northeast of Cirencester, this village is a favorite with British picnickers fond of strolling and fishing. Bibury (BYE-bree) offers some relaxing sights, including a row of very old weavers'

COTSWOLDS

cottages, a trout farm, a stream teeming with fat fish and proud ducks, and a church surrounded by rosebushes, each tended by a volunteer of the parish. A protected wetlands area on the far side of the stream hosts newts and water voles. Walk up the main street, then turn right along the old weavers' Arlington Row and back on the far side of the marsh, peeking into the rushes for wildlife.

For a closer look at the fish, cross the little bridge to the 15-acre **Trout Farm,** where you can feed them—or catch your own (£4 to walk the grounds, fish food-£0.50; daily March-Oct 8:00-18:00, Nov-Feb 8:00-16:00; catch-your-own only on weekends March-Oct 10:00-17:00, no fishing in winter, call or email to confirm fishing schedule, tel. 01285/740-215, www.biburytroutfarm.co.uk).

Drivers will enjoy exploring the scenic **Coln Valley** from A-429 to Bibury through the enigmatic villages of Coln St. Dennis, Coln Rogers, Coln Powell, and Winson.

Getting There: Bus #801 goes from Moreton-in-Marsh and Stow to Northleach. From there, you can transfer to bus #855 to reach Bibury.

Sleeping in Bibury: If you'd like to spend the night in tiny Bibury, consider **$$ The William Morris B&B,** named for the 19th-century designer and writer (small Db-£85, big Db-£95, 2 rooms, tearoom, 200 yards from the bridge toward the church at 11 The Street, tel. 01285/740-555, www.thewilliammorris.com, ian@ianhowards.wanadoo.co.uk).

▲Cirencester

Almost 2,000 years ago, Cirencester (SIGH-ren-ses-ter) was the ancient Roman city of Corinium. It's 20 miles from Stow down A-429, which was called Fosse Way in Roman times. The **TI,** in the shop at the Corinium Museum (described later), answers questions and sells a £0.50 town map and a £1.20 town walking-tour brochure (same hours as museum, tel. 01285/654-180).

Getting There: If traveling by bus, take #801 from Moreton-in-Marsh or Stow to Northleach, then transfer to bus #855 to Cirencester. Drivers follow *Town Centre* signs and find parking right on the market square; if it's parked up, retreat to the Waterloo pay-and-display lot (a 5-minute walk away).

Sights: In Cirencester, stop by the impressive **Corinium Museum** to find out why they say, "If you scratch Gloucestershire, you'll find Rome." The museum chronologically displays well-explained artifacts from the town's rich history, with a focus on Roman times—when Corinium was the second-biggest city in the British Isles (after Londinium). You'll see column capitals and fine mosaics, before moving on to the Anglo-Saxon and Middle Ages exhibits (£5; Mon-Sat 10:00-17:00, Sun 14:00-17:00, until 16:00 Nov-March; Park Street, tel. 01285/655-611, www.coriniummuseum.org).

Cirencester's church is the largest of the Cotswold "wool" churches. The cutesy New Brewery Arts crafts center entertains visitors with traditional weaving and potting, workshops, an interesting gallery, and a good coffee shop. Monday and Friday are general-market days, Friday features an antique market, and a crafts market is held on most Saturdays.

Moreton-in-Marsh

This workaday town—worth ▲—is like Stow or Chipping Campden without the touristy sugar. Rather than gift and antiques shops, you'll find streets lined with real shops: ironmongers selling cottage nameplates and carpet shops strewn with the remarkable patterns that decorate B&B floors. A traditional market of 100-plus stalls fills High Street each Tuesday, as it has for the last 400 years (8:00-15:30, handicrafts, farm produce, clothing, books, and people-watching; best if you go early). The Cotswolds has an economy aside from tourism, and you'll feel it here.

COTSWOLDS

Orientation to Moreton-in-Marsh

Moreton has a tiny, sleepy train station two blocks from High Street, lots of bus connections, and the best **TI** in the region. The TI offers a room-booking service, pay Internet access, and discounted tickets for major sights (such as Blenheim Palace and Warwick Castle). Peruse the racks of fliers, confirm rail and bus schedules, and consider the £0.50 *Town Trail* self-guided walking tour leaflet (Mon 8:45-16:00, Tue-Thu 8:45-17:15, Fri 8:45-16:45,

Sat 10:00-13:00—or until 12:30 in winter, closed Sun, good public WC, tel. 01608/650-881).

Helpful Hints

Internet Access: It's available for £0.50/15 minutes at the **TI** and free at the erratically open **library** (down High Street where it becomes Stow Road, tel. 0845-230-5420).

Baggage Storage: While there is no formal baggage storage in town, the **Black Bear Inn** (next to the TI) might let you leave bags there—especially if you buy a drink.

Laundry: The handy launderette is a block in front of the train station on New Road (daily 7:00-19:00, last wash at 18:00, £4-5 self-service wash, £2-3 self-service dry, or drop off Mon-Fri 8:00-11:00 for £3 extra and same-day service—pick up by 17:00, tel. 01608/650-888).

Bike Rental, Taxis, and Car Rental: See "Getting Around the Cotswolds" (page 527).

Parking: It's easy—anywhere on High Street is fine any time, as long as you want, for free (though there is a 2-hour parking limit for the small lot in the middle of the street). On Tuesdays, when the market makes parking tricky, you can park at the **Budgens** supermarket for £3—refundable if you spend at least £5 in the store (2-hour limit).

Hikes and Walks from Moreton-in-Marsh: As its name implies, Moreton-in-Marsh sits on a flat, boggy landscape, making it a bit less appealing for hikes; I'd bus to Chipping Campden or to Stow, both described earlier, for a better hike (this is easy, since Moreton is a transit hub). If you do have just a bit of time to kill in Moreton, consider taking a fun and easy walk a mile out to the arboretum and falconry center in **Batsford** (described later).

Sleeping in Moreton-in-Marsh

$$$ Manor House Hotel is Moreton's big old hotel, dating from 1545 but sporting such modern amenities as toilets and electricity. Its 35 classy-for-the-Cotswolds rooms and its garden invite relaxation (Sb-£120, standard Db-£158, superior Db-£178, four-poster Db-£200, family suite-£220, £40 more for Sat night, rates are soft—often a bit less, includes breakfast, elevator, free Wi-Fi, log fire in winter, attached restaurants, free parking, on far end of High Street away from train station, tel. 01608/650-501, www.cotswold-inns-hotels.co.uk, info@manorhousehotel.info).

$$ The Swan Inn is wonderfully perched on the main drag, with eight en suite rooms. Though the halls look a bit worn and you enter through a bar/restaurant (that can be noisy on weekends), the

Moreton-in-Marsh

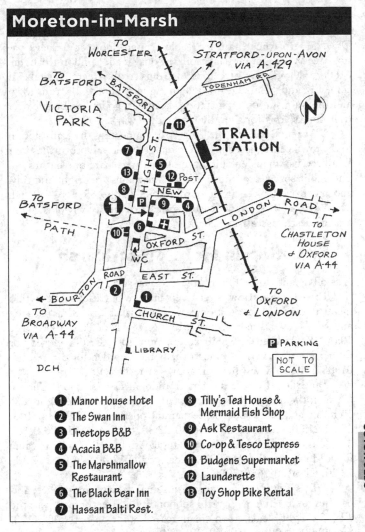

TO WORCESTER

TO STRATFORD-UPON-AVON VIA A-429

TO BATSFORD

BATSFORD

TODENHAM RD.

VICTORIA PARK

HIGH ST.

TRAIN STATION

❶❶

❼

❺

❶❸

❶❷ Post

❽

NEW

❾

❹

TO BATSFORD

PATH

❸

LONDON ROAD

TO CHASTLETON HOUSE & OXFORD VIA A-44

❶⓪

❻

OXFORD ST.

WC

ROAD

EAST ST.

❷

TO BROADWAY VIA A-44

BOURTON

TO OXFORD & LONDON

❶

CHURCH ST.

LIBRARY

DCH

P PARKING

NOT TO SCALE

❶ Manor House Hotel
❷ The Swan Inn
❸ Treetops B&B
❹ Acacia B&B
❺ The Marshmallow Restaurant
❻ The Black Bear Inn
❼ Hassan Balti Rest.
❽ Tilly's Tea House & Mermaid Fish Shop
❾ Ask Restaurant
❶⓪ Co-op & Tesco Express
❶❶ Budgens Supermarket
❶❷ Launderette
❶❸ Toy Shop Bike Rental

COTSWOLDS

renovated rooms themselves are classy and the bathrooms modern (Sb-£60, standard Db-£70-110, four-poster Db-£90-130, free Wi-Fi, free parking, restaurant gives guests 10 percent discount, High Street, tel. 01608/650-711, www.swanmoreton.co.uk, info@swan-moreton.co.uk, Sara and Terry Todd and their two sons). Terry can pick up guests from the train station and is willing to drive carless guests to various destinations within 20 miles if no public transport is available.

$ Treetops B&B is plush, with seven spacious, attractive rooms, a sun lounge, and a three-quarter-acre backyard. Liz and

Ben (the family dog) will make you feel right at home—if you meet the two-night minimum on weekends (large Db-£70, gigantic Db-£75, two wheelchair-accessible ground-floor rooms have patios, free Wi-Fi, set far back from the busy road, London Road, tel. 01608/651-036, www.treetopscotswolds.co.uk, treetops1@talk21. com, Liz and Brian Dean). It's an eight-minute walk from town and the train station (exit station, keep left, go left on bridge over train tracks, look for sign, then long driveway).

$ Acacia B&B, on the short road connecting the train station to the town center, is a convenient budget option. Dorothy has four small rooms: one is en suite, the other three share one bathroom. The public spaces are a bit tired, but the rooms are bright and tidy, and most overlook a lovely garden (S-£40, D-£55, Db-£60, tel. 01608/650-130, 2 New Road, www.acaciainthecotswolds.co.uk, acacia.guesthouse@tiscali.co.uk).

Eating in Moreton-in-Marsh

A stroll up and down High Street lets you survey your options.

The Marshmallow is relatively upscale but affordable, with a menu that includes traditional English dishes as well as lasagna and salads (£9-11 main dishes, £13 high tea, Mon 8:30-18:00, Tue 10:00-18:00, Wed-Sat 8:30-20:00, Sun 10:30-18:00, closed for dinner Jan, reservations smart, shady back garden for dining, tel. 01608/651-536, www.marshmallow-tea-restaurant.co.uk).

The Black Bear Inn offers traditional English food. Choose between the dining room on the left or the pub on the right (£8-14 meals and daily specials, restaurant open daily 12:00-14:00 & 18:30-21:00, pub open daily 10:30-23:30, tel. 01608/652-992).

Hassan Balti, with tasty Bangladeshi food, is a fine value for sit-down or takeout (£7-11 meals, daily 12:00-14:00 & 17:30-23:30, tel. 01608/650-798).

Tilly's Tea House serves fresh soups, salads, sandwiches, and pastries for lunch in a cheerful spot on High Street across from the TI (£5-7 light meals, good cream tea-£4.50, Mon-Sat 9:00-17:00, Sun 10:00-16:00, tel. 01608/650-000).

Ask, a chain restaurant across the street, has decent pastas, pizzas, and salads, and a breezy, family-friendly atmosphere (£9-12 pizzas, daily 11:30-23:00, takeout available, tel. 01608/651-119).

Mermaid fish shop is popular for its take-out fish and tasty selection of traditional savory pies (£5 fish-and-chips, £2 pies, Mon-Sat 11:30-14:00 & 17:00-22:30, closed Sun, tel. 01608/651-391).

Picnic: There's a small **Co-op** grocery on High Street (Mon-Sat 7:00-20:00, Sun 8:00-20:00), and a **Tesco Express** two doors down (Mon-Fri 6:00-23:00, Sat-Sun 7:00-23:00). The big

Budgens supermarket is indeed super (Mon-Sat 8:00-22:00, Sun 10:00-16:00, far end of High Street). You can picnic across the street, in pleasant Victoria Park (with a playground).

Nearby: The excellent **Horse and Groom** gastropub in Bourton-on-the-Hill is a quick drive or uphill two-mile walk away (see page 562).

Moreton-in-Marsh Connections

Moreton, the only Cotswold town with a train station, is also the best base for exploring the region by bus (see "Getting Around the Cotswolds," page 527).

From Moreton by Train to: London's Paddington Station (one-way-£32-33, every 1-2 hours, 1.5-2 hours), **Bath** (hourly, 2.5-3 hours, 1-2 transfers), **Oxford** (every 1-2 hours, 40 minutes), **Ironbridge Gorge** (hourly, 2.5-3 hours, 2 transfers; arrive Telford, then catch bus or cab 7 miles to Ironbridge Gorge—see page 623), **Stratford-upon-Avon** (almost hourly, 2.5-3 hours, 2-3 transfers, slow and expensive, better by bus). Train info: Tel. 0845-748-4950, www.nationalrail.co.uk.

From Moreton by Bus to: Stratford-upon-Avon (#21 and #22 go via Chipping Campden: Mon-Sat 8/day, none on Sun, 1-1.25 hours; #23 goes via Shipston-on-Stour: Mon-Sat 2/day, none on Sun, 1 hour; Johnsons Coaches, tel. 01564/797-070, www.johnsonscoaches.co.uk).

Near Moreton-in-Marsh

COTSWOLDS

▲Chastleton House

This stately home, located about five miles southeast of Moreton-in-Marsh, was actually lived in by the same family from 1607 until

1991. It offers a rare peek into a Jacobean gentry house. (Jacobean, which comes from the Latin for "James," indicates the style from the time of King James I—the early 1600s.) Built, like most Cotswold palaces, with wool money, it gradually declined with the fortunes of its aristocratic family until, according to the last lady of the house, it was "held together by cobwebs." It came to the National Trust on condition that they would maintain its musty Jacobean ambience. Wander on creaky floorboards, many of them original, and chat with volunteer guides stationed in each room. It's an uppity place that doesn't encourage spontaneity. The docents are proud to play on one of the best croquet teams in the region (the rules of croquet were formalized in this house in 1868). Page through the early 20th-century family photo albums in the room just off the entry.

Cost and Hours: £9.50; April-Sept Wed-Sat 13:00-17:00; mid- to late March and Oct Wed-Sat 13:00-16:00; closed Nov-mid-March and Sun-Tue year-round; ticket office opens at 12:30, last entry one hour before closing; recorded info tel. 01494/755-560, www.nationaltrust.org.uk/chastleton.

Getting In: Only 180 visitors a day are allowed into the home (25 people every 30 minutes), and reservations are not possible—it's first-come, first served. At the busiest times, you might have to wait a bit to enter the house. Wednesday and Thursday are the quietest days, with the shortest wait times.

Getting There: Chastleton House is well-signposted, about a 10-minute drive southeast of Moreton-in-Marsh off A-44. It's a five-minute hike to house from the free parking lot.

Batsford

This village has two side-by-side attractions that might appeal if you have a special interest or time to kill.

Getting There: Batsford is an easy 45-minute, one-mile country walk west of Moreton-in-Marsh. It's also connected to Moreton by buses #21 and #22.

Cotswold Falconry Centre

Along with the Cotswolds' hunting heritage comes falconry—and this place, with dozens of specimens of eagles, falcons, owls, and other birds, gives a sample of what these deadly birds of prey can do. You can peruse the cages to see all the different birds, but the demonstration, with vultures or falcons swooping inches over your head, is what makes it fun.

Cost and Hours: £8, ticket good for 10 percent discount at Batsford Arboretum; daily mid-Feb-mid-Nov 10:30-17:30, mid-Nov-mid-Feb 10:30-16:30, last entry 30 minutes before closing; flying displays at 11:30, 13:30, and 15:00, plus in summer at 16:30; Batsford Park, tel. 01386/701-043, www.cotswold-falconry.co.uk.

Batsford Arboretum

This sleepy grove, with 2,800 trees from around the world, pales in comparison to some of the Cotswolds' genteel manor gardens. But it's next door to the Falconry Centre, and handy to visit if you'd enjoy strolling through a diverse wood. The arboretum's café serves lunch and tea on a terrace with sweeping views of the Gloucestershire countryside.

Cost and Hours: £7, ticket good for 10 percent discount at Falconry Centre, daily 10:00-18:00, last entry at 16:45, tel. 01386/701-441, www.batsarb.co.uk.

STRATFORD-UPON-AVON

Stratford is Shakespeare's hometown. To see or not to see? Stratford is a must for every big bus tour in England, and one of the most popular side-trips from London. English majors and actors are in seventh heaven here. Sure, it's touristy, and non-literary types might find it's much ado about nothing. But nobody back home would understand if you skipped Shakespeare's house.

Shakespeare connection aside, the town's riverside and half-timbered charm, coupled with its hardworking tourist industry, make Stratford a fun stop. But the play's the thing to bring the Bard to life—and you've arrived just in time to see the Royal Shakespeare Company (the world's best Shakespeare ensemble) making the most of their state-of-the-art theater complex. If you'll ever enjoy  a Shakespeare performance, it'll be here...even if you flunked English Lit.

Planning Your Time

If you're just passing through Stratford, it's worth a half-day—stroll the charming core, visit your choice of Shakespeare sights (Shakespeare's Birthplace is best and easiest), and watch the swans along the river. But if you can squeeze it in, it's worth it to stick around to see a play; in this case, you'll need to spend the night here or drive in from the nearby Cotswolds (doable—just 30 minutes away; see previous chapter).

By Train or Bus: It's easy to stop in Stratford for a wander or an overnight. Stratford is well-connected by train to London and Oxford, and linked by bus and train to nearby towns (Warwick and Coventry to the north, and Moreton in the Cotswolds to the south).

By Car: Stratford, conveniently located at the northern edge of the Cotswolds, is made-to-order for drivers connecting the Cotswolds with points north (such as Ironbridge Gorge or North Wales). If you're driving north after you visit Stratford, you're within easy reach of two more worthwhile stop-offs: the impressive Warwick Castle and the evocative ruined cathedral at Coventry (both covered in the next chapter). Speedy travelers squeeze in all three of these towns (Stratford, Warwick, and Coventry) on a one-day drive-through: Leave the Cotswolds early, spend the morning exploring Stratford, have lunch and tour the castle in Warwick, visit Coventry's cathedral at the end of the day (it closes Mon-Sat at 16:30; Sun evensong at 16:00), and drive in the evening to your next stop (you'll find driving tips at the end of this chapter). If you're more relaxed, see a play and stay in Stratford, then stop at Warwick and/or Coventry the following morning en route to your next destination.

Orientation to Stratford

Stratford, with 26,500 people, has a compact old town, with the TI and theater along the riverbank, and Shakespeare's Birthplace a few blocks inland; you can easily walk to everything except Mary Arden's place. The core of the town is lined with half-timbered houses. The River Avon has an idyllic yet playful feel, with a park along both banks, paddleboats, hungry swans, and a fun old crank-powered ferry.

Tourist Information

The TI is in a small brick building on Bridgefoot, where the main street hits the river (Mon-Sat 9:00-17:30, Sun 10:00-16:00, tel. 01789/264-293, www.discover-stratford.com). It has a café and a couple of Internet terminals (£1/12 minutes, £5/hour).

Combo-Tickets: The TI sells the Shakespeare Birthplace Trust Five House combo-ticket at a discount, as well as a special any-three combo-ticket, which gives you entry into your pick of three of the five trust sights (see "Shakespearean Sights," later, for details).

Arrival in Stratford

By Train: Don't get off at the Stratford Parkway train station—you want Stratford-upon-Avon. Once there, exit straight ahead from the train station, bear right up the hill (alongside the parking lot), and follow the main drag straight to the river. (For the Grove Road B&Bs, turn right at the first big intersection.) If you need to buy a picnic for your return train trip, stop at the Morrison's grocery store nearby (you can see it across the tracks). Unfortunately, Stratford (as of this writing) does not have baggage storage—but ask the TI to see if any options have opened up.

By Car: If you're sleeping in Stratford, ask your B&B for arrival and parking details (many have a few free parking spaces, but it's best to reserve ahead). If you're just here for the day, and coming from the south (i.e., the Cotswolds), cross the big bridge and veer right for the best parking, following *Through Traffic, P,* and *Wark* (Warwick Road) signs. Go around the block—turning right and right and right—and enter the multistory Bridgefoot garage; first hour free, £6/9 hours, £10/24 hours, you'll find no place easier or cheaper. The City Sightseeing bus stop and the TI are a block away. Parking is free at the park-and-ride near the Stratford Parkway train station, just off the A-46—but it's less convenient because you have to ride a shuttle bus into town (£1.70 round-trip, 4/hour during the day, 2/hour in the evening, drops off near the river on Bridge Street).

Helpful Hints

Name That Stratford: If you're coming by train or bus, be sure to request a ticket for "Stratford-upon-Avon," not just "Stratford" (to avoid a mix-up with Stratford Langthorne, near London, which hosted the 2012 Olympics and now boasts a huge park where the games were held).

Festival: Every year on the weekend nearest to Shakespeare's birthday (traditionally considered to be April 23—also the day he died), Stratford celebrates. The town hosts free events, including activities for children.

Internet Access: Get online at the **TI** (described earlier) or the **library** (£2.50/30 minutes; Mon-Fri 10:00-17:00, Sat 10:00-15:00, closed Sun; if all computers are in use, reserve a time at the desk; tel. 01789/292-209).

Laundry: Silly Suds, on the road between the train station and the river, is run by kindly Jane. You can do self-service (wash-£3.60, dryer-£1/10 minutes, daily 8:00-21:00, last wash at 18:45), or pay Jane £12 to do the wash for you in a few hours (daily 9:00-16:00; if you're in a pinch, she may even be able to pick up or drop off at your B&B; 34 Greenhill Street, tel. 01789/417-766, mobile 07710-192-704). The other option in town is **Sparklean,** a 10-minute walk from the city center, or about five minutes from the Grover Road B&Bs (same

Stratford-upon-Avon

TO WORCESTER VIA A-46

TRAIN STATION

ALCESTER RD.

ARDEN ST.

GREENHILL

WINDMILL

□ PEDESTRIAN ZONE

Ⓟ PARKING

Ⓣ TAXI

-- FOOTPATH

❸

❽

⑰

❾

TO ANNE HATHAWAY'S COTTAGE

GROVE RD.

MARKET PLACE

❶

ROTHER

ELY

SHOTTERY

EVESHAM PL.

CHESTNUT

NASH'S HOUSE

⑬

CHURCH

BROAD WALK

T.O.P. (FORMER COURTYARD THEATRE)

TO OXFORD VIA A-439

⑰

HALL'S CROFT

OLD TOWN

❿

SOUTHERN

RIVER

HOLY TRINITY CHURCH (SHAKESPEARE'S GRAVE)

❶ Ambleside, Woodstock, Adelphi & Salamander Guest Houses

❷ Mercure Shakespeare Hotel

❸ The Emsley Guest House

❹ To Hemmingford House Hostel

❺ Le Bistro Pierre

❻ Lambs, The Opposition & Barnaby's Fish & Chips

❼ The Vintner Restaurant

❽ Avon Spice Restaurant

❾ The Old Thatch Tavern

❿ The Windmill Inn

⓫ The Garrick Tavern

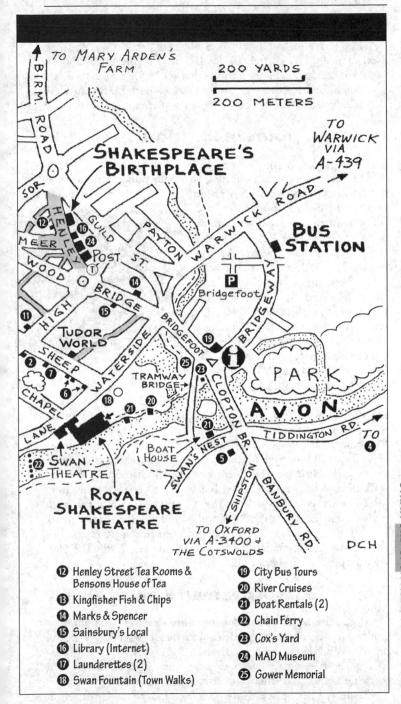

12 Henley Street Tea Rooms & Bensons House of Tea
13 Kingfisher Fish & Chips
14 Marks & Spencer
15 Sainsbury's Local
16 Library (Internet)
17 Launderettes (2)
18 Swan Fountain (Town Walks)
19 City Bus Tours
20 River Cruises
21 Boat Rentals (2)
22 Chain Ferry
23 Cox's Yard
24 MAD Museum
25 Gower Memorial

STRATFORD-UPON-AVON

self-service prices as above, no full-service option, daily 8:00-21:00, last wash at 20:00, 74 Bull Street, tel. 01789/296-075).

Taxis: Try **007 Taxis** (tel. 01789/414-007) or the taxi stand on Woodbridge, near the intersection with High Street. To arrange for a private car and driver, contact **Platinum Cars** (£25/hour, tel. 01789/264-626, www.platinum-cars.co.uk).

Tours in Stratford

Stratford Town Walks
These entertaining, award-winning two-hour walks introduce you to the town and its famous playwright. Tours run daily year-round, rain or shine. Just show up at the Swan fountain (on the waterfront, opposite Sheep Street) in front of the Royal Shakespeare Theatre and pay the guide (£5, kids-£2, ticket stub offers discounts to some sights and shops, Fri-Wed at 11:00, Fri-Sun also at 14:00, mobile 07855/760-377, www.stratfordtownwalk.co.uk). They also run an evening ghost walk led by a professional magician (£6, kids-£4, Mon and Thu-Sat at 19:30, 1.5 hours, must book in advance).

City Sightseeing Bus Tours
Open-top buses constantly make the rounds, allowing visitors to hop on and hop off at all the Shakespeare sights. Given the far-flung nature of two of the Shakespeare sights, and the value of the fun commentary provided, this tour makes the town more manageable. The full 11-stop circuit takes about an hour and comes with a steady and informative commentary (£12.50, discount with town walk ticket stub, buy tickets on bus or as you board, ticket good for 24 hours, buses leave from the TI every 20 minutes in high season from about 9:30-17:00, every 30 minutes and shorter hours off-season; buses alternate between recorded commentary and live guides—for the best tour, wait for a live guide; tel. 01789/412-680, www.citysightseeing-stratford.com).

Shakespearean Sights

Stratford's five biggest Shakespeare sights are run by the same organization, the Shakespeare Birthplace Trust (www.shakespeare. org.uk). While these sights are promoted as if they were tacky tourist attractions—and are designed to be crowd-pleasers rather than to tickle academics—they're well-run and genuinely interesting. Shakespeare's Birthplace, Nash's House, and Hall's Croft are in town; Mary Arden's Farm and Anne Hathaway's Cottage are just outside Stratford. Each has a tranquil garden and helpful, eager docents who love to tell a story; and yet, each is quite different, so visiting all five gives you a well-rounded look at the Bard.

If you're here for Shakespeare sightseeing—and have time to venture to the countryside sights—you might as well buy the "Five House" combo-ticket and drop into them all. If your time is more limited, visit only Shakespeare's Birthplace, which is the most convenient to reach (right in the town center) and offers the best historical introduction to the playwright.

Combo-Tickets: Admission to the three Shakespeare Birthplace Trust sights in town—Shakespeare's Birthplace, Hall's Croft, and Nash's House—requires a combo-ticket; no individual tickets are sold. To visit only these three sights, get the £14.95 **Shakespeare Birthplace combo-ticket,** which is sold at the participating sights. To add Anne Hathaway's Cottage and Mary Arden's Farm, you can buy the £22.50 **Shakespeare Five House combo-ticket** (sold at participating sights, good for one year; also available at a discount—£19.20—at the TI). You can also buy individual tickets for Anne Hathaway's Cottage and Mary Arden's Farm (see "Just Outside Stratford," later). Both tickets also include Holy Trinity Church, with Shakespeare's grave, which usually requests a £2 donation.

Another option is the £16.50 **any-three combo-ticket,** sold only at the TI. This ticket lets you choose which trio of sights you want to see—for instance, the birthplace, Anne Hathaway's Cottage, and Mary Arden's Farm (buy at TI; you'll get a receipt, then show it at the first sight you visit to receive your three-sight card).

Discounts: If you've taken a Stratford town walk (described under "Tours in Stratford," earlier), show your ticket stub to receive a 50 percent discount off any combo-ticket you buy at the sights. Also, ask your B&B owner if they have any discount vouchers— they often do.

Closing Times: What the Shakespeare sights list as their "closing time" is actually their last-entry time. If you show up at the closing time I've noted below, you'll still be able to get in, but with limited time to enjoy the sight (since they start closing things down soon after).

In Stratford
▲▲Shakespeare's Birthplace
Touring this sight, you'll experience a modern exhibit before seeing Shakespeare's actual place of birth. While the birthplace itself is a bit underwhelming, the exhibit, helpful docents, and sense that Shakespeare's ghost still haunts these halls make it a good introduction to the Bard.

William Shakespeare (1564-1616)

To many, William Shakespeare is the greatest author, in any language, period. In one fell swoop, he expanded and helped define modern English—the unrefined tongue of everyday people—and granted it a beauty and legitimacy that put it on par with Latin. In the process, he gave us phrases like "one fell swoop," which we quote without knowing that no one ever said it before Shakespeare wrote it.

Shakespeare was born in Stratford-upon-Avon in 1564 to John Shakespeare and Mary Arden. Though his parents were probably illiterate, Shakespeare is thought to have attended Stratford's grammar school, finishing his education at age 14. When he was 18, he married a 26-year-old local girl, Anne Hathaway (she was three months pregnant with their daughter Susanna).

The very beginnings of Shakespeare's writing career are shrouded in mystery: Historians have been unable to unearth any record of what he was up to in his early 20s. We only know that seven years after his marriage, Shakespeare was living in London as a budding poet, playwright, and actor. He soon hit the big time, writing and performing for royalty, founding (along with his troupe) the Globe Theatre (a functioning replica of which now stands along the Thames' South Bank—see page 138), and raking in enough dough to buy New Place, a swanky mansion back in his hometown. Around 1611, the rich-and-famous playwright retired from the theater, moving back to Stratford, where he died at the age of 52.

With plots that entertained both the highest and the lowest minds, Shakespeare taught the play-going public about human nature. His tool was an unrivaled linguistic mastery of English. Using borrowed plots, outrageous puns, and poetic language, Shakespeare wrote comedies (c. 1590—*Taming of the Shrew, As*

STRATFORD-UPON-AVON

Cost and Hours: Covered by combo-tickets, daily April-Oct 9:00-17:00, July-Aug until 18:00, Nov-March 10:00-16:00, café, in town center on Henley Street, tel. 01789/204-016.

Visiting Shakespeare's Birthplace: You'll begin by touring an exhibit that provides an entertaining and easily digestible introduction (or, for some, review) about what made the Bard so great. The new exhibit, planned to open in early 2014, is expected to include movie clips of his works and information about his upbringing in Stratford, his family life, and his career in London. Likely on display will be actual historic artifacts, including an original 1623 First Folio of Shakespeare's work. (If you're in a hurry, look for an

You Like It), tragedies (c. 1600—Hamlet, Othello, Macbeth, King Lear), and fanciful combinations (c. 1610—The Tempest), exploring the full range of human emotions and reinventing the English language.

Perhaps as important was his insight into humanity. His father was a glove-maker and wool merchant, and his mother was the daughter of a landowner from a Catholic family. Some scholars speculate that Shakespeare's parents were closet Catholics, practicing their faith during the rise of Protestantism. It is this tug-of-war between two worlds, some think, that helped enlighten Shakespeare's humanism. Think of his stock of great characters and great lines: Hamlet ("To be or not to be, that is the question"), Othello and his jealousy ("It is the green-eyed monster"), ambitious Mark Antony ("Friends, Romans, countrymen, lend me your ears"), rowdy Falstaff ("The better part of valor is discre-

tion"), and the star-crossed lovers Romeo and Juliet ("But soft, what light through yonder window breaks"). Shakespeare probed the psychology of human beings 300 years before Freud. Even today, his characters strike a familiar chord.

The scope of his brilliant work, his humble beginnings, and the fact that no original Shakespeare manuscripts survive raise a few scholarly eyebrows. Some have wondered if Shakespeare had help on several of his plays. After all, they reasoned, how could a journeyman actor with little education have written so many masterpieces? And he was surrounded by other great writers, such as his friend and fellow poet, Ben Jonson. Most modern scholars, though, agree that Shakespeare did indeed write the plays and sonnets attributed to him.

His contemporaries had no doubts about Shakespeare—or his legacy. As Jonson wrote in the preface to the First Folio, "He was not of an age, but for all time!"

express route—designed for groups—that lets you skip the main exhibit and head more directly for the garden and house.)

You'll exit the exhibit into the garden, where you can follow signs to the **birthplace,** a half-timbered Elizabethan building where young William grew up. I find the old house a bit disappointing, as if millions of visitors have rubbed it clean of anything authentic. It was restored in the 1800s, and, while the furnishings seem tacky and modern, they're supposed to be true to 1575, when William was 11. To liven up the otherwise dead-feeling house, chat up the well-versed, often-costumed attendants posted here and there, eager to answer your questions. You'll be greeted by a guide who offers an introductory talk, then set free to explore on your own. Look for the window etched with the names of decades of important visitors, from Water Scott to actor Henry Irving.

Shakespeare's father, John—who came from humble beginnings, but bettered himself by pursuing a career in glove-making (you'll see the window where he sold them to customers on the street)—provided his family with a comfortable, upper-middle-class existence. The guest bed in the parlor was a major status symbol: They must have been rich to afford such a nice bed that wasn't even used every day. This is also the house where Shakespeare and his bride, Anne Hathaway, began their married life together. Upstairs are the rooms where young Will, his siblings, and his parents slept (along with their servants). After Shakespeare's father died and William inherited the building, the thrifty playwright converted it into a pub to make a little money.

Exit into the fine **garden.** The ugly modern building in the middle of the complex houses a café and sometimes hosts temporary exhibits upstairs. If you hear a commotion, it's likely Shakespearean **actors,** who perform brief scenes in the garden (they may even take requests). Pull up a bench and listen, imagining the playwright as a young boy stretching his imagination in this very place.

Nash's House

Nash was the first husband of Shakespeare's granddaughter...not exactly a close connection. However, this house is next to the garden that was once the site of New Place, the house where Shakespeare retired. The sight features the dull parlor of Nash's House, along with the pretty Knott Garden and behind it, what was once Shakespeare's orchard. Upstairs are temporary exhibits, often featuring items that archaeologists have excavated in the adjacent New Place site.

Cost and Hours: Covered by combo-ticket; daily April-Oct 10:00-17:00, Nov-March 11:00-16:00; Chapel Street, tel. 01789/292-325.

Hall's Croft

This former home of Shakespeare's eldest daughter, Susanna, is in the Stratford town center. A fine old Jacobean house, it's the fanciest of the group. Since she married a doctor, the exhibits here are focused on 17th-century medicine. If you have time to spare and one of the combo-tickets, it's worth a quick pop-

in. To make the exhibits interesting, ask the docent for the 15- to 20-minute introduction, which helps bring the plague—and some of the bizarre remedies of the time—to life.

Cost and Hours: Covered by combo-ticket, same hours as Nash's House, on-site tearoom, between Church Street and the river on Old Town Street, tel. 01789/292-107.

Shakespeare's Grave

To see his final resting place, head to the riverside Holy Trinity Church. Shakespeare was a rector for this church when he died.

While the church is surrounded by an evocative graveyard, the Bard is entombed in a place of honor, right in front of the altar inside. The church marks the ninth-century birthplace of the town, which was once a religious settlement.

Cost and Hours: £2 donation, not covered by combo-ticket (but included in individual tickets to Anne Hathaway's Cottage or Mary Arden's Farm), April-Sept Mon-Sat 8:30-17:40, Sun 12:30-16:40; Oct-March until 16:40 or 15:40, 10-minute walk past the theater—see its graceful spire as you gaze down the river, tel. 01789/266-316, www.stratford-upon-avon.org.

Just Outside Stratford

To reach either of these sights, it's best to drive or take the hop-on, hop-off bus tour (see "Tours in Stratford," earlier)—unless you're staying at one of the Grove Road B&Bs, which are an easy 20-minute walk from Anne Hathaway's Cottage. Both sights are well-signposted (with brown signs) from the major streets and ring roads around Stratford. If driving between the sights, ask for directions at the sight you're leaving.

▲▲Mary Arden's Farm

Along with Shakespeare's Birthplace, this is my favorite of the Shakespearean sights. Famous as the girlhood home of William's mom, this homestead is in Wilmcote (about three miles from Stratford). Built around two historic farmhouses, it's an open-air folk museum depicting 16th-century farm life...which happens to have ties to Shakespeare. The Bard is basically an afterthought here.

Cost and Hours: £10, also covered by certain combo-tickets—see page 583, daily April-Oct 10:00-17:00, visitors must leave by 17:30, closed Nov-March, tel. 01789/293-455.

Getting There: The most convenient way to get here is by car (free parking) or the hop-on, hop-off bus tour, but it's also easy to reach by train. The Wilmcote train station is up the street, about

STRATFORD-UPON-AVON

a five-minute walk from Mary Arden's Farm (£1.80 round-trip fare, two stops from Stratford-upon-Avon on Birmingham- and London-bound trains, 1-2/hour, 5-minute trip, call London Midland to confirm departure time—tel. 0844-811-0133, www.londonmidland.com).

Visiting Mary Arden's Farm: The museum hosts many special **events,** including the falconry show described below. The day's events are listed on a chalkboard by the entry, or you can call ahead to find out what's on. There are always plenty of activities to engage kids: It's an active, hands-on place.

Follow the Tudor roses from building to building, through farmhouses with good displays about farm life. Throughout the complex, you'll see period interpreters in Tudor costumes. They'll likely be going through the day's chores as people back then would have done—activities such as milking the sheep and cutting wood to do repairs on the house. They're there to answer questions and provide fun, gossipy insight into what life was like at the time.

The first building, **Palmer's farm** (mistaken for Mary Arden's home for hundreds of years, and correctly identified in 2000), is furnished as it would have been in Shakespeare's day.

Mary Arden actually lived in the neighboring **farmhouse,** covered in brick facade and seemingly less impressive. The house is filled with kid-oriented activities, including period dress-up clothes, board games from Shakespeare's day, and a Tudor alphabet so kids can write their names in fancy lettering.

Of the many events here, the most enjoyable is the **falconry demonstration,** with lots of mean-footed birds (daily, usually at 11:30, 13:30, and 15:30). Chat with the falconers about their methods for earning the birds' trust. The birds' hunger sets them to flight (a round-trip earns the bird a bit of food; the birds fly when hungry—but don't have the energy if they're *too* hungry). Like Katherine, the wife described as "my falcon" in *The Taming of the Shrew,* these birds are tamed and trained with food as a reward. If things are slow, ask if you can feed one.

Stratford Thanks America

Residents of Stratford are thankful for the many contributions Americans have made to their city and its heritage. Along with pumping up the economy day in and day out with tourist visits, Americans paid for half the rebuilding of the Royal Shakespeare Theatre after it burned down in 1926. The Swan Theatre renovation was funded entirely by American aid. Harvard University inherited—you guessed it—the Harvard House, and it maintains the house today. London's much-loved theater, Shakespeare's Globe, was the dream (and gift) of an American. And there's even an odd but prominent "American Fountain" overlooking Stratford's market square on Rother Street, which was given in 1887 to celebrate the Golden Jubilee of the rule of Queen Victoria.

▲Anne Hathaway's Cottage

Located 1.5 miles out of Stratford (in Shottery), this home is a 12-room farmhouse where the Bard's wife grew up. William courted Anne here—she was 26, he was only 18—and his tactics proved successful. (Maybe a little too much, as she was several months pregnant at their wedding.) Their 34-year marriage produced two more children, and lasted until his death in 1616 at age 52. The Hathaway  family lived here for 400 years, until 1911, and much of the family's 92-acre farm remains part of the sight.

Cost and Hours: £9, also covered by certain combo-tickets—see page 583, daily April-Oct 9:00-17:00, Nov-March 10:00-16:00, tel. 01789/292-100.

Getting There: It's a 30-minute walk from central Stratford (20 minutes from the Grove Road B&Bs), a stop on the hop-on, hop-off tour bus, or a quick taxi ride from downtown Stratford (around £5). Drivers will find it well-signposted entering Stratford from any direction, with easy £1 parking.

Visiting Anne Hathaway's Cottage: After buying your ticket, turn left and head down through the garden to the thatch-roofed **cottage,** which looks cute enough to eat. The house offers an intimate peek at life in Shakespeare's day. In some ways, it feels even more authentic than his birthplace, and it's fun to imagine the writer of some of the world's greatest romances wooing his favorite girl right here during his formative years. Docents are posted in the first and last rooms to provide meaning and answer questions; while most tourists just stampede through, you'll have a more informative visit if you pause to listen to their commentary. (If the place shakes, a tourist has thunked his or her head on the low beams.)

Maybe even more interesting than the cottage are the **gardens**, which have several parts (including a prizewinning "traditional cottage garden"). If you head uphill, to the right from the entry, you'll find a "Woodland Walk" (look for the Singing Tree—touch it to hear a tune), along with a fun sculpture garden littered with modern interpretations of Shakespearean characters (such as Falstaff's mead gut, and a great photo-op statue of the British Isles sliced out of steel). From April through June, the gardens are at their best, with bulbs in bloom and a large sweet-pea display. You'll also find a music trail, a butterfly trail, and—likely—rotating exhibits, generally on a gardening theme.

The Royal Shakespeare Company

The Royal Shakespeare Company (RSC), undoubtedly the best Shakespeare company on earth, performs year-round in Stratford and in London. Seeing a play here in the Bard's birthplace is a must for Shakespeare fans, and a memorable experience for anybody. Between its excellent acting and remarkable staging, the RSC makes Shakespeare as accessible and enjoyable as it gets.

The RSC makes it easy to take in a play, thanks to their very user-friendly website (www.rsc.org.uk), painless ticket-booking system, and chock-a-block schedule that fills the summer with mostly big-name Shakespeare plays (plus a few more obscure titles to please the die-hard aficionados). Except in January and February, there's almost always something playing.

The RSC is enjoying new popularity after the 2011 opening of its cutting-edge Royal Shakespeare Theatre. Even if you're not seeing a play, exploring this cleverly designed theater building is well worth your time. The smaller, attached Swan Theatre hosts plays on a more intimate scale, with only about 400 seats.

▲▲▲Seeing a Play

Performances take place most days (Mon-Sat generally at 19:15 for the Royal Shakespeare Theatre or 19:30 at the Swan, matinees around 13:15 at the RST or 13:30 at the Swan, sporadic Sun shows). Shows generally last three hours or more, with one intermission; for an evening show, don't count on getting back to your B&B much before 23:00. There's no strict dress code—and people dress casually (nice jeans and short-sleeve shirts are fine)—but shorts are discouraged. You can buy a program for £4. If you're feeling bold, buy a £5 standing ticket and then slip into an open seat as the lights dim—if nothing is available during the play's first half, something might open up after intermission.

The Look of Stratford

There's much more to Stratford than Shakespeare sights. Take time to appreciate the look of the town itself. While the main street goes back to Roman times, the key date for the city was 1196, when the king gave the town "market privileges." Stratford was shaped by its marketplace years. The market's many "departments" were located on logically named streets, whose names still remain: Sheep Street, Corn Street, and so on. Today's street plan—and even the 57' 9" width of the lots—survives from the 12th century. (Some of the modern store-fronts in the town center are still that exact width.)

Starting in about 1600, three great fires gutted the town, leaving very few buildings older than that era. After those fires, tinderbox thatch roofs were prohibited—the Old Thatch Tavern on Greenhill Street is the only remaining thatch roof in town, predating the law and grandfathered in.

The town's main drag, Bridge Street, is the oldest street in town, but looks the youngest. It was built in the Regency style—a result of a rough little middle row of wattle-and-daub houses being torn down in the 1820s to double the street's width. Today's Bridge Street buildings retain that early 19th-century style: Regency.

Throughout Stratford, you'll see striking black-and-white, half-timbered buildings, as well as half-timbered structures that were partially plastered over and covered up in the 19th century. During Victorian times, the half-timbered style was considered low-class, but in the 20th century—just as tourists came, preferring ye olde style—timbers came back into vogue, and the plaster was removed on many old buildings. But any black and white you see is likely to be modern paint. The original coloring was "biscuit yellow" and brown.

Getting Tickets: Tickets range from £5 (standing) to £60, with most around £40. Saturday evening shows—the most popular—are most expensive. You can book tickets as you like it: online (www.rsc.org.uk), by phone (tel. 0844-800-1110), or in person at the box office (Mon-Sat 10:00-20:00, Sun 10:00-17:00). Pay by credit card, get a confirmation number, then pick up your tickets at the theater 30 minutes before "curtain up." Because it's so easy to get tickets online or by phone, it makes absolutely no sense to pay extra to book tickets through any other source.

Tickets go on sale months in advance. Saturdays and very famous plays (such as *Romeo and Juliet* or *Hamlet*)—or any play with a well-known actor—sell out the fastest; the earlier in the week the performance is, the longer it takes to sell out (Thursdays sell out faster than Mondays, for example). Before your trip, check the schedule on their website, and consider buying tickets if something strikes your fancy. But demand is difficult to predict, and some tickets do go unsold. On a recent visit, on a sunny Friday in June, the riverbank was crawling with tourists. I stepped into the RSC on a lark to see if they had any tickets. An hour later, I was watching King Lear lose his marbles.

Even if there aren't any seats available, you may be able to buy a returned ticket on the same day of an otherwise sold-out show. Also, the few standing-room tickets in the main theater are sold only on the day of the show. While you can check at the box office anytime during the day, it's best to go either when it opens at 10:00 (daily) or between 17:30 and 18:00 (Mon-Sat). Be prepared to wait.

Visiting the Theaters

▲▲The Royal Shakespeare Theatre

The RSC's main venue reopened in 2011 after it was updated head to toe, with both a respect for tradition and a sensitivity to the needs of contemporary theater-goers. You need to take a guided tour (explained later) to see the backstage areas, but you're welcome to wander the theater's public areas anytime the building is open. Interesting tidbits of theater history and easy-to-miss special exhibits make this one of Stratford's most fascinating sights. If you're seeing a play here, come early to poke around the building. Even if you're not, step inside and explore.

Cost and Hours: Free entry, Mon-Sat 10:00-20:00, Sun 10:00-17:00.

Guided Tours: Well-informed RSC volunteers lead entertaining, one-hour building tours. Some cover the main theater while others take you into behind-the-scenes spaces, such as the space-age control room (try for a £7.50 behind-the-scenes tour, but if those aren't running, consider a £5.50 front-of-the-house tour—which skips the backstage areas; tour schedule varies by day, depending on performances, but there's often one at 9:15—call, check online, or go to box office to confirm schedule; best to book ahead, tel. 0844-800-1110, www.rsc.org.uk).

Background: The recently remodeled flagship theater of the RSC has an interesting past. The original, Victorian-style theater was built in 1879 to honor the Bard, but it burned down in 1926. The big Art Deco-style building you see today was erected in 1932 and outfitted with a stodgy Edwardian "picture frame"-style stage, even though a more dynamic "thrust"-style stage—better for engaging the audience—was the actors' choice. (It's would also have been closer in design to Shakespeare's original Globe stage, which jutted into the crowd.)

The latest renovation addressed this ill-conceived design, adding an updated, thrust-style stage. They've left the shell of the 1930s theater, but given it an unconventional deconstructed-industrial style, with the seats stacked at an extreme vertical pitch. Though smaller, the redesigned theater can seat about the same size audience as before (1,048 seats), and now there's not a bad seat in the house—no matter what, you're no more than 50 feet from the stage (the cheapest "gallery" seats look down right onto Othello's bald spot). Productions are staged to play to all of the seats throughout the show. Those sitting up high appreciate different details from those at stage level, and vice versa.

Visiting the Theater: From the main lobby and box office/gift shop area, there's plenty to see. First head left. In the circular **atrium** between the brick wall of the modern theater and fragments of the previous theater, notice the ratty old floorboards. These were pried up from the 1932 stage and laid down here—so as you wait for your play, you're treading on theater history. Upstairs on level 2, find the **Paccar Room,** with generally excellent temporary exhibits assembled from the RSC's substantial collection of historic costumes, props, manuscripts, and other theater memorabilia. Continue upstairs to level 3 to the Rooftop Restaurant (described later). High on the partition that runs through the restaurant, facing the brick theater wall, notice the four **chairs** affixed to the wall. These are original seats from the earlier theater, situated where the back row used to be (90 feet from the stage)—illustrating how much more audience-friendly the new design is.

Back downstairs, pass through the box office/gift shop area to find the **Swan Gallery**—an old, Gothic-style Victorian space that survives from the original 1879 Memorial Theatre. Just past the bar, the Victorian reading room comes with borrowable binders filled with newspaper reviews of several decades of RSC performances. Upstairs is the Ferguson Room, with additional special exhibits.

Back outside, across the street from the theater, notice the building with the steep gable and huge door (marked *CFE 1887*). This was built as a **workshop** for building sets, which could be moved in large pieces to the main theater. To this day, all of the sets, costumes, and props are made here in Stratford. The row of **cottages** to the right is housing for actors. The RSC's reputation exerts enough pull to attract serious actors from all over the UK and beyond, who live here for the entire season. The RSC uses a repertory company approach, where the same actors appear in multiple shows concurrently. Today's Lady Macbeth may be tomorrow's Rosalind.

Tower View: For a God's-eye view of all of Shakespeare's houses, ride the elevator to the top of the RSC's **tower** (£2.50, buy ticket at box office, daily 10:00-19:00). Aside from a few sparse exhibits, the main attraction here is the 360-degree view over the theater building, the Avon, and the lanes of Stratford.

The Food's the Thing: The main theater has a casual café with a terrace overlooking the river (£3 sandwiches, daily 10:00-21:00), as well as the fancier Rooftop Restaurant, which counts the Queen as a patron (£11.50 lunch menu; dinner—£17.50 two-course meal, £22.50 three-course meal; Mon-Sat 11:30 until late, Sun 12:00-18:00, dinner reservations smart, tel. 01789/403-449).

The Swan Theatre

Adjacent to the RSC Theatre is the smaller (about 400 seats), Elizabethan-style Swan Theatre, named not for the birds that fill the park out front, but for the Bard's nickname—the "sweet swan of Avon." This galleried playhouse that opened in 1986, thanks to an extremely generous donation from an American theater lover. It has a vertical layout (with a thrust stage) similar to the RSC Theatre, but its wood trim and railings give it a cozier, more traditional feel. The Swan is used for lesser-known Shakespeare plays and alternative works. Occasionally, the lowest level of seats is removed to accommodate "groundling" (standing-only) tickets, much like at the Globe Theatre in London.

The Courtyard Theatre

A two-minute walk down Southern Lane from the original Royal Shakespeare Theatre, this theater (affectionately called the "rusty shed" by locals) was built as a replacement venue while the Royal Shakespeare Theatre was being renovated. It was used as a prototype for the main theater—a testing ground for the lights, seats, and structure of its big brother. Now it's being converted into an alternative, studio theater-type venue called The Other Place (TOP), which will showcase new writing and experimental works. Part of the building is also used for rehearsal space and a costume shop.

Other Stratford Sights

Avon Riverfront

The River Avon is a playground of swans and canal boats. The swans have been the mascots of Stratford since 1623, when, seven years after the Bard's death, Ben Jonson's poem in the First Folio dubbed him "the sweet swan of Avon." Join in the bird-scene fun and buy **swan food** to feed swans and ducks (sold at the TI for £1, and possibly by other vendors—ask around). Don't feed the Canada geese, which locals disdain (they say the geese are vicious and have been messing up the eco-balance since they were imported by a king in 1665).

The **canal boats** saw their workhorse days during the short window of time between the start of the Industrial Revolution

and the establishment of the railways. Today, they're mostly pleasure boats. The boats are long and narrow, so two can pass in the slim canals. There are 2,000 miles of canals in England's Midlands, built to connect centers of industry with seaports and provide vital transportation during the early days of the Industrial Revolution. Stratford was as far inland as you could sail on natural rivers from Bristol; it was the terminus of the man-made Birmingham Canal, built in 1816. Even today, you can motor your canal boat all the way to London from here. Along the embankment, look for the signs indicating how many hours it'll take—and how many locks you'll traverse—to go by barge to various English cities.

For a little bit of mellow river action, rent a **rowboat** (£5/hour per person) or, for more of a challenge, pole yourself around on a

Cambridge-style **punt** (canal is poleable—only 4 or 5 feet deep; same price as the rowboat and more memorable/embarrassing if you do the punting—don't pay £10/30 minutes per person for a waterman to do the punting for you). You can rent these boats at the Swan's Nest Boat-

house across the Tramway Footbridge; another rental station, along the river, next to the theater, has higher prices but is more conveniently located. Take a short stop on your lazy tour of the English countryside, and moor your canal boat at Stratford's Canal Basin.

You can also try a sleepy 40-minute **river cruise** (£5.50, includes commentary, Avon Boating, board boat in Bancroft Gardens near the RSC theater, tel. 01789/267-073, www.avon-boating.co.uk), or jump on the oldest surviving **chain ferry** (c. 1937)

in Britain (£0.50), which shuttles people across the river just beyond the theater.

Cox's Yard, a riverside timber yard until the 1990s, is a rare physical remnant of the days when Stratford was an industrial port. Today, Cox's has been taken over by the pricey, sprawling Lazy Cow restaurant complex, with a pricey steakhouse, a burger stand, a milkshake shop, lots of outdoor seating, and occasional live music. Upstairs is the Attic Theatre, which puts on fringe theater acts (www.treadthe-boardstheatre.co.uk).

In the riverfront park, roughly between Cox's Yard and the TI, the **Gower Memorial** honors the Bard and his creations. Named for Lord Ronald Gower, the man who paid for and sculpted the memorial, this 1888 work shows Shakespeare up top ringed by four of his most indelible creations, each representing a human pursuit: Hamlet (philosophy), Lady Macbeth (tragedy), Falstaff (comedy), and Prince Hal (history). Originally located next to the theater, it was moved here after the 1932 fire.

▲MAD Museum

A refreshing change of pace in Bard-bonkers Stratford, this museum's name stands for "Mechanical Art and Design." It celebrates machines as art, showcasing a changing collection of skillfully constructed robots, gizmos, and Rube-Goldberg machines that spring to entertaining life with the push of a button. Engaging for kids, riveting for engineers, and enjoyable to anybody, it's pricey but conveniently located near Shakespeare's Birthplace.

Cost and Hours: £6.80, daily April-Sept 10:30-17:30, Oct-March 11:00-17:00, 45 Hanley Street, tel. 01789/269-356, www.themadmuseum.co.uk.

Tudor World at the Falstaff Experience

This attraction is tacky, gimmicky, and more about entertainment than education. (And, while it's named for a Shakespeare character, the exhibit isn't about the Bard.) Filling Shrieve's House Barn with mostly kid-oriented exhibits (mannequins and descriptions, but few real artifacts), it sweeps through Tudor history from the plague to Henry VIII's privy chamber to a replica 16th-century tavern. If you're into ghost-spotting, their nightly ghost tours may be your best shot.

Cost and Hours: Museum-£5.50, daily 10:30-17:30, last entry 30 minutes before closing; ghost tours-£7.50, daily at 18:00, additional tours may be available Fri-Sat; Sheep Street, tel. 01789/298-070, www.falstaff-experience.co.uk.

Sleeping in Stratford

If you want to spend the night after you catch a show, options abound. Ye olde timbered hotels are scattered through the city center. Most B&Bs are a short walk away on the fringes of town, right on the busy ring roads that route traffic away from the center. (The

Sleep Code

(£1 = about $1.60, country code: 44, area code: 01789)
S = Single, **D** = Double/Twin, **T** = Triple, **Q** = Quad, **b** = bathroom, **s** = shower only. Unless noted otherwise, credit cards are accepted and breakfast is included.

To help you sort easily through these listings, I've divided the accommodations into three categories based on the price for a standard double room with bath:

$$$ Higher Priced—Most rooms £90 or more.
$$ Moderately Priced—Most rooms between £60-90.
$ Lower Priced—Most rooms £60 or less.

Prices can change without notice; verify the hotel's current rates online or by email. For the best prices, always book direct.

---

recommended places below generally have double-paned windows for rooms in the front, but still get some traffic noise.)

In general, the weekend on or near Shakespeare's birthday (April 23) is particularly tight, but Fridays and Saturdays are busy throughout the season. This town is so reliant upon the theater for its business that some B&Bs have secondary insurance covering their loss if the Royal Shakespeare Company ever stops performing in Stratford.

On Grove Road

These accommodations are at the edge of town on busy Grove Road, across from a grassy park. From here, it's about a 10-minute walk either to the town center or to the train station (opposite directions).

$$$ Adelphi Guest House is run by Shakespeare buffs Sue and Simon, who pride themselves on providing a warm welcome, homemade cakes, and original art in every room (S-£40-50, Db-£80-95, Tb-£130, Qb-£160, 2 percent surcharge on credit cards, 10 percent discount off these prices if you stay at least 2 nights—mention this book when you reserve, free Wi-Fi, free parking if booked  in advance, 39 Grove Road, tel. 01789/204-469, www.adelphi-guesthouse.com, info@adelphi-guesthouse.com).

$$ Ambleside Guest House is run with quiet efficiency and attentiveness by owners Peter and Ruth. Each of the seven rooms has been completely renovated, including the small but tidy bathrooms. The place has a homey, airy feel, with no B&B clutter (S-£35-40, Db-£60-80, Tb-£85-115, Qb-£100-140, ground-floor rooms, free Wi-Fi, free parking, 41 Grove Road, tel. 01789/297-239, www.amblesideguesthouse.com, peter@amblesideguesthouse.com—include your phone number in your request, since they like to call you back to confirm with a personal touch).

$$ Woodstock Guest House is a friendly, frilly, family-run, and flowery place with five comfortable rooms (Sb-£35-48, Db-£60-85, Tb-£90-120, can accommodate 4 people—ask, get Rick Steves discount if you stay 2 or more nights—mention this book when you reserve, 5 percent surcharge on credit cards, ground-floor room, free Wi-Fi, free parking, 30 Grove Road, tel. 01789/299-881, www.woodstock-house.co.uk, jackie@woodstock-house.co.uk, owners Denis and bubbly Jackie).

$ Salamander Guest House, run by gregarious Frenchman Pascal and his wife, Anna, rents eight simple rooms that are a bit cheaper than their neighbors (S-£39, Db-£50-65, Tb-£70-85, Qb-£80-95, free Wi-Fi, free on-site parking, 40 Grove Road, tel. 01789/205-728, www.salamanderguesthouse.co.uk, p.delin@btinternet.com).

Elsewhere in Stratford

$$$ Mercure Shakespeare Hotel, centrally located in a black-and-white building just up the street from Nash's House, has 78 business-class rooms, each one named for a Shakespearean play or character. Some of the rooms are old-style Elizabethan higgledy-piggledy (with modern finishes), while others are contemporary style—note your preference when you reserve (Sb-£80-100, standard Db-£110-140, deluxe Db-£140-170, prices soft depending on demand, breakfast-£15.50/person, free Wi-Fi, parking-£10/day, Chapel Street, tel. 01789/294-997, www.mercure.com, h6630-re@accor.com).

$$ The Emsley Guest House holds five bright, modern rooms named after different counties in England. It's conscientiously run by Melanie and Ray Coulson, who give it a homey and inviting atmosphere (Db-£70-90, Qb or Quint/b-£100-130, 5-person family room with extra bathroom, no kids under 5, free Wi-Fi, free off-street parking, 5 minutes from station at 4 Arden Street, tel. 01789/299-557, www.theemsley.co.uk, mel@theemsley.co.uk).

$ Hostel: Hemmingford House, with 134 beds in 2- to 6-bed rooms (half of them en suite), is a 10-minute bus ride from town (from £15/bed, breakfast-£5; take bus #15, #18, or #18A two miles to Alveston; tel. 01789/297-093 or 0845-371-9661, stratford@yha.org.uk).

Eating in Stratford

Restaurants

Stratford's numerous restaurants vie for your pre-theater business, with special hours and meal deals. (Most offer light two- and three-course menus before 19:00.) You'll find many hardworking places on Sheep Street and Waterside. Unfortunately, post-theater dinners are more challenging, as most places close early.

Le Bistro Pierre, across the river near the boating station, is a French eatery that's been impressing Stratford residents. They have indoor or outdoor seating and slow service (£11 two-course lunches; £14 two-course meals before 18:45, otherwise £13-17 main courses; Mon-Fri 12:00-15:00 & 17:00-22:30, Sat 12:00-16:00 & 17:00-23:00, Sun 12:30-16:30 & 18:00-22:00, Swan's Nest, Bridgefoot, tel. 01789/264-804). They also have a pub with a different menu.

Sheep Street Eateries: The next three places, part of the same chain, line up along Sheep Street, offering trendy ambience and modern English cuisine at relatively high prices (all three have pre-theater menus before 19:00—£13.50 two-course meal, £17 for three courses): **Lambs** is intimate and serves meat, fish, and veggie dishes with panache. The upstairs feels dressy, under low, half-timbered beams (£12-17 main courses, Mon-Fri 17:00-21:00, Wed-Fri also 12:00-14:00, Sat 12:00-21:30, Sun 12:00-15:00 & 18:00-21:00, 12 Sheep Street, tel. 01789/292-554). **The Opposition,** next door, has a less formal "bistro" ambience (£8-10 light meals, £13-16 main courses; Mon-Thu 12:00-14:00 & 17:00-21:00, Fri-Sat until 22:30, closed Sun, tel. 01789/269-980; book in advance if you want to have a post-theater dinner here on Fri or Sat). **The Vintner,** just up the street, has the best reputation and feels even trendier than its siblings, but still with old style. They're known for their £11 burgers (£7-11 light meals, £12-16 main courses, daily 9:30-21:00, until 22:00 Fri-Sat, 4-5 Sheep Street, tel. 01789/297-259).

Indian: **Avon Spice** has a good reputation and good prices (£7-9 main courses, daily 17:00-23:30, until later Fri-Sat, 7 Greenhill Street, tel. 01789/267-067).

Pubs

The Old Thatch Tavern is, according to natives, the best place in town for beer, serving up London-based Fuller's brews. The atmosphere is cozy, and the food is a cut above what you'll get in the other pubs; enjoy it either in the bar, in the tight, candlelit restaurant, or out on the quiet patio (£9-12 main courses, food served Mon-Sat 12:00-21:00, Sun 12:00-15:00, on Greenhill Street overlooking the market square, tel. 01789/295-216).

The Windmill Inn serves decent, modestly priced fare in a

17th-century inn. It combines old and new styles, and—since it's a few steps beyond the heart of the tourist zone—actually attracts some locals as well. Order drinks and food at the bar, settle into a comfy chair or head out to the half-timbered courtyard, and wait for your meal (£8-10 pub grub, food served daily 11:00-21:45, Church Street, tel. 01789/297-687).

The Garrick Inn bills itself as the oldest pub in town, and comes with a cozy, dimly lit restaurant vibe. Choose between the pub or table-service section; either way, you'll dine on bland, pricey pub grub (£9-13 dishes, food served daily 12:00-22:00, Sun until 21:00, 25 High Street, tel. 01789/292-186).

Picnics

With its sprawling and inviting riverfront park, Stratford is a particularly pleasant place to picnic. Choose a bench with views of the river or vacation houseboats, and munch your meal while tossing a few scraps into the river to attract swans. It's a fine way to spend a midsummer night's eve. For groceries or prepared foods, find **Marks & Spencer** on Bridge Street (Mon-Sat 9:00-18:00, Sun 10:30-16:30, small coffee-and-sandwiches café upstairs, tel. 01789/292-430). Across the street, **Sainsbury's Local** stays open later than other supermarkets in town (daily 7:00-22:00).

For fish-and-chips, you have a couple of options: **Barnaby's** is a greasy fast-food joint near the waterfront—but it's convenient if you want to get takeout for the riverside park just across the street (£4-7 fish-and-chips, daily 11:00-20:00, at Sheep Street and Waterside). For better food (but a less convenient location—closer to my recommended B&Bs than to the park), queue up with the locals at **Kingfisher,** then ask for the freshly battered haddock (£6-7 fish-and-chips, Mon 11:30-13:45 & 17:00-21:30, Tue-Sat 11:30-13:45 & 17:00-22:00, closed Sun, a long block up at 13 Ely Street, tel. 01789/292-513).

Tearoom

Henley Street Tea Rooms, across the street from Shakespeare's Birthplace, has indoor seating, outdoor tables right on the main pedestrian mall, and friendly service (£4.25 cream tea, £11 afternoon tea, teas available all day, daily 9:00-17:30, Sept-March until 17:00, 40 Henley Street, tel. 01789/415-572). The same people run Bensons House of Tea & Gift Shop, just down the street (at #33).

Stratford Connections

Remember: When buying tickets or checking schedules, ask for "Stratford-upon-Avon," not just "Stratford." Notice that a single train (running about every 2 hours) connects most of these destinations: Warwick, Leamington Spa (change for Coventry or Oxford), then London.

From Stratford-upon-Avon by Train to: London (5/day direct, more with transfers, 2.25 hours, to Marylebone Station), **Warwick** (10/day, 30 minutes), **Coventry** (at least hourly, 1.75 hours, change in Leamington Spa or Birmingham), **Oxford** (every 2 hours, 1.5 hours, change in Leamington Spa, Birmingham, or Banbury), **Moreton-in-Marsh** (almost hourly, 2.5-3 hours, 2-3 transfers, slow and expensive, better by bus). Train info: Tel. 0845-748-4950, www.nationalrail.co.uk.

By Bus to: Cotswolds towns (bus #21 or #22, Mon-Sat 8/day, none on Sun, 35 minutes to **Chipping Campden,** 1-1.25 hours to **Moreton-in-Marsh;** also stops at Broadway, Blockley, and Bourton-on-the-Hill; Johnsons Coaches, tel. 01564/797-070, www.johnsonscoaches.co.uk), **Warwick** (#16 is fastest, hourly, 20 minutes, tel. 01788/535-555, www.stagecoachbus.com), **Coventry** (hourly, 1.25 hours, same bus as Warwick). A direct bus runs to **Oxford** once a day (National Express, tel. 0871-781-8181, www. nationalexpress.com); otherwise 4/day with change in Chipping Norton (train is better). Most intercity buses stop on Stratford's Bridge Street (a block up from the TI). For bus info that covers all the region's companies, call Traveline at tel. 0871-200-2233 (www. travelinemidlands.co.uk).

By Car: Driving is easy and distances are short: **Stow-on-the-Wold** (22 miles), **Warwick** (8 miles), **Coventry** (19 miles).

Route Tips for Drivers

These tips assume you're heading north from Stratford and considering visits to Warwick and/or Coventry (both described in the next chapter).

Stratford to Points North via Warwick and Coventry: Leaving the Bridgefoot garage in downtown Stratford (see map on page 278), circle to the right around the same block, but stay on "the Wark" (Warwick Road, A-439). Warwick is eight miles away. The castle is just south of town on the right. (For parking advice, see page 579.) When you're trying to decide whether to stop in Coventry or not, factor in Birmingham's rush hour—try to avoid driving through that city between 14:00-20:00, if you can (worst on Fri-Sun; on Mon-Thu it generally gets better earlier, around 18:30).

If You're Including Coventry: After touring Warwick Castle, carry on through the center of Warwick town and follow signs to Coventry (still the A-439, then the A-46). If you're stopping in Coventry, follow signs painted on the road to the *City Centre,* and then to *Cathedral Parking.* Grab a place in the high-rise parking lot. Leaving Coventry, follow signs to *Nuneaton* and *M6 North* through lots of sprawl, and you're on your way. (See next page.)

If You're Skirting Coventry: Take the M-69 (direction: Leicester) and follow the M-6 as it threads through giant Birmingham.

Once You're on the M-6: The highway divides into the free M-6 and an "M-6 Toll" road (designed to help drivers cut through the Birmingham traffic chaos). Take the toll road—£5.50 is a small price to pay to avoid all the nasty traffic (www.m6toll.co.uk).

When battling through sprawling Birmingham, keep your sights on the M-6. If you're heading for any points north—Ironbridge Gorge (Telford), North Wales, Liverpool, Blackpool, or the Lakes (Kendal for the South Lake District, Keswick for the North Lake District)—just stay relentlessly on the M-6 (direction: North West). Each destination is clearly signed directly from the M-6. For specifics on getting to Ironbridge Gorge, see page 633.

STRATFORD-UPON-AVON

WARWICK AND COVENTRY

Just north of Stratford, you'll find England's single most spectacular castle: Warwick. This medieval masterpiece, which has been turned into a virtual theme park, is extremely touristy—but it's also historic and fun, and may well be Britain's most kid-friendly experience. The town of Warwick, huddled protectively against the castle walls, is a half-timbered delight—enjoyable for a lunch or dinner, or even for an overnight.

A bit farther north sits the decidedly *not* cute city of Coventry—a blue-collar burg that was notoriously obliterated by the Nazi Luftwaffe in World War II. While today's Coventry, having been rebuilt modern and drab, offers little charm, it does feature one of Britain's most poignant WWII sights: the charred husk of its once-grand cathedral, now left as a monument, with the inspiring new cathedral just next door. A few other intriguing museums round out Coventry's appeal.

Planning Your Time

Warwick and Coventry are both ideal on-the-way destinations—lash them onto your itinerary as you head north from Stratford. Warwick Castle deserves at least three hours for a quick visit, but it can be an all-day outing for families. Coventry's cathedral can be seen quickly—in about an hour, if that's all the time you have—though the city's other sights could fill an additional couple of hours. If you're prioritizing, Warwick is (for most) the better stop, with its grand castle and charming town; Coventry is worthwhile primarily for its iconic cathedral ruins and for the chance to see a real, struggling, industrial Midlands city.

Warwick and Coventry are both reachable by public trans-

Warwick and Coventry

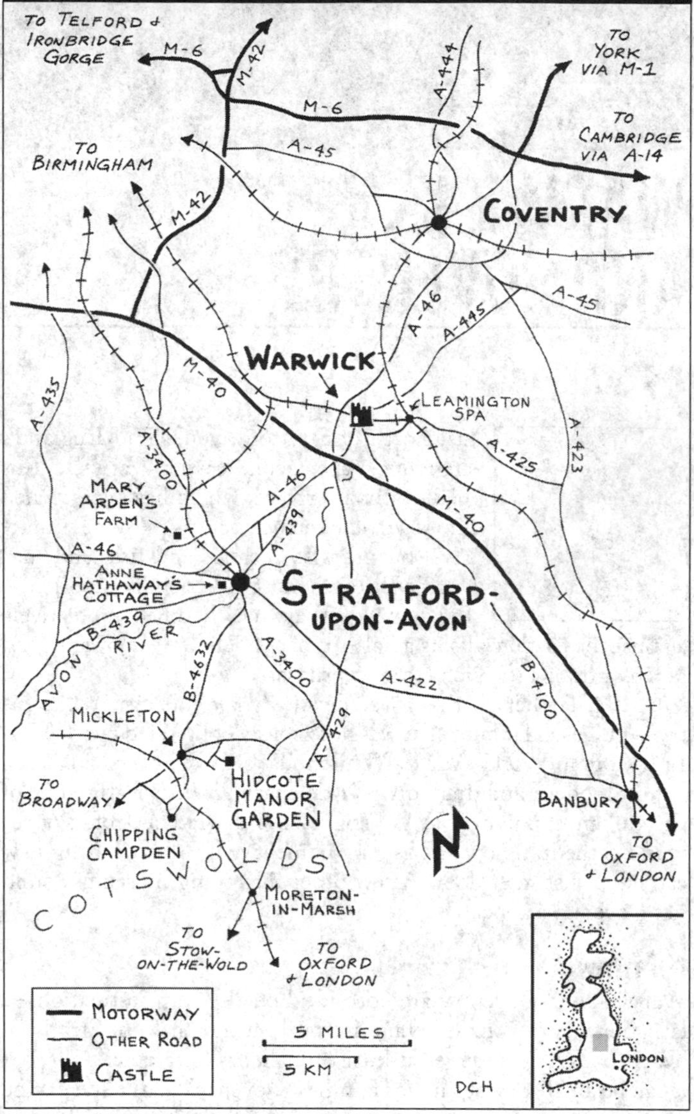

TO TELFORD &
IRONBRIDGE
GORGE

M-6

M-42

A-444

TO
YORK
VIA M-1

M-6

TO BIRMINGHAM

A-45

A-45

TO
CAMBRIDGE
VIA A-14

M-42

COVENTRY

A-435

M-40

WARWICK

A-46

A-445

A-45

A-425

A-423

A-3400

LEAMINGTON
SPA

MARY
ARDEN'S
FARM

A-46

A-439

A-46

ANNE
HATHAWAY'S
COTTAGE

**STRATFORD-
UPON-AVON**

B-439

AVON
RIVER

B-4632

A-3400

A-429

A-422

M-40

B-4100

MICKLETON

TO
BROADWAY

HIDCOTE
MANOR
GARDEN

BANBURY

TO
OXFORD
& LONDON

CHIPPING
CAMPDEN

C O T S W O L D S

MORETON-
IN-MARSH

N

TO
STOW-
ON-THE-WOLD

TO
OXFORD
& LONDON

	MOTORWAY
	OTHER ROAD
♜	CASTLE

5 MILES

5 KM

DCH

LONDON

portation, but easier for drivers. For tips on splicing Warwick and/ or Coventry into your northbound drive out of Stratford, see that chapter's "Planning Your Time" on page 577 and "Route Tips for Drivers" on page 601.

Warwick

The pleasant town of Warwick ("WAR-ick") is home to England's finest medieval castle, which dominates the banks of the River

Avon just upstream from Stratford. The castle is impressive in itself, but its lineup of theme-park-type experiences makes it particularly entertaining, especially for kids. The castle-related attractions, while pricey, offer something for everyone, and on a sunny day the grounds are a treat to explore.

Meanwhile, Warwick town—with a fine market square and some good eateries—goes about its business almost oblivious to the busloads of tourists passing through. While handy for an overnight, Warwick offers relatively little to see beyond its castle.

Orientation to Warwick

With about 24,000 people, Warwick is small and manageable. The castle and old town center sit side by side, with the train station about a mile to the north. From the castle's main gate, a lane leads into the old town center a block away, where you'll find the TI, plenty of eateries (see "Eating in Warwick," later), and a few minor sights.

Tourist Information

Warwick's TI sells same-day tickets to Warwick Castle for £15, an £8 savings over buying them at the castle (Mon-Fri 9:30-16:30, Sat 10:30-16:00, Sun 10:30-15:30, closes 30 minutes earlier Oct-May, The Court House, Jury Street, tel. 01926/492-212, www.visitwarwick.co.uk, info@visitwarwick.co.uk). The TI has computers with Internet access (£0.50 to get online for a few minutes) and a room-booking service (pay 10 percent here and the rest at your B&B).

Arrival in Warwick

By Train: Warwick has two train stations; you want the one called simply "Warwick" (Warwick Parkway Station is farther from the

Warwick

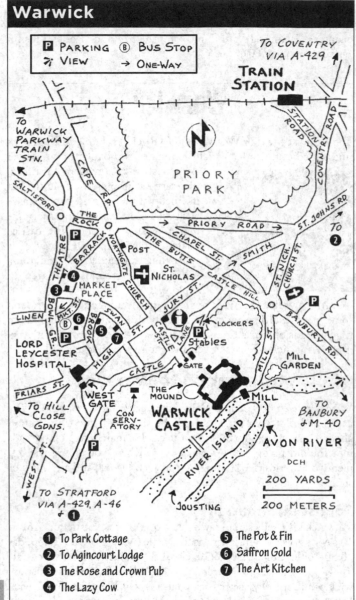

P PARKING　B BUS STOP
↗ VIEW　→ ONE-WAY

TO COVENTRY
VIA A-429

TRAIN STATION

TO WARWICK PARKWAY TRAIN STN.

SALTISFORD

CAPE RD.

THE ROCK

BARRACK

NORTHGATE

THEATRE

BOWL. GR.

LINEN ST.

MKT. ST.

BROOK

SWAN ST.

CHURCH ST.

HIGH ST.

Post

MARKET PLACE

St. Nicholas

THE BUTTS

CHAPEL ST.

PRIORY ROAD

PRIORY PARK

STATION ROAD

COVENTRY ROAD

ST. JOHNS RD.

TO ❷

SMITH ST.

CASTLE HILL

ST. NICH. CHURCH ST.

BANBURY RD.

JURY ST.

CASTLE ST.

CASTLE LANE

Stables

LOCKERS

GATE

MILL ST.

MILL GARDEN

Lord Leycester Hospital

FRIARS ST.

TO HILL CLOSE GDNS.

WEST ST.

WEST GATE

CONSERVATORY

THE MOUND

WARWICK CASTLE

MILL

RIVER ISLAND

JOUSTING

AVON RIVER

TO BANBURY & M-40

DCH

200 YARDS

200 METERS

TO STRATFORD VIA A-429, A-46 & ❶

❶ To Park Cottage
❷ To Agincourt Lodge
❸ The Rose and Crown Pub
❹ The Lazy Cow

❺ The Pot & Fin
❻ Saffron Gold
❼ The Art Kitchen

castle). Day-trippers might be able to leave bags at the train station's Castle Cars taxi office for an extortionate £10 a day (tel. 01926/494-989). It's much cheaper to carry your bags into town and use the £1 lockers near the castle (at the entrance to the Stables Car Park; if lockers are all taken—unlikely but possible—try asking very nicely at the castle information desk).

A **taxi** from the station to the castle or town center costs about £5. It's a 15-minute, one-mile **walk** from the station to the castle or town center: Exit straight ahead down the street, then bear right onto Coventry Road, where you'll start to see signs for the castle. From here, at the traffic light, turn right onto St. John's Road. At the three-way fork, take Smith Street (the middle fork), which leads you through the old gateway straight up Warwick's High Street. After a long block, the TI appears on your left, with the main castle gate just beyond (up Castle Street). To reach the market square and restaurants from the TI, go one more block and turn right.

By Car: The main Stratford-Coventry road cuts right through Warwick. Coming from Stratford (8 miles to the south), you'll hit the castle parking lots first (£6, buy token from machine to exit lot; if these are full, lurk until a few cars leave and they'll let you in). The four castle lots are expensive, and three of them are a 10- to 15-minute walk from the actual castle; the closest one, just off Castle Lane, is the Stables Car Park, which costs more (£10). Street parking in the town center is cheaper (less than £2), but there's a two- to three-hour maximum—not enough time to fully experience the castle.

Sights in Warwick

▲▲Warwick Castle

Almost too groomed and organized, this theme park of a castle gives its crowds of visitors a decent value for the stiff entry fee.

The cash-poor but enterprising Earl of Warwick hired the folks at Merlin Entertainments (which owns many other big-name British attractions) to wring maximum tourist dollars out of his castle. They've made the place entertaining indeed, and packed it with lively exhibits...but also watered down the history a bit, and added several layers of gift shops, overpriced concessions, and nickel-and-dime add-ons. The greedy feel of the place can be a little annoying, considering the already-steep admission. But—especially for kids—there just isn't a better medieval castle experience in England. With a lush, green, grassy moat and fairy-tale fortifications, Warwick Castle will entertain you from dungeon to lookout.

The castle is a 14th- and 15th-century fortified shell, holding an 18th- and 19th-century royal residence, surrounded by another one of dandy "Capability" Brown's landscape jobs (like at Blenheim Palace). You can tour the sumptuous staterooms, climb the towers and ramparts for the views, stroll through themed exhibits populated by aristocratic wax figures, explore the sprawling grounds and gardens, and—best of all—interact with costumed docents who explain the place and perform fantastic demonstrations of medieval weapons and other skills.

Cost: Steep £23 entry fee (£16 for kids under age 12, £17 for seniors) includes gardens and most castle attractions except for the gory Castle Dungeon (£9) and the *Merlin: The Dragon Tower* show (£4). Combo-tickets are available. English Heritage members get a 50 percent discount at the door.

Hours: Open daily April-Sept 10:00-18:00, Oct-March 10:00-17:00.

Advance Tickets: Booking in advance at www.warwick-castle.com saves substantial money and time waiting in the ticket line (even better, advance tickets bought at the Warwick TI let you avoid the line, and save you £8).

Audioguides and Guidebooks: The dry, nine-stop audioguide leads you through the state rooms (£2.50; £4/2 people), but the posted information is more concise and interesting. The £5 guidebook gives you nearly the same script in souvenir-booklet form. (A children's audioguide, called "A Knight's Tale," is £1.50.) The audioguides and the guidebook are available at the gift shop near the entrance (not the ticket booth). If you tour the castle without help, pick the brains of the earnest and talkative docents.

Information: Recorded info tel. 0871-265-2000, or call 01926/495-421 Mon-Fri 9:00-17:00, www.warwick-castle.com.

Demonstrations and Events: It's the well-presented demos and other events that make this castle particularly worthwhile. These can include jousting competitions, archers showing off their longbow skills, sword fights, jester acts, falconry shows, and demonstrations of the trebuchet (like a catapult) and ballista (a type of giant slingshot). They're offered year-round, but most frequently in summer and on weekends and school holidays. When you buy your castle ticket, be sure to pick up the daily events flier and plan your day around these events.

Eating at the Castle: Consider bringing your own picnic to enjoy at the gorgeous grounds. Otherwise you'll be left with over-priced concessions stands serving variations on the same mass-produced food. The stands are scattered around the castle grounds (and marked on the map you get with your ticket). **The Coach House** has cafeteria fare and grungy seating (located just before the turnstiles). **The Undercroft** has a sandwich buffet line (located inside, in basement of palace); you can sit under medieval vaults or escape with your food and picnic outside. The **riverside pavilion** sells sandwiches and fish-and-chips, and has fine outdoor seating (in park just before the bridge, behind castle). Fortunately, just 100 yards from the castle turnstiles—through a tiny gate in the wall—is Warwick town's workaday commercial district, with several better (and better-value) lunch options. It's worth the walk (see "Eating in Warwick," later).

○ **Self-Guided Tour:** Buy your ticket and head through the turnstile into the moat area, where you'll get your first view of the dramatic castle. In good weather, this lawn-like zone is filled with tents populated by costumed docents demonstrating every-day medieval lifestyles.

From the moat, two different entrance gateways lead to the castle's **inner courtyard.** Within these mighty walls, there's some-

thing for every taste (described next); look for signs for where to enter each one.

The bulge of land at the far end of the courtyard, called **The Mound,** is where the original Norman castle of 1068 stood. Under this "motte," the wooden stockade (the "bailey") defined the courtyard in the way the castle walls do today. You can climb up to the top for a view down into the castle courtyard (do this at the end, since you can exit down the other side, toward the riverbank).

The main attractions are in the largest buildings along the side of the courtyard: the Great Hall, five lavish staterooms, and the chapel. Progressing through these rooms, you'll see how the castle complex evolved over the centuries, from the militarized Middle Ages to

civilized Victorian times, from a formidable defensive fortress to a genteel manor home.

Enter through the cavernous **Great Hall,** decorated with suits of equestrian armor. Adjoining the Great Hall is the state dining room, with portraits of English kings and princes. Then follow the one-way route through the **staterooms,** keeping ever more esteemed company as you go—the rooms closest to the center of the complex were the most exclusive, reserved only for those especially close to the Earl of Warwick. You'll pass through a series of three drawing rooms (abbreviated from "withdrawing," from a time when these provided a retreat into a more intimate area after a to-do in the larger, more public rooms): first, one decorated in a deep burgundy; then the cedar drawing room, with  intricately carved wood paneling, a Waterford crystal chandelier, and a Carrara marble fireplace; and finally the green drawing room, with a beautiful painted coffered ceiling and wax figures of Henry VIII and his six wives. The sumptuous Queen Anne Room was decorated in preparation for a planned 1704 visit by the monarch (unfortunately, Queen Anne never came—she got wind that one of her ladies-in-waiting, with whom she was fiercely competitive, was also coming, so she canceled at the last minute). Finally comes the blue boudoir, an oversized closet decorated in blue silk wallpaper. The portrait of King Henry VIII over the fireplace faces a clock once owned by Marie-Antoinette.

On your way out, you'll pass the earl's private **chapel.** The earl's family worshipped in the pews in front of the stone screen, while the servants would stand behind it. Notice the ornate wood-carved relief depicting a scene of the Greeks fighting the Amazons, based on a painting by Peter Paul Rubens. The organ in the back of the chapel was powered by a hand-pumped bellows.

Back out in the courtyard, to the left of the staterooms, are the entrances to two other, less impressive exhibits. The **Kingmaker** exhibit (set in 1471) uses mannequins, sound effects, and smells to show how medieval townsfolk prepared for battle—from the blacksmiths and armory, to the wardrobe, to the final rallying cry, with costumed docents standing by. The **Secrets and Scandals of the Royal Weekend Party** exhibit lets you explore staterooms staged as they appeared in 1898, but with an added narrative element: The philandering

Daisy Maynard Greville, Countess of Warwick—considered the most beautiful woman in Victorian England—is throwing a party, and big-name aristocrats are in attendance, including a young Winston Churchill. Among the guests is the Prince of Wales (the future King Edward VII), with whom Daisy reportedly also had a long-time affair. Gossipy "servants" clue you in on who's flirting with whom. The rooms are populated by eerily convincing Madame Tussauds-style wax figures, and posted information and soundtracks loosely narrate the scandal. Unfortunately, it's more dry than titillating, and a bit hard to follow unless you're versed in the ins and outs of late-19th-century aristocratic intrigue.

You can climb up onto the **ramparts and tower**—a one-way, no-return route that leads you up and down (on very tight spiral stairs) the tallest tower, leaving you at a fun perch from which to fire your imaginary longbow. The halls and stairs can be very crowded with young kids, and—as the signs warn—it takes 530 steep steps (both up and down) to follow the whole route; claustrophobes should consider it carefully.

The **Princess Tower** offers children (ages 3-8) the chance to dress up as princesses and princes for a photo op. While it's included in the castle ticket, those interested must first sign up for a 15-minute time slot at the information tent in the middle of the courtyard, near the staterooms.

Two other pricey and skippable add-on attractions can also be entered from the courtyard (if you didn't buy a combo-ticket at the entrance, you can buy individual tickets at the information tent near the staterooms). **The Castle Dungeon,** a gory, tacky knock-off of the London Dungeon, features a series of costumed hosts who entertain and spook visitors on a 45-minute tour. *Merlin: The Dragon Tower,* a 20-minute live-action stage show with special effects, is based on a popular BBC television series.

Outside of the inner courtyard area are additional diversions. Surrounding everything is a lush, peacock-patrolled, picnic-perfect park, complete with a Victorian rose garden. The castle grounds are often enlivened by a knight in shining armor on a horse that rotates with a merry band of musical jesters. The grassy moat area is typically filled with costumed characters and demonstrations, including ar-  chery and falconry. Near the entrance to the complex is the **Pageant Playground,** with medieval-themed slides and climbing areas for kids. Down by the river is a bridge across to River Island, and—tucked around the back of the castle—a restored **mill and engine**

house, with an exhibit that explains how the castle was electrified in 1894.

More Sights in Warwick

While Warwick has a few attractions beyond the castle, most are not that exciting.

The most photogenic building in town (aside from the castle) is the **Lord Leycester Hospital,** a gaggle of adjoining 14th-century half-timbered houses next to the southern gate of High Street. Converted into a "hospital" (rest home for the elderly or ill) in 1571, it has a chapel, great hall, maze of old rooms, and pretty garden (overpriced at £5, borrow self-guided tour brochure at entry, Tue-Sun 10:00-17:00, until 16:30 in winter, closed Mon year-round except Bank Holidays, 60 High Street, tel. 01926/491-422, www.lordleycester.com).

Garden fans will find three good ones in Warwick. Most appealing is the **Mill Garden,** down the quaint and half-timbered Mill Street from the castle gate; this small garden, which adjoins the castle property, has fantastic views of the River Avon and castle (£2, April-Oct daily 9:00-18:00, closed Nov-March, 55 Mill Street, tel. 01926/492-877). **Hill Close Gardens,** at the other end of town near the racecourse, has 16 small Victorian garden plots and an erratically open café (£3.50, April-mid-Oct Mon-Thu 10:30-15:30, Fri 10:30-17:00, Sat 11:00-17:00, Sun 14:00-17:00; shorter hours and closed Sat-Sun off-season, Bread and Meat Close, tel. 01926/493-339, www.hillclosegardens.com). The garden at the **Lord Leycester Hospital** (described above) rounds out your options.

Sleeping in Warwick

(area code: 01926)

$$ Park Cottage fills a creaky 1521 half-timbered house (once the dairy for the castle) with seven rooms and teddy-on-the-beddy touches. It's on the main road at the opposite end of town from the train station (near the racecourse and the castle), but Stuart and Janet will pick you up if their schedule allows (Sb-£65, Db-£75-85, family room-£12.50 extra per child, free Wi-Fi, free parking, 113 West Street/A-429, tel. 01926/410-319, www.parkcottagewarwick. co.uk, janet@parkcottagewarwick.co.uk).

Several B&Bs line Emscote Road (A-445) at the train-station end of town. The closest to town—and best—is **$$ Agincourt Lodge,** renting six comfortable rooms in an 1854 Victorian house (S-£45, Sb-£50-58 depending on size, D with private b on the hall-£65, Db-£73, larger Db with four-poster bed-£83, Tb-£85, Qb-£95, free Wi-Fi, free parking, 36 Coten End, tel. 01926/499-399, www.agincourtlodge.co.uk, enquiries@agincourtlodge.co.uk, Mike and Marisa).

Eating in Warwick

All of these are on or within a short stroll of Market Place.

The Rose and Crown is a popular gastropub serving English food with a modern twist. Enjoy the cozy but not claustrophobic interior (order food at the bar, or dine in the table-service area), or sit outside (lunch—£5-7 light meals, £11-13 larger dishes; dinner—£11-18 main courses, £3 sides; food served daily 8:00-22:00, open longer for drinks, 30 Market Place, tel. 01926/411-117).

The Lazy Cow, a newer competitor a few doors down, is a bit more trendy and pricey, with a focus on steaks (in the open kitchen, see the aging cabinet and the indoor barbecue). Vegetarians may be put off by both the meat-heavy menu and the cow-themed decor (£6-8 starters, £10-20 main courses, open Mon-Thu 7:00-23:00, Fri-Sat until 24:00, Sun until 22:30, food served in bar until 19:00 Fri-Sat, in sit-down restaurant until closing, 10 Theatre Street, tel. 08451-200-666, www.thelazycowwarwick.co.uk).

The Pot & Fin serves up excellent fish-and-chips in a charming, rustic cottage setting a block off of Market Place (toward the castle). Everything is made fresh in-house. If you order takeaway (£4-7), you can grab one of the tables; or head upstairs for the pricier table-service menu, with £8 main courses (Tue-Sat 12:00-14:00 & 17:00-21:00, 48 Brook Street, tel. 01926/492-426).

Saffron Gold is a well-regarded Indian restaurant serving tasty £7-13 meals in an upscale setting with good service (Sun-Thu 17:30-23:30, Fri-Sat 17:30-24:00, just a block off Market Square but tricky to find—in drab Westgate House building near the Marks & Spencer, on Market Street, tel. 01926/402-061).

The Art Kitchen, right on the main pedestrian shopping street, is a mod Thai bistro surrounding a bar (£6-8 lunches, £8-17 dinners, daily 12:00-23:00, 7 Swan Street, tel. 01926/494-303).

Warwick Connections

Warwick is on the train line between Birmingham's Moor Street Station and London's Marylebone Station; most other connections require a change in the adjacent town of Leamington Spa.

From Warwick by Train to: Leamington Spa (about 2/hour, 3-10 minutes), **Stratford** (10/day, 30 minutes—buses are better, see below), **Coventry** (2/hour, 30-60 minutes, transfer in Leamington Spa), **Oxford** (2/hour, 50-70 minutes, transfer in Leamington Spa), **London**'s Marylebone Station (2/hour direct, 1.5 hours). Train info: Tel. 0845-748-4950, www.nationalrail.co.uk.

By Bus to: Stratford-upon-Avon (hourly, 20 minutes, bus #X17, also slower #15/ #18), **Coventry** (10/day, 1 hour, bus #X17, www.stagecoachbus.com).

Coventry

Coventry was bombed to smithereens in 1940 by the Nazi Luftwaffe (air force). From that point on, the German phrase for "to really blast the heck out of a place" was (roughly) "to coventrate" it. But Coventry rose from its ashes, and its message to our world is one of forgiveness, reconciliation, and the importance of peace.

Before it was infamous as a victim of World War II, Coventry had an illustrious history. According to legend, Coventry's most famous hometown girl, Lady Godiva, rode bareback and bare-naked through the town in the 11th century to convince her stubborn husband to lower taxes. You'll see her bronze statue on the market square a block from the cathedral, and a fun exhibit about her in the Herbert Museum.

The cloth trade made Coventry one of England's leading cities in the Middle Ages. Its fortunes rose and fell over time, and by the 20th century it had become a major industrial center—first as Britain's main bicycle manufacturer, later as its top car-making city, and eventually as a major center of armaments and aircraft assembly (making it a key target for the Nazis' Luftwaffe bombers). The city was utterly devastated by the Blitz; aside from the human toll, its greatest loss was its proud and famous St. Michael's Cathedral, which burned to the ground—the only English cathedral destroyed by the Nazis. Tellingly, Coventry's sister cities include two other places synonymous with horrific WWII destruction: Dresden, Germany, and Volgograd (formerly Stalingrad), Russia.

Today's Coventry isn't pretty. While many other WWII-damaged English towns were rebuilt quaint and cobbled, Coventry is all characterless modern concrete. But its cathedral—combining the still bombed-out shell of the old building, and a highly symbolic, starkly modern new one—is poignant and inspiring, and its other museums are quite good (and free). While I wouldn't go out of my way to visit Coventry, if you're passing by, consider stopping off to browse through a bit of normal, everyday, urban England.

Orientation to Coventry

Coventry is a big city—with about 310,000 people—but everything of interest to visitors is in the small central core, which is bound by a busy ring road. You can walk from one end of the ring to the other in about 15 minutes. The train station is just south of the ring; the cathedral, TI, St. Anne's Guildhall, and Herbert Museum are in the northeastern part of the ring; and the Transport Museum is about a 10-minute walk west of the cathedral.

Tourist Information

The TI, at the base of the cathedral tower, hands out free maps and brochures (April-Sept Mon-Fri 10:00-17:00, Sat 10:00-16:30, Sun 10:00-12:30 & 13:30-16:30, closes 30 minutes earlier Oct-March, may move in 2014—check online for location or call; tel. 024/7622-5616, www.visitcoventryandwarwickshire.co.uk, tic@coventry.gov.uk).

Arrival in Coventry

If you're passing through Coventry by public transportation, baggage storage is a problem—there's none at the train station. The cathedral and Transport Museum will store your bags while you visit each sight, but otherwise you're stuck. If your train route takes you through Birmingham's New Street Station (a transit hub for the area), consider using the left luggage desk there.

By Train: From the train station (which sits just outside the ring road), it's about a 15-minute walk to the cathedral. Exit straight ahead and find the blue line in the pavement, which leads you through the confusing maze of ring road overpasses to the edge of downtown; from there, simply follow signs for the cathedral (or the Transport Museum) through the modern shopping district. The cathedral is the taller of the two pointy spires.

By Car: Use the pay parking lot on Cox Street (just off of Fairfax Street), near the cathedral. From the ring road, take junction (exit) 2. The parking lot is basically under the ring road, across from the Coventry Sports and Leisure Centre.

Sights in Coventry

▲▲St. Michael's Cathedral

The symbol of Coventry is the bombed-out hulk of its old cathedral, with the huge new one adjoining it. This inspiring complex welcomes visitors.

Cost and Hours: The ruins of the old cathedral are free to enter (gates open daily roughly 9:00-17:00), though you'll pay to climb the tower (see below). Entering the new cathedral costs a hefty £8; consider it a donation to a worthwhile cause (Mon-Sat 10:00-17:00, Sun 12:00-16:00, last entry one hour before closing). During the afternoon service or evensong, admission is free (Mon-Fri at 17:15, Sat-Sun at 16:00, evensong predictable only on Sun, otherwise service may be spoken). The museum and café are closed on Sundays.

Services: The front desk will hold your bags while you visit.

Information: Tel. 024/7652-1200, www.coventrycathedral.org.uk.

Tower Climb: You can walk 181 steps up to the top of the tower for views over the cathedral complex and city. Buy your ticket and enter at the TI, at the base of the tower (£2.50, open same hours as TI, last entry 30 minutes before closing).

❍ Self-Guided Tour: A visit to the cathedral complex has two parts: First explore the ruins of the original building, then head into the new cathedral. You can pick up the free *Guide to the Ruined Cathedral* pamphlet at the TI; the new cathedral also hands out a floor plan that includes both the old and new churches.

Old Cathedral Ruins: Coventry's grand Perpendicular Gothic cathedral was the second to stand on this spot (built 1373-1460). Its towering, 303-foot-tall steeple—the third-highest in England—was a symbol for the city. On the night of November 14, 1940, Nazi Luftwaffe bombers filled the skies above Coventry. They dropped incendiary devices (firebombs) to light up the ground so they could see their targets. One of these hit the roof of the  cathedral, which was quickly consumed in flames. (The tower survived.) Today the footprint and surviving walls stand as a testament to the travesty of war.

At the apse of the ruined structure (far end from tower) is a replica of the **charred cross;** the original is inside the new ca-

thedral. While surveying the wreckage after the bombing, workers found these beams lying on the ground in the shape of a cross—so they lashed them together and erected it here. The message "Father Forgive" (spoken by Christ on the cross) makes it clear that this is a symbol not of anger, but of reconciliation. Every Friday at 12:00, the Coventry Litany of Reconciliation is said in these ruins—asking forgiveness for the seven deadly sins.

Various **monuments** are scattered around the ruins. Directly to the left of the charred cross is the bronze memorial to an early 20th-century bishop. In a chilling bit of irony, there's a swastika on his headband—dating from a time when this was just a good-luck symbol, before it had been appropriated by Hitler and painted on the planes that destroyed this place. Closer to the tower, you'll see the modern *Ecce Homo* sculpture (depicting Christ before Pilate) and a reconciliation monument, showing two people embracing across a gulf.

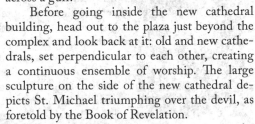

Before going inside the new cathedral building, head out to the plaza just beyond the complex and look back at it: old and new cathedrals, set perpendicular to each other, creating a continuous ensemble of worship. The large sculpture on the side of the new cathedral depicts St. Michael triumphing over the devil, as foretold by the Book of Revelation.

The cathedral's visitors center is to the right; in this undercroft is a museum about the history of all three cathedrals that have stood on this site, with artifacts from each one. (Also notice, to your left, the glassy entrance to the Herbert Art Gallery and Museum—a good post-cathedral stop, it's described later.)

• *Now head into the new cathedral interior. If the main door (up the stairs) is open, head inside and buy a ticket; otherwise, enter through the visitors center.*

New Cathedral: By the morning after the cathedral burned, the people of Coventry had already decided to rebuild it. The architect Basil Spence won the contest to design this re-imagining of the important church: The ruined old cathedral represents death and sacrifice, while the new structure—part of the same continuum—represents resurrection. While at first the cold gray walls inside the building make it feel gloomy and uninspired—almost (perhaps appropriately) like a giant bomb shelter—its highly symbolic design reveals itself to those who take the time to explore it.

Stand at the top of the main nave, on the giant letters that create a **gathering area** for the congregation. In the center of the

nave near these letters, look for the maple leaf embedded in the floor—a thank-you to Canadians whose donations helped fund this building. Looking down the nave, notice that the cathedral follows the same basic traditional layout of much older churches (long nave, choir area, high altar and apse at the far end) but features decidedly modern designs and decorations.

Turn right to take in the gigantic and gorgeous stained-glass window of the **baptistery**—a starburst with intensely warm colors

at the center, cool colors at the perimeter. Beneath this is the baptismal font, which is carved into a chunk of rock from the hills near Bethlehem. Looking down the nave, notice that otherwise, the cathedral has relatively little stained glass... from here, at least.

Across the nave from the baptistery, walk up the stairs into the **Chapel of Unity.** With its circular shape and floor mosaics depicting the five continents, this chapel preaches understanding among all Christian faiths—an ecumenism that echoes the cathedral's mission of reconciliation.

Back out in the main nave, walk down the central aisle. Notice the well-worn **copper coins** embedded in the floor. Dating from 1962 (when the cathedral was consecrated), these help choir members keep a straight line as they process into the church.

Pause in front of the **choir,** with its modern, dramatically prickly canopy, designed to evoke Jesus' crown of thorns—or possibly birds in flight. The Christmas-tree-shaped tower marks the seat of the bishop.

The green artwork that fills the far wall is not a fresco but a 74-foot-by-38-foot **tapestry** that depicts Jesus in a Byzantine Pantocrator ("creator of all") pose, surrounded by symbols of the four evangelists. Notice the faint outline of a small human being standing protected between Jesus' feet.

Turn around and look back down the **nave.** Remember how

stained glass seemed in short supply from the far end of the church? From this direction, you can clearly see how the sawtooth-shaped design allows for row after row of colorful glass to be seen by worshippers as they return to their seats after taking communion. At the far end, notice that instead of a wall sealing off the church, there's a giant glass window—to emphasize the connection between this new cathedral and the old one just outside. Both buildings also use the same local red sandstone. This is intended to be one big, unified space.

Now circle around the left side of the choir, to the back-left corner of the church, where stairs lead down to WCs, the church museum, and a café. Hanging at the top of the stairwell is the **original charred cross** that was found in the ruins of the cathedral after the bombing.

Now cross toward the other side of the church. Right in the middle, you'll pass a misshapen cross above the main altar; in its center is a smaller cross consisting of three nails from the medieval church, which were also found in the wreckage. This **"cross of nails"** has become a symbol worldwide for postwar reconciliation. Several such crosses have been made, many of them given to other cities that were devastated by the war; one stands above the high altar of the rebuilt Frauenkirche in Dresden, Germany. (You can buy a small replica of the cross of nails in the cathedral shop, across from the main door.)

Continue to the far side of the church. You'll pass the **Chapel of Gethsemane,** with a crown of thorns-shaped screen around the window. Beyond that, walk down the hallway and into the **Chapel of Christ the Servant.** The clear (rather than stained-glass) windows remind worshippers to extend their faith and stewardship outside the walls of this building. Also displayed here are fragments of the old cathedral's original stained-glass windows.

Near the Cathedral

▲Herbert Art Gallery and Museum

This expanded, impressive museum complex and cultural center combines town history exhibits and art collections. Since it's free and directly behind the cathedral, it's well worth dropping in if you have some time to spare. As there are several different exhibits—both permanent and temporary—be sure to explore the entire building (ask for a floor plan).

Cost and Hours: Free, Mon-Sat 10:00-16:00, Sun 12:00-16:00, Jordan Well, tel. 024/7683-2386, www.theherbert.org.

Visiting the Gallery: Near the entrance is the History Gallery, with enjoyable interactive exhibits that trace the city's story from its beginnings to the Blitz to today. You'll see actual artifacts from the Blitz and hear locals describe living through it. Beyond

the information desk are small exhibits on peace and reconciliation (Coventry has understandably become a very pacifist city), and the small but entertaining Discover Godiva exhibit, which examines the legend (and possible fact) of Lady Godiva. Her husband, Earl Leofric, increased taxes dramatically on his subjects. She pleaded with him for a tax cut, and he agreed—provided that she ride naked through town on horseback. A fun animated video shows how the legend evolved, with each generation of storytellers adding their own flourishes. One popular version says that the townspeople respectfully averted their eyes, except for one "Peeping Tom"—who was struck blind for his voyeurism. You'll also see paintings of the Lady, clips from movies about her, and companies that have appropriated her as a mascot. Upstairs is the museum's modest but enjoyable gallery of sculpture, Old Masters, modern and contemporary artwork, and temporary exhibits.

▲St. Mary's Guildhall

The origins of this fine half-timbered building, sitting next to the cathedral, are rooted in the fascinating history of England's often-overlooked King Henry VI

(r. 1422-1461). Afflicted with what today would be diagnosed as catatonic schizophrenia, Henry seemed to his medieval subjects to exist between our world and another—he'd drift into a trance and be unreachable for days or weeks at a time, and emerge reporting the vibrant visions he'd had. During the Wars of the Roses, Henry briefly moved the capital of England to Coventry, creating a special bond with the city. After his death, Henry's corpse reportedly bled in front of observers, leading them to conclude that he was miraculous. A cult of followers sprang up around Henry, centered here in Coventry.

People began to pray for divine intervention from the man they came to call "Saint Henry." One young girl, who had been crushed under a wagon wheel, was miraculously healed when her mother prayed to Henry. (The pope sent delegates to verify some 300 reported miracles, and Henry would likely have been formally canonized—if his son, Henry VII, hadn't refused to pay the hefty sum for sainthood. By the time his grandson, Henry VIII, broke away from the Vatican, all bets were off.) The local businessmen's guilds of Coventry built this fine hall to venerate their favorite king and unofficial saint.

Cost and Hours: Free, £0.50 pamphlet, £1 detailed descriptions, Easter-early Oct Sun-Thu 10:00-16:00, closed Fri-Sat, during events, and off-season, tel. 024/7683-3328, www.coventry.gov.uk/stmarys.

Visiting the Guildhall: While it's fun and a bit spooky to explore the maze of tight old rooms, the highlight here is the great hall. The semicircular stained-glass window traces Henry VI's royal lineage—that's him in the center, flanked by his supposed ancestors, William the Conqueror, King Arthur, and the Roman emperor Constantine (notice that Constantine's cross is bigger than the others'—his mother, St. Helen, supposedly discovered Jesus' "true cross"). Below the window is a remarkable, if faded, 14th-century tapestry that also honors Henry (ask the attendants to briefly turn on the light to see it better). More than 500 years old, this tapestry is still in situ—in the location for which it was intended. The hall is staffed by knowledgeable attendants who love to explain its history. If you dare, also ask them about the constant ghost sightings in this building—so frequent they've become routine.

▲Coventry Transport Museum

A 10-minute walk from the cathedral, this good museum pays

homage to Coventry's car-making heritage. For much of the 20th century, Coventry was the main auto production center of Britain, and in the 1950s and '60s, more than a third of the city's population built cars. On two floors of a sprawling modern building, you can see the first, fastest, and most famous cars that came from this "British Detroit." The museum also shows off a collection of tractors, bicycles, motorcycles, and tanks...if it had wheels, they made it here. For car lovers, it's worth ▲▲.

Cost and Hours: Free, good £5 souvenir guidebook, £1

lockers for use only while on the premises, daily 10:00-17:00, tel. 024/7623-4270, www.transport-museum.com.

Visiting the Museum: The exhibit focuses on local production (Daimler, Standard, Mandslay, and others), but a few famous non-Coventry cars are also included, such as Monty's staff car, Princess Di's modest Austin Metro car (a gift from Prince Charles before they married), a DeLorean, a 1949 Land Rover, and Ewan McGregor's motorcycle from the BBC series *Long Way Round*. Aside from the cars, you'll find the Landmarques Show (re-created streets of old-time Coventry, circa 1868-1948), the Coventry Blitz Experience (a low-tech, walk-through simulation of war-torn Coventry with sound and light effects), and—upstairs—the thought-provoking Ghost Town? exhibit (tracing the decline of the Coventry auto industry from 1980 to 2010).

Coventry Connections

From Coventry by Train to: Warwick (2/hour, 30-60 minutes, change in Leamington Spa), **Stratford-upon-Avon** (at least hourly, 1.75 hours, change in Leamington Spa or Birmingham), **Oxford** (hourly, 50 minutes), **London**'s Euston Station (6/hour, 1-2 hours), **Telford Central** (near Ironbridge Gorge; 2/hour, 1.5 hours, change in Birmingham). Train info: Tel. 0845-748-4950, www.nationalrail.co.uk.

IRONBRIDGE GORGE

The Industrial Revolution was born in the Severn River Valley. In its glory days, this valley (blessed with abundant deposits of iron ore and coal, and a river for transport) gave the world its first iron wheels, steam-powered locomotive, and cast-iron bridge (begun in 1779). The museums in Ironbridge Gorge, which capture the flavor of the Victorian Age, take you back into the days when Britain was racing into the modern era, and pulling the rest of the West with her.

Near the end of the 20th century, the valley went through a second transformation: Photos taken just 30 years ago show an industrial wasteland. Today the Severn River Valley is lush and lined with walks and parkland. Even its bricks, while still smoke-stained, seem warmer and more inviting.

Planning Your Time

Without a car, Ironbridge Gorge isn't worth the headache. Drivers can slip it in between the Cotswolds/Stratford/Warwick and points north (such as the Lake District or North Wales). Speed demons zip in for a midday tour of the Blists Hill Victorian Town, look at the famous Iron Bridge and quaint Industrial Age town that sprawls around it, and head out. For an overnight visit, arrive in the early evening to browse the town, see the bridge, and walk along the river. Spend the morning touring the Blists Hill Victorian Town, have lunch there, and head to your next destination.

With more time—say, a full month in Britain—I'd spend two nights and a leisurely day: 9:30-Iron Bridge and the town; 10:30-Museum of the Gorge; 11:30-Coalbrookdale Museum of

Iron; 14:30-Blists Hill Victorian Town; then dinner at the recommended Golden Ball Inn.

Orientation to Ironbridge Gorge

The town is just a few blocks gathered around the Iron Bridge, which spans the peaceful, tree-lined Severn River. While the smoke-belching bustle is long gone, knowing that this wooded, sleepy river valley was the "Silicon Valley" of the 19th century makes wandering its brick streets almost a pilgrimage. The actual museum sites are scattered over three miles. The modern cooling towers (for coal, not nuclear energy) that loom ominously over these red-brick remnants seem strangely appropriate.

Tourist Information

The TI is in the Museum of the Gorge, just west of the town center. It has lots of booklets for sale, including pamphlets describing nearby walks (daily 10:00-17:00, tel. 01952/433-424, www.ironbridge.org.uk or www.ironbridgeguide.info).

Getting Around Ironbridge Gorge

By Bus: Gorge Connect buses link the various museums, running every 30 minutes on weekends and Bank Holidays from Easter through October—and every day in late July and August (£1.50/ride, £2 day ticket, free with Passport Ticket—described on page 626; runs 9:30-17:00, no buses Nov-Easter; see schedule at www.telford.gov.uk—search site for "Gorge Connect"; tel. 01952/200-005).

If you're waiting for the Gorge Connect bus on the main road by the bridge, or at a stop for one of the less-popular museums, make sure the driver sees you or the bus may not stop. For connections from the Telford train or bus stations to the sights, see the end of this chapter.

Bus #88, operated by Arriva, connects the Museum of Iron (stop: Coalbrookdale School Road) and the TI in Ironbridge, but it runs infrequently (roughly 1/hour).

By Car: Routes to the attractions are well-signed, so driving should be a snap (museum parking described later).

By Taxi: Taxis will pick up at the museums, making this a good option if you don't have a car and the bus is not convenient. Call Central Taxis at tel. 01952/501-050.

By Bike: An eight-mile, relatively flat, circular bike path connects all of the museums except the Broseley Pipeworks. You can rent a bike from **The Bicycle Hub,** five miles north of Ironbridge in Telford (£15/day, helmet-£1, lock-£1; Mon-Sat 9:00-18:00, closed Sun; smart to book ahead, especially in nice weather—£25 refundable booking fee; international travelers must leave passport; within the Telford Town Park Visitor Centre—follow Hinkshay Road to Dark Lane, free parking at the Wonderland kiddie park, then 3-minute walk; tel. 01952/883-249; www.thebicyclehub.co.uk). If you're tempted to test a tandem, try their sister shop, **Bicycles by Design.** It's next to the Jackfield Tile Museum, about a mile from the bridge (£40/day; Mon-Fri 10:00-17:00, Sat 9:00-17:00, closed Sun; must leave passport, Church Road, tel. 01952/459-900, www. bicycles-by-design.co.uk).

Sights in Ironbridge Gorge

▲▲Iron Bridge

While England was at war with her American colonies, this first cast-iron bridge was built in 1779 to show off a wonderful new

building material. Lacking experience with cast iron, the builders erred on the side of sturdiness and constructed it as if it were made out of wood. Notice that the original construction used traditional timber-jointing techniques rather than rivets. (Any rivets are from later repairs.) The valley's centerpiece is free, open all the time, and thought-provoking. Walk across the bridge to the tollhouse. Inside, read the fee schedule and notice the subtle slam against royalty. (England was not immune to the revolutionary sentiment brewing in the colonies at this time.) Pedestrians paid half a penny to cross; poor people crossed cheaper by coracle—a crude tub-like wood-and-canvas shuttle ferry. Cross back to the town and enjoy a pleasant walk downstream along the towpath. Where horses once dragged boats laden with Industrial Age cargo, locals now walk their dogs.

Ironbridge Gorge Museums

Ten museums located within a few miles of each other focus on the Iron Bridge and all that it represents. Not all the sights are worth your time. The Blists Hill Victorian Town is by far the best. The Museum of the Gorge attempts to give a historical overview, but the displays are humble—its most interesting feature is the 12-minute video. The Coalbrookdale Museum of Iron tells the story of iron—interesting to metalheads. Enginuity is just for kids. And the original Abraham Darby Furnace (free to view, located across from the Museum of Iron) is a shrine to 18th-century technology. Before visiting any of these places, it helps to see the introductory movie at the Museum of the Gorge, to put everything into context.

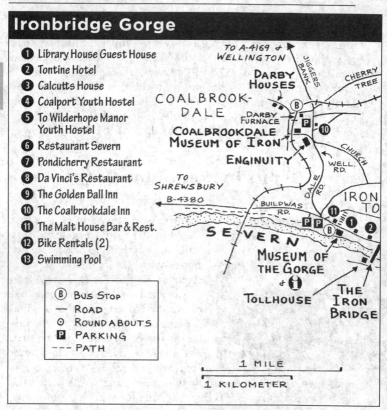

Ironbridge Gorge

1. Library House Guest House
2. Tontine Hotel
3. Calcutts House
4. Coalport Youth Hostel
5. To Wilderhope Manor Youth Hostel
6. Restaurant Severn
7. Pondicherry Restaurant
8. Da Vinci's Restaurant
9. The Golden Ball Inn
10. The Coalbrookdale Inn
11. The Malt House Bar & Rest.
12. Bike Rentals (2)
13. Swimming Pool

- Ⓑ BUS STOP
- — ROAD
- ⊙ ROUNDABOUTS
- Ⓟ PARKING
- --- PATH

1 MILE

1 KILOMETER

Cost: This group of widely scattered sights has varied admission charges (most sights £4-9; Blists Hill is £16); the £24 **Passport Ticket** (families-£65) covers admission to all of them and the Gorge Connect bus. If you're visiting the area's top three sights—Blists Hill Victorian Town, the Museum of the Gorge, and the Coalbrookdale Museum of Iron—you'll save about £4 with the Passport Ticket.

Hours: Unless otherwise noted, the sights share the same opening hours: daily 10:00-17:00.

Parking: To see the most significant sights by car, you'll park three times: once in town (either in the pay-and-display lot just over the bridge or at the Museum of the Gorge—the Iron Bridge and Gorge Museum are connected by an easy, flat walk); once at the Blists Hill parking lot; and once outside of the Coalbrookdale Museum of Iron (Enginuity is across the lot, and the Darby Houses are a three-minute uphill hike away). While you'll pay separately to park at the Museum of the Gorge, a single ticket is good for both pay-and-display lots at the Coalbrookdale Museum and Blists Hill.

Information: Tel. 01952/433-424, www.ironbridge.org.uk.

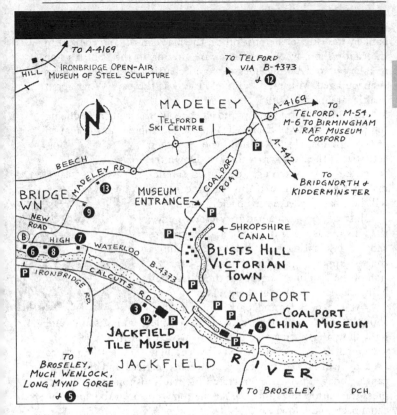

Museum of the Gorge

Orient yourself to the valley here in the Old Severn Warehouse. The 12-minute introductory movie (on a continuous loop) lays the groundwork for what you'll see in the other museums. Check out the exhibit and the model of the gorge in its heyday. Farther upstream from the museum parking lot is the fine riverside Dale End Park, with picnic areas and a playground.

Cost: £4, 500 yards upstream from the bridge, parking-£1.50 (3-hour maximum).

▲▲Blists Hill Victorian Town

Save most of your time and energy for this wonderful town—an immersive, open-air folk museum. You'll wander through 50 acres of Victorian industry, factories, and a re-created community from the 1890s. Pick up the Blists Hill guidebook for a good step-by-step rundown.

Cost and Hours: £16, closes at 16:00 Nov-March.

Visiting Blists Hill: The map you're given when entering is very important—it shows which stops in the big park are staffed with lively docents in Victorian dress. Pop in to say hello to the banker, the lady in the post office, the blacksmith, and the girl in the candy shop. Maybe the boys are singing in the pub. It's fine to take photos. Asking questions and chatting with the villagers is encouraged. What's a shilling? How was the pay? What about health care in the 1800s?

Stop by the pharmacy and check out the squirm-inducing setup of the dentist's chair—it'll make you appreciate the marvel of modern dental care. Check the hands-on activities in the barn across the way. Down the street, kids like watching a costumed candle-maker at work, as he explains the process and tells how candles were used back in the day.

Just as it would've had in Victorian days, the village has a working pub, a greengrocer's shop, a fascinating squatter's cottage, and a snorty, slippery pigsty. Don't miss the explanation of the "winding engine" at the Blists Hill Mine (demos throughout the day).

At the back of the park, you can hop aboard a train and enter a clay mine, complete with a sound and light show illustrating the dangers of working in this type of environment (£2, 10 minutes). Nearby, the Hay Inclined Plane was used to haul loaded tub boats between the river and the upper canal. Today, a passenger-operated lift hauls visitors instead (just press the button to call for it). At the top, you can walk along the canal back to the town.

Eating in Blists Hill: Several places serve lunch: a café near the entrance, the New Inn Pub for beer and pub snacks, a traditional fish-and-chips joint, and the cafeteria near the children's old-time rides.

▲Coalbrookdale Museum of Iron and Abraham Darby's Old Furnace

The Coalbrookdale neighborhood is the birthplace of modern technology—the place where locals like to claim that mass production was invented. The museum and furnace are located on either side of a parking lot.

Cost: Museum—£8.25, £9 combo-ticket includes the Darby Houses—listed later; furnace—free, volunteer tour guides sometimes lead free guided walks to the furnace (ask at museum info desk for times).

Museum: While old-school, this museum does a fine job of explaining the original iron-smelting process and how iron (which makes up 95 percent of all industrial metal) changed our world. But compared to the fun and frolicking Blists Hill village, this museum is sleepy. There's a café inside the museum.

Abraham Darby Furnace: Across from the museum, standing like a shrine to the Industrial Revolution, is Darby's blast furnace, sitting inside a big glass pyramid and surrounded by evocative Industrial Age ruins (info sheets on the furnace available at museum). It was here that, in 1709, Darby first smelted iron, using coke as fuel. To me, "coke" is a drink, and "smelt" is the past tense of smell...but around here, these words recall the event that kicked off the modern Industrial Age.

All the ingredients of the recipe for big industry were here in abundance—iron ore, top-grade coal, and water for power and shipping. Wander around Abraham Darby's furnace. Before this furnace was built, iron ore was laboriously melted by charcoal. With huge waterwheel-powered bellows, Darby burned top-grade coal at super-hot temperatures (burning off the impurities to make "coke"). Local iron ore was dumped into the furnace and melted. Impurities floated to the top, while the pure iron sank to the bottom of a clay tub in the bottom of the furnace. Twice a day, the plugs were knocked off, allowing the "slag" to drain away on the top and the molten iron to drain out on the bottom. The low-grade slag was used locally on walls and paths. The high-grade iron trickled into molds formed in the sand below the furnace. It cooled into pig iron (named because the molds look like piglets suckling their mother). The pig-iron "planks" were broken off by sledgehammers and shipped away. The Severn River became one of Europe's busiest, shipping pig iron to distant foundries, where it was melted again and made into cast iron (for projects such as the Iron Bridge), or to forges, where it was worked like toffee into wrought iron.

Enginuity

Enginuity is a hands-on funfest for kids. Riffing on Ironbridge's engineering roots, this converted 1709 foundry is full of entertaining-to-kids water contraptions, pumps, magnets, and laser games. Build a dam, try your hand at earthquake-proof construction, navigate a water maze, operate a remote-controlled robot, or power a turbine with your own steam.

Cost: £8.50, across the parking lot from the Coalbrookdale Museum of Iron.

Darby Houses

The Darby family, Quakers who were the area's richest residents by far, lived in these two homes located just above the Coalbrookdale Museum.

The 18th-century Darby mansion, **Rosehill House,** features a collection of fine china, furniture, and trinkets from various family members. It's decorated in the way the family home would have been in 1850. If the gilt-framed mirrors and fancy china seem a little ostentatious for the normally wealth-shunning Quakers, keep in mind that these folks were rich beyond reason, and—as docents will assure you—considering their vast wealth, this was relatively modest.

Skip the adjacent **Dale House.** Dating from the 1780s, it's older than Rosehill, but almost completely devoid of interior furniture, and its exhibits are rarely open.

Cost and Hours: £5, £9 combo-ticket includes Coalbrookdale Museum of Iron, closed Nov-March for lack of light.

Coalport China Museum, Jackfield Tile Museum, and Broseley Pipeworks

Housed in their original factories, these showcase the region's porcelain, decorated tiles, and clay tobacco pipes. These industries were developed to pick up the slack when the iron industry shifted away from the Severn Valley in the 1850s. Each museum features finely decorated pieces, and the china and tile museums offer low-energy workshops.

Cost and Hours: £5-8.25 each; Broseley Pipeworks open afternoons only late spring through summer (mid-May-mid-Sept 13:00-17:00, closed mid-Sept-mid-May).

Near Ironbridge

Ironbridge Open-Air Museum of Steel Sculpture

This park is a striking tribute to the region's industrial heritage. Stroll the 10-acre grounds and spot works by Roy Kitchin and other sculptors stashed in the forest and perched in rolling grasslands.

Cost and Hours: £3, March-Nov Tue-Sun 10:00-17:00, closed Mon except Bank Holidays, closed Dec-Feb, free parking, (2 miles from Ironbridge, Moss House, Cherry Tree Hill, Coalbrookdale, Telford, tel. 01952/433-152).

Skiing and Swimming

There's a small, brush-covered **ski and snowboarding slope** with two Poma lifts at Telford Snowboard and Ski Centre in Madeley, two miles from Ironbridge Gorge; you'll see signs for it as you drive into Ironbridge Gorge (£13/hour including gear, less for kids, open practice times vary by day—schedule posted online, tel. 01952/382-688, www.telford.gov.uk/skicentre). A public **swimming pool** is in Madeley (5-minute drive from town on Ironbridge Road, Abraham Darby Sports and Leisure Centre, tel. 01952/382-770).

Royal Air Force (RAF) Museum Cosford

This Red Baron magnet displays more than 80 aircraft, from warplanes to rockets. Get the background on ejection seats and a primer on the principles of propulsion.

Cost and Hours: Free, daily March-Oct 10:00-18:00, Nov-Feb 10:00-17:00, last entry one hour before closing, parking-£2.50/3 hours, Shifnal, Shropshire, on the A-41 near junction with the M-54, tel. 01902/376-200, www.rafmuseum.org.uk/cosford.

More Sights

If you're looking for reasons to linger in Ironbridge Gorge, these sights are all within a short drive: the medieval town of Shrewsbury, the abbey village of Much Wenlock, the scenic Long Mynd gorge at Church Stretton, the castle at Ludlow, and the steam railway at the river town of Bridgnorth. Shoppers like Chester (en route to points north).

Sleeping in Ironbridge Gorge

$$$ Library House Guesthouse is *Better Homes and Gardens*-elegant. Located in the town center, a half-block downhill from the bridge, it's a classy, friendly gem that actually used to be the village library. Each of its four rooms is a delight. The Chaucer Room, which includes a small garden, is the smallest and least expensive. Lizzie Steel offers a complimentary drink upon arrival (small Db-£85, larger Db-£95, twin Db-£105, take £10 off these prices for Sb, DVD library, free Wi-Fi, free parking just up the road, 11 Severn Bank, Ironbridge Gorge, tel. 01952/432-299, www.libraryhouse.com, info@libraryhouse.com). Lizzie may be able to pick you up from the Telford train station if you request it in advance.

$$ Tontine Hotel is the town's big, 12-room, musty, Industrial Age hotel. Check out the historic photos in the bar (S-£30, Sb-£45, D-£46, Db-£62, Tb-£70, Qb-£80, if booking in advance ask about discount with this book, restaurant, The Square, tel. 01952/432-127, www.tontine-hotel.com, tontinehotel@tiscali.co.uk).

Outside of Town

$$$ Calcutts House rents seven rooms in their 18th-century ironmaster's home and adjacent coach house. Rooms in the main house are elegant, while the coach-house rooms are bright, modern, and less expensive. Their inviting garden is a plus. Ask the owners, James and Sarah Pittam, how the rooms were named (Db-£55-95, price depends on room size, free Wi-Fi, Calcutts Road, tel. 01952/882-631, www.calcuttshouse.co.uk, info@calcuttshouse.

Sleep Code

(£1 = about $1.60, country code: 44, area code: 01952)
S = Single, **D** = Double/Twin, **T** = Triple, **Q** = Quad, **b** = bathroom, **s** = shower only. Unless otherwise noted, credit cards are accepted and breakfast is included.

To help you sort easily through these listings, I've divided the accommodations into three categories based on the price for a standard double room with bath during high season:

$$$ Higher Priced—Most rooms £65 or more.
 $$ Moderately Priced—Most rooms between £45-65.
  $ Lower Priced—Most rooms £45 or less.

Prices can change without notice; verify the hotel's current rates online or by email. For the best prices, always book direct.

co.uk). From Calcutts House, it's a delightful 15-minute stroll down a former train track into town.

$ Coalport Youth Hostel, plush for a hostel, fills an old factory at the China Museum in Coalport (£13-22 bunks in mostly 4-bed dorms, bunk-bed Db-£36-48, £3 less for members, includes sheets, reception open 7:30-23:00, no lockout, kitchen, restaurant, self-service laundry, High Street, tel. 01952/588-755 or 0845-371-9325, www.yha.org.uk, coalport@yha.org.uk). Don't confuse this hostel with another area hostel, Coalbrookdale, which is only available for groups.

$ Wilderhope Manor Youth Hostel, a beautifully remote Elizabethan manor house from 1586, is one of Europe's best hostels—and recently refurbished (it even has a bridal suite). On Wednesday and Sunday afternoons, tourists actually pay to see what hostelers get to sleep in (£18.50-25 bunks, under 18-£17-19, £3 less for members, single-sex dorms, family rooms available, reservations recommended, reception closed 10:00-15:00, restaurant open 18:00-20:30, laundry, kitchen, tel. 01694/771-363 or 0845-371-9149, www.yha.org.uk, wilderhope@yha.org.uk). It's in Longville-in-the-Dale, six miles from Much Wenlock, down the B-4371 toward Church Stretton.

Eating in Ironbridge Gorge

Restaurant Severn is the local favorite for a place with style that serves contemporary dishes. Choose from a £24-27 two-course fixed-price meal or a £26-29 three-course offering (evenings Wed-Sat, lunch only on Sun, closed Mon-Tue, across from the Iron

Bridge in the town center, reservations smart—especially on weekends, 33 High Street, tel. 01952/432-233, www.restaurantseven. co.uk).

Pondicherry, in a renovated former police station, serves delicious Indian curries and a few British dishes to keep the less adventurous happy. The mixed vegetarian sampler is popular even with meat-eaters. The basement holding cells are now little plush lounges—a great option if you'd like your pre-dinner drink "in prison" (£10-16 plates, daily 17:00-23:00, starts to get hopping after 19:00, 57 Waterloo Street, tel. 01952/433-055).

Da Vinci's serves good, though pricey, Italian food and has a dressy ambience (£15-20 main courses, Tue-Sat 19:00-22:00, closed Sun-Mon, 26 High Street, tel. 01952/432-250).

The Golden Ball Inn, a brewery back in the 18th century, is a popular pub known for its quality food and great atmosphere. You can dine with the friendly local crowd in the "bar," eat in back with the brewing gear in the more quiet—and formal—dining room, or munch on the lush garden patio. This place is serious about their beer, listing featured ales daily (£10-15 meals, food served Mon-Fri 12:00-14:30 & 18:00-21:00, Sat 12:00-21:00, Sun 12:00-19:45, reservations smart on weekends, 8-minute hike up Madeley Road from the town roundabout, 1 Newbridge Road, tel. 01952/432-179).

The Coalbrookdale Inn is filled with locals enjoying excellent ales and good food. This former "best pub in Britain" has a tradition of offering free samples from a lineup of featured beers. Ask which real ales are available (daily 12:00-24:00, food served only until 16:00) lively ladies' loo, across street from Coalbrookdale Museum of Iron, 1 mile from Ironbridge, 12 Wellington Road, tel. 01952/432-166).

The Malt House, located in an 18th-century beer house, is a very popular scene with the local twentysomething gang (£9-20 main courses, bar menu at their Rock Bar, food served daily 12:30-22:00, near Museum of the Gorge, 5-minute walk from center, The Wharfage, tel. 01952/433-712). For nighttime action, The Malt House is *the* vibrant spot in town, with live rock music and a fun crowd (generally Thu-Sat).

Ironbridge Gorge Connections

Ironbridge Gorge is five miles southwest of Telford, which has the nearest train station.

Getting between Telford and Ironbridge Gorge: To go by **bus** from Telford's train station to the center of Ironbridge Gorge, you'll first have to zip over to the Telford bus station—any northbound bus that stops at the train station will take you there (every

5-10 minutes; some buses drive by without stopping—don't be alarmed—just wait for one that stops). From the Telford bus station, take bus #77, #88, or #99 into Ironbridge (roughly 1/hour, usually at :30 or :45 after the hour, 30 minutes, none on Sun). The Telford bus station is attached to a large modern mall, making it an easy place to wait—ask at the info office when the next bus is leaving and from which door. The bus drops you off in Ironbridge at the TI or the bridge—tell the driver which stop you want (pay per leg or buy "Day Saver" pass—only cost-effective if you take the bus at least three times). Buses are run by Arriva (www.arrivabus.co.uk), but you can also call Traveline for departure times and other information (tel. 0871-200-2233, www.traveline.org.uk).

If the Gorge Connect bus is running (generally April-Oct on weekends and Bank Holidays, plus some weeks in summer; see page 624) you can take bus #44 (2-5/hour) direct from the Telford train station to High Street in the town of Madeley. This is where the Gorge Connect bus originates and ends. Hop on it to ride to one of the museums, the TI, or the bridge.

A **taxi** from Telford train station to Ironbridge costs about £10.

By Train from Telford to: Birmingham (2/hour, 30-50 minutes), **Stratford-upon-Avon** (roughly hourly, 2.5 hours, 1-2 changes), **Moreton-in-Marsh** (hourly, 2.5-3 hours, 2 transfers), **Conwy** in North Wales (10/day, 2.5-3 hours, some change in Chester or Shrewsbury), **Blackpool** (hourly, 2.5 hours, 2 changes), **Keswick/Lake District** (hourly, 4 hours total; 3 hours to Penrith with 1-2 changes, then catch a bus to Keswick—see page 716), **Edinburgh** (hourly, 4-5 hours, 1-2 changes). **Train info:** Tel. 0845-748-4950, www.nationalrail.co.uk.

Route Tips for Drivers

Driving in from the Cotswolds and Stratford, take the M-40 to Birmingham, then the M-6 (direction northwest) through Birmingham. Be aware that traffic northbound through Birmingham is miserable from 14:00 to 20:00, especially on Fridays. Take one of two M-6 options: free with traffic through the city center; or the M-6 Toll, which, for around £5.50, skirts you north of the center with nearly no traffic—a very good bet during rush hour.

After Birmingham, follow signs to *Telford* via the M-54 (if on toll road, it'll be via the A-5). Leave the M-54 at the Telford/Ironbridge exit (Junction 4). Follow the brown *Ironbridge* signs through several roundabouts to Ironbridge Gorge. (Note: On maps, Ironbridge Gorge is often referred to as "Iron Bridge" or "Iron-Bridge.")

LIVERPOOL

Wedged between serene North Wales and the even-more-serene Lake District, Liverpool provides an opportunity to sample the "real" England. It's the best look at urban England outside of London.

Beatles fans flock to Liverpool to learn about the Fab Four's early days, but the city has much more to offer—most notably, a wealth of free and good museums, a pair of striking cathedrals, a dramatic skyline mingling old red-brick maritime buildings and glassy new skyscrapers, and—most of all—the charm of the Liverpudlians.

Sitting at the mouth of the River Mersey in the metropolitan county of Merseyside, Liverpool has long been a major shipping center. Its port played a key role in several centuries of world history—as a point in the "triangular trade" of African slaves, a gateway for millions of New World-bound European emigrants, and a staging ground for the British Navy's Battle of the Atlantic against the Nazi's U-boat fleet. But Liverpool was devastated physically by WWII bombs, then economically by the advent of container shipping in the 1960s. Liverpudlians looked on helplessly as postwar recovery resources were steered elsewhere, the city's substantial wartime contributions seemingly ignored.

Despite the pride and attention garnered in the 1960s by a certain quartet of favorite sons, Liverpool continued to decline through the 1970s and '80s. The Toxteth Riots of 1981, sparked by the city's dizzyingly high unemployment, brought worldwide attention to Liverpool's troubles.

But finally, things started looking up. The city's status as the 2008 European Capital of Culture spurred major gentrification, EU funding, and a cultural renaissance. And, with some 50,000

On the Scouse

Nicknamed "Scousers" (after a traditional local stew, originally brought here by Norwegian immigrants), the people of Liverpool have a reputation for being relaxed, easygoing, and welcoming to visitors. The Scouse dialect comes with a distinctive lilt and quick wit (the latter likely a means of coping with long-term hardship)—think of the Beatles' familiar accents, and all their famously sarcastic off-the-cuff remarks, and you get the picture. Many Liverpudlians attribute these qualities to the Celtic influence here: Liverpool is a melting pot of not only English culture, but also loads of Irish and Welsh, as well as arrivals from all over Europe and beyond (Liverpool's diverse population includes many of African descent). Liverpudlians are also famous for their passion for football (i.e., soccer), and the Liverpool FC team—as locals will be quick to tell you—is one of England's best.

students attending three universities in town, Liverpool is also a youthful city, with a pub or nightclub on every corner. Anyone who still thinks of Liverpool as a depressed industrial center is behind the times.

Planning Your Time

Liverpool deserves at least a few hours, but those willing to give it a full day or more won't be disappointed.

For the quickest visit, focus your time at the Albert Dock, home to The Beatles Story, Merseyside Maritime Museum, Tate Gallery (for contemporary art lovers), and Museum of Liverpool. If time allows, consider a Beatles bus tour (departs from the Albert Dock).

A full day buys you time either to delve into the rest of the city (the rejuvenated urban core, the cathedrals, and the Walker Art Gallery near the train station), to binge on more Beatles sights (the boyhood homes of John and Paul), or a bit of both.

If you're here just for the Beatles, you can easily fill a day with Fab Four sights: Do the tour of John and Paul's homes in the morning, then return to the Albert Dock to visit The Beatles Story. Take an afternoon bus tour from the Albert Dock to the other Beatles sights in town, winding up at the Cavern Quarter to enjoy a Beatles cover band in the reconstructed Cavern Club. (Beatles bus tours zip past the John and Paul houses from the outside, but visiting the interiors takes more time and should be reserved well in advance.)

International Beatles Week, celebrated in late August, is a very busy time in Liverpool, with lots of live musical performances.

Orientation to Liverpool

With nearly a half-million people, Liverpool is Britain's fifth-biggest city. But for visitors, most points of interest are concentrated in the generally pedestrian-friendly downtown area. You can walk from one end of this zone to the other in about 25 minutes. Since interesting sights and colorful neighborhoods are scattered throughout this area, it's enjoyable to connect your sightseeing on foot. (Beatles sights, however, are spread far and wide—it's much easier to connect them with a tour.)

Tourist Information

Liverpool's TI is at the **Albert Dock** (daily April-Oct 10:00-17:30, Nov-March 10:00-17:00, just inland from The Beatles Story, tel. 0151/707-0729, www.visitliverpool.com). Pick up the free, good city map and the comprehensive *Liverpool Visitor Guide,* crammed with updated lists of museums, hotels, restaurants, shops, and more.

Arrival in Liverpool

By Train: Most trains use the main **Lime Street train station.** The station has eateries, shops, and baggage storage (per item:

£3/3 hours, £5/6 hours, £7/24 hours, Mon-Thu 7:00-21:00, Fri-Sun 7:00-23:00; most bus tours and private minivan/car tours are able to accommodate people with luggage). Note that regional trains also arrive at the much smaller, confusingly named **Central Station,** located just a few blocks south.

Getting to the Albert Dock: From Lime Street Station to the Albert Dock is about a 20-minute walk or a quick trip by bus, subway, or taxi.

To **walk,** exit straight out the front door. On your right, you'll see the giant, Neoclassical St. George's Hall; the Walker Art Gallery is just beyond it. To reach the Albert Dock, go straight ahead across the street, then head down the hill between St. George's

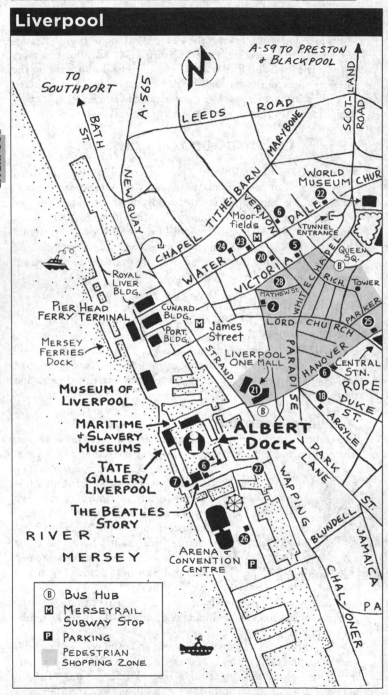

Liverpool

TO SOUTHPORT

A-59 TO PRESTON & BLACKPOOL

BATH ST.

A-565

NEW QUAY

LEEDS ROAD

MARYBONE

SCOT-LAND ROAD

TITHE-BARN

VERNON

DALE

WORLD MUSEUM   CHUR

22

CHAPEL

Moor-fields

6

Tunnel Entrance

WATER

23   M

24

20

VICTORIA

5

QUEEN SQ.

B

RICH.   Tower

Royal Liver Bldg.

28

MATHEW ST.

WHITECHAPEL

Pier Head Ferry Terminal

Cunard Bldg.

2

Port Bldg.

M   James Street

LORD

CHURCH

PARKER

25

Mersey Ferries Dock

STRAND

Liverpool One Mall

PARADISE

Hanover

6   Central Stn.

ROPE

21

B

18

DUKE ST.

ARGYLE

MUSEUM OF LIVERPOOL

MARITIME & SLAVERY MUSEUMS

i

ALBERT DOCK

PARK LANE

WAPPING

TATE GALLERY LIVERPOOL

7   6

27

THE BEATLES STORY

26

BLUNDELL

JAMAICA

PA

CHALONER

RIVER

MERSEY

Arena & Convention Centre

P

B   BUS HUB

M   MERSEYRAIL SUBWAY STOP

P   PARKING

PEDESTRIAN SHOPPING ZONE

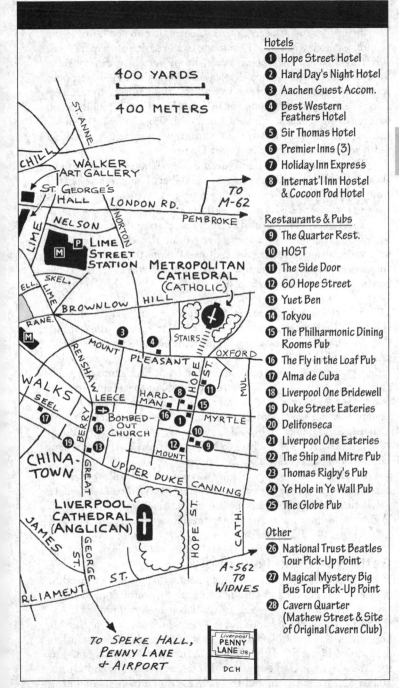

LIVERPOOL

Hotels
1. Hope Street Hotel
2. Hard Day's Night Hotel
3. Aachen Guest Accom.
4. Best Western Feathers Hotel
5. Sir Thomas Hotel
6. Premier Inns (3)
7. Holiday Inn Express
8. Internat'l Inn Hostel & Cocoon Pod Hotel

Restaurants & Pubs
9. The Quarter Rest.
10. HOST
11. The Side Door
12. 60 Hope Street
13. Yuet Ben
14. Tokyou
15. The Philharmonic Dining Rooms Pub
16. The Fly in the Loaf Pub
17. Alma de Cuba
18. Liverpool One Bridewell
19. Duke Street Eateries
20. Delifonseca
21. Liverpool One Eateries
22. The Ship and Mitre Pub
23. Thomas Rigby's Pub
24. Ye Hole in Ye Wall Pub
25. The Globe Pub

Other
26. National Trust Beatles Tour Pick-Up Point
27. Magical Mystery Big Bus Tour Pick-Up Point
28. Cavern Quarter (Mathew Street & Site of Original Cavern Club)

Hall (on your right) and the big blob-shaped mall (on your left). This brings you to Queen Square Centre, a hub for buses. (The round pavilion with the "i" symbol is a transit info center—see "Getting Around Liverpool," later.) From here, you can continue by bus (see below) or take a pleasant walk through Liverpool's spiffed-up central core: Head around the right side of the transit-info pavilion, then turn left onto Whitechapel Street, which soon becomes a slick pedestrian zone lined with shopping malls. Follow this all the way down to the waterfront, where you'll see the big red-brick warehouses of the Albert Dock.

To ride the **bus,** walk to Queen Square Centre (see directions above); for the most direct route to the Albert Dock, take bus #C5 from stall 9 (2/hour—see schedule posted next to stall, bus prices vary—from about £1.10/ride, £3.60 for all-day ticket).

You can also take a **subway** from Lime Street Station to James Street Station, then walk about five minutes to the Albert Dock (about £2, also covered by BritRail pass). Note that some regional trains may pass through James Street Station before reaching Lime Street Station; if so, you can hop out here rather than riding to Lime Street.

A **taxi** from Lime Street Station to the Albert Dock costs about £5. Taxis wait outside either of the side doors of the station.

By Plane: From Liverpool John Lennon Airport (code: LPL, tel. 0871-521-8484, www.liverpoolairport.com) is about eight miles southeast of downtown, along the river. Buses into town depart regularly from the bus stalls just outside the main terminal doors. Bus #500 to the city center is quickest, stopping at Queen Square Centre, Liverpool One bus hub, and Lime Street Station (2/hour, 35 minutes, about £3, covered by all-day ticket). Buses #80A, #82A, and #86A also go from the airport to the Liverpool One bus hub, but these take a bit longer.

By Car: Drivers approaching Liverpool first follow signs to *City Centre* and *Waterfront,* then brown signs to *Albert Dock,* where you'll find a huge pay parking lot at the dock. If coming from Wales, take the toll tunnel under the River Mersey (£1.60) and follow signs for *Albert Dock.*

Getting Around Liverpool

The city is walkable (and fun to explore), so you may not need to take advantage of the local bus network. But if your feet need a rest, several city center buses swing around Liverpool, stopping at major sights. Of these, the most useful is #C3, which loops from the Albert Dock, up the hill to Chinatown and the Liverpool Cathedral, down Hope Street (with many recommended restaurants) to the Metropolitan Cathedral, past Lime Street Station and Queen Square Centre bus hub, and through the downtown area and the

Beatles-focused Cavern Quarter (#C1 does a similar circle in the opposite direction). For more public-transit information, visit a Merseytravel center—there's one at the main bus hub on Queen Square Centre (near Lime Street Station) and another at the Liverpool One bus station (1 Canning Place), across the busy street from the Albert Dock (both open Mon-Sat 8:30-18:00, Sun 10:00-17:00, tel. 0871-200-2233, www.merseytravel.gov.uk).

Tours in Liverpool

Beatles Bus Tours

If you want to see as many Beatles-related sights as possible in a short time, these tours are the way to go. Each drives by the houses where the Fab Four grew up (exteriors only), places they performed, and spots made famous by the lyrics of their hits ("Penny Lane," "Strawberry Fields," the Eleanor Rigby graveyard, and so on). Even lukewarm fans will enjoy the commentary and seeing the shelter on the roundabout, the barber who shaves another customer, and the banker who never wears a mack in the pouring rain. (Very strange.)

Magical Mystery Big Bus Tour

Beatles fans enjoy loading onto this old, psychedelically painted bus for a spin past Liverpool's main Beatles landmarks, with a few photo ops off the bus. With an enthusiastic, live commentary and Beatles tunes cued to famous landmarks, it leaves people happy (£16, daily year-round at 14:00; also at 11:30 daily April-Oct, off-season weekends, and school holidays; often at other times as well—ask TI, call, or check online for schedule; 1.75 hours, buses depart from the Albert Dock near The Beatles Story and TI, tel. 0151/236-9091, www.cavernclub.org). As these tours often fill up, you'd be wise to book at least a day ahead by phone or through the TI (tel. 0151/707-0729).

Phil Hughes Minibus Beatles and Liverpool Tours

For something more extensive, fun, and intimate, consider a four-hour minibus Beatles tour from Phil Hughes. It's longer because it includes information on historic Liverpool, along with the Beatles stuff and a couple of *Titanic* and *Lusitania* sights. Phil organizes his tour to fit your schedule and will do his best to accommodate you (£20/person, private group tour with 5-person minimum, can coordinate tour to include pickup from end of National Trust tour of Lennon and McCartney homes or drop-off for late-day tour starting at Speke Hall, 8-seat minibus, tel. 0151/228-4565, mobile 07961-511-223, www.tourliverpool.co.uk, tourliverpool@hotmail.com).

Jackie Spencer Private Tours

To tailor a visit to your schedule and interests, Jackie Spencer is at your service...just say when and where you want to go (up to 5 people in her chauffeur-driven minivan—£150, 2.5 hours, longer tours available, will pick you up at hotel or train station, mobile 0799-076-1478, www.beatleguides.com, jackie@beatleguides.com).

Other Tours

City Bus Tour

Two different hop-on, hop-off bus tours cruise around town, offering a quick way to get an overview that links all the major sights. The options are **City Sightseeing** (£10, buy ticket from driver, valid 24 hours, recorded commentary, 14 stops, April-Oct Mon-Sat 10:00-17:00, 3/hour, less frequent Sun and Nov-March, tel. 0151/203-3920, www.citysightseeingliverpool.com) and **City Explorer** (£8, buy ticket from driver, valid 24 hours, live guides, 13 stops; April-Aug daily 10:00-16:30, 2/hour; Sept-March generally daily 10:00-16:00, until 15:00 in winter, 1-2/hour; tel. 0151/933-2324, www.cityexplorerliverpool.co.uk).

Ferry Cruise

Mersey Ferries offers narrated cruises that depart from the Pier Head ferry terminal, an easy five-minute walk north of the Albert Dock. The 50-minute cruise makes two brief stops on the other side of the river; you can hop off and catch the next boat back (£8 round-trip, ask about £4.80 All-Areas Saveaway ticket if you plan to get off, runs year-round, Mon-Fri 10:00-15:00, Sat-Sun 10:00-18:00, leaves Pier Head at top of hour, café, WCs onboard, tel. 0151/330-1000, www.merseyferries.co.uk).

Sights in Liverpool

On the Waterfront

In its day, Liverpool was England's greatest seaport, but trade declined after 1890, as the port wasn't deep enough for the big new ships. The advent of mega container ships in the 1960s put the final nail in the port's coffin, and by 1972 it was closed entirely.

But over the last couple of decades, this formerly derelict and dangerous area has been the focus of the city's rejuvenation efforts. Liverpool's waterfront is now a venue for some of the city's top attractions. Three zones interest tourists (from south to north): the Wapping Dock area, with Liverpool's futuristic new arena, conference center, and adjacent Ferris wheel; the red-brick Albert Dock complex, with some of the city's top museums and lively restaurants

Liverpool at a Glance

▲▲**Museum of Liverpool** Three floors of intriguing exhibits, historical artifacts, and fun interactive displays tracing the port city's history, culture, and contributions to the world. **Hours:** Daily 10:00-17:00. See page 649.

▲▲**Liverpool Cathedral** Huge Anglican house of worship—the largest cathedral in Great Britain—with cavernous interior and tower climb. **Hours:** Daily 8:00-18:00. See page 656.

▲**Lennon and McCartney Homes** The 1950s boyhood homes of Beatles John Lennon and Paul McCartney, with restored interiors viewable on a National Trust minibus tour. Advance reservations smart. **Hours:** Tours run four times a day Wed-Sun in summer. See page 658.

▲**The Beatles Story** Well-done if overpriced exhibit about the Fab Four, with a great audioguide narrated by John Lennon's sister, Julia Baird. **Hours:** Daily May-Sept 9:00-19:00, Oct-April 10:00-18:00. See page 644.

▲**Merseyside Maritime Museum and International Slavery Museum** Duo of thought-provoking museums exploring Liverpool's seafaring heritage and the city's role in the African slave trade. **Hours:** Daily 10:00-17:00. See page 645.

▲**Walker Art Gallery** Enjoyable, easy-to-appreciate collection of European paintings, sculptures, and decorative arts. **Hours:** Daily 10:00-17:00. See page 652.

▲**Metropolitan Cathedral of Christ the King** Striking, daringly modern Catholic cathedral with a story as fascinating as the building itself. **Hours:** Daily 8:00-18:00, until 17:00 on Sun in winter; after 17:15 (during Mass), you can't walk around. See page 654.

Tate Gallery Liverpool Prestigious modern art gallery with a rotating collection of 20th-century statues and paintings. **Hours:** Daily 10:00-18:00, except closes at 17:00 Nov-Easter. See page 649.

World Museum Family-oriented museum with five floors of kid-friendly exhibits, including dinosaurs and an aquarium. **Hours:** Daily 10:00-17:00. See page 653.

and nightlife; and Pier Head, with the Museum of Liverpool, ferries across the River Mersey, and buildings both old/stately and new/glassy. Below are descriptions of the main sights at the Albert Dock and Pier Head.

At the Albert Dock

Opened in 1852 by Prince Albert, and enclosing seven acres of water, the Albert Dock is surrounded by five-story brick warehouses. A half-dozen trendy eateries are lined up here, protected from the rain by arcades and padded by lots of shopping mall-type distractions. There's plenty of pay parking.

▲The Beatles Story

It's sad to think the Beatles are stuck in a museum. Still, this exhibit—while overpriced and a bit small—is well-done, the story's a fascinating one, and even an avid fan will pick up some new informa-

tion. The Beatles Story has two parts: the original, main exhibit at the south end of the Albert Dock; and a much smaller branch in the Pier Head ferry terminal, near the Museum of Liverpool just to the north. A free shuttle runs between the two locations every 30 minutes.

Cost and Hours: £13 covers both parts, tickets good for 48 hours, includes audioguide, daily May-Sept 9:00-19:00, Oct-April 10:00-18:00, last entry at 17:00 year-round, tel. 0151/709-1963, www.beatlesstory.com.

Visiting the Museum: Start in the **main exhibit** with a chronological stroll through the evolution of the Beatles, focusing on their Liverpool years: meeting as schoolboys, performing at (and helping decorate) the Casbah Coffee Club, making a name for themselves in Hamburg, meeting their manager Brian Epstein, and the advent of worldwide Beatlemania (with some help from Ed Sullivan). There are many actual artifacts (from George Harrison's first boyhood guitar to John Lennon's orange-tinted "Imagine" glasses), as well as large dioramas celebrating landmarks in Beatles lore (a reconstruction of the Cavern Club, a life-size re-creation of the *Sgt. Pepper* album cover, and a walk-through yellow submarine). The last rooms trace the members' solo careers, and the final few steps are reserved for reverence about John's peace work, including a replica of the white room he used while writing "Imagine." Rounding out the exhibits are a "Discovery Zone" for kids and (of course) the "Fab 4 Store," with an impressive pile of Beatles buyables.

The great audioguide, narrated by Julia Baird (John Lennon's little sister), captures the Beatles' charm and cheekiness in a way the stiff wax mannequins can't. You'll hear clips of interviews from the actual participants in the Beatles' story—their families, friends, and collaborators. Cynthia Lennon, John's first wife, still marvels at the manic power of Beatlemania.

While this is a fairly sanitized look at the Fab Four (LSD and Yoko-related conflicts are glossed over), the exhibits remind listeners of all that made the group earth-shattering—and even a little edgy—at the time. For example, performing before the Queen Mother, John Lennon famously quips: "Will the people in the cheaper seats clap your hands? And the rest of you, if you'll just rattle your jewelry."

The **Pier Head exhibit** is less interesting, but since it's included with the ticket, it's worth dropping into if you have the time. You'll find it upstairs in the Pier Head ferry terminal—a quick trip on the free shuttle bus (runs every 30 minutes) or about a 10-minute walk north (at the opposite end of the Albert Dock, then another 5-minute walk across the bridge and past the Museum of Liverpool). The main attraction here is a corny "Fab 4D Experience," an animated movie that strings together Beatles tunes into something resembling a plot while mainly offering an excuse to play around with 3-D effects and other surprises (such as the smell of strawberries when you hear "Strawberry Fields Forever"). The Hidden Gallery displays recently rediscovered early photos of the moptops by then-teenaged photographer Paul Berriff. Through fall of 2014, the museum also features the temporary exhibit Elvis and Us, about the relationship between the Beatles and their fellow 1960s music icon (£3 extra).

▲Merseyside Maritime Museum and International Slavery Museum

These museums tell the story of Liverpool, once the second city of the British Empire. The third floor covers slavery, while the first, second, and basement handle other maritime topics.

Cost and Hours: Free, donations accepted, daily 10:00-17:00, café, tel. 0151/478-4499, www.liverpoolmuseums.org.uk.

Background: Liverpool's port prospered in the 18th century as one corner of a commerce triangle with Africa and America. British shippers profited greatly through exploitation: About 1.5 million enslaved African people passed through Liverpool's docks (that's 10 percent of all African slaves). From Liverpool, the British exported manufactured goods to Africa in exchange for enslaved

LIVERPOOL

The Beatles in Liverpool

The most iconic rock-and-roll band of all time was made up of four Liverpudlians who spent their formative years amid the bombed-out shell of WWII-era Liverpool. The city has become a pilgrimage site for Beatlemaniacs, but even those with just a passing interest in the Fab Four are likely to find themselves humming their favorite tunes around town. Most Beatles sights in Liverpool relate to their early days, before the psychedelia, transcendental meditation, Yoko, and solo careers. Because these sights are so spread out, the easiest way to connect all of them in one go is by tour (see "Tours in Liverpool").

All four of the Beatles were born in Liverpool, and any tour of town glides by the **home** most identified with each one's childhood: John Lennon at "Mendips," Paul McCartney at 20 Forthlin Road, George Harrison at 12 Arnold Grove, and Ringo Starr (a.k.a. Richard Starkey) at 10 Admiral Grove.

Behind John's house at Mendips is a wooded area called **Strawberry Field** (he added the "s" for the song). This surrounds a Victorian mansion that was, at various times, a Salvation Army home and an orphanage. John enjoyed sneaking into the trees around the mansion to play. Today visitors pose in front of Strawberry Field's red gate (a replica of the original).

During the Beatles' formative years in the mid-1950s, skiffle music (American-inspired rockabilly/folk) swept through Liverpool. As a teenager, John formed a skiffle band called the Quarrymen. Paul met John for the first time when he saw the Quarrymen on July 6, 1957, at **St. Peter's Church** in Woolton. After the show, in the social hall across the street, Paul noted that John played only banjo chords (his mother had taught him to play on a banjo rather than a guitar—he didn't even know how to tune a guitar), and improvised many lyrics. John, two years older, realized he was a better improviser than a musician, so he was impressed when Paul borrowed a guitar, tuned it effortlessly, and played a note-perfect rendition of Eddie Cochran's "Twenty Flight Rock." Before long, Paul had joined the band.

In the St. Peter's Church graveyard is a headstone for a woman named **Eleanor Rigby.** But to this day, Paul swears that he never saw it, and made up the name for that famous song. Either he's lying, the name crept into his subconscious, or it's a truly remarkable coincidence.

The boys went to school on **Mount Street** in the center of Liverpool (near Hope Street, between the two cathedrals). John and his friend Stuart Sutcliffe attended the Liverpool College of Art, and Paul and his pal George Harrison went to Liverpool Institute High School for Boys. (When Paul introduced George to John as a possible new member for the band, John dismissed him as being too young...until he heard George play. He immediately became the lead guitarist.) Paul later bought his old school build-ing and turned it into the Liverpool Institute for Performing Arts (LIPA)—nicknamed the "Fame Academy" for the similar school on the American TV series.

As young men, the boys rode the bus together to school—waiting at a bus stop in the **Penny Lane** neighborhood. Later they wrote a nostalgic song about the things they would observe while waiting there: the shelter by the roundabout, the barbershop, and so on. (While they also sing about the fireman with the clean machine, the firehouse itself is not actually on Penny Lane, but around the corner.)

After a series of lineup shuffles, by 1960 the group had offi-cially become The Beatles: John Lennon, Paul McCartney, George Harrison, and...Pete Best and Stu Sutcliffe. The quintet gradually built a name for themselves in Liverpool's "Merseybeat" scene, performing at local clubs. While the famous **Cavern Club** is gone

(the one you see advertised is a re-construction, but does offer similar ambience and good cover bands), the original **Casbah Coffee Club**—which the group felt more attached to—still exists and is open for tours (3.5 miles northwest of downtown in Pete Best's former basement, prebook by calling the TI at tel. 0151/707-0729 or online at www.petebest.com).

The group went to Hamburg, Germany, to cut their teeth in the thriving music scene there. They wound up performing as the backing band for Tony Sheridan's single "My Bonny." When this caught on back in Liverpool, promoter Brian Epstein took note, and signed the act. His shrewd management would eventually propel the Beatles to superstardom.

Many different people could be considered the "Fifth Bea-tle." John's friend Stu, who performed with the group in Ham-burg, left to pursue his own artistic interests. Pete Best was the band's original drummer, but he was a loner and producers ques-tioned his musical chops, so he was replaced with Ringo Starr. (John later said, "Pete Best was a great drummer, but Ringo was a Beatle.") Brian Epstein, the manager who marketed the Beatles brilliantly before his untimely death, is another candidate. But—in terms of long-term musical influence—it's hard to ignore the case for George Martin, who produced all of the Beatles' albums ex-cept *Let It Be*, and was instrumental in both forging and develop-ing the Beatles sound.

By 1963, the Beatles were already world famous—but, as evi-denced by their songs about Penny Lane and Strawberry Fields, they never forgot their Merseyside home.

Africans; the slaves were then shipped to the Americas, where they were traded for raw material (cotton, sugar, and tobacco); and the goods were then brought back to Britain. While the merchants on all three sides made money, the big profit came home to England (which enjoyed substantial income from customs, duties, and a thriving smugglers' market). As Britain's economy boomed, so did Liverpool's.

After participation in the slave trade was outlawed in Britain in the early 1800s, Liverpool kept its port busy as a transfer point for emigrants. If your ancestors came from Scandinavia, Ukraine, or Ireland, they likely left Europe from this port. Between 1830 and 1930, nine million emigrants sailed from Liverpool to find their dreams in the New World.

Visiting the Museums: Begin by riding the elevator up to floor 3—we'll work our way back down.

On floor 3, three galleries make up the **International Slavery Museum.** First is a description of life in West Africa, which re-creates traditional domestic architecture and displays actual artifacts. Then comes a harrowing exhibit about enslavement and the Middle Passage. The tools of the enslavers—chains, muzzles, and a branding iron—and the intense film about the Middle Passage sea voyage to America drive home the horrifying experience of being abducted from your home and taken in wretched, life-threatening conditions thousands of miles away to toil for a wealthy stranger. Finally, the museum examines the legacy of slavery—both the persistence of racism in contemporary society and the substantial positive impact that people of African descent have had on European and American cultures. Walls of photos celebrate important people of African descent, and a music station lets you sample songs from a variety of African-influenced genres.

Continue down the stairs to the **Maritime Museum,** on floor 2. This celebrates Liverpool's shipbuilding heritage and displays actual ship components, model boats, and a gallery of nautical paintings.

Floor 1 shows footage and artifacts of three big Liverpool-related **shipwrecks:** the *Lusitania,* the *Empress of Ireland,* and the *Titanic* (all of which were destroyed—by a German U-boat, accidental collision with a coal freighter, and iceberg, respectively—in a tragically short span of time between 1912 and 1915). Also on this floor, an extensive exhibit traces the **Battle of the Atlantic** (during World War II, Nazi U-boats attacked merchant ships bringing supplies to Britain, in an attempt to cripple this island nation). You'll see how crew members lived aboard merchant ships. The **Hello Sailor!** exhibit explains how gay culture flourished at sea at a time where it was taboo in almost every other walk of British life.

Make your way to the basement, where exhibits describe the tremendous wave of **emigration** through Liverpool's port. And the **Seized!** exhibit looks at the legal and illegal movement of goods through that same port, including thought-provoking displays on customs, taxation, and smuggling.

Tate Gallery Liverpool

This prestigious gallery of modern art is near the Maritime Museum. It won't entertain you as well as its London sister, the Tate Modern, but if you're into modern art, any Tate's great. Its two airy floors, dedicated to the rotating collection of statues and paintings from the 20th century, are free; the top and ground floors are devoted to special exhibits. The Tate also has an inexpensive, recommended café.

Cost and Hours: Free, donations accepted, £7-13 for special exhibits, daily Easter-Oct 10:00-18:00, Nov-Easter 10:00-17:00, tel. 0151/702-7400, www.tate.org.uk/liverpool.

At Pier Head, North of the Albert Dock

A five-minute walk across the bridge north of the Albert Dock takes you to the Pier Head area, with the following sights.

▲▲Museum of Liverpool

This museum, which opened in 2011 in the blocky white building just across the bridge north of the Albert Dock, does a good job of fulfilling its goal to "capture Liverpool's vibrant character and demonstrate the city's unique contribution to the world." The museum is full of interesting items, fun interactive displays (great for kids), and fascinating facts that bring a whole new depth to your Liverpool experience.

Cost and Hours: Free, donations accepted, daily 10:00-17:00, guidebook-£1, café, Mann Island, Pier Head, tel. 0151/478-4545, www.liverpoolmuseums.org.uk/mol.

Visiting the Museum: First, stop by the information desk to check on the show times for the museum's various videos. If you have kids age six and under, you can also get a free timed-entry ticket for the hands-on Little Liverpool exhibit on the ground floor.

Ground Floor: On this level, **The Great Port** details the story of Liverpool's defining industry and how it developed through the Industrial Revolution. On display is an 1838 steam locomotive that was originally built for the Liverpool and Manchester Railway. The **Global City** exhibit focuses on how Liverpool's status as a major

British shipping center made it the gateway to a global empire and features a 20-minute video, *Power and the Glory,* about Liverpool's role within the British Empire.

First Floor: Don't miss the **Liverpool Overhead Railway** exhibit, which features the only surviving car from this 19th-century elevated railway. You can actually jump aboard and take a seat to watch 1897 movie footage shot from the train line. A huge interactive model shows the railway's route. Also on this floor is the **History Detectives** exhibit, which covers Liverpool's history and archaeology.

Second Floor: If you're short on time, spend most of it here. The **People's Republic** exhibit examines what it means to be a Liverpudlian (a.k.a. "Scouser") and covers everything from housing and health issues to military and religious topics. As industrialized Liverpool has long been a hotbed of the labor movement, exhibits here also detail the political side of the city, including child labor issues and women's suffrage.

One fascinating display is the re-creation of Liverpool's 19th-century court housing, which consisted of a series of tiny dwellings bunched around a narrow courtyard. With more than 60 people sharing two toilets, this was some of the most overcrowded and unsanitary housing in Britain at the time.

Next, the exhibit skips to religion and the centerpiece of this room: a 10-foot-tall model of Liverpool's Catholic cathedral that was never built. In 1932, Archbishop Richard Downey and architect Sir Edwin Lutyens commissioned this model to showcase their grandiose plans for constructing the world's second-largest cathedral. Their vision never came to fruition, and the Metropolitan Cathedral was built instead (for more on what happened, see page 654).

On the other side of the floor, the **Wondrous Place** exhibit celebrates the arts, cultural, and sporting side of Liverpool. An exhibit on the city's famous passion for soccer features memorabilia and the 17-minute video *Kicking and Screaming,* about the rivalry between the Everton and Liverpool football teams and the sometimes tragic history of the sport (such as when 96 fans were crushed to death at a Liverpool match).

Music is the other big focus here, with plenty of fun, interactive stops that include music quizzes, a karaoke booth, and listening stations featuring artists with ties to Liverpool (from Elvis Costello to Echo & the Bunnymen). And, of course, you'll see plenty of Beatles mania, including their famous suits, the original stage from St. Peter's Church (where John Lennon was performing the first time Paul McCartney laid eyes on him; located in the theater), and an eight-minute film on the band.

Finally, in the **Skylight Gallery,** look for Ben Johnson's painting *The Liverpool Cityscape, 2008*, a remarkable and fun-to-examine melding of old and new art styles. At first glance, it's a typical skyline painting, but Johnson used computer models to create perfect depictions of each building before he put brush to canvas. This method allows for a photorealistic, highly detailed, but completely sanitized portrait of a city. Notice there are no cars or people.

The Three Graces

Three towering buildings near the Museum of Liverpool, remnants of a time of great seafaring prosperity, are known collec-

tively as Liverpool's Three Graces: the double-clock-towered **Royal Liver Building,** with spires topped by the city's mythical mascot, the "Liver birds"; the relatively dull and boxy **Cunard Building;** and the domed **Port of Liverpool Building,** which strains to evoke memories of St. Paul's Cathedral in London. A 2002 plan to create a Fourth Grace—a metallic, glassy, and yellow blob called The Cloud—never panned out, and that site is now home to the Museum of Liverpool (described previously). While you can see the Three Graces from along the embankment—which is also lined with monuments to important Liverpudlians—the best views are from across the River Mersey (see page 666 for details on riding the ferry; note that the Pier Head ferry terminal also hosts some exhibits from The Beatles Story).

Downtown

Beatles Sights in the Cavern Quarter

The narrow, bar-lined Mathew Street, right in the heart of downtown, is ground zero for Beatles fans. The Beatles frequently performed in their early days together at the original Cavern Club, deep in a cellar along this street. While that's long gone, a mock-up of the historic nightspot (built with many of the original bricks) lives on a few doors down. Still billed as "the **Cavern Club,**" this is worth a visit to see the reconstructed cellar that's often filled by Beatles cover bands. While touristy, dropping by in the afternoon for a live Beatles tribute act in the Cavern Club somehow just feels right. You'll have Beatles songs stuck in your head all

day anyway, so you might as well see a wannabe John and Paul strumming and harmonizing a close approximation of the original (open daily 10:00-24:00, later Thu-Sat; live music daily from 14:00,

Sat from 12:00, cover charge Thu-Fri and Sun after 20:00 and Sat after 14:00, tel. 0151/236-9091, www.cavernclub.org).

Across the street and run by the same owners, the **Cavern Pub** lacks its sibling's troglodyte aura, but makes up for it with walls lined with old photos and memorabilia from the Beatles and other bands who've performed here. Like the Cavern Club, the pub features frequent performances by Beatles cover bands and other acts (no cover, Mon-Wed 11:00-24:00, later Thu-Sun, tel. 0151/236-4041).

Out front is the Cavern's **Wall of Fame,** with a too-cool-for-school bronze John Lennon leaning up against a wall of bricks engraved with the names of musical acts that have graced the Cavern stage.

At the corner is the recommended **Hard Day's Night Hotel,** decorated inside and out to honor the Fab Four. Notice the statues of John, Paul, George, and Ringo on the second-story corners, and the Beatles gift shop (one of many in town) on the ground floor.

Museums near the Train Station
Both of these museums are just a five-minute walk from the Lime Street train station.

▲Walker Art Gallery
Though it has few recognizable works, Liverpool's main art gallery offers an enjoyable walk through an easy-to-digest collection

of European (mostly British) paintings, sculpture, and decorative arts. There's no audioguide, but many of the works are well-explained by posted descriptions.

Cost and Hours: Free, donations accepted, daily 10:00-17:00, William Brown Street, tel. 0151/478-4199, www.liverpoolmuseums.org.uk.

Visiting the Museum: The ground floor has an information desk, café, children's area, small decorative arts collection, and sculpture gallery focusing on British Neoclassical works from the 19th century. The sculpture gallery has many works by John Gibson, a Welshman who grew up in Liverpool, and later studied under the Italian master Antonio Canova. Gibson's *Tinted Venus* (in the case in the middle) was considered scandalous to Victorian mores because of the nude sculpture's lifelike pinkish tint.

Upstairs is a concise 15-room painting gallery. For a general chronological spin, from the top of the stairs head straight back to find Room 1. Because of various special exhibits that rotate in and out, the following paintings may be located in other rooms or not on display.

Room 1 (actually two adjoining rooms) has a famous Nicholas Hilliard portrait of Queen Elizabeth I (nicknamed "The Pelican," for her brooch) and a well-known royal portrait of Henry VIII by Hans Holbein. Room 3 has bombastic Baroque works by Rubens and Murillo, Room 4 features a Rembrandt self-portrait, while Room 5 focuses on 18th-century English painting, including canvases by Gainsborough, Hogarth (find the painting of the great actor David Garrick in the role of Richard III), and lots of George Stubbs. Rooms 6-8 showcase a delightful array of Pre-Raphaelite works, among them Millias' evocative portrait of Isabella (Room 6). You'll find some Turners (a mushy landscape and a more sharp-focus Linlithgow Castle) in Room 7.

For a counterpoint to the lyrical, mystical Pre-Raphaelite works, step into Room 9, with very literal Victorian narrative paintings depicting slices of English life, such as Sadler's *Friday* (showing Dominican monks feasting on fish) and Yeams' *And When Did You Last See Your Father?* On this chilling canvas, showing a scene from the English Civil War, authorities are slyly interrogating a naive, cherubic boy while his family watches from behind, terrified that the child will reveal where his father is hiding.

Room 10 makes the transition to the 20th century and Impressionism, while modern British art dominates the rest of the gallery. In Room 11, Bernard Fleetwood-Walker's *Amity* shows a pair of chaste but (apparently) sexually charged teenagers relaxing in the grass.

World Museum

This catchall family museum offers five floors of kid-oriented exhibits. You'll see dinosaurs, an aquarium, artifacts from the ancient world, a planetarium and theater (get free tickets at the info desk in the lobby for these), and more.

Cost and Hours: Free, donations accepted, daily 10:00-17:00, William Brown Street, tel. 0151/478-4393, www.liverpoolmuseums.org.uk.

Cathedrals

Liverpool has not one but two notable cathedrals—one Anglican, the other Catholic. (As the Spinners song puts it, "If you want a cathedral, we've got one to spare.") Both are huge, architecturally significant, and well worth visiting. Near the eastern edge of downtown, they're connected by a 10-minute, half-mile walk on pleasant Hope Street, which is lined with theaters and good restaurants (see "Eating in Liverpool," later).

Liverpudlians enjoy pointing out that they have not only the world's only Catholic cathedral designed by a Protestant architect, but also the only Protestant one designed by a Catholic. With its large Irish-immigrant population, Liverpool suffered from tension between its Catholic and Protestant communities for much of its history. But during the city's darkest stretch of the depressed 1970s, the bishops of each church—Anglican Bishop David Sheppard and Catholic Archbishop Derek Worlock—came together and worked hard to reconcile the two communities for the betterment of Liverpool. (Liverpudlians nicknamed this dynamic duo "fish and chips" because they were "always together, and always in the newspaper.") It worked: Liverpool is a bold new cultural center, and relations between the two faiths remain healthy here. Join in this ecumenical spirit by visiting both of their main churches.

▲Metropolitan Cathedral of Christ the King (Catholic)

This daringly modern building, a cone topped with a crowned cylinder, seems almost out of place in its workaday Liverpool neighborhood. But the cathedral you see today bears no resemblance to Sir Edwin Lutyens' original 1930s plans for a stately Neo-Byzantine cathedral, which was to take 200 years to build and rival St. Peter's Basilica in Vatican City. (Lutyens was desperate to one-up the grandiose plans of Sir Giles Gilbert Scott, who was  building the Anglican Cathedral down the street.) The crypt for the ambitious church was excavated in the 1930s, but World War II (during which the crypt was used as an air-raid shelter) stalled progress for decades. In the 1960s, the plans were scaled back, and this smaller (but still impressive) house of worship was completed in 1967.

Cost and Hours: Cathedral—free entry but donations accepted, daily 8:00-18:00 (until 17:00 on Sun in winter)—but after 17:15 (during Mass), you won't be able to walk around; crypt—£3, Mon-Sat 10:00-16:00, closed Sun, last entry 45 minutes before closing, enter from inside church near organ; visitors center/café/gift shop—Mon-Sat 9:00-17:30, Sun 9:00-16:00; Mount Pleasant, tel. 0151/709-9222, www.liverpoolmetrocathedral.org.uk.

Visiting the Cathedral: On the stepped plaza in front of the church, you'll see the entrance to the cathedral's visitors center and café (on your right). You're standing on a big concrete slab that provides a roof to the humongous Lutyens Crypt, underfoot. The existing cathedral occupies only a small part of the would-be cathedral's footprint. Imagine what might have been—"the greatest building never built." Because of the cathedral's tent-like appearance and ties to the local Irish community, some Liverpudlians dubbed it "Paddy's Wigwam."

Climb up the stairs to the main doors, step inside, and let your eyes adjust to this magnificent, dimly lit space. Unlike a typical nave-plus-transept cross-shaped church, this cathedral has a round footprint, with seating for a congregation of 3,000 fully surrounding the white marble altar. Like a theater in the round, it was designed to involve worshippers in the service. Suspended above the altar is a stylized crown of thorns.

Spinning off from the round central sanctuary are 13 smaller chapels, many of them representing different stages of Jesus' life. Each chapel is different. Explore, tuning into the symbolic details in each one. Also keep an eye out for the 14 exquisite bronze Stations of the Cross by local artist Sean Rice (on the wall).

The massive **Lutyens Crypt** (named for the ambitious original architect)—the only part of the originally planned cathedral to be completed—is massive, with huge vaults and vast halls lined with six million bricks. The crypt contains a chapel—with windows by Lutyens—that's still used for Sunday Mass, the tombs of three archbishops, a treasury, and an exhibit about the cathedral's construction.

Hope Street

The street connecting the cathedrals is the main artery of Liverpool's "uptown," a lively and fun-to-explore district loaded with dining and entertainment options. In addition to well-respected theaters, this street is home to the Philharmonic and its namesake pub (see "Eating in Liverpool," later). At the intersection with Mount Street is a monument consisting of concrete suitcases; just down this street are the high schools that Paul, George, and John attended (for details, see "The Beatles in Liverpool" sidebar, earlier).

▲▲Liverpool Cathedral (Anglican)

The largest cathedral in Great Britain, this gigantic house of worship hovers at the south end of downtown. Tour its cavernous interior and consider scaling its tower.

Cost and Hours: Free, £3 suggested donation, daily 8:00-18:00; £5 ticket includes tower climb (2 elevators and 108 steps), audioguide, and 10-minute *Great Space* film; tower—Mon-Fri 10:00-16:30 (last ascent), Thu until sunset March-Oct, Sat 9:00-16:30, Sun 12:00-15:30 (changes possible depending on bell-ringing schedule); film—Mon-Sat 9:00-15:45 (last showing), Sun 12:00-13:30 (depending on services); St. James Mount, tel. 0151/709-6271, www.liverpoolcathedral.org.uk.

❍ Self-Guided Tour: Over the main door is a modern *Risen Christ* statue by Elisabeth Frink. Liverpudlians, not thrilled with the featureless statue and always quick with a joke, have dubbed it **"Frinkenstein."**

Stepping inside, pick up a floor plan at the information desk, go into the main hall, and take in the size of the place. When Liverpool was officially designated a "city" (seat of a bishop), they wanted to build a huge house of worship as a symbol of Liverpudlian pride. Built in bold Neo-Gothic style (like London's Parliament), it seems to trumpet with modern bombast the importance of this city on the Mersey. Begun in 1904, the cathedral's construction was interrupted by the tumultuous 20th century, and not completed until 1973.

Go to the big, circular tile in the very center of the cathedral, under the highest tower. This is a plaque for the building's archi-

tect, **Sir Giles Gilbert Scott** (1880-1960). While the church you're surrounded by may seem like his biggest legacy, he also designed an icon that's synonymous with Britain: the classic red telephone box. Flanking this aisle, notice the highly detailed sandstone carvings.

Take a counterclockwise spin around the church interior. Head up the right aisle until you find the **model** of the original plan for the cathedral (press the button to light it up). Scott was a very young architect, and received the commission with the agreement that he work closely under the wing of his more established mentor, George Bodley. These two architects' visions clashed, and Bodley usually won...until he died early in the planning stages, leaving Scott to pursue his own muse.

If Bodley had survived, the cathedral would probably look more like this model. As it was, only one corner of the complex (the Lady Chapel, which we're about to see) was completed before Giles changed plans to create the version you see today.

Nearby, the **"whispering arch"** spanning over the sarcophagus has remarkable acoustics, carrying voices from one end to the other. Try it.

Continuing down the church, notice the very colorful, modern painting of *The Good Samaritan* (by Adrian Wiszniewski, 1995),

 high above on the right. The naked crime victim (who has been stabbed in his side, like the Crucifixion wound of Jesus) has been ignored by the well-dressed yuppies in the foreground, but the female Samaritan is finally taking notice. The canvas is packed with symbolism (for example, the Swiss Army knife, in a pool of blood in the left foreground, is open in the 3 o'clock position—the time that Jesus was crucified). This contemporary work of art demonstrates that this is a new, living church. But the congregation has its limits. This painting used to hang closer to the front of the church, but now they've moved it here, out of sight.

Proceeding to the corner, you'll reach the entrance to the oldest part of the church (1910): the **Lady Chapel,** with stained-glass windows celebrating important women. (Sadly, the original windows were destroyed in World War II; these are replicas.)

Back up in the main part of the church, continue behind the main altar, to the **Education Centre,** with a fun, sped-up video showing all of the daily work it takes to make this cathedral run.

Circling around the far corner of the church, you'll pass the children's chapel and chapterhouse, and then pass under another modern Wiszniewski painting *(The House Built on Rock).* Across from that painting, go into the choir to get a good look at the Last Supper altarpiece above the **main altar.**

Continuing back up the aisle, you'll come to the **war chapel.** At its entrance is a book listing Liverpudlians lost in war. Battle flags fly high on the wall above.

You'll wind up at the gift shop, where you can buy a ticket to climb up to the top of the tower. The cathedral's café is up the stairs, above the gift shop.

▲Lennon and McCartney Homes

John and Paul's boyhood homes are now owned by the National Trust and have both been restored to how they looked during the lads' 1950s childhoods. While some Beatles bus tours stop here for photo ops, only the National Trust minibus tour gets you inside the homes. This isn't Graceland—you won't find an over-the-top rock-and-roll extravaganza here. If you don't know the difference between John and Paul, you'll likely be bored. But for die-hard Beatles fans who want to get a glimpse into the time and place that created these musical masterminds, the National Trust tour is worth ▲▲▲.

Because the houses are in residential neighborhoods—and still share walls with neighbors—the National Trust runs only four tours per day (Wed-Sun) in summer, limited to 15 or so Beatlemaniacs each.

Cost and Reservations: Tickets are £20. Because so few people are allowed on each tour, it's strongly advised to make a reservation ahead of time, especially in summer and on weekends or holidays. It's a good idea to book as soon as you know your Liverpool plans (or at least two weeks ahead)—though at times, you may be able to get tickets a couple of days in advance. (On the flip side, tours can be booked up months in advance, such as during Beatles week in August.) You can reserve online (www.nationaltrust.org.uk/beatles) or by calling 0151/427-7231. If you haven't reserved ahead, you can try to book a same-day tour (for the morning tours, call 0151/707-0729). The last tour is less likely to be full because it takes 30 minutes (by car or taxi) to reach the tour's starting point from central Liverpool—see below.

Tour Options: A minibus takes you to the homes of John and Paul, with about 45 minutes inside each. From late Feb-Nov, tours run from the Albert Dock Wed-Sun at 10:00, 11:00, and 14:15 (no tours Mon-Tue or Dec-late Feb). They depart from the Jurys Inn (south across the bridge from The Beatles Story, near the Ferris wheel) and follow a route that includes a quick pass by Penny Lane.

From mid-March-Oct, an additional tour leaves at 15:00 from Speke Hall, an out-of-the-way National Trust property located eight miles southeast of Liverpool. Drivers should allow 30 minutes from the city center to Speke Hall—follow the brown *Speke Hall* signs through dozens of roundabouts, heading in the general direction of the airport. If you don't have a car, hop in a taxi.

From either starting point, the entire visit takes about 2.5 hours.

Guides: Each home has a live-in caretaker who acts as your guide. These folks give an entertaining, insightful-to-fans 20- to 30-minute talk, and then leave you time (10-15 minutes) to wander through the house on your own. Ask lots of questions if their spiel peters out early—these docents are a wealth of information.

Mendips (John Lennon's Home)

Even though he sang about being a working-class hero, John grew up in the suburbs of Liverpool, surrounded by doctors, lawyers,

and—beyond the back fence—Strawberry Field.

This was the home of John's Aunt Mimi, who raised him in this house from the time he was five years old and once told him, "A guitar's all right, John, but you'll never earn a living by it." (John later bought Mimi a country cottage with those fateful words etched over the fireplace.) John moved out at age 23, but his first wife, Cynthia, bunked here for a while when John made his famous first trip to America. Yoko Ono bought the house in 2002 and gave it as a gift to the National Trust (generating controversy among the neighbors). The house's stewards make this place come to life.

On the surface, it's just a 1930s house carefully restored to how it would have been in the past. But delve deeper. It's been lovingly cared for—restored to be the tidy, well-kept place Mimi would have recognized (down to her apron hanging in the kitchen). It's a lucky quirk of fate that the house's interior remained mostly unchanged after the Lennons left: The bachelor who owned it decades after them didn't upgrade much, so even the light switches are true to the time.

If you're a John Lennon fan, it's fun to picture him as a young boy drawing and imagining at his dining room table. It also makes for an interesting comparison to Paul's humbler home, which is the second part of the tour.

20 Forthlin Road (Paul McCartney's Home)

In comparison to Aunt Mimi's house, the home where Paul grew up is simpler, much less "posh," and even a little ratty around the edges. Michael, Paul's brother, wanted it that way—their mother, Mary (famously mentioned in "Let It Be"), died when the boys were young, and it never had the tidiness of a woman's touch. It's been intentionally scuffed up around the edges to preserve the historical accuracy. Notice the differences—Paul has said that John's house was vastly different and more clearly middle class; at Mendips, there were books on the bookshelves.

More than a hundred Beatles songs were written in this house (including "I Saw Her Standing There") during days Paul and John spent skipping school. The photos from Michael, taken in this house, help make the scene of what's mostly a barren interior much more interesting.

Nightlife in Liverpool

Liverpool hops after hours, especially on weekends. The most happening zone is the area called **Ropewalks,** just east of the downtown shopping district and Albert Dock. Part of the protected historic area of Liverpool's docklands, the Ropewalks area has been redeveloped over the last few years and is now filled mostly with trendy pubs, nightclubs, and lounges—some of them rough around the edges, others posh and sleek. While this area is aimed primarily at the college-age crowd, it's still worth a stroll, and has a few eateries worth considering.

Pubs

The "Eating in Liverpool" section, later, lists several pubs good for either a drink or a meal. Liverpool also has a wide range of watering holes best for serious drinkers and beer aficionados. The food at these palaces, all in the city center, is an afterthought, but they're a great spot for a pint: **The Ship and Mitre,** overlooking an off-ramp at the edge of downtown, has perhaps Liverpool's best selection of beers—with 30-plus types on tap—as well as frequent beer festivals; it can get very crowded (133 Dale Street, tel. 0151/236-0859, see festival schedule at www.theshipandmitre.com). **Thomas Rigby's** has hard-used wooden floors that spill out into a rollicking garden courtyard (21 Dale Street). Around the corner and much more sedate, **Ye Hole in Ye Wall** brags that it's Liverpool's oldest pub, from 1726. Notice the men's room on the ground floor—the women's room, required by law to be added in the 1970s, is upstairs (just off Dale Street on Hackins Hey). A few blocks over, right in the heart of downtown and surrounded by modern mega-malls, is **The Globe**—a tight, cozy, local-feeling pub with five real ales and sloping floors (17 Cases Street).

Sleeping in Liverpool

Your best budget options in this thriving city are the boring, predictable, and central chain hotels—though I've listed a couple of more colorful options also worth considering. Many hotels, including the ones listed below, charge more on weekends (particularly Sat), especially when the Liverpool FC soccer team plays a home game. Rates shoot up even higher two weekends a year: during

Sleep Code

(£1 = about $1.60, country code: 44, area code: 0151)
S = Single, **D** = Double/Twin, **T** = Triple, **Q** = Quad, **b** = bathroom, **s** = shower only. Unless noted otherwise, credit cards are accepted.

To help you sort easily through these listings, I've divided the accommodations into three categories based on the price for a standard double room with bath:

$$$ **Higher Priced**—Most rooms £90 or more.
$$ **Moderately Priced**—Most rooms between £45-90.
$ **Lower Priced**—Most rooms £45 or less.

Prices can change without notice; verify the hotel's current rates online or by email. For the best prices, always book direct.

the Grand National horse race (long weekend in April) and during Beatles Week in late August—avoid these times if you can. Prices plummet on Sunday nights.

$$$ Hope Street Hotel is a class act that sets the bar for Liverpool's hotels. Located across from the Philharmonic on Hope Street (midway between the cathedrals, in an enticing dining neighborhood), this stylish and contemporary hotel has 89 luxurious rooms with lots of hardwood, exposed brick, and elegant little extras (standard Db-officially £190, but often £120-160 Fri-Sat and £87-107 Sun-Thu; fancier and pricier deluxe rooms and suites available, breakfast-£10 if you prebook, elevator, free Wi-Fi, parking-£10, 40 Hope Street, tel. 0151/709-3000, www.hopestreethotel.co.uk, sleep@hopestreethotel.co.uk).

$$$ Hard Day's Night Hotel is the ideal splurge for Beatles pilgrims. Located in a carefully restored old building smack in the heart of the Cavern Quarter, its decor is purely Beatles, from its public spaces (lobby, lounge, bar, restaurant) to its 110 rooms, each with a different original Beatles portrait by New York artist Shannon. What could have been a tacky travesty is instead tasteful, with a largely black-and-white color scheme and subtle nods to the Fab Four (standard Db-£90-150, deluxe Db-£20 more, prices can spike dramatically during peak times, especially busy for Sat weddings in their own wedding chapel/reception hall, breakfast-£10 if

you prebook, air-con, elevator, Internet-enabled TVs with music playlists, free Wi-Fi, Central Building, North John Street, tel. 0151/236-1964, www.harddaysnighthotel.com, enquiries@harddaysnighthotel.com).

$$ Aachen Guest Accommodations has 15 modern, straightforward rooms in an old Georgian townhouse on a pleasant street just uphill from the heart of downtown (Sb-£45-55, D-£49-75, Db-£59-85, Tb-£95-125, rates depend on demand—higher price is usually for weekends, includes breakfast, free Wi-Fi, 89-91 Mount Pleasant, tel. 0151/709-3477, www.aachenhotel.co.uk, enquiries@aachenhotel.co.uk).

$$ Best Western Feathers Hotel, nearly next door in a stately old Georgian building, has tight hallways and 82 small rooms with mod decor and amenities (Db-generally around £69-79 Sun-Thu, £99-109 Fri, £149-159 Sat, breakfast-£10 if you prebook, no elevator and six floors, guest computer, free Wi-Fi, parking-£10, 115-125 Mount Pleasant, tel. 0151/709-9655, www.feathers.uk.com, feathershotel@feathers.uk.com).

$$ Sir Thomas Hotel is a centrally located hotel that was once a bank. The lobby has been redone in trendy style, and the 39 rooms are comfortable. As windows are thin and it's a busy neighborhood, ask for a quieter room (Db-£69-85 Sun-Thu, £91-151 Fri-Sat, little difference between "standard" and "superior" rooms, one stately "luxury" room with heavy decor available, some rates include breakfast—otherwise £4, elevator, free Wi-Fi, 10-minute walk from station, 24 Sir Thomas Street at the corner of Victoria Street, tel. 0151/236-1366, www.sirthomashotel.co.uk, reservations@sirthomashotel.co.uk).

$$ Premier Inn, which has 186 pleasant, American-style rooms and a friendly staff, is inside the giant converted warehouses on the Albert Dock; many rooms have exposed brick from the original structure (Db-£68-140, averages £70-80 on weekdays, check website for specific rates and special deals, breakfast-£8.25, elevator, pay Wi-Fi, discounted parking in nearby garage-£7.50/day, next to The Beatles Story, tel. 0151/702-6320, www.premierinn.com). There's also a second, downtown **$$ Premier Inn** with 165 rooms. While it's farther from the Albert Dock sights, it's just a 10-minute walk from the Lime Street train station and handy to downtown (Db-£53-141, Vernon Street, just off Dale Street, tel. 0151/242-7650). A third location is on Hanover Street, near the Liverpool One mall. These places can fill up quickly on weekends.

$$ Holiday Inn Express has a branch at the Albert Dock, next door and nearly identical to the Premier Inn described above. Its 135 rooms are a smidge more basic—and cheaper—than the Premier Inn's; you might as well check both hotels' websites to see which has the better deal going (Db-generally around £70-100

Sun-Thu, £125-135 Fri-Sat, includes buffet breakfast, pay Wi-Fi, nearby parking-£7.50/day, beyond The Beatles Story at the Albert Dock, tel. 0844-875-7575, www.holidayinnexpressliverpool.com, enquiries@exliverpool.com).

$ International Inn Hostel, run by the daughter of the Beatles' first manager, rents 100 budget beds in a former Victorian warehouse (Db-£38-47, bed in 2- to 10-bed room-£17-22, includes sheets, all rooms have bathrooms, guest kitchen with free toast and tea/coffee available 24 hours, free Wi-Fi, laundry room, game room/TV lounge, video library, 24-hour reception, café next door has pay Internet access, 4 South Hunter Street, tel. 0151/709-8135, www.internationalinn.co.uk, info@internationalinn.co.uk).

In the hostel's basement is the **$$ Cocoon Pod Hotel,** offering 32 small, no-nonsense, modern rooms for people who have outgrown hosteling. As all the rooms are underground, there are no windows, which can make rooms a bit stuffy, though very quiet (except on weekends, when the hotel attracts some rowdy stag and hen parties). Choose either two twins or a king (Sb or Db-£45 Sun-Thu, £55 Fri-Sat; 1- and 3-bedroom apartments from £65; same location, amenities, and contact info as hostel; 2-night minimum on weekends; www.cocoonliverpool.co.uk). From the Lime Street Station, the hostel/Cocoon Pod are an easy 15-minute walk; if taking a taxi, tell them it's on South Hunter Street near Hardman Street.

Eating in Liverpool

Liverpool has an exciting and quickly evolving culinary scene; as a rollicking, youthful city, it's a magnet for creative chefs as well as upscale chain restaurants. I've arranged my listings by neighborhood. Consider my suggestions, but also browse the surrounding streets. This is a city where restaurant-finding is a joy rather than a chore.

On and near Hope Street

Hope Street, which connects the two cathedrals, is also home to several excellent restaurants. The Quarter, HOST, and 60 Hope Street—which cluster near the corner of Hope and Falkner streets—are owned by brothers.

The Quarter serves up Mediterranean food at rustic tables that sprawl through several connected houses. It's trendy but cozy. They also serve breakfast and have carryout coffee, cakes, pasta, and sandwiches in their attached deli (£4-7 starters, £7-10 pizzas and pastas, chalkboard specials, Mon-Fri 8:00-23:00, Sat 9:00-23:00, Sun 9:00-22:30, 7 Falkner Street, tel. 0151/707-1965).

HOST (short for "Hope Street") features Asian fusion dishes in a casual, colorful, modern atmosphere (£4-6 small plates, £10-13 big plates, Mon-Sat 11:00-23:00, Sun 11:00-22:00, 31 Hope Street, tel. 0151/708-5831).

The Side Door is a tight, upscale, and inviting little one-room bistro with a constantly changing menu of highly regarded modern English food. While this place is pricey, their "pre-theatre menu" is a good value (£17-19 two-course meals, £19-21 three-course meals, available before 18:30; open Mon-Sat 12:00-14:30 & 17:00-21:30, closed Sun, 29a Hope Street, tel. 0151/707-7888).

60 Hope Street has modern English cuisine made with "as locally sourced as possible" ingredients in an upscale atmosphere. While the prices are high (£8-9 starters, £19-30 main dishes), their fixed-price meals are a good deal (£20/two courses, £25/three courses, prices include half-carafe of wine on Mon-Thu; open Mon-Sat 12:00-14:30 & 17:00-22:30, Sun 12:00-20:00, reservations smart—especially on weekends, 60 Hope Street, tel. 0151/707-6060, www.60hopestreet.com).

Chinatown: A few blocks southwest of Hope Street is Liverpool's thriving Chinatown neighborhood, with the world's biggest

Chinese arch. Lots of enticing options dishing up Chinese grub line up along Berry Street in front of the arch and Cornwallis Street behind it. Among these, **Yuet Ben** is one of the most established (Tue-Sun 17:00-23:00, until 24:00 Fri-Sat, closed Mon, facing the arch at 1 Upper Duke Street, tel. 0151/709-5772). Or you can line up with the Liverpudlians at **Tokyou,** featuring tasty £5 noodle and rice dishes (Cantonese, Japanese, Malaysian, etc.), with service that's fast and furious (daily 12:30-23:00, 7 Berry Street, tel. 0151/445-1023).

Pubs near Hope Street

The Philharmonic Dining Rooms, kitty-corner from the actual Philharmonic, is actually a pub—but what a pub. This place wins the "atmosphere award" for its old-time elegance. The bar is a work of art, the marble urinals are downright genteel, and the three sitting areas on the ground floor (including the giant hall) are an enticing place to sip a pint. This is a better place to drink than to eat, as food is usually served in the less-atmospheric upstairs (Mon-

Fri evenings and all day Sat-Sun, £6-11 pub grub). John Lennon once said that his biggest regret about fame was "not being able to go to the Phil for a drink" (open for drinks daily 11:00-24:00, corner of Hope and Hardman streets, tel. 0151/707-2837).

The Fly in the Loaf has a classic pub exterior and interior, with efficient service, eight hand pulls for real ales, and good food (£3-4 sandwiches, £6-7 meals, open daily 12:00-23:00; food served Tue-Sat until 19:00, Sun until 17:00, no food on Mon; 13 Hardman Street, tel. 0151/708-0817).

Ropewalks

While primarily a nightlife zone (see "Nightlife in Liverpool," earlier), this gentrified area also has a smattering of unique restaurants—including one in a former church, and another in a former police station.

Alma de Cuba is housed in the former Polish Catholic Church of St. Peter's with a trendy bar (downstairs, in the nave and altar

area) and restaurant (upstairs, looking down into the nave). While the food (an eclectic international mix) is an afterthought, the "hedonists' church" atmosphere is nothing short of remarkable—at least, to those who don't find it all a bit sacrilegious (£3-7 starters, £10-18 main dishes; food served daily 12:00-22:00, Fri-Sat until 23:00, bar stays open later; live music Thu from 22:30, live DJ with flower-petal shower and samba dancers Fri-Sat from 23:00, gospel brunch with small gospel choir Sun 13:30-17:00; Seel Street, tel. 0151/702-7394).

Liverpool One Bridewell pub fills a circa-1850 police station with a lively pub atmosphere. Downstairs, past the bar, several jail cells have been converted into cozy seating areas, while another bar and dining area sprawl upstairs (£7-10 meals; open daily 12:00-23:00, until 24:00 Fri-Sat; food served Tue-Sat until 21:00, Sun-Mon until 18:00; 1 Campbell Square, Argyle Street, tel. 0151/709-7000).

On Duke Street: A few big, modern, popular, chain-feeling restaurants—Japanese, Mexican, Italian, and more—line up along Duke Street in the heart of the Ropewalks area (concentrated on the block between Kent Street and the Chinatown arch). While not high cuisine, these crowd-pleasers are close to the nightlife action.

Downtown

Delifonseca is a trendy delicatessen with two parts. In the cellar is the picnic-perfect deli counter, with prepared salads sold by weight, a wide range of meats and cheeses, and made-to-order £3 sandwiches. Upstairs is a casual bistro serving British, Mediterranean, and international cuisine (£7-10 sandwiches and salads, £10-13 chalkboard main dishes). While not cheap, the food here is high quality (both open Mon-Sat 8:00-21:00, closed Sun, 12 Stanley Street, tel. 0151/255-0808).

Liverpool One: This shopping center, right in the heart of town, is nirvana for British chain restaurants. The upper Leisure Terrace has a row of some popular chains—including **Café Rouge** (French), **Wagamama Noodle Bar, Gourmet Burger Company, Pizza Express,** and more—all with outdoor seating. If you want to dine on predictable mass-produced food, you'll have a wide selection here.

At the Albert Dock

The eateries at the Albert Dock aren't high cuisine, but they're handy to your sightseeing. A slew of trendy restaurants come alive with club energy at night, but are sedate and pleasant in the afternoon and early evening. For lunch near the sights, consider the café in the **Tate Gallery** (£3-4 sandwiches and soups, £6-9 main dishes, daily 10:00-17:30 except closes at 16:30 Nov-March).

Liverpool Connections

By Train

Note that many connections from Liverpool transfer at the Wigan North Western Station, which is on a major north-south train line.

From Liverpool by Train to: Blackpool (1/hour direct, 1.5 hours), **Keswick/Lake District** (train to Penrith—roughly hourly with change in Wigan and possibly elsewhere, 2.25 hours; then bus to Keswick), **York** (1/hour direct, 2.25 hours, more with transfer), **Edinburgh** (1-2/hour, 3.5-4.5 hours, most change in Wigan or Manchester), **Glasgow** (1/hour, 3.5-4.5 hours, change in Wigan and possibly elsewhere), **London**'s Euston Station (1/hour direct, 2 hours, more with changes), **Crewe** (2/hour, 45 minutes), **Chester** (4/hour, 45 minutes). Train info: tel. 0845-748-4950, www.nationalrail.co.uk.

By Ferry

By Ferry to Dublin, Republic of Ireland: P&O Irish Sea Ferries runs a car ferry only—no foot passengers (1-3/day, 8-hour trip, prices vary widely—roughly £150 for car and 2 passengers, overnight ferry includes berth and meals, 20-minute drive north of the city center at Liverpool Freeport—Gladstone dock, check in 1-2 hours before departure, tel. 0871-664-4777, www.poirishsea.com). Those without cars can take a ferry to Dublin via the Isle of Man (www.steam-packet.com), or ride the train to North Wales, and catch the Dublin ferry from Holyhead (www.stenaline.co.uk).

By Ferry to Belfast, Northern Ireland: Ferries sail from nearby Birkenhead roughly twice a day (8 hours, fares vary widely, tel. 0871-230-0330, www.stenaline.co.uk). Birkenhead's dock is a 15-minute walk from Hamilton Square Station on Merseyrail's Wirral Line.

Route Tips for Drivers
From Liverpool to Blackpool: Leaving Liverpool, drive north along the waterfront, following signs to the M-58 (Preston). Once on the M-58 (and not before), follow signs to the M-6, and then the M-55 into Blackpool.

LIVERPOOL

BLACKPOOL

Blackpool is Britain's tacky, laid-back underbelly. It's one of England's most-visited attractions, the private domain of its working class, a faded and sticky mix of Coney Island, Las Vegas, and Denny's. Some people love it...others hate it. But it is, without a doubt, a spectacle.

Blackpool grew up with the Industrial Revolution. In the mid-1800s, entire mill towns would close down and take a two-week break here. They came to drink in the fresh air (much needed after a hard year in the mills) and—literally—the seawater. (Back then they figured it was healthy.)

Blackpool's heyday is long past now, as more and more working people can afford cheap flights to sunny Spain. The resort has become popular for "stag" and "hen" (bachelor and bachelorette) parties—basically a cheap drunk weekend for the twentysomething crowd. Consequently, there are two Blackpools: the daytime Blackpool of kids riding roller coasters and grannies tucking into early-bird specials; and the drunken, debauched, late-night Blackpool of glass-dance-floor clubs and bars.

Blackpool is working to reinvent itself and draw more visitors. An overhaul of The Promenade wrapped up in 2011, and Merlin Entertainments (the deep-pocketed owner of Madame Tussauds, the London Eye, and Warwick Castle) has recently invested heavily here—buying and completely rehabbing Blackpool Tower, and opening a new Madame Tussauds just down the street. And yet the town remains an accessible and affordable fun zone for the Flo and Andy Capps of northern England. People come year after year. They stay for a week, and they love it.

Be warned: Some of you will get to Blackpool and wonder,

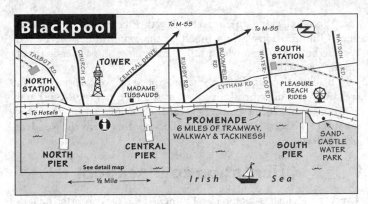

Blackpool

To M-55 · To M-55

TALBOT RD. · CHURCH ST. · **TOWER** · CENTRAL DRIVE · RUGBY RD. · BLOOMFIELD RD. · WATERLOO RD. · WATSON RD.

NORTH STATION · **SOUTH STATION**

MADAME TUSSAUDS · LYTHAM RD. · **PLEASURE BEACH RIDES**

← To Hotels

PROMENADE
6 MILES OF TRAMWAY, WALKWAY & TACKINESS!

NORTH PIER · **CENTRAL PIER** · **SOUTH PIER** · **SANDCASTLE WATER PARK**

See detail map · ½ Mile · *Irish Sea*

"Why did Rick send me *here*?" Most Americans don't even consider a stop in Blackpool. Many won't like it. It's an ears-pierced-while-you-wait, tipsy-toupee kind of place. Tacky, yes. Lowbrow, OK. More than a little run-down in parts, sure. If you're before or beyond kids, and not into kitsch and greasy spoons, skip it. But if you have kids, they'll enjoy Blackpool (hey, it's cheaper than Disneyland). And for those who are

into nightlife, this town delivers. If you believe (as I do) that an itinerary should feature as many different facets of a culture as possible, consider a stop here. Blackpool is as English as the Queen—and considerably more fun.

A million greedy doors try every trick to get you inside. Huge arcade halls advertise free toilets and broadcast bingo numbers into the streets; the wind machine under a wax Marilyn Monroe blows at a steady gale; and the smell of fries, tobacco, and sugar is everywhere. Spend the day "muckin' about" the beach promenade of fortune-tellers, fish-and-chips joints, amusement piers, warped mirrors, and Englanders wearing hats with built-in ponytails. Scream down roller coasters and eat "candy floss" until you're deliriously queasy.

Planning Your Time

Ideally, get to Blackpool around lunchtime for an afternoon and evening of making bubbles in this cultural mud puddle. A good overall plan is to ride the tram down to Pleasure Beach, and then walk back along the waterfront to the North Pier and Blackpool Tower, dipping into whatever fun zones appeal. To find a more pristine beach, just keep walking north.

The evening light here is great, with the sun setting over the sea. Walk out along the peaceful North Pier at twilight. Blackpool's Illuminations, when much of the waterfront is decorated with lights, draws crowds in fall, particularly on weekends (Sept through early Nov).

Blackpool is easy by car or train. Speed demons with a car can treat it as a midday break (it's just off the M-6, on the M-55) and continue north. If the weather's great and you love nature, the lakes are just two hours north. A visit to Blackpool sharpens the wonders of Windermere.

Orientation to Blackpool

Everything clusters along The Promenade, a tacky, glittering six-mile-long beachfront good-time strip mall punctuated by three fun-filled piers reaching out into the sea. The Pleasure Beach rides are near the South Pier. Jutting up near the North Pier is Blackpool's stubby Eiffel-type tower. The most interesting shops, eateries, and theaters are inland from the North Pier. For a break from glitz, walk north along The Promenade or the sandy beach—a residential neighborhood stretches for miles. When you've had enough, just hop on the tram or a bus for a quick ride back.

Tourist Information

The TI is in a building on The Promenade, across from Blackpool Tower (Mon-Sat 9:00-17:00, Sun 10:00-16:00; tel. 01253/478-222—answered during the day, recorded entertainment info after hours; www.visitblackpool.com). There you'll find a city map, brochures on the amusement centers, and a helpful staff. The free *Events Programme* lists local happenings; the TI can book shows for you for a £2.50 fee (no fee for Grand Theatre shows). The TI books rooms for no fee (but collects a 10 percent deposit, which hotels don't recoup).

Discount Tickets: The TI sells tickets to many of Blackpool's attractions—including Blackpool Tower and its various sights, Sandcastle Waterpark, and Madame Tussauds—often at a significant discount. It's worth visiting the TI first to see what kinds of prices you can score.

Combo-Tickets: The **Resort Pass** includes the Tower Eye, Madame Tussauds, and an unlimited ticket to Pleasure Beach (usually £30), and is good for seven days (£57.50, £52.50 if you buy in advance, tel. 01253/478-222, www.blackpoolresortpass.com). The **Big Ticket** gives you access to the Blackpool Tower Eye and circus, Madame Tussauds, and more for one high price (£50, £45 if you buy online, details at www.theblackpooltower.com).

Arrival in Blackpool

By Train: The main (north) train station is three blocks from the town center (no maps given, but one is posted). Exiting the station, turn right and look for the pedestrian underpass. Go left up the ramp, then make your first right and walk straight into town on Talbot Road, which ends at the North Pier and The Promenade (lots of construction; you may have to zigzag your way down).

The only **baggage storage** in Blackpool is about a 15-minute walk southwest of the train station, at the National Express bus office, in the big parking lot at the corner of New Bonny Street and Central Drive, behind the row of pay toilets (£1.50-2/day per item depending on size, Mon-Sat 7:30-17:00, closed Sun).

By Car: The motorway funnels you down Yeadon Way into a giant parking zone. If you're just here for the day, head for one of the huge pay garages. If you're spending the night, drive to the waterfront and head north. My top accommodations are north of the center, on The Promenade (easy parking). Leaving Blackpool to go anywhere, follow signs to *M-55*, which starts at Blackpool and zips you to the M-6 (for points north or south).

Helpful Hints

Markets: At the indoor **Abingdon Street Market,** vendors sell baked goods, fruit, bras, jewelry, eggs, and more (Mon-Sat 9:00-17:00, closed Sun). Eight miles north, the **Fleetwood Market** is huge, with two buildings full of produce, clothes, and crafts spilling out onto the street (Tue and Thu-Sat 9:00-16:30, closed Wed and Sun-Mon, www.fleetwoodmarket.co.uk; catch tram marked *Fleetwood*, 30 minutes, £2.50 one-way).

Tipping: The pubs of Blackpool have a unique tradition of "and (name an amount) your own, luv." Say that here, and your barmaid will add that amount to your bill and drop it into her tip jar. (Say it anywhere else...and they won't know what you mean.)

Internet Access: The public library, in the big domed building on Queen Street, lets visitors use its computers for up to one hour for free (Mon-Thu 9:30-19:00, Fri-Sat 9:30-17:00, closed Sun, can be busy so you may want to book a machine in advance, tel. 01253/478-080 or 01253/478-070).

Post Office: The main P.O. is in the basement of the WH Smith store, at 12-16 Bank Hey Street (Mon-Sat 9:00-17:30, closed Sun).

Car Rental: If you decide to tour the Lake District by car, you'll find plenty of rental agencies in Blackpool, such as **Avis** (closed Sat afternoon and Sun, at the airport—just south of the South Pier, tel. 0844-544-6029).

Getting Around Blackpool

By Public Transportation: Trams trundle up and down the waterfront, connecting all the sights. This electric tramway—the first in Europe—dates from 1885 (about £2/ride depending on length of trip, pay conductor; trams come every 12-20 minutes or so year-round 5:00-23:45, shorter hours on Sun). You can also purchase a day pass that covers both trams and buses (£4.50 if you buy it on board, £3.50 at the Blackpool Transport office described below or at various corner stores around town—ask at your hotel for the nearest location).

Many **buses** also run along The Promenade—make sure you're not standing at a tram stop if you're waiting for a bus (similar prices to tram, buy on board, covered by day pass described above). Buses that run south to St. Annes depart from Market Street, in front of the BHS store; buses going north toward Cleveleys leave from Clifton Street. For bus information, visit the Blackpool Transport office on Market Street (Mon-Sat 8:45-17:15, Sun 10:30-15:00, tel. 01253/473-001, www.blackpooltransport.com).

By Taxi: Cabs are easy to snare in Blackpool, and three to five people travel cheaper in a taxi than by tram. Hotels can get you a taxi by phone within a few minutes (no extra charge).

Sights in Blackpool

▲▲▲People-Watching

Blackpool's top sight is its people. You'll see England here as nowhere else. Grab someone's hand and a big baton of "rock" (candy), and stroll. Grown men walk around with huge teddy bears looking for places to play "bowlingo," a short-lane version of bowling. "Gypsy" psychics with celebrity photos in their windows promise to reveal your future. Ponder the thought of actually retiring here and spending your last years, day after day, wearing plaid pants and a bad toupee, surrounded by Blackpool. This place puts people in a talkative mood. Start up conversations. Ask a young couple on the street, "What's there to do here?" Find someone to explain the difference between tea and supper. Back at your hotel, join in the chat sessions in the lounge.

▲▲The Piers

Blackpool's famous piers were originally built for Victorian landlubbers who wanted to go to sea but were afraid of getting seasick. Each of the three amusement piers has its own personality and is a joy to wander (all are free and open with demand Easter-early Nov). The rides you'll see operate on a token system (buy tokens from kiosks along the pier). Each pier has its own family-friendly bar, where kids are welcome all the time (typically open from about 12:00 until 17:00 or 18:00, but much later—about 23:00—in summer and on weekends).

The sedate **North Pier** is most traditional and refreshingly uncluttered. Dance down its empty planks at twilight to the early

English rock playing on its speakers. Its Carousel Bar at the end has a free kids' DJ nightly in summer (parents drink good beer while the kids bunny-hop and boogie). At its tip is a big theater offering corny shows.

The something-for-everyone **Central Pier** is lots of fun. Ride its great Ferris wheel for the best view in Blackpool (rich photography at twilight; get the operator to spin you as you bottom out). The Family Bar at the end of the pier is a hit with kids.

The rollicking **South Pier** has classic carnival rides, such as bumper cars and carousels. The two very pricey adventure rides—Skycoaster and Skyscreamer—treat riders like rocks in a giant slingshot. This pier is also home to the Laughing Donkey Family Bar.

From the far end of any pier, look out at the horizon to see the natural-gas drilling platforms in the Irish Sea. In the distance, off the North Shore, castaway wind turbines capture energy.

▲Blackpool Tower

This mini-Eiffel Tower is a 100-year-old vertical fun center. Refurbished from head to toe, the tower has added some glitzy new attractions while preserving some of its oldies-but-goodies. Work

your way up from the bottom through layer after layer of noisy entertainment: a circus (1-3 acts a day, runs Easter-first weekend in Nov); Jungle Jim's kiddie area; a gory "Blackpool Dungeon" attraction; and a wonderful old ballroom with barely live music and golden oldies dancing to golden oldies all day. Enjoy a break at the dance-floor-level pub or on a balcony perch. Kids love this place. With a little marijuana, adults would, too. Ride the elevator to the "Blackpool Tower Eye" viewpoint at the tip of this 518-foot-tall symbol of Blackpool, where you can stroll across the "Sky-Walk" glass floor and enjoy a smashing view, especially at sunset. Also up top is a "4D" cinema (3-D plus other startling effects).

Cost and Hours: It's free to go inside and wander around, but tickets are required to enter the attractions. Pricing is à la carte, depending on which sights you choose. Admission to the Eye alone is £13; for all five, it's £30 (see website for complete pricing options, kid and family tickets available, cheaper if you buy online or at TI). Open daily from 10:00, closing times vary per attraction and with the season, some attractions may close for events, top of tower closes when excessively windy, tel. 01253/622-242, www. theblackpooltower.co.uk. Heritage tours of the tower are available on certain Fridays and Saturdays from April-Sept (£10, 1.5 hours, tel. 0871-222-9929).

▲Madame Tussauds Blackpool

Just south of the Blackpool Tower along The Promenade, this kid-sister to the famous waxworks in London features eerily realistic wax copies of famous people with whom you can pose for a hundred goofy photos. However, while the London Tussauds focuses on international stars, the one in Blackpool (understanding its target audience) focuses on British celebs. Reality-TV stars, comedians, and other media personalities from the UK are featured, as well as such icons as a replica of the Rovers Return pub from the beloved-by-Brits soap opera *Coronation Street*. A kids' area features *Shrek* and *Spider-Man*, among other favorites. The average American likely won't recognize the vast majority of the waxy faces in here (with a few exceptions—notably Simon Cowell and Susan Boyle—plus international guest-stars such as Michael Jackson, Lady Gaga, Britney Spears, and Tiger Woods), and the price tag is hefty. But fans of British pop culture will enjoy seeing Graham Norton, Gok Wan, Alan Carr, and superstar competitive dart-thrower Phil Taylor. And anyone will be impressed by the remarkably lifelike features of the figures.

Cost and Hours: Adults-£16, kids-£12.50, cheaper if you buy in advance (online or over the phone) or from the TI, Mon-Fri 10:00-16:00, Sat-Sun 10:00-17:00, hours can vary—check website, near the Central Pier on The Promenade, tel. 0871-282-9200, www. madametussauds.com.

▲Pleasure Beach

Rated ▲▲▲ for roller-coaster enthusiasts, these 42 acres across The Promenade from the beach attract nearly six million visitors annually and are littered with rides galore, an ice show, circus and illusion shows, and varied amusements. The Nickelodeonland area features rides and characters tied into the American children's TV network (also popular in the UK). Many rides are tame enough for the under-10 set, but the top few offer some of the best thrills in Europe: the Pepsi Max Big One (with a peak of 235 feet and 85 mph, it's one of the world's fastest, highest, and steepest roller coasters), the Infusion (a twisty, loopy speed rush that you ride with your feet dangling), and the Ice Blast (which rockets you straight up before letting you bungee down). Also memorable is the Steeplechase—carousel horses stampeding down a roller-coaster track (a dream come true for *Mary Poppins* fans). The Irn Bru Revolution speeds you over a steep drop and upside-down in a loop, then does it again backward, while the Valhalla ride zips you on a Viking boat in watery darkness past scary Nordic things like lutefisk. With two 80-foot drops and lots of hype, first you're scared, then you're soaked, and—finally—you're just glad you survived. A recent addition—the Wallace and Gromit Thrill-O-Matic—zips you through some of the duo's most iconic adventures. The park also offers several old wooden-framed rides full of historic charm—but brittle travelers will want to consider their necks and backs. The tame-looking Wild Mouse, built in 1958, is the jerkiest and has no doubt kept generations of Blackpool chiropractors in the money.

Cost: £6 admission includes a few attractions, then you can pay individually for rides with £1 tickets (2-8 tickets per ride). For unlimited rides, get a wristband (adults-£30, kids-£27, family ticket available, cheaper if purchased in advance on their website, covered by Resort Pass—see page 670). If you haven't pre-purchased your pass, pay the £6 entry fee and have a look around (figure out how long lines are for the top rides)—once you've paid admission to the park, you can upgrade to the wristband by paying the difference.

Hours: Daily Easter-early Nov, also open some weekends in Nov and Feb-Easter; opens at about 10:00 and closes as early as 17:00 or as late as 20:00 (and possibly later) depending on season, weather, and demand—check website; closed entirely Dec-Jan, tel. 0871-222-1234, www.blackpoolpleasurebeach.com.

Avoiding Lines: The park can be jam-packed in summer (July-Aug) and on school holidays, causing long ticket lines from about 10:30 to 13:00; during these times, try to arrive early (ticket office opens at 9:30). If lines are horrendous, consider a £10 Speedy Pass, which lets you book a spot in line with a pager device or even your mobile phone, then go off and do other things until it's time to board the ride. More expensive Speedy Passes also allow you to reduce your wait times (www.speedypassmobile.com).

Getting There: Pleasure Beach is about two miles (a 45-minute walk) south of the North Pier, so consider taking the tram or bus.

Sandcastle Waterpark

This popular indoor attraction, across the street from Pleasure Beach, has a big pool, long slides, a wave machine, and water, water, everywhere, at a constant temperature of 84 degrees. Featuring the longest tube waterslide in the world (called "Masterblaster")—and some newer rides (Montazooma and Aztec Falls)—this is a place where most kids could easily spend a day. It's not so bad for parents, either—thanks to the Sea Breeze Spa, which has a sauna, steam room, heated loungers, and other amenities (extra fee applies).

Cost and Hours: Basic adult admission-£13.50, kids under age 12-£11; pay £6 extra for Hyperzone area with the best rides; family passes and discount tickets available online and at TI; daily April-Oct but hours vary depending on the day and season—opening between 9:30 and 10:30 and closing between 16:30 and 18:00 (late July-Aug), possibly open on weekends Nov-March; last admission one hour before closing, tel. 01253/343-602, www.sandcastle-waterpark.co.uk.

▲Illuminations

Blackpool was the first town in England to "go electric" in 1879. Now, every fall, from early September through early November, Blackpool stretches its tourist season by illuminating its six miles of waterfront with countless lights, all blinking and twinkling. People here speak with wonder about these lights. The American in me kept saying, "I've seen bigger, and I've seen better," but I stuffed his mouth with cotton candy and just had some simple fun like everyone else on my specially decorated tram. Look for the animated tableaux up along the North Shore (www.blackpool-illuminations.net).

St. Annes-on-Sea

Had enough greasy food and flashing lights? The seaside village of St. Annes is an easy 20-minute bus ride away to the south and offers a welcome break (buses #7 and #11 run from Market Street in front of the BHS store every 15 minutes, covered by the all-day tram/bus pass). Get off at St. Annes Square, which is the first stop after the bus turns left following the long, dune-side straightaway. The town's promenade and the end of the simple Victorian pier (once you pass the noisy game arcade) feel like a breath of sanity. The broad sand beach is perfect for flying a kite, building a sandcastle, or watching happy dogs play in the surf. Consider strolling the beach northward all the way to the southern edge of The Promenade (about three miles—you can see the Pleasure Beach roller coasters from here); if you max out on sand and sea before that, simply cross the dunes back to the seaside road and find the nearest bus stop.

Nightlife in Blackpool

▲Showtime
Blackpool always has a few razzle-dazzle music, dancing-girl, racy-humor, magic, and tumbling shows. Box offices around town can give you a rundown on what's available (£10-50 tickets). Your hotel has the latest. Blackpool is also a staging ground for some London West End plays—giving you a chance to enjoy a show for a fraction of the London cost. You might try the Opera House for musicals (booking tel. 0844-856-1111, info tel. 01253/625-252) and the Grand Theatre for drama, ballet, and musicals (£15-30, tel. 01253/290-190, www.blackpoolgrand.co.uk). Both are on Church Street, a couple of blocks behind the tower. For the latest in evening entertainment, see the window displays at the TI on The Promenade (www.blackpoollive.com).

▲▲Funny Girls
Blackpool's hot bar is in a dazzling venue a couple of blocks from

the tower. Most nights from 20:00 to 23:30, Funny Girls puts on a "glam bam thank you ma'am" burlesque-in-drag show that delights footballers and grannies alike. A troupe of a dozen or so gorgeous guys go through an entire wardrobe, putting on skits and dances that range from the Charleston to Beyoncé to a very vampy *Sound of Music*. Between songs, the high-heeled MC entertains.

Get your drinks at the bar...unless the transvestites are dancing on it. The show, while racy, is not raunchy. The music is very loud. The crowd is young, old, straight, gay, very down-to-earth, and fun-loving. A weeknight is both a less-expensive and less-crushed experience, as Fridays and Saturdays are jammed. While the area up front can be a mosh pit, there are more sedate tables in back, where service comes with a vampish smile. If you want to experience the show without standing, immersed in a bar crowd, pay extra to sit at a table (4- to 6-person minimum, depending on the night they may sell you a couple of seats at a table, reservations smart).

Getting Tickets: Admission is charged according to whether you're sitting or standing (Sun £4 to stand, £12-14.50 to sit; Tue-Thu £3.50 to stand, £9-12 to sit; Fri £6 to stand, £16-19 to sit; Sat £8.50 to stand, £19-22 to sit; no shows Mon; £4 fee if you reserve by phone). Getting dinner in the adjacent restaurant before the show runs about £17 (dinner reservations required 2 weeks in advance, does not include show ticket). You must be 18 to enter, and standing-room tickets are usually available at the door (doors open at 19:00, 5 Dickson Road). To reserve in advance, buy from the TI, call 01253/624-901 or 01253/649-190, or visit the box office (44 Queen Street, find door next to the Flying Handbag—open Mon-Fri 9:30-17:15, Sat 10:00-14:00, closed Sun, www.funnygirl-sonline.co.uk).

Birley Street Light Show

This recently pedestrianized street, right in the heart of town, has silver arches bunny-hopping up and down its length. From September to early November, a sound-and-light display called "Brilliance" enlivens the street after dark with flashing lights and music (possibly weekends only).

Other Nightspots

More than 100 years old, **The Mitre** pub serves beer in a cozy, truly rare, old-time Blackpool ambience. Drop in anytime to survey the fun photos of old Blackpool and for the great people scene (real ales and £4-7 meals, daily 11:00-1:00 in the morning, 3 West Street, tel. 01253/623-718). Other pubs in the center that are more traditional than rowdy (though admittedly touristy) are **The Pump and Truncheon** on Bonny Street behind Madame Tussauds (real ales and basic £5 pub grub with exposed brick and a billiards table, tel. 01253/624-099), and **Scruffy Murphy's** on Corporation Street (food only at lunchtime in summer, live music most weekends, tel. 01253/624-538).

Blackpool's clubs and discos are cheap, with live bands and an interesting crowd (nightly 22:00-2:00 in the morning). With all the stag and hen parties, the late-night streets can be clotted with rude rowdies.

Sleeping in Blackpool

Blackpool's 140,000 people provide 120,000 beds in 3,500 mostly dumpy, cheap, nondescript hotels and B&Bs. Remember, this town's in the business of accommodating the people who can't afford to go to Spain. Empty beds abound except summer weekends and from September through early November (during Illuminations, when everyone bumps up prices). With the huge number of hotels in town, prices get really soft off-season. I've listed regular high-season prices. A launderette is likely within a five-minute walk of your hotel; ask your host.

North of the Tower

These listings are on or near the waterfront in the quiet area they call "the posh end," a mile or two north of Blackpool Tower, with easy parking and easy access to the center by tram or bus. The first

Central Blackpool

NOT TO SCALE
NORTH PIER TO CENTRAL PIER
IS ABOUT ½ MILE (800 METERS)

+—+ TRAM LINE

P PARKING

▨ PEDESTRIAN ZONE

BLACKPOOL
NORTH
**TRAIN
STN.**

TO
❷

❶₆ DICKSON

❶₅

LIBRARY

ABINGDON

QUEEN ST.

KING

TOPPING
MARKET

❻ ❼ ❽

❹

❾ ❶₇ ❸

❶₄ ❺

CORPORATION ST.

❶₀

TALBOT SQ.

MARKET

❶₉

POST

CORONATION STREET

OPERA HOUSE &
WINTER GARDENS

NATL EXPRESS
BUS STN.

GRAND
THEATRE

TOWER

❶₂

❶₈

❶₃

MADAME
TUSSAUDS

TO
M-55

TO
SOUTH
PIER →

P R O M E N A D E

❶ ❶₁ TRAMWAY ❰ BEACH ❱ 𝒊 ❰ BEACH ❱

NORTH PIER

I R I S H ⛵ S E A

**CENTRAL
PIER**

BLACKPOOL

❶ To Hotels North of the Tower
❷ To The Lonsdale & Valdene Hotels
❸ St. John's Square Eateries
❹ Abingdon Barbeque
❺ Marks & Spencer
❻ AJ's Bistro
❼ Yorkshire Fisheries
❽ Kwizeen
❾ Sapori
❿ Michael Wan's Mandarin Restaurant
⓫ To Red Bank Road Eateries
⓬ The Mitre Pub
⓭ The Pump and Truncheon
⓮ Scruffy Murphy's Pub
⓯ Funny Girls (Bar & Show)
⓰ Funny Girls (Box Office)
⓱ Co-op Supermarket
⓲ Nat'l Express Bus Station, Bag Storage & WCs
⓳ Blackpool Transport Office

two listings have classy extras you wouldn't expect in Blackpool and aren't far from the North Pier. The last two are B&Bs with welcoming owners and lots of stairs, a short tram ride or approximately 35-minute walk from the North Pier.

$$$ The Imperial Hotel would like to brag that it's where the Queen would stay in Blackpool. (They boast that every prime minister since they opened has visited their #10 Bar.) With 180 rooms, it's the kind of grand, monumental hotel they don't make anymore, with a dark-paneled Old World elegance (standard Db-£95-170 depending on size of room, season, and day of week, average is

Sleep Code

(£1 = about $1.60, country code: 44, area code: 01253)
S = Single, **D** = Double/Twin, **T** = Triple, **Q** = Quad, **b** = bathroom, **s** = shower only. Unless otherwise noted, credit cards are accepted.

To help you sort easily through these listings, I've divided the accommodations into three categories based on the price for a standard double room with bath:

$$$ **Higher Priced**—Most rooms £90 or more.
$$ **Moderately Priced**—Most rooms between £45-90.
$ **Lower Priced**—Most rooms £45 or less.

Prices can change without notice; verify the hotel's current rates online or by email. For the best prices, always book direct.

about Db-£112, check website for deals but call front desk for best standard room available, seaview rooms-£30-60 extra, children 16 and under stay free, rates may include breakfast—otherwise breakfast is £10, elevator, gym, spa, pool, free Wi-Fi, parking-£3.50/day, tram stop: Wilton Parade, North Promenade, tel. 01253/623-971, www.pumahotels.co.uk, imperialblackpool@pumahotels.co.uk).

$$$ The **Hilton Hotel** is good if you need a splurge. Yes, I know, staying at the Hilton in Blackpool is like wearing a tux to eat a corndog. But this is a grand 274-room place with lots of views, a pool, sauna, gym, and comfortable rooms (Db-£110-184, "club deal" Db with lots of extras-£25 more, ask about "special rates," best deals online, some rates include breakfast and/or dinner—otherwise £14.50 for breakfast, call front desk to request view room for no extra charge, free Wi-Fi in lobby, expensive Wi-Fi in rooms, tram stop: Wilton Parade, North Promenade, tel. 01253/623-434, www.hilton. com).

$$ **Beechcliffe Private Hotel** has seven clean rooms run by a friendly couple, Ken and Carol Selman. The rooms are tight and simple, but this place has a homey touch (Sb-£25, Db-£50, extra person-£25 but kids half-price, free Wi-Fi, tram stop: Cabin—turn left from tram stop, then right at Shaftesbury Avenue, and walk a block away from the beach; 16 Shaftesbury Avenue, North Shore, tel. 01253/353-075, www.beechcliffe.co.uk, info@beechcliffe.co.uk). Ken offers guests rides to or from the train station for no charge.

$$ **Robin Hood Hotel** is a cheery place with a big, welcoming living room and nine spacious rooms with big beds and some sea views. If you don't mind the stairs, ask for a top-floor room, which features great views over the beach and sea (Sb-£28, Db-£56, extra person-£25 but kids half-price, under 6 free, may serve afternoon tea and evening meals for a fee, free Wi-Fi, tram stop: Lowther Avenue, 30 yards north of hotel, 1.5 miles north of tower across from a peaceful stretch of beach, 100 Queens Promenade, North Shore, tel. 01253/351-599, www.robinhoodhotel. co.uk, info@robinhoodhotel.co.uk, Paul and Kathy).

Near the Train Station

Both of these hotels are located on quiet Cocker Street, which provides an oasis of sanity and affordable comfort in a handy, if rough, neighborhood just a few short blocks from the train station and the Blackpool Tower and North Pier. These hotels are family-run, have strict security and noise standards, and cater to couples and families rather than to revelers. To reach these places by tram, get off at the Pleasant Street stop, head right along the promenade (toward the tower), then turn left on Cocker Street.

$$ **The Lonsdale Hotel** offers five rooms in an oasis of peace behind a lush front porch garden. The plush lounge—with Edwardian paintings, furnishings, and a grand piano—takes you to another era. Steve has managed the place for more than 25 years (Sb-£45-60, Db-£60-85, 2-night minimum on weekends, free Wi-Fi, free parking, at the corner of Lord Street and Cocker Street at 25 Cocker Street, tel. 01253/621-628, www.blackpoolaccommodation.net, lonsdalehotel@hotmail.co.uk).

$$ **The Valdene Hotel,** with a small garden facing the street, rents 10 rooms above its generous and inviting lounge. Old-time Blackpool photos on the walls create a peaceful and nostalgic atmosphere (Db-£45-55, 16 Cocker Street, tel. 01253/291-080, www. valdene-hotel.co.uk, valdenehotel@aol.com, Dave and Sarah).

Eating in Blackpool

Considering what's in demand here, I wouldn't hope for great food in Blackpool. Generally, food in the tower and along The Promenade is terrible. But if you explore the streets in the real town center, a few blocks up from The Promenade, you'll find some decent options. Because there's no real "destination" restaurant in town, I've organized them by streets that are worth browsing—just select whichever place appeals to you.

St. John's Square and Nearby

This recently pedestrianized square is fronted by several popular eateries. Trendy cafés—including Lounge, Number Five, and Sugar[3]—line the top of the square (all open only until about 17:00, no dinner except at Lounge on weekends). To fill the tank, head to **Quilligans,** a local favorite, across the square from the church. This kitschy, retro Blackpool diner suits the city's lowbrow aesthetic perfectly, with huge portions of comfort food (£3-5 light meals, £6-7 bigger meals, tel. 01253/293-894). At the bottom of the square, **West Coast Rock Café** is popular with teens for its gigantic portions.

Carryout Options near St. John's Square: These places are good options for picking up some take-away food; you can sit on a bench on St. John's Square, or—better yet—head for the beach. **Abingdon Barbeque,** with its expansive deli counter, is mobbed with hungry locals at lunch, munching on cheap roasted chicken and meat pies (Mon-Sat 8:00-17:00, Sun 10:00-16:00 July-Dec only, takeaway only, 44 Abingdon Street, tel. 01253/621-817). **Marks & Spencer** has a big supermarket in its basement (Mon-Sat 8:00-18:00, Sun 10:30-16:30, just south of St. John's Square on Church Street, tel. 01253/623-831). A **Co-op** supermarket is at the corner of Birley and Abingdon streets (daily 7:00-22:00).

Topping Street and Nearby

This somewhat dingy, urban-feeling street sits about halfway between the train station and The Promenade. But its lack of glitz helps keep some of the tourists away, making this a relatively local-feeling strip. Your options here include a pair of Thai restaurants, two pubs with great old-fashioned ambience and passable food (The Washington and Churchills), an Italian joint, and the places listed below.

AJ's Bistro, named for owners Andrew and Julie, features quality modern English cuisine (with an emphasis on seafood and steaks, and mostly gluten-free) in a casual atmosphere. Their £10.50 "evening menu"—like an early-bird deal but available anytime (except Sat)—includes two courses and a drink. Or you can order from the pricey à la carte menu (£5-7 starters, £13-19 main dishes, Tue-Sun 17:30-23:00, closed Mon, 65 Topping Street, tel. 01253/626-111).

Fish-and-Chips: **Yorkshire Fisheries,** the locals' choice for best chippy, promises better-quality fish-and-chips than the greasy joints that line The Promenade. Order at the counter, then either take it away or eat there (£4-7 meals, Mon-Sat 11:30-19:00, Sun 12:00-18:00 Easter-Dec only, 16 Topping Street, tel. 01253/627-739).

Near Topping Street: **Kwizeen,** on a dingy street a block up from Topping Street, is an elegant bistro that serves Mediterranean and modern English dishes with a focus on locally sourced and creatively prepared food (£6-7 starters, £13-16 main dishes, £16 two-course and £19 three-course early-bird specials 18:00-19:00; open Mon-Fri 12:00-13:30 & 18:00-21:00, Sat 18:00-21:00, closed Sun; 47-49 King Street, tel. 01253/290-045).

Clifton Street

Stretching up from the Promenade and the TI, this street has a few ethnic offerings, including Italian, Indian, and Chinese. These two have the best reputation.

Sapori offers good Italian food in a sophisticated atmosphere that makes you forget that the tackiness of Blackpool is just outside the front door (£7-8 pizzas and pastas, £12-19 main dishes, daily 17:00-23:00, 36 Clifton Street, tel. 01253/627-440).

Michael Wan's Mandarin Restaurant is a local fixture that's been providing Blackpool with authentic Chinese cuisine since 1961 (£8-15 meals, Mon-Sat 12:00-14:00 & 17:30-23:00—open later Fri-Sat nights, Sun 17:30-22:30, free Wi-Fi, 27 Clifton Street, tel. 01253/622-687).

In the North End: Red Bank Road

If you're staying at the hotels at the north end of The Promenade and don't want to venture into the rowdy downtown for dinner, locals recommend riding the tram north to Bispham. From here, Red Bank Road has several acceptable eateries including Indian, Italian, fish-and-chips, and steakhouse choices. The basic, diner-style **Bispham Kitchen** has stick-to-your-ribs English comfort food, including good fish-and-chips (£5-7 meals, Sun-Thu 8:30-20:30, Fri-Sat 8:30-21:00, open later late July-early Nov, at #14-16, tel. 01253/592-514). None of these places is high cuisine—the pickings are slim—but it's relatively convenient to accommodations in the north end.

Blackpool Connections

If you're heading to (or from) Blackpool by train, you'll usually need to transfer at **Preston** (4/hour, 25 minutes). The following trains leave from Blackpool's main (north) station. The information desk can print you a schedule for your requested journey.

From Blackpool to: Liverpool (1/hour direct, 1.5 hours), **Keswick/Lake District** (nearly hourly, allow 3-3.5 hours total for journey: 2-hour train to Penrith with transfer in Preston, then bus to Keswick; alternatively, you could take the train to Windermere—every 1-2 hours with a change in Preston and sometimes also Oxenholme, 1.5-2 hours—and ride the bus from there to Keswick), **Conwy** in North Wales (roughly hourly, 3 hours,

3 transfers), **Edinburgh** (roughly hourly, 3.5 hours, transfer in Preston), **Glasgow** (hourly, 3.5 hours, transfer in Preston), **York** (1/hour direct, 3 hours, more with change in Manchester), **Moreton-in-Marsh/Cotswolds** (hourly, 4.25-5 hours, 3 transfers), **Bath** (hourly, 4.5-5 hours, 2-3 transfers), **London**'s Euston Station (1-2/hour, 3-3.5 hours, 1-2 transfers), Telford near **Ironbridge Gorge** (hourly, 2.5 hours, 2 transfers), **Oban** (1/day, 7.75 hours, 3 transfers). Train info: Tel. 0845-748-4950, www.nationalrail.co.uk.

BLACKPOOL

THE LAKE DISTRICT

Keswick • North Lake District • Ullswater Lake • South Lake District

In the pristine Lake District, William Wordsworth's poems still shiver in trees and ripple on ponds. Nature rules this land, and humanity keeps a wide-eyed but low profile. Relax, recharge, take a cruise or a hike, and maybe even write a poem. Renew your poetic license at Wordsworth's famous Dove Cottage.

The Lake District, about 30 miles long and 30 miles wide, is nature's lush, green playground. Explore it by foot, bike, bus, or car. While not impressive in sheer height (Scafell Pike, the tallest peak in England, is only 3,206 feet), there's a walking-stick charm about the way nature and the culture mix here. Locals are fond of declaring that their mountains are older than the Himalayas and were once as tall, but have been worn down by the ages. Walking along a windblown ridge or climbing over a rock fence to look into the eyes of a ragamuffin sheep, even tenderfeet get a chance to feel very outdoorsy. The tradition of staying close to the land remains true—albeit in an updated form—in the 21st century; you'll see restaurants serving organic food as well as stickers advocating for environmental causes in the windows of homes.

Dress in layers, and expect rain mixed with brilliant "bright spells" (pubs offer atmospheric shelter at every turn). Drizzly days can be followed by delightful evenings.

Plan to spend the majority of your time in the unspoiled North Lake District. In this chapter, I focus on the town of Keswick, the lake called Derwentwater, and the vast, time-passed Newlands Valley. The North Lake District works great by car or by bus (with easy train access via Penrith), delights nature lovers, and has good accommodations to boot.

The South Lake District—slightly closer to London—is famous

primarily for its Wordsworth and Beatrix Potter sights, and gets the promotion, the tour crowds, and the tackiness that comes with them. While the slate-colored towns (Ambleside, Windermere, Bowness-on-Windermere, and so on) are cute, they're also touristy—which means crowded and overpriced. I strongly recommend that you buck the trend and focus on the north. Ideally, enter the region from the north, via Penrith. Make your home base in or near Keswick, and side-trip from here into the South Lake District only if you're interested in the Wordsworth and Beatrix Potter sights. Dipping into the South Lake District also works well en route if you're driving between Keswick and points south.

Planning Your Time

I'd suggest spending two days and two nights in this area. Penrith is the nearest train station, just 45 minutes by bus or car from Keswick. Those without a car will use Keswick as a springboard: Cruise the lake and take one of the many hikes in the Catbells area. Non-hikers can hop on a minibus tour. If great scenery is commonplace in your life, the Lake District can be more soothing (and rainy) than exciting. If you're rushed, you could make this area a one-night stand—or even a quick drive-through. But since the towns themselves are unexceptional, a visit here isn't worth it unless you have time to head up into the hills or out on the water at least once.

Two-Day Driving Plan: Here's the most exciting way for drivers coming from the south—who'd like to visit South Lake District sights en route to the North Lake District—to max out their time here:

Day 1: Get an early start, aiming to leave the motorway at Kendal by 10:30; drive along Windermere, the lake, and through the town of Ambleside.

11:30   Tour Dove Cottage and the Wordsworth Museum.

13:00   Backtrack to Ambleside, where a small road leads up and over the dramatic Kirkstone Pass (far more scenic northbound than southbound—get out and bite the wind) and down to Glenridding on Lake Ullswater.

15:00   Catch the next Ullswater boat and ride to Howtown. Hike six miles (3-4 hours) from Howtown back to Glenridding. Or, for a shorter Ullswater experience, hike up to the Aira Force waterfall (1 hour) or up and around Lanty's Tarn (2-2.5 hours).

19:00   Drive to your Keswick hotel or farmhouse B&B near Keswick, with a stop as the sun sets at Castlerigg Stone Circle.

Day 2: Spend the morning (3-4 hours) splicing the Catbells high-ridge hike into a circular boat trip around Derwentwater. In the afternoon, make the circular drive from Keswick through the Newlands Valley, Buttermere, Honister Pass, and Borrowdale. You could tour the Honister Slate Mine en route (last tour at 15:30) and/or pitch-and-putt nine holes in Keswick before a late dinner.

Getting Around the Lake District
With a Car

Nothing is very far from Keswick and Derwentwater. Pick up a good map (any hotel can loan you one), get off the big roads, and leave  the car, at least occasionally, for some walking. In summer, the Keswick-Ambleside-Windermere-Bowness corridor (A-591) suffers from congestion. Back lanes are far less trampled and lead you through forgotten villages, where sheep outnumber people and stone churchyards are filled with happily permanent residents.

To **rent a car** here, try Enterprise in Penrith. They'll pick you up in Keswick and drive you back to their office to get the car, and also drive you back to Keswick after you've dropped it off (Mon-Fri 8:00-18:00, Sat 9:00-12:00, closed Sun, requires drivers license and second form of ID, reserve a day in advance, tel. 01768/893-840). Larger outfits are more likely to have a branch in Carlisle, which is a bit to the north but well-served by train (on the same Glasgow-Birmingham line as Penrith) and only a few minutes farther from the Keswick area.

Parking is tight throughout the region. It's easiest to park in the pay-and-display lots (generally about £3/2-3 hours, £5/4-5 hours, and £7/12 hours; have coins on hand, as most machines don't make change). If you're parking for free on the roadside, don't block vital turnouts. Never park on double yellow lines.

Without a Car

Those based in Keswick without a car manage fine. Because of the region's efforts to "green up" travel and cut down on car traffic, the bus service is quite efficient for hiking and sightseeing. (Consider leaving your car in town and using the bus for many sightseeing and hiking agendas.)

By Bus: Keswick has no real bus station; buses stop at a turnout in front of the Booths Supermarket. Local buses take you quickly and easily (if not always frequently) to all nearby points of interest. Check the schedule carefully to make sure you can catch the last bus home. The *Lakes Connection* booklet explains the schedules (available at TIs or on any bus). On board, you can purchase an Explorer pass that lets you ride any Stagecoach bus throughout the

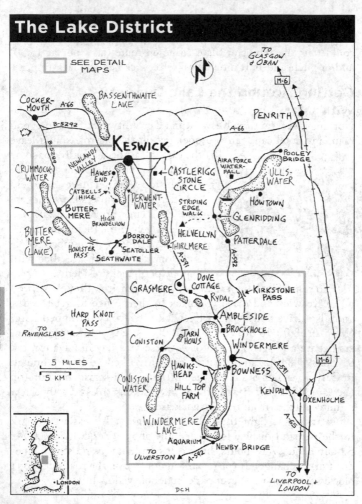

The Lake District

SEE DETAIL MAPS

LAKE DISTRICT

area (£10.30/1 day, £22/3 days), or you can get one-day passes for certain routes. For bus and rail info, visit www.traveline.org.uk.

Buses **#X4** and **#X5** connect Penrith train station to Keswick (hourly Mon-Sat, every 2 hours Sun, 45 minutes, £6.20).

Bus **#77/#77A,** the Honister Rambler, makes the gorgeous circle from Keswick around Derwentwater, over Honister Pass, through Buttermere, and down the Whinlatter Valley (4/day clockwise, 4/day "anticlockwise," daily Easter-Oct, 1.5-hour loop, £7 Honister & Borrowdale Dayrider all-day pass).

Bus **#78,** the Borrowdale Rambler, goes topless in the summer, affording a wonderful sightseeing experience in and of itself, heading from Keswick to Lodore Hotel, Grange, Rosthwaite, and

Seatoller at the base of Honister Pass (nearly hourly, more frequent late July-Aug, 30 minutes each way, £7 Honister & Borrowdale Dayrider all-day pass).

Buses **#108** and **#508,** the Kirkstone Rambler, run between Penrith and Glenridding (near the bottom of Ullswater), stopping in Pooley Bridge (4/day, 45 minutes). On weekends and in late July-Aug, bus #508 also connects Glenridding and Windermere (4/day, 1 hour). The £14.80 Ullswater Bus & Boat all-day pass covers buses #108 and #508 as well as steamers on Ullswater.

Bus **#505,** the Coniston Rambler, connects Windermere with Hawkshead (about hourly, daily Easter-Oct, 35 minutes).

Bus **#555** connects Keswick with the south (hourly, more frequent in summer, one hour to Windermere).

Bus **#599,** the open-top Lakeland Experience, runs along the main Windermere corridor, connecting the big tourist attractions in the south: Grasmere and Dove Cottage, Rydal Mount, Ambleside, Brockhole, Windermere, and Bowness Pier (3/hour Easter-late Sept, 2/hour late Sept-Oct, 50 minutes each way, £7 Central Lakes Dayrider all-day pass).

By Bike: Keswick works well as a springboard for several fine days out on a bike; consider a three-hour loop trip up Newlands Valley, following the Railway Path up a former train track (now a biking path), and returning via Castlerigg Stone Circle.

Several shops in Keswick rent road bikes and mountain bikes. Bikes come with helmets, touring maps, and advice for good trips. Try **Whinlatter Bikes** (£15/day, daily 10:00-17:00, 82 Main Street, tel. 017687/73940, www.whinlatterbikes.com) or **Keswick Bikes** (from £12/half-day, £15/day, daily 9:00-17:30, 133 Main Street, tel. 017687/73355, www.keswickbikes.co.uk).

By Boat: A circular boat service glides you around Derwentwater, with several hiker-aiding stops along the way (for a cruise/hike option, see "Derwentwater Lakeside Walk" on page 700).

By Foot: Hiking information is available everywhere. Don't hike without a good, detailed map (wide selection at Keswick TI and at the many outdoor gear stores, or borrow one from your B&B). Helpful fliers at TIs and B&Bs describe the most popular routes. For an up-to-date weather report, ask at a TI or call 0844-846-2444. Wear suitable clothing and footwear (you can rent boots in town; B&Bs can likely loan you a good coat or an umbrella if weather looks threatening). Plan for rain. Watch your footing. Injuries are common. Every year, several people die while hiking in the area (some from overexertion; others are blown off ridges).

By Tour: For organized bus tours that run the roads of the Lake District, see "Tours in Keswick," later.

The Lake District at a Glance

North Lake District

In Keswick
▲▲**Theatre by the Lake** Top-notch theater a pleasant stroll from Keswick's main square. **Hours:** Shows generally at 20:00 in summer, possibly earlier fall through spring; box office open daily 9:30-20:00. See page 707.

▲**Derwentwater** Lake immediately south of Keswick, with good boat service and trails. See page 697.

▲**Pencil Museum** Paean to graphite-filled wooden sticks. **Hours:** Daily 9:30-17:00. See page 698.

▲**Pitch-and-Putt Golf** Cheap, easygoing nine-hole course in Keswick's Hope Park. **Hours:** Daily from 10:00, last start at 18:00 but possibly later in summer, closed Nov-Feb. See page 698.

Near Keswick
▲▲▲**Scenic Circle Drive South of Keswick** Hour-long drive through the best of the Lake District's scenery, with plenty of fun stops (including the fascinating Honister Slate Mine) and short side-trip options. See page 704.

▲▲**Castlerigg Stone Circle** Evocative and extremely old (even by British standards) ring of Neolithic stones. See page 699.

▲▲**Catbells High Ridge Hike** Two-hour hike along dramatic ridge southwest of Keswick. See page 700.

▲▲**Buttermere Hike** Four-mile, low-impact lakeside loop in a gorgeous setting. See page 701.

▲▲**More Hikes from Keswick** Scenic hikes with varying degrees of difficulty: Latrigg Peak, Railway Path, and Walla Crag. See page 704.

▲**Honister Slate Mine Tour** A 1.5-hour guided hike through a 19th-century mine at the top of Honister Pass. **Hours:** Daily at 10:30, 12:30, and 15:30; also at 14:00 in summer; Dec-Jan 12:30 tour only. See page 705.

Ullswater Lake Area

▲▲**Ullswater Hike and Boat Ride** Long lake best enjoyed via steamer boat and seven-mile walk. **Hours:** Boats generally daily 9:45-16:45, 6-9/day April-Oct, fewer off-season. See page 717.

▲▲**Lanty's Tarn and Keldas Hill** Moderately challenging 2.5-mile loop hike from Glenridding with sweeping views of Ullswater.

▲**Aira Force Waterfall** Easy uphill hike to thundering waterfall. See page 718.

South Lake District

▲▲**Dove Cottage and Wordsworth Museum** The poet's humble home, with a museum that tells the story of his remarkable life. **Hours:** Daily March-Oct 9:30-17:30, Nov-Feb 9:30-16:30 except closed Jan. See page 720.

▲**Rydal Mount** Wordsworth's later, more upscale home. **Hours:** March-Oct daily 9:30-17:00; Nov-Dec and Feb Wed-Sun 11:00-16:00, closed Mon-Tue; closed Jan. See page 722.

▲**Hill Top Farm** Beatrix Potter's painstakingly preserved cottage. **Hours:** June-Aug Sat-Thu 10:00-17:30, April-May and Sept-Oct Sat-Thu 10:30-16:30, mid-Feb-March Sat-Thu 10:30-15:30, closed Nov-mid-Feb and Fri year-round, often a long wait to visit—call ahead. See page 724.

▲**Beatrix Potter Gallery** Collection of artwork by and background on the creator of Peter Rabbit. **Hours:** April-Oct Sat-Thu 10:30-17:00, mid-Feb-March Sat-Thu 10:30-15:30, closed Fri (except possibly in summer) and Nov-mid-Feb. See page 724.

The World of Beatrix Potter Touristy exhibition about the author. **Hours:** Daily April-Sept 10:00-18:00, Oct-March 10:00-17:00. See page 725.

Brockhole National Park Visitors Centre Best place to gather info on Lake Windermere and the surrounding area, grandly situated in a lakeside mansion. **Hours:** Daily April-Oct 10:00-17:00, Nov-March 10:00-16:00. See page 726.

Keswick and the North Lake District

As far as touristy Lake District towns go, Keswick (KEZ-ick, population 5,000) is far more enjoyable than Windermere, Bowness, or Ambleside. Many of the place names around Keswick have Norse origins, inherited from the region's 10th-century settlers. Notice that most lakes in the region end in either *water* (e.g., Derwentwater) or *mere* (e.g., Windermere), which is related to the German word for lake, *Meer.*

An important mining center for slate, copper, and lead through the Middle Ages, Keswick became a resort in the 19th century. Its fine Victorian buildings recall those Romantic days when city slickers first learned about "communing with nature." Today, the compact town is lined with tearooms, pubs, gift shops, and hiking-gear shops. The lake called Derwentwater is a pleasant 10-minute walk from the town center.

Orientation to Keswick

Keswick is an ideal home base, with plenty of good B&Bs, an easy bus connection to the nearest train station at Penrith, and a prime location near the best lake in the area, Derwentwater. In Keswick, everything is within a 10-minute walk of everything else: the pedestrian town square, the TI, recommended B&Bs, grocery stores, the wonderful municipal pitch-and-putt golf course, the main bus stop, a lakeside boat dock, the post office (with Internet access upstairs), and a central parking lot. Thursdays and Saturdays are market days in the town square, but the square is lively every day throughout the summer.

Keswick town is a delight for wandering. Its centerpiece, Moot Hall (meaning "meeting hall"), was a 16th-century copper warehouse upstairs with an arcade below (closed after World War II; most Lake District towns and villages have similar meeting halls). "Keswick" means "cheese farm"—a legacy from the time when the town square was the spot to sell cheese. When the town square went pedestrian-only, locals were all abuzz about people tripping over the curbs. (The English, seemingly thrilled by ever-present danger, are endlessly warning visitors to "watch your head," "duck or grouse," "watch the step," and "mind the gap.")

Keswick and the Lake District are popular with English holidaymakers who prefer to bring their dogs with them on vacation. The town square in Keswick can look like the Westminster Dog Show, and the recommended Dog and Gun pub, where "well-behaved dogs are welcomed," is always full of patient pups. If you are shy about connecting with people, pal up to an English pooch—you'll often find they're happy to introduce you to their owners.

Tourist Information

The National Park Visitors Centre/TI is in Moot Hall, right in

the middle of the town square (daily Easter-Oct 9:30-17:30, Nov-Easter 9:30-16:30, tel. 017687/72645, www.lakedistrict.gov.uk and www.keswick.org). Staffers are pros at advising you about hiking routes. They can also help you figure out public transportation to outlying sights, book rooms (you'll pay a £4 booking fee; it's cheaper to call B&Bs direct), and tell you about the region's various adventure activities.

The TI sells theater tickets, Keswick Launch tickets (at a £1 discount), fishing licenses, and brochures and maps that outline nearby hikes (£0.60-2, including a very simple and driver-friendly £2 *Lap Map* featuring sights, walks, and a mileage chart). The TI also has books and maps for hikers, cyclists, and drivers (more books are sold at shops all over town).

Check the boards inside the TI's foyer for information about walks, talks, and entertainment. You can also pick up the *Events and Guided Walks* guide. The daily weather forecast is posted just outside the front door (weather tel. 0844-846-2444). For information about the TI's guided walks, see "Tours in Keswick," later.

Helpful Hints

Book in Advance: Keswick hosts a variety of festivals and conventions, especially during the summer, so it's smart to book ahead. Please honor your bookings—the B&B proprietors here lose out on much-needed business if you don't show up.

A sampling of events: The Keswick Jazz Festival mellows out the town in early May (www.keswickjazzfestival.co.uk), followed immediately by the Mountain Festival (www.keswickmountainfestival.co.uk), then a beer festival in early June (www.keswickbeerfestival.co.uk). The Keswick Convention packs the town with 4,000 evangelical Christians for three weeks each summer (sometime in July-Aug, www.keswickministries.org).

Keswick

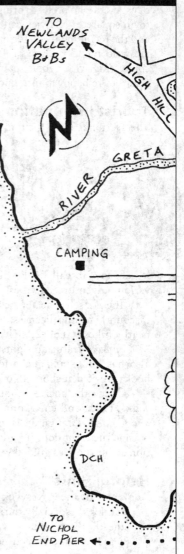

TO NEWLANDS VALLEY B&Bs

HIGH HILL

RIVER GRETA

CAMPING

DCH

TO NICHOL END PIER

DERWENTWATER

TO ASHNESS GATE PIER

P PARKING

PEDESTRIAN ZONE

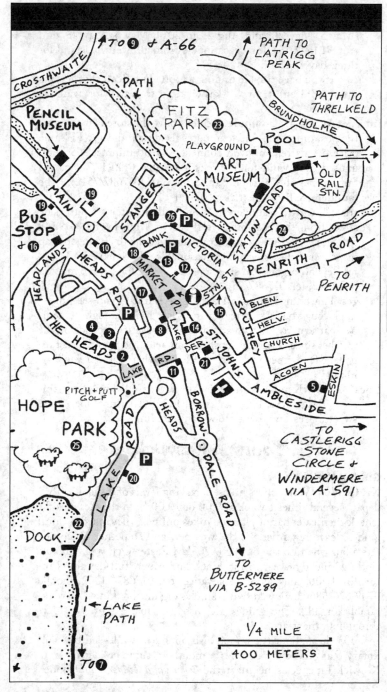

LAKE DISTRICT

Several Bank Holiday Mondays in spring and summer (May 5, May 26, and Aug 25 in 2014; May 4, May 25, and Aug 31 in 2015) draw vacationers from all over the island for three-day weekends.

If you have trouble finding a room (or a B&B that accepts small children), try www.keswick.org to search for available rooms.

Internet Access: U-Compute, located above the store that contains the post office, provides computer terminals and Wi-Fi (same price no matter how you connect—£2/30 minutes, £3/hour, unused time valid for 2 weeks, Mon-Sat 9:00-17:30, closed Sun, corner of Main and Bank streets, tel. 017687/75127). The **launderette** listed next also has Wi-Fi.

Laundry: The town's launderette is on Bank Street, just up the side street from the post office (self-service Mon-Fri 8:00-19:00, Sat-Sun 9:00-18:00, about £6/load wash and dry, coin-op soap dispenser; full-service for a reasonable additional £1.40-2.80 fee depending on load size; tea and Wi-Fi for £2, see map on page 692, tel. 017687/75448).

Midges: Tiny biting insects called midges—similar to no-see-ums—might bug you in this region from late May through September, particularly at dawn and dusk. The severity depends on the weather since wind and sunshine can deter them, and insect repellant fends them off: Ask the locals what works if you'll be hiking.

Local Candy: Kendal mint cakes are advertised throughout this area. Basically a big, flat, mint-flavored sugar cube, these sweet, refreshing treats are worth sampling.

Tours in Keswick

Guided Walks
KR Guided Walks offers hikes of varying levels of difficulty. They depart several times a week at 9:00 or 10:00 from the Keswick TI (check their calendar of planned hikes online). They're led by local guides, leave regardless of the weather, and sometimes incorporate a bus ride into the outing (£20/day, Easter-Oct, wear suitable clothing and footwear, bring lunch and water, full-day tours return by 17:00, must book in advance, tel. 017687/71302, mobile 0709-176-5860, www.keswickrambles.org.uk, booking@keswick-rambles.org.uk). The guides are also available for private tours throughout the year.

TIs throughout the region also offer **free walks** led by "Voluntary Rangers" several times a month in summer (depart from Keswick TI; check schedule in the *Events and Guided Walks* guide).

Bus Tours

These are great for people with bucks who'd like to wring maximum experience out of their limited time and see the area without lots of hiking or messing with public transport. For a cheaper alternative, take public buses.

Mountain Goat Tours is the region's dominant tour company. Unfortunately, they run their minibus tours out of Windermere, with pick-ups in Bowness, Ambleside, and sometimes in Grasmere. For those based in Keswick, add about an extra hour of driving or bus riding, round-trip, if you join their tours in Windermere, though they may be able to arrange tours from Keswick if you contact them in advance (tours run daily, £28/half-day, £39/day, year-round if there are sufficient sign-ups, minimum 4 people to a maximum of 16 per hearty bus, book in advance by calling 015394/45161, www.mountain-goat.com, enquiries@mountaingoat.com).

Show Me Cumbria Private Tours runs personalized tours all around the Lake District, and can pick you up in Keswick and other locations. They charge per hour, not per person, so their tours are a fine value for small groups (£30/hour, 1-6 people per tour, room for 2 small children in built-in child seats, tel. 01768/864-825, mobile 0780-902-6357, based in Penrith, www.showmecumbria.co.uk, andy@showmecumbria.co.uk).

Sights in Keswick

▲Derwentwater

One of Cumbria's most photographed and popular lakes, Derwent-

water has four islands, good circular boat service, and plenty of trails. The pleasant town of Keswick is a short stroll from the shore, near the lake's north end. The roadside views aren't much, and while you can walk around the lake (fine trail, floods in heavy rains, 9 miles, 4 hours), much of the walk is boring. You're better off mixing a hike and boat ride (see "Hikes and Drives in the North Lake District," later), or simply enjoy the circular boat tour of the lake.

Boating on Derwentwater: Keswick Launch runs two **cruises** an hour, alternating clockwise and "anticlockwise" (boats depart on the half-hour, daily 10:00-16:30, July-Aug until 17:30, in winter 5-6/day generally weekends and holidays only, at end of Lake Road, tel. 017687/72263, www.keswick-launch.co.uk). Boats make seven stops on each 50-minute round-trip (may skip some stops or not run at all if the water level is very high—such as after a heavy rain). The boat trip costs about £2 per segment (cheaper the more segments you buy) or £9.50 per circle (£1 less if you book through TI) with free stopovers; you can get on and off all you want, but tickets are collected on the boat's last leg to Keswick, marking the end of your ride. If you want to be picked up at a certain stop, stand at the end of the pier Gilligan-style, or the boat may not stop. Keswick Launch also rents **rowboats** for up to three people (£8/30 minutes, £12/hour, open Easter-Oct, larger rowboats and motor boats available). Keswick Launch also has a delightful **evening cruise** (see page 707).

▲Pencil Museum

Graphite was first discovered centuries ago in Keswick. A hunk of the stuff proved great for marking sheep in the 15th century. In 1832, the first crude Keswick pencil factory opened, and the rest is history (which is what you'll learn about here). While you can't actually tour the 150-year-old factory where the famous Derwent pencils were made, you can enjoy the smell of thousands of pencils getting sharpened for the first time. The adjacent charming and kid-friendly museum is a good way to pass a rainy hour; you may even catch an artist's demonstration. Take a look at the exhibit on "war pencils," which were made for WWII bomber crews (filled with tiny maps and compasses). Relax in the theater with a 10-minute video on the pencil-manufacturing process, followed by a sleepy animated-snowman short (drawn with Rexel Cumberland pencils).

Cost and Hours: £4.25, daily 9:30-17:00, last entry one hour before closing, humble café, 3-minute walk from the town center, signposted off Main Street, tel. 017687/73626, www.pencilmuseum.co.uk.

Fitz Park

An inviting, grassy park stretches alongside Keswick's tree-lined, duck-filled River Greta. There's plenty of room and a playground for kids to burn off energy. Consider an after-dinner stroll on the footpath. You may catch men in white (or frisky schoolboys in uniform) playing a game of cricket. There's the serious bowling green (where you're welcome to watch the experts play and enjoy the cheapest cuppa—i.e., tea—in town), and the public one where tourists are welcome to give lawn bowling a go (£3.50/person per hour). You can try tennis on a grass court (£7/hour for 2 people, includes rackets) or enjoy the putting green (£2.80/person). Find the rental pavilion across the road from the art gallery (open daily Easter-Sept 10:00-17:30, longer hours July-Aug, mobile 07976/573-785).

▲Golf

A lush nine-hole pitch-and-putt golf course near the gardens in Hope Park separates the town from the lake and offers a classy, cheap, and convenient chance to golf near the birthplace of the sport. This is a great, fun, and inexpensive experience—just right after a day of touring and before dinner (£4.50 for pitch-and-putt, £2.80 for putting, £3.10 for 18 tame holes of "obstacle golf," daily from 10:00, last round starts around 18:00, possibly later in summer, café, tel. 017687/73445).

Swimming

While the leisure center doesn't have a serious adult pool, it does have an indoor pool kids love, with a huge waterslide and wave machine (swim times vary by day and by season—call or check website, no towels or suits for rent, lockers-£1 deposit, 10-minute walk from town center, follow Station Road past Fitz Park and veer left, tel. 017687/72760, www.carlisleleisure.com).

Near Keswick

▲▲Castlerigg Stone Circle

For some reason, 70 percent of England's stone circles are here in Cumbria. Castlerigg is one of the best and oldest in Britain, and an easy stop for drivers. The circle—90 feet across and 5,000 years old—has 38 stones mysteriously laid out on a line between the two tallest peaks on the horizon. They served as a celestial calendar for ritual celebrations. Imagine the ambience here, as ancient people filled this clearing in spring to celebrate fertility, in late summer to commemorate the harvest, and in the winter to celebrate the winter solstice and the coming renewal of light. Festival dates were dic-

tated by how the sun rose and set in relation to the stones. The more that modern academics study this circle, the more meaning they find in the placement of the stones. The two front stones face due north, toward a cut in the mountains. The rare-for-stone-circles "sanctuary" lines up with its center stone to mark where the sun rises on May Day. (Party!) For maximum "goose pimples" (as they say here), show up at sunset (free, open all the time, 1-mile hike from town; by car it's a 3-mile drive east of Keswick—follow brown signs, 3 minutes off the A-66, easy parking).

LAKE DISTRICT

Hikes and Drives in the North Lake District

From Keswick

Derwentwater Lakeside Walk

A trail runs all along Derwentwater, but much of it (especially the Keswick-to-Hawes End stretch) is not that interesting. The best hour-long section is the 1.5-mile path between the docks at High Brandelhow and Hawes End in Keswick, where you'll stroll a level trail through peaceful trees. This walk works best in conjunction with the lake boat (see "Boating on Derwentwater," earlier).

▲▲Catbells High Ridge Hike

For a great "king of the mountain" feeling, 360-degree views, and a close-up look at the weather blowing over the ridge, hike above

Derwentwater about two hours from Hawes End up along the ridge to Catbells (1,480 feet) and down to High Brandelhow. Because the mountaintop is basically treeless, you're treated to dramatic panoramas the entire way up. From High Brandelhow, you can catch the boat back to Keswick or take the easy path along the shore of Derwentwater to your Hawes End starting point. (Extending the hike farther around the lake to Lodore takes you to a waterfall, rock climbers, a fine café, and another boat dock for a convenient return to Keswick—see page 704). Note: When the water level is very high (for example, after a heavy rain), boats can't stop at Hawes End—ask at the TI or boat dock before setting out.

Catbells is probably the most dramatic family walk in the area (but wear sturdy shoes, bring a raincoat, and watch your footing). From Keswick, the lake, or your farmhouse B&B, you can see silhouetted figures hiking along this ridge.

Getting There: To reach the trailhead from Keswick, catch the "anticlockwise" boat (see "Boating on Derwentwater," earlier) and ride for 10 minutes to the second stop, Hawes End. (You can also ride to High Brandelhow and take this walk in the other direction, but I don't recommend it—two rocky scrambles along the way are easier and safer to navigate going uphill from Hawes End.) Note the schedule for your return boat ride. Drivers can park free at Hawes End, but parking is limited and the road can be hard to find—get very clear directions in town before heading out. (Hardcore hikers can walk to the foot of Catbells from Keswick via Portinscale, which takes about 40 minutes—ask your B&B or the TI for directions). The Keswick TI sells a *Catbells* brochure about the hike (£1).

The Route: The path is not signposted, but it's easy to follow, and you'll see plenty of other walkers. From Hawes End, walk away from the lake, through a kissing gate to the turn just before the car park. Then turn left and go up, up, up. After about 20 min-

utes, you'll hit the first of two short scrambles (where the trail vanishes into a cluster of steep rocks), which leads to a bluff. From the first little summit (great for a picnic break), and then along the ridge, you'll enjoy sweeping views of the lake on one side and of Newlands Valley on the other. The bald peak in the distance is Catbells. Broken stones crunch under each step, wind buffets your ears, clouds prowl overhead, and the sheep baa comically. To anyone looking up from the distant farmhouse B&Bs, you are but a stick figure on the ridge. Just below the summit, the trail disintegrates into another short, steep, scramble. Your reward is just beyond: a magnificent hilltop perch.

After Catbells summit, descend along the ridge to a saddle ahead. The ridge continues much higher, and while it may look like your only option, at its base a small, unmarked lane with comfortable steps leads left. Unless you're up for extending the hike (see "Longer Catbells Options," next), take this path down to the lake. To get to High Brandelhow Pier, take the first left fork you come across down through a forest to the lake. When you reach Abbot's Bay, go left through a swinging gate, following a lakeside trail around a gravelly bluff, to the idyllic High Brandelhow Pier, a peaceful place to wait for your boat back to Keswick. (You can pay your fare when you board.)

Longer Catbells Options: Catbells is just the first of a series of peaks, all connected by a fine ridge trail. Hardier hikers continue up to nine miles along this same ridge, enjoying valley and lake views as they arc around the Newlands Valley toward (and even down to) Buttermere. After High Spy, you can descend an easy path into Newlands Valley. The ultimate, very full day-plan would be to take a bus to Buttermere, climb Robinson, and follow the ridge around to Catbells and back to Keswick.

▲▲Buttermere Hike

The ideal little lake with a lovely, circular four-mile stroll offers nonstop, no-sweat Lake District beauty. If you're not a hiker (but kind of wish you were), take this walk. If you're very short on time, at least stop here and get your shoes dirty.

Buttermere is connected with Borrowdale and Derwentwater by a great road that runs over rugged Honister Pass. Buses #77/#77A make a 1.5-hour round-trip loop between Keswick and

LAKE DISTRICT

Derwentwater & Newlands Valley

Accommodations
1. Uzzicar Farm
2. Ellas Crag Guest House
3. Gill Brow Farm
4. Keskadale Farm
5. Bridge Hotel
6. Buttermere Hostel
7. Ashness Farm
8. Seatoller Farm B&B
9. Borrowdale Hostel

1 MILE

1 KM

TO COCKERMOUTH

B-5292

(B) 77

WHIN-LATTER PASS

BRAITH-WAITE

PORTIN-SCALE

A-66

N

NEWLANDS VALLEY

① STAIR

SKEL-GILL

TO COCKERMOUTH

NEWLANDS PASS

④

③ ②

CRUMMOCK WATER

B-5289

⑤

⑥ BUTTERMERE VILLAGE

(B) 77

LITTLE TOWN

CATBELLS RIDGE HIKE

GRANGE

BUTTER-MERE

P GATESGARTH FARM

SEATOLLER
(B) 78
(END POINT)

HONISTER PASS

B-5289 ⑧ P

SLATE MINE P

SEATHWAITE P

Derwentwater Piers
Ⓐ Keswick Launch Pier
Ⓑ Ashness Gate Pier
Ⓒ Lodore Pier
Ⓓ High Brandelhow Pier
Ⓔ Low Brandelhow Pier
Ⓕ Hawes End Pier
Ⓖ Nichol End Pier

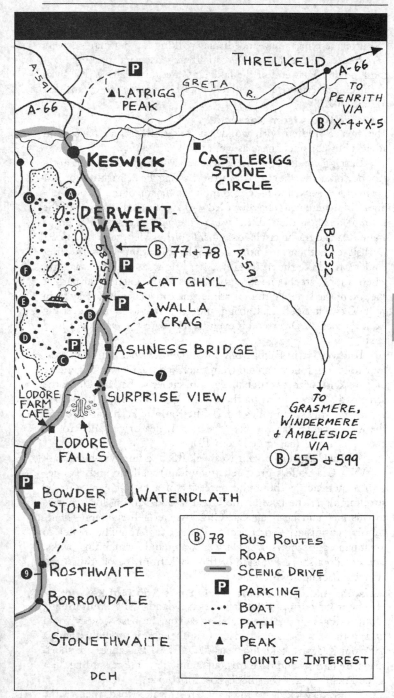

THRELKELD

A-66

TO PENRITH VIA Ⓑ X-4 & X-5

A-541

A-66

LATRIGG PEAK

GRETA R.

Ⓟ

KESWICK

CASTLERIGG STONE CIRCLE

Ⓖ Ⓐ

DERWENT-WATER

B-5289

← Ⓑ 77 & 78

Ⓟ

CAT GHYL

A-591

B-5532

Ⓟ

WALLA CRAG

Ⓕ

Ⓔ Ⓑ

Ⓓ

Ⓟ ASHNESS BRIDGE

Ⓒ

❼

SURPRISE VIEW

LODORE FARM CAFE

LODORE FALLS

TO GRASMERE, WINDERMERE & AMBLESIDE VIA Ⓑ 555 & 599

Ⓟ BOWDER STONE WATENDLATH

❾ ROSTHWAITE

BORROWDALE

STONETHWAITE

DCH

Ⓑ 78	BUS ROUTES
—	ROAD
▬	SCENIC DRIVE
Ⓟ	PARKING
⋯	BOAT
- - -	PATH
▲	PEAK
■	POINT OF INTEREST

Buttermere that includes a trip over this pass. The two-pub hamlet of Buttermere has a pay-and-display parking lot, but many drivers park free along the side of the road. There's also a pay parking lot at the Honister Pass end of the lake (at Gatesgarth Farm). The Syke Farm in Buttermere is popular for its homemade ice cream (tel. 01768/77022).

▲▲More Hikes from Keswick

The area is riddled with wonderful hikes. B&Bs all have good advice, but consider these as well:

Latrigg Peak: For the easiest mountain-climbing sensation around, take the short drive to the Latrigg Peak parking lot just north of Keswick, and hike 15 minutes to the top of the 1,200-foot-high hill, where you'll be rewarded with a commanding view of the town, lake, and valley, all the way to the next lake over (Bassenthwaite). At the traffic circle just outside of Keswick, take the A-591 Carlisle exit, then an immediate right (direction: Ormathwaite/Underscar). Take the next right, a hard right, at the *Skiddaw* sign, where a long, steep, one-lane road leads to the Latrigg car park at the end of the lane. With more time, you can walk all the way from your Keswick B&B to Latrigg and back (it's a popular evening walk for locals). Or extend it even farther with the walk described next.

Railway Path: Right from downtown Keswick, this flat, easy, four-mile trail follows an old train track and the river to the village of Threlkeld (with two pubs). You can either walk back along the same path, or loop back via the Castlerigg Stone Circle (described earlier, roughly seven miles total). The Railway Path starts behind the leisure center (as you face the center, head right and around back; pick up £1 map/guide from TI).

Walla Crag: From your Keswick B&B, a fine two-hour walk to Walla Crag offers great fell (mountain) walking and a ridge-walk experience without the necessity of a bus or car. Start by strolling along the lake to the Great Wood parking lot (or drive to this lot), and head up Cat Ghyl (where "fell runners"—trail-running enthusiasts—practice) to Walla Crag. You'll be treated to great panoramic views over Derwentwater and surrounding peaks. You can do a shorter version of this walk from the parking lot at Ashness Packhorse Bridge.

▲▲▲Car Hiking: A Scenic Circle Drive South of Keswick

This hour-long drive, which includes Newlands Valley, Buttermere, Honister Pass, and Borrowdale, gives you the best scenery you'll find in the North Lake District. (To do a similar route without a car from Keswick, take loop bus #77/#77A.) Distances are short, roads are narrow and have turnouts, and views are rewarding. Get a good map and ask your B&B host for advice.

From Keswick, leave town on Crosthwaite Road, then, at the

roundabout, head west on Cockermouth Road (A-66, following *Cockermouth* and *Workington* signs). Don't take the first Newlands Valley exit, but do take the second one (through Braithwaite), and follow signs up the majestic Newlands Valley (also signed for *Buttermere*).

If the **Newlands Valley** had a lake, it would be packed with tourists. But it doesn't—and it isn't. The valley is dotted with

500-year-old family-owned farms. Shearing day is reason to rush home from school. Sons get school out of the way ASAP and follow their dads into the family business. Neighbor girls marry those sons and move in.

Grandparents retire to the cottage next door. With the price of wool depressed, most of the wives supplement the family income by running B&Bs (virtually every farm in the valley rents rooms). The road has one lane, with turnouts for passing. From the Newlands Pass summit, notice the glacial-shaped wilds, once forested, now not.

From the parking lot at **Newlands Pass,** at the top of Newlands Valley (unmarked, but you'll see a waterfall on the left), an easy 300-yard hike leads to a little waterfall. On the other side of the road, an easy one-mile hike climbs up to **Knottrigg,** which probably offers more TPCB (thrills per calorie burned) than any walk in the region. If you don't have time for even a short hike, at least get out of the car and get a feel for the setting.

After Newlands Pass, descend to **Buttermere** (scenic lake, tiny hamlet with pubs and an ice-cream store—see "Buttermere Hike," earlier), turn left, drive the length of the lake, and climb over rugged **Honister Pass**—strewn with glacial debris, remnants from the old slate mines, and curious, shaggy Swaledale sheep (looking more like goats with their curly horns). The U-shaped valleys you'll see are textbook examples of those carved out by glaciers. Look high on the hillsides for "hanging valleys"—small glacial-shaped scoops cut off by the huge flow of the biggest glacier, which swept down the main valley.

The **Honister Slate Mine,** England's last still-functioning slate mine (and worth ▲), stands at the summit of Honister Pass. The youth hostel next to it was originally built to house miners in the 1920s. The mine offers worthwhile tours (perfect for when it's pouring outside): You'll put on a hardhat, load onto a bus for a short

climb, then hike into a shaft to learn about the region's slate industry. It's a long, stooped hike into the mountain, made interesting
by the guide and punctuated by the sound of your helmet scraping
against low bits of the shaft. Standing deep in the mountain, surrounded by slate scrap and the beams of thirty headlamps fluttering
around like fireflies, you'll learn of the hardships of miners' lives
and how "green gold" is trendy once again, making the mine viable.
Even if you don't have time to take the tour, stop here for its slate-
filled shop (café and nice WCs, £10, 1.5-hour tour; departs daily
at 10:30, 12:30, and 15:30; additional tour at 14:00 in summer;
Dec-Jan 12:30 tour only; call ahead to confirm times and to book
a spot, helmets and lamps provided, wear good walking shoes and
bring warm clothing—even in summer, tel. 017687/77230, www.
honister-slate-mine.co.uk).

After stark and lonely Honister Pass, drop into sweet and
homey **Borrowdale,** with a few lonely hamlets and fine hikes from
Seathwaite. Circling back to Keswick past Borrowdale, the B-5289
(a.k.a., the Borrowdale Valley Road) takes you past the following
popular attractions.

A set of stairs leads to the top of the house-size **Bowder Stone**
(signposted, a few minutes' walk off the main road). For a great
lunch or snack, including tea and homemade quiche and cakes,
drop into the much-loved **High Lodore Farm Café** (Easter-Oct
daily 9:00-18:00, closed Nov-Easter, short drive uphill from the
main road and over a tiny bridge, tel. 017687/77221). Farther along,
Lodore Falls is a short walk from the road, behind Lodore Hotel (a
nice place to stop for tea and beautiful views). **Shepherds Crag,** a
cliff overlooking Lodore, was made famous by pioneer rock climbers. (Their descendants hang from little ridges on its face today.)
This is serious climbing, with several fatalities a year.

A very hard right off the B-5289 (signposted *Ashness Bridge,
Watendlath*) and a steep half-mile
climb on a narrow lane takes you to
the postcard-pretty **Ashness Packhorse Bridge,** a quintessential Lake
District scene (parking lot just above
on right). A half-mile farther up,
park the car and hop out (parking lot
on left, no sign). You'll be startled
by the "surprise view" of Derwentwater—great for a lakes photo op.
Continuing from here, the road gets

extremely narrow en route to the hamlet of **Watendlath,** which has
a tiny lake and lazy farm animals.

Return to the B-5289 and head back to Keswick. If you have

yet to see it, cap your drive with a short detour from Keswick to the Castlerigg Stone Circle (described earlier).

Nightlife in Keswick

▲▲Theatre by the Lake
Keswickians brag that they enjoy "London theater quality at Keswick prices." Their theater offers events year-round and a wonderful rotation of six plays from late May through October (plays vary throughout the week, with music concerts on Sun in summer). There are two stages: The main one seats 400, and the smaller "studio" theater seats 100 (and features edgier plays that may involve rough language and/or nudity). Attending a play here is a fine opportunity to enjoy a classy night out.

Cost and Hours: £10-32, discounts for old and young, shows generally at 20:00, possibly earlier fall through spring, café, restaurant (pre-theater dinners must be booked 24 hours ahead by calling 017687/81102), smart to buy tickets in advance, parking at the adjacent lot is free after 19:00, tel. 017687/74411; book at box office (daily 9:30-20:00), by phone, at TI, or at www.theatrebythelake. com.

▲▲Evening Activities
For a small and remote town, Keswick has lots going on in the evening. Remember, at this latitude it's light until 22:00 in midsummer.

In Hope Park: Along with the Theatre by the Lake (described above), you can do some early evening **golfing** (fine course, pitch-and-putt, goofy golf, or just enjoy the putting green—see "Golf" under "Sights in Keswick," earlier) or **walk** among the grazing sheep as the sun gets ready to set (between the lake and the golf course, access from just above the beach, great photo ops on balmy evenings).

Keswick Launch's **evening lake cruise** comes with a glass of wine and a mid-lake stop for a short commentary. You're welcome to bring a picnic dinner and munch scenically as you cruise (£9.50, £23.50 family ticket, 1 hour, daily mid-July-Aug at 18:30 and 19:30—weather permitting and if enough people show up).

In the Town Center: To socialize with locals, head to a pub for one of their special evenings: There's **quiz night** at The Dog and Gun (21:30 on most Thu; £1, proceeds go to Keswick's Mountain Rescue team, which rescues hikers and the occasional sheep). At a quiz night, tourists are more than welcome. Drop in, say you want to join a team, and you're in. If you like trivia, it's a great way to get to know people here.

The Oddfellows Arms has free **live music** (often classic rock) just about every night in summer (April-Oct, from 21:30).

The **Keswick Street Theatre**—a theatrical walk through Keswick and its history—takes place on Tuesday evenings in summer (£3, 1.5 hours, usually starts at 19:30, weekly late May–early July, details at TI). Or you could catch a **movie** at the Lonsdale Alhambra Cinema (St. Johns Street, tel. 017687/72195, www.keswick-alhambra.co.uk), a restored old-fashioned movie theater a few minutes' walk from the town center.

Sleeping in Keswick

The Lake District abounds with attractive B&Bs, guesthouses, and hostels. It needs them all when the summer hordes threaten the serenity of this Romantic mecca.

Reserve your room in advance in high season. From November through March, you should have no trouble finding a room. But to get a particular place (especially on Saturdays), call ahead. If you're using public transportation, you should sleep in Keswick. If you're driving, staying outside Keswick is your best chance for a remote farmhouse experience. Lakeland hostels offer inexpensive beds and come with an interesting crowd of all ages.

For Keswick, I've featured B&Bs and small hotels mainly on two streets, each within three blocks of the bus station and town square. Stanger Street, a bit humbler but quiet and handy, has smaller homes and more moderately priced rooms. "The Heads" is a classier area lined with proud Victorian houses, close to the lake and theater, overlooking the golf course. In addition to these two streets, Keswick abounds with many other options that are equally good; for example, the southeast area of the town center (around Eskin, Blencathra, and Helvellyn streets) is a few minutes' walk farther out, but has several B&Bs with easier parking.

Many of my Keswick listings charge extra for a one-night stay. Most won't book one-night stays on weekends (but if you show up and they have a bed free, it's yours) and don't welcome young children (generally under ages 8-12). Owners are enthusiastic about offering plenty of advice to get you on the right walking trail. Most accommodations have inviting lounges with libraries of books on the region and loaner maps. Take advantage of these lounges to transform your humble B&B room into a suite.

This is still the countryside—expect huge breakfasts (often with a wide selection, including vegetarian options), no phones in the rooms, and shower systems that might need to be switched on to get hot water. Parking is pretty easy (each place has a line on parking).

Sleep Code

(£1 = about $1.60, country code: 44, area code: 017687)
S = Single, **D** = Double/Twin, **T** = Triple, **Q** = Quad, **b** = bathroom, **s** = shower only. Unless otherwise noted, credit cards are accepted and breakfast is included.

To help you sort easily through these listings, I've divided the accommodations into three categories based on the price for a double room with bath:

 $$$ **Higher Priced**—Most rooms £80 or more.
  $$ **Moderately Priced**—Most rooms between £60-80.
   $ **Lower Priced**—Most rooms £60 or less.

Prices can change without notice; verify the hotel's current rates online or by email. For the best prices, always book direct.

On Stanger Street

This street, quiet but just a block from Keswick's town center, is lined with B&Bs situated in Victorian slate townhouses. Each of these places is small and family-run. They are all good, offering comfortably sized rooms and a friendly welcome.

$$ Ellergill Guest House has five spic-and-span rooms with an airy, contemporary feel—several with views (Db-£65-80 depending on room size, 1 with private bath down the hall, 2 percent surcharge for credit cards, 2-night minimum, no children under age 10, free Wi-Fi, private parking, 22 Stanger Street, tel. 017687/73347, www.ellergill.co.uk, stay@ellergill.co.uk, Clare and Robin Pinkney).

$$ Badgers Wood B&B, at the top of the street, has six modern, bright, un-frilly view rooms, each named after a different tree (Sb-£40, Db-£74-78, cash only, 2-night minimum, no children under age 10, special diets accommodated, free Wi-Fi, free parking, 30 Stanger Street, tel. 017687/72621, www.badgers-wood.co.uk, enquiries@badgers-wood.co.uk, Andrew and Anne).

$$ Dunsford Guest House rents four recently updated rooms at a good price. Stained glass and wooden pews give the blue-and-cream breakfast room a country-chapel vibe (Db-£70, this price promised with this book when you book direct, cash only, free Wi-Fi, parking, 16 Stanger Street, tel. 017687/75059, www.dunsford.net, enquiries@dunsford.net, Deb and Keith).

$$ Abacourt House, with a daisy-fresh breakfast room, has five pleasant doubles (Db-£74-78, 3 percent surcharge for credit cards, no children, free Wi-Fi, £5 sack lunches available,

26 Stanger Street, tel. 017687/72967, www.abacourt.co.uk, aba-court.keswick@btinternet.com, John and Heather).

On The Heads

These B&Bs are in an area known as The Heads. This area is class-ier, with bigger and grander Victorian architecture and great views overlooking the pitch-and-putt range and out into the hilly distance. The golf-course side of The Heads has free parking, if you can snare a spot (easy at night). A single yellow line on the curb means you're allowed to park there for free, but only overnight (16:00-10:00).

$$$ Howe Keld has the pol-ished feel of a boutique hotel, but of-fers all the friendliness of a B&B. Its 14 contemporary-posh rooms, two on the ground floor, are spacious and tastefully decked out in native woods and slate. It's warm, welcoming, and family-run, with one of the best breakfasts I've had anywhere in England (Sb-£55-65, standard Db-£95-110, superior Db-£100-125, cash and 2-night minimum preferred, discount for 2 or more nights, family deals, free Wi-Fi, tel. 017687/72417 or toll-free 0800-783-0212, www.howekeld.co.uk, david@howekeld.co.uk, run with care by David and Valerie Fisher).

$$$ Parkfield House, thoughtfully run and decorated by John and Susan Berry, is a big Victorian house with a homey lounge. Its six rooms, some with fine views, are bright and classy (Sb-£70, Db-£80, superior king Db-£95-100, these prices promised with this book, 2-night minimum, no children under age 16, free Wi-Fi, free parking, tel. 017687/72328, www.parkfield-keswick.co.uk, parkfieldkeswick@hotmail.co.uk).

$$$ Burleigh Mead B&B is a slate mansion from 1892 with wild carpeting. Gill (pronounced "Jill," short for Gillian) rents seven lovely rooms and offers a friendly welcome, as well as a lounge and peaceful front-yard sitting area that's perfect for enjoying the view (north-facing Db with lesser views-£78-84, south-facing Db with grander views-£82-90, Db suite-£96-106, rate depends on length of stay, cash only, no children under age 8, free Wi-Fi, tel. 017687/75935, www.burleighmead.co.uk, info@burleighmead.co.uk).

$$$ Hazeldene Hotel, on the corner of The Heads, rents 10 spacious rooms, many with commanding views. It's run with care by delightful Helen and Howard (Db-£75-100 depending on view, Tb-£120, free guest computer, free Wi-Fi, free parking, tel. 017687/72106, www.hazeldene-hotel.co.uk, info@hazeldene-hotel.co.uk).

$$ Brundholme Guest House has four bright and comfy rooms, most with sweeping views—especially from the front side—and a friendly and welcoming atmosphere (Db-£70, free Wi-Fi, tel. 017687/73305, mobile 0773-943-5401, www.brundholme.co.uk, bazaly@hotmail.co.uk, Barry and Allison Thompson).

On Eskin Street

The area just southeast of the town center has several streets lined with good B&Bs, and is still within easy walking distance of downtown and the lake.

$$ Allerdale House, a classy, nicely decorated stone mansion, holds six rooms and is well-run by Barbara and Paul (Sb-£39.50, standard Db-£79, superior Db-£93, these prices promised with this book, cash only, free Wi-Fi, private parking, 1 Eskin Street, tel. 017687/73891, www.allerdale-house.co.uk, reception@allerdale-house.co.uk).

Hostels in and near Keswick

The Lake District's inexpensive hostels, mostly located in great old buildings, are handy sources of information and social fun.

$ Keswick Youth Hostel, with 85 beds in a converted old mill that overlooks the river, has a big lounge and great riverside balcony. Travelers of all ages feel at home here, but book ahead—family rooms can be especially hard to come by from July through September (£13-22 beds in mostly 3- to 6-bed rooms, members pay £3 less, breakfast-£5, family rooms, includes sheets, pay guest computer, pay Wi-Fi, kitchen, laundry, café, bar, office open 7:00-23:00, center of town just off Station Road before river, tel. 017687/72484, www.yha.org.uk, keswick@yha.org.uk).

$ Derwentwater Hostel, in a 220-year-old mansion on the shore of Derwentwater, is two miles south of Keswick and has 88 beds (£19-21 beds in 4- to 22-bed rooms, family rooms, breakfast-£5.25, free Wi-Fi, kitchen, laundry, 23:00 curfew; follow B-5289 from Keswick—entrance is 2 miles along the Borrowdale Valley Road about 150 yards after Ashness exit—look for cottage and bus stop at bottom of the drive; tel. 017687/77246, www.derwentwater.org, contact@derwentwater.org).

West of Keswick, in the Newlands Valley

If you have a car, drive 10 minutes past Keswick down the majestic Newlands Valley (described earlier, under "Car Hiking: Scenic Circle Drive South of Keswick"). This valley is studded with 500-year-old farms that have been in the same family for centuries and now rent rooms to supplement the family income. Each place offers easy parking, grand views, and perfect tranquility. Most of these rooms tend to be plainer and generally more dated than the B&Bs in town, and come with steep and gravelly roads, plenty of dogs, and an earthy charm. Traditionally, farmhouses lacked central heating, and while they are now heated, you can still request a hot-water bottle to warm up your bed.

Getting to the Newlands Valley: Leave Keswick via the roundabout at the end of Crosthwaite Road, and then head west on Cockermouth Road (A-66). Take the second Newlands Valley exit through Braithwaite, and follow signs through Newlands Valley (drive toward Buttermere). All of my recommended B&Bs are on this road: Uzzicar Farm (under the shale field, which local kids love hiking up to glissade down; a 10-minute drive from Keswick), Ellas Crag Guest House, then Gill Brow Farm, and finally—the last house before the stark summit—Keskadale Farm (about four miles before Buttermere at the top of the valley— about a 15-minute drive from Keswick). The one-lane road has turnouts for passing.

$$ Uzzicar Farm is a big, rustic place with two comfy guest rooms in a low-ceilinged, 16th-century farmhouse—watch out for ducks. It's a particularly intimate and homey setting, where you'll feel like part of the family (Db-£70-80, family rooms, cash or check only, tel. 017687/78026, www.uzzicarfarm.co.uk, stay@uzzicarfarm.co.uk, Helen, David, and three daughters).

$$ Ellas Crag Guest House, with three rooms—each with a great view—is a comfortable stone house with a contemporary feel and tranquil terrace overlooking the valley. This homey B&B offers a good mix of modern and traditional decor, including beautifully tiled bathrooms (Sb-£55-65, Db-£68-72, these prices good with this book, singles available Mon-Thu only, cash only, 2-night minimum, local free-range meats and eggs for breakfast, sack lunches available, huge DVD library, laundry-£10/load, tel. 017687/78217, www.ellascrag.co.uk, info@ellascrag.co.uk, Jane and Ed Ma and their children).

$$ Keskadale Farm is another good farmhouse experience, with Ponderosa hospitality. One of the valley's oldest, the house— with two guest rooms and a cozy lounge—is made from 500-year-old ship beams. This working farm is an authentic slice of Lake District life and is your chance to get to know lots of curly-horned sheep and the dogs that herd them. Now that her boys are old enough to help Dad in the fields, Margaret Harryman runs the B&B (Db-£70-80, £2 extra for one-night stays, cash only, closed Dec-Feb, sack lunches available, tel. 017687/78544, www.keskadalefarm.co.uk, info@keskadalefarm.co.uk). They also rent a two-bedroom apartment (£450/week).

$ Gill Brow Farm is a rough-hewn, working farmhouse more than 300 years old where Anne Wilson rents two simple but fine rooms, one with an en-suite bathroom, the other with a private bathroom down the hall (Db-£64, discount with 3-night stay, self-catering cottage also available, tel. 017687/78270, www.gillbrow-keswick.co.uk, info@gillbrow-keswick.co.uk).

Southwest of Keswick, in Buttermere

$$$ Bridge Hotel, just beyond Newlands Valley at Buttermere, offers 21 beautiful rooms—most of them quite spacious—and a classic Old World countryside-hotel experience. On Fridays and Saturdays, dinner is required (standard Db-£90-130 Sun-Thu, £130-180 Fri-Sat with dinner, fancier rooms for £10-20 more, apartments available, check website for specials, minimum 2-night stay on weekends, free Wi-Fi in lobby, tel. 017687/70252, www. bridge-hotel.com, enquiries@bridge-hotel.com). There are no shops within 10 miles—only peace and quiet a stone's throw from one of the region's most beautiful lakes. The hotel has a dark-wood pub/restaurant on the ground floor.

$ Buttermere Hostel, a quarter-mile south of Buttermere village on Honister Pass Road, has good food, 70 beds, family rooms, and a peacefully rural setting (£15-22 beds in mostly 4- to 6-bed rooms, members pay £3 less, breakfast-£5, inexpensive dinners and packed lunches, laundry, office open 8:30-10:00 & 17:00-22:30, 23:00 curfew, reservation tel. 0845-371-9508, hostel tel. 017687/70245, www.yha.org.uk, buttermere@yha.org.uk).

South of Keswick, near Borrowdale

$$$ Ashness Farm sits alone, ruling its valley high above Derwentwater. If you want to be immersed in farm sounds and lakeland beauty, this is the place. On this 750-acre working farm, now owned by the National Trust, people have raised sheep and cattle for centuries. Today Anne and her family are "tenant farmers," keeping this farm operating and renting five rooms to boot (Sb-£56-58, Db-£82-94, discount with stays of 2 or more nights, cozy lounge, eggs and sausage literally fresh off the farm for breakfast, sack lunches available, just above Ashness Packhorse Bridge, tel. 017687/77361, www.ashnessfarm.co.uk, enquiries@ashnessfarm. co.uk).

$$ Seatoller Farm B&B is a rustic 16th-century house on another working farm owned by the National Trust. Christine Simpson rents three rooms in her B&B, one of five buildings in this hamlet. The old windows are small, but the abundant flower boxes keep things bright (Db-£78, discount with stays of 2 or more nights, cottage available, closed mid-Dec-mid-Jan, tel. 017687/77232, www. seatollerfarm.co.uk, info@seatollerfarm.co.uk).

$ Borrowdale Hostel, in secluded Borrowdale Valley just

south of Rosthwaite, is a well-run place surrounded by many ways to immerse yourself in nature. The hostel offers cheap dinners and sack lunches (86 beds—mostly bunks, £18-23 beds in mostly 2- to 6-bed dorms, D-£50-60, members pay £3 less, family rooms, breakfast-£5, pay guest computer, pay Wi-Fi, laundry, office open 7:00-23:00, 23:00 curfew, reservation tel. 0845-371-9624, hostel tel. 017687/77257, www.yha.org.uk, borrowdale@yha.org.uk). To reach this hostel from Keswick by bus, take #78, the Borrowdale Rambler. Note that the last bus from Keswick departs around 17:00-17:30 most of year (see page 687 for bus details).

Eating in Keswick

Keswick has a huge variety of eateries catering to its many visitors, but I've found nothing particularly enticing at the top end; the places listed here are just good, basic values. Most stop serving by 21:00.

The Dog and Gun serves good pub food (I love their rump of lamb) with great pub ambience. Upon arrival, muscle up to the bar to order your beer and/or meal. Then snag a table as soon as one opens up. Mind your head, and tread carefully: Low ceilings and wooden beams loom overhead, while paws poke out from under tables below, as Keswick's canines wait patiently for their masters to finish their beer (£6-10 meals, food served daily 12:00-21:00, goulash, no chips and proud of it, dog treats, 2 Lake Road, tel. 017687/73463).

The Pheasant is a walk outside town, but locals trek here regularly for the food. The menu offers Lake District pub standards (fish pie, Cumbrian sausage, guinea fowl), as well as more inventive choices. Check the walls for caricatures of pub regulars, sketched at these tables by a Keswick artist. While they have a small restaurant section, I much prefer eating in the bar (£9-13 meals, daily 12:00-14:00 & 18:00-21:00, light bites served 14:00-16:00 on spring and summer weekends, Crosthwaite Road, tel. 017687/72219). From the town square, walk past the Pencil Museum, hang a right onto Crosthwaite Road, and walk 10 minutes. For a more scenic route, cross the river into Fitz Park, go left along the riverside path until it ends at the gate to Crosthwaite Road, turn right, and walk five minutes.

Star of Siam serves authentic Thai dishes in a tasteful dining room (£8-11 plates, daily 12:00-14:30 & 17:30-22:30, 89 Main Street, tel. 017687/71444).

Abraham's Tea Room, popular with townspeople, is a fine value for lunch. It's tucked away on the upper floor of the giant George Fisher outdoor store (£4-8 soups, salads, and sandwiches;

Mon-Fri 10:00-17:00, Sat 9:30-17:00, Sun 10:30-16:30, on the corner where Lake Road turns right, tel. 017687/71811).

The Lakeland Pedlar, a wholesome, pleasant café, serves freshly baked vegan, gluten-free, and vegetarian fare, including soups, organic bread, and daily specials. Their interior is cute. Outside tables face a big parking lot (£8 meals, Sun-Wed 9:00-17:00, Thu-Sat 9:00-20:30, Hendersons Yard, find the narrow walkway off Market Street between pink Johnson's sweet shop and The Golden Lion, tel. 017687/74492).

Bryson's Bakery and Tea Room has an enticing ground-floor bakery, with sandwiches and light lunches. The upstairs is a popular tearoom. Order lunch to go from the bakery, or for a few pence more, eat there, either sitting on stools or at a couple of sidewalk tables. Consider their £22.50 two-person Cumberland Cream Tea, which is like afternoon tea in London, but cheaper, and made with local products. Sandwiches, scones, and little cakes are served on a three-tiered platter with tea (£4-8 meals, daily 9:00-17:00, 42 Main Street, tel. 017687/72257).

Pumpkin has a small café space but a huge following, and is known for its fresh ingredients. Stop by for a light snack of homemade muffins and an espresso, or try a lamb burger (prices higher if you eat in, Mon-Sat 8:30-16:00, Sun 10:00-16:00, 19 Lake Road, tel. 017687/75973).

Eateries on Station Road: The street leading from the town square to the leisure center has several restaurants, including **Casa Bella,** a popular and packed Italian place that's good for families—reserve ahead (£8-11 pizzas and pastas, daily 17:00-21:15, 24 Station Street, tel. 017687/75575).

Picnic: The fine **Booths supermarket** is right where all the buses arrive (Mon-Sat 8:00-21:00, Sun 9:30-16:00, The Headlands). The recommended **Bryson's Bakery** does good sandwiches to go (described earlier). **The Old Keswickian,** on the town square, serves up old-fashioned fish-and-chips to go (Sun-Thu 11:00-22:30, Fri-Sat 11:00-23:30, closes at 22:00 in winter, upstairs restaurant closes earlier). Just around the corner, **The Cornish Pasty** offers an enticing variety of fresh meat pies to go (£2-3 pies, daily 9:00-17:30 or until the pasties are all gone, across from The Dog and Gun on Borrowdale Road, tel. 017687/72205).

In the Newlands Valley

The farmhouse B&Bs of Newlands Valley don't serve dinner, so their guests have two good options: Go into Keswick, or take the lovely 10-minute drive to Buttermere for an evening meal at **The Fish Inn** pub, which has fine indoor and outdoor seating, but takes no reservations (£8-10 meals, food served daily 12:00-14:00 & 18:00-21:00, family-friendly, good fish and daily specials with fresh vegetables, tel. 017687/70253). The neighboring **Bridge Hotel Pub** is a bit cozier and serves "modern-day nibbles and good classic pub grub" (£10-12 meals, food served daily 9:30-21:30, tel. 017687/70252).

Keswick Connections

The nearest train station to Keswick is in Penrith (ticket window open Mon-Sat 5:30-21:00, Sun 11:30-21:00, no lockers). For train and bus info, check at a TI, visit www.traveline.org.uk, or call 0845-748-4950 (for train), or 0871-200-2233. Most routes run less frequently on Sundays.

From Keswick by Bus: For connections, see page 687.

From Penrith by Bus to: Keswick (hourly Mon-Sat, every 2 hours on Sun, 45 minutes, £6.20, pay driver, Stagecoach bus #X4 or #X5), **Ullswater** and **Glenridding** (4/day, 45 minutes, bus #108 or #508). The Penrith bus stop is just outside the train station (bus schedules posted inside and outside station).

From Penrith by Train to: Blackpool (nearly hourly, 2 hours, change in Preston), **Liverpool** (nearly hourly, 2.25 hours, change in Wigan or Preston), **Birmingham**'s New Street Station (5/day direct, more with transfer, 2.5-3 hours), **Durham** (hourly, 3 hours, change in Carlisle and Newcastle), **York** (roughly 2/hour, 3.5-4 hours, 1-2 transfers), **London**'s Euston Station (4/day direct, more with transfer, 3-4 hours), **Edinburgh** (9/day direct, 1.75 hours), **Glasgow** (roughly hourly direct, 1.75 hours), **Oban** (2/day, 6 hours, transfer in Glasgow).

Route Tips for Drivers

From Points South (such as Blackpool, Liverpool, or North Wales) to the Lake District: The direct, easy way to Keswick is to leave the M-6 at Penrith, and take the A-66 motorway for 16 miles to Keswick. For a scenic sightseeing drive through the south lakes to Keswick, exit the M-6 on the A-590/A-591 through the towns of Kendal and Windermere to reach Brockhole National Park Visitors Centre. From Brockhole, the A road to Keswick is fastest, but the high road—the tiny road over Kirkstone Pass to Glenridding and lovely Ullswater—is much more dramatic.

Coming from (or Going to) the West: Only 1,300 feet above sea level, Hard Knott Pass is still a thriller, with a narrow, winding, steeply graded road. Just over the pass are the scant but evocative remains of the Hard Knott Roman fortress. The great views can come with miserable rainstorms, and it can be very slow and frustrating when the one-lane road with turnouts is clogged by traffic. Avoid it on summer weekends.

Ullswater Lake Area

For advice on the Ullswater area, visit the **TI** at the pay parking lot in the heart of the lakefront village of Glenridding (daily 9:30-17:30, tel. 017684/82414, www.visiteden.co.uk).

▲▲Ullswater Hike and Boat Ride

Long, narrow Ullswater, which some consider the loveliest lake in the area, offers eight miles of diverse and grand Lake District scenery. While you can drive it or cruise it, I'd ride the boat from the south tip halfway up (to Howtown—which is nothing more than

a dock) and hike back. Or walk first, then enjoy an easy ride back.

An old-fashioned **"steamer" boat** (actually diesel-powered) leaves Glenridding regularly for Howtown (departs daily generally 9:45-16:45, 6-9/day April-Oct, fewer off-season, 40 minutes; £6.20 one-way, £9.80 round-trip, £13.20 round-the-lake ticket lets you hop on and off, covered by £14.80 Ullswater Bus & Boat day pass, family rates, drivers can use safe pay-and-display parking lot, by public transit take bus #108 or #508 from Penrith, café at dock, £4 walking route map, tel. 017684/82229, www.ullswater-steamers.co.uk).

From Howtown, spend three to four hours hiking and dawdling along the well-marked path by the lake south to Patterdale, and then along the road back to Glenridding. This is a serious seven-mile walk with good views, varied terrain, and a few bridges and farms along the way. For a shorter hike from Howtown Pier, consider a three-mile loop around Hallin Fell. A rainy-day plan is to ride the covered boat up and down the lake to Howtown and Pooley Bridge at the northern tip of the lake (£13.20, 2.25 hours). Boats don't run in really bad weather—call ahead if it looks iffy.

▲▲Lanty's Tarn and Keldas Hill

If you like the idea of an Ullswater-area hike, but aren't up for the long huff from Howtown, consider this shorter (but still moderately challenging and plenty scenic) loop that leaves right from the TI's pay parking lot in Glenridding (about 2.5 miles, allow 2-2.5 hours; before embarking, buy the well-described leaflet for this walk in the TI).

From the parking lot, head to the main road, turn right to cross the river, then turn right again immediately and follow the river up into the hills. After passing a row of cottages, turn left,

LAKE DISTRICT

cross the wooden bridge, and proceed up the hill through the swing gate. Just before the next swing gate, turn left (following *Grisedale* signs) and head to yet another gate. From here you can see the small lake called Lanty's Tarn.

While you'll eventually go through this gate and walk along the lake to finish the loop, first you can detour to the top of the adjacent hill, called Keldas, for sweeping views over the near side of Ullswater (to reach the summit, climb over the step gate and follow the faint path up the hill). Returning to—and passing through— the swing gate, you'll walk along Lanty's Tarn, then begin your slow, steep, and scenic descent into the Grisedale Valley. Reaching the valley floor (and passing a noisy dog breeder's farm), cross the stone bridge, then turn left and follow the road all the way back to the lakefront, where a left turn returns you to Glenridding.

▲Aira Force Waterfall

At Ullswater, there's a delightful little park with parking, a ranger trailer, and easy trails leading half a mile uphill to a powerful 60-foot-tall waterfall. You'll read about how Wordsworth was inspired to write three poems here...and after taking this little walk, you'll know why. The pay-and-display car park is just where the Troutbeck road from the A-66 hits the lake, on the A-592 between Pooley Bridge and Glenridding.

Helvellyn

Considered by many the best high-mountain hike in the Lake District, this breathtaking round-trip route from Glenridding includes the spectacular Striding Edge—about a half-mile along the ridge. Be careful; do this six-hour hike only in good weather, since the wind can be fierce. While it's not the shortest route, the Glenridding ascent is best. Get advice from the Ullswater TI in Glenridding or look for various books on this hike at any area TI.

South Lake District

The South Lake District has a cheesiness that's similar to other popular English resort destinations. Here, piles of low-end vacationers suffer through terrible traffic, slurp ice cream, and get candy floss caught in their hair. The area around Windermere is worth a drive-through if you're a fan of Wordsworth or Beatrix Potter, but you'll still want to spend the majority of your Lake District time (and book your accommodations) up north.

South Lake District

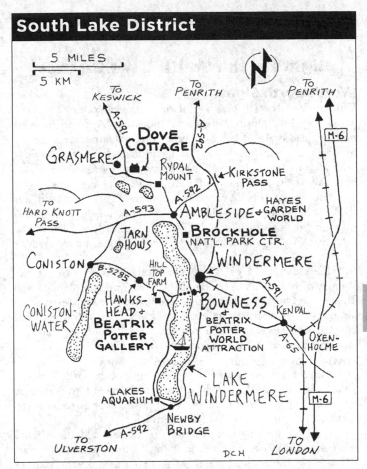

5 MILES
5 KM

TO KESWICK
TO PENRITH
TO PENRITH
M-6
DOVE COTTAGE
GRASMERE
RYDAL MOUNT
KIRKSTONE PASS
TO HARD KNOTT PASS
A-593
AMBLESIDE
HAYES GARDEN WORLD
BROCKHOLE NAT'L. PARK CTR.
TARN HOWS
WINDERMERE
CONISTON
B-5285
HILL TOP FARM
A-591
HAWKS-HEAD & BEATRIX POTTER GALLERY
BOWNESS
KENDAL
CONISTON-WATER
BEATRIX POTTER WORLD ATTRACTION
A-65
OXEN-HOLME
LAKE WINDERMERE
M-6
LAKES AQUARIUM
NEWBY BRIDGE
TO ULVERSTON
A-592
TO LONDON
DCH

LAKE DISTRICT

Getting Around

By Car: Driving is your best option to see the small towns and sights clustered in the South Lake District; consider combining your drive with the bus trip mentioned below. If you're coming to or leaving the South Lake District from the west, you could take the Hard Knott Pass for a scenic introduction to the area.

By Bus: Buses are a fine and stress-less way to lace together this gauntlet of sights in the congested Lake Windermere neighborhood. The open-top Lakeland Experience bus #599 stops at Bowness Pier (lake cruises), Windermere (train station), Brockhole (National Park Visitors Centre), Ambleside, Rydal Mount, and Grasmere (Dove Cottage). Consider leaving your car at Grasmere and enjoying the breezy and extremely scenic ride, hopping off and on as you like (3/hour Easter-late Sept, 2/hour late Sept-Oct, 50 minutes each way, £7 Central Lakes Dayrider all-day pass). Bus #555 runs between Windermere and Keswick.

Sights in the South Lake District

Wordsworth Sights

William Wordsworth was one of the first writers to reject fast-paced city life. During England's Industrial Age, hearts were muzzled and brains ruled. Science was in, machines were taming nature, and factory hours were taming humans. In reaction to these brainy ideals, a rare few—dubbed Romantics—began to embrace untamed nature and undomesticated emotions.

Back then, nobody climbed a mountain just because it was there—but Wordsworth did. He'd "wander lonely as a cloud" through the countryside, finding inspiration in "plain living and high thinking." He soon attracted a circle of like-minded creative friends.

The emotional highs the Romantics felt weren't all natural. Wordsworth and his poet friends Samuel Taylor Coleridge and Thomas de Quincey got stoned on opium and wrote poetry, combining their generation's standard painkiller drug with their tree-hugging passions. Today, opium is out of vogue, but the Romantic movement thrives as visitors continue to inundate the region.

▲▲Dove Cottage and Wordsworth Museum

For poets, this two-part visit is the top sight of the Lake District. Take a short tour of William Wordsworth's humble cottage, and be inspired in its excellent museum, which displays original writings, sketches, personal items, and fine paintings.

The poet whose appreciation of nature and a back-to-basics lifestyle put this area on the map spent his most productive years (1799-1808) in this well-preserved stone cottage on the edge of Grasmere. After functioning as the Dove and Olive Bow pub for almost 200 years, it was bought by his family. This is where Wordsworth got married, had kids, and wrote much of his best poetry. Still owned by the Wordsworth family, the furniture was his, and the place comes with some amazing artifacts, including the poet's passport and suitcase (he packed light). Even during his lifetime, Wordsworth was famous, and Dove Cottage was turned into a museum in 1891—predating even the National Trust, which protects the house today.

Cost and Hours: £7.50, daily March-Oct 9:30-17:30, Nov-Feb 9:30-16:30 except closed Jan, last entry 30 minutes before closing, café, bus #555 from Keswick, bus #555 or #599 from Windermere, tel. 015394/35544, www.wordsworth.org.uk. Parking costs £1 in the Dove Cottage lot off the main road (A-591), 50 yards from the site.

Wordsworth at Dove Cottage

William Wordsworth (1770-1850) was a Lake District home-boy. Born in Cockermouth (in a house now open to the public), he was schooled in Hawkshead. In adulthood, he married a local girl, settled down in Grasmere and Ambleside, and was buried in Grasmere's St. Oswald's churchyard.

But the 30-year-old man who moved into Dove Cottage in 1799 was not the carefree lad who'd once roamed the district's lakes and fields. At Cambridge University, he'd been a C student, graduating with no job skills and no interest in a nine-to-five career. Instead, he and a buddy hiked through Europe, where Wordsworth had an epiphany of the "sublime" atop Switzerland's Alps. He lived a year in France, watching the Revolution rage. It stirred his soul. He fell in love with a Frenchwoman who bore his daughter, Caroline. But lack of money forced him to return to England, and the outbreak of war with France kept them apart.

Pining away in London, William hung out in the pubs and coffeehouses with fellow radicals, where he met poet Samuel Taylor Coleridge. They inspired each other to write, edited each other's work, and jointly published a groundbreaking book of poetry.

In 1799, his head buzzing with words and ideas, William and his sister (and soul mate) Dorothy moved into the white-washed, slate-tiled former inn now known as Dove Cottage. He came into a small inheritance, and dedicated himself to poetry full time. In 1802, with the war over, William returned to France to finally meet his daughter. (He wrote of the rich experience: "It is a beauteous evening, calm and free... / Dear child! Dear Girl! that walkest with me here, / If thou appear untouched by solemn thought, / Thy nature is not therefore less divine.")

Having achieved closure, Wordsworth returned home to marry a former kindergarten classmate, Mary. She moved into Dove Cottage, along with an initially jealous Dorothy. Three of their five children were born here, and the cottage was also home to Mary's sister, the family dog Pepper (a gift from Sir Walter Scott; see Pepper's portrait), and frequent house-guests who bedded down in the pantry: Scott, Coleridge, and Thomas de Quincey, the Timothy Leary of opium.

After almost nine years here, Wordsworth's family and social status had outgrown the humble cottage. They moved first to a house in Grasmere before settling down in Rydal Hall. Wordsworth was changing. After the Dove years, he would write less, settle into a regular government job, quarrel with Coleridge, drift to the right politically, and endure criticism from old friends who branded him a sellout. Still, his poetry—most of it written at Dove—became increasingly famous, and he died honored as England's Poet Laureate.

Visiting the Cottage and Museum: Even if you're not a fan, Wordsworth's appreciation of nature, his Romanticism, and the ways his friends unleashed their creative talents with such abandon are appealing. The 25-minute cottage tour (which departs regularly—you shouldn't have to wait more than 30

minutes) and adjoining museum, with lots of actual manuscripts handwritten by Wordsworth and his illustrious friends, are both excellent. In dry weather, the garden where the poet was much inspired is worth a wander. (Visit this after leaving the cottage tour, and pick up the description at the back door. The garden is closed when wet.) Allow 1.5 hours for this visit.

Poetry Readings: On some Tuesday evenings in summer, the Wordsworth Trust puts on poetry readings, where national poets read their own works. They're hoping to continue the poetry tradition of the Lake District. Readings are held in Grasmere Village either at St. Oswald's Church or at the Daffodil Hotel (£8 at the door, £7 if prebooked, every other Tue at 19:30, generally May-mid-Oct, same contact info as above).

▲Rydal Mount

Located just down the road from Dove Cottage, this sight is worthwhile for Wordsworth fans. The poet's final, higher-class home, with

a lovely garden and view, lacks the humble charm of Dove Cottage, but still evokes the time and creative spirit of the literary giant who lived here for 37 years. His family repurchased it in 1969 (after a 100-year gap), and his great-great-great-granddaughter still calls it home on occasion, as shown by recent family photos sprinkled throughout the house. After a short intro by the attendant, you'll be given an explanatory flier and are welcome to roam. Wander through the garden William himself designed, which has changed little since then. Surrounded by his nature, you can imagine the poet enjoying them with you. "O happy garden! Whose seclusion deep, hath been so friendly to industrious hours; and to soft slumbers, that did gently steep our spirits carrying with them dreams of flowers, and wild notes warbled among leafy bowers."

Cost and Hours: £6.75; March-Oct daily 9:30-17:00; Nov-Dec and Feb Wed-Sun 11:00-16:00, closed Mon-Tue; closed Jan, occasionally closed for private functions—check website, tearoom, 1.5 miles north of Ambleside, well-signed, free and easy parking,

Wordsworth's Poetry at Dove

At Dove Cottage, Wordsworth was immersed in the beauty of nature and the simple joy of his young, growing family. It was here that he reflected on both his idyllic childhood and his troubled twenties. The following are select lines from two well-known poems from this fertile time.

Ode: Intimations of Immortality

There was a time when meadow, grove, and stream,
The earth, and every common sight, to me did seem
Apparelled in celestial light, the glory and the freshness of
    a dream.
It is not now as it hath been of yore; turn wheresoe'er I
    may, by night or day,
The things which I have seen I now can see no more.
Now while the birds thus sing a joyous song...
To me alone there came a thought of grief...
Whither is fled the visionary gleam?
Where is it now, the glory and the dream?
Our birth is but a sleep and a forgetting:
The Soul...cometh from afar...
Trailing clouds of glory do we come
From God, who is our home.

I Wandered Lonely as a Cloud

I wandered lonely as a cloud
That floats on high o'er vales and hills,
When all at once I saw a crowd,
A host, of golden daffodils;
Beside the lake, beneath the trees,
Fluttering and dancing in the breeze...
For oft, when on my couch I lie
In vacant or in pensive mood,
They flash upon that inward eye
Which is the bliss of solitude;
And then my heart with pleasure fills,
And dances with the daffodils.

bus #555 from Keswick, tel. 015394/33002, www.rydalmount. co.uk.

Beatrix Potter Sights

Of the many Beatrix Potter commercial ventures in the Lake District, there are two serious Beatrix Potter sights: her farm (Hill Top Farm) and her husband's former office, which is now the Beatrix Potter Gallery, filled with her sketches and paintings. The sights are two miles apart, in or near Hawkshead, a 20-minute drive south of Ambleside. If you're coming from Windermere, take bus

#505 to Hawkshead or catch the little 15-car ferry from Bowness (runs constantly except when it's extremely windy, 10-minute trip, £4.30 car fare includes all passengers, £3.80 if you buy ticket at TI). If you have questions, call the Hawkshead TI at tel. 015394/36946. Note that both of the major sights are closed on Friday (though the Beatrix Potter Gallery may be open on Fridays in summer—call ahead).

On busy summer days, the wait to get into Hill Top Farm can last several hours (only 8 people are allowed in every 5 minutes, and the timed-entry tickets must be bought in person). If you like cutesy tourist towns (Hawkshead), this can be a blessing. Otherwise, you'll wish you were in the woods somewhere with Wordsworth.

▲Hill Top Farm

A hit with Beatrix Potter fans (and skippable for others), this dark and intimate cottage, swallowed up in the inspirational and rough nature around it, provides an enjoyable if quick experience. The six-room farm was left just as it was when she died in 1943. At her request, the house is set as if she had just stepped out—flowers on the tables, fire on, low lights. While there's no printed information here, guides in each room are eager to explain things. Call the farm for the current tour-wait times (if no one answers, leave a message for the administrator; someone will call you back).

Cost and Hours: Farmhouse-£8.50, tickets often sell out by 14:00 or even earlier during busy times; gardens-free; June-Aug Sat-Thu 10:00-17:30, April-May and Sept-Oct Sat-Thu 10:30-16:30, mid-Feb-March Sat-Thu 10:30-15:30, closed Nov-mid-Feb and Fri year-round; last entry 30 minutes before closing, tel. 015394/36269, www.nationaltrust.org.uk/hill-top.

Getting There: The farm is located in Near Sawrey village, 2 miles south of Hawkshead. Mountain Goat Tours runs a shuttle bus from across from the Hawkshead TI to the farm every 40 minutes (tel. 015394/45161). Drivers can take the B-5286 and B-5285 from Ambleside or the B-5285 from Coniston. Park and buy tickets 150 yards down the road, and walk back to tour the place.

▲Beatrix Potter Gallery

Located in the cute but extremely touristy town of Hawkshead, this gallery fills Beatrix's husband's former law office with the wonderful and intimate drawings and watercolors that she did to illustrate her books. Each year the museum highlights a new theme and brings out a different set of her paintings, drawings, and other items. The best of the Potter sights, the gallery has plenty of explanation about her life and work, including touchscreen displays and information panels. Even non-Potter fans will find this museum rather charming and her art surprisingly interesting.

Cost and Hours: £4.80, April-Oct Sat-Thu 10:30-17:00, mid-Feb-March Sat-Thu 10:30-15:30, closed Fri except possibly in

Beatrix Potter (1866-1943)

As a girl growing up in London, Beatrix Potter vacationed in the Lake District, where she became inspired to write her popular children's books. Unable to get a publisher, she self-published the first two editions of *The Tale of Peter Rabbit* in 1901 and 1902. When she finally landed a publisher, sales of her books were phenomenal. With the money she made, she bought Hill Top Farm, a 17th-century cottage, and fixed it up, living there from 1905 until she married in 1913. Potter was more than a children's book writer; she was a fine artist, an avid gardener, and a successful farmer. She married a lawyer and put her knack for business to use, amassing a 4,000-acre estate. An early conservationist, she used the garden-cradled cottage as a place to study nature. She willed it—along with the rest of her vast estate—to the National Trust, which she enthusiastically supported.

summer (June-Aug; call or check online), closed Nov-mid-Feb, last entry 30 minutes before closing, Main Street, drivers use the nearby pay-and-display lot and walk 200 yards to the town center, tel. 015394/36355, www.nationaltrust.org.uk/beatrix-potter-gallery.

Hawkshead Grammar School Museum

The town of Hawkshead is engulfed in Potter tourism, and the extreme quaintness of it all is off-putting. Just across from the pay-and-display parking lot is the interesting Hawkshead Grammar School Museum, founded in 1585, where William Wordsworth studied from 1779 to 1787. It shows off old school benches and desks whittled with penknife graffiti.

Cost and Hours: £2.50 includes guided tour; April-Sept Mon-Sat 10:00-12:30 & 13:30-17:00, Sun 13:00-17:00; Oct until 16:30, closed Nov-March, tel. 015394/36735, www.hawkshead-grammar.org.uk.

The World of Beatrix Potter

This tour, a hit with children, is a gimmicky exhibit with all the historical value of a Disney ride. The 45-minute experience features a four-minute video trip into the world of Mrs. Tiggywinkle and company, a series of Lake District tableaux starring the same imaginary gang, and an all-about-Beatrix section, with an eight-minute video biography.

Cost and Hours: £7, kids-£3.65, daily April-Sept 10:00-18:00, Oct-March 10:00-17:00, last entry 30 minutes before closing, tearoom, on Crag Brow in Bowness-on-Windermere, tel. 08445-041-233, www.hop-skip-jump.com.

More Sights at Lake Windermere

Brockhole National Park Visitors Centre

Look for a stately old lakeside mansion between Ambleside and Windermere on the A-591. Set in a nicely groomed lakeside park, the center offers a free video on life in the Lake District, an information desk, organized walks (see the park's free *Visitor Guide*), exhibits, a shop (excellent selection of maps and guidebooks), a cafeteria, gardens, and nature walks. It's also a great place to bring kids for its free indoor play space, six-foot-tall climbing wall, and fun adventure playground with slides, swings, zip lines, nets, and swinging bridges. Other family activities, including an aerial treetop trek, mini-golf, and pony rides, have a fee.

Cost and Hours: Free, pay-when-you-leave parking (coins only); daily April-Oct 10:00-17:00, Nov-March 10:00-16:00, bus #555 from Keswick, bus #599 from Windermere, tel. 015394/46601, www.lakedistrict.gov.uk.

Cruise: For a joyride around famous Lake Windermere, you can catch the Brockhole "Green" cruise here (£7.40, runs daily 10:00-16:00, 2/hour mid-July-Aug, hourly April-mid-July and Sept-Oct, 45-minute circle, scant narration, tel. 015394/43360, www.windermere-lakecruises.co.uk).

Lakes Aquarium

This aquarium gives a glimpse of the natural history of Cumbria. Exhibits describe the local wildlife living in lake and coastal environments, including otters, eels, pike, and sharks. A rainforest exhibit features reptiles and marmoset monkeys. Experts give various talks throughout the day.

Cost and Hours: £9, £6 for kids under age 16, cheaper online, family deals, daily 9:00-18:00, until 17:00 in winter, last entry one hour before closing, in Lakeside, one mile north of Newby Bridge, at south end of Lake Windermere, tel. 015395/30153, www.lakesaquarium.co.uk.

Hayes Garden World

This extensive gardening center, a popular weekend excursion for locals, offers garden supplies, a bookstore, a playground, and gorgeous grounds. Gardeners could wander this place all afternoon. Upstairs is a fine cafeteria-style restaurant.

Cost and Hours: Mon-Sat 9:00-18:00, Sun 10:00-17:00, at south end of Ambleside on main drag, see *Garden Centre* signs, located at north end of Lake Windermere, tel. 015394/33434, www.hayesgardenworld.co.uk.

YORK

Historic York is loaded with world-class sights. Marvel at the York Minster, England's finest Gothic church. Ramble The Shambles, York's wonderfully preserved medieval quarter. Enjoy a walking tour led by an old Yorker. Hop a train at one of the world's greatest railway museums, travel to the 1800s in the York Castle Museum, head back 1,000 years to Viking times at the Jorvik Viking Centre, or dig into the city's buried past at the Yorkshire Museum.

York has a rich history. In A.D. 71, it was Eboracum, a Roman provincial capital—the northernmost city in the empire. Constantine was proclaimed emperor here in A.D. 306. In the fifth century, as Rome was toppling, the Roman emperor sent a letter telling England it was on its own, and York—now called Eoforwic—became the capital of the Anglo-Saxon kingdom of Northumbria.

The city's first church was built here in 627, and the town became an early Christian center of learning. The Vikings later took the town, and from the 9th through the 11th century, it was a Danish trading center called Jorvik. The invading and conquering Normans destroyed, then rebuilt the city, fortifying it with a castle and the walls you see today.

Medieval York, with 9,000 inhabitants, grew rich on the wool trade and became England's second city. Henry VIII used the city's fine Minster as the northern capital of his Anglican Church. (In today's Anglican Church, the Archbishop of York is second only to the Archbishop of Canterbury.)

In the Industrial Age, York was the railway hub of northern England. When it was built, York's train station was the world's largest. During World War II, Hitler chose to bomb York by pick-ing the city out of a travel guidebook (not this one).

Today, York's leading industry is tourism. It seems like ev-erything that's great about Britain finds its best expression in this manageable town. While the city has no single claim to fame, York is more than the sum of its parts. With its strollable cobbles and half-timbered buildings, grand cathedral and excellent museums, thriving restaurant scene and welcoming locals, York delights.

Planning Your Time

After London, York is the best sightseeing city in England. On even a 10-day trip through England, it deserves two nights and a day. For the best 36 hours, follow this plan: Arrive early enough to catch the 17:15 evensong service at the Minster, then take the free city walking tour at 18:45 (evening tours offered June-Aug only). Splurge on dinner at one of the city's creative bistros. The next morning at 9:00, take my self-guided walk, interrupting it midway with a tour of the Minster. Finish the walk and grab lunch near The Shambles. To fill your afternoon, choose among the town's many important sights (such as the York Castle Museum—open until 17:00; or the Railway Museum—open until 18:00). Spend the eve-ning enjoying a ghost walk of your choice (they depart at different times between 18:45 and 20:00) and another memorable dinner.

This is a packed day; as you review this chapter, you'll see that there are easily two days of sightseeing fun in York.

Orientation to York

York has roughly 195,000 people; about one in ten is a student. But despite the city's size, the sightseer's York is small. Virtually everything is within a few min-utes' walk: sights, train station, TI, and B&Bs. The longest walk a visitor might take (from a B&B across the old town to the York Castle Museum) is about 25 minutes.

Bootham Bar, a gate in the medieval town wall, is the hub of your York visit. (In York, a "bar" is a gate and a "gate" is a street. Blame the Vikings.) At Bootham Bar and on Exhibition Square, you'll find the starting points for most walking tours and bus tours, handy access to the medieval town wall, a public WC, and Bootham Street (which leads to my recommended B&Bs). To find your way around York, use the Minster's towers as a navigational landmark, or follow the strategically placed signposts, which point out all places of interest to tourists.

Tourist Information

York's TI, a block in front of the Minster, sells a £1 *York Map and Guide*. Ask for the free monthly *What's On* guide and the *York MiniGuide*, which includes a map (Mon-Sat 9:00-17:00, Sun 10:00-16:00, 1 Museum Street, tel. 01904/550-099, www.visity-ork.org). The TI books rooms for a £4 fee and has an Internet terminal (£1.50/30 minutes). A screen lists upcoming events.

York Pass: The TI sells an expensive pass that covers most sights in York, along with a few regional sights, including the North Yorkshire Moors Railway and Castle Howard (both described in the next chapter); it also gives discounts on the City Sightseeing hop-on, hop-off bus tours. You'd have to be a very busy sightseer to make this pass worth it (£36/1 day, £48/2 days, £58/3 days, www.yorkpass.com).

Arrival in York

By Train: The train station is a 10-minute walk from town. Day-trippers can store baggage at the window next to the Europcar office on platform 1 (£5/24 hours, baggage window open Mon-Sat 8:00-20:30, Sun 9:00-20:30).

Recommended B&Bs are a 5- to 15-minute walk (depending on where you're staying) or a £6 taxi ride from the station. For specific walking directions to the B&Bs, see page 760.

To walk downtown from the station, turn left down Station Road, veer through the gap in the wall and then left across the river, and follow the crowd toward the Gothic towers of the Minster. After the bridge, a block before the Minster, you'll come upon the TI on your right.

By Car: Driving and parking in York is maddening. Those day-tripping here should follow signs to one of the several park-and-ride lots ringing the perimeter. At these lots, parking is free, and cheap shuttle buses go every 10 minutes into the center.

If you're sleeping here, park your car where your B&B advises and walk. As you near York (and your B&B), you'll hit the A-1237 ring road. Follow this to the A-19/Thirsk roundabout (next to river on northeast side of town). From the roundabout, follow signs for *York*, traveling through Clifton into Bootham. All recommended B&Bs are four or five blocks before you hit the medieval city gate (see neighborhood map on page 762). If you're approaching York from the south, take the M-1 until it becomes the A-1M, exit at junction 45 onto the A-64, and follow it for 10 miles until you reach York's ring road (A-1237), which allows you to avoid driving

York

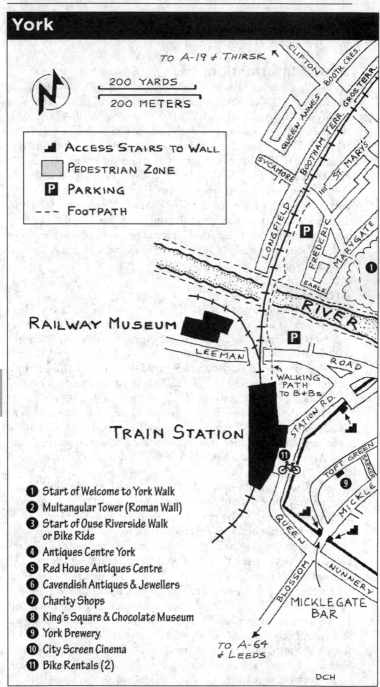

TO A-19 & THIRSK ↑

200 YARDS

200 METERS

- Access Stairs to Wall
- Pedestrian Zone
- **P** Parking
- - - - Footpath

YORK

RAILWAY MUSEUM

LEEMAN

RIVER

P

P

WALKING PATH TO B&Bs

ROAD

STATION RD.

TRAIN STATION

❶❶

TOFT GREEN

BARKER

❾

MICKLE

CLIFTON

BOOTH. CRES.

QUEEN ANNE'S

BOOTHAM TERR.

GROS. TERR.

SYCAMORE

ST. MARY'S

LONGFIELD

FREDERIC

MARYGATE

EARLS

❶

QUEEN

BLOSSOM

NUNNERY

MICKLEGATE BAR

TO A-64 & LEEDS

❶ Start of Welcome to York Walk
❷ Multangular Tower (Roman Wall)
❸ Start of Ouse Riverside Walk or Bike Ride
❹ Antiques Centre York
❺ Red House Antiques Centre
❻ Cavendish Antiques & Jewellers
❼ Charity Shops
❽ King's Square & Chocolate Museum
❾ York Brewery
❿ City Screen Cinema
⓫ Bike Rentals (2)

DCH

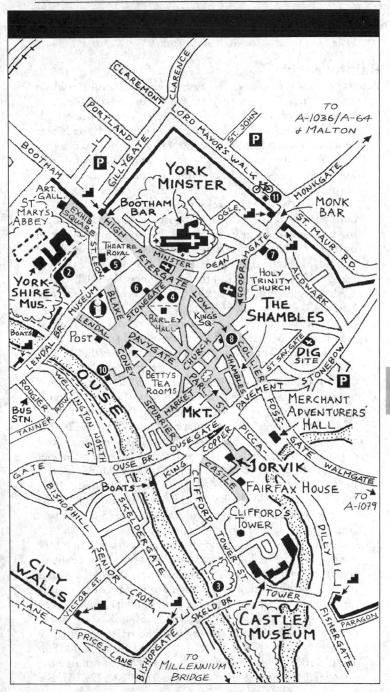

through the city center. If you have more time, the A-19 from Selby is a slower and more scenic route into York.

Helpful Hints

Festivals: Book a room well in advance during festival times and on weekends any time of year. The **Viking Festival** features *lur* horn-blowing, warrior drills, and re-created battles in mid-February (www.jorvik-viking-centre.co.uk). The **Early Music Festival** (medieval minstrels, Renaissance dance, and so on) zings its strings in early July (www.ncem.co.uk/yemf.shtml). York claims to be the "Ascot of the North," and the town fills up on horse-race weekends (once a month May-Oct, check schedules at www.yorkracecourse.co.uk); it's especially busy during the **Ebor Races** in mid-August. (Many avoid York during this period, as prices go up and the streets are filled with drunken revelers. Others find that attractive.) The **York Food and Drink Festival** takes a bite out of late September (www.yorkfoodfestival.com). And the St. Nicholas Fayre Christmas market jingles its bells in late November. For a complete list of festivals, see www.yorkfestivals.com.

Internet Access: The **TI** has one Internet terminal (see "Tourist Information," earlier). **Evil Eye Lounge** has six terminals in a hip bar (£1/30 minutes, free Wi-Fi, Mon-Sat 10:00-23:00, Sun 11:00-23:00, upstairs at 42 Stonegate, tel. 01904/640-002). The **York Public Library**'s reference desk, on the first floor up, provides computer terminals for visitors (£1/2 hours, free Wi-Fi, Mon-Thu 9:00-20:00, Fri 9:00-18:00, Sat 9:00-17:00, Sun 11:00-16:00, Museum Street, tel. 01904/552-828).

Laundry: The nearest place is **Haxby Road Launderette,** a long 15-minute walk north of the town center (self-service–about £6/load, about £1.50 more for drop-off service, Mon-Wed and Fri 9:00-17:45, Thu 10:00-18:00, Sat 9:00-17:00, Sun 9:00-16:00, start last loads 1.5 hours before closing, drop off 3 hours before closing, 124 Haxby Road, tel. 01904/623-379). Some B&Bs will do laundry for a reasonable charge.

Bike Rental: With the exception of the pedestrian center, the town's not great for biking. But there are several fine countryside rides from York, and the riverside New Walk bike path is pleasant. **Giant York** is just outside Monk Bar (£15/day, helmet and map free with this book, Mon-Sat 9:00-18:00, closed Sun, 13-15 Lord Mayor's Walk, tel. 01904/622-868, www.giant-york.co.uk). **Cycle Heaven** is at the train station (£10/half-day, £15/day, Mon-Fri 8:30-17:30, Sat 9:00-18:00, Sun 11:00-16:00, closed Sun off-season, to the left as you face the main station entrance from outside, tel. 01904/622-701). For locations, see map on page 730.

Taxi: From the train station, taxis zip new arrivals to their B&Bs for £6. Queue up at the taxi stand, or call 01904/638-833; cabbies don't start the meter until you get in.

Car Rental: If you're nearing the end of your trip, consider dropping your car upon arrival in York. The money saved by turning it in early just about pays for the train ticket that whisks you effortlessly to London. In York, you'll find these agencies: **Avis** (3 Layerthorpe, tel. 0844-544-6117); **Hertz** (at train station, tel. 01904/500-193); **Budget** (near the National Railway Museum behind the train station at 75 Leeman Road, tel. 01904/644-919); and **Europcar** (train station platform 1, tel. 0844-846-4003). Beware: Car-rental agencies close early on Saturday afternoons and all day Sunday—when dropping off is OK, but picking up is only possible by prior arrangement (and for an extra fee).

Updates to this Book: For news about changes to this book's coverage since it was published, see www.ricksteves.com/update.

Tours in York

▲▲▲Walking Tours

Free Walks with Volunteer Guides

Charming locals give energetic, entertaining, and free two-hour walks through York (April-Oct daily at 10:15 and 14:15, June-Aug also at 18:45; Nov-March daily at 10:15 and also at 13:15 on weekends; depart from Exhibition Square in front of the art gallery, tel. 01904/550-098, www.avgyork.co.uk). These tours often go long because the guides love to teach and tell stories. You're welcome to cut out early—but let them know, or they'll worry, thinking they've lost you.

Yorkwalk Tours

These are more serious 1.5- to 2-hour walks with a history focus. They do four different walks—Essential York, Roman York, Secret York, and The Snickelways of York—as well as a variety of "special walks" on more specific topics (£6, Feb-Nov daily at 10:30 and 14:15, Dec-Jan weekends only, depart from Museum Gardens Gate, just show up, tel. 01904/622-303, www.yorkwalk.co.uk—check website, ask TI, or call for schedule). Tours go rain or shine, with as few as two participants.

Ghost Walks

Each evening, the old center of York is crawling with creepy ghost walks. These are generally 1.5 hours long, cost £5, and go every evening, rain or shine. There are no reservations (you simply show up) and no tickets (just pay at the start). At the advertised time and place, your black-clad guide appears, and you follow him or her to

YORK

the first stop. Your guide gives a sample of the entertainment you have in store, humorously collects the "toll," and you're off.

You'll see fliers and signboards all over town advertising the many ghost walks. Companies come and go, but I find there are three general styles of walks: historic, street theater, and storytelling. Here are three reliably good walks, one for each style. Each gives a £1 discount (limit two "victims" per book) off full price for Rick Steves readers with this book:

The **Terror Trail Walk** is more historic, "all true," and a bit more intellectual (18:45, meet at The Golden Fleece at bottom of The Shambles, www.yorkterrortrail.co.uk).

The **Ghost Hunt** is comedic street theater produced and usually performed by Andy Dextrous, who introduces himself by saying, "My name is...unimportant" (19:30, meet at the bottom of The Shambles, www.ghosthunt.co.uk).

The **Original Ghost Walk** was the first of its kind, dating back to the 1970s, and is more classic, spooky storytelling rather than comedy (20:00, meet at The Kings Arms at Ouse Bridge, www.theoriginalghostwalkofyork.co.uk).

▲City Bus Tours

City Sightseeing's half-enclosed, double-decker, hop-on, hop-off buses circle York, taking tourists past secondary sights that the city walking tours skip—the mundane perimeter of town. While you can hop on and off all day, York is so compact that these have no real transportation value. If taking a bus tour, I'd catch either one at Exhibition Square (near Bootham Bar) and ride it for an orientation all the way around. Consider getting off at the National Railway Museum, skipping the last five minutes. Once or twice an hour, they run a "Heritage Tour" route with a live guide (£12, £13.50 combo-ticket with York Boat cruise—described next, pay driver, cash only, ticket valid 24 hours, Easter-Oct departs every 10-15 minutes, daily 9:00-17:30, less frequent off-season, about 1 hour, tel. 01904/633-990, www.yorkbus.co.uk).

Boat Cruise

York Boat does a lazy, narrated 45-minute lap along the River Ouse (£7.50, £13.50 combo-ticket with City Sightseeing bus tours—see above, April-Sept runs every 30 minutes, daily 10:30-15:00, off-season 4/day; leaves from Lendal Bridge and King's Staith landings, near Skeldergate Bridge; also 1.25-hour evening cruise at 21:15 for £9.50, leaves from King's Staith; tel. 01904/628-324, www.yorkboat.co.uk).

York at a Glance

▲▲▲**York Minster** York's pride and joy, and one of England's finest churches, with stunning stained-glass windows, textbook Decorated Gothic design, and glorious evensong services. **Hours:** Open for worship daily from 7:00 and for sightseeing Mon-Sat 9:00-18:30, Sun 12:30-18:30; shorter hours for tower and undercroft; evensong services Tue-Sat at 17:15, Sun at 16:00, occasionally on Mon at 17:15. See page 741.

▲▲**Yorkshire Museum** Sophisticated archaeology and natural history museum with York's best Viking exhibit, plus Roman, Saxon, Norman, and Gothic artifacts. **Hours:** Daily 10:00-17:00. See page 749.

▲▲**Jorvik Viking Centre** Entertaining and informative Disney-style exhibit/ride exploring Viking lifestyles and artifacts. **Hours:** Daily April-Oct 10:00-17:00, Nov-March until 16:00. See page 752.

▲▲**York Castle Museum** Far-ranging collection displaying everyday objects from Victorian times to the present. **Hours:** Daily 9:30-17:00. See page 754.

▲▲**National Railway Museum** Train buff's nirvana, tracing the history of all manner of rail-bound transport. **Hours:** Daily 10:00-18:00. See page 755.

▲**The Shambles** Atmospheric old butchers' quarter, with colorful, tipsy medieval buildings. **Hours:** Always open. See page 740.

▲**Ouse Riverside Walk** Bucolic path along river to a mod pedestrian bridge. **Hours:** Always open. See page 757.

▲**York Brewery** Honest, casual tour through an award-winning microbrewery with the guy who makes the beer. **Hours:** Mon-Sat at 12:30, 14:00, 15:30, and 17:00. See page 757.

▲**Fairfax House** Glimpse into an 18th-century Georgian family house, with enjoyably chatty docents. **Hours:** Tue-Sat 10:00-17:00, Sun 12:30-16:00, Mon by tour only at 11:00 and 14:00, closed Jan-mid-Feb. See page 753.

YORK

Self-Guided Walk

Welcome to York

Get a taste of Roman and medieval
York on this easy stroll. The walk begins in the gardens just in front of the
Yorkshire Museum, covers a stretch
of the medieval city walls, and then
cuts through the middle of the old
town. Start at the ruins of St. Mary's
Abbey in the Museum Gardens.

St. Mary's Abbey: This abbey
dates to the age of William the
Conqueror—whose harsh policies (called the "Harrowing of the
North") consisted of massacres and destruction, including the
burning of York's main church. His son Rufus, who tried to im-
prove relations in the 11th century, established a great church here.
The church became an abbey that thrived from the 13th century until the Dissolution of the Monasteries in the 16th century.
The Dissolution, which accompanied the Protestant Reformation
and break with Rome, was a power play by Henry VIII. The king
wanted much more than just a divorce: He wanted the land and
riches of the monasteries. Upset with the pope, he demanded that
his subjects pay him taxes rather than give the Church tithes. (For
more information, see the sidebar on page 744.)

As you gaze at this ruin, imagine magnificent abbeys like this
scattered throughout the realm.
Henry VIII destroyed most of
them, taking the lead from their
roofs and leaving the stones to
scavenging townsfolk. Scant as
they are today, these ruins still
evoke a time of immense monastic power. The one surviving
wall was the west half of a very

long, skinny nave. The tall arch marked the start of the transept.
Stand on the plaque that reads *Crossing beneath central tower*, and
look up at the air that now fills the space where a huge tower once
stood. (Fine carved stonework from the ruined abbey is on display
in a basement room of the adjacent Yorkshire Museum.)

Beyond the abbey, laid out like a dozen stone eggs, are 12 ancient **Roman sarcophagi** that were excavated at the train station.
You'll also see a bowling green and the abbey's original wall (not
part of the city walls).

• *With your back to the abbey, see the fine Neoclassical building housing
the* ***Yorkshire Museum*** *(well worth a visit and described later, under*

"Sights in York"). Walk past this about 30 yards to a corner of the city's **Roman wall.** *A tiny lane through the garden (past a yew tree) leads through a small arch, giving a peek into the ruined tower.*

Multangular Tower: This 12-sided tower (c. A.D. 300) was likely a catapult station built to protect the town from enemy river traffic. The red ribbon of bricks was a Roman trademark—both structural and decorative. The lower stones are Roman, while the upper, bigger stones are medieval. After Rome fell, York suffered through two centuries of a dark age. Then, in the ninth century, the Vikings ruled. They built with wood, so almost nothing from that period remains. The Normans came in 1066 and built in stone, generally atop Roman structures (like this wall). The wall that defined the ancient Roman garrison town worked for the Norman town, too. But after the English Civil War in the 1600s and Jacobite rebellions in the 1700s, fortified walls were no longer needed in England's interior.

• *Now, return 10 steps down the lane and turn right, walking between the museum and the Roman wall. Continuing straight, the lane goes between the abbot's palace and the town wall. This is a "snickelway"—a small, characteristic York lane or footpath. The snickelway pops out on...*

Exhibition Square: With Henry VIII's Dissolution of the Monasteries, the abbey was destroyed and the Abbot's Palace became the **King's Manor** (from the snickelway, make a U-turn to the left and through the gate). Enter the building under the coat of arms of Charles I, who stayed here during the English Civil War in the 1640s. Today, the building is part of the University of York. Because the northerners were slow to embrace the king's reforms, Henry VIII came here to enforce the Dissolution. He stayed 17 days in this mansion and brought along

1,000 troops to make his determination clear. You can wander into the grounds and building. The Refectory Café serves cheap cakes, soup, and sandwiches to students, professors, and visitors like you (Mon-Fri 9:30-15:30, closed Sat-Sun).

Exhibition Square is the departure point for various walking and bus tours. You can see the towers of the Minster in the distance. Travelers in the Middle Ages could see the Minster from miles away as they approached the city. Across the street is a public WC and **Bootham Bar**—one of the fourth-century Roman gates in York's wall—with access to the best part of the city walls (free, walls open 8:00-dusk).

• *Climb up the bar.*

Walk the Wall: Hike along the top of the wall behind the Minster to the first corner. York's 13th-century walls are three miles long. This stretch follows the original Roman wall. Norman kings built the walls to assert control over northern England. Notice the pivots in the crenellations (square notches

at the top of a medieval wall), which once held wooden hatches to provide cover for archers. The wall was extensively renovated in the 19th century (Victorians added Romantic arrow slits).

At the corner with the benches—**Robin Hood's Tower**—you can lean out and see the moat outside. This was originally the Roman ditch that surrounded the fortified garrison town. Continue walking for a fine view of the Minster, with its truncated main tower and the pointy rooftop of its chapter house.

• *Continue on to the next gate...*

Monk Bar: This fine medieval gatehouse is the home of the quirky **Richard III Museum.** Run by eccentric enthusiasts of the last king of England's Plantagenet dynasty (the Tudors took over after Richard was killed in 1485), it's filled with high-schoolish exhibits and lacks any historic artifacts. But with fun architecture to explore, it's mildly entertaining. Especially since the sensational discovery of Richard III's remains in Leicester in 2013, this king—demonized as a hunchbacked monster by Shakespeare—fascinates the English (£3, daily 9:00-17:00, Monk Bar, tel. 01904/634-191, www.richardiiimuseum.co.uk).

• *Descend the wall at Monk Bar, and step past the portcullis (last lowered in 1953 for the Queen's coronation) to emerge outside the city's protective wall. Take 10 paces and gaze up at the tower. Imagine 10 archers behind the arrow slits. Keep an eye on the 17th-century guards, with their stones raised and primed to protect the town.*

Return through the city wall. After a short block, turn right on Ogleforth. ("Ogle" is the Norse word for owl, hence our word "ogle"—to look at something fiercely.)

York's Old Town: Walking down Ogleforth, ogle (on your left) a charming little brick house called the **Dutch House.** Designed by an apprentice architect who was trying to show off for his master, it's from the 17th century. It was the first entirely brick house in town, a sign of opulence. Next, also of brick, is a former brewery, with a 19th-century, industrial feel.

Ogleforth jogs left and becomes **Chapter House Street,** passing the Treasurer's House to the back side of the Minster. Circle around the left side of the church, past the stonemasons' lodge (where craftsmen are chiseling local limestone for the church, as has been done here since the 13th century), to the statue of Roman Emperor Constantine and an ancient Roman column.

Step up to lounging **Constantine.** Five emperors visited York when it was the Roman city of Eboracum. Constantine was here when his father died. The troops declared him the Roman emperor in A.D. 306 at this site, and six years later, he went to Rome to claim his throne. In A.D. 312, Constantine legalized Christianity, and in A.D. 314, York got its first bishop. The thought-provoking plaque reads: "His recognition of the civil liberty of his Christian subjects and his personal conversion established the religious foundation of Western Christendom."

The **ancient column,** across the street from Constantine, is a reminder that the Minster sits upon the site of the Roman headquarters, or *principia*. The city placed this column here in 1971, just before celebrating the 1,900th anniversary of the founding of Eboracum—a.k.a. York.

• *If you want to visit* **York Minster** *now, find the entrance on its west side (see description on page 741). Otherwise, head into the town center. From opposite the Minster's south transept door (by Constantine), take a narrow pedestrian walkway—which becomes Stonegate—into the tangled commercial center of medieval York. Walk straight down Stonegate, a street lined with fun and inviting cafés, pubs, and restaurants. Just before the* Ye Olde Starre Inne *banner hanging over the street, turn left down the snickelway called Coffee Yard. (It's marked by a red devil.) Enjoy strolling York's...*

"Snickelways": This is a made-up York word combining "snicket" (a passageway between walls or fences), "ginnel" (a narrow passageway between buildings), and "alleyway" (any narrow passage)—snickelway. York—with its population packed densely inside its protective walls—has about 50 of these public passages. In general, when exploring the city, you should duck into these—both for the adventure and to take a shortcut. While some of York's history has been bulldozed by modernity, bits of it hide and survive in the snickelways.

Coffee Yard leads past Barley Hall, popping out at the corner of Grape Lane and Swinegate. Medieval towns named streets for the business done there. Swinegate, a lane of pig farmers, leads to the market. Grape Lane is a polite version of that street's original, crude name, Gropec*nt Lane. If you were here a thousand years ago, you'd find it lined by brothels. Throughout England, streets for prostitutes were called by this graphic name. Today, if you see a street named Grape Lane, that's usually its heritage.

Skip Grape Lane and turn right down Swinegate to a market (which you can see in the distance). The frumpy **Newgate Market,** popular for cheap produce and clothing, was created in the 1960s with the demolition of a bunch of colorful medieval lanes.

• *In the center of the market, tiny "Little Shambles" lane (on the left) dead-ends into the most famous lane in York.*

The Shambles: This colorful old street (rated ▲) was once the "street of the butchers." The name is derived from "shammell"—a butcher's bench upon which he'd cut and display his meat. In the 16th century, this lane was dripping with red meat. Look for the hooks under the eaves; these were once used to hang rabbit, pheasant, beef, lamb, and pigs' heads. Fresh slabs were displayed on the fat sills, while people lived above the shops. All the garbage and sewage flushed down the street to a mucky pond at the end—a  favorite hangout for the town's cats and dogs. Tourist shops now fill these fine, half-timbered Tudor buildings. Look above the modern crowds and storefronts to appreciate the classic old English architecture. Unfortunately, the soil here isn't great for building; notice how the structures have settled in the absence of a solid foundation.

Turn right and slalom down The Shambles. At the Mr. Sandwich shop, pop into the snickelway and look for very old **woodwork.** Study the 16th-century carpentry—mortise-and-tenon joints with wooden plugs rather than nails.

Next door (on The Shambles) is the **shrine of St. Margaret Clitherow,** a 16th-century Catholic crushed by Protestants under her own door (as was the humiliating custom when a city wanted to teach someone a lesson). She was killed for hiding priests in her home here. Stop into the tiny shrine for a peaceful moment to ponder Margaret who, in 1970, was sainted for her faith.

At the bottom of The Shambles is the cute, tiny **St. Crux Parish Hall,** which charities use to raise funds by selling light meals (see "Eating in York," later). Take some time to chat with the volunteers.

With blood and guts from The Shambles' 20 butchers all draining down the lane, it's no wonder The Golden Fleece, just below, is considered the most haunted pub in town.

• *Your town walk is finished. From here, you're just a few minutes from plenty of fun: street entertainment and lots of cheap eating options on King's Square, good restaurants on Fossgate, the York Castle Museum (a few blocks farther downhill), and the starting point for my Ouse Riverside Walk.*

Sights in York

▲▲▲York Minster

The pride of York, this largest Gothic church north of the Alps (540 feet long, 200 feet tall) brilliantly shows that the High Middle Ages were far from dark. The word "minster" means an important church chartered with a mission to evangelize. As it's the seat of a bishop, York Minster is also a cathedral. While Henry VIII destroyed England's great abbeys, this was not part of a monastery and was therefore left standing. It seats 2,000 comfortably; on Christmas and Easter, at least 4,000 worshippers pack the place. Today, more than 250 employees and 500 volunteers work to preserve its heritage and welcome 1.3 million visitors each year.

YORK

Cost: £10 includes guided tour, undercroft museum, and crypt; free for kids under age 16; tower climb-£5.

Hours: The cathedral is open for sightseeing Mon-Sat 9:00-18:30, Sun 12:30-18:30. It opens for worship daily at 7:00. Closing time flexes with activities, but last entry is generally at 17:30—call or look online to confirm. Sights within the Minster have shorter hours (listed below). The Minster may close for special events (check calendar on website).

Information: Pick up the worthwhile *Welcome to the York Minster* flier. Helpful Minster guides stationed throughout are happy to answer your questions. Tel. 01904/557-217 or 0844-393-0011, www.yorkminster.org.

Tower Climb: It costs £5 for 30 minutes of exercise (275 steps) and forgettable views. The tower opens at 10:00 (later on Sun), with ascents every 45 minutes; the last ascent is generally at 16:00—later in peak season and earlier in winter (no children under 8, not good

York Minster

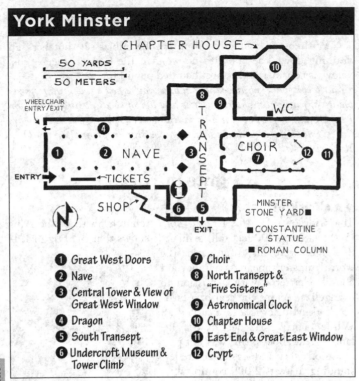

WHEELCHAIR ENTRY/EXIT

CHAPTER HOUSE

WC

NAVE

TRANSEPT

CHOIR

ENTRY

TICKETS

SHOP

EXIT

MINSTER STONE YARD

CONSTANTINE STATUE

ROMAN COLUMN

50 YARDS
50 METERS

1. Great West Doors
2. Nave
3. Central Tower & View of Great West Window
4. Dragon
5. South Transept
6. Undercroft Museum & Tower Climb
7. Choir
8. North Transept & "Five Sisters"
9. Astronomical Clock
10. Chapter House
11. East End & Great East Window
12. Crypt

YORK

for acrophobes, closes in extreme weather). Be sure to get your ticket upon arrival, as only 50 visitors are allowed up at once; you'll be assigned an entry time. It's a tight, spiraling, claustrophobic staircase with an iron handrail. You'll climb about 150 steps to the top of the transept, step outside to cross a narrow walkway, then go back inside for more than 100 steps to the top of the central tower. From here (while caged in), you can enjoy views of rooftops and the flat countryside.

Undercroft Museum: This new museum focuses on the history of the site and its origins as a Roman fortress (Mon-Sat 10:00-17:00, Sun 12:30-16:00).

Tours: Free guided tours depart from the ticket desk every hour on the hour (Mon-Sat 10:00-15:00, can be more frequent during busy times, none on Sun, one hour, they go even with just one or two people). You can join a tour in progress, or if none is scheduled, request a departure.

Stained-Glass Tours: Glass enthusiasts can take a special behind-the-scenes tour to learn about the restoration of the Minster's glass masterpiece, the Great East Window (£7.50; Mon, Wed, and Fri at 14:00; one hour, 15-person maximum).

Evensong: To experience the cathedral in musical and spiritual action, attend an evensong (Tue-Sat at 17:15, Sun at 16:00). On Mondays, visiting choirs fill in about half the time (otherwise it's a spoken service, also at 17:15). Visiting choirs also perform when the Minster's choir is on summer break (mid-July-Aug, confirm at church or TI). Arrive 15 minutes early and wait just outside the choir in the center of the church. You'll be ushered in and can sit in one of the big wooden stalls. As evensong is a worship service, attendees enter the church free of charge. For more on evensong, see page 164.

Church Bells: If you're a fan of church bells, you'll experience ding-dong ecstasy daily except Mon (Sun morning about 10:00, Tue practice 19:30-21:30, and Tue-Sat at 16:45 to announce evensong). These performances are especially impressive, as the church holds a full carillon of 35 bells (it's the only English cathedral to have such a range). Stand in front of the church's west portal and imagine the gang pulling on a dozen ropes (halfway up the right tower—you can actually see the ropes through a little window) while one talented carillonneur plays 22 more bells with a keyboard and foot pedals.

● Self-Guided Tour: Enter the great church through the west portal (under the twin towers). Upon entering, decide if you're climbing the tower. If so, get a ticket (with an assigned time).

• *Entering the church, turn 180 degrees and look back at the...*

Great West Doors: These are used only on special occasions. Flanking the doors is a list of archbishops (and other church of-

ficials) that goes unbroken back to the 600s. The statue of Peter with the key and Bible is a reminder that the church is dedicated to St. Peter, and the key to heaven is found through the word of God. While the Minster sits on the remains of a Romanesque church (c. 1100), today's church was begun in 1220 and took 250 years to complete. Up above, look for the female, headless "semaphore saints," using semaphore flag code to spell out a message with golden discs: "Christ is here."

• *Grab a chair and enjoy the view down the...*

Nave: Your first impression might be of its spaciousness and brightness. One of the widest Gothic naves in Europe, it was built between 1280 and 1360—the middle period of the Gothic style, called "Decorated Gothic." Rather than risk a stone roof, builders spanned the space with wood. Colorful shields on the arcades are

YORK

England's Anglican Church

The Anglican Church (a.k.a. the Church of England) came into existence in 1534 when Henry VIII declared that he, and not Pope Clement VII, was the head of England's Catholics. The pope had refused to allow Henry to divorce his wife to marry his mistress Anne Boleyn (which Henry did anyway, resulting in the birth of Elizabeth I). Still, Henry regarded himself as a faithful Catholic—just not a *Roman* Catholic—and made relatively few changes in how and what Anglicans worshipped.

Henry's son, Edward VI, later instituted many of the changes that Reformation Protestants were bringing about in continental Europe: an emphasis on preaching, people in the pews actually reading the Bible, clergy being allowed to marry, and a more "Protestant" liturgy in English from the revised Book of Common Prayer (1549). The next monarch, Edward's sister Mary I, returned England to the Roman Catholic Church (1553), earning the nickname of "Bloody Mary" for her brutal suppression of Protestant elements. When Elizabeth I succeeded Mary (1558), she soon broke from Rome again. Today, many regard the Anglican Church as a compromise between the Catholic and Protestant traditions. In the US, Anglicans split off from the Church in England after the American Revolution, creating the Episcopal Church that still thrives today.

Ever since Henry VIII's time, the York Minster has held a special status within the Anglican hierarchy. After a long feud over which was the leading church, the archbishops of Canterbury and York agreed that York's bishop would have the title "Primate of England" and Canterbury's would be the "Primate of All England," directing Anglicans on the national level.

the coats of arms of nobles who helped tall and formidable Edward I, known as "Longshanks," fight the Scots in the 13th century.

The coats of arms in the clerestory (upper-level) glass represent the nobles who helped his son, Edward II, in the same fight. There's more medieval glass in this building than in the rest of England combined. This precious glass survived World War II—hidden in stately homes throughout Yorkshire.

Walk to the very center of the church, under the **central tower.** Look up. An exhibit in the undercroft explains how gifts and skill saved this 197-foot tower from collapse. Use the neck-saving mirror to marvel at it.

Look back at the west end to marvel at the **Great West Window,** especially the stone tracery. While its nickname is the "Heart of Yorkshire," it represents the sacred heart of Christ, meant to remind people of his love for the world.

Find the **dragon** on the right of the nave (two-thirds of the way up the wall). While no one is sure of its purpose, it pivots and has a hole through its neck—so it was likely a mechanism designed to raise a lid on a baptismal font.

• *Facing the altar, turn right and head into the...*

South Transept: Look up. The new "bosses" (carved medallions decorating the point where the ribs meet on the ceiling) are a reminder that the roof of this wing of the church was destroyed by fire in 1984, caused when lightning hit an electricity box. Some believe the lightning was God's angry response to a new bishop, David Jenkins, who questioned the literal truth of Jesus' miracles. (Jenkins had been interviewed at a nearby TV studio the night before, leading locals to joke that the lightning occurred "12 hours too late, and 17 miles off-target.") Regardless, the entire country came to York's aid. *Blue Peter* (England's top kids' show) conducted a competition among their young viewers to design new bosses. Out of 30,000 entries, there were six winners (the blue ones—e.g., man on the moon, feed the children, save the whales).

Two other sights can be accessed through the south transept: the **Undercroft Museum** (explained later) and the **tower climb** (explained earlier). But for now, stick with this tour; we'll circle back to the south transept at the end, before exiting the church.

• *Head back into the middle of the nave and face the front of the church. You're looking at the...*

Choir: Examine the choir screen—the ornate wall of carvings separating the nave from the choir. It's lined with all the English

kings from William I (the Conqueror) to Henry VI (during whose reign it was carved, in 1461). Numbers indicate the years each reigned. It is indeed "slathered in gold leaf," which sounds impressive, but the gold is very thin...a nugget the size of a sugar cube is pounded into a sheet the size of a driveway.

Step into the choir, where a service is held daily. All the carving was redone after an 1829 fire, but its tradition of glorious evensong services (sung by choristers from the Minster School) goes all the way back to the eighth century.

• *To the left as you face the choir is the...*

YORK

North Transept: In this transept, the grisaille windows—dubbed the **"Five Sisters"**—are dedicated to British servicewomen who died in wars. Made in 1260, before colored glass was produced in England, these contain more than 100,000 pieces of glass.

The 18th-century **astronomical clock** is worth a look (the sign helps you make sense of it). It's dedicated to the heroic Allied aircrews from bases here in northern England who died in World War II (as Britain kept the Nazis from invading in its "darkest hour"). The Book of Remembrance below the clock contains 18,000 names.

• A corridor leads to the Gothic, octagonal...

Chapter House: This was the traditional meeting place of the governing body (or chapter) of the Minster. On the pillar in the middle of the doorway, the Virgin holds Baby Jesus while standing on the devilish serpent. The Chapter House, without an interior support, is remarkable (almost frightening) for its breadth. The fanciful carvings decorating the canopies above the stalls date from 1280 (80 percent are originals) and are some of the Minster's finest. Stroll slowly around the entire room and imagine that the tiny sculpted heads are a 14th-century parade—a fun glimpse of medieval society. Grates still send hot air up robes of attendees on cold winter mornings. A model of the wooden construction illustrates the impressive 1285 engineering.

The Chapter House was the site of an important moment in England's parliamentary history. Fighting the Scots in 1295, Edward I (the "Longshanks" we met earlier) convened the "Model Parliament" here, rather than down south, in London. (The Model Parliament is the name for its early version, back before the legislature was split into the Houses of Commons and Lords.) The government met here through the 20-year reign of Edward II, before moving to London during Edward III's rule in the 14th century.

• Go back out into the main part of the church, turn left, and continue all the way down the nave (behind the choir) to the...

East End: This part of the church is square, lacking a semi-circular apse, typical of England's Perpendicular Gothic style (15th century). Monuments (almost no graves) were once strewn throughout the church, but in the Victorian Age, they were gathered into the east end, where you see them today.

The **Great East Window,** the size of a tennis court, is currently under restoration. Under it, three exhibits—"Stone by Stone,"

"Let There Be Light," and "The Orb"—give an intimate look at Gothic stone- and glasswork.

Let There Be Light explains the significance of the window and the scope of the conservation project. It illustrates the painstaking process of removing, dismantling, cleaning, and restoring each of the 311 panels. Interactive computers let you zoom in on each panel, read about the stories depicted in them, and explore the codes and symbols that are hidden in the window.

The Orb, a futuristic dome that seems out of place in a medieval cathedral, offers a close-up look at several restored and exquisite stained-glass panels. Photos show what the windows looked like before, and information boards explain the challenges involved in restoring each one. This is a unique opportunity to see how exquisitely detailed the panels are. When they're back in their proper location, their minute features will be invisible from the floor of the church and therefore will be "for God's eyes only."

Because of the Great East Window's immense size, the east end has an extra layer of supportive stonework, parts of it wide enough to walk along. In fact, for special occasions, the choir has been known to actually sing from the walkway halfway up the window. But just as the window has deteriorated over time, so too has the stone. Nearly 3,500 stones need to be replaced or restored (as explained in the "Stone by Stone" exhibit). On some days, you may even see masons in action in the stone yard behind the Minster.

• *Below the choir (on either side), steps lead down to the...*

Crypt: Here you can view the boundary of the much smaller, but still huge, Norman church from 1100 that stood on this spot (look for the red dots, marking where the Norman church ended, and note how thick the wall was). You can also see some of the old columns and additional remains from the Roman fortress that once stood here, the tomb of St. William of York (actually a Roman sarcophagus that was reused), and the modern concrete save-the-church foundations (much of this church history is covered in the undercroft museum).

• *You'll exit the church through the south transept. If you've yet to climb the **tower,** the entrance is in the south transept. Also before leaving, look for the entrance to the...*

Undercroft Museum: Well-described exhibits follow the history of the site from its origins as a Roman fortress to the founding of an Anglo-Saxon/Viking church, the shift to a Norman place of worship, and finally the construction of the Gothic structure that stands today. Videos re-create how the fortress and Norman structure would have been laid out, and various artifacts and remains provide an insight into each period. The museum fills a space that was excavated following the near collapse of the central tower in 1967.

Highlights include the actual remains of the Roman fort's basilica, which are viewable through a see-through floor. There are also patches of Roman frescoes from what was the basilica's anteroom. One remarkable artifact is the Horn of Ulf: an intricately carved elephant's tusk presented to the Minster in 1030 by Ulf, a Viking nobleman, as a symbol that he was dedicating his land to God and the Church. Also on view is the York Gospels manuscript, a thousand-year-old text containing the four gospels. Made by Anglo-Saxon monks at Canterbury, it's the only book in the Minster's collection that dates prior to the Norman Conquest. It is still used to this day to swear in archbishops. Your last stop in the undercroft is a small and comfortable theater where you can enjoy three short videos (10 minutes total) showing the Minster in action.

• *This finishes your visit. Before leaving, take a moment to just be in this amazing building. Then, go in peace.*

Nearby: As you leave through the south transept, notice the people-friendly plaza created here and how effectively it ties the church in with the city that stretches before you. To your left are the Roman column from the ancient headquarters, which stood where the Minster stands today (and from where Rome administered the northern reaches of Britannia 1,800 years ago); a statue of Emperor Constantine; and the covered York Minster Stone Yard, where masons are chiseling stone—as they have for centuries—to keep the religious pride and joy of York looking good.

Other Sights Inside York's Walls

I've listed these roughly in geographical order, from near the Minster at the northwest end of town to the York Castle Museum at the southeast end.

Note that several of York's glitzier and most heavily promoted sights (including Jorvik Viking Centre, Dig, and Barley Hall) are run by the York Archaeological Trust (YAT). While rooted in real history, YAT attractions are geared primarily for kids and work hard (some say too hard) to make the history entertaining. If you like their approach and plan to visit several, ask about the various combo-ticket options.

▲▲Yorkshire Museum

Located in a lush, picnic-perfect park next to the stately ruins of St. Mary's Abbey (described in the self-guided walk, earlier), the Yorkshire Museum is the city's serious "archaeology of York" museum. You can't dig a hole in York without hitting some remnant of the city's long past, and most of what's found ends up here. While the hordes line up at Jorvik Viking Centre, this museum has no crowds and provides a broader historical context, with more real artifacts. The three main collections—Roman, medieval, and natural history—are well-described, bright, and kid-friendly.

Cost and Hours: £7.50, kids under 16 free with paying adult, £13 combo-ticket with York Castle Museum, daily 10:00-17:00, within Museum Gardens, tel. 01904/687-687, www.yorkshiremuseum.org.uk.

Visiting the Museum: At the entrance, you're greeted by an original, early fourth-century A.D. Roman statue of the god Mars. If he could talk, he'd say, "Hear me, mortals. There are three sections here: Roman (on this floor), medieval (downstairs), and natural history (a kid-friendly wing on this floor). Start first with the 10-minute video for a sweeping history of the city."

The **Roman** collection surrounds a large map on the floor of the Roman Empire. You'll see slice-of-life exhibits about Roman baths, a huge floor mosaic, and skulls accompanied by artists' renderings of how the people originally looked. (One man was apparently killed by a sword blow to the head—making it graphically clear that the struggle between Romans and barbarians was a violent one.) These artifacts are particularly interesting when you consider that you're standing in one of the farthest reaches of the Roman Empire.

The **medieval** collection is in the basement. During the Middle Ages, York was England's second city. One large room is dominated by ruins of the St. Mary's Abbey complex (described on page 736; one wall still stands just out front—be sure to see it before leaving). You'll also see old weapons, glazed vessels, and a well-preserved 13th-century leather box.

The museum's prized pieces are in this section: a helmet and a pendant. The eighth-century Anglo-Saxon helmet (known as the York Helmet or the Coppergate Helmet) shows a bit of barbarian refinement. Examine the delicate carving on its brass trim. The exquisitely etched 15th-century pendant—called

YORK

the Middleham Jewel—is considered the finest piece of Gothic jewelry in Britain. The noble lady who wore this on a necklace believed that it helped her worship and protected her from illness. The back of the pendant, which rested near her heart, shows the Nativity. The front shows the Holy Trinity crowned by a sapphire (which people believed put their prayers at the top of God's to-do list).

In addition to the Anglo-Saxon pieces, the Viking collection is one of the best England. Looking over the artifacts, you'll find that the Vikings (who conquered most of the Anglo-Saxon lands) wore some pretty decent shoes and actually combed their hair. The Cawood Sword, nearly 1,000 years old, is one of the finest surviving swords from that era.

The **natural history** exhibit (titled Extinct) is back upstairs, showing off skeletons of the extinct dodo and ostrich-like moa birds, as well as an ichthyosaurus.

Barley Hall
Uncovered behind a derelict office block in the 1980s, this medieval house has been restored to replicate a 1483 dwelling. It's designed to resurrect the Tudor age for visiting school groups, but feels soulless to adults.

Cost and Hours: £5, includes audioguide, kids under 5-free, combo-tickets with Jorvik Viking Centre and/or Dig, daily April-Oct 10:00-17:00, Nov-March 10:00-16:00, 2 Coffee Yard off Stonegate, tel. 01904/615-505, www.barleyhall.org.uk.

Holy Trinity Church
Built in the late Perpendicular Gothic style, this church has windows made of precious clear and stained glass from the 13th to 15th centuries. It holds rare box pews, which rest atop a floor that is sinking as bodies rot and coffins collapse. Enjoy its peaceful picnic-friendly gardens.

Cost and Hours: Free, Tue-Sat 10:00-16:00, Sun-Mon 12:00-16:00, 70 Goodramgate, tel. 1904/613-451, www.holytrinityyork.org.

King's Square
This lively people-watching zone, with its inviting benches, once hosted a church. Then it was the site for the town's gallows. Today, it's prime real estate for buskers and street performers. Just hanging out here can be very entertaining. Just beyond is the most characteristic and touristy street in old York: The Shambles. Within sight of this lively square are plenty of cheap eating options (for tips, see "Eating in York," later).

Chocolate: York's Sweet Story
Though known mainly for its Roman, Viking, and medieval past, York also has a rich history in chocolate-making. Throughout the 1800s and 1900s, York was home to three major confectionaries—

including Rowntree's, originators of the venerable Kit Kat. However, this chocolate "museum" is childish and overpriced. The building has no significance, and there are almost no historic artifacts. If you come, the visits are by tour only; your guide gives you lots of chocolate as you learn of York's confectionary past and watch brief videos.

Cost and Hours: £10, 30-minute tours run every 15 minutes daily 10:00-17:00 (last tour at 17:00), King's Square, tel. 0845-498-9411, www.yorksweetstory.com.

Dig

This hands-on, kid-oriented archaeological site gives young visitors an idea of what York looked like during Roman, Viking, medieval, and Victorian eras. Sift through "dirt" (actually shredded tires), dig up reconstructed Roman wall plaster, and take a look at what archaeologists have found recently. Entry is possible only with a one-hour guided tour (departures every 30 minutes); pass any waiting time by looking at the exhibits near the entry. The exhibits fill the haunted old St. Saviour's Church.

Cost and Hours: £5.50, kids under 5-free, combo-tickets with Jorvik Viking Centre and/or Barley Hall, daily 10:00-17:00, last tour departs one hour before closing, Saviourgate, tel. 01904/615-505, www.digyork.com.

Merchant Adventurers' Hall

Claiming to be the finest surviving medieval guildhall in Britain (from 1357-1361), this vast half-timbered building with marvelous exposed beams contains about 15 minutes' worth of interest-

ing displays about life and commerce in the Middle Ages. You'll see three original, large rooms that are still intact: the great hall itself, where meetings took place; the undercroft, which housed a hospital and alms-house; and a chapel. Several smaller rooms are filled with exhibits about old York. Sitting by itself in its own little park, this classic old building is worth a stop even just to see it from the outside. Remarkably, the hall is still owned by the same Merchant Adventurers society that built it 650 years ago (now a modern charitable organization).

Cost and Hours: £6, includes audioguide, March-Oct Mon-Thu 9:00-17:00, Fri-Sat 9:00-15:30, Sun 11:00-16:00, shorter hours and closed Sun off-season, south of The Shambles between Fossgate and Piccadilly, tel. 01904/654-818, www.theyork company.co.uk.

▲▲Jorvik Viking Centre

Take the "Pirates of the Caribbean," sail them northeast and back in time 1,000 years, sprinkle in some real artifacts, and you get

Jorvik (YOR-vik)—as much a ride as a museum. Between 1976 and 1981, more than 40,000 artifacts were dug out of the peat bog right here in downtown York— the UK's largest archaeological dig of Viking-era artifacts. When the archae-ologists were finished, the dig site was converted into this attraction. Innovative in 1984, the commercial success of Jorvik inspired copycat ride/museums all over England. Some love Jorvik, while others call it gimmicky and overpriced. If you think of it as Disneyland with a splash

of history, Jorvik's fun. To me, Jorvik is a commercial venture de-signed for kids, with too much emphasis on its gift shop. But it's also undeniably entertaining, and—if you take the time to peruse its exhibits—it can be quite informative.

Cost and Hours: £10, various combo-tickets with Dig and/or Barley Hall, daily April-Oct 10:00-17:00, Nov-March until 16:00, these are last-entry times, tel. 01904/615-505, www.jorvik-viking-centre.co.uk.

Crowd-Beating Tips: This popular attraction can come with long lines. At the busiest times (roughly 11:00-15:00), you may have to wait an hour or more—especially on school holidays. For £1 extra, you can book a slot in advance, either over the phone or on their website. Or you can avoid the worst lines by coming early or late in the day (when you'll more likely wait just 10-15 minutes).

Visiting Jorvik: First you'll walk down stairs (marked with the layers of history you're passing) and explore a small **museum.** Under the glass floor is a re-creation of the archaeological dig that took place right here. Surrounding that are a few actual artifacts (such as a knife, comb, shoe, and cup) and engaging videos detail-ing the Viking invasions, longships, and explorers, and the history of the excavations. Next to where you board your people-mover is the largest Viking timber found in the UK (from a wooden build-ing on Coppergate). Don't rush through this area: These exhibits offer historical context to your upcoming journey back in time. Viking-costumed docents are happy to explain what you're seeing.

When ready, board a theme-park-esque **people-mover** for a 12-minute trip through the re-created Viking street of Coppergate. It's the year 975, and you're in the village of Jorvik. You'll glide past reconstructed houses and streets that sit atop the actual excavation site, while the recorded commentary tells you about everyday life in

Viking times. Animatronic characters jabber at you in Old Norse, as you experience the sights, sounds, and smells of yore. Everything is true to the original dig—the face of one of the mannequins was computer-modeled from a skull dug up here.

Finally, you'll disembark at the **hands-on area,** where you can actually touch original Viking artifacts. You'll see several skeletons, carefully laid out and labeled to point out diseases and injuries, along with a big gob of coprolite (fossilized feces that offer archeologists invaluable clues about long-gone lifestyles). Next, a gallery of everyday items (metal, glass, leather, wood, and so on) provides intimate glimpses into that redheaded culture. Take advantage of the informative touchscreens. The final section is devoted to swords, spears, axes, and shields. You'll also see bashed-in skulls (with injuries possibly sustained in battle) and a replica of the famous Coppergate Helmet (the original is in the Yorkshire Museum).

▲Fairfax House

This well-furnished home, supposedly the "first Georgian townhouse in England," is perfectly Neoclassical inside. Each room is staffed by wonderfully pleasant docents eager to talk with you. They'll explain how the circa-1760 home was built as the dowry for an aristocrat's daughter. The house is compact and bursting with stunning period furniture (the personal collection of a local chocolate magnate), gorgeously restored woodwork, and lavish stucco ceilings that offer clues as to each room's purpose. For example, stuccoed philosophers look down on the library, while the goddess of friendship presides over the drawing room. Taken together, this house provides fine insights into aristocratic life in 18th-century England.

Cost and Hours: £6, Tue-Sat 10:00-17:00, Sun 12:30-16:00, Mon by guided tour only at 11:00 and 14:00—the one-hour tours are worthwhile, closed Jan-mid-Feb, near Jorvik Viking Centre at 29 Castlegate, tel. 01904/655-543, www.fairfaxhouse.co.uk.

Clifford's Tower

Perched high on a knoll across from the York Castle Museum, this ruin is all that's left of York's 13th-century castle—the site

of the gruesome 1190 mass-suicide of local Jews (they locked themselves inside and set the castle afire rather than face death at the hands of the bloodthirsty townspeople; read the whole story on the sign at the base of the hill). If you go inside, you'll see a model of the original castle complex as it looked in the Middle Ages, and you can climb up to enjoy fine city views from the top of the ramparts—but neither is worth the cost of admission.

Cost and Hours: £4.20, daily April-Sept 10:00-18:00, closes earlier off-season, last entry 15 minutes before closing, tel. 01904/646-940.

▲▲York Castle Museum

This fascinating museum is a Victorian home show, possibly the closest thing to a time-tunnel experience England has to offer. The

one-way plan assures that you'll see everything, including remakes of rooms from the 17th to 20th centuries, a re-creation of a Victorian street, interesting military exhibits, and some eerie prison cells.

Cost and Hours: £8.50, kids under 16 free with paying adult, £13 combo-ticket with Yorkshire Museum, daily 9:30-17:00, cafeteria at entrance, tel. 01904/687-687, www.yorkcastlemuseum.org.uk. It's at the bottom of the hop-on, hop-off bus route. The museum can call you a taxi (worthwhile if you're hurrying to the National Railway Museum, across town).

Information: The museum's £4 guidebook isn't necessary, but it makes a fine souvenir. The museum proudly offers no audioguides, as its roaming guides are enthusiastic about talking—engage them.

❍ Self-Guided Tour: The exhibits are divided between two wings: the North Building (to the left as you enter) and the South Building (to the right).

Follow the one-way route through the complex, starting in the **North Building.** You'll first visit the Period Rooms, illuminating Yorkshire lifestyles during different time periods (1600s-1950s) and among various walks of life. The excellent From Cradle to Grave exhibit traces the rites of passage of a typical lifetime during the Victorian Age. For example, most women mourned their husbands for two and a half years, reflected by the color of their clothes. (Queen Victoria, who was famously an extra-credit mourner, dressed in black for four decades after the death of her beloved Prince Albert; for more on Victoria, see sidebar on page 840.) The Hearth and Home exhibit showcases fireplaces and kitchens from the 1600s to the 1980s, and the Barn Gallery explains farming in Yorkshire.

Next, stroll down the museum's re-created Kirkgate, a street from the Victorian era, when Britain was at the peak of its power. It features old-time shops and storefronts, including a pharmacist, sweet shop, school, and grocer for the working class, along with

roaming live guides in period dress. Around the back is a slum area depicting how the poor lived in those times.

Circle back to the entry and cross over to the **South Building.** A new World War I exhibit marks the war's centennial. Because of the reorganization, parts of the following exhibits may be closed, in flux, or missing. The military section includes displays about the Merchant Adventurers (traders and buccaneers on the high seas), Elizabethan soldiers of York, Yorkshire's role in the English Civil War (tracing the events of 1642-1651), and a powerful exhibit called Seeing It Through in York, explaining both the military and civilian experience here during World War II. The Costume Gallery features 250 years of clothes and textiles, and the Toy Gallery takes you from dollhouses to Transformers.

Exit outside and cross through the castle yard. A detour to the left leads to a flour mill (open sporadically). Otherwise, your

tour continues through the door on the right, where you'll find another reconstructed historical street, this one capturing the spirit of the swinging 1960s—"a time when the cultural changes were massive but the cars and skirts were mini." Slathered with DayGlo colors, this street scene examines fashion, music, and television (including clips of beloved kids' shows and period news reports).

Finally, head into the York Castle Prison, which recounts the experiences of actual people who were thrown into the clink here. Videos, eerily projected onto the walls of individual cells, show actors telling tragic stories about the cells' one-time inhabitants.

Across the River

▲▲National Railway Museum

If you like model railways, this is train-car heaven. The thunderous museum shows 200 illustrious years of British railroad history. This biggest and best railroad museum anywhere is interesting even to people who think "Pullman" means "don't push."

Cost and Hours: Free but £3 suggested donation, daily 10:00-18:00, café, restaurant, tel. 0844-815-3139, www.nrm.org.uk.

Getting There: It's about a 15-minute walk from the Minster (southwest of town, up the hill behind the train station). From the train station itself, the fastest approach is to go all the way to the back of the station (using the overpass to cross the tracks), exit out the back door, and turn right up the hill. To skip the walk, a cute little "road train" shuttles you more quickly between the Minster and the Railway Museum (£2 each way, runs daily Easter-Oct, leaves museum every 30 minutes 11:00-16:00 at :00 and :30 past each hour; leaves town—from Duncombe Place, 100 yards in front of the Minster—at :15 and :45 past each hour).

Visiting the Museum: Pick up the floor plan to locate the various exhibits, which sprawl through several gigantic buildings on both sides of the street. Throughout the complex, red-shirted "explainers" are eager to talk trains.

The museum's most impressive room is the **Great Hall** (head right from the entrance area; it's across the street). Fanning out from this grand roundhouse is an array of historic cars and engines, starting with the very first "stagecoaches on rails," with a crude steam engine from 1830. You'll trace the evolution of steam-powered transportation, from the Flying Scotsman (the first London-Edinburgh express rail service), to the era of the aerodynamic Mallard (famous as the first train to travel at a startling two miles per minute—a marvel back in 1938) and the striking Art Deco-style Duchess of Hamilton. (The Flying Scotsman and other trains may not be on display, as they are sometimes on loan or under maintenance—ask an explainer if you can't find something.) The collection spans to the present day, with a replica of the Eurostar (Chunnel) train and the Shinkansen Japanese bullet train. Other exhibits include a steam engine that's been sliced open to show its cylinders, driving wheels, and smoke box, as well as a working turntable that's put into action twice a day. The Mallard Experience simulates a ride on the Mallard.

The Works is an actual workshop where engineers scurry about, fixing old trains. Live train switchboards show real-time rail traffic on the East Coast Main Line. Next to the diagrammed screens, you can look out to see the actual trains moving up and down the line. **The Warehouse** is loaded with more than 10,000 items relating to train travel (including dinnerware, signage, and actual trains). Exhibits feature dining cars, post cars, sleeping cars, train posters, and more info on the Flying Scotsman.

Crossing back to the entrance side, continue to the **Station Hall,** with a collection of older trains, including ones that the royals have used to ride the rails (including Queen Victoria's lavish royal car). Behind that are the South Yard and the Depot, with actual, working trains in storage.

▲York Brewery

This intimate, tactile, and informative 45-minute-long tour gives an enjoyable look at how this charming little microbrewery produces 5,500 pints per batch. Their award-winning Ghost Ale is strong, dark, and chocolaty. You can drink their beer throughout town, but to get it as fresh as possible, drink it where it's birthed, in their cozy Tap Room.

Cost and Hours: £6, includes a pint of the best beer—ale not lager—in town; tours Mon-Sat at 12:30, 14:00, 15:30, and 17:00—just show up; cross the river on Lendal Bridge and walk 5 minutes to Toft Green just below Micklegate, tel. 01904/621-162, www.york-brewery.co.uk.

Outside of Town

▲Ouse Riverside Walk or Bike Ride

The New Walk is a mile-long, tree-lined riverside lane created in the 1730s as a promenade for York's dandy class to stroll, see, and be seen—and is a fine place for today's visitors to walk or bike. This hour-long walk is a delightful way to enjoy a dose of countryside away from York. It's paved, illuminated in the evening, and a popular jogging route any time of day.

Start from the riverside under Skeldergate Bridge (near the York Castle Museum), and walk south away from town for a mile. Notice modern buildings across the river, with their floodwalls. Shortly afterwards, you cross the tiny Foss River on Blue Bridge, originally built in 1738. The easily defended confluence of the Foss and the Ouse is the reason the Romans founded York in A.D. 71. Look back to see the modern floodgate (built after a flood in 1979) designed to stop the flooding Ouse from oozing up the Foss. At the bridge, a history panel describes this walk to the Millennium Bridge.

Stroll until you hit the striking, modern **Millennium Bridge.** Sit a bit on its reclining-lounge-chair fence and enjoy the vibrations of bikes and joggers as they pass. There's a strong biking trend in Britain these days. In recent Olympics, the British have won most of the gold medals in cycling. In 2012, Bradley Wiggins became Sir Bradley Wiggins by winning the Tour de France; his countryman, Chris Froome, won it in 2013. You'll see lots of locals riding fancy bikes and wearing high-tech gear while getting into better shape. (Energetic bikers can continue past the Millennium Bridge 14 miles to the market town of Selby.)

Cross the river and walk back home, passing **Rowntree Park.** After the skateboard court, enter the park through its fine old gate.

This park was financed by Joseph Rowntree, a wealthy chocolate baron with a Quaker ethic of contributing to his community. In the 19th century, life for the poor was a Charles Dickens-like struggle. A rich man building a park for the working class, which even had a swimming pool, was quite progressive. Victorian England had a laissez-faire approach to social issues. Then, like now, many wealthy people believed things would work out for the poor if the government just stayed out of it. However, others, such as the Rowntree family, felt differently. Their altruism contributed to the establishment of a society that now takes care of its workers and poor much better.

Walk directly into the park toward the evocative Industrial Age housing complex capping the hill beyond the central fountain. In the park's brick gazebo are touching memorial plaques to WWI and WWII deaths. Rowntree gave this park to York to remember those lost in the "Great War." Stroll along the delightful, duck-filled pond near the Rowntree Park Café, return to the riverside lane, and continue back into York. You're almost home.

Shopping in York

With its medieval lanes lined with classy as well as tacky little shops, York is a hit with shoppers. I find two kinds of shopping in York particularly interesting: antique malls and charity shops.

Antique Malls: Three places within a few blocks of each other are filled with stalls and cases owned by antique dealers from the countryside (all open daily). The malls, a warren of rooms on three floors with cafés buried deep inside, sell the dealers' bygones on commission. Serious shoppers do better heading for the country, but York's shops are a fun browse: The **Antiques Centre York** (41 Stonegate, www.theantiquescentreyork.co.uk), the **Red House Antiques Centre** (a block from the Minster at Duncombe Place, www.redhouseyork.co.uk), and **Cavendish Antiques and Jewellers** (44 Stonegate, www.cavendishjewellers.co.uk).

Charity Shops: In towns all over Britain, it seems one low-rent street is lined with charity shops, allowing locals to both donate their junk and buy the junk of others in the name of a good cause. (Talk about a win-win.) It's great for random shopping. And, as the people working there are often volunteers involved in that cause, it can lead to some interesting conversations. In York, on Goodramgate (stretching a block or so in from the town wall), you'll find "thrift shops" run by the British Heart Foundation, Save the Children, Mind, and Oxfam. Good deals abound on clothing, purses, accessories, children's toys, books, CDs, and maybe even a guitar. If you buy something, you're getting a bargain and at the same time helping the poor, mentally ill, elderly, or even a pet in need of a vet (stores generally open between 9:00 and 10:00 and close between 16:00 and 17:00, with shorter hours on Sun).

Nightlife in York

Pubs

Even more than chocolate, York likes its beer. It has its own award-winning microbrewery, the York Brewery (which offers fine tours daily—see page 757), along with countless atmospheric pubs for memorable and convivial eating or drinking. Many pubs serve inexpensive plates at lunch, then focus on selling beer in the evening. Others offer lunch and early dinner. You can tell by their marketing how enthusiastic they are about cooking versus drawing pints.

The York Brewery Tap Room, a private club, feels like a fraternity of older men. But if you drop in, you can be an honorary guest. It's right at the microbrewery, with five beloved varieties on tap as fresh as you'll find anywhere (14 Toft Green, just below Micklegate, tel. 01904/621-162, www.york-brewery.co.uk).

The Maltings, just over Lendal Bridge, has classic pub ambience and serves good meals at lunch only. Local beer purists swear by this place (£6-7 pub lunches, open for drinks nightly, cross the bridge and look down and left to Tanners Moat, tel. 01904/655-387).

The Blue Bell is one of my favorites for old-school York vibes. This tiny, traditional establishment with a time-warp Edwardian interior is the smallest pub in York. It has two distinct and inviting little rooms (limited food served at lunch only, east end of town at 53 Fossgate, tel. 01904/654-904).

The House of the Trembling Madness is another fine watering hole with a cozy atmosphere above a "bottle shop" selling a stunning variety of beers by the bottle to go (48 Stonegate; also described later, under "Eating in York").

Evil Eye Lounge, a hit with York's young crowd, is a creaky, funky, hip space famous for its strong cocktails and edgy ambience. There are even beds to drink in. You can order downstairs at the bar (with a small terrace out back), or head upstairs (42 Stonegate; also a restaurant—described later, under "Eating in York").

The Golden Fleece is a sloppy, dingy place with tilty floors that make you feel drunk even if you aren't. Its wooden frame has survived without foundations for 500 years. Originally owned by wool traders, it's considered the oldest and most haunted coaching inn in York (16 Pavement, across the street from the southern end of The Shambles, tel. 01904/625-171).

The Last Drop is a solid, basic pub—no music, no game machines, no children. It's owned by the York Brewery, so it always has their ales on tap (27 Colliergate facing King's Square, tel. 01904/621-951).

Student Pub Crawl: The **"Micklegate Run"** is a ritual for students all over Yorkshire. As this pub crawl starts just below the train station, students ride the train into York and then have a pint in each pub or club along Micklegate. You'll pass at least eight pubs as the street runs downhill from Micklegate Bar to the river. It can be lowbrow and sloppy. You'll see lots of hen-party and stag-party spectacles, and what local guys rudely call "mutton dressed as lamb"—older women trying to look young.

Riverside Eating and Drinking: On sunny days, there are several pubs with riverside tables just below Ouse Bridge, starting with **The Kings Arms,** which boasts flood marks inside its door and has a rougher local crowd than other recommended pubs (3 King's Staith, tel. 01904/659-435).

Entertainment

Theatre Royal
A full variety of dramas, comedies, and works by Shakespeare entertain the locals in either the main theater or the little 100-seat theater-in-the-round (£10-22, usually Tue-Sat at 19:30, tickets easy to get, on St. Leonard's Place near Bootham Bar and a 5- to 10-minute walk from recommended B&Bs, booking tel. 01904/623-568, www.yorktheatreroyal.co.uk). Those under 25 and students of any age can get tickets for only £8.

Ghost Tours
You'll see fliers, signs, and promoters hawking a variety of entertaining after-dark tours. For a rundown on this scene, see page 733.

Movies
The centrally located **City Screen Cinema,** right on the river, plays both art-house and mainstream flicks. They also have an enticing café/bar overlooking the river that serves good food (13 Coney Street, tel. 0871-902-5726).

Sleeping in York

I've listed peak-season, book-direct prices; July through October are the busiest (and usually most expensive) months. B&Bs often charge more for weekends and sometimes turn away one-night bookings, particularly for peak-season Saturdays. (York is worth two nights anyway.) Prices may spike up for horse races and Bank Holidays (about 20 nights a season). Remember to book ahead during festival times (see "Helpful Hints," page 732) and weekends year-round.

Sleep Code

(£1 = about $1.60, country code: 44, area code: 01904)
S = Single, **D** = Double/Twin, **T** = Triple, **Q** = Quad, **b** = bathroom, **s** = shower only. Unless otherwise noted, credit cards are accepted and breakfast is included.

To help you sort easily through these listings, I've divided the accommodations into three categories based on the price for a standard double room with bath (during high season):

$$$ **Higher Priced**—Most rooms £100 or more.
  $$ **Moderately Priced**—Most rooms between £75-100.
    $ **Lower Priced**—Most rooms £75 or less.

Prices can change without notice; verify the hotel's current rates online or by email. For the best prices, always book direct.

B&Bs and Small Hotels

These B&Bs are all small and family-run. They come with plenty of steep stairs (and no elevators) but no traffic noise. Rooms can be tight; if maneuverability is important to you, say so when booking. For a good selection, contact them well in advance. B&B owners will generally hold a room with an email or phone call and work hard to help their guests sightsee and eat smartly. Most have permits to lend for street parking. Please honor your bookings—the B&B proprietors here lose out on much-needed business if you don't show up.

The handiest B&B neighborhood is the quiet residential area just outside the old town wall's Bootham gate, along the road called Bootham. All of these are within a 10-minute walk of the Minster and TI, and a 5- to 15-minute walk or £6 taxi ride from the station. If driving, head for the cathedral and follow the medieval wall to the gate called Bootham Bar. The street called Bootham leads away from Bootham Bar.

Getting There: Here's the most direct way to walk to this B&B area from the train station: Head to the north end of the station, to the area between platforms 2 and 4. Shoot through the gap between the men's WC and the York Tap pub, into the short-stay parking lot. Walk to the end of the lot to a pedestrian ramp, and zigzag your way down. At the bottom, head left, following the sign for the riverside route. When you reach the river, cross over it on the footbridge. At the far end of the bridge, the Abbey Guest House is a few yards to your right, facing the river. To reach The Hazelwood and Ardmore Guest House (closer to the town wall), walk from the bridge along the river until just before the short ruined tower, then turn inland up

YORK

York Accommodations

TO A-19 & THIRSK

CLIFTON
BOOTH. CRES.
GROS. TERR.
QUEEN ANNES
BOOTHAM TERR.
ST. MARY'S
SYCAMORE
LONGFIELD
FREDERIC
MARYGATE
EARLS.
STATION RD.
LEEMAN
ROAD
WALKING PATH TO B+Bs
TOFT GREEN
BARKER
MICKLE
QUEEN
BLOSSOM
NUNNERY
MICKLEGATE BAR

RAILWAY MUSEUM

RIVER

TRAIN STATION

① Hedley House Hotel
② Abbeyfields Guest House
③ St. Raphael Guesthouse
④ Arnot House
⑤ Amber House & Number 34
⑥ Bootham Guest House
⑦ Queen Annes Guest House
⑧ Abbey Guest House
⑨ Number 23 St. Mary's B&B
⑩ Crook Lodge B&B
⑪ Airden House
⑫ The Hazelwood
⑬ Ardmore Guest House
⑭ Dean Court Hotel
⑮ Grays Court Hotel
⑯ Premier Inns (2)
⑰ Travelodge York Central
⑱ Travelodge York Central Micklegate
⑲ Ace York Hostel
⑳ Internet Café
㉑ Library (Internet)
㉒ To Launderette

200 YARDS
200 METERS

TO A-64 & LEEDS

Access Stairs to Wall
Pedestrian Zone
P Parking
--- Footpath

YORK

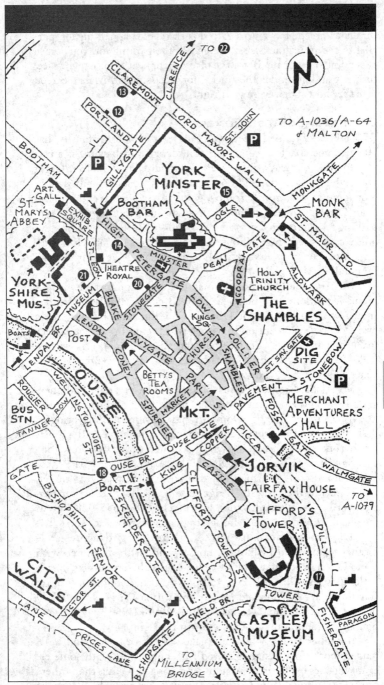

onto Marygate. For other B&Bs, at the bottom of the footbridge, turn left immediately onto a path that skirts the big parking lot (parallel to the train tracks). At the end of the parking lot, you'll turn depending on your B&B: for the places on or near Bootham Terrace, turn left and go under the tracks; for B&Bs on St. Mary's Street, take the short stairway on your right.

On or near Bootham Terrace

$$$ Hedley House Hotel, well-run by a wonderful family, has 30 clean and spacious rooms. The outdoor hot tub/sauna is a fine way to end your day (Sb-£75-105, standard Db-£80-135, larger Db-£90-155, rates depend on demand, ask for a deal with stay of 3 or more nights, family rooms, good two-course evening meals from £18, free Wi-Fi, in-house massage and beauty services, free parking, 3 Bootham Terrace, tel. 01904/637-404, www.hedley-house.com, greg@hedleyhouse.com, Greg and Louise Harrand). They also have nine luxury studio apartments—see their website for details.

$$ Abbeyfields Guest House has eight comfortable, bright rooms. This doily-free place lacks B&B clutter and has been designed with care (Sb-£55; Db-£84 Sun-Thu, £89 Fri-Sat; these prices good if you mention this book when reserving direct, homemade bread, free Wi-Fi, free parking, 19 Bootham Terrace, tel. 01904/636-471, www.abbeyfields.co.uk, enquire@abbeyfields.co.uk, charming Al and Les).

$$ At St. Raphael Guesthouse, young, creative, and energetic Dom and Zoe (and son Ollie) understand a traveler's needs. You'll be instant friends. Dom's graphic design training brings a dash of class to their seven comfy rooms, each themed after a different York street, and each lovingly accented with a fresh rose (Sb-£75 Sun-Thu, £85 Fri-Sat; Db-£82 Sun-Thu, £94 Fri-Sat; these prices promised if you mention this book when reserving direct, free drinks in their guests' fridge, family rooms, guest computer, free Wi-Fi, 44 Queen Annes Road, tel. 01904/645-028, www.straphaelguesthouse.co.uk, info@straphaelguesthouse.co.uk).

$$ Arnot House, run by a hardworking daughter-and-mother team, is old-fashioned, homey, and lushly decorated with Victorian memorabilia. The three well-furnished rooms even have little libraries (Db-£80-85 if you book direct, 2-night minimum stay unless it's last-minute, no children, free Wi-Fi, huge DVD library, 17 Grosvenor Terrace, tel. 01904/641-966, www.arnot-houseyork.co.uk, kim.robbins@virgin.net, Kim).

$ Amber House is a small place with three breezy and well-tended rooms (one Asian-inspired). It's homey, but with some elegant touches—a bit more tasteful and upscale-feeling than others in this price range (Db-£66 Sun-Thu, £74 Fri-Sat; Tb-£93; mention this book when reserving direct for these prices, free Wi-Fi, free parking, 36 Bootham Crescent, tel. 01904/620-275, www. amberhouse-york.co.uk, amberhouseyork@hotmail.co.uk, John and Linda).

$ Bootham Guest House features gregarious and welcoming Emma. Public spaces are ho-hum, but the eight rooms (six are en-suite, two share a bath) are cheery and stylish (S-£40, Sb-£50, D-£65, Db-£75, Tb-£95, mention this book when reserving direct for these prices, free Wi-Fi, 56 Bootham Crescent, tel. 01904/672-123, www.boothamguesthouse.com, boothamguesthouse1@hotmail.com).

$ Number 34, run by hardworking Amy and Jason, has five simple, light, and airy rooms at fair prices. It's a bit masculine-feeling, with modern decor (Sb-£35-45, Db-£60-66, Tb-£85-90, price depends on season and day of week, mention Rick Steves when reserving to get best rates, ground-floor room, free Wi-Fi, 34 Bootham Crescent, tel. 01904/645-818, www.number34york.co.uk, enquiries@number34york.co.uk).

$ Queen Annes Guest House has eight basic rooms in two adjacent houses at some of the best prices in the neighborhood. While it doesn't have the plushest beds or richest decor, this is a respectable, affordable, and clean place to sleep (S-£35, Db-£72, Tb-£108, 10 percent discount if you mention this book and reserve direct, cheaper if you stay 2 nights, family room, free Wi-Fi, lounge, 24 and 26 Queen Annes Road, tel. 01904/629-389, www.queen-annes-guesthouse.co.uk, info@queen-annes-guesthouse.co.uk, Phil).

On the River

$$ Abbey Guest House is a peaceful refuge overlooking the River Ouse, with five cheerful, beautifully updated, contemporary-style rooms and a cute little garden (Db-£78, four-poster Db with river view-£83, ask for Rick Steves discount when you book direct, free Wi-Fi, free parking, £7 laundry service, 13-14 Earlsborough Terrace, tel. 01904/627-782, www.abbeyghyork.co.uk, info@abbeyghyork.co.uk, delightful couple Gill—pronounced "Jill"—and Alec Saville, and a dog aptly named Loofah).

On St. Mary's Street

$$ Number 23 St. Mary's B&B is extravagantly decorated. Chris and Julie Simpson have done everything just right and offer nine spacious and tastefully comfy rooms, a classy lounge, and all the doily touches (Sb-£50-60, Db-£80-100 depending on room size and season, discount for longer stays, family room, honesty box for drinks and snacks, free Wi-Fi, 23 St. Mary's, tel. 01904/622-738, www.23stmarys.co.uk, stmarys23@hotmail.com).

YORK

$$ Crook Lodge B&B, with seven tight but elegantly charming rooms, serves breakfast in an old Victorian kitchen. The 21st-century style somehow fits this old house (Db-£75-80, cheaper off-season, check for online specials, one ground-floor room, guest computer, free Wi-Fi, parking, quiet, 26 St. Mary's, tel. 01904/655-614, www.crooklodge.co.uk, crooklodge@hotmail.com, Brian and Louise Aiken).

$ Airden House rents 10 nice, mostly traditional rooms, though the two basement-level rooms are more mod. One comes with a sauna, and the other, decorated in bright, feminine hues, has a space-age-looking Jacuzzi and a separate room with twin bed (standard Db-£68-72, traditional Db-£74-78, sauna Db-£78-82, Jacuzzi Db-£84-92, Tb-£94-100, these prices with 2-night minimum if you mention this book when reserving, higher prices are for weekends, lounge, free Wi-Fi, free parking, 1 St. Mary's, tel. 01904/638-915, www.airdenhouse.co.uk, info@airdenhouse.co.uk, Emma and Heather).

Closer to the Town Wall

$$$ The Hazelwood, more formal than a B&B, rents 14 rooms. The "standard" rooms have bright, cheery decor and small bathrooms, while the bigger "superior" rooms come with newer bathrooms and handcrafted furniture. Ask about their bright top-floor two-bedroom apartment good for families (Sb-£70, standard Db-£80-100, superior Db-£100-130, price depends on season and day of week, guest computer, free Wi-Fi, homemade biscuits on arrival, free laundry service for Rick Steves readers, free parking, garden patio; fridge, ice, and travel library in pleasant basement lounge; 24 Portland Street, tel. 01904/626-548, www.thehazelwoodyork.com, reservations@thehazelwoodyork.com; Ian and Carolyn, along with Sharon and Emma).

$ Ardmore Guest House is a fine little three-room place enthusiastically run by Irishwoman Vera. It's about 15 minutes' walk from the station, but only five minutes from Bootham Bar (Sb-£40, smaller Db-£60, larger Db-£75, Tb-£75, discount off-season for 3 or more nights, cash only, free Wi-Fi, parking, 31 Claremont Terrace, tel. 01904/622-562, mobile 0793-928-3588, www.ardmoreyork.co.uk, ardmoreguesthouse@crwprojects.co.uk).

Large Hotels

$$$ Dean Court Hotel, a Best Western facing the Minster, is a big, stately hotel with classy lounges and 37 comfortable rooms. A few have views for no extra charge—try requesting one (Sb-£115, small Db-£150, standard Db-£180, superior Db-£210, spacious deluxe Db-£230; cheaper midweek, off-season, and on Sun—check specific rates online; elevator, guest computer, free Wi-Fi,

bistro, restaurant, Duncombe Place, tel. 01904/625-082, www. deancourt-york.co.uk, sales@deancourt-york.co.uk).

$$$ Grays Court Hotel is a historic mansion—the home of dukes and archbishops since 1091—that now rents seven rooms to tourists. While its public spaces and gardens are lavish, its rooms are elegant yet modest. The creaky, historic nature of the place makes for a memorable stay. If it's too pricey for lodging, consider coming here for its tearoom—described later, under "Eating in York" (Db-£160-200, free Wi-Fi, Chapter House Street, tel. 01904/612-613, www.grayscourtyork.com).

$$$ Premier Inn offers 200 rooms in two side-by-side hotels that I hate to recommend, but it's a workable option if York's B&Bs have filled up, or if you can score a deep advance discount. They have little character (at one, you enter through a coffee shop), but they offer industrial-strength efficiency and a decent value (Db-£75-141, usually £80-95 Sun-Thu, £90-141 Fri-Sat; check for specials online—occasional deals as low as £29 if you book far enough ahead; up to 2 kids stay free, continental breakfast-£5.25, full breakfast-£8.25, elevator in one building, pay guest computer, pay Wi-Fi, parking-£8.50/24 hours, 5-minute walk to train station, 20 and 28-40 Blossom Street, tel. 0871-527-9194 and 0871-527-9196, www.premierinn.com).

$$ Travelodge York Central offers 93 affordable, recently renovated rooms near the York Castle Museum. If you book long in advance on their website, this can be amazingly cheap. River views make some rooms slightly less boring—after booking online, call the front desk to try to arrange a view (rates vary wildly depending on demand—as cheap as £19 for a fully prepaid "saver rate" 21 days ahead; for best rates, book online; cheapest rates are first-come, first-served; continental breakfast-£4.50, elevator, pay guest computer, pay Wi-Fi, parking-£7.50/24 hours and a 5-minute walk away, 90 Piccadilly, central reservations tel. 0871-984-8484, front desk tel. 0203-195-4978, www.travelodge.co.uk). A second location, **Travelodge York Central Micklegate,** has 104 rooms at the train station end of the Ouse Bridge (similar rates, Micklegate, tel. 0203-195-4976).

Hostel

$ Ace York is a boutique hostel on a rowdy street, which can be very noisy late at night on Fridays and Saturdays. It's in a big, old Georgian house that provides a much-needed option for backpackers. They rent 158 beds in 2- to 14-bed rooms, with great views, private prefab "pod" bathrooms, and reading lights for each bed. They also offer fancier, hotel-quality doubles (£16-25/bed, twin Db-£60-68, king Db-£80-84, family room for up to four-£120-128, rates depend on day and size of room, includes continental breakfast; four

YORK

floors, no elevator, air-con, free Wi-Fi, self-service laundry-£3, TV lounge, game room, bar, lockers, no curfew, 5-minute walk from train station at 88 Micklegate, tel. 01904/627-720, www.acehotelyork.co.uk, reception@ace-hotelyork.co.uk, Brian).

Eating in York

York is touting its new reputation as a foodie city. It claims to be rated "#5 in Europe" by some social media—but that's a stretch. Still, the local high-tech industry and university—combined with all the tourists—build a demand that sustains lots of creative and fun eateries. There's also a wide range of ethnic food (including several good choices for Indian, Thai, Italian, Spanish tapas, and so on). While there's plenty of decent pub grub served in the bars, York still has no great gastropubs. (For pubbing advice, see "Nightlife in York," earlier.)

If you're in a hurry or on a tight budget, picnic and light-meals-to-go options abound, and it's easy to find a churchyard, bench, or riverside perch upon which to munch cheaply. On a sunny day, perhaps the best picnic spot in town is under the evocative 12th-century ruins of St. Mary's Abbey in the Museum Gardens (near Bootham Bar).

Upscale Bistros: As these trendy, pricey eateries are a York forte, I've listed four of my favorites: Café No. 8, Café Concerto, The Blue Bicycle, and Ambience Café Bistro. These places are each romantic, laid-back, and popular with locals (so reservations are wise for dinner). They also have good-quality, creative vegetarian options. Most offer economical lunch specials and early dinners. After 19:00 or so, main courses cost £15-25 and fixed-price meals (two or three courses) go for around £25. On Friday and Saturday evenings, many offer special, more expensive menus.

Cheap Eats Around King's Square

King's Square is about as central as can be for sightseers. And from here, you can actually see several fine quick-and-cheap lunch options. After buying your take-out food, sit on the square and enjoy the street entertainers. Or, for a peaceful place to munch more prayerfully, find the Holy Trinity Church yard, with benches amid the old tombstones on Goodramgate (half a block to the right of York Roast Company).

York Roast Company is a local fixture, serving delicious and hearty £4-6 pork sandwiches with applesauce, stuffing, and "crackling" (roasted bits of fat and skin). Other meats are also available. You can even oversee the stuffing of your own Yorkshire pudding (£6-7). If Henry VIII wanted fast food, he'd eat here (corner of Low Petergate and Goodramgate, order at counter then dine upstairs or

take away, daily 10:00-23:00, 74 Low Petergate, tel. 01904/629-197).

Drakes Fish-and-Chips, across the street from York Roast Company, is a local favorite chippy (daily 11:00-22:30, 97 Low Petergate, tel. 01904/624-788).

The Cornish Bakery, facing King's Square, cooks up £3 pasties to eat in or take away (30 Colliergate, tel. 01904/671-177).

The Newgate Market, just past The Shambles, has several stalls offering fun and nutritious light meals. On The Shambles, **Mr. Sandwich** is famous for its £1 sandwiches.

St. Crux Parish Hall is a medieval church now used by a medley of charities that sell tea, homemade cakes, and light meals. They each book the church for a day, often a year in advance (usually open Tue-Sat 10:00-16:00, closed Sun-Mon, at bottom of The Shambles at its intersection with Pavement, tel. 01904/621-756).

For a nice finish, consider the **Harlequin Café,** a charming place loved by locals for its good coffee and homemade cakes, as well as its light meals. It's up a creaky staircase overlooking the square (daily 10:00-16:00, 2 King's Square, tel. 01904/630-631).

On or near Swinegate

Strolling this street, you can just take your pick of the various tempting bars and eateries. Some are trendy, with thumping music, while others are tranquil; some have elaborately decorated dining rooms, while others emphasize heated courtyards. This corner of town has two similar, fiercely competitive, American-style bar/brasserie/lounges (both open daily and serving £8-12 meals): **Oscar's,** right on Swinegate, has a mod interior and good burgers; **Stonegate Yard,** around the corner on Little Stonegate, in a delightful, ivy-covered courtyard. Others enjoy the courtyard and Mediterranean food at **Lucia** (£4 small plates, £10-15 meals, daily, 12-13 Swinegate).

Vegetarian: **El Piano Restaurant,** just off Swinegate on charming Grape Lane, is a popular place serving only vegan, gluten-free, and low-sodium dishes. Their meals are made with locally sourced ingredients and Indian/Asian/Middle Eastern/East African flavors. The inside ambience is bubble gum with blinking lights. If you don't want to feel that you're eating inside a sombrero, they also have a pleasant patio out back (£3 starters, £10 meals, £30 2-or-3-person sampler, Mon-Sat 11:00-23:00, Sun 12:00-21:00, between Low Petergate and Swinegate at 15-17 Grape Lane, tel. 01904/610-676). Save money at the takeaway window (£4-5 boxes).

On Stonegate

The House of the Trembling Madness, considered by some to be the best pub in town, is easy to miss. Enter through The Bottle, a

YORK

York Restaurants

1 King's Square Eateries
2 York Roast Co.
3 Drakes Fish & Chips
4 Newgate Market
5 St. Crux Parish Hall Café
6 Swinegate Eateries
7 Stonegate Yard
8 El Piano Restaurant
9 The House of the Trembling Madness & Bottle Shop
10 Evil Eye Lounge
11 Café Concerto
12 Café No. 8
13 Ambience Café Bistro
14 The Exhibition Hotel Pub
15 Sainsbury's Local Grocery
16 Rustique French Bistro
17 The Blue Bicycle
18 Melton's Too
19 Mumbai Lounge
20 Il Paradiso del Cibo Rist. Pizzeria
21 Ristorante Bari
22 Mamma Mia
23 Ask Restaurant
24 Bettys Café Tea Rooms
25 Grays Court Tea Rooms
26 York Brewery Tap Room
27 The Maltings Pub
28 The Blue Bell Pub
29 The Golden Fleece Pub
30 The Last Drop Pub
31 "Micklegate Run" Pub Crawl
32 The Kings Arms Pub

TO A-19 & THIRSK

CLIFTON
BOOTH CRES.
QUEEN ANNES
BOOTHAM TERR.
GROS TERR.
SYCAMORE
ST. MARYS
LONGFIELD
FREDERIC
MARYGATE
EARLS.
P

RAILWAY MUSEUM

RIVER

LEEMAN

ROAD
P

WALKING PATH TO B+Bs

STATION RD.

TRAIN STATION

TOFT GREEN
BARKER
26
MICKLE
31

QUEEN

BLOSSOM
NUNNERY

MICKLEGATE BAR

TO A-64 & LEEDS

ACCESS STAIRS TO WALL

PEDESTRIAN ZONE

P **PARKING**

- - - **FOOTPATH**

YORK

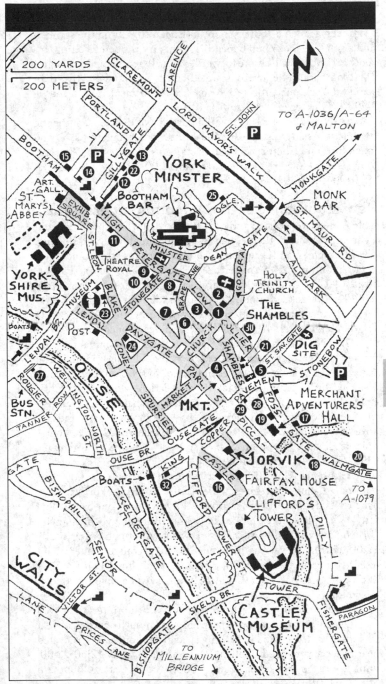

ground-floor shop selling an astonishing number of different take-away beers (called a "bottle shop" in England). Climb the stairs to find a small but cozy pub beneath a high, airy timbered ceiling. It's youthful and a bit fashion-forward, yet still accessible to all ages. The food tries to be locally sourced and is far more creative than standard York pub grub (£3-6 snacks, £8-10 meals, daily 10:00-24:00, 48 Stonegate, tel. 01904/640-009).

Evil Eye Lounge serves large portions of delicious, authentic Southeast Asian cuisine. But the hipster space may be a bit too much for some. There's food and drinks on several levels (£8 meals, food served Mon-Fri 12:00-21:00, Sat 12:00-19:00, 42 Stonegate, tel. 01904/640-002).

Near Bootham Bar and Recommended B&Bs

Café Concerto, a casual and cozy bistro with wholesome food and a charming musical theme, has an understandably loyal following. The fun menu features updated English favorites with some international options (£4-8 starters; £9-12 soups, sandwiches, and salads; £12-17 main dishes; vegetarian and gluten-free options; daily 9:00-21:00, weekends until 22:00, smart to reserve for dinner—try for a window seat, also offers takeaway, facing the Minster at 21 High Petergate, tel. 01904/610-478, http://cafeconcerto.biz).

Café No. 8 feels like Café Concerto but is more romantic, with jazz, modern art, candles, and hardworking Martin bringing it all together. Grab one of the tables in front or in the sunroom, or enjoy a shaded little garden out back if the weather's good. Chef Chris Pragnell uses what's fresh in the market to shape his menu. The food—mod cuisine with veggie options—is simple, elegant, and creative (£6-10 lunches, £16.50 two-course dinners, £22 three-course dinners, about £5 more Fri-Sat; daily 10:00-22:00, 8 Gillygate, tel. 01904/653-074, www.cafeno8.co.uk).

Ambience Café Bistro serves modern English and international dishes with seven cute tables in front. You can also dine in its delightful garden under the town wall out back. Chef Guy Whapples serves lunch daily and dinners—with a fancier "bistro" menu—only two nights a week (£7 lunch plates, daily 12:00-17:00; £21 two-course and £24 three-course dinners, a bit less if you come before 19:00, dinner served Thu-Fri only 18:00-20:30; 40 Gillygate, tel. 01904/652-500, www.ambiencecafebistro.co.uk).

The Exhibition Hotel pub has a classic pub interior, as well as a glassed-in conservatory and beer garden out back that's great for kids. While the food is nothing special, it's conveniently located near my recommended B&Bs (£8-11 pub grub, daily 12:00-23:00, until 24:00 on weekends, facing Bootham Bar at 19 Bootham Street, tel. 01904/641-105).

Supermarket: **Sainsbury's Local** grocery store is handy and open late (daily 6:00-24:00, 50 yards outside Bootham Bar, on Bootham).

At the East End of Town

This neighborhood is across town from my recommended B&Bs, but still central (and a short walk from the York Castle Museum). These places are all hits with local foodies; reservations are smart for all.

Rustique French Bistro has one big room of tight tables and walls decorated with simple posters. The place has good prices and is straight French—right down to the welcome (£6 starters, £15 main dishes, £13 two-course and £15 three-course meals available except after 19:00 Fri-Sat, open Mon-Sat 12:00-22:00, Sun 12:00-19:00, across from Fairfax House at 28 Castlegate, tel. 01904/612-744, www.rustiquey-ork.co.uk).

The Blue Bicycle is no longer a brothel (but if you explore downstairs, you can still imagine when the tiny privacy-snugs needed their curtains). Today, it is passionate about fish. The energy of its happy eaters, its charming canalside setting, and its tasty Anglo-French cuisine make it worth the splurge. It's a velvety, hardwood scene, a little sultry but fresh...like its fish. The basement, while *très romantique,* may be a bit hot and stuffy (£6-12 starters, £16-24 main dishes, vegetarian and meat options, daily 18:00-21:30, also open for lunch Thu-Sun 12:00-14:30, 34 Fossgate, tel. 01904/673-990, www.thebluebicycle.com).

Melton's Too is a fun and casual place to eat. This homey, spacious, youthful restaurant (combining old timbers and plastic chairs) serves up elegantly simple traditional and international meals and a nice a selection of £5-8 tapas, all with a focus on local ingredients. The seating sprawls on several floors: ground-floor pub, upstairs bistro, and top-floor loft (£7 lunches, £11-14 dinners, £11.50 two-course and £13 three-course meals; Mon-Sat 10:30-22:30, Sun 10:30-21:30, just past Fossgate at 25 Walmgate, tel. 01904/629-222).

Mumbai Lounge (named for its top-floor lounge) is considered the best place in town for Indian food, so it's very popular. The space is big and high-energy, with a hardworking team of waiters in black T-shirts. I'd call to reserve a table on the ground floor—but avoid the basement (£10 plates, £7 lunch special, daily 12:00-14:30 & 17:30-23:30, 47 Fossgate, tel. 01904/654-155, www.mumbai-loungeyork.co.uk).

Ethnic on Walmgate: The emerging bohemian-chic street called Walmgate has several quality little restaurants within a few steps of each other. Each is small, feels real, and has a local, untouristy energy: **Il Paradiso del Cibo Ristorante Pizzeria** (described next), **Khao San Thai Bistro** (52 Walmgate, tel. 01904/635-599), and **The Barbakan Polish Restaurant** (58 Walmgate, tel. 01904/672-474).

Italian

Il Paradiso del Cibo Ristorante Pizzeria just feels special. It's a small place with tight seating, no tourists, and a fun bustle, run by a Sardinian with attitude (£7 pastas and pizzas, £15 main dishes, £7 lunch/early dinner special Mon-Fri only, open daily 12:00-15:00 & 18:00-22:00 except closed Sun off-season, 40 Walmgate, tel. 01904/611-444).

Ristorante Bari has perhaps the most touristy location in York, right in the middle of The Shambles—but it also has a loyal local following that has kept it in business for more than 50 years. This family-run place has red rustic chairs and an accessible menu of Italian classics (£8-11 pizzas and pastas, £12-20 main dishes, daily 11:30-14:30 & 18:00-22:00, The Shambles, tel. 01904/633-807).

Mamma Mia is another popular choice for functional, affordable Italian. The casual, garlicky eating area features a tempting gelato bar, and in nice weather the back patio is *molto bello* (£8-10 pizza and pasta, daily 11:30-14:00 & 17:30-23:00, 20 Gillygate, tel. 01904/622-020).

Ask Restaurant is a cheap and cheery Italian chain, similar to those found in historic buildings all over Britain. But York's version lets you dine in the majestic Neoclassical yellow hall of its Grand Assembly Rooms, lined with Corinthian marble columns. The food may be Italian-chain dull—but the atmosphere is 18th-century deluxe (£9-12 pizza, pastas, and salads; Sun-Wed 11:00-22:00, Thu-Sat 11:00-23:00, Blake Street, tel. 01904/637-254). Even if you're just walking past, peek inside to gape at the interior.

Tearooms

York is famous for its elegant teahouses. These two places serve traditional afternoon tea as well as light meals in memorable settings. In both cases, the food is pricey and comes in small portions—I'd come here at 16:00 for tea and cakes, but dine elsewhere. It's permissible for travel partners on a budget to enjoy the experience for about half the price by having one person order "full tea" (with enough little sandwiches and sweets for two to share) and the other a simple cup of tea.

Bettys Café Tea Rooms is a destination restaurant for many ladies. You pay £9 for a Yorkshire Cream Tea (tea and scones with clotted Yorkshire cream and strawberry jam) or £18 for a full traditional English afternoon tea (tea, delicate sandwiches, scones, and sweets). Your table is so full of doily niceties that the food is served on a little three-tray tower. While you'll pay a little extra here (and the food's nothing special), the ambience and people-watching are hard to beat. When there's a line, it moves quickly (except at dinnertime). They'll offer to seat you sooner in the bigger and less atmospheric basement, but I'd be patient and wait for a place upstairs—ideally by the window (daily 9:00-21:00, "afternoon tea" served all day; on weekends the special £26 afternoon tea includes fresh-from-the-oven scones served 12:30-17:00 in upstairs room with pianist; piano music nightly 18:00-21:00 and Sun 10:00-13:00, tel. 01904/659-142, St. Helen's Square, fine view of street scene from a window seat on the main floor). Near the WC downstairs is a mirror signed by WWII bomber pilots—read the story. For those just wanting to buy a pastry to go, it's fine to go directly to the bakery counter.

Grays Court, tucked away behind the Minster, holds court over its own delightful garden just inside the town wall. (You'll look down into its inviting oasis as you walk along the top of the wall.) For centuries, this was the residence of the Norman Treasurers of York Minster. Today it's home to a pleasant tearoom, small hotel, and bar. In summer, you can either sit outside, at tables scattered in the pleasant garden; or inside, in their elegant dining room or Jacobean gallery—a long wood-paneled hall with comfy sofas (£37 for 2-person "afternoon tea" served all day, £6 sandwiches, £6-11 light meals, daily 9:00-17:00, Chapter House Street, tel. 01904/612-613).

York Connections

From York by Train to: Durham (3-4/hour, 45 minutes), **London**'s King's Cross Station (2/hour, 2 hours), **Bath** (hourly with change in Bristol, 4.5 hours, more with additional transfers), **Oxford** (1/hour direct, 3.5 hours), **Cambridge** (roughly 2/hour, 2.5-3 hours, 1-2 transfers), **Birmingham** (2/hour, 2-2.5 hours), **Keswick/Lake District** (train to Penrith: roughly 2/hour, 3.5-4 hours, 1-2 transfers; then bus, allow about 4.5 hours total), **Manchester Airport** (2/hour, 1.75 hours), **Edinburgh** (2/hour,

2.5-2.75 hours). Train info: tel. 0845-748-4950, www.national-rail.co.uk.

Connections with London's Airports: Heathrow (allow 3 hours minimum; from airport take Heathrow Express train to London's Paddington Station, transfer by Tube to King's Cross, train to York—2/hour, 2 hours; for details on cheaper but slower Tube or bus option from airport to London King's Cross, see page 212), **Gatwick** (allow 3 hours minimum; from Gatwick South, catch First Capital Connect train to London's St. Pancras Station; from there, walk to neighboring King's Cross Station, and catch train to York—2/hour, 2 hours).

NORTH YORKSHIRE

Near York • North York Moors
• The North Yorkshire Coast

The countryside to the north of York—dubbed "North Yorkshire"—is speckled with pleasant attractions: the house and office of the "real" rural vet James Herriot, the desolately beautiful North York Moors, an eclectic mansion often used in movies, an engaging folk museum, a quirky World War II museum at a former POW camp, a kitschy scenic steam train, and several looming skeletons of destroyed abbeys. On the Yorkshire coast, you'll find an appealing pair of salty seaside towns. While none of these is a top-tier sight in itself, they complement each other nicely, so a day driving to several is time well spent.

Getting Around North Yorkshire

By Car: Driving is the best option—distances are short, the towns are small and easy to navigate, and there are plenty of tempting stopovers along the way. Get a good map, and use it thoughtfully to craft an efficient itinerary. As you drive, watch out for "wild" pheasants absentmindedly crossing the road. These birds are bred and fed by locals, and left to range freely through the woods...until autumn, when hunting season begins, and the fat, tame, and naive pheasants become easy prey.

By Public Transportation: You can reach most of these destinations by public transportation, but it requires patience (and, in some cases, a long walk from where the bus or train drops you off). York serves as a fine hub. I've explained particularly handy connections with each listing. As bus schedules change frequently with the season or simply on a whim, always confirm details at the York TI.

York has decent **bus** connections to Thirsk, Castle Howard,

North Yorkshire

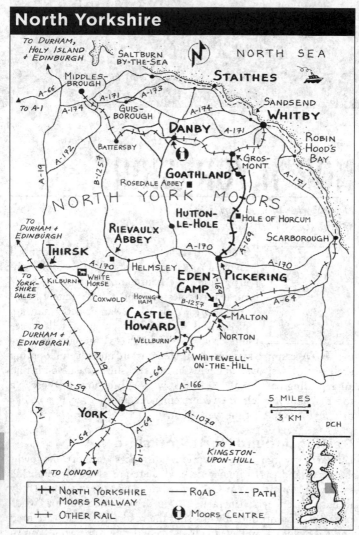

Eden Camp, Pickering, and Whitby. Reliance bus #30 or #30X departs York from near the train station and/or Exhibition Square and heads to Thirsk. Stephensons bus #181 leaves from Piccadilly or Stonebow in York and runs to Castle Howard. Coastliner bus #840 goes from York's train station to Eden Camp and Pickering; some runs continue on to Whitby. Once on the north coast, buses follow the coastal road north and south of Whitby, including Staithes. For most connections, use the route planner at www. yorkshiretravel.net.

A fun old **steam train** chugs through the middle of the North York Moors, from Pickering to Grosmont, with some continuing on to Whitby. Other trains can also be helpful (such as the Esk Valley Railway, which goes from Whitby to Grosmont and to Danby on the moors).

By Tour: Various tour companies offer guided bus excursions from York, focusing on Yorkshire Dales/James Herriot country, the North York Moors, Castle Howard, and more (ask at the York TI or try Eddie Brown, tel. 01423/321-248, www.eddiebrowntours.com).

Near York

The following sights are between York and the North York Moors. I've listed them in order from west to east. If you have a car, pick the ones that appeal to you and link them with a lazy countryside drive. If taking public transportation, sparse connections limit you to just one or two sights.

▲World of James Herriot

Devotees of the *All Creatures Great and Small* books, movies, and BBC TV series should visit the folksy veterinarian's digs in Thirsk,

a pleasant market town 23 miles north of York.

James Herriot was an autobiographical character created by Alfred Wight, once the Thirsk town vet. Today, Wight's home and office have been converted into a museum that painstakingly re-creates the 1940s Skeldale House featured in the novels, and also explores the development of veterinary science. The museum holds the world's largest James Herriot memorabilia collection, including the original Austin 7 car from the TV show. Even non-fans will find the slice-of-1940s-life decor fascinating and the trivia intriguing. (For example, Alf Wight couldn't use his own name for his autobiographical protagonist without violating an anti-advertising law...so instead he named "himself" for his favorite Scottish soccer goalie, James Herriot.) Fans will be tickled by the museum's reverence for all things Herriot.

In the barn, watch the 15-minute documentary about the TV series; even the studio sets from the show have been re-created.

NORTH YORKSHIRE

The interactive children's section is particularly engaging, even for adults: Try your hand at horse dentistry and find out if you're strong enough to calve a cow.

Cost and Hours: £8.50, daily April-Oct 10:00-17:00, Nov-March 10:00-16:00, last entry one hour before closing, 23 Kirkgate, tel. 01845/524-234, www.worldofjamesherriot.org.

Getting There: From the market square in Thirsk, the museum is just a block up Kirkgate. Reliance bus #30 or #30X connects York with Thirsk (nearly hourly Mon-Sat, none on Sun, 1 hour, leaves from near York train station and/or Exhibition Square, http://reliancebuses.co.uk). There are more connections by train, but the train station is about a mile outside of Thirsk, whereas the bus drops you at the main square. Drivers can zip here from York on the A-19 in about 40 minutes and park free for two hours (get the disc in the visitors center).

Nearby: Die-hard Herriot fans might enjoy exploring the **Yorkshire Dales,** westward from and much tamer than the North York Moors. Get details about the region—and information about guided tours—at the York TI. Approaching Thirsk, keep an eye out on the right side of the road for the **White Horse**—a gigantic image in the hillside that overlooks the town of Kilburn. The figure was created by a schoolmaster and his students in 1857, who removed the soil to expose the light-colored bedrock.

▲Rievaulx Abbey

Rievaulx (ree-VOH) is the sprawling ruins of a 12th-century abbey. Since it's not near any major towns, its pre-cut stones were less susceptible to plunder—so it's been left a bit more intact than many other ruined abbeys. Its beautiful and secluded setting—tucked away in a gentle, sheep-speckled valley—is appealing, but if you've seen other fine old abbeys, this is a rerun. Start with the little museum, then follow the included audioguide through the ruins. You'll learn how monastic life changed during the four centuries between its founding and its destruction by Henry VIII.

Cost and Hours: £6, includes audioguide, £4 parking fee is refunded when you buy abbey ticket; generally April-Sept daily 10:00-18:00; Oct Thu-Mon 10:00-17:00, closed Tue-Wed; Nov-March Sat-Sun 10:00-16:00, closed Mon-Fri; café, tel. 01439/798-228, www.english-heritage.org.uk.

Getting There: Drivers get there in a snap (just a short detour from the A-170). It's possible, but complicated, to get there by public transportation—ask for advice at the York TI. From York, first catch Stephensons bus #31 or #31X to Helmsley (4/day Mon-Sat, none on Sun, 1 hour, leaves from York Exhibition Square, confirm bus goes all the way to Helmsley, www.stephensonsofeasingwold. co.uk). From Helmsley, you can get to the abbey on foot (3 miles) or by taxi (the information center at Helmsley Castle, a short walk from Market Place, can help you with a taxi).

▲▲Castle Howard

Made popular by the filming of the *Brideshead Revisited* TV mini-series here in 1981, this fine, palatial, 300-year-old home (more

a manor than a "castle") is impressive. Taking more than 100 years to complete, it was commissioned in 1699 by Charles Howard, 3rd Earl of Carlisle. Howard chose John Vanbrugh, a playwright with no previous architectural training whatsoever, to design the house. This may explain some of the home's unique flourishes (like the grand, domed Great Hall—once the main entryway—which might be more at home in a Baroque church). Vanbrugh went on to build the even grander Blenheim Palace near Oxford (which is at least twice as interesting, if you're choosing between them—see page 519).

After being damaged in a 1940 fire, Castle Howard lay in ruins for years before being refurbished in the 1960s and opened to the public. The Howard family, whose precocious daughters are pictured throughout the place, still lives in one wing—and in winter, when the place is closed to the public, they use the rooms that are normally on the tour route. Fancy houses run in the family: Another branch of Howards currently reside at Arundel Castle, near the south coast (see page 340).

Cost and Hours: £14 for manor and grounds, £9.50 for grounds only in winter, when the manor is closed. Gardens open daily 10:00-17:30, last entry at 16:30, open until 15:30 in winter; manor open daily late March-Oct 11:00-17:00, closed Nov-late March except late Nov-late-Dec—when it's decorated for Christmas, last entry at 16:00, cafés and fresh produce store, tel. 01653/648-333, www.castlehoward.co.uk.

Tours: Free 40-minute outdoor tours cover various themes, including the gardens and the house's architecture (March-Oct, ask at ticket desk for times).

Getting There: It's in the countryside, 15 miles northeast of York, between Helmsley and Malton, off the A-64. It's ideal by car. You can get here from York on Stephensons bus #180 or #181 (3/day Mon-Sat, none on Sun, 1.25 hours, leaves from Piccadilly or Stonebow in York; show bus ticket for a discount on manor admission). Additional connections, through Malton, are more complicated (for details, see the castle's website or www.stephen-sonsofeasingwold.co.uk).

Visiting the House: As you follow the one-way tour route, read the English descriptions in each room. Chatty docents posted in key rooms explain what you're seeing. Many of the decorations are "souvenirs" from the Howards' travels—such as replicas of Roman busts and  Greek statues, or paintings that attempt to jam several of a Grand Tour city's landmarks onto a single canvas, much like today's collage postcards.

Visitors enter the house through the **West Wing.** After climbing the Grand Staircase, you'll veer into a series of bedrooms built in the mid-1700s in the Palladian style (constructed later than the other wings, and more staid and subdued than the flashy Baroque you'll see later). Starting in the 1830s, these bedrooms became the private apartments of George Howard and Lady Georgiana, whose marriage marked the union of two powerful families—the Howards and the Chatsworths. These days, the bedrooms are still used by guests when the house is closed to visitors. From here stretches the **Antique Passage,** lined with busts, sculptures, tables, and other items collected from Italy during the 4th Earl's visit there in the 1730s.

The passage leads from the West Wing into the **Great Hall,** the centerpiece of the house. The gigantic columns and tall arches draw your eye straight up to the highlight of the hall: the 70-foot tall dome adorned with the work of the Venetian artist Pellegrini. Above the columns are paintings of the four elements (Earth, Fire, Air, and Water). The dome depicts the tale of Apollo's son Phaeton as he falls from his father's chariot and plummets to earth. The Great Hall and dome were destroyed in the 1940 fire, so what you see here has been rebuilt (which explains why the colors in the paintings are so vivid).

Now head upstairs to view **exhibits** on the manor's restoration after the fire and the filming of *Brideshead Revisited* (both the original TV miniseries and the 2008 big-screen version, starring Emma Thompson and Michael Gambon).

Once back downstairs, you'll continue on to the **South Front,** with an impressive string of rooms built in the early 1700s in the Baroque style. Look up and notice the carved wood molding in these rooms, made from pine trees straight from the grounds. The Music Room features two pianos dating back to 1796 and 1805.

NORTH YORKSHIRE

The Crimson Dining Room's highlight is a large Canaletto painting depicting a view of Venice. The Turquoise Drawing Room showcases numerous paintings, including Thomas Gainsborough's *Girl with Pigs* and his portrait of Isabella Byron, mother of the 5th Earl and great aunt of the poet Lord Byron. In the Museum Room, look for the elaborate, multistory, blue Delft porcelain tulip vase—dating from the "Tulip Fever" era of the late 17th century, when a single flower could cost £1,000. Imagine the extravagance of filling this whole vase.

From the Museum Room, the Long Gallery leads back through the West Wing and to the **chapel.** The chapel was renovated in 1870-1875, when the floor was lowered and the ceiling and pillars redone to resemble those in the Royal Chapel at St. James's Palace in London. The stained-glass windows, showing scenes from the life of Christ, were produced by Morris & Co. in 1872. The chapel is still used for services and ceremonies, such as weddings and baptisms.

The chapel marks the end of the manor tour. From here, feel free to roam the sprawling grounds. The mini-pyramid on the horizon—behind the big Atlas Fountain—was inspired by a trip to Egypt. The grounds also include several pools, lakes, and fountains, a rose garden, and a quiet wood.

Eden Camp

Once an internment camp for German and Italian POWs during World War II, this is now a theme museum on Britain's war experience. Sprawling, cluttered, pleasantly low-tech, and a bit hokey, the exhibit works best for Brits who want to help their kids (or grandkids) understand the war years. But even though it's overpromoted, its earnestness will win over WWII buffs, as it energetically tries to convey the spirit of a country Hitler couldn't conquer.

Cost and Hours: £6, daily 10:00-17:00, closed for a few weeks late-Dec-mid-Jan, last entry at 16:00, cash only, mess-kitchen cafeteria, tel. 01653/697-777, www.edencamp.co.uk.

Getting There: It's near Malton, 18 miles northeast of York. From York, drivers take the A-169 toward Scarborough, then follow signs to the camp (notice its proximity to Castle Howard—it's easy to combine these two and more on a day's drive). Or, from York, you can catch Coastliner bus #840 (every 1-2 hours Mon-Sat, limited on Sun, 1 hour, leaves from York train station, www.coastliner.co.uk).

Visiting Eden Camp: The comprehensive exhibits investigate a wide range of World War II and postwar topics. Various barracks detail the rise of Hitler, the fury of the Blitz, and the efforts on the home front—such as rationing and the Local Defense Volunteers, affectionately dubbed "Dads Army." A detailed map and ample

NORTH YORKSHIRE

posted information are helpful, if a bit overwhelming. Focus your visit on the topics that interest you most. An intense exhibit on the Blitz comes with the sound of bombs, the acrid smell of burning, and wartime mottos such as, "Hitler will send no warning—so always carry your gas mask." Don't miss hut #10, which details the actual purpose of the camp—a prison for captured Nazis and Italians during World War II (think *Hogan's Heroes* in reverse). Enjoy the quirky handmade items—such as a miniature pair of shoes carved out of bread—created by bored POWs who were killing time. Consider the relative delight of being in the care of the gentlemanly English rather than in a Russian camp. It's no wonder the Germans and Italians settled right in.

North York Moors

In the lonesome North York Moors, sheep seem to outnumber people. Upon this high, desolate-feeling plateau, with spongy and in-

hospitable soil, bleating flocks jockey for position against scrubby heather for control of the terrain. Although the 1847 novel *Wuthering Heights* was set 60 miles to the southwest, you can almost imagine the mysterious Heathcliff plodding across this countryside. As you pass through this haunting landscape, crisscrossed by only a few roads, notice how the gloomy brown heather—which blooms briefly with purple flowers at summer's end—is burned back by wardens to clear the way for new growth. The vast, undulating expanses of nothingness are punctuated by greener, sparsely populated valleys called dales. Park your car and take a hike across the moors on any small road. You'll come upon a few tidy villages and maybe even old Roman roads.

For information on the moors, you can stop at the TI in Pickering (at the south end) and/or the excellent Moors Centre (near Danby, at the north end). Pick up the annual magazine *Out and About in the North York Moors*. Either place can give you hiking tips and sell you essential maps. Popular walks include a 5.5-mile loop near the Hole of Horcum, the 4.5-mile walk between Goathland and Grosmont, or the brief stroll to the waterfall near Goathland. Most villages have at least one general store where you can buy a basic brochure suggesting local hikes.

NORTH YORKSHIRE

Getting Around the North York Moors

If you're **driving,** the easiest route across the moors is the A-169, which roughly parallels the steam-train line north to Grosmont; it passes the Hole of Horcum and comes close to Grosmont, before heading northeast to Whitby. To the west, smaller roads head north through Hutton-le-Hole (with its folk museum) and the village of Rosedale Abbey. While less straightforward—you'll need a very good map and an even better navigator—this western zone really gets you deep into the moors.

Those relying on **public transportation** will primarily use the North Yorkshire Moors Railway (explained later).

Sights on the Moors

These locations are listed roughly from south to north (as you'd approach them coming from York).

Pickering

This functional town, the southern gateway to the North York Moors, is a major crossroads and a proud hub for this region's meager public transit. A parking lot, the train station, and the TI all cluster on the same block. The helpful **TI** can provide advice for driving and hiking on the moors, and has a room-booking service (March-Oct Mon-Sat 9:30-17:00, Sun 9:30-16:00; Nov-Feb Mon-Sat 9:30-16:00, closed Sun; tel. 01751/473-791, www.discovernorthyorkshire.co.uk, pickeringtic@btconnect.com).

The main reason to visit Pickering is to catch the **North Yorkshire Moors Railway** steam train into the moors. Otherwise, you can browse its Monday market (produce, knickknacks) and consider its rural-life museum (Hutton-le-Hole's is better)—but don't bother visiting Pickering unless you're passing through anyway.

With more time, consider stopping by Pickering's ruined 13th-century Norman **castle,** built on the site of a wooden castle from William the Conqueror's 11th-century heyday. Appreciate its textbook motte-and-bailey (stone fort on a grassy hilltop) design, and climb to the top to understand its strategic location (£4; July-Aug daily 10:00-18:00; April-June and Sept Thu-Mon 10:00-17:00, closed Tue-Wed; Oct Sat-Sun only 10:00-16:00; closed Nov-March; on the ridge above town, tel. 01751/474-989, www.english-heritage.org.uk).

Getting There: Drivers find Pickering right on the A-169, 25 miles north of York (en route to the coast). Two-hour parking is across from the TI; an all-day parking lot is on Vivis Lane, a couple of blocks south of the TI (£4/6 hours, £5.50 for over 6 hours). Those relying on public transportation can catch Coastliner bus #840 from York (every 1-2 hours Mon-Sat, limited on Sun,

1.5 hours, leaves from York train station, www.coastliner.co.uk); alternatively, you can shave a few minutes off the trip by taking the train to Malton, then catching bus #840 from there.

▲North Yorkshire Moors Railway

This 18-mile, one-hour steam-engine ride between Pickering and Grosmont (GROW-mont) runs through some of the best parts of the moors. Some trains continue from Grosmont on to the seaside town of Whitby; otherwise, you might be able to transfer in Grosmont to another, non-steam train to reach Whitby (check schedules as you plan your trip). Once in Whitby, you can use the bus to connect to other towns along the coast (such as to Staithes) or to return to York.

Even with the small and dirty windows (try to wipe off the outside of yours before you roll), and with the track situated mostly in a scenic gully, it's a good ride. You can stop along the way for a walk on the moors (or at the appealing village of Goathland) and catch the next train (£18 round-trip to Grosmont, £24 round-trip to Whitby, includes hop-on, hop-off privileges; runs daily late March-Oct, may run on some weekends in winter—check timetable online, schedule flexes with season but first train generally departs Pickering at 9:00, last train departs Grosmont between 17:00 and 18:00; trip takes about 1 hour one-way to Grosmont, 1.5 hours to Whitby; tel. 01751/472-508—press 1 for 24-hour timetable info, www.nymr.co.uk). There's no baggage storage at any stop on the steam-train line (but you can leave your bag for free at the Pickering TI until 17:00)—pack light if you decide to hike.

▲Hutton-le-Hole

This postcard-pretty town, lining up along a river as if posing for its close-up, is an ideal springboard for a trip into the North York Moors. It has some touristy shops and inviting picnic benches, but Hutton-le-Hole's biggest attraction is its engaging folk museum.

Ryedale Folk Museum

This open-air complex illustrates farm life in the moors through reconstructed and furnished historic buildings. The line of shops includes a village store, which served as one-stop shopping (the original Costco) to save locals the long trek into the closest market town. A humble cluster of traditional thatch-roof cottages have a genuine, lived-in feeling. If the beds are unmade,  notice the "mattress" is made of rope stretched across a frame, which could be tightened for a firmer night's sleep (giving us the phrase "sleep tight"). A small-scale model of a traditional York-shire village features adorable miniature houses. The Harrison Collection holds items representing English domestic life through the centuries, such as an early 1900s gramophone, a late Victorian sewing machine, a two-foot-tall gingerbread mold, and a blanket smoother (like a giant rolling pin). The museum is most worth-while during frequent special weekends, when lively costumed do-cents explain what you're seeing along the way—check the online schedule or call ahead.

Cost and Hours: £7; mid-March–late Oct daily 10:00-17:30, last entry at 16:30; late Oct–mid-March 10:00-16:30, closes early Dec–mid-Jan; tel. 01751/417-367, www.ryedalefolkmuseum.co.uk.

Getting There: Drivers find it just north of the A-170. From Hutton-le-Hole, you can plunge northward directly into the North York Moors (which begin suddenly as you leave town). Without a car, you may be out of luck, as public transportation is limited—call the museum or check its website for the latest options.

In the Heart of the Moors

The Hole of Horcum

This huge sinkhole was supposedly scooped out by a giant. While not too exciting, it offers a good excuse to get out of your car and appreciate the moorland scenery (at the Saltergate car park).

Rosedale Abbey

A tranquil village on the west side of the moors (north of Hutton-le-Hole and far from the Hole of Horcum and Goathland), Rose-dale Abbey offers a good dose of small-town moor life. Nestled between hills, it also provides pleasing moor views.

Goathland

This village, huddled along a babbling brook, is worth considering for a sleepy stopover, either on the steam-train trip or for drivers (it's

an easy detour from the A-169). Movie buffs enjoy Goathland's train station, which was used to film scenes at "Hogsmeade Sta-tion" for the early Harry Potter movies (for more on Harry Pot-ter sights, see page 890). But Brits know and love Goathland as the setting for the beloved, long-running TV series *Heartbeat,* about a small Yorkshire town in the 1960s. You'll see TV sets intermingled with real buildings, and some shops are even labeled "Aidensfield," for the TV town's fictional name.

▲The Moors Centre

This expanded and refurbished visitors center near Danby provides the best orientation for exploring North York Moors National Park. (Unfortunately, it's at the northern end of the park—not as convenient if you're coming from York.) The grand old lodge offers excellent exhibits on various moorland topics, informative films about the landscape, an art gallery showcasing works by local artists inspired by these surroundings, a children's play area, an information desk, plenty of books and maps, guided nature walks, brass rubbing, a cheery cafeteria, and brochures on several good walks that start right outside the front door.

Cost and Hours: Free entry, parking-£2.20/up to 2 hours, £4/day; March-Oct daily 10:00-17:00; Nov-Feb Sat-Sun 11:00-16:00, may be open shorter hours during the week—phone ahead; café, tel. 01439/772-737, www.northyorkmoors.org.uk.

Getting There: The Moors Centre is three-fourths of a mile from Danby in Esk Valley, in the northern part of the park (follow signs from Danby, which is a short drive from the A-171, running along the northern edge of the park). Danby is on the Esk Valley rail line, with connections to Grosmont and Whitby (4/day, 20 minutes from Danby to Grosmont, 40 minutes from Danby to Whitby, www.eskvalleyrailway.co.uk). From the Danby train station, it's a 15-minute walk to the visitors center.

North Yorkshire Coast

Two salty Yorkshire towns—one big (Whitby) and one small (Staithes)—are seaside escapes worth a stop for the seagulls, surf, and Captain Cook lore. If you're not seeing the English coast anywhere else on your trip, and you have an extra day in York, side-tripping here is worthwhile.

Getting to the North Yorkshire Coast

Yorkshire Coastliner bus #840 connects **York** to Whitby (4/day Mon-Sat, limited on Sun, 2.5 hours, leaves from York train station, www.coastliner.co.uk). Alternatively, you can ride the train to Scarborough (hourly, 50 minutes), then catch bus #93 or #X93 to Whitby (2/hour in summer, hourly in winter, 1 hour).

To connect Whitby to the **North York Moors,** you can take the historic steam train from Pickering to Grosmont, with some trains continuing into Whitby (otherwise you may be able to transfer in Grosmont to a Whitby-bound train).

From **Durham,** you can get to Whitby by train with transfers in Darlington and Middlesbrough (3/day, 2.5-3 hours, Middlesbrough-Whitby leg also stops at Grosmont, where you can catch the Moors steam train south to Pickering and Danby, near The Moors Centre).

Getting Around the North Yorkshire Coast

From Whitby, Arriva buses #5 and #5a run up and down the coast north of town, connecting you to Sandsend and Staithes en route to Middlesbrough (2/hour in summer, hourly on Sun and in winter); south of Whitby, bus #93 and #X93 runs to Robin Hood's Bay (2/hour in summer, hourly in winter, 20 minutes, www.arrivabus. co.uk).

Whitby

An important port since the 12th century, Whitby is today a fun coastal resort town with about 14,000 people, a gaggle of steep  and salty old streets, and enjoyable nautical ambience. Its busy harbor, bristling with ships' masts, is squeezed into a narrow canyon flanked on one side by the stately skeleton of its 11th-century abbey, and on the other by the bluff-topping West Cliff neighborhood. The harborfront zone is a carousel of Coney Island-type amusements and city dwellers from inland Yorkshire whooping it up. Rounding out Whitby's claim to fame are its connections to Captain Cook and Bram Stoker (whose *Dracula* was partly written here).

Orientation to Whitby

Tourist Information

The TI is on the harbor next to the train and bus stations (daily May-June 9:30-18:00, July-Sept 9:30-19:00, Oct-April 10:00-16:30, tel. 01723/383-636, www.discoveryorkshirecoast.com).

Arrival in Whitby

If driving, consider first stopping by the hilltop sights (the abbey on one side of town, and West Cliff on the other). Then drive down into the old town center and drop your car in the pay-and-display parking lot across the street from the TI and near the train and bus stations. Walk about 200 yards toward the harbor—and the lone bridge spanning it—to get oriented.

From the bridge, face the sea to consider your options (described in more detail below): On the left is the waterfront promenade called Pier Road/Fish Quay, lined with tacky carnival distractions, as well as the recommended Magpie Café (popular fish-and-chips) and a tacky Dracula exhibit (skip it); above this scene is the West Cliff area, with fine views over town. On the right (across the bridge) is a warren of touristy lanes filled with hard-candy stores, knickknack shops, and the Captain Cook Memorial Museum; overhead (but not quite visible from here) is the ruined abbey.

Sights in Whitby

▲Abbey

Whitby's main landmark is its ruined abbey, set on a bluff overlooking the harbor. Built on the site of a seventh-century monastic settlement, the remains of this 11th-century version echo with the chants of ages past...enough to raise goose bumps even on a vampire (*Dracula* was partly set here). Many of the stones from this formerly grand abbey were used to build houses in the town below.

Cost and Hours: £6.40, includes audioguide; April-Sept daily 10:00-18:00; Oct Thu-Mon 10:00-16:00, closed Tue-Wed; Nov-March Sat-Sun 10:00-16:00, closed Mon-Fri; last entry 30 minutes before closing, pay-and-display parking, tel. 01947/603-568, www.english-heritage.org.uk.

Getting There: The abbey is connected to the streets below by a **staircase** of 199 steps at the end of the old town. In the olden days, poor people would carry the coffins of the departed up these steps, resting occasionally on broader steps called "coffin rests"... which, for practical reasons, are more frequent near the top. An alternate route up is via the path called Caedmon's Trod.

Captain Cook Memorial Museum

This small museum, in an old shipowner's house where Cook lodged for a few years, offers a dull look at the famous hometown sailor and his exotic voyages. The most interesting bit is the Voyages Room, with a cutaway model of one of Cook's ships, and miniature replicas of everything that went on board. Two of Cook's boats (*Resolution* and *Endeavour*) were built in the Whitby shipyards; a full-size replica of the *Endeavour*, which has been used in many swashbuckling films, is often moored in Whitby.

Cost and Hours: £4.80, pick up free pamphlet as you enter, daily mid-Feb-March 11:00-15:00, April-Oct 9:45-17:00, last entry 30 minutes before closing, closed Nov-mid-Feb unless reserved for

£7.50/person; tucked down little Grape Lane behind the Dolphin Hotel, near the bridge on the abbey side of town; tel. 01947/601-900, www.cookmuseumwhitby.co.uk.

West Cliff
Across the harbor from the abbey is this fun little hilltop park, with inviting benches and a lively kids' area. Supposedly it was from this vantage point that Bram Stoker contemplated Whitby's abbey...and inspiration bit him in the neck. In *Dracula,* a boat docks at the long pier, and a black dog—the Count in disguise—jumps off the boat and runs up the 199 steps to the abbey (where he hides out for the next three chapters, until he takes to the sea again). Nearby, the whale bones forming an archway over the path recall Whitby's former status as a major whaling city. When whalers returned to port, they'd prop up bones like these on their ships, as a sign to their wives and mothers (who were anxiously waiting ashore) that the trip had gone safely.

Beach Walks
To go for a walk along the beach, consider strolling to nearby villages, then walking or catching an Arriva bus back: Sandsend to the north (buses #5 and #5a) is closer than Robin Hood's Bay to the south (bus #93 and #X93, www.arrivabus.co.uk). Before heading out, check the tide tables carefully (posted in the TI window).

Sleeping in Whitby

A collection of inviting B&Bs perches atop the plateau behind West Cliff. Among these, **$$ Crescent Lodge B&B** is a good choice (6 rooms, Db-£68, just off the main drag as you enter the upper part of town at 27 Crescent Avenue, tel. 01947/820-073, http://crescentlodgewhitby.com, carol@carolyates.wanadoo.co.uk, Carol).

$ Whitby's **Abbey House youth hostel** is one of England's most impressive. Right on the abbey grounds above town—and literally built with bits and pieces of that abbey—this 17th-century building has undergone an extensive restoration. It now houses 132 beds in 26 rooms, most of them 4- to 6-bed dormitories with bathrooms (and many bookable as private rooms). Many rooms have information plaques on the walls explaining the architecture and renovation (£11-23/bed, Db twin-£35-55, price depends on day and season, discount for members, price includes ticket to the abbey, breakfast-£5, reception open 7:30-10:00 & 14:00-22:30, no curfew, family rooms, fully wheelchair-accessible rooms, pay guest computer, pay Wi-Fi—or free for members, laundry, kitchen, cafeteria-style restaurant, reservation tel. 0845-371-9049, reception tel. 01947/602-878, www.yha.org.uk, whitby@yha.org.uk).

Sleep Code

(£1 = about $1.60, country code: 44, area code: 01947)
S = Single, **D** = Double/Twin, **T** = Triple, **Q** = Quad, **b** = bathroom, **s** = shower only. Unless otherwise noted, breakfast is included and credit cards are accepted.

To help you sort easily through these listings, I've divided the accommodations into two categories based on the price for a standard double room with bath (during high season):

$$ **Moderately Priced**—Most rooms £50 or more.
$ **Lower Priced**—Most rooms less than £50.

Prices can change without notice; verify the hotel's current rates online or by email. For the best prices, always book direct.

Eating in Whitby

In this nautical town, fish-and-chips are on everybody's mind. The **Magpie Café** is a local institution, generally marked by a line of loyal eaters waiting to get in; the carryout window is to the right (£7 for takeaway; in the restaurant: £10-12 fish-and-chips, £11-18 fish dinners; daily 11:30-21:00 except until 20:00 Mon-Thu in winter, closed much of Jan, 14 Pier Road, tel. 01947/602-058).

If the Magpie is too crowded—which is quite likely—try these local-approved alternatives: **Quayside,** nearly next door to the Magpie (takeaway counter with £6 fish-and-chips, sit-down restaurant with £8-14 meals, daily 11:00-19:00, until 20:00 in summer, tel. 01947/602-059); and, across the harbor, the simpler **Mister Chips,** just down the street from the Captain Cook Museum (£5-7 fish-and-chips, takeaway or restaurant, daily 11:30-22:00, 68-69 Church Street, tel. 01947/604-683).

Staithes

A ragamuffin village where the boy who became Captain James Cook got his first taste of the sea, Staithes (pronounced "staythz,"

about 10 miles north of Whitby) is a salty jumble of cottages bunny-hopping down a ravine into a tiny harbor. About a tenth the size of its big sister down the coast, Staithes is the yang to Whitby's yin. This refreshingly unpretentious town is gloriously stubborn about not wooing tourists (www.staithes-town.info).

While dead as a doornail today, in 1816 Staithes was home to 70 boats and the busiest fishing station on the northeast coast of England. Ten years ago, the town supported 20 fishing boats—today, only three. But fishermen (who pronounce their town's name "steers" in the local dialect) still outnumber tourists in undiscovered Staithes. The out-of-towners who do come here rent cottages in the old center and settle in for a long stay as temporary locals. The town has changed little since Captain Cook's days. Lots of flies and seagulls seem to have picked the barren cliffs raw. There's nothing to do

but stroll the beach and enjoy a harborside beer or ice cream. As you gaze out at the scenery and rich light, imagine Staithes in the early 20th century, when a small artists' colony called the "Staithes Group" enjoyed painting this same scene.

For a bit more activity, drop by the **lifeboat station,** operated by the Royal National Lifeboat Institution (RNLI)—Britain's entirely volunteer answer to the Coast Guard. Entering the big barn, notice the boards up on the eaves with not-quite-stirring accounts of the boats being called to duty. As this organization—England's sole method for responding to maritime emergencies—is entirely funded by donations, consider supporting the cause with a coin or two (flexible hours—typically open daily 10:00-16:00 in summer, most days in winter; tel. 01947/840-141, shop tel. 01947/840-587, www.rnli.org.uk or www.staithes-lifeboat.org.uk).

Getting to Staithes

Staithes is an easy **drive** north of Whitby. Parking is tough—generally, you can drive in only to unload. Service trucks clog the windy main (and only) lane much of the day. A pay-and-display lot is at the top of the town—an easy downhill walk to the action (but a more strenuous hike back up). While the **bus** #5 and #5a connection from Whitby to Staithes is fairly straightforward, there's not much in low-key Staithes to justify the trip (2/hour in summer, hourly on Sun and in winter, 30 minutes; 10-minute walk from bus stop into town, www.arrivabus.co.uk).

Eating in Staithes

A pair of lowbrow pubs serve lunch and dinner: **The Royal George,** along the main drag, has well-worn, basic decor (daily 12:00-23:00, tel. 01947/841-432). **The Cod & Lobster,** overlooking the harbor, has scenic outdoor seating and a cozy indoor space warmed by a couple of fireplaces. Drop in to see its old-time Staithes photos (daily 11:00-23:00, tel. 01947/840-330).

In nice weather, the best option is to enjoy a drink, snack, or light meal (i.e., fish-and-chips) sitting at an outdoor table fronting the harbor. Try the friendly **Seadrift Café,** which specializes in sweets, but also does basic grub (Sun-Thu 10:00-16:00, last order at 15:30, closed Fri, tel. 01947/841-345).

DURHAM AND NORTHEAST ENGLAND

Durham • Beamish Museum • Hadrian's Wall • Holy Island • Bamburgh Castle

Northeast England harbors some of the country's best historical sights. Go for a Roman ramble at Hadrian's Wall, a reminder that Britain was an important Roman colony 2,000 years ago. Make a pilgrimage to Holy Island, where Christianity gained its first toehold in Britain. Marvel at England's greatest Norman church—Durham's cathedral—and enjoy an evensong service there. At the excellent Beamish Museum, travel back in time to the 18th and 19th centuries.

Planning Your Time

For **train** travelers, Durham is the most convenient overnight stop in this region. But it's problematic to see en route to another destination, since there's no baggage storage in Durham: Either stay overnight, or do Durham as a day trip from York. If you like Roman ruins, visit Hadrian's Wall (tricky but doable by public transportation—see page 820). The Beamish Museum is an easy day trip from Durham (less than an hour by bus).

By **car,** you can easily visit everything in this chapter. Spend a night in Durham and a night near Hadrian's Wall. With a car, you can easily visit Beamish Museum on the way to Hadrian's Wall.

For the best quick visit to Durham, arrive by mid-afternoon, in time to tour the cathedral and enjoy the evensong service (Tue-Sat at 17:15, Sun at 15:30; limited access and no tours during June graduation ceremonies). Sleep in Durham. Visit Beamish the next morning before continuing on to your next destination.

Durham

Without its cathedral, Durham would hardly be noticed. But this magnificently situated structure is hard to miss (even if you're zooming by on the train). Seemingly happy to go nowhere, Durham sits along the tight curve of its river, snug below its castle and famous church. It has a medieval, cobbled atmosphere and a scraggly peasant's indoor market just off the main square. Durham is the home to England's third-oldest university, with a student vibe jostling against its lingering working-class mining-town feel. You'll see tattooed and pierced people in search of job security and a good karaoke bar. Yet Durham has a youthful liveliness and a small-town warmth that shines—especially on sunny days, when most everyone is out licking ice cream cones.

Orientation to Durham

As it has for a thousand years, tidy little Durham (pop. 30,000) clusters everything safely under its castle, within the protective hairpin bend of the River Wear.
Because of the town's hilly to-
pography, going just about anywhere involves a lot of up and
down...and back up again. The
main spine through the middle
of town (Framwellgate Bridge,
Silver Street, and Market Place)
is level to moderately steep, but

walking in any direction from that area involves some serious up-
hill climbing. Take advantage of the handy Cathedral Bus to avoid the tiring elevation changes—especially up to the cathedral and castle area, or to the train station (perched high on a separate hill).

Tourist Information

Due to funding cuts, Durham no longer has a physical TI, but the town does maintain a call center and website (calls answered Mon-Sat 9:30-17:30, Sun 11:00-16:00, tel. 03000-262-626, www.thisisdurham.com, visitor@thisisdurham.com).

Though not an official TI, the Durham World Heritage Site Visitor Centre, near the Palace Green, can offer some guidance, including brochures on things to see and a 12-minute video on the town. They also sell tickets to tour the castle (center open daily April-Sept 9:30-17:00, until 18:00 July-Aug, Oct-March 9:30-16:30, 7 Owengate, tel. 0191/334-3805, www.durhamworldheritagesite.com). You can also ask for advice at your B&B or hotel.

Durham

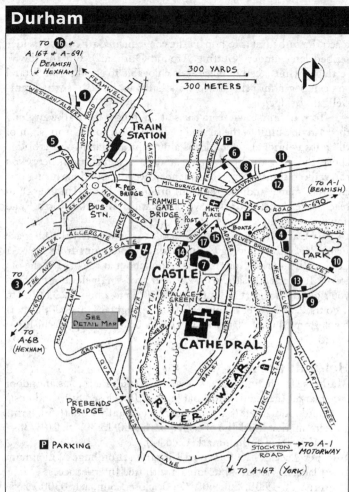

P PARKING

1. Victorian Town House B&B
2. Castleview Guest House
3. To Farnley Tower B&B
4. Durham Marriott Hotel Royal County
5. Kingslodge Hotel & Rest.
6. Premier Inn Durham City Center
7. Durham Castle Rooms
8. Oldfields Restaurant
9. The Court Inn Pub
10. The Dun Cow
11. Claypath Deli
12. The Capital Indian Rest.
13. Zen Restaurant
14. Café Rouge & Bella Italia
15. Bells Fish & Chips
16. To Bistro 21
17. Marks & Spencer; Tesco Metro

Arrival in Durham

By Train: From the train station, the fastest and easiest way to reach the cathedral is to hop on the convenient **Cathedral Bus** (described later, under "Getting Around Durham"). But the town's setting—while steep in places—is enjoyable to stroll through (and you can begin my self-guided walk halfway through, at the Framwellgate Bridge).

To **walk** into town from the station, follow the walkway along the road downhill to the second pedestrian turnoff (within sight of the railway bridge), which leads almost immediately over a bridge above the busy road called Alexander Crescent. From here, you can walk to some of my recommended accommodations (using this chapter's map—and the giant rail bridge as a handy landmark); to reach other hotels—or the river and cathedral—take North Road down into town.

By Car: Drivers simply surrender to the wonderful 400-space Prince Bishops Shopping Centre parking lot (coming from the M-1 exit, you'll run right into it at the roundabout at the base of the old town). It's perfectly safe, with 24-hour access. An elevator deposits you right in the heart of Durham (£2.10/up to 2 hours, £3.30/up to 4 hours, £11.50/over 6 hours, £1.50/overnight 18:00-8:00; a short block from Market Place, tel. 0191/375-0416, www.princebishops.co.uk).

Helpful Hints

Markets: The main square, known as Market Place, has an indoor market (generally Mon-Sat 9:00-17:00, closed Sun) and hosts outdoor markets (Sat retail market generally 9:30-16:30, farmers' market third Thu of each month 9:30-15:30, tel. 0191/384-6153, www.durhammarkets.co.uk).

Internet Access: The **Clayport Library,** set on huge Millennium Place, has about 40 terminals with free Internet access (Mon-Fri 9:30-19:00, Sat 9:00-17:00, closed Sun, tel. 03000/265-524).

Laundry: Durham has none within walking distance; ask your B&B host for recommendations if you're willing to drive or take a taxi.

Tours: Blue Badge guides offer 1.5-hour city walking tours on weekends in peak season (£4, usually May-Sept Sat-Sun at 14:00, meet outside Town Hall in Market Square, contact TI call center to confirm schedule, tel. 03000-262-626). **David Butler,** the town historian, gives excellent private tours (reasonable prices, tel. 0191/386-1500, www.dhent.co.uk, dhent@dhent.fsnet.co.uk) as well as a weekly Durham Ghost Tour in summer (£5, July-Sept Mon at 19:00).

Getting Around Durham

While all my recommended hotels, eateries, and sights are doable by foot, if you don't feel like walking Durham's hills, hop on the convenient **Cathedral Bus.** Bus #40A runs between the train station, Market Place, and the Palace Green (£1 all-day ticket, those over 60 ride free most of the day; daily 3/hour Mon-Fri about 8:30-17:00, from 9:00 on Sat, none on Sun; tel. 0191/372-5386, www.thisisdurham.com). A different bus #40A goes from Freeman's Place (near the Premier Inn) to Market Place and the Palace Green (2/hour Mon-Sat about 10:00-15:45). Confirm the route when you board.

Taxis zip tired tourists to their B&Bs or back up to the train station (about £5 from city center, wait on west side of Framwellgate Bridge at the bottom of North Road or on the east side of Elvet Bridge).

Self-Guided Walk

Welcome to Durham

• *Begin at Framwellgate Bridge (down in the center of town, halfway between the train station and the cathedral).*

Framwellgate Bridge was a wonder when it was built in the 12th century—much longer than the river is wide and higher than seemingly necessary. It was well-designed to connect stretches of solid high ground and to avoid steep descents toward the marshy river. Note how elegantly today's Silver Street (which leads toward town) slopes into the Framwellgate Bridge. (Imagine that until the 1970s, this people-friendly lane was congested with traffic and buses.)

• *Follow Silver Street up the hill to the town's main square.*

Durham's **Market Place** retains the same plotting the prince bishop gave it when he moved villagers here in about 1100. Each long and skinny plot of land was the same width (about eight yards), maximizing the number of shops that could have a piece of the Market Place action. Find today's distinctly narrow buildings (Thomas Cook, Whittard, and Thomson)—

DURHAM & NE ENGLAND

they still fit the 900-year-old plan. The widths of the other buildings fronting the square are multiples of that original shop width.

Examine the square's **statues.** Coal has long been the basis of this region's economy. The statue of Neptune was part of an ill-fated attempt by a coal baron to bribe the townsfolk into embracing a canal project that would make the shipment of his coal more efficient. The statue of the fancy guy on the horse is Charles Stewart Vane, the Third Marquess of Londonderry. He was an Irish aristocrat and a general in Wellington's army who married a local coal heiress. A clever and aggressive businessman, he managed to create a vast business empire by controlling every link in the coal business chain—mines, railroads, boats, harbors, and so on.

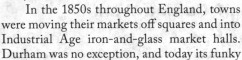

In the 1850s throughout England, towns were moving their markets off squares and into Industrial Age iron-and-glass market halls. Durham was no exception, and today its funky 19th-century **indoor market** (which faces Market Place) is a delight to explore (closed Sun). There are also outdoor markets here on Saturdays and the third Thursday of each month.

Do you enjoy the sparse traffic in Durham's old town? It was the first city in England to institute a "congestion fee." When drivers enter, a camera snaps a photo of each car's license plate, and mails them a bill for £5. This has cut downtown traffic by more than 50 percent. Locals brag that London (which now has a similar congestion fee) was inspired by their success.

• *Head up the hill on Saddler Street toward the cathedral, stopping where you reach the chunk of wall at the top of a stairway. On the left, you'll see a bridge.*

A 12th-century construction, **Elvet Bridge** led to a town market over the river. Like Framwellgate, it's very long (17 arches) and designed to avoid riverside muck and steep inclines. Even today, Elvet Bridge leads to an unusually wide road—once swollen to accommodate the market action. Shops lined the right-hand side of Elvet Bridge in the 12th century, as they do today. An alley separated the bridge from the buildings on the left. When the bridge was widened, it met the upper stories of the buildings on the left, which became "street level."

Turn back to look at the chunk of **wall** by the top of the stairs—a reminder of a once-formidable fortification. The Scots, living just 50 miles from here, were on the rampage in the 14th century. After their victory at Bannockburn in 1314, they pushed farther south and actually burned part of Durham. Wary of this new threat,

Central Durham

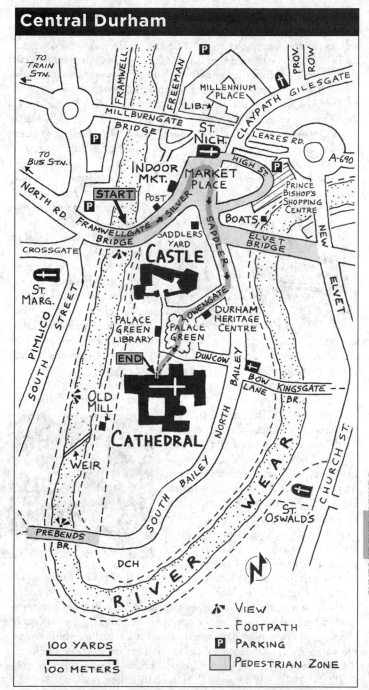

TO TRAIN STN.

FRAMWELL.

FREEMAN

P

MILLENNIUM PLACE

CLAYPATH

GILESGATE

PROV. ROW

MILLBURNGATE

BRIDGE

LIB.

ST. NICH.

LEAZES RD.

A-690

P

TO BUS STN.

NORTH RD.

FRAMWELLGATE BRIDGE

INDOOR MKT.

MARKET PLACE

HIGH ST.

START

P

Post

SILVER

SADDLERS YARD

SADDLER

BOATS

ELVET BRIDGE

PRINCE BISHOP'S SHOPPING CENTRE

NEW

CROSSGATE

CASTLE

OWENGATE

ST. MARG.

PIMLICO

SOUTH STREET

PALACE GREEN LIBRARY

PALACE GREEN

DURHAM HERITAGE CENTRE

ELVET

END

DUNCOW

NORTH BAILEY

BOW LANE

KINGSGATE BR.

OLD MILL

CATHEDRAL

CHURCH ST.

WEIR

SOUTH BAILEY

RIVER WEAR

ST. OSWALD'S

PREBENDS BR.

DCH

N

👁 VIEW

--- FOOTPATH

P PARKING

PEDESTRIAN ZONE

100 YARDS

100 METERS

Durham built thick city walls. As people settled within the walls, the population density soared. Soon, open lanes were covered by residences and became tunnels (called "vennels"). A classic vennel leads to Saddlers Yard, a fine little 16th-century courtyard (opposite the wall). While the vennels are cute today, centuries ago they were Dickensian nightmares—the filthiest of hovels.

• *Continue up Saddler Street. Just before the fork at the top of the street, duck through the purple door below the* Georgian Window *sign. You'll see a bit of the medieval wall incorporated into the brickwork of a newer building and a turret from an earlier wall. Back on Saddler Street, you can see the ghost of the old wall. (It's exactly the width of the building now housing the Salvation Army.) Veer right at Owengate as you continue uphill to the Palace Green. (The Durham World Heritage Site Visitor Centre is near the top of the hill, on the left.)*

The **Palace Green** was the site of the original 11th-century Saxon town, filling this green between the castle and an earlier church. Later, the town made way for 12th-century Durham's defenses, which now enclose the green. With the threat presented by the Vikings, it's no wonder people found comfort in a spot like this.

The **castle** still stands—as it has for a thousand years—on its motte (man-made mound). Like Oxford and Cambridge, Durham University is a collection of colleges scattered throughout the town, and even this castle is now part of the school. Look into the old courtyard from the castle gate. It traces the very first and smallest bailey (protected area). As future bishops expanded the castle, they left their coats of arms as a way of "signing" the wing they built. Because the Norman kings appointed prince bishops here to rule this part of their realm, Durham was the seat of power for much of northern England. The bishops had their own army and even minted their own coins. You can enter the castle only with a 45-minute guided tour, which includes the courtyard, kitchens, great hall, and chapel (£5, open most days when school is in session—but schedule varies so call ahead, buy tickets at Durham World Heritage Site Visitor Centre or Palace Green Library—described next, tel. 0191/334-2932, www.dur.ac.uk/university.college/tours).

Durham's Early Years

Durham's location, tucked inside a tight bend in the River Wear, was practically custom-made for easy fortifications. But it wasn't settled until A.D. 995, with the arrival of St. Cuthbert's body (buried in Durham Cathedral). Shortly after that, a small church and fortification were built upon the site of today's castle and church to house the relic. The castle was a classic "motte-and-bailey" design (with the "motte," or mound, providing a lookout tower for the stockade encircling the protected area, or "bailey"). By 1100, the prince bishop's bailey was filled with villagers—and he wanted everyone out. This was *his* place! He provided a wider protective wall, and had the town resettle below (around today's Market Place). But this displaced the townsfolk's cows, so the prince bishop constructed a fine stone bridge (today's Framwellgate) to connect the new town to grazing land he established across the river. The bridge had a defensive gate, with a wall circling the peninsula and the river serving as a moat.

• *Turning your back to the castle and facing the cathedral, on the right is the university's Palace Green Library.*

The **Palace Green Library** hosts rotating exhibits on everything from rare books to robots in its Wolfson Gallery and Dunelm Gallery. Pop in or check online for current exhibits (generally £3, Tue-Sun 10:00-16:45, closed Mon, Palace Green, tel. 0191/334-2932, www.dur.ac.uk/library/asc).

• *This walk ends at Durham's stunning **cathedral**, described next.*

Sights in Durham

▲▲▲Durham's Cathedral

Built to house the much-venerated bones of St. Cuthbert from Lindisfarne (known today as Holy Island), Durham's cathedral offers the best look at Norman architecture in England. ("Norman" is British for "Romanesque.") In addition to touring the cathedral, try to fit in an evensong service.

Cost: Entry to the cathedral itself is free, though a donation is requested, and you must pay to climb the tower and possibly to enter the Treasures of St. Cuthbert exhibit (if open).

Hours: The cathedral is open to visitors Mon-Sat 9:30-18:00,

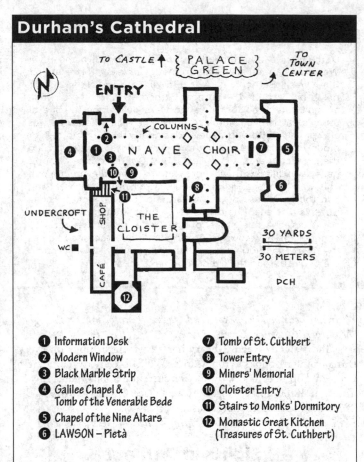

Durham's Cathedral

TO CASTLE ↑ { PALACE GREEN } TO TOWN CENTER

ENTRY

COLUMNS

NAVE   **CHOIR**

UNDERCROFT

SHOP

THE CLOISTER

WC ■

CAFÉ

30 YARDS
30 METERS

DCH

1 Information Desk
2 Modern Window
3 Black Marble Strip
4 Galilee Chapel & Tomb of the Venerable Bede
5 Chapel of the Nine Altars
6 LAWSON – Pietà

7 Tomb of St. Cuthbert
8 Tower Entry
9 Miners' Memorial
10 Cloister Entry
11 Stairs to Monks' Dormitory
12 Monastic Great Kitchen (Treasures of St. Cuthbert)

DURHAM & NE ENGLAND

Sun 12:30-18:00, daily until 20:00 mid-July-Aug, sometimes closes for special services, opens daily at 7:15 for worship and prayer. Access is limited for a few days in June, when the cathedral is used for graduation ceremonies (check online).

Information: The £1 pamphlet, *A Short Guide to Durham Cathedral,* is informative but dull. Tel. 0191/386-4266, www.durhamcathedral.co.uk.

Tours: Regular tours run Monday through Saturday. If one is already in session, you're welcome to join (£5; tours start at 10:30, 11:00, and 14:00; fewer in winter, call or check website to confirm schedule).

Services: A shop, café, and WC are tucked away in the cloister.

Photography: No photos, videos, or mobile phones are allowed inside the cathedral.

Evensong: For a thousand years, this cradle of English Christianity has been praising God. To really experience the cathedral, attend an evensong service. Arrive early and ask to be seated in the choir. It's a spiritual Oz, as the choristers (12 men and 40 youngsters—now girls as well as boys) sing psalms—a red-and-white-robed pillow of praise, raised up by the powerful pipe organ. If you're lucky and the service goes well, the organist will run a spiritual musical victory lap as the congregation breaks up (Tue-Sat at 17:15, Sun at 15:30, 1 hour, sometimes sung on Mon; visiting choirs nearly always fill in when choir is off on school break mid-July-Aug; tel. 0191/386-4266). For more on evensong, see page 164.

Organ Recitals: The organ plays most Wednesday evenings in July and August (£8, 19:30).

Tower Climb: The view from the tower will cost you 325 steps and £5 (Mon-Sat 10:00-16:00, closes at 15:00 in winter, sometimes open Sun outside of services, last entry 30 minutes before closing; closed during services, events, and bad weather; must be at least 4'3" tall, no backless shoes; enter through south transept).

◑ Self-Guided Tour: Begin your visit outside the cathedral. From the Palace Green, notice how this fortress of God stands boldly opposite the Norman keep of Durham's fortress of man.

Look closely: The **exterior** of this awe-inspiring cathedral has a serious skin problem. In the 1770s, as the stone was crumbling, they crudely peeled it back a few inches. The scrape marks give the cathedral a bad complexion to this day. For proof of this odd "restoration," study the masonry 10 yards to the right of the door. The L-shaped stones in the corner would normally never be found in a church like this—they only became L-shaped when the surface was cut back.

At the cathedral **door,** check out the big, bronze, lion-faced knocker (this is a replica of the 12th-century original, which should be in the Treasures of St. Cuthbert exhibit when reopened). The knocker was used by criminals seeking sanctuary (read the explanation).

Inside, purple-robed church attendants are standing by to happily answer questions. Ideally, follow a church tour. A handy information desk is at the back (right) end of the nave.

Notice the **modern window** with the novel depiction of the Last Supper (above and to the left of the entry door). It was given to the church by the local Marks & Spencer department store in 1984. The shapes of the apostles represent worlds and persons of every kind, from the shadowy Judas to the brightness of Jesus. This window is a good reminder that the cathedral remains a living part of the community.

Spanning the nave (toward the altar from the info desk), the **black marble strip** on the floor was as close to the altar as women were allowed in the days when this was a Benedictine church (until 1540). Sit down (ignoring the black line) and let the fine proportions of England's best Norman nave—and arguably Europe's best Romanesque nave—stir you. All the frilly woodwork and stonework were added in later centuries.

The architecture of the **nave** is particularly harmonious because it was built in a mere 40 years (1093-1133). The round arches and zigzag-carved decorations are textbook Norman. The church was also proto-Gothic, built by well-traveled French masons and architects who knew the latest innovations from Europe. Its stone and ribbed roof, pointed arches, and flying buttresses were revolutionary in England. Notice the clean lines and simplicity. It's not as cluttered as other churches for several reasons: For centuries—out of respect for St. Cuthbert—no one else was buried here (so it's not filled with tombs). During Reformation times, sumptuous Catholic decor was removed. Subsequent fires and wars destroyed what Protestants didn't.

Head to the back of the nave and enter the **Galilee Chapel** (late Norman, from 1175). Find the smaller altar just to the left of the main altar. The paintings of St. Cuthbert and St. Oswald (seventh-century king of Northumbria) on the side walls of the niche are rare examples of Romanesque (Norman) paintings. Facing this altar, look above to your right to see more faint paintings on the upper walls above the columns. On the right side of the chapel, the upraised tomb topped with a black slab contains the remains of the **Venerable Bede,** an eighth-century Christian scholar who wrote the first history of England. The Latin reads, "In this tomb are the bones of the Venerable Bede."

Back in the main church, stroll down the nave to the center, under the highest **bell tower** in Europe (218 feet). Gaze up. The ropes turn wheels upon which bells are mounted. If you're stirred by the cheery ringing of church bells, tune in to the cathedral on Sunday (9:15-10:00 & 14:30-15:30) or Thursday (19:30-21:00 practice, trained bell ringers welcome, www.durhambellringers.org.

uk) when the resounding notes tumble merrily through the entire town.

Continuing east (all medieval churches faced east), enter the **choir.** Monks worshipped many times a day, and the choir in the center of the church provided a cozy place to gather in this vast, dark, and chilly building. Mass has been said daily here in the heart of the cathedral for 900 years. The fancy wooden benches are from the 17th century. Behind the altar is the delicately carved Neville Screen from 1380 (made of Normandy stone in London, shipped to Newcastle by sea, then brought here by wagon). Until the Reformation, the niches contained statues of 107 saints. Exit the choir from the far right side (south). Look for the stained-glass window (to your right) that commemorates the church's 1,000th anniversary in 1995. The colorful scenes depict England's history, from coal miners to cows to computers.

Step down behind the high altar into the east end of the church, which contains the 13th-century **Chapel of the Nine Altars.** Built later than the rest of the church, this is Gothic—taller, lighter, and relatively more extravagant than the Norman nave. On the right, see the powerful modern *pietà* made of driftwood, with brass accents by local sculptor Fenwick Lawson.

Climb a few steps to the **tomb of St. Cuthbert.** An inspirational leader of the early Christian Church in north England, St. Cuthbert lived in the Lindisfarne monastery (100 miles north of Durham, today called Holy Island—see page 831). He died in 687. Eleven years later, his body was exhumed and found to be miraculously preserved. This stoked the popularity of his shrine, and pilgrims came in growing numbers. When Vikings raided Lindisfarne in 875, the monks fled with his body (and the famous illuminated Lindisfarne Gospels, now in the British Library in London). In 995, after 120 years of roaming, the monks settled in Durham on an easy-to-defend tight bend in the River Wear. This cathedral was built over Cuthbert's tomb.

Throughout the Middle Ages, a shrine stood here and was visited by countless pilgrims. In 1539, during the Reformation—whose proponents advocated focusing on God rather than saints—the shrine was destroyed. But pilgrims still come, especially on St. Cuthbert's feast day (March 20).

Turn around and walk back the way you came. In the **south transept** (to your left) is the entrance to the tower (described on next page), as well as an astronomical clock and the Chapel of the Durham Light Infantry, a regiment of the British Army (1881-1968). The old flags and banners hanging above were actually carried into battle.

Return along the left side of the nave toward the entrance. Across from the entry is the door to the cloister. Along the wall by the door to the cloister, notice the **memorial honoring coal miners** who died, and those who "work in darkness and danger in those pits today." (This message is a bit dated—Durham's coal mines closed down in the 1980s.) The nearby book of remembrance lists mine victims. As an ecclesiastical center, a major university town and a gritty, blue-collar coal-mining town, Durham's population has long been a complicated mix: priests, academics, and the working class.

Sights in the Cloister: The following sights are within the cloister (which provides a fine view back up to the church towers—made briefly famous in the Harry Potter films, described on page 890).

Enter the cloister, go through a door on the right and up some stairs to the **Monks' Dormitory,** a long, impressive room that stretches out under an original 14th-century timber roof. Formerly the monks' sleeping quarters, the room now holds a library with a small exhibit of Anglo-Saxon stones such as old Celtic crosses (donation suggested, Mon-Sat 10:00-16:00, Sun 13:00-16:00).

The reshuffled **Treasures of St. Cuthbert** collection recently moved to the Monastic Great Kitchen. It may be reopened by the time you visit. Filled with medieval bits and holy pieces, it contains the actual relics from St. Cuthbert's tomb—his coffin, vestments, and cross—as well as items from the Norman/medieval period (when the monks of Durham busily copied manuscripts), the Reformation, and the 17th century (check exhibit status, prices and times at info desk or by calling the cathedral).

In the newly renovated undercroft, you'll find a **shop** and a **café** (daily 10:00-16:30, tel. 0191/386-3721).

More Sights in Durham

There's little to see in Durham beyond its cathedral, but it's a pleasant place to go for a stroll and enjoy its riverside setting.

Durham Heritage Centre Museum

Situated in the old Church of St. Mary-le-Bow near the cathedral, this modest, somewhat hokey, but charming little museum does its best to illuminate the city's history, and is worthwhile on a rainy day. The exhibits, which are scattered willy-nilly throughout the old nave, include a reconstructed Victorian-era prison cell; a look at Durham industries past and present, especially coal mining (in Victorian times, the river was literally black from coal); and a 10-minute movie about 20th-century Durham. In the garden on the side of the church are two modern sculptures by local artist Fenwick Lawson, whose work you'll also see in the cathedral.

Cost and Hours: £2; July-Sept daily 11:00-16:30; June daily 14:00-16:30; April-May and Oct Sat-Sun 14:00-16:30, closed

Mon-Fri; closed Nov-March; corner of North Bailey and Bow Lane, tel. 0191/384-5589, www.durhamheritagecentre.org.uk.

Riverside Path

For a 20-minute woodsy escape, walk Durham's riverside path from busy Framwellgate Bridge to sleepy Prebends Bridge.

Boat Cruise and Rental

Hop on the *Prince Bishop* for a relaxing one-hour narrated cruise of the river that nearly surrounds Durham (£7, Easter-Oct; for schedule, call 24-hour info line at 0191/386-9525, check their website or go down to dock at Brown's Boat House at Elvet Bridge, just east of old town; www.princebishoprc.co.uk). Sailings vary based on weather and tides. For some exercise with identical scenery, you can rent a rowboat at the same pier (£5/hour per person, £10 deposit, late-March-Oct daily 10:00-18:00, last rental at 17:00, tel. 0191/386-3779).

Sleeping in Durham

(area code: 0191)

Close-in pickings are slim in Durham. Because much of the housing is rented to students, there are only a handful of B&Bs. Otherwise, there are a few hotels within easy walking distance of the town center. During graduation (typically the last two weeks of June), everything books up well in advance and prices increase dramatically. Rooms can be tight on weekends any time of year. If the B&Bs are full, Durham could be a good place to resort to a bigger chain hotel (Premier Inn or Marriott).

B&Bs

$$$ **Victorian Town House B&B** offers three spacious, boutique-like rooms in an 1853 townhouse. It's in a nice residential area just down the hill from the train station and is handy to the town center (Sb-£55-65, Db-£85-90, family room for up to 4 people-£85-120, cash only, 2-night minimum preferred April-Oct, some view rooms, free Wi-Fi, check-in 16:00-19:00 or by prior arrangement, 2 Victoria Terrace, 10-minute walk from train or bus station, tel. 0191/370-9963, www.durhambedandbreakfast.com, stay@durhambedandbreakfast.com, friendly Jill and Andy).

$$$ **Castleview Guest House** rents five airy, restful rooms in a well-located, 250-year-old guesthouse next door to a little church. Located on a charming cobbled street, it's just above Silver Street and the Framwellgate Bridge (Sb-£70, Db-£100, cash preferred, guest computer, free Wi-Fi, free street-parking permit, 4 Crossgate, tel. 0191/386-8852, www.castle-view.co.uk, info@guesthousesdurham.co.uk, Anne and Mike Williams).

$$ **Farnley Tower,** a decent but impersonal B&B, has 13 large

Sleep Code

(£1 = about $1.60, country code: 44)

S = Single, **D** = Double/Twin, **T** = Triple, **Q** = Quad, **b** = bathroom, **s** = shower only. Unless otherwise noted, credit cards are accepted and breakfast is included.

To help you sort easily through these listings, I've divided the accommodations into three categories based on the price for a standard double room with bath (during high season):

$$$ Higher Priced—Most rooms £90 or more.

$$ Moderately Priced—Most rooms between £50-90.

$ Lower Priced—Most rooms £50 or less.

Prices can change without notice; verify the hotel's current rates online or by email. For the best prices, always book direct.

rooms and a quirky staff. On a quiet street at the top of a hill, it's a 15-minute hike up from the town center. Though you won't find the standard B&B warmth and service, this is a suitable alternative when the central hotels are booked (Sb-£65, Db-£85, superior Db-£95—some with cathedral view, family room-£120, 2 percent fee for credit cards, free Wi-Fi, phones in rooms, easy free parking, inviting yard, The Avenue—hike up this steep street and look for the sign on the right, tel. 0191/375-0011, www.farnley-tower. co.uk, enquiries@farnley-tower.co.uk, Raj and Roopal Naik). The Naiks also run the inventive Gourmet Spot fine-dining restaurant, in the same building.

Hotels

$$$ Durham Marriott Hotel Royal County scatters its 150 posh, four-star, but slightly scruffy rooms among several buildings sprawling across the river from the city center. The Leisure Club has a pool, sauna, Jacuzzi, spa, and fitness equipment (prices vary, standard Db-about £94-114, supreme Db with separate seating area-about £119-129, check website for exact prices and deals, breakfast included in some rates but otherwise £15.50 extra, elevator, pay guest computer, free Wi-Fi in public areas, pay Wi-Fi in rooms, restaurant, bar, parking-£5/overnight, Old Elvet, tel. 0191/386-6821 or tel. 0870-400-7286, www.marriott.co.uk).

$$ Kingslodge Hotel & Restaurant is a slightly worn but comfortable 21-room place with charming terraces, an attached restaurant, and a pub. Located in a pleasantly wooded setting, it's convenient for train travelers (Sb-£60-65, Db-£75-85, family room-£109-115, free Wi-Fi, free parking, Waddington Street,

Flass Vale, tel. 0191/370-9977, www.kingslodge.info, kingslodge-hotel@yahoo.co.uk).

$$ Premier Inn Durham City Center, squeezed between Clayport Library and the river, has 103 cookie-cutter purple rooms in a very convenient central location (Sb/Db-generally around £70-95, check online for prepaid deals as low as £29, continental breakfast-£5.25, full English breakfast-£8.25, air-con, elevator, pay guest computer, pay Wi-Fi, validated parking for guests at Walkergate car park behind hotel-£7.70/24 hours, Freemans Place, tel. 0871-527-8338 or 0191/374-4400, www.premierinn.com).

$$ *Student Housing Open to Anyone:* Durham Castle, a student residence actually on the castle grounds facing the cathedral, rents rooms during the summer break (generally July-Sept). Request a room in the stylish main building, which is more appealing than the modern dorm rooms (S-£36.50, Sb-£61, Db-£92, fancier Db-£150-200, elegant breakfast hall, Palace Green, tel. 0191/334-4106, www.dur.ac.uk/university.college, durham.castle@durham.ac.uk). Note that the same office also rents rooms in other university buildings, but most are far less convenient to the city center—make sure to request the Durham Castle location when booking.

Eating in Durham

Durham is a university town with plenty of lively, inexpensive eateries, but there's not much to get excited about. Especially on weekends, the places downtown are crowded with noisy college kids and rowdy townies. Stroll down North Road, across Framwellgate Bridge, up through Market Place, and up Saddler Street, and consider the options suggested below. The better choices are about a five-minute walk from this main artery and worth the short trek.

Updated British Food: **Oldfields** serves pricey, updated British classics made from locally sourced ingredients. The inviting dining room feels upscale but not snooty, and there's another, more traditional dining room upstairs. While the service can be spotty and some locals wonder if this place is resting on its laurels, it remains one of the best options in town (£5-7 starters, £13-18 main dishes; lunch and early bird specials—£12/two courses, £15/three courses; Mon-Sat 12:00-22:00, Sun 12:00-21:00, 18 Claypath, tel. 0191/370-9595).

Pubs Across the Elvet Bridge: Two good options are within a five-minute walk of the Elvet Bridge (just east of the old town). **The**

Court Inn offers an eclectic menu of pub grub and an open, lively atmosphere (£4-6 sandwiches, £8-12 meals, Spanish-style tapas, food served daily 11:00-22:00; cross the Elvet Bridge, turn right, walk several blocks, and then look left; Court Lane, tel. 0191/384-7350). For beer and ales, locals favor **The Dun Cow.** There's a cozy "snug bar" up front and a more spacious lounge in the back. Read the legend behind the pub's name on the wall along the outside corridor. More sedate than the student-oriented places in the town center, this pub serves only snacks and light meals (£2-4)—come here to drink and nibble, not to feast (Mon-Sat 11:00-23:00, Sun 12:00-23:00; from the Elvet Bridge, walk five minutes straight ahead to Old Elvet 37; tel. 0191/386-9219).

Deli Lunch: Claypath Delicatessen is worth the five-minute uphill walk above Market Place. Not just any old sandwich shop, this creative place assembles fresh ingredients into tasty sandwiches, salads, sampler platters, and more. While carryout is possible, most people eat in the casual, comfortable café setting (£4-6 light meals, Tue-Sat 10:00-17:00, closed Sun-Mon; from Market Place, cross the bridge and walk up Claypath to #57; tel. 0191/340-7209).

Indian: The Capital, a five-minute uphill walk above Market Place (and across the street from Claypath Deli), has well-executed Indian food in a contemporary setting (£8-12 meals, daily 18:00-23:30, 69 Claypath, tel. 0191/386-8803).

Thai: Zen is a trendy, modern, dark-wood place serving curries, noodles, fried rice, and other Asian fare. It's popular with students, so it's best to book a table or go early and sit in the bar (£9-11 meals, daily 12:00-22:00, Court Lane, tel. 0191/384-9588, www. zendurham.co.uk).

Chain Restaurants with a Bridge View: Two chain places (that you'll find in every British city) are worth considering in Durham only because of their delightful setting right at the Old Town end of the picturesque Framwellgate Bridge. **Café Rouge** has French-bistro food and decor (£5-9 starters and light meals, £11-14 main dishes, Mon-Sat 9:00-22:30, Sun 10:00-22:00, 21 Silver Street, tel. 0191/384-3429). **Bella Italia,** next door and down the stairs, has a terrace overlooking the river and surprisingly good food (£5-6 starters, £7-10 pizzas and pastas, Tue-Sat 10:00-23:00, Sun-Mon 10:00-22:30, reservations recommended, 20 Silver Street, tel. 0191/386-1060).

Fish-and-Chips: Bells, just off Market Place toward the cathedral, is a standby for carryout fish-and-chips. I'd skip their fancier dining room (£5-7, hours vary but likely Mon-Thu 11:00-21:00, Fri-Sat 11:00-2:00 in the morning, Sun 12:00-16:00).

Splurge Outside Town: Bistro 21, an untouristy splurge serving modern French/Mediterranean fare and good seafood, is one of Durham's top restaurants. Unfortunately, it's about 1.5 miles out of Durham—practical only for drivers (£6-7 starters, £15-22 main dishes; dinner special available Mon-Sat 17:30-19:00—£16.50/two courses, £19/three courses; open Mon-Sat 12:00-14:00 & 17:30-22:00, Sun 12:00-15:00, northwest of town, Aykley Heads, tel. 0191/384-4354).

Supermarket: **Marks & Spencer** is in the old town, just off Market Place (Mon-Sat 8:00-18:00, Sun 11:00-17:00, 4 Silver Street, across from post office). Next door is a **Tesco Metro** (Mon-Sat 7:00-22:00, Sun 11:00-17:00). You can **picnic** on Market Place, or on the benches and grass outside the cathedral entrance (but not on the Palace Green, unless the park police have gone home).

Durham Connections

From Durham by Train to: York (3-4/hour, 45 minutes), **Keswick/ Lake District** (train to Penrith—hourly, 3 hours, change in New-castle and Carlisle; then bus to Keswick), **London** (1/hour direct, 3 hours, more with changes), **Hadrian's Wall** (take train to New-castle—4/hour, 15 minutes, then a bus or a train/bus combination to near Hadrian's Wall—see "Getting Around Hadrian's Wall" on page 820), **Edinburgh** (1/hour direct, 2 hours, more with changes, less frequent in winter). **Train info:** tel. 0845-748-4950, www.nationalrail.co.uk.

Route Tips for Drivers

As you head north from Durham on the A-1 motorway, you'll pass a famous bit of public art: **The Angel of the North,** a modern, rusted-metal angel standing 65 feet tall with a wingspan of 175 feet (wider than a Boeing 757). While initially controversial when it was erected in 1998, it has since become synonymous with Northeast England, and is a beloved local fixture.

Beamish Museum

This huge, 300-acre open-air museum, which re-creates the years 1825 and 1913 in northeast England, is England's best museum of its type. It takes at least three hours to explore its four sections: Pit Village (a coal-mining settlement with an actual mine), The Town (a 1913 street lined with actual shops), Pockerley Old Hall (a "gentleman farmer's" manor house), and Home Farm (a preserved

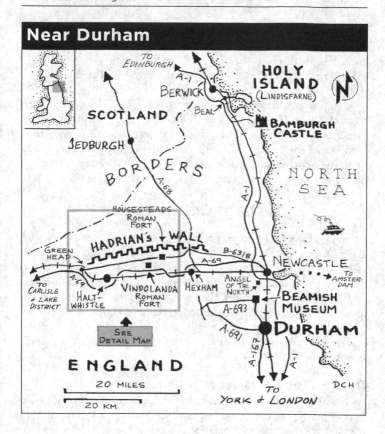

Near Durham

farm and farmhouse). This isn't a wax museum. If you touch the exhibits, they may smack you. Attendants at each stop happily explain everything. In fact, the place is only really interesting if you talk to the attendants—who make it worth ▲▲▲.

Cost and Hours: £17.50, children 5-16–£10, under 5-free, 25 percent discount with bus ticket—see below; to visit over several days, choose the "Beamish Unlimited Pass" at no extra charge (makes your ticket valid for a year); Easter-Oct open daily 10:00-17:00; Nov-Easter only The Town and Pit Village are open but vintage trams still run, Tue-Thu and Sat-Sun 10:00-16:00, closed Mon and Fri, half-price on weekdays; check events schedule on chalkboard as you enter, last tickets sold at 15:00 year-round, tel. 0191/370-4000, www.beamish.org.uk.

Getting There: By **car,** the museum is five minutes off the A-1/M-1 motorway (one exit north of Durham at Chester-le-Street/Junction 63, well-signposted, 12 miles, 25-minute drive northwest of Durham).

Getting to Beamish from Durham by **bus** is a snap on peak-season Saturdays via direct bus #128 (£3.70 day pass, 8/day, 30 minutes, runs April-Oct only, stops at Durham train and bus stations). Otherwise, catch bus #21 or #50 from the Durham bus station (£3.70 day pass, 3-4/hour, 25 minutes) and transfer at Chester-le-Street to bus #28 or #28A, which take you right to the museum entrance (2/hour Mon-Sat, hourly Sun, 15 minutes, leaves from central bus kiosk a half-block away, tel. 0845-606-0260, www.simplygo.com). Show your bus ticket for a 25 percent museum discount.

Getting Around the Museum: Pick up a free map at the entry to help navigate the four different zones; while some are side-by-side, others are up to a 15-minute walk apart. Vintage trams and cool, circa-1910 double-decker buses shuttle visitors around the grounds, and their attendants are helpful and knowledgeable. Signs on the trams advertise a variety of 19th-century products, from

"Borax, for washing everything" to "Murton's Reliable Travelling Trunks."

Eating at Beamish: There are several eateries scattered around Beamish, including a pub and tearooms (in The Town), a fish-and-chips stand (in the Pit Village), and various cafeterias and snack stands. Or bring a picnic.

❍ **Self-Guided Tour:** I've described the four areas in counterclockwise order from the entrance.

From the entrance building, bear left along the road, then watch for the turnoff on the right to the **Pit Village.** This is a

company town built around a coal mine, with a schoolhouse, a Methodist chapel, and a row of miners' homes with long, skinny pea-patch gardens out front. Poke into some of the homes to see their modest interiors. In the Board School, explore the different classrooms, and look for the interesting poster with instructions for avoiding consumption (a.k.a. tuberculosis, a huge public-health crisis back then).

Next, cross to the adjacent **Colliery** (coal mine) where you can take a fascinating—if claustrophobic—20-minute tour into the drift mine (check in at the "lamp camp"—tours depart when enough people gather, generally every 5-10 minutes). Your guide will tell you stories about beams collapsing, gas exploding, and flooding; after that cheerful speech, you'll don a hard hat as you're led into the mine. Nearby (across the tram tracks) is the fascinating **engine works,** where you can see the actual steam-powered winding engine used to operate the mine elevator. The "winderman" demonstrates how he skillfully eases both coal and miners up and down the tight shaft of the mine. This delicate, high-stakes job was one of the most sought-after at the entire Colliery—passed down from father to son—and the winderman had to stay in this building for his entire shift (the seat of his chair flips up to reveal a built-in WC).

A path leads through the woods to Georgian-era **Pockerley,** which has two parts. First you'll see the **Waggonway,** a big barn filled with steam engines, including the re-created, first-ever passenger train from 1825. (Occasionally this train takes modern-day visitors for a spin on 1825 tracks—a hit with railway buffs.)

Then, climb the hill to **Pockerley Old Hall,** the manor house of a gentleman farmer and his family. The house dates from the

1820s, and—along with the farmhouse described later—is Beamish's only vintage building still on its original site (other buildings at Beamish were relocated from elsewhere and reconstructed here). While not extremely wealthy, the farmer who lived here owned large tracts of land and could afford to hire

help to farm it for him. This rustic home is no palace, but it was comfortable for the period. Costumed docents in the kitchen often bake delicious cookies from old recipes...and hand out samples.

The small garden terrace out front provides beautiful views across the pastures. From the garden, turn left and locate the narrow stairs up to the "old house." Actually under the same roof as the gentleman farmer's family, this space consists of a few small rooms that were rented by some of the higher-up workers to shelter their entire families of up to 15 children (young boys worked on the farm, while girls were married off early). While the parents

had their own bedroom, the children all slept in the loft up above (notice the ladder in the hall).

From the manor house, hop on a vintage tram or bus, or walk 10 minutes, to the Edwardian-era **The Town** (c. 1913).

This bustling street features several working shops and other buildings that are a delight to explore. In the Masonic Hall, ogle the grand, high-ceilinged meeting room, and check out the fun old metal signs inside the garage. Across the street, poke into the courtyard to find the stables, which are full of carriages. The heavenly smelling candy store sells old-timey sweets, and has an actual workshop in back with trays of free samples. The newsagent sells stationery, cards, and old toys, while in the grocery, you can see old packaging and the scales used for weighing out products. Other buildings include a clothing store, a working pub (The Sun Inn, Mon-Sat 11:00-16:30, Sun 12:00-16:30, tel. 01913/702-908), Barclays Bank, and a hardware store featuring a variety of "toilet sets" (not what you think).

For lunch, try the Tea Rooms cafeteria (upstairs, daily 10:00-16:00). Or, if the weather is good, picnic in the grassy park with the gazebo next to the tram stop. The row of townhouses includes both homes and offices (if the dentist is in, chat with him to hear some harrowing stories about pre-Novocain tooth extraction). At the circa-1913 railway station at the far end of The Town, you can stand on the bridge over the tracks to watch old steam engines go back and forth—along with a carousel of "steam gallopers." Nearby, look for the "Westoe netty," a circa 1890 men's public urinal. This loo became famous in 1972 as the subject in a nostalgic Norman Rockwell-style painting of six miners and a young boy doing their business while they read the graffiti.

Finally, walk or ride a tram or bus to the **Home Farm.** (This is the least interesting section—if you're running short on time,

it's skippable.) Here you'll get to experience a petting zoo and see a "horse gin" (a.k.a. "gin gan")—where a horse walking in a circle turned a crank on a gear to amplify its "horsepower," helping to replace human hand labor. Near the cafeteria, you can cross a busy road (carefully) to the old farmhouse, still on its original site, where attendants sometimes bake goodies on a coal fire.

DURHAM & NE ENGLAND

Hadrian's Wall

Cutting across the width of the isle of Britain, this ruined Roman wall is one of England's most thought-provoking sights. Once a towering 20-foot-tall fortification, these days "Hadrian's Shelf," as some cynics call it, is only about three feet wide and three to six feet high. (The conveniently pre-cut stones of the wall were carried away by peasants during the post-Rome Dark Ages and now form the foundations of many local churches, farmhouses, and other structures.) In most places, what's left of the wall has been covered over by centuries of sod...making it effectively disappear into the landscape. But for those intrigued by Roman history, Hadrian's Wall provides a fine excuse to take your imagination for a stroll. Pretend

you're a legionnaire on patrol in dangerous and distant Britannia, at the empire's northernmost frontier...with nothing but this wall protecting you from the terrifying, bloodthirsty Picts just to the north.

Today, several chunks of the wall, ruined forts, and museums thrill history buffs. While a dozen Roman sights cling along the wall's route, I've focused my coverage on an easily digestible six-mile stretch right in the middle, where you'll find the best museums and some of the most enjoyable-to-hike stretches of the wall. Three top sights are worth visiting: Housesteads Roman Fort shows you where the Romans lived; Vindolanda's museum shows you how they lived; and the Roman Army Museum explains the empire-wide military organization that brought them here.

A breeze for drivers, this area can also be seen fairly easily in summer by bus for those good at studying timetables (see "Getting Around Hadrian's Wall," later).

Hadrian's Wall is in vogue as a destination for multi-day hikes through the pastoral English countryside. The Hadrian's Wall National Trail runs 84 miles, following the wall's route from coast to coast (for details, go to www.nationaltrail.co.uk/HadriansWall). Through-hikers (mostly British) can walk the wall's entire length in four to ten days. You'll see them bobbing along the ridgeline, drying out their socks in your B&B's mudroom, and recharging at local pubs in the evening. For those with less time, the brief ridge walk next to the wall from Steel Rigg to Sycamore Gap to Housesteads Roman Fort gives you a perfect taste of the scenery and history.

The History of Hadrian's Wall

In about A.D. 122, during the reign of Emperor Hadrian, the Romans constructed this great stone wall. Stretching 73 miles

coast to coast across the narrowest stretch of northern England, it was built and defended by some 20,000 troops. Not just a wall, it was a military complex that included forts, ditches, settlements, and roads. At every mile of the wall, a castle guarded a gate, and two turrets stood between each castle. The mile-castles are numbered. (Eighty of them cover the 73 miles, because a Roman mile was slightly shorter than our mile.)

In cross-section, Hadrian's Wall consisted of a stone wall—around 15 to 20 feet tall—with a ditch on either side. The flat-bottomed ditch on the south side of the wall, called the vallum, was flanked by earthen ramparts and likely demarcated the "no-man's land" beyond which civilians were not allowed to pass. Between the vallum and the wall ran a service road called the Military Way. Another less-elaborate ditch ran along the north side of the wall. In some areas—including the region that I describe—the wall was built upon a volcanic ridgeline that provided a natural fortification.

The wall's actual purpose is still debated. While Rome ruled Britain for 400 years, it never quite ruled its people. The wall may have been used for any number of reasons: to protect Roman Britain from invading Pict tribes from the north (or at least cut down on pesky border raids); to monitor the movement of people as a show of Roman strength and superiority; or to simply give an otherwise bored army something to do. (Emperors understood that nothing was more dangerous than a bored army.) Or perhaps the wall represented Hadrian's tacit admission that the empire had reached its maximum extent; Hadrian was known for consolidating his territory, in some cases giving up chunks of land that had been conquered by his predecessor, Trajan, to create an easier-to-defend (if slightly smaller) empire. His philosophy of "defense before expansion" is embodied by the impressive wall that still bears his name.

Orientation to Hadrian's Wall

The area described in this section is roughly between the mid-size towns of Bardon Mill and Haltwhistle, which are located along the busy A-69 highway. Each town has a train station and some handy B&Bs, restaurants, and services. However, to get right up close to the wall, you'll need to head a couple of miles north to the adjacent villages of Once Brewed and Twice Brewed (along the B-6318 road).

Tourist Information

Portions of the wall are in Northumberland National Park. The **Once Brewed National Park Visitor Centre** lies along the Hadrian's Wall bus #AD122 route and has information on the area, including walking guides to the wall. (Note that this center may undergo a major renovation and could be in a temporary location when you visit). The TV, set in front of a cozy couch, plays a variety of interesting movies about the wall and the surrounding landscape—ideal for a rainy day (Easter-Oct daily 9:30-17:00; Nov-Easter 10:00-15:00 Sat-Sun only, closed Mon-Fri; parking-£4/day, Military Road/B-6318, tel. 01434/344-396, www.northumberlandnationalpark.org.uk, tic.oncebrewed@nnpa.org.uk).

The helpful **TI** in Haltwhistle, a block from the train station inside the library, has a good selection of maps and guidebooks, and schedule information for Hadrian's Wall bus #AD122 (Easter-Oct Mon-Sat 10:00-13:00 & 13:30-16:30, closed Sun and Nov-Easter, The Library, Westgate, tel. 01434/322-002, www.hadrians-wall.org).

Getting Around Hadrian's Wall

Hadrian's Wall is anchored by the big cities of Newcastle to the east and Carlisle to the west. Driving is the most convenient way to see Hadrian's Wall. If you're coming by train, consider renting a car for the day at either Newcastle or Carlisle; otherwise, you'll need to rely on the bus to connect the sights. If you're just passing through for the day using public transportation, it's challenging to stop and see more than just one or two of the sights—study the bus schedule carefully and prioritize. Non-drivers who want to see everything—or even hike part of the wall—will need to stay at least one night along the bus route.

By Car

Zip to this "best of Hadrian's Wall" zone on the speedy A-69; when you get close, head a few miles north and follow the B-6318, which parallels the wall and passes several viewpoints, minor sights, and "severe dips." (These road signs add a lot to a photo portrait.) Buy a good local map to help you explore this interesting area more easily and thoroughly. Official Hadrian's Wall parking lots (including the Once Brewed National Park Visitor Centre, Housesteads Roman Fort, and the trailhead at Steel Rigg) are covered by a single one-day £4 parking pass (coin-op pay-and-display machines at all lots).

By Public Transportation

To reach the Roman sights without a car, take the made-for-tourists Hadrian's Wall **bus #AD122** (named for the year the wall was built; runs only in peak season—see below). Essential resources for navigating the wall by public transit include the *Hadrian's Wall Country Map,* the bus #AD122 schedule, and a local train timetable for Northern Line #4—all available at local visitors centers and train stations (also see www.visithadrianswall.co.uk). If you arrive by train during the off-season, you'll need to rely on taxis or long walks to visit the wall (see "Off-Season Options," later).

By Bus: Bus #AD122 connects the Roman sights (and several recommended accommodations) with the following train stations, listed west to east: **Carlisle, Haltwhistle, Hexham,** and **Newcastle** (from £2/ride, £9 unlimited Day Rover ticket, buy tickets on board, Day Rover also available at TI, tel. 01434/322-002).

Due to funding cuts, the bus schedule has been scaled back. It runs most frequently between Haltwhistle and Hexham (7/day in each direction late May-Aug, less frequent and possibly weekends only Easter-late May and Sept-Oct, no service Nov-Easter). From Carlisle, it runs three times a day late May-Aug (less frequently outside those times). From Newcastle, the bus leaves just once a day (at 9:30—if you miss this bus, take the train to Haltwhistle and pick up the bus there). If you're planning to take this bus, it's smart to confirm online whether it'll be running during your visit (www.visithadrianswall.co.uk).

By Train: Northern Line's train route #4 runs parallel to and a few miles south of the wall much more frequently than the bus. While the train stops at stations in larger towns—including (west to east) **Carlisle, Haltwhistle, Hexham,** and **Newcastle**—it doesn't take you near the actual Roman sights. You can catch bus #AD122 at all four stations, though bus service is best from Hexham and Haltwhistle (no bus service off-season; train runs daily 1/hour; Carlisle to Haltwhistle—30 minutes; Haltwhistle to Hexham—20 minutes; Hexham to Newcastle—40 minutes; www.northernrail.org). Note: To get to or from Newcastle on this line, you must transfer in Hexham.

By Taxi: These Haltwhistle-based taxi companies can help you connect the dots: Melvin's Taxi (tel. 01434/320-632, mobile 07903-760-230), Sprouls (tel. 01434/321-064, mobile 07712-321-064), or Diamond (mobile 07597/641-222). It costs about £11 one-

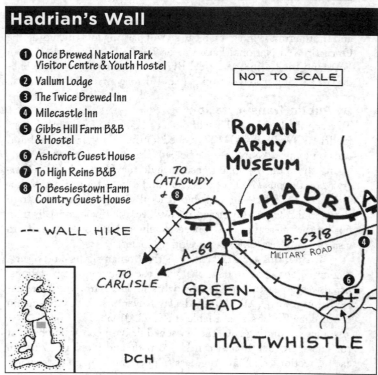

Hadrian's Wall

1. Once Brewed National Park Visitor Centre & Youth Hostel
2. Vallum Lodge
3. The Twice Brewed Inn
4. Milecastle Inn
5. Gibbs Hill Farm B&B & Hostel
6. Ashcroft Guest House
7. To High Reins B&B
8. To Bessiestown Farm Country Guest House

NOT TO SCALE

ROMAN ARMY MUSEUM

TO CATLOWDY

HADRIA

B-6318 MILITARY ROAD

--- WALL HIKE

A-69

TO CARLISLE

GREEN-HEAD

HALTWHISTLE

DCH

way from Haltwhistle to Housesteads Roman Fort (arrange for return pickup or have museum staff call a taxi). Note that on school days, all of these taxis are busy shuttling rural kids to class in the morning (about 8:00-10:00) and afternoon (about 14:30-16:30), so you may have to wait.

Off-Season Options: Bus #AD122 doesn't run off-season (Nov-Easter) and may operate only on weekends in spring and fall, so you can only get as far as the train will take you (i.e., Haltwhistle)—from there, you'll have to take a taxi (described earlier) to the sights. Or, if you're a hardy hiker, take the Northern Line train to Bardon Mill, then walk about two miles to Vindolanda and another 2.5 miles to Housesteads Roman Fort.

Baggage Storage: It's difficult to bring your luggage along with you. If you're day-tripping, you can store your luggage in **Carlisle** (across the street from the train station at Bar Solo, £2/ bag per day, daily 9:00-22:30, tel. 01228/631-600) or possibly at the **Newcastle** train station left-luggage office (may be closed; if open, £5/bag per day, Mon-Sat 8:00-20:00, Sun 9:00-20:00, platform 12; call or email Newcastle TI to confirm if it's open—tel. 01912/778-000, visitorinfo@ngi.org.uk). If you must travel with

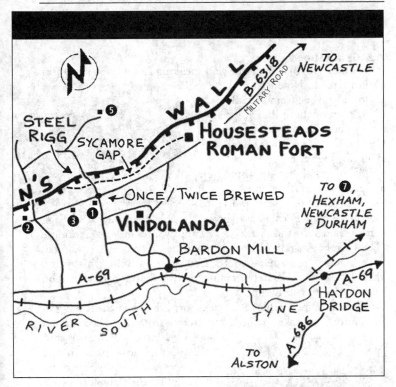

luggage, Housesteads Roman Fort and Vindolanda will most likely let you leave your bags at the sight entrance while you're inside. If you want to walk the wall, various baggage-courier services will send your luggage ahead to your next B&B in the region for about £5 per bag (contact Hadrian's Haul, mobile 07967-564-823, www.hadrianshaul.com; or Walkers', tel. 0871-423-8803, www.walkers-bags.co.uk).

By Private Tour

Peter Carney, a former history teacher, leads guided walks and tours around Hadrian's Wall, including an all-day walk that starts at the Roman Army Museum and then connects Vindolanda and Housesteads via a seven-mile hike (£100/person, £125 for 2 people, £150 for up to 6 people, does not include museum admission). His Roman Fort Tour includes the same sights but without the hike (£80/person, £90 for 2 people, £100 for up to 6 people). He can also customize tours to suit your time frame and interests (£50/half-day or £90/day for 2 people, happy to pick you up from your B&B or hotel, mobile 07585/139-016, 07810-665/733, or 07757/420-672, www.hadrianswall-walk.com, petercarney@hadrianswall-walk.com).

Sights at Hadrian's Wall

▲▲Hiking the Wall

It's enjoyable to hike along the wall speaking Latin, even if only for a short stretch. Note that park rangers forbid anyone from actually walking on top of the wall, except along a very short stretch at Housesteads. On the following hikes, you'll walk alongside the wall.

For a good, craggy, three-mile, up-and-down walk along the wall, hike between Steel Rigg and Housesteads Roman Fort. For a shorter stretch, begin at Steel Rigg (where there's a handy parking lot) and walk a mile to Sycamore Gap, then back again (described next; the Once Brewed National Park Visitor Centre hands out a free sheet outlining this walk). These hikes are moderately strenuous and are best for those in good shape and with sturdy shoes.

To reach the trailhead for the short hike from **Steel Rigg to Sycamore Gap,** take the little road across from the Once Brewed National Park Visitor Centre and park in the pay-and-display parking lot on the right at the crest of the hill. Walk through the gate to the shoulder-high stretch of wall, go to the left, and follow the wall running steeply down the valley below you. Ahead of you are dramatic cliffs, creating a natural boundary made-to-order for this Roman fortification. Walk down the steep slope into the valley, then back up the other side (watch your footing on the stone stairs). Following the wall, you'll do a similar up-and-down routine three more times, like a slow-motion human roller coaster. In the second gap is one of the best-preserved milecastles, #39 (called Castle Nick because it sits in a nick in a crag).

Soon after, you'll reach the third gap, called Sycamore Gap for the large symmetrical tree in the middle. (Do you remember the 1991 Kevin Costner movie *Robin Hood: Prince of Thieves*? Locals certainly do—this tree was featured in it, and tourists frequently ask for directions to the

"Robin Hood Tree.") You can either hike back the way you came, or cut down toward the main road to find the less strenuous Roman Military Way path, which skirts the bottom of the ridge (rather than following the wall); this leads back to the base of the Steel Rigg hill, where you can huff back up to your car.

▲▲Housesteads Roman Fort

With its recently revamped museum, powerful scenery, and the best-preserved segment of the wall, this is your best single stop at Hadrian's Wall. It requires a steep hike up from the parking lot, but once there it's just you, the bleating sheep, and memories of ancient Rome.

Cost and Hours: £6.20 for site and museum; April-Sept daily 10:00-18:00; Oct daily 10:00-17:00; Nov-March Sat-Sun 10:00-16:00, closed Mon-Fri though visitors center may be open during the week; last entry 45 minutes before closing, parking-£4/day, same parking ticket also good for the Once Brewed National Park Visitor Centre and Steel Rigg parking lots, bus #AD122 stops here.

Information: Museum tel. 01434/344-363, info tel. 0870-333-1181, gift shop tel. 01434/344-525, www.english-heritage.org.uk/housesteads.

Services: At the car park is a visitors center with WCs, a snack bar, and a gift shop. They sell a £3.50 guidebook about the fort or a £5 guidebook covering the entire wall. If you're traveling by bus and want to leave your luggage, ask at the visitors center if they'll stow it for a bit.

Visiting the Museum and Fort: From the visitors center, head outside and hike about a half-mile uphill to the fort. At the top of the hill, duck into the **museum** (on the left) before touring the site. While smaller and housing fewer artifacts than the museum at Vindolanda (explained next), it's interesting nonetheless. Look for the giant Victory statue, which once adorned the fort's East Gate; her foot is stepping on a globe, serving as an intimidating reminder to outsiders of the Romans' success in battle. A good seven-minute film shows how Housesteads (known back them as Vercovicium) would have operated.

Artifacts offer more insights into those who lived here. A cooking pot from Frisia (Northern Holland) indicates the presence of women, showing that soldiers came with their families in tow. A tweezer, probe, spoons, and votive foot (that would have been offered to the gods in exchange for a cure for a foot ailment) reveal the type of medical care you could expect. And a weighted die and a coin mold—perhaps used to make counterfeit money—show what may have been the less-than-savory side of life at the fort.

After exploring the museum, head out to the sprawling ruins of the **fort**. Interpretive signs and illustrations explain what you're seeing. All Roman forts were the same rectangular shape and design, containing a commander's headquarters, barracks, and latrines (Housesteads has the best-preserved Roman toilets found anywhere—look for them at the lower-right corner). This fort even had a hospital. The fort was built right up to the wall, which runs along its upper end. (This is the one place along the wall where you're actually allowed to get up and walk on top of it for a photo op.) Visually trace the wall to the left to see how it disappears into a bank of overgrown turf.

▲▲Vindolanda

This larger Roman fort (which actually predates the wall by 40 years) and museum are just south of the wall. Although Housesteads has better ruins and the wall, Vindolanda has the more impressive museum, packed with artifacts that reveal intimate details of Roman life.

Cost and Hours: £6.50, £10 combo-ticket includes Roman Army Museum, guidebook-£4, daily April-Sept 10:00-18:00, mid-Feb-March and Oct 10:00-17:00, Nov 10:00-16:00, may be open on weekends Dec-mid-Feb, last entry 45 minutes before closing, call first during bad weather, free parking with entry, bus #AD122 stops here, café.

Information: Tel. 01434/344-277, www.vindolanda.com.

Tours: Guided tours run twice daily on weekends only (typically at 10:45 and 14:00); in high season, archaeological talks and tours may be offered on weekdays as well. Both are included in your ticket.

Archaeological Dig: The Vindolanda site is an active dig—from Easter through September, you'll see the excavation work in progress (usually Mon-Fri, weather permitting). Much of the work is done by volunteers, including armchair archaeologists from the US.

Visiting the Site and Museum: After entering, stop at the model of the entire site as it was in Roman times (c. 213-276). Notice that the site had two parts: the fort itself, and the town just outside that helped to supply it.

Head out to the **site,** walking through 500 yards of grassy parkland decorated by the foundation stones of the Roman fort and a full-size replica chunk of the wall. Over the course of 400 years, at least nine forts were built on this spot. The Romans, by lazily sealing the foundations from each successive fort, left modern-day archaeologists with a 20-foot-deep treasure trove of remarkably well-preserved artifacts: keys, coins, brooches, scales, pottery, glass, tools, leather shoes, bits of cloth, and even a wig. Many of these are now displayed in the museum, well-described in English, German, French, and...Latin.

At the far side of the site, pass through the pleasant riverside garden area on the way to the museum. The well-presented **museum** pairs actual artifacts with insightful explanations—such as a collection of Roman shoes with a description about what each one tells us about its wearer. The weapons (including arrowheads and spearheads) and fragments of armor are a reminder that Vindolanda was an important outpost on Rome's northern boundary—look for the Scottish skull stuck on a pike to discourage rebellion. You'll also see lots of leather; tools that were used for building and expanding the fort; locks and keys (the fort had a password that changed daily—jotting it on a Post-It note wasn't allowed); a large coin collection; items imported here from the far corners of the vast empire (such as fragments of French pottery and amphora jugs from the Mediterranean); beauty aids such as combs, tools for applying makeup, and hairpins; and religious pillars and steles.

But the museum's main attraction is its collection of writing tablets. A good video explains how these impressively well-preserved examples of early Roman cursive were discovered here in 1973. Displays show some of the actual letters—written on thin pieces of wood—alongside the translations. These letters bring Romans to life in a way that ruins alone can't. The most famous piece (described but not displayed here) is the first known example of a woman writing to a woman (an invitation to a birthday party).

Finally, you'll pass through an exhibit about the history of the excavations, including a case featuring the latest discoveries, on your way to the shop and cafeteria.

▲▲Roman Army Museum

This museum, a few miles farther west at Greenhead (near the site of the Carvoran Roman fort), was fully renovated in 2011. Its cutting-edge, interactive exhibit illustrates the structure of the Roman Army that built and monitored this wall, with a focus on the everyday lifestyles of the Roman soldiers stationed here. Bombastic displays, life-size figures, and several different films—but few actual artifacts—make this entertaining museum a good complement to the archaeological emphasis of Vindolanda. If visiting all three Roman sights, this is a good one to start at, as it sets the stage for what you're about to see.

Cost and Hours: £5.25, £10 combo-ticket includes Vindolanda, daily April-Sept 10:00-18:00, mid-Feb-March and Oct-mid-Nov 10:00-17:00, may be open on weekends mid-Nov-mid-Feb, last entry 30 minutes before closing, free parking with entry, bus #AD122 stops here.

Information: Tel. 01697/747-485; if no answer, call Vindolanda tel. 01434/344-277; www.vindolanda.com.

Visiting the Museum: In the first room, a video explains the complicated structure of the Roman Army—legions, cohorts, centuries, and so on. While a "legionnaire" was a Roman citizen, an "auxiliary" was a non-citizen specialist recruited for their unique skills (such as horsemen and archers). A video of an army recruiting officer delivers an "Uncle Caesar wants YOU!" speech to prospective soldiers. A timeline traces the history of the Roman Empire, especially as it related to the British Isles.

The good 20-minute *Edge of Empire* 3-D movie offers an evocative look at what life was like for a Roman soldier marking time on the wall, and digital models show reconstructions of the wall and forts. In the exhibit on weapons, shields, and armor (mostly replicas), you'll learn how Roman soldiers trained with lead-filled wooden swords, so that when they went into battle, their steel swords felt light by comparison. Another exhibit explains the story of Hadrian, the man behind the wall.

Sleeping and Eating near Hadrian's Wall

If you want to spend the night in this area, set your sights on the adjacent villages of Once Brewed and Twice Brewed, with a few accommodations options, a good pub, and easy access to the most important sights. I've also listed some other accommodations scattered around the region.

In and near Once Brewed and Twice Brewed
(area code: 01434)

These two side-by-side villages, each with a handful of houses, sit at the base of the volcanic ridge along the B-6318 road. (While the mailing address for these hamlets is "Bardon Mill," that town is actually about 2.5 miles away, across the busy A-69 highway.) The Twice Brewed Inn, Once Brewed Youth Hostel, and Milecastle Inn are reachable with Hadrian's Wall bus #AD122 (described earlier). Bus drivers can drop you off at Vallum Lodge by request (but they won't pick up).

$$ Vallum Lodge is a cushy, comfortable, nicely renovated base situated near the vallum (the ditch that forms part of the fortification a half-mile from the wall itself). Its six cheery rooms are all on the ground floor, and a separate guesthouse called the Snug has one bedroom and a kitchen. It's just up the road from The Twice Brewed Inn—a handy dinner option (Sb-£70, Db-£85, Db in Snug-£98, free Wi-Fi, lounge, Military Road, tel. 01434/344-248, www.vallum-lodge.co.uk, stay@vallum-lodge.co.uk, Clare and Michael).

$$ The Twice Brewed Inn, two miles west of Housesteads and a half-mile from the wall, rents 16 workable rooms, including en-suite rooms that have been recently renovated (S-£37, D-£59, Db-£76-90, ask for a room away from the road, free Wi-Fi, Military Road, tel. 01434/344-534, www.twicebrewedinn.co.uk, info@twicebrewedinn.co.uk). The inn's friendly **pub** serves as the community gathering place (free Wi-Fi), and is a hangout for hikers and the archaeologists digging at the nearby sites. It serves real ales and large portions of good pub grub (£9-12 meals, vegetarian options, fancier restaurant in back with same menu, food served daily 12:00-20:30, Fri-Sat until 21:00).

$ Once Brewed Youth Hostel is a comfortable, institutional place next door to the Once Brewed National Park Visitor Centre, though it may be closed for renovation when you visit (£18-22/bed with sheets in 2- to 6-bed rooms, private rooms available, members pay £3 less, breakfast-£5, packed lunch-£5.50, dinner-£7.50-12, reception open daily 8:00-10:00 & 16:00-22:00, must reserve ahead in Dec-Jan, guest kitchen, laundry, Military Road, tel. 01434/344-360 or 0845-371-9753, www.yha.org.uk, oncebrewed@yha.org.uk).

West of Once/Twice Brewed: **Milecastle Inn,** two miles to the west, cooks up all sorts of exotic game and offers the best dinner around, according to hungry national park rangers. You can order food at the counter and sit in the pub, or take a seat in the table-service area (£9-13 meals, food served daily Easter-Sept 12:00-20:45, Oct-Easter 14:30 & 18:00-20:30, smart to reserve in summer, North Road, tel. 01434/321-372).

Rural and Remote, North of the Wall: **$$ Gibbs Hill Farm B&B and Hostel** is a friendly working sheep-and-cattle farm set on 700 acres in the stunning valley on the far side of the wall (only practical for drivers). The B&B offers four big, airy double en-suite rooms in the main house, while the three 6-bed dorm rooms are in a restored hay barn (hostel bed/bedding-£16, Sb-£50, Db-£75, packed lunch-£5, laundry facilities, 5-minute drive from Once Brewed National Park Visitor Centre, tel. 01434/344-030, www.gibbshillfarm.co.uk, val@gibbshillfarm.co.uk, warm Val). They also rent several cottages for two to six people by the week (£280-600).

In Haltwhistle
(area code: 01434)

The larger town of Haltwhistle has a train station, along with stops for Hadrian's Wall bus #AD122 (at the train station and a few blocks east, at Market Place). It also has a helpful TI (see "Tourist Information," on page 820), a launderette, several eateries, and a handful of B&Bs, including this one.

$$ Ashcroft Guest House, a large Victorian former vicarage, is 400 yards from the Haltwhistle train station and 200 yards from the Market Place bus stop. It has six big, luxurious rooms, huge terraced gardens, and views from the comfy lounge, along with a two-bedroom apartment with kitchen (Sb-£55, Db-£85, super king or four-poster Db-£95, ask about family deals, 2-night minimum for apartment, guest computer, free Wi-Fi, 1.5 miles from the wall, Lanty's Lonnen, tel. 01434/320-213, www.ashcroftguesthouse. co.uk, info@ashcroftguesthouse.co.uk, helpful Geoff and Christine James).

Near Hexham
(area code: 01434)

$$ High Reins offers four rooms in a stone house built by a shipping tycoon in the 1920s (Sb-£46, Db-£72, cash only, 2-bedroom apartment also available, lounge, 1 mile south of train station on the western outskirts of Hexham, Leazes Lane, tel. 01434/603-590, pwalton@highreins.co.uk, Jan and Peter Walton).

Near Carlisle
(area code: 01228)

$$$ Bessiestown Farm Country Guest House, located far northwest of the Hadrian sights, is convenient for drivers connecting the Lake District and Scotland. It's a quiet and soothing stop in the middle of sheep pastures, with four bedrooms in the main house and two 2-bedroom apartments in the former stables (Sb-£59, Db-£90, Tb-£120, honeymoon suite-£150, discount with 3-night stay; in Catlowdy, midway between Gretna Green and Hadrian's Wall, 14 miles (20-minute drive) north of Carlisle; tel. 01228/577-219, www.bessiestown.co.uk, info@bessiestown. co.uk, gracious Margaret and John Sisson).

Holy Island and Bamburgh Castle

This remote area is worthwhile only for those with a car. It's out of the way for most itineraries—unless you're driving between Durham and Edinburgh on the A-1 highway, in which case Holy Island and Bamburgh Castle (and Beamish Museum, described earlier) are easy stop-offs. If you're determined to reach these sights by public transportation, you can go to Newcastle, then take bus #501 to Bamburgh Castle (2-3/day, 2.5 hours); or bus #505 to Beal (6/day Mon-Sat, none direct on Sun, 2 hours), where you can walk a level six miles or catch Perrymans bus #477 to Holy Island (2/day Mon-Sat late-July-Aug, Wed and Sat only Sept-mid-July, none on Sun year-round, described under "Getting There," below).

Holy Island (Lindisfarne)

Twelve hundred years ago, this "Holy Island"—then known as Lindisfarne—was Christianity's tenuous toehold on England. In

the A.D. 680s, Holy Island was the home and original burial ground of St. Cuthbert (he's now in Durham). We know it as the source of the magnificent Lindisfarne Gospels (A.D. 698; now in London's British Library), decorated by monks with some of the finest art from Europe's "Dark Ages." By the ninth century, Viking raids forced the monks to take shelter in Durham, but they returned centuries later to re-establish a church on this holy site.

Today Holy Island—worth ▲▲—makes a pleasant stop for modern-day pilgrims: You'll cross a causeway to a quiet town with a striking castle and the ruins of an evocative priory that was originally founded in 635.

Getting There: Holy Island is reached by a two-mile causeway that's cut off twice a day by high tides. Safe crossing times are posted at each end of the causeway (and at www.lindisfarne.org.uk), warning **drivers** when this holy place becomes Holy Island—and you become stranded. Once on the island, signs direct you to a well-marked, mandatory parking lot at the entrance to town (£2.40/3 hours).

It's also possible to reach Holy Island by **bus** from the nearby town of Beal, but it's not worth the effort unless you're a determined pilgrim (Perrymans bus #477, 2/day Mon-Sat late July-Aug, Wed and Sat only Sept-mid-July, none on Sun year-round; if coming on the bus from Newcastle, get off at Beal to transfer to this bus—but carefully confirm schedule for the complete connection before you head out).

Getting Around Holy Island: From the parking lot, it's an easy 10-minute **walk** into town and to the priory; the castle is about a 20-minute walk away. To save time, ride the convenient **shuttle bus,** which makes a circuit from the parking lot to the village green (next to the priory entrance), then out to the castle, and back again (£1, 3/hour, runs only when castle is open).

Sights on Holy Island

The two main attractions on Holy Island are the ruins of the old priory and the castle outside of town. The town itself is a charming little community of about 150 residents.

Holy Island Town

The town has B&Bs and cafés catering to tourists, a tiny post office, a fire station (with no firefighters—they're helicoptered in when the need arises), a six-student schoolhouse, and a tiny winery offering free tastes of their Lindisfarne mead. There's no official TI, but the **Lindisfarne Centre**—with a well-presented, kid-friendly history exhibit—acts as an unofficial information point and is proudly staffed by native Holy Islanders (£3 to tour the exhibit, daily April-Sept 10:00-17:00, Oct 10:00-16:00, open sporadically Nov-March, Marygate, tel. 01289/389-004, www.lindisfarne.org.uk).

Lindisfarne Priory

The priory has an evocative field of ruined church walls and a tiny but instructive museum. (A priory—run by a prior rather than an abbot—is similar to an abbey, but smaller.)

Cost and Hours: £5.20 ticket includes both museum and priory ruins, guidebook-£4; April-Sept daily 10:00-18:00; Oct daily 10:00-16:00; Nov-March Sat-Sun 10:00-16:00, closed Mon-Fri, shorter winter hours possible; tel. 01289/389-200, www.english-heritage.org.uk/lindisfarne.

Visiting the Priory: In the **museum,** you'll see exhibits about Holy Island's Anglo-Saxon culture, from stonework to manuscripts—including the famous Lindisfarne Gospels. The Gospels' text was in Latin, the language of scholars ever since the Roman Empire, but the illustrations—with elaborate tracery and interwoven decoration—are a mix of Irish, classical, and even Byzantine forms. These Gospels are a reminder that Christianity almost didn't make it in Europe. After the fall of Rome (which had established

Christianity as the Empire's official religion), much of Europe reverted to its pagan ways. In that chaotic era, Lindisfarne—an obscure monastery of Irish monks on a remote island—was one of the few beacons of light, tending the embers of civilization through the long night of the Dark Ages.

You can visit the adjacent church and churchyard without paying, but you need a ticket to get into the actual **priory ruins.** The

Lindisfarne monks fled the island in A.D. 875 to escape Viking raids. They made their way to Durham, and built a cathedral to hold the tomb of St. Cuthbert (see page 803). Centuries later, in 1082, the monks returned to Holy Island to re-found the priory and build a fine church in a Norman (Romanesque) style similar to the one in Durham. They fended off invasions by Picts and Scots throughout the 14th century, and fortified the great church. But when Henry VIII "dissolved" (destroyed) the monasteries in the 1530s, the priory was one of his victims. The forgotten ruins were later excavated in the 1850s as an important example of early English (Anglo-Saxon) history.

As you walk through this site, you're stepping on several layers of history: a ruined Norman church sitting on the ruins of an earlier Anglo-Saxon one (where Cuthbert served as bishop), next to the still-standing Parish Church of St. Mary's, where Holy Islanders worship today. The priory ruins are well-explained by posted plaques and floor plans that help resurrect the rubble.

Lindisfarne Castle

Faintly visible from the priory ruins, the dramatically situated Lindisfarne Castle is enticing from afar, and makes for a fine photo op. But inside, there's little of interest. Built in 1549—many centuries after the heyday of Cuthbert and the monks—the castle never really saw much action, and it was converted into a holiday home for an aristocratic publisher in the early 1900s. If you do visit, you'll wander

through sparsely furnished rooms and stroll out onto the upper battery—an outdoor terrace with views of the priory ruins.

Cost and Hours: £6.50; mid-Feb-Oct Tue-Sun 10:00-15:00 or 12:00-17:00 depending on tides—confirm times at the National Trust shop on Marygate in town before heading out, closed Mon except on Bank Holidays and in Aug; Jan-mid-Feb Sat-Sun 10:00-15:00 twice per month, closed Mon-Fri and every other weekend;

also closed Nov-Dec; tel. 01289/389-244, www.nationaltrust.org.uk/lindisfarne.

Bamburgh Castle

About 10 miles south of Holy Island, this grand castle—worth
▲—dominates the Northumbrian countryside and overlooks

Britain's loveliest beach. Bamburgh
(BOMB-ruh) was bought and pas-
sionately refurbished by Lord William George Armstrong, a wealthy
industrialist, in the 1890s. While
it's one of England's most dramatic
castles from the outside, the interior
(a 19th-century rebuild) lacks soul,
barely cracking the country's top ten.
But if you're passing by or visiting nearby Holy Island, Bamburgh
may be worth a stop.

Cost and Hours: £9.75 includes staterooms and grounds,
daily mid-Feb-Oct 10:00-17:00, winter Sat-Sun only 11:00-16:30,
last entry one hour before closing, parking-£2, tel. 01668/214-515,
www.bamburghcastle.com.

Touring the Castle: Bamburgh's main attraction is its staterooms; as you explore the rest of the grounds, you'll also have the
chance to see several smaller exhibits. If arriving late in the day,
go directly to the staterooms, which may close early. There's virtually no information inside the castle, aside from a few docents; to
give meaning to your visit, either rent the £1 audioguide (with two
hours of commentary) or buy the £1 guidebook.

The **staterooms** feel lived-in because they still are—with
Armstrong family portraits and aristocratic-yet-homey knick-

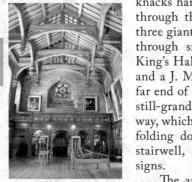

knacks hanging everywhere. You'll enter
through the medieval kitchen, with its
three giant fireplaces, and work your way
through smaller storage rooms to the
King's Hall, with a fantastic teak ceiling
and a J. M. W. Turner painting. At the
far end of the great hall is a smaller (but
still-grand) alcove separated by an archway, which could be sealed off by gigantic
folding doors. Continuing through the
stairwell, notice the *private apartment*
signs.

The armory once had a very differ-
ent purpose—you can still see the apse of what was once a chapel.
In the keep is a 145-foot-deep Anglo-Saxon well. The scullery (a

medieval utility room) includes a long row of sinks and an alcove where they make fresh fudge. You'll wind up in the gift shop; before leaving, check out the archaeology room, with exhibits about the castle's history; and the dungeon, with cheesy mannequins being tortured.

Exploring the **grounds,** you enjoy fine views over the sea and

beach, and get a good look at the stout 12th-century keep that's the castle's centerpiece. In the former stables is an art gallery displaying works by local artists. The Armstrong and Aviation Artefacts Museum features the inventions of the family that has owned the castle through modern times. Lord William George Armstrong (1810-1900) was a pioneer in aviation and a clever innovator, creating (among other things) the first all-steel aircraft structure, a method for in-flight refueling, and the ejector seat. You'll see several of his inventions, along with exhibits on cars, shipbuilding, and more. While the museum is fun for aviation-history buffs, it may be dull to others.

Nearby: The village of Bamburgh is pleasant enough, with tourist-oriented cafés and fine views over a manicured cricket pitch of the looming castle. Better yet, go for a walk on the beach: Crisscrossed by walking paths, rolling dunes lead to a vast sandy beach and lots of families on holiday.

BRITAIN: PAST AND PRESENT

Britain was created by force and held together by force. It's a nation shaped by the 19th century, when its rich Victorian-era empire reached a financial peak. Its traditional industry, buildings, and the pervasive notion of "Great" Britain are the products of its past wealth.

To best understand the many fascinating tour guides you'll encounter in your travels, have a basic handle on the sweeping story of this land and its capital, London. (Generally speaking, the nice and bad stories guides tell are not true...and the boring ones are.)

Basic British History for the Traveler

When Julius Caesar landed on the misty and mysterious isle of Britain in 55 b.c., England entered the history books. The primitive Celtic tribes Caesar fought were themselves invaders (who had earlier conquered the even more mysterious people who built Stonehenge). About 90 years later, the Romans came back, building towns and roads and establishing their capital at Londinium. The Celtic natives in Scotland and Wales—consisting of Gaels, Picts, and Scots—were not easily subdued. The Romans built Hadrian's Wall near the Scottish border as protection against their troublesome northern neighbors. Even today, the Celtic language and influence are strongest in these far reaches of Britain.

As Rome fell, so fell Roman Britain—a victim of invaders and internal troubles. Barbarian tribes from Germany and Denmark, called Angles and Saxons, swept through the southern part of the island, establishing Angle-land. These were the days of the real King Arthur, possibly a Christianized Roman general who fought valiantly—but in vain—against invading barbarians. In 793, England was hit with the first of two centuries of savage invasions by

> ## Get It Right
>
> Americans tend to use "England," "Britain," and the "United Kingdom" (or "UK") interchangeably, but they're not quite the same.
> - **England** is the country occupying the center and southeast part of the island.
> - **Britain** is the name of the island.
> - **Great Britain** is the political union of the island's three countries: England, Scotland, and Wales.
> - The **United Kingdom (UK)** adds a fourth country, Northern Ireland.
> - The **British Isles** (not a political entity) also includes the independent Republic of Ireland.
> - The **British Commonwealth** is a loose association of possessions and former colonies (including Canada, Australia, and India) that profess at least symbolic loyalty to the Crown.
>
> You can call the modern nation either the United Kingdom ("the UK"), "Great Britain," or simply "Britain."

barbarians from Norway, called the Vikings or Norsemen. The island was plunged into 500 years of Dark Ages—wars, plagues, and poverty—lit only by the dim candle of a few learned Christian monks and missionaries trying to convert the barbarians. The sightseer sees little from this Anglo-Saxon period.

Modern England began with yet another invasion. William the Conqueror and his Norman troops crossed the English Channel from France in 1066. William crowned himself king in Westminster Abbey (where all subsequent coronations would take place) and began building the Tower of London. French-speaking Norman kings ruled the country for two centuries. Then followed two centuries of civil wars, with various noble families vying for the crown. In the bitterest feud, the York and Lancaster families fought the Wars of the Roses, so-called because of the white and red flowers the combatants chose as their symbols. Rife with battles, intrigues, and kings, nobles, and ladies imprisoned and executed in the Tower, it's a wonder the country survived its rulers.

England was finally united by the "third-party" Tudor family. Henry VIII, a Tudor, was England's Renaissance king. He was handsome, athletic, highly sexed, a poet, a scholar, and a musician. He was also arrogant, cruel, gluttonous, and paranoid. He went through six wives in 40 years, divorcing, imprisoning, or executing them when they no longer suited his needs. (To keep track of each one's fate, British kids learn this rhyme: "Beheaded, divorced, died; beheaded, divorced, survived.")

Henry "divorced" England from the Catholic Church, estab-

PAST & PRESENT

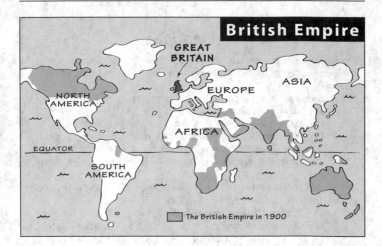

lishing the Protestant Church of England (the Anglican Church) and setting in motion years of religious squabbles. He also "dissolved" the monasteries (c. 1540), left just the shells of many formerly glorious abbeys dotting the countryside, and pocketed their land and wealth for the crown (for more on Henry, see the sidebar on page 130).

Henry's daughter, Queen Elizabeth I, who reigned for 45 years, made England a great trading and naval power (defeating the Spanish Armada) and presided over the Elizabethan era of great writers (such as William Shakespeare) and scientists (such as Sir Francis Bacon). But Elizabeth never married, so the English Parliament asked the Protestant ruler to the north, Scotland's King James (Elizabeth's first cousin twice removed), if he'd like to inherit the English throne. The two nations have been tied together, however fitfully, ever since (though recent stirrings toward Scottish independence may indeed shake up this long-standing union).

The enduring quarrel between England's divine-right kings and Parliament's nobles finally erupted into a civil war (1643). Parliament forces under the Protestant Puritan farmer Oliver Cromwell defeated—and beheaded—King Charles I. This civil war left its mark on much of what you'll see in Britain. Eventually, Parliament invited Charles' son to take the throne. This "restoration of the monarchy" was accompanied by a great colonial expansion and the rebuilding of London (including Christopher Wren's St. Paul's Cathedral), which had been devastated by the Great Fire of 1666. Parliament gained ultimate authority over the throne when it deposed Catholic James II and imported the Dutch monarchs William and Mary in 1688, guaranteeing a Protestant succession.

Britain grew as a naval superpower, colonizing and trading with all parts of the globe (although it lost its most important colony to those ungrateful Americans in 1776). Admiral Horatio Nelson's victory over Napoleon's fleet at the Battle of Trafalgar secured her naval superiority ("Britannia rules the waves"), and 10 years later, the Duke of Wellington stomped Napoleon on land at Waterloo. Nelson and Wellington—both buried in London's St. Paul's Cathedral—are memorialized by many arches, columns, and squares throughout England.

Economically, Britain led the world into the Industrial Age with her mills, factories, coal mines, and trains. By the time of Queen Victoria's reign (1837-1901), Britain was at its zenith of power, with a colonial empire that covered one-fifth of the world (for more on Victoria, see sidebar, later).

The 20th century was not kind to Britain. After decades of rebellion, Ireland finally gained its independence—except for the more Protestant north. Two world wars devastated Britain's population. The Nazi Blitz of World War II reduced much of London to rubble, although the freedom-loving world was inspired by Britain's determination to stand up to Hitler. Britain was rallied through difficult times by two leaders: Prime Minister Winston Churchill, a remarkable orator, and King George VI, who overcame a persistent stutter. After the war, the colonial empire dwindled to almost nothing, and Britain lost its superpower economic status.

One post-Empire hot spot—Northern Ireland, plagued by the "Troubles" between Catholics and Protestants—heated up, and then finally started cooling off. In the spring of 2007, the unthinkable happened when leaders of the ultra-nationalist party sat down with those of the ultra-unionist party. London returned control of Northern Ireland to the popularly elected Northern Ireland Assembly. Perhaps most important of all, after almost 40 years, the British Army withdrew from Northern Ireland that summer.

The tradition (if not the substance) of greatness continues, presided over by Queen Elizabeth II, her husband, Prince Philip, and their son Prince Charles. It seems you can't pick up a British newspaper without some mention of the latest event, scandal, or oddity involving the royal family.

The sons of Prince Charles and the late Princess Diana generate the biggest tabloid buzz. The older son, Prince William (b. 1982), is a graduate of Scotland's St. Andrews University and served as a search-and-rescue helicopter pilot with the Royal Air Force. In 2011, William married Catherine "Kate" Middleton, who is now the Duchess of Cambridge and will eventually become Britain's queen. Their son, Prince George Alexander Louis, born in 2013, will ultimately succeed William as sovereign. (A conveniently timed change in the law ensured that William and Kate's firstborn would inherit the throne, regardless of gender.)

William's brother, redheaded Prince Harry (b. 1984), has

Queen Victoria (1819-1901)

Plump, pleasant, and barely five feet tall, Queen Victoria, with her regal demeanor and 64-year reign, came to symbolize the global dominance of the British Empire during its greatest era.

Born in Kensington Palace, Victoria was the granddaughter of "Mad" King George III, the tyrant who sparked the American Revolution. Her domineering mother raised her in sheltered seclusion, drilling into her the strict morality that would come to be known as "Victorian." At 18, she was crowned queen. Victoria soon fell madly, deeply in love with Prince Albert, a handsome German nobleman with mutton-chop sideburns. They married and set up house in Buckingham Palace (the first monarchs to do so) and at Windsor Castle. Over the next 17 years, she and Albert had nine children, whom they eventually married off to Europe's crowned heads. Victoria's royal descendants include Kaiser Wilhelm II of Germany (who started World War I); the current monarchs of Spain, Norway, Sweden, and Denmark; and England's Queen Elizabeth II, who is Victoria's great-granddaughter.

Victoria and Albert promoted the arts and sciences, organizing a world's fair in Hyde Park (1851) that showed off London as the global capital. Just as important, they were role models for an entire nation; this loving couple influenced several generations with their wholesome middle-class values and devoted parenting. Though Victoria is often depicted as dour and stuffy—she supposedly coined the phrase "We are not amused"—in private she was warm, easy to laugh, plainspoken, thrifty, and modest, with a talent for sketching and journal writing.

In 1861, Victoria's happy domestic life ended. Her mother's death was soon followed by the sudden loss of her beloved Albert to typhoid fever. A devastated Victoria dressed in black for the funeral—and for her remaining 40 years never again wore any other color. She hunkered down at Windsor with her family. Critics complained she was an absentee monarch. Rumors swirled that her kilt-wearing servant, John Brown, was not only her close friend but also her lover. For two decades, she rarely appeared in public.

Over time, Victoria emerged from mourning to assume her role as one of history's first constitutional monarchs. She had

mostly shaken his reputation as a bad boy: He's proved his mettle as a career soldier, completing a tour in Afghanistan, doing charity work in Africa, and serving as an Apache aircraft commander pilot with the Army Air Corps. Nonetheless, Harry's romances and high-wire party antics are popular tabloid topics.

For years, their parents' love life was also fodder for the British press: Charles' marriage to Princess Di, their bitter divorce, Diana's dramatic death, and the ongoing drama with Charles' longtime girlfriend—and now wife—Camilla Parker Bowles. Camilla,

inherited a crown with little real power. But beyond her ribbon-cutting ceremonial duties, Victoria influenced events behind the scenes. She studiously learned politics from powerful mentors (especially Prince Albert and two influential prime ministers) and kept well-informed on what Parliament was doing. Thanks to Victoria's personal modesty and honesty, the British public never came to disdain the monarchy, as happened in other countries.

Victoria gracefully oversaw the peaceful transfer of power from the nobles to the people. The secret ballot was introduced during her reign, and ordinary workers acquired voting rights (though this applied only to men—Victoria opposed women's suffrage). The traditional Whigs and Tories morphed into today's Liberal and Conservative parties. Victoria personally promoted progressive charities, and even paid for her own crown.

Most of all, Victoria became the symbol of the British Empire, which she saw as a way to protect and civilize poorer peoples. Britain enjoyed peace at home, while its colonial possessions doubled to include India, Australia, Canada, and much of Africa. Because it was always daytime someplace under Victoria's rule, it was often said that "the sun never sets on the British Empire."

The Victorian era saw great changes. The Industrial Revolution was in full swing. When Victoria was born, there were no trains. By 1842, when she took her first train trip (with much fanfare), railroads crisscrossed Europe. The telegraph, telephone, and newspapers further laced the world together. The popular arts flourished—it was the era of Dickens novels, Tennyson poems, Sherlock Holmes stories, Gilbert and Sullivan operettas, and Pre-Raphaelite paintings. Economically, Britain saw the rise of the middle class. Middle-class morality dominated—family, hard work, honor, duty, and sexual modesty.

By the end of her reign, Victoria was wildly popular, both for her personality and as a focus for British patriotism. At her Golden Jubilee (1887), she paraded past adoring throngs to Westminster Abbey. For her Diamond Jubilee (1897), she did the same at St. Paul's Cathedral. Cities, lakes, and military medals were named for her. When she passed away in 1901, it was literally the end of an era.

trying to gain the respect of the Queen and the public, doesn't call herself a princess—she uses the title Duchess of Cornwall. (And even when Charles becomes king, she will not be Queen Camilla—instead she plans to call herself the "Princess Consort.")

Charles' siblings are occasionally in the news: Princess Anne, Prince Andrew (who married and divorced Sarah "Fergie" Ferguson), and Prince Edward (who married Di look-alike Sophie Rhys-Jones).

Through it all, Queen Elizabeth has stayed above the fray,

Britain's Royal Families

Royal Lineage

802-1066	Saxon and Danish kings
1066-1154	Norman invasion (William the Conqueror), Norman kings
1154-1399	Plantagenet (kings with French roots)
1399-1461	Lancaster
1462-1485	York
1485-1603	Tudor (Henry VIII, Elizabeth I)
1603-1649	Stuart (civil war and beheading of Charles I)
1649-1653	Commonwealth, no royal head of state
1653-1659	Protectorate, with Cromwell as Lord Protector
1660-1714	Restoration of Stuart dynasty
1714-1901	Hanover (four Georges, William IV, Victoria)
1901-1910	Saxe-Coburg (Edward VII)
1910-present	Windsor (George V, Edward VIII, George VI, Elizabeth II)

Royal Sightseeing

You can see the trappings of royalty at Buckingham Palace (the Queen's London residence) with its Changing of the Guard; Kensington Palace—with a wing that's home to Will, Kate, and baby George, and a cottage that serves as Harry's bachelor pad—plus good exhibits on Victoria, William and Mary, and the Hanovers); Clarence House, the London home of Prince Charles and Camilla; Althorp Estate (80 miles from London), the childhood home and burial place of Princess Diana; Windsor Castle, a royal country home near London; and the crown jewels in the Tower of London.

Your best chances to actually see the Queen are on three public occasions: State Opening of Parliament (mid-May, next in 2015), Remembrance Sunday (early November, at the Cenotaph), or Trooping the Colour (one Saturday in mid-June, parading down Whitehall and at Buckingham Palace).

Otherwise, check the "Latest news and diary" section of www.royal.gov.uk, where you can search for future royal events.

and most British people still jump at an opportunity to see royalty. With the worldwide hubbub surrounding Prince William's marriage to Kate (more than two billion people tuned in to watch) and the birth of their son, it is clear that the concept of royalty is still alive and well in the third millennium. (And, according to pollsters, just one-fifth of the Queen's subjects are in favor of abolishing the monarchy.)

In 2012, Queen Elizabeth marked her 60th year on the throne—her Diamond Jubilee. Only her great-great-grandmother, Queen Victoria (see sidebar on page 840), had a longer reign—but Elizabeth is on pace to overtake her in September of 2015. While many wonder who will succeed her—and when—the situation is straightforward: The Queen sees her job as a lifelong position, and legally, Charles (who wants to be king) cannot be skipped over for his son William. Given the longevity in the family (the Queen's mum, born in August of 1900, made it to a ripe old age of 101), Charles may be in for a long wait.

For more on the monarchy, see www.royal.gov.uk.

Architecture in Britain

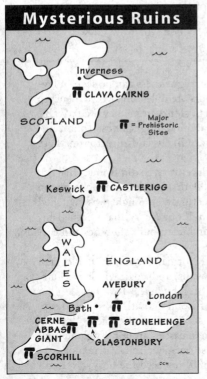

Mysterious Ruins

From Stonehenge to Big Ben, travelers are storming castle walls, climbing spiral staircases, and snapping the pictures of 5,000 years of architecture. Let's sort it out.

The oldest ruins—mysterious and prehistoric—date from before Roman times back to 3000 B.C. The earliest sites, such as Stonehenge and Avebury, were built during the Stone and Bronze ages. The remains from these periods are made of huge stones or mounds of earth, even man-made hills, and were created as celestial calendars and for worship or burial. Britain is crisscrossed with imaginary lines said to connect these mysterious sights (ley lines). Iron Age people (600 B.C.-A.D. 50) left desolate stone forts. The Romans thrived in Britain from A.D. 50 to 400, building cities,

Typical Church Architecture

History comes to life when you visit a centuries-old church. Even if you wouldn't know your apse from a hole in the ground, learning a few simple terms will enrich your experience. Note that not every church has every feature, and that a "cathedral" isn't a type of church architecture, but rather a designation for a church that's a governing center for a local bishop.

Aisles: The long, generally low-ceilinged arcades that flank the nave.

Altar: The raised area with a ceremonial table (often adorned with candles or a crucifix), where the priest prepares and serves the bread and wine for Communion.

Apse: The space beyond the altar, often bordered with small chapels.

Barrel Vault: A continuous round-arched ceiling that resembles an extended upside-down U.

Choir ("quire" in British English): A cozy area, often screened off, located within the church nave and near the high altar where services are sung in a more intimate setting.

Cloister: Covered hallways bordering a (usually square shaped) open-air courtyard, traditionally where monks and nuns got fresh air.

Facade: The exterior surface of the church's main (west) entrance, viewable from outside and usually highly decorated.

Groin Vault: An arched ceiling formed where two equal barrel

walls, and roads. Evidence of Roman greatness can be seen in lavish villas with ornate mosaic floors, temples uncovered beneath great English churches, and Roman stones in medieval city walls. Roman roads sliced across the island in straight lines. Today, unusually straight rural roads are very likely laid directly on these ancient roads.

As Rome crumbled in the fifth century, so did Roman Britain. Little architecture survives from Dark Ages England, the Saxon period from 500 to 1000. Architecturally, the light was switched on with the Norman Conquest in 1066. As William earned his title "the Conqueror," his French architects built churches and castles in the European Romanesque style.

English Romanesque is called Norman (1066-1200). Norman churches had round arches, thick walls, and small windows; Durham Cathedral and the Chapel of St. John in the Tower of London are prime examples. The Tower of London, with its square keep, small windows, and spiral stone stairways, is a typical Norman castle. You can see plenty of Norman castles around England—all built to secure the conquest of these invaders from Normandy.

Gothic architecture (1200-1600) replaced the heavy Norman

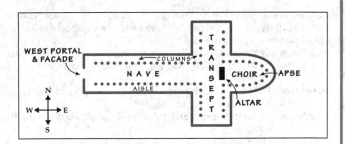

vaults meet at right angles. Less common usage: term for a medieval jock strap.

Narthex: The area (portico or foyer) between the main entry and the nave.

Nave: The long, central section of the church (running west to east, from the entrance to the altar) where the congregation sits or stands through the service.

Transept: In a traditional cross-shaped floor plan, the transept is one of the two parts forming the "arms" of the cross. The transepts run north-south, perpendicularly crossing the west-east nave.

West Portal: The main entry to the church (on the west end, opposite the main altar).

style with light, vertical buildings, pointed arches, soaring spires, and bigger windows. English Gothic is divided into three stages. Early English Gothic (1200-1300) features tall, simple spires; beautifully carved capitals; and elaborate chapter houses (such as the Wells Cathedral). Decorated Gothic (1300-1400) gets fancier, with more elaborate tracery, bigger windows, and ornately carved pinnacles, as you see at Westminster Abbey. Finally, the Perpendicular Gothic style (1400-1600, also called "rectilinear") returns to square towers and emphasizes straight, uninterrupted vertical lines from ceiling to floor, with vast windows and exuberant decoration, including fan-vaulted ceilings (King's College Chapel at Cambridge). Through this evolution, the structural ribs (arches meeting at the top of the ceilings) became more and more decorative and fanciful (the most fancy being the star vaulting and fan vaulting of the Perpendicular style).

As you tour the great medieval churches of Britain, remember that almost everything is symbolic. For instance, on the tombs of knights, if the figure has crossed legs, he was a Crusader. If his feet rest on a dog, he died at home; but if the legs rest on a lion, he died

Typical Castle Architecture

Castles were fortified residences for medieval nobles. Castles come in all shapes and sizes, but knowing a few general terms will help you understand them.

The Keep (or Donjon): A high, strong stone tower in the center of the castle complex that was the lord's home and refuge of last resort.

Great Hall: The largest room in the castle, serving as throne room, conference center, and dining hall.

The Yard (or Bailey or Ward): An open courtyard inside the castle walls.

Loopholes: Narrow slits in the walls (also called embrasures, arrow slits, or arrow loops) through which soldiers could shoot arrows at the enemy.

Towers: Tall structures serving as lookouts, chapels, living quarters, or the dungeon. Towers could be square or round, with either crenellated tops or conical roofs.

Turret: A small lookout tower projecting up from the top of the wall.

Moat: A ditch encircling the wall, often filled with water.

Motte-and-Bailey: A traditional form for early English castles, with a small fort on top of a hill (motte) next to an enclosed and fortified yard (bailey).

Wall Walk (or Allure): A pathway atop the wall where guards could patrol and where soldiers stood to fire at the enemy.

Parapet: Outer railing of the wall walk.

Crenellation: A gap-toothed pattern of stones atop the parapet.

Hoardings (or Gallery or Brattice): Wooden huts built onto the upper parts of the stone walls. They served as watch towers,

in battle. Local guides and books help us modern pilgrims understand at least a little of what we see.

Wales is particularly rich in English castles, which were needed to subdue the stubborn Welsh. Edward I built a ring of powerful castles in North Wales, including Conwy and Caernarfon.

Gothic houses were a simple mix of woven strips of thin wood, rubble, and plaster called wattle and daub. The famous black-and-white Tudor (or "half-timbered") look came simply from filling in heavy oak frames with wattle and daub.

The Tudor period (1485-1560) was a time of relative peace (the Wars of the Roses were finally over), prosperity, and renaissance. But when Henry VIII broke with the Catholic Church and disbanded its monasteries, scores of Britain's greatest churches were left as gutted shells. These hauntingly beautiful abbey ruins (Glastonbury, Tintern, Whitby, Rievaulx, Battle, St. Augustine's

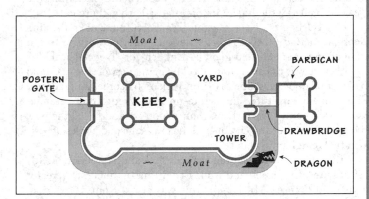

living quarters, and fighting platforms.

Machicolation: A stone ledge jutting out from the wall, fitted with holes in the bottom. If the enemy was scaling the walls, soldiers could drop rocks or boiling oil down through the holes and onto the enemy below.

Barbican: A fortified gatehouse, sometimes a stand-alone building located outside the main walls.

Drawbridge: A bridge that could be raised or lowered, using counterweights or a chain-and-winch.

Portcullis: A heavy iron grille that could be lowered across the entrance.

Postern Gate: A small, unfortified side or rear entrance used during peacetime. In wartime, it could become a "sally-port" used to launch surprise attacks, or as an escape route.

in Canterbury, St. Mary's in York, and lots more), surrounded by lush lawns, are now pleasant city parks.

Although few churches were built during the Tudor period, this was a time of house and mansion construction. Heating a home was becoming popular and affordable, and Tudor buildings featured small square windows and many chimneys. In towns, where land was scarce, many Tudor houses grew up and out, getting wider with each overhanging floor.

The Elizabethan and Jacobean periods (1560-1620) were followed by the English Renaissance style (1620-1720). English architects mixed Gothic and classical styles, then Baroque and classical styles. Although the ornate Baroque never really grabbed Britain, the classical style of the Italian architect Andrea Palladio did. Inigo Jones (1573-1652), Christopher Wren (1632-1723), and those they inspired plastered Britain with enough columns, domes, and symmetry to please a Caesar. The Great Fire of London (1666) cleared the way for an ambitious young Wren to put his mark on London forever with a grand rebuilding scheme, including the great St. Paul's Cathedral and more than 50 other churches.

The celebrants of the Boston Tea Party remember Britain's Georgian period (1720-1840) for its lousy German kings. But in architectural terms, "Georgian" is English for "Neoclassical." Its architecture was rich and showed off by being very classical. Grand ornamental doorways, fine cast-ironwork on balconies and railings, Chippendale furniture, and white-on-blue Wedgwood ceramics graced rich homes everywhere. John Wood Sr. and Jr. led the way, giving the trendsetting city of Bath its crescents and circles of aristocratic Georgian row houses.

The Industrial Revolution shaped the Victorian period (1840-1890) with glass, steel, and iron. Britain had a huge new erector set (so did France's Mr. Eiffel). This was also a Romantic period, reviving the "more Christian" Gothic style. London's Houses of Parliament are Neo-Gothic—they're just 140 years old but look 700, except for the telltale modern precision and craftsmanship. Whereas Gothic was stone or concrete, Neo-Gothic was often red brick. These were Britain's glory days, and there was more building in this period than in all previous ages combined.

The architecture of the mid-20th century obeyed the formula "form follows function"—it worried more about your needs than your eyes. But more recently, the dull "international style" has been nudged aside by a more playful style, thanks to cutting-edge architects such as Lord Norman Foster and Renzo Piano. In the last several years, London has added several creative buildings to its skyline: the City Hall (nicknamed "the Armadillo"), the Swiss Re Tower ("the Gherkin"), and the tallest building in the European Union, the pointy Shard London Bridge (called...um, "the Shard").

Even as they set trends for the 21st century, Britain treasures its heritage and takes great pains to build tastefully in historic districts and to preserve its many "listed" (government-protected) buildings. With a booming tourist trade, these quaint reminders of its past—and ours—are becoming a valuable part of the British economy.

Britain Today

Regardless of the revolution we had 230-some years ago, many American travelers feel that they "go home" to Britain. This most popular tourist destination has a strange influence and power over us. The more you know of Britain's roots, the better you'll get in touch with your own.

What's So Great About Britain?

Geographically, the Isle of Britain is small (about the size of Uganda or Idaho)—600 miles long and 300 miles at its widest point (and just 75 miles at its narrowest). Similar in size to Louisiana, England occupies the southeastern part of Britain (with about 60 percent of its land and 80 percent of its population). England's highest mountain (Scafell Pike in the Lake District) is 3,206 feet, a foothill by our standards. The population is a fifth that of the United States. At its peak in the mid-1800s, Britain owned one-fifth of the world and accounted for more than half the planet's industrial output. Today, the Empire is down to the Isle of Britain itself and a few token, troublesome scraps, such as the Falklands, Gibraltar, and Northern Ireland (though many larger nations—including Canada and Australia—still consider themselves part of the "British Commonwealth").

Economically, Great Britain's industrial production is about 5 percent of the world's total. After emerging from a recession in 1992, Britain's economy enjoyed its longest period of expansion on record. But in 2008, the global economic slowdown, tight credit, and falling home prices pushed Britain back into a recession.

Culturally, Britain is still a world leader. Her heritage, culture, and people cannot be measured in traditional units of power. London is a major exporter of actors, movies, and theater; of rock and classical music; and of writers, painters, and sculptors.

Ethnically, the British Isles are a mix of the descendants of the early Celtic natives (in Scotland, Ireland, Wales, and Cornwall), the invading Anglo-Saxon "barbarians" who took southeast England in the Dark Ages, and the conquering Normans of the 11th century...not to mention more recent immigrants from around the world. Cynics call the United Kingdom an English Empire ruled by London, whose dominant Anglo-Saxon English (50 million) far outnumber their Celtic brothers and sisters (10 million).

Politically, Britain is ruled by the House of Commons, with some guidance from the mostly figurehead Queen and House of Lords. Just as the United States Congress is dominated by Democrats and Republicans, Britain's Parliament has traditionally been dominated by two parties: left-leaning Labour and right-leaning Conservative ("Tories"). But recently the center-left Liberal Democrats ("Lib Dems") have made inroads, and the current administration is a coalition between the Lib Dems and Tories.

Strangely, Britain's "constitution" is not one single document; the government's structures and policies are based on centuries of tradition, statues, and doctrine, and much of it is not actually in writing. While this might seem potentially troublesome—if not dangerous—the British body politic takes pride in its ethos of civility and mutual respect, which has long made this arrangement work.

The prime minister is the chief executive. He or she is not elected directly by voters; rather, he or she assumes power as the head of the party that wins a majority in Parliamentary elections. In the interest of protocol, the Queen symbolically invites the winner to form a "government" (administration). Instead of imposing term limits, the Brits allow their prime ministers to choose when to leave office. The ruling party also gets to choose when to hold elections, as long as it's within five years of the previous one—so prime ministers carefully schedule elections for times that (they hope) their party will win. (Breaking with tradition, David Cameron's government announced their election date as soon as they took office: May 7, 2015.) When an election is announced, the Queen dissolves the Parliament so the parties can focus on a short-and-sweet, one-month campaign.

In the 1980s, Conservatives were in charge under Prime Minister Margaret Thatcher and Prime Minister John Major. As proponents of traditional, Victorian values—community, family, hard work, thrift, and trickle-down economics—they took a Reagan-esque approach to Britain's serious social and economic problems. In ending costly government subsidies to old-fashioned heavy industries, they caused many dated factories to close (earning working-class ire), but also nudged Britain toward a more 21st-century economy.

In 1997, a huge Labour victory brought Tony Blair to the prime ministership. Labour began shoring up a social-service system (health care, education, minimum wage) undercut by years of Conservative rule. Blair started out as a respected and well-liked PM, but his legacy became tarnished after he followed US President George W. Bush into war with Iraq. In 2007, Blair's Chancellor of the Exchequer and longtime colleague, Gordon Brown, succeeded him as prime minister. Elections in May of 2010 pitted a floundering Brown (who never achieved Blair's level of popularity) against a Conservative opponent, David Cameron, and a third-party Liberal Democrat challenger, Nick Clegg. No party won the number of seats needed for a majority, but the Conservatives and the Lib Dems formed a coalition government (the first since World War II)—vaulting David Cameron into the prime ministership. While Cameron's push for "austerity" (government-spending cutbacks) were initially met with approval, the promised results have not materialized; the election scheduled for May of 2015 will be a referendum on his approach.

In 2012, the Brits hosted two huge events: the Olympics and the Queen's Diamond Jubilee. The flurry of investment that swept Britain in the lead-up to that summer has left this already spruced-up country looking better than ever. This is the icing on top of a decades-long effort to rejuvenate some of Britain's former urban wastelands; cities like Liverpool and Cardiff have reclaimed their deserted, industrial waterfronts and converted them into hip, thriving people zones.

Current Challenges

From early 2008 to late 2009, the British economy shrank more than 6 percent—the largest decline since the Great Depression. Facing a huge—and growing—budget deficit, soon after his election Prime Minister Cameron announced an austerity program that dramatically cut back spending and increased the VAT (Value-Added Tax—the national sales tax) to 20 percent. The prime minister's budget eliminated more than 500,000 public-sector jobs, shortened long-term unemployment benefits to 12 months, imposed higher rents on public housing, slashed funding for the arts and the BBC, cut police services, and raised the retirement age to 66 by 2020. (Visitors might notice reduced bus schedules and unexpected closures of TIs or minor sights.) The initial result of these efforts was a double-dip recession (in 2012). The economy showed some signs of recovery in early 2013—but skeptics remain concerned that the growth isn't sustainable.

Other hot-button topics in Britain include terrorism, immigration, and binge-drinking.

Like the US, Britain has been coping with its own string of terrorist threats and attacks. On the morning of July 7, 2005, London's commuters were rocked by four different bombs that killed dozens across the city. In the summer of 2006, authorities foiled a plot to carry liquid bombs onto a plane (resulting in the liquid ban air travelers are still experiencing today). On June 29, 2007, two car bombs were discovered (and defused) near London's Piccadilly Circus, and the next day, a flaming car drove into the baggage-claim level at Glasgow Airport. Most Brits have accepted that they now live with the possibility of terrorism at home—and that life must go on.

Britain has taken aggressive measures to prevent future attacks, such as installing CCTV (closed-circuit television) surveillance cameras everywhere, in both public and private places. (You'll frequently see signs warning you that you're being recorded.) As Brits trade their privacy for security, many wonder if they've given up too much.

The terrorist threats have also highlighted issues relating to Britain's large immigrant population (nearly 4 million). Three of the four suicide bombers responsible for the July 2005 attacks were second-generation Muslims, born in Britain. Some Brits reacted to the event known as "7/7" as if all the country's Muslims were

PAST & PRESENT

Prime Minister David Cameron

David Cameron succeeded Gordon Brown as prime minister in May of 2010, and lives at #10 Downing Street with his wife, Samantha, and their young children. Elected at age 43, Cameron was the youngest PM in two centuries. He heads the Conservative Party (the "Tories"), but has never quite fit the stodgy Conservative image. Rumors still swirl of wild parties and illicit drugs in his student days at Oxford. He's known as "Dave" to his friends, and he developed a habit of riding his bike to work. Cameron rose quickly through the political ranks: He worked to re-elect Conservative PM John Major (1992), assisted the finance minister at #11 Downing Street (1992-1994), and was himself elected to Parliament in 2001, becoming head of the Conservative Party in 2005. By 2008, he was on the cover of *Time* magazine, which hailed him as the future of conservatism.

In 2010, Cameron's Conservative Party came to power, but it was hardly a sweeping Conservative mandate: Three parties split the vote, forcing Cameron's Conservatives to form a coalition with the (more left-leaning) Liberal Democrat Party. The Labour Party, which had held power in Britain for 13 years under Gordon Brown and Tony Blair, is the coalition's chief opposition.

Politically, Cameron is a moderate Conservative who is more pragmatic than ideological. Socially, he's "liberal" in the classical sense, advocating for personal freedoms—gay rights, decriminalization of drugs, allowing hunting and smoking, and ensuring citizens' privacy against government intrusion. Fiscally, he rails against big-government waste. His fiscal policies have emphasized austerity and belt-tightening in order to get the budget under control. The immediate result was a double-dip recession. His most right-of-center stance is his support for distancing Britain from the euro and the European Union; his veto of EU treaty amendments during the euro crisis led some to predict "the beginning of the end" of Britain's EU membership.

Despite his personal appeal, Cameron can't quite shake the Conservatives' image as the party of the upper class. Cameron was born rich, married rich, and has worked within the corporate culture. His colleagues form an old boys' network from his days at Eton, England's most exclusive prep school. The mayor of London, Boris Johnson, is not only an old Oxford frat buddy but also a distant cousin. Cameron's reputation has been tarnished by his links to discredited media mogul Rupert Murdoch, and some have questioned his handling of riots in London and other urban centers in the summer of 2011.

As the Conservatives try to unite the country to solve Britain's severe economic and cultural problems, it remains to be seen whether David Cameron has brought a fresh enough approach to #10. The people of Britain will get a chance to weigh in on May 7, 2015, when Cameron's party is up for re-election.

to blame. At the same time, a handful of radical Islamic clerics attempted to justify the bombers' violent actions.

The large Muslim population is just one thread in the tapestry of today's Britain. While nine out of ten Brits are white, the country has large minority groups, mainly from Britain's former colonies: India, Pakistan, Bangladesh, Africa, the Caribbean, and many other places. Despite the tensions between some groups, for the most part Britain is relatively integrated, with minorities represented in most (if not all) walks of life.

But unemployment, the economic downturn, and cuts to programs for the working class have strained relations between communities within Britain. In August of 2011, London police shot and killed a young black man named Mark Duggan, inflaming tensions between the police and the black community. A peaceful protest against the police was followed by violent riots and looting. British society as a whole was left to grapple with its causes and social implications: Were the riots a sign of rising racial and economic tensions, or simply a chance for poor young people to grab a shiny new smartphone?

Throughout the British Isles, you'll also see many Eastern Europeans (mostly Poles, Slovaks, and Lithuanians) working in restaurants, cafés, and B&Bs. These transplants—who started arriving after their home countries joined the EU in 2004—can make a lot more money working here than back home. British small-business owners have found these new arrivals to be polite, responsible, and affordable. While a few Brits complain that the new arrivals are taking jobs away from the natives, and others are frustrated that their English can be far from perfect, for the most part Britain has absorbed this new set of immigrants gracefully.

In 2003, Tony Blair's Licensing Act deregulated alcohol sales and did away with the government-mandated 23:00 closing time for pubs. The goal was to encourage a lively, late-night café culture in Britain, but an unintended consequence has been an epidemic of binge-drinking among young people. A 2007 study revealed that one out of every three British men, and one out of every five British women, routinely drinks to excess. It's become commonplace for young adults (typically from their mid-teens to mid-20s) to spend weekend nights drinking at pubs and carousing in the streets. (And they ratchet up the debauchery even more when celebrating a "stag night" or "hen night"—bachelor and bachelorette parties.) While sociologists and politicians scratch their heads about this phenomenon, tourists are complaining about weekend noise and obnoxious (though generally harmless) young drunks on the streets.

British TV

Although it has its share of lowbrow reality programming, much British television is still so good—and so British—that it deserves a mention as a sightseeing treat. After a hard day of castle climbing, watch the telly over tea in the living room of your village B&B.

For many years there were only five free channels, but now nearly every British television can receive a couple dozen. BBC television is government-regulated and commercial-free. Broadcasting of its eight channels (and of the five BBC radio stations) is funded by a mandatory £145.50-per-year-per-household television and radio license (hmmm, 60 cents per day to escape commercials and public-broadcasting pledge drives...not bad). Channels 3, 4, and 5 are privately owned, are a little more lowbrow, and have commercials—but those "adverts" are often clever and sophisticated, providing a fun look at British life. About 60 percent of households pay for cable or satellite television.

Whereas California "accents" fill our airwaves 24 hours a day, homogenizing the way our country speaks, Britain protects and promotes its regional accents by its choice of TV and radio announcers. See if you can tell where each is from (or ask a local for help).

Commercial-free British TV, while looser than it used to be, is still careful about what it airs and when. But after the 21:00 "watershed" hour, when children are expected to be in bed, some nudity and profanity are allowed, and may cause you to spill your tea.

American programs (such as *Game of Thrones, CSI, Friends, Frasier, How I Met Your Mother, The Simpsons, Family Guy*, and trash-talk shows) are very popular. But the visiting viewer should be sure to tune the TV to more typically British shows, including a dose of British situation- and political-comedy fun, and the top-notch BBC evening news. British comedies have tickled the American funny bone for years, from sketch comedy *(Monty Python's Flying Circus)* to sitcoms (*Are You Being Served?, Fawlty Towers, Absolutely Fabulous*, and *The Office*). Quiz shows and reality shows are taken very seriously here (*American Idol, America's Got Talent, Dancing with the Stars, Who Wants to Be a Millionaire?*, and *The X Factor* are all based on British shows). Jonathan Ross is the David Letterman of Britain for sometimes edgy late-night talk. Other popular late-night "chat show" hosts include Graham Norton and Alan Carr. For a tear-filled, slice-of-life taste of British soaps dealing in all the controversial issues, see the popular and remarkably long-running *Emmerdale, Coronation Street*, or *EastEnders*. The costume drama *Downton Abbey*, the long-running sci-fi serial *Doctor Who*, and the small-town dramedy *Doc Martin* have all become hits on both sides of the Atlantic.

Notable Brits of Today and Tomorrow

Only history can judge which British names will stand the test of time, but these days big names in the UK include politicians (David Cameron, Nick Clegg, Ed Miliband), actors (Helen Mirren, Emma Thompson, Helena Bonham Carter, Jude Law, Stephen Fry, Ricky Gervais, Robert Pattinson, Daniel Radcliffe, Kate Winslet), musicians (Adele, Chris Martin of Coldplay, James Arthur, Emeli Sandé), writers (J. K. Rowling, Hilary Mantel, Tom Stoppard, Nick Hornby, Ian McEwan, Zadie Smith), artists (Damien Hirst, Rachel Whiteread, Tracey Emin, Anish Kapoor), athletes (David Beckham, Bradley Wiggins), entrepreneurs (Sir Richard Branson, Lord Alan Sugar)...and, of course, William and Kate.

APPENDIX

Contents

Tourist Information

Tourist Information Offices

The Visit Britain website contains a wealth of knowledge on destinations, activities, accommodations, and transport in Great Britain. Families will especially appreciate the "Britain for Kids" travel suggestions. Maps, airport transfers, sightseeing tours, and theater tickets can be purchased online (www.visitbritain.com, www.visitbritainshop.com/usa for purchases).

In England, your best first stop in every town is generally the tourist information office—abbreviated **TI** in this book (and abbreviated locally as "TIC," for "tourist information centre"). In London, the City of London Information Centre is helpful; see page 50.

TIs are good places to get a city map, information on public transit (including bus and train schedules), walking tours, special events, and nightlife. Due to funding constraints, some of Britain's TIs are struggling; village TIs may be staffed by volunteers who need to charge you for maps and informational brochures that more fully funded TIs give out for free.

Many TIs have information on the entire country or at least the region, so try to pick up maps for destinations you'll be visiting later in your trip. If you're arriving in town after the TI closes, call ahead to get your questions answered and try to pick up a map in a neighboring town.

For all the help TIs offer, steer clear of their room-finding services (bloated prices, booking fees, and commissions that come from the pocket of your B&B host).

Communicating

Telephones

Smart travelers use the telephone to book or reconfirm rooms, get tourist information, reserve restaurants, confirm tour times, or phone home. Generally, it's cheapest to use an international phone card in Britain. This section covers dialing instructions, phone cards, and types of phones (for more in-depth information, see www.ricksteves.com/phoning).

How to Dial

Calling from the US to Britain, or vice versa, is simple—once you break the code. The European calling chart in this chapter will walk you through it.

Dialing Domestically Within Britain

The following instructions apply whether you're dialing from a landline (such as a pay phone or your hotel-room phone) or a British mobile phone.

Britain, like the US, uses an area-code dialing system. To make domestic calls within Britain, punch in just the phone number if you're dialing locally, and add the area code (which starts with 0) if calling long distance.

Area codes are listed (with phone numbers) in this book, displayed by city on phone-booth walls, and available from directory assistance (dial 118-500, £0.64/minute). Certain phone numbers, however, are considered "nongeographical" and don't have area codes. These include mobile phone, toll-free, and toll numbers.

Mobile phone numbers begin with 074, 075, 076, 077, 078, and 079 (and are more expensive to call than a landline). Numbers starting with 080 are toll-free, but those beginning with 084, 087, or 03 are inexpensive toll numbers (£0.10/minute maximum from a landline, £0.20-40/minute from a mobile). Numbers beginning with 09 are pricey toll lines. If you have questions about a prefix, call 100 for free help.

The English Accent

In the olden days, an English person's accent indicated his or her social standing. Eliza Doolittle had the right idea—elocution could make or break you. Wealthier families would send their kids to fancy private schools to learn proper pronunciation. But these days, in a sort of reverse snobbery that has gripped the nation, accents are back. Politicians, newscasters, and movie stars have been favoring deep accents over the Queen's English. While it's hard for American ears to pick out all of the variations, most English can determine where a person is from based on his or her accent...not just the region, but often the village, and even the part of town.

If you're dialing within Britain using your US mobile phone, you may need to dial as if it's a domestic call, or you may need to dial as if you're calling from the US (see "Dialing Internationally," next). Try it one way, and if it doesn't work, try it the other way.

Dialing Internationally to or from Britain

If you want to make an international call, follow these steps:

• Dial the international access code (00 if you're calling from Britain, 011 from the US or Canada). If you're dialing from a mobile phone, you can replace the international access code with +, which works regardless where you're calling from. (On most mobile phones, you can insert a + by pressing and holding the 0 key.)

• Dial the country code of the country you're calling (44 for Britain, or 1 for the US or Canada).

• Dial the area code (without the initial zero) and the local number. (The European calling chart on page 864 lists specifics per country.)

Calling from the US to Britain: To call a London hotel from the US, dial 011 (US access code), 44 (Britain's country code), 20 (London's area code without its initial 0), then 7730-8191 (the hotel's number).

Calling from any European Country to the US: To call my office in Edmonds, Washington, from anywhere in Europe, I dial 00 (Europe's access code), 1 (US country code), 425 (Edmonds' area code), and 771-8303.

Mobile Phones

Traveling with a mobile phone is handy and practical. There are two basic options: roaming with your own phone (expensive but easy) or buying and using SIM cards with an unlocked phone (a bit more hassle, but potentially much cheaper).

Roaming with Your US Mobile Phone: This pricier option

can be worthwhile if you won't be making or receiving many calls, don't want to bother with SIM cards, or want to stay reachable at your US number. Start by calling your mobile-phone service provider to ask whether your phone works in Europe and what the rates are (likely $1.29-1.99 per minute to make or receive calls, and 20–50 cents to send or receive text messages). Tell them to enable international calling on your account, and if you know you'll be making multiple calls, ask your carrier about any global calling deals to lower the per-minute costs. When you land in Europe, turn on your phone and—bingo!—you have service. Because you'll pay for receiving calls and texts, be sure your family knows to call only in an emergency. Note that Verizon and Sprint use a different technology than European providers, so their phones are less likely to work abroad; if yours doesn't, your provider may be able to send you a loaner phone (arrange in advance).

Buying and Using SIM Cards in Europe: If you're comfortable with mobile-phone technology, will be making lots of calls, and want to save some serious money, consider this very affordable alternative: Carry an unlocked mobile phone, and use it with a European SIM card to get much cheaper rates.

Getting an **unlocked phone** may be easier than you think. You may already have an old, unused mobile phone in a drawer somewhere. When you got the phone, it was probably "locked" to work only with one company—but if your contract is now up, your provider may be willing to send you a code to unlock it. Just call and ask. Otherwise, you can simply buy an unlocked phone: Search your favorite online shopping site for an "unlocked quad-band phone" before you go, or wait until you get to Europe and buy one at a mobile-phone shop there. Either way, a basic model costs less than $50.

Once in Europe, buy a **SIM card**—the little chip that inserts into your phone (either under the battery, or in a slot on the side)—to equip the phone with a European number. (Note that smaller "micro-SIM" or "nano-SIM" cards—used in some iPhones—are less widely available.) SIM cards are sold at mobile-phone shops, department-store electronics counters, and some newsstand kiosks for $5-10, and usually include about that much prepaid calling credit (making the card itself virtually free). In most places, buying a SIM card is as easy as buying a pack of gum—and almost as cheap. (In some countries—including Italy, Germany, and Hungary—it can take a bit longer, because you have to show your passport and be registered.) Because SIM cards are prepaid, there's no contract and no commitment (in fact, they expire after just a few months of disuse); I buy one even if I'm in a country for only a few days.

When using a SIM card in its home country, it's free to receive calls and texts, and it's cheap to make calls—domestic calls average 20-30 cents per minute (though toll lines can be substantially more). Rates are higher if you're roaming in another country, but as long as you stay within the European Union, these fees are capped (about 30 cents per minute for making calls or 10 cents per minute for receiving calls). Texting is cheap even if roaming in another country. Particularly inexpensive SIM card brands (such as Lebara) let you call either within Europe or to the US for less than 10 cents per minute.

When purchasing a SIM card, always ask about fees for domestic and international calls, roaming charges, and how to check your credit balance and buy more time. If text or voice prompts are in another language, ask the clerk whether they can be switched to English.

It's also possible to buy an **inexpensive mobile phone in Europe** that already comes with a SIM card. While these phones are generally locked to work with just one provider (and therefore can't be reused on future trips), they may be less hassle than buying an unlocked phone and a SIM card separately.

Mobile-Phone Calling Apps: If you have a smartphone, you can use it to make free or cheap calls in Europe by using a calling app such as Skype or FaceTime when you're on Wi-Fi; for details, see the next section.

Calling over the Internet

Some things that seem too good to be true...actually are true. If you're traveling with a smartphone, tablet, or laptop, you can make free calls over the Internet to another wireless device, anywhere in the world, for free. (Or you can pay a few cents to call from your computer or smartphone to a telephone). The major providers are Skype, Google Talk, and (on Apple devices) FaceTime. You can get online at a Wi-Fi hotspot and use these apps to make calls without ringing up expensive roaming charges (though call quality can be spotty on slow connections). You can make Internet calls even if you're traveling without your own mobile device: Many European Internet cafés have Skype, as well as microphones and webcams, on their terminals—just log on and chat away.

Landline Telephones

Just like Americans, these days most Europeans make the majority of their calls on mobile phones. But you'll still encounter landlines in hotel rooms and at pay phones.

Hotel-Room Phones: Calling from your hotel room can be great for local calls, and for international calls if you have an international phone card (described later). Otherwise, hotel-room phones can be an almost criminal rip-off for long-distance or in-

Smartphones and Data Roaming

I take my smartphone to Europe, using it to make phone calls (sparingly) and send texts, but also to check email, listen to audio tours, and browse the Internet. You may have heard horror stories about people running up outrageous data roaming bills on their smartphones. But if you understand the options, it's easy to avoid these fees and still stay connected. Here's how.

For voice calls and text messaging, smartphones work like any mobile phone (as described under "Roaming with Your US Mobile Phone," earlier). To avoid roaming charges, connect to free Wi-Fi, and use Skype, FaceTime, or other apps to make cheap or free calls (see "Calling over the Internet," earlier).

To get online with your phone, you have two options: Wi-Fi and mobile data. Because free Wi-Fi hotspots are generally easy to find in Europe (at most hotels, many cafés, and even some public spaces), the cheap solution is to use Wi-Fi wherever possible.

But what if you just can't get to a hotspot? Fortunately, most providers offer an affordable, basic data-roaming package for Europe: $25 or $30 buys you about 100 megabytes—enough to view 100 websites or send/receive 1,000 text emails. If you don't buy a data-roaming plan in advance, but use data in Europe anyway, you'll pay staggeringly high rates—about $20 per megabyte, or about 80 times what you'd pay with a plan.

While a data-roaming package is handy, your allotted megabytes can go quickly—especially if you stream videos or music.

ternational calls. Many hotels charge a fee for local and sometimes even "toll-free" numbers—always ask for the rates before you dial.

Phones are rare in **B&Bs,** but if your room has one, the advice above applies. If there's no phone in your B&B room, and you have an important, brief call to make, politely ask your hosts if you can use their personal phone. Ideally use a cheap international phone card with a toll-free access number, or offer to pay your host for the call.

Public Pay Phones: These are relatively easy to find in Britain, but they're expensive. Unlike phones in most of Europe, British pay phones don't use dedicated, insertable phone cards; instead, you'll pay with a major credit card (which you insert into the phone—minimum charge for a credit-card call is £1.20) or coins (have a bunch handy; minimum fee is £0.60). The phone clearly shows how your money supply's doing. Only unused coins will be returned, so put in biggies with caution. Avoid using an international phone card at a pay phone (see next page).

To keep a cap on usage and avoid incurring overage charges, I manually turn off data roaming on my phone whenever I'm not actively using it. (To turn off data and voice roaming, look in your phone's menu—try checking under "Cellular" or "Network," or ask your mobile-phone provider how to do it.) As I travel through Europe, I jump from hotspot to hotspot. But if I need to get online at a time when I can't easily access Wi-Fi—for example, to download driving directions when I'm on the road to my next hotel—I turn on data roaming just long enough for that task, then turn it off again. You can also limit how much data your phone uses by switching your email settings from "push" to "fetch" (you choose when to download messages rather than having them automatically "pushed" to your device). By carefully budgeting my data this way, my 100 megabytes last a long time.

If you want to use your smartphone exclusively on Wi-Fi—and not worry about either voice or data charges—simply turn off both voice and data roaming (or put your phone in "Airplane Mode" and then turn your Wi-Fi back on). If you're on a long trip, are positive you won't be using your phone for voice or data roaming, and want to save some money, ask your provider about suspending those services altogether while you're gone.

By sticking with Wi-Fi wherever possible and budgeting your use of data, you can easily and affordably stay connected while you travel.

Telephone Cards

International phone cards can be used with any type of phone (and will generally save you plenty of money, especially on overseas calls). With these cards, phone calls from Great Britain to the US can cost less than 10 cents a minute, as long as you don't call from a phone booth. British Telecom levies a hefty surcharge for using international phone cards from a pay phone (so instead of 100 minutes for a £5 card, you'll get less than 10 minutes—a miserable deal). But they're still a good value if you use them when calling from your hotel-room phone or mobile phone with a European SIM card.

To use the card, dial a toll-free access number, then enter your scratch-to-reveal PIN code. (If you have several access numbers listed on your card, you'll save money overall if you choose the toll-free one starting with 0800.) To call the US or Britain, see "How to Dial," earlier. To make calls within Britain using an international calling card, you must dial the area code even if you're just calling across the street. These cards, which are sold at newsstands, work only within the country of purchase (e.g., one bought in Britain

European Calling Chart

Just smile and dial, using this key:
AC = Area Code, LN = Local Number.

European Country	Calling long distance within ...	Calling from the US or Canada to ...	Calling from a European country to ...
Austria	AC + LN	011 + 43 + AC (without initial zero) + LN	00 + 43 + AC (without initial zero) + LN
Belgium	LN	011 + 32 + LN (without initial zero)	00 + 32 + LN (without initial zero)
Bosnia-Herzegovina	AC + LN	011 + 387 + AC (without initial zero) + LN	00 + 387 + AC (without initial zero) + LN
Croatia	AC + LN	011 + 385 + AC (without initial zero) + LN	00 + 385 + AC (without initial zero) + LN
Czech Republic	LN	011 + 420 + LN	00 + 420 + LN
Denmark	LN	011 + 45 + LN	00 + 45 + LN
Estonia	LN	011 + 372 + LN	00 + 372 + LN
Finland	AC + LN	011 + 358 + AC (without initial zero) + LN	999 (or other 900 number) + 358 + AC (without initial zero) + LN
France	LN	011 + 33 + LN (without initial zero)	00 + 33 + LN (without initial zero)
Germany	AC + LN	011 + 49 + AC (without initial zero) + LN	00 + 49 + AC (without initial zero) + LN
Gibraltar	LN	011 + 350 + LN	00 + 350 + LN
Great Britain & N. Ireland	AC + LN	011 + 44 + AC (without initial zero) + LN	00 + 44 + AC (without initial zero) + LN
Greece	LN	011 + 30 + LN	00 + 30 + LN
Hungary	06 + AC + LN	011 + 36 + AC + LN	00 + 36 + AC + LN
Ireland	AC + LN	011 + 353 + AC (without initial zero) + LN	00 + 353 + AC (without initial zero) + LN
Italy	LN	011 + 39 + LN	00 + 39 + LN

APPENDIX

European Country	Calling long distance within ...	Calling from the US or Canada to ...	Calling from a European country to ...
Latvia	LN	011 + 371 + LN	00 + 371 + LN
Montenegro	AC + LN	011 + 382 + AC (without initial zero) + LN	00 + 382 + AC (without initial zero) + LN
Morocco	LN	011 + 212 + LN (without initial zero)	00 + 212 + LN (without initial zero)
Netherlands	AC + LN	011 + 31 + AC (without initial zero) + LN	00 + 31 + AC (without initial zero) + LN
Norway	LN	011 + 47 + LN	00 + 47 + LN
Poland	LN	011 + 48 + LN	00 + 48 + LN
Portugal	LN	011 + 351 + LN	00 + 351 + LN
Russia	8 + AC + LN	011 + 7 + AC + LN	00 + 7 + AC + LN
Slovakia	AC + LN	011 + 421 + AC (without initial zero) + LN	00 + 421 + AC (without initial zero) + LN
Slovenia	AC + LN	011 + 386 + AC (without initial zero) + LN	00 + 386 + AC (without initial zero) + LN
Spain	LN	011 + 34 + LN	00 + 34 + LN
Sweden	AC + LN	011 + 46 + AC (without initial zero) + LN	00 + 46 + AC (without initial zero) + LN
Switzerland	LN	011 + 41 + LN (without initial zero)	00 + 41 + LN (without initial zero)
Turkey	AC (if there's no initial zero, add one) + LN	011 + 90 + AC (without initial zero) + LN	00 + 90 + AC (without initial zero) + LN

- The instructions above apply whether you're calling to or from a European landline or mobile phone.

- If calling from any mobile phone, you can replace the international access code with "+" (press and hold 0 to insert it).

- The international access code is 011 if you're calling from the US or Canada.

- To call the US or Canada from Europe, dial 00, then 1 (country code for US and Canada), then the area code and number. In short, 00 + 1 + AC + LN = Hi, Mom!

won't work in France). Buy a lower denomination in case the card is a dud.

US calling cards, such as the ones offered by AT&T, Verizon, or Sprint, are a rotten value and are being phased out. Try any of the options outlined earlier.

Useful Phone Numbers and Websites
Emergencies
Police and Ambulance: Tel. 999

Embassies and Consulates in London
US Consulate and Embassy: Tel. 020/7499-9000 (all services), no walk-in passport services; for emergency 36-hour passport service, email LondonEmergencyPPT@state.gov or call all-services number, 24 Grosvenor Square, Tube: Bond Street, www.usembassy.org.uk

Canadian High Commission: Tel. 020/7258-6600, passport services available Mon-Fri 9:30-13:00, 38 Grosvenor Street, Tube: Bond Street, www.unitedkingdom.gc.ca

Travel Advisories
US Department of State: Tel. 888-407-4747, from outside US tel. 1-202-501-4444, www.travel.state.gov

Canadian Department of Foreign Affairs: Canadian tel. 800-387-3124, from outside Canada tel. 1-613-996-8885, www.travel.gc.ca

US Centers for Disease Control and Prevention: US tel. 800-CDC-INFO (800-232-4636), www.cdc.gov/travel

Directory Assistance
Operator Assistance: Tel. 100 (free)

Directory Assistance: Toll tel. 118-500 (£0.64/minute, plus £0.23/minute connection charge from fixed lines)

International Directory Assistance: Toll tel. 118-505 (£1.99/minute, plus £0.69 connection charge)

Trains and Buses
Train information for Trips within Britain: Tel. 0845-748-4950, overseas tel. 011-44-20-7278-5240, www.nationalrail.co.uk

Eurostar (Chunnel Info): Tel. 0843-218-6186, overseas tel. 011-44-12-3361-7575, www.eurostar.com

National Express Buses: Tel. 0871-781-8178, www.nationalexpress.com

Airports
Heathrow (LHR): Tel. 0870-000-0123, www.heathrowairport.com

Gatwick (LGW): Tel. 0844-892-0322, www.gatwickairport.com

Stansted (STN): Tel. 0844-335-1803, www.stanstedairport.com

Luton (LTN): Tel. 01582/405-100, www.london-luton.com

London City Airport (LCY): Tel. 020/7646-0088, www.london-cityairport.com

Southend Airport (SEN): Tel. 01702/608-100,www.southendairport.com

Airlines
Aer Lingus: Tel. 0871-718-2020, www.aerlingus.com

Air Canada: Tel. 0871-220-1111, www.aircanada.com

Alitalia: Tel. 0871-424-1424, www.alitalia.com

American: Tel. 0844-499-7300, www.aa.com

British Airways: Tel. 0844-493-0787, www.ba.com

Brussels Airlines: Toll tel. 0905-609-5609 (40p/minute), www.brusselsairlines.com

easyJet: Tel. 0870-600-0000, www.easyjet.com

KLM Royal Dutch: Tel. 0871-231-0000, www.klm.com

Lufthansa: Tel. 0871-945-9747, www.lufthansa.com

Ryanair: Tel. 0871-246-0000, www.ryanair.com

Scandinavian Airlines (SAS): Tel. 0871-226-7760, www.flysas.com

United Airlines: Tel. 0845-607-6760, www.united.com

US Airways: Tel. 0845-600-3300, www.usairways.com

Heathrow Airport Car-Rental Agencies
Avis: Tel. 0844-581-0147, www.avis.co.uk

Budget: Tel. 0844-544-3439, www.budget.co.uk

Enterprise: Tel. 0800-800-227, www.enterprise.co.uk

Europcar: Tel. 0871-384-1087, www.europcar.co.uk

Hertz: Tel. 0870-844-8844, www.hertz.co.uk

Internet Access

It's useful to get online periodically as you travel—to confirm trip plans, check train or bus schedules, get weather forecasts, catch up on email, blog or post photos from your trip, or call folks back home (explained earlier, in "Calling over the Internet").

Your Mobile Device: The majority of accommodations in Britain offer Wi-Fi, as do many cafés, making it easy for you to get online with your laptop, tablet, or smartphone. Access is often free, but sometimes there's a fee. At hotels that charge for a certain number of hours, save money by logging in and out of your account on an as-needed basis. You should be able to stretch a two-hour Wi-Fi pass over a stay of a day or two.

Some hotel rooms and Internet cafés have high-speed Internet jacks that you can plug into with an Ethernet cable.

Public Internet Terminals: Many accommodations offer a guest computer in the lobby with Internet access. If you ask politely, smaller places may let you sit at their desk for a few minutes just to check your email. If your hotelier doesn't have access, ask to be directed to the nearest place to get online.

Security: Whether you're accessing the Internet with your own device or at a public terminal, using a shared network or computer comes with the potential for increased security risks. If you're not convinced a connection is secure, avoid accessing any sites (such as your bank's) that could be vulnerable to fraud.

Mail

You can mail one package per day to yourself worth up to $200 duty-free from Europe to the US (mark it "personal purchases"). If you're sending a gift to someone, mark it "unsolicited gift." For details, visit www.cbp.gov and search for "Know Before You Go."

The British postal service works fine, but for quick transatlantic delivery (in either direction), consider services such as DHL (www.dhl.com).

Transportation

By Car or Public Transportation?

If you're debating between public transportation and car rental, consider these factors: Cars are best for three or more traveling together (especially families with small kids), those packing heavy, and those scouring the countryside. Trains and buses are best for solo travelers, blitz tourists, city-to-city travelers, and those who don't want to drive in Europe. While a car gives you more freedom, trains and buses zip you effortlessly and scenically from city to city, usually dropping you in the center, often near a TI. Cars are an expensive headache in places like London.

In England, my choice is to connect big cities by train and to explore rural areas (Cornwall, Dartmoor, the Cotswolds, and the Lake District) footloose and fancy-free by rental car. The mix works quite efficiently (e.g., London, Bath, and York by train, with a rental car for the rest). You might consider a BritRail & Drive

APPENDIX

Public Transportation Routes in Britain

Legend:
- Rail
- Eurostar
- Bus
- (8H) Ferry with crossing time

Ferry Note:
Dover - Calais–1.5H
Dover - Boul–1.5 H

Orkney Islands
Burwick
Thurso
John o' Groats
Lewis
Elgin
Skye
Portree
Inverness
Culloden
Kyle
Loch Ness
Aviemore
Aberdeen
Mallaig
Fort William
SCOTLAND
Pitlochry
Mull
Iona
Perth
Dundee
Leuchars
Oban
St. Andrews
Stirling
Edinburgh
Berwick
Glasgow
Holy Island
Larne (2H)
(2-3H)
Cairnryan
Hexham
Newcastle
To Amsterdam (15H)
Stranraer
Carlisle
Durham
Belfast
Keswick
Penrith
NORTHERN IRELAND
Danby
Whitby
North Sea
Windermere
North York Moors
Scarborough
Isle of Man
ENGLAND
Irish Sea
Blackpool
York
Hull
To Zeebrugge (10H)
Leeds
Preston
Dublin
(7H)
Liverpool
Grimsby
Dun Laoghaire
(2-3H)
Holyhead
Conwy
Manchester
Lincoln
Bangor
Chester
Caernarfon
Betws-y-Coed
Stoke
Peter-borough
King's Lynn
REPUBLIC OF IRELAND
Pwllheli
Blaenau Ffest.
Derby
Norwich
Harlech
Telford
Wolv.
Birmingham
Ely
(3.5H)
Aberystwyth
Ironbridge Gorge
Coventry
Cambridge
Esbjerg (18 H)
Rosslare
Stratford
Warwick
Harwich
WALES
Cheltenham
Moreton
To Hoek van Holland (6H)
Fishguard
Carmarthen
Stow
Oxford
Newport
London
Ebbs-fleet
Canterbury
Swansea
Reading
Woking
Dover (1.5H)
Cardiff
Bath
STONE-HENGE
Ashford
Bristol
Westbury
Salisbury
Brighton
Calais
Wells
Glastonbury
Newhaven
Atlantic Ocean
Exeter
Southampton
Portsmouth
To Dieppe (4H)
EUROSTAR (2.5H)
Dartmoor
St. Ives
Truro
Plymouth
English Channel
To Cherbourg (3H)
To Ouistreham (6H)
Penzance
Falmouth
To Paris & Brussels
To Roscoff (6H)
FRANCE

50 Kilometers
50 Miles

Sample Train Journey

Here is a typical example of a personalized train schedule printed out at Britain's train stations. At the Salisbury station, I told the clerk that I wanted to leave after 16:30 for Moreton-in-Marsh in the Cotswolds.

Stations	Arrive	Depart	Class
Salisbury	—	16:41	Standard
Bristol	17:48	18:28	1st/Standard
Cheltenham Spa	19:10	19:29	1st/Standard
Worcester	19:52	20:05	1st/Standard
Moreton-in-Marsh	20:42	—	

Even though the trip involved three transfers, this schedule allowed me to easily navigate the rails.

In many stations, train departures are listed on overhead boards by their final destination; intermediate stops typically are not listed. Ask at the info desk—or any conductor—for the final destination of your next train so you can quickly figure out which platform it's departing from. For example, after checking with the conductor, I know that I'll need to look for *Oxford* to catch the train for Moreton-in-Marsh.

Often the conductor on your previous train can even tell you which platform your next train will depart from, but it's wise to confirm. The platforms often display scrolling screens that list the next train that's arriving and all its intermediate stops.

Britain's train system can experience delays, so don't schedule your connections too tightly if you need to reach your destination at a specific time.

Pass, which gives you various combinations of rail days and car days to use within two months' time.

Public Transportation

Trains

Regular tickets on Britain's great train system (15,000 departures from 2,400 stations daily) are the most expensive per mile in all of Europe. For the greatest savings, either book in advance or leave after rush hour (after 9:30).

Now that Britain has privatized its railways, it can be tricky to track down all your options; a single train route can be operated by several companies. However, one British website covers all train lines (www.nationalrail.co.uk), and another covers all bus and train routes (www.traveline.org.uk—for information, not ticket sales). Another good resource, which also has schedules for trains throughout Europe, is German Rail's timetable (www.bahn.com).

As with airline tickets, British train tickets can come at many different prices for the same journey. A clerk at any station can figure out the cheapest fare for your trip (or call the helpful National Rail folks at tel. 0845-748-4950, 24 hours daily). Savings can be significant. For a London-York round-trip (standard class), the full fare is about £98; if you book the day of departure for travel after 9:30, it may be around £87; and the cheapest fare, booked a couple of months in advance as two one-way tickets, can cost as little as £30.

While not required on British trains, reservations are free and can normally be made well in advance. They are an especially good idea for long journeys or for travel on Sundays or holidays. Make reservations at any train station or over the phone or Internet when you buy your ticket. With a point-to-point ticket, you can reserve up to two hours before train time, but railpass holders should book seats at least 24 hours in advance.

For information on the high-speed Eurostar train through the "Chunnel" to Paris or Brussels, see page 222.

Buying Train Tickets in Advance: The best fares go to those who book their trips well in advance of their journey. (While only a 7-day minimum advance booking is officially required for the cheapest fares, these sell out fast—especially in summer—so booking 6-8 weeks in advance is often necessary.) Keep in mind that when booking in advance, "return" (round-trip) fares are not always cheaper than buying two "single" (one-way) tickets. Cheap advance tickets often come with the toughest refund restrictions, so be sure to nail down your travel plans before you reserve. To book ahead, go in person to any station, book online at www.nationalrail.co.uk, or call 0845-748-4950 (from the US, dial 011-44-20-7278-5240, phone answered 24 hours) to find out the schedule and best fare for your journey; you'll then be referred to the appropriate vendor—depending on the particular rail company—to book your ticket. If you order online, be sure you know what you want; it's tough to reach a person who can change your online reservation. You'll pick up your ticket at the station, or you may be able to print it at home. (BritRail passholders, however, cannot use the Web to make reservations.)

A company called **Megabus** (through their subsidiary Mega-train) sells some discounted train tickets well in advance on a few specific routes, though their focus is mainly on selling bus tickets (info tel. 0871-266-3333, www.megatrain.com).

Buying Train Tickets as You Travel: If you'd rather have the flexibility of booking tickets as you go, you can save a few pounds by buying a round-trip ticket, called a "return ticket" (a same-day

Railpasses

Prices listed are for 2013 and are subject to change. For the latest prices, details, and train schedules (and easy online ordering), see my comprehensive *Guide to Eurail Passes* at www.ricksteves.com/rail.

"Standard" is the polite British term for "second" class. "Senior" refers to those age 60 and up. No senior discounts for standard class. "Youth" means under age 26. For each adult or senior BritRail or BritRail England pass you buy, one child (5–15) can travel free with you (ask for the **"Family Pass,"** not available with all passes). Additional kids pay the normal half-adult rate. Kids under 5 travel free.

Note: Overnight journeys begun on the final night of your pass can be completed the day after your pass expires—only BritRail allows this trick. A bunk in a twin sleeper costs $75.

BRITRAIL CONSECUTIVE PASS

	Adult 1st Class	Adult Standard	Senior 1st Class	Youth 1st Class	Youth Standard
3 consec. days	$319	$215	$269	$255	$169
4 consec. days	395	265	339	319	215
8 consec. days	565	375	479	455	305
15 consec. days	839	565	715	675	455
22 consec. days	1065	709	909	855	569
1 month	1259	839	1075	1009	675

BRITRAIL FLEXIPASS

	Adult 1st Class	Adult Standard	Senior 1st Class	Youth 1st Class	Youth Standard
3 days in 2 months	$395	$269	$339	$319	$215
4 days in 2 months	495	335	419	395	269
8 days in 2 months	719	479	615	575	385
15 days in 2 months	1079	725	919	865	585

BRITRAIL & DRIVE PASS

Any 4 rail days and 2 car days in 2 months.

	1st Class	2nd Class	Extra Car Day
Mini	$610	$430	$48
Economy	619	439	57
Compact	627	447	65
Compact Auto	658	478	96
Intermed. Auto	672	492	110
Minivan Auto	755	560	193

Prices are per person, two traveling together. Third and fourth persons sharing car buy a regular BritRail pass. To order a Rail & Drive pass, call Rail Europe at 800-438-7245. *Not sold by Europe Through the Back Door.*

Map key:

Approximate point-to-point one-way standard-class fares in US dollars by rail (solid line) and bus (dashed line). First class costs 50 percent more. Add up fares for your itinerary to see whether a railpass will save you money.

BRITRAIL ENGLAND CONSECUTIVE PASS

	Adult 1st Class	Adult Standard	Senior 1st Class	Youth 1st Class	Youth Standard
3 consec. days	$255	$169	$219	$205	$139
4 consec. days	319	215	269	255	169
8 consec. days	449	305	385	365	245
15 consec. days	675	449	575	539	365
22 consec. days	855	569	729	685	459
1 month	1009	675	859	809	539

Covers travel only in England, not Scotland, Wales, or Ireland.

BRITRAIL ENGLAND FLEXIPASS

Type of Pass	Adult 1st Class	Adult Standard	Senior 1st Class	Youth 1st Class	Youth Standard
3 days in 2 months	$319	$215	$269	$255	$175
4 days in 2 months	395	269	339	319	215
8 days in 2 months	575	385	489	465	309
15 days in 2 months	865	585	735	695	469

Covers travel only in England, not Scotland, Wales, or Ireland.

BRITRAIL LONDON PLUS PASS

	Adult 1st Class	Adult Standard
2 out of 8 days	$225	$149
4 out of 8 days	309	239
7 out of 15 days	385	285

Covers much of SE England (see London Plus Coverage Map, online). Includes vouchers to cover two trips on the Heathrow, Stansted, or Gatwick Express, separate from your counted travel days, which can be used up to 6 months from the date you validate the pass in Britain (but not before pass is validated for the 8- or 15-day travel window). Many trains are standard class only. The 7 p.m. rule for night trains does not apply. Kids 5–15 half price; under 5 free.

BRITRAIL SOUTH WEST CONSECUTIVE PASS

	Adult 1st Class	Adult Standard	Senior 1st Class	Youth 1st Class	Youth Standard
3 consec. days	$225	$149	$189	$179	$125
4 consec. days	279	189	239	225	149
8 consec. days	395	265	339	319	215
15 consec. days	589	395	505	475	319
22 consec. days	749	499	639	599	399
1 month	885	589	755	709	475

BRITRAIL SOUTH WEST FLEXI PASS

	Adult 1st Class	Adult Standard	Senior 1st Class	Youth 1st Class	Youth Standard
3 days in 2 months	$279	$189	$239	$225	$155
4 days in 2 months	349	235	295	279	189
8 days in 2 months	505	339	429	405	275
15 days in 2 months	759	509	645	609	409

Covers most trains in SW England operated by First Great Western (but not east of Portsmouth), South West Trains, and Heathrow Express (see coverage map online); not other operators. Includes Newport-Cardiff-Swansea main line trains in Wales. Many trains offer Standard class only.

round-trip, called a "day return," is particularly cheap); buying before 18:00 the day before you depart; traveling after the morning rush hour (this usually means after 9:30 Mon-Fri); and going standard class instead of first class. Preview your options at www. nationalrail.co.uk.

Senior, Youth, and Family Deals: To get a third off the price of most point-to-point rail tickets, seniors can buy a Senior Railcard (for ages 60 and above), and younger travelers can buy a 16-25 Railcard (for ages 16-25, or for full-time students 26 and above with a valid ISIC card). A Family and Friends Railcard allows adults to travel about 33 percent cheaper while their kids ages 5 to 15 receive a 60 percent discount for most trips (maximum of 4 adults and 4 kids). Each Railcard costs £30; see www.railcard. co.uk. Any of these cards are valid for a year on almost all trains except special runs, such as the Heathrow Express or the Eurostar to Paris or Brussels (fill out application at station, brochures on racks in info center, need to show passport; passport-type photo needed for 16-25 Railcard).

Railpasses: Consider getting a railpass, which offers hop-on flexibility and no need to lock in reservations, except for overnight sleeper cars. The BritRail pass comes in "consecutive day" and "flexi" versions, with price breaks for youths, seniors, off-season travelers, and groups of three of more. Most allow one child under 16 to travel free with a paying adult. If you're exploring England's backcountry with a BritRail pass, standard class is a good choice since many of the smaller train lines don't even offer first-class cars. Choose between England-only BritRail passes and ones that cover Scotland and Wales as well.

More BritRail options include Britain/Ireland passes, "London Plus" passes (good for travel in most of southeast England but not in London itself), South West passes (good for the Cotswolds, Bath, Dorset, Devon, Cornwall, plus part of South Wales), and BritRail & Drive passes (which offer you some rail days and some car-rental days). These BritRail passes, as well as Eurail passes, get you a discount on the Eurostar train that zips you to continental Europe under the English Channel. These passes are sold outside of Europe only. For specifics, see www.ricksteves.com/rail.

Buses

Although buses are about a third slower than trains, they're also a lot cheaper. Most buses are operated by **National Express** (tel. 0871-781-8178, www.nationalexpress.com). Note that Brits distinguish between "buses" (for in-city travel with lots of stops) and "coaches" (long-distance cross-country runs)—though for simplicity in this book, I call both "buses."

Round-trip bus tickets usually cost less than two one-way

fares. And buses go many places that trains don't. Budget travelers can save a wad with a bus pass. National Express sells **Brit Xplorer bus passes** for unlimited travel on consecutive days (£79/7 days, £139/14 days, £219/28 days, sold over the counter, non-UK passport required, tel. 0871-781-8178, www.nationalexpress.com). Check their website to learn about online deals; senior/youth/family cards and fares; and discounts for advance booking.

If you want to take a bus from your last destination to the nearest airport, you'll find that National Express often offers **airport buses**. Bus stations are normally at or near train stations (in London, the main bus station is a block southwest of Victoria Station).

Megabus sells very cheap promotional fares on certain routes, often beating National Express in price. But you have to book far ahead for the best rates, and journey times tend to be longer than those on National Express (info tel. 0871-266-3333, www.megabus.com). Megabus also sells discounted train tickets on selected routes.

Renting a Car

If you're renting a car in Britain, bring your driver's license. It's recommended, but not required, that you also have an International Driving Permit (sold at your local AAA office for $15 plus the cost of two passport-type photos; see www.aaa.com); however, I've frequently rented cars in Britain and traveled problem-free with just my US license.

Rental companies in Britain require you to be at least 23 years old. Drivers under the age of 25 or over the age of 70 may incur a young- or older-driver surcharge (some rental companies do not rent to anyone 75 or older). If you're considered too young or old, look into leasing (covered later), which has less-stringent age restrictions.

Research car rentals before you go. It's cheaper to arrange most car rentals from the US. Call several companies and look online to compare rates, or arrange a rental through your hometown travel agent.

Most of the major US rental agencies (including Avis, Budget, Enterprise, Hertz, and Thrifty) have offices throughout Europe. It can be cheaper to use a consolidator, such as Auto Europe (www.autoeurope.com) or Europe by Car (www.ebctravel.com), which compares rates at several companies to get you the best deal. However, my readers have reported problems with consolidators, ranging from misinformation to unexpected fees; because you're going through a middleman, it can be more challenging to resolve disputes that arise with the rental agency.

Regardless of the car-rental company you choose, always read

British Radio

Local radio broadcasts can be a treat for drivers sightseeing in Britain. While most rental cars have CD players, very few have adapter ports for portable media players—so you may wind up listening to a lot of British radio, whether you want to or not.

Many British radio stations broadcast nationwide; your car radio automatically detects the local frequency a station plays on and displays its name (not its frequency) on your radio's digital readout.

The BBC has five nationwide stations, which you can pick up in most of the country. These government-subsidized stations have no ads.

BBC **Radio 1** plays today's pop music, with youthful DJs spinning top 40 hits and interviewing big-name bands. Many of the same songs and artists air stateside, but Radio 1 will acquaint you with British acts that aren't yet known "across the pond." And many hit singles (even those by American groups) get a lot of play here months before they turn up on US radios. You'll be ahead of the curve when you get home, hear a hot "new" song on the radio, and wink knowingly to your friends, "This was a huge hit in the UK last summer."

BBC **Radio 2**—the highest-rated station nationwide—aims at a slightly more mature audience, with adult contemporary, retro pop, and other "middle of the road" music with broad popular appeal.

the fine print carefully for add-on charges—such as one-way drop-off fees, airport surcharges, or mandatory insurance policies—that aren't included in the "total price." You may need to query rental agents pointedly to find out your actual cost.

For the best deal, rent by the week with unlimited mileage. To save money on fuel, ask for a diesel car. I normally rent the smallest, least-expensive model with a stick shift (generally much cheaper than automatic). Almost all rentals are manual by default, so if you need an automatic, request one in advance; be aware that these cars are usually larger models (not as maneuverable on narrow, winding roads). But weigh this against the fact that in Britain you'll be sitting on the right side of the car, and shifting with your left hand... while driving on the left side of the road. The floor pedals are in the same locations as in the US, and the gears are found in the same basic "H" pattern as at home.

For a one-week rental, allow roughly $150 per person (based on two people sharing) for a small economy car with unlimited mileage. Allow extra for insurance, fuel, tolls, and parking. For trips of three weeks or more, look into leasing; you'll save money on insurance and taxes.

BBC **Radio 3** features mostly classical music (including live broadcasts of all the concerts in the annual BBC-sponsored Proms music festival), with some jazz and world music.

BBC **Radio 4** is all talk. It's reminiscent of public radio back home—current events, entertaining chat shows, special-interest topics such as cooking and gardening, and lots of radio plays.

BBC **Radio 5 Live**—less widely broadcast than the "big four"—features sporting events, as well as news and sports talk programs.

You'll encounter regional variations of BBC stations, such as BBC London, Radio York, or BBC Scotland. At the top of the hour, many BBC stations broadcast the famous "pips" (indicating Greenwich Mean Time) and a short roundup of the day's news.

Beyond the BBC offerings, several private stations broadcast music and other content with "adverts" (commercials). While many of these are unique to a specific city or region, others are nationwide, including **XFM** (alternative rock), **Classic FM** (classical), **Absolute Radio** (pop), and **Capital FM** (pop).

Traffic Alerts: If you want to stay up-to-date on traffic conditions, ask your rental-car company about turning on automatic traffic alerts that play on the car radio. Once these are enabled (look for the letters *TA* or *TP* on the radio readout), traffic reports for the area you are driving in will periodically interrupt programming.

You can usually get a GPS unit with your rental car or leased vehicle for an additional fee (around $15/day; be sure it has all the maps you need before you drive off). Or, if you have a portable GPS device at home, consider taking it with you to Europe (buy and upload European maps before your trip). GPS apps are also available for smartphones, but downloading maps in Europe could lead to an exorbitant data-roaming bill (for more details, see the sidebar on page 862).

Big companies have offices in most cities; ask whether they can pick you up at your hotel. Small local rental companies can be cheaper but aren't as flexible. If you pick up the car in a smaller city, such as Bath, you'll more likely survive your first day on the English roads.

Compare pickup costs (downtown can be less expensive than the airport) and explore drop-off options. Always check the hours of the location you choose: Many rental offices close from midday Saturday until Monday morning and, in smaller towns, at lunchtime.

When selecting a location, don't trust the agency's description of "downtown" or "city center." In some cases, a "downtown" branch can be on the outskirts of the city—a long, costly taxi ride from the center. Before choosing, plug the addresses into a mapping website. You may find that the "train station" location is handier. But returning a car at a big-city train station or downtown agency can be tricky; get precise details on the car drop-off location and hours, and allow ample time to find it.

When you pick up the rental car, check it thoroughly and make sure any damage is noted on your rental agreement. Find out how your car's lights, turn signals, wipers, and fuel cap function. Ask what type of fuel your car takes before you fill up. When you return the car, make sure the agent verifies its condition with you.

Car Insurance Options

When you rent a car, you are liable for a very high deductible, sometimes equal to the entire value of the car. Limit your financial risk with one of these three options: Buy Collision Damage Waiver (CDW) coverage from the car-rental company, get coverage through your credit card (free, if your card automatically includes zero-deductible coverage), or buy coverage through Travel Guard.

CDW includes a very high deductible (typically $1,000-1,500). Though each rental company has its own variation, basic CDW costs $15-35 a day (figure roughly 25 percent extra) and reduces your liability, but does not eliminate it. When you pick up the car, you'll be offered the chance to "buy down" the basic deductible to zero (for an additional $10-30/day; this is sometimes called "super CDW").

If you opt for **credit-card coverage,** there's a catch. You'll technically have to decline all coverage offered by the car-rental company, which means they can place a hold on your card (which can be up to the full value of the car). In case of damage, it can be time-consuming to resolve the charges with your credit-card company. Before you decide on this option, quiz your credit-card company about how it works.

Finally, you can buy collision insurance from **Travel Guard** ($9/day plus a one-time $3 service fee covers you for up to $35,000, $250 deductible, tel. 800-826-4919, www.travelguard.com). It's valid everywhere in Europe except the Republic of Ireland, and some Italian car-rental companies refuse to honor it. Note that various states differ on which products and policies are available to their residents—check with Travel Guard *before* you rent your car.

For more on car-rental insurance, see www.ricksteves.com/cdw.

Leasing

For trips of three weeks or more, consider leasing (which automatically includes zero-deductible collision and theft insurance). By technically buying and then selling back the car, you save lots of money on tax and insurance. Leasing provides you a brand-new car with unlimited mileage and a 24-hour emergency assistance program. You can lease for as little as 21 days to as long as six months. Car leases must be arranged from the US. One of many reliable companies offering affordable lease packages is Europe by Car (US tel. 800-223-1516, www.ebctravel.com).

Driving in Britain

Driving in Britain is basically wonderful—once you remember to stay on the left and after you've mastered the roundabouts. Every year, however, I get a few notes from traveling readers advising me that, for them, trying to drive in Britain was a nerve-racking and regrettable mistake. If you want to get a little slack on the roads, drop by a gas station or auto shop and buy a green *P* (probationary driver with license) sign to put in your car window (don't get the red *L* sign, which means you're a learner driver without a license and thus prohibited from driving on motorways).

Many Yankee drivers find the hardest part isn't driving on the left, but steering from the right. Your instinct is to put yourself on the left side of your lane, which means you may spend your first day or two constantly drifting into the left shoulder. It can help to remember that the driver always stays close to the center line.

Road Rules: Be aware of Britain's rules of the road. Seat belts are mandatory for all, and kids under age 12 (or less than about 4.5 feet tall) must ride in an appropriate child-safety seat. It's illegal to use a mobile phone while driving—pull over or use a hands-free device. In Britain, you're not allowed to turn left on a red light unless a sign or signal specifically authorizes it. For more information about driving in Britain, ask your car-rental company, read the Department for Transport's *Highway Code* (www.direct.gov.uk—click on "Motoring" and look for "The Highway Code" link), or check the US State Department website (www.travel.state.gov, click on "International Travel," then specify your country of choice and click "Traffic Safety and Road Conditions").

STOP AND LEARN THESE ROAD SIGNS

Speed Limit (mph) · Yield · No Passing · End of No Passing Zone

One Way · Intersection · Main Road · Freeway

Danger · No Entry · No Entry for cars · All Vehicles Prohibited

Parking · No Parking · Customs · Peace

Speed Limits: Speed limits are 30 mph in town, 70 mph on the motorways, and 50 or 60 mph elsewhere (though, as back home, many British drivers consider these limits advisory). The national sign for 60 mph is a white circle with a black slash. Motorways have electronic speed limit signs; posted speeds can change depending on traffic or the weather. Follow them accordingly.

Note that road-surveillance cameras strictly enforce speed limits. Any driver (including foreigners renting cars) photographed speeding will get a nasty bill in the mail. (Cameras—in foreboding gray boxes—flash on rear license plates to respect the privacy of anyone sharing the front seat with someone he or she shouldn't.) Signs (an image of an old-fashioned camera) alert you when you're entering a zone that may be monitored by these "camera cops." Heed them.

Roundabouts: Don't let a roundabout spook you. After all, you routinely merge into much faster traffic on American highways back home. Traffic flows clockwise, and cars already in the roundabout have the right-of-way; entering traffic yields (look to your right as you merge). You'll probably encounter "double-round-abouts"—figure-eights where you'll slingshot from one roundabout directly into another. Just go with the flow and track signs carefully. When approaching an especially complex roundabout, you'll first pass a diagram showing the layout and the various exits. And in many cases, the pavement is painted to indicate the lane you should be in for a particular road or town.

Freeways (Motorways): The shortest distance between any two points is usually the motorway (what we'd call a "freeway"). In Britain, the smaller the number, the bigger the road. For example, the M-4 is a freeway, while the B-4494 is a country road.

Motorway road signs can be confusing, too few, and too late. Miss a motorway exit and you can lose 30 minutes. Study your map before taking off. Know the cities you'll be lacing together, since road numbers are inconsistent. British road signs are never marked with compass directions (e.g., *A-30 West*); instead, you need to know what major town or city you're heading for *(A-30 Penzance)*. The driving directions in this book are intended to be used with a good map. Get a road atlas, easily purchased at gas stations in Britain, or download digital maps before your trip.

Unless you're passing, always drive in the "slow" lane on motorways (the lane farthest to the left). The British are very disciplined about this; ignoring this rule could get you a ticket (or into a road-rage incident). Remember to pass on the right, not the left.

How to Navigate a Roundabout

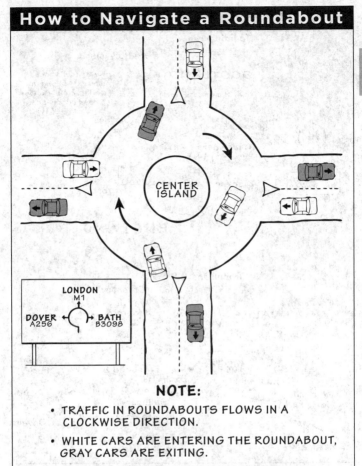

NOTE:

- TRAFFIC IN ROUNDABOUTS FLOWS IN A CLOCKWISE DIRECTION.
- WHITE CARS ARE ENTERING THE ROUNDABOUT, GRAY CARS ARE EXITING.
- VEHICLES ENTERING A ROUNDABOUT MUST YIELD TO VEHICLES IN THE ROUNDABOUT.
- LOOK TO YOUR RIGHT AS YOU MERGE! ☺

Rest areas are called "services" and often have a number of useful amenities, such as restaurants, cafeterias, gas stations, shops, and motels.

Fuel: Gas (petrol) costs about $10 per gallon and is self-serve. Pump first and then pay. Diesel rental cars are common; make sure you know what kind of fuel your car takes before you fill up. Unleaded pumps are usually green. Note that self-service gas pumps and automated toll booths and parking garages often accept only a chip-and-PIN credit card or cash. It might help if you know the PIN for your US credit and debit cards, but just in case a machine

England by Car: Mileage & Time

To Edinburgh

130m 3h

75m · 2h → Holy Island

SCOTLAND

Note: Your times may vary based on traffic, construction & road conditions.

Hadrian's Wall
(Housesteads Fort)

80m · 2h

50m · 1h → Durham

65m · 1.75h

85m · 2h

Keswick
(North Lake Dist.)

20m · .5h

120m · 3h

75m · 1.5h

Windermere
(South Lake Dist.)

Whitby

m = miles
h = hours

60m · 1.25h

120m · 2.5h

35m · 1h

Blackpool

90m · 1.75h

York

55m · 1.25h

130m · 3.5h

Liverpool

90m · 1.75h

Conwy

ENGLAND

60m
1.25h

75m · 2h

140m · 2.5h

160m · 3h

220m · 4h

Ironbridge
Gorge

10m · .25h

70m · 1.75h

10m
.25h

Coventry

WALES

Warwick

110m
2h

Stratford

Cambridge

Cotswolds
(Stow)

10m · .5h

4m
1h

90m · 2h

60m
1.25h

55m
1.25h

65m · 1.75h

60m · 1.5h

Oxford

Cardiff

20m · .75h

65m · 1.5h

London

Canter-
bury

Wells

50m

60m · 1.5h

Glastonbury

1.25h

Bath

115m · 2.5h

Dartmoor
Nat'l Park

80m · 1.5h

10m
.25h

100m · 2h

75m · 1.5h

115m · 2.5h

Salisbury

55m · 1.75h

85m · 3h

45m
1h

50m · 1.5h

Dover

100m · 2h

Portsmouth

Brighton

Penzance

rejects them, be sure to carry sufficient cash. For more on chip and PIN, see page 15.

Driving in Cities: Whenever possible, avoid driving in cities. Be warned that London assesses a congestion charge (see page 67). Most cities have modern ring roads to skirt the congestion. Follow signs to the parking lots outside the city core—most are a 5- to 10-minute walk to the center—and avoid what can be an unpleasant grid of one-way streets (as in Bath) or roads that are only available to public transportation during the day (as in Oxford).

Driving in Rural Areas: Outside the big cities and except for the motorways, British roads tend to be narrow. In towns, you may have to cross over the center line just to get past parked cars. Adjust your perceptions of personal space: It's not "my side of the road" or "your side of the road," it's just "the road"—and it's shared as a cooperative adventure. If the road's wide enough, traffic in both directions can pass parked cars simultaneously, but frequently you'll have to take turns—follow the locals' lead and drive defensively. Some narrow country lanes are barely wide enough for one car. Go slowly, and if you encounter an oncoming car, look for the nearest pullout (or "passing place")—the driver who's closest to one is expected to use it, even if it means backing up to reach it. If another car pulls over and blinks its headlights, that means, "Go ahead; I'll wait to let you pass." British drivers—arguably the most courteous on the planet—are quick to offer a friendly wave to thank you for letting them pass (and they appreciate it if you reciprocate). Pull over frequently—to let faster locals pass and to check the map.

Parking: Parking can be confusing. One yellow line marked on the pavement means no parking Monday through Saturday during work hours. Double yellow lines mean no parking at any time. Broken yellow lines mean short stops are OK, but you should always look for explicit signs or ask a passerby. White lines mean you're free to park.

In towns, rather than look for street parking, I generally just pull into the most central and handy pay-and-display parking lot I can find. To pay and display, feed change into a machine, receive a timed ticket, and display it on the dashboard or stick it to the driver's-side window. Rates are reasonable by US standards, and locals love to share stickers that have time remaining. If you stand by the machine, someone on their way out with time left on their sticker will probably give it to you. Keep a bag of coins in the console or glove box for these machines and for parking meters.

In some municipalities, drivers will see signs for "disc zone" parking. This is free, time-limited parking. But to use it, you must obtain a clock parking disc from a shop and display it on the dashboard (set the clock to show your time of arrival). Return within the signed time limit to avoid being ticketed.

The AA: The services of Britain's Automobile Association are included with most rentals (www.theaa.com), but check for this when booking to be sure you understand its towing and emergency road-service benefits.

Cheap Flights

London is the hub for many cheap, no-frills airlines, which affordably connect the city with other destinations in the British Isles and throughout Europe. If you're considering a train ride that's more than five hours long, a flight may save you both time and money. When comparing your options, factor in the time it takes to get to the airport and how early you'll need to arrive to check in.

The best comparison search engine for both international and intra-European flights is www.kayak.com. For inexpensive flights within Europe, try www.skyscanner.com or www.hipmunk.com. If you're not sure who flies to your destination, check its airport's website for a list of carriers.

The low-cost airline **easyJet** flies from London (Gatwick, Luton, Southend, and Stansted airports) as well as Liverpool. Prices are based on demand, so the least popular routes make for the cheapest fares, especially if you book early (tel. 0870-600-0000, www.easyjet.com).

Irish-owned **Ryanair** flies from London (mostly Stansted Airport, though also Gatwick and Luton), Liverpool, and Glasgow to often obscure airports near Dublin, Frankfurt, Stockholm, Oslo, Venice, Turin, and many others (Irish toll tel. 0818-303-030, British tel. 0871-246-0000, www.ryanair.com). However, be warned that Ryanair charges additional fees for nearly everything. Online check-in is mandatory (£7 charge), from 15 days to four hours before your flight (no airport check-in). You must also print a boarding pass before going to the airport; if you show up without it, there's an additional £70 charge. You can carry on only a small day bag; you'll pay a fee for each checked bag (price depends on the season; up to two bags allowed per passenger).

Brussels Airlines (formerly Virgin Express) is a Brussels-based company with good rates and hubs in Bristol, Birmingham, Heathrow, and Manchester (US tel. 516/296-9500, British toll tel. 0905-609-5609—£0.40/minute, www.brusselsairlines.com).

Be aware of the potential drawbacks of flying on the cheap: nonrefundable and nonchangeable tickets, minimal or nonexistent customer service, treks to airports far outside town, and stingy baggage allowances with steep overage fees. If you're traveling with lots of luggage, a cheap flight can quickly become a bad deal. To avoid unpleasant surprises, read the small print before you book.

Resources

Resources from Rick Steves

Rick Steves' England is one of many books in my series on European travel, which includes country guidebooks, city guidebooks (London, Paris, Rome, Florence, etc.), Snapshot Guides (excerpted chapters from my country guides), Pocket Guides (full-color little books on big cities, including London), and my budget-travel skills handbook, *Rick Steves' Europe Through the Back Door*. Most of my titles are available as ebooks. My phrase books—for Italian, French, German, Spanish, and Portu-

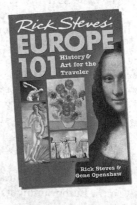

guese—are practical and budget-oriented. My other books include *Europe 101* (a crash course on art and history designed for travelers), *Mediterranean Cruise Ports* and *Northern European Cruise Ports* (how to make the most of your time in port), and *Travel as a Political Act* (a travelogue sprinkled with tips for bringing home a global perspective). A more complete list of my titles appears near the end of this book.

Video: My public television series, *Rick Steves' Europe*, covers European destinations in 100 shows, including 10 episodes on Great Britain. To watch episodes online, visit www.hulu.com; for scripts and local airtimes, see www.ricksteves.com/tv.

Audio: My weekly public radio show, *Travel with Rick Steves*, features interviews with travel experts from around the world. I've also produced free self-guided audio tours of the top sights and neighborhoods in London (and other great cities). All of this audio content is available for free at Rick Steves Audio Europe, an extensive online library organized by destination. Choose whatever interests you, and download it for free via the Rick Steves Audio Europe smartphone app, www.ricksteves.com/audioeurope, iTunes, or Google Play.

Maps

The black-and-white maps in this book are concise and simple, designed to help you locate recommended places and get to local TIs, where you can pick up more in-depth maps of towns or regions (usually free). Better maps are sold at newsstands and bookstores. Before you buy a map, make sure it has the level of detail you want.

If you'll be lingering in London, buy a city map at a London newsstand; the red *Benson's Handy London Map & Guide* is excellent. Even the vending-machine maps sold in Tube stations are good. The *Rough Guide* map to London is well-designed (sold at London and US bookstores). The *Rick Steves' Britain, Ireland & London City Map* has a good map of London (www.ricksteves. com). Many Londoners, along with obsessive-compulsive tourists, rely on the highly detailed *London A-Z* map book (called "A to Zed" by locals, available at newsstands and www.a-zmaps.co.uk).

If you're driving, get a road atlas covering all of England. Ordnance Survey, AA, and Bartholomew editions are all available at tourist information offices, gas stations, and bookstores. Drivers, hikers, and cyclists may want more in-depth maps for the Cotswolds and the Lake District.

Begin Your Trip at www.ricksteves.com

At our travel website, you'll discover a wealth of free information on European destinations, including fresh monthly news and helpful tips from thousands of fellow travelers. You'll find my latest guidebook updates (www.ricksteves.com/update), a monthly travel enewsletter, my personal travel blog, and my free Rick Steves Audio Europe smartphone app (if you don't have a smartphone, you can access the same content via podcasts). You can also follow me on Facebook and Twitter.

Our **online Travel Store** offers travel bags and accessories that I've designed specifically to help you travel smarter and lighter. These include my popular bags (rolling carry-on and backpack versions), money belts, totes, toiletries kits, adapters, other accessories, and a wide selection of guidebooks, planning maps, and DVDs.

Choosing the right **railpass** for your trip—amid hundreds of options—can drive you nutty. Our website will help you find the perfect fit for your itinerary and budget.

Want to travel with greater efficiency and less stress? We organize **tours** with more than three dozen itineraries and 600 departures reaching the best destinations in this book...and beyond. We offer a 14-day England tour, a 10-day Scotland tour, and a 7-day in-depth London city tour. You'll enjoy great guides, a fun bunch of travel partners (with small groups of 24 to 28 travelers), and plenty of room to spread out in a big, comfy bus when touring between towns. You'll find European adventures to fit every vacation length. For all the details, and to get our Tour Catalog and a free Rick Steves Tour Experience DVD (filmed on location during an actual tour), visit www.ricksteves.com or call us at 425/608-4217.

Other Guidebooks

If you're like most travelers, this book is all you need. But if you're heading beyond my recommended destinations, $40 for extra maps and books can be money well spent. If you'll be focusing on London or traveling elsewhere in Britain, consider *Rick Steves' London 2014* or *Rick Steves' Great Britain*.

The following books are worthwhile, though most are not updated annually; check the publication date before you buy. The *Lonely Planet* and *Let's Go* guidebooks on London and on Britain are fine budget-travel guides. *Lonely Planet*'s guidebooks are more thorough and informative; *Let's Go* books are youth-oriented, with good coverage of nightlife, hostels, and cheap transportation deals. For cultural and sightseeing background, look into *Michelin* and *Cadogan* guides to London, England, and Britain. *Secret London* by Andrew Duncan leads the reader on unique walks through a less touristy London.

Recommended Books and Movies

To learn more about England past and present, check out a few of these books or films.

Nonfiction

For a serious historical overview, wade into *A History of Britain,* a three-volume collection by Simon Schama. *Literary Trails* (Hardyment) reunites famous authors with the environments that inspired them.

In *Notes from a Small Island,* American expat Bill Bryson records his witty notes about every British foible. For more good memoirs, pick up any of the books by Susan Allen Toth on her British travels. If you'll be spending time in the Cotswolds, try *Cider with Rosie,* Laurie Lee's boyhood memoir set just after World War I. Animal lovers enjoy James Herriot's adventures as a Yorkshire vet, told in *All Creatures Great and Small* and its sequels. And the obsessive world of English soccer is illuminated in Nick Hornby's memoir, *Fever Pitch.*

Fiction

For the classics of British fiction, read anything—and everything—by Charles Dickens, Jane Austen, and the Brontës.

Pillars of the Earth (Follett) traces the building of a fictional 12th-century cathedral in southern England. For a big book on the era of King Richard III, try *The Sunne in Splendour,* one in a series by Sharon Kay Penman. *Wolf Hall* and *Bring Up the Bodies* (Mantel) transport readers to the court of Henry VIII through the eyes of Thomas Cromwell, while *Restoration* (Tremain) returns readers to the time of King Charles II.

Set in the 19th-century Anglican church, *The Warden* (Trollope) dwells on moral dilemmas. *Brideshead Revisited* (Waugh) satirizes the British obsession with class and takes place between the World Wars. A rural village in the 1930s is the social battlefield for E. F. Benson's *Mapp and Lucia.* A family saga spanning the interwar years and beyond, *Atonement* (McEwan) takes an intense look at England's upper-middle class. For evocative Cornish settings, try Daphne du Maurier's *Rebecca* or *The House on the Strand.*

Mystery novels have a long tradition in Britain. *A Morbid Taste for Bones* (Peters) features a Benedictine monk-detective in 12th-century Shropshire. Agatha Christie's Miss Marple was introduced in 1930 in *The Murder at the Vicarage.* And Ian Rankin's troubled Inspector Rebus first gets his man in *Knots and Crosses,* set in present-day Edinburgh. For other modern mysteries, try any of the books in the Inspector Lynley series by Elizabeth George.

For a more contemporary read, check out *Bridget Jones's Diary* (Fielding), *Behind the Scenes at the Museum* (Atkinson), *White Teeth*

(Smith), *Saturday* (McEwan), or anything by Nick Hornby *(High Fidelity, About a Boy)*.

Film and Television

In terms of world influence, Britain's filmmaking rivals its substantial literary contributions. Here are some films that will flesh out your understanding of this small island, past and present.

For a taste of Tudor-era London, try *Shakespeare in Love* (1999), which is set in the original Globe Theatre. In *A Man for All Seasons* (1966), Sir Thomas More faces down Henry VIII. Showtime's racy, lavish series *The Tudors* (2007-2010) is an entertaining, loosely accurate chronicle of the marriages of Henry VIII. For equally good portraits of Elizabeth I, try *Elizabeth* (1998) and its sequel *Elizabeth: The Golden Age* (2007), or the BBC/HBO miniseries *Elizabeth I* (2005).

Written and set in the early 19th century, the works of Jane Austen have fared well in film. Among the many versions of *Pride and Prejudice,* the 1995 BBC miniseries starring Colin Firth is the winner. *Persuasion* (1995) was partially filmed in Bath. Other Austen adaptations include *Sense and Sensibility* (1995, with Emma Thompson, Hugh Grant, and Kate Winslet) and *Emma* (1996, with Gwyneth Paltrow). The 1995 SoCal teen comedy *Clueless* also (freely) reinterprets *Emma*. Charlotte Brontë's *Jane Eyre* has been made into a movie at least nine times, most recently in 2011 (with Mia Wasikowska and Michael Fassbender).

In *The Elephant Man* (1980), the cruelty of Victorian London is starkly portrayed in black and white. *Sweeney Todd* (2007) captures the gritty Victorian milieu, as do two highly stylized *Sherlock Holmes* films (2009 and 2011). Sherlock shows up again in an excellent British TV update of the detective's story, set in present-day London (2010-present).

The upstairs-downstairs Edwardian era of the early 20th century has inspired many films. Producer Ismail Merchant and director James Ivory teamed up to create many well-regarded films about this era, including *Howard's End* (1992, which captures the stifling societal pressure underneath the gracious manners), *A Room with a View* (1985), and *The Remains of the Day* (1993).

The all-star *Gosford Park* (2001) is part comedy, part murder mystery, and part critique of England's stratified class system in the 1930s. Its screenwriter, Julian Fellowes, went on to create the wildly popular *Downton Abbey* (2011-present), a spot-on portrayal of aristocratic life before and after World War I (filmed at Highclere Castle, about 70 miles west of London). *Chariots of Fire* (1981), about British track stars competing in the 1924 Paris Olympics, ran away with the Academy Award for Best Picture.

Wartime London has been captured in many fine movies. *The*

King's Speech (2010) won the Best Picture Oscar, with Colin Firth named Best Actor for his portrayal of King George VI on the eve of World War II. *Hope and Glory* (1987) is a semi-autobiographical story of a boy growing up during WWII's Blitz. In *Foyle's War,* a BBC series (2002-2013), detective Christopher Foyle solves crime amid wartime in southern England.

British acts became all the rage in the States in the 1960s, thanks to a little band called the Beatles, whose *A Hard Day's Night* (1964) is filled with wit and charm. During this time, "swinging London" also exploded on the international scene, with films such as *Alfie* (1966), *Blowup* (1966), and *Georgy Girl* (1966). For a swinging spoof of this time, try the Austin Powers comedies.

England goes mainstream in a series of 1990s hits: Hugh Grant charms the ladies in *Four Weddings and a Funeral* (1994) and *Notting Hill* (1999); Gwyneth Paltrow lives two lives in *Sliding Doors* (1998); and John Cleese, Jamie Lee Curtis, and Kevin Kline hilariously double-cross one another in *A Fish Called Wanda* (1988).

For a departure from the typical Hollywood fare, see *My Beautiful Laundrette* (1986), a gritty story of two gay men (with Daniel Day-Lewis). For another portrayal of urban London—and the racial tensions found in its multiethnic center—look for *Sammy and Rosie Get Laid* (1987). *Lock, Stock and Two Smoking Barrels* (1998) is a violent crime caper set in the city.

Billy Elliot (2000), about a young boy ballet dancer, and *Bend It Like Beckham* (2003), about a young girl of Punjabi descent who plays soccer, were both huge crowd-pleasers. *An Education* (2009), about a bright schoolgirl who falls for an older man, takes place in 1960s London. *V for Vendetta* (2006), based on a British graphic novel, shows a sci-fi future of a London ruled with an iron fist. Alfonso Cuarón's *Children of Men* (2006) takes place in a dystopian future London.

In *The Queen* (2006), Helen Mirren expertly channels Elizabeth II during the days after Princess Diana's death. If you enjoy *The Queen*, don't miss two other reality-based films by the same screenwriter and with many of the same cast members (most notably Michael Sheen as Tony Blair): *The Special Relationship* (2010, about the friendship between Tony Blair and Bill Clinton) and *The Deal* (2003, about Tony Blair's early relationship with Gordon Brown).

Britain has offered up plenty of comedy choices over the years. If you're in the mood for something completely different, try *Monty Python and the Holy Grail* (1975), a surreal take on the Arthurian legend. The BBC's deeply irreverent "mockumentary" series *The Office* (by Ricky Gervais and Stephen Merchant) inspired the gentler US television show. In *The Full Monty* (1997), some working-class Yorkshire lads take it all off to pay the bills.

Harry Potter Sights

Harry Potter's story is set in a magical Britain, and all the places mentioned in the books, except London, are fictional, but you can visit many real film locations. Many of the locations are closed to visitors, though, or are an un-magical disappointment in person, unless you're a huge fan. For those diehards, here's a sampling.

Spoiler Alert: The information below will ruin surprises for the three of you who haven't yet read or seen the Harry Potter series.

London

In the first film, *The Sorcerer's Stone* (2001), Harry first realizes his wizard powers when talking with a boa constrictor, filmed at the **London Zoo's Reptile House** in Regent's Park (Tube: Great Portland Street). Hagrid takes Harry shopping for school supplies in the glass-roofed **Leadenhall Market** (Tube: Bank). The goblin-run Gringotts Wizarding Bank was filmed in the marble-floored Exhibition Hall of **Australia House** (Tube: Temple), home of the Australian Embassy.

Harry catches the train to Hogwarts, the wizarding prep school, at **King's Cross Station.** The fanciful exterior in *The Chamber of Secrets* (2002) was actually shot at nearby **St. Pancras International Station.** Inside, Harry heads to platform 9¾. (For a fun photo-op, head to the station's western departures concourse to find the *Platform 9¾* sign and the luggage cart that looks like it's disappearing into the wall, between tracks 8 and 9.)

In *The Prisoner of Azkaban* (2004), Harry careens through London on a three-decker bus that dumps him at the Leaky Cauldron pub. The exterior was shot on rough-looking Stoney Street at the southeast edge of **Borough Street Market,** by The Market Porter pub (Tube: London Bridge).

In *The Order of the Phoenix* (2007), the Order takes to the night sky on broomsticks over London, passing over plenty of identifiable landmarks, including the **London Eye, Big Ben,** and **Buckingham Palace.** The **Millennium Bridge** is attacked and collapses into the Thames in the dramatic finale to *The Half-Blood Prince* (2009). For *Order of the Phoenix* and the first *Deathly Hallows* (2010), the real government offices of **Whitehall** serve as exteriors for the Ministry of Magic. Harry, Ron, and Hermione fight off disguised Death Eaters in a Muggle café, filmed in the West End's bustling **Piccadilly Circus.** Other London settings, like Diagon Alley, only exist at **Leavesden Film Studios** (20 miles north of London), where most of the films' interiors were shot. Leavesden recently opened its doors to Harry Potter pilgrims (see page 151).

Near Bath

Many scenes showing Hogwarts were filmed in the elaborate corridors of the **Gloucester Cathedral** cloisters, 50 miles north of Bath. In *The Sorcerer's Stone*, the scene showing Harry being chosen for Gryffindor's Quidditch team was shot in the halls of the 13th-century **Lacock Abbey,** 13 miles east of Bath. Harry attends Professor Snape's class in one of the Abbey's peeling-plaster rooms. (Mad Max tours include Lacock; see page 413.)

Outdoor scenes from the first *Deathly Hallows,* in which Harry, Ron, and Hermione take refuge in the woods, were filmed in the Swinley Forest area of Windsor's **Great Park.**

Oxford

Hogwarts is a composite of several locations, many of them in Oxford. (For information on Harry Potter tours

in Oxford, see page 499.) **Christ Church College** provided the model for Hogwarts' Great Hall, with its **stone staircase,** and for the high-ceilinged **dining hall** seen throughout the films.

In *The Sorcerer's Stone,* Harry sneaks into the restricted section of Hogwarts Library under a cloak of invisibility. This scene was filmed inside Oxford's **Duke Humfrey's Library.** At the end of *The Sorcerer's Stone,* Harry awakens in the Hogwarts infirmary, filmed in the big-windowed **Divinity School,** on the ground floor of the Bodleian Library. In *The Goblet of Fire* (2005), Mad-Eye Moody turns Draco into a ferret in the **New College cloister.**

Durham and Northeast England

In *The Sorcerer's Stone,* Harry walks with his white owl, Hedwig, through a snowy cloister courtyard located in **Durham's Cathedral** (see listing on page 803). Harry first learns to fly a broomstick on the green grass of Hogwarts' school grounds, filmed inside the walls of **Alnwick Castle,** 30 miles from Newcastle. In *The Chamber of Secrets,* this is where the Weasleys' flying car crashes into the Whomping Willow.

Southeast England

In the second *Deathly Hallows* (2011), the pivotal scene at Lily and James Potter's home—when Harry becomes the "Boy Who Lived"—was shot in the medieval town of **Lavenham,** Suffolk.

Northwest England

Fleeing a pack of eager Death Eaters, Harry and Hagrid speed through **Liverpool's Queensway Tunnel** on Sirius Black's flying motorcycle in *Deathly Hallows: Part I.*

For Kids: If you're traveling to London or Great Britain with children, consider watching *Mary Poppins* (1964), *My Fair Lady* (1964), *A Little Princess* (1995), the Wallace & Gromit movies, Rowan Atkinson's *Mr. Bean* television series and movies, and the Harry Potter films (adults can watch them, too).

Holidays and Festivals

This list includes national holidays observed throughout Great Britain plus selected festivals. Many sights and banks close on national holidays—keep this in mind when planning your itinerary. Throughout Britain, hotels get booked up during Easter week; over the Early May, Spring, and Summer Bank Holidays; and during Christmas, Boxing Day, and New Year's Day. On Christmas, virtually everything shuts down, even the Tube in London. Museums also generally close December 24 and 26.

Many British towns have holiday festivals in late November and early December, with markets, music, and entertainment in the Christmas spirit (for instance, Keswick's Victorian Fayre).

Before planning a trip around a festival, make sure to verify its dates by checking the festival website or the Visit Britain website (www.visitbritain.com).

Here are some major holidays:

Jan 1	New Year's Day
Mid-Feb	London Fashion Week (www.londonfashionweek.co.uk)
Mid-Feb	Jorvik Viking Festival, York (costumed warriors, battles; www.jorvik-viking-centre.co.uk)
Early March	Literature Festival, Bath (www.bathlitfest.org.uk)
Easter Sunday	April 20 in 2014, April 5 in 2015
Easter Monday	April 21 in 2014, April 6 in 2015
Early May	Bank Holiday: May 5 in 2014, May 4 in 2015
Early May	Jazz Festival, Keswick (www.keswickjazzfestival.co.uk)
Late May	Chelsea Flower Show, London (www.rhs.org.uk/chelsea)
Late May	Bank Holiday: May 26 in 2014, May 25 in 2015
Late May-early June	International Music Festival, Bath (www.bathmusicfest.org.uk)
Late May-early June	Fringe Festival, Bath (alternative music, dance, and theater; www.bathfringe.co.uk)

Early June	Beer Festival, Keswick (music, shows; www.keswickbeerfestival.co.uk)
Early-mid June	Trooping the Colour, London (military bands and pageantry, Queen's birthday parade; www.trooping-the-colour.co.uk)
Late June	Royal Ascot Horse Race, Ascot (near Windsor; www.ascot.co.uk)
Mid-late June	Golowan (Midsummer) Festival, Penzance (www.golowan.org)
Late June-early July	Wimbledon Tennis Championship, London (www.wimbledon.org)
Mid-July	Early Music Festival, York (www.ncem.co.uk)
Late July-early Aug	Cambridge Folk Festival (www.cambridgefolkfestival.co.uk)
Late Aug	Notting Hill Carnival, London (costumes, Caribbean music, www.thenottinghillcarnival.com)
Late Aug	Bank Holiday: Aug 25 in 2014, Aug 31 in 2015 (England and Wales only)
Late Aug-late Oct	Illuminations, Blackpool (waterfront light festival, www.visitblackpool.com/illuminations)
Mid-Sept	London Fashion Week (www.londonfashionweek.co.uk)
Mid-Sept	Jane Austen Festival, Bath (www.janeausten.co.uk)
Late Sept	York Food and Drink Festival (www.yorkfoodfestival.com)
Nov 5	Bonfire Night, or Guy Fawkes Night, Britain (fireworks, bonfires, effigy-burning of 1605 traitor Guy Fawkes)
Dec 24-26	Christmas holidays

Conversions and Climate

Numbers and Stumblers

- In Europe, dates appear as day/month/year, so Christmas is 25/12/15.
- What Americans call the second floor of a building is the first floor in Britain.
- On escalators and moving sidewalks, Brits keep the left "lane" open for passing. Keep to the right.
- To avoid the British version of giving someone "the finger," don't hold up the first two fingers of your hand with your palm facing you. (It looks like a reversed victory sign.)
- And please...don't call your waist pack a "fanny pack" (see the British-Yankee Vocabulary list at the end of this appendix).

Metric Conversions

Britain uses the metric system for nearly everything. Weight and volume are typically calculated in metric: A kilogram is 2.2 pounds, and one liter is about a quart (almost four to a gallon). Temperatures are generally given in Celsius, although some newspapers also list them in Fahrenheit.

1 foot = 0.3 meter	1 square yard = 0.8 square meter
1 yard = 0.9 meter	1 square mile = 2.6 square kilometers
1 mile = 1.6 kilometers	1 ounce = 28 grams
1 centimeter = 0.4 inch	1 quart = 0.95 liter
1 meter = 39.4 inches	1 kilogram = 2.2 pounds
1 kilometer = 0.62 mile	32°F = 0°C

Imperial Weights and Measures

Britain hasn't completely gone metric. Driving distances and speed limits are measured in miles. Beer is sold as pints (though milk can be measured in pints or liters), and a person's weight is measured in stone (a 168-pound person weighs 12 stone).

1 stone = 14 pounds
1 British pint = 1.2 US pints
1 imperial gallon = 1.2 US gallons or about 4.5 liters

Clothing Sizes

When shopping for clothing, use these US-to-Britain comparisons as general guidelines (but note that no conversion is perfect).
- Women's dresses and blouses: Add 4
  (US women's size 10 = UK size 14)
- Men's suits, jackets, and shirts: US and UK sizes are the same
- Women's shoes: Subtract 2½ (US size 8 = UK size 5½)
- Men's shoes: Subtract about ½ (US size 9 = UK size 8½)

England's Climate

First line, average daily high; second line, average daily low; third line, average days without rain. For more detailed weather statistics for destinations in this book (as well as the rest of the world), check www.wunderground.com.

	J	F	M	A	M	J	J	A	S	O	N	D
LONDON												
	43°	44°	50°	56°	62°	69°	71°	71°	65°	58°	50°	45°
	36°	36°	38°	42°	47°	53°	56°	56°	52°	46°	42°	38°
	16	15	20	18	19	19	19	20	17	18	15	16
YORK												
	43°	44°	49°	55°	61°	67°	70°	69°	64°	57°	49°	45°
	33°	34°	36°	40°	44°	50°	54°	53°	50°	44°	39°	36°
	14	13	18	17	18	16	16	17	16	16	13	14

Fahrenheit and Celsius Conversion

Britain uses both Celsius and Fahrenheit to take its temperature. For a rough conversion from Celsius to Fahrenheit, double the number and add 30. For weather, remember that 28°C is 82°F—perfect. For health, 37°C is just right.

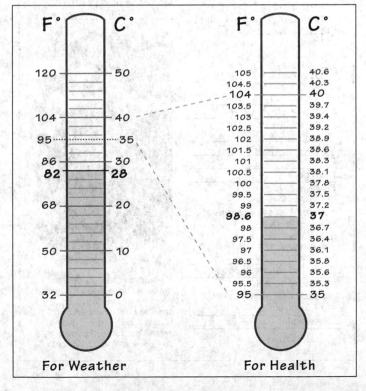

Packing Checklist

Whether you're traveling for five days or five weeks, here's what you'll need to bring. Pack light to enjoy the sweet freedom of true mobility. Happy travels!

- ❑ 5 shirts: long- & short-sleeve
- ❑ 1 sweater or lightweight fleece
- ❑ 2 pairs of pants
- ❑ 1 pair of shorts
- ❑ 5 pairs of underwear & socks
- ❑ 1 pair of shoes
- ❑ 1 rainproof jacket with hood
- ❑ Tie or scarf
- ❑ Swimsuit
- ❑ Sleepwear
- ❑ Money belt
- ❑ Money—your mix of:
  - ❑ Debit card
  - ❑ Credit card(s)
  - ❑ Hard cash ($20 bills)
- ❑ Documents plus photocopies:
  - ❑ Passport
  - ❑ Printout of airline eticket
  - ❑ Driver's license
  - ❑ Student ID, hostel card, etc.
  - ❑ Railpass/train reservations/ car-rental voucher
  - ❑ Insurance details
- ❑ Guidebooks & maps
- ❑ Address list (for sending emails & postcards)
- ❑ Notepad & pen
- ❑ Journal
- ❑ Daypack
- ❑ Toiletries kit:
  - ❑ Toiletries
  - ❑ Medicines & vitamins
  - ❑ First-aid kit
  - ❑ Glasses/contacts/ sunglasses (with prescriptions)
- ❑ Small towel/washcloth
- ❑ Laundry supplies:
  - ❑ Laundry soap
  - ❑ Clothesline
- ❑ Sewing kit

- ❑ Electronics—your choice of:
  - ❑ Camera (& related gear)
  - ❑ Mobile phone
  - ❑ Portable media player (iPod or other)
  - ❑ Laptop/netbook/ tablet
  - ❑ Ebook reader
  - ❑ Headphones or earbuds
  - ❑ Chargers for each of the above
  - ❑ Plug adapter(s)
- ❑ Alarm clock
- ❑ Earplugs
- ❑ Sealable plastic baggies
- ❑ Empty water bottle
- ❑ Postcards & photos from home

If you plan to carry on your luggage, note that all liquids must be in 3.4-ounce or smaller containers and fit within a single quart-size sealable baggie. For details, see www.tsa.gov/travelers.

British-Yankee Vocabulary

For a longer list, plus a dry-witted primer on British culture, see *The Septic's Companion* (Chris Rae). Note that instead of asking, "Can I help you?" many Brits offer a more casual, "You alright?" or "You OK there?"

APPENDIX

advert: advertisement

afters: dessert

anticlockwise: counterclockwise

Antipodean: an Australian or New Zealander

aubergine: eggplant

banger: sausage

bangers and mash: sausage and mashed potatoes

Bank Holiday: legal holiday

bap: small roll

bespoke: custom-made

billion: a thousand of our billions (a million million)

biro: ballpoint pen

biscuit: cookie

black pudding: sausage made from dried blood

bloody: damn

blow off: fart

bobby: policeman ("the Bill" is more common)

Bob's your uncle: there you go (with a shrug), naturally

boffin: nerd, geek

bollocks: all-purpose expletive (a figurative use of testicles)

bolshy: argumentative

bomb: success or failure

bonnet: car hood

boot: car trunk

braces: suspenders

bridle way: path for walkers, bikers, and horse riders

brilliant: cool

brolly: umbrella

bubble and squeak: cabbage and potatoes fried together

bum: butt

candy floss: cotton candy

caravan: trailer

car-boot sale: temporary flea market, often for charity

car park: parking lot

cashpoint: ATM

casualty: emergency room

cat's eyes: road reflectors

ceilidh (KAY-lee): informal evening of song and folk fun (Scottish and Irish)

cheap and cheerful: budget but adequate

cheap and nasty: cheap and bad quality

cheers: good-bye or thanks; also a toast

chemist: pharmacist

chicory: endive

Chinese whispers: playing "telephone"

chippie: fish-and-chips shop; carpenter

chips: French fries

chock-a-block: jam-packed

chuffed: pleased

chunter: mutter

cider: alcoholic apple cider

clearway: road where you can't stop

coach: long-distance bus

concession: discounted admission

concs (pronounced "conks"): short for "concession"

coronation chicken: curried chicken salad

cos: romaine lettuce

cot: baby crib

cotton buds: Q-tips

courgette: zucchini

craic (pronounced "crack"): fun, good conversation (Irish/Scottish and spreading to England)

crisps: potato chips

cuppa: cup of tea

dear: expensive

dicey: iffy, risky

digestives: round graham cookies

dinner: lunch or dinner

diversion: detour

dogsbody: menial worker

donkey's years: ages, long time

draughts: checkers

draw: marijuana

dual carriageway: divided highway (four lanes)

dummy: pacifier

elevenses: coffee-and-biscuits break before lunch

elvers: baby eels

face flannel: washcloth

fag: cigarette

fagged: exhausted

faggot: sausage

fancy: to like, to be attracted to (a person)

fanny: vagina

fell: hill or high plain (Lake District)

first floor: second floor

fiver: £5 bill

fizzy drink: pop or soda

flutter: a bet

football: soccer

force: waterfall (Lake District)

fortnight: two weeks (shortened from "fourteen nights")

fringe: hair bangs

Frogs: French people

fruit machine: slot machine

full Monty: whole shebang, everything

gallery: balcony

gammon: ham

gangway: aisle

gaol: jail (same pronunciation)

gateau (or gateaux): cake

gear lever: stick shift

geezer: "dude"

give way: yield

glen: narrow valley (Scotland)

goods wagon: freight truck

gormless: stupid

goujons: breaded and fried fish or chicken sticks

green fingers: green thumbs

half eight: 8:30 (not 7:30)

hard cheese: bad luck

heath: open treeless land

hen night: bachelorette party

holiday: vacation

homely: homey or cozy

hoover: vacuum cleaner

ice lolly: Popsicle

interval: intermission

ironmonger: hardware store

ish: more or less

jacket potato: baked potato

jelly: Jell-O

jiggery-pokery: nonsense

Joe Bloggs: John Q. Public

jumble (sale): rummage sale

jumper: sweater

just a tick: just a second

kipper: smoked herring

knackered: exhausted (Cockney: cream crackered)

knickers: ladies' panties

knocking shop: brothel

knock up: wake up or visit (old-fashioned)

ladybird: ladybug

lady fingers: flat, spongy cookie

lady's finger: okra

lager: light, fizzy beer

left luggage: baggage check

lemonade: lemon-lime pop like 7-Up, fizzy

lemon squash: lemonade, not fizzy

let: rent

licenced: restaurant authorized to sell alcohol

lift: elevator

listed: protected historic building

loo: toilet or bathroom

lorry: truck

mack: mackintosh raincoat

mangetout: snow peas

marrow: summer squash

mate: buddy (boy or girl)

mean: stingy

mental: wild, memorable

mews: former stables converted to two-story rowhouses

mobile (MOH-bile): cell phone

moggie: cat

motorway: freeway

naff: tacky or trashy

nappy: diaper

natter: talk on and on

neep: Scottish for turnip

newsagent: corner store

nought: zero

noughts & crosses: tic-tac-toe

off-licence: liquor store

on offer: for sale

OTT: over the top, excessive

panto, pantomime: fairy-tale play performed at Christmas (silly but fun)

pants: (noun) underwear, briefs; (adj.) terrible, ridiculous

pasty (PASS-tee): crusted savory (usually meat) pie from Cornwall

pavement: sidewalk

pear-shaped: messed up, gone wrong

petrol: gas

piccalilli: mustard-pickle relish

pillar box: mailbox

pissed (rude), **paralytic, bevvied, wellied, popped up, merry, trollied, ratted, rat-arsed, pissed as a newt:** drunk

pitch: playing field

plaster: Band-Aid

plonk: cheap, bad wine

plonker: one who drinks bad wine (a mild insult)

prat: idiot

publican: pub owner

public school: private "prep" school (e.g., Eton)

pudding: dessert in general

pukka: first-class

pull, to be on the: on the prowl

punter: customer, especially in gambling

put a sock in it: shut up

queue: line

queue up: line up

quid: pound (£1)

randy: horny

rasher: slice of bacon

redundant, made: laid off

Remembrance Day: Veterans' Day

return ticket: round trip

revising; doing revisions: studying for exams

ring up: call (telephone)

roundabout: traffic circle

rubber: eraser

rubbish: bad

sausage roll: sausage wrapped in a flaky pastry

Scotch egg: hard-boiled egg wrapped in sausage meat

Scouser: a person from Liverpool

self-catering: accommodation with kitchen

Sellotape: Scotch tape

services: freeway rest area

serviette: napkin

setee: couch

shag: intercourse (cruder than in the US)

shambolic: chaotic

shandy: lager and 7-Up

silencer: car muffler

single ticket: one-way ticket

skip: Dumpster

sleeping policeman: speed bumps

smalls: underwear

snap: photo (snapshot)

snogging: kissing, making out

sod: mildly offensive insult

sod it, sod off: screw it, screw off

sod's law: Murphy's law

soda: soda water (not pop)

soldiers (food): toast sticks for dipping

solicitor: lawyer

spanner: wrench

spend a penny: urinate

stag night: bachelor party

starkers: buck naked

starters: appetizers

state school: public school

sticking plaster: Band-Aid

sticky tape: Scotch tape

stone: 14 pounds (weight)

stroppy: bad-tempered

subway: underground walkway

suet: fat from animal rendering (sometimes used in cooking)

sultanas: golden raisins

surgical spirit: rubbing alcohol

suspenders: garters

suss out: figure out

swede: rutabaga

ta: thank you

take the mickey/take the piss: tease

tatty: worn out or tacky

taxi rank: taxi stand

telly: TV

tenement: stone apartment house (not necessarily a slum)

tenner: £10 bill

theatre: live stage

tick: a check mark

tight as a fish's bum: cheapskate (watertight)

tights: panty hose

tin: can

tip: public dump

tipper lorry: dump truck

top hole: first rate

top up: refill (a drink, mobile-phone credit, petrol tank, etc.)

torch: flashlight

towel, press-on: panty liner

towpath: path along a river

trainers: sneakers

Tube: subway

twee: quaint, cutesy

twitcher: bird-watcher

Underground: subway

verge: grassy edge of road

verger: church official

way out: exit

wee (adj.): small (Scottish)

wee (verb): urinate

Wellingtons, wellies: rubber boots

whacked: exhausted

whinge (rhymes with hinge): whine

wind up: tease, irritate

witter on: gab and gab

wonky: weird, askew

yob: hooligan

zebra crossing: crosswalk

zed: the letter Z

INDEX

INDEX

INDEX

MAP INDEX